D1805035

ECONOMICS
Concepts, Analysis,
and Applications

ECONOMICS
Concepts, Analysis, and Applications

Orley M. Amos, Jr.
Oklahoma State University

HB
171.5
A48
1987

Wadsworth Publishing Company
Belmont, California
A Division of Wadsworth, Inc.

Economics Editor: Stephanie Surfus
Special Projects Editor: Judith McKibben
Editorial Assistant: Cynthia Haus
Production Editor: Sandra Craig
Text and Cover Designer: MaryEllen Podgorski
Print Buyer: Ruth Cole
Art Editor: Marta Kongsle
Copy Editor: Thomas L. Briggs
Technical Illustrator: Lori Heckelman
Compositor: Graphic Typesetting Service
Signing Representative: Steve Jones

© 1987 by Wadsworth, Inc. All rights reserved. No part of this book may be reproduced, stored in a retrieval system, or transcribed, in any form or by any means, electronic, mechanical, photocopying, recording, or otherwise, without the prior written permission of the publisher, Wadsworth Publishing Company, Belmont, California 94002, a division of Wadsworth, Inc.

Printed in the United States of America   34

1 2 3 4 5 6 7 8 9 10—91 90 89 88 87

Library of Congress Cataloging-in-Publication Data

Amos, Orley M., 1954–
   Economics : concepts, analysis, and applications.
   Includes index.
   1. Economics.   I. Title.
HB171.5.A48   1987   330   86-24569
ISBN 0-534-06948-7

For Pam, Chris, and Holly

Contents in Brief

PART I · INTRODUCTION 1

SECTION 1 · BASIC ECONOMIC CONCEPTS 3

Unit 1.1 An Introduction to Economics 4
Unit 1.2 The Economic Problem of Scarcity 12
Unit 1.3 The Mixed Economy 18
Unit 1.4 Graphs and Economics 25
Unit 1.5 The Economy's Production Possibilities 34

Section Inquiry: Military Spending 45

SECTION 2 · THE MARKET 47

Unit 2.1 An Introduction to the Market 48
Unit 2.2 Demand 52
Unit 2.3 Supply 62
Unit 2.4 Market Equilibrium 72
Unit 2.5 Government and the Market 85
Unit 2.6 Elasticity 92
Unit 2.7 Elasticity and the Market 102

Section Inquiry: The Used Textbook Market 111

PART II · MACROECONOMICS: THE NATIONAL ECONOMY 113

SECTION 3 · MACROECONOMIC FOUNDATIONS 115

Unit 3.1 The Circular Flow of Economic Activity 116
Unit 3.2 National Product 126
Unit 3.3 National Income 140
Unit 3.4 Unemployment 152
Unit 3.5 Inflation 161
Unit 3.6 The Aggregate Market 170
Unit 3.7 The Business Cycle 180

Section Inquiry: The Underground Economy 192

SECTION 4 · KEYNESIAN ECONOMICS 193

Unit 4.1 An Introduction to Keynesian Economics 194
Unit 4.2 Consumption 203
Unit 4.3 Investment 213
Unit 4.4 Government Purchases and Taxes 224
Unit 4.5 Determining National Income and Output 232
Unit 4.6 The Multiplier 242
Unit 4.7 Fiscal Policy Applications of Keynesian Economics 251

Section Inquiry: Balancing the Budget 263

SECTION 5 · MONEY 264

Unit 5.1 An Introduction to Money 265
Unit 5.2 Money Creation 273
Unit 5.3 The Federal Reserve System 281
Unit 5.4 The Money Market and Output Determination 293
Unit 5.5 Comparing Monetarist and Keynesian Policies 303

Section Inquiry: Return to a Gold Standard   314

SECTION 6 · A CLOSER LOOK AT INFLATION   315

Unit 6.1   The Causes of Inflation   316
Unit 6.2   Inflation and Unemployment   324
Unit 6.3   Inflation Control Policies   335

Section Inquiry: Inflation and Productivity   344

PART III · MICROECONOMICS: OUTPUT MARKETS   347

SECTION 7 · A CLOSER LOOK AT DEMAND   349

Unit 7.1   Consumer Behavior   350
Unit 7.2   Utility and Demand   358
Unit 7.3   Indifference Curves and Demand   366
Unit 7.4   Applications of Consumer Demand   375

Section Inquiry: Consumer Demand for Television Programming   381

SECTION 8 · A CLOSER LOOK AT SUPPLY   383

Unit 8.1   The Firm   384
Unit 8.2   Production   394
Unit 8.3   The Costs of Production   401
Unit 8.4   Perfect Competition and Supply   411
Unit 8.5   Problems in the Supply of Agricultural Goods   423

Section Inquiry: The Supply of Airline Services   433

SECTION 9 · MONOPOLY AND IMPERFECT COMPETITION   435

Unit 9.1   Market Power   437
Unit 9.2   Monopoly   444
Unit 9.3   Natural Monopolies and Public Utilities   455
Unit 9.4   Monopolistic Competition   462
Unit 9.5   Oligopoly   467
Unit 9.6   Controlling Imperfect Competition with Antitrust Legislation   476
Unit 9.7   Market Power in the Health Care Industry   484

Section Inquiry: Market Power in the World Petroleum Market   492

PART IV · MICROECONOMICS: RESOURCE MARKETS   495

SECTION 10 · THE FACTOR MARKET   497

Unit 10.1   Factor Demand   498
Unit 10.2   Factor Supply   505
Unit 10.3   Factor Market Equilibrium   511
Unit 10.4   The Effect of Unions on the Labor Market   518

Section Inquiry: Comparable Worth   530

SECTION 11 · THE DISTRIBUTION OF FACTOR INCOMES   531

Unit 11.1   Wages   532
Unit 11.2   Interest   542
Unit 11.3   Rent and Profit   549
Unit 11.4   Income Distribution   557
Unit 11.5   Poverty   565

Section Inquiry: Minimum Wage for Teenagers   574

PART V · SELECTED TOPICS IN ECONOMICS   577

SECTION 12 · GOVERNMENT AND ALLOCATION   580

Unit 12.1   Public Choice   581
Unit 12.2   The Market Failure of Public Goods   590
Unit 12.3   Principles of Taxation   598
Unit 12.4   Government Regulation of Economic Activity   610

Section Inquiry: A Flat Rate Tax   619

SECTION 13 · THE NATURAL ENVIRONMENT   621

Unit 13.1 The Market Failure of Externalities   622
Unit 13.2 The Costs of Pollution   631
Unit 13.3 Pollution Control Policies   638
Unit 13.4 The Economics of Energy Resources   645

Section Inquiry: The Limits to Growth   653

SECTION 14 · THE WORLD ECONOMY   655

Unit 14.1 International Trade   656
Unit 14.2 International Finance   667
Unit 14.3 Economic Growth   676
Unit 14.4 Economic Development   685

Section Inquiry: The Third World Debt   694

SECTION 15 · ALTERNATIVE ECONOMIC SYSTEMS   695

Unit 15.1 An Introduction to Economic Systems   696
Unit 15.2 Marxian Economics   703
Unit 15.3 The Soviet Economy   709
Unit 15.4 The Chinese Economy   718

Section Inquiry: Market Socialism in Yugoslavia   725

Contents

Preface xxi

PART I

Introduction 1

SECTION 1 · BASIC ECONOMIC CONCEPTS 3

UNIT 1.1 · AN INTRODUCTION TO ECONOMICS 4

What Is Economics? 5
Why Do We Study Economics? 7
How Do We Study Economics? 7
The Economist's View of the World 9
In Summary 10
Questions for Study and Analysis 11
Review Glossary 11

UNIT 1.2 · THE ECONOMIC PROBLEM OF SCARCITY 12

Limited Resources and Goods 12
Factors of Production 14
Unlimited Wants 16
In Summary 17
Questions for Study and Analysis 17
Review Glossary 17

UNIT 1.3 · THE MIXED ECONOMY 18

Two Methods of Resource Allocation 18
The Range of Government-Market Orientation 19
The Mixed U.S. Economy 20
Goals of a Market-Oriented Economy 21
Tradeoffs Between Goals 23
In Summary 23
Questions for Study and Analysis 24
Review Glossary 24

UNIT 1.4 · GRAPHS AND ECONOMICS 25

Reading and Interpreting a Graph 25
The Components of a Straight Line 27
A Curve 29
Intersection Between Two Lines 29
Tangency Between Two Lines 31
The Misuse of Graphs 31
In Summary 32
Questions for Study and Analysis 33
Review Glossary 33

UNIT 1.5 · THE ECONOMY'S PRODUCTION POSSIBILITIES 34

Production Possibilities: A Student Example 34
Production Possibilities for the Economy 35
Production Possibilities Frontier 36
Opportunity Costs 37

The Law of Increasing Opportunity Costs   37
Full Employment and Unemployment   39
Economic Growth   40
The Three Questions of Allocation   42
In Summary   43
Questions for Study and Analysis   43
Review Glossary   44

SECTION INQUIRY: MILITARY SPENDING   45

Questions for Discussion   46

SECTION 2 · THE MARKET   47

UNIT 2.1 · AN INTRODUCTION TO THE MARKET   48

The Market   48
Three Characteristics of a Market   49
The Important Role of Price in the Market   50
The Market as an Allocative Mechanism   50
Ideal Markets and the Real World   51
In Summary   51
Questions for Study and Analysis   51
Review Glossary   52

UNIT 2.2 · DEMAND   52

The Law of Demand   52
The Demand Curve   53
A Change in the Quantity Demanded and a Change in Demand   54
The Determinants of Demand   56
In Summary   60
Questions for Study and Analysis   60
Review Glossary   61

UNIT 2.3 · SUPPLY   62

The Law of Supply   62
The Supply Curve   63
A Change in the Quantity Supplied and a Change in Supply   64
The Determinants of Supply   65
In Summary   70
Questions for Study and Analysis   70
Review Glossary   71

UNIT 2.4 · MARKET EQUILIBRIUM   72

Determining the Market Equilibrium   72
Surplus and Shortage   74
Shocks to the Market   75
Changes in Both Demand and Supply   80
In Summary   82
Questions for Study and Analysis   83
Review Glossary   84

UNIT 2.5 · GOVERNMENT AND THE MARKET   85

Price Floor   85
Price Ceiling   86
Black Markets   87
A Tax on the Market   88
In Summary   90
Questions for Study and Analysis   91
Review Glossary   91

UNIT 2.6 · ELASTICITY   92

Elasticity   92
Price Elasticity of Demand   92
Income Elasticity of Demand   97
Cross Price Elasticity of Demand   98
Price Elasticity of Supply   98
Determinants of Elasticity   99
In Summary   100
Questions for Study and Analysis   100
Review Glossary   101

UNIT 2.7 · ELASTICITY AND THE MARKET   102

Price Floor   102
Price Ceiling   104

CONTENTS

Tax Incidence   105
Price Elasticity of Gasoline Demand   106
Price Elasticity of Water Demand   107
Income Elasticity of Fuel Oil and Coal Demand   108
Cross Price Elasticity of Demand for Timber Production   108
In Summary   109
Questions for Study and Analysis   110
Review Glossary   110

SECTION INQUIRY: THE USED TEXTBOOK MARKET   111

Questions for Discussion   111

PART II

Macroeconomics: The National Economy   113

SECTION 3 · MACROECONOMIC FOUNDATIONS   115

UNIT 3.1 · THE CIRCULAR FLOW OF ECONOMIC ACTIVITY   116

The Simple Circular Flow   116
The Circular Flow with Financial Markets   119
The Circular Flow with the Government   120
The Circular Flow with the Foreign Sector   122
In Summary   124
Questions for Study and Analysis   124
Review Glossary   125

UNIT 3.2 · NATIONAL PRODUCT   126

Gross National Product   126
Gross National Product and Welfare   130
Real Gross National Product   131
Expenditures on Gross National Product   133
Net National Product   136
In Summary   138
Questions for Study and Analysis   138
Review Glossary   139

UNIT 3.3 · NATIONAL INCOME   140

National Income   140
Personal Income   146
Disposable Personal Income   146
Another Visit to the Circular Flow   147
In Summary   150
Questions for Study and Analysis   151
Review Glossary   151

UNIT 3.4 · UNEMPLOYMENT   152

The Nature of Unemployment   152
Measuring Unemployment   154
Costs of Unemployment   157
In Summary   158
Questions for Study and Analysis   159
Review Glossary   160

UNIT 3.5 · INFLATION   161

A Definition of Inflation   161
Measures of Inflation   161
The Effects of Inflation   165
In Summary   168
Questions for Study and Analysis   169
Review Glossary   169

UNIT 3.6 · THE AGGREGATE MARKET   170

Aggregate Demand   170
Aggregate Supply   172
The Aggregate Market   174
Shocks to the Aggregate Market   175
In Summary   178
Questions for Study and Analysis   178
Review Glossary   179

UNIT 3.7 · THE BUSINESS CYCLE   180

Business Cycles   180
Business Cycles Since 1919   181
Business Cycles and the Aggregate Market   183
Alternative Theories of the Business Cycle   186
Cyclical Trends in Unemployment and Inflation   188
In Summary   190
Questions for Study and Analysis   190
Review Glossary   191

SECTION INQUIRY: THE UNDERGROUND ECONOMY   192

Questions for Discussion   192

SECTION 4 · KEYNESIAN ECONOMICS   193

UNIT 4.1 · AN INTRODUCTION TO KEYNESIAN ECONOMICS   194

Keynesian Economics   194
Classical Economics   195
The Depression   198
The Keynesian Answer to the Depression   200
In Summary   202
Questions for Study and Analysis   202
Review Glossary   203

UNIT 4.2 · CONSUMPTION   203

The Disposition of Disposable Personal Income   203
Consumption Function   206
Saving Function   207
Determinants of Consumption   209
Change in Amount Consumed and Change in Consumption   209
In Summary   211
Questions for Study and Analysis   211
Review Glossary   212

UNIT 4.3 · INVESTMENT   213

Planned and Realized Investment   213
Investment, Output, and the Interest Rate   213
Consumption and Investment   217
Recent Data on Investment Expenditures   221
In Summary   221
Questions for Study and Analysis   222
Review Glossary   223

UNIT 4.4 · GOVERNMENT PURCHASES AND TAXES   224

The Government's Budget   224
Aggregate Expenditures   227
The Circular Flow   229
In Summary   231
Questions for Study and Analysis   231
Review Glossary   232

UNIT 4.5 · DETERMINING NATIONAL INCOME AND OUTPUT   232

The Ground Rules   232
Equilibrium with Aggregate Expenditures   233
Equilibrium with Leakages and Injections   236
The Keynesian Cross and the Aggregate Market   239
In Summary   240
Questions for Study and Analysis   241
Review Glossary   241

UNIT 4.6 · THE MULTIPLIER   242

Shifts in the Aggregate Expenditures Line   242
The Multiplier Effect   244
Paradox of Thrift   247
In Summary   249

Questions for Study and Analysis   250
Review Glossary   250

UNIT 4.7 · FISCAL POLICY APPLICATIONS OF KEYNESIAN ECONOMICS   251

Full Employment Output   252
Fiscal Policy and Full Employment Output   253
Fiscal Policy and the Aggregate Market   257
Automatic Stabilizers   258
High Employment Budget   259
Recent Fiscal Policy   259
In Summary   260
Questions for Study and Analysis   261
Review Glossary   262

SECTION INQUIRY: BALANCING THE BUDGET   263

Questions for Discussion   263

SECTION 5 · MONEY   264

UNIT 5.1 · AN INTRODUCTION TO MONEY   265

Functions of Money   265
Characteristics of Money   267
Types of Money   267
Money in the U.S. Economy   268
In Summary   271
Questions for Study and Analysis   272
Review Glossary   272

UNIT 5.2 · MONEY CREATION   273

The Goldsmith   273
Modern Banking and Money Creation   275
In Summary   279

Questions for Study and Analysis   280
Review Glossary   280

UNIT 5.3 · THE FEDERAL RESERVE SYSTEM   281

The Origin of the Federal Reserve System   281
Structure of the Federal Reserve System   282
The Tools of Monetary Policy   286
Monetary Policy and the Money Supply   288
In Summary   290
Questions for Study and Analysis   291
Review Glossary   291

UNIT 5.4 · THE MONEY MARKET AND OUTPUT DETERMINATION   293

Money Demand   293
Money Supply   295
Money Market Equilibrium   296
The Money Market and National Output   297
Recent Monetary Policy   300
In Summary   301
Questions for Study and Analysis   302
Review Glossary   302

UNIT 5.5 · COMPARING MONETARIST AND KEYNESIAN POLICIES   303

Differences Between Monetarists and Keynesians   303
Monetary Policy   304
Fiscal Policy   308
In Summary   312
Questions for Study and Analysis   312
Review Glossary   313

SECTION INQUIRY: RETURN TO A GOLD STANDARD   314

Questions for Discussion   314

SECTION 6 · A CLOSER LOOK AT INFLATION 315

UNIT 6.1 · THE CAUSES OF INFLATION 316

The Dynamics of Inflation 316
Determinants of Aggregate Demand 318
Determinants of Aggregate Supply 321
In Summary 322
Questions for Study and Analysis 323
Review Glossary 323

UNIT 6.2 · INFLATION AND UNEMPLOYMENT 324

The Phillips Curve 324
Historical Evidence of the Phillips Curve 326
Aggregate Supply and the Phillips Curve 327
Inflationary Expectations 329
Rational Expectations 333
In Summary 333
Questions for Study and Analysis 334
Review Glossary 334

UNIT 6.3 · INFLATION CONTROL POLICIES 335

Contractionary Fiscal and Monetary Policy 335
Balanced Budget and Constant Growth of the Money Supply 337
Wage and Price Controls/Guidelines 338
Indexing 339
Supply-Side Policies 340
In Summary 342
Questions for Study and Analysis 343
Review Glossary 343

SECTION INQUIRY: INFLATION AND PRODUCTIVITY 344

Questions for Discussion 345

PART III
Microeconomics: Output Markets 347

SECTION 7 · A CLOSER LOOK AT DEMAND 349

UNIT 7.1 · CONSUMER BEHAVIOR 350

The Consumer 350
Utility 351
The Choice Between Two Goods 353
In Summary 355
Questions for Study and Analysis 356
Review Glossary 357

UNIT 7.2 · UTILITY AND DEMAND 358

The Law of Diminishing Marginal Utility 358
Utility and the Law of Demand 359
Income and Substitution Effects 360
Consumer Surplus 361
Diamond/Water Paradox 361
In Summary 364
Questions for Study and Analysis 264
Review Glossary 365

UNIT 7.3 · INDIFFERENCE CURVES AND DEMAND 366

Indifference Curves 366
The Budget Line 369
The Choice Between Two Goods 371
The Demand Curve 372
In Summary 373
Questions for Study and Analysis 374
Review Glossary 374

UNIT 7.4 · APPLICATIONS OF CONSUMER DEMAND 375

The Relative Price of Diesel Fuel 375
The Slump in Liquor Industry Sales 376

The Choice of Savings Accounts   377
The Price of a Personal Foul   378
In Summary   379
Questions for Study and Analysis   379

SECTION INQUIRY: CONSUMER DEMAND FOR TELEVISION PROGRAMMING   381

Questions for Discussion   381

SECTION 8 · A CLOSER LOOK AT SUPPLY   383

UNIT 8.1 · THE FIRM   384

The Firm   384
Legal Forms of the Firm   385
Firms in the United States   386
Market Structures   387
Objectives of the Firm   390
Natural Selection   391
In Summary   391
Questions for Study and Analysis   392
Review Glossary   392

UNIT 8.2 · PRODUCTION   394

Production   394
The Principles of Short-Run Production   395
The Law of Diminishing Marginal Returns   396
In Summary   399
Questions for Study and Analysis   399
Review Glossary   400

UNIT 8.3 · THE COSTS OF PRODUCTION   401

Opportunity Cost   401
Total Cost   402
Average Cost   406
Marginal Cost   407
The Law of Diminishing Marginal Returns   407
In Summary   408
Questions for Study and Analysis   409
Review Glossary   410

UNIT 8.4 · PERFECT COMPETITION AND SUPPLY   411

Nature of Perfect Competition   411
The Perfectly Competitive Firm's Demand   412
Short-Run Output   414
Price and Average Cost: Minimizing Losses   417
The Perfectly Competitive Firm's Supply Curve   419
Perfect Competition and Resource Allocation   420
In Summary   421
Questions for Study and Analysis   421
Review Glossary   422

UNIT 8.5 · PROBLEMS IN THE SUPPLY OF AGRICULTURAL GOODS   423

The Farm Problem   423
Agricultural Policies   427
An Evaluation of Agricultural Policies   430
In Summary   431
Questions for Study and Analysis   431
Review Glossary   432

SECTION INQUIRY: THE SUPPLY OF AIRLINE SERVICES   433

Questions for Discussion   434

SECTION 9 · MONOPOLY AND IMPERFECT COMPETITION   435

UNIT 9.1 · MARKET POWER   437

Characteristics of Monopoly, Monopolistic Competition, and Oligopoly   437

Market Power   438
Barriers to Entry   439
Product Differentiation   441
Market Power and Demand   442
In Summary   442
Questions for Study and Analysis   443
Review Glossary   444

UNIT 9.2 · MONOPOLY   444

Real World Monopolies   444
The Monopolist's Demand   445
Short-Run Output   448
The Monopolist's Supply Curve   450
Monopoly and Resource Allocation   452
In Summary   453
Questions for Study and Analysis   453
Review Glossary   454

UNIT 9.3 · NATURAL MONOPOLIES AND PUBLIC UTILITIES   455

The Natural Monopoly   455
Regulatory Pricing   458
In Summary   460
Questions for Study and Analysis   460
Review Glossary   461

UNIT 9.4 · MONOPOLISTIC COMPETITION   462

Characteristics of Monopolistic Competition   462
The Monopolistically Competitive Firm's Demand   462
Short-Run Output   463
Monopolistic Competition and Resource Allocation   465
In Summary   466
Questions for Study and Analysis   466
Review Glossary   467

UNIT 9.5 · OLIGOPOLY   467

Oligopoly and Concentration in U.S. Industries   468
Oligopolistic Behavior   469
The Kinked Demand Curve   471
Collusion and Cartels   472
Oligopoly and Resource Allocation   474
In Summary   474
Questions for Study and Analysis   475
Review Glossary   475

UNIT 9.6 · CONTROLLING IMPERFECT COMPETITION WITH ANTITRUST LEGISLATION   476

Market Structures   477
Market Power and Its Misuse   477
Antitrust Legislation in the United States   479
An Evaluation of Antitrust Legislation   481
In Summary   481
Questions for Study and Analysis   482
Review Glossary   483

UNIT 9.7 · MARKET POWER IN THE HEALTH CARE INDUSTRY   484

Recent Trends in Health Care   484
The Structure of the Health Care Industry   484
Market Power   486
The Demand for Health Care   488
Policies for Controlling Health Care Prices   490
In Summary   490
Questions for Study and Analysis   491
Review Glossary   491

SECTION INQUIRY: MARKET POWER IN THE WORLD PETROLEUM MARKET   492

Questions for Discussion   492

PART IV

Microeconomics: Resource Markets 495

SECTION 10 · THE FACTOR MARKET 497

UNIT 10.1 · FACTOR DEMAND 498

Derived Demand 498
Marginal Productivity Theory 499
Determinants of Factor Demand 501
In Summary 503
Questions for Study and Analysis 504
Review Glossary 504

UNIT 10.2 · FACTOR SUPPLY 505

Market and Firm Supply 505
Marginal Factor Cost 506
Factor Supply Curves 507
Differences in Labor, Capital, Land, and Entrepreneurship 508
Mobility 509
In Summary 510
Questions for Study and Analysis 510
Review Glossary 511

UNIT 10.3 · FACTOR MARKET EQUILIBRIUM 511

Perfect Competition 511
Monopsony 513
Monopoly 514
Bilateral Monopoly 514
In Summary 516
Questions for Study and Analysis 517
Review Glossary 517

UNIT 10.4 · THE EFFECT OF UNIONS ON THE LABOR MARKET 518

Types of Labor Unions 518
Union Membership in the United States 518
Role of Labor Unions in the Labor Market 519
A Brief History of Labor Unions in the United States 522
Craft Unions 524
Industrial Unions 525
Stimulating Demand 525
How a Union Affects a Nonunion Labor Market 526
In Summary 527
Questions for Study and Analysis 528
Review Glossary 595

SECTION INQUIRY: COMPARABLE WORTH 530

Questions for Discussion 530

SECTION 11 · THE DISTRIBUTION OF FACTOR INCOMES 531

UNIT 11.1 · WAGES 532

Wage Differentials 532
Human Capital 536
The Labor-Leisure Tradeoff 539
In Summary 540
Questions for Study and Analysis 540
Review Glossary 541

UNIT 11.2 · INTEREST 542

Investment in Physical Capital 542
The Financial Market 543
Financial Market Equilibrium and Capital 545
Interest Rate Differentials 545
In Summary 547

Questions for Study and Analysis   547
Review Glossary   548

UNIT 11.3 · RENT AND PROFIT   549

Land and Space   549
The Supply of Land   550
The Market for Land   550
Rent   551
Profit   553
Causes of Economic Profit   554
Resource Allocation and Economic Profit   555
Real World Profits and the Reward to Entrepreneurs   555
In Summary   555
Questions for Study and Analysis   556
Review Glossary   556

UNIT 11.4 · INCOME DISTRIBUTION   557

Personal and Functional Income Distributions   557
Measures of the Distribution of Income   558
Causes of Income Inequality   561
Equity and Efficiency   563
In Summary   564
Questions for Study and Analysis   564
Review Glossary   565

UNIT 11.5 · POVERTY   565

Absolute and Relative Poverty   565
Antipoverty Policies   568
Poverty Programs in the United States   570
An Evaluation of Poverty Programs   572
In Summary   572
Questions for Study and Analysis   573
Review Glossary   574

SECTION INQUIRY: MINIMUM WAGE FOR TEENAGERS   574

Questions for Discussion   575

PART V
Selected Topics in Economics   577

SECTION 12 · GOVERNMENT AND ALLOCATION   580

UNIT 12.1 · PUBLIC CHOICE   581

The Political Entrepreneur   582
The Principle of the Median Voter   582
Voting and Rational Ignorance   584
Logrolling   584
The Voting Paradox   586
Special Interest Groups   587
In Summary   588
Questions for Study and Analysis   589
Review Glossary   590

UNIT 12.2 · THE MARKET FAILURE OF PUBLIC GOODS   590

What Makes a Public Good?   590
The Free Rider Problem   593
The Demand for Public Goods   593
Optimal Production of Public Goods   594
Benefit-Cost Analysis   595
In Summary   596
Questions for Study and Analysis   597
Review Glossary   598

UNIT 12.3 · PRINCIPLES OF TAXATION   598

A Few Basics   598
Taxation and Equity   600
Tax Reform and the Federal Income Tax System   600
Taxation and Efficiency   601
Tax Incidence and Welfare Loss   602
The Wide World of Taxes   604
In Summary   607

CONTENTS

Questions for Study and Analysis   608
Review Glossary   609

UNIT 12.4 · GOVERNMENT REGULATION OF ECONOMIC ACTIVITY   610

A Short List of Regulatory Agencies   610
Reasons for Regulation   612
Reasons Against Regulation   614
An Evaluation of Government Regulation   617
In Summary   617
Questions for Study and Analysis   618
Review Glossary   618

SECTION INQUIRY: A FLAT RATE TAX   619

Questions for Discussion   620

SECTION 13 · THE NATURAL ENVIRONMENT   621

UNIT 13.1 · THE MARKET FAILURE OF EXTERNALITIES   622

What Is an Externality?   622
Optimal Production with Externalities   625
Two Reasons for Externalities   627
In Summary   629
Questions for Study and Analysis   630
Review Glossary   630

UNIT 13.2 · THE COSTS OF POLLUTION   631

Water Pollution   632
Air Pollution   633
Policy Considerations   634
The Materials Balance Concept   634
In Summary   636
Questions for Study and Analysis   637
Review Glossary   637

UNIT 13.3 · POLLUTION CONTROL POLICIES   638

Pigouvian Tax   638
Alternative Pollution Control Policies   639
Environmental Legislation   642
In Summary   643
Questions for Study and Analysis   643
Review Glossary   644

UNIT 13.4 · THE ECONOMICS OF ENERGY RESOURCES   645

Energy Resources in the United States   645
The Supply of Fossil Fuels   646
Recent Energy Policies   649
Alternative Energy Resources   651
In Summary   652
Questions for Study and Analysis   653
Review Glossary   653

SECTION INQUIRY: THE LIMITS TO GROWTH   653

Questions for Discussion   654

SECTION 14 · THE WORLD ECONOMY   655

UNIT 14.1 · INTERNATIONAL TRADE   656

Patterns of International Trade   656
Comparative Advantage   659
The International Market   660
Tariffs   662
An Evaluation of Arguments in Favor of Tariffs   663
The Costs of Trade Restrictions   664
In Summary   665
Questions for Study and Analysis   665
Review Glossary   666

UNIT 14.2 · INTERNATIONAL FINANCE 667

International Trade and Foreign Exchange 667
The Foreign Exchange Market 668
The Exchange Rate 670
Balance of Payments 672
In Summary 674
Questions for Study and Analysis 674
Review Glossary 675

UNIT 14.3 · ECONOMIC GROWTH 676

The Nature of Economic Growth 676
The Sources of Economic Growth 677
The Costs of Economic Growth 681
In Summary 683
Questions for Study and Analysis 683
Review Glossary 684

UNIT 14.4 · ECONOMIC DEVELOPMENT 685

The Nature of Economic Development 685
Economic Development Throughout the World 685
Problems of LDCs 686
Policies for LDCs 691
In Summary 692
Questions for Study and Analysis 693
Review Glossary 693

SECTION INQUIRY: THE THIRD WORLD DEBT 694

Questions for Discussion 694

SECTION 15 · ALTERNATIVE ECONOMIC SYSTEMS 695

UNIT 15.1 · AN INTRODUCTION TO ECONOMIC SYSTEMS 696

Two Characteristics of Economic Systems 696
Three Alternative Economic Systems 697
Other Considerations 698
The Convergence Hypothesis 700
In Summary 701
Questions for Study and Analysis 702
Review Glossary 702

UNIT 15.2 · MARXIAN ECONOMICS 703

The Background of Marxian Economics 703
Marx's View of the World 704
Marx's Economic Theory 705
An Evaluation of Marxian Economics 707
In Summary 707
Questions for Study and Analysis 708
Review Glossary 708

UNIT 15.3 · THE SOVIET ECONOMY 709

The Background of the Soviet Economy 709
The Structure of the Soviet Economy 711
An Evaluation of the Soviet Economy 713
In Summary 716
Questions for Study and Analysis 717
Review Glossary 717

UNIT 15.4 · THE CHINESE ECONOMY 718

The Background of the Chinese Economy 718
The Structure of the Chinese Economy 720
An Evaluation of the Chinese Economy 721
In Summary 724
Questions for Study and Analysis 724
Review Glossary 725

SECTION INQUIRY: MARKET SOCIALISM IN YUGOSLAVIA 725

Questions for Discussion 726

ANSWERS TO SELECTED QUESTIONS 727

GLOSSARY / INDEX 753

Preface

Like everyone in high school, I took standard science courses in biology, chemistry, and physics. I enjoyed these courses, but I understood very little about the hows and whys of science. They became clear to me when I later discovered the writings of Isaac Asimov, the noted science fiction author. Not only is Isaac Asimov a master at writing science *fiction* but he is also a master at explaining science *fact*. What I admired most about his writing was his ability to explain extremely complex scientific facts and theories in a simple, straightforward manner.

Unfortunately, Isaac Asimov does not write about economics. In college I learned the discipline by working my way through economic principles with very little help from the textbook. As an instructor, I have found it difficult to teach economics from the textbooks currently available. Many books are well written but are constructed in a way that imbeds the basic economic concepts and principles within news articles, "real world" examples, applications, cartoons, pro/con debates. . . . The list goes on.

I decided to write *Economics: Concepts, Analysis, and Applications* because I wanted a textbook that would cover the important content in depth but would do it in a simple and straightforward manner. I constructed this text with a purposeful sequencing of topics within a standard organization so that the relationships between fundamental concepts and economic analysis and applications are clearer and more helpful to students.

APPROACH

To understand economic theory and the operation of the economy, students first need to grasp and comprehend fully the fundamental economic principles. These principles, made up of individual concepts and their relationships, form the building blocks of theory. Only when the conceptual tools have been learned and understood can students begin to use theory to analyze economic problems and issues.

With this fact in mind, *Economics: Concepts, Analysis, and Applications* was written using a slightly altered structure. The text is composed of units of material grouped by theme into fifteen sections. For example, the units dealing with consumer behavior, utility, and indifference curves appear in Section 7, A Closer Look at Demand. Each section begins with units that clearly *identify* and *explain* basic economic concepts, such as demand, supply, consumption, production, and monopoly. Once students have a firm grasp of the basic concepts, they can undertake units of material dealing with standard economic *analysis*, such as determining market equilibrium and examining the aggregate market. And they can *apply* the concepts to important issues in the economy, such as those presented in the units on agricultural production and health care.

CONTENT

This particular structuring of the content is pedagogically advantageous because it provides for increased flexibility without really deviating from the standard organization of a principles course or sacrificing depth of coverage. I have striven to be eclectic and balanced in the presentation of topics while demonstrating to students the nature of theory and its role in economics.

Introduction

Part I of *Economics: Concepts, Analysis, and Applications* is an introduction to the basic conceptual tools of general economic analysis, such as scarcity, demand, supply, and equilibrium. Unit 1.4, Graphs and Economics, illustrates how graphs are used to represent important economic concepts and shows how graphs that are technically correct can be misused in the representation of economic concepts.

The concept of elasticity is also introduced in Part I, providing a complete and thorough explanation of the mechanisms of the market before the presentation of microeconomic theory *or* macroeconomic theory. Presenting and analyzing elasticity in Section 2, The Market, in addition to the concepts of scarcity, demand, supply, and equilibrium, makes the discussion of the market in *Economics: Concepts, Analysis, and Applications* the most comprehensive available.

Macroeconomics

The basic concepts of macroeconomics, such as national production, unemployment, inflation, consumption, investment, and the multiplier, are presented in Part II. The circular flow model is used to introduce and integrate these and other important macroeconomic concepts by building upon the simplest possible circular flow model—two sectors, two markets—and adding additional markets and sectors throughout Part II. The simple circular flow provides a foundation on which to build more complex and realistic models of the macro economy.

Part II examines the Keynesian theory of aggregate demand in Section 4, Keynesian Economics, and the monetarist theory in Section 5, Money. I have also included discussions of more current theories, such as supply-side economics and rational expectations, in Section 6, A Closer Look at Inflation, to enhance the presentation of standard economic theory. This section centers around the youth of the aggregate-demand, aggregate-supply model.

Microeconomics

Parts III and IV introduce the basics of microeconomics: output and resource markets. These sections cover consumer behavior, utility, production, monopoly, competition, and factor market equilibrium. A simple, intuitive example is used to explain indifference curve analysis in a way students can understand, making the overall discussion of consumer demand more interesting and pertinent. Part IV includes one of the most comprehensive examinations of factor markets and factor payments currently available. I have also included many timely applications, such as problems in the supply of agricultural goods and market power in the health care industry.

Special Topics

Part V builds upon concepts, principles, and analyses from the first four parts to analyze important issues and problems, such as the role of public choice in government decision making, the pros and cons of government regulation, recent energy problems, and the move by the Chinese economy toward a greater reliance on the market.

LEARNING AIDS

Economics: Concepts, Analysis, and Applications contains several elements designed to enhance learning.

Part and Section Introductions

Each of the five major parts of the book begins with an introduction that places economics in a broad historical and political perspective. The section introductions are also an important feature of the text because they preview the material contained within each section and illustrate how the individual units work together.

Graphs, Figures, and Tables

All graphs, figures, and tables provide students with a quick, concise review of the material through clear, detailed captions tied specifically to key points in the text. Special care was taken to make sure that the graphs are clear, concise, and informative.

Summaries

End-of-unit summaries highlight pertinent definitions and explanations and provide students with another means of reviewing the material.

Questions for Study and Analysis

More than four hundred questions for study and analysis appear at the ends of the units. These questions encourage students to test their comprehension of the basic concepts. Many questions are analytical and applied in nature. Answers to selected questions appear at the end of the book.

Section Inquiries

Each section ends with a timely, multipart problem that requires students to use the conceptual tools learned within the section to actually *do* economic analysis.

Glossary/Index

The comprehensive glossary/index at the end of the book provides definitions and references for all key terms.

SUPPLEMENTS

Economics: Concepts, Analysis, and Applications is the centerpiece of a complete package designed to help instructors teach and students learn economics effectively. This package includes:

- Student Guide
- Instructor's Resource Manual
- Transparency Masters
- Test Items
- Computerized Test Bank

Student Guide

The Student Guide was prepared by Dr. Edward O. Price of Oklahoma State University and myself. It is organized by units that correspond to the text and contains a number of features making it particularly useful. Each unit of the Student Guide contains a brief outline, matching exercises, multiple-choice questions, and true-false questions. The Student Guide also parallels the text in its inclusion of two unique features—additional Questions for Study and Analysis at the end of each unit and more Section Inquiries.

Instructor's Resource Manual/Transparency Masters

The Instructor's Resource Manual was written with one idea in mind—to reduce instructors' preparation time as much as possible. Its organization parallels that of the text and includes a section overview, a brief statement about unit organization, a description of the unit's main objective, unit highlights, an outline of the unit, answers to all of the Questions for Study and Analysis that appear in the text, and answers to the Section Inquiries. Transparency Masters are also available upon adoption.

Test Items and Wadsworth Testing Service

Approximately 2000 test items, keyed to units of material, have been written. Test items include drill and practice problems and questions requiring analysis. The test items are available on diskette (IBM PC, Apple II series) or on a mainframe tape. You can select from the data bank of test items, edit any of these items, add any of your own items, and print out reproduction-ready tests in as many versions as you want. The program also allows you to construct your own tests and store your questions by unit and by question type (drill or concept).

ACKNOWLEDGMENTS

In closing, there are several people I'd like to thank for providing valuable assistance and contributions during the preparation of this text. At the top of the list is Stephanie Surfus, economics editor, who never lost her enthusiasm for the project. I would also like to thank a score of other people at Wadsworth who took a large stack of manuscript pages and turned it into a first-class text, especially Sandra Craig, the production editor, who put the manuscript together, MaryEllen Podgorski, who designed the book, Judith McKibben, who provided welcome comments, and Marty Kongsle, who coordinated the art program.

I would like to thank my colleague, Ed Price, for preparing the Student Guide and giving insightful comments, criticisms, and feedback on the project from the beginning. Several other members of the Oklahoma State University economics department provided welcome comments and encouragement, especially John Rea, Kent Olson, and Keith Willet. The contribution of hundreds of students in my introductory classes must also be acknowledged.

Even with the assistance of so many people, this text was possible only through the patience and understanding of my wife, Pam, and our two children, Christopher and Holly.

And finally, I would like to thank the following reviewers for their valuable assistance in developing *Economics: Concepts, Analysis, and Applications:*

Torben Andersen, Red Deer College; Marirose Arendale, Chattanooga State Technical Community College; Daniel Christiansen, Albion College; Paul Grimes, Western Illinois University; Yoseph Gutema, San Francisco State University; John W. Hambleton, San Diego State University; Rick Hansen, University of Northern Iowa; James Horner, Cameron University; Parviz Jenab, West Virginia University; Glenn Knowles, University of Wisconsin; Jim Love, Valdosta State College; Herb Milikien, American River College; Rahmat Mozayan, Monmouth College; Martin Perline, Wichita State University; Leonard Peterson, Lansing Community College; Rex Pulley, Arkansas State University; Michael Rendich, Westchester Community College; Lawrence G. Smith, Grossmont College; Steve Smith, Rose State College; Abdol Soofi, University of Wisconsin; Allan Stone, Southwest Missouri State University; Robert Thomas, Iowa State University; Gordon Weil, Wheaton College; Nan Wilson, Johnson County Community College; Ernest Zampelli, University of Maryland.

Orley M. Amos, Jr.

PART I

Introduction

In the beginning there were neither economists, economic textbooks, nor economic classes. However, the subject matter studied in economics has been around as long as humanity has consciously thought about its next meal. In fact, the first "economic concept" entered a human mind even before fire was discovered, for example, when cave dwellers realized that it was easier to hunt with spears than with bare hands. In modern terminology the cave dwellers recognized that hunting productivity could be increased by using part of their labor to produce capital goods (spears) instead of spending all of their time producing consumer goods (meat from the hunt). As we will see throughout this text, economics deals with many topics that relate to human existence.

While the *act* of switching labor from hunting to spear production was very important to the development of humanity, the *economic concept* underlying the act (that productivity could be increased by shifting labor from the production of consumer goods to capital goods) was even more important. For instance, fishing productivity could be increased by using labor to make nets and boats, and farming productivity could be increased by using labor to make plows.

Economic concepts and principles always have been, and always will be, an integral part of our life. While the historical origin of economic concepts is difficult to pinpoint, we can single out 1776 as the time in which the modern study of economic concepts began. In the same year that Thomas Jefferson and Benjamin Franklin signed the Declaration of Independence in Philadelphia, Adam Smith (1723–1790), a professor of logic and moral philosophy at the University of Glasgow in Scotland, published *The Nature and Causes of the Wealth of Nations*. Because *The Wealth of Nations* was the first book to bring the wide range of economic concepts and principles affecting human activity together into a single volume, it is considered the cornerstone of modern economics.

In Part I of this text we examine several of the most important and fundamental concepts in economics, concepts first discovered by cave dwellers as they fought each day for existence, and later discussed by Adam Smith in *The Wealth of Nations*. Indeed you have probably come face to face with most of the concepts in your life, though the terminology of economics may be new. In fact, we might even say that some of the concepts represent nothing more than plain common sense.

But if economic concepts are simply common sense, why do we bother studying what we already know? Because while the concepts may be obvious, as a part of our daily lives, the consequences of applying them may not be.

Let's illustrate this point with a concept from physics, gravity. From infancy we know that objects fall to the earth. We may not know *what* this concept is until we study physics, but we certainly know *how* it works. However, apples falling from trees is merely the tip of the iceberg. The study of physics suggests that gravity is only one part of the interaction between matter, energy, and time. Understanding gravity helps us to undertake flights to the moon, calculate the beginning of the universe, and develop nuclear weapons. The same is true for economic concepts. We may know that people buy fewer goods if the price goes up. But this simple concept also helps us understand why people are unemployed, why inflation occurs, and why one country exchanges goods with another.

Later, in Parts II through V of this text, we delve into the more complex consequences of applying basic economic concepts. However, in Part I our primary goal is to understand these basic concepts and the accompanying terminology, a first and necessary step in the study of economics.

SECTION 1

Basic Economic Concepts

In this section we are introduced to many fundamental concepts that underlie the study of economics. Like any other subject, economics relies on its own set of terms and concepts and views things differently from other academic disciplines. That is, economists look at the world from a different perspective and explain it in a different language than sociologists, biologists, or philosophers. And when we are finished with Section 1 we will have a basic understanding of the nature of economics and how economists view our world.

Unit 1.1, An Introduction to Economics, gives us our first taste of economics and the subject matter it studies. This unit answers three questions that must be addressed any time a new subject is studied: What is it? Why is it studied? How is it studied? The answers to these three questions provide respectively a definition of economics, a preview of the types of topics studied in economics, and the nature of economics as a social science.

Unit 1.2, The Economic Problem of Scarcity, introduces the basic problem of scarcity facing societies in the past, present, and future. Scarcity occurs because people have unlimited wants, yet the resources used to satisfy those wants are limited. In this unit we learn about the four basic factors of production: labor, capital, land, and entrepreneurship.

Unit 1.3, The Mixed Economy, takes a brief look at the U.S. economy. In this unit, we see that the U.S. economy, like all other economies in the world, is a mixed economy, an economy resulting from a combination of individual decisions in markets and collective decisions by the government used to determine the employment of the economy's limited resources.

Unit 1.4, Graphs and Economics, illustrates how graphs are used to represent important economic concepts. Furthermore we see how graphs that are technically correct can be misused in the representation of economic concepts. Since this unit presents basic information concerning graphs, it can either be used for review or omitted if you are familiar with the topic.

Unit 1.5, The Economy's Production Possibilities, presents us with our first example of economic analysis, unlike the first four units, which merely introduce many important concepts. In this unit we see how limited resources, discussed in Unit 1.2, lead to the limited production of goods and services. In addition we see that limited production is the basis for the concept of cost used throughout our study of economics.

UNIT 1.1

An Introduction to Economics

Economic topics receive daily coverage on television and in the newspapers. The topics range from wheat production and the price of bread to the federal deficit and its effect on the future price of gold. More often than not the topics seem complicated and confusing. However, the topics are much like a lock without the key; once we have the key, the lock is easily opened. The purpose of this text is to present the key to these economic topics. This unit provides a definition of economics, suggests a few reasons why the study of economics is important, and indicates how the subject matter is structured. But first, to get a sense of the types of issues to be discussed, let's look at five general economic topics that have been in the news in recent years and ask a few questions about them.

- In the 1970s the price per gallon of gasoline tripled, from 40¢ to over $1.20. But during the first half of the 1980s the price per unit of personal computers declined, from about $3,000 to under $1,000. What in particular caused these price changes, and what in general determines the price of any good?

- During the early 1980s the unemployment rate was over 10 percent, the highest it had been since the Depression of the 1930s, and the economy was in one of the worst recessions since the Second World War. In fact, it seems that every four or five years the U.S. economy takes a downturn and the unemployment rate takes an upturn. Why does the economy continue to experience these frequent but irregular fluctuations, and what can be done about them?

- On January 1, 1984, after a ten-year court battle, AT&T was officially broken up by the federal government from one large company into several smaller companies. Why was AT&T the only supplier of telephone services in the economy, how is the allocation of resources affected with a single producer in a given market, and why did the government want to break up AT&T?

- Every few months we hear that negotiations between a labor union and management are at a standstill. A labor union official invariably says that the union doesn't want to go on strike but it will if necessary. The first half of the 1980s was marked by several notable strikes, including air traffic controllers and professional football players. Why do labor unions go out on strike, and how does this affect the allocation of resources?

- About once a week on the nightly newscast and in most major newspapers we hear or read about the exchange rates between the U.S. dollar and any number of foreign currencies. What are these exchange rates, how are they determined, and how do they relate to the growing interdependence of economies throughout the world?

WHAT IS ECONOMICS?

Before we answer these questions we need to look more closely at the specific nature of economics. In particular we want to ask what any beginning student should ask: What is economics? Perhaps the best way to answer this question is with a formal definition.

Economics Defined

Economics is a social science that studies the allocation of resources to the production of goods and services used to satisfy consumers' unlimited wants.

In a sense we could say that economics studies the problem of **scarcity,** a condition that exists when there is an insufficient quantity of resources to produce all of the goods desired by people. We examine scarcity in more detail in the next unit, but at this point think of scarcity as meaning that society just does not have enough of *everything* for *everybody*. And economics studies what we do about this problem.

To put this definition of economics into perspective, let's examine its three aspects—social science, allocation, and consumer satisfaction—to give us insight into the basic nature of economics.

Social Science Economics, like sociology and political science, studies the social relationship of individuals. And as a science economics represents an abstract way of looking at society. In its abstraction economics identifies concepts and principles that govern economic behavior in society, in the same way that astronomy, as a science, identifies the laws that govern planetary bodies.

But unlike other social sciences, the primary focus of economics is on that part of society called the economy. An **economy** is a system of production, distribution, and consumption of goods and services. In the complex U.S. economy businesses and firms employ millions of workers, billions of dollars worth of factories and equipment, and countless tons of raw materials in the production of goods and services. These **resources,** the materials available to an economy for the production of goods and services, are used to produce over $4 trillion worth of goods and services, which are ultimately distributed to over 230 million people. Economics is concerned with how the economy organizes the production and distribution of these resources and goods.

Allocation Allocation is the process of distributing resources for the production of the goods and services, and of distributing goods and services for consumer use. Economics wants to know why and how resources are allocated to the production of some goods and not others. It also wants to know why and how goods and services are allocated to some people and not others. Although problems in production and allocation, such as labor strikes, transportation tie-ups, or raw material shortages, often make newspaper headlines, we should note that the economy operates smoothly most of the time. While we are certainly interested in the various problems of allocation that make the headlines, we should be equally interested in determining why the economy runs smoothly the rest of the time. If we know why it works as well as why it doesn't, then we are better able to prevent these problems of allocation.

In studying economics we want to know what governs the production decisions for a business, for example, why it decides to use more equipment and fewer workers. We also want to know what governs the distribution of goods that are produced, for example, why some consumers drive Cadillacs and live on spacious estates, while others ride buses and live in rat-infested slums.

Underlying the allocation of resources and goods is the need for choices. If a resource is used to produce one good, it cannot be used to produce another. Moreover, goods that are purchased and consumed by one person cannot be consumed by another. Because consumers have limited incomes, they have to make a choice between buying one good or another. Similarly, businesses have to determine the best way to divide their limited expenditures among labor, advertising, and factory construction. Even governments have to decide how to spend their limited tax revenues on a wide assortment of public goods.

Consumer Satisfaction Economics is ultimately concerned with the satisfaction of consumers. The production and allocation of goods and resources is not an end unto itself. The ultimate goal of an economy is to provide its members with goods and services to satisfy their wants and needs. The better the economy performs this function, the closer the allocation process is to being efficient. The key word in economics is **efficiency,** which is simply the process of obtaining the highest level of consumer satisfaction from the available resources. If resources are allocated such that one consumer cannot have more satisfaction without reducing the satisfaction of another consumer, then the economy is efficient.

Macroeconomics and Microeconomics

Economics is divided into two branches: macroeconomics and microeconomics. **Macroeconomics is the branch of economics that studies the entire economy.** If we are concerned about the overall level of production in an economy, the average level of prices, or the total number of workers that are unemployed, then we are dealing with macroeconomics. **Microeconomics is the branch of economics that studies parts of the economy.** If we want to know what determines the price of gasoline, the surplus of wheat, or the proportion of income a family spends on medical care, then we are dealing with microeconomics.

The difference between macroeconomics and microeconomics can be illustrated by a simple analogy. Macroeconomics is much like a puzzle; the more pieces that we obtain, understand, and set in place, the better we will be able to comprehend the puzzle as a whole. Microeconomics is analogous to a tree rather than a puzzle. In microeconomics we study a limited number of very important concepts, which represent the trunk of the tree. And then we apply these concepts to various aspects of life as symbolized by the numerous branches of the tree.

While macroeconomics studies the entire economy and microeconomics studies only parts of it, there is a great deal of overlap. The operation of the overall economy depends on the operation of separate parts of the economy, so these parts cannot be studied in isolation. The total output in the economy is based on the decisions of thousands of businesses throughout the United States. Conversely, individual decisions are based in part on the activity of the entire economy.

UNIT 1.1 • AN INTRODUCTION TO ECONOMICS

WHY DO WE STUDY ECONOMICS?

The study of economics can help explain the five economic topics and accompanying questions listed at the beginning of this unit. Let's look at each topic individually and relate it to the study of economics. In Part I, Introduction (in particular Section 2), we learn how the price of a good is determined. The price of gasoline increased in the 1970s because OPEC (the Organization of Petroleum Exporting Countries) raised the price of crude petroleum, which increased the cost of refining gasoline and caused sellers to charge a higher price. But the price of personal computers declined because advances in technology made them less expensive to produce, so that sellers were willing to charge a lower price.

In Part II, Macroeconomics: The National Economy, we see that the national economy fluctuates because households, businesses, and government increase or decrease the amount of goods that they buy. If fewer goods are being sold, producers need fewer workers, and unemployment goes up.

Part III, Microeconomics: Output Markets, explains why AT&T was broken up from one large company into several smaller ones. As a single producer of telephone services AT&T had a great deal of control over prices. By breaking up AT&T the government was trying to increase the amount of competition in this industry and consequently reduce prices paid by anyone using telephone services.

Part IV, Microeconomics: Resource Markets, discusses the importance of labor as a resource in the production of goods and services. Moreover, we see that labor unions are organizations of groups of workers, the union's main purpose being to increase the price of this resource. If the union doesn't get the price it is asking, then it might decide to go on strike; in other words, it might refuse to sell any labor at the existing price. But if labor stops producing goods, then fewer goods are available for consumer satisfaction.

In Part V, Selected Topics in Economics, we learn how exchange rates are determined and how they affect the relationship between economies throughout the world. Changes in exchange rates affect the amount of goods that are produced in the United States and sold to other countries, and the amount of goods that are produced in other countries and sold in the United States. On the one hand, the more goods we produce in the United States, the more employment we have. On the other hand, if consumers in the United States have more goods available from other countries, then they are likely to be more satisfied because of the greater variety.

Economics studies many topics that are important to our daily lives. As consumers we are concerned about inflation and prices. As employees and employers we are concerned about wages, salaries, and unemployment. As taxpayers we are concerned about government spending and budget deficits. Each of these topics is better understood through the study of economics. And as we understand economics we can make more informed decisions as consumers, employees, employers, and taxpayers.

The impact of economics on our everyday lives is often as obvious as paying more for gasoline or telephone services. However, the impact also can be subtle and indirect. For example, how will exchange rates influence consumer satisfaction, and what effect will a labor union strike in the rubber industry have on the availability of automobiles? Economics can help us understand why the airline industry was deregulated, or why trading with Japan is important. The first step in eliminating economic problems such as unemployment or inflation is to understand them.

HOW DO WE STUDY ECONOMICS?

As a social science, economics isolates principles that explain the behavior of people and society—purchases by consumers, production by firms, even the overall operation of the economy. For example, economics tries to explain why consumers buy more beef at a lower price, or alternatively why farmers grow more wheat at a higher price.

Theory

To explain the behavior of people and society, economic principles are combined into theories. A **theory** is a set of general principles used to explain activity in the world. In astronomy the law of gravity is a principle that explains planetary activity. In chemistry the laws of thermodynamics are principles that explain molecular activity. For instance, the Theory of Relativity in physics constitutes a set of principles that explain a wide range of activity. While each principle by itself deals with only a small piece of the world, the combination of several principles forms a larger theory.

However, we should note that theories are merely tools, or abstractions, to help us understand the world. Principles and theories are abstractions because they are incomplete representations of the world. An economic theory does not try, nor does it need, to explain *every* aspect of economic activity. For example, Keynesian macroeconomic theory deals with the *overall* performance of the economy, including production and unemployment. It does not try to explain why a General Motors factory in Kansas City decides to produce five thousand station wagons rather than three thousand convertibles, or why you have a job but your neighbor is unemployed. These types of details are not considered within the Keynesian macroeconomic theory because the theory would become so bogged down by detail that it would become meaningless.

Economic theories, like all scientific theories, resemble road maps. A road map represents an abstraction of the world, effectively guiding a motorist from one city to the next. A motorist does not want a map that is a *complete* representation of the world, that contains every tree and bush along the highway; this level of detail is unnecessary. In the same way that a road map identifies the major highways, economic theory identifies the main principles of economic activity. We use economics as a road map guiding us through the economy. But don't expect a complete, detailed description of the world, only the highlights.

Hypotheses

Economic theories are developed through a continual process of trial and error. Economists have spent a great deal of time determining if particular principles actually explain activities in the world. The day-to-day function of science is to test its theories. And this function is accomplished through the use of hypotheses. A **hypothesis** is a prediction obtained directly from a theory that can be compared with observations in the real world. A hypothesis is derived from economic principles that make up the economic theory. Usually it takes the form of "If A happens, then B also happens." For example, a hypothesis might be "If tuition increases, fewer students will go to college." This hypothesis can be tested by looking at tuition and the number of students going to college. If fewer students go to college when tuition has increased, then the hypothesis is supported.

Ceteris Paribus

The process of testing hypotheses necessarily employs what is called the *ceteris paribus* assumption. ***Ceteris paribus*** is a Latin phrase meaning that all other factors are held unchanged. To test the hypothesis "If A happens, then B also happens," we need to be sure that A is the *only* factor that *can* cause B to happen. Suppose tuition has increased and college enrollment has declined. Does this necessarily mean that the higher tuition has caused the decline in enrollment? If other relevant factors have also changed, then we don't know for certain that higher tuition is responsible for the decline. For example, a decrease in government support for colleges may mean fewer courses are offered, which might discourage some students from enrolling. Likewise, the decline in enrollment might result from a decline in the number of people in the college-age bracket.

In addition, if overall employment in the economy has increased, many potential college students may have decided to work rather than go to school.

Without using the *ceteris paribus* assumption, which holds these other factors unchanged, it would be impossible to determine if tuition *alone* has caused a decline in enrollment. In laboratory sciences such as chemistry and physics it is usually possible to perform experiments that specifically hold all of the other factors unchanged. However, in economics and other social sciences we cannot easily perform laboratory-type experiments. To test hypotheses, economists have to use whatever information happens to be available.

Principles

All economic principles begin as hypotheses. An **economic principle** is a hypothesis that has been tested many times and that consistently agrees with the real world. Once a hypothesis becomes accepted as an economic principle, it is added to the original economic theory, thus creating a new and expanded theory that better explains activity in the world. This process of testing hypotheses, establishing principles, and expanding the theory is a constant and ongoing process. Even as we study economics in this unit, economists are expanding and modifying economic theories and principles. However, for the most part the adjustments are minor. The economic principles we study in this textbook are well founded and have been tested and confirmed many times over the past two hundred years.

Positive and Normative Economics

This process of testing hypotheses with observations of the real world comes under the heading of positive economics. **Positive economics** is a branch of economics that tries to explain the way the economy actually operates. But economists do not spend all of their time testing hypotheses; some is spent practicing normative economics. **Normative economics** is a branch of economics that states the way the economy should operate. That is, part of economics is aimed at improving the world in general and the economy in particular. However, an important aspect of normative economics is that it is based on the specific values, beliefs, or norms of the person trying to "improve" the world. To some people an action may be an improvement, while to others it may not be.

For example, if you say, "The quantity of health care services demanded will increase if the price declines," then you are practicing positive economics. This statement can be tested against the activity in the real world and refuted by observation. But if you say, "The price of health care services should be reduced," then you are practicing normative economics. Whether the price of health care services should or should not be reduced is based on a value judgment. Reduction of health care prices must be based on some criterion. Is the criterion related to the performance of the economy? Or is it based on the value judgment that doctors are too rich? Without knowing the criterion you cannot properly decide what should be done with health care prices.

A positive statement can be proved right or wrong. But a normative statement can be argued over for generations. Two well-trained and highly respected economists can disagree over whether health care prices are too high. And neither is necessarily right or wrong, because their positions are based on their beliefs and values.

THE ECONOMIST'S VIEW OF THE WORLD

To close this introductory unit, let's consider the economist's view of the world. Economics is as much a way of looking at the world as it is a well-defined set of theories and principles. Our study of economics will show us that almost everything that happens in the world has both good and bad effects, or *benefits* and *costs*. In some cases, the benefits are clearly defined and self-evident, but the costs are hidden. In other cases, the inverse is true. Knowing this fundamental fact of life, the obligation of an economist is to identify and weigh the benefits and the costs of any action.

Another important part of the economist's view of the world is the *marginal* nature of the decisions people make. For example, producers usually don't decide between producing five thousand units of a good or none at all, they decide whether to produce one additional unit. By the same token, consumers decide what to do with the extra dollar remaining at the end of the month, or whether to purchase one more loaf of bread. An economist is typically concerned with the benefits and costs of *one additional* unit of production, *one additional* dollar of income, or *one additional* loaf of bread rather than the total amount of a firm's production, a consumer's total income, or the total amount of bread purchased. Obviously the total amounts are important, but the *marginal* amounts are where the choices lie.

Economists are also concerned with *economic policies* designed to improve the economy or society or both. Using economic principles and theories, economists make policy evaluations for the government. The evaluations are *positive* in nature, as when economists state the likely outcome of a proposed action by the government. For example, if the government proposes a higher tax on automobiles imported from Japan, then economists could indicate how and why the price of automobiles would be affected. However, economists often make recommendations that are *normative* in nature, as when economists suggest what *should* be done based on some particular criterion. For example, economists might recommend a higher tax on imported automobiles, believing that it is better to have more domestic production of automobiles and fewer imports. Throughout this text we find that much of our discussion centers around economic policies.

And finally we should note that economists are often grouped into different *schools of thought*, which can affect their policy recommendations. While economists agree with the majority of the principles and theories we examine in this text,

there are also areas of disagreement. Often the disagreement centers on which principles and theories are most important in explaining the operation of the economy. Economists who adhere to one set of principles and theories are often grouped into a school of thought, while those who adhere to another set are separated into another school. Two important schools of thought we encounter in our study of macroeconomics are Keynesian economics and monetarism. Often these schools of thought recommend different, often opposing, economic policies. These different views not only generate lively debate but also test the underlying economic principles and help us better understand the actual operation of the economy.

IN SUMMARY
An Introduction to Economics

- Economics is a social science that studies the way society allocates its available resources in the production of goods and services consumed by people. Economics, and the subject matter of economics, touches our lives daily. If we shop for groceries, go to work, or pay taxes, economics can help us to better understand our world.

- Macroeconomics is the study of the entire economy. Microeconomics is the study of parts of the economy. While they view the economy from different perspectives, both are important.

- Scientific theories are used to explain economic activity in the world. The theories consist of sets of economic principles that abstract from the real world, similar to the way a road map abstracts from the world. A principle is obtained by continuously testing a hypothesis to see if it corresponds to activity in the world.

- Positive economics describes the way the world actually operates, and normative economics suggests how the world should operate. Positive economics is based on testable hypotheses, which can be proved false. Normative economics is based on an individual's values, which cannot be proved either right or wrong.

- The economist seeks to identify the benefits and costs of any activity. Since marginal changes in benefits and costs from an activity are the basis for most choices, such changes tend to attract the economist's attention. Economists also use economic theories to recommend policies to the government.

QUESTIONS FOR STUDY AND ANALYSIS

1. Explain why an economist would be more interested in studying the price of butter than the distribution of votes cast in the last election.

2. Discuss three ways that you think economics can benefit you in the future.

3. Suppose you are given the following economic principles:
   a. "If consumers receive additional income, they spend more on goods and services."
   b. "If businesses build more factories, consumers will receive more income."
   c. "If the interest rate increases, businesses will build fewer factories."
   From these three principles, derive a hypothesis relating consumer spending on goods and services to the interest rate. The hypothesis should take this form: "If the interest rate increases, then consumer spending will . . ."

4. What *ceteris paribus* problems might be encountered if you tried to test this hypothesis: "A student who attends class more often will receive a higher grade."

5. Explain why this statement would fall under the heading of positive economics: "The price of oranges will increase if the federal deficit is eliminated."

6. Explain why this statement would fall under the heading of normative economics: "The price of oranges is too high." Would an orange buyer view this statement differently than an orange grower would? Explain.

REVIEW GLOSSARY

allocation The process of distributing resources for the production of goods and services, and of distributing goods and services for consumer use.

ceteris paribus A Latin phrase meaning that all other factors are held unchanged. The *ceteris paribus* assumption is used to isolate the effect one economic factor has on another. Without this assumption it would be difficult to determine cause and effect in the economy.

economic principle A hypothesis that has been tested many times and that consistently agrees with the real world.

economics A social science that studies the allocation of resources to the production of goods and services used to satisfy consumers' unlimited wants and needs. As a social science economics studies the social relationship of individuals. But unlike other social sciences, economics concentrates its study on the economy.

economy A system of production, distribution, and consumption of goods and services.

efficiency The process of obtaining the highest level of consumer satisfaction from the available resources.

hypothesis A prediction obtained directly from a theory that can be compared with observations in the real world. Hypotheses usually take the form "If A, then also B."

macroeconomics The branch of economics that studies the entire economy. Macroeconomics examines such topics as the total amount of output in the economy, the rate of inflation, and the number of unemployed workers.

microeconomics The branch of economics that studies parts of the economy. Microeconomics examines the individual consumers, businesses, and industries that make up the economy.

normative economics A branch of economics that states the way the economy should operate. A normative statement is based on values and cannot be proved right or wrong.

positive economics A branch of economics that tries to explain the way the economy actually operates. Positive economics is concerned with the process of testing hypotheses. A positive statement can be refuted by looking at the real world.

resources The materials available to an economy for the production of goods and services.

scarcity The condition that exists when there is an insufficient quantity of resources to produce all of the goods and services desired by people.

theory A set of general principles used to explain activity in the world. Economic theories abstract from the world in the same way a road map abstracts from the world. Both highlight important features and neither attempts total description.

UNIT 1.2

The Economic Problem of Scarcity

In this unit we look at scarcity—the economic problem. This problem occurs because human desires are virtually limitless in a world of limited means. More specifically <u>**scarcity** is the condition that exists when there is an insufficient quantity of resources to produce all of the goods desired by people</u>. Quite simply, this means there is not enough of *everything* for *everybody*. This problem has arisen in every past civilization, confronts every nation today, and will be encountered by all future societies.

Scarcity derives from the combination of limited resources and unlimited wants. If either resources are unlimited or demand for them is limited, then scarcity is not a problem. For example, if resources are *unlimited* and someone wants another good, then enough resources are always available to produce it. By the same token, if people have *limited* wants and needs, then they are soon satisfied, and scarcity will not exist.

In this unit we start with a detailed look at the two factors that lead to scarcity: limited resources and unlimited wants. Then we see how they combine to cause scarcity.

LIMITED RESOURCES AND GOODS

Let's begin our discussion of the economic problem with a look at resources. <u>**Resources** are the materials available to an economy for the production of goods and services</u>. At this point we should note the relationship between resources and goods and services. Goods and services are what people use to directly satisfy their wants; resources are used to produce those goods and services. The availability of goods and services is based on the availability of resources. With this in mind, let's distinguish between three related terms: limited resource (or good), scarce resource (or good), and free resource (or good).

Limited Resource (Good)

The first term that we want to identify is limited resource (good). A **limited resource (good)** is a resource (or good) that has a finite quantity. Clearly, most of the materials that we have on the planet are limited resources. And since the resources are limited, the goods produced from the resources are also limited. There is only so much soil, water, iron ore, petroleum, and oxygen, and only so many factories and people on this planet. And because of the limited resources, there are only so many typewriters, automobiles, potato chips, and digital watches that people can produce to satisfy their wants.

Scarce Resource (Good)

While limited resources and goods are important, we are more concerned about a subset of limited resources (goods) called scarce resources (goods). A **scarce resource (good)** is a resource (or good) with an available quantity less than its desired use. A limited resource or good becomes scarce if there is not enough of it to go around. A good is scarce if it is limited relative to the amount people directly need to satisfy their wants. A resource is scarce if it is limited relative to the amount people indirectly need in order to produce the goods and services that they directly use. For example, suppose that the number of students wanting to take a class such as computer programming in BASIC is greater than the classroom capacity. In this case the seats in the classroom are scarce goods, since there are not enough seats for everyone who would like to (or need to) take the class. And a resource such as iron ore is scarce if there is not enough of it to produce all of the automobiles and kitchen appliances that people need to directly satisfy their wants.

Free Resource (Good)

While almost all resources, and thus goods, are limited, they are not necessarily scarce. In fact a limited resource (good) can also be a free resource (good). A **free resource (good)** is a resource (or good) with an available quantity greater than its desired use. An uncongested park is an example of a free resource (good). On a cold January day, a park in North Dakota has enough space for everyone who wants to use it. Keep in mind that space in the park is as limited in January as it is on a warm Memorial Day weekend. However, with fewer people wanting to use the park, it becomes a free resource (good). For the most part *free resources (goods)* are literally *free of charge*. Since a free resource (good) is abundantly available, one person cannot sell it to another.

Another example of a free resource (good) is clean, fresh air in Wyoming. While clean air in the city of Los Angeles is rapidly becoming a scarce resource (good), because of pollution and smog, there is more than enough clean air for everyone in Wyoming. In many cases water is also an example of a free resource (good). While water is definitely a *scarce* resource (good) during the summer months in the Midwest, during the rainy spring months it is a *free* resource (good). The scarcity of a resource (good) depends on both availability and desirability.

Changes in Scarce Resources (Goods) over Time

A limited resource (good) is not necessarily a scarce resource (good). A scarce resource (good) depends on both availability and the amount desired. This point is illustrated by the fact that, over time, a free resource (good) can become a scarce resource (good), or vice versa.

In the early 1800s petroleum often bubbled to the surface of the Texas plains, but no one knew what to do with it. At that time the greatest modern-day use for petroleum, the automobile, had not been developed. The few uses people had for petroleum were more than satisfied by the amount available. In other words there was more than enough to go around, and petroleum was a free resource. However, the status of petroleum has clearly changed since the 1800s, and today it is a scarce resource. This change in status results not so much from its limited availability as from its increased use. But times can change. If a new form of transportation is developed tomorrow that does not use petroleum as a fuel, then petroleum could once again become a free resource.

FACTORS OF PRODUCTION

Another, more descriptive, term for resources is **factors of production,** which consist of four major categories of resources: labor, capital, land, and entrepreneurship.

To illustrate these four factors of production, let's look at a simple example. Suppose we want to build a computer. To do so we need the materials that comprise the computer itself. We need workers, technicians, and engineers to design and assemble it. We need tools and equipment to build with and buildings to work in. And we need someone to organize the operation and take the risk of getting production started. Each of these resources can be classified as one of the four factors of production.

Labor

The workers, technicians, and engineers who produce the computer are generally referred to as human labor. **Labor** is the human resource used to produce goods and services. From the production of agricultural products to telephone services, human labor plays a crucial role. As a factor of production, labor is not limited to workers and technicians, but also includes a wide range of human resources necessary to the production process, such as managers, accountants, secretaries, supervisors, and executives.

Capital

For computer production workers employ different types of tools and equipment, including other computers, complex and specialized machinery, buildings, and factories, all of which are referred to as capital. **Capital** is the synthetic resources used to produce goods and services. Capital does not occur naturally, but rather, like consumer goods and services, is produced by the four factors of production. For example, the screwdriver used to assemble a computer is itself produced by the four factors of production.

There is an important characteristic of capital that distinguishes it from raw materials. A capital good can be used over and over again in the production of goods, whereas raw materials become part of each specific good produced. Once a material, such as a screw, is used in one computer, it cannot be used in another. But a piece of capital, such as a screwdriver, can be used to produce many computers. The screw leaves the factory with the computer, the screwdriver does not.

An important distinction should also be made between physical and financial capital. When the term *capital* is used in economics, it refers to the physical, synthetic capital employed in the production of goods and services. The term *capital* as used in financial markets refers to financial assets, such as stocks and bonds. Although financial capital often implies ownership of physical capital, it need not. For example, corporate stock representing the ownership of a corporation actually reflects ownership of the corporation's physical capital. However, financial capital representing ownership of commodity futures does not reflect capital ownership.

Land

A third factor in the production of a computer includes a wide variety of materials, such as silicon, metals, plastics, and glass. These materials all have their origins with the land. **Land is the natural resource used to produce goods and services, including the land itself; the minerals and nutrients in the ground; the water, wildlife, and vegetation on the surface; and the air above**. Metals such as steel, aluminum, and copper are all processed and refined from mineral resources found in the land. Synthetic plastics are processed from petroleum found in the ground, or from agricultural commodities such as soybeans. Some land, like capital, can also be used over and over again in the production of goods. However, the important difference between land and capital is that capital is produced, while land is naturally occurring.

Entrepreneurship

The fourth factor of production, **entrepreneurship, is the specialized type of human resource that assumes the risk of combining the other three factors in the production of goods and services**. While entrepreneurs represent a type of labor, their function is important enough to the economy to warrant a separate discussion. Without someone to assume the responsibility and risk of bringing labor, capital, and land together, capital would be untapped, and labor and land would remain idle. For example, Steve Jobs and Steve Wozniak began production of Apple computers in a living room, bringing together labor, capital, and land factors and investing their time and money to produce microcomputers. If they had not taken the risk, and brought together the other factors, people would not be using Apple computers today.

Factors of Production in the United States

The United States has large quantities of all four factors of production, as Table 1.2.1 shows. While the total amount of labor in the United States is relatively easy to identify, the amount of capital, land, and entrepreneurship is not. Capital comes in many different forms. At best we can only identify the value of the capital, since any measure of quantity would be meaningless. Land is even more diverse than capital; moreover, most land is not valued. Entrepreneurship is the most difficult of the four to measure, and no attempt is even made to do so in Table 1.2.1. The problem is that a unit of labor today may be an entrepreneur tomorrow, and vice versa. However, let's look at some of the best measures of the factors of production that are available.

In 1985 the total labor force in the United States, the number of people willing and able to work, was 115 million people. The stock of capital in 1983 was valued at $9098 billion. Businesses owned $5921 billion worth, while government and households owned the other $3178 billion (primarily houses). Capital owned by businesses broke down into $1451 billion worth of equipment, $1634 billion worth of nonresidential structures (factories), and $2836 billion worth of residential structures (apartment buildings).

Land is a more difficult factor of production to quantify. While land contains a vast array of natural resources, the area of land can give us an indication of the quantity of this factor. The United States has 3.6 million square miles of surface area. This is divided into 3.5 million square miles of land area, and 79,481 square miles of water. The 3.5 million square miles of land area equals about 2264 million acres. Over half of this land, 1329 million acres, is owned by private individuals. Fifty-one million acres are owned by Indians. The rest is owned by various levels of government. The federal government owns 730 million acres, and state and local governments 155 million acres.

While the quantities of these factors are quite large, it is important to note that they are still limited. Moreover, for the most part they are also scarce, because they are used to produce goods and services for over 230 million people. This brings us to the last topic we want to discuss in this unit, unlimited wants.

Table 1.2.1

Factors of Production in the United States

This table indicates the quantities of labor, capital, and land available as factors of production of the U.S. economy. While there appears to be an abundance of each, they are limited, so that the quantity of output the economy can produce is also limited.

Factor	Quantity	
Labor		
Labor force (1985)	115	million people
Capital		
Net stocks (1983)		
Total	9098	billion dollars
Business	5921	"
Equipment	1451	"
Nonresidential	1634	"
Residential	2836	"
Government	2014	"
Households	1164	"
Land		
Total area (1980)	3.618	million square miles
Land	3.539	"
Water	79,481	square miles
Ownership (1982)		
Private	1329	million acres
Indian	51	"
Federal government	730	"
State and local governments	155	"

Sources: U.S. Bureau of the Census, *Statistical Abstract of the United States*, 1985; and U.S. Bureau of Economic Analysis, *Survey of Current Business*, February 1986.

UNLIMITED WANTS

In addition to limited resources, unlimited wants also cause the economic problem of scarcity. The 230 million people in the United States need food, clothing, and shelter in order to survive. However, even when they have these basic necessities, there is a wide, seemingly endless, range of additional goods that they would like to have, such as entertainment, sports cars, and vacations in the Bahamas. **Unlimited wants** is a characteristic of people such that they are never totally satisfied with the quantity and variety of goods and services. There is always *one* more good that a person would like to have. However, when that "one more good" is obtained, another one beckons.

If the world possessed the mythical horn of plenty, there would be no need for economics because everyone would have all that they desire. Unfortunately there is no horn of plenty, and we must produce any goods and services we desire from limited resources. Together, unlimited wants and limited resources create the economic problem of scarcity.

IN SUMMARY

The Economic Problem of Scarcity

- The economic problem of scarcity results from the combination of unlimited wants and limited resources. People have virtually unlimited desires for goods and services. However, the resources needed to produce the goods and services are limited.

- Resources are the materials available for the production of goods and services. Most resources, and thus the goods they produce, are limited. However, limited resources (goods) are scarce only if their quantity is less than the amount people want. Free resources (goods), on the other hand, are greater than the amount people want.

- Resources are also called factors of production and are divided into four categories: labor, capital, land, and entrepreneurship. Labor consists of the human resources, including workers, technicians, and managers, used to produce goods. Capital is the synthetic factor, including buildings, factories, machinery, and equipment. Land is the natural resources of the earth, such as air, water, and minerals, and the land itself. Entrepreneurship is the human resource that takes the risk of bringing the other three factors together.

- People are generally never fully satisfied with the available quantity and variety of goods and services. If people could be satisfied, scarcity would not be a problem.

QUESTIONS FOR STUDY AND ANALYSIS

1. Under what circumstances could scarcity and the economic problem be eliminated? Are these circumstances realistic?

2. The amount of sunshine falling anywhere on the earth is limited to at most twenty-four hours per day, yet it is a free good. Why is a limited good, such as sunshine, not necessarily a scarce good? Describe a situation in which sunshine would be a scarce good.

3. Explain why an acre of farmland in Illinois might be considered a capital good rather than a natural resource.

4. Why are the owners of the United States Football League teams entrepreneurs? Explain.

5. Some economists argue that there are only two factors of production—capital and natural resources. Capital is anything that is synthetic or manufactured, and natural resources are everything that is naturally occurring.
   a. With this division in mind, how would you categorize labor? Why?
   b. In which category would you place entrepreneurship? Why?

6. The production of a Hollywood movie includes many different resources. Give some specific examples of each of the four factors of production used to make a movie, and explain each selection.

REVIEW GLOSSARY

capital The synthetic resources used to produce goods and services. Capital is a factor of production that has been previously produced. In addition, capital does not become a part of the product, unlike other types of material items.

entrepreneurship The specialized type of human resource that assumes the risk of combining the other three factors in the production of a good.

factors of production The four basic factors used to produce goods in the economy are labor, capital, land, and entrepreneurship.

free resource (good) A resource (or good) with an available quantity greater than its desired use. Free resources or goods can be limited, but people want less than is available.

labor The human resources used to produce goods and services.

land The natural resource used to produce goods and services, including the land itself; the minerals and nutrients in the ground; the water, wildlife, and vegetation on the surface; and the air above.

limited resource (good) A resource (or good) that has a finite quantity.

resources The materials available to an economy for the production of goods and services.

scarce resource (good) A resource (or good) with an available quantity less than its desired use. All scarce resources and goods are also limited. However, a limited resource or good is scarce only if people want more than is available.

scarcity The condition that exists when there is an insufficient quantity of resources to produce all of the goods and services desired by people. The economic problem of scarcity has always faced humanity and always will.

unlimited wants A characteristic of people such that they are never totally satisfied with the quantity and variety of goods and services.

UNIT 1.3

The Mixed Economy

There are two basic methods of allocating resources and addressing the economic problem of scarcity. One method employs private markets, the second the government. Private markets are analyzed in detail in Section 2, The Market, and are the main focus of most of this text. The role played by the government in resource allocation pops up throughout the text, particularly in Section 12, Government and Allocation.

The U.S. economy relies primarily on private markets for resource allocation, but government resource allocation also plays a part. In fact most economies throughout the world are mixed economies, relying on a combination of markets and government for resource allocation. In this unit we look at mixed economies in general, and the degree of government involvement in the U.S. economy in particular. We examine not only how the government is involved in the economy but also why. First, let's see how markets and government allocate resources differently.

TWO METHODS OF RESOURCE ALLOCATION

As mentioned previously, the two basic methods of allocating resources are the market, which is extensively used in the United States, and the government, which is also used in the United States but is more predominant in other countries.

Markets

A **market** is the organized exchange of commodities (goods, services, or resources) between buyers and sellers, where each individual participant decides whether or not to engage in the exchange. For our purposes in this unit the most important aspect of allocation by markets is the individual decision. In the market each buyer decides whether he or she wants to buy the good at the existing price. Likewise, each seller decides whether he or she wants to sell the good at the existing price.

Resource allocation by markets also depends on individual decisions. Individual buyers determine which goods are produced based on which ones they are willing to buy. For example, suppose individuals decide that they would rather buy more rye bread and less wheat bread. This decision causes the economy to devote fewer resources to the production of wheat and more to the production of rye. Furthermore, decisions by individual suppliers help determine which resources are used to produce which goods. (In Section 7, A Closer Look at Demand and Section 8, A Closer Look at Supply, we see how the individual decisions are made.)

Government

A **government** is a political body exercising control and authority over a group of individuals. In the United States we have three distinct levels of government: federal, state, and local. At the federal level are all of the agencies and political bodies associated with the legislative, administrative, and judicial branches. At the state level are the governments for each of the fifty states. At the local level are municipal and county governing bodies.

The government can become involved in the allocation process in three ways. First, it can directly own and thus control the resources, as exemplified by government ownership of parks, universities, or public utilities. In each case the government decides how the resources are used, for example, leasing government-owned land to private companies for energy exploration. Second, the government can influence private markets through various laws and regulations, for example, prohibiting the production and exchange of a product such as a dangerous pesticide or nuclear weapons through markets.

Third, the government can affect resource allocation through its powers of taxation and spending. Since the government controls its tax revenues, it can influence resource allocation by purchasing goods private individuals would not purchase, for example, national defense or space exploration.

The government allocates resources by law. If the federal government decides to raise taxes and apply the revenue to defense spending, people have to pay the taxes, and thus indirectly purchase the defense goods. Herein lies the important difference between market and government allocation. With markets, if someone doesn't want to engage in the exchange, they usually don't have to unless a contract has been signed. With government allocation people are usually forced to engage in the exchange determined by the political authority, whether they want to or not, though in a democracy people have some control over the government.

Generally speaking, real world economies allocate resources by a combination of individual decisions in markets and command decisions by governments. All economies represent a mix of government and markets because, as we see at the end of this unit, there are five goals of a market economy that require some type of government involvement.

THE RANGE OF GOVERNMENT-MARKET ORIENTATION

All economies in the world today have goods allocated by some mixture of markets and government. The United States is an example of a predominately market-oriented economy, with a degree of government involvement. By contrast, the Soviet Union is an example of a government-dominated economy, with a small degree of market reliance.

Figure 1.3.1 shows the possible degree of government-market orientation. At the far left is the pure market economy. A **pure market economy** is an economy that relies exclusively on markets for the allocation of resources. There is *no* government in a pure market economy, not even to enforce

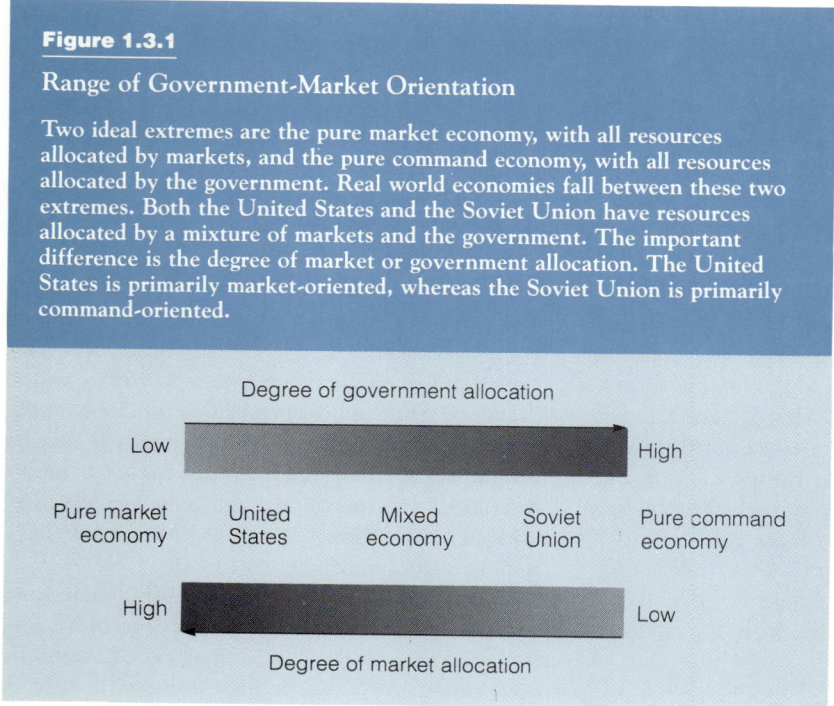

Figure 1.3.1

Range of Government-Market Orientation

Two ideal extremes are the pure market economy, with all resources allocated by markets, and the pure command economy, with all resources allocated by the government. Real world economies fall between these two extremes. Both the United States and the Soviet Union have resources allocated by a mixture of markets and the government. The important difference is the degree of market or government allocation. The United States is primarily market-oriented, whereas the Soviet Union is primarily command-oriented.

contracts between buyers and sellers. A pure market economy represents an ideal extreme rather than a realistic possibility. Real world economies that rely heavily on markets are *market-oriented economies,* not pure market economies.

At the far right of Figure 1.3.1 is the pure command economy. A **pure command economy** is **an economy that relies totally on the government to allocate all resources.** A pure command economy is also not a realistic possibility. In this type of economy the government decides on all phases of resource allocation. The government tells each person how much of every good they may consume, supervises every phase of the production process, and determines how much of each resource is used in producing each good.

All economies in the world fall somewhere between these two extremes, with a mixture of market and government allocation. A **mixed economy** **is an economy that relies on both markets and** government to allocate resources. The main difference among economies in the world is not whether resources are allocated by markets or government but rather to what degree each is involved. At the far right of Figure 1.3.1 lie the Soviet Union and most communist countries. At the far left lie the market-oriented economies of the United States, Canada, and many western democracies. At various points in between lie the rest of the countries in the world.

THE MIXED U.S. ECONOMY

The mixed U.S. economy is predominately a market-oriented economy, but there is a significant amount of government involvement in the allocation process. We can get a good idea of the degree of market and government allocation by looking at Table 1.3.1. Here we see three indications of

> **Table 1.3.1**
>
> **Markets and Government Involvement in the U.S. Economy, 1985 (percent)**
>
> Although the government sector plays an important role in our economy, markets and the private sector play an even bigger role. Here we see that 89 percent of domestic production, 83 percent of nonagricultural employment, and 82 percent of purchases are by the private sector.
>
> | Activity | Government | Private Sector (Households and Business) |
> |---|---|---|
> | Domestic production | 10.6 | 89.3 |
> | Nonagricultural employment | 16.7 | 83.3 |
> | Purchases of GNP* | 20.4 | 81.5 |
>
> *Percentages do not add up to 100 due to purchases of imports by both sectors.
> Source: U.S. Bureau of Economic Analysis, *Survey of Current Business*, February 1986.

market and government allocation: direct production of output, employment, and expenditures on production.

The first row lists the proportion of production in the United States in 1985 that was directly undertaken by the government, about 11 percent, and the proportion undertaken by the private sector, which includes private businesses and households, about 89 percent. The second row shows the proportion of nonagricultural employment by the government and the private sector. In this case the government employs about 17 percent, while the private sector employs about 83 percent. And finally, the last row shows the proportion of purchases by the government sector, about 20 percent, and by the private sector, about 82 percent.

While Table 1.3.1 does not indicate how extensively the government is involved in the allocation of resources through the use of laws and regulations, it does suggest that despite the government's significant participation in the allocation process, we clearly have a market-oriented economy in the United States.

GOALS OF A MARKET-ORIENTED ECONOMY

A market-oriented economy has five basic goals: full employment, price stability, economic growth, efficiency, and equity. Markets alone are often not able to achieve these goals. As such, pursuit of these goals requires a mixed economy, with government involvement. The best way to discuss these goals is to group them as either macroeconomic or microeconomic in nature. The first three goals are macroeconomic and deal with the overall performance of the economy, and the last two goals are microeconomic and deal with individual parts of the economy.

Macroeconomic

The three most important goals of a market-oriented economy at the macroeconomic level are full employment, price stability, and economic growth.

Full Employment <u>**Full employment** is a condition of the economy in which all available resources are used in the production of goods and services.</u> An economy that relies exclusively on markets to allocate resources does not necessarily keep its resources fully engaged in the production of goods and services. In the 1930s, during the Great Depression, up to one-fourth of the labor in the United States was not working, and factories and farmland remained idle. A pure market economy produces goods desired by consumers; if consumers want fewer goods, then fewer goods are produced. But the quantity of goods that *are produced* is not necessarily the same as the quantity that *could be produced* with the amounts of labor, capital, land, and entrepreneurship available to the economy. Thus, one reason for the government to enter a market-oriented economy is to buy enough goods to achieve full employment. (The government's role in promoting full employment is the central theme in Section 4, Keynesian Economics.)

Price Stability Price stability is a condition in which the average level of prices in the economy does not change or changes very slowly. If prices change abruptly, buyers and sellers are not sure what to expect the next time they engage in an exchange, creating a great deal of confusion and uncertainty in markets. Moreover, if prices continually and rapidly rise (*inflation*), the purchasing power of income falls, since the same amount of income buys fewer goods and services. With its centralized control, the government can stabilize the average price level of a market-oriented economy. (Price stability and inflation are examined more closely in Section 6, A Closer Look at Inflation.)

Economic Growth Economic growth is the process of increasing the economy's ability to produce goods and services. The economy is closer to solving the economic problem with the additional goods and services that can be obtained through economic growth. However, producing more or better labor, capital, land, or entrepreneurship means other goods and services cannot be consumed by people. In essence the economy has to give up some goods today so that more goods can be produced in the future. In some cases a market-oriented economy might not expand and improve these resources without a little encouragement from the government. (Section 14, The World Economy, discusses the role of the government in promoting economic growth.)

Microeconomic

The two main microeconomic goals for a market-oriented economy are efficiency and equity. Both efficiency and equity deal with individual parts of the economy rather than the entire economy.

Efficiency As we saw in Unit 1.1, efficiency means getting the highest level of consumer satisfaction from the available resources. A market-oriented economy may fail to achieve the goal of efficiency in one of three ways: public goods, externalities, and market power.

A **public good** is a good that is nonrival in consumption and that nonpayers cannot be excluded from consuming. National defense and education are two examples of public goods because nonpayers cannot be easily excluded from consuming them. By contrast, automobiles and donuts are private goods, because nonpayers can be excluded from consuming the good. A market can efficiently allocate private goods, but not public goods, from which people benefit without paying. As such, people are not likely to exchange a public good through a market, so the government assumes a part in its production or allocation. (Unit 12.2, The Market Failure of Public Goods, discusses the efficient allocation of public goods.)

Externalities are costs or benefits that affect someone not directly involved in the production or exchange of a good, and that are incurred without compensation. Pollution is a good example of an externality. Water pollution is generated when paper products are produced and sold to consumers, but consumers buying the products are usually not the ones harmed by the pollution. The prices of the products do not cover the full costs of their production, and thus the prices tend to be too low to achieve an efficient allocation of resources. This means too many resources are being used to produce paper products. In general it is not possible to exclude people from sharing either the costs or benefits of an externality. Once again the government needs to enter the market to achieve an efficient allocation. (Section 13, The Natural Environment, discusses the efficient resource allocation of externalities.)

Market power is the ability of buyers or sellers to control or influence the price and/or quantity exchanged in the market. If buyers or sellers have a great deal of market power they can prevent resources from being allocated efficiently. For example, a monopoly is a market with a single firm selling output. With one firm in the market, buyers have to pay the price charged by *that* firm if they want the good. As with the AT&T breakup, if the government feels the allocation is not efficient, it can take corrective action. (Section 9, Monopoly and Imperfect Competition, illustrates how market power can lead to an inefficient allocation of resources.)

Equity A second microeconomic goal of a market-oriented economy is equity. **Equity is the fairness with which income or wealth is distributed within a society.** A market-oriented economy that is relatively competitive typically, but not always, pays its resources based on their contribution to the production of goods and services. Owners of more productive, or higher quality, resources receive larger incomes. In addition, people who have larger quantities of resources also receive more income. Furthermore, discrimination by some members of society can cause other members of society to have a relatively smaller quantity and quality of resources, or to receive a smaller reward for the same resources. Clearly, income is not always distributed equally to all members of society.

Problems occur when some members of society do not own any productive resources and thus receive no income. For example, some physically and mentally disabled people are completely unable to produce goods and services; consequently, they can't earn income. The government's role is to provide minimum support for these people. And if the unequal distribution is caused by discrimination, then the government needs to step in to alleviate the inequity. (The problems of an unequal distribution of income are discussed in more detail in Unit 11.4, Income Distribution.)

TRADEOFFS BETWEEN GOALS

Each of these five basic economic goals is important to achieve in its own right. In general people are better off if the economy has full employment, stable prices, economic growth, an efficient allocation of resources, and an equitable distribution of income. Unfortunately these goals are often at odds with each other, meaning the pursuit of one goal is at the expense of other goals.

Two important tradeoffs are between full employment and price stability and between efficiency and equity. In our study of macroeconomics we see that pursuing full employment can often lead to the instability of prices associated with inflation, while trying to reduce inflation can inhibit the full employment of resources. In our study of microeconomics we see that an efficient allocation of resources does not necessarily lead to an equitable distribution of income, and if the government tries to make the distribution of income more equitable, resource allocation can become inefficient.

The tradeoffs that exist between these five goals reflect back to the economic problem introduced in the previous unit and illustrate a fundamental principle in economics—we cannot have everything we want. Whether we are concerned with the satisfaction of unlimited wants or the pursuit of the goals of a market-oriented economy, we cannot have it all. Our economy must decide between automobiles and food, stable prices and full employment, efficiency and equity.

IN SUMMARY

The Mixed Economy

- There are two basic methods of allocating resources: markets and government. Allocation by markets is based on individual decisions and free choice. Governments can affect resource allocation through direct ownership of resources, by laws and regulations imposed on markets, and by taxation and spending. In each case the resource allocation by the government carries the weight of the law.

- The economies in the world fall between two ideal extremes. A pure market economy has all resources allocated by markets. A pure command economy has all resources allocated by the government or a central authority. All economies in the real world are mixed economies, with resource allocation by both markets and government.

- In the United States there are three main levels of government: federal, state, and local. Together they produce 10 percent of the nation's output, employ 17 percent of the labor, and purchase 20 percent of the goods and services.

- There are five goals of a market-oriented economy, which often require some degree of government intervention. The three macroeconomic goals are full employment, price stability, and economic growth. The two microeconomic goals are efficiency (in terms of public goods, externalities, and market power) and equity.

QUESTIONS FOR STUDY AND ANALYSIS

1. Would a political democracy be more compatible with a market economy or a command economy? Explain.

2. Do you think that a pure command economy can be a practical and effective system for allocating resources? Describe the type of society that might result if all allocation decisions were made by the government.

3. Some people feel that the best government is no government at all. List five goods provided by the government that would not be provided, or would be provided at a substantially higher price, if the government was not involved in the economy. Explain each.

4. Discuss why you think each of the three macroeconomic and two microeconomic goals justifies or does not justify the involvement of the government in a market-oriented economy.

5. In the United States education is primarily funded by federal, state, and local governments. Why is education not funded exclusively through private markets? Which, if any, of the five goals would you say justifies public funding of education? Explain.

REVIEW GLOSSARY

economic growth The process of increasing the economy's ability to produce goods and services.

efficiency The process of obtaining the highest level of consumer satisfaction from the available resources.

equity The fairness with which income or wealth is distributed within a society.

externality A cost or benefit that affects someone not directly involved in the production or exchange of a good and that is incurred without compensation.

full employment A condition of the economy in which all available resources are used in the production of goods and services.

government A political body exercising control and authority over a group of individuals. Governments allocate resources based on laws and the command of the government.

market An organized exchange of commodities (goods, services, or resources) between buyers and sellers. Markets allocate resources based on the individual decisions of buyers and sellers.

market power The ability of buyers or sellers to control or influence the price and/or quantity exchanged in the market.

mixed economy An economy that relies on both markets and government for the allocation of resources. The United States is an example of a primarily market-oriented mixed economy.

price stability A condition in which the average level of prices in the economy does not change or changes very slowly.

public good A good that is nonrival in consumption and that nonpayers cannot be excluded from consuming.

pure command economy An economy that relies exclusively on the government for the allocation of resources.

pure market economy An economy that relies exclusively on markets for the allocation of resources.

UNIT 1.4

Graphs and Economics

In Unit 1.1 we saw that economics, like other sciences, abstracts from the real world, studying only the most important relationships between economic concepts. One common method of abstraction in economics is the graph. A **graph** is two or more lines, with each line representing a relationship between two variables. Graphs serve as an easy method of presenting economic principles by isolating relationships between economic concepts. For example, Unit 2.2 studies the demand curve, a graph that represents the relationship between the amount of a good demanded and the price of the good.

Without graphs (or even more sophisticated mathematical techniques) we would have to rely exclusively on words to explain economic principles. However, words can be vague and misleading. A graph helps us think more precisely about an underlying economic principle. Moreover, a graph can often generate hypotheses that are not evident in the written word. In this unit we see how graphs are used, and sometimes misused, in the study of economics.

READING AND INTERPRETING A GRAPH

To begin our study of graphs, let's first cover a few basic concepts. Figure 1.4.1 presents a graph that can help us understand some useful concepts in our study of economics. The first item we should note are the axes of the graph. The axes in Figure 1.4.1 are the two lines joined at right angles, with numerical scales marked on each. The vertical line

Figure 1.4.1

Reading and Interpreting a Graph

Points *J, K, L, M, N* all fall on a straight line. A straight line can be identified by its slope and intercept. The intercept is the value of *Y* where the line cuts the *Y*-axis, which is equal to 2 for this line. The slope of the line is 1. If *X* increases by 1 unit, *Y* also increases by 1 unit. The equation for this line is $Y = 2 + 1X$. Since the slope is positive, the two variables are directly related.

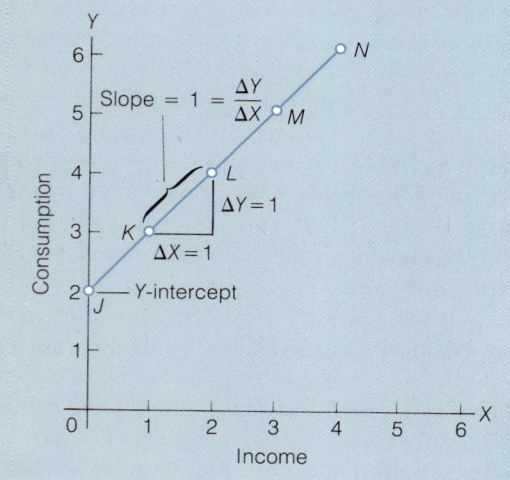

is labeled with a *Y* and called the *Y*-axis; the horizontal line is labeled with an *X* and called the *X*-axis. An important feature of the *X*- and *Y*-axes is that they are joined at the point of origin, where the numerical scales of both axes are equal to zero.

These axes are used to measure one or more economic variables. A **variable** is a quantity that can take on a series of different values. For example, the price of a good is an economic variable that we will be using quite extensively in this text. Price is a variable because it can take on a wide range of different values. In fact Section 2, The Market, investigates why the price of a good takes on the particular value that it does.

Now let's look at the line labeled *JKLMN* in Figure 1.4.1 to provide some insight into how graphs are used in the study of economics. This line depicts the relationship between the variable measured on the *Y*-axis and the variable measured on the *X*-axis. If the variable on the *Y*-axis is the price of a good and the variable on the *X*-axis is the quantity of the good supplied by producers, then this line represents a supply curve. But if the *Y*-axis variable is consumption and the *X*-axis variable is income, then the line represents a consumption function. In either case the line indicates how one variable (*Y*) is related to the other variable (*X*).

Let's see how this relationship works. At point *J* the value of the *X*-axis variable (income) is 0 and the value of the *Y*-axis variable (consumption) is 2. But at point *N* income (*X*) is 4 and consumption (*Y*) is 6. If we follow this line, we can determine the amount of consumption associated with each level of income. For example, if we know that the income is 2, then we can easily see that consumption is 4.

Line *JKLMN* in Figure 1.4.1 is a good example of abstraction in economics. Let's say that we identified this consumption/income relationship by asking five people how much income they have and how much they spend on consumption. In this case the first person, *J*, has no income but spends $2 on consumption. The second person, *K*, has $1 but spends $3 on consumption. Points *L*, *M*, and *K* represent the income and consumption of third, fourth, and fifth persons.

Line *JKLMN* is an abstraction because it only "represents" the five people, it is not actually the five people. In essence we have focused on only two important characteristics, consumption and income, while ignoring a great number of other characteristics, such as hair color, age, IQ, and waist size, because these are the two characteristics that concern us. In other situations their IQ or waist size might be more important. However, since we limited ourselves to only *two* characteristics, we abstracted from the real world.

But with our abstraction we are able to learn something relatively interesting: the amount of consumption associated with each level of income. If we had included hair color, age, waist size, and so on, then this relationship may have been less obvious. And if we had tried to include every single detail we could find about each of the five people, the relationship between the two central variables might have gone completely unnoticed. This is why we abstract in economics, to isolate an important relationship.

THE COMPONENTS OF A STRAIGHT LINE

The line in Figure 1.4.1 is a straight line. A **straight line** is a line with a constant slope. There are two important characteristics of a straight line: slope and intercept.

Slope

Note that the line in Figure 1.4.1 runs diagonally from the lower left part of the graph to the upper right part. That is, higher values of consumption (Y) are associated with the higher values of income (X). The line depicts a positive, or direct, relationship between income and consumption, or between X and Y. A **positive (direct) relationship** exists when the values of two variables increase together. An easy method of identifying a positive relationship is by the slope of the line.

The **slope** of a line is the change in the variable on the vertical axis divided by the change in the variable on the horizontal axis. For example, let's move from point K to point L on the line. At point K income is 1 and consumption is 3. At point L income is 2 and consumption is 4. Income increases from 1 to 2 as we move from point K to point L. At the same time, consumption increases from 3 to 4. As we move from point K to point L, income increases by 1 and consumption also increases by 1. The change in Y, the variable on the vertical axis, is 1 (= 4 − 3). The change in X, the variable on the horizontal axis, is also 1 (= 2 − 1). This means the slope of the line from K to L is 1 (= 1/1).

We can also calculate the slope between any other pair of points in Figure 1.4.1, and in each case we see that the slope is equal to 1. Income changes by the same amount as consumption. The slope of the line is *constant* and is the same everywhere along the line, whether income and consumption are large or small. In fact, *every straight line has a constant slope.*

Intercept

The second important characteristic of the line in Figure 1.4.1 is the intercept term. The **intercept** term (or more appropriately the Y-intercept term) is the value of the variable on the Y-axis when the value of the variable on the X-axis is zero. In Figure 1.4.1 this occurs at point J, where income (X) is 0 and consumption (Y) is 2. The intercept term is always defined as the value of Y, in this case 2, when the value of X is zero. Recall that the Y-axis cuts through the X-axis at the zero value of X. Therefore, when the line cuts through the Y-axis, the value on the X-axis is zero.

The Equation of a Straight Line

Knowing the slope and intercept of a straight line, we can write a simple expression relating the two variables. An **equation** is a formal statement showing the equality between two variables. An equation is much like a sentence, only written in numbers and symbols instead of words. An equation tells us that variable Y is related to variable X in a specific manner. For example, the equation of the line in Figure 1.4.1 is:

$$Y = 2 + 1X$$

This equation tells us how income (X) and consumption (Y) are related. It tells us that each value of Y is 2 units greater than each value of X. Let's see how we interpret and determine this relationship. First, what is consumption if income is zero? If we insert $X = 0$ into the equation, we have

$$Y = 2 + 1(0)$$

Since 1 times 0 is 0, the term to the right of the plus sign drops off, leaving us with $Y = 2$. This is the Y-intercept term we identified. The value of the term to the left of the plus sign (2) is the intercept term of the equation.

The number multiplied times X is the slope of the line. So in the equation, 1 is the value of the slope. The slope tells us how consumption is affected if we change income by one unit. We know that $Y = 2$ when $X = 0$. But what is the value of Y if $X = 1$? If we plug $X = 1$ into the equation we have

$$Y = 2 + 1(1)$$

And when $X = 1$, then $Y = 3 (= 2 + 1)$. When X increases from 0 to 1, then Y increases from 2 to 3. As X increases by 1, so does Y. This is what the value of the slope tells us.

If we know the slope and intercept of a straight line, we can find any point on the line. An equation is a short-cut method of describing a line.

Negative Slope

So far we have only dealt with a positive relationship between two variables, that is, an increase in one variable associated with an increase in the other variable. For a direct relationship the value of the slope is positive, but for a negative or inverse relationship the slope is negative. A **negative (inverse) relationship** exists when the value of one variable increases as the value of the other variable decreases. Figure 1.4.2 depicts the graph of a straight line with a negative slope. Notice that the line moves from the top left of the graph to the bottom right. If X represents the quantity of videocassette tapes demanded and Y the price of videotapes, then Figure 1.4.2 is a demand curve.

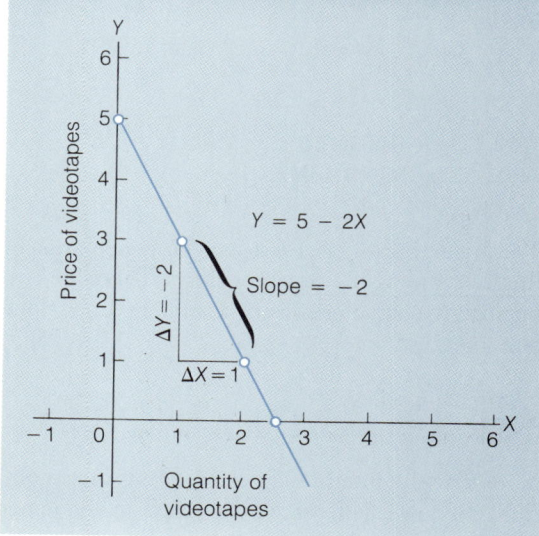

Figure 1.4.2

Negative Slope

This graph represents a negative relationship between two variables, price and quantity demanded. As variable X increases, variable Y decreases. The slope of the line is -2, meaning variable Y decreases by 2 units when variable X increases by 1 unit.

The equation for the line in Figure 1.4.2 is

$$Y = 5 - 2X$$

The intercept term is 5, and the slope is -2. Again, the intercept term is the value of Y (price), when X (quantity demanded) is zero, or the point where the line cuts the vertical axis. The slope tells us the change in price as we change the quantity demanded. Suppose we start at the Y-intercept, where $Y = 5$ and $X = 0$. If we increase the value of X to 1, the value of Y decreases by 2, and $Y = 3$. Thus high prices are associated with small quantities demanded, and low prices are associated with large quantities demanded.

UNIT 1.4 • GRAPHS AND ECONOMICS

Figure 1.4.3
A Curve

A line with a changing slope is a curve. If X changes from 0 to 1, Y changes from 1 to 1.1, and the slope of the line is 0.1. However, if X changes from 10 to 11, Y changes from 7 to 10, and the slope is 3. For greater values of X the slope of the line is also greater.

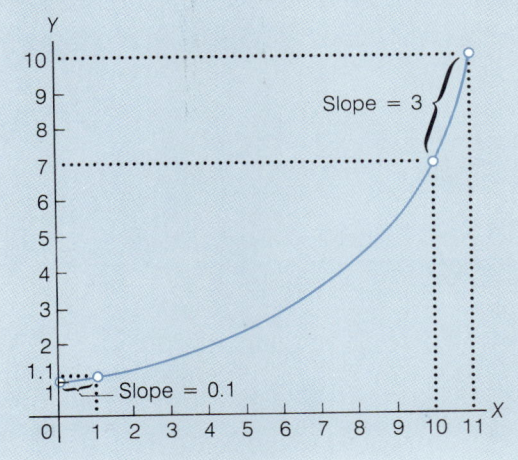

A CURVE

Not all lines are straight lines. A straight line is characterized by a constant slope. If a line is *not* a straight line, it does *not* have a constant slope. The line in Figure 1.4.3 is a curve. A **curve** is a line that does not have a constant slope.

At low values of X the line is relatively flat, which means the slope of the line is relatively small. By contrast, for larger values of X the line is relatively steep, so the slope is greater. If X increases from 0 to 1, Y increases from 1 to 1.1. The change in Y over the change in X is 0.1/1, and the slope of the line is 0.1. However, the slope of the line as X increases from 10 to 11 is much greater. Notice that when X is 10, Y is 7, but when X is 11, Y is 10. The change in Y is 3 and the change in X is 1, so the slope of the line is 3 (3/1).

Whenever the slope of a line changes, the line is curved. The slope could *increase* from left to right, as in Figure 1.4.3, or it could *decrease* from left to right while still remaining positive, as illustrated in panel a of Figure 1.4.4. In panel b the curve has a negative slope, but the slope becomes flatter from left to right. In panel c the slope is also negative, but it becomes steeper from left to right.

INTERSECTION BETWEEN TWO LINES

A single line, whether straight or curved, describes a relationship between two variables. However, often in economics two different relationships exist between the same variables. For example, if we look at the relationship between the price and quantity of a good, we find one relationship between price and the quantity a buyer would like to buy, and a second relationship between the price and the quantity a seller would like to sell.

With two distinct relationships we can gain more information by plotting both lines on the same graph, as in Figure 1.4.5. Here we see that line 1 (demand curve) has a negative slope and line 2 (supply curve) has a positive slope.

With two lines depicted in Figure 1.4.5, one point stands out, the intersection of line 1 and line 2. An **intersection** is the point at which the values of both variables are the same for both lines. At point E the two lines cross, and the values of X (quantity) and Y (price) are the same for both relationships, that is, for line 1, $X = 100$ and $Y = 5$, and for line 2, $X = 100$ and $Y = 5$.

For the two lines in Figure 1.4.5, E is the only point at which price *and* quantity are the same for both relationships. So, if we want to know when the relationship depicted by line 1 holds *and* the relationship depicted by line 2 also holds, we only have to find the intersection of the lines.

Figure 1.4.4

Curves and Slopes

Panel a illustrates a curve with a positive slope, but it decreases and becomes flatter with larger values of X. Compare this curve to the curve in Figure 1.4.3, which also has a positive slope but which increases and becomes steeper with larger values of X. Panel b illustrates a curve with a negative slope that becomes flatter with larger values of X. Panel c illustrates another curve with a negative slope that becomes steeper with larger values of X.

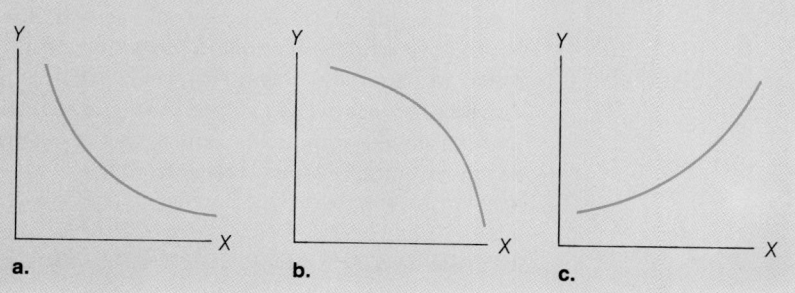

a.   b.   c.

Figure 1.4.5

Intersection Between Lines

An intersection occurs when two lines cross. At point E the Y value (price) for line 1 is equal to the Y value for line 2. Likewise, the X value (quantity) for line 1 is equal to the X value for line 2. The intersection tells us when the relationships underlying both lines hold at the same time.

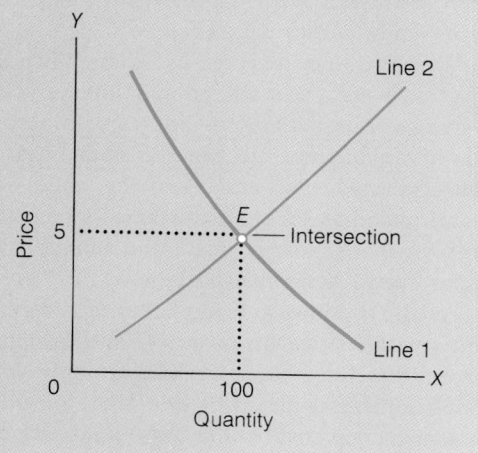

Figure 1.4.6

Tangency Between Lines

A tangency exists when two lines touch at a single point and the slopes of both lines are the same. Not only are the X and Y values the same for both lines at point E but also the slopes are equal.

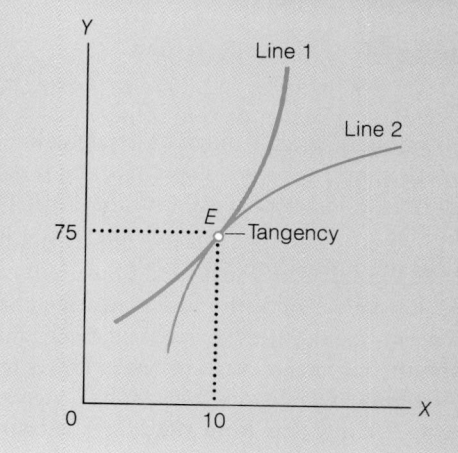

TANGENCY BETWEEN TWO LINES

A tangency is similar to an intersection but with one important difference, equal slopes. A **tangency** is the point at which the slopes of two lines are the same and the values of the variables are the same. Figure 1.4.6 presents a tangency between two lines.

Line 1 is a positively sloped curve, and the slope is increasing from left to right. Line 2 is also a positively sloped curve, but the slope is decreasing from left to right. At lesser values of X the slope of line 1 is relatively small, while the slope of line 2 is relatively large. At greater values of X the slope of line 1 is relatively large, while the slope of line 2 is relatively small.

At point E the slopes of the two lines are equal. But point E also lies on both line 1 and line 2. The values of X and Y for line 1 at point E are 10 and 75. The values of X and Y for line 2 at point E are also 10 and 75. Therefore point E represents a tangency between line 1 and line 2.

THE MISUSE OF GRAPHS

Although graphs are extremely helpful in depicting economic principles, they can also be misused, causing distortions of the very principles we are trying to identify and ultimately doing more harm than good. For example, let's look at the relationship between the price of record albums and the quantity of albums demanded by buyers. In particular, we want to know what effect changes in price have on the quantity demanded. Figure 1.4.7 gives us three alternative views of this relationship.

Let's look first at panel a. Our initial observation would indicate that the price needs to change a great deal before there is much of a change in the quantity demanded, at least based on the steepness of the slope. However, if we look more closely at the Y-axis in panel a we notice that measurement of price is discontinuous, that is, the Y-axis omits the range of prices between $0 and $6. This suggests that changes in the price are somewhat exaggerated.

However, if we turn to panel b, we see a slightly different graph of the relationship between the price of record albums and the quantity demanded. In panel b measurement is continuous between $0 and $7, and the line appears to be much flatter and less steeply sloped than the line in panel a. But both lines are measuring the exact same relationship between the price of albums and the quantity demanded. If we looked at panel b, we might conclude that only very small changes in the price are needed to obtain relatively large increases in the quantity demanded.

When using a graph, always be aware of the units of measurement on the axes, because these measures can easily be adjusted to visually amplify or dampen the relationship between two variables. In Unit 2.6 we see how to compute a measure of elasticity that helps prevent this type of distortion and allows us to determine the "true" relationship between two variables.

Graphs can also distort a relationship by presenting only part of the picture. In both panels a and b we saw only the relationship that exists if the price changes between $6 and $7. Might it not also be useful to see this relationship for other prices? Panel c indicates the quantity of record albums demanded if the price is less than $6. While panels a and b indicate that this relationship is a straight line, panel c suggests that the slope of the line actually changes over the entire range of prices. Panel c presents an entirely different picture of the relationship between the price of albums and the quantity demanded.

In many cases it is appropriate to concentrate on only part of a relationship. For example, if the price of record albums has always remained between $6 and $7, then we probably don't need to know the quantity of record albums demanded at $1. However, if we have only the information contained in panels a or b, then we have to be careful about predicting the quantity demanded if the price declines to $1.

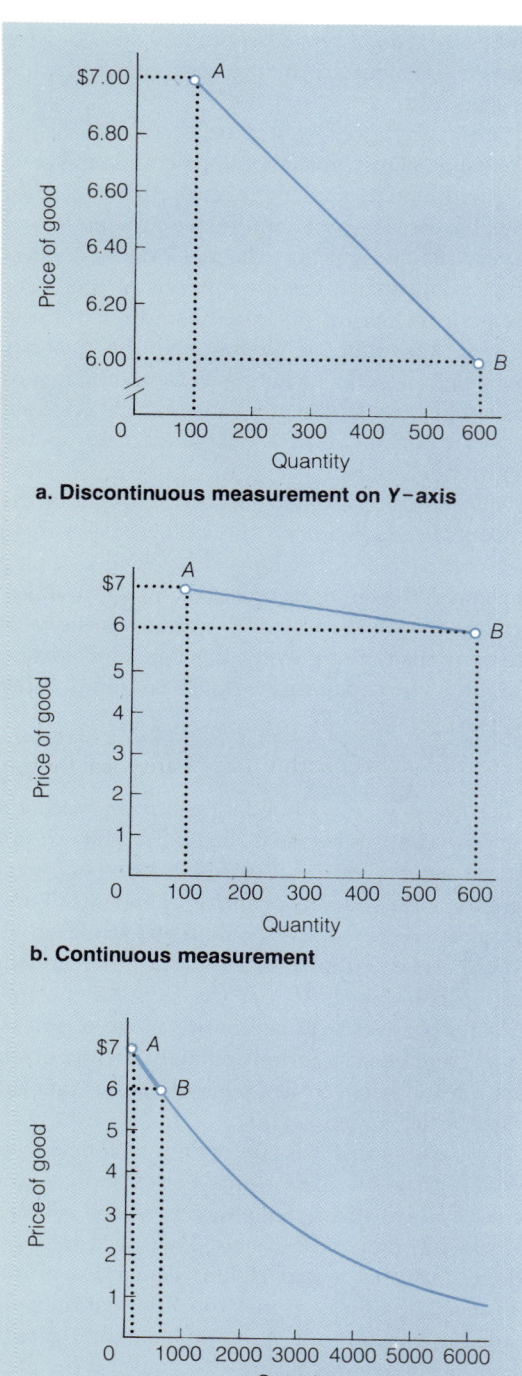

a. Discontinuous measurement on Y-axis

b. Continuous measurement

c. Complete relationship

Figure 1.4.7

The Misuse of Graphs

Panel a displays a line that seems to indicate that the quantity of record albums demanded is not very sensitive to the price, but because the range of values between $0 and $6 is omitted, this is misleading. Panel b presents the exact same relationship, but it seems to indicate that quantity demanded is more sensitive to the price. However, even this can be misleading, because only part of the relationship between price and quantity is presented. Panel c presents a more complete relationship and gives us fuller information.

IN SUMMARY

Graphs and Economics

- Graphs are one way economics abstracts from the real world. They allow the depiction of important principles more clearly than other methods. Graphs can easily illustrate the relationship between two economic variables, such as price and quantity or income and consumption.

- A straight line is identified by its slope and intercept. The slope is the change in the variable on the vertical Y-axis divided by the change in the variable on the horizontal X-axis. A straight line has a constant slope. The intercept is the value of the variable on the vertical Y-axis when the value of the variable on the horizontal X-axis is zero. If the slope of a line is positive, then the relationship depicted by the line is positive, or direct. If the slope is negative, then the relationship is negative, or inverse.

- A curve is a line with a changing slope. The slope of a curve can be positive or negative, but it is different at different points on the curve.

- An intersection occurs when two lines cross. The importance of the intersection is that the values of both variables are equal for both lines. This means the relationships represented by both lines hold at the same time. A tangency occurs when the two lines touch at a single point and the slopes of both lines are the same.

- Graphs can also be misused in the representation of economic principles. This can happen if measurement is discontinuous or if only part of the relationship between the variables is presented. Any time graphs are used, attention must be given not only to simple appearance but also to the units of measurement on the axes.

QUESTIONS FOR STUDY AND ANALYSIS

1. **a.** Plot the following three observations in a graph and connect the points with a line.

Observation	X	Y
a	0	10
b	5	20
c	−15	−20

   b. What is the slope of the line? Is it constant? Is it positive or negative?
   c. What is the Y-intercept of the line?
   d. What is the equation for the line?
   e. If the variable X took on the value of 2, what would be the value of variable Y?

2. Let's say that you hear on the nightly news that the interest rate is falling. Furthermore, the newscaster comments that this should be very helpful to the housing industry because more people will want to buy houses. Explain how you would use a graph to isolate the relationship between the interest rate and the number of houses sold. Based on the newscaster's comments, do you think the relationship depicted is direct or inverse? Explain.

3. Some people feel that abstraction prevents a "true" understanding of the real world. Discuss how abstraction through the use of graphs can help us better understand the real world.

4. Discuss how the misuse of graphs can prevent us from understanding the real world.

REVIEW GLOSSARY

curve A line that does not have a constant slope.

equation A formal statement showing the equality between two variables.

graph A diagram of two or more lines, with each line representing the relationship between two variables. Graphing is a method of abstraction that helps isolate important economic principles.

intercept (Y-intercept) The value of the variable on the vertical axis when the variable on the horizontal axis equals zero. The intercept is where the line cuts the vertical axis.

intersection The point at which two lines cross, where the values of both variables are equal for the two relationships depicted in the graph.

negative (inverse) relationship A relationship that exists when the value of one variable increases as the value of the other variable decreases.

positive (direct) relationship A relationship that exists when the values of two variables increase together.

slope The change in the variable on the vertical axis divided by the change in the variable on the horizontal axis.

straight line A line with a constant slope.

tangency The point at which the slopes of two lines are the same and the values of the variables are the same.

variable A quantity that can take on a series of different values.

UNIT 1.5

The Economy's Production Possibilities

When resources are limited, an economy's output is limited. In this unit we examine how limited resources affect the production possibilities of an economy. **Production possibilities are the alternative combinations of goods and services an economy can produce if it fully and efficiently uses all available resources.**

Since the total amount of production is limited, the economy must make a choice between the goods produced. Should it produce automobiles or designer jeans? Nuclear reactors or solar water heaters? The choice lies at the heart of the production possibilities concept. In this unit we look at the production possibilities frontier, a graphic representation of the limits on production of various combinations of goods and services. In addition, we see how the concepts of full employment and cost are related to limited production. And finally, we see how economic growth expands production through increases in the quantity or quality of resources. To illustrate the production possibilities concept, let's start with a simple example.

PRODUCTION POSSIBILITIES: A STUDENT EXAMPLE

A student has a choice between the production of two alternative "goods": high grades and recreational activities. Both goods are produced using the student's labor resource, or, more specifically, the amount of time. As more time is spent producing high grades, less time is spent producing recreational activities, and vice versa.

Table 1.5.1 presents some hypothetical numbers for a student faced with a choice between the production of grades or recreational activities (measured with a hypothetical fun index). Six options are shown (A through F). In option A we see the proverbial diligent student, who spends all available time studying and none engaging in recreational activities. The grade point average of 3.8 reflects the student's diligence, but the fun index is zero. In option B, where the student becomes less studious and takes a few hours away from studying to engage in recreational activities, the grade point average falls to 3.7, but the fun index increases to 10 units. As the student moves down the table to option F, the grade point average steadily drops, but the fun index increases. The student is exchanging time spent studying and good grades for time spent in recreational activities.

Table 1.5.1

Hypothetical Production Possibilities for a Student

A tradeoff exists in the production of two "goods" by a student, grades and fun. If more effort is used to produce grades, then very little fun is produced. If effort is diverted from the production of higher grades, then more fun can be produced. However, because of the student's limited time, the highest grade point average is 3.8 and the most units of fun are 50.

Option	Grade Point Average	Units of Fun
A	3.8	0
B	3.7	10
C	3.4	20
D	2.6	30
E	1.4	40
F	0.0	50

Table 1.5.1 reflects the tradeoff faced by a student in the production of grades or recreation. As the student moves from option A to option F, higher grades are given up in return for recreation; if the student initially began at point F, recreation is traded for higher grades. But notice that the student's limited time prevents an increase in the fun index while achieving higher grades. Even if all available time is devoted to studying, the student can do no better than a 3.8 grade point average. By the same token, if all time is spent on recreational activities, the fun index cannot exceed 50. Since the student's labor resource is limited, the quantity of goods produced (grades and recreation) with the available time is also limited.

PRODUCTION POSSIBILITIES FOR THE ECONOMY

Like the student, the economy has a limited amount of resources available for the production of alternative goods. Limited quantities of labor, capital, land, and entrepreneurship prevent the economy from producing enough goods to totally satisfy everyone. And even though the United States has enormous quantities of resources, these resources are ultimately as limited as the twenty-four hours available to the student.

If the U.S. economy devotes all resources to the production of one good, it can certainly produce a large quantity of that good. For example, suppose the economy concentrates solely on building factories, and is able to produce 650 per month. But no matter how hard the economy tries, its limited resources prevent the production of any more. Or suppose the economy opts to produce agricultural goods instead of factories. If all available resources are applied in this direction, 5.3 million tons of food can be produced per month. But like the 650 factories, this is the maximum amount of food the economy can produce with available resources. And keep in mind that as the economy produces 5.3 million tons of food, it is producing no factories.

Table 1.5.2

Hypothetical Production Possibilities for the Economy

The economy is faced with a tradeoff between the production of different goods. In this table the economy can produce factories but no food (option A), food but no factories (option F), or some combination in between. However, for any combination the total production of both goods is limited because the economy's resources are limited.

Option	Number of Factories	Millions of Tons of Food
A	650	0
B	640	1.0
C	510	3.6
D	410	4.6
E	100	5.2
F	0	5.3

Table 1.5.2 shows several possibilities open to the economy for the production of factories and food. With option A the economy produces 650 factories but no food. With option F it produces 5.3 million tons of food but no factories. A number of other food/factory combinations can be generated: a great deal of food and very few factories (option E); or more factories and very little food (option B); or some factories and some food (options C or D). The economy's range of combinations of factories and food represent its production possibilities.

While we have only looked at two goods, the economy has a wide range of production possibilities for all of its goods. For example, one production possibility for the economy might be 10,000 automobiles, 600 houses, 1000 tractors, 500 pairs of jeans, 9000 light bulbs, and so on. But whether we are looking at two goods or two thousand goods, the principles are the same.

PRODUCTION POSSIBILITIES FRONTIER

A tool used to graphically represent the economy's production possibilities is the production possibilities frontier. A **production possibilities frontier (PPF)** is a curve that illustrates the alternative combinations of two goods that can be produced with the existing quantity and quality of resources and current level of technology. An example is presented in Figure 1.5.1 using the hypothetical numbers from Table 1.5.2. The vertical axis of Figure 1.5.1 measures the number of factories that the economy can produce each month; the horizontal axis measures million of tons of food.

In Figure 1.5.1 point A represents an economy devoting all its resources to produce factories, and point F represents exclusive production of food. Each factory/food production combination presented in Table 1.5.2 is plotted in Figure 1.5.1, and all six points (A through F) are connected by a line.

The line in Figure 1.5.1 is the *production possibilities frontier (PPF)*, which represents a *boundary* for the economy. While the economy can produce any factory/food combination that lies between the frontier and the axes, it cannot produce at any

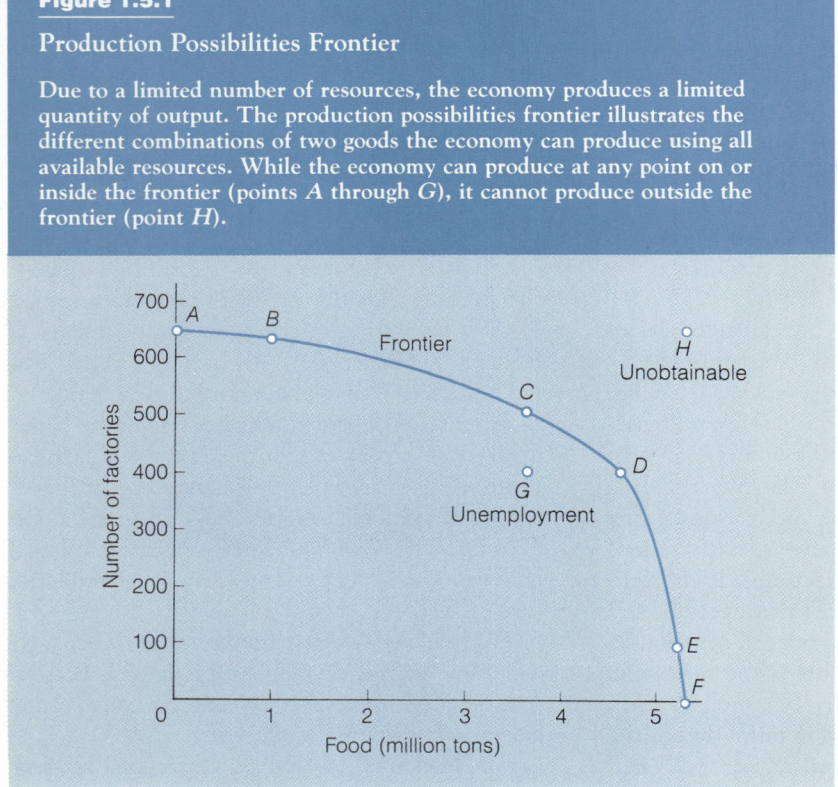

Figure 1.5.1

Production Possibilities Frontier

Due to a limited number of resources, the economy produces a limited quantity of output. The production possibilities frontier illustrates the different combinations of two goods the economy can produce using all available resources. While the economy can produce at any point on or inside the frontier (points A through G), it cannot produce outside the frontier (point H).

point above and to the right of the frontier. It is possible to produce 410 factories and 3.6 million tons of food at point G, but it is impossible to produce 650 factories and 5.3 million tons of food at point H. Because of the economy's limited resources and existing technology, the curve represents a boundary that cannot be crossed.

OPPORTUNITY COSTS

If the economy is at point C in Figure 1.5.1, then it is producing 510 factories and 3.6 million tons of food. What happens if it decides to produce more food? To produce more food, the economy must increase the amounts of labor, capital, land, and entrepreneurship. But at point C on the production possibilities frontier the economy is already using all factors either in the production of food or in the production of factories. The economy cannot produce more than 3.6 million tons of food if it continues to produce 510 factories. The only way to increase food production is to reduce the production of factories. Consequently, the economy has to shift resources from factory production to food production.

What are the results of this action? Suppose the economy moves to point D on the production possibilities frontier, increasing food production from 3.6 million tons to 4.6 million tons but decreasing factory production from 510 to 410. The economy is producing 1.0 million tons more food at the expense of producing 100 fewer factories.

For every factory given up, the economy receives 10,000 tons of food. Every 10,000 tons of food cost the economy exactly 1 factory, thus illustrating the idea of opportunity cost. **Opportunity cost is the highest value of goods or other benefits given up when a good is produced or any action is taken.** When the economy produces less of one good in order to produce more of another, it incurs an opportunity cost. If the economy moves from point D to point C, it gives up 1.0 million tons of food in order to produce 100 more factories, and each factory costs the economy 10,000 tons of food.

THE LAW OF INCREASING OPPORTUNITY COSTS

Notice that the PPF in Figure 1.5.1 is bowed away from the origin. This shape reflects the law of increasing opportunity cost. The **law of increasing opportunity cost is a principle that states the opportunity cost of producing a good increases as the economy moves along the production possibilities frontier and more of the good is produced.** Between points A and B the economy is devoting most of its resources to the production of factories, and the frontier is nearly horizontal. But between points E and F the economy is concentrating on the production of food, and the frontier is nearly vertical. If the economy moves along the curve from point A to point F, its slope changes from nearly horizontal to nearly vertical. Why?

To illustrate the law of increasing opportunity cost, let's look at Figure 1.5.2. If the economy is at point M, then every resource in the economy is used to produce factories. All resources specifically designed to produce factories are included. However, the economy also employs resources that are less suited for the production of factories, such as tractors, farmhands, wheat combines, and a variety of other agricultural resources. These resources are great at making food but not as good at producing factories. So while at point M all resources are being used to produce factories, some are not doing a very good job.

What happens if the economy moves along the curve from point M to point N? The economy diverts some resources from the production of factories to the production of food, and the first resources to be diverted are those *best* suited to food production and *least* suited to factory production. So the opportunity cost of producing an additional 1.0 million tons of food, as the economy moves from point M to point N is only 10 factories. Or, for each single factory given up by the economy from points M to N, an additional 100,000 tons of food are produced.

Compare the move from points M to N, where *10* factories are given up by the economy to pro-

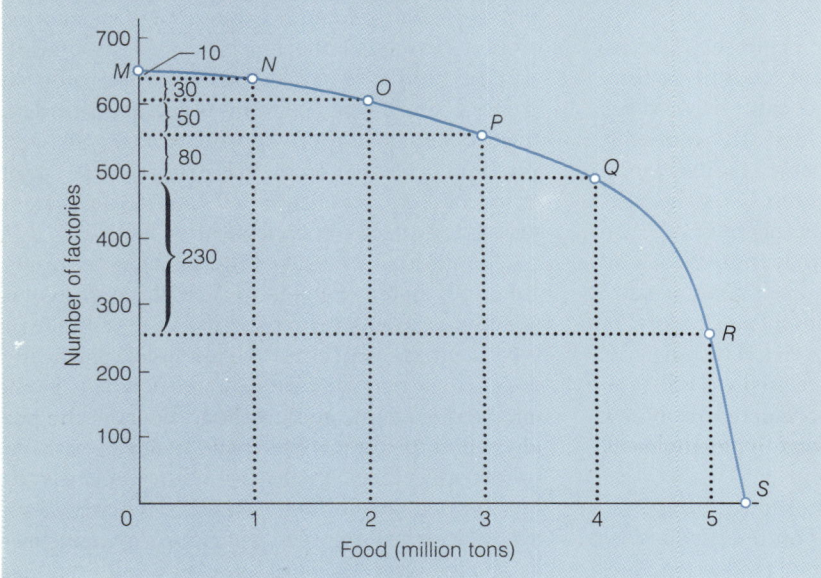

Figure 1.5.2

Increasing Opportunity Costs

Here, the opportunity cost of a good increases as more of the good is produced. The first million tons of food means the economy must forego only 10 factories. However, the economy must forego 30 factories for the second million tons, 50 factories for the third million tons, and so on. Increasing opportunity costs cause the curve to become more steeply sloped from left to right.

duce 1.0 million tons of food, with a similar move along the frontier from point O to point P, where 50 factories are given up in order to produce 1.0 million tons of food. The opportunity cost in the move from point O to P is thus 50 factories. Between points O and P a further reduction in factory production is possible only by removing resources that are more suited to this task. Therefore, the opportunity cost of food production is greater.

As the economy moves even further along the frontier, between points Q and R, it must give up 230 factories in order to produce 1.0 million tons of food. It is evident that as the economy increases the production of food, the opportunity cost of the food production increases.

The law of increasing opportunity cost holds when the economy is on the *PPF*. However, if the economy is inside the *PPF*, for example at point

G in Figure 1.5.1, then all resources are *not* being fully used to produce goods and services, and the law of increasing opportunity cost does not hold. Let's turn our attention to the employment of resources and how it relates to the *PPF*.

FULL EMPLOYMENT AND UNEMPLOYMENT

Full employment is a condition of the economy in which all available resources are used in the production of goods and services. Full employment occurs when the economy is on the production possibilities frontier. If the economy is at points A, B, C, D, E, or F on the frontier, it is at full employment, and all resources are *fully employed*.

Full employment does not mean every factor of production is working twenty-four hours a day in the production of goods and services. It does mean, however, that all labor that is willing and able works a standard forty-hour week. More specifically full employment is considered to exist if only 5 percent of the labor force is unemployed. Full employment also means that factories are operating three eight-hour work shifts a day if that's how the work load is arranged. It means all agricultural land is planted to crops unless the land needs to be idle to enrich the soil. Full employment does not mean that all mineral resources and fossil fuel reserves are extracted from the ground, nor that all timber is harvested, but it does mean that oil wells and lumber companies are operating at full capacity.

However, it is possible that the economy is not using all its resources in the production of goods and services. If this is the case, then some resources are unemployed. **Unemployment** is a condition of the economy in which some available resources are not being used in the production of goods and services. If the economy is at point G inside the production possibilities frontier, the economy is not fully utilizing its resources. Although the term *unemployment* usually refers to labor that is not employed, any factor of production can be unemployed. Unemployment exists if labor is not working, if factories are shut down, or if agricultural land is not planted to crops even though the soil doesn't need enrichment.

Unemployment means resources are not engaged in the production of any goods or services. However, if resources produce some goods and services but not as many as they could, this is called underemployment. **Underemployment** is a condition of the economy in which resources are engaged in the production of goods and services, but they are operating below capacity or potential. Resources are underemployed if they work less than they could. For example, labor that works twenty hours a week or a factory that operates only during two out of three shifts are both underemployed. In addition, resources can be underemployed if they are not operating up to their potential skill level, for example, an electrical engineer who is washing dishes.

If the economy has unemployed or underemployed resources, it can use them to increase the production of one good without reducing the production of the other. For example, if the economy is at point G in Figure 1.5.1, it is producing 3.6 million tons of food and 410 factories. However, since all resources are not fully employed at point G, it is possible to use these resources to increase the number of factories produced without reducing the quantity of food. This is seen as a move from point G to point C. Or the economy can increase the quantity of food without reducing the number of factories, a move from point G to point D. However, this does *not* mean no opportunity costs are incurred, since labor foregoes the benefits of leisure time as we move from G to D.

Full employment means the economy is getting the most goods and services with the available resources. The economy is better off on the *PPF* than inside, and better off still if it can shift the frontier further out and increase the amount of goods and services available, which is economic growth.

ECONOMIC GROWTH

Economic growth is the process of increasing the economy's ability to produce goods and services. The production possibilities frontier graphically demonstrates the limited amount of output that the economy can produce with its available resources. At any one time the quantity and quality of resources available to an economy are fixed, dictating where the production possibilities frontier lies. If the economy has more or better resources, then it can produce more goods, and the frontier lies further from the origin. For example, if the economy doubles all of its resources, including labor, capital, land, and entrepreneurship, then it can produce more output. Figure 1.5.3 illustrates the type of shift in the frontier that results from an increase in resources; *PPF* II represents more output than *PPF* I. If the economy continues to shift its production possibilities frontier outward over a period of years or decades, then we have economic growth.

There are four ways to shift out the production possibilities frontier. First, the quantity or quality of labor resources can increase. We should note we are also including entrepreneurship in this discussion of labor, since everything that is said about labor also applies to entrepreneurship. One way labor resources can increase is through growth of the population. However, even with a fixed population the quantity of labor can be increased. Every person in the economy is not necessarily part of the labor force. Some people may be mentally or physically incapable of working or simply unwilling to work. The production possibilities frontier can be shifted out by increasing the proportion of the population willing and able to work. In addition, the quality of labor can be improved through education and training. This means the same amount of labor is more productive, and the *PPF* is shifted out.

Second, the amount of land resources available to the economy can increase. At any one time the economy has a limited amount of land or natural resources available for the production of goods

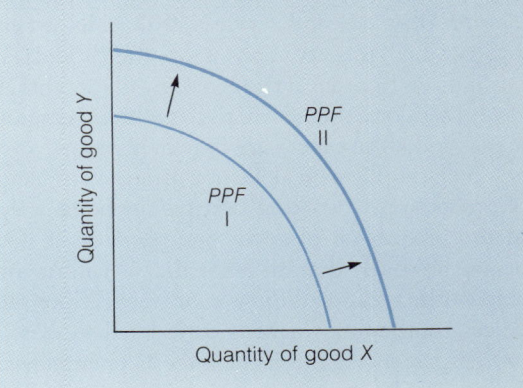

Figure 1.5.3

Economic Growth and the Production Possibilities Frontier

Economic growth can be seen on the *PPF* as an outward shift in the frontier. As resources are increased or the level of technology is expanded, the *PPF* shifts out from frontier I to frontier II. Economic growth occurs as the *PPF* continues to shift outward, and the economy is able to produce a greater number of all goods.

and services. Additional land and natural resources exist, but if their location is unknown or if they are not available to the economy, then they cannot be used to produce output and have no effect on the production possibilities frontier. As land resources are discovered through exploration for such resources as petroleum, iron ore, and other minerals, the production possibilities frontier shifts out.

Third, the level of technology can increase. Technology is the economy's combined body of knowledge of alternative and new methods of production. If a new production method enables the economy to use the same quantities of scarce resources to produce a larger quantity of output, then the level of technology increases. For example, the development of computers has technologically increased the production possibilities of the economy. Businesses throughout the economy can more efficiently manage many phases of production with the help of computers. The reduction in waste and inefficiency means the economy produces more output with its available resources.

Fourth, the economy's stock of capital can increase, a possibility that requires some elaboration. As we saw earlier in this unit, the economy can choose between the production of capital goods (factories) and consumption goods (food). While it is important to produce consumption goods to satisfy the wants and needs of the economy, the production of capital goods also enables the economy to produce more consumption goods as well as capital goods in the future. For example, if we build more automobile factories, then we can produce more automobiles. Since capital goods, such as automobile factories, are part of the economy's resources, an increase in the quantity of capital causes the production possibilities frontier to shift out in the same way as an increase in labor causes the frontier to shift out.

Let's look at panel a of Figure 1.5.4. On the vertical axis we are measuring capital goods, and

Figure 1.5.4

Economic Growth and the Tradeoff Between Capital and Consumption Goods

Although consumption goods provide current satisfaction to the economy, capital goods contribute to economic growth and allow the economy to produce more goods in the future. If the economy selects point *F* on the *PPF* 1990 in panel **a**, the lack of capital goods prevents the *PPF* from shifting out in the future. If the economy trades consumption goods for capital goods (point *E* in panel **a** in 1990, in 1995 the *PPF* shifts out to 1995*E*. If even more capital goods are produced (point *D* in panel **b**), the *PPF* can shift out to 1995*D*.

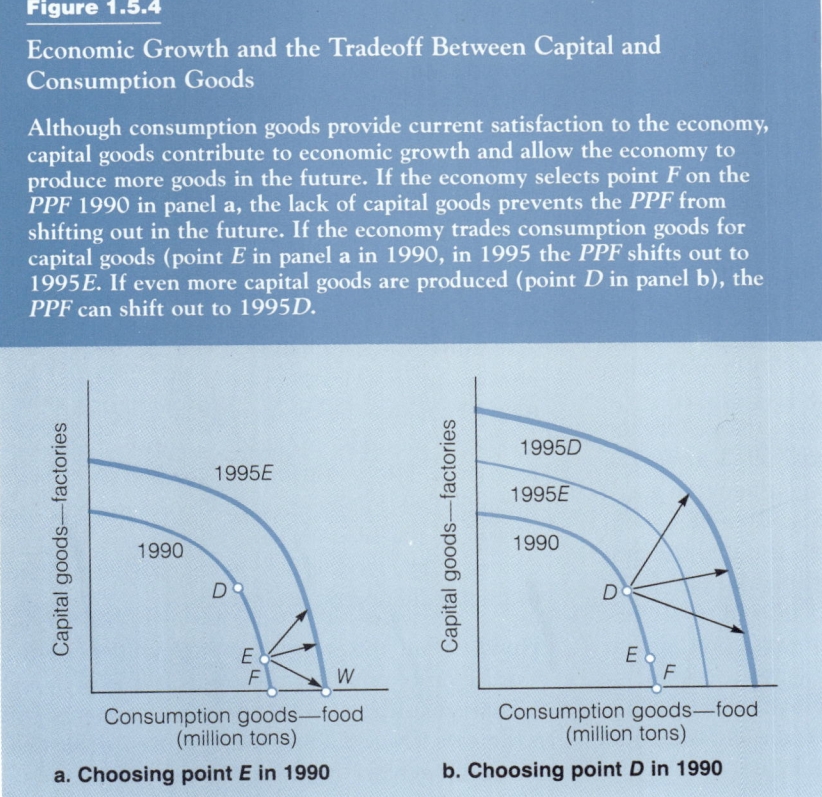

a. Choosing point *E* in 1990

b. Choosing point *D* in 1990

on the horizontal axis consumption goods. The economy can devote its resources to the production of any combination of capital goods (factories) and consumption goods (food) on the frontier labeled 1990, which is the *PPF* curve from Figure 1.5.1. If the economy chooses point F, it is producing 5.3 million tons of food and nothing else. Since no factories are produced, there is no addition to the existing stock of capital, and the *PPF* does not shift. Five years in the future, the economy is on the same frontier.

What happens if the economy chooses a point other than F? Suppose the economy produces at point E, which includes a large quantity of consumption goods (5.2 million tons of food) and a small quantity of capital goods (100 factories). At point E the economy has given up 100,000 tons of food, but it does have 100 more factories. At point E the people may not be as satisfied as they were at point F, since they have less food, but they can be more satisfied in the future. The addition of 100 factories to the existing stock of capital means more food can be produced in 1995. The *PPF* shifts to 1995E, and the economy can be at any point on this new frontier, including point W, which has more food than point F.

If the economy remains at point F, it can *never* produce more consumption goods than it does at point F. However, if it decides in the present to forego a few consumption goods and produce a few capital goods, then it can have more consumption and capital goods in the future.

Let's look at panel b. If the economy decides to produce at point D on curve 1990 instead of point E, then it produces fewer consumption goods (4.6 million tons of food) and more capital goods (410 factories) in the present. In this case the production possibilities frontier shifts outward even more in the future, to 1995D instead of 1995E. With more capital goods and fewer consumption goods produced by the economy in the present, it can shift the production possibilities curve further outward in the future, and even more consumption goods will be available.

THE THREE QUESTIONS OF ALLOCATION

With scarce resources the production possibilities of the economy are limited, and the economy must decide which goods to produce. It must decide, for example, between factories and food, or more generally between capital and consumption goods. At various times the economy has had to make difficult choices between defense and consumption goods, between goods produced by the government and goods produced by privately owned business, and between a clean environment and more automobiles.

In fact, limited resources force the economy to answer three related questions concerning the allocation of resources and goods: What? How? For whom? All three questions must be addressed by every economy, regardless of political philosophy or economic system.

What? The economy must decide what goods to produce. In other words, which point on the production possibilities frontier does the economy want? Should it only produce goods desired by consumers? Should it only produce goods that political leaders want in their respective jurisdictions? Should it produce goods deemed morally justified in religious terms? Or should it produce goods that the nation's largest corporations think the public will buy?

While we have talked about the production possibilities frontier for two goods, the economy must choose among thousands of different types of goods. It must determine the quantity of automobiles, beef, cloth, donuts, eggs, and so on through the alphabet to wheat, xylophones, yogurt, and zippers. If the economy uses resources in the production of one good, it cannot use the same resources in the production of other goods.

How? While the production of goods requires the four factors of production—labor, capital, land, and entrepreneurship—each good can be produced in a variety of ways. The economy must determine how resources are combined in the production of goods and services. Automobiles can be made entirely by hand or produced in highly automated factories. Cattle can be grazed on the open plains or raised in feed lots. Should resources be organized in production based on government decree or should production be based on the costs of each resource? Every economy must decide how each unit of labor, capital, land, and entrepreneurship is brought together in the production of each good.

For Whom? In conjunction with the other two questions the economy must also decide who receives the goods produced. What criteria are used? Do the people most able to buy the goods receive them? Or is the allocation based on those with the greatest needs? Is the decision based on a random characteristic of the person, such as the last digit on their license plate, on political affiliation, or on the performances in the last Olympic games? Whatever the criterion the decision must be made.

Every economic system, regardless of political philosophy, must answer all three questions. In the United States these three questions are answered primarily through the market system. Markets for goods and services tell producers *what* goods to produce. If the price of one good increases relative to the other goods, businesses will tend to direct resources toward the production of that good. Markets for resources tell producers *how* to combine each of the resources into the production of a good. If the price of labor increases relative to the price of capital, businesses will tend to increase the use of capital and reduce the use of labor. Markets for goods also tell *who* receives the goods produced. If the price of one good is high, fewer people are able to buy the good.

IN SUMMARY

The Economy's Production Possibilities

- The limited resources available to the economy restrict the quantity of goods that can be produced. This limit makes it necessary to choose which goods to produce. The production possibilities frontier (*PPF*) illustrates the alternative production possibilities for goods and shows a tradeoff in the production of the goods.

- If the economy wishes to remain on the frontier and tries to produce more of one good, then it must divert resources from the production of another good. The amount of other goods given up to produce one good is the opportunity cost.

- The production possibilities curve for the economy is bowed away from the origin due to increasing opportunity costs. The opportunity cost of a good increases as more of the good is produced. This is the law of increasing opportunity cost. Opportunity costs increase when the economy is on the production possibilities frontier because resources are not equally suited to the production of all goods.

- Full employment of resources exists when the economy lies *on* the frontier. If the economy is producing inside the frontier, then some resources are unemployed or underemployed.

- While the production possibilities frontier is fixed at any one time, it can shift outward with increases in the quantity or quality of limited resources. Economic growth occurs when the frontier continues to shift out over time and can be caused by increases in the quantity or quality of labor, capital, land, and technology.

- The three questions every economic system faces are what to produce, how to produce, and for whom to produce.

QUESTIONS FOR STUDY AND ANALYSIS

1. Why is the production possibilities frontier a boundary? What would happen if the economy tried to produce at a point inside the frontier? Outside the frontier?

2. How is opportunity cost related to the production possibilities frontier? Is it possible to produce a good *without* incurring an opportunity cost? How is the law of increasing opportunity cost related to the shape of the production possibilities frontier?

3. How do we know if the economy is at full employment?

4. Suppose you are given the following information concerning the production of two goods by the economy if it fully uses all resources.

Textbooks	YoYos
500	0
400	1000
300	2000
200	3000
100	4000
0	5000

   a. What is the opportunity cost per YoYo if YoYo production is increased from 2000 to 3000? What is the opportunity cost per YoYo if production is increased from 3000 to 4000?
   b. Does the production possibilities for textbooks and YoYos reflect the law of increasing opportunity cost? Would you say that resources are equally suited for the production of textbooks and YoYos? Explain.
   c. Draw the economy's production possibilities frontier for these two goods. What is the slope of the frontier? How is the slope of any *PPF* related to the law of increasing opportunity cost?

5. Using question 4, suppose a technological advancement is made in the production of YoYos such that it is possible to double the number of YoYos produced. The economy can now produce 400 textbooks and 2000 YoYos or 100 textbooks and 8000 YoYos and so on.
   a. How many textbooks are produced if no YoYos are produced?
   b. What is the opportunity cost of producing an additional YoYo? How does this compare to the opportunity cost of producing an additional YoYo in question 4?
   c. Draw the new production possibilities frontier. How does it compare to the original frontier?

6. The war in the Middle East, like every war, has led to the loss of many lives and the destruction of buildings and equipment. Construct two production possibilities frontiers. Let the first *PPF* represent the production possibilities of the Middle East before war began. Let the second *PPF* reflect the production possibilities of the Middle East after several years of war. How do they compare? Why?

7. During the Reagan administration the government made a concerted effort to increase defense spending and reallocated resources from nondefense goods to defense goods. What do you think happened to the opportunity costs of producing defense goods during this period?

REVIEW GLOSSARY

economic growth The process of increasing the economy's ability to produce goods and services. Economic growth can be achieved by increases in labor, land, capital, and technology. Economic growth is seen as an outward shift of the production possibilities frontier.

full employment A condition of the economy in which all available resources are used in the production of goods and services. Full employment exists when the economy is on the production possibilities frontier.

opportunity costs The highest value of goods or other benefits given up when a good is produced or other action is taken. When the economy is on the production possibilities frontier, to produce more of one good it must produce less of another by reallocating resources. The value of other goods given up is the opportunity cost of increasing the production of a good.

production possibilities The alternative combinations of goods produced if the economy fully uses all resources. The production possibilities of an economy are limited because resources used to produce goods and services are limited.

production possibilities frontier (*PPF*) The curve that illustrates the alternative combinations of goods that can be produced with the existing quantity of resources and current level of technology. The economy can produce at any point on or inside the frontier, but it cannot produce at any point outside the frontier.

the law of increasing opportunity cost A principle that states the opportunity cost of producing a good increases as the economy moves along the production possibilities frontier and more of the good is produced. The production possibilities frontier is bowed away from the origin due to the law of increasing opportunity costs. The law of increasing opportunity cost holds because all resources are not equally suited to the production of all goods.

three questions of allocation The three questions every economy has to address are What goods should be produced? How will the goods be produced with the available resources? Who will get the goods once they are produced?

underemployment A condition of the economy in which resources are engaged in the production of goods and services, but they are operating below capacity or potential. Underemployment of resources means the economy is operating inside the production possibilities frontier.

unemployment A condition of the economy in which some available resources are not being used in the production of goods and services. When unemployment exists the economy is producing inside the production possibilities frontier.

SECTION INQUIRY

Military Spending

It is a basic fact of life, as well as a fundamental principle of economics, that societies must make choices. Every society must determine what goods to produce with its available resources. One of the most important choices societies have made throughout history is the allocation of resources between military goods and nonmilitary goods. Early cave dwellers probably chose between searching for wild berries and making spears to protect themselves from attacking animals. During the height of the Roman Empire, debates were undoubtedly heated when members of the Senate discussed the costs of supplies for Julius Caesar's army. In every war throughout history, participating countries have been forced to give up nonmilitary goods to allow the production of military goods. And today, even in periods of relative peace, this basic choice remains.

An important part of Ronald Reagan's campaign for president in 1980 centered on the lack of expenditures for national defense. In 1980 5.2 percent of the U.S. economy's total production of goods and services (gross national product) consisted of national defense goods, meaning that the remaining 94.8 percent was nondefense goods. In contrast, in 1945, during World War II, 34.5 percent of gross national product was for national defense; in 1955, during the Korean War, 11.2 percent of gross national product was national defense; and near the height of the Vietnam War, in 1970, 7.6 percent of gross national product was national defense. Under the Reagan administration the economy has used more resources for the production of defense goods and fewer for the production of nondefense goods. By 1985 6.6 percent of gross national product was national defense goods and 93.4 was nondefense goods. In the first half of the 1980s the choice was to reallocate resources from nondefense goods to defense goods. While this has sparked controversy in the political arena, it is just one of the basic choices made by any economy.

QUESTIONS FOR DISCUSSION

1. Would the allocation of resources between nondefense and defense goods be most likely studied under the heading of macroeconomics or microeconomics? Explain.

2. Are defense goods scarce or free goods? Explain. What role does the economic problem of scarcity play in the production of defense goods? Explain.

3. Discuss whether it would be necessary to produce defense goods if the economic problem of scarcity did not exist.

4. Which of the goals of a market-oriented economy is related to government production of defense goods? Explain. Would markets be able to produce a sufficient amount of defense goods to prevent the United States from being invaded by another country? Why or why not?

5. Discuss some of the specific opportunity costs of producing more defense goods. What do you think has happened to the opportunity costs of producing defense goods since 1980? Why?

6. Explain how economic growth and unemployment would affect the reallocation of resources from nondefense to defense goods.

Division of Expenditures Between Defense and Nondefense Goods

Year	Defense	Nondefense
	(Percent of *GNP*)	
1940	2.3	97.7
1945	34.5	65.5
1950	5.0	95.0
1955	11.1	88.9
1960	8.8	91.2
1965	7.2	92.8
1970	7.6	92.4
1975	5.6	94.4
1976	5.2	94.8
1977	5.1	94.9
1978	4.8	95.2
1979	4.9	95.1
1980	5.2	94.8
1981	5.5	94.5
1982	6.1	93.9
1983	6.3	93.7
1984	6.3	93.7
1985	6.6	93.4

Source: *Economic Report of the President*, 1986.

SECTION 2

The Market

In Section 1, Basic Economic Concepts, we saw that limited resources lead to limited production possibilities for the economy. When there are unlimited wants but limited resources and therefore limited production, the economy must determine how goods and services are to be allocated. In Unit 1.3 we learned that the two most important methods of allocation are markets and government. In the U.S. economy markets are the predominate method of allocation, which in itself lends significance to our study of markets. However, we should note also that the principles underlying the study of the market constitute the single most important set of principles in economics. The remainder of this text builds on the concepts introduced here.

Unit 2.1, An Introduction to the Market, begins our study of markets with a brief introduction to the two sides of the market: demand (the buyers' side) and supply (the sellers' side). We see that the fundamental purpose of markets is to exchange commodities (goods, services, or resources) between buyers and sellers. We also examine the crucial role price plays in the market, and the process of allocation.

Unit 2.2, Demand, illustrates how buyers respond to changes in the price of a good; this response is expressed in the law of demand and the demand curve. However, we also see that price is not the only factor that affects demand. Unit 2.2 introduces the five most important determinants of demand: buyers' income, prices of other goods, buyers' tastes and preferences, buyers' future expectations, and number of buyers in the market.

Unit 2.3, Supply, explains how sellers respond to changes in the price of a good. The discussion of supply in this unit parallels the discussion of demand in Unit 2.2. We are introduced to the law of supply, the supply curve, and the five most important determinants of supply: factor prices, level of technology, prices of other goods, sellers' future expectations, and number of sellers in the market.

Unit 2.4, Market Equilibrium, applies the principles introduced in the first three units of this section, showing how demand and supply come together to form the market. We see that equilibrium in the market is achieved through the independent decisions of buyers and sellers, and also the part that the price of a good plays in achieving and maintaining market equilibrium. And Unit 2.4 introduces the technique of comparative statics, an analytical tool used throughout the study of economics.

Unit 2.5, Government and the Market, looks at three important applications of the market. In this unit we see how equilibrium in a freely operating market is prevented by price floors, price ceilings, and taxes. This unit not only reinforces the concepts covered in the first four units but also delves into four important issues: agricultural price floors, minimum wage legislation, rent controls, and natural gas regulation.

Unit 2.6, Elasticity, introduces the concept of elasticity. Here we also look at four specific measures of elasticity that relate to the study of the market: the price elasticity of demand, the income elasticity of demand, the cross price elasticity of demand, and the price elasticity of supply. The unit then examines three key determinants of elasticity: availability of substitutes, time period, and proportion of income.

Unit 2.7, Elasticity and the Market, illustrates how elasticity measures are used. In particular, we see how the price elasticities of demand and supply affect markets with price floors, price ceilings, and taxes. We then focus on specific estimates of elasticity for four goods—gasoline, water, fuel oil and coal, and timber—to see how elasticity enhances our understanding of the market and economic activity.

UNIT 2.1

An Introduction to the Market

Solving the economic problem of scarcity requires an answer to the three questions of allocation: What? How? For whom? In the United States allocation is achieved primarily through markets, which determine what goods are produced, how resources are combined to produce the goods, and who receives the goods that are produced. Indeed markets are involved in almost every phase of production, distribution, and consumption in the economy. Thus, in order to understand the operation of the economy, it is essential to understand markets.

By way of introduction to markets, we define a market, which is characterized by the type of commodity exchange, the geographic locale of the exchange, and the time period over which the exchange occurs. In this unit the function of a market is discussed, the concepts of supply and demand are introduced, and the role price plays in the market is developed. And finally, we see how the market functions as a method of allocation.

THE MARKET

Let's start our study of markets with a definition. A **market** is the organized exchange of a commodity between buyers and sellers within a specific geographic area and in a given period of time. The commodities exchanged in a market can be goods, services, or resources. There are markets for labor and capital, and markets for tennis rackets and legal services. Whatever the nature of the commodity, the function of the market is the exchange of a commodity between the people who have it and the people who want it, or between buyers and sellers.

On the buyers' side of the market is the demand for the commodity. **Demand** is the range of quantities of a commodity that buyers are willing and able to buy at different prices in a given period of time. This definition of demand reflects two important features. First, buyers must be willing to buy a commodity. For example, there is no demand for organic waste if no one wants it, can use it, or derives satisfaction from it. However, if someone develops a use for organic waste, such as an agricultural fertilizer, then a demand arises. Second, buyers must be able to buy a commodity. For example, a lot of people would like to have a Mercedes-Benz automobile, but at $50,000 per car, few can afford one. They are willing, but unable, to buy.

On the sellers' side of the market is the supply of the commodity. **Supply** is the range of quantities of a commodity that sellers are willing and able to sell at different prices in a given period of time. As with demand, sellers must be both willing and able to supply a commodity. If the seller is also the producer of a commodity, then the ability to supply is usually based on the ability to cover the costs of producing the commodity. However, if the seller is a private owner, such as an art collector or homeowner, then covering costs may not be enough. The seller may be unwilling to sell at any price because of a personal attachment to the commodity.

THREE CHARACTERISTICS OF A MARKET

There are many different types of markets in the economy. Most of us are aware of the stock market, which is designed to exchange corporate stocks signifying legal ownership of corporations. There are many other relatively well known markets. On the financial side is the gold market, the Eurodollar market, and the treasury bills market. Each market is designed to facilitate the exchange of a commodity, whether gold, Eurodollars, or treasury bills. But few people participate directly in one of these financial markets; most of the participants are banks, financial institutions, or wealthy individuals.

However, everyone takes part in other types of markets on a daily basis. A trip to the grocery store places a person in the retail market for food. Anyone holding a job is in the labor market. A car buyer is in the automobile market. Anytime someone buys or sells any type of commodity, then that person is participating in a market.

A wide range of markets are used to allocate resources, goods, and services. However, with all of this variety, we can still isolate three characteristics required of every market. The **characteristics of a market** are type of commodity, geographic area, and period of time. First and most obvious is the type of commodity exchanged. The market for automobiles and the market for breakfast cereal are clearly different because the commodity exchanged is different. However, the market for sports cars and the market for station wagons also constitute two markets that are different because the commodities exchanged are physically different.

However, identifying the type of commodity is not enough to identify the market. We also need to know the geographic area of the market. The market for houses in Ferndale, Michigan, is not the same as the market for houses in Lubbock, Texas. The price in one market might be rising while the price in the other is falling. There could be an abundance of supply in one and a lack of supply in the other. In short, a market has to be characterized by its geographic area, though that area can be as limited as a small town or as large as the entire planet.

A market must also be characterized by the period of time in which exchange occurs. In general, the longer the time period, the greater the exchange that can occur. For example, the New York Stock Exchange trades around 100 million shares of stock each day and around 20 billion shares in a year. Clearly, the substantial difference in quantity exchanged suggests the importance of specifying the time period for each market.

THE IMPORTANT ROLE OF PRICE IN THE MARKET

Price is the amount of money or other commodity given up to buy a commodity in a market. The price of a commodity is what the buyer pays to the seller in exchange for the commodity. In most modern market-oriented economies the commodity is exchanged for a certain amount of money, that is, the buyer gives the seller money in exchange for the commodity. However, money is not, and need not be, the only denomination used to express a price. For example, in the early history of the United States trappers traded furs for food and supplies. The price of the food and supplies was stated in terms of number of furs rather than dollars, francs, or pounds sterling.

Whatever the unit of measurement, the price of exchange for a commodity plays a significant role in a market, a market-oriented economy, and the process of allocation, providing information and incentives to both buyers and sellers.

Information

The price conveys important information about both buyers and sellers. The price that buyers are willing and able to pay for a commodity indicates how highly they value it. Likewise, the sellers' price tells how much they value the commodity. If they are willing to pay or accept a relatively high price, they must value the commodity a great deal. But if they are willing to exchange it for a relatively low price, then they must not value the commodity quite as much.

Incentives

The price also provides important incentives to buyers and sellers. If the price is relatively high, buyers have an incentive to buy less of the commodity. Only the buyers who value it most, and who are willing to pay a high price, buy the commodity. Thus a relatively high price tends to ration a commodity. The price also provides incentives for the seller. If the price is relatively high, the seller has the incentive to sell more of the commodity. And if the seller also produces the commodity, then there is an incentive to increase production.

THE MARKET AS AN ALLOCATIVE MECHANISM

The two functions of price make the market an excellent tool for allocation of goods. In fact the market answers the three questions of allocation: What? How? For whom? Let's see how each is answered.

Markets determine what commodities are produced by responding to relative prices. If the price of one commodity is high or increasing relative to other prices, then sellers have the incentive to offer more for sale, which directly or indirectly encourages producers to increase production of the commodity by obtaining more resources. But these additional resources are generally being used to produce other commodities, so there is a reallocation of resources from one commodity to another. For example, if the price of corn increases, farmers have the incentive to produce more corn by removing farmland, tractors and equipment, and labor from the production of another crop, such as soybeans, that has a relatively lower price.

Markets also determine how commodities are produced. If the price of one resource is relatively high, producers try to substitute a resource that has a relatively low price. For example, in the United States the price of labor is relatively high compared to the price in India. Thus, farmers in the United States tend to use very little labor but more capital and land in the production of agricultural products. In India agricultural products are produced using relatively more labor and less capital and land.

Markets also determine who receives the commodities that are produced. Markets allocate commodities to the buyers willing and able to pay the highest prices. For example, suppose a potential buyer offers to pay a car dealer $5000 for a used

Camaro. If someone else offers $7000, the car dealer would undoubtedly take the higher offer.

IDEAL MARKETS AND THE REAL WORLD

At this point we need to distinguish between real world markets and theoretical markets. In this section we are building a theory of the market, an abstract, analytical tool that enables us to study economic activity in the world. As an abstract representation of the real world, it does not contain all of the details that exist in an actual market.

In the theoretical market a distinct type of commodity is identified, for example, automobiles. However, in the real world the market for automobiles is not clear-cut, because it may not be evident exactly what types of vehicles are considered to be automobiles. Of course the basic four-door sedans are included, but what about trucks, four-wheel drive vehicles, or vans? In the real world commodities are not easily classified.

In addition, in the theoretical market a geographic area is specified, such as the market for swimsuits in Ferndale, Michigan. But even a geographic area may not be distinct. Suppose a tourist from Florida buys a swimsuit while traveling through Ferndale. Since the tourist does not live in Ferndale, should this sale be included or excluded from the market? Or suppose a resident of Ferndale goes to Detroit to buy a swimsuit. Should this sale be included as part of the Ferndale market for swimsuits? Furthermore, suppose a Ferndale resident meets a Ferndale swimsuit sales representative in Pocatello, Idaho. If they make an exchange there, is it part of the Ferndale swimsuit market?

In the real world it is not easy to isolate distinct markets. However, the theoretical market does give us a good understanding of allocation and exchange in the real world. While the theoretical market is an abstract representation of the world, it does identify and provide insight into the two most important features of every market, supply and demand.

IN SUMMARY

An Introduction to the Market

- A market is the organized exchange of a commodity between buyers and sellers, within a specific geographic area and for a given period of time. The primary function of the market is to facilitate the exchange of commodities between demanders (buyers) and suppliers (sellers). Demanders are the ones who want the commodity, and suppliers are the ones who have it.

- There are many different types of markets, but all markets are characterized by type of commodity, geographic area, and period of time.

- The price paid to the seller by the buyer in exchange for the commodity is an important part of the market. The price, whether in monetary units or in terms of another good, has two functions: information and incentives.

- As a mechanism for allocating resources, the market answers the three questions of allocation: What? How? For whom? The price determines what goods to produce by signaling producers to allocate resources to the production of goods with relatively high or rising prices. The market also determines how goods are produced based on the relative prices of resources. And the market determines who receives the goods based on which buyers are willing and able to pay the highest prices.

- The theoretical market is an abstraction from markets in the real world. However, the theory identifies the principles of demand and supply that are the basis of exchange in the real world.

QUESTIONS FOR STUDY AND ANALYSIS

1. Over the past two decades the price of medical care has increased faster than the price of food. Based on the allocative function of markets

and prices, what do you think happened to the allocation of resources between the production of medical care and food over this period of time? How might this affect a college student's decision whether to study biology or agronomy?

2. Rent controls on apartments in many major cities have prevented rental payments from increasing, or at least increasing as fast as other prices. Explain how this would affect the incentive to build new apartments in these cities. Explain how the allocation of resources between the construction of apartments and uncontrolled owner-occupied houses would be affected.

3. Suppose that Ben trades a peanut butter and jelly sandwich to Joey for two Twinkies. What is the price of a Twinkie? If Joey trades the sandwich to Susan for a litter of six kittens, now what is the price of a Twinkie (in terms of kittens)?

REVIEW GLOSSARY

characteristics of a market There are three important characteristics of a market: type of commodity, geographic area, and period of time.

demand The range of quantities of a commodity that buyers are willing and able to buy at different prices in a given period of time.

market The organized exchange of a commodity between buyers and sellers within a specific geographic area and in a given period of time. The market facilitates the exchange of a commodity between those who have it and those who want it.

price The amount of money or other commodity given up to buy a commodity in a market. While the price is usually in monetary units, it can also be in terms of another commodity. The price of a commodity provides information and incentives to both buyers and sellers.

supply The range of quantities of a commodity that sellers are willing and able to sell at different prices in a given period of time.

UNIT 2.2

Demand

Demand represents the buyers' side of the market, and reflects buyers' willingness and ability to purchase goods and services. More specifically, **demand** is the range of quantities of a commodity that buyers are willing and able to buy at different prices in a given period of time. In this unit we first examine the law of demand, which is embodied in a graph called the demand curve. The demand curve illustrates how quantity demanded is related to the price of a good, but it can also be used to show how other factors, called determinants, affect the demand for a good.

THE LAW OF DEMAND

The **law of demand** is a principle that states an inverse relationship exists between the price of a commodity and the quantity of the commodity that buyers are willing and able to purchase in a given period of time if other factors are held constant. Let's illustrate the law of demand with a simple example. Suppose you want a midmorning, between-class snack. If you discover that the price of a donut in the cafeteria is 10 cents, you might be so pleased that you buy several donuts. But if you discover that the price of a donut is 60 cents, you will probably be less willing and able to buy as many donuts. Table 2.2.1 presents what we call the demand schedule for donuts. A **demand schedule** is a table that illustrates the alternative quantities of a commodity demanded at different prices. We can see that as the price of donuts increases from 10 cents to 60 cents, the quantity of donuts demanded decreases from 5 donuts to no donuts. The relationship between the quantity of donuts demanded and the price of donuts illustrates the law of demand.

UNIT 2.2 • DEMAND

Table 2.2.1

Hypothetical Demand Schedule for Donuts

The law of demand states that the price of a good and the quantity of the good demanded are inversely related. In this table, as the price of donuts declines from 60 cents to 10 cents, the quantity demanded increases from no donuts to 5 donuts.

Price in Cents	Quantity
60	0
50	1
40	2
30	3
20	4
10	5

The law of demand holds for two reasons. First, if the price of a good rises, buyers tend to buy less of that good and more of other goods because of the substitution effect. The **substitution effect** is the change in quantity demanded that results because the price of the good changes relative to the prices of other goods. As the price of donuts rises, you are likely to purchase another good, such as cinnamon rolls. If cinnamon rolls sell for 40 cents, they are relatively expensive compared to donuts that sell for only 10 cents. Even if you like cinnamon rolls more than donuts, you might be willing to buy 4 donuts instead of 1 cinnamon roll. But if the price of donuts rises to 20 cents, you may not be willing to buy only 2 donuts instead of 1 cinnamon roll. Although donuts are still cheaper than cinnamon rolls, the price of a donut has increased *relative* to the price of cinnamon rolls, so you substitute cinnamon rolls for donuts.

Second, because of limited income, buyers tend to buy less of a good when the price rises. This is the **income effect,** which is the change in quantity demanded that results because a change in the price gives a buyer more real income, even though money income remains unchanged. If you have only 1 dollar to spend on a midmorning, between-class snack, 5 donuts are easily purchased for 10 cents each, with change left over. However, if the price rises to 50 cents, your limited income prevents you from purchasing 5 donuts.

THE DEMAND CURVE

The **demand curve** is the graphical representation of the law of demand. Figure 2.2.1 presents a demand curve, which is obtained by plotting the price/quantity combinations from the demand schedule in Table 2.2.1. If the price of donuts is 20 cents, the quantity demanded in Figure 2.2.1 is 4 donuts (point A), but if the price increases to 40 cents,

Figure 2.2.1

Demand Curve for Donuts

A demand curve has a negative slope because of the law of demand. An inverse relationship exists between price and quantity demanded. If the price of donuts rises from 20 cents to 40 cents, the quantity demanded falls from 4 donuts to 2 donuts.

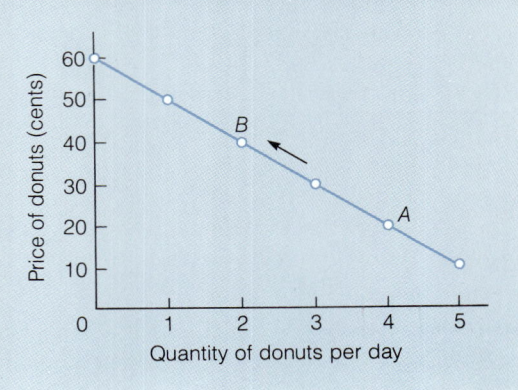

the quantity demanded decreases to 2 donuts (point B). The demand curve in Figure 2.2.1 has a negative slope, because higher prices lead to smaller quantities demanded; this negative slope demonstrates the law of demand.

Figure 2.2.1 shows the demand curve for donuts for a single individual. However, we are primarily concerned with market demand. The **market demand** is the total demand of every individual willing and able to buy the good. To get the market demand for donuts, we have to combine the demand curves of every individual in the market for donuts.

Table 2.2.2 illustrates how we obtain the market demand for donuts if there are only two buyers in the market. The first column lists the price of donuts. The second column lists the corresponding quantity of donuts demanded by buyer A and the third column lists the quantities demanded by buyer B. Note that as the price decreases from 80 cents to 10 cents, the quantity of donuts demanded by buyer B increases from 2 to 9.

If the donut market consists only of buyers A and B, we can find the *total* market demand by determining how much both demand at a given price. If the price of donuts is 80 cents, and buyer A demands no donuts and buyer B demands 2, then the total market demand is 2 donuts. If the price of donuts decreases to 10 cents, and buyer A demands 5 donuts and buyer B demands 9 donuts, then the total market demand is 14 donuts. Each number in the fourth column of Table 2.2.2 is obtained in the same manner. Whether the market contains two buyers or two thousand, the total market demand is obtained by combining the quantities demanded by each buyer at each price.

Figure 2.2.2 illustrates the relationship between the individual demand curves for buyers A and B and the market demand curve. Panel a presents the demand curve for buyer A, and panel b the demand curve for buyer B. In panel c the market demand curve is obtained by the horizontal addition of the two individual demand curves. If we start with a price of 80 cents, we see from the demand curve in panel a that buyer A demands no donuts. However, in panel b we see that buyer B demands 2 donuts at the same price. If the total quantity demanded by both buyers is plotted in panel c, we have one point on the market demand curve.

If the price is 10 cents, buyer A demands 5 donuts, as shown in the demand curve in panel a, and buyer B demands 9 donuts, as shown in panel b. The total is plotted in panel c, giving us another point on the market demand curve.

A CHANGE IN THE QUANTITY DEMANDED AND A CHANGE IN DEMAND

We need to make an important distinction between the price of a good, and other factors that affect demand. A change in the price of a good causes a change in the quantity demanded. A **change in**

Table 2.2.2

Derivation of Market Demand for Donuts

The market demand for a good is found by adding the quantity demanded by each buyer at each price. If the price is 80 cents, then buyer A demands no donuts and buyer B demands 2 donuts, for a total market demand of 2 donuts. If the price is 10 cents, buyer A demands 5 donuts and buyer B demands 9 donuts, for a total market demand of 14 donuts.

Price in Cents	Quantity Demanded		Market Demand
	Buyer A	Buyer B	
80	0	2	2
70	0	3	3
60	0	4	4
50	1	5	6
40	2	6	8
30	3	7	10
20	4	8	12
10	5	9	14

Figure 2.2.2

Market Demand Curve

The market demand curve is obtained by horizontally adding all individual demand curves. The quantity of the good demanded by buyer A and buyer B at a given price is added; the total is the market demand at that price. This procedure is repeated for each price, and the quantities are plotted in panel c.

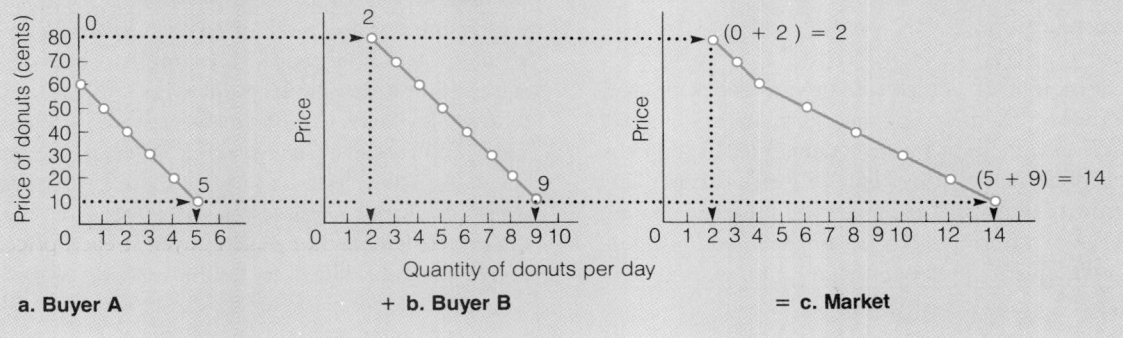

a. Buyer A   + b. Buyer B   = c. Market

Quantity of donuts per day

quantity demanded is a movement along a demand curve caused by a change in the price of the good. In Figure 2.2.3 an increase in price causes the movement from point A to point B along demand curve D. As the price of donuts increases from 10 cents to 20 cents, the quantity of donuts demanded falls from 140 to 100. Moreover, a change in the price is the only factor that can cause a change in quantity demanded.

However, other factors can also affect demand. A change in any factor, other than the price of the good, that affects demand causes an overall change in demand. A **change in demand** is a shift in the entire demand curve resulting from a change in any of the determinants of demand. Suppose buyers suddenly have an overwhelming urge to buy donuts. In Figure 2.2.3 buyers are willing to buy 170 donuts if the price is 20 cents (point B'), and 230 donuts if the price is 10 cents (point A'). In both cases buyers are willing to buy more donuts after this new urge has hit them than before. In fact, at every price buyers are willing to buy more donuts. The sudden urge for donuts causes the demand curve to shift rightward from D to D'.

Figure 2.2.3

A Change in Quantity Demanded and a Change in Demand

A change in price causes a change in quantity demanded and a movement along a given demand curve, such as from A to B. A change in any other factor causes the entire demand curve to shift, such as from D to D'.

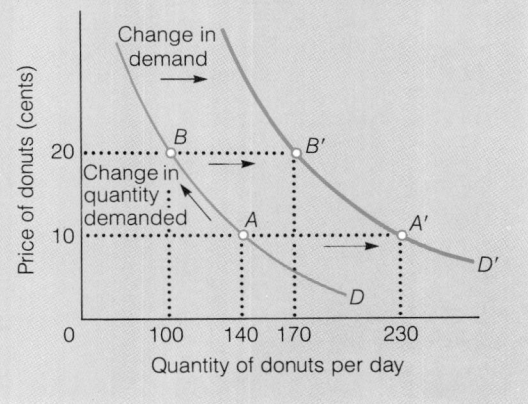

THE DETERMINANTS OF DEMAND

The five key factors in determining demanders' willingness and ability to buy goods in the market are income, prices of other goods, tastes and preferences, expectations, and number of buyers. These factors are called the **determinants of demand,** and each of them can cause a shift in the market demand curve.

Income

The ability of demanders to buy goods is based directly on their income. Usually as income increases, more of a good is demanded at the existing price. Panel a in Figure 2.2.4 illustrates how an increase in income affects the market demand curve of a normal good. A **normal good** is a good for which an increase in income causes an increase in demand, or a rightward shift in the demand curve. For example, buyers initially demand 75 stereo record albums at $10 each (point A), but if their income rises, they demand 110 albums at the same price (point B). At every price more albums are demanded with the higher income level.

Panel b in Figure 2.2.4 illustrates the effect of income on an inferior good. An **inferior good** is a good for which an increase in income causes a decrease in demand, or a leftward shift in the demand curve. Inferior goods are often less expensive substitutes for another good. For example, people with relatively low income levels may buy 30 black and white televisions even though they would rather have color television sets. But if their income increases, they can afford to buy more desired, yet more expensive, color television sets. Consequently, this group of people may buy only 10 black and white television sets at the existing price of

Figure 2.2.4

Income and the Demand Curve

In panel a an increase in income causes the demand curve to shift rightward because stereo albums are a normal good. In panel b an increase in income causes the demand curve to shift leftward because black and white televisions are an inferior good.

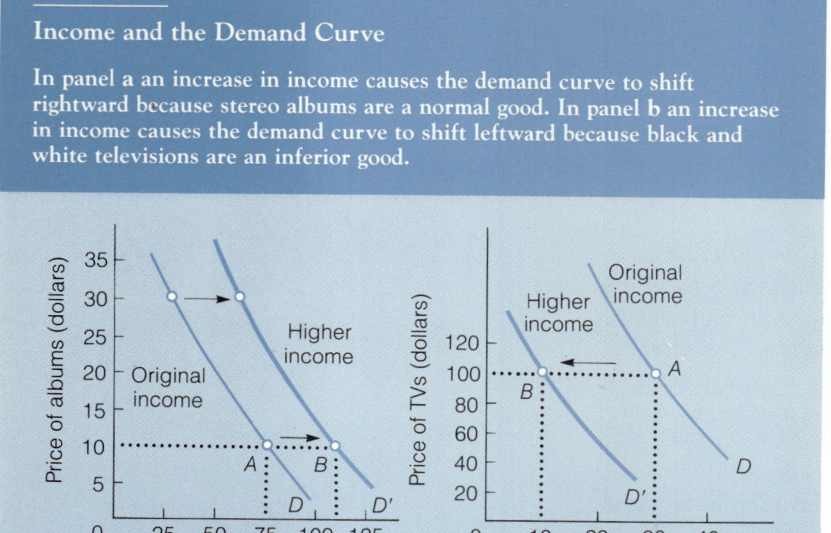

a. Normal good—stereo albums

b. Inferior good—black and white TVs

$100, causing the demand curve for black and white television sets to shift leftward.

Prices of Other Goods

A change in the price of one good can cause a shift in the demand curve of another good. When an increase in the price of one good causes an increase in demand and a rightward shift in the demand curve for a second good, the two goods are **substitutes** in consumption. For example, the price of long-distance telephone services affects the demand for postage stamps. If the price of a long-distance call increases from 25 cents to 50 cents per minute, the quantity (both the number and the length) of long-distance telephone calls demanded decreases as people write more letters. In panel a of Figure 2.2.5 this effect is shown as a rightward shift in the market demand for postage stamps. At every price the demand for postage stamps is greater because people are making fewer long-distance telephone calls and writing more letters.

Another type of relationship is also possible. When an increase in the price of one good causes a decrease in demand and a leftward shift in the demand curve for a second good, the two goods are **complements** in consumption. Take the case of golf clubs and golf balls, both of which are necessary to play golf. If the price of golf clubs increases, the quantity demanded decreases, and fewer people play golf. But if fewer people play golf, fewer golf balls are needed, and the number of golf balls purchased declines without a change in price. In panel b of Figure 2.2.5 this is seen as a leftward shift of the demand curve.

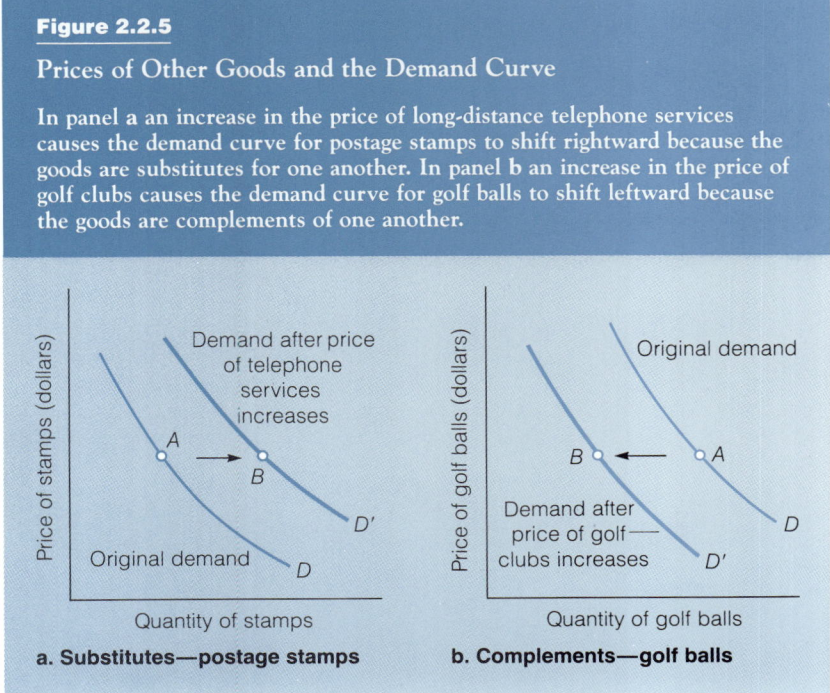

Figure 2.2.5

Prices of Other Goods and the Demand Curve

In panel a an increase in the price of long-distance telephone services causes the demand curve for postage stamps to shift rightward because the goods are substitutes for one another. In panel b an increase in the price of golf clubs causes the demand curve for golf balls to shift leftward because the goods are complements of one another.

a. Substitutes—postage stamps
b. Complements—golf balls

Tastes and Preferences

Market demand is affected by buyers' willingness to purchase different goods. Tastes and preferences, which affect this willingness, change over time. For example, in the mid-1970s the movie *Saturday Night Fever*, starring John Travolta, started the disco craze. Sparked by the movie, the demand for disco clothes increased tremendously, and stores were unable to maintain their inventories. Panel a in Figure 2.2.6 illustrates how the demand curve for disco clothes shifted from almost nothing (D) before the movie, to the far right (D') after the movie was released. This shift was due to changing tastes and preferences on the part of clothing buyers.

The story does not end here. A few years after the success of *Saturday Night Fever,* Travolta appeared in another movie, entitled *Urban Cowboy,* which sparked a second fashion trend in the United States, the western look. The demand curve for disco clothes shifted almost all the way back to D in panel a, while the demand curve for western fashions shifted from curve D to D' in panel b.

Changes in tastes and preferences are very evident in the fashion industry. However, tastes in many different types of goods undergo changes, though not quite as abruptly. Over the years tastes in automobiles have changed, from chrome and large tail fins to well-defined European styles. Football has replaced baseball as the national pastime. Hula-hoops, pet rocks, and miniskirts have all come and gone and may even come back again.

Expectations

The market demand today can be greatly affected by buyers' future expectations. If buyers expect market conditions to change in the near future,

Figure 2.2.6

Tastes and Preferences and the Demand Curve

A change in the tastes and preferences of buyers causes the demand curve to shift. In panel a the demand curve for disco clothes shifted rightward from D to D' after the movie *Saturday Night Fever* started a new fashion trend. However, after the movie *Urban Cowboy* was released, the demand for disco clothes in panel a shifted leftward, back close to $D,$ and the demand for cowboy clothes shifted rightward in panel b.

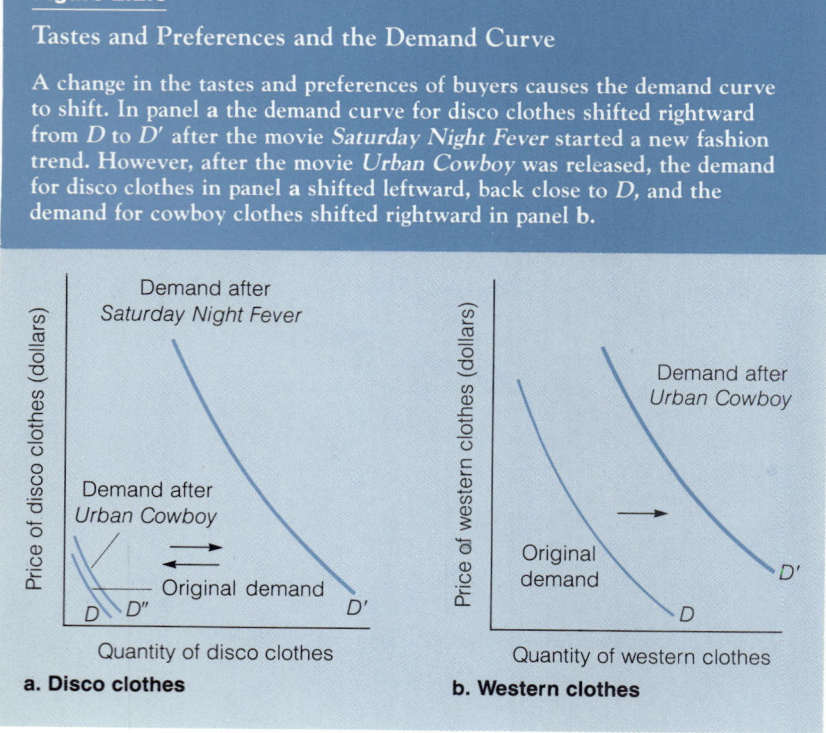

a. Disco clothes

b. Western clothes

then they adjust their demand in the present accordingly. If buyers expect lower prices in the future, the demand curve shifts leftward. If they expect higher prices in the future, the demand curve shifts rightward. For example, conditions in the market for personal computers changed rapidly in the early 1980s as newer and less expensive machines were constantly being introduced. Anyone who bought a personal computer usually saw the price of their machine fall by 10 percent to 30 percent within a few months. In fact, the manufacturer of Osborne computers, the first portable computer, went out of business because of changes in expectations.

Osborne was successfully producing and selling their portable computer when they announced they would introduce a newer, faster, and cheaper portable computer in the near future. Everyone who was considering buying an Osborne decided to wait for the new machine; this is seen in Figure 2.2.7 as a leftward shift in the demand curve from D to D'. Meanwhile, Osborne had a lot of the existing computers that they couldn't sell. Indeed, their sales became so slow that they went out of business before they could introduce their newer machine.

Number of Buyers

An increase in the number of buyers in the market causes the demand curve to shift rightward. A decrease in the number of buyers causes the demand curve to shift leftward. As we saw in Figure 2.2.2, the market demand is composed of the individual demands of every buyer in the market. If more buyers enter the market, the market demand curve shifts rightward. The market demand for notebooks in a college town during the summer, when most students and many of the faculty are gone, might look like curve D in Figure 2.2.8. When the

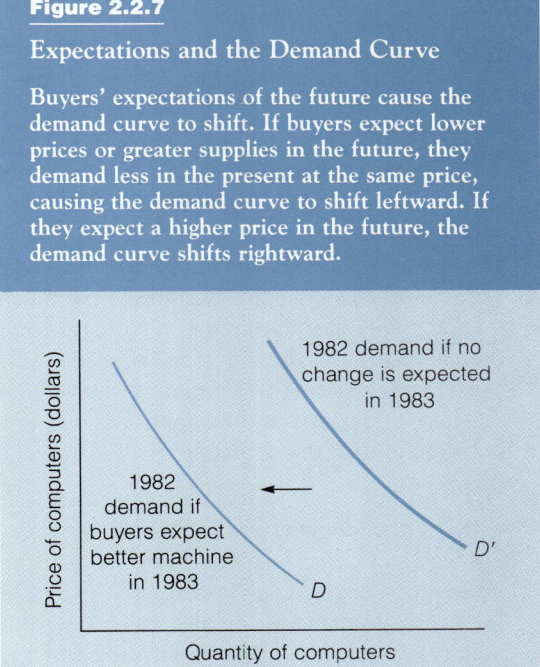

Figure 2.2.7

Expectations and the Demand Curve

Buyers' expectations of the future cause the demand curve to shift. If buyers expect lower prices or greater supplies in the future, they demand less in the present at the same price, causing the demand curve to shift leftward. If they expect a higher price in the future, the demand curve shifts rightward.

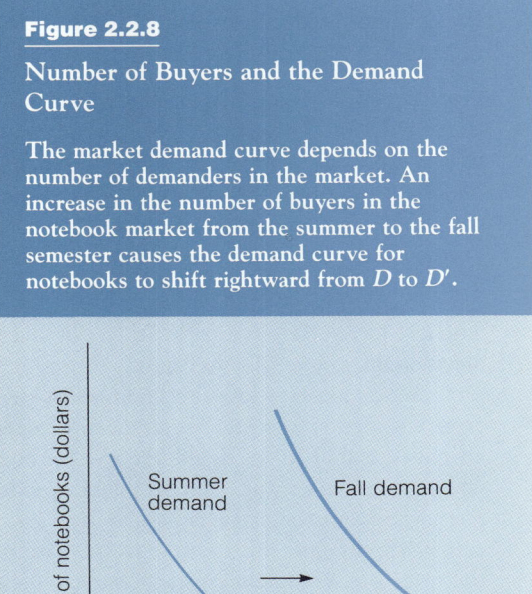

Figure 2.2.8

Number of Buyers and the Demand Curve

The market demand curve depends on the number of demanders in the market. An increase in the number of buyers in the notebook market from the summer to the fall semester causes the demand curve for notebooks to shift rightward from D to D'.

semester begins and the students and faculty return to campus, the market demand for notebooks shifts rightward to D' because the number of buyers in the market has increased.

IN SUMMARY
Demand

- Demand, the buyers' side of the market, constitutes the range of quantities that buyers are willing and able to purchase at alternative prices. According to the law of demand, higher prices decrease the quantity demanded as buyers are constrained by their income or switch to other goods.

- The demand curve is the graphical representation of the law of demand, and has a negative slope. A higher price causes a movement up along the demand curve, resulting in a decrease in the quantity demanded. The market demand for a good is obtained by horizontally adding all individual demand curves.

- A change in the quantity demanded can only be caused by a change in the price of the good, which represents movement along a demand curve. If any other factors affecting demand, called the determinants of demand, change, then the entire demand curve shifts, which is a change in demand.

- The five key determinants that affect demand are income, prices of other goods, tastes and preferences, expectations, and number of buyers in the market. An increase in income causes a rightward shift in the demand curve for normal goods and a leftward shift for inferior goods. An increase in the price of a substitute good causes a rightward shift, while an increase in the price of a complement good causes a leftward shift. Tastes and preferences and expectations can cause either increases or decreases in demand, and more buyers cause a rightward shift.

QUESTIONS FOR STUDY AND ANALYSIS

1. Suppose you are given the following information concerning price and the quantity of bestseller novels demanded:

Price	Quantity Demanded
$10	100
9	200
8	300
7	400
6	500
5	600
4	700
3	800
2	900
1	1000

   a. Construct the demand curve. What is the numerical value of the slope of the demand curve? Is it positive or negative?
   b. Suppose this is a normal good and buyers have a decrease in income. If buyers are willing and able to purchase 100 fewer novels of the good at each price, construct the new demand curve. In which direction did the demand curve shift when income declined?
   c. Suppose the price of the good increases from $2 to $8 at the same time buyers experience the decrease in income as described in part b. How much of the good do buyers demand before the change in price and income? How much is demanded after the change in both price and income? What is the difference between these two? How much of this difference is due to a change in demand and how much is due to a change in quantity demanded?

2. Explain how each of the following situations affects the demand for computer software. Indicate whether there is a change in quantity demanded or a change in demand. If there is a change in demand, discuss which determinant is involved and in which direction the demand curve shifts.

a. IBM announces a 23 percent reduction in the price of personal computers.
b. The top three computer software producers go bankrupt.
c. The government passes legislation giving tax breaks to anyone buying computers or computer software.
d. The price of electricity increases.
e. The price of admission to movies decreases.
f. Everyone in the country realizes that personal computers are just a passing fad and that a Ph.D. in computer science is needed to operate one.
g. Computer software companies decide to sell their operating manuals separately from their floppy disks and at a higher price.

3. Prior to the 1984 Olympics in Los Angeles, local store merchants began to stock up for what they thought would be two weeks of lucrative sales. However, most merchants found that sales were actually less than normal during the Olympics. Explain how buyers' expectations might have kept the merchants from getting as much gold as the athletes.

4. If the law of demand states that price and quantity are inversely related, why do people buy luxury goods only when they are priced higher than other goods? For example, many people who would buy a Mercedes-Benz when priced at $35,000 would not buy it if priced at $10,000. Does this violate the law of demand?

REVIEW GLOSSARY

change in demand A shift of the entire demand curve resulting from a change in any of the determinants of demand.

change in quantity demanded The movement along a demand curve, caused by a change in the price of the good. A change in quantity demanded can only result from a change in price.

complements Two goods that are used together, and an increase in the price of one good leads to a decrease in demand and a leftward shift in the demand curve of the other good.

demand The range of quantities of a commodity that buyers are willing and able to buy at different prices in a given period of time.

demand curve A graphical representation of the law of demand. A demand curve has a negative slope due to the law of demand.

demand schedule A table that illustrates the alternative quantities of a commodity demanded at different prices.

determinants of demand The five key factors that affect market demand are income, prices of other goods, tastes and preferences, expectations, and number of buyers in the market.

income effect The change in quantity demanded that results because a change in the price gives a buyer more real income, even though money income remains unchanged.

inferior good A good for which an increase in income causes a decrease in demand, or a leftward shift in the demand curve.

law of demand The principle that states an inverse relationship exists between the price of a commodity and the quantity of the commodity that buyers are willing and able to purchase in a given period of time if other factors are held constant. One reason the law of demand holds is that buyers substitute similar goods that become relatively cheaper as the price of one good rises. A second reason is that buyers are constrained by the amount of income they have to spend on a good.

market demand The total demand of every individual willing and able to buy the good. The market demand curve is found by horizontally adding all individual demand curves.

normal good A good for which an increase in income causes an increase in demand, or a rightward shift in the demand curve.

substitutes Two goods that have similar uses, where an increase in the price of one good leads to an increase in demand and a rightward shift in the demand curve of the other good.

substitution effect The change in quantity demanded that results because the price of the good changes relative to the prices of other goods.

UNIT 2.3

Supply

Supply represents the sellers' side of the market and reflects sellers' willingness and ability to sell goods and services. **Supply** is the range of quantities of a commodity that sellers are willing and able to sell at different prices in a given period of time. In this unit we first examine the law of supply, which, like the law of demand, is one of the most important principles in economics. The law of supply is graphically presented as the supply curve, illustrating the relationship between the price of a commodity and the quantity of the commodity supplied. The supply curve is also used to illustrate the determinants of supply.

THE LAW OF SUPPLY

The **law of supply** is a principle that states a direct relationship exists between the price of a commodity and the quantity of the commodity that sellers are willing and able to supply in a given period of time if other factors are held constant. Let's illustrate the law of supply with a simple example. Suppose a barber is willing and able to produce 25 haircuts per day at $10 per haircut, but at $12 per haircut the barber is willing and able to produce 30 haircuts per day. In short, higher prices encourage the barber to produce more haircuts. Table 2.3.1 presents a supply schedule for this barber. A **supply schedule** is a table that illustrates the alternative quantities of a commodity supplied at different prices. As the price of haircuts increases from $2 to $16, the quantity supplied increases from 5 haircuts to 40 haircuts. The direct relationship between price and quantity supplied in Table 2.3.1 results from the law of supply.

UNIT 2.3 ▪ SUPPLY

Table 2.3.1

Hypothetical Supply Schedule for Haircuts

The law of supply states that the price of a good and the quantity of the good supplied are directly related. In this table, as the price of haircuts decreases from $16 to $2, the quantity supplied also decreases from 40 haircuts to 5 haircuts.

Price	Quantity
$16	40
14	35
12	30
10	25
8	20
6	15
4	10
2	5

The law of supply holds because of the costs of production. The barber is willing and able to sell 5 haircuts for $2 if the costs of production can be covered. However, to produce 30 haircuts, more factors of production must be purchased, and the additional factors may be less productive than the existing factors. For example, if a second barber is less efficient, and spends more time on each haircut, then the cost per haircut rises. Or the barber may have to bid factors away from the production of another good, which also increases the cost of producing additional haircuts. Higher costs mean the barber needs to receive a higher price to be willing and able to sell haircuts.

Although the law of supply does not always hold in the production of all goods at all times, in general, higher prices are required for producers to supply more goods. In some circumstances producers are willing and able to supply more output at the same price, or even at a lower price; we discuss some of these cases in detail in Section 9, Monopoly and Imperfect Competition.

THE SUPPLY CURVE

The **supply curve** is the graphical representation of the law of supply. It is obtained by plotting the price/quantity combinations from the supply schedule in Table 2.3.1. Figure 2.3.1 presents a supply curve, showing the direct relationship between price and quantity supplied. If haircuts sell for $4 each, then the barber is willing to supply 10 haircuts (point A), but if the price increases to $8 per haircut, the barber offers 20 haircuts for sale (point B). Higher prices lead to larger quantities supplied, in accordance with the law of supply. As the price of a haircut changes, the barber moves up and down along the supply curve in Figure 2.3.1,

Figure 2.3.1

Supply Curve for Haircuts

A supply curve is positively sloped because of the law of supply. A direct relationship exists between price and the quantity supplied. If the price of haircuts rises from $4 to $8, the quantity supplied rises from 10 haircuts to 20 haircuts.

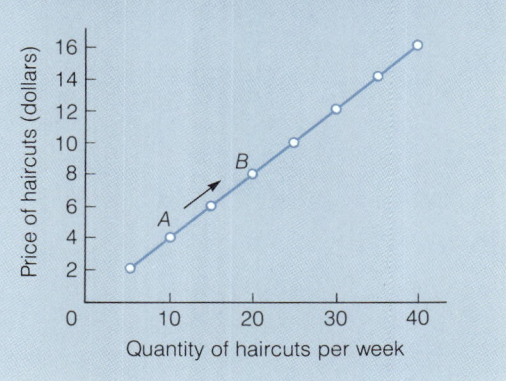

increasing or decreasing the quantity of haircuts supplied.

In most markets output is supplied by more than one seller, which means our primary concern is with the market supply. **Market supply is the total supply of every individual seller willing and able to sell the good at alternative prices.** To obtain the market supply, the supply curves of all individual sellers in the market are combined.

Table 2.3.2 illustrates how we can determine the total market supply for haircuts if we have a market consisting of two suppliers. The first column lists the price of haircuts, ranging from $16 to $2. The second column lists the quantities supplied by barber A, and the third column the quantities supplied by barber B. Note that the first two columns are identical to Table 2.3.1. For prices less than $8, barber B does not supply any haircuts, because any amount less than $8 is not enough to cover the costs of producing haircuts. However, at $8 and above barber B follows the law of supply, offering more haircuts for sale at higher prices.

The fourth column lists the total quantity of haircuts supplied in the market, a figure obtained by adding the numbers in the second and third columns. With two barbers in the market, we can determine the market supply by adding together the quantity each barber supplies at each price.

Figure 2.3.2 illustrates the relationship between the supply curves for barbers A and B and the market supply. Panel a presents the supply curve for barber A, and panel b the supply curve for barber B. As with market demand, the market supply curve is obtained by the horizontal addition of both supply curves. If we start with a price of $16, we can horizontally move across Figure 2.3.2, noting that barber A supplies 40 haircuts and barber B supplies 50 haircuts, for a total market supply, plotted in panel c, of 90 haircuts. Each point on the market supply curve is obtained in the same way.

A CHANGE IN THE QUANTITY SUPPLIED AND A CHANGE IN SUPPLY

A change in the price of a good causes a change in the quantity supplied. A **change in quantity supplied is a movement along a supply curve caused by a change in the price of the good,** seen in Figure 2.3.3 as a movement along supply curve S from point A to point B. As the price of haircuts increases from $8 to $12, the quantity of haircuts supplied increases from 30 to 60.

However, supply is also affected by several determinants of supply. A change in any of these determinants causes a change in supply. A **change in supply is a shift in the entire supply curve resulting from a change in any of the determinants of supply.** For example, suppose that the two barbers underlying market supply curve S in Figure 2.3.3 are joined by a new barber, who is willing to supply

Table 2.3.2
Derivation of Market Supply for Haircuts

The market supply for a good is found by adding the quantity supplied by each seller at each price. If the price is $16, then barber A supplies 40 haircuts and barber B supplies 50 haircuts, for a total market supply of 90 haircuts. If the price is $2, barber A supplies 5 haircuts and barber B supplies no haircuts, for a total market supply of 5 haircuts.

	Quantity Supplied		
Price	Barber A	Barber B	Market Total
$16	40	50	90
14	35	40	75
12	30	30	60
10	25	20	45
8	20	10	30
6	15	0	15
4	10	0	10
2	5	0	5

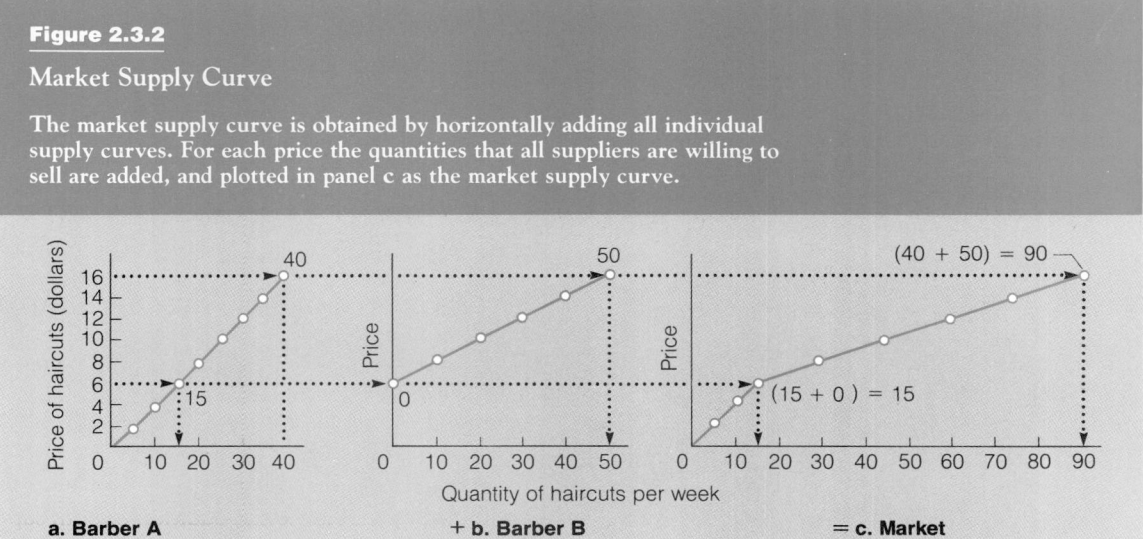

Figure 2.3.2
Market Supply Curve

The market supply curve is obtained by horizontally adding all individual supply curves. For each price the quantities that all suppliers are willing to sell are added, and plotted in panel c as the market supply curve.

a. Barber A + b. Barber B = c. Market

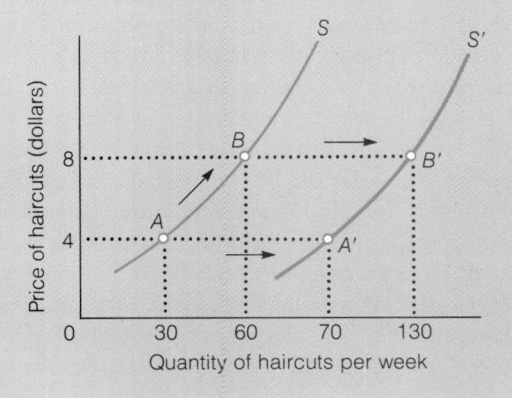

Figure 2.3.3

A Change in Quantity Supplied and a Change in Supply

A change in the price causes a change in the quantity supplied and a movement along a given supply curve, such as from A to B. A change in any of the determinants causes the entire supply curve to shift, in this case, from S to S'.

40 haircuts at $8, and 70 haircuts at $12. The three barbers now supply 70 haircuts at $8, and 130 haircuts at $12, plotted in Figure 2.3.3 as market supply curve S'. A change in the price is the only factor that causes a change in the quantity supplied and a movement along a supply curve. But a change in one of the determinants causes the supply curve itself to shift.

THE DETERMINANTS OF SUPPLY

Other than price, the five key factors in determining suppliers' willingness and ability to offer goods for sale are factor of production prices, technology, prices of other goods, expectations, and number of suppliers. These are called the **determinants of supply**, and all can cause the supply curve to shift.

Factor Prices

The price at which producers are willing and able to sell output depends on the costs of factors, including wages, rent payments, and material prices. If factor prices increase, then the cost of producing

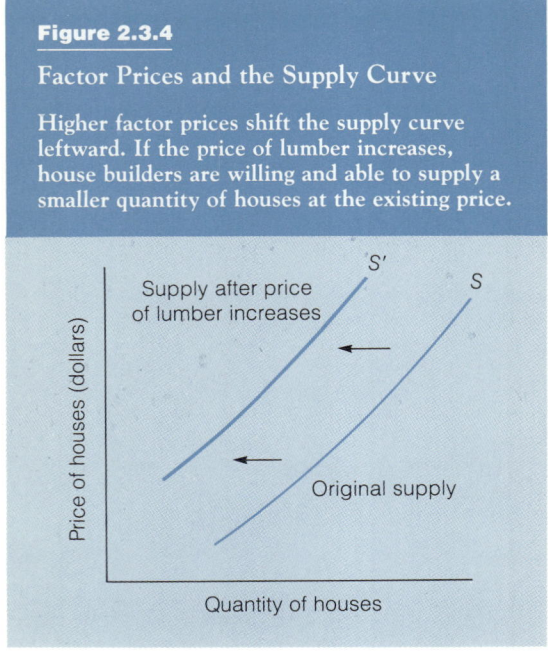

Figure 2.3.4

Factor Prices and the Supply Curve

Higher factor prices shift the supply curve leftward. If the price of lumber increases, house builders are willing and able to supply a smaller quantity of houses at the existing price.

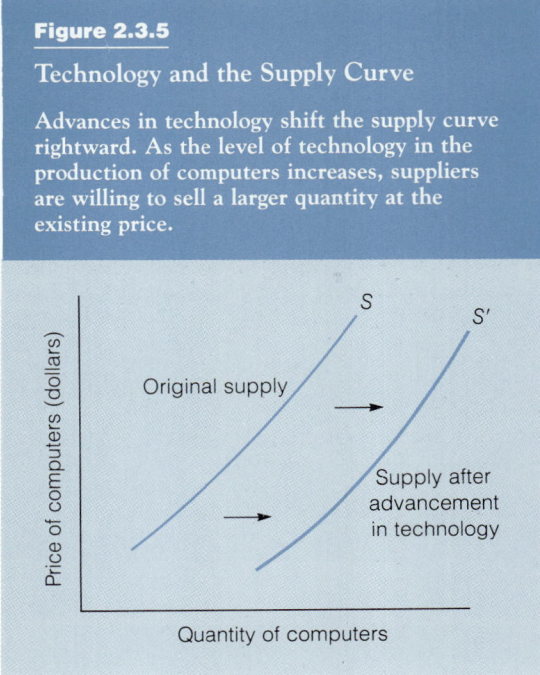

Figure 2.3.5

Technology and the Supply Curve

Advances in technology shift the supply curve rightward. As the level of technology in the production of computers increases, suppliers are willing to sell a larger quantity at the existing price.

the same quantity of the good also increases, so that producers need to charge a higher price to continue producing the same quantity. For example, lumber is an important factor in the production of houses. If the price of lumber increases, house builders are unwilling to charge the same price for the same number of houses. Figure 2.3.4 illustrates how a change in the cost of lumber causes the market supply curve for houses to shift leftward. Note that at every price, house builders offer a smaller quantity for sale, shifting the supply curve leftward from S to S'.

Technology

Technology is the economy's combined knowledge and information of alternative methods for using factors in the production of goods and services. Technology determines the alternative methods of combining labor, capital, and land in the production of output. Technology is important in the supply of goods because it improves over time. That is, the methods of production become more efficient, enabling more output to be produced with the same quantity of factors, or the same quantity of output to be produced with fewer factors.

The production of computers provides a good example of how technology affects the supply of a good. Thirty years ago computers were big, slow, and expensive. A computer that could store 64,000 characters (letters or numbers) cost well over $1 million. Today a smaller, faster computer with that amount of memory can be purchased for under $200. The reason for the lower price is the tremendous advancement in the technology of making computers. Today, computers use silicon chips, which perform the same function that transistors and glass tubes once did. The advent of the silicon chip has shifted the supply curve for computers rightward, as illustrated in Figure 2.3.5. At each price computer producers are willing and able to supply a larger number of computers.

Prices of Other Goods

If two goods use the same types of resources in production, then a change in the price of one good can cause the supply curve of the other to shift. <u>Substitutes in production are goods that are produced with the same resources such that resources used to produce one good cannot be used to produce the other.</u> For example, if farmers plant land with corn, they can neither use that land nor the labor and capital to produce soybeans. Producing corn with those resources excludes the production of soybeans with the same resources.

The relationship between the production of corn and soybeans means a change in the price of one can shift the supply curve of the other. For example, if the price of corn increases, the law of supply tells us that the quantity of corn supplied also increases. But to increase corn production, farmers have to divert some soybean resources to the production of corn. Therefore the production of soybeans declines. Note that fewer soybeans are produced because the price of corn has risen, not because the price of soybeans has declined.

The relationship between goods that are substitutes in production is illustrated in Figure 2.3.6. Panel a shows the supply curve for corn. At the original price of corn farmers produce 1000 bushels (point C). However, with the higher price farmers

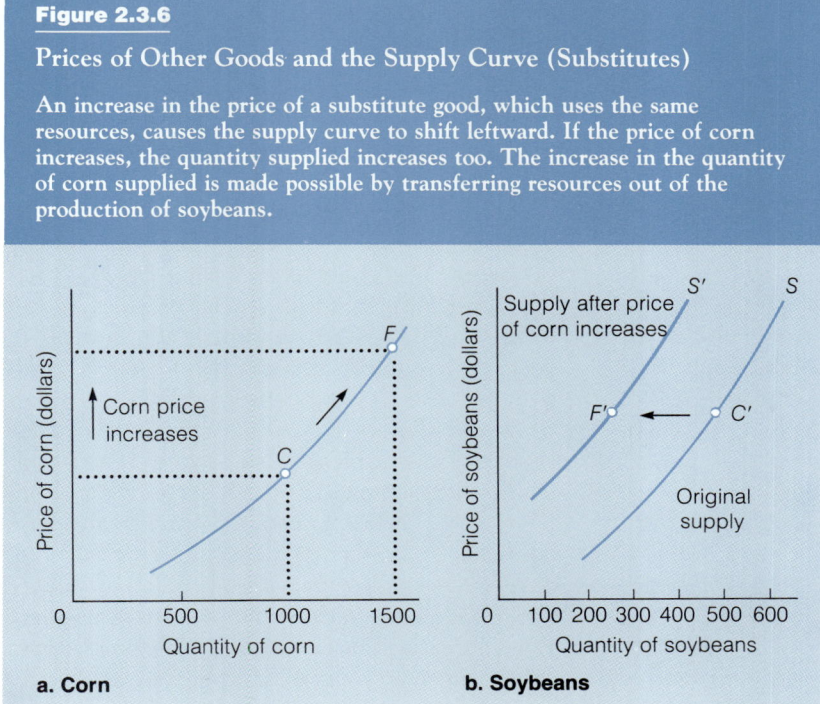

Figure 2.3.6

Prices of Other Goods and the Supply Curve (Substitutes)

An increase in the price of a substitute good, which uses the same resources, causes the supply curve to shift leftward. If the price of corn increases, the quantity supplied increases too. The increase in the quantity of corn supplied is made possible by transferring resources out of the production of soybeans.

a. Corn

b. Soybeans

increase production to 1500 bushels, moving up the supply curve to point F in accordance with the law of supply.

In panel b, at the existing price of soybeans farmers supply 500 bushels of soybeans before the price of corn changes (point C' on curve S). However, after the price of corn changes, farmers switch soybean resources into the production of corn, leaving fewer resources available for the production of soybeans. At the original price of soybeans farmers are now willing and able to supply fewer soybeans than before (point F' on curve S').

Goods also may be **complements in production,** which are goods that are produced jointly with the same resources. Common examples of joint products are gasoline and petrochemicals, beef and leather, and lumber and paper.

Figure 2.3.7 illustrates how a change in the price of one good affects the supply curve of a complement good. Panel a presents the supply curve for beef. An increase in the price of beef causes a movement along the beef supply curve from point C to point G, leading to an increase in the quantity of beef supplied.

Panel b presents the supply curve for leather, a joint product with beef. An increase in the price of beef, in addition to increasing the quantity of beef supplied, also increases the supply of leather at the existing price of leather, a shift from point C' on curve S to point G' on curve S'. At every price of leather, more leather is supplied, causing the supply curve to shift from S to S'. An increase in the price of one good causes a rightward shift in the supply curve of a complement good.

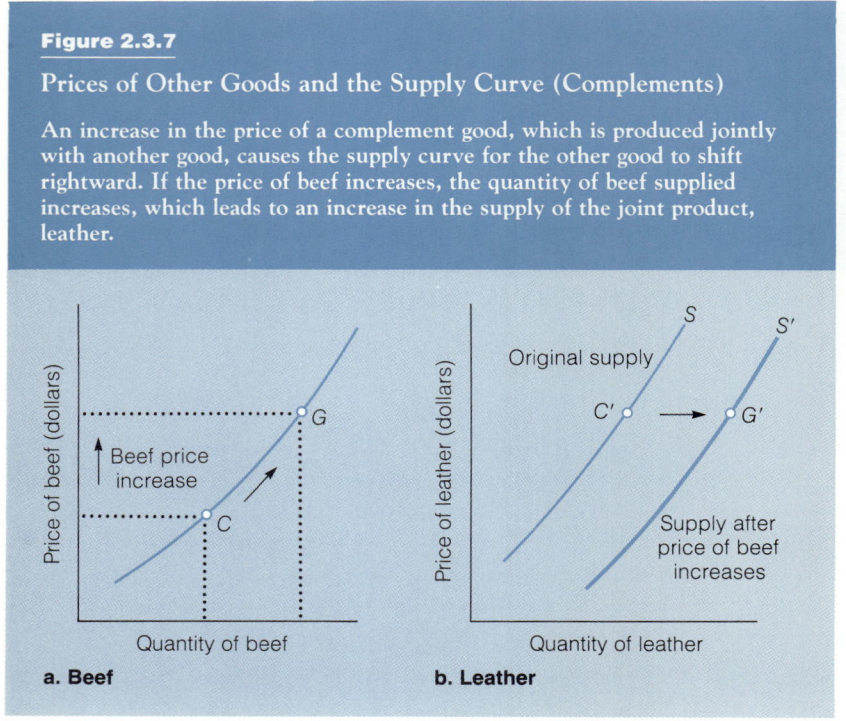

Figure 2.3.7

Prices of Other Goods and the Supply Curve (Complements)

An increase in the price of a complement good, which is produced jointly with another good, causes the supply curve for the other good to shift rightward. If the price of beef increases, the quantity of beef supplied increases, which leads to an increase in the supply of the joint product, leather.

a. Beef

b. Leather

Expectations

Suppliers' expectations of future conditions relating to their good can also cause the supply curve to shift. For example, suppose suppliers of natural gas, anticipating legislation that deregulates the price, offer less natural gas for sale today, expecting to sell it at a higher price in the future. Therefore, the supply decreases.

In general, if suppliers expect a higher price for their product in the future, they offer less for sale at the existing price. But if they expect a lower price in the future, they offer more of the good for sale in the present. In both cases they try to supply more of the good at the higher price. In Figure 2.3.8, panel a illustrates the rightward shift of the current supply curve if sellers expect a lower price in the future. Panel b illustrates the leftward shift of the current supply if sellers expect a higher price in the future.

Number of Sellers

In Figure 2.3.2 we saw that the market supply is composed of the supply of the individual sellers in the market. If more sellers enter the market, the market supply curve shifts rightward. The supply of personal computers illustrates how the number of sellers affects the supply curve. Figure 2.3.9 presents the supply curve for personal computers when they were first introduced by Apple Computers in 1975 (curve S). Today, however, IBM, Radio Shack, and Atari are but a few of the many companies producing personal computers. The supply curve

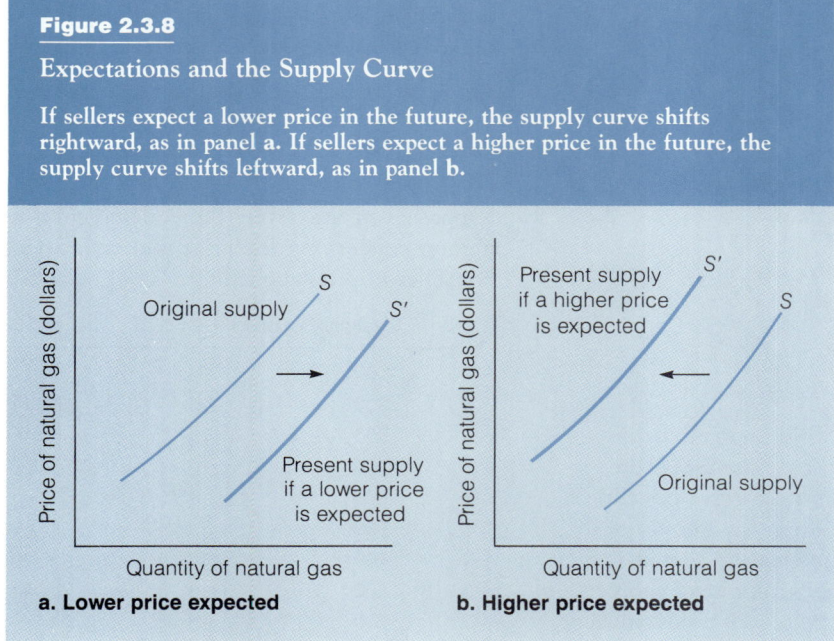

Figure 2.3.8

Expectations and the Supply Curve

If sellers expect a lower price in the future, the supply curve shifts rightward, as in panel a. If sellers expect a higher price in the future, the supply curve shifts leftward, as in panel b.

Figure 2.3.9

Number of Sellers and the Supply Curve

The market supply curve depends on the number of suppliers in the market. An increase in the number of sellers in the computer market shifts the supply curve rightward from S to S'.

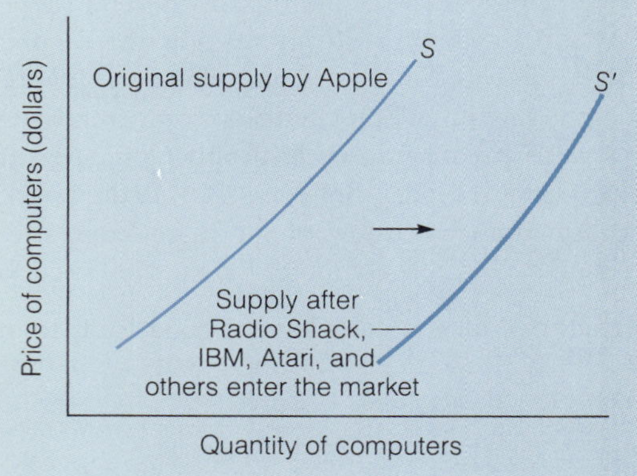

[Graph: Price of computers (dollars) vs. Quantity of computers, showing original supply curve S (Original supply by Apple) and a rightward-shifted curve S' (Supply after Radio Shack, IBM, Atari, and others enter the market)]

for personal computers is now curve S'. At each price more personal computers are offered for sale because more firms are in the market, causing a rightward shift in the supply curve.

IN SUMMARY

Supply

- Supply, the sellers' side of the market, is the quantity of a commodity that producers are willing and able to sell at alternative prices. According to the law of supply, higher prices result in an increase in the quantity supplied. Suppliers need higher prices to produce more of a commodity because the cost of producing additional units also increases.

- A graphical representation of the law of supply is a positively sloped supply curve. At higher prices more of a commodity is supplied as we move along a given supply curve. The market supply curve is obtained by horizontally adding all individual supply curves.

- A change in quantity supplied can only be caused by a change in the price of the good, which represents a movement along a supply curve. If the determinants of supply change, the entire supply curve shifts. This is a change in supply.

- The five key determinants that affect supply are factor prices, technology, prices of other goods, expectations, and number of sellers in the market. Higher factor prices cause a decrease in supply. Increases in technology cause an increase in supply. Increases in the prices of other goods can cause an increase or decrease in supply, depending on whether the goods are complements or substitutes in production. Expectations can cause either an increase or decrease in supply. And an increase in the number of sellers leads to an increase in supply.

QUESTIONS FOR STUDY AND ANALYSIS

1. Suppose you are given the following information concerning the price and quantity of bestseller novels supplied:

Price	Quantity Supplied
$10	1000
9	900
8	800
7	700
6	600
5	500
4	400
3	300
2	200
1	100

a. Construct the supply curve. What is the slope of the supply curve? Is it positive or negative?

b. What happens to the supply curve if all authors band together and form a union, demanding twice their current royalty rate (which is 10 percent of the sales price)? Construct the new supply curve. In which direction does the supply curve shift?

c. Construct a new supply curve reflecting advances in technology and the use of computers that make it possible to produce twice as many novels at the same price. Compared to part a, in which direction does the supply curve shift?

2. Explain how each of the following situations affects the supply of leather belts. Indicate whether there is a change in quantity supplied or a change in supply. If there is a change in supply, discuss which determinant is involved and in which direction the supply curve shifts.

a. The United States signs a trade agreement with Canada allowing for the first time the sale of Canadian leather belts in the United States.

b. The price of beef declines.

c. A new leather tanning machine is developed that works twice as fast and is cheaper than earlier machines.

d. The price of leather boots increases.

e. The government imposes a price ceiling on leather belts, preventing the sale of any belts above 50 percent of the existing price.

f. The government announces that in two years it will impose a 10 percent tax on all leather belts sold.

g. The leather workers labor union receives a 25 percent boost in wages.

3. Explain how expectations lead toy stores to increase their stock of toys several months before Christmas.

4. What happens to the supply curve of computers if technology increases *and* more sellers enter the market?

5. What happens to the supply curve for airline services if pilots receive a higher wage *and* half of the companies go out of business?

REVIEW GLOSSARY

change in quantity supplied The movement along a supply curve caused by a change in the price of the good. A change in the quantity supplied can only result from a change in the price of the good.

change in supply A shift in the entire supply curve resulting from a change in any of the determinants of supply.

complements in production Goods that are produced jointly with the same resources. An increase in the price of one complement good leads to an increase in the supply of the other good and a rightward shift of the supply curve.

determinants of supply The five most important factors that affect market supply are factor prices, technology, prices of other goods, expectations, and number of sellers in the market.

law of supply The principle that states a direct relationship exists between the price of a commodity and the quantity of the commodity that suppliers are willing and able to supply in a given period of time if other factors are held constant. The law of supply holds because the cost of producing additional units increases.

market supply The total supply of every seller willing and able to sell the good at alternative prices. The market supply curve is found by horizontally adding all individual supply curves.

substitutes in production Goods that are produced with the same resources, such that resources used to produce one good cannot be used to produce the other. An increase in the price of one substitute good leads to a decrease in the supply of the other good and a leftward shift of the supply curve.

supply The range of quantities of a commodity that sellers are willing and able to sell at different prices in a given period of time.

supply curve A graphical representation of the law of supply, with a positive slope due to the law of supply.

supply schedule A table that illustrates the alternative quantities of a commodity supplied at different prices.

technology The economy's combined knowledge and information of alternative methods for using factors in the production of goods and services. An increase in the level of technology shifts the supply curve rightward.

UNIT 2.4

Market Equilibrium

In Unit 2.1 we saw that a **market** is the organized exchange of a commodity between buyers and sellers within a specific geographic area and for a given period of time. On one side of the market are the demanders, willing and able to buy larger quantities at lower prices. On the other side of the market are the suppliers, willing and able to sell larger quantities at higher prices. In this unit we are ready to put the two sides of the market—supply and demand—together to provide us with a powerful tool for studying the economy.

Our specific goal in this unit is to identify the market equilibrium that occurs when demand and supply come together, and to examine how market equilibrium is achieved and maintained. We also see what happens to market equilibrium when the determinants of demand or supply cause either curve to shift by itself, or both curves to shift at the same time.

DETERMINING THE MARKET EQUILIBRIUM

To begin, let's define the term **equilibrium,** which is the state that exists when opposing forces exactly offset each other and there is no inherent tendency for change. A good example of a state of equilibrium can be seen in a simple game of tug-of-war. Suppose we put six people on each end of a long rope and let them pull. If neither group is stronger than the other, they continue to pull, but nothing happens; they are in a state of equilibrium.

We want to achieve a similar state of equilibrium for the two opposing forces of the market—demand and supply—and determine the point at which the forces of demand exactly offset the forces of supply, such that nothing changes. **Market equilibrium** occurs when the demanders and suppliers come together and exchange a mutually agreeable quantity at a mutually agreeable price. In equilibrium the market is at rest, with no reason for either the quantity exchanged or the price to change. If both sides of the market do not agree on the quantity and price, then market equilibrium is not achieved.

To illustrate market equilibrium, Table 2.4.1 presents a hypothetical market for housing. As the price of a house ranges from $200,000 to $20,000, the quantity demanded ranges from 45 houses to 240 houses per year, while the quantity supplied varies from 250 houses to 10 houses per year.

By analyzing the interaction of demand and supply in the market, we can identify market equilibrium—a price and quantity agreeable to both demanders and suppliers. Market equilibrium is agreeable to buyers as a group because the quantity they demand (or want to buy) at the market price is the quantity they actually buy. Likewise, the market equilibrium is agreeable to sellers as a group because the entire quantity they supply (or are willing to sell) at the market price is the quantity they actually sell. In market equilibrium the quantity demanded at the market price is exactly the same as the quantity supplied.

In Table 2.4.1 only a price of $100,000 per house satisfies both demanders and suppliers. Suppliers sell every house that they offer for sale at that price, and demanders buy the number of houses that they want to buy at that price. At no other price does this occur. The **equilibrium price,** the

Table 2.4.1

Hypothetical Market for Houses

Market equilibrium is found by identifying the price at which the quantity demanded and the quantity supplied are equal. In this table market equilibrium is achieved at $100,000, with 100 houses demanded and 100 houses supplied. If the price is greater than $100,000, the quantity demanded is less than the quantity supplied, but if the price is less than $100,000, the quantity demanded is greater than the quantity supplied.

Price	Quantity Demanded	Quantity Supplied	Surplus (+) or Shortage (−)
$200,000	45	250	+ 205
180,000	50	240	+ 190
160,000	55	210	+ 155
140,000	65	170	+ 105
120,000	80	130	+ 50
100,000	100	100	0
80,000	120	70	− 50
60,000	150	45	− 105
40,000	190	20	− 170
20,000	240	10	− 230

price that equates the quantity demanded and supplied in the market, is $100,000. The **equilibrium quantity,** the quantity exchanged between buyers and sellers in equilibrium, is 100 houses per year. To see why $100,000 is the equilibrium price, let's look at some alternative prices.

For $160,000 per house, buyers demand 55 houses per year, whereas suppliers are willing to sell 210 houses per year, leaving 155 houses that they are unable to sell. And if suppliers have more houses than they can sell, then the market price is too high. Conversely, at a price of $40,000 per house, the quantity demanded by buyers is 190 houses per year, whereas the quantity supplied is only 20 houses per year. The suppliers can easily sell all 20 houses produced, but demanders are left wanting an additional 170 houses. In this case the suppliers are satisfied, but the demanders are not. If demanders are not getting all of the houses they want, then the market price is too low. Only when a price is found at which the quantity supplied equals the quantity demanded is the market in equilibrium. At any other price one side of the market is not satisfied.

Figure 2.4.1 illustrates market equilibrium using demand and supply curves, which were discussed in Unit 2.2 and Unit 2.3, respectively. The demand schedule in Table 2.4.1 has been graphed in Figure 2.4.1 as the negatively sloped demand curve D, and the supply schedule as the positively sloped supply curve S. The intersection of the demand curve D and the supply curve S is the market equilibrium (point E).

Only at point E is the quantity demanded equal to the quantity supplied. The equilibrium price is $100,000 per house, and the equilibrium quantity exchanged between buyers and sellers is 100 houses per year. At any other price the quantities demanded and supplied are not the same. At prices above $100,000 the supply curve lies to the right of the demand curve, indicating that demanders are buying less than the suppliers are trying to sell. At prices below $100,000 the demand curve lies to the right of the supply curve, indicating that suppliers are offering less for sale than the demanders would like.

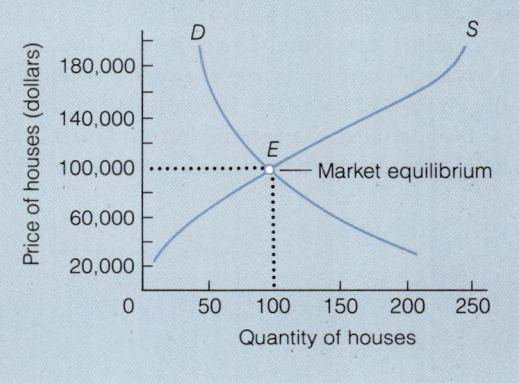

Figure 2.4.1

Market Equilibrium

The intersection of demand and supply curves is the market equilibrium. At a price of $100,000 per house, the quantity demanded equals the quantity supplied, and the demand and supply curves intersect at point E. Both buyers and sellers are satisfied, because they can buy or sell all that they want at that price.

SURPLUS AND SHORTAGE

At the market equilibrium demanders and suppliers agree on both the quantity exchanged and the price. However, markets are not always in equilibrium. In the news we constantly hear about a surplus of one good, or a shortage of another, which means that a market is not in equilibrium. Let's first analyze a market that contains a surplus, and then one with a shortage, to see how it eliminates each and returns to equilibrium.

Surplus

A **surplus** exists when the quantity supplied is greater than the quantity demanded at the existing price. Suppose the existing market price in Figure 2.4.2 is $160,000 per house. We saw earlier that suppliers are not able to sell all that they want at that price, and thus the market has a surplus, or an excess supply.

What happens when the market has a surplus? Since suppliers are trying to sell 210 houses but demanders are willing to buy only 55, the sellers try to get rid of their excess supply. One way is to lower the price; suppliers are not going to maintain a price of $160,000 if they cannot sell all that they produce.

This downward pressure on price has two effects. First, as the price falls, demanders are willing and able to purchase a larger quantity of houses. A decline in price from $160,000 to $140,000 causes buyers to demand 65 houses instead of 55 houses, which helps reduce the surplus of houses. Second, as the price falls, suppliers are willing and able to supply a smaller quantity. The decline in price to $140,000 decreases the quantity supplied to 170 houses per year, which also helps reduce the surplus.

As long as the price is above the equilibrium price, the market has a surplus, and prices are driven downward. A price above the equilibrium tends to move down toward the equilibrium, a mechanism of the market that ensures that the market equilibrium is reached if the price is too high. But what if the price is too low?

Shortage

A **shortage** exists when the quantity demanded is greater than the quantity supplied at the existing price. Again looking at Figure 2.4.2, suppose the existing price is $40,000 per house. In this case the quantity demanded is 190 houses and the quantity supplied is 20 houses, creating a shortage of 170 houses. If the market has a shortage, or excess demand, buyers are not able to purchase all that they want at the existing price.

Buyers unable to purchase houses at $40,000 because of a shortage will bid up the price, affecting both supply and demand. Higher prices give suppliers incentive to increase the quantity that they are willing and able to sell, in part because they are able to hire resources away from the production of other goods by paying them more. But higher prices also reduce the quantity demanded. Some buyers willing to buy a house at $40,000 are not willing to purchase it at $60,000.

At $60,000 the quantity demanded is 150 houses and the quantity supplied is 45 houses. A shortage still exists, but the difference between supply and demand is less at $60,000 than it is at $40,000. As long as the shortage exists, unsatisfied demanders bid up the price. Only when the price rises to $100,000, which is the market equilibrium, is the shortage completely eliminated.

SHOCKS TO THE MARKET

What if the market is shocked away from equilibrium because of a change in one of the determinants of demand or supply? Does the market reach a new equilibrium after a shift in the demand or

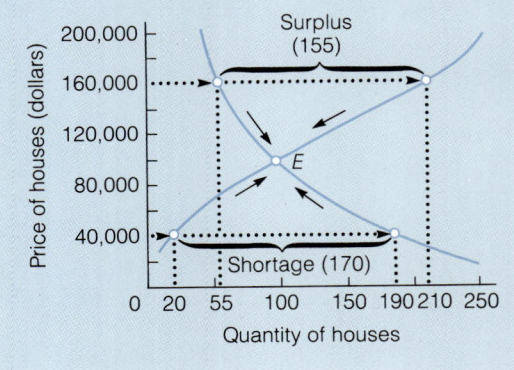

Figure 2.4.2

Surpluses and Shortages

If surpluses or shortages exist, either buyers or sellers are unsatisfied. With a surplus some sellers cannot sell all that they want, so they lower the price, leading to a reduction in the surplus. With a shortage some buyers cannot buy all that they want, so they bid up the price, leading to a reduction of the shortage. In either case the price tends to move toward the equilibrium level (point E).

supply curve? To answer this question, an analysis called comparative statics is applied. **Comparative statics** is the technique of comparing the equilibrium resulting from a change in a determinant with the equilibrium existing prior to the change. Recall that both demand and supply have important determinants that are held constant under the *ceteris paribus* assumption when the demand and supply curves are drawn. The technique of comparative statics allows us to relax the *ceteris paribus* assumption and identify how each determinant affects the market through shifts in either the demand curve or the supply curve.

In the following analyses we use comparative statics to see what happens when the market is shocked by determinants. There are four basic ways a market can be shocked: an increase in demand, a decrease in demand, an increase in supply, and a decrease in supply. Each of these shocks has a different effect on the market.

Increase in Demand

Suppose buyers in the housing market expect the interest rate to increase in the near future. Since most houses are purchased with loans from mortgage companies, expecting a higher interest rate is the same as expecting an increase in the price of a house. Because expectations are a determinant of demand, if buyers expect a higher price in the future, they will tend to demand more in the present, shown in Figure 2.4.3 as a rightward shift of the demand curve from D to D'.

Prior to the change in expectations concerning the interest rate, the housing market achieves equilibrium at point E with the exchange of 100

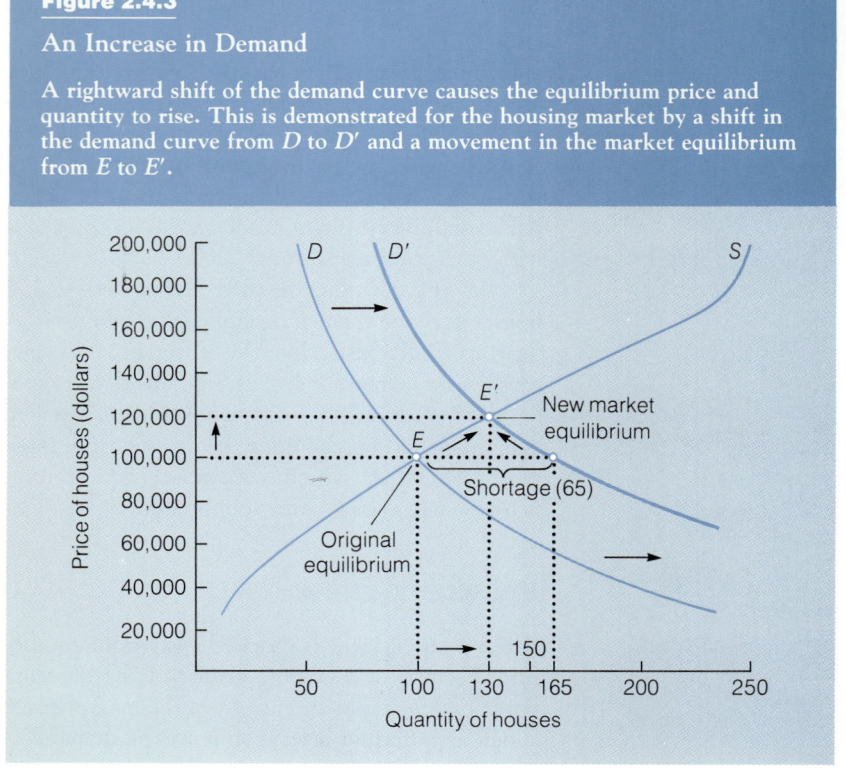

Figure 2.4.3

An Increase in Demand

A rightward shift of the demand curve causes the equilibrium price and quantity to rise. This is demonstrated for the housing market by a shift in the demand curve from D to D' and a movement in the market equilibrium from E to E'.

houses at $100,000 each. However, after the change in expectations buyers are willing and able to purchase 165 houses at $100,000 each, but the house builders are still only willing to supply 100 houses at that price. Nothing has affected the quantity of houses supplied in the market up to this point.

At the price of $100,000 the market has an excess demand of 65 houses, so the original equilibrium price of $100,000 no longer holds. But not everyone in the market is satisfied, and dissatisfied buyers in particular place upward pressure on the price, as always occurs when the market has a shortage.

The market price continues to rise until the shortage created by the shift of the demand curve to D' is eliminated. Only at point E' is the quantity supplied equal to the quantity demanded. When the price rises to $120,000 per house, the quantity supplied, moving up the original supply curve S, is 130 houses. In addition, the quantity demanded, moving up the new demand curve D', is also 130 houses. Both sides of the market once again agree on the price and quantity, and the market has achieved a new equilibrium, one in which the price is higher and the quantity exchanged greater.

Decrease in Demand

An increase in demand leads to a higher price and a greater quantity exchanged, whether the demand curve shifts due to tastes and preferences, income, expectations, prices of other goods, or number of buyers in the market. A decrease in demand has the opposite effect on the market. Figure 2.4.4 illustrates how a leftward shift of the demand curve affects the equilibrium price and quantity.

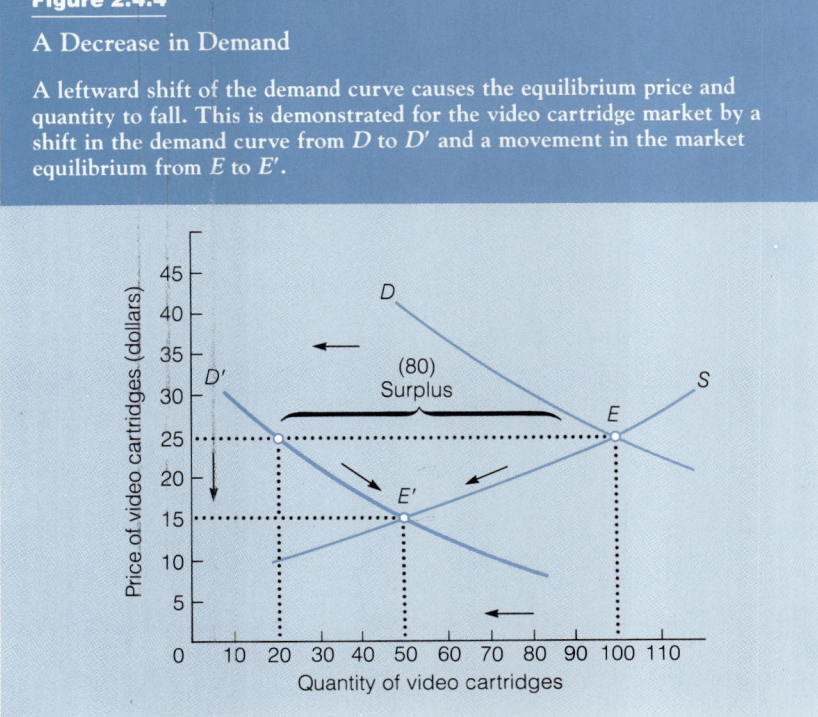

Figure 2.4.4

A Decrease in Demand

A leftward shift of the demand curve causes the equilibrium price and quantity to fall. This is demonstrated for the video cartridge market by a shift in the demand curve from D to D' and a movement in the market equilibrium from E to E'.

Suppose the market for video game cartridges (such as Atari or Coleco) is depicted by demand curve D and supply curve S. The equilibrium is at point E, with each of the 100 cartridges selling for $25. What happens if people become tired of playing video games? Instead of being willing to buy 100 cartridges at $25 each, they are willing to buy only 20 cartridges at that price, so the demand curve shifts leftward to D'.

At $25 the market has a surplus of cartridges. As with any surplus there is a downward pressure on the price until a new equilibrium is reached at E', with 50 cartridges exchanged for $15 each. In comparison to the original equilibrium, the price and quantity exchanged are both less. Since people are no longer willing to buy the cartridges, fewer are sold, and at a lower price.

Increase in Supply

The supply curve shifts because of a change in one of the determinants of supply. Figure 2.4.5 illustrates how the market is affected if supply is increased, whether due to lower factor prices, an increase in the level of technology, or comparable changes in the other determinants of supply.

Suppose the level of technology advances in the computer market. The original market is given

Figure 2.4.5

An Increase in Supply

A rightward shift of the supply curve causes the equilibrium price to fall and the equilibrium quantity to rise. This is demonstrated for the computer market by a shift in the supply curve from S to S' and a movement in the market equilibrium from E to E'.

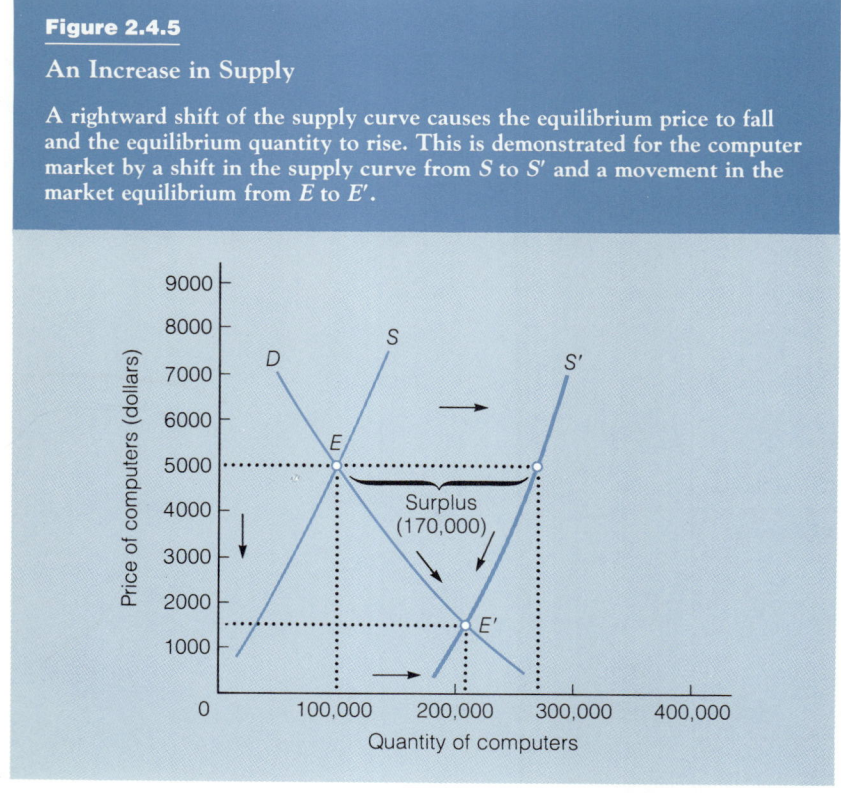

by curves D and S, and the original equilibrium is at point E, with 100,000 computers sold for $5000 each. However, the increase in technology shifts the supply curve rightward to S'. Sellers are now willing to supply 270,000 computers at $5000 each, creating a surplus at the original equilibrium price.

As with any surplus, there is downward pressure on the price. The price declines until a new equilibrium is reached at point E', where 210,000 computers are sold for $1500 each. The advancement in technology leads to an increase in the quantity of computers exchanged, and a reduction in the price. Anytime the supply curve shifts rightward, the price is lower and the quantity exchanged greater.

Decrease in Supply

A decrease in supply has the opposite effect on the market. Remember that factor prices constitute one of the determinants of supply. If prices of the factors used to produce a good increase, then the supply curve of the good shifts leftward. For example, an important factor in the production of gasoline is crude petroleum. Figure 2.4.6 illustrates how the market for gasoline was affected when the price of petroleum was raised by OPEC in 1973, causing the supply curve of gasoline to shift leftward.

Before the increase in the price of petroleum, the price of gasoline was 40 cents, and 100 million gallons were exchanged (point E). After the supply

Figure 2.4.6

A Decrease in Supply

A leftward shift of the supply curve causes the equilibrium price to rise and the equilibrium quantity to fall. This is demonstrated for the gasoline market by a shift in the supply curve from S to S' and a movement in the market equilibrium from E to E'.

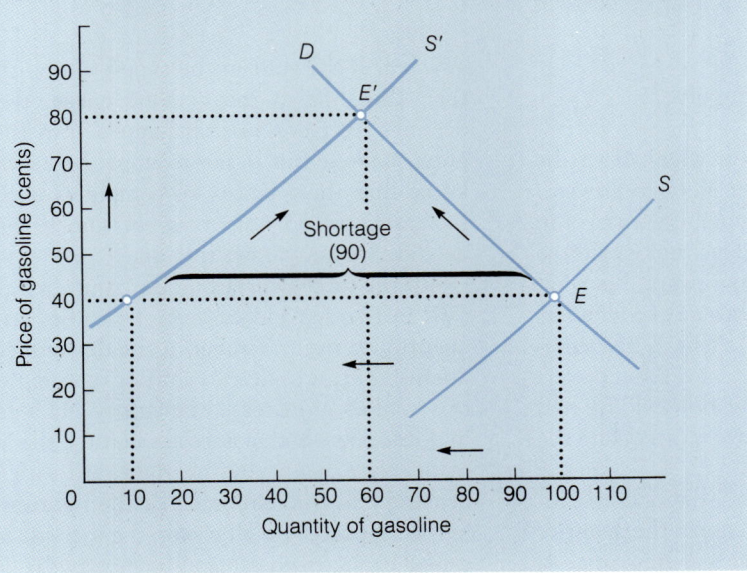

curve shifted leftward, sellers were willing to supply only 10 million gallons of gasoline at 40 cents a gallon, and a shortage was created. But, as with any shortage, upward pressure was placed on the price, until a new equilibrium was reached (point E'), with 60 million gallons exchanged at 80 cents per gallon. Note that the new equilibrium has a higher price and a lower quantity exchanged than the original equilibrium. Whenever the supply decreases, the price rises and the quantity exchanged falls.

CHANGES IN BOTH DEMAND AND SUPPLY

Many times a market experiences simultaneous shifts in both demand and supply curves. Whenever both curves shift, it is not possible to determine the changes in both the equilibrium quantity and the equilibrium price. If we can determine the direction of the change in price, we cannot determine the direction of the change in quantity. Likewise, if we can determine the direction of the change in quantity, we cannot determine the direction of the change in price. If both the supply and demand curves shift, either price or quantity is indeterminate.

An Increase in Demand and Supply

Figure 2.4.7 illustrates a case in which both the supply and demand curves shift rightward. Remember the example of the computer market in Figure 2.4.5, where advances in technology shifted the supply curve for computers rightward. But what happens if people become more aware of computers and find that anyone can use them? This represents, in effect, a change in the tastes and preferences of the buyers. People are now willing and able to buy more computers at every price, and the demand curve shifts rightward.

In Figure 2.4.7 the rightward shift of both supply and demand leads to an increase in the quantity exchanged. However, it is not clear how price is

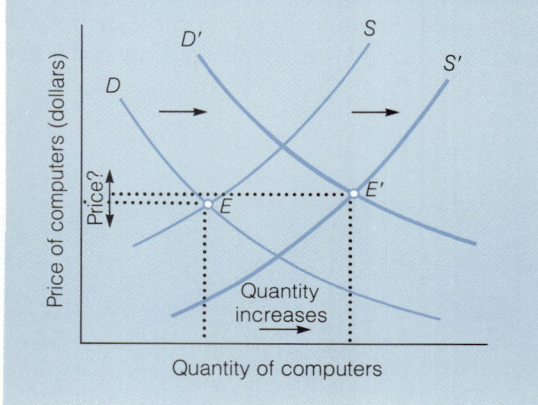

Figure 2.4.7

An Increase in Demand and an Increase in Supply

If the demand and supply curves both shift rightward, the equilibrium quantity increases. However, the new equilibrium price is indeterminate. Although E' is to the right of E, it could be above or below E, depending on the relative shifts of the demand and supply curves.

affected. If the shift in the supply curve is greater than the shift in the demand curve, the price declines. In fact, this has happened in the computer market. But in our example here, while we know that the quantity of computers exchanged increases, we do not know for sure if the price declines, rises, or stays the same.

If the supply curve S doesn't shift, a rightward shift in the demand curve to D' causes price and quantity to rise. However, if the demand curve D doesn't shift, a rightward shift of the supply curve to S' causes an increase in quantity, but a decrease in price. Since both curves are shifting, the increase in quantity caused by the rightward shift in the demand curve is reinforced by the rightward shift in the supply curve. However, the increase in price caused by increased demand is offset by the decrease in price caused by increased supply. Without more information we cannot know if the price is ultimately higher or lower.

A Decrease in Demand and Supply

A second alternative that illustrates what happens when both the demand and supply curves shift in the same direction is presented in Figure 2.4.8. Let's return to the housing market. If there is widespread unemployment of labor, the income of house buyers is likely to decline. This means people are willing and able to buy fewer houses at the existing price, which causes a leftward shift in the demand curve from D to D'. In addition, a lumber shortage causes the price of wood, an important factor in the production of houses, to rise, and the supply curve for houses shifts leftward from S to S'.

The combination of leftward shifts in both the demand and the supply curves causes the quantity exchanged in the market to decline. However, the effect on the price is not clear. Fewer houses are constructed, and fewer houses bought, but the price of each house might decline, rise, or remain the same. Once again the demand and supply shifts reinforce the effect on quantity but have offsetting effects on price. As Figures 2.4.7 and 2.4.8 indicate, if the demand and supply curves shift in the same direction, the quantity exchanged in the market also changes in that direction, but the price is indeterminate.

An Increase in Demand and a Decrease in Supply

Let's look at a third example to see what happens when demand increases but supply decreases. Suppose the most influential fashion designers in the country decide the next fashion trend will be the 100-percent cotton denim look. As the trend catches on, the demand for cotton increases, shifting the demand curve in Figure 2.4.9 rightward. However, at the same time this fashion revolution is beginning to take hold of the country, a new type of boll weevil attacks the nation's cotton crops, cutting cotton production in half, and causing the supply curve for cotton to shift leftward.

As we saw earlier, an increase in demand with no change in supply causes both price and quantity to increase, whereas a decrease in supply with no change in demand causes an increase in price but a decrease in quantity. How do both changes together affect the market?

Both an increase in demand and a decrease in supply cause the price to rise. These changes reinforce each other, leading to a higher price. At the same time, the increase in demand leads to a larger quantity, while the decrease in supply leads to a smaller quantity. These changes do not reinforce each other, but work in opposite directions. While it is clear that the price increases in the cotton

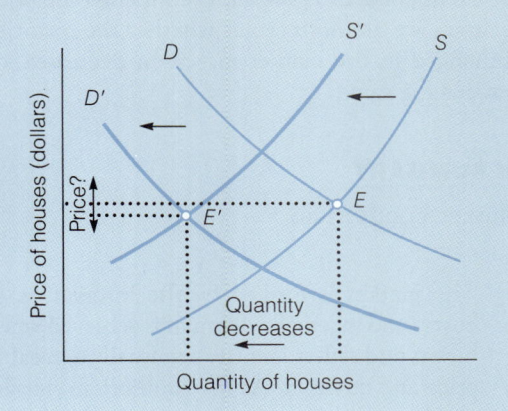

Figure 2.4.8

A Decrease in Demand and a Decrease in Supply

If the demand and supply curves both shift leftward, the equilibrium quantity falls. However, the new equilibrium price is indeterminate. Although E' is to the left of E, it could be above or below E, depending on the relative shifts of the demand and supply curves.

Figure 2.4.9

An Increase in Demand and a Decrease in Supply

If the demand curve shifts rightward and the supply curve shifts leftward, the equilibrium price rises. However, the new equilibrium quantity is indeterminate. Although E' is above E, it could be to the right or left of E, depending on the relative shifts of the demand and supply curves.

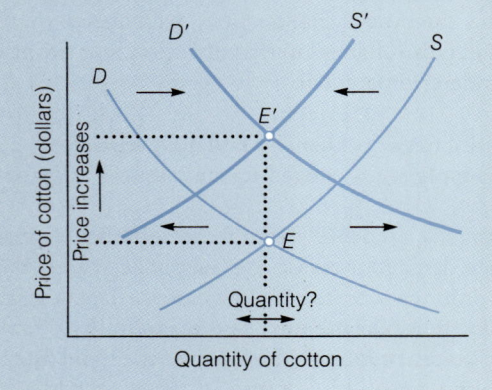

Figure 2.4.10

A Decrease in Demand and an Increase in Supply

If the demand curve shifts leftward and the supply curve shifts rightward, the equilibrium price falls. However, the new equilibrium quantity is indeterminate. Although E' is below E, it could be to the right or left of E, depending on the relative shifts of the demand and supply curves.

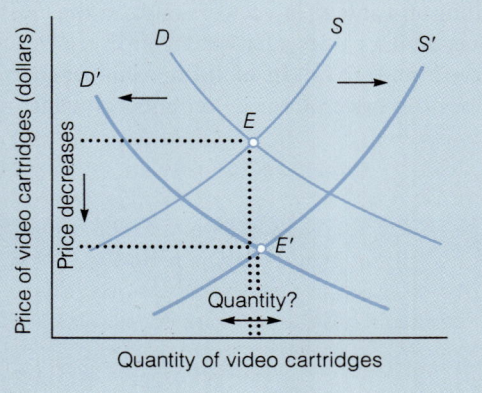

market, whether more or less cotton is exchanged depends on the relative shifts in the demand and supply curves. The quantity exchanged is indeterminate.

A Decrease in Demand and an Increase in Supply

Let's return to the market for video game cartridges. In Figure 2.4.4 we saw that a change in the tastes of buyers causes a leftward shift in the demand curve. In Figure 2.4.10, what happens to the market if the leftward shift in the demand curve from D to D' is accompanied by a rightward shift in the supply curve from S to S' as the number of producers of video game cartridges increases?

With more sellers in the market at the same time fewer people are willing to buy video game cartridges, the price declines. The new equilibrium at point E' has a lower price than the original equilibrium at point E. However, even though the price declines, we are not certain whether the quantity exchanged in the market increases, decreases, or remains the same.

IN SUMMARY

Market Equilibrium

- The market is formed by the interaction of buyers and sellers. Equilibrium is achieved when buyers and sellers identify a mutually agreeable price and quantity. At the equilibrium, buyers purchase all of the good that they are willing and able to buy at that price, and sellers sell all that they are willing and able to sell at the same price.

- Once equilibrium in the market is reached, it remains. If the price is greater than the equilibrium level, a surplus is created, forcing the price down to the equilibrium level and eliminating the surplus. If the price is below the equilibrium level, a shortage is created, forcing the price up to the equilibrium level and eliminating the shortage.

- Even if the market is shocked by a shift in either the supply curve or the demand curve, the market adjusts to a new equilibrium. Comparative statics of the market indicate distinct changes in price and quantity if either the demand curve or the supply curve shifts by itself. An increase in demand leads to an increase in price and quantity; a decrease in demand leads to a decrease in price and quantity. But an increase in supply leads to a decrease in price and an increase in quantity. A decrease in supply has the opposite effect.

- If both demand and supply shift at the same time, some results are not as clear. An increase in demand together with an increase in supply leads to an increase in the quantity but has an indeterminate effect on the price. Whenever both the supply and demand curves shift, the effect on either price or quantity cannot be determined.

QUESTIONS FOR STUDY AND ANALYSIS

1. Suppose you are given the following information concerning market supply and demand:

Price	Quantity Demanded	Quantity Supplied	Surplus or Shortage
$10	1000	100	
20	800	200	
30	600	300	
40	400	400	
50	200	500	
60	0	600	

a. Complete the table by computing the surplus or shortage at each price. What is the equilibrium price and quantity?
b. Construct the demand and supply curves for this market. Label the equilibrium point, including price and quantity.
c. If the number of firms in the market doubles such that twice as much of the good is supplied at each price, what is the new equilibrium price and quantity? How does this compare with the original equilibrium?

2. a. If Ronald Reagan, a lover of jellybeans, proclaims Wednesdays national jellybean day and requires everyone in the country to have three meals of jellybeans every Wednesday, what happens to the price of jellybeans and the quantity exchanged in the market?
b. After national jellybean day has been established, suppose OJEC (Organization of Jellybean Exporting Countries) cuts off all sales of jellybeans to the United States. If OJEC supplies half of all jellybeans eaten in the United States, what happens to the equilibrium price and quantity? Compare this new equilibrium to the jellybean market both before and after national jellybean day was declared.

3. Prior to the boycott of the 1984 Olympic Games in Los Angeles by the Soviet Union and its allies, ticket scalpers and speculators purchased tickets at regular prices, hoping for a windfall once the games began. However, after the boycott was announced, ticket scalpers became very concerned that they might not receive the expected higher price or even recoup the original price.
a. Which determinant(s) of demand or supply changed, and how were the demand and supply curves affected?
b. Using comparative statics of the market, demonstrate the market equilibrium before and after the Soviet boycott.
c. After the games began, ticket scalpers received more than the original price. Explain why.

4. Explain how each of the following situations affects the market for automobiles. Indicate whether there is a shift in the demand curve or the supply curve (or both), what direction the shift(s) takes, and which determinant causes the shift(s).
   a. The tax rate on income is reduced, meaning everyone in the country pays less income tax and has more income to spend on goods and services.
   b. The number of foreign automobiles imported into the country is restricted.
   c. The price of gasoline increases.
   d. The price of pickup trucks increases.
   e. OPEC announces that they will double the price of petroleum in one year.
   f. The minimum driving age is raised to eighteen nationwide.
   g. The Environmental Protection Agency requires stricter pollution control devices on every new automobile.
   h. Everyone in the country becomes more health conscious and takes up jogging, walking, and riding bicycles.

REVIEW GLOSSARY

comparative statics A technique of comparing the equilibrium resulting from a change in a determinant with the equilibrium prior to the change.

equilibrium The state that exists when opposing forces exactly offset each other and there is no inherent tendency for change.

equilibrium price The price that equates the quantity demanded and supplied in the market.

equilibrium quantity The quantity exchanged between buyers and sellers in equilibrium.

market The organized exchange of a commodity between buyers and sellers within a specific geographic area and for a given period of time.

market equilibrium The state of the market that occurs when the demanders and suppliers come together and exchange a mutually agreeable quantity at a mutually agreeable price. Graphically, equilibrium is determined by the intersection of the demand and supply curves.

shortage A condition in the market in which the quantity demanded is greater than the quantity supplied at the existing price. A shortage causes the price to rise.

surplus A condition in the market in which the quantity supplied is greater than the quantity demanded at the existing price. A surplus causes the price to fall.

UNIT 2.5

Government and the Market

The market is one of the economist's most useful tools for examining economic activity. Up to this point we have looked at the unrestricted operation of the market, that is, the market left free to achieve its equilibrium price and quantity. In the last unit we saw that if either the demand curve or the supply curve shifted, the market adjusted to a new market equilibrium. But now we want to place constraints on the market and see how it reacts if we *prevent* it from reaching the equilibrium price and quantity given by the intersection of the demand and supply curves. In particular, we want to consider how the government can, and has, restricted the free operation of the market and prevented it from reaching equilibrium by imposing price floors, price ceilings, and taxes.

PRICE FLOOR

A **price floor** is a legally established minimum price above the market equilibrium. Common examples of price floors are minimum wages and agricultural price floors. In both of these cases the government restricts any sales below the floor. The minimum wage prevents employers from hiring any workers at a lower wage, and agricultural price floors prevent the buyer of agricultural goods from offering less than a specified price.

The United States has a long history of imposing price floors on agricultural products ranging from tobacco to milk, primarily to maintain farmers' incomes. If the price of wheat declines, clearly income received by wheat farmers also declines. Over the past century farmers have become more productive, and thus have been able to increase the supply of agricultural products. However, the demand for agricultural products has not risen as fast, leading to a decline in agricultural prices and, consequently, farmers' incomes. In response, the government establishes price floors in agriculture.

Minimum wages are justified for a similar reason. However, minimum wages are designed to maintain incomes of unskilled or semiskilled workers rather than farmers. Most workers covered by minimum wages are near the poverty level; the wage floors try to prevent them from dipping below that level.

Both agricultural price floors and minimum wages have the noble goal of trying to achieve greater equity in the economy. However, as we will see, these attempts to improve equity lead to an inefficient allocation of goods.

Let's see how a price floor affects the market. Figure 2.5.1 presents the market for a good that is subject to a price floor. If the market is left alone, it reaches an equilibrium price of $10, and 100 units of the good are exchanged between buyer and seller, shown by point E, the intersection of the demand and supply curves. But what happens if a price floor is established above the market equilibrium, at $15?

The first, and most obvious, effect of a price floor is the creation of a surplus. At $15 the quantity supplied is 125 units, but the quantity demanded is only 75 units. Suppliers are willing and able to sell more than demanders are willing and able to buy at $15.

In an uncontrolled market a surplus causes downward pressure on the price, as suppliers lower their price to sell their surplus. However, with the government-imposed price floor suppliers cannot sell any of the good at less than $15, and they are stuck with the surplus. The surplus remains until the price floor is removed, the demand curve shifts rightward, or the supply curve shifts leftward. Note that the price floor must be above the market equilibrium price. If the price floor is set below the market equilibrium, it has no effect, as the market simply adjusts to the equilibrium price.

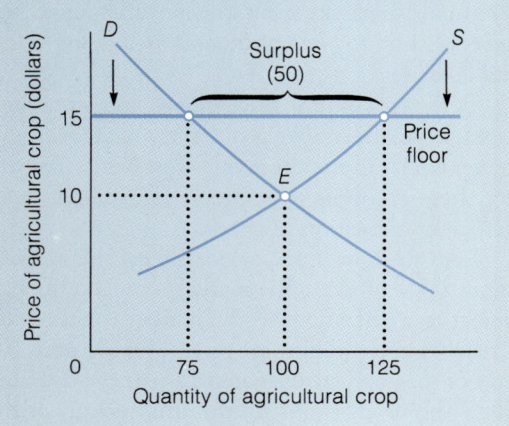

Figure 2.5.1

Price Floor

A price floor is a legally established minimum price above the equilibrium price. If the market equilibrium price is $10, a price floor of $15 creates a surplus of 50 units. This surplus remains as long as the price floor remains, and neither curve shifts.

What does a surplus mean in terms of either agricultural price floors or the minimum wage? In the agricultural industry price floors lead to a surplus of agricultural production. If the price of milk is maintained above its market equilibrium, dairy producers are willing to produce more milk than consumers are willing to buy. The same is true for price floors for wheat, cotton, or sugar. And while the agricultural industry may be happy to receive the relatively high price, they are not happy about unsold production. Usually the government steps in to buy up the surplus, or else guarantees the farmer a specific price if the farmer agrees to produce less output. Agricultural production and price floors are discussed in more detail in Unit 8.5.

The minimum wage has a similar impact on the market for labor. The surplus of labor is unemployment. More people are willing to supply their labor at the minimum wage than there are employers demanding that labor. Some of the surplus of labor is "bought up" by the government in much the same way as surplus agricultural goods are purchased, in this case through unemployment compensation or welfare payments. Unfortunately, a great deal of the surplus labor, especially teenaged, receives neither unemployment compensation nor welfare payments, and simply remains idle.

PRICE CEILING

A price ceiling is very similar to a price floor. A **price ceiling** is a legally established maximum price below the market equilibrium. It is not legal for exchange to occur at a price above the price ceiling. Common examples of price ceilings are rent controls and natural gas regulation. In both cases the government restricts any sales above the ceiling.

Many major cities throughout the United States have rent controls, which limit the payments made by tenants for rented apartments. Like price floors, rent controls have a noble objective, to prevent apartment dwellers from being overcharged. Usually rent controls are established when the demand for rental units is rising faster than supply and rental payments are increasing as well.

Natural gas regulation is also designed to prevent buyers from paying "too much" for the good. Natural gas regulation was an outgrowth of the economywide wage and price controls implemented during the early 1970s, when inflation was becoming a serious problem. However, while controls on most other prices were removed later in the decade, they were left on natural gas.

As with price floors, price ceilings reflect the government's efforts to achieve equity in the market. However, price ceilings also affect the allocation process, as illustrated by Figure 2.5.2. Once again the unconstrained market equilibrium price is $10, and 100 units are exchanged. A price ceiling is set at $5, below the market equilibrium price. Note that the price ceiling is not effective if it is above the equilibrium price.

If the legal price is $5, suppliers are willing and able to sell only 50 units, which is less than the equilibrium quantity exchanged at the higher price. However, at $5 demanders are willing and able to buy 150 units, which is greater than the quantity demanded in equilibrium. The price ceiling creates a shortage of 100 units in this market.

Price ceilings have had a noticeable impact on the markets for natural gas and housing. For example, the price ceiling on natural gas contributed to devastating shortages during several cold winters in the late 1970s. The natural gas was available in wells throughout the country, but producers were not willing and able to supply it at the controlled price. Rent controls have also created shortages in the housing markets in many major cities. Landlords faced with rents below the market price have been unable and unwilling to provide as much housing as demanded, or they simply let existing apartments deteriorate.

BLACK MARKETS

Price ceilings can also generate black markets. A **black market** is a market that exchanges goods above a legally restricted maximum price. A black market occurs when a price ceiling is established.

Let's look again at Figure 2.5.2 to see why. The shortage places upward pressure on the price, because people are willing and able to buy more of the good than the available supply. However, some demanders must do without, even though they are also willing to pay a higher price. If only 50 units of the good are supplied, some demanders are willing and able to pay $20 per unit. In fact, a lot of demanders are willing to pay more than $5 to obtain more than the 50 units supplied with the price ceiling.

The demander unable to get enough output at $5 might illegally offer the supplier a "slight premium" to obtain a larger quantity. But the "slight premium" is in effect a higher price. As demanders offer the premium, suppliers take this as a signal to increase the quantity supplied from 50 units.

Thus, 50 units are exchanged legally at the price of $5, but in addition, some suppliers might illegally sell more at a slightly higher price. Keep in mind that these exchanges above the price ceiling are illegal, and that the suppliers and demanders are making the exchanges as discreetly as possible.

Because of the discreet and illegal nature of exchanges above the equilibrium price, not all demanders and suppliers are going to participate. Therefore, as the illegal premium raises the price received by suppliers above $5, the increase in the quantity supplied is not going to follow the unconstrained supply curve. Likewise, the demand curve in the black market does not follow the unconstrained demand curve.

Figure 2.5.3 illustrates the effect of the black market on demand and supply. As the price rises above $5, the supply curve S_{bm} is steeper than the normal supply curve, whereas the demand curve D_{bm} is flatter than the normal demand curve. In both cases there are fewer participants in the market at higher prices.

Figure 2.5.2

Price Ceiling

A price ceiling is a legally established maximum price below the equilibrium price. If the market equilibrium price is $10, a price ceiling of $5 creates a shortage of 100 units. This shortage remains as long as the price ceiling remains, and neither curve shifts.

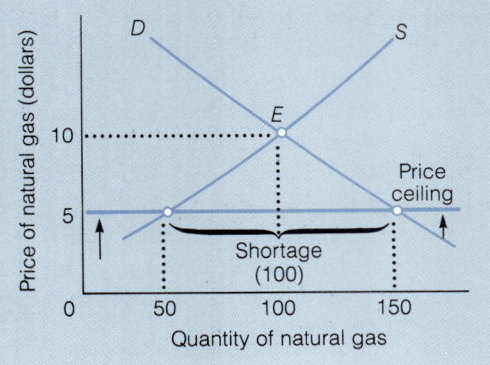

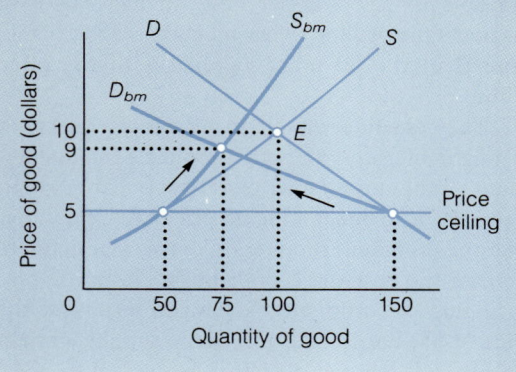

Figure 2.5.3

Black Market

A price ceiling can often lead to a black market, an exchange of goods above the legal price ceiling. In a black market some buyers who are unable to purchase the good are willing to pay a premium (higher price). This signals some suppliers to illegally offer more for sale. However, the illegal nature of these transactions means less output is exchanged than in the unconstrained market.

Equilibrium in the black market is reached by the intersection of the black market demand and supply curves. The black market price is $9, and the quantity exchanged is 25 units. With 50 units legally exchanged, this means a total of 75 units of the good are exchanged. Note that while the black market price can be above or below the original, preceiling price, the total quantity exchanged is always less than the preceiling equilibrium.

A TAX ON THE MARKET

The goods in many different markets are subject to taxes. Some specific goods, such as tires, cigarettes, and gasoline, are taxed as they are sold. Many state and local governments levy general sales taxes on most goods purchased by consumers. How does a tax affect the operation of a market?

Per Unit Tax

Let's first distinguish between two different types of taxes. A **per unit tax** is a fixed amount of tax levied on each unit sold. For example, cigarettes and gasoline have per unit taxes. If the per unit tax on gasoline is 10 cents, you pay 10 cents tax on each and every gallon purchased, regardless of the price charged by suppliers. If the price per gallon charged by suppliers is 30 cents, you pay a total of 40 cents per gallon. If the suppliers' price is $1.20, you pay that amount plus the 10-cent tax.

Ad Valorem Tax

A second type of tax is the **ad valorem tax,** which is a percentage of the price. Most sales taxes in the country are *ad valorem* taxes. If the sales tax is 3 percent and you buy $1 of goods, then you pay $1.03. If you buy $100 worth of goods, you pay $103. If the tax on gasoline is *ad valorem*, then the amount of tax paid is higher as the suppliers' price increases.

In most cases the supplier collects the taxes for the government. That is, the government actually taxes suppliers for the quantity sold. It is then the suppliers' responsibility to charge buyers the appropriate tax. From the suppliers' point of view, the tax is just another cost of doing business. If the suppliers want to sell the good, they have to pay for labor, capital, land, entrepreneurship, and the taxes, so they have to charge a higher price for each quantity sold. Figure 2.5.4 illustrates how per unit and *ad valorem* taxes affect the market supply.

In panel a, per unit tax is shown. Suppose suppliers are willing and able to sell 10 units for $1 each without a tax, point A on supply curve S. If a $1 tax is levied on the sale of the good, suppliers charge $2 for the 10 units, $1 to cover the supply price plus $1 for the tax.

UNIT 2.5 · GOVERNMENT AND THE MARKET

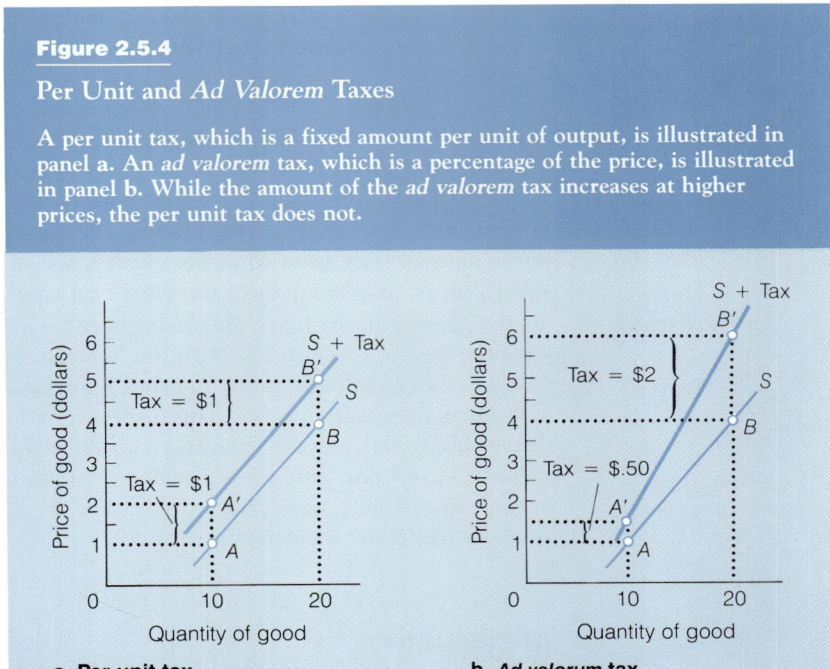

Figure 2.5.4

Per Unit and *Ad Valorem* Taxes

A per unit tax, which is a fixed amount per unit of output, is illustrated in panel a. An *ad valorem* tax, which is a percentage of the price, is illustrated in panel b. While the amount of the *ad valorem* tax increases at higher prices, the per unit tax does not.

a. Per unit tax

b. *Ad valorum* tax

If suppliers are willing to sell 20 units for $4, the $1 tax means they have to collect $5 for each unit. We can construct a line, S + Tax, which represents the relationship between the quantity of output supplied and the overall price charged by the seller. Note that the S + Tax line is parallel to the original supply curve, because the tax is a constant amount per unit.

An *ad valorem* tax is presented in panel b. Remember that an *ad valorem* tax is not a constant amount on each unit, but depends on the price of the product. If suppliers receive a higher price, then the tax on each unit is also higher. Let's say a 50 percent *ad valorem* tax is levied on the good. If the price is $1 for 10 units, the tax is 50 cents, and the supplier needs to collect $1.50. However, if the supply price is $4 for 20 units, then the tax is $2, and the supplier needs to collect $6. The tax on each unit is higher if the price is higher. Thus, the S + Tax line in panel b is *not* parallel to the original supply curve, and the gap between the two curves widens as the price increases.

Tax Incidence

Tax incidence is the division of a tax between buyers and sellers. Whether a per unit or an *ad valorem* tax is levied on the market, the effect is the same. Figure 2.5.5 presents a market with a per unit tax. Without the tax the market is in equilibrium at the intersection of the demand and supply curves, point E, where 20 units are exchanged for $5.

However, this equilibrium is based on the condition that suppliers only need to collect $5 for 20 units. But if a $1 tax is levied on each good sold, suppliers need to collect $6. Since this is a per unit

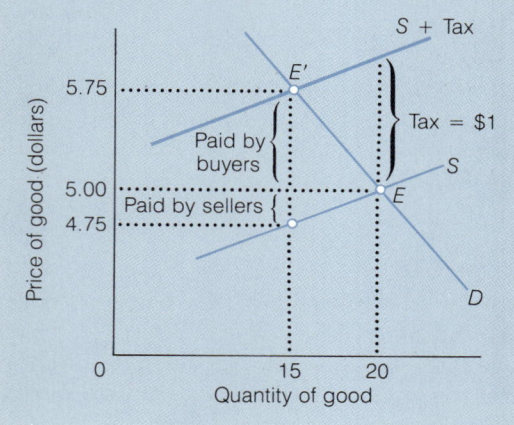

Figure 2.5.5

Tax Incidence

In general, buyers and sellers both pay a portion of a tax. If the original price is $5, buyers pay $5.75 after a $1 tax is levied, while sellers have $4.75 remaining after the tax is paid to the government. The incidence of the $1 tax is divided between both buyers and sellers, with buyers paying 75 cents and sellers paying 25 cents.

tax, the S + Tax line runs parallel to the original supply curve, and effectively assumes the role of the market supply curve.

If suppliers charge $6, demanders do not continue to buy 20 units. The law of demand takes over, and buyers reduce the quantity demanded, creating a surplus at $6, and forcing the price downward. The surplus is eliminated after the price falls to $5.75. At point E', which is the intersection of the demand curve and the S + Tax line, the market is back in equilibrium.

Let's compare the new equilibrium at E' with the original equilibrium at E to determine the impact of the tax. The quantity exchanged in the market is less, declining from 20 units to 15 units. And more importantly, the price is higher. Buyers pay $5.75 for each unit, after the tax, compared to $5 before the tax. So buyers are paying an additional 75 cents.

But suppliers are not getting the additional 75 cents. Remember suppliers are merely collecting a $1 tax for the government. While suppliers collect $5.75 on each unit sold, $1 of that goes to the government. The suppliers keep only $4.75, which is the amount they need to receive if they are to sell 15 units. While suppliers receive $5 on each good sold without the tax, they receive only $4.75 with the tax, or 25 cents less with the imposition of the tax. In effect, buyers pay 75 cents of the tax, and sellers the other 25 cents. This is the tax incidence. In general, the tax levied on a good is paid by both buyers and sellers; very seldom is it paid entirely by suppliers, nor by buyers. We spend more time discussing tax incidence in Unit 12.3.

IN SUMMARY

Government and the Market

- A price floor is a legally established minimum price, such as the minimum wage or agricultural price floors. A price floor creates a surplus. In the agricultural industry the surplus is often purchased by the government. The surplus created by the minimum wage is unemployment.

- A price ceiling is a legally established maximum price, such as rent controls or natural gas regulation. A price ceiling creates a shortage, for example, the lack of housing in major cities or natural gas shortages.

- Price ceilings can also lead to black markets. Black markets are markets that have illegal exchanges of goods above the legally established maximum.

- The goods exchanged in many different markets are taxed. The tax could be a fixed amount on each unit sold (per unit tax). Or it could be a percentage of the price (*ad valorem* tax). With either type of tax, buyers generally pay a higher price, and sellers receive a lower price. The division of the tax between buyers and sellers is the tax incidence.

QUESTIONS FOR STUDY AND ANALYSIS

1. Suppose you have the following demand and supply schedules:

Price	Quantity Demanded	Quantity Supplied
$10	100	20
20	90	30
30	80	40
40	70	50
50	60	60
60	50	70
70	40	80

   a. What is the market equilibrium price and quantity?
   b. If a price floor is established at $60, is a surplus or shortage created? How much of a surplus or shortage? What happens if the floor is set at $30?
   c. If a price ceiling is established at $20, is a surplus or shortage created? How much of a surplus or shortage? What happens if the ceiling is set at $70?
   d. If a per unit tax of $20 is levied on the market, what is the quantity exchanged? What price is paid by the buyers? What price is received by sellers (after the tax is paid to the government)? What is the tax incidence (how much is paid by buyers and how much by sellers)?

2. With a graph, demonstrate a price floor that has no effect on the market. To be effective, where must a price floor lie relative to the market equilibrium price? Above? Below?

3. In many major cities landlords require a substantial, nonrefundable "finders fee" before they will rent out an apartment. Based on our study of price ceilings and black markets, explain why this occurs.

4. Evaluate this statement: Retail stores need not be concerned about sales taxes, because they can simply pass them on to consumers.

REVIEW GLOSSARY

ad valorem tax A tax that is a percentage of the price.

black market A market that exchanges goods above the legally restricted maximum price. A black market is created by a price ceiling because some buyers are left without goods and are willing to pay a premium above the ceiling.

per unit tax A tax that is a fixed amount on each unit sold.

price ceiling A legally established maximum price below the market equilibrium. Rent controls and natural gas regulation are two examples of price ceilings. A price ceiling established below the market equilibrium price creates a shortage.

price floor A legally established minimum price above the market equilibrium. Minimum wages and agricultural price supports are two examples of price floors. A price floor established above the market equilibrium price creates a surplus.

tax incidence The division of a tax between buyers and sellers.

UNIT 2.6

Elasticity

So far in this section we have seen that buyers and sellers are responsive to changes in the price. A price increase leads to a decrease in the quantity demanded and an increase in the quantity supplied. However, it is also important to know how much the quantity increases or decreases. The responsiveness of quantity demanded and supplied to price changes is termed elasticity.

In this unit the concept of elasticity is introduced, and we see how it relates to the market. In particular, we look at four important measures of elasticity: price elasticity of demand, income elasticity of demand, cross price elasticity of demand, and price elasticity of supply. The unit ends by examining three determinants of elasticity: availability of substitutes, time period, and proportion of budget. This study of elasticity enhances our ability to use the market as a tool for economic analysis, as will be demonstrated in Unit 2.7, Elasticity and the Market.

ELASTICITY

In this unit we look at the relative response of quantity demanded (or demand) and quantity supplied (or supply) to changes in price, income, or price of another good, or elasticity. **Elasticity is the relative response of one variable to changes in another variable**. The term *relative response* simply refers to the percentage change. For example, the price elasticity of demand, which is formally defined in a moment, represents the percentage change in quantity demanded measured against the percentage change in price.

A simple example will help illustrate the general concept of elasticity. Suppose you tell your instructor that the dog ate your homework assignment (or a similar unsubstantiated story), and your grade is raised from a D to an A. Since very little effort went into your grade change, the instructor can be considered very elastic (or responsive to your plea). Now let's consider the alternative. Suppose you document your story with eyewitness accounts from the five most reputable citizens in town, provide an affidavit from your veterinarian, and replay a videotape of the actual event, but your grade is raised only from a D to a D+. In this case the instructor is not very elastic.

Let's apply this concept of elasticity to the market depicted in Figure 2.6.1. In both panels a and b the supply curve undergoes identical shifts from S to S', but the demand curve in panel a is steeper than the curve in panel b. When the market moves down the relatively steep demand curve in panel a from point E to E', the equilibrium price falls from $10 to $5 and the equilibrium quantity increases from 100 to 110 units. Compare this to panel b, where the equilibrium price decreases from $10 to $8 and the equilibrium quantity increases from 100 to 150 units.

Note that the demand curve in panel b results in a smaller decrease in the price and a larger increase in the quantity demanded. The demand curve in panel b is *more responsive* to changes in price than the demand curve in panel a. In other words D_b is more elastic than D_a.

PRICE ELASTICITY OF DEMAND

A detailed look at the price elasticity of demand will help illuminate how the elasticity concept works in practice. **Price elasticity of demand is the relative response of quantity demanded to a change in price**. More specifically, it is measured as

$$\text{price elasticity of demand} = \frac{\text{percentage change in quantity demanded}}{\text{percentage change in price}}$$

UNIT 2.6 ELASTICITY

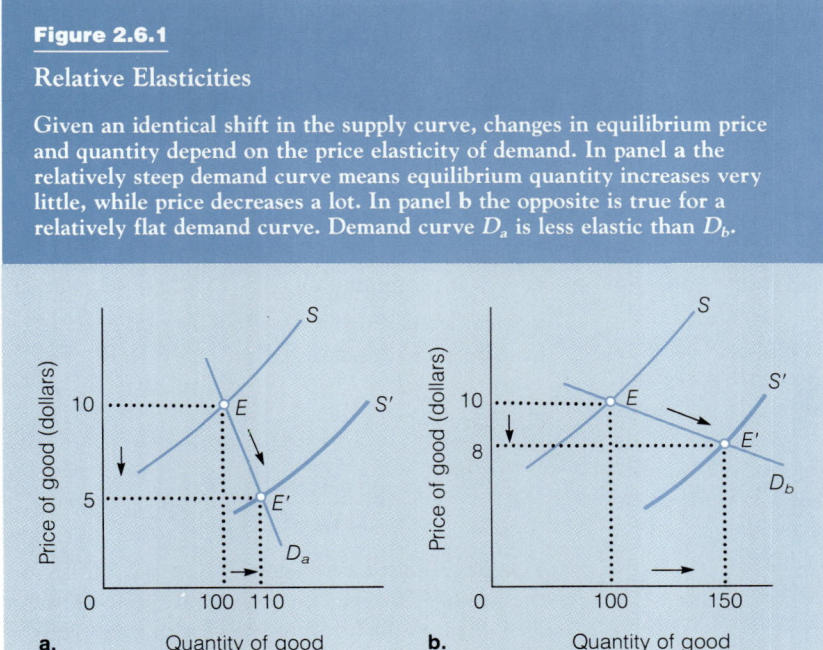

Figure 2.6.1

Relative Elasticities

Given an identical shift in the supply curve, changes in equilibrium price and quantity depend on the price elasticity of demand. In panel a the relatively steep demand curve means equilibrium quantity increases very little, while price decreases a lot. In panel b the opposite is true for a relatively flat demand curve. Demand curve D_a is less elastic than D_b.

Table 2.6.1 presents a hypothetical demand schedule that can be used to calculate a numerical value of the price elasticity of demand. If the price decreases from $5 to $4, the quantity demanded increases from 60 units to 70 units. The percentage change in price is measured as

$$\text{percentage change in price} = \frac{\$4 - \$5}{\$5}$$

$$= -0.20 \text{ or } -20 \text{ percent}$$

The percentage change in quantity demanded is measured as

$$\text{percentage change in quantity demanded} = \frac{70 - 60}{60}$$

$$= 0.17 \text{ or } 17 \text{ percent}$$

Table 2.6.1.

Hypothetical Demand Schedule

Price	Quantity
$10	10
9	20
8	30
7	40
6	50
5	60
4	70
3	80
2	90
1	100

Hence the price elasticity of demand is measured as

$$\text{elasticity} = \frac{17 \text{ percent}}{-20 \text{ percent}} = -0.85$$

A 1 percent *increase* in the price results in a 0.85 percent *decrease* in quantity demanded, or a price elasticity of demand of -0.85. The negative sign reflects the inverse relationship between price and quantity demanded. Since demand curves are negatively sloped, price and quantity demanded move in opposite directions. If the percentage change in one is *positive*, the change in the other is *negative*.

Knowing that the price elasticity of demand is always negative, we can usually concentrate on just the magnitude, or absolute value, of the number. From a practical standpoint this allows us to say that a very elastic demand has a very large absolute value, thus avoiding the mental gymnastics of trying to associate a very small number (one that is very negative) to a highly elastic demand. Confining ourselves to absolute values of the price elasticity of demand enables us to say that the larger the number, the more elastic the demand. While we will carry along the negative sign, we will concentrate on only the absolute magnitude of the number.

Midpoints Formula

There is a problem in calculating elasticity as we have done in this example. If the price decreases from $5 to $4, elasticity is -0.85, but if the price rises from $4 to $5, elasticity is -0.56. Although we are moving along the same portion of the demand curve, a price increase results in a different elasticity than a price decrease.

Why would elasticity be different? Note that the percentage decrease in price from $5 to $4 is 20 percent, but the percentage increase from $4 to $5 is 25 percent. The base price is different for a price decrease than for a price increase. The same is true for quantity; the percentage change in quantity demanded from 60 to 70 units is different than from 70 to 60 units.

To correct for this, we use the midpoints formula for calculating elasticity. The **midpoints formula** is a method of calculating elasticity that uses the average, or midpoint, price and quantity over the range of the change. The midpoints formula for calculating elasticity is measured as

$$\text{midpoint elasticity} = \frac{Q_2 - Q_1}{(Q_2 + Q_1)/2} \bigg/ \frac{P_2 - P_1}{(P_2 + P_1)/2}$$

In our example the price elasticity of demand for a price decrease from $5 to $4 *or* a price increase from $4 to $5 is measured as

$$\text{elasticity} = -\frac{10/(60+70)/2}{1/(5+4)/2}$$

$$= -\frac{15 \text{ percent}}{22 \text{ percent}} = -0.68$$

The price elasticity of demand is -0.68, or, on the average, a 1-percent change in price between $5 and $4 results in a 0.68 percent change in quantity demanded.

Elastic, Inelastic, and Unit Elastic

In the previous example the percentage change in the quantity demanded is less than the percentage change in the price, so the absolute value of the price elasticity of demand is less than 1.0. In fact, when the percentage change in quantity demanded is less than the percentage change in price, the absolute value of the price elasticity of demand is less than 1.0, and demand is **inelastic.** An inelastic demand means that the quantity demanded is not very responsive to the price. A 1 percent change in the price results in a less than 1 percent change in quantity demanded.

Let's take another example. Suppose the price decrease from $5 to $4 causes the quantity demanded to increase from 60 units to 100 units. In this case price elasticity of demand (using the midpoints formula) is 50 percent/-22 percent, or -2.27; the absolute value is obviously greater than 1.0. When the absolute value of the price elasticity of demand is greater than 1.0, and the percentage change in quantity demanded is greater than the percentage change in the price, demand is **elastic**. Elastic demand means that the quantity demanded is very responsive to price. In fact, the larger the elasticity, the more responsive quantity demanded is to price.

If the percentage change in the quantity demanded is exactly the same as the percentage change in the price, and the absolute value of the price elasticity of demand is zero, demand is **unit elastic**. Suppose that a price decrease from $5 to $4 results in a quantity increase from 80 to 100 units. The elasticity in this case is 22 percent/−22 percent, or −1.0.

There are also two extreme possibilities representing the endpoints for the entire range of price elasticities of demand. If the quantity demanded is totally unresponsive to changes in price, then demand is **perfectly inelastic**. No matter how much price changes, quantity demanded does not change. A vertical demand curve is perfectly inelastic. Since the percentage change in the quantity demanded is zero, elasticity is zero for a perfectly inelastic demand curve. At the other extreme, if there is an infinitesimally small change in price, and the quantity demanded either falls to zero or increases to an infinitely large value, then demand is **perfectly elastic**. A horizontal demand curve is perfectly elastic. These five alternatives are summarized in Table 2.6.2.

Slope and Elasticity

Even though more steeply sloped demand curves tend to be relatively less elastic, it is impossible to determine if a demand curve is elastic or inelastic from the slope alone. For example, consider the straight line demand curve in Figure 2.6.2, which is a plot of the demand schedule given in Table 2.6.1. The midpoints formula reveals an elasticity between points C and D of −0.68. However, the absolute value of the slope between C and D, as well as for the entire curve, is 0.1.

Table 2.6.2

Elasticity Alternatives

Demand can be classified as perfectly elastic, elastic, unit elastic, inelastic, or perfectly inelastic depending on the absolute value of the price elasticity of demand.

Demand	Absolute Value of Elasticity (E)
Perfectly elastic	$E = \infty$
Elastic	$E > 1.0$
Unit elastic	$E = 1.0$
Inelastic	$E < 1.0$
Perfectly inelastic	$E = 0$

Even though the slope is constant, elasticity is not. Between points A and B the elasticity is −6.33, which means price is very responsive to demand. If we decrease the price in increments of $1, we see that the absolute value of elasticity declines from point A to point E. A demand curve with a constant slope has a constantly changing elasticity. In fact, a straight line demand curve has segments that are elastic, unit elastic, and inelastic, as Figure 2.6.2 illustrates.

Total Expenditure and Elasticity

The price elasticity of demand has implications about total expenditures on a good. In particular, the price elasticity of demand indicates whether a price change leads to an increase, a decrease, or no change in total expenditures. For example, suppose an urban transit authority wants to increase its revenues. One recommendation is to raise fares, the price charged to users. If the initial fare is 40 cents, and 2000 people use the system daily, the total expenditures by users is $.40 × 2000, or $800 per day. And for

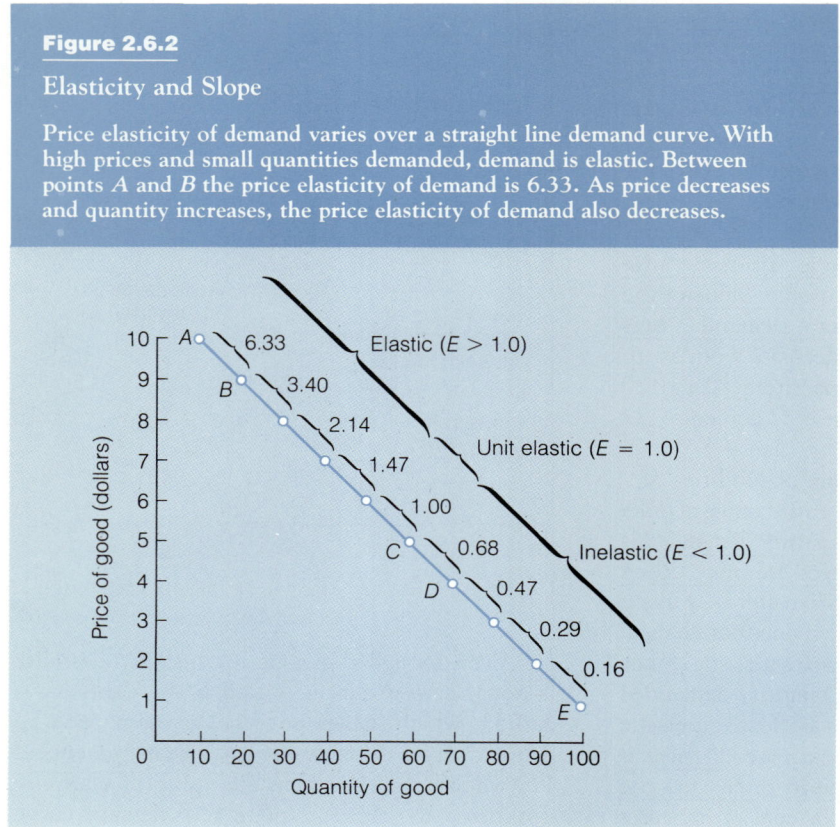

Figure 2.6.2

Elasticity and Slope

Price elasticity of demand varies over a straight line demand curve. With high prices and small quantities demanded, demand is elastic. Between points A and B the price elasticity of demand is 6.33. As price decreases and quantity increases, the price elasticity of demand also decreases.

our purposes, assume the transit authority wants more than $800 per day in revenues.

Let's say the fare is raised to 60 cents. If 2000 people continue to use the service, revenue increases. However, the law of demand tells us that price and quantity are inversely related, and the higher price leads to a smaller quantity demanded. If the quantity demanded falls to 1200 people per day, the total revenue received by the transit authority is only $.60 × 1200, or $720 per day. The higher price results in a decrease in revenues.

We can see where the transit authority went wrong by looking at the price elasticity of demand. The price increase from 40 to 60 cents led to a decrease in the quantity demanded from 2000 to 1200. Using the midpoints formula, we calculate

$$\text{elasticity} = -\frac{800/(2000 + 1200)/2}{0.20/(0.60 + 0.40)/2}$$

$$= -\frac{50 \text{ percent}}{40 \text{ percent}} = -1.125$$

The midpoints formula reveals that the demand curve is elastic, or that the quantity demanded is very responsive to price. The decrease in quantity demanded is relatively greater than the increase in price. The additional revenue received by the transit authority from the price increase is more than offset by the revenue lost from a decrease in the number of users.

In this case a price increase results in a decrease in total expenditures; price and total expenditures move in opposite directions. Indeed, when the absolute value of the price elasticity of demand is greater than 1.0, meaning demand is elastic, price and total expenditures always move in opposite directions. The transit authority is actually better off with a price decrease than with an increase. Since the demand is elastic, a lower price results in a relatively larger increase in quantity demanded, and thus an increase in revenues.

Table 2.6.3 summarizes the relationship between elasticity and total expenditures. If demand is inelastic (the absolute value of the price elasticity of demand is less than 1.0), total expenditures and price move in the same direction, and a price increase causes total expenditures to increase. For an inelastic demand the additional revenue from increasing the price is not entirely offset by the revenue lost due to the reduction in the quantity demanded.

But when demand is unit elastic, total expenditures do not change. If the absolute value of the price elasticity of demand is equal to 1.0, additional revenues from a price increase are exactly offset by less revenues from the equivalent percentage decrease in the quantity demanded. Total expenditures on the good do not change. With unit elasticity, the transit authority is unable to affect revenues one way or the other by a price change.

INCOME ELASTICITY OF DEMAND

Price is not the only variable that affects demand. One of the more important determinants of demand is income. The **income elasticity of demand** is the relative response of demand to changes in income. It is measured as

$$\text{income elasticity} = \frac{\text{percentage change in demand}}{\text{percentage change in income}}$$

Different types of goods can respond differently to changes in income. There are two types of goods that are singled out in this regard. If the quantity of a good demanded increases as income increases, it is a **normal good.** In terms of the measure of income elasticity, both the numerator and the denominator have the same sign, meaning the income elasticity of demand is positive (greater than zero).

If the quantity of a good demanded decreases with increases in income, it is an **inferior good.** For an inferior good, quantity demanded always moves in the opposite direction of the change in income, and the income elasticity of demand is negative (less than zero). Table 2.6.4 summarizes the income elasticity of demand for normal and inferior goods. In calculating income elasticity, the minus sign becomes important because it tells us that a good is income inferior.

Table 2.6.3

Elasticity and Total Expenditures

The price elasticity of demand determines the relationship between total expenditures and price. If demand is elastic, total expenditures decrease when the price increases. If demand is inelastic, total expenditures increase when the price increases. If demand is unit elastic, total expenditures do not change.

Demand	Elasticity (E)	Price and Total Expenditures
Elastic	$E > 1.0$	Change in different directions
Unit elastic	$E = 1.0$	Total expenditures do not change
Inelastic	$E < 1.0$	Change in same direction

Table 2.6.4

Income Elasticity of Demand

The income elasticity of demand indicates whether a good is normal or inferior. A normal good has a positive income elasticity, whereas an inferior good has a negative income elasticity.

Type of Good	Income Elasticity (N)
Normal	$N > 0$
Inferior	$N < 0$

Table 2.6.5

Cross Price Elasticity of Demand

The cross price elasticity of demand indicates whether goods are substitutes or complements. Substitutes have a positive cross price elasticity, whereas complements have a negative cross price elasticity.

Type of Good	Cross Price Elasticity (C)
Substitute	$C > 0$
Complement	$C < 0$

CROSS PRICE ELASTICITY OF DEMAND

Another important measure of elasticity is the cross price elasticity of demand. **Cross price elasticity of demand** is the relative response of the demand of one good to changes in the price of another good. Prices of other goods have an important influence on demand. For example, if the price of gasoline increases, the demand for automobiles is affected. Or if the price of pork changes, the demand for chicken is affected. Cross price elasticity is measured as

$$\text{cross price elasticity} = \frac{\text{percentage change in demand of good 1}}{\text{percentage change in price of good 2}}$$

If two goods are **substitutes** in consumption, then an increase in the price of one good results in an increase in the demand for the other good. According to the definition of cross price elasticity, the numerator and denominator move in the same direction. The cross price elasticity for substitute goods is positive (greater than zero).

If two goods are **complements** in consumption, then an increase in the price of one good results in a decrease in the demand for the other good. The cross price elasticity for complement goods is negative (less than zero). As with the income elasticity of demand, a minus sign in the calculation of the cross price elasticity of demand tells us that the goods are complements. Table 2.6.5 summarizes the cross price elasticities for complements and substitutes.

PRICE ELASTICITY OF SUPPLY

Up to this point we have discussed the three most important elasticity measures associated with demand, but supply is also responsive to price. Indeed, the price elasticity of supply is analogous to the price elasticity of demand. The **price elasticity of supply** is the relative response in quantity supplied to changes in price. It is measured as

$$\text{price elasticity of supply} = \frac{\text{percentage change in quantity supplied}}{\text{percentage change in price}}$$

Since price and quantity supplied are directly related, the price elasticity of supply is positive. Thus, there is no need to worry about the absolute value. However, like the absolute value of the price elasticity of demand, the price elasticity of supply ranges from zero to infinity. The price elasticity of supply can also be classified as perfectly inelastic, inelastic, unit elastic, elastic, and perfectly elastic.

If the supply curve is perfectly inelastic, quantity supplied is completely unresponsive to price changes, and the price elasticity of supply is zero, as indicated by a vertical supply curve. If the supply curve is inelastic, the price elasticity of supply is greater than zero but less than 1.0. If the supply curve is unit elastic, the price elasticity of supply is equal to 1.0. If the supply curve is elastic, the price elasticity of supply is greater than 1.0. If the supply curve is perfectly elastic, then the price elasticity of supply is infinite, as indicated by a horizontal supply curve. For immeasurably small changes in price, the quantity supplied will either fall to zero or increase to an infinitely large number.

DETERMINANTS OF ELASTICITY

Different goods have different demand and supply elasticities. The price elasticity of demand for a life support system is different than for a hamburger. The three key **determinants of elasticity** are availability of substitutes, time period of analysis, and proportion of budget. The first two determinants are important for both the demand and supply, while the last determinant relates only to the price elasticity of demand.

Availability of Substitutes

A consumption good with many close substitutes tends to have a very elastic demand curve. For example, a good with several close substitutes, such as a specific brand of cola, is very elastic. If the price of Coca-Cola increases, buyers can switch to another brand of cola, a noncola soft drink, tea, coffee, or any number of other beverages. The price increase results in a large decrease in demand as buyers switch to similar goods. But if a good has very few close substitutes, then demand tends to be highly inelastic. For example, if the price of medical services increases, buyers have few options available. They can either pay the higher price, try to cure themselves, see a witch doctor, or do without. There are no close substitutes.

The availability of substitutes is also important in determining the price elasticity of supply. However, instead of substitutes in consumption, the important determinant of supply elasticity is the substitution of factors of production between two goods. For example, the supply of soybeans is relatively elastic because factors are easily switched from corn production. A small increase in the price of soybeans results in relatively large increases in the quantity supplied, since factors are easily hired away from corn production. The supply of doctors is less elastic, however, because factors such as education and training are not as easily substituted from another production process.

Time Period

The longer the time period of analysis, the greater the price elasticities of demand and supply are. Brief periods do not allow consumers and producers time to adjust consumption and production decisions, to find substitutes for the consumption good or alternative factors to be used in production. Even the supply of soybeans is highly inelastic over a short period of time (one month). Given a longer period of time (a year), soybean production becomes more elastic. The supply of doctors, although very inelastic, grows more elastic if the time period of analysis is extended to a decade or more.

Proportion of Budget

The price elasticity of demand is also determined by the proportion of the consumer's budget devoted to buying a good. The larger the proportion of the budget, the more elastic demand is. For example, the demand for automobiles, which are a very large proportion of the budget for most consumers, tends to be very elastic. A 10 percent price increase on a $10,000 car amounts to $1000, enough to take many people out of the market. But the demand for a good that requires only a small proportion of the budget, such as salt, tends to be very inelastic. Even if the price of salt doubles, the impact on the consumer's budget is so small that very little reduction in quantity demanded is likely.

IN SUMMARY

Elasticity

- Elasticity is the relative response of one variable to changes in another variable. In terms of the market it is the change in quantities demanded or supplied relative to changes in prices and income. There are four important elasticity measures: price elasticity of demand, income elasticity of demand, cross price elasticity of demand, and price elasticity of supply.

- The price elasticities of demand and supply are said to be inelastic, unit elastic, or elastic, depending on whether elasticity is less than 1.0, equal to 1.0, or greater than 1.0, respectively.

- A demand curve with a constant slope does not have a constant elasticity. Slope and elasticity are two different concepts. A straight line demand curve has a constantly changing elasticity. At high prices and small quantities, the demand curve is very elastic. At lower prices and larger quantities, the demand curve is inelastic.

- The price elasticity of demand affects changes in total expenditures on a good that result from a price change. For an inelastic good, total expenditures increase if the price increases. For an elastic good, total expenditures decrease if the price increases. For a unit elastic good, total expenditures do not change.

- Income elasticity of demand tells us whether a good is normal or inferior, depending on whether the coefficient is greater than or less than zero, respectively.

- Cross price elasticity of demand tells us whether goods are substitutes or complements, depending on whether the coefficient is greater than or less than zero, respectively.

- Elasticity is influenced by three determinants: availability of substitutes, time period of analysis, and proportion of budget. While the first two determinants, substitutes and time period, affect the elasticities of both demand and supply, the proportion of budget affects only the elasticity of demand.

QUESTIONS FOR STUDY AND ANALYSIS

1. Let's say that you are given the following demand schedule:

Price	Quantity
$ 0	210
10	160
20	120
30	90
40	70
50	60

    Using the elasticity midpoints formula, would you classify the demand schedule as elastic, unit elastic, inelastic, or a combination of the three? How would your calculations of elasticity change if the price were expressed in cents rather than dollars?

2. Suppose you are given two demand curves. The first has a constant slope of 1.0, and the second a constant slope of 2.0. Which is more elastic? Would you consider the demand curves as elastic, unit elastic, or inelastic? Why or why not?

3. The president of Econa-Cola Soft Drink Company has placed you in charge of pricing Econa-Cola. Knowing that there are a large number of very good substitutes available, would you raise or lower the price if you wanted to increase the revenues received by the firm?

4. The dean of your school decides to raise tuition from the fall to the spring term. Revenues collected in the spring term are higher than the fall. However, revenues decrease in the following year. What does this say about the price elasticity of demand for higher education in the short and long run?

5. You are given the following information about price, quantity demand, and income:

Price	Income	Quantity
$10	$5000	200
10	8000	150
20	5000	170
20	8000	120
30	5000	140
30	8000	90

Is the income elasticity for this good positive or negative? Would you consider this a normal or inferior good?

REVIEW GLOSSARY

complements Two goods with a negative cross price elasticity. If demand of good 1 decreases as the price of good 2 increases, the goods are complements.

cross price elasticity of demand The relative response of demand to a change in the price of another good. It is defined as the percentage change in the demand of good 1 divided by a percentage change in the price of good 2.

determinants of elasticity The three key determinants of elasticity are availability of substitutes, time period of analysis, and proportion of budget. While the first two apply to the price elasticities of both demand and supply, the last applies primarily to the price elasticity of demand.

elastic A condition of elasticity in which the percentage change in quantity demanded (or supplied) is greater than the percentage change in price, and the absolute value of the price elasticity of demand (or supply) is greater than 1.0. An elastic curve is very responsive to changes in price.

elasticity A measure of the relative response of one variable to changes in another variable. In terms of the market it is the relative response of quantity demanded, or supplied, to a change in price, income, or the price of another good. Elasticity is determined by the percentage change in quantity divided by the percentage change in the variable stimulating the change in quantity.

income elasticity of demand The relative response of demand to changes in income, defined as the percentage change in demand divided by the percentage change in income.

inelastic A condition of elasticity in which the percentage change in quantity demanded (or supplied) is less than the percentage change in price, and the absolute value of the price elasticity of demand (or supply) is less than 1.0. An inelastic curve is not very responsive to changes in price.

inferior good A good with a negative income elasticity. If demand decreases as income increases, it is an inferior good.

midpoints formula A method of calculating elasticity that uses the average, or midpoint, price and quantity over the range of the change.

normal good A good with a positive income elasticity. If demand increases as income increases, it is a normal good.

perfectly elastic A condition of elasticity in which there is an infinitely large change in quantity demanded (or supplied) for a small percentage change in price, and the absolute value of the price elasticity of demand (or supply) is infinity. A perfectly elastic curve is extremely responsive to any changes in price, and is depicted by horizontal demand and supply curves.

perfectly inelastic A condition of elasticity in which quantity demanded (or supplied) does not change regardless of the percentage change in price, and the absolute value of the price elasticity of demand (or supply) is zero. A perfectly inelastic curve is not responsive to any changes in price, and is depicted by vertical demand and supply curves.

price elasticity of demand The relative response of quantity demanded to a change in price, defined as the percentage change in quantity demanded divided by the percentage change in price.

price elasticity of supply The relative response of quantity supplied to a change in price, defined as the percentage change in quantity supplied divided by the percentage change in price. Like the price elasticity of demand, the price elasticity of supply can be greater than, equal to, or less than 1.0, indicating a supply that is elastic, unit elastic, or inelastic.

substitutes Two goods with a positive cross price elasticity. If demand of good 1 increases as the price of good 2 increases, the goods are substitutes.

unit elastic A condition of elasticity in which the percentage change in quantity demanded (or supplied) is equal to the percentage change in price, and the absolute value of the price elasticity of demand (or supply) is equal to 1.0. A unit elastic curve is neutral in its response to changes in price.

UNIT 2.7

Elasticity and the Market

Knowledge of elasticity is important when using the market as an analytical tool. This unit investigates how price and income elasticities affect simple market analyses. While differing elasticities do not affect the direction of shocks to a market, they do affect the magnitude of the changes. Here we examine how elasticity affects the analysis of price floors, price ceilings, and taxes. Then we turn our attention to specific estimates of elasticities for gasoline, water, fuel oil and coal, and timber. Let's look first at price floors.

PRICE FLOOR

A **price floor** is a legally established minimum price above the market equilibrium. As we saw in Unit 2.5, price floors have been commonly used in the United States in the agricultural sector to support farm incomes, and in the labor sector in the form of minimum wages to bolster labor incomes. Panel a in Figure 2.7.1 illustrates how a simple price floor works. If the market is left unrestrained, it will reach an equilibrium price at P_e. The price floor is established above P_e at P_f, creating the surplus AB.

The surplus exists because both demand and supply respond to the higher price. The quantity demanded decreases from E to A, and the quantity supplied increases from E to B. This is where the concept of elasticity becomes important. We realize there is a surplus. We know that farmers are unable to sell as much output as they want, and that in the labor market fewer workers are employed

Figure 2.7.1

Price Floors

The price floor P_f in panel a creates the surplus AB, the size of the surplus depending on the price elasticities of demand and supply. In panel b demand and supply are inelastic, and the size of the surplus AB is smaller than in panel a. With elastic demand and supply curves such as those in panel c, the surplus is even greater.

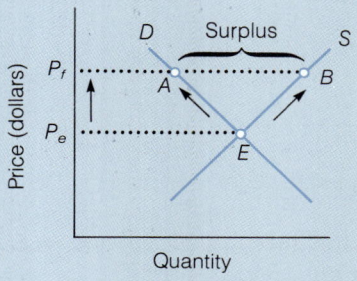

a.

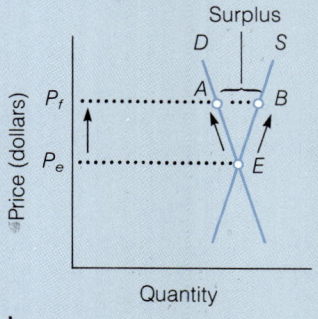

b.

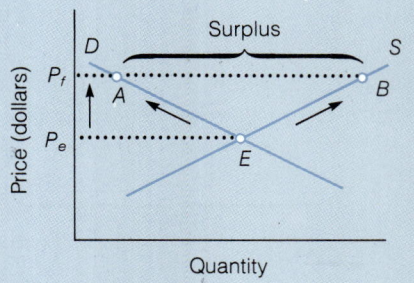

c.

than seek jobs. Now, by using elasticity, we can calculate the relative size of the resulting surplus.

Let's look at the first of two extreme possibilities. If demand and supply are both unresponsive to price changes, or highly inelastic, a market such as the one depicted in panel b of Figure 2.7.1 exists. Note that the demand and supply curves in panel b are nearly vertical. But if the same price floor as in panel a is applied, the price floor P_f reduces the quantity demanded and increases the quantity supplied, just as in panel a. However, the changes are not as great. The surplus AB created by the price floor is small relative to the surplus in panel a.

If the objective of the price floor is to maintain farmers' income, it succeeds. Remember that if demand is inelastic, revenue and price move in the same direction, and the quantity demanded decreases relatively less than price rises. A large surplus is not created because, in addition to the small decrease in quantity demanded, the quantity supplied increases very little. In short, the more inelastic demand is, the more effective a price floor is in maintaining the income of farmers and labor.

Let's look at the other extreme. Panel c illustrates a market with relatively high price elasticities of demand and supply. Since both the demand and supply curves are relatively flat, the price increase from P_e to P_f creates the large surplus AB. Because demand and supply are both very responsive, quantity demanded decreases and quantity supplied increases more than in either panel a or panel b. If the objective is to increase farm income, a relatively high price elasticity of demand defeats the purpose. An elastic demand means price and revenue move in opposite directions, or as prices rise, farmers' income declines.

All three panels in Figure 2.7.1 tell the same qualitative story. As the price floor is established, the quantity demanded decreases and the quantity supplied increases, creating a surplus. However, the price elasticities of demand and supply add an extra dimension by determining the relative size of the surplus created. And the price elasticity of demand determines the effect of the price floor on the total revenue received by the suppliers.

PRICE CEILING

A **price ceiling** is a legally established maximum price below the market equilibrium, and is designed to prevent the price of a commodity from becoming too high. We saw in Unit 2.5 that price ceilings have been used in the United States in recent years to regulate the price of natural gas and to control rents in major urban areas. The objective of a price ceiling is to prevent buyers from spending "too much" on the good. While an artificially low price supposedly keeps buyers' expenditures down, this is not necessarily true.

Panel a in Figure 2.7.2 depicts the simple price ceiling P_c, which is below the unrestrained equilibrium price P_e. The price ceiling creates a shortage because the quantity demanded increases while the quantity supplied decreases. In panel a we cannot tell if the objective of limiting buyer spending is accomplished, since we know nothing about the price elasticities of demand and supply.

Panel b illustrates one extreme in which both demand and supply are relatively inelastic. The shortage CD created by the price ceiling is relatively less than the shortage in panel a because both demand and supply are relatively price inelastic. In fact, the more inelastic demand and supply are, the smaller the shortage created by a price ceiling is. This means that the government least distorts the allocation of resources if it places price ceilings on goods with relatively inelastic demand and supply. This conclusion is reinforced by noting the size of the shortage in panel c, where the demand and supply curves are both relatively elastic, and the resulting shortage is relatively large.

However, the primary reason for establishing a price ceiling is to help out buyers of the good. Note that the quantity demanded in each of the three panels in Figure 2.7.2 depends on the price elasticity of demand, which is not the key element in determining if buyers are actually helped by the price ceiling. In fact, we have to consider the price elasticity of supply, because buyers are able to buy only the amount supplied by sellers, and that is based on the price elasticity of supply. If the supply is relatively inelastic, as in panel b, then buyers

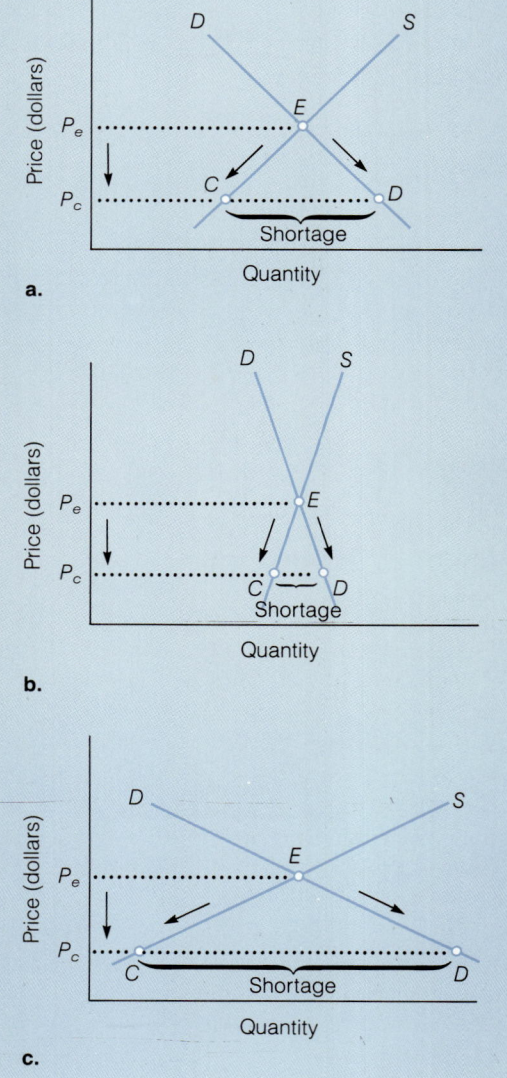

Figure 2.7.2

Price Ceilings

The price ceiling P_c in panel a creates the shortage CD, the size of the shortage depending on the price elasticities of demand and supply. In panel b demand and supply are inelastic, and the size of the shortage CD is smaller than in panel a. With elastic demand and supply curves such as those in panel c, the shortage is even greater.

can obtain nearly as much of the good after the price ceiling is imposed as they could in the unrestricted market. However, in panel c, where supply is relatively elastic, buyers can obtain a great deal less of the good under the price ceiling.

Without information on the price elasticities of demand and supply it could be disastrous to establish a price ceiling with the intent of helping the buyers. The more elastic supply is, the less of the good is produced, and the more buyers have to do without.

TAX INCIDENCE

Tax incidence is the division of a tax between buyers and sellers. As discussed in Unit 2.5, both buyers and sellers generally pay a portion of the tax, whether it is a per unit or an *ad valorem* tax. Common examples of per unit taxes on goods are taxes on tires, gasoline, and cigarettes; *ad valorem* taxes are sales taxes at the state and local levels.

Figure 2.7.3 illustrates the general effect of a per unit tax on the market. Suppose the initial equilibrium price is P_e and the equilibrium quantity is Q_e, seen at the intersection of the demand and supply curves at point E. A simple per unit tax drives a wedge between demand and supply in the amount of the tax YZ. The after-tax quantity exchanged in the market falls to Q_t, and the price paid by buyers is P_t, which is equal to the costs of production P_s plus the tax YZ.

When we analyze the effect of a tax on a market such as the one presented in Figure 2.7.3, our main concern is with the incidence of the tax YZ. Based on the original equilibrium price (P_e), we see that buyers pay a higher price (P_t) with the tax than without. But sellers receive a lower price (P_s) with the tax than without (P_e). The incidence of the tax is divided between that portion paid by the buyers ($P_t - P_e$) and that portion paid by the sellers ($P_e - P_s$). While the tax is usually paid jointly by buyers and sellers, the relative price elasticities of demand and supply can indicate which side pays more.

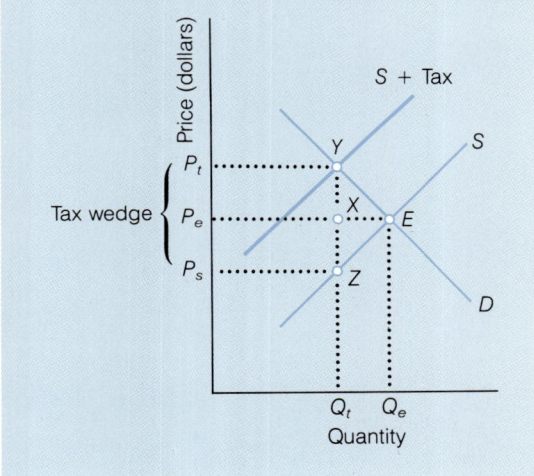

Figure 2.7.3

Tax Incidence

A per unit tax drives a wedge between the price paid by buyers and the price received by sellers. The tax YZ increases the price paid by buyers from P_e to P_t and reduces the price received by sellers from P_e to P_s. In general, a tax is paid by both buyers and sellers in the market. The incidence of tax YZ is divided between the buyers YX (equal to $P_t - P_e$) and the sellers XZ (equal to $P_t - P_s$). The quantity exchanged is also reduced by the tax from Q_s to Q_t.

Figure 2.7.4 illustrates a market in which the tax incidence is not equally shared by buyers and sellers, as it is in Figure 2.7.3. The supply curve in Figure 2.7.4 is very inelastic, and the demand curve is very elastic. This means the quantity supplied is not very responsive to price, but the quantity demanded is.

Using the same logic as employed in Figure 2.7.3, we can see that the sellers in Figure 2.7.4 pay the vast majority of the tax. The difference between the original equilibrium price P_e and the after-tax price received by sellers P_s is much greater than the difference between the original price and the after-tax price paid by buyers, P_t.

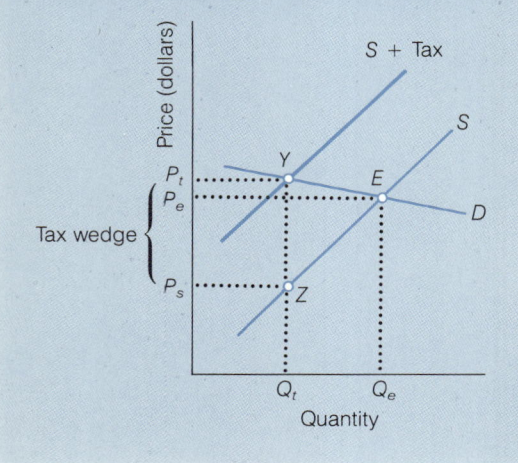

Figure 2.7.4

Elastic Demand, Inelastic Supply, and Tax Incidence

The tax incidence depends on the elasticities of demand and supply. In this case the demand curve is more elastic, and the supply curve is more inelastic. This causes sellers to pay a larger share of the tax than buyers.

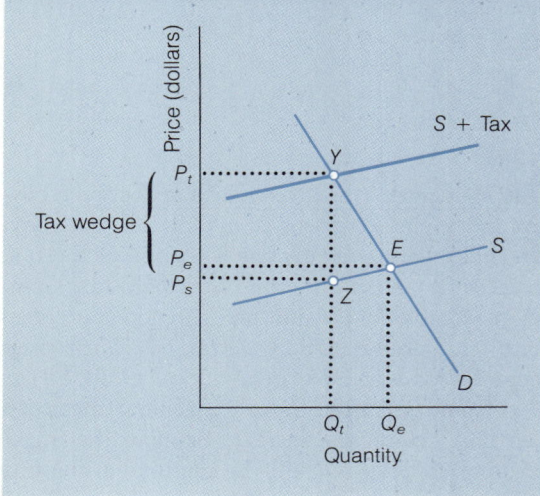

Figure 2.7.5

Inelastic Demand, Elastic Supply, and Tax Incidence

The tax incidence depends on the elasticities of demand and supply. In this case the demand curve is more inelastic, and the supply curve is more elastic. This causes buyers to pay a larger share of the tax than sellers.

The more elastic the demand and the more inelastic the supply, the larger the portion of the tax paid by sellers. Conversely, the more inelastic the demand and the more elastic the supply, the larger the portion paid by the buyers. Figure 2.7.5 illustrates a market in which the demand curve is relatively inelastic and the supply curve is relatively elastic, so the buyers pay the larger portion of the tax. If we take this point to its logical end, it means sellers pay the entire tax if the demand curve is perfectly elastic or the supply curve is perfectly inelastic. And buyers pay the entire tax if the demand curve is perfectly inelastic or the supply curve is perfectly elastic.

PRICE ELASTICITY OF GASOLINE DEMAND

A graphic illustration of price elasticity of demand occurred in the United States in the 1970s, when the price of gasoline increased by 34 percent from 1973 to 1974. What effect did this increase have on the quantity of gasoline demanded?

We can answer that question by looking at the price elasticity of demand for gasoline. The short-run price elasticity is about -0.15, as presented in Table 2.7.1. A 34 percent increase in the price of gasoline leads to a 5 percent decrease in the quantity of gasoline demanded. So in the short run

Table 2.7.1
Price Elasticity of Gasoline

Time Period	Elasticity
Short run	−0.15
Long run	−0.46

Source: H. S. Hothakker and Lester D. Taylor, *Consumer Demand in the United States, 1929–1970* (Cambridge, MA: Harvard University Press, 1966), p. 116.

Table 2.7.2
Price Elasticity of Water Demand

Water Use	Elasticity
Overall	−1.0
Indoors	−0.2 to −0.6
Outdoors	−1.4 to −1.6

Source: S. H. Hanke, "A Method for Integrating Engineering and Economic Planning," *Journal of AWWA* 70, no. 9 (September 1978): 487–491.

the demand for gasoline is inelastic, or unresponsive to price.

After the price increase people were still willing and able to buy almost as much gasoline as before the price increase. Although gasoline was in short supply, people lined up at the pumps to fill up their tanks. Why? Because in the short run very few substitutes for gasoline are available. Gasoline is the predominant fuel for powering motor vehicles in the United States, and if the price of gasoline increases, drivers cannot immediately switch to other sources of fuel. People can choose either to pay the higher price or to use an alternative, and usually less desirable, form of transportation.

While a 5 percent reduction in demand in the short run results primarily from people driving less, in the long run the situation becomes more complicated as substitutes for gasoline are developed. The midseventies saw a great deal of research on battery- and liquid-propane-powered automobiles, and people began to buy lighter, smaller, more fuel-efficient cars. A longer period of time, perhaps five to ten years, allows more time to identify, and even invent, substitutes. Thus, the long-run price elasticity of gasoline rises to about −0.46. Gasoline is still an inelastic good, but in the long run buyers have more time to adjust, and demand becomes somewhat less inelastic.

PRICE ELASTICITY OF WATER DEMAND

Water in the United States is primarily supplied by municipal governments. Because the price of water is usually not set by the forces of the market, many people discount the importance of price on the demand for water. In times of water shortages, alternative rationing plans are usually proposed before a price increase is considered.

Like any other economic good, water is responsive to the price. Table 2.7.2 presents alternative estimates of the price elasticity of water. Overall (considering all types of household demand), the price elasticity is about −1.0; if the price of water increases by 1 percent, the quantity of water demanded decreases by 1 percent.

In times of a serious drought a price increase can effectively reduce demand and eliminate the shortage. Let's suppose that a particularly dry summer reduces the supply of water by 20 percent. To eliminate this shortage, the quantity demanded must decrease by an equivalent 20 percent. Based on the overall price elasticity of water demand in Table

2.7.2, this can be quickly accomplished by raising the price 20 percent.

Some people might argue that the price increase causes a reduction in many essential uses of water, that people cook, bathe, and drink 20 percent less if the price rises. Further examination of Table 2.7.2 indicates that this is not so. Indoor demand for water for use in cleaning, cooking, and drinking is very inelastic, ranging from -0.2 to -0.6. Indoor demand could appropriately be termed necessary uses of water, and it does not decrease much if the price rises.

Now let's look at the price elasticity of outdoor water demand for such activities as watering lawns and washing cars. The price elasticity of outdoor water use ranges from -1.4 to -1.6, and is thus more elastic than indoor use. If the price increases, households reduce outdoor use of water much more than indoor use. If a community is facing a water shortage, most people would agree that outdoor uses should be eliminated before indoor uses. This is exactly what the price elasticities tell us will happen.

Table 2.7.3
Income Elasticity of Selected Energy

Energy Good	Elasticity
Fuel oil and coal	-0.57
Electricity	3.58
Natural gas	4.76

Source: H. S. Hothakker and Lester D. Taylor, *Consumer Demand in the United States, 1929–1970* (Cambridge, MA: Harvard University Press, 1966), pp. 88, 89, 91.

INCOME ELASTICITY OF FUEL OIL AND COAL DEMAND

Two examples of income inferior goods are fuel oil and coal. As seen in Table 2.7.3, the combined income elasticity of these goods is -0.57, meaning that a 1 percent increase in income results in a 0.57 decrease in demand. As income rises, buyers tend to switch from fuel oil and coal to natural gas and electricity, because fuel oil and coal are not as desirable, clean, or convenient as electricity and natural gas. In short, they are **inferior goods, with a negative income elasticity.**

As their incomes increase, consumers can afford to buy more electricity and natural gas. Both electricity and natural gas are extremely responsive to changes in income, with income elasticities of 3.58 and 4.76, respectively.

CROSS PRICE ELASTICITY OF DEMAND FOR TIMBER PRODUCTION

The cross price elasticity of demand can give us insight into the timber industry. In a study of the timber industry, Peter Berck looked at the demand for Douglas fir production; his cross price elasticity estimates are given in Table 2.7.4.

The price elasticity of demand for Douglas fir is -0.62, implying an inelastic demand, which seems reasonable. But note the cross price elasticity estimates in Table 2.7.4. For example, structural concrete has a cross price elasticity of -1.39. Since the elasticity is negative, this means Douglas fir production and structural concrete are **complements, two goods with a negative cross price elasticity.** An increase in the price of structural concrete reduces the quantity of concrete demanded, and with it the demand for Douglas fir. The erection of most structures requires concrete for the foundation and timber for the walls and roof.

But the cross price elasticity of structural steel is 1.39. Since the elasticity is positive, steel and wood are **substitutes, two goods with a positive cross price elasticity.** If the price of steel increases, the quantity of steel demanded falls as it is replaced with wood.

Table 2.7.4
Cross Price Elasticity of Timber Demand

Good	Elasticity
Douglas fir	−0.62
Structural concrete	−1.39
Structural steel	1.39
Wallboard and structural paper	0.03

Source: Peter Berck, "The Economics of Timber Production: A Renewable Resource in the Long Run," *The Bell Journal of Economics* 10, no. 2 (Autumn 1979): 447–462.

Looking at cross price elasticities provides insight into relationships that may not be intuitively obvious. For example, the third cross price elasticity in Table 2.7.4, for wallboard and structural paper, falls into this category. The elasticity is estimated at 0.03, indicating that this good is a substitute for Douglas fir production, which may not be as obvious as with the other two goods. One reason is that the size of the elasticity is very small; while it is a substitute for Douglas fir, it is not a close substitute. Without knowing the cross price elasticity in this case, it might be difficult to say whether the two goods are complements or substitutes.

IN SUMMARY
Elasticity and the Market

- Elasticity is important to the market for several reasons. A price floor, which is a legally established minimum price above the market equilibrium, creates a larger surplus if the demand and supply curves are more elastic. A price ceiling, which is a legally established maximum price below the equilibrium, creates a larger shortage if the demand and supply curves are more elastic.

- Tax incidence is also affected by demand and supply elasticities. The incidence of the tax falls more heavily on sellers with an elastic demand and an inelastic supply. Conversely, buyers pay a larger share of the tax if the demand curve is more price inelastic and the supply curve is more price elastic. At the extreme, buyers will pay the entire tax with a perfectly inelastic demand or a perfectly elastic supply. The sellers will pay the entire tax if the demand curve is perfectly elastic or the supply curve perfectly inelastic.

- An interesting case study of price elasticity of demand is seen with the gasoline market in the 1970s. The short-run price elasticity of demand for gasoline is about −0.15. After the first OPEC price increase the demand for gasoline fell only slightly. However, the long-run price elasticity of gasoline is about −0.46. Over a period of several years gasoline demanders have more time to adjust to higher prices.

- The price elasticity of water demand is an often overlooked policy tool in times of water shortages. While the overall price elasticity of demand for water use is about −1.0, indoor use is more inelastic than outdoor use. A price increase in times of drought will reduce outdoor water demand more than indoor use.

- The income elasticity of fuel oil and coal illustrates the case of an inferior good. The combined income elasticity of these products is −0.57. These goods are inferior because higher incomes lead consumers to switch to electricity and natural gas, both of which are cleaner and more convenient to use.

- Estimates of cross price elasticity indicate whether goods are complements or substitutes. For example, the demand for Douglas fir production has a complement in structural concrete, but substitutes in structural steel and wallboard.

QUESTIONS FOR STUDY AND ANALYSIS

1. Would a price floor be effective (that is, keep the price below the equilibrium level) if demand or supply is perfectly inelastic? What if demand or supply is perfectly elastic?

2. How is the tax incidence distributed if demand is elastic and supply is inelastic? What if demand is inelastic and supply is elastic?

3. Under what conditions would buyers pay the entire tax? When would the seller pay the entire tax?

4. Why is the price elasticity of demand for gasoline greater in the long run than the short run? Explain why the price elasticity of demand for automobiles is less in the short run than the long run.

5. Suppose you are faced with a market that has an elastic demand and an inelastic supply. What effect will a price ceiling have on this market? If the ceiling is established to prevent buyers from paying "too high" a price for the good, is it successful?

6. The county tax commissioner has assigned you the job of raising additional tax revenues through a per unit sales tax. There are two goods sold in the county, gasoline and Caribbean cruises. The demand and supply of gasoline are both inelastic. The demand for cruises is very elastic, while the supply is unit elastic. If the same quantities of both goods are sold, which good would you tax? Why? What would happen to the relative quantities exchanged in each market after the tax?

7. Many people have called for some type of regulation of the medical profession, such as a price ceiling. Considering that the demand for medical services is price inelastic, would a price ceiling prevent consumers from paying "too much" for this good? What do you think would happen to the quantity of medical services exchanged? How much would the market be disrupted by the price ceiling?

REVIEW GLOSSARY

complements Two goods with a negative cross price elasticity.

inferior good A good with a positive income elasticity.

price ceiling A legally established maximum price below the market equilibrium. A price ceiling creates a shortage, or excess demand, the size of which depends on the elasticities of demand and supply. The more elastic demand and supply are, the greater the shortage is.

price floor A legally established minimum price above the market equilibrium. A price floor creates a surplus, or excess supply, the size of which depends on the elasticities of demand and supply. The more elastic are demand and supply the greater is the surplus.

substitutes Two goods with a positive cross price elasticity.

tax incidence The division of a tax between buyers and sellers. Generally, the tax is paid by both buyers and sellers in a market. However, the tax incidence is not necessarily divided equally between the two, but depends on the price elasticities of demand and supply. The more elastic demand is, the larger the share paid by sellers is. The more elastic supply is, the larger the share paid by buyers is.

SECTION INQUIRY

The Used Textbook Market

An interesting type of market that exists on college campuses across the nation is the market for used textbooks. Like any market, the used textbook market consists of the demand for and supply of textbooks. The demand for used textbooks depends on a number of factors. The first is the number of students in college. If college enrollment increases, then the number of used textbooks demanded is also likely to increase. A second factor is the price of the used textbooks. In particular, it is the price of the used textbooks relative to the price of new textbooks. That is, most textbooks are available as either brand new copies or used copies. The used copies are typically priced lower than the new copies because of the wear and tear inflicted on the books by previous owners, ranging from doodles, scribbles, and highlighting to torn or missing pages. But for most students, the used copy works just as well as the new copy, so why not save a few dollars?

The supply of used textbooks is also an interesting part of this market and depends on a number of factors as well. The first is the number of textbooks students have but are willing to part with. While many students keep their textbooks for a lifetime of continuous learning, others must pay the rent after the semester ends. The supply of used textbooks depends on the number of students who are willing to part with this "close friend" when they no longer need to spend exciting but seemingly endless nights together. Of course a student's attachment to a particular textbook probably depends on the grade received in the course, whether or not the course is part of the student's major, and how much the bookstore is willing to pay to buy the textbook back.

A second important factor affecting the overall supply of used textbooks involves college instructors. Most textbook publishers provide complimentary copies of textbooks to instructors who are actually teaching or even thinking about teaching a particular course. While there may be only a few free copies given to teachers at any one college, nationwide the number of complimentary copies reaches into the thousands. Publishers are more than willing to undertake this expense because this allows instructors a chance to examine their product and decide whether or not it should be the required textbook for the course. However, these complimentary textbooks can often work their way into the supply of used textbooks when instructors no longer need them.

QUESTIONS FOR DISCUSSION

1. Discuss how the price of a used textbook is likely to provide information and/or incentives to both the demand and supply sides of the market.

2. Would you say that the demand for textbooks follows the law of demand? Why or why not? Would you say that the supply of textbooks follows the law of supply? Why or why not?

3. Are new textbooks and used textbooks complements or substitutes? How would an increase in the price of new textbooks affect the demand curve for used textbooks? What is likely to happen to the price of used textbooks if the price of new textbooks increases? Explain.

4. Discuss how each of the determinants of supply—factor prices, technology, prices of other goods, expectations, and number of suppliers—will affect the supply of used textbooks. Give specific examples of each type of determinant.

5. What effect would an increase in college enrollment have on the price of used textbooks and the quantity of used textbooks exchanged? Which curve is affected by increased enrollment—demand, supply, or both?

6. Which curve, demand or supply, would you say is relatively more elastic? Explain.

PART II

Macroeconomics: The National Economy

The study of economics over the past two hundred years has evolved into two separate but related branches—microeconomics and macroeconomics. The study of microeconomics is analogous to the study of individual trees in a forest, while the study of macroeconomics considers the entire forest. In effect, it is important to study the characteristics and growth not only of each individual tree but also of the forest as a whole. This analogy is quite appropriate to microeconomics and macroeconomics. If we concentrate too much on the details of microeconomics, we may miss valuable knowledge provided by the overall macroeconomic picture. In Part II our attention is directed toward the study of macroeconomics.

Perhaps the most valuable knowledge we can obtain from the study of macroeconomics relates directly to the economic problem. In macroeconomics we are, first and foremost, concerned with the aggregate, or total, amount of goods and services produced in the economy, the amount available for the satisfaction of people's wants and needs. If the economy has more goods and services, then it is closer to solving the economic problem. Throughout our study of the national economy in Part II, we focus on the aggregate amount of goods and services produced in the economy.

Our study of macroeconomics cannot begin without acknowledging the contributions of two eonomists: John Maynard Keynes (1883–1946) and Milton Friedman (1912–). If Adam Smith is the father of the modern study of economics, then John Maynard Keynes is the father of macroeconomics. In 1936 Keynes, a British economist, published the cornerstone of modern macroeconomics, entitled *The General Theory of Employment, Interest, and Money*. *The General Theory* (as it is commonly called) represented a clear break from conventional economic thought. While economists of the early 1900s argued that an economy would always tend toward full employment of the factors of production, Keynes argued that the economy could have persistent periods of unemployment. We should note that his revolutionary theory of macroeconomics was influenced, at least in part, by the Great Depression of the 1930s. As we move into Section 4, Keynesian Economics, we will see why Keynes's economic theory revolutionized our study of the macroeconomy.

Although Keynes was the father of macroeconomics, numerous aunts, uncles, and cousins have continuously modified our view of the national economy. But among all of these relatives, the one who stands out is Milton Friedman. While his contributions to economics in general, and macroeconomics in particular, are numerous, he is probably best known as the father of monetarism. He has been a severe critic of Keynesian economics and the types of government policies recommended by Keynesian economics. And he has argued successfully over the past several decades that money is fundamentally important to the total production of goods and services in the economy. In Section 5, Money, we examine the role money plays in the economy, and how an awareness of that role has modified the simple Keynesian view of the macroeconomy.

It is difficult to function in today's world without at least a basic understanding of the national economy. While we can study each individual household, firm, and market in isolation from the others, in reality they all interweave to form the fabric of the national economy. Changes in unemployment, inflation, or aggregate production are likely to affect our lives in one way or another. As we study the operation of the national economy in the next twenty-two units, we see how that operation affects our daily lives.

SECTION 3

Macroeconomic Foundations

This section begins our study of macroeconomics, the branch of economics that deals with the entire economy. In particular, our objective is to examine the basic concepts, terms, and principles that form the foundation of macroeconomics; we will apply this information throughout Part II.

In this section we not only build on the principles that relate to our study of the market in Section 2 but also introduce principles that apply strictly to the macroeconomy. Much of our discussion of the macroeconomy is based on the aggregate (or total) demand and supply of output in the economy. However, some of the principles that apply to a single individual, firm, or market do not necessarily apply to the entire economy. For example, while a firm can increase production by hiring more factors, the entire economy cannot do this if all factors in the economy are already fully employed.

Unit 3.1, The Circular Flow of Economic Activity, discusses the simplest, but perhaps most important, concept of macroeconomic analysis, the circular flow. In this unit we see how each of the four major macroeconomic sectors (household, business, government, and foreign) interact through product, factor, and financial markets. And through this study of interaction we identify the two sides of the circular flow: national product and national income.

Unit 3.2, National Product, looks at the first half of the circular flow. In particular, this unit examines the two official government measures of national product: gross national product and net national product. We see what is measured, what is not measured, and what should be measured.

Unit 3.3, National Income, looks at the second half of the circular flow. In this unit we study what goes into the official measurement of national income, and we also identify two related measures of income: personal income and disposable personal income. We see not only how each of these three measures of income are related but also how they are related to gross national product and net national product, as discussed in Unit 3.2.

Unit 3.4, Unemployment, examines the use, and lack of use, of labor resources. This unit discusses the various types of unemployment, including cyclical, seasonal, frictional, and structural. We also see how the unemployment rate is used as the official measure of unemployment in the economy. And finally, the unit ends by looking at the costs of unemployment.

Unit 3.5, Inflation, examines the nature and consequences of inflation. We discuss how inflation is related to the overall price level in the economy. We also focus on three of the most common measures of the price level: consumer price index, GNP price deflator, and producer price index. The unit concludes with a look at the effects of inflation, including the hidden redistribution of income and wealth and the reduction in production.

Unit 3.6, The Aggregate Market, presents a simple framework for analyzing the level of national product in the economy. This simple framework applies many of the principles underlying our study of an individual market in Section 2. However, in this unit we are concerned with *all* goods and services in the economy, rather than just a single good. First, the aggregate demand and supply curves are introduced, then we see how their interaction determines the price level and the level of national product.

Unit 3.7, The Business Cycle, applies the discussions of national product and the aggregate market to the recurring fluctuations of economic activity. This unit introduces the peaks, contractions, troughs, and expansions of the business cycle. We also see how the aggregate market can be used to illustrate the business cycle, and we examine the two most important macroeconomic problems resulting from the business cycle: inflation and unemployment.

UNIT 3.1

The Circular Flow of Economic Activity

The best way to begin the study of macroeconomics is with a look at the circular flow of economic activity, which provides a simple way of viewing the operation of the national economy. The circular flow describes how the services of the factors of production move from households to businesses through factor markets, and how the goods and services produced with these factors move from businesses to households through product markets.

The circular flow of economic activity also provides us with an introduction to many of the fundamental concepts of macroeconomics. In particular, we identify the four major sectors that participate in the operation of the macroeconomy: household, business, government, and foreign. Then we look at the concepts of national product and national income, which are essential to the study of the national economy.

In this study of the circular flow we begin with the simplest possible case—an economy with only two sectors (household and business) and two types of markets (product and factor). From this simple case we build the circular flow into a more complete description of the economy's operation, first by adding financial markets, then by including the other two sectors in the economy (government and foreign).

THE SIMPLE CIRCULAR FLOW

Let's begin with a definition. The **circular flow** is the continuous and simultaneous flow of final goods and services and factors of production in exchange for the payments for the goods, services, and factors. An interesting aspect of the circular flow is that it really consists of a combination of two flows moving in opposite directions. In one direction flows goods, services, and factors of production, and in the other direction the payments for these commodities. To isolate these two flows, let's look at an economy with two sectors (household and business) and two types of markets (product and factor).

Structure of a Simple Economy

For our purposes here, the simplest type of economy we can examine contains two major sectors, household and business. The **household sector** is composed of all households in the economy, as well as nonprofit organizations. These households can contain any number of people, related or unrelated, who live under the same roof. The nonprofit organizations range from local arts associations to large charitable groups such as the United Way. Even though some nonprofit organizations look, and act, like profit-seeking business firms, most behave more like households. For this reason official statistics include nonprofit organizations in the household sector.

The **business sector** contains all of the privately owned firms engaged in the production of goods and services in the economy, including corporations, partnerships, and proprietorships. Clearly, the most important function of the business sector is to sell goods and services to the household sector through product markets. **Product markets** are markets used to exchange final goods and services. This first interaction between the household and business sectors through the product markets is the most obvious and easily recognized interaction.

However, the household and business sectors also interact in other types of markets. In order to produce the goods and services supplied to households, the business sector must hire the four factors of production: labor, capital, land, and entrepreneurship. Because these factors of production are owned or controlled by the household sector, the business sector must obtain their services through factor markets. **Factor markets** are markets used to exchange the services of the factors of production. Note that with the factor markets the business and household sectors are exchanging the services of the factors, and not the actual factors. For example, a firm hires the services of labor; it does not buy the actual worker.

Now that we have defined the components of this simple economy, we can put them together and see how the circular flow emerges. Let's first isolate the physical flow of commodities through the economy, and then trace the flow of payments. This two-way flow is illustrated in Figure 3.1.1.

The Physical Flow

The counterclockwise flow in Figure 3.1.1 depicts the physical flow of commodities in this economy. In the upper half of the diagram we see the flow of final goods and services from the business sector to the household sector, goods and services obtained by consumers through the product markets. Note that in the product markets the consumers in the household sector are demanders, while firms in the business sector are suppliers. This is consistent with our earlier study of markets in Section 2.

In the lower half of the diagram, the counterclockwise flow depicts the flow of factors of production. The business sector hires the services of the factors of production from the household sector through factor markets. Thus, in factor markets the firms in the business sector are demanders, while the consumers in the household sector are now suppliers.

The interesting aspect of the physical flow is that the household sector ends up with goods and services that are produced with the factors of production it supplies to the business sector. For example, picture an autoworker for Ford buying a car that he or she helped to produce.

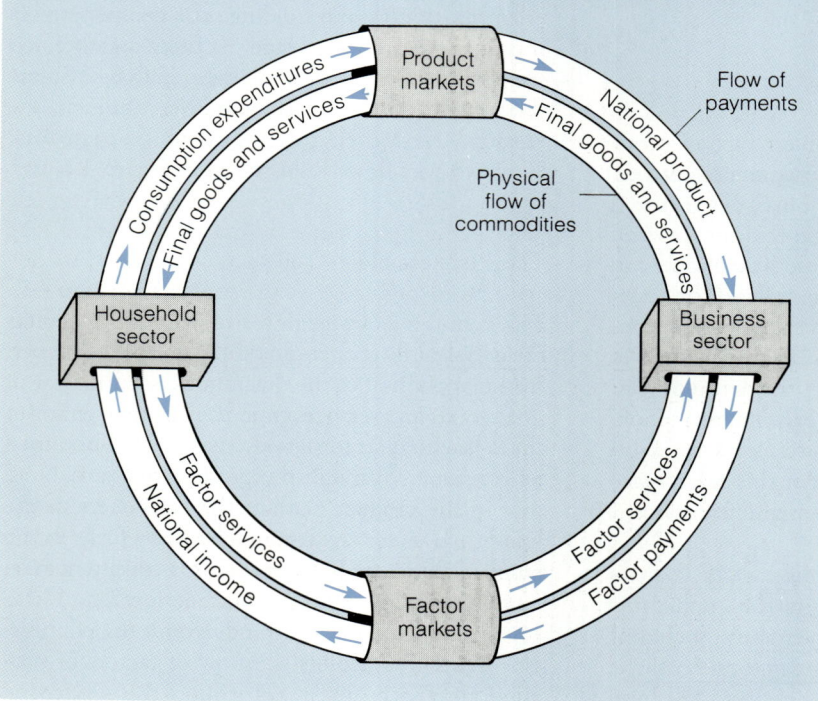

Figure 3.1.1

The Simple Two-Sector Circular Flow

The simplest circular flow contains two sectors (household and business) and two markets (product and factor). The business sector hires factors of production from households through the factor markets, and uses those factors of production to produce final goods and services purchased by the household sector through product markets. The physical flow of commodities is in one direction, while the flow of payments for these commodities is in the opposite direction.

The Flow of Payments

While the physical flow of commodities is important, we can gain more understanding of the economy by looking at the flow of the payments for the commodities. In Figure 3.1.1, the clockwise flow represents this flow of payments. There are four segments of the circular flow of payments that we particularly want to discuss: consumption expenditures, national product, factor payments, and national income.

Let's begin with a look at consumption expenditures, the flow of payments between the household sector and product markets in the upper left-hand corner of the diagram. **Consumption expenditures** are expenditures by households for goods and services purchased through the product markets. Consumption expenditures are viewed from the demand side of the product markets. On the supply side of the product market, the exchange of goods and services yields the revenue received by firms in the business sector. In this simple economy the expenditures made by households equal the revenue received by the firms. In essence, we are simply looking at two sides of the same coin.

The revenue received by the business sector for the sale of goods and services represents the value of the national product sold in the economy, or more simply, national product. **National product** is the total value of final goods and services produced in the economy and sold through the product markets. Because this flow reflects the national product, it tells us, in general, how well the economy is functioning, and how many goods and services are available to solve the economic problem.

As we continue clockwise around the circular flow of payments, we come to payments in the factor markets. The payments made by the business sector as it hires the services of factors of production are called factor payments. **Factor payments** are payments made by firms for the services of the four factors of production. These payments include wages, salaries, rent, interest, and profit, and are represented by the flow of payments from the business sector to the factor markets in the lower right-hand portion of the diagram.

While on the demand side of the factor markets factor payments represent expenditures by firms for the factors of production, on the supply side these payments become the income received by households in exchange for supplying the factors. This income is termed national income. **National income** is the total income earned by the factors of production.

Starting with the household sector, note that consumers buy final goods and services through the product market in the form of consumption expenditures, which constitutes the revenue received by firms in the business sector. But what do the firms do with the revenue? They use it to pay the factors of production that are hired through the factor markets. And these factor payments are the income received by households, which use it for consumption expenditures to purchase goods and services through product markets. This is the essence of the circular flow—revenue going from the household sector to the business sector, back to the household sector, and so on in a continuous cycle.

THE CIRCULAR FLOW WITH FINANCIAL MARKETS

While this simple circular flow captures the essence of the economy, the picture of the economy is far from complete. We must now complicate matters by adding a few real world complexities. First, we should note that households do not spend all of their income on goods and services, but rather divert some to saving. Furthermore, we must point out that the business sector as well as the household sector buys final goods and services in the product markets. Therefore, a third set of markets must be added to the circular flow, financial markets. **Financial markets** are markets used to exchange financial capital.

Figure 3.1.2 illustrates how financial markets affect the circular flow of the economy. Note that we are concentrating exclusively on the flow of payments; the flow of commodities has been omitted to simplify the diagram. The main function of financial markets is to divert income from consumption expenditures and make it available to the business sector. Let's examine this function.

Figure 3.1.2 illustrates two uses that consumers have for their income: consumption expenditures and saving. **Saving** is that part of household income not used for consumption expenditures. While there are many ways that consumers can save their income, most consumers save income by placing it in a bank, savings and loan, or other financial institution. The financial institutions in turn use the funds supplied by households to make loans.

Although financial institutions make loans to consumers for consumption expenditures, our primary concern here is with the loans that are made

Figure 3.1.2

The Two-Sector Circular Flow with Financial Markets

The household and business sectors also interact through financial markets. A portion of the national income received by the household sector is diverted to financial markets as saving. The business sector then borrows these funds to use for investment expenditures on capital goods.

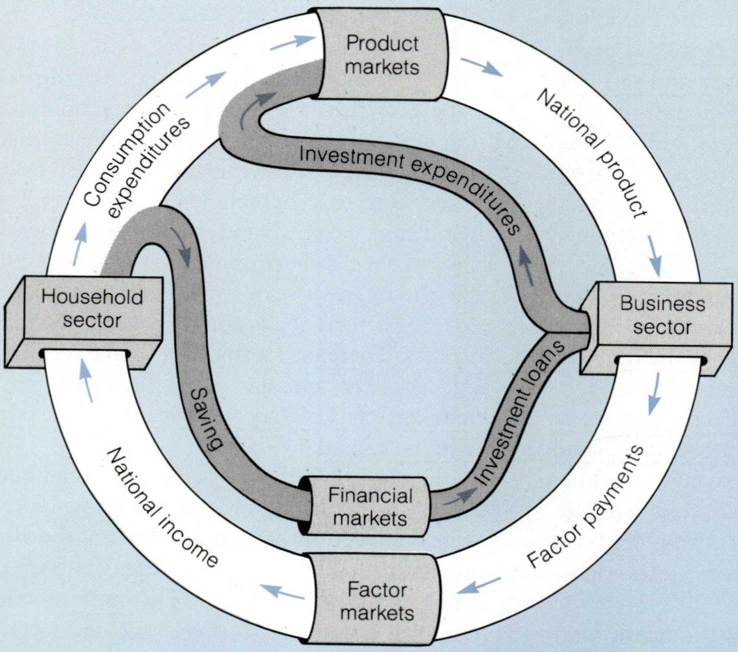

to the business sector. The business sector borrows funds for a very important reason—to purchase capital goods, such as factories, buildings, and machinery. This process of buying capital goods is commonly termed investment. **Investment expenditures** are expenditures by firms for capital goods purchased through product markets. In Figure 3.1.2 we see that the business sector obtains funds through financial markets for investment expenditures in the product markets.

THE CIRCULAR FLOW WITH THE GOVERNMENT

Thus far our circular flow has considered only two of the four sectors in the economy, households and business. It's now time to add a third important sector, the government. The **government sector** is the combination of all levels of government: federal, state, and local. Figure 3.1.3 illustrates how the circular flow is affected by including the gov-

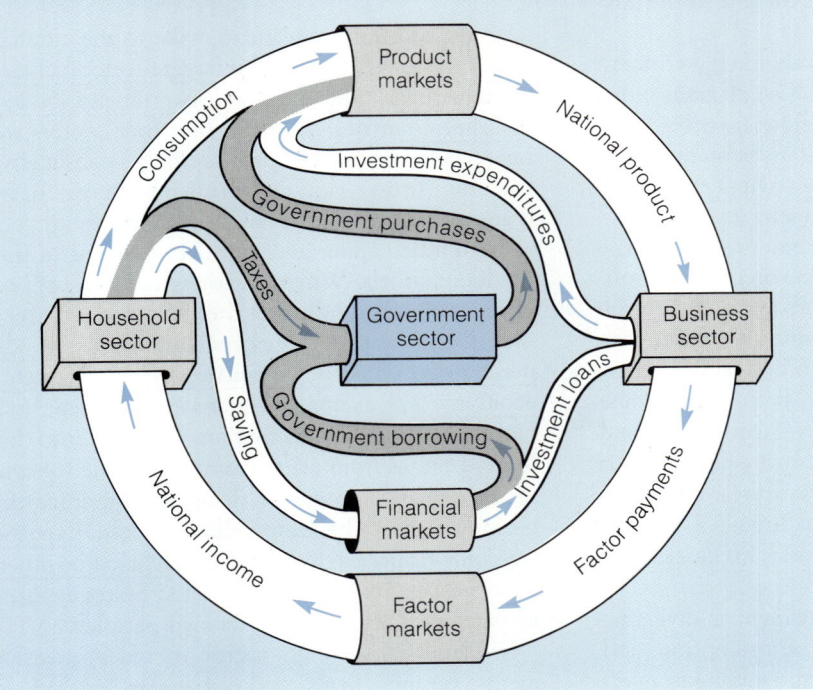

Figure 3.1.3

The Three-Sector Circular Flow

The government sector enters into the circular flow in three important ways. First, it receives taxes from the household sector. Second, it purchases final goods and services through the product markets. And third, if its purchases are greater than its tax receipts, it borrows the needed funds through the financial markets.

ernment sector. Although the government is involved in a market-oriented economy in many ways, such as imposing price floors and ceilings and regulating economic activity, we are concerned here with its involvement as a third buyer in the product markets.

When the Department of Defense buys a new aircraft carrier or a state university buys a personal computer for a faculty member, the government is purchasing a final good, which is essentially the same as the purchase of a personal computer by a consumer or a firm. In either case the computer is purchased through the product markets, the only difference being the sector that makes the purchase. If the household sector makes the purchase, it is a consumption expenditure; if the business sector makes the purchase, it is an investment expenditure. And if the government sector makes the purchase, it is a government purchase. **Government purchases** are expenditures by the government for goods and services purchased through the product markets.

To fund the purchase of goods and services, the government draws on two sources of revenues, which are depicted in the circular flow of Figure 3.1.3. The first, and most obvious, source is taxation. Note that in addition to consumption and saving, households divert their income to the government sector.

The second source of funds for government purchases is financial markets. The diagram shows that the household saving that flows into the financial markets can be used to fund investment expenditures by the business sector or to finance government purchases by the government sector.

The inclusion of the government sector in the circular flow leads us to an interesting observation. Taxation and government borrowing divert the circular flow of household income away from consumption and investment expenditures. If the government collects more taxes, then less income remains for both consumption expenditures and saving. With less saving, there are fewer funds available for investment expenditures. Likewise, government borrowing through financial markets also reduces the availability of funds for investment expenditures.

However, while the government is diverting the circular flow away from consumption and investment expenditures, it is also adding to overall expenditures through government purchases. In essence, the government is taking away some of the control of the economy's resources from the private (household and business) sector and diverting it to the government sector. The private sector has less say about the types of goods and services produced, while the government has more say.

As we continue our study of the macroeconomy, the diversion of the circular flow between the alternative paths created by the government becomes very important. The total amount of the flow, or the national product, can be affected by the amount of the flow along each of the paths seen in Figure 3.1.3. A greater flow along one path and a smaller flow along another path can increase or decrease national product. This possibility is discussed in more detail in Section 4, Keynesian Economics.

THE CIRCULAR FLOW WITH THE FOREIGN SECTOR

The last addition we want to make to the circular flow is the foreign sector. The **foreign sector** includes all households, businesses, and governments located in other countries. Thus far the three sectors we have included in the circular flow—consumers, business firms, and government—have been domestic sectors. However, the foreign sector acts as both a demander and supplier of output in the product markets. When the foreign sector supplies output purchased by any of the three domestic sectors, these are called imports. **Imports** are goods purchased from other countries by the domestic economy. For example, bananas, petroleum, and Hondas are three goods that are imported into the United States from other countries. If the foreign sector demands output produced by the domestic business sector, these are called exports. **Exports** are domestically produced goods purchased by other countries. For example, the United States exports wheat, Fords, and some of its own petroleum.

While the foreign sector includes governments, business firms, and consumers, in essence we can consider the foreign sector to be the world that exists beyond our national boundaries. Figure 3.1.4 illustrates how the foreign sector is included in the circular flow. While the vast majority of expenditures made by consumers, business firms, and the government are for domestically produced goods and services (and thus go through the domestic product market), some of these expenditures are for imported goods. This is seen as the import flow to the foreign sector. Moreover, some of the goods produced by domestic firms are sold to other countries, seen as the export flow from the foreign sector. Keep in mind that the export and import flows

UNIT 3.1 • THE CIRCULAR FLOW OF ECONOMIC ACTIVITY

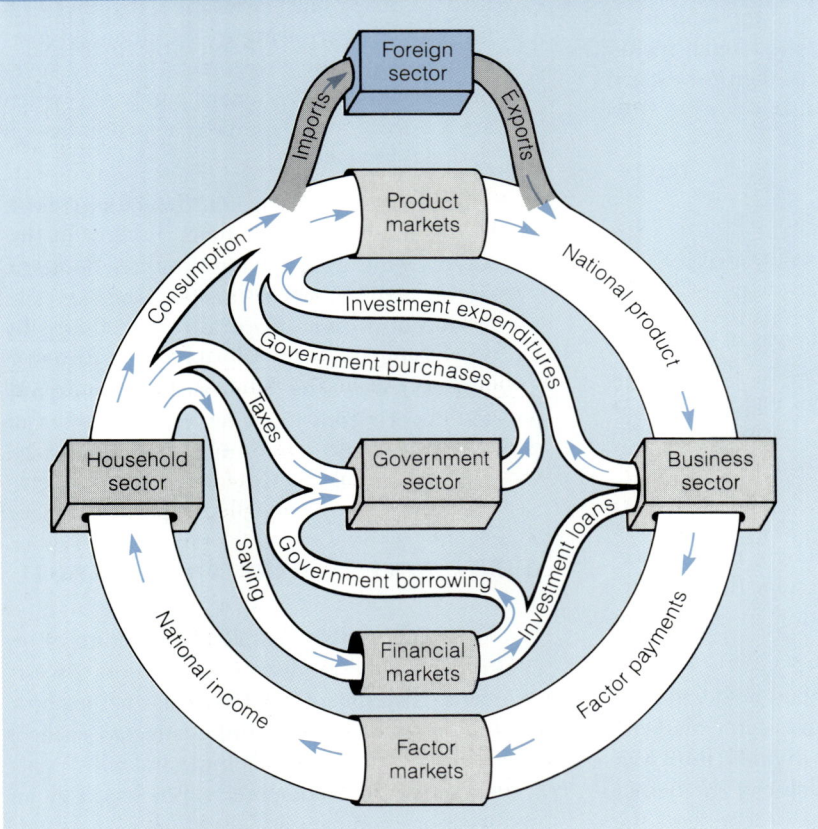

Figure 3.1.4

The Four-Sector Circular Flow

The foreign sector enters into the circular flow through the product markets. On one hand, it supplies final goods and services, or imports, to the three domestic sectors. On the other hand, it buys domestic production, or exports. Imports reduce national product, while exports increase national product. In many cases we simply consider the difference between exports and imports, which are net exports.

presented in this diagram represent the flow of payments, and that in both cases there is a physical flow of goods in the opposite direction.

It is important to note the balance of imports and exports. If the economy imports more goods, then the flow through the domestic product market is reduced, fewer domestically produced goods are demanded, and national product is less. But if the economy exports more goods, then the demand for domestically produced goods is greater, and national product is more. And if national product is greater, the overall amount in the circular flow, including factor payments, national income, and consumption, saving, and/or taxes, is also greater.

Because of this we often limit our attention to net exports, which are measured as exports minus imports. **Net exports are expenditures by the foreign sector on domestically produced goods and services minus the expenditures by the three domestic sectors on foreign-produced goods and services.** Net exports tell us the difference between the amount of goods our economy produces that are sold to the foreign sector and the amount of goods that are purchased from the foreign sector. If exports are greater than imports, then net exports are positive, and national product is greater than it would otherwise be.

IN SUMMARY

The Circular Flow of Economic Activity

- The circular flow is a simple way of looking at the operation of the economy. The circular flow illustrates how the four major sectors in the economy—household, business, government, and foreign—are linked together through product, factor, and financial markets. While the circular flow represents the physical flow of commodities in one direction, more importantly it represents the circular flow of payments for the commodities in the other direction.

- In a simple economy with household and business sectors and product and factor markets, the circular flow can be divided into four important segments. The value of the output produced by the business sector represents the national product, which in turn flows to the factors of production as factor payments. However, the factor payments are merely the national income earned by the household sector, income that is used as consumption expenditures to purchase the national product of the business sector.

- Saving is a part of national income not used for consumption expenditures. Saving flows through the financial markets and becomes a source of funding for investment expenditures by the business sector. The investment expenditures, like consumption expenditures, are expenditures on national product.

- Including the government sector in the circular flow highlights national income that is used for taxes. The tax revenue, together with government borrowing in the financial markets, provides the government with the revenue needed for government purchases, which are the third major source of expenditures on national product.

- The foreign sector is the fourth sector included in the circular flow. It enters the flow in two ways. One is by supplying the three domestic sectors with imports of final goods and services produced in other countries. The other is by purchasing exports produced by the domestic business sector. The difference between exports and imports constitutes net exports, and that difference indicates the net expenditures on national product by the foreign sector.

QUESTIONS FOR STUDY AND ANALYSIS

1. There are four categories of expenditures on gross national product: consumption, investment, government purchases, and net exports. Indicate which expenditure category each of the following items falls into, and why.
   a. A new IBM computer is purchased by an insurance company in Des Moines, Iowa.
   b. A new IBM computer is purchased by the U.S. Defense Department.
   c. A new IBM computer is purchased by your economics instructor to play video games and keep track of personal finances.
   d. A new IBM computer is purchased by the prime minister of Canada.

e. A new IBM computer is purchased by the U.S. secretary of defense to play video games and keep track of personal finances.

f. A new IBM computer is purchased by a state-funded university and used in an economics class.

2. The circular flow presented in Figure 3.1.4 contains three sets of markets: product, factor, and financial. For each of the following items indicate which market would be involved, and why.

   a. Exxon hires a geologist who specializes in locating oil deposits.

   b. Exxon sells corporate bonds to raise funds used for exploration of oil deposits.

   c. Exxon uses some of the funds raised from selling the corporate bonds to buy new drilling equipment.

   d. Exxon pays for the right to drill on land that contains oil deposits.

   e. Exxon sells the gasoline produced from the oil at its service stations.

   f. Exxon pays dividends to its corporate shareholders based on the profit received from its oil discovery.

   g. Exxon's corporate shareholders deposit their newly received dividends in their local bank.

3. Why are national product and national income considered "two sides of the same coin"? Explain.

4. Why would both the president's budget director and the business sector be interested in the amount of saving by the household sector?

5. Why might saving, taxes, and imports be considered leakages from the circular flow?

6. Why might investment, government purchases, and exports be considered injections into the circular flow?

7. In terms of the circular flow, explain why an unemployed autoworker might be interested in the sale of grain to the Soviet Union. Also explain why a farmer might be concerned with the sale of Japanese automobiles in the United States.

REVIEW GLOSSARY

business sector All of the privately owned firms engaged in the production of goods and services in the economy, including corporations, partnerships, and proprietorships.

circular flow The continuous and simultaneous flow of final goods and services and factors of production in exchange for the payments for the goods, services, and factors. The circular flow is the simplest, yet most fundamental, way of looking at the operation of the macroeconomy.

consumption expenditures Expenditures by households for goods and services purchased through product markets.

exports Domestically produced goods purchased by other countries.

factor markets Markets used to exchange the services of the factors of production. In factor markets the business sector is the demander, and the household sector the supplier. In factor markets only the services of the factors are exchanged, not the factors themselves.

factor payments Payments made by firms for the services of the four factors of production. Factor payments are the expenditures by firms on the demand side of the factor markets.

financial markets Markets used to exchange financial capital. Financial markets are used to divert saving from the household sector to the business and government sectors for investment expenditures and government purchases, respectively.

foreign sector Households, businesses, and governments located in other countries.

government purchases Expenditures by the government for goods and services through the product markets.

government sector The combination of all levels of government: federal, state, and local.

household sector All households and nonprofit organizations in the economy.

imports Goods purchased from other countries by the domestic economy.

investment expenditures Expenditures by firms for capital goods purchased through product markets.

national income The total income earned by the factors of production. National income is the revenue received by households on the supply side of the factor markets.

national product The total value of final goods and services produced in the economy and sold through product markets. National product indicates the total amount of output available to the economy, and is the revenue received by firms on the supply side of the product markets.

net exports Expenditures by the foreign sector on domestically produced goods and services minus the expenditures by the three domestic sectors on foreign-produced goods and services.

product markets Markets used to exchange final goods and services. In product markets the household sector is the demander, and the business sector the supplier.

saving The part of household income not used for consumption expenditures.

UNIT 3.2

National Product

The concept of national product is central to the study of the macroeconomy. As explained in Unit 3.1, **national product** is the total value of final goods and services produced in the economy and sold through product markets. Because national product tells us the amount of goods and services that are available in the economy, it also indicates how far the economy goes toward addressing the economic problem. A larger national product makes it possible to satisfy more consumer wants.

This unit examines the concept of national product. In particular, we look at two official measurements of national product: gross national product (*GNP*) and net national product (*NNP*). We see what *GNP* does measure, what it doesn't measure, and what it should measure. We then discuss an important distinction between real *GNP* and nominal *GNP*. And after dividing *GNP* into the four expenditures on national product—consumption, investment, government purchases, and net exports—we look at a second measure of national product, net national product, and see how it relates to gross national product.

GROSS NATIONAL PRODUCT

As previously discussed, national product is the value of the goods and services that flow through the product markets in the upper loop of the circular flow diagram. In this unit we introduce a more specific concept, gross national product. **Gross national product (*GNP*)** is the total market value of all final goods and services produced in the economy in a given period of time (usually one year). *GNP* is the most comprehensive and aggregate measure of production for the economy. To get a better understanding of gross national product, let's see exactly what it measures.

What GNP Does Measure

If we dissect our definition of GNP, we can see the three items of interest included in this measure of national production: market value, final goods and services, and current production. Let's look at each.

Market Value First, GNP is a measure of the value of production in the economy. That is, GNP is expressed in monetary, or dollar, terms, not as a measure of the quantities of goods and services produced, but rather of the value of those goods and services. And the best, and usually easiest, way to measure the value of a commodity is to determine the dollar amount that demanders are willing to pay for it in the market.

By measuring market value in dollars, the measure of GNP becomes more meaningful. For example, if GNP is $4 trillion, we know that demanders value the nation's production at $4 trillion. But if the same GNP were measured exclusively in physical quantities, it would consist of 10,000 automobiles, 300,000 apples, 10 million toothpicks, and so on. Not only is GNP impossible to measure in these terms, it is also meaningless to equate the value of automobiles with the value of toothpicks.

Final Goods and Services Gross national product is also a measure of final goods and services produced in the economy. **Final goods** are goods that are purchased for final use and are not transformed and resold. Note that our measure of GNP does not directly include the production of intermediate goods. **Intermediate goods** are goods that are transformed and ultimately resold. When intermediate goods are processed and resold as final goods, they are included in GNP. Otherwise, the value of these goods would be counted twice, once as an intermediate good and once as a final good.

To illustrate why the market transactions of intermediate goods are not included in GNP, let's look at a simple example. Suppose you buy a package of notebook paper from the college bookstore for $1. This market transaction is included in GNP because it represents the sale of a final good. However, before the notebook paper is sold as a final good, there are a number of intermediate transactions at different stages of production, as illustrated in Table 3.2.1.

The first transaction is the sale of the tree from the timber company to the pulp and paper mill. To produce one package of paper, the mill needs $.05 worth of trees, which it transforms into paper and sells to the wholesaler for $.60. The wholesaler sells the paper to the bookstore for $.75, and you buy it from the bookstore for $1.00. While these four transactions total $2.40, if they were all included in GNP, the value of the product would be overstated by $1.40, because the actual value of the paper produced is $1.00. Why then is the total of all market transactions involved in the production of this good $2.40?

The reason is **double counting,** the process in which the value of an intermediate good is counted once when it is sold to a firm and again to a household as a final good. Each of the intermediate transactions in Table 3.2.1 are included in the price of the notebook paper when you buy it from the bookstore. When the paper mill sells the paper for $.60, this amount also includes the cost of the intermediate good ($.05). When the wholesaler sells the paper to the bookstore for $.75, this amount includes the cost of the paper purchased from the paper mill ($.60). And when you buy the paper from the bookstore for $1.00, this amount includes the cost of the paper purchased from the wholesaler ($.75).

Another way to consider this is to look at the value added in the production of the good. **Value added** is the increase in the value of a good at each stage of the production process. The value of a good is increased at each stage as it is transformed into a good that can provide people with more satisfaction. For example, the third column of Table 3.2.1 lists the value added by the timber company, the pulp and paper mill, the wholesaler, and the

Table 3.2.1

Intermediate Stages in the Production of Notebook Paper

The production of a final good typically involves several intermediate stages and transactions. If all market transactions, including intermediate ones, were included in *GNP*, double counting would result. Therefore, *GNP* only includes transactions for final goods, in this case $1.00 for the notebook paper. Alternatively, *GNP* can be measured by identifying the value added at each stage of the production process, the last column in the table, which is also $1.00.

Intermediate Stage	Amount of Transaction	Cost of Intermediate Goods	Value Added
Tree sold to pulp company	$0.05	$0.00	$0.05
Pulp sold to wholesaler	0.60	0.05	0.55
Paper sold to bookstore	0.75	0.60	0.15
Paper sold to student	1.00	0.75	0.25
Total	$2.40	$1.40	$1.00

bookstore, respectively. In each case the firm transforms the good in such a way that it becomes more valuable. For example, the timber company adds $.05 to the value of the product by taking natural resources (land, water, and air) and producing a tree. The pulp and paper company takes $.05 worth of timber and, by transforming it into notebook paper, makes a good worth $.60, thus adding $.55 to the value of the good. The wholesaler, by making the paper more accessible to the bookstore, adds $.15 to its value. And the bookstore, by making the paper available to you, adds another $.25 to its value.

The value added at various stages of the production process totals $1.00. In essence, the value added approach indicates that the total value of the notebook paper ($1.00) is simply the sum of the value contributed by each stage of the production process. In fact, we can measure the market value of the good as either the value of the final sale or the value added at each stage of production.

Current Production Gross national product is also a measure of current production, which suggests that the value of all final goods and services exchanged in a market in a given period is not necessarily included in *GNP*. Indeed, some market transactions are excluded if they do not involve current production. For example, let's say that you purchase the package of notebook paper in February of 1988. The value of this notebook paper is not included in *GNP* for 1988 if the notebook paper was actually produced in 1987 but remained on the bookstore's shelf until 1988. The 1988 *GNP* includes only final goods and services that were produced in 1988. So the notebook paper was already included in the 1987 *GNP*, even though it had not been sold as a final good in a market during that year.

This concept also applies to the sale of a used good. For example, the value of a three-year-old car is not included in the current year's GNP, because the market transaction does not represent current production. The car was already included in GNP in the year it was produced. Remember that if noncurrent production is included in GNP, then we are double counting.

What GNP Does Not Measure

Now that we have an idea of what GNP measures, let's look at several items that are excluded from GNP. Keep in mind that while GNP tries to measure the production of final goods and services, as a first approximation it tries to identify all market transactions in the economy.

Here we are distinguishing between two sets of activities in the economy: market transactions and production of final goods and services. Figure 3.2.1 illustrates these two sets of activities. On the right side of the figure is the set of all market transactions that occur in the economy. On the left side is the set that includes the production of final goods and services, or economic production. Ideally, we want GNP to measure the economic production set on the left. But since market transactions are easily observed, this is where our measure starts, though in so doing, we have to throw out several items and include several others. Let's look at these more closely.

Market Transactions Excluded from GNP Let's start with area A, which represents the set of market transactions that do not involve the production of final goods and services. We have already seen that intermediate goods, which fall into this set, are excluded from GNP. In addition, market transactions involving noncurrent production also fall into area A, and are excluded from GNP. And the exchange of existing financial assets, such as stocks and bonds, are included in area A but excluded from GNP, since these transactions are for the exchange of financial capital rather than physical capital.

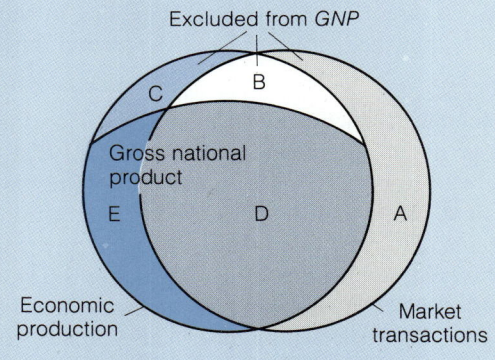

Figure 3.2.1
The Ins and Outs of GNP

The first place to begin measuring GNP is with all market transactions. However, some market transactions are excluded because they do not involve the production of final goods and services (area A). Other market transactions are excluded, even though they include production, because of accounting difficulties (area B). Other production that does not involve market transactions is also excluded because of accounting difficulties (area C). This leaves us with a GNP consisting of market transactions that involve production (area D) and production without market transactions (area E).

A Excluded market transactions: used assets intermediate goods stocks and bonds

B Excluded market transactions and economic production: illegal drugs gambling prostitution

C Excluded economic production: home repairs housework

D Included market transactions and economic production: manufactured goods

E Included economic production: payments-in-kind rent on owner-occupied housing

Market Transactions and Economic Production Excluded from *GNP* A second set of market transactions, represented by area B, are also excluded from *GNP*, even though they involve the production of final goods and services. Examples of this set include illegal transactions such as gambling, drug sales, and prostitution. They are excluded from *GNP* for a simple reason—it is almost impossible to keep track of the value of this production. Obviously, a drug dealer is not likely to report the value of transactions to the federal government just so we can have a more valid measure of *GNP*. But these illegal activities do for the most part constitute the production of final goods and services. The biggest difference between the production and distribution of marijuana and tobacco is that one is illegal and the other is not. Gambling in Las Vegas is essentially the same as gambling in Minnesota, but the first is legal and the second is not.

Economic Production Excluded from *GNP* A third set of activities, represented by area C, that is excluded from *GNP* is the production of some types of final goods that do not involve market transactions. The best example of this set is any work performed around the house, including the work of housewives, househusbands, treeshade mechanics, and do-it-yourself plumbers. Like area B, this set is excluded because it is nearly impossible to measure its value.

Economic Production Included in *GNP* This leaves areas D and E, which constitute *GNP* in this diagram. Area D represents the vast majority of the market transactions that involve the production of final goods and services, while area E contains economic production that is included in *GNP* even though no market transactions are involved. The two best examples of items in this latter set are payments-in-kind and the services provided by owner-occupied housing.

Payments-in-kind include any payments to the factors of production in the form of physical goods rather than money, for example, food consumed by farmers on the farm, or housing services provided to an apartment manager. In both cases economic production occurs, but there is no market transaction. However, unlike work around the house, it is possible to estimate the value of payments-in-kind.

GNP also includes the value of services provided by owner-occupied houses. A house is included in *GNP* in the year that it is produced, just like a new factory or a new apartment building. And after the house is built, the services it provides (protection from the weather, a place to sleep, and so on) continue to enter into *GNP*, much like the services provided by a hotel, motel, hospital, or nursing home, which are also included in *GNP*. While motel services involve market transactions, this is typically not the case for owner-occupied housing, since the owner also lives in the house. The value of the services provided by owner-occupied housing is estimated, by comparison with similar structures that are rented out, and included in *GNP*.

GROSS NATIONAL PRODUCT AND WELFARE

GNP is a measure of the economy's economic production. It is not a measure of society's welfare, which reflects the total satisfaction received by people, and which is based on more than the economic production included in *GNP*. However, economic production is an important part of this total satisfaction. Generally speaking, people are better off if they have more goods and services to consume. Greater production of final goods and services moves the economy closer to solving the economic problem of scarcity. So while *GNP* does not measure society's welfare, it does make an important contribution to this welfare. Apart from *GNP*, there are at least three other aspects of society's welfare that must also be considered: environmental quality, leisure time, and population.

Environmental Quality

One aspect of society's welfare that is not included in the measurement of GNP is environmental quality. Note that in many cases the production of GNP leads to reductions in environmental quality. The production of most goods and many services causes the emission of pollutants and waste materials into the air and water, which reduces environmental quality and adversely affects people who use, enjoy, or otherwise "consume" the environment. Since there are usually no market transactions involved when people enjoy the environment, its value does not appear in GNP. Moreover, increases in production of goods and services often lead to increases in pollution, meaning we might find that a higher GNP is actually associated with a reduction in society's welfare.

Leisure Time

GNP also excludes any welfare obtained by society through the enjoyment of leisure time. If labor and entrepreneurship (the two human factors) decide to spend less time working and more time in leisure activities, then GNP is reduced. This does not necessarily mean that society's welfare is reduced. People can also be satisfied with goods and services that are not contained in GNP, such as spending time with family and friends, walking through a park, or simply relaxing on a sunny Saturday afternoon. With more leisure time GNP is less, but society's welfare may actually be greater.

Population

Although GNP measures total production in the economy, it does not indicate how much of the production each person in society receives. For example, if two nations have the same GNP, but one has twice the population of the other, it is hard to argue that both nations have equal welfare. Therefore, we often look at per capita GNP. **Per capita GNP** is the average gross national product per person in the economy. It is found by dividing GNP by total population. However, per capita GNP is only an average measure of production; not every person in the economy actually receives this level of production. Some people typically receive a lot of the production, while others receive very little. In fact, if the economy has an extremely unequal distribution of GNP, the combined welfare of the members of society might be relatively low, even though per capita GNP is relatively high.

REAL GROSS NATIONAL PRODUCT

Measuring GNP in terms of the market value of final goods and services can create another type of problem. The market value of a good depends on both the quantity produced and the price. If the prices of all goods and services in the economy rise, then GNP is greater, though no change in the quantity of goods and services produced or the overall level of national production has occurred. This is particularly evident in inflationary times, when prices of all goods increase dramatically.

This discrepancy can be easily corrected by computing real GNP. **Real GNP is the total market value of all final goods and services produced in the economy in a given period of time, expressed in constant dollars.** Real GNP estimates the value of national production in terms of a constant set of prices. For example, in the United States real GNP is estimated based on prices in 1982. This allows us to see how national production itself changes from year to year by eliminating any changes in prices.

Let's look at a simple example of how real GNP is estimated. Suppose an economy produces only one good, notebook paper. Table 3.2.2 presents the information needed to compute the economy's GNP in 1972 and 1988. In 1982, 200 packages of notebook paper are produced and sold for $1 each; in 1988, 400 packages of paper are produced and sold for $3 each. With this information it is relatively easy to calculate nominal GNP for each year.

Table 3.2.2
Nominal and Real *GNP* and *GNP* Price Deflator

Nominal *GNP* is production measured with current prices, and real *GNP* is production measured with constant prices. The nominal *GNP* of notebook paper is $200 in 1982 and $1200 in 1988. However, real *GNP* measured in 1982 prices is $200 in 1982 and $400 in 1988. Real *GNP* is less than nominal *GNP* because the price of notebook paper tripled from 1982 to 1988. The *GNP* price deflator, which measures the average level of prices in the economy, is 100 in 1982 and 300 in 1988.

Item	1982	1988
Price of notebook paper	$1	$3
Quantity of notebook paper	200	400
Nominal *GNP*	$200	$1200
	(= $1 × 200)	(= $3 × 400)
Real *GNP* (1972 prices)	$200	$400
	(= $1 × 200)	(= $1 × 400)
GNP price deflator	100	300
	(= $200/$200 × 100)	(= $1200/$400 × 100)

<u>**Nominal *GNP*** is the total market value of all final goods and services produced in the economy in a given period of time, expressed in current dollars.</u> Nominal GNP is simply the value of production expressed in terms of the prices that exist when the goods and services are actually produced (in current dollars). So in Table 3.2.2, nominal GNP is $200 in 1982 and $1200 in 1988.

Now let's look at real GNP, and exclude any changes in the price of notebook paper. To calculate real GNP, multiply the quantity of paper produced in 1988 by the price of paper in 1982. Real GNP in 1988, expressed in constant 1982 dollars, is $400. While nominal GNP is six times greater in 1988 than 1982, real GNP is only twice as much. The rest of the increase in nominal GNP is caused by a three-fold increase in the price of paper.

In this example it is easy to see that the average level of prices in the economy tripled during this period of time, since the table lists only one good. However, the real world economy is far more complex, because thousands of prices are changing in various ways, making it difficult to determine changes in the overall level of prices. But by separately calculating real and nominal GNP, we can estimate the average change in the level of prices in the economy. If we divide nominal GNP by real GNP, we have the GNP price deflator, or average price level. The <u>**GNP price deflator** is a price index computed from the ratio of nominal GNP to real GNP.</u> The GNP price deflator is presented for the simple economy in Table 3.2.2. In 1982 the price deflator is 100, and in 1988 it is 300, meaning that prices tripled from 1982 to 1988. The price deflator

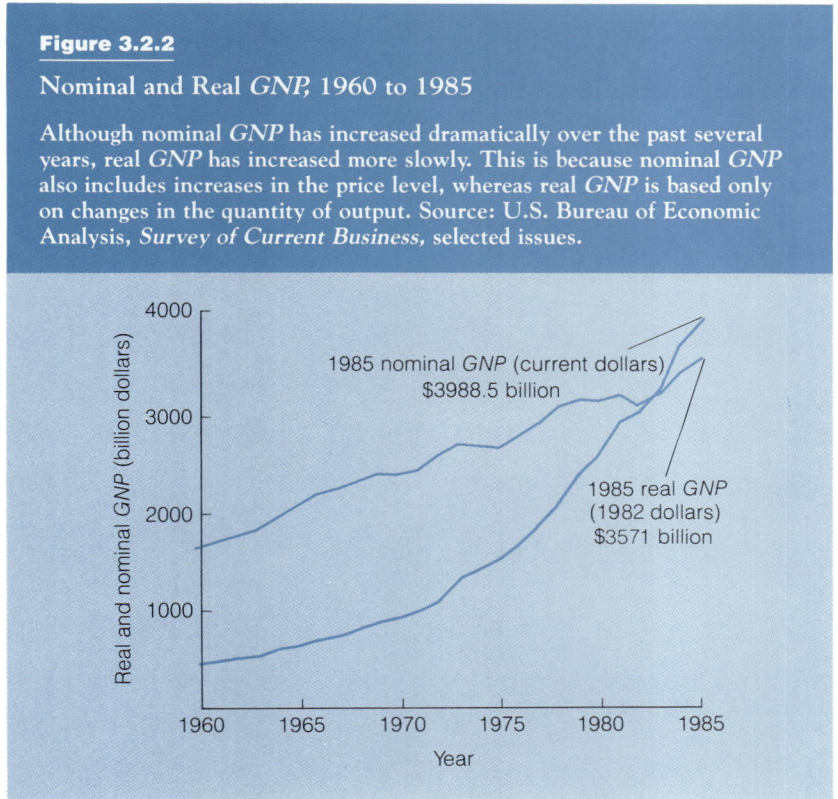

Figure 3.2.2

Nominal and Real *GNP*, 1960 to 1985

Although nominal *GNP* has increased dramatically over the past several years, real *GNP* has increased more slowly. This is because nominal *GNP* also includes increases in the price level, whereas real *GNP* is based only on changes in the quantity of output. Source: U.S. Bureau of Economic Analysis, *Survey of Current Business,* selected issues.

is equal to 100 in 1982 because 1982 prices are used to compute real *GNP*.

To illustrate why it is important to adjust for inflation and price changes, let's look at nominal and real *GNP* for the United States in recent years. Figure 3.2.2 and Table 3.2.3 present this information. The graph in Figure 3.2.2 shows that nominal *GNP* has increased dramatically since the mid-1960s, partly due to inflation. Note that the increase in real *GNP* was much less dramatic over this period of time. In fact, real *GNP* even declined in several instances, as the figures in Table 3.2.3 also indicate. If we look at only nominal *GNP*, we can easily overestimate national production, and thus the economy's ability to solve the economic problem.

EXPENDITURES ON GROSS NATIONAL PRODUCT

As we saw in the study of the circular flow in the previous unit, the production of final goods and services is only one way of looking at national product. We can also look at expenditures on national production. In general, we separate expenditures into four types, based on the four sectors in the economy: consumption expenditures, investment expenditures, government purchases, and net exports.

Figure 3.2.3 and Table 3.2.3 present *GNP* and expenditures on *GNP* over the past several years. Consumption expenditures by households are the

Table 3.2.3

Gross National Product and Related Measures, 1929 to 1985 (billions)

Year	Gross National Product	Consumption	Investment	Government Purchases	Net Exports	Net National Product	Capital Consumption Allowance	Real Gross National Product 1982 Prices	GNP Price Deflator 1982 = 100
1929	$ 103.4	$ 77.2	$ 16.2	$ 8.8	$ 1.1	$ 93.7	$ 7.9	$ 710	$ 14.6
1930	90.4	69.9	10.3	9.4	1.0	82.4	8.0	644	14.2
1931	75.9	60.5	5.6	9.2	0.5	68.0	7.9	588	13.0
1932	58.0	48.6	1.0	8.1	0.4	50.7	7.4	509	11.5
1933	55.8	45.8	1.4	8.2	0.4	48.4	7.0	499	11.2
1934	65.1	51.3	3.3	9.8	0.6	58.2	6.8	537	12.2
1935	72.2	55.7	6.4	10.0	0.1	65.4	6.9	580	12.5
1936	82.5	61.9	8.5	12.0	0.1	75.4	7.0	662	12.5
1937	90.4	66.5	11.8	11.9	0.3	83.3	7.2	695	13.1
1938	84.7	63.9	6.5	13.0	1.3	77.4	7.3	664	12.8
1939	90.9	66.8	9.3	13.5	1.2	82.2	7.3	717	12.7
1940	100.0	71.0	13.1	14.2	1.8	91.0	9.1	773	13.0
1941	125.1	80.8	17.9	24.9	1.5	115.0	10.0	909	13.8
1942	158.5	83.6	9.9	59.8	0.2	147.3	11.2	1080	14.7
1943	192.1	99.4	5.8	88.9	−1.9	180.7	11.5	1276	15.1
1944	210.6	108.2	7.2	97.0	−1.7	198.9	11.7	1381	15.3
1945	212.4	119.5	10.6	82.8	−0.5	200.2	12.2	1355	15.8
1946	209.8	143.8	30.7	27.5	7.8	195.8	14.0	1097	19.3
1947	233.4	161.7	34.0	25.5	11.9	215.7	17.3	1067	22.0
1948	259.5	174.7	45.9	32.0	6.9	239.3	20.2	1109	23.6
1949	258.3	178.1	35.3	38.4	6.5	236.5	21.8	1109	23.5
1950	286.5	192.0	53.8	38.5	2.2	263.0	23.5	1204	24.0
1951	330.8	207.1	59.2	60.1	4.4	303.6	27.2	1328	25.1
1952	348.0	217.1	52.1	75.6	3.2	318.7	29.3	1380	25.5
1953	366.8	229.7	53.3	82.5	1.3	335.8	31.0	1435	25.9
1954	366.8	235.8	52.7	75.8	2.5	334.1	32.7	1416	26.3
1955	400.0	253.7	68.4	75.0	3.0	365.3	34.8	1495	27.2
1956	421.7	266.0	71.0	79.4	5.3	383.0	38.7	1526	28.1
1957	444.0	280.4	69.2	87.1	7.3	402.3	41.7	1551	29.1

Continued

Table 3.2.3
Gross National Product and Related Measures, 1929 to 1985 (billions) (*continued*)

Year	Gross National Product	Consumption	Investment	Government Purchases	Net Exports	Net National Product	Capital Consumption Allowance	Real Gross National Product (1982 Prices)	GNP Price Deflator (1982 = 100)
1958	449.7	289.5	61.9	95.0	3.3	406.2	43.5	1539	29.7
1959	487.9	310.8	78.1	97.6	1.4	443.0	44.9	1629	30.4
1960	506.5	324.9	75.9	100.3	5.5	460.2	46.3	1665	30.9
1961	524.6	335.0	74.8	108.2	6.6	477.0	47.5	1709	31.2
1962	565.0	355.2	85.4	118.0	6.4	516.1	49.0	1799	31.9
1963	596.7	374.6	90.9	123.7	7.6	546.1	50.6	1873	32.4
1964	637.7	400.5	97.4	129.8	10.1	584.8	52.9	1973	32.9
1965	691.1	430.4	113.5	138.4	8.3	635.0	56.0	2088	33.8
1966	756.0	465.1	125.7	158.7	6.5	695.3	60.7	2208	35.0
1967	799.6	490.3	122.8	180.2	6.3	733.7	65.9	2271	35.9
1968	873.4	536.9	133.3	199.0	4.3	801.3	72.1	2366	37.7
1969	944.0	581.8	149.3	208.8	4.2	864.0	80.0	2423	39.8
1970	992.7	621.7	144.2	220.1	6.7	904.7	88.1	2416	42.0
1971	1077.6	672.2	166.4	234.9	4.1	981.1	96.5	2485	44.4
1972	1185.9	737.1	195.0	253.1	0.7	1079.5	106.4	2609	46.5
1973	1326.4	812.0	229.8	270.4	14.2	1209.9	116.3	2744	49.5
1974	1434.2	888.1	228.7	304.1	13.4	1298.2	136.0	2729	54.0
1975	1549.2	976.4	206.1	339.9	26.8	1389.9	159.3	2695	59.3
1976	1718.0	1084.3	257.9	362.1	13.8	1543.0	175.0	2827	63.1
1977	1918.0	1205.5	322.3	394.5	−4.2	1722.0	196.0	2959	67.3
1978	2156.1	1348.7	375.3	432.6	−0.6	1934.9	221.2	3115	72.2
1979	2413.9	1510.9	415.8	473.8	13.4	2160.3	253.6	3192	78.6
1980	2631.8	1668.1	401.9	537.8	23.9	2338.5	293.2	3187	85.7
1981	2957.8	1849.1	484.2	596.5	28.0	2627.5	330.3	3249	94.0
1982	3166.0	2050.7	447.3	641.7	26.3	2782.8	383.2	3166	100.0
1983	3401.6	2229.3	501.9	675.7	−5.3	3007.6	394.0	3278	103.8
1984	3774.7	2423.0	674.0	736.8	−59.2	3368.8	405.9	3492	108.1
1985	3988.5	2582.3	669.3	815.4	−78.5	3565.3	423.2	3571	111.7

Source: U.S. Bureau of Economic Analysis, *Survey of Current Business*, selected issues.

most stable of the four expenditures on GNP, usually about 63 percent of GNP. Investment expenditures fluctuate much more, ranging from 15 to 18 percent of GNP in recent years. Government purchases, however, have shown a steady increase as a percentage of GNP in the 1980s, rising to over 20 percent. And net exports, which also fluctuate a great deal from year to year, are usually less than 1 percent of GNP.

NET NATIONAL PRODUCT

The last topic in our examination of national product is net national product (NNP). Although GNP is the most comprehensive and widely used measure of national product, it represents a gross measure of production. In particular, GNP includes the total production of all capital goods, even though some of the capital goods are being produced to

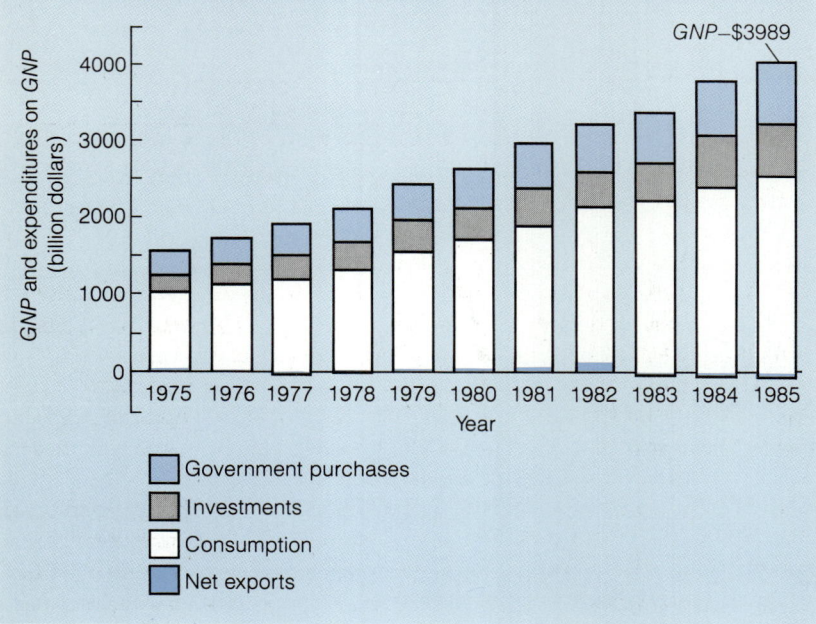

Figure 3.2.3

Expenditures on GNP, 1975 to 1985

Of the four expenditures on GNP, consumption is by far the largest, accounting for over 60 percent of all GNP. Investment expenditures fluctuate from year to year, but have tended to become a relatively smaller part of GNP in recent years, around 15 to 20 percent. Government purchases, however, have tended to become a larger part of GNP in recent years, around 20 percent. Net exports also tend to fluctuate from year to year, but are usually less than 1 percent of GNP. Source: U.S. Bureau of Economic Analysis, *Survey of Current Business*, selected issues.

replace worn-out capital. Net national product, while similar to GNP, excludes these capital goods used for replacement. **Net national product (NNP) is the total market value of final goods and services produced in the economy in a given period of time, excluding the depreciation of capital.** NNP is instructive because it tells us the net increase in national production from one year to the next. By excluding worn-out or depreciated capital, we have the total value of the additional final goods and services produced in a given year that are actually available for the direct or indirect satisfaction of consumer wants.

From a practical standpoint NNP is calculated by subtracting the capital consumption allowance from GNP. The **capital consumption allowance is the amount of the capital stock worn out, or depreciated, in the production of goods and services.** Figure 3.2.4 and Table 3.2.3 present recent information concerning the capital consumption allow-

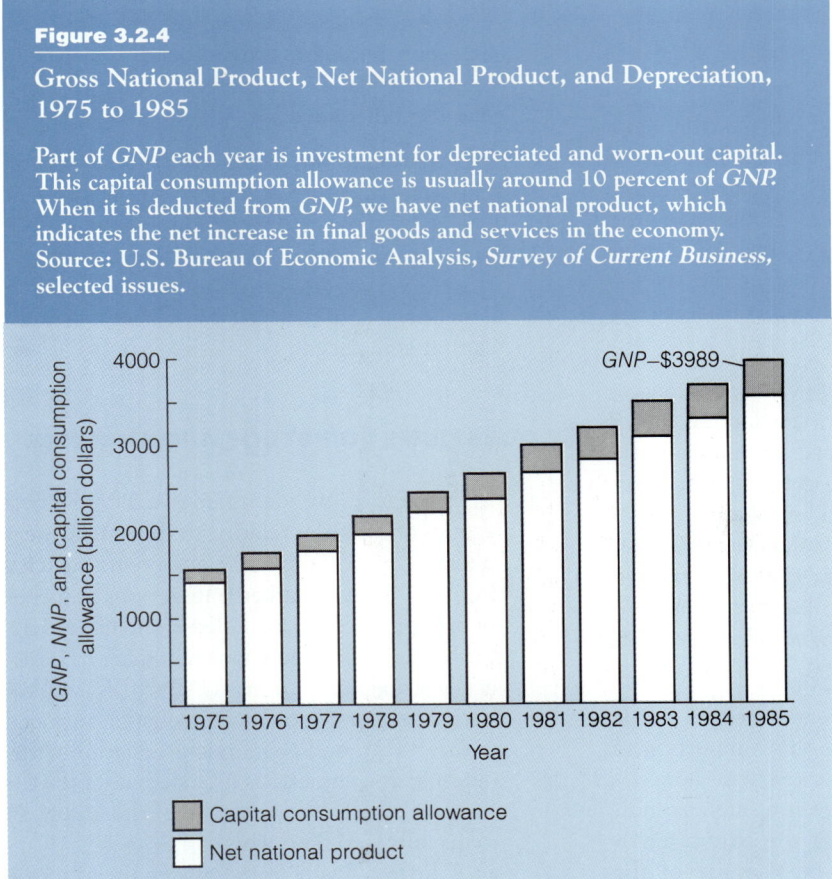

Figure 3.2.4

Gross National Product, Net National Product, and Depreciation, 1975 to 1985

Part of *GNP* each year is investment for depreciated and worn-out capital. This capital consumption allowance is usually around 10 percent of *GNP*. When it is deducted from *GNP*, we have net national product, which indicates the net increase in final goods and services in the economy.
Source: U.S. Bureau of Economic Analysis, *Survey of Current Business*, selected issues.

ance and the relationship between GNP and NNP.

In this figure we see that the capital consumption allowance is 10 to 11 percent of GNP each year, meaning 10 to 11 percent of GNP goes toward replacing worn-out capital. But recall from Figure 3.2.3 that the overall level of investment expenditures each year is only 15 to 18 percent of GNP. In other words, over half of all investment expenditures on capital goods simply go for replacement of worn-out capital. Thus, the U.S. economy spends only 5 to 8 percent of its GNP on the expansion of its stock of capital.

IN SUMMARY
National Product

- Gross national product (GNP) is the most comprehensive, and best-known, measure of national product. GNP is the total market value of final goods and services produced in the economy in a given period of time. GNP measures production in terms of market value, includes only final goods, and considers only current production.

- In addition to intermediate goods and market transactions of noncurrent production, GNP also excludes the exchange of financial and used physical assets, the exchange and production of illegal goods and services, and economic production that is difficult to measure, such as housework or home repairs. But GNP does include payments-in-kind and the estimated value of the services provided by owner-occupied housing.

- GNP is not a measure of society's welfare. While production measured by GNP is important to society's welfare, there are three items not considered in GNP that make it a dubious indicator of welfare: quality of the natural environment, leisure time, and the size of the population in the economy.

- GNP is also sensitive to changes in the overall price level in the economy. If prices increase without an increase in production, then the market value also increases, even though the availability of goods and services is the same. To compensate for this, real GNP is often used. Real GNP measures market value computed with a constant set of prices, in contrast to nominal GNP, which measures market value with the current year's prices.

- Expenditures on GNP can be divided into consumption, investment, government purchases, and net exports. Consumption is the largest and most stable of the expenditures; investment fluctuates from year to year; government purchases have steadily grown in recent years; and net exports are relatively small but also fluctuate a lot.

- Net national product (NNP) is a second important measure of national production. It is GNP minus the depreciation of the economy's capital stock. NNP is often more useful than GNP because it tells us how much of the economy's output is left over after worn-out capital is replaced.

QUESTIONS FOR STUDY AND ANALYSIS

1. In Figure 3.2.1 we identified five different categories of activities relating to the official measurement of GNP: market transactions excluded from GNP (A), market transactions and economic production excluded from GNP (B), economic production without market transactions excluded from GNP (C), market transactions and economic production included in GNP (D), and economic production without market transactions included in GNP (E). Indicate which category each of the following items falls into, and why.

   a. A little old lady from Pasadena buys a new Camaro.

b. The little old lady gives the car a do-it-yourself tune-up.
c. She illegally wins $25 in a drag race with a Porsche.
d. She then goes to Las Vegas and loses the $25, and more, at the blackjack table.
e. On her way back from Las Vegas she takes a job as a migrant farm worker and receives food and lodging in lieu of a wage payment.
f. Penniless and dejected, she sells the now used Camaro to a Wall Street investment broker.
g. Based on a tip from the broker, she uses all of her funds to buy swampland in Florida.
h. When a shopping center is built on the swampland, she uses her new-found wealth to construct a chain of "Granny's Tune-up Shops" all across the country.

2. If you could change the official measures of GNP in any way, what would you do to make it more accurately reflect the level of national production? What would you do to make it a better measure of welfare? Are both of these changes compatible? Why or why not?

3. Let's say that we have an economy that produces only two goods: food and houses. The following table presents the quantities and prices for each of these goods over a period of four years:

Year	Food Price	Food Quantity	Houses Price	Houses Quantity
1988	$100	20	$200	40
1989	$120	15	$250	35
1990	$125	40	$300	50
1991	$ 80	50	$150	50

a. Compute the nominal GNP for each year.
b. Compute the real GNP for each year, using 1988 prices.
c. Compute the GNP price deflator for each year.

4. In terms of solving the economic problem, would it be better to look at GNP or NNP? Why?

5. Is a 3 percent tax on the value added at each stage of production the same as a 3 percent tax on the sale of final goods? Explain.

REVIEW GLOSSARY

capital consumption allowance The amount of capital stock worn out, or depreciated, in the production of goods and services.

double counting The process in which the value of an intermediate good is counted once when it is sold to a firm and again when it is sold as the final good to a household. GNP includes only the market transactions of final goods to avoid double counting.

final goods Goods that are purchased for final use and are not transformed and resold.

GNP price deflator A price index computed from the ratio of nominal GNP to real GNP. The GNP price deflator is an important method of measuring changes in the economy's average price level.

gross national product (GNP) The total market value of final goods and services produced in the economy in a given period of time (usually one year).

intermediate goods Goods that are transformed and ultimately resold.

national product The total value of final goods and services produced in the economy and sold through product markets.

net national product (NNP) The total market value of all final goods and services produced in the economy in a given period of time, excluding the depreciation of capital.

nominal *GNP* The total market value of all final goods and services produced in the economy in a given period of time, expressed in current dollars.

per capita *GNP* The average gross national product per person in the economy. While per capita GNP indicates the amount of output that is available for each person in the economy, it doesn't indicate whether or not each person receives this output.

real *GNP* The total market value of all final goods and services produced in the economy in a given period of time, expressed in constant dollars.

value added The increase in the value of a good at each stage of the production process. The value of a final good can be divided between the value that each stage of the production process adds to the good.

UNIT 3.3

National Income

In the last unit we examined national production, as depicted in the upper loop of the circular flow. In this unit we complete the circular flow by examining national income, as depicted in the lower loop. While national income is equated with national production, it should also be viewed separately. As the income generated in the production of goods and services, national income in one sense represents the cost of supplying national production. But national income also represents the income earned by factors of production and households, income that gives households command over the purchase of goods and services, either directly through consumption expenditures or indirectly through saving and taxation.

Our study of national income leads us to three related but distinct measures of income: national income, personal income, and disposable personal income. First, we look at the broadest of the three measures, national income. In particular, we want to identify the numerous components of national income. Second, we study personal income, which is related to, but slightly different from, national income. Then we turn our attention to disposable personal income and see how it relates to personal income. And finally, we take another look at the circular flow of the economy to see how each of the three measures of income, and the two measures of national product, are related.

NATIONAL INCOME

As we saw in Unit 3.1, **national income (*NI*)** is the income earned by the factors of production. Before we begin a detailed look at national income, let's see how it relates to our discussion of national product in Unit 3.2. One way of defining national income is as the value of output at factor costs. In contrast, net national product would be considered the value of output at market prices. Since the business sector does not own any of the factors of production, all revenues received by firms for the production of the output goes toward paying the factors of production, with one exception, indirect business taxes.

In fact, national income is equal to net national product minus indirect business taxes. An **indirect business tax** is a tax levied on business firms, but indirectly paid by households through higher prices. Sales and excise taxes are two common examples of indirect business taxes. Note that while the government actually charges firms the tax, the firms merely add the tax onto the price of the product.

For example, let's say that there is a 5 percent sales tax on all food sold. If a consumer buys $1.00 worth of food, the store charges $1.05, including the 5 percent ($.05) sales tax. But the price paid by the consumer is greater than the price received by the store, which receives $1.00 and sends the remaining $.05 to the government.

From the consumer's side of the market, the food is worth $1.05, which is the market value of the food included in net national product. From the store's side of the market, it must be willing to supply the food for only $1.00, because that is all that it receives from the consumer. In other words the factors of production must be willing to accept $1.00 in payment for producing the food. Thus, $1.00 constitutes the factor payment and is part of national income, and the indirect business tax of $.05 becomes the difference between net national product and national income. Figure 3.3.1 and Table 3.3.1 present the relationship between net national product, indirect business taxes, and national income for recent years.

Let's now turn our attention to the components of national income—the income earned by factors of production—as shown in Figure 3.3.2. This income consists of payments to each of the four factors of production: labor, capital, land, and entrepreneurship. These payments fall into one of the following categories: wages paid to labor, interest paid to capital, rent paid to land, and profit paid to entrepreneurs. However, in actual practice it is usually not that easy to separate all of these payments.

Compensation to Employees

This first component of national income consists essentially of the wages earned by labor, including the hourly wages paid to blue-collar workers, the salaries paid to white-collar workers, and the supplements to wages and salaries that are earned by labor but not paid directly to the employees. These supplements include private pension plans, health benefits, and social security taxes. Compensation to employees usually comprises about 75 percent of national income.

Net Interest

The second component of national income, net interest, is considered the income earned by capital, and comprises between 5 and 10 percent of national income. Net interest includes the interest payments made by firms for borrowed funds, but not interest payments made by the government on the public debt or interest paid by households on funds borrowed for consumption expenditures. While funds borrowed by firms are used to purchase productive capital, funds borrowed by government and households are usually not.

Rental Income

The third component of national income is rental income—the income earned by landowners for rented property, and royalty payments to resource owners—which comprises about 2 percent of national income. We should note that rental income includes not only rent on land but also rent on many capital goods. For example, the rent paid for an apartment is considered rental income, even though part of the payment is for the land and part for the building. The portion of the rent for the building actually represents a payment for capital.

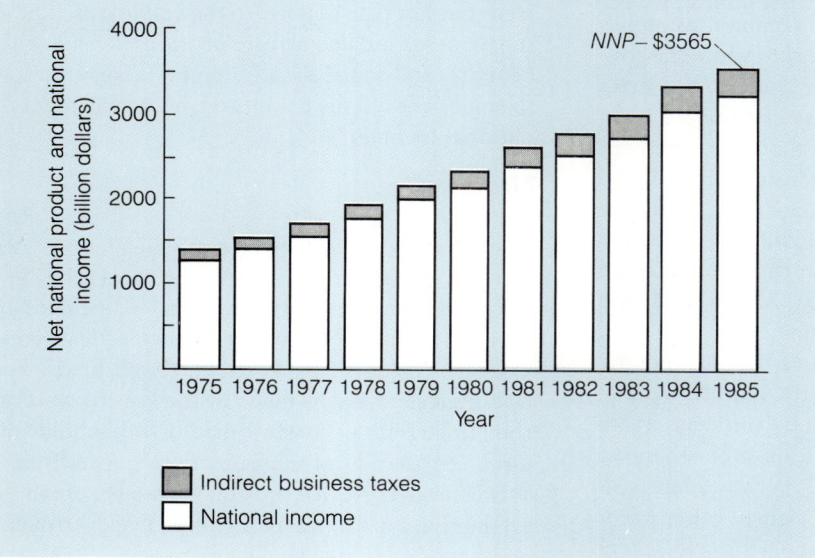

Figure 3.3.1

Net National Product, National Income, and Indirect Business Taxes, 1975 to 1985

Indirect business taxes drive a wedge between the price paid for final goods and services and the price received by the sellers. This means that net national product, which is output valued at market prices, is greater than national income, which is output valued at factor prices; the difference between the two is indirect business taxes. In recent years indirect business taxes have been a little less than 10 percent of net national product.
Source: U.S. Burueau of Economic Analysis, *Survey of Current Business*, selected issues.

However, since it is difficult to separate the two payments, they are grouped together as rental income.

Corporate Profit

The fourth component of national income is corporate profit, which is one portion of the profit earned by entrepreneurs. In recent years these profits have comprised between 5 and 10 percent of national income. Corporate profits can be divided into three separate categories—dividends, undistributed corporate profits, and corporate income tax—each of which becomes important in our discussion of national income. Dividends are that portion of corporate profits paid to the corporate stockholders. However, corporations usually pay only a part of the dividends to stockholders, with the rest either paid to the government as corporate income tax or retained by the firm for reinvestment. The profit retained by the firm is termed undistributed corporate profits.

UNIT 3.3 ■ NATIONAL INCOME

Table 3.3.1
National Income and Related Measures, 1929 to 1985 (billions)

Year	Net National Product	Indirect Business Taxes	National Income	Income Earned but not Received	Income Received but not Earned	Personal Income	Personal Taxes	Desirable Personal Income
1929	$ 93.7	$ 7.1	$ 84.8	$ 3.5	$ 0.9	$ 85.0	$ 2.6	$ 83.3
1930	82.4	7.2	75.4	−1.5	0.9	77.0	2.5	74.5
1931	68.0	6.9	59.7	−4.1	1.3	65.9	1.9	64.0
1932	50.7	6.8	42.8	−4.5	1.4	50.2	1.5	48.7
1933	48.4	7.1	39.9	−3.5	1.5	47.0	1.5	45.5
1934	58.2	7.8	49.5	0.0	1.8	54.0	1.6	52.4
1935	65.4	8.2	57.2	1.1	2.0	60.4	1.9	58.5
1936	75.4	8.7	65.0	2.4	2.2	68.6	2.3	66.3
1937	83.3	9.2	73.6	2.9	2.4	74.1	2.9	71.2
1938	77.4	9.2	67.4	1.5	2.4	68.3	2.9	65.5
1939	82.2	9.4	71.4	2.3	2.5	72.4	2.4	70.3
1940	91.0	10.1	79.7	5.3	2.7	77.9	2.6	75.3
1941	115.0	11.3	102.7	10.5	2.6	95.4	3.3	92.2
1942	147.3	11.8	135.9	16.2	2.7	122.6	5.9	116.6
1943	180.7	12.8	169.3	22.0	2.5	150.8	17.8	133.0
1944	198.9	14.2	182.1	21.2	3.1	164.5	18.9	145.6
1945	200.2	15.5	180.7	14.9	5.6	170.0	20.8	149.1
1946	195.8	17.1	178.6	15.8	10.8	177.6	18.7	158.9
1947	215.7	18.4	194.9	23.4	11.2	190.1	21.4	168.7
1948	239.3	20.1	219.9	24.3	10.6	209.0	21.0	188.0
1949	236.5	21.3	213.6	20.7	11.7	206.4	18.5	187.9
1950	263.0	23.4	237.6	28.0	14.4	227.2	20.6	206.9
1951	303.6	25.3	274.1	33.6	11.6	254.9	28.9	226.0
1952	318.7	27.7	287.9	31.4	12.1	271.8	34.0	237.7
1953	335.8	29.7	302.1	31.5	12.9	287.7	35.5	252.2
1954	334.1	29.6	301.1	30.6	15.1	289.6	32.5	257.1
1955	365.3	32.2	330.5	40.3	16.2	310.3	35.4	275.0
1956	383.0	35.1	349.4	38.5	17.3	332.6	39.7	292.9
1957	402.3	37.5	365.2	38.4	20.1	351.0	42.4	308.6
1958	406.2	38.7	366.9	34.1	24.3	351.1	42.1	319.0
1959	443.0	41.8	400.4	35.3	25.2	384.4	46.0	338.4
1960	460.2	45.4	415.7	44.1	27.0	402.3	50.4	352.0
1961	477.0	48.0	428.8	55.0	30.8	417.8	52.1	365.8

Continued

Table 3.3.1

National Income and Related Measures, 1929 to 1985 (billions) (*continued*)

Year	Net National Product	Indirect Business Taxes	National Income	Income Earned but not Received	Income Received but not Earned	Personal Income	Personal Taxes	Desirable Personal Income
1962	516.1	51.6	462.0	52.5	31.6	443.6	56.8	386.8
1963	546.1	54.6	488.5	58.4	33.4	466.2	60.3	405.9
1964	584.8	58.8	524.9	64.5	34.8	499.2	58.6	440.6
1965	635.0	62.6	572.4	74.2	37.6	540.7	64.9	475.8
1966	695.3	65.3	628.1	83.5	41.6	588.2	74.5	513.7
1967	733.7	70.2	662.2	82.8	49.5	630.0	82.1	547.9
1968	801.3	78.9	722.5	90.0	56.4	690.6	97.2	593.4
1969	864.0	86.6	779.3	88.8	62.8	754.7	115.7	638.9
1970	904.7	94.9	810.7	76.9	76.1	811.1	115.8	695.3
1971	981.1	103.7	871.5	91.0	90.0	868.4	116.7	751.8
1972	1079.5	111.5	963.6	106.6	99.8	951.4	141.0	810.3
1973	1209.9	120.9	1086.2	123.6	114.0	1065.2	150.7	914.5
1974	1298.2	129.1	1160.7	111.9	135.4	1188.8	170.2	998.3
1975	1389.9	140.1	1239.4	130.1	170.9	1285.0	168.9	1096.1
1976	1543.0	151.7	1379.2	156.2	186.4	1391.2	196.8	1194.4
1977	1722.0	166.0	1546.5	186.0	199.3	1588.0	226.5	1311.5
1978	1934.9	178.1	1745.4	210.5	214.6	1721.1	258.8	1462.9
1979	2160.3	188.4	1963.3	217.3	239.9	1943.8	302.0	1641.7
1980	2338.5	213.3	2116.6	291.0	297.6	2165.3	336.5	1828.9
1981	2627.5	251.2	2363.8	286.8	337.3	2429.5	387.7	2041.7
1982	2782.8	258.8	2518.4	240.4	410.6	2670.8	409.3	2261.4
1983	3007.6	282.5	2718.3	314.0	442.2	2836.4	411.1	2425.4
1984	3368.8	310.6	3039.3	388.0	454.7	3111.9	441.8	2670.2
1985	3565.3	328.4	3212.8	419.3	484.5	3293.5	492.7	2800.8

Source: U.S. Bureau of Economic Analysis, *Survey of Current Business*, selected issues.

Proprietors' Income

The fifth component of national income is proprietors' income, which is actually a composite of payments to all of the factors of production (labor, capital, land, and entrepreneurship). A large percentage of the business firms in the economy are owner-operated proprietorships. Proprietorships differ from corporations in that the owner often supplies all of the factors of production.

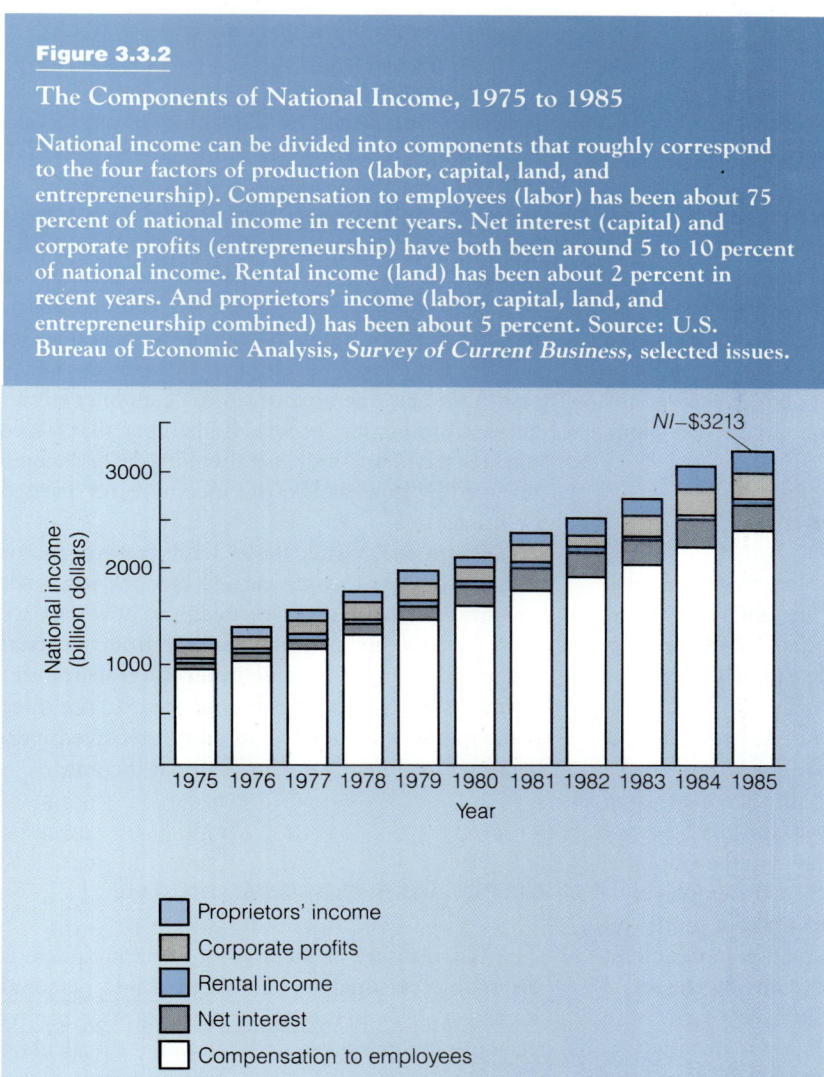

Figure 3.3.2

The Components of National Income, 1975 to 1985

National income can be divided into components that roughly correspond to the four factors of production (labor, capital, land, and entrepreneurship). Compensation to employees (labor) has been about 75 percent of national income in recent years. Net interest (capital) and corporate profits (entrepreneurship) have both been around 5 to 10 percent of national income. Rental income (land) has been about 2 percent in recent years. And proprietors' income (labor, capital, land, and entrepreneurship combined) has been about 5 percent. Source: U.S. Bureau of Economic Analysis, *Survey of Current Business,* selected issues.

Moreover, any "profit" earned by the owner is simply treated as the owner's income. Since it is impossible to determine how much of the income is actually a wage payment for the labor supplied by the owner, and how much is a payment for capital, land, and entrepreneurship, such payments are lumped together as proprietors' income. In recent years proprietors' income has comprised between 5 and 7 percent of national income.

PERSONAL INCOME

While national income is a very useful measure of economic activity, a second measure, personal income, is often more useful. **Personal income (*PI*) is the income received by households.** There is a slight, but important, difference between national income and personal income. National income is *earned* by the factors of production, whereas personal income is the income *received* by households that own the factors. This means that some income earned by the factors is not received by households, and conversely, that some income received by households is not earned by the factors. Let's look at both types of income.

Income Earned but not Received

There are three categories of income that are earned by factors of production but are not received by households: contributions to social security, corporate income tax, and undistributed corporate profits.

The first category, contributions to social security, is set up such that employees pay half of the tax and employers the other half. However, from the perspective of the employer, the total cost of hiring the employee is the wage paid to the employee plus the social security tax paid by the employer to the government. For a firm to make a profit, an employee's contribution to production must at least equal the total cost of the wages paid plus the social security tax. So while the employee "earns" the social security tax, he or she does not "receive" it.

The second and third categories of income earned but not received, corporate income tax and undistributed corporate profits, were introduced earlier. In both cases profit is earned by corporate stockholders, but in neither case do the stockholders receive the income. For the corporate income tax, the profit is paid to the government as a tax. For the undistributed corporate profit, the profit is simply retained by the firm for future investment.

Income Received but not Earned

The main type of income that is received by households but not earned by the factors of production is transfer payments from the government. A **transfer payment is a payment from one sector in the economy to another sector that does not result in current production.** The most common transfer payments from the government to households are welfare payments, unemployment compensation, interest paid on the government debt, and social security benefits. In each of these cases income is transferred between sectors in the economy but no current production occurs. Remember that while transfer payments increase the amount of income received by households, the income is not earned by the factors.

Figure 3.3.3 and Table 3.3.1 present recent information on income earned but not received, income received but not earned, and how they are used to compute personal income from national income. Note that because in recent years transfer payments have been roughly equivalent to the three categories of income earned but not received, personal income nearly equals national income.

DISPOSABLE PERSONAL INCOME

The last measure of income we want to discuss is disposable personal income. **Disposable personal income (*DPI*) is income remaining after paying personal income taxes.** It is very easy to calculate disposable personal income. Simply subtract personal income taxes from personal income. Figure 3.3.4 and Table 3.3.1 present recent information on the relationship between personal income, personal taxes, and disposable personal income.

Disposable personal income indicates the amount of income that households have to spend. In a very real sense disposable personal income is discretionary income. All of the items substracted from national income before identifying disposable

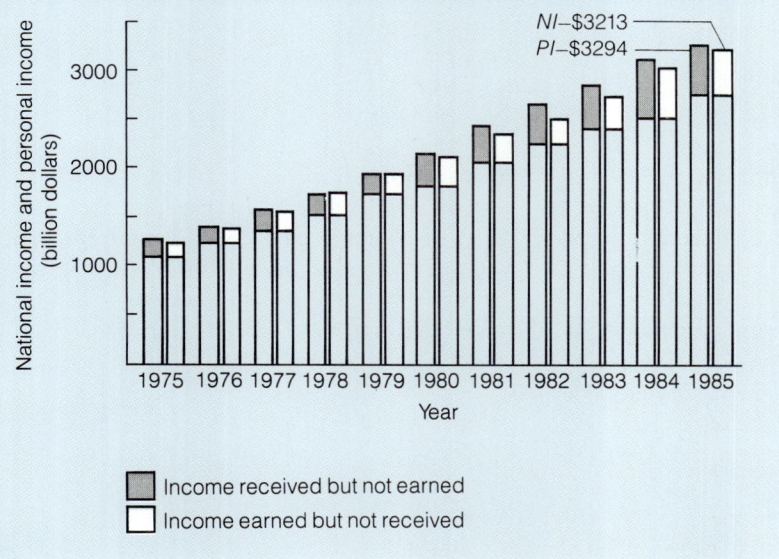

Figure 3.3.3

Differences Between National Income and Personal Income, 1975 to 1985

The income earned by factors of production is not necessarily received by households, and income received by households is not necessarily earned in the production of goods and services. Historically, income earned but not received (social security contributions, corporate income taxes, and undistributed corporate profits) have been about the same as income received but not earned (transfer payments). Therefore, national income has been nearly equal to personal income. Source: U.S. Bureau of Economic Analysis, *Survey of Current Business*, selected issues.

personal income, including corporate income taxes, undistributed corporate profits, social security contributions, and personal taxes, are more or less beyond the control of the household. But with disposable personal income households are essentially free to spend or save as they see fit. The discretionary character of this income plays an important role in the discussion of the principles underlying the operation of the economy in Section 4, Keynesian Economics.

ANOTHER VISIT TO THE CIRCULAR FLOW

Now that we have identified the two measures of national product in Unit 3.2 and the three measures of income in this unit, let's take another look at the circular flow of the economy and see how each of the five measures are related. Figure 3.3.5 illustrates this circular flow.

If we trace the flow of payments from the product market at the top of the diagram, we see the

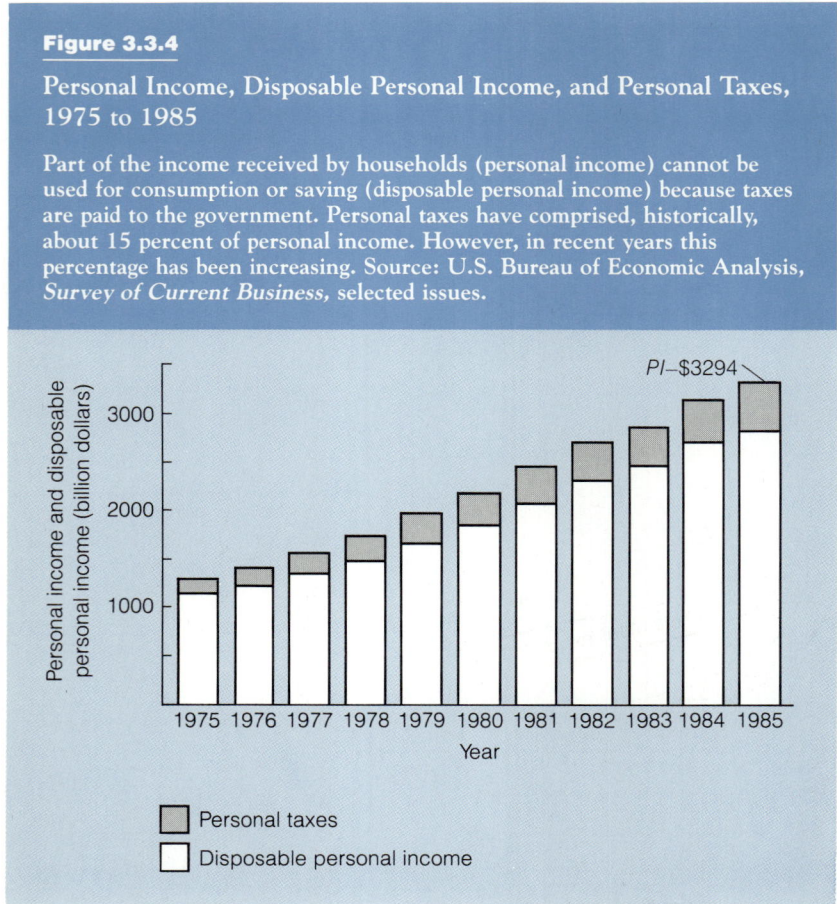

Figure 3.3.4

Personal Income, Disposable Personal Income, and Personal Taxes, 1975 to 1985

Part of the income received by households (personal income) cannot be used for consumption or saving (disposable personal income) because taxes are paid to the government. Personal taxes have comprised, historically, about 15 percent of personal income. However, in recent years this percentage has been increasing. Source: U.S. Bureau of Economic Analysis, *Survey of Current Business*, selected issues.

four basic expenditures on gross national product: household, business, government, and foreign. These are consumption expenditures (C), investment expenditures (I), government purchases (G), and net exports (X − M), respectively. What flows out of the product markets is gross national product (GNP), which can be stated as

$$GNP = C + I + G + (X - M)$$

Moving clockwise around the circular flow, the capital consumption allowance (CCA) is subtracted out, leaving us with net national product (NNP), which can be summarized as

$$NNP = GNP - CCA$$

Note that the capital consumption allowance is one of the sources of funds used by firms for investment expenditures. The net national product is the market value of the production received by the firms.

As the net national product flow leaves the firms, indirect business taxes (IBT) are subtracted,

UNIT 3.3 ▪ NATIONAL INCOME

Figure 3.3.5

The Circular Flow and Official Measures of Income and Product

Each of the official measures of national income and national product fit into the circular flow. Gross national product and net national product are both measures of national production. National income is the income earned by the factors of production, personal income is the income actually received by households and disposable personal income is the income available after taxes for either consumption or saving.

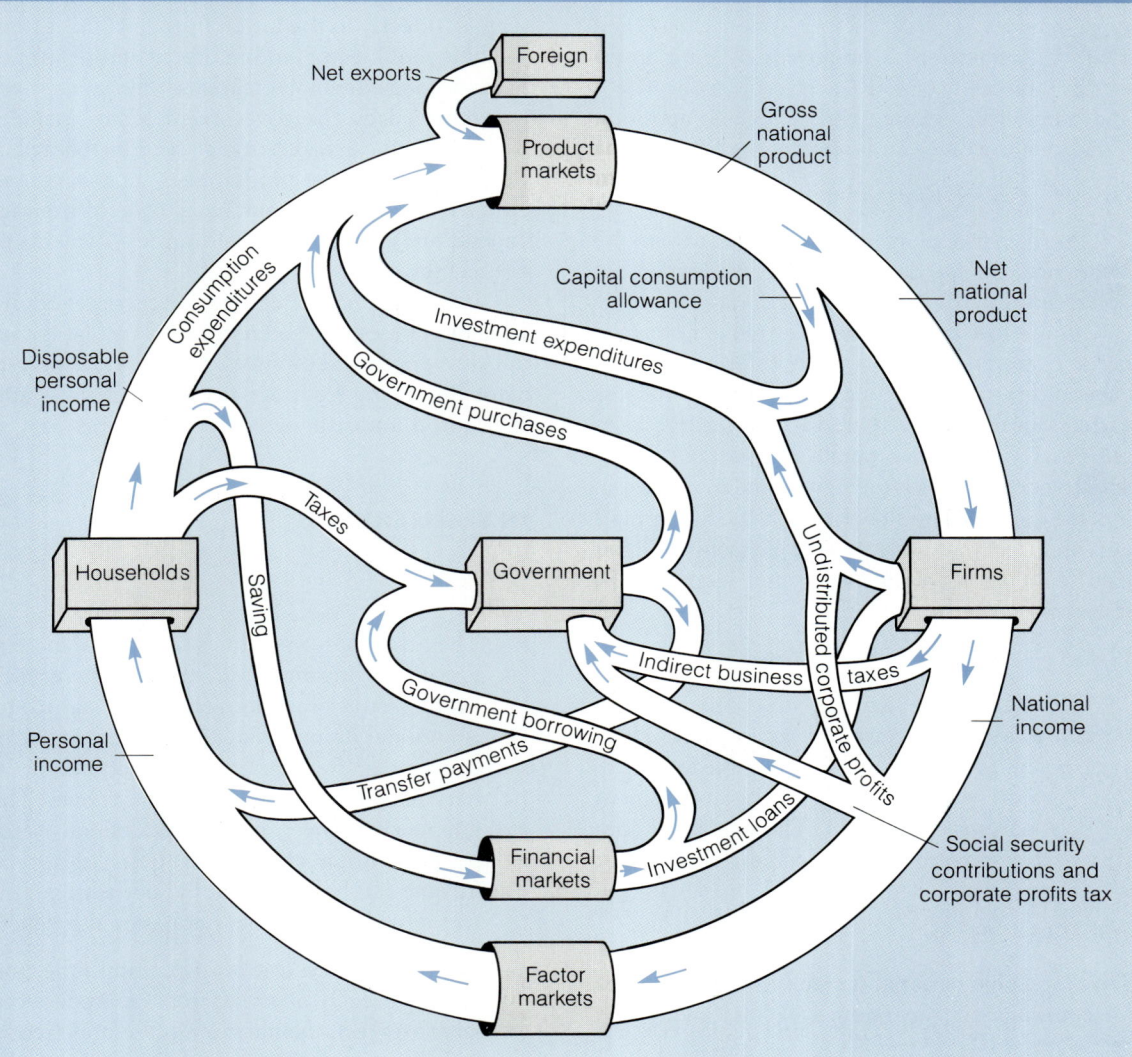

leaving national income (NI), the income earned by the factors of production, or production valued at factor prices rather than market prices. Note how the indirect business taxes quickly work their way over to the government sector. The basic relationship between national income and net national product can be stated as

NI = NNP − IBT

We should also note that national income at this stage includes five basic factor payments: wage and salary compensation to employees (W), net interest (IN), rental income (RI), corporate profits (CP), and proprietors' income (PRI). The composition of national income can be summarized as

NI = W + IN + RI + CP + PRI

As the national income flow moves toward the factor markets, we deduct the income earned but not received. The undistributed corporate profits (UCP) are the first to leave; they move upward to become another source of funds for investment expenditures. The second two types of income earned but not received are social security contributions (SSC) and corporate profits tax (CPT), which both flow to the government. National income continues to flow through the factor markets and, together with transfer payments (TP), is paid to the households as personal income (PI), stated as

PI = NI − UCP − SSC − CPT + TP

Personal income flows into the household sector as the income received by households. However, not all personal income is available for spending, because part of it flows to the government sector as personal taxes (PT). The remainder constitutes disposable personal income (DPI), which is summarized as

DPI = PI − PT

The disposable personal income can then be used for consumption expenditures (C) or saving (S), as shown by

DPI = C + S

If disposable personal income is used as saving, it flows to the financial markets, where it becomes loans to either firms or the government. If it is used as consumption expenditures, it represents one of the four demands for gross national production, and it has come full circle back to the product markets.

In the middle of the circular flow we see how the government sector diverts various portions of the flow away from the household and business sectors, directly in the form of personal taxes from the household sector, and indirectly in the form of loans from the financial markets. The other revenue received by the government sector includes indirect business taxes, social security contributions, and corporate profits taxes, and it is used either for government purchases (one of the four expenditures for GNP) or for transfer payments to households.

In closing, note the three basic sources of revenue for investment expenditures. The first is capital consumption allowances, the second is investment borrowing from the financial markets, and the third is undistributed corporate profits.

IN SUMMARY

National Income

- The first of three measures of national income is national income itself, the income earned by the factors of production. National income is national product valued at factor prices, in contrast to net national product, which is national product valued at product prices. The difference between product prices and factor prices is indirect business taxes. National income can be calculated by subtracting indirect business taxes from net national product.

- National income can be divided into the payments to each of the factors of production: labor (wages), capital (interest), land (rent), and entrepreneurship (profit). However, in the official measurement of national income payments, proprietors' income (containing wages, interest, rent, and profit payments received by proprietorships) is listed as a separate item.

- Personal income is the second measure of the economy's income. It is the income received by households, as opposed to national income, which is the income earned by the factors of production. To compute personal income, we need to take national income and subtract income earned but not received, and then add income received but not earned. Income earned but not received consists of social security contributions, corporate income taxes, and undistributed corporate profits. Income received but not earned, which consists of social security benefits, welfare payments, unemployment compensation, and so on, is known as transfer payments.

- Disposable personal income is the last measure of the economy's income. It is the income left for consumption and/or saving after personal taxes are paid. It is easily calculated by subtracting personal taxes from personal income.

QUESTIONS FOR STUDY AND ANALYSIS

1. Explain why net national product is output valued through the product markets and national income is output valued through the factor markets. Also explain how indirect business taxes make the market price of a good different from the costs of its production.

2. What is the difference between personal income and national income? Which of the following items would be included in national income but not personal income? Which would be included in personal income but not national income? Which would be included in both?
   a. Social security contributions
   b. Welfare payments to the poor
   c. Corporate dividends
   d. Undistributed corporate profits
   e. Corporate profits tax
   f. Proprietors' income

3. Explain how and why consumption expenditures are affected in each of the following cases:
   a. Decrease in transfer payments
   b. Increase in undistributed corporate profits
   c. Decrease in capital consumption allowance
   d. Decrease in social security contributions
   e. Increase in indirect business taxes

4. Political leaders usually favor the use of sales, excise, or corporate profit taxes rather than personal income taxes. In terms of the circular flow explain how these taxes are actually taxes on household income. Why do you think these types of taxes are often referred to as "hidden" taxes? Explain.

REVIEW GLOSSARY

disposable personal income (*DPI*) Income remaining after paying personal taxes. Disposable personal income is found by subtracting taxes from personal income, and represents the income that households can use for either consumption or saving.

indirect business tax A tax levied on business firms, but indirectly paid by households through higher prices. Indirect business taxes are the difference between net national product and national income.

national income (*NI*) Income earned by the factors of production. National income can be viewed as national production valued at factor prices, while net national product is national production valued at product prices.

personal income (*PI*) Income received by households. Personal income is found by subtracting social security contributions, corporate income taxes, and undistributed corporate profits from, and adding transfer payments to, national income.

transfer payment A payment from one sector of the economy to another sector that does not result in current production. Transfer payments are income received by the households, but not earned.

UNIT 3.4

Unemployment

In the last unit we concentrated on the lower loop of the circular flow, national income. In this unit we focus on the physical flow of labor services that generate a large part of national income. In particular, we examine the nature and causes of the unemployment of labor, for three reasons. First, as we saw in the last unit, labor receives about 75 percent of national income, making it a very important factor in terms of contribution to national product. Second, for many people labor represents the sole source of income; for these people unemployment can mean serious personal hardships. Third, the unemployment of labor is commonly used as an indicator of the overall health of the economy. As we see in our discussion of business cycles in Unit 3.7, more people tend to be unemployed during bad economic times than during good economic times.

Our examination of unemployment begins with a look at the nature of unemployment, which can be either voluntary or involuntary. We divide unemployment into four different types: cyclical, seasonal, frictional, and structural. We then study the official measurement of unemployment in the United States, the unemployment rate. We see how the official unemployment rate is obtained, and we look at some problems in its measurement. Finally, after examining recent trends in the unemployment rate, we discuss the costs of unemployment.

THE NATURE OF UNEMPLOYMENT

To begin, let's consider our definition of unemployment. As we saw in Unit 1.5, **unemployment** is the condition of the economy in which some factors of production are not being used in the production of goods and services. The factor of production we are concerned with here is labor. Note that people are considered labor, and thus a factor of production, only if they are willing and able to work. In fact, some members of society are either unwilling or unable to work, and thus are not part of the labor force.

Voluntary and Involuntary Unemployment

Let's first concern ourselves only with people who are both willing and able to work. While 90 to 95 percent of the labor force is employed in the production of goods and services at any one time, 5 to 10 percent is not, which suggests that labor can be either voluntarily or involuntarily unemployed.

Voluntary unemployment is unemployment created when labor chooses not to take available employment, anticipating that better jobs can be found. This type of unemployment might occur because a worker quits one job and begins looking for another. Or a worker might decide not to take an existing but relatively low-paying job, hoping eventually to find a higher-paying job. For example, an unemployed autoworker could take a job as a convenience store clerk at $3.50 per hour, but instead continues to look for a job in the automobile industry at $10.00 per hour.

But there is also involuntary unemployment. **Involuntary unemployment** is unemployment created when labor is willing and able to work, but cannot find an available job. For example, involuntary unemployment would exist if the autoworker is willing to work in the convenience store, but no job is available there, or anywhere else.

There is a fine line between voluntary and involuntary unemployment. For example, suppose the unemployed worker is a highly skilled and specialized automotive engineer. Technically, if the engineer did not take the convenience store job, this would be voluntary unemployment. However, if the engineer did take the job, then his or her skills would be underused, which would constitute underemployment. **Disguised unemployment,** or **underemployment,** is when labor is engaged in the production of goods and services, but is not being used to its full potential. In principle, disguised unemployment is no different than involuntary unemployment. If a worker is not employed at all, then he or she is totally unemployed. However, with disguised unemployment the worker may be, in effect, only partially employed, and producing only part of the goods and services that he or she could produce. Disguised unemployment may comprise 25, 50, or 75 percent unemployment, but it is unemployment nonetheless.

Types of Unemployment

With this distinction between voluntary and involuntary unemployment in mind, let's look at four common types of unemployment in the economy: cyclical, seasonal, frictional, and structural.

Cyclical Unemployment The first type of unemployment to consider, and perhaps the most important type in terms of our future discussions, is cyclical unemployment. **Cyclical unemployment is unemployment created by irregular declines in overall economic activity.** As we see in Unit 3.7, the economy is faced with recurring but irregular declines in economic activity. During these declines national product falls because expenditures on national product fall. And because business firms are producing less output, they employ fewer workers. If automobile factories, steel mills, and retail stores do not have sufficient demand for their product, then they are likely to lay off some of their labor. In other words cyclical unemployment is involuntary unemployment. An important aspect of cyclical unemployment is that it occurs at irregular intervals; firms are never quite sure when economic activity will decline.

Seasonal Unemployment The irregularity associated with cyclical unemployment does not occur with the second type of unemployment, seasonal unemployment. **Seasonal unemployment is unemployment created by relatively regular, or seasonal, declines in business activity.** Seasonal unemployment is similar to cyclical unemployment, but with one important difference—it is regular and predictable. For example, construction workers, lifeguards, and professional baseball players are typically unemployed during the winter months, and ski instructors and department store Santas during the summer. Another example of seasonal unemployment that is relatively regular and predictable is the unemployment created when teenagers enter the job market during summer months. In many cases the regularity of seasonal unemployment is built into the terms of employment. If a worker knows that the job involves employment only nine out of twelve months, then a higher wage may be necessary during the nine months of employment to offset the three months of unemployment. For this reason, seasonal unemployment is more often voluntary unemployment. Even though no job exists for the worker in the off season, the worker generally knows this before accepting the job.

Frictional Unemployment The third type of unemployment, frictional unemployment, also constitutes voluntary unemployment. **Frictional unemployment is unemployment created by imperfections in the labor market.** Frictional unemployment occurs because it takes time for an unemployed worker to find a job, even though the job is available. This might be due to lack of information concerning job opportunities, or the time lag involved in moving to a new location. With frictional unemployment people are typically moving from one job to another, so they are voluntarily unemployed from their previous job, even though they have yet to find another job. Frictional unemployment is a basic fact of the economy, and even when the economy is in what we would consider full employment, frictional unemployment still exists. In short, every member of the economy's labor force is not going to be employed at the same time.

Structural Unemployment The last type of unemployment, structural unemployment, is best considered as involuntary. **Structural unemployment** is unemployment created by changes in the types of skills required in the production of goods and services. This type of unemployment occurs because the basic structure of the economy changes, such that the skills possessed by unemployed workers may not be the skills needed by firms. For example, as more firms computerize their operations, many of the skills associated with the operation of machinery are no longer needed. If firms need workers who possess computer-oriented skills, then the machine operators are structurally, and therefore involuntarily, unemployed. Structural unemployment is usually long-lasting, and requires retraining and reeducation.

MEASURING UNEMPLOYMENT

The official measurement of the unemployment of labor in the economy is the unemployment rate. The **unemployment rate** is the percentage of the total labor force that is unemployed. In principle, the unemployment rate is easily determined by identifying the number of people willing and able to work who are not employed and dividing that number by the total size of the labor force. This is stated as

$$\text{unemployment rate} = \frac{\text{unemployed}}{\text{labor force}} \times 100$$

In practice, it becomes more difficult to identify the unemployment rate. With this in mind, we need to consider some problems in measuring the unemployment rate. First, let's examine how to determine if a worker is unemployed, and then let's see how to identify the size of the economy's labor force.

Unemployment

According to official statistics, workers are unemployed if they meet one of the following two criteria. One, they were not employed, but were available for work and had actively looked for employment within the previous four weeks. Two, they were not employed, but did not look for work within the previous four weeks because they were either laid off or waiting to start a new job within thirty days. According to these criteria, most of the unemployed workers in the economy—the laid-off autoworker, the out-of-work carpenter, and the teenager looking for summer employment—are officially counted as unemployed.

However, some unemployed workers will not fall into these categories. Workers are not considered unemployed if they have not actively looked for work in the past four weeks, were not laid off, or were not about to start a new job. In other words, if someone has given up looking for a job because they have not been employed in recent months and have no prospects for a job, then they would not be considered unemployed. But clearly, they are unemployed; they are simply discouraged workers. **Discouraged workers** are unemployed workers who have given up looking for employment because of their inability to find work. Although discouraged workers are not officially considered in the calculation of the unemployment rate because they are difficult to identify, they should be included.

Labor Force

Once we have determined the number of workers who are unemployed, we have to determine the size of the labor force. The **labor force** is the portion of the population that is willing and able to work, including those actively engaged in the production of goods and services and those who are unemployed. This definition includes everyone in the economy who is willing and able to produce goods and services, whether or not they are actually doing so. The size of the labor force has a direct bearing on the unemployment rate. For example, if unemployed workers become discouraged and decide to leave the labor force, and also the ranks of the unemployed, then the unemployment rate declines, because the relative decline in the number of workers unemployed is greater than the relative decline in the labor force.

Note that every member of a society is not considered part of the labor force, because everyone in the economy is not necessarily willing and able to engage in production. For example, in 1984 the population of the United States was more than 230 million people. However, the official civilian labor force was only 114 million people, meaning that less than half of the population was considered part of the labor force. To more precisely identify the fraction of the population willing and able to work, we must look at the labor force participation rate. The **labor force participation rate** is the percentage of the population that is willing and able to work, and thus is a part of the labor force. The labor force participation rate is obviously important in determining the size of the labor force. Even without changes in a country's population, the labor force can increase if the labor force participation rate increases. And since the size of the labor force is extremely important in determining the unemployment rate, the participation rate is worth further consideration.

We should start by noting that the labor force participation rate is never 100 percent, because for one reason or another, part of the population is unwilling or unable to work. There are four basic reasons why people are not part of the labor force: age, school, institutionalization, and home responsibilities.

First, legal restraints prevent people below the age of sixteen from working, except under certain circumstances, so the labor force participation rate is measured for the population sixteen years and older. Since the participation rate of people under sixteen years is minimal, the inclusion of this age group would have little bearing on the participation rate anyway.

Second, many people sixteen and older are not in the labor force because they are going to school. Students in the last few years of high school and in college are not part of the labor force unless they work part-time after school. But for many students, it is an either/or choice—either work or go to school. And when they choose school, they may be physically able to work, but are unwilling to work, and thus are not in the labor force.

Third, people who are institutionalized are also excluded from the labor force. The institutionalized population, which includes people in prisons, mental hospitals, nursing homes, or hospitals, are excluded from the labor force because they are unable to work.

And fourth, a large number of people are not officially part of the labor force because of responsibilities around the house. That is, the typical homemaker, either housewife or househusband, might choose not to be a member of the labor force in order to take care of household duties and raise a family. We should note that housewives and househusbands are not officially members of the labor force, and therefore are not officially either employed or unemployed. But this doesn't mean that they are not engaged in the production of goods and services. As we saw in our discussion of gross national product in Unit 3.2, work performed around the house does constitute economic production, it just doesn't involve a market transaction, and is difficult to include in official measurements. The same reasoning applies to homemakers.

Household responsibilities also deserve special consideration in today's economy. In the past the traditional situation in which the husband went to work while the wife remained at home to raise the family kept two-thirds of women out of the labor force. Today this traditional situation is breaking down, as women are becoming active members of the labor force in addition to their roles as housewives.

Recent Trends of Unemployment

Let's now examine some of the recent trends in unemployment in the United States. Figure 3.4.1 depicts the unemployment rate for the past several years. First, note the peaks and valleys of this curve.

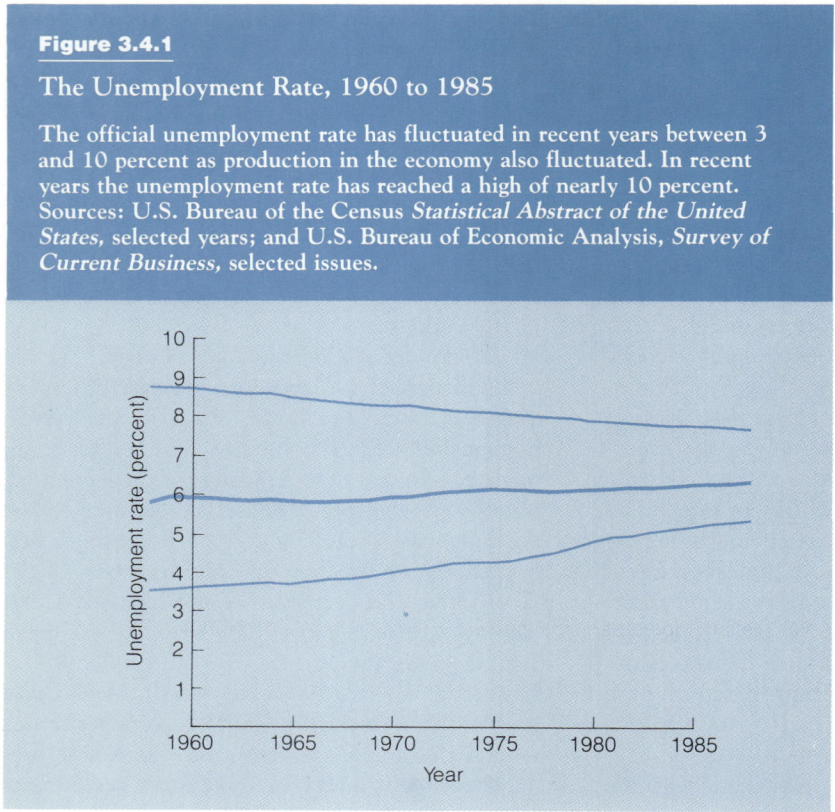

Figure 3.4.1

The Unemployment Rate, 1960 to 1985

The official unemployment rate has fluctuated in recent years between 3 and 10 percent as production in the economy also fluctuated. In recent years the unemployment rate has reached a high of nearly 10 percent. Sources: U.S. Bureau of the Census *Statistical Abstract of the United States*, selected years; and U.S. Bureau of Economic Analysis, *Survey of Current Business*, selected issues.

In 1975 there was a relatively high unemployment rate, over 8 percent; it declined to under 6 percent in 1979, and then rose again in 1982 to over 10 percent. In Unit 3.7, our discussion of business cycles sheds some light on this pattern. For the moment we can note that this pattern of peaks and valleys is typical of the unemployment rate.

It is also interesting to look at trends in the labor force participation rates for the past decade. Figure 3.4.2 shows the participation rate for the entire economy (center line), and the participation rates for males (top line) and females (bottom line). In all three cases we are looking at the official participation rates of the population sixteen years and older.

The center line indicates a historical participation rate of around 60 to 65 percent of the population. However, in the past few years the participation rate has increased, reversing a slight declining trend of earlier years. If we look at the participation rates for each of the sexes, we can see why this has happened. While the participation rate for males has been declining in recent years, the participation rate for females has steadily increased. At one time the female participation rate was only 30 percent, but it has increased to over 50 percent and is apparently still on the rise. This rise in the female rate has led to the increase in the overall participation rate for the economy.

And finally, let's look at the unemployment

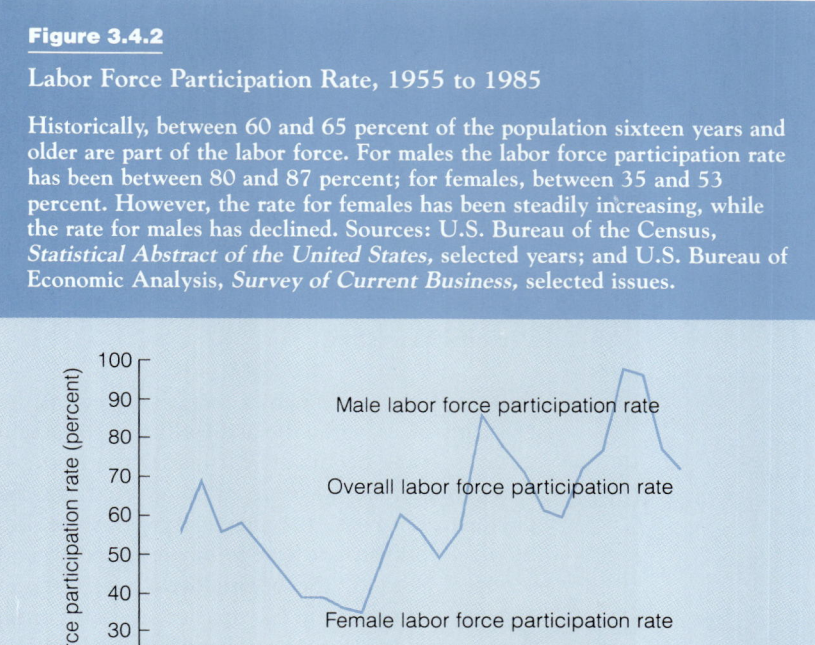

Figure 3.4.2

Labor Force Participation Rate, 1955 to 1985

Historically, between 60 and 65 percent of the population sixteen years and older are part of the labor force. For males the labor force participation rate has been between 80 and 87 percent; for females, between 35 and 53 percent. However, the rate for females has been steadily increasing, while the rate for males has declined. Sources: U.S. Bureau of the Census, *Statistical Abstract of the United States*, selected years; and U.S. Bureau of Economic Analysis, *Survey of Current Business*, selected issues.

rates for different groups in the economy, as listed in Table 3.4.1, for males and females by race and age. As a benchmark, note that the overall unemployment rate in the economy is 9.6 percent. However, all groups in the economy do not have the same unemployment rate. For example, males twenty years and older tend to have a lower unemployment rate than that of the entire economy, whereas females twenty years and older tend to have an unemployment rate about equal to the national level. But teenagers of either sex between the ages of sixteen and nineteen tend to have unemployment rates much greater than the national average.

If we compare the unemployment rates between whites and nonwhites, we see that whites in all sexes and age groups have lower unemployment rates than nonwhites. In fact, while teenagers of any race have high unemployment rates, the highest unemployment rates in the economy are for nonwhite teenagers, who have an unemployment rate of about 40 percent.

COSTS OF UNEMPLOYMENT

If labor is unemployed, it is not producing output and not receiving income. Both of these are important costs of unemployment. To close this unit, let's

Table 3.4.1

Unemployment Rates for Selected Groups (percent)

The unemployment rate varies for different members of the labor force. Whites typically have a lower unemployment rate than blacks. People over twenty also have much lower unemployment rates than teenagers between sixteen and nineteen years of age.

Group	1970	1985
Total	4.9	7.2
White	4.5	6.2
Males 20 and over	3.2	5.4
Females 20 and over	4.4	5.7
Males 16 to 19	13.7	16.5
Females 16 to 19	13.4	14.8
Nonwhite	8.2	15.1
Males 20 and over	5.6	13.2
Females 20 and over	6.8	13.1
Males 16 to 19	25.0	41.0
Females 16 to 19	34.5	39.2

Sources: Economic Report of the President, 1984; and U.S. Department of Labor, *Monthly Labor Review*, March 1986.

---

a 1 percent increase in the unemployment rate leads to a 3 percent decline in gross national product. If the unemployment rate increases from 5 to 6 percent, then gross national product declines by 3 percent. In terms of a $4 trillion *GNP*, this means the decline in output consists of $120 billion worth of goods and services. Based on a population of 230 million, this averages out to about $520 per person. Even at today's prices this is a significant reduction in goods and services.

Personal Hardships

Although unemployment affects everyone in the economy by reducing the availability of goods and services, some people are hit harder than others. Obviously, those who are most affected are the unemployed. First, the unemployed receive less income, and thus are able to buy fewer goods and services. Second, the unemployed suffer mental anguish and other psychic damage, not only from the uncertainty of not knowing when work will be found, but also from the stigma of failure often associated with unemployment. While we can easily measure the costs to the economy of lost output, it is far more difficult to measure the costs in human suffering experienced by the unemployed.

IN SUMMARY
Unemployment

- Unemployment, and in particular the unemployment of labor, is an important problem facing the macroeconomy. If labor is unemployed, it is not being used to produce goods and services, and thus the economy is further from solving the economic problem. Moreover, unemployed workers receive less income and experience various personal hardships.

- Unemployment occurs when factors of production are not engaged in the production of

---

briefly discuss the two basic costs of unemployment—the loss of national production and the incidence of personal hardships.

National Production

The relationship is very straightforward; unemployed labor does not produce output. If less output is produced, then consumers are able to satisfy fewer wants and needs and are further from solving the economic problem. According to some estimates, goods and services. Labor can be either voluntarily unemployed, as when a worker chooses not to take an existing job, or involuntarily unemployed, as when no jobs are available. Disguised unemployment, or underemployment, occurs when someone has a job, but the job does not use the worker's full potential.

- Unemployment can be divided into four types, cyclical, seasonal, frictional, and structural. Cyclical unemployment is created by the irregular declines in economic activity associated with business cycles. Seasonal unemployment is created by relatively regular and predictable declines in economic activity. Frictional unemployment is created when workers do not take available jobs because they do not know about them or because they are waiting for something better. Structural unemployment is created because workers do not have the skills required for the production of goods and services.

- Unemployment of labor is commonly measured with the unemployment rate, the percentage of the labor force that is unemployed. Officially, the unemployment rate is based only on people who have actively looked for work. This does not include discouraged workers who are willing and able to work but have given up looking because of their inability to find work.

- Officially, the labor force contains people both willing and able to work. A member of the population may not be part of the labor force for various reasons. The labor force participation rate indicates the fraction of the population that is part of the labor force, and has historically been around 60 to 65 percent.

- The two most important costs of unemployment are the reduction of national output and personal hardships experienced by the unemployed. These costs have made reductions in unemployment a major goal of the macroeconomy.

QUESTIONS FOR STUDY AND ANALYSIS

1. Total unemployment can be divided into four basic types: cyclical, seasonal, frictional, and structural. For each of the following cases of unemployment indicate which type of unemployment is involved, and why. Also indicate whether each case is voluntary or involuntary unemployment.
   a. Referees for the National Basketball Association are unemployed during the summer months.
   b. Airline pilots are laid off due to a slowdown in business.
   c. Coal miners are unemployed in the Appalachian region.
   d. A computer programmer leaves a job in Detroit to seek a fortune in Silicon Valley.

2. Why are discouraged workers omitted from official measures of the unemployment rate? Do you think that they should be included? Do you think that voluntary unemployment should be included or excluded? Do you think disguised unemployment, or underemployment, should be included or excluded?

3. Presently, institutionalized people, including prison inmates, are not considered part of the labor force. However, some people have proposed turning prisons into factories and allowing prisoners to produce and sell goods. In this case what changes, if any, do you think would need to be made in our measurement of the labor force?

4. In recent years the labor force participation rate for men has declined, while the rate for women has increased. Discuss why you think this has occurred. How has this affected the official unemployment rate?

5. Why are we less concerned with the unemployment of capital and land than with labor? Should we be less concerned with the unemployment of these other factors? Explain.

REVIEW GLOSSARY

cyclical unemployment Unemployment created by frequent but irregular declines in economic activity associated with business cycles.

discouraged workers Unemployed workers who have given up looking for employment because of their inability to find work.

disguised unemployment (underemployment) Unemployment created when labor is engaged in the production of goods and services but is not being used to its full potential.

frictional unemployment Unemployment created by imperfections in the labor market. With frictional unemployment, jobs are available, but workers are not employed because they do not know about the jobs or are waiting to find better jobs.

involuntary unemployment Unemployment created when labor is willing and able to work, but cannot find an available job.

labor force The portion of the population that is willing and able to work, including those actively engaged in the production of goods and services and those who are unemployed.

labor force participation rate The percentage of the population that is willing and able to work, and thus is a part of the labor force. Officially, the labor force participation rate is based on the fraction of the population sixteen years and older that is part of the labor force.

seasonal unemployment Unemployment created by relatively regular, or seasonal, declines in economic activity. Since seasonal unemployment is regular and predictable, it is usually incorporated into the wages paid to labor.

structural unemployment Unemployment created by changes in the types of skills required in the production of goods and services.

unemployment The condition of the economy in which some factors of production are not being used in the production of goods and services.

unemployment rate The percentage of the total labor force that is unemployed.

voluntary unemployment Unemployment created when labor chooses not to take available employment, anticipating that better jobs can be found.

UNIT 3.5

Inflation

Inflation is one of the most discussed topics in economics. When the economy is gripped by inflation, as it was in the 1970s, almost everyone has an opinion as to its causes and effects. The inflation of the 1970s was attributed to everything from OPEC to inefficiencies in government to greedy consumers. Our objective in this unit is to lay the foundation needed to understand this topic. In Section 6, A Closer Look at Inflation, we discuss the causes of, and solutions to, inflation; in this unit we concern ourselves with the nature and consequences of inflation.

First, we define inflation. In particular, we want to contrast the terms *inflation* and *price level*, which, while related, refer to different concepts. We then look at the three most common measures of the price level used to estimate inflation: consumer price index, GNP price deflator, and producer price index. As we look at these three measures, we see that inflation is not all that easy to measure. And finally, we discuss several of the adverse consequences of inflation, noting that while inflation can be harmless, it can also be devastating. The two main problems created by inflation are redistribution of wealth and income and reduction of production.

A DEFINITION OF INFLATION

The best way to start is with a simple definition. **Inflation** is an increase in the average price level. The **price level** is simply the average of all prices for goods and services in the economy. The relationship between inflation and the price level is much like the relationship between investment and the stock of capital. Investment is a change in the stock of capital, and inflation is a change in the price level. In examining the three most common measures used to estimate inflation, keep in mind that each is a measure of the price level. To measure inflation, we have to identify *changes* in the price level.

MEASURES OF INFLATION

The three most common measures of the price level used to estimate inflation are the consumer price index, the GNP price deflator, and the producer price index. Since each measure indicates the average level of prices in the economy, changes in these measures indicate inflation in the economy. However, we should point out that each measure is designed for a slightly different set of prices, which means we sometimes get conflicting indications of inflation in the economy.

Consumer Price Index

The **consumer price index (CPI)** is an index of the prices of goods and services purchased by families in urban areas. This index is by far the most common measure of the price level and inflation in the economy. It is determined by comparing the prices of a set of goods and services purchased in a given year to the prices of the same set in 1967. For example, if the CPI is equal to 200 for a given year, then the prices of goods purchased by urban families, on average, have doubled since 1967. The first column of Table 3.5.1 lists the value of the CPI for the past several years. The CPI is equal to 100 for 1967, since this is the comparison year, and increases to 322.2 in 1985, meaning that in 1985 prices were 222.2 percent greater than in 1967.

In terms of the average price level for the economy, the CPI has two significant features. First, the CPI measures only the prices paid by *urban* families. While urban families comprise about three-fourths of the total population in the United States, the goods and services purchased by the remaining one-fourth of the population, who live in rural areas, are not necessarily included in the CPI.

Table 3.5.1

Three Measures of the Price Level, 1967 to 1985

The three most common measures of the price level are the consumer price index (*CPI*), *GNP* price deflator (*GNP-PD*), and producer price index (*PPI*). The *CPI* measures the prices of goods purchased by urban families, the *GNP-PD* measures the prices of all final goods produced in the economy, and the *PPI* measures the prices of inputs purchased by producers.

Year	Consumer Price Index (CPI)	GNP Price Deflator (GNP-PD)	Producer Price Index (PPI)
1967	100.0	35.9	100.0
1968	104.2	37.7	102.9
1969	109.8	39.8	106.6
1970	116.3	42.0	110.3
1971	121.3	44.4	113.7
1972	125.3	46.5	117.2
1973	133.1	49.5	127.9
1974	147.7	54.0	147.5
1975	161.2	59.3	163.4
1976	170.5	63.1	170.6
1977	181.5	67.3	181.7
1978	195.4	72.2	195.9
1979	217.4	78.6	217.7
1980	246.8	85.7	247.0
1981	272.4	94.0	269.8
1982	289.1	100.0	280.7
1983	298.4	103.8	284.6
1984	311.1	108.1	290.3
1985	322.2	111.7	291.9

Source: U.S. Bureau of Economic Analysis, *Survey of Current Business*, selected issues.

Second, the *CPI* uses a fixed set of goods and services, particularly those purchased by urban families in 1967. The problem is that urban families do not necessarily buy the same types of goods and services in 1987 as they did in 1967. The *CPI* includes prices of goods and services that are no longer purchased, while excluding others that are purchased. For example, microcomputers, calculators, and electronic games were not around in 1967, but they certainly are important to today's economy.

One reason that consumers change the types of goods purchased is because relative prices change. If the price of one good increases relatively more than the price of another, then people will tend to buy the good with the relatively lower price. However, the CPI assumes that people continue to buy the same amount of the higher priced good, thus tending to overstate the actual amount of inflation in the economy.

GNP Price Deflator

The second measure of the economy's price level, the *GNP* price deflator, does not have the deficiencies inherent in the *CPI*. The **GNP price deflator (*GNP-PD*)** is a price index computed from the ratio of nominal *GNP* to real *GNP*. As we saw in Unit 3.2, the economy's gross national product is computed using two different sets of prices. Nominal *GNP* is computed with the actual prices in the year that the national product is sold, whereas real *GNP* is computed based on the price levels of 1982. The ratio of nominal *GNP* to real *GNP* gives the *GNP-PD*, which represents a measure of the relative price level in the economy. The second column of Table 3.5.1 lists the *GNP-PD* for recent years. Because 1982 is the base year, the *GNP-PD* for that year is 100. In 1985 the *GNP-PD* is equal to 111.7, meaning the price level increased by 11.7 percent since 1982.

For our purposes the *GNP-PD* provides a much better measure than the *CPI* of the overall price level in the economy. Since the *GNP-PD* is derived from the measurement of *GNP*, it pertains to *all* final goods and services in the economy, unlike the *CPI*. The *GNP-PD* is the price of the economy's current production, and thus the average price level in the economy.

Although the *GNP-PD* is a better measure of the price level, and thus inflation, the *CPI* is more commonly used simply because it is reported more often. The *CPI* comes out once a month, usually within two to three weeks after the month has ended, whereas the *GNP-PD* comes out only once every three months, at the same time all of the official measures of national output and income are reported. Moreover, the *GNP-PD* is not reported until two to four months after the period it covers has ended. Thus, the *GNP-PD* might not tell us the rate of inflation for January, February, and March until sometime in May. But the *CPI* gives us an idea of the rate of inflation in January *before* the end of February.

Producer Price Index

The third measure of price level is the producer price index. The **producer price index (*PPI*)** is a price index based on the prices of selected raw materials and intermediate goods purchased by producers. Since the *PPI* measures the prices of materials purchased by producers, it is not, strictly speaking, a measure of the overall price level in the economy. However, it is still important to our study of inflation.

The *PPI* measures the prices of the raw materials and intermediate goods that will be transformed in some manner and ultimately resold as final goods. Therefore, a higher *PPI* generally indicates that the *CPI* and *GNP-PD* will increase in later periods. Clearly, if producers have to pay more for their raw materials and intermediate goods, they are likely to pass these higher costs on to the consumer in the form of higher prices for final goods. For this reason the *PPI* is a good indicator of the economy's price level in periods to come. Like the *CPI*, the *PPI* uses 1967 as its base year. The third column of Table 3.5.1 lists recent numbers for the *PPI*.

Inflation and the Price Level

Let's now see how inflation can be computed from these three measures of the price level. Table 3.5.2 presents the three measures of the price level from Table 3.5.1, with the percentage change in the index for each year next to each measure. For example, the *CPI* is 100 in 1967, and 104.2 in 1968. This means that the price level in 1968 is

Table 3.5.2

Three Measures of the Price Level and Inflation, 1967 to 1985

Each measure of the price level can also be used to estimate the rate of inflation. Estimates based on the *GNP-PD* are probably better indicators of inflation because they include only goods and services actually sold in the economy.

Year	CPI	Change in CPI	GNP-PD	Change in GNP-PD	PPI	Change in PPI
1967	100.0	2.9	35.9	2.6	100.0	0.2
1968	104.2	4.2	37.7	5.0	102.9	2.9
1969	109.8	5.4	39.8	5.6	106.6	3.6
1970	116.3	5.9	42.0	5.5	110.3	3.5
1971	121.3	4.3	44.4	5.7	113.7	3.1
1972	125.3	3.3	46.5	4.7	117.2	3.1
1973	133.1	6.2	49.5	6.5	127.9	9.1
1974	147.7	11.0	54.0	9.1	147.5	15.3
1975	161.2	9.1	59.3	9.8	163.4	10.8
1976	170.5	5.8	63.1	6.4	170.6	4.4
1977	181.5	6.5	67.3	6.7	181.7	6.5
1978	195.4	7.7	72.2	7.3	195.9	7.8
1979	217.4	11.3	78.6	8.9	217.7	11.1
1980	246.8	13.5	85.7	9.0	247.0	13.5
1981	272.4	10.4	94.0	9.7	269.8	9.2
1982	289.1	6.1	100.0	6.4	280.7	4.0
1983	298.4	3.2	103.8	3.8	284.6	1.4
1984	311.1	4.3	108.1	4.1	290.3	2.0
1985	322.2	3.6	111.7	3.3	291.9	0.6

Source: U.S Bureau of Economic Analysis, *Survey of Current Business*, selected issues.

4.2 percent greater than in 1967. Furthermore, in 1969 the *CPI* was 109.8, a 5.4 percent increase from 1968 [(109.8 − 104.2)/104.2 × 100].

The numbers in the second column of Table 3.5.2 represent the percentage change in the *CPI* from one year to the next, those in the fourth column the percentage change in the *GNP-PD* for each year, and those in the sixth column the percentage change in the *PPI*. As measures of inflation, these three columns indicate how the price level in the economy has changed over time. Note that in years with relatively high rates of inflation, from 1974 to 1981, the percentage change in the *CPI* is consistently greater than the percentage change in the *GNP-PD*, in part because energy prices increased relatively faster than other prices. Even though consumers reduced energy purchases, the *CPI* assumes they purchased the same quantity. Thus, the rate of inflation is overstated by the *CPI* for these years.

THE EFFECTS OF INFLATION

To begin a discussion of the effects of inflation, let's consider the case of pure inflation. **Pure inflation** is an equal proportional increase in all nominal values in the economy. This means that nominal prices, nominal wages and income, and the nominal amount of money in the economy all increase by the same relative amounts. For example, if prices increase by 10 percent, then wages and income increase by 10 percent, and the amount of money in the economy also increases by 10 percent. Furthermore, the prices of all goods and services, including factors of production, also increase by 10 percent.

Pure inflation gives us an important benchmark for comparison with inflation that is not quite so pure. Note that this idealized, pure inflation has no actual effect on the economy, because although prices are 10 percent higher, consumers also have 10 percent more income. Consumers can buy exactly the same quantities of goods and services after the increase in prices as before.

As long as *all* prices and nominal values in the economy increase proportionally, inflation does not affect the economy. Unfortunately, in the real world this seldom occurs. Usually, the price of one good increases more than the price of another good, or the nominal value of one item does not increase as much as the nominal value of another item. If inflation is not pure, then two basic types of problems are created. The first is a distribution effect that transfers existing wealth, real output, or resources among members of the economy. The second is a production effect that reduces the total quantity of real output in the economy.

Distribution Effect

Inflation can lead to a redistribution of existing wealth, real output, or resources among members of the economy, if all prices and/or nominal values do not increase proportionally. Let's first see what happens if prices do not increase proportionally.

Different Increases in the Prices of Goods To illustrate this effect, let's take a simple example. Suppose that an economy produces only two goods, timber and wheat, and each good comprises 50 percent of real GNP. Assume that labor is the only factor used to produce each good, and that it is relatively specialized, such that it cannot switch from the production of one good to the other. If the price of wheat increases by 10 percent each year, and the price of timber increases by 20 percent, the total revenue received by wheat producers also increases by 10 percent each year, while the revenue received by timber producers increases by 20 percent. But the revenue received by the producers goes to pay the factors of production, which in this case is labor. Therefore, the labor used to produce wheat receives 10 percent more income each year, and the labor used to produce timber receives 20 percent more income.

Table 3.5.3 illustrates the redistribution of income between labor for two years. In year 1 the price of timber and wheat are both equal to $100. Moreover, the real quantity of output by both is equal to 5, meaning that the labor used to produce timber receives $500 in total income, the same as the income received by the labor used to produce wheat. In short, both types of labor receive exactly 50 percent of the total income in the economy.

In year 2 the price of timber increases by 20 percent to $120, while the price of wheat increases by only 10 percent to $110. Since there are no changes in real output, the quantity of timber and wheat produced remains at 5. With the higher prices the income received by the timber labor increases to $600, while income received by the wheat labor increases to only $550. Note that the two types of labor no longer receive an equal share of the economy's total income. Timber labor now receives 52 percent, and wheat labor 48 percent.

Wheat labor is losing out because it receives only 10 percent more income, although the average price level in the economy has increased by 15 percent. Wheat labor is not able to buy the same goods and services after prices rise as they could

Table 3.5.3

Different Price Increases and the Distribution of Income

If the prices of goods increase at different rates, then income earned by factors producing the goods also increases at different rates. Here, the price of timber increases relatively more than the price of wheat, indicating a redistribution of income in favor of labor producing timber.

		Timber				Wheat			
Year	Price	Quantity of Output	Income	Percentage of Income	Price	Quantity of Output	Income	Percentage of Income	Total Income
1	$100	5	$500	50	$100	5	$500	50	$1000
2	120	5	600	52	110	5	550	48	1500

before. By contrast, timber labor is doing a lot better, because while average prices have risen by 15 percent, they are receiving 20 percent more income.

During the 1970s the prices of health care, real estate, and petroleum increased faster than the overall price level, meaning there was a redistribution of income toward factors of production in these industries. But the prices of higher education and agricultural products increased more slowly than the overall price level, leading to a redistribution away from these factors.

Different Increases in the Value of Assets Inflation can also lead to a redistribution of the economy's income and wealth if the value of assets does not increase proportionally. One of the major problems associated with inflation is that all nominal values do not increase proportionally. In particular, the value of financial assets typically increases less than the value of physical assets. Real assets include real estate, gold, silver, gems, works of art, and many other types of commodities used by people to store their wealth. Financial assets include money, savings deposits, and corporate bonds. The basic difference between physical and financial assets is that the quantity of a financial asset is tied to the monetary unit. For example, a $5 bill or a $500 deposit at the bank are stated in terms of the monetary unit (dollars), whereas the quantity of a physical asset is stated in terms of a physical unit, such as acres of land. Thus, the value of the asset depends on both the quantity and the market price.

This difference is crucial, because prices of physical assets are part of the overall price level. With inflation, the value of physical assets increase, but the value of financial assets do not. If inflation is 10 percent, the price of an acre of land increases from $1000 to $1100. However, a $5 bill does not become worth $5.50.

To see how wealth can be redistributed from inflation, let's look at a simple example in which all the wealth in the economy is held by two people, one in the form of money, and the other in land. Assume that both have the same amount of wealth, equal to $100, in the first year, giving each 50 percent of the economy's wealth. This is shown in the first row of Table 3.5.4.

If inflation is 10 percent, the price and value of land increases from $100 to $110 in the second year, which gives the landlord a total wealth of

Table 3.5.4

Different Value Increases and the Distribution of Wealth

A redistribution of wealth can occur if physical assets increase in value along with inflation but financial assets (especially money) do not. In this example the value of land increases with the price level, while the value of money does not. This leads to a redistribution of wealth in favor of the landowner.

Year	Banker		Landowner		Total Wealth
	Money	Percentage of Wealth	Land	Percentage of Wealth	
1	$100	50	$100	50	$200
2	100	48	110	52	210

$110. But since the value of money does not increase, the banker still has $100 of wealth. The total financial wealth in the economy increases to $210, with the banker holding 48 percent and the landlord holding 52 percent, but there has been a redistribution of wealth from the banker (holding the financial asset) to the landlord (holding the physical asset). This is one reason why many people invest in gold, silver, and other physical assets when the rate of inflation is high.

There is a way to avoid this redistribution of wealth. In Table 3.5.4 there would be no redistribution of wealth if the banker could also increase the value of the nominal asset to $110 in the second year. While there is very little that can be done for someone holding currency, if the nominal asset is an interest-paying financial asset, its value can be increased to $110. That is, if the person holding the nominal asset receives a 10 percent interest payment, then its value in the second year increases to $110, and there is no redistribution of wealth.

Let's also consider the function of an interest payment. People receive an interest payment as an incentive to forego current consumption. In other words, people give up $100 worth of goods and services today only if they can have *more* than $100 worth of goods and services at some time in the future. With inflation, the payment for sacrificing current consumption becomes even more important. Not only is payment needed to forego current consumption, but an additional payment is needed to compensate for the loss of purchasing power. In Table 3.5.4 the necessary compensation for the loss of purchasing power is equal to 10 percent, which is the rate of inflation. Therefore, if people are willing to loan funds for a 5 percent interest rate with *no* inflation, they would be willing to loan the same funds for 15 percent if inflation were 10 percent.

This points out an important difference between the nominal interest rate and the real interest rate. The **nominal interest rate** is the interest rate actually paid for borrowed funds, in current prices, and is the interest rate observed in the economy. If you agree to pay 15 percent to a bank for a new car loan, the nominal interest rate is 15 percent. The **real interest rate** is the difference between the nominal interest rate and the rate of inflation. For example, if the rate of inflation is 10 percent, then the real interest rate on the 15 percent new car loan is only 5 percent. The real interest rate reflects the purchasing power of the interest income received. If the real interest rate is 5 percent, then the bank receives 5 percent in additional purchasing power when the loan is repaid.

Production Effect

The second type of effect that can be caused by inflation in the economy is a reduction in the overall production of goods and services. If the economy does not have pure inflation of all prices and nominal values, then real output in the economy is likely to decline due to increases in transaction costs.

Once again, let's consider how inflation affects the purchasing power of money. Since most money, especially currency and checking accounts, consists of financial assets that do not receive interest payments, the amount of real output that can be purchased with a given amount of money declines as the price level increases. Therefore, people find it worthwhile to hold as little money, for as short a period of time, as possible. The alternatives to holding money are buying commodities whose values rise with inflation or transferring funds to interest-paying financial assets whose nominal interest rate is adjusted for the rate of inflation.

Since buying final goods and services represents the ultimate use of money, one alternative is simply to spend the money on these commodities. Because many goods and services are perishable, this often entails making purchases more frequently. In essence, people tend to go to the grocery store more often to buy goods and services before prices rise. But these more frequent trips are not free. Resources that could be used to produce goods and services are being used in the exchange of goods and services in the form of transaction costs, and so the overall level of production declines.

Transaction costs also become important when people hold financial or real assets instead of money. If people try to preserve their purchasing power by shifting their wealth between money and interest-paying financial assets (such as money market certificates, savings accounts, or bonds), then they also incur transaction costs, including brokerage fees and the time and effort needed to visit the bank. The transaction costs for exchanging between money and real assets (such as land, jewelry, or works of art) are usually even more pronounced than the costs of exchanging between money and financial assets. But in either case resources that could be used to produce goods and services are being used for transactions, and the overall level of output is less.

IN SUMMARY

Inflation

- Inflation is a continuous increase in the price level.

- The three most common measures of the price level are the consumer price index (*CPI*), the *GNP* price deflator (*GNP-PD*), and the producer price index (*PPI*). The *CPI* measures the price level in urban areas. While it is the most common measure, it is limited because it excludes rural areas and is based on goods and services purchased in 1967. The *GNP-PD* avoids these two limitations because it is based on the ratio of nominal *GNP* to real *GNP* and thus includes all final goods and services currently produced. However, it is available less frequently than the *CPI* and therefore is less used. The *PPI* is based on the raw materials and intermediate goods purchased by producers. While this is not a measure of the economy's price level, it does foreshadow changes in the price level by keeping track of changes in the costs of production.

- Inflation affects the economy adversely in two ways, the redistribution of income and wealth and the reduction of production. Both effects occur because inflation is not pure, meaning all nominal values in the economy do not change proportionally. The distribution effect occurs because prices of different goods increase at different rates or because the value of physical assets increases while the value of financial assets does not. The production effect occurs because resources are used in transferring wealth from one asset to another rather than in producing output.

QUESTIONS FOR STUDY AND ANALYSIS

1. Under what circumstances would the consumer price index overstate the actual price level and thus the rate of inflation in the economy? Under what circumstances would the CPI understate the price level and rate of inflation?

2. What are the adverse effects of pure inflation? Explain.

3. If the rate of inflation is 15 percent, what is the real interest rate on funds borrowed at 18 percent? What is the real interest rate on a savings account that pays $5\frac{1}{4}$ percent?

4. In the 1970s the rate of inflation was as high as 18 percent, and was over 10 percent for several years. In the early 1980s the rate of inflation was less than 5 percent. In light of this, explain why the price of gold was high in the 1970s but declined throughout the first half of the 1980s.

5. How might the widespread use of computers and computer shopping reduce the adverse consequences of the production effect? Explain.

REVIEW GLOSSARY

consumer price index (*CPI*) An index of the prices of goods and services purchased by families in urban areas. The *CPI* is the most common measure of the price level and inflation. It is limited because it is based only on the goods and services purchased by urban families in 1967.

***GNP* price deflator (*GNP-PD*)** A price index computed from the ratio of nominal *GNP* to real *GNP*. Since the *GNP-PD* is based on gross national product, it is based on all final goods and services currently produced in the economy, thus avoiding limitations of the *CPI*. However, while the *CPI* is available every month, the *GNP-PD* is only available once every three months.

inflation An increase in the average price level.

nominal interest rate The interest rate actually paid on borrowed funds.

price level The average of all prices of goods and services in the economy.

producer price index (*PPI*) A price index based on the prices of selected raw materials and intermediate goods purchased by producers. While the *PPI* is not a measure of the economy's price level, it typically indicates whether the price level is likely to rise or fall in the near future.

pure inflation An equal proportional increase in all nominal values in the economy. With pure inflation there are no distribution or production effects.

real interest rate The purchasing power of the nominal interest rate. The real interest rate can be found by subtracting the rate of inflation from the nominal interest rate.

UNIT 3.6

The Aggregate Market

The circular flow introduced in Unit 3.1 gives us a simple, descriptive view of the economy. In this unit we move beyond a description and attempt to explain the operation of the economy by examining the aggregate market. The **aggregate market** is the combined product markets for all final goods and services produced in the economy. In terms of the circular flow, the aggregate market constitutes the upper loop connecting national product and the four expenditures on national product: consumption, investment, government purchases, and net exports.

We study the aggregate market for final goods and services much like we studied any market in Section 2. We begin with the demand side of the market, or more appropriately, the aggregate demand for output. We see why the aggregate demand curve has a negative slope. To complete the aggregate market, we examine the aggregate supply of final goods and services, and we identify the shape of the aggregate supply curve. We then focus on the operation of the aggregate market to see how the price level and production of final goods and services is determined.

AGGREGATE DEMAND

Let's begin with aggregate demand. **Aggregate demand** is the total demand by the household, business, government, and foreign sectors for final goods and services produced in the economy, at alternative price levels. The aggregate demand indicates the aggregate expenditures of all four sectors for national product. However, an essential feature of aggregate demand is how aggregate expenditures are affected by changes in the price level, the average level of prices in the economy.

Aggregate demand and aggregate expenditures are closely related, but with an important difference. Aggregate expenditures comprise the total expenditures by all four sectors on final goods and services, while aggregate demand comprises the expenditures on final goods and services at alternative price levels. Thus, aggregate demand considers the economy's price level, or more appropriately, changes in the price level; aggregate expenditures does not.

The relationship between aggregate expenditures and price level is shown by the aggregate demand curve. The **aggregate demand curve** is a curve representing the relationship between aggregate demand for final goods and services and the average price level. Figure 3.6.1 presents an aggregate demand curve, which looks much like the demand curves for any of the products discussed in Section 2. Let's look at the similarities and differences between the aggregate demand curve in this figure and the demand curve for a single product.

First, note the labels on each axis. The horizontal axis in Figure 3.6.1 measures the total quantity of final goods and services produced in the economy, or real *GNP*, whereas the demand curves in Section 2 were concerned only with the quantity of a single product. Furthermore, instead of the price of a single product on the vertical axis, we are measuring the overall price level in the economy, or the *GNP* price deflator as introduced in Unit 3.2.

Second, note the negative slope of the aggregate demand curve. Remember that demand curve for a single good is negatively sloped for two basic reasons. One, higher prices mean a consumer can afford to buy a smaller quantity with the same amount of income (income effect). Two, as the price of one good increases relative to the price of substitute goods, consumers buy more of the substitute goods (substitution effect). But the negative slope of the aggregate demand curve is fundamentally different from the negative slope of a single

> **Figure 3.6.1**
>
> **The Aggregate Demand Curve**
>
> The aggregate demand curve depicts the relationship between the average price level (*GNP* price deflator) in the economy and aggregate expenditures for real *GNP*. The aggregate demand curve has a negative slope resulting from the real balance and interest rate effects. If the price level increases, consumption and investment expenditures on real *GNP* decline because of limited financial wealth (real balance effect) and higher interest rates (interest rate effect).

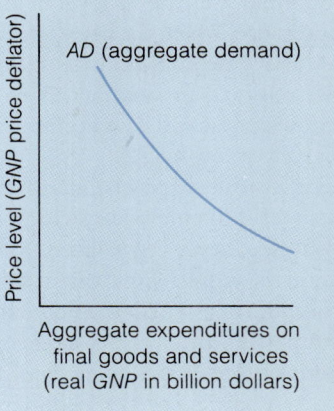

afford to buy fewer goods and services, so that consumption expenditures on real *GNP* decline. Thus, the economy's limited financial wealth acts to constrain consumption expenditures when the price level rises. On the surface limited financial wealth plays a similar constraining role with the aggregate demand curve that individuals' income plays with the demand for a single good. However, keep in mind that income (the flow of revenue received by a household in a given period of time) is fundamentally different from financial wealth (the overall stock of financial assets that accumulate up to a point in time).

A second basic reason for the negative slope of the aggregate demand curve is the interest rate effect. The **interest rate effect** is the change in consumption and investment expenditures caused by a change in the interest rate. The interest rate effect occurs because a change in the price level generally leads to a change in the interest rate, which is also related to limited financial wealth. Since limited financial wealth means households cannot purchase as much output with higher prices as they did with lower prices, the only way they can continue purchasing the same output is to borrow funds or to buy on credit. However, a greater demand for borrowed funds causes the interest rate to increase, which results in a reduction in both investment and consumption expenditures. For example, households buy durable goods, such as automobiles, furniture, and appliances, with borrowed funds. An increase in the interest rate increases the overall cost of buying these goods, and thus reduces the amount purchased. Businesses also depend on borrowed funds for investment expenditures, so if the interest rate increases, the overall cost of building a factory or buying a piece of equipment also increases, leading to a reduction in the amount purchased. In short, an increase in the interest rate, caused by a higher price level, decreases the aggregate expenditures of both households and businesses.

Although the interest rate and real balance effects play the most important roles in the negative slope of the aggregate demand curve, there is

good in that it is based on the real balance effect and the interest rate effect.

The **real balance effect** is the change in consumption expenditures caused by a change in the purchasing power of financial wealth (real balance). An increase in the price level causes a decline in the real value of households' financial wealth, including money, savings accounts, and other financial assets that can be used directly to buy output or easily converted to assets that can. With the same amount of financial wealth, especially money, a higher price level means households can also a minor substitution effect, similar to the substitution effect for a single good. Since the aggregate demand curve deals with *all* goods and services produced by the domestic economy, the only possible substitute goods come from the foreign sector. A change in the price level in the economy relative to changes in price levels in other countries, will likely lead to substitution between domestic production and imports. If the price level of domestically produced goods in the economy increases, then goods produced in other countries become relatively cheaper, and relatively more imports will be purchased by the three domestic sectors. Moreover, the higher price of domestic production leads to fewer exports to the foreign sector. But if the price level in the economy declines, then we are likely to see fewer imports and even more exports. In short, a higher price level on the aggregate demand curve indicates a decline in net exports, and in aggregate expenditures; a lower price level has the opposite effect.

AGGREGATE SUPPLY

In our discussions of macroeconomics throughout Section 3, we have been concerned almost exclusively with aggregate expenditures on national product. However, to complete our examination of the aggregate market, we now turn our attention to the aggregate supply of output in the economy. **Aggregate supply** is the total amount of final goods and services produced in the economy, at alternative price levels. Aggregate supply reflects the ability of the economy to produce final goods and services with the available factors of production. The best way to discuss aggregate supply is to introduce the aggregate supply curve. The **aggregate supply curve** is a curve depicting the relationship between the average price level and the quantity of final goods and services produced in the economy. Figure 3.6.2 shows an aggregate supply curve. While the aggregate supply curve generally slopes upward like the supply curve for a single product, it has three segments with distinctly different slopes.

In Figure 3.6.2 the **Keynesian range** is the horizontal segment of the aggregate supply curve, up to the quantity Y_1 of real GNP. In the Keynesian range the supply of output can be increased without changes in the average price level in the economy, which remains at P_1. Furthermore, a reduction in output in this range is not associated with a reduction in the price level. The **intermediate range** is the positively sloped segment of the aggregate supply curve, between Y_1 and Y_2 in the figure. Over this segment an increase in the supply of output leads to an increase in the average price level in the economy. Moreover, a reduction in output in this range leads to a reduction in the price level. Finally, at the Y_2 level of production is the **classical range,** where the aggregate supply curve is vertical, above P_2. In this range it is not possible to increase national production. Any attempt to produce more output will cause only an increase in the average price level.

The key to the shape of the aggregate supply curve rests with full employment in the economy. For the aggregate supply curve given in Figure 3.6.2 the economy is at full employment when it produces Y_2 output. In essence, the economy is on the production possibilities frontier at this point. **Full employment output** is the quantity of final goods and services produced by the economy when all factors of production are engaged in production, which occurs when unemployment is about 5 percent.

Since Y_2 is based on full employment in the economy, if the economy produces less than Y_2, there must be unemployment. This is especially true in the Keynesian range of the aggregate supply curve. The economy can easily increase national production up to Y_1 by drawing on the unemployed factors of production. A firm can increase production by hiring unemployed factors at the going factor costs, but it does not need to raise the price of its product, and the average price level in the economy does not change. We should also note that a reduction in output in the Keynesian range does not lead to a decline in the price level, either. Due to contractual arrangements with buyers and resource

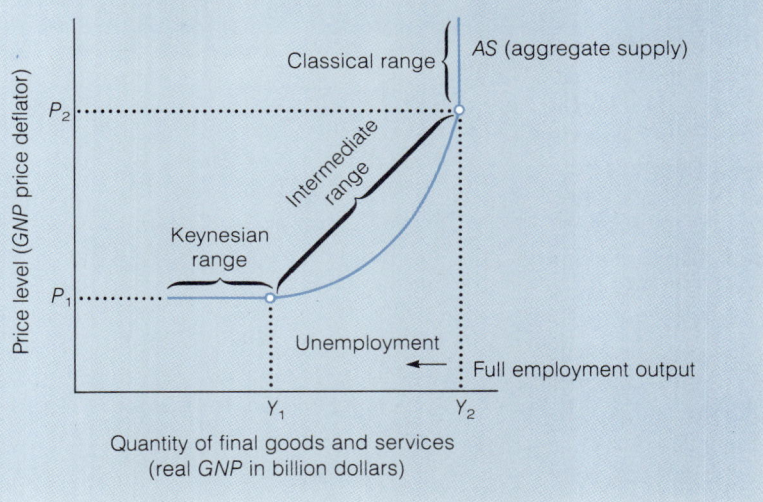

Figure 3.6.2

The Aggregate Supply Curve

The aggregate supply curve depicts the relationship between the average price level in the economy and the production of final goods and services (real *GNP*). The aggregate supply curve has three distinct ranges: Keynesian, intermediate, and classical. The Keynesian range is horizontal, the intermediate range is positively sloped, and the classical range is vertical at the full employment level of real *GNP*.

suppliers, firms are more likely to temporarily reduce output than to reduce their prices. In particular, labor (especially unionized labor) is more willing to accept temporary unemployment associated with a reduction in output than the reduction in wages necessary to maintain full employment. The inflexibility of wages and prices in the Keynesian range underlies our discussion of Keynesian economics throughout Section 4.

Let's return to the classical range and full employment. If all factors are fully employed in the production of Y_2, then any attempt to increase output will only lead to increases in the price level. A firm that wants to increase output must hire factors of production that are currently employed by another firm. To accomplish this, the firm must pay the factors higher prices, and subsequently raise the price of its product to cover the extra costs. Since firms are merely bidding factors away from one another, there is no net increase in national production, but the prices charged by each firm are higher, and thus the average price level in the economy is higher.

Now let's look at the positively sloped intermediate range of the aggregate supply curve between Y_1 and Y_2. Over this range of output the entire economy is not yet in full employment, but many industries are. If firms in these industries try to increase production, they must hire currently employed factors at higher prices, forcing the firms to charge higher prices, and leading to an increase in the overall price level. But since some industries are operating below full employment, it is still possible to increase the supply of output. Along this segment the economy is nearing full employment, and thus begins to feel upward pressures on the price level.

THE AGGREGATE MARKET

The combination of the aggregate demand and aggregate supply curves forms the aggregate market. The aggregate market determines two important variables in the economy, the quantity of output produced (or real *GNP*) and the average price level. Let's take a look at Figure 3.6.3 to see how the aggregate market operates.

The equilibrium level of national production is given by the intersection of the *AD* and *AS* curves, point E at price level P_e and quantity Y_e. At P_e the four sectors in the economy want to buy Y_e quantity of goods and services, and firms want to produce Y_e output. At a price above P_e, the amount demanded is less than the amount supplied; at a price lower than P_e, the amount demanded is greater than the amount supplied.

As with the markets discussed in Section 2, if the price is above P_e, suppliers are unable to sell all of their output, so they lower their prices. As the price level in the economy falls, aggregate expenditures on real *GNP* increase due to the real balance and interest rate effects, causing a movement down the *AD* curve toward equilibrium point E. If the price is below P_e, this mechanism operates in the opposite direction. The price level rises because the demand is greater than the supply. The higher price means aggregate expenditures on real *GNP* decline and the economy moves up the *AD* curve toward equilibrium point E.

The most important feature of the aggregate market is not how it achieves equilibrium, but the fact that the equilibrium can be achieved at *any point* on the *AS* curve. In Figure 3.6.3 the intersection just happens to occur at Y_e, the full employ-

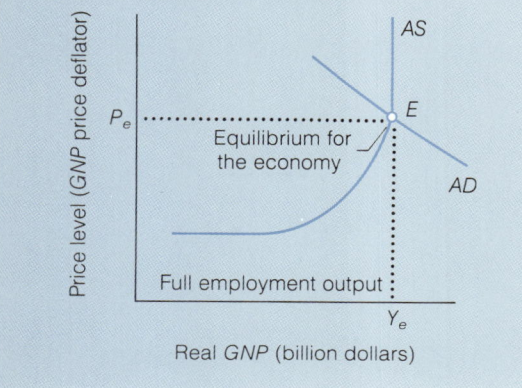

Figure 3.6.3
The Aggregate Market

The aggregate market is the combined product markets for all final goods and services. It can be used to identify the equilibrium level of real *GNP* by identifying the intersection of the aggregate demand and aggregate supply curves (point E). As with any market, if demand is not equal to supply, then the market is not in equilibrium. With the aggregate market the average price level in the economy adjusts to equate aggregate demand with aggregate supply.

ment level of output, and P_e, the lowest price level that can be achieved at the full employment level of output. However, if the intersection of the *AD* and *AS* curves occurs at a lower price level, then production is less than Y_e, and the economy has unemployment.

Figure 3.6.4 illustrates several other possible equilibria for the economy. If aggregate demand is AD', and intersects the *AS* curve in the horizontal segment of the Keynesian range, then the economy produces Y_1 output at price level P_1. The significance of equilibrium E' is that some of the factors of production are unemployed, so the economy is producing below the full employment level of output. However, since this is an equilibrium for the

UNIT 3.6 ■ THE AGGREGATE MARKET

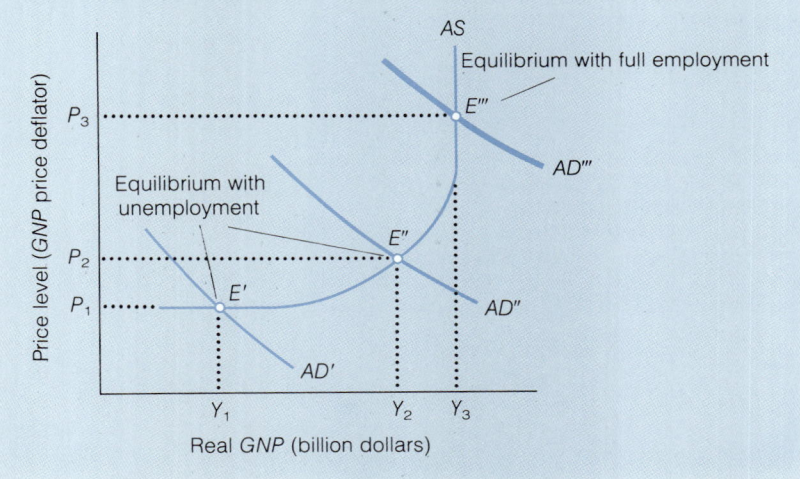

Figure 3.6.4

Alternative Equilibria in the Aggregate Market

The aggregate market can be in equilibrium in any range of the aggregate supply curve. At point E, the aggregate demand curve intersects the aggregate supply curve in its horizontal, Keynesian range, meaning real GNP is below the full employment level of output, and the economy has unemployment. If the intersection takes place in the intermediate range at point E'', the economy still has unemployment, but now there are inflationary pressures on the price level. If the intersection is in the classical range at point E''', the economy is at full employment, but there are inflationary pressures.

aggregate market, the economy will continue to produce Y_1, with the accompanying unemployment, until either the AD or AS curve shifts to a new location.

The equilibrium given by the intersection of AD'' and AS is a second possibility. At E'' the economy is still producing below the full employment level of output at Y_2, in the intermediate range, yet there is upward pressure on the price level. If the aggregate demand is AD'', the economy is beginning to feel constraints on its production capacity, as some industries are operating at full employment.

If the economy's aggregate demand is AD''', and thus intersects the AS curve in the vertical segment, or classical range, then the price level is P_3 and the quantity of production is Y_3, full employment output. However, this level of output is being produced at a price level higher than needed.

SHOCKS TO THE AGGREGATE MARKET

In the same way that the demand and supply curves in the market for a single good can shift because of changes in the determinants, the aggregate demand and aggregate supply curves can also shift. In subsequent units we will examine some of the specific reasons for shifts in each curve; here, let's see how the shifts affect aggregate production and the price level.

Shifts in the Aggregate Demand Curve

Shifts in the aggregate demand curve have a different effect on the economy in different ranges of the aggregate supply curve. Figure 3.6.5 illustrates three alternative shifts in the AD curve. In the first case the AD curve shifts between AD_1 and AD_1'. Since the AD curve is in the Keynesian range of the AS curve, output either increases or decreases (depending on the direction of the shift in the AD curve), but the price level does not change. Remember that changes in aggregate demand in the Keynesian range lead to changes in production but not in the price level.

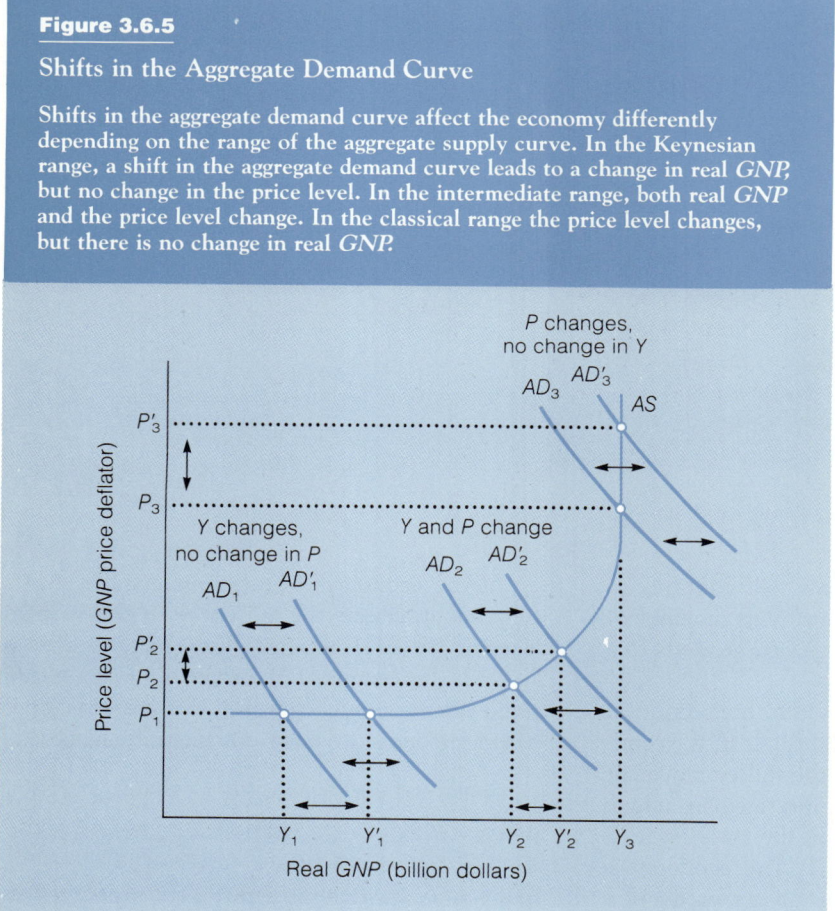

Figure 3.6.5

Shifts in the Aggregate Demand Curve

Shifts in the aggregate demand curve affect the economy differently depending on the range of the aggregate supply curve. In the Keynesian range, a shift in the aggregate demand curve leads to a change in real GNP, but no change in the price level. In the intermediate range, both real GNP and the price level change. In the classical range the price level changes, but there is no change in real GNP.

However, this is not the case for the second alternative presented in Figure 3.6.5. If the AD curve shifts between AD_2 and AD_2', the quantity of output changes between Y_2 and Y_2', but the price level also changes between P_2 and P_2'. Since the AD curve is in the intermediate range of the AS curve, changes in aggregate demand lead to changes in both price level and output.

The third alternative is given by the shift of the AD curve between AD_3 and AD_3'. While the quantity produced remains at Y_3, the price level changes between P_3 and P_3'. Since Y_3 represents full employment output, production does not change. Changes in aggregate demand in the classical range of the AS curve lead to changes in the price level, but not output.

Shifts in the Aggregate Supply Curve

Because of its distinct segments, the AS curve can have two basic types of shifts. Figure 3.6.6 illustrates the first type, a shift in the Keynesian range, without a change in full employment output and the classical range. If the AD curve intersects the AS curve in the Keynesian or intermediate ranges, then price level and output both change, but in opposite directions. This situation is illustrated by the shift in the AS curve if the aggregate demand curve is AD.

However, if the AD curve intersects the AS curve in the classical range, then the economy is not affected. For the AD' curve the shift in the AS curve leads to the same price level and quantity of output as before the shift. This happens because the shift of the AS curve does not affect the full employment level of output. If this full employment level of output is reduced, then the price level and quantity of production also change.

A second type of shift in the AS curve is illustrated in Figure 3.6.7. In this case the full employment level of output changes and the classical range shifts, but the Keynesian range does not. If

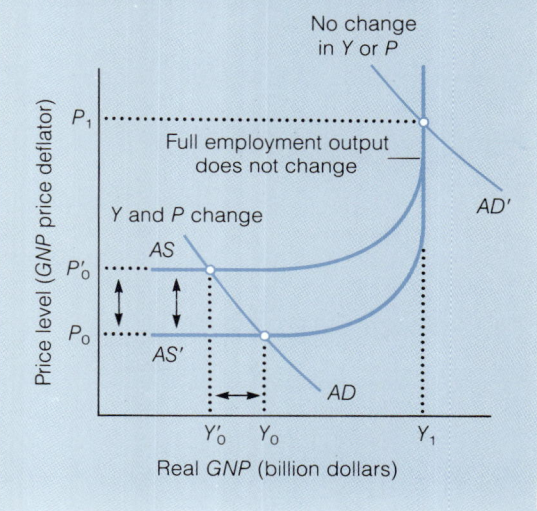

Figure 3.6.6

An Upward Shift in the Aggregate Supply Curve

An upward shift in the aggregate supply curve affects the economy differently depending on the relative position of the aggregate demand curve. If the economy is in equilibrium in the Keynesian or intermediate ranges, then the price level increases and real GNP falls. If the equilibrium is in the classical range, then the price level and real GNP might not change.

the AD curve is in the Keynesian range, then neither output nor the price level changes. However, if the AD curve is in the classical range, then the price level and output change in opposite directions.

While we have isolated separate shifts in the Keynesian and classical ranges, in many cases both ranges shift together. However, we isolate these separate shifts, because determinants of the full employment level of output need not cause the Keynesian range to shift, and vice versa.

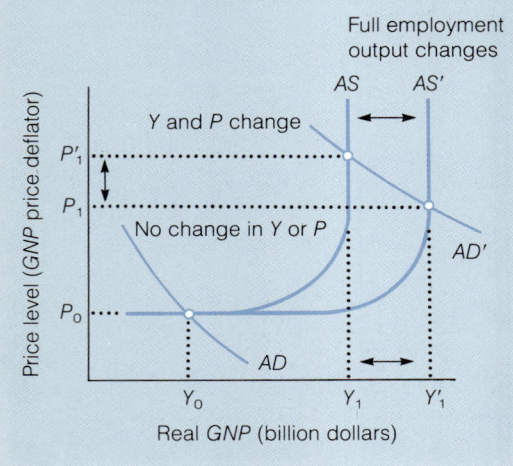

Figure 3.6.7

A Rightward Shift in the Aggregate Supply Curve

A rightward shift in the aggregate supply curve resulting from a change in the full employment level of output causes the price level to fall and real *GNP* to increase if the original equilibrium is in the classical or intermediate ranges. However, if the equilibrium is in the Keynesian range, then neither the price level nor real *GNP* changes.

IN SUMMARY

The Aggregate Market

- The aggregate market is a method of looking at the level of national production and the average price level in the economy. The aggregate market combines product markets for all final goods and services in the economy. As with the market for a single good, the aggregate market is based on demand and supply. Aggregate demand is the aggregate expenditures by all four sectors: household (consumption), business (investment), government (purchases), and foreign (net exports). Aggregate supply is based on the ability of the economy to produce output.

- Aggregate demand is aggregate expenditures on final goods and services at alternative price levels, and is embodied in the aggregate demand curve. The aggregate demand curve has a negative slope resulting from the real balance and interest rate effects, which indicate that consumption and investment expenditures decline as the price level increases.

- Aggregate supply is the total amount of final goods and services produced in the economy at alternative price levels. The aggregate supply curve, which embodies this relationship, has three distinct segments. In the horizontal, Keynesian range the economy can increase production without an increase in the price level, because factors of production are unemployed. The vertical, classical range occurs at the full employment level of output, and any attempt to increase production only leads to a higher price level. In the intermediate range between the Keynesian and classical ranges, the economy can increase national product, but the price level also increases. This occurs because some industries in the economy are at full employment output.

- The aggregate market is in equilibrium at the intersection of the aggregate demand and aggregate supply curves. The most important conclusion reached from the study of the aggregate market is that the economy can be in equilibrium in any of the three segments of the aggregate supply curve—the Keynesian, intermediate, or classical ranges—even though factors of production are unemployed.

QUESTIONS FOR STUDY AND ANALYSIS

1. Explain how the circular flow introduced in Unit 3.1 is affected if the aggregate market is

in equilibrium in the Keynesian range rather than in the classical range.

2. How are aggregate expenditures and aggregate demand related? What are the differences between the aggregate demand curve and the demand curve for a single good? Explain how aggregate expenditures are affected if the average price level in the economy decreases.

3. Under what circumstances could we have a completely vertical aggregate supply curve, with nothing but the classical range? Under what circumstances could we have a completely horizontal aggregate supply curve, with nothing but the Keynesian range? Do either of these sound plausible? Does one sound more plausible than the other? Explain.

4. If the aggregate market is in equilibrium in the Keynesian range, how is the economy affected if business firms decide to reduce investment expenditures? What would happen if the government sector decides to increase government purchases?

5. If the aggregate market is in equilibrium in the classical range, how is the economy affected if the government sector decides to increase government purchases? What would happen if the full employment level of output is reached because of a cutoff in the amount of petroleum imports?

REVIEW GLOSSARY

aggregate demand The total demand by the household, business, government, and foreign sectors for final goods and services produced in the economy, at alternative price levels.

aggregate demand curve A curve representing the relationship between aggregate demand for final goods and services and the average price level. The aggregate demand curve has a negative slope resulting from the real balance effect and the interest effect. If the price level rises, these two effects lead to a reduction in consumption and investment expenditures.

aggregate market The combined product markets for all final goods and services in the economy. The aggregate market combines the aggregate demand and aggregate supply curves to analyze equilibrium national production and the price level.

aggregate supply The total amount of final goods and services produced in the economy, at alternative price levels.

aggregate supply curve A curve representing the relationship between the average price level and the quantity of final goods and services produced in the economy. The aggregate supply curve has three distinct segments. The vertical (classical) slope occurs when all factors of production in the economy are fully employed. The positively sloped intermediate range occurs when the economy is getting close to full employment. And the horizontal (Keynesian) slope occurs when there is unemployment throughout the economy.

classical range The vertical segment of the aggregate supply curve. In this segment all factors of production are fully employed. The classical range occurs when the economy is on the production possibilities frontier.

full employment output The quantity of final goods and services produced by the economy when all factors of production are engaged in production. Full employment output occurs in the classical range of the aggregate supply curve. It is generally considered to occur when the unemployment rate is 5 percent.

interest rate effect The change in consumption and investment expenditures caused by a change in the interest rate. The interest rate effect is one reason the aggregate demand curve is negatively sloped. Changes in the price level lead to changes in the interest rate, which affects consumption and investment expenditures.

intermediate range The positively sloped segment of the aggregate supply curve. In this segment some, but not all industries, are at full employment. Therefore, national production can be increased, but the price level also increases.

Keynesian range The horizontal segment of the aggregate supply curve. In this segment factors of production are unemployed.

real balance effect The change in consumption expenditures caused by a change in the purchasing power of financial wealth (real balance). The real balance effect is one reason the aggregate demand curve is negatively sloped. Changes in the price level have an inverse effect on the real value of financial wealth, and thus on the output it can purchase.

UNIT 3.7

The Business Cycle

Our analysis of shocks to the aggregate market in the previous unit gives us an important insight into the operation of the economy. In fact, the economy is in an almost continual state of fluctuation because of shifts in either the aggregate demand curve or the aggregate supply curve. Furthermore, these fluctuations in the economy follow a relatively consistent pattern, one in which production increases, then declines, then increases once again. While the fluctuations are irregular, the consistency of expansion and decline has led these fluctuations to be termed business cycles. A **business cycle** is the pattern of expansion and contraction of economic activity.

In this unit we first look at the nature of a business cycle, a "first look" only because the fluctuation of economic activity is central to our entire study of macroeconomics. In general, if the economy is declining, factors of production are unemployed, but if the economy is expanding, the upward pressure of the price level leads to inflation.

Indeed, much of our study of macroeconomics is ultimately concerned with the unemployment or inflation associated with business cycles. After studying the nature of the business cycle and noting the historical trend in economic activity in the United States, we use the aggregate market introduced in the last unit to examine the causes underlying business cycles, and we discuss several alternative explanations for business cycles. And finally we see how unemployment and inflation are related to business cycles.

BUSINESS CYCLES

The pattern followed by business cycles can be divided into four different phases: peak, contrac-

UNIT 3.7 ▪ THE BUSINESS CYCLE

> **Figure 3.7.1**
>
> **The Phases of the Business Cycle**
>
> A business cycle is the expansion and contraction of economic activity. It can be divided into four phases: peak, contraction, trough, and expansion. The peak is the highest phase of the business cycle. In the contraction phase economic activity is declining. The trough is the lowest phase of the business cycle. And in the expansion phase economic activity is increasing.

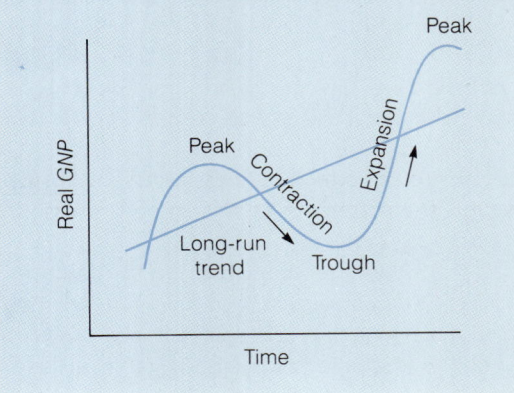

tion, trough, and expansion. Figure 3.7.1 illustrates these four phases in terms of real *GNP*. A business cycle combines the four phases, either from one peak to another, or from one trough to another.

While we can enter the business cycle in Figure 3.7.1 at any point, let's begin with the peak. The **peak** is the highest phase of the business cycle, in which the factors of production are at or near full employment. At the peak, the economy has just undergone a period of high growth. However, since it is the peak, a period of decline in the economy is also beginning.

The second phase of the business cycle is the contraction. The **contraction** is the declining phase of the business cycle, in which economic activity is falling. The contraction phase of the business cycle is commonly referred to as a recession; these two terms will be used interchangeably to refer to a decline in economic activity.

The third phase of the business cycle is the trough. The **trough** is the lowest phase of the business cycle, in which many of the factors of production are unemployed. The trough represents the turning point for the contraction, when the decline in activity has stopped and the economy is beginning the expansion phase.

The fourth phase of the business cycle is the expansion. The **expansion** is the growing phase of the business cycle, in which economic activity is increasing. In this phase the factors of production are being put back to work, and production is growing rapidly.

BUSINESS CYCLES SINCE 1919

In the real world, business cycles do not follow the rather simplified pattern shown in Figure 3.7.1. In the first place the different phases are usually of unequal duration. Each of the phases can be either short and fleeting or maintained for several years. For example, the Great Depression in the 1930s represented an extended trough, and the 1960s a period of sustained expansion.

The irregularity of business cycles in the United States is seen in Table 3.7.1, which presents the peaks and troughs of business cycles since 1919. In between the peaks and troughs are phases of expansion and contraction of differing lengths.

Note that many of the expansions and peaks in Table 3.7.1 are associated with periods of war, mainly because during wars the government increases expenditures on goods and services used in the war. As we see in Section 4, these expenditures help stimulate the economy, contributing to the expansionary phase of the business cycle. World War I, World War II, the Korean War, and the Vietnam War were all associated with expansions of economic activity. And after the wars ended, the economy typically went into a contractionary period as government purchases declined.

Table 3.7.1

Business Cycles Since 1919 (months)

The U.S. economy has experienced fourteen complete business cycles since 1919. The average length of contraction has been about 15 months, and the average length of expansion has been about 40 months. In general, a complete cycle lasts a little over four years.

Trough	Peak	Contraction (from last peak)	Expansion (from trough)	Length of Cycle Trough to Trough	Length of Cycle Peak to Peak
March 1919	January 1920	7	10	51	17
July 1921	May 1923	18	22	28	40
July 1924	October 1926	14	27	36	41
November 1927	August 1929	13	21	40	34
March 1933	May 1937	43	50	64	93
June 1938	February 1945	13	80	63	93
October 1945	November 1948	8	37	88	45
October 1949	July 1953	11	45	48	56
May 1954	August 1957	10	39	55	49
April 1958	April 1960	8	24	47	32
February 1961	December 1969	10	106	34	116
November 1970	November 1973	11	36	117	47
March 1975	January 1980	16	58	52	74
July 1980	July 1981	6	12	64	18
November 1982	NA	16	NA	28	NA
Average, all cycles:					
1919–1945 (6 cycles)		18	35	53	53
1945–1982 (8 cycles)		11	45	56	55
Average, peacetime cycles:					
1919–1945 (5 cycles)		20	26	46	45
1945–1982 (6 cycles)		11	34	46	44

Source: U.S. Bureau of the Census, *Statistical Abstract of the United States*, 1985.
NA—not applicable.

BUSINESS CYCLES AND THE AGGREGATE MARKET

A study of business cycles using the aggregate market indicates that business cycles can be caused in two ways, by changes in aggregate demand and changes in aggregate supply. A **demand-driven business cycle** is a business cycle caused by changes in aggregate demand. Most of the business cycles in Table 3.7.1 were demand-driven. However, in the 1970s we discovered that business cycles could also be caused by changes in aggregate supply. A **supply-driven business cycle** is a business cycle caused by changes in aggregate supply. In the 1970s our economy was thrown into the contractionary phase of a business cycle by increases in the prices of petroleum and agricultural products. The higher prices of these materials then caused the aggregate supply curve to shift, throwing the economy into the contractionary phase of the business cycle. Before we discuss the supply-driven business cycle, let's see how the typical demand-driven business cycle operates.

Aggregate Demand and Contraction

As before, let's enter the business cycle at a peak. Figure 3.7.2 illustrates what the aggregate market might look like at the peak of a business cycle, with AD_1 the relevant aggregate demand curve. In this case the economy is producing Y_1 real GNP, and the economy is at full employment.

However, from this peak level of full employment, activity in the economy begins to decline in the contractionary phase. This is seen as a leftward shift of the aggregate demand curve to AD_2, causing real GNP in the economy to decline to Y_2. If the contractionary phase continues, the aggregate demand curve might continue to shift to AD_3, causing real GNP to fall to Y_3. However, as real GNP moves from Y_1 toward Y_2 and Y_3, employment in the economy also declines.

What circumstances might cause the aggregate demand curve to shift leftward from AD_1? Recall that aggregate demand combines the expenditures of all four sectors: household, business, government, and foreign. Therefore, a reduction in the expenditures by any of the four sectors can cause a leftward shift, though net exports are a relatively small component of aggregate demand and probably would not shift the AD curve enough to cause the contractionary period.

However, expenditures by the three domestic sectors can cause such a contraction. For example, if the business sector decides to reduce investment expenditures on capital goods, the AD curve will shift. Firms expecting a downturn in the economy are not likely to expand the size of their factories or otherwise increase their capital stock. This expectation will likely be reflected in a downturn in the economy and a leftward shift in the AD curve.

Figure 3.7.2

Aggregate Demand and Contraction

The contractionary phase of a demand-driven business cycle is caused by leftward shifts in the aggregate demand curve, seen here as shifts from AD_1 to AD_2 to AD_3. In the contractionary phase of a demand-driven business cycle, the price level tends to fall, while unemployment increases.

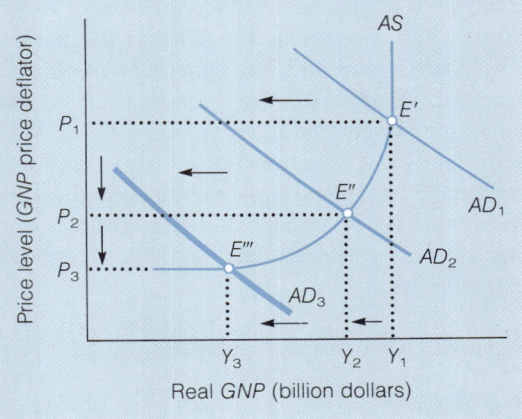

Government purchases can also provide for large leftward shifts in the AD curve. Recall that periods of war are often associated with peaks of the business cycle. However, when the war is over, the government reduces expenditures, because it no longer needs new battleships, tanks, and soldiers. Thus, the economy tends to contract at the end of wars.

If households decide to spend a smaller portion of their income, reducing consumption expenditures, the AD curve also shifts leftward. While this is a possibility, consumption expenditures are the most stable of the four expenditures, and generally one of the more stable features of the economy. Over several decades consumers have consistently spent about 90 percent of their disposable income on final goods and services.

We should mention that the amount of money circulating in the economy also affects the position of the AD curve. If there is less money available, fewer goods and services can be purchased at the existing price level. Thus, a reduction in the total amount of money in the economy can also shift the AD curve leftward and lead to a contraction.

While we have discussed each of these possible causes separately, in most recessions the AD curve shifts leftward due to a combination of factors. For example, if the amount of money in the economy is reduced, leading to a leftward shift, this might indicate to business firms that a downturn is around the corner, so the firms reduce investment expenditures. But as economic activity in the business sector falls, state and local governments may be forced to reduce spending, because their tax revenues are closely tied to economic activity. Many state and local governments are constitutionally constrained to spend only the amount that they receive in tax revenues, so if the economy contracts, their revenues decline, and so do their expenditures.

Aggregate Demand and Expansion

The expansionary phase of the business cycle can also be seen using the aggregate market. Let's start

Figure 3.7.3

Aggregate Demand and Expansion

The expansionary phase of a demand-driven business cycle is caused by rightward shifts in the aggregate demand curve, seen here as shifts from AD_3 to AD_6. In the expansionary phase of a demand-driven business cycle, the price level tends to rise, while unemployment decreases.

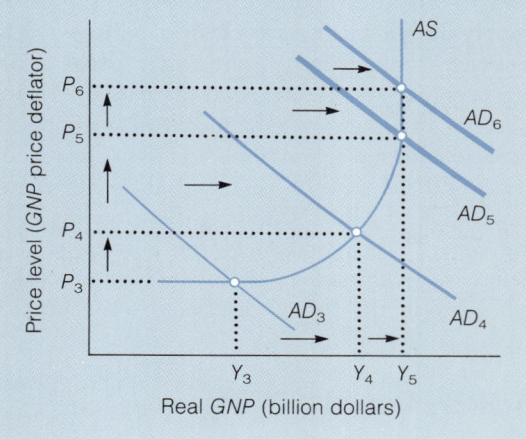

in Figure 3.7.3 where we left off in Figure 3.7.2. At aggregate demand curve AD_3, the economy has unemployment and is at the trough of the business cycle. The expansionary phase can occur if the AD curve shifts rightward to AD_4 and AD_5, and for the exact opposite reasons as for the leftward shifts. For example, business firms might increase investment expenditures, the government might increase government purchases, or the amount of money in the economy might be increased. And once again these factors often reinforce each other.

In part because of the tendency for each of these causes to reinforce one another, the AD curve often shifts "too far." In Figure 3.7.3 the ideal location of the AD curve is AD_5, where the economy has full employment output at the lowest possible price level. However, if the AD curve shifts to AD_6, the economy still produces Y_5, the full employment output, but the price level P_6 is higher.

When the expansionary phase of the economy is too strong, the AD curve continues to shift rightward and the price level continues to rise. If the price level continues to rise over time, then the economy has inflation. Inflation caused by a continuous rightward shift in the AD curve is demand-pull inflation. **Demand-pull inflation** is the inflation that is caused by increases in aggregate demand without comparable increases in aggregate supply.

Aggregate Supply and Contraction

So far we have only looked at the role aggregate demand plays in the business cycle. However, shifts in the aggregate supply curve can also contribute to business cycles. Once again, let's begin at the peak of the business cycle and see how the contractionary phase might begin, as depicted in Figure 3.7.4.

For the initial aggregate supply curve AS_1, the economy is at its peak producing the full employment output Y_1. However, if the aggregate supply curve shifts up and to the left, output is reduced to Y_2 and the price level increases to P_2. While a shift of both classical and Keynesian ranges is shown, the same results can be achieved with separate shifts of either range. Figure 3.7.4 illustrates a condition of the economy in which there is unemployment at the same time the price level is rising; this is stagflation. **Stagflation** is a condition of the economy characterized by a decline in economic activity together with inflation.

Prior to the 1970s this condition was rarely, if ever, seen in the economy. Experience indicated that higher prices were only associated with an expanding economy, and not with a contracting one. However, in the 1970s, as OPEC raised petroleum prices and curtailed shipments to the United States, business firms found they were unable to supply the same quantity of final goods and services at the same prices, since petroleum was such an important factor in the production of many goods. This caused the AS curve shift seen in Figure 3.7.4. In particular, if inflation results from a continuous upward shift of the Keynesian range of the AS curve, it is cost-push inflation. **Cost-push inflation** is the inflation that is caused by increases in factor costs without comparable increases in the production of final goods and services.

Aggregate Supply and Expansion

Shifts in the aggregate supply curve can also lead to the expansionary phase of the business cycle. Figure 3.7.5 illustrates the aggregate market when the economy is at the trough of a business cycle, with an aggregate supply curve AS_1, the price level

Figure 3.7.4

Aggregate Supply and Contraction

The contractionary phase of a supply-driven business cycle is caused by leftward/upward shifts in the aggregate supply curve, seen here as a shift from AS_1 to AS_2. In the contractionary phase of a supply-driven business cycle, both the price level and unemployment increase, resulting in stagflation.

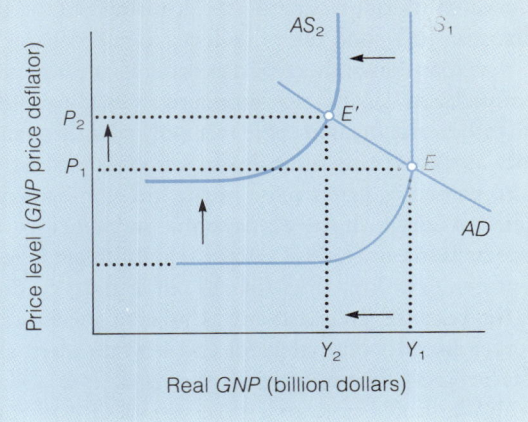

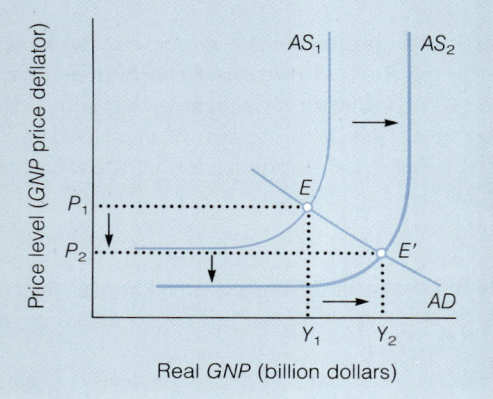

Figure 3.7.5

Aggregate Supply and Expansion

The expansionary phase of a supply-driven business cycle is caused by a rightward shift in the aggregate supply curve, seen here as a shift from AS_1 to AS_2. In the expansionary phase of a supply-driven business cycle, both the price level and unemployment decrease.

P_1, and output Y_1. Note that the output is below the full employment output for the economy. Expansion of the economy can begin if the AS curve shifts rightward to AS_2, causing output to increase to Y_2 and the price level to fall to P_2.

Expansion of this type can occur if factor prices are reduced, or if factor productivity is increased; in either case firms are able to supply a larger quantity at the existing price level. A rightward shift is also caused by an increase in the full employment level of output. If the economy has more factors of production, including labor, capital, land, or entrepreneurship, then the AS curve shifts to the right because the economy is able to produce a larger quantity of final goods and services when all factors are fully employed.

We should note that this type of shift of the AS curve might lead to the expansionary phase of the busines cycle, but it is much more important for longer-run growth of the economy. It is mentioned here as a possible cause of the expansionary phase of the business cycle. However, we devote more attention to this shift of the aggregate supply curve in Section 6, A Closer Look at Inflation, and Section 14, The World Economy.

ALTERNATIVE THEORIES OF THE BUSINESS CYCLE

Our analysis of the aggregate market, and of shifts in the aggregate demand and supply curves, indicates the mechanism underlying the business cycle. The aggregate market illustrates *how* the business cycle is generated, but it does not indicate *why* the business cycle occurs. At this point let's turn our attention to three theories designed to explain why the business cycle does occur.

Investment Expenditures: The Accelerator Theory

One of the most widely accepted theories of the business cycle is based on changes in investment expenditures. This theory suggests that the business sector follows a cyclical pattern of investment expenditures, at one time spending a great deal on capital goods, then subsequently spending very little. These changes in investment expenditures stimulate widespread changes in national production for the rest of the economy as the aggregate demand curve shifts.

But what would cause investment expenditures to follow the pattern of decreasing, increasing, decreasing, and so on needed to stimulate the contraction-expansion-contraction pattern of the business cycle? One explanation is based on the relationship between capital goods and the production of output. This theory suggests that businesses need a relatively fixed amount of capital to produce a dollar's worth of output. In the United

States we have historically needed about $3 worth of capital for every $1 of output produced, meaning a $1 increase in national production stimulates $3 worth of investment expenditures on capital goods. But since this $3 worth of capital goods are also part of national production, this stimulates $9 worth of additional investment expenditures, which then stimulates $27 worth of investment, and so on.

It is easy to see how these accelerating investment expenditures can lead to the booming economy associated with the expansionary phase. However, the expansionary phase cannot continue forever, because the economy eventually reaches the full employment level of output. If production does not increase at full employment, then the business sector does not need to continue purchasing capital goods, and investment expenditures decline from their previous levels. This decline in investment causes a leftward shift of the aggregate demand curve, as illustrated in Figure 3.7.2, and the economy enters the contractionary phase of the business cycle.

While the economy is contracting, the existing stock of capital wears out (which is the capital consumption allowance introduced in Unit 3.2). Eventually, the business sector begins to replace the worn-out capital, which creates additional national production and starts the expansionary phase of the business cycle once again. Then the economy reaches full employment, and begins to contract.

The Political Cycle

A second theory of the business cycle is based on a perception of the influence on the economy exercised by political leaders, particularly presidential administrations. This theory derives from the idea that voters tend to reelect incumbent political leaders during good economic conditions, and that political leaders are able to exert control over the economy through government purchases and the money supply.

According to this theory of the political cycle, in the year before a presidential election the incumbent administration stimulates the economy by increasing government purchases and/or the money supply, causing the aggregate demand curve to shift to the right, as in Figure 3.7.3. This sends the economy into the expansionary phase of the business cycle, and the incumbent administration hopes that the resulting low rate of unemployment and high level of national production will sway the voters at election time. Unfortunately, such actions often overstimulate the economy and lead to inflation. Therefore, after the election the government typically "bites the bullet" by reducing government purchases and the money supply, causing the aggregate demand curve to shift leftward, and sending the economy into the contractionary phase of the business cycle until the next presidential election comes around.

It is interesting to note that the average length of business cycles from peak to peak, as seen in Table 3.7.1, is about four years. Moreover, since the Second World War, with only a few exceptions, per capital real GNP has increased faster in the years before a presidential election than in the years after the election.

Sunspot Theory

While theories based on investment expenditures and political cycles to explain fluctuations in economic activity are the most commonly accepted, other theories have also been developed. One of the seemingly wildest-sounding theories is based on sunspots. However, close inspection of this theory gives it some credibility. This theory suggests that the pattern of sunspots on the sun affects weather conditions on the earth. The change in weather conditions affects the growth of agricultural crops, which subsequently affects the aggregate supply of output. If the weather is good, crops are plentiful, and the economy expands; if the weather is bad, crops fail, and the economy contracts. In many agricultural-based economies this theory has some validity, but it does not satisfactorily explain business cycles in industrialized economies such as the United States.

CYCLICAL TRENDS IN UNEMPLOYMENT AND INFLATION

Let's now turn our attention to the two major problems caused by the business cycle: unemployment and inflation. As we saw in Unit 3.4, unemployment is the condition in which some factors of production are not being used in the production of goods and services. During the contraction and trough periods of a business cycle, labor and the other factors of production are unemployed. While unemployment of nonlabor factors of production is important, at this point let's focus on the unemployment of labor.

The historical rates of unemployment in the United States are presented in Figure 3.7.6. Note the tremendous peak in the unemployment rate during the Great Depression of the 1930s, which rose to as high as 25 percent of the labor force.

After the Depression the unemployment rate fluctuated between 3 and 7 percent until the mid-1970s. In the troughs of the business cycle the unemployment rate was high, and at the peaks the

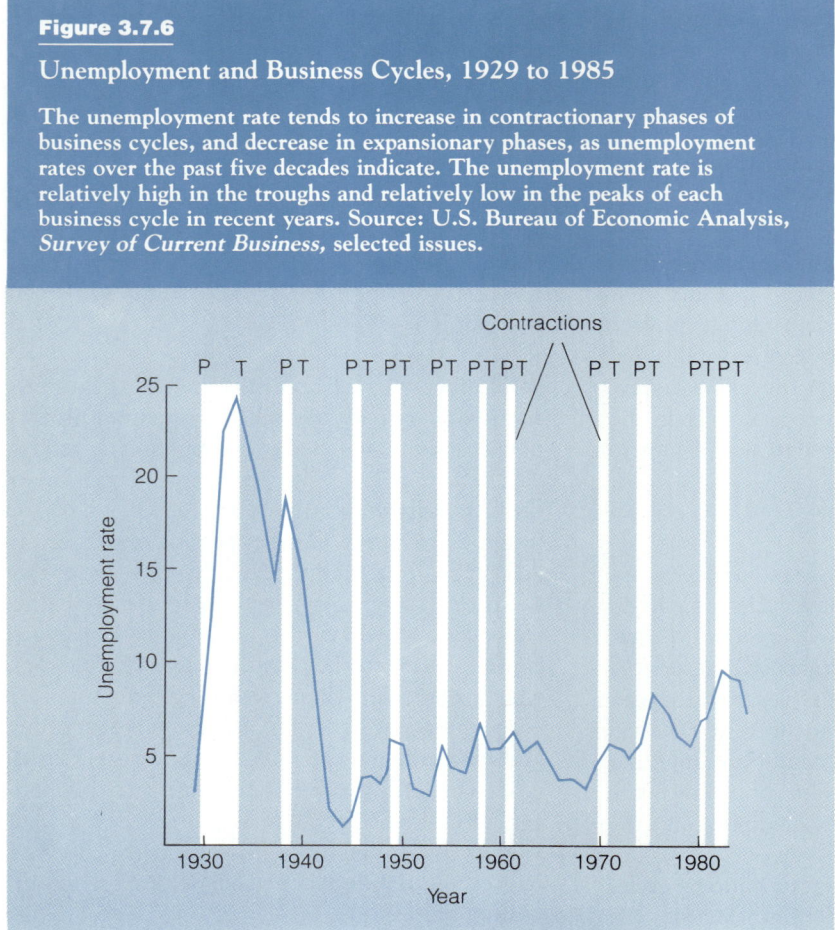

Figure 3.7.6

Unemployment and Business Cycles, 1929 to 1985

The unemployment rate tends to increase in contractionary phases of business cycles, and decrease in expansionary phases, as unemployment rates over the past five decades indicate. The unemployment rate is relatively high in the troughs and relatively low in the peaks of each business cycle in recent years. Source: U.S. Bureau of Economic Analysis, *Survey of Current Business,* selected issues.

UNIT 3.7 • THE BUSINESS CYCLE

unemployment rate was low. However, in the mid-1970s the unemployment rate jumped to 10 percent. To relate the unemployment rate to the business cycle, the official peaks and troughs from Table 3.7.1 are presented in Figure 3.7.6.

We should note that even during the peaks of a business cycle, the rate of unemployment does not fall to zero. That is, the economy always experiences some degree of unemployment. At the peaks the economy has frictional and structural unemployment, and in the troughs cyclical unemployment increases. In fact, this is exactly why it is called cyclical unemployment, because it is caused by the business cycle.

Although we will be studying inflation in detail in Section 6, let's briefly see how inflation is associated with the business cycle. While the economy has had continuous inflation since the mid-1960s, in the past there have been periods of decline in the price level. Figure 3.7.7 depicts changes in the price level, and the official peaks and troughs of business cycles, since 1930.

As you might expect, the price level had periods of continuous increase during each of the three

Figure 3.7.7

Inflation and Business Cycles, 1930 to 1985

The rate of inflation tends to be higher in the expansionary phase and peak of a business cycle, and lower in the contractionary phase and trough of a demand-driven business cycle. However, in the 1970s a supply-driven contractionary phase led to higher rates of inflation rather than lower.
Source: U.S. Bureau of Economic Analysis, *Survey of Current Business*, selected issues.

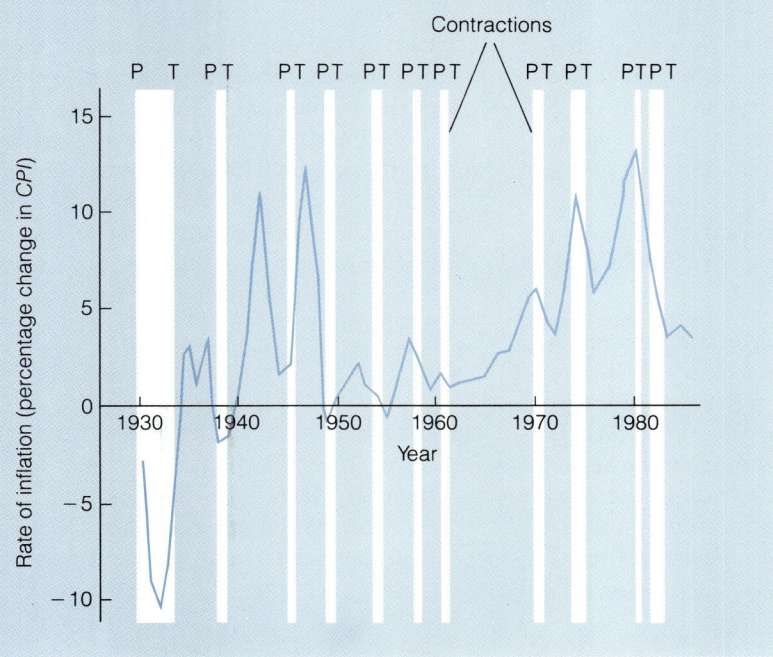

major wars since the 1930s: World War II, the Korean War, and the Vietnam War. As we saw earlier, these periods of expansion were caused, at least in part, by increases in government purchases.

However, we also see some periods of decline in the price level. One such period occurred during the Great Depression. And a second one occurred during a recession just before the Vietnam War began to intensify. These price declines were probably caused by contractions resulting from reductions in aggregate demand. However, the contractions that occurred during the 1970s, when energy prices soared and the aggregate supply curve shifted, led to an increase in the price level, and inflation.

IN SUMMARY

The Business Cycle

- Business cycles are the consistent but irregular fluctuations of economic activity, characterized by periods of expansion, then contraction, then expansion again. A business cycle can be divided into four phases. The peak is the highest point of the business cycle, in which the factors of production are at or near full employment. The contractionary phase, or recession, is a period of decline in real *GNP* and increase in unemployment. The trough is the lowest point of the business cycle, with the highest levels of unemployment. The expansionary phase is a period of increase in real *GNP* as the economy approaches the peak once again.

- The aggregate market indicates two basic causes of a business cycle, shifts in the aggregate demand curve and shifts in the aggregate supply curve. A demand-driven business cycle is seen as a series of leftward shifts in the aggregate demand curve, which leads to the contraction. This is followed by a series of rightward shifts, which leads to the expansion.

- A supply-driven business cycle is seen by an upward/leftward shift in the aggregate supply curve, leading to the contraction. A rightward/downward shift of the aggregate supply curve could then lead to an expansion. In the contractionary phase of a supply-driven business cycle, unemployment and the price level both increase. With a demand-driven business cycle, unemployment and higher prices occur in different phases.

- Two theories of the business cycle are based on accelerating investment expenditures and the political cycle. The first theory states that investment expenditures stimulate the economy, which leads to more investment and further stimulation of the economy, until the economy reaches full employment. Then investment expenditures decline, causing the economy to contract. The political cycle theory states that incumbent political leaders stimulate the economy before presidential elections in order to gain reelection, then contract the economy to do away with problems caused by the stimulation.

- Unemployment is high at the troughs of the business cycle and low at the peaks. But inflation has historically been greater in the peaks of the business cycle and less in the troughs. From time to time the price level even declines in the troughs. However, using the aggregate market we can see that demand-pull inflation, caused by increases in aggregate demand, is less in recessions, while cost-push inflation, caused by higher factor prices, is greater in recessions.

QUESTIONS FOR STUDY AND ANALYSIS

1. Business cycles have been part of the U.S economy for the past 200 years. Do you think business cycles are an inherent part of eco-

nomic activity? Explain. Ideally, if you could implement any policies or restructure the economy in any way, what would you do to eliminate business cycles? Is this a realistic possibility?

2. How do demand-driven and supply-driven business cycles differ? In terms of the components of aggregate demand, what can bring about a demand-driven business cycle? In terms of the aggregate supply curve, what needs to happen to bring about a supply-driven business cycle? Which is more likely to occur? Why?

3. During the early 1980s the price of petroleum declined from over $30 per barrel to about $15 per barrel. Explain how you would expect this to affect the economy in terms of business cycles.

4. During the first half of the 1980s the federal deficit was at an all-time high. This meant that the government was spending more on goods and services than it was taking away from consumers in taxes. Explain how you would expect this to affect the economy in terms of business cycles. If the federal government was forced to maintain a balanced budget, how would this affect the economy in terms of business cycles?

5. During the 1970s we had a very serious round of stagflation. Many people saw this as an indication that the U.S. economy was on the verge of collapse or that we were about to become a postindustrialized, second-class nation. Explain why this was in fact just another part of the business cycle. Also indicate what we can do to avoid stagflation in the future.

6. During the most recent presidential election, was the unemployment rate relatively high or relatively low? Was the economy in a contractionary or expansionary phase? Was the winner of the election a member of the incumbent political party? Explain.

REVIEW GLOSSARY

business cycle The pattern of expansion and contraction of economic activity. Business cycles are the frequent but irregular fluctuations in national production in the economy.

contraction The declining phase of the business cycle, in which economic activity is falling. In the contraction phase unemployment increases.

cost-push inflation The inflation caused by increases in factor costs without comparable increases in the production of final goods and services.

demand-driven business cycle A business cycle caused by changes in aggregate demand. Historically, business cycles in the United States are demand-driven.

demand-pull inflation The inflation that is caused by increases in aggregate demand without comparable increases in aggregate supply.

expansion The growing phase of the business cycle in which economic activity is increasing. In the expansion phase unemployment declines.

peak The highest phase of the business cycle, in which the factors of production are at or near full employment.

stagflation A condition of the economy characterized by a decline in economic activity together with inflation.

supply-driven business cycle A business cycle caused by changes in aggregate supply. The best example of a supply-driven business cycle occurred in the 1970s, when the prices of petroleum and agricultural products increased.

trough The lowest phase of the business cycle, in which many of the factors of production are unemployed.

SECTION INQUIRY

The Underground Economy

The vast majority of economic activity occurring in the economy is reflected in the various measures of output, income, and employment reported by the government. Most, but not all. A significant portion of economic activity slips through the official measures of gross national product, national income, and the unemployment rate. This activity, often termed the underground economy, has been estimated by some economists to be between 10 and 20 percent of the official *GNP* measurement. The underground economy consists of two types of activities: illegal activities, which are difficult for the government to measure for obvious reasons, and legal activities that are simply not reported to the government. The illegal activities include drugs, gambling, and prostitution. Unreported legal activities range from corporations understating profits to babysitters who fail to report wages received. A substantial fraction of the legal but unreported activities consists of the services of professionals and others who sell their output "off the books." The sales are almost always for cash (with a discounted price), and often the services are performed after normal working hours.

Many economists and policymakers believe that the underground economy has grown substantially in recent years. This growth means that official estimates of output, income, and employment are increasingly less accurate, as more economic activity goes from the "aboveground" economy to the underground economy. Moreover, while the growth of the underground economy is greater than the growth of the rest of the economy, it is generally countercyclical. When the economy is in a contractionary phase, the underground economy has its greatest growth. When the economy is in an expansionary phase, the underground economy has its lowest growth.

QUESTIONS FOR DISCUSSION

1. Explain how excluding the underground economy causes the official unemployment rate to overstate the fraction of the labor force that is actually unemployed.

2. Discuss the relationship that might exist between the underground economy and discouraged workers.

3. Discuss why the underground economy tends to be countercyclical.

4. In a demand-driven business cycle, inflation and unemployment usually occur at different times. Considering the nature of the underground economy, discuss why higher rates of inflation might begin even though officially the economy still has a relatively high rate of unemployment.

5. Since official measures of output and income are typically understated and the underground economy generally moves in the opposite direction to the phases of the business cycle, discuss why policymakers should be careful when trying to stimulate the economy out of contractionary phases or limiting the inflationary pressures in expansionary phases.

SECTION 4

Keynesian Economics

In this section we undertake the study of one of the major cornerstones of macroeconomics, Keynesian economics, named after John Maynard Keynes (1883–1946), who developed the basic theoretical framework. The Keynesian approach to the macroeconomy is particularly relevant to recessionary periods with high rates of unemployment. This is primarily because Keynes developed his theory during the Great Depression of the 1930s, when unemployment was as high as 25 percent in the United States and the economy showed few signs of emerging from a business cycle trough that lasted nearly a decade. In these circumstances, Keynes focused on the lack of aggregate demand in general and in particular the lack of investment expenditures by the business sector, which kept the economy from entering the expansionary phase. While Keynesian economics is also applicable to an economy with full employment and inflation, we should note that it presents only a partial picture and must be considered with other aspects of the economy.

Unit 4.1, An Introduction to Keynesian Economics, provides an introduction to the Keynesian view of the economy's operation. To put Keynesian economics into perspective, this unit looks at its theoretical predecessor, classical economics. By studying classical economics, we can see why Keynesian economics was developed and why it is so concerned with unemployment and recessions.

Unit 4.2, Consumption, looks more closely at the first component of aggregate demand. In particular, we see how income is divided between consumption expenditures and saving. The unit also introduces the consumption function, which illustrates the relationship between consumption and income, and which plays a central role in Keynesian economics.

Unit 4.3, Investment, examines the second major component of aggregate demand and suggests that investment expenditures planned by the business sector are not always realized. These unplanned investment expenditures, which involve changes in inventories, play an important role in guiding an economy toward equilibrium. In this unit we also discuss how income and the interest rate can affect investment expenditures.

Unit 4.4, Government Purchases and Taxes, divides the government's budget into two categories that affect aggregate demand. The first is government purchases, which directly add to the total expenditures in the economy. The second is taxes, which indirectly affect aggregate demand by changing household income and thus consumption expenditures.

Unit 4.5, Determining National Income and Output, is the first of three units that combine the components of aggregate demand and provide a basic Keynesian analysis of the operation of the economy. In particular, we see how the economy determines the level of national output by equating aggregate expenditures with the supply of output.

Unit 4.6, The Multiplier, asks a simple question: What happens to national output if aggregate expenditures change? In answering this question we see that national output usually changes by a multiple of the change in expenditures. The key concept in this unit is the multiplier, which is used to measure this effect on output when expenditures change.

Unit 4.7, Fiscal Policy Applications of Keynesian Economics, applies the concepts and relationships derived in the first six units of this section to the government's use of fiscal policy. At last we see the thrust of Keynes's approach to the economy—that the equilibrium level of output is not necessarily full employment output. In particular, we learn that full employment output can be achieved through the use of the spending and taxation powers of the government, which constitutes fiscal policy.

UNIT 4.1

An Introduction to Keynesian Economics

From the mid-1930s to the late 1970s, Keynesian economics dominated the way we viewed the macroeconomy. And though recently other economic theories have offered challenges to the Keynesian view, it is still the cornerstone in the study of macroecnomics. In Section 5, Money, and Section 6, A Closer Look at Inflation, we discuss some of these alternative theories. But first, in this unit we begin our study of the Keynesian view.

To understand why Keynesian economics is still the dominant theory of the macroeconomy, it is instructive to see why and when it was developed. So after a brief introduction to Keynesian economics, we look at classical economics, which was the prevailing economic theory before Keynes came along. We also examine the Great Depression of the 1930s, which, according to classical economics, should not have happened. The study of classical economics and the Depression sheds light not only on why Keynesian economics was developed but also on how it views the macroeconomy.

KEYNESIAN ECONOMICS

The best way to start a study of Keynesian economics is with a definition. **Keynesian economics is a body of economic thought, first developed by John Maynard Keynes, built on the idea that the aggregate expenditures on output are not necessarily equal to the economy's full employment level of output.** The basic structure of Keynesian economics was first presented in John Maynard Keynes's masterwork, entitled *The General Theory of*

Employment, Interest, and Money, published in 1936. Although the concepts and principles first introduced by Keynes have been modified over the past fifty years, the basic thrust of the theory remains the same.

According to Keynes, the economy can achieve a state of equilibrium at any level of output. In particular, the economy can achieve equilibrium at output levels less than the output produced if all factors are fully employed. Note that *The General Theory* was published in the middle of the Depression, when the United States and rest of the world were six years into the worst contractionary period, with the highest unemployment rates, in recorded history. Moreover, because in the mid-1930s there seemed to be no end to the Depression in sight, Keynes concluded that the economy had reached equilibrium at a level of output that did not require the full employment of the factors.

CLASSICAL ECONOMICS

In order to see why the proposition that the economy can be in equilibrium below the full employment level of output was so important, we need to turn our attention to classical economics. **Classical economics is a body of economic thought, originating with the pioneering work of Adam Smith, that built on the idea that freely operating markets would lead to production that always tended to the full employment level of output.** Classical economics dominated the study of the economy during the late 1700s, through the 1800s, and into the early 1900s.

The theory of classical economics was based on the relatively simple principles discussed in Section 2 underlying the operation of the market. Classical economists believed that if markets were allowed to operate freely, without government intervention, then the forces of demand and supply would lead to equilibrium in each market. This means that the labor market would also be in equilibrium, and that everyone who wanted to work at the existing wage would be able to. Therefore, no one would be involuntarily unemployed, and the economy would be at full employment. However, the key to market equilibrium, as we saw in Section 2, is the flexibility of prices. In terms of classical economics and the labor market, this also means the flexibility of wages. Let's now dig a little deeper into the principles of classical economics, which appear intuitively obvious, making it easy to see why classical economics prevailed for more than 150 years.

Say's Law

The single most important principle underlying the classical economic view of the macroeconomy was Say's law. **Say's law is a principle stating that supply creates its own demand.** According to its originator, French economist Jean Baptiste Say (1767–1832), the total amount of output produced in the economy generates an equivalent amount of demand for the output.

Let's reconsider the diagram of the circular flow of the economy, in which the production of output leads to an equivalent amount of income paid to the factors of production. But what do the factors of production do with this income? They use it to buy goods and services, which represents the main reason people work in the first place. And in the process of earning income, the factors contribute to the production of goods and services. If more output is produced, then there is more income that can be used to purchase the output. Thus, the production of output generates the income needed to buy the output.

Flexible Wages and Prices

The second principle of classical economics concerns the flexibility of wages and prices. With flexible wages and prices markets can freely adjust to a new equilibrium, which is always at full employment. Let's consider the market for a single good to see how flexible wages and prices would always move the economy back to full employment.

Figure 4.1.1 presents the market for wheat, initially in equilibrium at price P_0 and quantity Q_0.

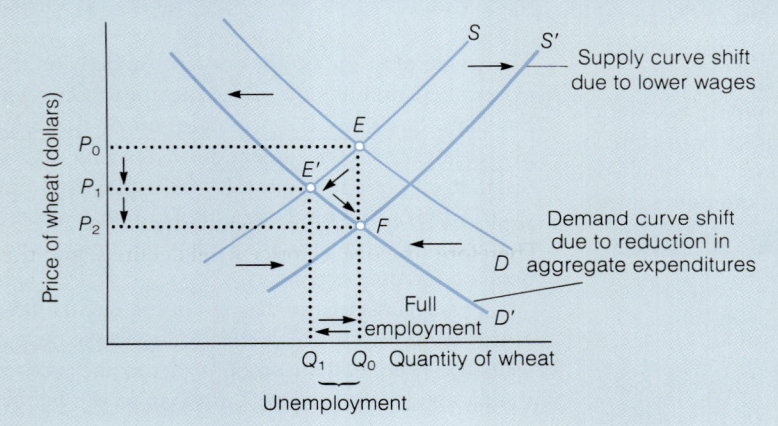

Figure 4.1.1

Full Employment and Flexible Wages and Prices

According to classical economics, flexible wages and prices will always move the economy back to full employment. For example, if the demand for a good declines, the price of the good and the quantity supplied also decline. The reduction in output leads to unemployment of labor, and the unemployed labor accepts lower wages, thus reducing the costs of production and shifting the supply curve to the right, once again achieving full employment.

This equilibrium is given by the intersection of supply curve S and demand curve D, at point E. According to classical economics, Q_0 represents full employment output for this market. But what happens to the market if demand declines, causing output to fall and unemployment to rise?

Suppose there is a decline in the export demand for wheat, seen as a shift in the demand curve from D to D'. With this shift in the demand curve the market adjusts to a new equilibrium at point E', with price P_1 and quantity Q_1. However, this quantity of wheat is less than the quantity that can be produced by fully employing all of the factors, so there is unemployment in this market. Furthermore, if all markets experience a decline in demand at the same time, which occurs during a recession, then there is unemployment throughout the economy.

According to classical economists, this would be a temporary situation, because flexible wages and prices would lead the economy back to full employment. In Figure 4.1.1, wages in the labor market adjust due to the increase in unemployment. Remember that in effect, unemployment results from a surplus in the labor market, meaning the surplus of labor causes the flexible price of labor to decline. But the price of labor is a cost of producing wheat, and when the cost of a factor of production declines, the supply curve for the product shifts, in this case from S to S'.

With the rightward shift in the supply curve, the wheat market obtains a new equilibrium at point

F, which happens to be at the quantity Q_0, full employment output. The supply curve must shift all the way down to S', which leads to equilibrium at full employment. If it shifts less than S', then unemployment remains, there is a surplus of labor, wages continue to fall, and the supply curve continues to shift.

While we have only looked at a single market so far, we can also apply this view to the entire economy. In Figure 4.1.2, using the aggregate market type of analysis presented in Unit 3.6, we see how flexible wages and prices enable the entire economy to maintain full employment. While the aggregate demand curve is identical to the one in Figure 3.6.1, the aggregate supply curve is a little different—it is a vertical line. In particular, this constitutes the classical range of the aggregate in supply curve and does not include the Keynesian range. The reason for this will be evident shortly.

With the economy in equilibrium at point E, based on the aggregate demand and aggregate supply curves AD and AS, the price level is P_0 and the amount of national product is Y_f, the full employment level of output. Let's see how the economy adjusts if it experiences unemployment resulting from a reduction in demand, seen as a leftward shift of the aggregate demand curve from AD to AD'. This shift could be caused by a reduction in any of the components of aggregate demand. At the existing price level P_0, we see that demand Y_1 is less than the full employment level of output. However, in the classical view, this situation will not persist because firms in the economy have a surplus of their output and will reduce their prices. Therefore, the overall price level declines, and the economy moves down AD' until point F is reached, at the intersection of AD' and AS.

Note that flexible prices once again allow the economy to obtain equilibrium at the full employment level of output, Y_f. In fact, the flexibility of prices is what makes the aggregate supply curve in Figure 4.1.2 completely vertical. By contrast, the aggregate supply curve in Unit 3.6 also contains the horizontal Keynesian range, because prices are not flexible in the downward direction. Without flexible prices, the decline in aggregate demand would leave the economy at point E' at the original price level, meaning that in the Keynesian range the economy maintains the existing price level but at the expense of unemployment. It should now be evident why the vertical part of the aggregate supply curve is called the classical range.

Saving and Investment

Because of a potential flaw in Say's law, one last principle is needed to complete the classical view of the economy. Even though people work and produce goods in order to earn income for consumption, they do not necessarily spend all of their income

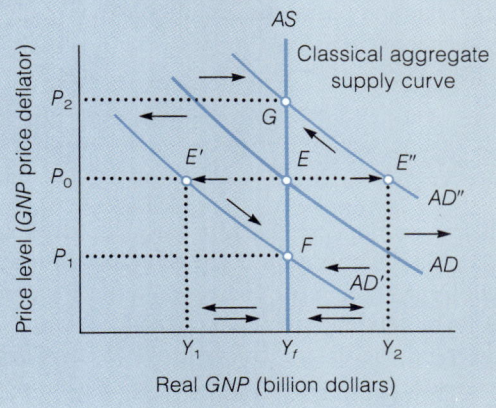

Figure 4.1.2

The Classical Aggregate Supply Curve

In classical economics the aggregate supply curve constitutes a vertical line at the full employment level of output. If aggregate demand declines, markets throughout the economy have surpluses. Therefore, prices throughout the economy, and thus the average price level, decline until the surpluses are eliminated and full employment is once again achieved at point E.

on consumption, but may in fact save part of it. If people do save part of their income, then consumption expenditures will be less than the amount of output produced, in which case the demand for the output will be less than the supply, and unemployment will occur.

However, the classical economists stated that the amount of output not purchased with consumption expenditures would be purchased with investment expenditures by business firms using household savings. And with flexible prices, the amount of saving would always equal the amount of investment.

To understand why this is so, let's turn to Figure 4.1.3. The classical economists argued that household saving was directly related to the interest rate, as depicted by curve S, and that investment expenditures were indirectly related to the interest rate, as depicted by curve I. In this theory, higher interest rates encourage households to save more of their income, rather than spend it on current consumption of goods and services. The only way to get people to postpone consumption is to pay them an interest, and the higher the interest, the more people will save.

The classical economists also stated that the interest rate determines the level of investment. If the interest rate increases, firms will undertake fewer investment projects and thus need fewer investment funds. Note that the interest payment on borrowed funds represents a cost of buying the capital goods, so if the interest rate increases, the cost of the goods increases, and firms demand less capital.

Based on the classical view of saving and investment, saving would always equal investment, because the concept of flexible prices also applies to the interest rate. One way to consider this equality is to consider the workings of a simple financial market. Firms need, or demand, investment funds, and are willing to pay an interest for them. If households are not supplying as many funds as firms demand, the firms offer a higher interest rate, which encourages more saving, until the firms' demands are satisfied. In this way the financial market ensures that the amount of income not used for consumption expenditures is simply turned over to firms to be converted into investment expenditures. Consequently, aggregate expenditures by households and businesses are always equal to full employment output.

THE DEPRESSION

Classical economics seemed to do a good job of explaining the operation of the economy until the Great Depression in the 1930s, when the economy showed no tendency to reach full employment. To understand the extent and severity of the Great Depression, let's look at two indicators of a business cycle. Panel a of Figure 4.1.4 depicts one impor-

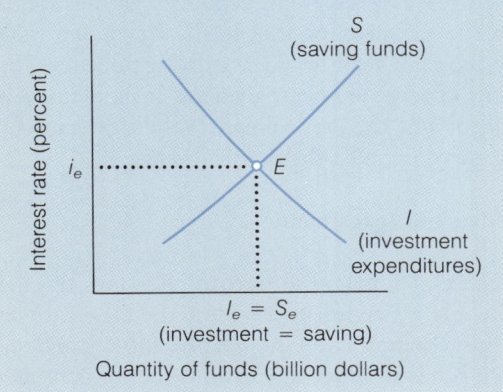

Figure 4.1.3

Investment and Saving

Classical economists argued that the interest rate (i) would adjust such that investment (I) and saving (S) would always be equal ($I_e = S_e$). If investment is less than saving, then the total expenditures on output is less than the amount of output produced, resulting in unemployment.

UNIT 4.1 ▪ AN INTRODUCTION TO KEYNESIAN ECONOMICS

Figure 4.1.4

Economic Activity and Unemployment During the Depression

The Depression of the 1930s was a period in the United States in which economic activity, as seen in panel **a**, was extremely low, and showed few signs of moving into a strong expansionary phase of the business cycle until 1940. Furthermore, the unemployment rate in the economy was over 14 percent for most of the Depression, reaching a high of 25 percent, as seen in panel **b**. Clearly, this did not constitute a temporary departure from full employment. Source: U.S. Bureau of Economic Analysis, *Survey of Current Business*, selected issues.

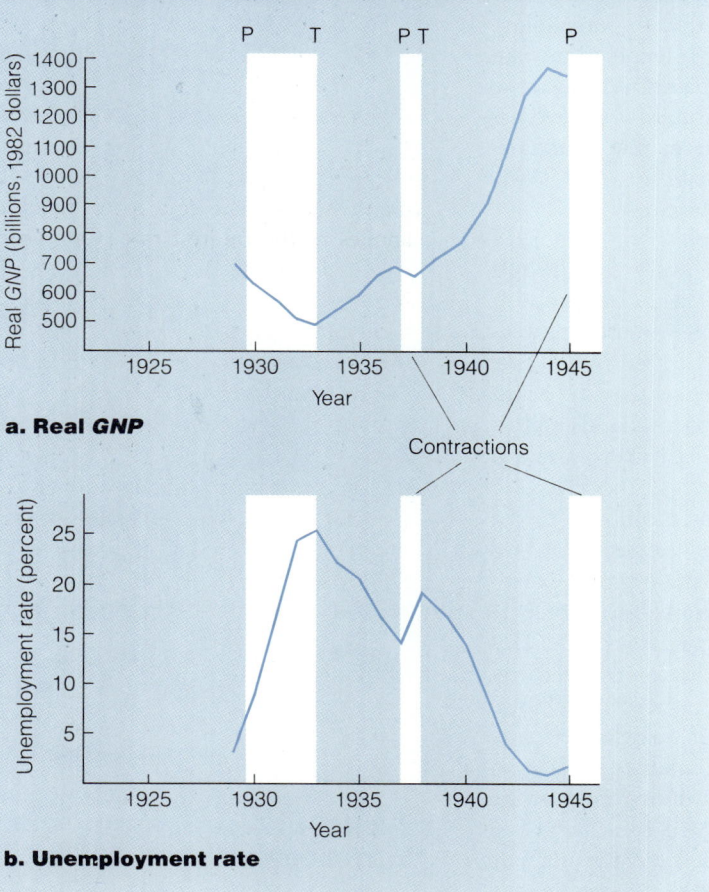

a. Real *GNP*

b. Unemployment rate

tant indicator of the economy during the Depression, real *GNP* measured in 1982 dollars. If we start at 1929, we see that the economy takes a nosedive as national production declines. Not only does national production decline, but it remains relatively low for the entire decade. It is not until the beginning of the Second World War that real *GNP* reaches its pre-Depression level. This trough of the business cycle was so deep and sustained that most people wondered if the economy would ever recover.

Panel b of Figure 4.1.4 depicts another indicator of the Depression's severity, the unemployment rate of labor. In 1929 the unemployment rate was a very respectable 3.2 percent. Within three years it was over 20 percent, and it stayed over 20 percent until 1936. Furthermore, the unemployment rate remained over 14 percent until 1941, when the Second World War began.

At the height of the Depression, from 1932 to 1935, nearly one out of every four people was unemployed. And during the entire decade at least one out of every six people was unemployed. Based on this record, it is easy to see why people found fault with the classical view that the economy would achieve full employment. If full employment was not reached within ten years, would it ever be?

Perhaps the most important epilogue to the Depression is the role played by the Second World War. Clearly, the economy did not begin its expansionary phase until the country began to prepare for the war in the late 1930s and early 1940s. This preparation is significant in that it involved tremendous increases in government purchases, including a wide assortment of weapons and supplies and the services of thousands of soldiers as Figure 4.1.5 shows. Note that during most of the Depression, government purchases were about $10 billion, but that in 1941 these purchases jumped to nearly $25 billion, and in 1942 they were nearly $60 billion. As we see later in this section, government purchases play an important role in the Keynesian view of the economy.

Figure 4.1.5

Government Purchases During the Depression

Government purchases during the Depression did not offset the reduction in private expenditures by the business and household sectors, which contributed to the length and severity of the Depression. It wasn't until the Second World War that the economy began to come out of the Depression. This expansionary phase was caused, at least in part, by the tremendous increase in government purchases associated with the war. Source: U.S. Bureau of Economic Analysis, *Survey of Current Business*, selected issues.

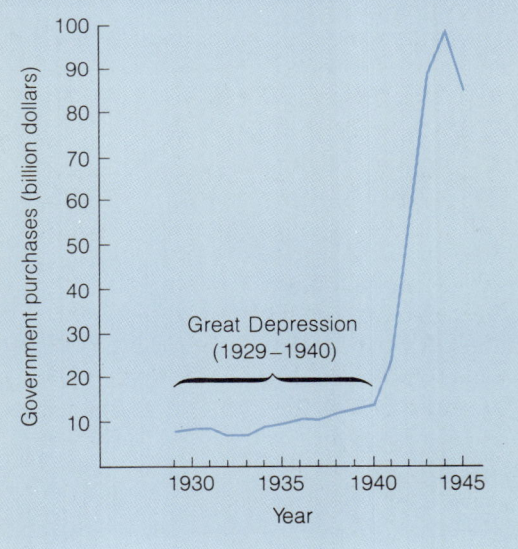

THE KEYNESIAN ANSWER TO THE DEPRESSION

To Keynes, the Depression was obviously caused by a lack of demand for the economy's output. Consider that in 1929 GNP was $103 billion and the unemployment rate was 3.2 percent, but by 1933 consumption expenditures had fallen by $22 billion and investment had fallen by $15 billion. These declines, together with a slight decline in government purchases, meant GNP had fallen to $56 billion, an almost 50 percent decline in four years. And according to the Keynesian view, this decline in GNP resulted from a decline in expenditures by the private sector (household and business).

But where did classical economics go wrong? Why didn't markets adjust to regain full employment? Keynes thought classical economics was wrong in two regards. First, prices, and especially wages, were not flexible in the downward direction. And second, saving and investment were not necessarily equal.

Although union contracts and government minimum wage legislation tend to restrict wages in the downward direction, there is also a natural tendency on the part of workers to oppose a lower wage. An unemployed worker who is making $5 an hour is likely to resist taking a new job for less than that amount, in part because the worker sees the wage as a reflection of ability. If the worker is "worth" $5 an hour, then taking a job at anything less is equivalent to a slap in the face. Firms also tend to resist lower prices, often finding it easier to reduce production than to lower the price.

Furthermore, Keynes argued, saving does not necessarily equal investment. He felt that the interest rate had very little impact on the amount of saving, and that saving was based more on the level of income than on the interest rate. If income was greater, then saving would be greater, regardless of the interest rate. And he questioned the sensitivity of investment to the interest rate, arguing that decreases in already low interest rates might not stimulate any additional investment, meaning the interest rate might not be able to decline enough to equate saving with investment.

In other words, if saving is greater than investment, then expenditures on output are less than the amount of output produced. This, according to Keynes, is where the government becomes important. When the private sector is not able to purchase all of the output produced, the government sector needs to come in and add to the overall level of expenditures. Remember that the economy did not climb out of the Depression until the government sector doubled, tripled, and quadrupled its purchases during the war.

The Keynesian view of the Depression can be seen with the aggregate market, especially the aggregate supply curve, in Figure 4.1.6. This aggregate supply curve is fundamentally different from the one presented in Figure 4.1.2 in that it has two basic sections, a vertical segment at the full employment level of output and a horizontal segment. The classical aggregate supply curve has only one section, because it is completely vertical at the full employment level of output. In fact, the horizontal segment embodies the basic difference between classical economics and the Keynesian view of the macroeconomy, and exists because prices and wages are inflexible in the downward direction.

In the Keynesian view the Depression occurred, and persisted, because the aggregate demand curve shifted from AD to AD', the result of a reduction in aggregate expenditures. But with the inflexibility of wages and prices the economy reached a new equilibrium along the horizontal Keynesian range at E', with real GNP equal to Y_1, an amount less than full employment output Y_f. We should note that in Figure 4.1.2, a similar shift from AD to AD' led only to a temporary reduction of output to Y_1, as wages and prices declined to reachieve equilibrium. However, in the Keynesian view this does not happen. Inflexible wages and prices, and the horizontal segment of the aggregate supply curve, make it necessary to increase aggregate demand before full employment is once again reached. This conclusion gives rise to the major policy prescription of Keynesian economics—if the household and business sectors do not have sufficient aggregate demand to reach full employment, it is up to the government sector to provide the additional stimulus.

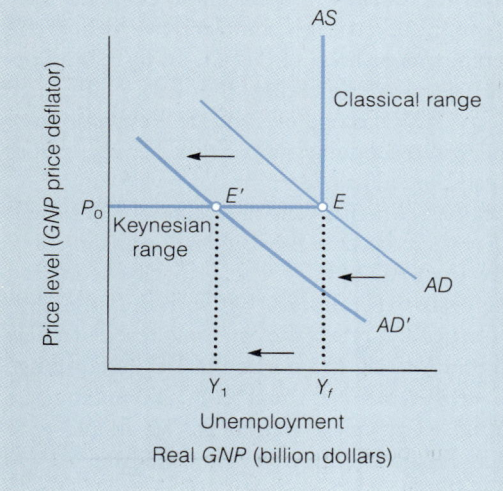

Figure 4.1.6

The Keynesian View of the Depression

The Keynesian view of the Depression is seen by a fundamental change in the aggregate supply curve. While the classical supply curve is completely vertical at the full employment level of output, the Keynesian aggregate supply curve has a horizontal segment caused by inflexible wages and prices. A reduction in aggregate demand means the economy can reach equilibrium at E', corresponding with a level of output below full employment. And the way to reachieve full employment is by increasing aggregate demand.

first developed in the mid-1930s, during the worst contractionary period, with the highest unemployment rates, ever experienced in the United States.

- Keynesian economics can be better understood through the study of its predecessor, classical economics. Classical economists argued that the economy would always tend toward full employment output. Classical economics rests on three propositions: Say's law, which states that the act of supplying national production creates its own demand; the flexibility of wages and prices, which allows all markets in the economy to move toward full employment; and the equality between saving and investment, which guarantees that the economy will have sufficient aggregate demand, even if households save part of the income they receive for producing output.

- The Great Depression of the 1930s made the classical view of the macroeconomy suspect, and opened the door for Keynesian economics. During the Great Depression, unemployment of the labor force was over 14 percent for the entire decade, reaching a high of 25 percent in 1933. National production declined by almost half, due in large part to the lack of aggregate demand of the private sector. Keynes's view of the economy was further reinforced by the beginning of the Second World War, at which time government purchases increased and the economy entered into an expansionary period.

IN SUMMARY

An Introduction to Keynesian Economics

- Keynesian economics is the body of thought first developed by John Maynard Keynes. The main thrust of Keynesian economics concerns unemployment of factors of production caused by a lack of aggregate demand. This should not be surprising, because his theories were

QUESTIONS FOR STUDY AND ANALYSIS

1. Explain why classical economists believed that the aggregate supply curve was completely vertical at the full employment level of output. Based on the Depression of the 1930s, do you think the aggregate supply curve is vertical? Explain.

2. During the Depression of the 1930s, aggregate demand in the economy was less than the full employment level of output. Explain how each of the four components of aggregate demand (consumption, investment, government purchases, and net exports) might contribute to an equilibrium that is less than full employment. Also discuss how each of the components could be used to achieve equilibrium at the full employment level of output.

3. According to Say's law, supply creates its own demand. Under what circumstances would this law hold? Under what circumstances would this law not hold? Explain.

4. Based on today's economy, how valid is the assumption of flexible wages and prices? Discuss two examples in which wages or prices are flexible and two in which they are not.

REVIEW GLOSSARY

classical economics A body of economic thought, originating with the pioneering work of Adam Smith, that built on the idea that freely operating markets would lead to production that always tended to the full employment level of output.

Keynesian economics A body of economic thought, first developed by John Maynard Keynes, built on the idea that aggregate expenditures on output are not necessarily equal to the economy's full employment level of output.

Say's law A principle that states supply creates it own demand. Say's law was a key ingredient for the classical view of the economy. Together with flexible wages and prices and the equality between saving and investment, Say's law meant the economy would always tend toward full employment.

UNIT 4.2

Consumption

In this unit we examine consumption expenditures by households. Although several factors affect the level of consumption expenditures by households, one stands above the rest—income. Our primary objective here is to see how consumption expenditures are related to income.

The relationship between income and consumption is probably the single most important relationship underlying Keynesian economics and the study of macroeconomics. Not only do consumption expenditures represent the largest of the four components of aggregate demand, they also increase as national income increases, which leads to further increases in national income. As we will discuss in Unit 4.6, this relationship between income and consumption is expressed in the multiplier analysis, which is the core of macroeconomics.

To begin our study of consumption, we examine the two basic uses for disposable household income—consumption and saving—and how the household sector divides its income between these two uses. In doing so we are able to identify both the consumption function, which graphically relates consumption expenditures to disposable income, and the saving function, which is the graphical relationship between saving and income. The unit ends by making a useful distinction between a change in consumption and a change in the amount consumed.

THE DISPOSITION OF DISPOSABLE PERSONAL INCOME

Disposable personal income (or simply disposable income) received by households can be used for consumption expenditures or saving. Recall that

Table 4.2.1
Consumption, Saving, and Income (billions)

Disposable Income	Consumption	Saving	APC	APS	MPC	MPS
$ 100	$175	$ −75	1.75	−0.75		
					0.75	0.25
200	250	−50	1.25	−0.25		
					0.75	0.25
300	325	−25	1.08	−0.08		
					0.75	0.25
400	400	0	1.00	0.00		
					0.75	0.25
500	475	25	0.95	0.05		
					0.75	0.25
600	550	50	0.92	0.08		
					0.75	0.25
700	625	75	0.89	0.11		
					0.75	0.25
800	700	100	0.88	0.12		
					0.75	0.25
900	775	125	0.86	0.14		
					0.75	0.25
1000	850	150	0.85	0.15		

disposable income is the discretionary income received by households after personal taxes are paid.

Let's look at Table 4.2.1, which presents a consumption/saving schedule, containing numerical information about disposable income, consumption, and saving by the household sector. A **consumption/saving schedule** is a table that illustrates the division of disposable income between consumption and saving. This table lists figures for disposable income ranging from $100 to $1000; the question is how much of the disposable income do households use for consumption, and how much for saving? (To simplify the discussion in this and subsequent units, we will omit "billion" in dollar amounts.)

For example, if households receive $100 in disposable income, they spend $175 on consumption expenditures and save $−75. We might wonder how households can spend $75 more than their income. Recall that the income received by households is the income received in a single year. Households are able to spend more than they earn by withdrawing part of their savings accumulated in past years or by borrowing funds against future income, which accounts for the $−75. The negative number indicates that households are not saving current income but actually spending income earned, or income to be earned, in other periods; they are dissaving. **Dissaving** is the process of spending more on consumption than is available in current disposable income.

As we can see in Table 4.2.1, households have dissaving up to the $400 disposable income level—with $400 of disposable income households are spending as much as they have available. As income increases beyond $400, households do not spend all of their income, but direct positive amounts to saving.

The key point in this table is the relationship between consumption, saving, and disposable income. Note that increases in income lead to increases in both consumption and saving. For example, as disposable income increases from $100 to $1000, consumption increases from $175 to $850, and saving increases from $−75 to $150. Another important point is that as income increases, consumption increases, but at a slower rate than income. The same is true for income and saving. This sim-

UNIT 4.2 • CONSUMPTION

ply means that any additional income received by households is used partly for consumption and partly for saving.

Average Propensities to Consume and Save

From the total levels of consumption and saving presented in Table 4.2.1 we can calculate two related and important measures of consumption and saving, average propensity to consume (APC) and average propensity to save (APS). **Average propensity to consume (APC)** is the proportion of disposable income used for consumption expenditures. The APC is specified as

$$APC = \frac{\text{consumption}}{\text{disposable income}}$$

Average propensity to save (APS) is the proportion of disposable income used for saving. The APS is specified as

$$APS = \frac{\text{saving}}{\text{disposable income}}$$

The APC and APS for each level of disposable income are calculated and listed in the fourth and fifth columns of Table 4.2.1, respectively. Two aspects in particular of the APC and APS numbers should be noted. First, the APC declines as disposable income increases, and the APS increases. Second, the total of APC and APS at every level of income can be stated as

$$APC + APS = 1$$

The reason for this should be obvious. Because there are only two specific uses for income, the portion applied to consumption plus the portion applied to saving must equal the total disposable income.

Marginal Propensities to Consume and Save

A second pair of measures of consumption and saving are even more instructive than the APC and APS. Note in Table 4.2.1 that every $100 increase in disposable income leads to $75 in additional consumption and $25 in additional saving. As we study the operation of the macroeconomy, we will find it extremely useful to determine changes in consumption or saving resulting from changes in disposable income. The changes in consumption and saving due to changes in disposable income constitute the marginal propensity to consume (MPC) and the marginal propensity to save (MPS), respectively. The **marginal propensity to consume (MPC)** is the proportion of each additional dollar of disposable income used for consumption expenditures. It is specified as

$$MPC = \frac{\text{change in consumption}}{\text{change in disposable income}}$$

The **marginal propensity to save (MPS)** is the proportion of each additional dollar of disposable income used for saving. It is specified as

$$MPS = \frac{\text{change in saving}}{\text{change in disposable income}}$$

Let's calculate the MPC and MPS for the change in disposable income from $100 to $200, as shown in the sixth and seventh columns of Table 4.2.1, respectively. As income increases by $100, households increase consumption expenditures by $75 and saving by $25. Thus, the MPC is $75/$100 = 0.75, and the MPS is $25/$100 = 0.25. If we compute the MPC and MPS for the change in income from $200 to $300, we find that again MPC = 0.75 and MPS = 0.25. In fact, for every change in disposable income in this table, MPC = 0.75 and MPS = 0.25, unlike the average propensities.

However, there is also a similarity between the marginal propensities and the average propensities. As with the APC and APS, the total of MPC and MPS at every level of income can be stated as

$$MPC + MPS = 1$$

Once again, because each additional dollar received is divided between consumption and saving, this equation tells us that the change in consumption plus the change in saving must equal one.

CONSUMPTION FUNCTION

Throughout our study of economics it is useful to transfer numbers from a table into a graph. For example, we can better investigate the operation of the macroeconomy if we graphically depict the relationship between consumption and disposable income shown in the consumption/saving schedule in Table 4.2.1. Later in this unit we construct a similar relationship between saving and disposable income.

Figure 4.2.1 presents the relationship between consumption and disposable income. Line C is obtained by plotting the level of consumption for each level of disposable income. For example, if disposable income is $200 (on the horizontal axis), consumption is $250 (on the vertical axis); if disposable income is $300, consumption is $325; and so on. The line formed is called the consumption function. The **consumption function** is a line that depicts the relationship between consumption and disposable income.

The consumption function in Figure 4.2.1 illustrates what we have already said about the relationship between consumption and income. First, note that the consumption function has a positive

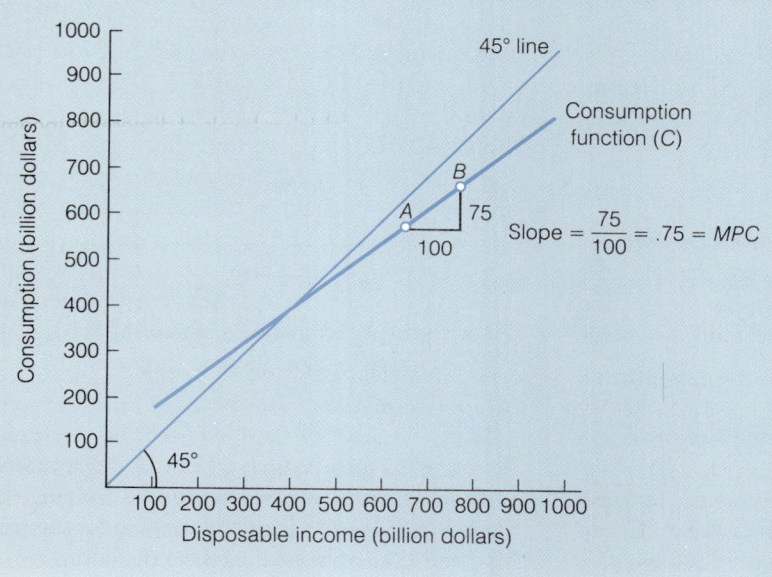

Figure 4.2.1

The Consumption Function

The consumption function shows the relationship between consumption expenditures and disposable income. The slope of the consumption function is the marginal propensity to consume. The positive slope indicates that consumption expenditures are higher at higher levels of income. And the slope of less than one indicates that the increase in consumption is less than the increase in income. In other words, households spend only a fraction of any additional income.

slope, meaning that increases in income lead to increases in consumption. However, let's take a closer look at the slope.

For reference purposes a 45° line is included in Figure 4.2.1 to represent all points in which consumption is equal to disposable income. Note that the slope of the 45° line is equal to one. A comparison between the slope of the 45° line and the consumption function indicates that the consumption function has a lesser slope. Let's calculate the value of the slope of the consumption function.

Remember that the slope of a line is calculated by dividing the change in the variable on the vertical axis by the change in the variable on the horizontal axis. In this case we are looking at a change in the value of consumption (vertical axis) divided by a change in the value of disposable income (horizontal axis). If disposable income increases from $700 to $800, from point A to point B, the change is $100. However, from point A to point B, consumption increases from $625 to $700, a change of $75. The slope between points A and B is therefore $75/$100 = 0.75. Moreover, since the consumption function is a straight line, the slope is the same between any two points, and is always equal to 0.75. And as suggested earlier, the slope of the consumption function is less than one.

What does the slope of the consumption function tell us? It tells us that a $1 increase in disposable income leads to a $0.75 increase in consumption, which is simply the definition of the marginal propensity to consume (MPC). In fact, the slope of the consumption function *is* the marginal propensity to consume.

SAVING FUNCTION

A second important relationship can also be graphed from the information contained in Table 4.2.1—the saving function. The **saving function** is a line depicting the relationship between saving and disposable income. If we plot saving on the vertical axis and disposable income on the horizontal axis, as in panel b of Figure 4.2.2, line S becomes the saving function. The first thing to observe about line S is that it too has a positive slope, meaning that increases in disposable income lead to increases in saving. We can also see that households do not always save positive amounts. If income is less than $400, households are dissaving, and the saving function lies below the horizontal axis. Only after disposable income becomes greater than $400 do households save positive amounts.

While we can construct the saving function from the information in Table 4.2.1, we can also derive it directly from the consumption function. Recall that households have two uses for income, consumption and saving. If we turn our attention to panel a in Figure 4.2.2, which shows the consumption function from Figure 4.2.1, we can also identify saving.

In this discussion of the relationship between the consumption and saving functions, the 45° line in panel a tells us all of the points at which consumption on the vertical axis is equal to disposable income on the horizontal axis. Therefore, when the consumption function line C crosses the 45° line, consumption is equal to disposable income. This intersection occurs at point N, at which consumption and disposable income are both equal to $400. But if consumption and disposable income are both $400, then saving must be equal to zero. In panel b this corresponds to point N', where the saving function crosses the horizontal axis.

If we move to higher levels of disposable income, such as $700, we see that the consumption function at point O is below the 45° line, meaning that consumption is less than disposable income and there is a positive level of saving. In fact, the vertical difference between the consumption function and the 45° line *is* the level of saving. But if disposable income is less than $400, the consumption function at point M lies above the 45° line, indicating that consumption is greater than disposable income. In this case households have a negative level of saving, or dissaving. Remember that saving is the vertical difference between the consumption function and the 45° line. This is important because it tells us that whenever we have the consumption

Figure 4.2.2

Consumption and Saving Functions

The consumption function in panel **a** can be used to directly derive the saving function in panel **b**. The 45° line in panel **a** indicates all of the points at which consumption is equal to income. This means the vertical distance at any given point between the consumption function and the 45° line constitutes saving.

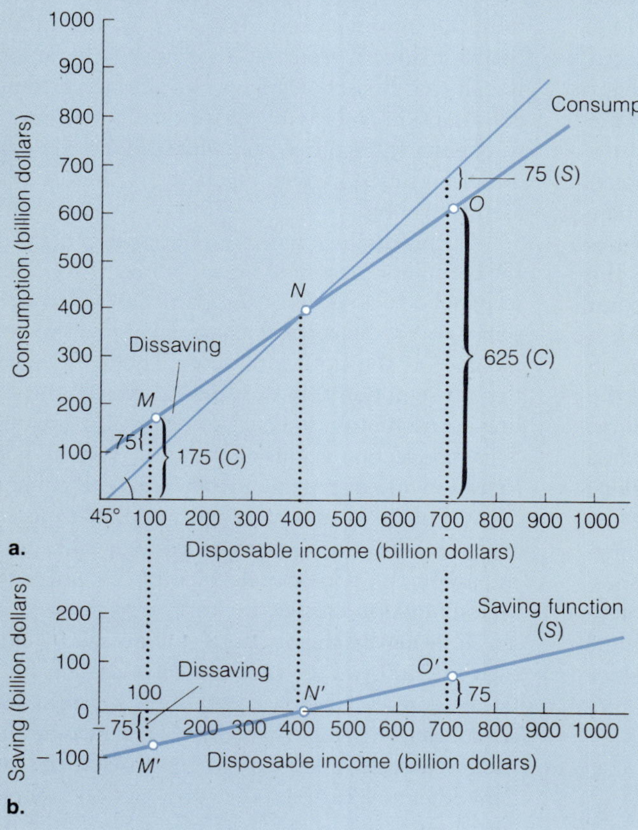

function, we also know all that we need to know about saving. We can always determine the level of saving from the consumption function.

Before we leave the saving function, there is one more topic we need to consider. Recall that the slope of the consumption function is also the marginal propensity to consume. For similar reasons, the slope of the saving function is the marginal propensity to save. If we compute the value of the slope between any two points on the saving function in panel b, we come up with 0.25. For example, if income increases from $400 to $700, saving increases from $0 to $75. Therefore the slope is $75/$300 = 0.25, which is the value of the MPS in Table 4.2.1.

DETERMINANTS OF CONSUMPTION

So far in this unit we have considered only the relationship between consumption expenditures and income. While income is the most important factor, three other factors can also affect consumption. The **determinants of consumption** are interest rate, wealth, and expectations.

Interest Rate

Durable consumption goods, such as automobiles, furniture, and appliances, are particularly sensitive to changes in the interest rate. Since most durable goods are purchased with borrowed funds, an increase in the interest rate leads to an increase in the overall cost of the good. Therefore, higher interest rates tend to reduce household consumption, while lower interest rates tend to increase consumption expenditures. We should note that, as we saw in Unit 3.6, the relationship between the interest rate and consumption expenditures is an important part of the interest rate effect underlying the negative slope of the aggregate demand curve.

Wealth

The effect of wealth on consumption is not as clear-cut as the effect of the interest rate, because wealth can cause either increases or decreases in consumption expenditures. If households have an increase in physical wealth in the form of physical assets or durable goods, the tendency to purchase these assets is reduced, so overall consumption expenditures are likely to decline as households save more income. But, an increase in financial wealth, including money, savings accounts, stocks, bonds, and other various types of financial assets, typically leads to an increase in consumption expenditures. If households are saving their income to reach a certain level of wealth, then an increase in financial wealth moves them closer to their desired goal, reducing the need to save, and increasing consumption. The relationship between financial wealth and consumption expenditures, in terms of the real balance effect, is also an important factor underlying the slope of the aggregate demand curve.

Expectations

Households' expectations concerning future conditions in the economy can also lead to changes in consumption expenditures. If the future of the economy looks good, then households are also likely to expect that their own situations will improve, and are more likely to make long-term commitments to buy durable goods or otherwise increase consumption expenditures. If they expect a downturn in the economy, then they are more likely to save rather than consume, in order to provide a safety net in case of a downturn.

CHANGE IN AMOUNT CONSUMED AND CHANGE IN CONSUMPTION

When we are using the consumption function, it is important to distinguish between changes in disposable income and changes in one of the determinants. A change in disposable income leads to a **change in amount consumed,** which represents nothing more than a movement along the consumption function.

However, a change in the interest rate, wealth, or expectations leads to a **change in consumption.** A change in consumption represents a shift in the entire consumption function, as illustrated in panel a of Figure 4.2.3. In this case, with an upward shift in the consumption function, consumption is greater at every level of income. We should note that when the consumption function shifts upward, the saving function must necessarily shift downward, as seen in panel b. If households are spending more of their income for consumption, then they must be saving less.

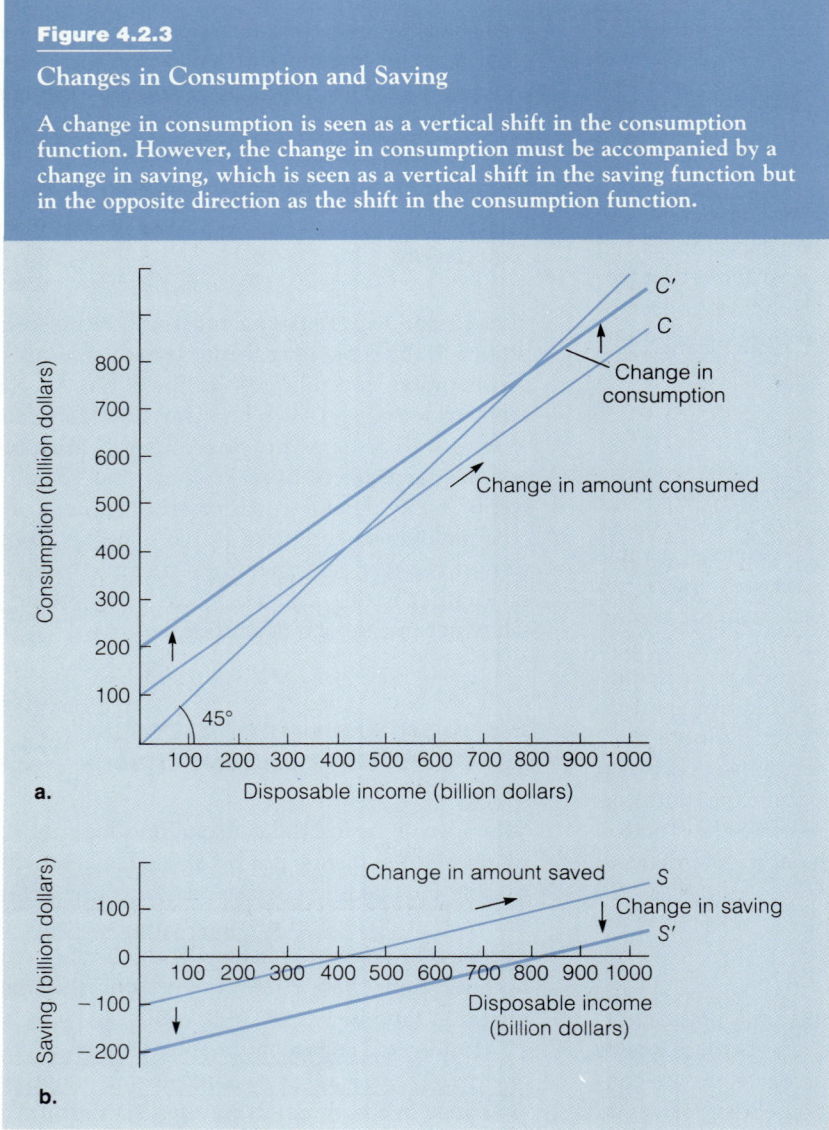

Figure 4.2.3

Changes in Consumption and Saving

A change in consumption is seen as a vertical shift in the consumption function. However, the change in consumption must be accompanied by a change in saving, which is seen as a vertical shift in the saving function but in the opposite direction as the shift in the consumption function.

An upward shift in the consumption function can be caused by a reduction in the interest rate, by additional financial wealth, or perhaps by favorable expectations concerning the future of the economy. And as the consumption function shifts up, the saving function shifts down. Conversely, an increase in the interest rate, a decline in wealth, or lowered expectations leads to a downward shift in the consumption function and an upward shift in the saving function.

IN SUMMARY
Consumption

- Consumption is the largest of the four expenditures on national product in the economy. Moreover, the relationship between consumption and income, seen by looking at the disposition of disposable income between consumption and saving, is the single most important relationship underlying the study of Keynesian economics. As household income increases, the income is divided between both consumption and saving.

- Four important measures of the relationship between income, consumption, and saving are the average propensity to consume (APC), the average propensity to save (APS), the marginal propensity to consume (MPC), and the marginal propensity to save (MPS). The average propensities to consume and save are found by dividing consumption or saving by disposable income. The marginal propensities to consume and save are found by dividing the change in consumption or saving by the change in disposable income.

- The consumption function is a line depicting the relationship between consumption and disposable income. The slope of the consumption function is the marginal propensity to consume.

- The saving function is a line depicting the relationship between saving and disposable income. The slope of the saving function is the marginal propensity to save. Although the saving function can be graphed directly from the numbers in a consumption/saving schedule, it can also be graphed from the consumption function. The vertical distance at any given point between the consumption function and the 45° line is saving.

- The three most important determinants of consumption are the interest rate, wealth, and expectations. A change in any of these determinants causes a shift in the consumption function. But a change in income causes a movement along a given consumption function and a change in the amount consumed.

QUESTIONS FOR STUDY AND ANALYSIS

1. Suppose you have uncovered the following levels of consumption expenditures and corresponding levels of disposable income:

Income	$10	20	30	40	50	60	70	80
Consumption	18	26	34	42	50	58	66	74

   a. Compute the level of saving for each level of income.
   b. Compute the average propensity to consume and the average propensity to save for each level of income. Compute the sum of the APC and APS at each level of income. What is this sum equal to?
   c. Compute the marginal propensity to consume and the marginal propensity to save for each level of income. Compute the sum of the MPC and MPS at each level of income. What is this sum equal to?

2. Would you say that your marginal propensity to consume is constant? If your income increased from $1000 to $1100 per month, what would you do with the additional $100? Explain.

3. Have you or your family ever personally experienced a year of dissaving? Explain.

4. In the late 1970s the federal government implemented policies that caused the interest rate to increase. How do you think the economy's consumption function was affected from this action? Why?

5. Let's say that the savings you have accumulated over a period of several years is suddenly doubled, from $5000 to $10,000. How is this likely to affect your consumption expenditures, assuming there is no change in your

income? How would your answer differ if you were accumulating the savings to buy a $7500 car, or merely putting funds aside for your future retirement?

6. If you expect the rate of inflation will be twice as high next year, what is likely to happen to your consumption expenditures this year? Explain.

7. How is the consumption function related to the circular flow discussed in Unit 3.1?

REVIEW GLOSSARY

average propensity to consume (*APC*) The proportion of disposable income used for consumption expenditures. The APC is found by dividing consumption by disposable income.

average propensity to save (*APS*) The proportion of disposable income used for saving. The APS is found by dividing saving by disposable income.

change in amount consumed A movement along the consumption function caused by a change in disposable income.

change in consumption A shift in the consumption function caused by a change in one of the determinants of consumption—interest rate, wealth, or expectations.

consumption function A line that depicts the relationship between consumption and disposable income. The slope of the consumption function is the marginal propensity to consume.

consumption/saving schedule A table that illustrates the division of disposable income between consumption and saving.

determinants of consumption The three factors (other than income) that have the most important effects on consumption are the interest rate, wealth, and expectations. A change in any of these determinants leads to a shift in the consumption (and saving) function.

dissaving The process of spending more on consumption than is available in current disposable income. Dissaving is made possible by spending either past income (from accumulated savings) or future income (through borrowing).

marginal propensity to consume (*MPC*) The proportion of each additional dollar of disposable income used for consumption expenditures. The MPC is found by dividing the change in consumption by the change in disposable income.

marginal propensity to save (*MPS*) The proportion of each additional dollar of disposable income used for saving. The MPS is found by dividing the change in saving by the change in disposable income.

saving function A line that depicts the relationship between saving and disposable income. The slope of the saving function is the marginal propensity to save.

UNIT 4.3

Investment

In this unit we examine investment expenditures by the business sector. While consumption expenditures constitute the largest and most stable expenditure on national product, investment expenditures are the least stable, fluctuating widely from month to month and from year to year. These fluctuations in investment can stimulate the contractions and expansions of business cycles.

Our study of investment begins by distinguishing between planned and realized investment. Although the business sector may plan to invest a lot or a little in the coming year, unforeseen circumstances can alter its investment plans. We then look at two of the most important factors affecting planned investment, income and the interest rate, and how changes in those factors affect decisions by individual firms. Finally, we examine investment expenditures and consumption expenditures as the first two components of aggregate expenditures for the economy's production.

PLANNED AND REALIZED INVESTMENT

Investment by business consists of expenditures on equipment and structures (including residential structures) and changes in business inventories. Changes in inventories become important to our analysis in later units, but for now let's just say that inventories consist of accumulated stocks of raw materials, intermediate goods, and final goods associated with production. And unplanned changes in inventories play a key role in determining the difference between planned and realized investment expenditures.

Planned investment is the investment expenditure that business firms would like to make over a period of time, based on conditions in the economy. Business firms plan to invest varying amounts based on the interest rate, the position in the business cycle, the cost of capital goods, and other relevant factors. Investment expenditures might include new equipment, structures, or even planned changes in inventories.

However, business firms are not always able to realize their expectations. **Realized investment** is the investment expenditure that business firms actually make over a period of time. The difference between planned and realized investment is based on unplanned changes in inventories. When business firms are able to buy all of the capital goods that they plan to buy, then planned and realized investment are equal, unless inventories change. If firms produce more output than they are able to sell, their inventories increase, which represents unplanned investment. But if firms sell more output than they produce, then these sales come from stocks of inventories accumulated in past years, in which case inventories decline and negative unplanned investment exists. In short, planned investment is greater than realized investment when inventories fall, and planned investment is less than realized investment when inventories rise.

INVESTMENT, OUTPUT, AND THE INTEREST RATE

While this difference between planned and realized investment is extremely important to the operation of the economy, let's limit our discussion here to a closer examination of planned investment. Numerous factors can affect planned investment expenditures; two of the most important factors are output and the interest rate.

Output

The simplest view of the relationship between output and investment is that output has no effect on investment. That is, the planned investment expenditures by business firms are not affected by the level of output in the economy. Such investment expenditures are called autonomous investment. **Autonomous investment expenditures** are investment expenditures that do not depend on the current level of national income and output.

Although this view of the investment-output relationship simplifies some of the analysis in later units, it is basically valid. Most of our subsequent analysis concerns the operation of the economy over a period of a few years. However, many investment expenditures undertaken by business firms, especially expenditures for structures and equipment, are based on a more distant time horizon. For example, a firm will build a new factory if it will be profitable over the coming decade, even though it might not be profitable in the short run. Such an investment will probably be made even as the economy enters into an unforeseen contractionary phase of the business cycle, and national production falls.

The autonomous investment view of the relationship between investment and output is graphically presented in Figure 4.3.1 as line I. Note that line I is horizontally sloped, meaning the same amount is invested regardless of the level of national output. However, realistically investment expenditures might increase slightly as the level of national output increases, because the economy needs more capital to produce more output. This is shown as the positively sloped line I'. If output increases, business firms need to expand the stock of capital through investment expenditures. However, this increase is so slight as to be negligible. Therefore, assume for the sake of our later discussions that investment expenditures are autonomous and do not depend on the level of national output.

Interest Rate

The interest rate charged on borrowed funds is also an important factor affecting investment expenditures. The **interest rate** is the charge for the use of borrowed funds over a period of time, expressed as a percentage. This means that if $100 is bor-

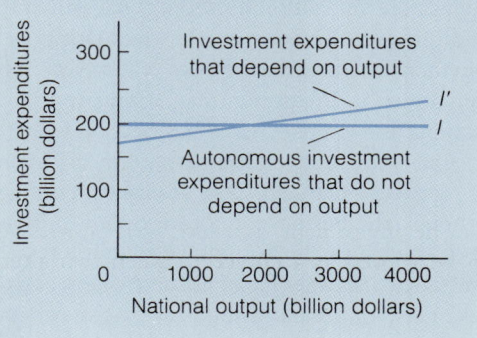

Figure 4.3.1

Investment and Output

Autonomous investment expenditures are investment expenditures that do not depend on the level of income or output, indicated by the horizontal investment line I. However, if investment depends on the level of income, then the investment line has a slightly positive slope, as indicated by line I'.

rowed for one year and the lender charges $10 for this service, the interest rate is 10 percent.

The interest rate affects investment expenditures because in one way or another it affects the cost of investment. For example, suppose a firm is planning to build a new factory at a construction cost of $1 million. If the firm borrows the funds to pay for this investment, the cost of the factory is more than $1 million. At an interest rate of 10 percent, the firm will have to pay an additional $100,000 each year until the loan is repaid, meaning the actual cost of the factory is greater than $1 million.

But even though the firm has funds available to purchase the factory, and therefore does not need to borrow the funds and pay interest on them, the interest rate still increases the cost of the factory. If the firm spends $1 million on the factory, then it cannot loan out those funds to someone else, so it is losing the interest that could be earned on the $1 million. At an interest rate of 10 percent, the firm is losing $100,000 per year, which constitutes the opportunity cost of investing in the factory.

While it should be clear that the interest rate affects the cost of investment, let's see how changes in the interest rate affect the overall level of investment in the economy. Figure 4.3.2 illustrates the relationship between the interest rate on the vertical axis and investment expenditures on the horizontal axis. Note that the curve has a negative slope, meaning at higher interest rates investment expenditures are lower, and at lower interest rates investment expenditures are higher. The inverse relationship between the interest rate and investment expenditures is an important part of the interest rate effect underlying the negative slope of the aggregate demand curve.

The investment decision by a business firm can be viewed as a choice between two alternatives. Firms can purchase capital goods and receive the additional profit generated, which is often expressed as an annual rate of return. The **rate of return** is the additional profit generated by an investment expenditure over a period of time, expressed as a percentage. Or firms can place funds in the financial markets and earn interest. Here firms are not borrowing funds from the financial markets, and thus not paying interest.

If the rate of return on the capital is greater than the interest rate, meaning the capital is earning more than if the funds were placed in the financial markets, then the firm should make the investment expenditure. Alternatively, the capital is earning enough to cover the cost of borrowing from the financial markets. If the rate of return is less than the interest rate, then the firm should not make the investment expenditure.

Firms throughout the economy have many investment expenditures to choose from. Some of these expenditures are for highly profitable capital goods, with high rates of return, while other investment expenditures are for capital goods with relatively low rates of return. This suggests that when interest rates are relatively low, perhaps 10 percent, a wide range of investment expenditures will be made, as shown in Figure 4.3.2 by point B on line I. But as the interest rate increases to 15 percent, at point A, some of the less profitable investment expenditures will not be made. For example, expenditures for capital goods that have a rate of return of only 11 or 12 percent are not made if the interest rate is 15 percent, because the firms place the funds in the financial markets and earn the 15 percent.

Shifts in the Investment Curves

So far we have two separate graphs depicting investment in the economy. Figure 4.3.1 illustrates the relationship between investment and output, and Figure 4.3.2 the relationship between investment and the interest rate. In fact, either figure can give us all of the information we need con-

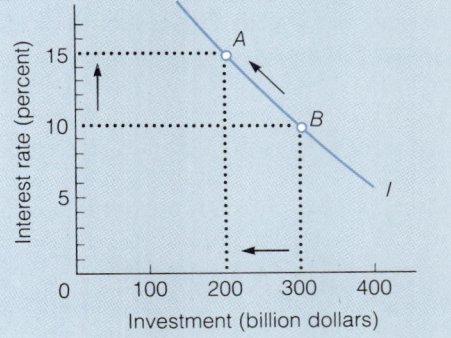

Figure 4.3.2

Investment and the Interest Rate

Investment expenditures are inversely related to the interest rate. An increase in the interest rate leads to a reduction in the level of investment expenditures.

cerning investment, output, and the interest rate, as Figure 4.3.3 shows.

Panel a in Figure 4.3.3 depicts *only* the relationship between investment and output, shown by curve I; all other factors affecting investment, including the interest rate, are held constant. But, we can see what happens to investment in panel a as the interest rate changes. If the interest rate declines, investment increases at every level of output, and the investment curve shifts upward from I to I'.

In panel b, which depicts the relationship between investment and the interest rate, all factors other than the interest rate are held unchanged, including output. But if the level of output increases, investment also increases, meaning at every interest rate investment is greater, and the investment curve shifts rightward from I to I'.

Both panels in Figure 4.3.3 are depicting the same two relationships, one between output and investment and one between the interest rate and investment. The only difference is that in each case one relationship is highlighted by being placed on the axes, and the other is placed in the background. In later discussions we find it useful to use each graph separately. But keep in mind that both tell the same story.

Determinants of Investment

While output and the interest rate have a strong effect on investment expenditures, there are four other **determinants of investment:** technology, cost of capital goods, government policies, and expectations. Each of these determinants can cause a shift in the investment curves in Figure 4.3.3.

Technology Change in technology is one determinant of investment expenditures. As new technology becomes available, existing capital is usu-

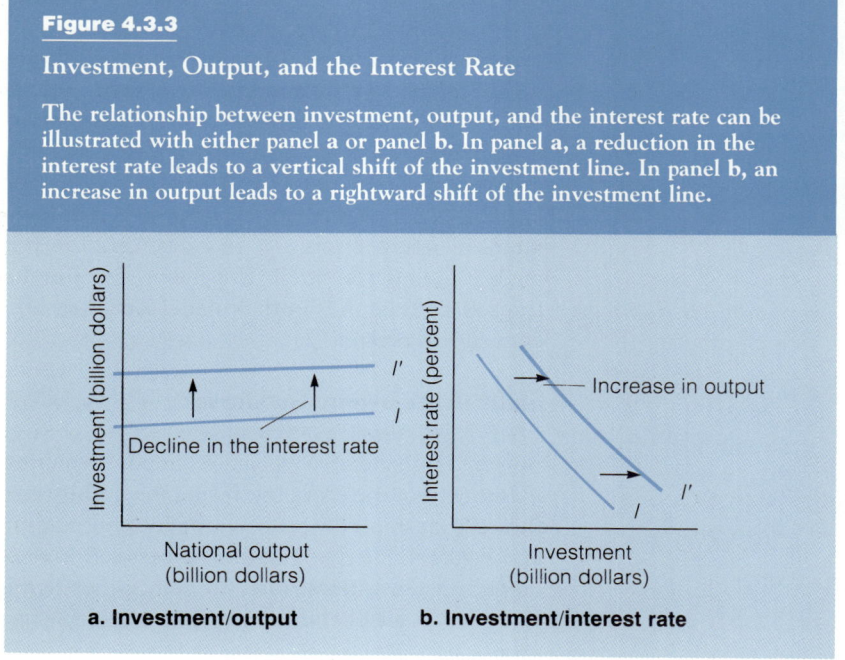

Figure 4.3.3

Investment, Output, and the Interest Rate

The relationship between investment, output, and the interest rate can be illustrated with either panel **a** or panel **b**. In panel **a**, a reduction in the interest rate leads to a vertical shift of the investment line. In panel **b**, an increase in output leads to a rightward shift of the investment line.

a. **Investment/output**

b. **Investment/interest rate**

ally outdated, causing firms to invest in new capital. For example, when a new generation of computers is introduced, existing computers need to be replaced to keep pace. In addition, the introduction of new types of products developed through technological innovations usually leads to investment in new factories required to make the new products.

Cost of Capital Goods Changes in the cost of capital goods, relative to the price of the product they produce, lead to changes in investment. If the cost becomes relatively cheaper, then firms will tend to buy more, and investment expenditures are increased. But if the cost becomes relatively higher, the opposite will likely occur.

Government Policies A wide variety of government policies can also affect investment expenditures. If the government provides investment tax credits, reduces laws and regulations, or otherwise provides a favorable climate for business, then investment expenditures are likely to increase.

Expectations Firms' expectations concerning the economy can affect investment. If firms expect an expansion in the economy, they are likely to increase investment expenditures to prepare for an anticipated increase in sales, but if they expect a downturn, then they are likely to decrease investment expenditures.

CONSUMPTION AND INVESTMENT

To conclude our discussion of investment in this unit, let's relate investment expenditures to the consumption expenditures discussed in the previous unit. We can do this in two ways. First, by noting that investment and consumption both constitute expenditures on final goods and services, we can add investment to the consumption function introduced in the last unit. Second, we need to take another look at the circular flow of the economy discussed in Section 3. In doing both, we will see how investment resembles consumption in one way, but differs from it in another.

Aggregate Expenditures with Two Sectors

Aggregate expenditures are the total expenditures on final goods and services by all relevant sectors in the economy. If the economy has only two sectors, household and business, aggregate expenditures on national product are the sum of consumption and investment. If we want to understand aggregate expenditures, the consumption function graph from Unit 4.2 needs to be slightly modified.

Figure 4.3.4 reproduces the consumption function C from Figure 4.2.1. Recall that the consumption function represents the expenditures by the household sector at each level of income or output, with no distinction made between income and output. Because we are considering only two sectors, household and business, all revenue received by firms is used to pay income to the factors of production.

Now let's look at the aggregate expenditures at each level of output (income) by including investment expenditures with consumption expenditures. Here we simplify matters by saying that investment is autonomous, and equal to $200 at every level of output. Therefore, if consumption expenditures are $175 when output is $100, aggregate expenditures are $375, including the $200 of investment. By the same logic, aggregate expenditures are $600 if output is $400, and $1200 if output is $1200.

Thus, the highest line in Figure 4.3.4 is the aggregate expenditures line, labeled $C + I = AE$, which tells us the total expenditures on national product at every level of output. Note that since we are now considering both investment and consumption, the vertical axis has been relabeled as aggregate expenditures. Furthermore, since investment expenditures are autonomous in this analysis, the AE line is parallel to the consumption function C. At every level of output the distance between, and the slopes of, the two lines are the same because investment expenditures are the same. But recall that the slope of the consumption function is the marginal propensity to consume, meaning that the slope of the AE line is also equal to the MPC.

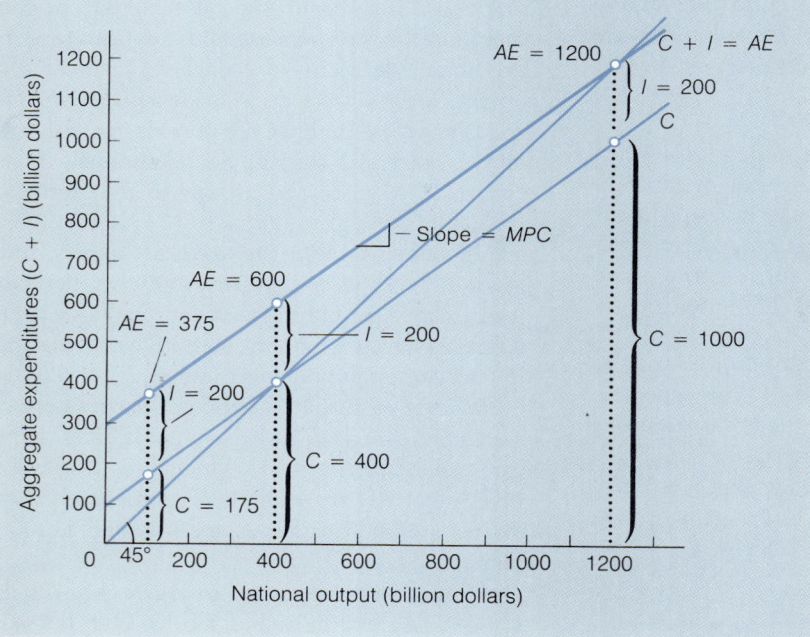

Figure 4.3.4

Aggregate Expenditures for a Two-Sector Economy

Aggregate expenditures for a two-sector economy are the total of consumption and investment expenditures. The aggregate expenditures line can be found by adding investment expenditures to the consumption function. If investment expenditures are autonomous, the aggregate expenditures line is parallel to the consumption function, and the slope of the aggregate expenditures line is equal to the marginal propensity to consume.

The Circular Flow

Now that we have seen how investment is similar to consumption in terms of aggregate expenditures, let's look at the circular flow to see how they differ. Figure 4.3.5 shows a simplified version of the circular flow, with only two sectors, household and business. We have also eliminated the financial markets to make an important point.

In this circular flow revenue from the sale of national product is used to pay factors of production, becoming the national income of households. Remember that households use their income in two ways, consumption and saving. The consumption expenditures remain in this circular flow to purchase national product, which ultimately ends up as household income, and thus is used again for consumption expenditures. This relationship

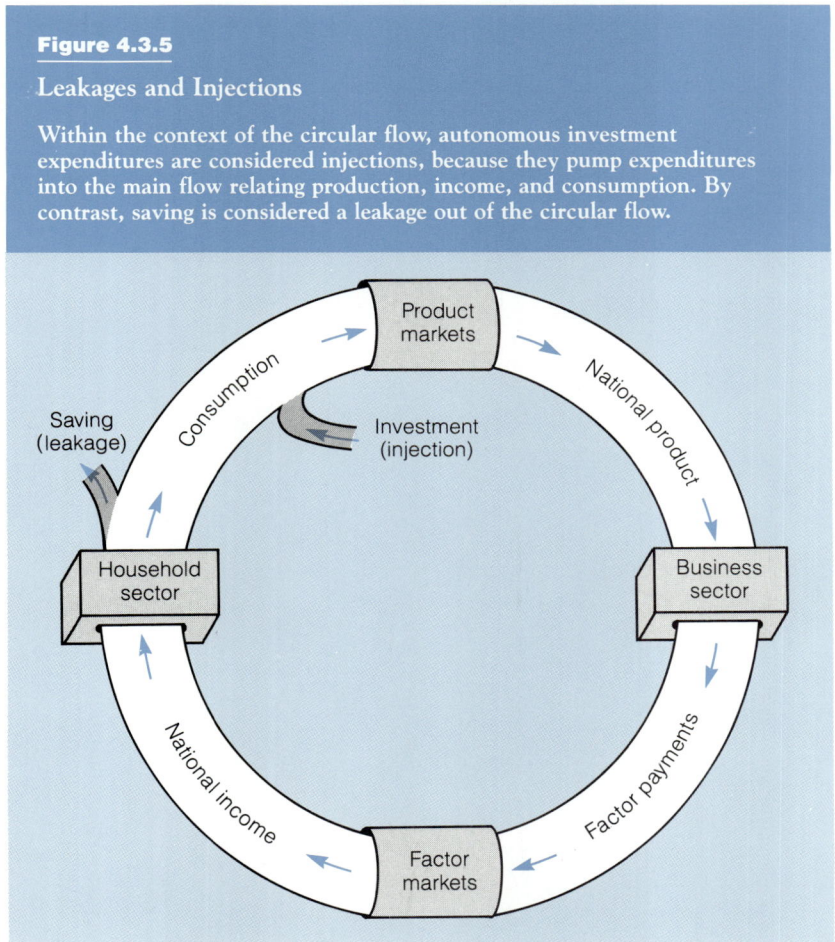

Figure 4.3.5

Leakages and Injections

Within the context of the circular flow, autonomous investment expenditures are considered injections, because they pump expenditures into the main flow relating production, income, and consumption. By contrast, saving is considered a leakage out of the circular flow.

between consumption and income forms the foundation of the economy's circular flow, because consumption expenditures continue to circle their way through the economy. But in a sense, saving leaks out of the circular flow. In fact, a **leakage** is a nonconsumption use of income that diverts funds away from the main flow relating national product, factor payments, national income, and expenditures.

Now let's look at investment. If investment is autonomous, and does not depend on output or income, the investment expenditures enter the circular flow only once. Once investment expenditures are made, no more will be made if output or income increases. This is fundamentally different from the consumption expenditures, which continue to increase as long as income continues to increase. In fact, the investment expenditures are used to purchase national product, and ultimately generate household income and thus consumption. Therefore, investment expenditures are often considered injections into the economy, which stimulate the circular flow. An **injection** is an expen-

Figure 4.3.6

Quarterly Change in Investment and Consumption, 1980 to 1985

This diagram indicates the instability of investment expenditures. The percentage change in investment expenditures from one quarter to the next is often very large, and many times negative. In contrast, the percentage change in consumption expenditures is relatively small, and seldom negative. These fluctuations in investment expenditures contribute to the economy's instability. Source: U.S. Bureau of Economic Analysis, *Survey of Current Business*, selected issues.

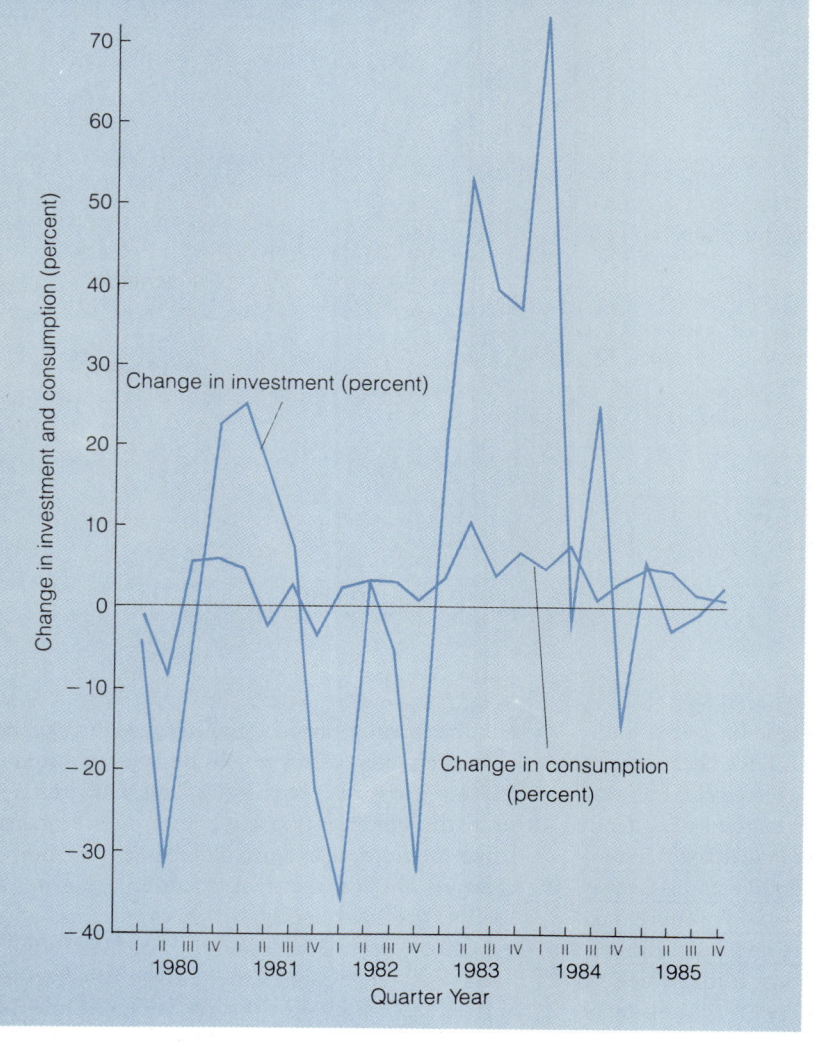

diture on national product that is outside the main flow relating national product, factor payments, national income, and expenditures.

RECENT DATA ON INVESTMENT EXPENDITURES

Investment expenditures are the most variable of the three domestic expenditures on national production. The variability of investment expenditures, as we saw in Unit 3.7, is often cited as one reason for the fluctuations of the business cycle. Figure 4.3.6 depicts recent information concerning changes in investment expenditures to indicate the extent of its variability. The lines plot the percentage change of investment expenditures and consumption expenditures from one quarter (three-month period) to the next, for the years 1980 to 1985.

The most noticeable feature of Figure 4.3.6 is the wide fluctuations of the line for investment. Note that the change in investment continually goes from a large positive percent to a large negative percent, and back again. The largest positive change is 71.6 percent, and the largest negative change is −36.5. By contrast, the line representing the percentage change in consumption from one quarter to the next shows very few fluctuations; it is negative for only a few quarters, and never rises over 10 percent.

IN SUMMARY
Investment

- There is an important distinction between planned and realized investment. Planned investment is the expenditure that the business sector would like to make; realized investment is the expenditure that firms end up making. Unplanned changes in inventories represent the difference between planned and realized investment.

- One of the two most important factors affecting investment is the level of national income and output. Investment expenditures are typically autonomous, but can change slightly because of changes in national output.

- The interest rate is the second factor affecting investment. Regardless of the source of funding for investment expenditures, a higher interest rate increases the opportunity cost of the expenditure. Therefore, investment expenditures are reduced at higher interest rates.

- The relationship between output and investment can be depicted in one graph, and the relationship between the interest rate and investment can be depicted in another. However, either graph can be used to provide the same information concerning output, the interest rate, and investment. A change in the interest rate shifts the investment/output curve, and a change in output shifts the interest rate/investment curve.

- After output and the interest rate, the four most important determinants of investment are technology, cost of capital goods, government policies, and expectations. A change in any of these determinants can cause a shift in both of the investment curves.

- In terms of the household and business sectors, aggregate expenditures are the total of consumption and investment. This means the aggregate expenditure line for the economy can be found by simply adding investment expenditures, at every level of income, to the consumption function. If investment expenditures are autonomous, then the aggregate expenditures line is parallel to the consumption function, and has a slope equal to the marginal propensity to consume.

- Autonomous investment expenditures can be considered an injection (nonconsumption expenditure) into the circular flow. Saving can be considered a leakage (nonconsumption use of income) out of the circular flow.

- Investment expenditures are more variable than consumption expenditures. They show relatively large percentage changes from one quarter to the next. The variability of investment is often cited as an underlying cause of business cycles.

QUESTIONS FOR STUDY AND ANALYSIS

1. Suppose you have the following schedule of investment expenditures and the associated level of national output:

Output	$100	200	300	400	500	600	700	800
Investment	120	140	180	200	220	240	260	280

a. Construct the investment curve relating investment to national output.
b. Assume the interest rate declines from 10 to 5 percent, leading to a $100 increase in investment expenditures at every level of income. Construct the new investment curve based on the lower interest rate. How does it compare to the original curve?
c. Based on this change in the interest rate, construct an investment curve relating investment and the interest rate, assuming the level of output is $500.
d. Now construct a second curve relating investment to the interest rate that assumes the level of output is $200. How does this second curve compare with the curve in question 1c?

2. To see why investment is inversely related to the interest rate, let's look at the following table of investment opportunities for Keynes Communications Co. In each of the seven projects, Keynes invests exactly $1000, which provides the annual return indicated.

Project	Annual Return
1	$ 50
2	75
3	100
4	125
5	150
6	175
7	200

a. If Keynes can borrow as many funds from the bank as it wants for a 9 percent annual interest charge, which projects are undertaken? What is the total amount of investment undertaken?
b. If the bank raises the interest rate it charges Keynes from 9 percent to 14 percent, which projects are now undertaken? What is the total amount of investments undertaken? How has the change in the interest rate affected investment expenditures by the Keynes Communications Co.?

3. For each of the following items indicate which determinant of investment is involved, whether it will cause investment to increase or decrease, and why.
a. The federal government eliminates sales taxes on the sale of all capital goods.
b. The federal government announces that next year it will eliminate sales taxes on the sale of all capital goods.
c. A practical, safe, and commercial method of generating electricity using fusion energy is discovered.
d. Leading economic indicators predict that the economy is headed into a recession in six months.
e. The president dismantles several government regulatory agencies, including the Environmental Protection Agency, the Consumer Product Safety Commission, and the Occupational Safety and Health Administration.
f. Labor unions involved in the production of capital goods receive a 10 percent wage increase.

4. In Unit 3.7 we discussed how investment expenditures might lead to the contractions and expansions of the business cycle. Explain the role changes in business inventories play in changes of realized investment and the business cycle.

5. If investment expenditures are autonomous, how is the slope of the aggregate expenditures line related to the slope of the consumption function? Explain.

REVIEW GLOSSARY

aggregate expenditures The total expenditures on final goods and services for all relevant sectors. If the only two sectors in the economy are the household and business sectors, then aggregate expenditures are the total of consumption and investment expenditures. The aggregate expenditure line is found by adding investment to the consumption function.

autonomous investment expenditures Investment expenditures that do not depend on the current level of national income and output.

determinants of investment Other than output and the interest rate, the four most important factors that affect investment are technology, cost of capital goods, government policies, and expectations. A change in these determinants causes either of the investment curves to shift.

injection A nonconsumption expenditure on national product that is outside of the main flow relating national product, factor payments, national income, and expenditures.

interest rate The charge for the use of borrowed funds over a period of time, expressed as a percentage.

leakage A nonconsumption use of income that diverts funds away from the main flow relating national product, factor payments, national income, and expenditures. Saving is one important type of leakage in the economy.

planned investment Investment expenditures that business firms would like to make over a period of time, based on conditions in the economy.

rate of return The additional profit generated by an investment expenditure over a period of time, expressed as a percentage.

realized investment Investment expenditures that business firms actually make over a period of time.

UNIT 4.4

Government Purchases and Taxes

In this unit we focus on the expenditures made by the government sector for the purchase of final goods and services. However, our concern with the government sector does not stop with these purchases. Note that the government's effect is dual. The government can influence aggregate expenditures not only directly through purchases but also indirectly through taxes. On the one hand, government purchases contribute to the aggregate expenditures, but on the other hand, taxes used to finance these purchases reduce disposable income and thus consumption expenditures.

In studying the government sector and aggregate expenditures, we first examine the basic components of the government's budget, expenditures and taxes. We then see how government purchases directly affect aggregate expenditures, and how taxes affect consumption and thus, indirectly, aggregate expenditures. And finally we revisit the circular flow to see similarities between government purchases and investment, and between saving and taxes.

THE GOVERNMENT'S BUDGET

The best place to begin a study of the government sector is with the budget. In general, a **budget** is a listing of all revenues and expenditures for a given period of time. The two basic expenditures in the government's budget are purchases of final goods and services and transfer payments; the two basic types of revenue are taxes and government borrowing. Table 4.4.1 presents a listing of the federal government's budget components for recent years.

Table 4.4.1

The Federal Government's Budget (billions)

The federal government's budget consists of two main types of expenditures, purchases of final goods and transfer payments. Revenues come primarily from tax receipts, but deficit borrowing is becoming increasingly more important.

	1965	1975	1985
Expenditures	$118.5	$328.8	$984.7
Purchases of goods	64.6	117.9	355.4
Transfer payments	30.6	134.5	379.8
Other*	23.3	76.1	249.5
Tax receipts	120.0	283.4	785.4
Deficit borrowing (−) or surplus (+)	+1.5	−45.4	−199.3

Source: U.S. Bureau of Economic Analysis, *Survey of Current Business*, selected issues.

*Includes grants to state and local governments, net interest paid, and subsidies of government enterprises.

As Table 4.4.1 shows, the difference between expenditures and tax receipts has become more important in recent years. Note that in 1965 expenditures were slightly less than tax receipts, causing a budget surplus. A **budget surplus** exists when the government's expenditures are less than taxes. But by 1985 expenditures were far greater than tax receipts, causing a budget deficit. A **budget deficit** exists when the government's expenditures are greater than taxes. To finance a budget deficit, the government borrows funds through the financial markets, as mentioned in our discussion of the circular flow. The government typically borrows funds by issuing various types of bonds, rang-

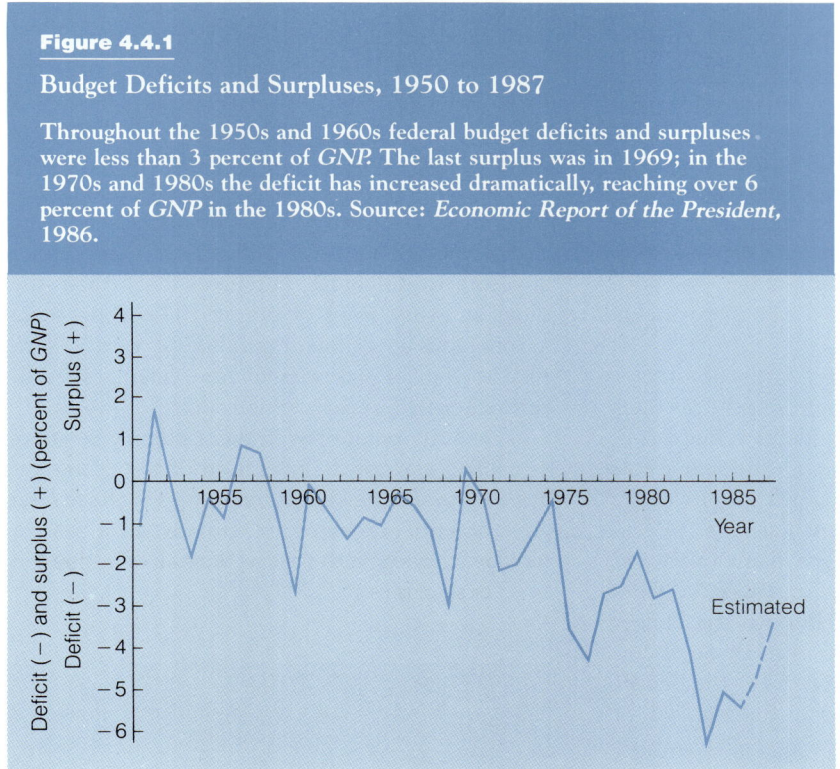

Figure 4.4.1

Budget Deficits and Surpluses, 1950 to 1987

Throughout the 1950s and 1960s federal budget deficits and surpluses were less than 3 percent of *GNP*. The last surplus was in 1969; in the 1970s and 1980s the deficit has increased dramatically, reaching over 6 percent of *GNP* in the 1980s. Source: *Economic Report of the President,* 1986.

ing from $25 and $50 savings bonds purchased by households to $100,000 treasury bills purchased by commercial banks.

Figure 4.4.1 places the government's budget deficits and surpluses into historical perspective. Throughout the 1950s and 1960s the government had deficits in some years and surpluses in others, but never more than 3 percent of *GNP*. However, the last surplus was in 1969. Throughout the 1970s the government maintained a budget deficit, and in the 1980s the deficit dramatically increased, to over 6 percent of *GNP*, stimulating lively debate among economists and policymakers concerning its adverse effects. In Unit 4.7, we see how the budget deficit relates to economic activity.

Discretionary and Nondiscretionary Expenditures

In connection with the government budget an important distinction should be made between discretionary and nondiscretionary expenditures and revenues. Although it is possible to have discretionary revenues, discretionary expenditures are more common, and can better illustrate this concept. **Discretionary expenditures** are expenditures that must be periodically (annually) appropriated by legislative and political bodies. Discretionary expenditures include most federal purchases appropriated by Congress, which each year must pass new legislation for the appropriations. In this way the government has some control over how much is spent on each expenditure. By contrast, **nondiscretionary expenditures** are expenditures that depend on established laws and that must be made unless new laws are passed. Transfer payments, such as unemployment compensation, social security benefits, and welfare payments, are examples of nondiscretionary expenditures. Once a law is passed guaranteeing social security benefits to anyone over sixty-five, the payments are automatic. The government has no control over the total payments unless the law is changed.

In this sense taxes are primarily nondiscretionary revenue. The government sets the tax rates and determines the payment guidelines, but it does not directly control the amount of tax revenue collected, which depends on how much activity meets the tax guidelines for that particular year.

While we distinguish between discretionary and nondiscretionary expenditures, in reality there is a thin line between the two. Although the budget for the Defense Department is considered a discretionary expenditure, a large portion of the budget is automatic and really beyond the control of Congress. The same is true for most government agencies.

The distinctions between discretionary and nondiscretionary expenditures by state and local governments are also blurred. Because funds have to be appropriated each year, state and local governments have a large share of discretionary expenditures. By the same token, many state and local governments have balanced budget constraints in their constitutions or charters, and are able to spend only the amount received in tax revenues. This means that they have discretionary power over *how* to spend the revenues, but little or no discretionary power over *how much* to spend. Therefore, a great deal of the expenditures by state and local governments can also be considered nondiscretionary.

Government Purchases

Based on the distinction between discretionary and nondiscretionary government purchases, we need to consider the relationship between government purchases and output. For most of our analysis in later units it will be sufficient to say that government purchases are unrelated to output. In this case we can say that government purchases are autonomous. **Autonomous government purchases** are purchases by the government sector that do not depend on the current level of national income and output. Figure 4.4.2 illustrates autonomous government purchases, purchases that remain the same at every level of output. The concept of autonomous government purchases is nearly identical to that of autonomous investment expenditures discussed in the previous unit.

Do autonomous government purchases reflect a realistic view of the operation of the economy? Yes and no. In the budgetary process of the federal government, purchases are initially set a year or more in advance, as the budget works its way through

Figure 4.4.2

Government Purchases and Output

Government purchases that do not depend on the level of income, indicated here by the horizontal line G, are particularly relevant at the federal level. However, at the state and local level government purchases are likely to increase as output increases, giving the government purchases line a positive slope, as seen by G'.

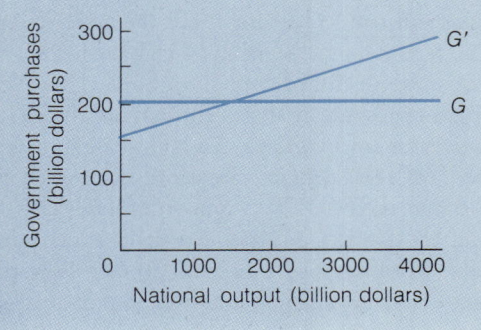

the various branches of government. This means that purchases at the federal level are not sensitive to fluctuations of output in the economy. The economy may be in a contractionary phase, but the level of government purchases was established before the level of output began to decline.

However, it is a little different at the state and local level. Recall that many state and local governments operate under constitutionally constrained balanced budgets, meaning they can spend only the revenues that they receive. For some governments this represents a month-to-month constraint; others have to balance their budget over the course of a year.

When we consider that the tax revenues received by state and local governments are tied to the income of the taxpayers, we begin to see that their expenditures are likely to depend on the overall level of output in the economy. As income drops, households pay fewer taxes to state and local governments. With lower tax revenues, state and local governments are constrained to spend less, and government purchases fall. Alternatively, as output increases, tax revenues and government purchases also increase. Since state and local purchases account for almost two-thirds of government purchases, increases in output are likely to lead to increases in government purchases.

Net Taxes

Let's now turn our attention to the taxes received by the government sector, particularly net taxes. **Net taxes** are the difference between taxes and transfer payments. Throughout our discussion of macroeconomics, we consider only net taxes, because taxes and transfer payments represent essentially identical, but opposite, flows in the economy.

For example, taxes are payments from the household sector to the government sector, so if taxes increase, households have less disposable income. Transfer payments are payments from the government sector to the household sector, so if transfer payments increase, households have more disposable income. This means that if the household sector pays $100 in taxes and receives $100 in transfer payments, it has no change in disposable income. And if the household sector pays $100 in taxes and receives $80 in transfer payments it has net tax payments of only $20 to the government. In effect, taxes take money from one pocket of the household sector, and transfer payments put the money back into another pocket.

Another similarity between taxes and transfer payments is that both are related to the level of output in the economy. An increase in the economy's output means households pay more income taxes, so net taxes increase. And an increase in the economy's output also means that the government makes fewer transfer payments to the households, because unemployment declines, and unemployment compensation payments are less. In addition, more poor people are able to find jobs and no longer require welfare payments. Moreover, workers at or near retirement age may continue to work or go back to work, and thus receive fewer social security benefits.

AGGREGATE EXPENDITURES

At this point let's identify the aggregate expenditures by the three sectors of the economy we have discussed thus far: household, business, and government. To isolate the effect of government purchases and net taxes on aggregate expenditures, let's consider each separately.

Government Purchases

Government purchases enter into aggregate expenditures in much the same way that investment enters into aggregate expenditures. To illustrate this point, let's look at Figure 4.4.3, which duplicates the graph in Figure 4.3.4, but includes some additional information.

First, we can identify the consumption function, labeled C. Second, we can identify the aggre-

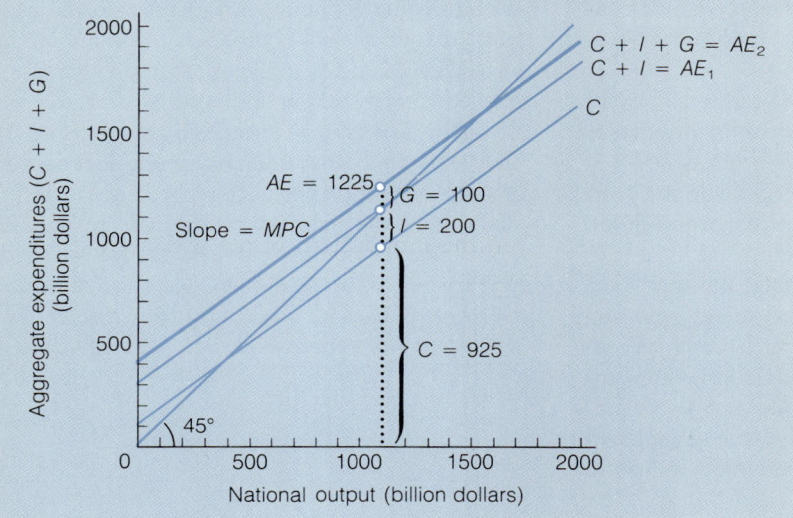

Figure 4.4.3

Aggregate Expenditures for a Three-Sector Economy

Aggregate expenditures for a three-sector economy are the total of consumption, investment, and government purchases. The aggregate expenditures line can be found by adding government purchases and investment to the consumption function. If government purchases and investment are autonomous, then the aggregate expenditures line is parallel to the consumption function, and the slope of the aggregate expenditures line is equal to the marginal propensity to consume.

gate expenditures line based on the household and business sectors, labeled AE_1. Note that AE_1 is parallel to the consumption function, meaning that investment expenditures are autonomous. AE_1 tells us the total level of consumption and investment expenditures at every level of output. However, since we are now including the government sector in the economy, the aggregate expenditures line is incomplete.

Aggregate expenditures for a three-sector economy are consumption, investment, and government purchases, so aggregate expenditures in Figure 4.4.3 are given by the line AE_2. Let's say that government purchases are equal to $100 at every level of output. In this case we can see that if output is $1100, aggregate expenditures are $1225, composed of $925 in consumption, $200 in investment, and $100 in government purchases. Since government purchases are autonomous, AE_2 is parallel to AE_1, and since investment is also autonomous, AE_1 is parallel to the consumption function. The aggregate expenditures line AE_2 has the same slope as the consumption function, which equals the marginal propensity to consume.

Net Taxes

As mentioned earlier, net taxes affect aggregate expenditures through consumption. If net taxes are increased, then households have less disposable income and fewer consumption expenditures. To illustrate how net taxes affect consumption expenditures and the consumption function, let's consider a lump sum tax.

A lump sum tax does not depend on the level of output and might take the form of charging every person in the economy a specific amount, such as $100, regardless of income. Figure 4.4.4 illustrates how a lump sum tax affects the consumption function. The consumption function with no taxes is labeled C. However, with taxes the consumption function shifts down to C'. Let's see why.

Suppose that the economy's output is $1000 and that consumption expenditures are $850, if there are no taxes. Remember that without taxes the economy's national output is also the disposable income received by households. This is not the case if taxes are introduced.

If net taxes are $100 at every level of income, then disposable income is $100 less than national output at all levels. But consumption expenditures depend on disposable income, not on national output. Therefore, if national output in Figure 4.4.4 is $1000, disposable income declines to $900 because taxes are $100. If the marginal propensity to consume is 0.75, this means consumption declines by $75, so consumption is only $775 (= $850 − $75) when taxes are equal to $100. And since the MPC is the same at every level of income, and taxes are the same at every level of income, consumption is $75 less at every level of output, based on the introduction of net taxes. The new consumption function with net taxes, labeled C', is vertically lower and parallel to the old consumption function. Moreover, the new consumption function has the same slope as the old, the marginal propensity to consume.

We should note that consumption declines by only $75 when taxes are $100 because saving declines by the additional $25. Remember that disposable income is divided between consumption and saving. When disposable income changes, consumption and saving change based on the marginal propensities to consume and save.

In reality, taxes are not lump sum, but increase as the level of income increases. If the economy has more income, the government receives more tax revenues. In this case the consumption function *with taxes* is not parallel to the consumption function *without taxes*.

Figure 4.4.4

Net Taxes and the Consumption Function

This diagram illustrates the relationship between lump sum taxes and the consumption function. Since lump sum taxes are the same at every level of income, disposable income is less than national income by an equal amount at every level of income. The consumption function with lump sum taxes is parallel to the consumption function without the taxes.

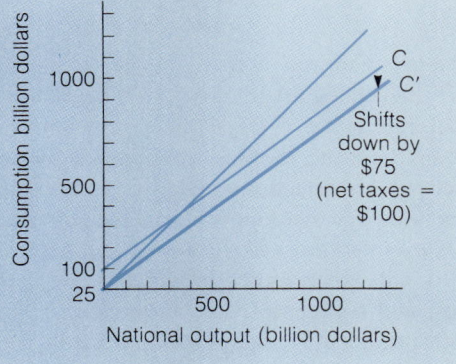

THE CIRCULAR FLOW

Let's return once again to the economy's circular flow. Figure 4.4.5 presents a simplified depiction of the circular flow, much like Figure 4.3.5 from

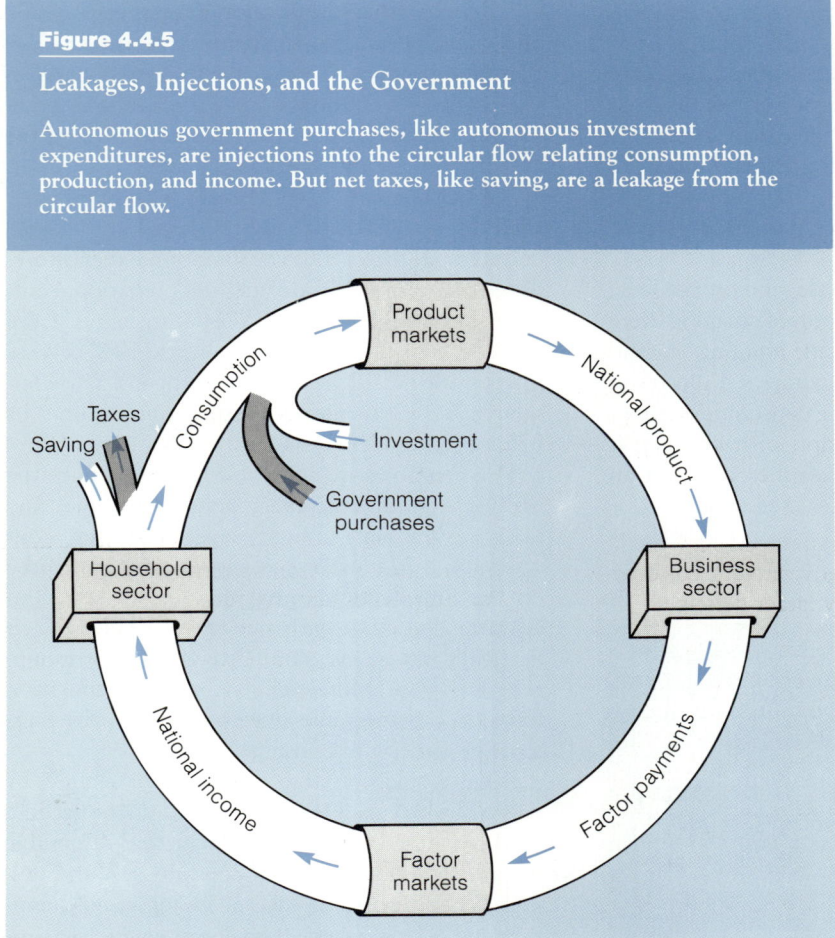

Figure 4.4.5

Leakages, Injections, and the Government

Autonomous government purchases, like autonomous investment expenditures, are injections into the circular flow relating consumption, production, and income. But net taxes, like saving, are a leakage from the circular flow.

the previous unit. Here we see the flow of national product going to the business sector, factor payments going through the factor markets and becoming national income, and consumption expenditures going from the household sector to the product markets. Also, investment expenditures are being injected into the circular flow, and saving is being leaked out of the circular flow.

However, we need to consider two additional flows, net taxes and government purchases. In the context of the circular flow, net taxes, when they depend on the level of income, are a nonconsumption use of income that leaks away. In this sense net taxes resemble saving. In fact, both net taxes and saving are considered leakages from the circular flow.

By the same token, autonomous government purchases are injections into the economy in the same way that autonomous investment expenditures are injections. Government purchases inject additional expenditures on final goods and services, and stimulate the subsequent circular flow relating national product, factor payments, national income, and expenditures.

The point that needs to be stressed here is that government purchases and investment expenditures affect the circular flow in essentially the same manner. It doesn't matter which injection occurs, because both stimulate the flow. The same is true for saving and net taxes, which leak away income that would otherwise stay in the circular flow.

IN SUMMARY

Government Purchases and Taxes

- The government's budget consists of two basic expenditures (purchases of goods and transfer payments) and two sources of revenue (tax receipts and borrowing). If expenditures are less than tax receipts, there is a budget surplus. If expenditures are greater than tax receipts, there is a budget deficit, and the government must borrow through the financial markets. In recent years the federal government has operated with an increasingly larger deficit.

- The government sector can affect expenditures in two basic ways, government purchases and net taxes. Government purchases directly affect aggregate expenditures because, like consumption and investment, they represent an expenditure on final goods and services. Net taxes indirectly affect aggregate expenditures because they change disposable income and, consequently, consumption expenditures.

- Discretionary expenditures (and revenue) have to be approved each year, and thus can be controlled or adjusted by the government. Nondiscretionary expenditures (and revenue) are more or less automatic because, though the government establishes the guidelines, it is unable to control the annual totals.

- Net taxes are taxes minus transfer payments. Taxes and transfer payments are combined in this manner because both affect aggregate expenditures in similar, but opposite, ways. Taxes decrease disposable income and thus consumption, whereas transfer payments increase disposable income and consumption.

- Aggregate expenditures for a three-sector economy are found by adding government purchases to consumption and investment. Graphically, this is shown by adding government purchases to the two-sector aggregate expenditures line $(C + I)$ from Unit 4.3. However, net taxes cause the consumption function to shift downward.

- In the circular flow, net taxes, like saving, are a leakage, or nonconsumption use of income. Furthermore, government purchases, like investment, are an injection, or nonconsumption expenditure.

QUESTIONS FOR STUDY AND ANALYSIS

1. Indicate whether each of the following activities of the government would tend to be more discretionary or nondiscretionary, and why.
   a. State sales tax revenue
   b. Federal appropriations to the military
   c. Unemployment compensation payments
   d. Federal income tax revenue
   e. Municipal appropriations to the fire department

2. If the MPC is equal to 0.8 and net taxes are increased by $1000 at every level income, what happens to the consumption function? Why?

3. Explain why autonomous investment and government purchases are injections, and why net taxes and saving are leakages.

4. For each of the following items, explain which aggregate expenditure is affected and the direction of the shift in the aggregate expenditures line.
   a. Households expect a higher rate of inflation in the future.
   b. The government increases the income tax rate from 10 to 20 percent.
   c. The interest rate declines.
   d. The federal government finally decides to eliminate the deficit and balance the budget.
   e. The marginal propensity to save increases.

5. If the federal government operated under a constitutional constraint to balance its bud-

get, would government purchases be discretionary or nondiscretionary? Explain.

6. During the Depression of the 1930s, investment expenditures declined by about $15 billion. How did this decline affect the aggregate expenditures line? During most of the 1930s government purchases remained unchanged or even declined slightly. What could the government have done to maintain aggregate expenditures at their pre-1930s level?

REVIEW GLOSSARY

autonomous government purchases Government purchases that do not depend on the current level of national income and output.

budget A listing of all revenues and expenditures for a given period of time. The basic components of the government's budget include government purchases and transfer payments on the expenditures side, and taxes and borrowing on the revenues side.

budget deficit A situation that exists when a government's expenditures are greater than taxes.

budget surplus A situation that exists when a government's expenditures are less than taxes.

discretionary expenditures Expenditures that must be periodically (annually) appropriated by legislative and political bodies. Discretionary expenditures give the government a great deal of control over the total amount of the expenditures.

net taxes The difference between taxes and transfer payments. Net taxes are the amount of tax revenues remaining for government purchases after transfer payments are made.

nondiscretionary expenditures Expenditures that depend on established laws and that must be made unless new laws are passed. Nondiscretionary expenditures limit the amount of control over the total amount of the expenditures.

UNIT 4.5

Determining National Income and Output

The time has now come for us to put together the components of aggregate expenditures discussed in the last three units and examine the overall operation of the economy. In particular, we want to see how the level of national income and output is determined. The analysis in this unit illustrates how the economy achieves equilibrium by producing an output sufficient to satisfy aggregate expenditures.

First, we have to lay some ground rules to let us see where this simple analysis of income and output determination fits into the more detailed analyses of later units. Our initial analysis is based on the equality of aggregate expenditures and output. Here we see how equilibrium output is determined in a three-sector economy containing household, business, and government sectors. W' then discuss how equilibrium can be viewed through the equality of leakages and injections. And finally we examine how this equilibrium analysis relates to the aggregate market.

THE GROUND RULES

Before we get into the details of determining the equilibrium level of output in the economy, it is important to specify some of the assumptions used in this unit.

First, we ignore many of the complexities of the economic flows between sectors that were illustrated in Figure 3.3.5, primarily to simplify our analysis. Since most of the flows are relatively small,

UNIT 4.5 ▪ DETERMINING NATIONAL INCOME AND OUTPUT

and affect only the relative levels of each measure of income and output and not the totals, we can concentrate for now on the most important flows. Therefore, the first four measures of income and output—gross national product, net national product, national income, and personal income—are set equal to each other. For purposes of notation, let Y represent this overall measure of income and output in the economy.

One of the flows that we retain in this analysis is net taxes, or taxes minus transfer payments. This means that the fifth measure of income, disposable income, is *not* equal to the other measures of income and output. The notation for disposable income, to distinguish it from output Y, is DY.

Second, in this analysis we assume that investment, government purchases, and net taxes are not related to output, so the slope of the aggregate expenditures line equals the marginal propensity to consume. This assumption allows us to look at the fundamental problem of determining equilibrium without complicating our analysis unnecessarily.

Third, we eliminate the foreign sector, once again allowing ourselves to concentrate on the relevant analysis, though none of the conclusions reached in this unit are fundamentally changed by including the foreign sector. A more detailed study of the foreign sector is taken up in Units 14.1 and 14.2.

EQUILIBRIUM WITH AGGREGATE EXPENDITURES

Before we examine how to determine the equilibrium level of output in the economy, let's review the concept of equilibrium introduced in Unit 2.4. **Equilibrium** is a state in which opposing forces exactly offset each other, and there is no inherent tendency for change. Unit 2.4 discussed equilibrium in the context of the market for a single good, but the concept of equilibrium can also be applied to the entire economy. That is, we can identify equilibrium between the supply of national product and the expenditures on national product. And in terms of the national economy, equilibrium occurs when national product does not change.

In fact, there are two separate ways to view equilibrium in the economy. The first approach, which concerns us in the next few pages, looks at the overall level of production and expenditures. The second approach, which will attract our attention later in the unit, looks at leakages and injections. To see how the economy can achieve equilibrium, let's examine a three-sector economy containing household, business, and government sectors.

Equilibrium in a three-sector economy occurs when aggregate expenditures on output are equal to the amount of output produced. In equilibrium all of the output produced is purchased by one of the sectors, and there is no surplus. In addition, the sectors obtain the output that they want to purchase, and there is no shortage. Table 4.5.1 presents the information needed to illustrate equilibrium for a three-sector economy.

Aggregate Expenditures

The first column of Table 4.5.1 lists the level of national output, which is equal to the level of national income. However, since the government sector and net taxes are included, national income is not equal to disposable income, which is listed in the second column. The third and fourth columns list the disposition of disposable income between consumption and saving. If households have $500 of income, they spend $475 on consumption and save $25. The fifth column lists the level of investment expenditures. To keep this analysis simple, assume that investment expenditures are autonomous, in this case equal to $200. But note, the basic procedure used for finding the equilibrium level of output does not change if investment increases with the level of output. The sixth and seventh columns list government purchases and net taxes, which again, for simplicity's sake, are assumed to be autonomous and are equal to $100. Note that the level of net taxes is equal

Table 4.5.1

Equilibrium in a Three-Sector Economy (billions)

Equilibrium in a three-sector economy is found by equating the level of national output to aggregate expenditures. Here this occurs when national output is equal to $1300. If output is less than $1300, aggregate expenditures are greater than production. If output is greater than $1200, aggregate expenditures are less than production.

National Output (Y)	Disposable Income (DY)	Consumption (C)	Saving (S)	Investment (I)	Government Purchases (G)	Net Taxes (T)	Aggregate Expenditures (AE)
$ 600	$ 500	$ 475	$ 25	$200	$100	$100	$ 775
700	600	550	50	200	100	100	850
800	700	625	75	200	100	100	925
900	800	700	100	200	100	100	1000
1000	900	775	125	200	100	100	1075
1100	1000	850	150	200	100	100	1150
1200	1100	925	175	200	100	100	1225
1300	1200	1000	200	200	100	100	1300
1400	1300	1075	225	200	100	100	1375
1500	1400	1150	250	200	100	100	1450
1600	1500	1225	275	200	100	100	1525
1700	1600	1300	300	200	100	100	1600

to the difference between national output and disposable income.

To find equilibrium, we need to identify the level of output that is equal to the total of consumption expenditures, investment expenditures, and government purchases. Here the eighth and final column becomes extremely important, because it totals the aggregate expenditures made by the household (consumption), business (investment), and government (purchases) sectors by adding the third, fifth, and sixth columns.

By comparing aggregate expenditures in the eighth column with output in the first column, we can easily see if the economy is in equilibrium. If output is $600, consumption is $475, investment is $200, government purchases are $100, and aggregate expenditures are $775. At this level of output aggregate expenditures are greater than production, and current production of final goods and services is not sufficient to satisfy these expenditures.

As we move down the table, we see that aggregate expenditures are greater than output until we reach $1300 in output. At this level, consumption is $1000, investment is $200, and government purchases are $100, so aggregate expenditures total $1300 and are equal to current production. All three sectors are able to obtain all of the production they are willing to buy. But if output is greater than

$1300, aggregate expenditures fall short of production, and part of the current production remains unsold. Only at the $1300 level is the economy in equilibrium; at any other level either producers or buyers are not satisfied.

Changes in Inventories

Although $1300 is clearly the equilibrium level, is there any guarantee that the economy will reach this level? In our study of individual markets we saw that the price of a good changed if there was a surplus or shortage. However, we have yet to consider price in this analysis. What then is the mechanism guiding the economy to equilibrium?

The mechanism lies in the changes in inventories component of investment. **Changes in inventories are the increases or decreases in the business sector's accumulated stocks of raw materials, intermediate goods, and final goods**. Changes in inventories, while a part of realized investment, are not part of the $200 in planned investment expenditures presented in the fifth column of Table 4.5.1.

An analysis of Table 4.5.1 indicates why changes in inventories are unplanned. When output is $600, aggregate expenditures are $775, but it is not possible to satisfy $775 worth of expenditures when current production falls $175 short. When current production cannot satisfy all expenditures, part of the expenditures can be satisfied from past production. In essence, producers can sell more than current production by using inventories built up from past production, thus causing inventories to decline. In fact, whenever aggregate expenditures are greater than output, inventories necessarily decline, signaling producers to increase their level of production to meet demand. The exact opposite occurs if aggregate expenditures are less than production, in which case producers find that their inventories are increasing. Since they are producing more than they are selling, the unplanned inventory changes signal producers to reduce production.

In both cases the economy moves toward equilibrium; once it reaches the equilibrium, aggregate expenditures equal national output, and there are no unplanned changes in inventories. With no changes in inventories, producers have no signal, or reason, to change their level of production.

Keynesian Cross

We can also determine the equilibrium level of income using the graph presented in Figure 4.5.1, which is called the Keynesian cross. The **Keynesian cross is a graph containing the Keynesian aggregate expenditures line that is used to illustrate equilibrium between aggregate expenditures and national output**. The Keynesian cross embodies the essence of the Keynesian economics studied in this section. In the Keynesian cross in this figure, the consumption function relationship, labeled C, is plotted using the consumption numbers from Table 4.5.1. At each level of income we can add the autonomous level of investment expenditures ($200), giving us the line labeled C + I. And finally, if we add autonomous government purchases ($100), we have the aggregate expenditures line for a three-sector economy, labeled AE.

We also need to consider the 45° line in Figure 4.5.1, which takes on new importance in the Keynesian cross. The 45° line tells us every point at which the value on the horizontal axis (output) is equal to the value on the vertical axis (aggregate expenditures). This means that the interesection between the aggregate expenditures line and the 45° line represents equilibrium for the economy. This intersection occurs at point E, where aggregate expenditures are equal to output, at $1300.

If output is less than $1300, the aggregate expenditures line lies above the 45° line, meaning aggregate expenditures are greater than production, and inventories are declining. If output is greater than $1300, the aggregate expenditures line lies below the 45° line, meaning aggregate expenditures are less than production, and inventories are increasing.

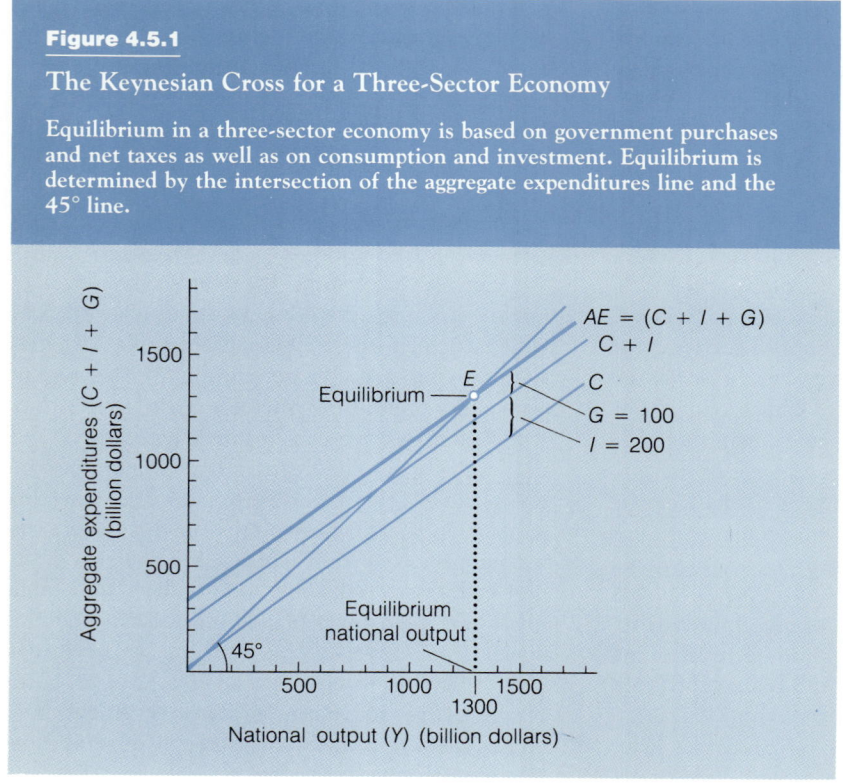

Figure 4.5.1

The Keynesian Cross for a Three-Sector Economy

Equilibrium in a three-sector economy is based on government purchases and net taxes as well as on consumption and investment. Equilibrium is determined by the intersection of the aggregate expenditures line and the 45° line.

EQUILIBRIUM WITH LEAKAGES AND INJECTIONS

Another way of viewing the economy's equilibrium is with leakages and injections. As a simple rule, whenever the economy is in equilibrium, planned leakages are equal to planned injections. Recall that two types of leakages (saving and taxes) and two types of injections (investment and government purchases) were identified in the previous units.

In Table 4.5.1 we saw that, in equilibrium, aggregate expenditures are equal to output. However, we may have overlooked the fact that the equilibrium level of output also occurs when total leakages are equal to total injections, at $300. In fact, this is the only level of output in which planned leakages are equal to planned injections.

To see why leakages equal injections, let's look at this simple relationship:

$$C + S + T = Y = AE = C + I + G$$

This means that income (Y) generated in the production of the economy's output is divided between net taxes (T) and the two uses of disposable income, consumption (C) and saving (S). However, in equilibrium output (Y) is equal to aggregate expenditures (AE), which are composed of consumption (C), planned investment (I), and government purchases (G). Another way of stating this equilibrium relationship is

$$C + S + T = C + I + G$$

But since consumption is the same on both sides of this equation, we can simply state that

$$S + T = I + G$$

In other words, in equilibrium, nonconsumption uses of income (saving and net taxes) are equal to nonconsumption expenditures on output (investment and government purchases).

This relationship cannot be overemphasized. Since part of the income received by households is used for saving and net taxes, consumption expenditures alone are not sufficient to purchase all of the output produced in the economy. However, this deficiency is corrected through investment expenditures and government purchases. The economy is in equilibrium when the output not purchased by households is purchased by the business and government sectors. Note that saving does not need to equal investment, and government expenditures do not need to equal taxes. It is only necessary that the sum of saving and taxes equal the sum of investment and government purchases.

This particular point can be seen in Table 4.5.2, which is identical to Table 4.5.1 except for one change. Instead of government purchases being equal to taxes at $100, government purchases are $200, while taxes remain at $100. If we equate aggregate expenditures with output, we see that equilibrium is $1700. At this level of output saving is $300, investment is $200, government purchases

Table 4.5.2
Equivalence Between Leakages and Injections (billions)

In equilibrium, leakages (saving and taxes) are equal to injections (investment and government purchases). However, saving need not equal investment and government purchases need not equal taxes, as long as in equilibrium ($1700) saving ($300) plus taxes ($100) are equal to investment ($200) plus government purchases ($200).

National Output (Y)	Disposable Income (DY)	Consumption (C)	Saving (S)	Investment (I)	Government Purchases (G)	Net Taxes (T)	Aggregate Expenditures (AE)
$ 600	$ 500	$ 475	$ 25	$200	$200	$100	$ 875
700	600	550	50	200	200	100	950
800	700	625	75	200	200	100	1025
900	800	700	100	200	200	100	1100
1000	900	775	125	200	200	100	1175
1100	1000	850	150	200	200	100	1250
1200	1100	925	175	200	200	100	1325
1300	1200	1000	200	200	200	100	1400
1400	1300	1075	225	200	200	100	1475
1500	1400	1150	250	200	200	100	1550
1600	1500	1225	275	200	200	100	1625
1700	1600	1300	300	200	200	100	1700

are $200, and taxes are $100. In this case saving is not equal to investment, and government purchases are not equal to taxes, but leakages are equal to injections. The total amount of leakages (saving and taxes) is $400, and the amount of injections (investment and government purchases) is also $400.

Figure 4.5.2 graphically illustrates the leakages and injections approach to income determination. Here we start with the saving function (S) graphed with the numbers given in Table 4.5.1. We then add net taxes to the saving function to give us total leakages (S + T). We also have the investment line (I), which is horizontal at $200. To the investment line we add government purchases to give us total injections (I + G). The economy's equilibrium is seen at the intersection of the S + T and I + G lines, where output is $1300. This corresponds to the equilibrium level of output that we identified earlier.

While equilibrium is important, it is also interesting to examine leakages and injections at nonequilibrium levels of output. If output is below the equilibrium level, then leakages are less than injections. If output is above the equilibrium level, then leakages are greater than injections.

At output levels greater than $1300, leakages are greater than injections, meaning more is coming out of the circular flow, in terms of nonconsumption uses of income, than is going back into the circular flow, in terms of nonconsumption expenditures. Under these circumstances the circular flow cannot maintain the same level, and output declines. But if leakages are less than injections, then more nonconsumption expenditures are entering the circular flow than are coming out, and the level of the flow increases.

Moreover, a larger amount of potential expenditures are being leaked from the economy (as saving and net taxes) than are being injected back

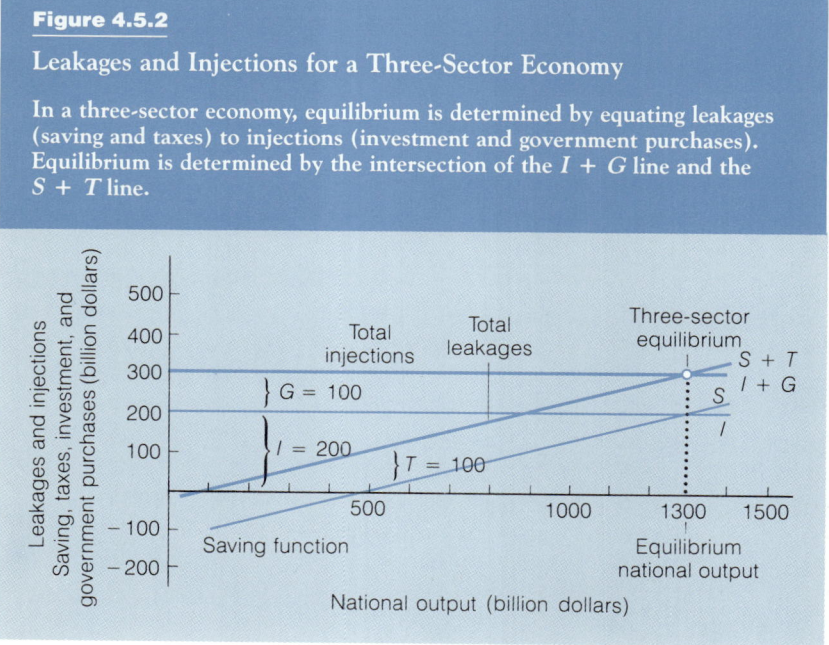

Figure 4.5.2

Leakages and Injections for a Three-Sector Economy

In a three-sector economy, equilibrium is determined by equating leakages (saving and taxes) to injections (investment and government purchases). Equilibrium is determined by the intersection of the *I + G* line and the *S + T* line.

into it (as investment and government purchases). This leads to a deficiency in aggregate demand, causing inventories to build up by the difference between leakages and injections. The change in inventories can be identified as the vertical difference between the $S + T$ and $I + G$ lines in Figure 4.5.2. If leakages are greater than injections, inventories are increasing. If leakages are less than injections, inventories are decreasing.

THE KEYNESIAN CROSS AND THE AGGREGATE MARKET

Now that we have examined the two basic methods of determining equilibrium output (aggregate expenditures and leakages/injections), let's see how Keynesian economics relates to the more general view of the economy based on the aggregate market. An important difference between our discussion of Keynesian economics in this section and our discussion of the aggregate market in Section 3 pertains to the economy's price level. The price level is an integral part of the aggregate market, but in our examination of Keynesian economics up to this point, we have not allowed the price to change. In Figure 4.5.3 we remedy that situation.

Panel a presents the Keynesian cross diagram with two separate aggregate expenditures line, AE and AE'. Both aggregate expenditures lines are found by adding the level of consumption, investment, and government purchases at every level of output. Aggregate expenditures line AE is based on expenditures, especially consumption and investment expenditures, undertaken if the price level is P_0, at which level the economy achieves equilibrium at output level Y_0.

Panel b presents the aggregate demand curve introduced in Section 3. The price level P_0 and the equilibrium output level Y_0 generated in the Keynesian cross in panel a give us one point on this aggregate demand curve. But what happens if the price level changes?

Recall from our earlier discussions of consumption and investment in Units 4.2 and 4.3 that

Figure 4.5.3

The Keynesian Cross and the Aggregate Demand Curve

The aggregate demand curve is negatively sloped as a result of the real balance and interest rate effects. In panel a a decrease in the price level leads to an increase in consumption and investment expenditures, causing an upward shift in the aggregate expenditures line and an increase in national output. In panel b the lower price level, which generates an increase in national output, causes a movement along the aggregate demand curve.

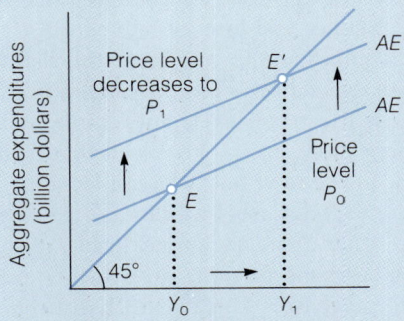

a. Keynesian cross

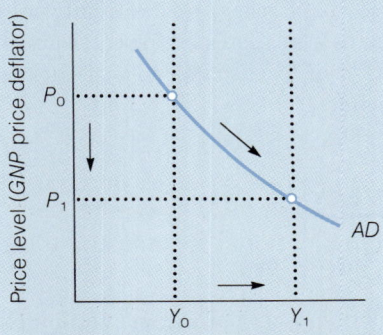

b. Aggregate demand curve

a change in the price level, through the real balance and interest rate effects, changes the level of consumption and investment expenditures. Changes in these two expenditures are caused by changes in the interest rate and wealth. In this case let's say that the price level declines from P_0 to P_1, leading to an increase in aggregate expenditures and an upward shift in the aggregate expenditures line from AE to AE'. The economy then achieves equilibrium at output Y_1, where AE' intersects the 45° line. In panel b price level P_1 and output Y_1 give us a second point on the aggregate demand curve. In essence, the aggregate demand curve slopes negatively because the changes in the price level cause changes in the aggregate expenditures line through the real balance and interest rate effects.

It is important to note that the *shift* in the aggregate expenditures line in panel a is due to a change in the price level, and corresponds to a movement along the aggregate demand curve in panel b. In the next unit we see that shifts in the aggregate expenditures line can also be caused by factors, other than the price level, that affect autonomous consumption, investment, and government purchases. This means that if the aggregate expenditures line in panel a shifts with no initial change in the price level, then the aggregate demand curve in panel b also shifts. An increase in aggregate expenditures (upward shift) leads to an increase in aggregate demand (rightward shift). And a decrease in aggregate expenditures (downward shift) leads to a decrease in aggregate demand (leftward shift).

IN SUMMARY
Determining National Income and Output

- Equilibrium national income and output can be determined using Keynesian economics in two different, but related ways. The first is with aggregate expenditures and national product, the second with leakages and injections.

- With the aggregate expenditures approach, the economy is in equilibrium when aggregate expenditures are equal to the level of national production. When this occurs, buyers purchase all the output they want, and producers sell all of the output they produce.

- In equilibrium there are no changes in inventories. Changes in inventories act as the signal to producers to either increase or decrease production. If inventories are increasing, because aggregate expenditures are less than national production, then producers are signaled to reduce production. If inventories are decreasing, because aggregate expenditures are greater than national production, producers are signaled to increase production. When aggregate expenditures equal national product, there are no changes in inventories, and thus producers are given no signal to change their level of production.

- The Keynesian cross illustrates equilibrium using the aggregate expenditures line. The level of output given by the intersection of the aggregate expenditures line and the 45° line is equilibrium. Only at this level of output are aggregate expenditures equal to national product.

- Equilibrium can also be identified using the leakages (saving and net taxes) and injections (investment and government purchases) approach. In equilibrium, and only in equilibrium, the total level of planned leakages is equal to the total level of planned injections. If planned leakages are not equal to planned injections, then inventories are changing and producers are signaled to change their level of production.

- The negative slope of the aggregate demand curve introduced in Section 3 can be identified using the Keynesian cross diagram. A decrease in the price level, due to the real balance and interest rate effects, causes the aggregate expenditures line to shift upward as consumption and investment expenditures increase. Therefore, aggregate expenditures on national output increase as the price level declines.

QUESTIONS FOR STUDY AND ANALYSIS

1. Let's look at an economy with three sectors: household, business, and government. Investment expenditures are equal to $1000, government purchases are equal to $1500, and net taxes are equal to $1000. The consumption function relationship among consumption, national income, and disposable income is given by the following table:

National output	$2000	3000	4000	5000	6000	7000
Disposable income	1000	2000	3000	4000	5000	6000
Consumption	2000	2500	3000	3500	4000	4500

   a. Determine the level of aggregate expenditures for each level of national output.
   b. What is the equilibrium level of national output?
   c. What is the equilibrium level of disposable income?
   d. What is the equilibrium level of consumption?
   e. What is the equilibrium level of saving?
   f. Are leakages equal to injections in equilibrium? Explain.

2. Using the information from question 1, construct a Keynesian cross depicting the equilibrium for the economy.

3. Based on the results obtained from Table 4.5.2, how would equilibrium be affected if investment expenditures declined to $50 and government purchases increased to $250? What does this say about the government's role during the Depression of the 1930s, as discussed in Unit 4.1?

4. What role do changes in inventories play in determining the equilibrium level of output? How do inventories change if output is less than the equilibrium level? How do inventories change if output is greater than the equilibrium level?

5. Suppose that you have the following relationship between saving, disposable income, and national income for a three-sector economy:

National output	$15	20	25	30	35	40	45	50
Disposable income		5	10	15	20	25	30	35	40
Saving	−4	−2	0	2	4	6	8	10

   a. Determine the total level of leakages at each level of national output.
   b. If autonomous investment expenditures are equal to $9 and autonomous government purchases are equal to $5, what is the equilibrium level of national output? Explain how you arrive at this answer.

6. How is the exchange of national production similar to, and different from, the exchange of a single good in markets such as those discussed in Section 2?

REVIEW GLOSSARY

changes in inventories The increases or decreases in the business sector's accumulated stocks of raw materials, intermediate goods, and final goods. Unplanned changes in inventories are an important part of the equilibrium mechanism for the macroeconomy. If inventories are increasing, then producers are signaled to reduce production. If inventories are decreasing, then producers are signaled to increase production. The only time there are no unplanned changes in inventories is when aggregate expenditures are equal to national production.

equilibrium A state in which opposing forces exactly offset each other and there is no inherent tendency for change. In terms of the macroeconomy, equilibrium is reached when aggregate expenditures on national output are equal to the amount of national output produced.

Keynesian cross A graph containing the Keynesian aggregate expenditures line that is used to illustrate equilibrium between aggregate expenditures and national output. The Keynesian cross contains the essence of Keynesian economics.

UNIT 4.6

The Multiplier

Determining the equilibrium level of output for the economy, as we did in the previous unit, is only a beginning for understanding the Keynesian explanation of the economy, because the equilibrium level constantly changes due to shocks in the economy. As we saw in our study of business cycles in Unit 3.7, production usually increases or decreases from one year to the next. In this unit we look at the mechanism underlying these fluctuations.

The key concept in this mechanism is the multiplier. A **multiplier** is the ratio of the change in national output to the change in an autonomous component of aggregate expenditures. The most important feature of a multiplier is that a change in aggregate expenditures can cause an overall change in output that is several times larger. In other words, the change in output is a multiple of the initial change in expenditures. The multiplier helps explain how the economy can steamroll its way into the expansionary phase of the business cycle following increases in investment or government spending. By the same token, the multiplier also illustrates why the contractionary phase can be so severe if aggregate expenditures decline.

In studying the multiplier we first look at its basic mechanism. We see how the economy adjusts from one equilibrium to another after a shift in the aggregate expenditures line. And we examine how two different multipliers are calculated, one based on changes in aggregate expenditures, and the other based on changes in taxes.

SHIFTS IN THE AGGREGATE EXPENDITURES LINE

In order to understand the multiplier and its significance in our study of the macroeconomy, let's consider the situation depicted in Figure 4.6.1. The

UNIT 4.6 • THE MULTIPLIER

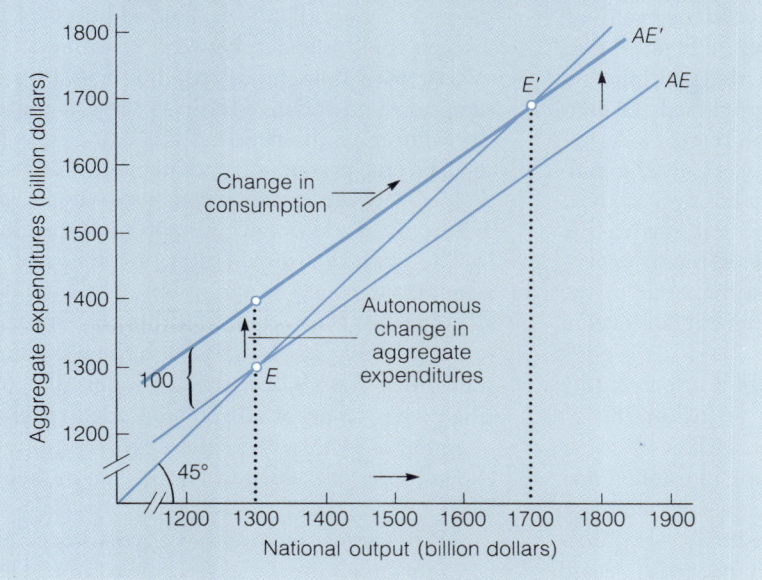

Figure 4.6.1

The Keynesian Cross and the Multiplier

The multiplier effect can be illustrated by a vertical shift in the aggregate expenditures line. If aggregate expenditures increase by $100, the aggregate expenditures line shifts vertically from AE to AE'. This increase in expenditures leads to additional production, which increases consumption expenditures. Therefore, the increase in output is greater than the initial increase in aggregate expenditures.

economy is initially in equilibrium at point E, based on the aggregate expenditures line AE; the equilibrium level of output is $1300.

Suppose that aggregate expenditures increase by $100, causing a shift in the aggregate expenditures line. At this point it doesn't matter which expenditure—consumption, investment, or government purchases—increases, only that the overall level of aggregate expenditures has in fact increased.

Under these circumstances, the aggregate expenditures line shifts vertically to AE'. The new aggregate expenditures line is parallel to the old line because expenditures are $100 more at every level of output. But what happens to the economy if aggregate expenditures are now $100 greater?

When expenditures first increase by $100, output remains at $1300, but expenditures are now $1400. Recall that when expenditures are greater than production, inventories decline because buyers' demands are satisifed from inventories of past production. As inventories are reduced, producers are signaled to increase production, which they continue to do as long as expenditures are greater than production. Expenditures equal production at the intersection of the new aggregate expenditures line, AE', and the 45° line, at point E'. Point E' becomes the new equilibrium for the economy based on the new level of expenditures, and the new level of output is $1700.

This is where the multiplier comes in. Using comparative statics, we can calculate how the level of output changes. The $100 increase in aggregate expenditures causes the output to increase from $1300 to $1700, a change of $400. In other words, output has changed by 4 times the initial change in aggregate expenditures, meaning the multiplier has a numerical value of 4.

The multiplier is a handy tool for determining changes in aggregate expenditures. In Figure 4.6.1, if we had known the value of the multiplier in advance, then we could have predicted the new level of output based solely on the change in aggregate expenditures. For example, let's say the multiplier is 4, and we hear that the business sector is a little skeptical about future conditions in the economy and plans to reduce investment expenditures by $10 billion. Knowing the value of the multiplier, we can predict that the overall level of output will fall by $40 billion.

This information can be useful in preventing a contraction in the economy, or in limiting an expansion in inflationary times. However, so far we have obtained the value of the multiplier *after* the fact. In Figure 4.6.1 we actually computed the value of the multiplier by determining how much output changed as a result of change in aggregate expenditures. What we want to do is compute the value of the multiplier *before* a change in expenditures.

THE MULTIPLIER EFFECT

First, let's trace the $100 increase in aggregate expenditures through the economy and see why it causes output to increase by $400. Initially, the $100 increase in expenditures for the purchase of final goods and services causes production to increase by $100. But as production increases by $100, households in turn have an additional $100 in income. Remember that in moving through the circular flow, households divide income between consumption and saving based on the marginal propensities to consume and save. In this case assume that the MPC is 0.75 and the MPS is 0.25, meaning households use $75 for consumption expenditures and save $25. This initial trip through the circular flow is presented as round 1 in Table 4.6.1.

But what happens to the $75 households spend on goods and services? As this $75 of consumption expenditures is used to purchase output, it works its way through the circular flow, and income increases by another $75. This additional $75 in income is also divided between consumption and saving, with households spending $56.3 on consumption and saving $18.7, as seen in round 2. But when households spend this $56.3, this leads to additional production and income, which is also divided between consumption and saving in round 3. And these additional consumption expenditures lead to additional production, income, and consumption in round 4, and so on.

The first seven rounds of this process are presented in Table 4.6.1, along with the totals for the subsequent rounds and the totals for all rounds. The combination of all rounds leads to a change in output of $400, with an increase in consumption expenditures of $300, and an increase in saving of $100.

While it may seem as though this process could continue indefinitely, it does come to an end. Note that the changes in consumption over each subsequent round continue to grow smaller and smaller. Eventually the process stops when the changes in consumption are so small that there is no noticeable impact on production and income.

Let's look closely at what has happened to the economy. Initially, aggregate expenditures increase by $100, and consumption expenditures are stimulated by the additional income. Once the consumption expenditures are increased, they continued to stimulate additional income and thus additional consumption expenditures. That is, the initial aggregate expenditures merely get the circular flow for the economy started; consumption expenditures keep the circular flow going for several more rounds.

Table 4.6.1

The Multiplier Effect (billions)

An autonomous change in aggregate expenditures stimulates a change in output and income leading to a change in consumption. However, the change in consumption stimulates an additional change in output, income, and consumption. This process means that the total change in output is a multiple of the initial change in aggregate expenditures.

Round	Initial Change in Aggregate Expenditures	Change in Output	Change in Consumption	Change in Saving
1	$100	$100	$ 75	$ 25
2		75	56.3	18.7
3		56.3	42.2	14.1
4		42.2	31.6	10.6
5		31.6	23.7	7.9
6		23.7	17.8	5.9
7		17.8	13.3	4.5
Subtotal (1–7)		346.6	259.9	86.7
Other rounds		53.4	40.1	13.3
Total	$100	$400	$300	$100

Overall production, which increases by $400, can be divided between the initial increase in aggregate expenditures and the subsequent increases in consumption expenditures. The first $100 increase in production is purchased by the initial $100 expenditures. The subsequent $300 in production is purchased by the consumption expenditures that were stimulated by increases in income. Figure 4.6.1 illustrates how these increases in expenditures are divided. The initial increase is the vertical shift in the aggregate expenditures line. The increase in consumption is due to a movement along the new aggregate expenditures line.

We can also divide the $400 increase in income between consumption and saving. Households, through all rounds, end up with $400 in additional income, of which they spend $300 on consumption expenditures and save $100. Note that this division of additional income corresponds with our marginal propensities to consume (0.75) and save (0.25).

We should point out that it is no coincidence that the overall increase in saving is equal to the original increase in aggregate expenditures. Saving represents the amount of income that is leaked away from the circular flow each time consumption increases. Since some of the income is leaked away, there is less remaining in the flow to stimulate further production and income. In fact, the circular flow continues only as long as income remains in the circular flow, meaning the process stops when all of the initial injection is leaked away into saving. Thus, the process shown in Table 4.6.1 stops when the additional saving is equal to the initial increase in expenditures.

Expenditures Multiplier

Our analysis thus far indicates that the overall size of the multiplier depends on the amount that is leaked out during each round of the circular flow. If more is leaked out on each round, then less remains for continued expenditures, and the overall change in output is less. If less is leaked out on each round, then more remains, and the overall increase in output is greater.

The amount leaked into saving on each round is simply the marginal propensity to save. And the reciprocal of the MPS is the value of the expenditures multiplier. The **expenditures multiplier** is the ratio of the change in national output to the change in consumption, investment, or government purchases. It is specified as

$$\text{expenditures multiplier} = \frac{1}{MPS}$$

In our example the MPS is 0.25, and its reciprocal is 4, the value of the multiplier that we calculated when we knew the change in output was $400 and the change in expenditures was $100. Moreover, since the sum of the MPC and MPS is equal to 1, MPS = 1 − MPC. Therefore, the expenditures multiplier can also be specified as

$$\text{expenditures multiplier} = \frac{1}{1 - MPC}$$

We should note that this is the simplest multiplier we can consider because in our model of the economy, consumption is the only expenditure depending on the level of income. If we wanted to complicate the multiplier, we could have investment, government expenditures, or net taxes depend on the level of income.

It is interesting to note that the expenditures multiplier is the same for changes in consumption, investment, and government purchases. An autonomous increase in each of these expenditures affects output in the same way, regardless of what causes the aggregate expenditures line to shift. The fact that the multiplier for government purchases is equal to the multiplier for investment expenditures becomes important in our discussion of fiscal policy in the next unit.

Tax Multiplier

Although the expenditures multiplier applies to changes in consumption, investment, or government purchases, it does not apply to changes in taxes. The **tax multiplier** is the ratio of the change in national output to the change in net taxes. It is specified as

$$\text{tax multiplier} = -MPC \times \frac{1}{MPS}$$

The only difference between the expenditures multiplier and the tax multiplier is $-MPC$. If the MPS is 0.25 and the MPC is 0.75, the expenditures multiplier is 4 and the tax multiplier is -3 ($= -0.75 \times 4$). In other words, when taxes *increase* by $100, output *decreases* by $300.

The reasoning behind this difference between the expenditures and tax multipliers is simple enough. If taxes increase, then aggregate expenditures decline because of a decrease in disposable income and consumption, causing the aggregate expenditures line to shift down. This is where the negative sign comes into play. An increase in any of the aggregate expenditures leads to an increase in output, and the multiplier is *positive*. But an increase in taxes leads to a decrease in output, so the multiplier is *negative*.

The marginal propensity to consume is included in the tax multiplier because an increase in taxes does not lead to an equivalent decrease in aggregate expenditures. For example, if taxes increase by $1, then the disposable income received by households decreases by $1. But this $1 decline in disposable income is not reflected only in a decline in consumption; saving is also affected. This is where the MPC comes into play. For a $1 decline in disposable income, consumption expenditures decrease by only 75 cents, or $0.75 \times \$1$. And because consumption expenditures are part of aggregate expenditures, aggregate expenditures also decline by only 75 percent of the initial change in taxes. This is why the tax multiplier is equal to $-MPC \times$ the expenditures multiplier.

Multipliers in the Real World

The expenditures and tax multipliers discussed in this unit are the simplest multipliers we can consider, simple because they isolate only the most important principle underlying the multiplier effect—the circular flow relationship between expenditures, income, and consumption. However, in the real world the circular flow (as seen in Figure 3.3.5) contains many secondary flows, notably personal taxes and imports, that can also affect the value of the multiplier by leaking income away and thus reducing the size of the multiplier. By contrast, investment and government purchases realistically depend on the level of income, and thus tend to increase the size of the multiplier. In our discussions of multipliers we have identified values of 4 for the expenditures multiplier and -3 for the tax multiplier, for purposes of illustration. However, when considering these additional flows, the actual values are closer to 2.5 for the expenditures multiplier and -2.0 for the tax multiplier.

Another item that can affect the actual value of the multipliers is the price level, as Figure 4.6.2 illustrates. Panel a depicts an autonomous increase in aggregate expenditures (for example, government purchases), similar to the shift in Figure 4.6.1. Using the simple expenditures multiplier, this shift leads to an increase in the equilibrium level of national output from Y_0 to Y_1.

Panel b depicts how the upward shift in the aggregate expenditures line from AE to AE' causes the aggregate demand curve to shift rightward from AD to AD'. With no change in the price level, the equilibrium level of national output in panel b also increases from Y_0 on AD to Y_1 on AD'. At this point we can see that the simple expenditures multiplier effectively calculates the horizontal shift in the aggregate demand curve. But remember that aggregate demand constitutes only half of the aggregate market. If the economy is operating in the Keynesian range of the aggregate supply curve, the price level does not change from P_0, and the overall change in the level of national output is from Y_0 to Y_1.

However, if the economy is operating in the intermediate or classical ranges, the price level increases, and the economy moves up the new aggregate demand curve AD' from point E'. If Y_0 is full employment output, and the economy is in the classical range, then the price level increases to P_1. However, if the economy is in the intermediate range, the price level increases to some level between P_0 and P_1, with a level of national output between Y_0 and Y_1.

But recall that an increase in the price level, through the real balance and interest rate effects, causes the aggregate expenditures line to shift down. Therefore, in panel a, aggregate expenditures line AE' shifts back down if the price level increases. If the price level increases to P_1 in panel b, then the aggregate expenditures line shifts down to AE, the original line, and there is no net change in national output. If the price level is between P_0 and P_1, then the aggregate expenditures line is somewhere between AE and AE'.

When we consider the price level, it is clear that the actual value of the expenditures multiplier is likely to be less than the simple expenditures multiplier discussed in this unit. In particular, the actual value of the expenditures multiplier will vary depending on the range of the aggregate supply curve, potentially declining all the way to zero in the classical range.

PARADOX OF THRIFT

An interesting illustration of the multiplier lies in the paradox of thrift. The **paradox of thrift** is an analysis that indicates an increase in saving by the entire economy is not likely to make the economy better off. The paradox of thrift suggests that a

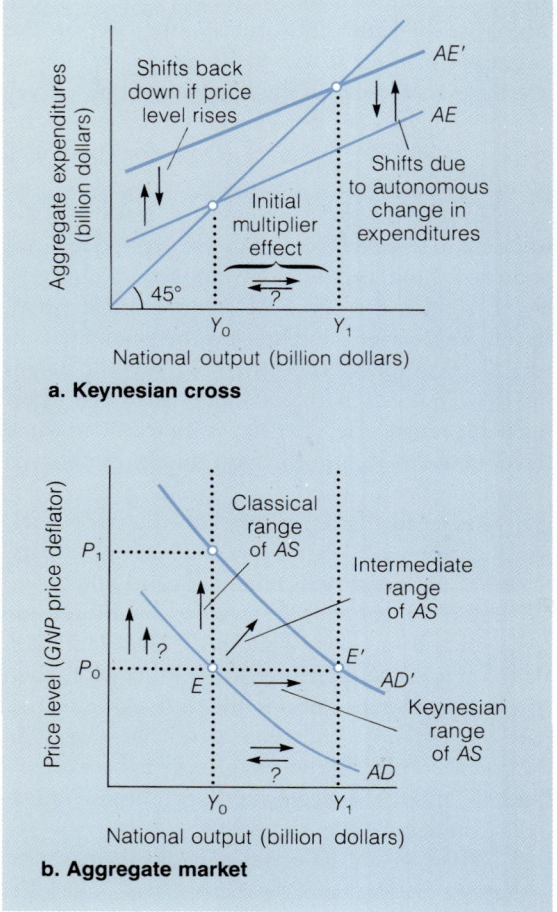

a. Keynesian cross

b. Aggregate market

Figure 4.6.2

The Multiplier and the Aggregate Market

An upward shift in the aggregate expenditures line in panel a illustrates the simple multiplier effect, where an autonomous change in expenditures leads to a change in national output. However, this does not consider the price level. In panel b a rightward shift in the aggregate demand curve corresponds to the autonomous change in aggregate expenditures. There are three alternative effects on the price level. In the Keynesian range of the aggregate supply curve the price level does not change, and there is no further shift of the aggregate expenditures line in panel a. But in the intermediate and classical ranges the price level increases, leading to a downward shift in the aggregate expenditures line in panel a, and a lower value for the multiplier.

prudent bit of advice for an individual is not necessarily good advice for the economy. An individual is usually better off by saving a larger percentage of income. However, if the economy saves a larger percentage of its income, it is usually worse off in the short run.

This is illustrated in Figure 4.6.3. Panel a depicts the economy in equilibrium at point E, where the saving function and investment line intersect. However, suppose that everyone in the economy decides to save more, so that saving increases by $100 at every level of income and the saving function shifts upward to S'. This is equivalent to consumption expenditures declining by $100 at every level of income; if households are saving more, they must be consuming less.

Applying the leakages (saving) and injections (investment) approach, we can see how the economy is affected. A new equilibrium is reached at the intersection of S' and the investment line. However, in reaching the new equilibrium, output declines to $900.

If the MPC is 0.75, the multiplier is equal to 4, and the $100 decrease in autonomous consumption leads to a $400 decrease in output. In other words, when everyone in the economy decides to save more, output declines, and everyone is really worse off.

However, the real paradox of thrift comes into play in panel b, where a more realistic version of the investment line is employed, one in which investment expenditures decrease as the level of output decreases. In this case the reduction in income also reduces investment. And since investment is equal to saving in equilibrium, saving also

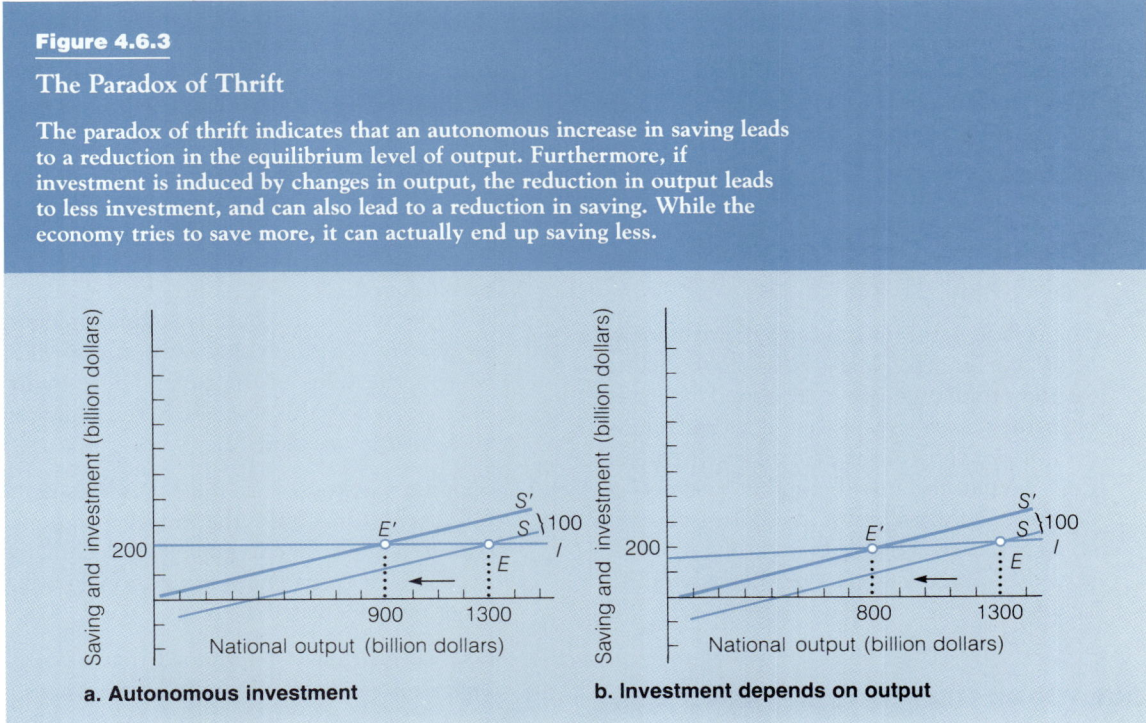

Figure 4.6.3

The Paradox of Thrift

The paradox of thrift indicates that an autonomous increase in saving leads to a reduction in the equilibrium level of output. Furthermore, if investment is induced by changes in output, the reduction in output leads to less investment, and can also lead to a reduction in saving. While the economy tries to save more, it can actually end up saving less.

a. Autonomous investment

b. Investment depends on output

falls, from $200 to $175. This is the paradox. Although everyone in the economy tries to save more, they actually end up saving less.

IN SUMMARY

The Multiplier

- The multiplier indicates how the equilibrium level of national output is affected if there is a change in aggregate expenditures. It is called the multiplier because national output changes by a multiple of the initial change in aggregate expenditures. Graphically, the multiplier indicates the effect of a vertical shift in the aggregate expenditures line.

- The change in output is a multiple of the initial change in aggregate expenditures because consumption is stimulated by the circular flow of income and output. Once aggregate expenditures stimulate the circular flow, total production continues to increase as consumption, production, and income increase in each subsequent round of the circular flow.

- The value of the expenditures multiplier depends on the marginal propensity to save. If a larger fraction of income is saved during each round of the circular flow, then less consumption remains in the flow, and production increases less each round. For this reason the expenditures multiplier is equal to 1/MPS, or 1/(1 − MPC).

- The tax multiplier tells us the change in output resulting from a change in net taxes, and is equal to $-MPC \times 1/MPS$. The tax multiplier differs from the expenditures multiplier by the term $-MPC$. The minus sign ($-$) indicates that an increase in taxes leads to a decrease in aggregate expenditures and output. The MPC indicates that only a fraction of the tax affects consumption and aggregate expenditures.

- The paradox of thrift indicates that what may be best for an individual is not necessarily best for the economy. People are generally better off if they are able to increase saving. However, if everyone in the economy saves more, then output declines because consumption decreases. Furthermore, if investment depends on output, then everyone in the economy might actually end up saving less as they attempt to save more.

QUESTIONS FOR STUDY AND ANALYSIS

1. What is the relationship between the multiplier effect and the circular flow? How does the MPC affect the amount in the circular flow? How does the MPC affect the size of the multiplier?

2. If the $MPC = 1$, what is the value of the expenditures multiplier? If the $MPC = 0$, what is the value of the expenditures multiplier? Explain.

3. Let's say that investment expenditures equal $50, government purchases equal $100, and net taxes equal $50. Furthermore, assume you have the following information concerning the relationship among consumption, disposable income, and national output:

National output	$100	200	300	400	500	600	700
Disposable income		50	150	250	350	450	550	650
Consumption	100	150	200	250	300	350	400

   a. Based on this information, what is the equilibrium level of national output?
   b. If investment expenditures increase to $150, what is the new equilibrium level of national output?
   c. What is the resulting change in national output? What is the value of the expenditures multiplier, computed as the ratio of the change in output to the change in investment expenditures?
   d. What is the value of the marginal propensity to save? Based on this value of the MPS, what is the value of the expenditures multiplier? How does this compare to the value you computed in question 3c?

4. Suppose you know that the MPC is equal to 0.8. In this case what is the change in national output if government purchases decline by $100? What is the change in national output if net taxes increase by $100?

5. Let's say you have determined that a $5000 increase in investment expenditures causes a $25,000 increase in national output. What change in net taxes is needed to increase national output from $900,000 to $1,000,000?

6. Explain how knowledge of the multiplier and the multiplier effect could have helped alleviate the Depression of the 1930s.

REVIEW GLOSSARY

expenditures multiplier The ratio of the change in national output to the change in consumption, investment, or government purchases. The expenditures multiplier is equal to 1/MPS.

multiplier The ratio of the change in national output to the change in a component of aggregate expenditures. The multiplier indicates how national output is affected by a change in aggregate expenditures.

paradox of thrift An analysis indicating that an increase in saving by the entire economy leads to a decline in output and possibly a decrease in saving.

tax multiplier The ratio of the change in national output to the change in net taxes. The tax multiplier is equal to $-MPC \times 1/MPS$. The MPC indicates that only a fraction of the change in taxes leads to a shift in the aggregate expenditures line. The minus sign ($-$) indicates that an increase in taxes leads to a decrease in aggregate expenditures and output.

UNIT 4.7

Fiscal Policy Applications of Keynesian Economics

Unit 4.3 discussed how the government sector can affect aggregate expenditures directly by purchasing final goods and services and indirectly by taxing away income otherwise used for consumption expenditures. In this unit we want to examine these two functions of government more closely. In particular, we study how these two components of fiscal policy, government purchases and taxation, can be used to stabilize the economy. **Fiscal policy** is the discretionary use of the two components of the government's fiscal budget, purchases and net taxation, to stabilize aggregate expenditures.

The stabilization of aggregate expenditures can have a strong effect on the business cycle discussed in Unit 3.7. The peaks and troughs of the business cycle (which are usually but not always associated with inflation and unemployment, respectively) are caused in part by fluctuations in aggregate expenditures. One way to stabilize aggregate expenditures is through discretionary control of government purchases and taxation.

We direct our attention first to the full employment level of output to see what happens if aggregate expenditures are too small or too large to achieve this level of production. We see how both types of fiscal policy (government purchases and taxation) can move the economy to full employment output. Then we discuss how nondiscretionary expenditures, also known as automatic stabilizers, tend to reduce the fluctuations in economic activity, without discretionary action by the government, and how this relates to the high employment budget.

And finally we examine implementation of fiscal policy in recent years.

FULL EMPLOYMENT OUTPUT

First, we need to relate aggregate expenditures (and the resulting equilibrium level of output) in the Keynesian cross diagram to the economy's full employment level of output. In this way we see how aggregate expenditures can be too little, or too much, to obtain full employment output with stable prices.

The Recessionary Gap

Let's look at a situation in which aggregate expenditures are not large enough to obtain the full employment level of output. In panel a of Figure 4.7.1 the aggregate expenditures line labeled AE_1 intersects the 45° line at point E, and the equilibrium level of output is Y_1. Our analysis is the same as in Unit 4.5, except that we are now taking into account the full employment level of output. In panel a the full employment level of output is identified as Y_f, the level of output produced if the factors of production are fully employed. It corre-

Figure 4.7.1

Recessionary and Inflationary Gaps

The recessionary gap in panel a and the inflationary gap in panel b are both identified as the difference between the existing level of aggregate expenditures and the level of aggregate expenditures needed to achieve full employment. However, the recessionary gap occurs because actual expenditures are less than those needed for full employment, whereas the inflationary gap occurs because actual expenditures are more than those needed for full employment.

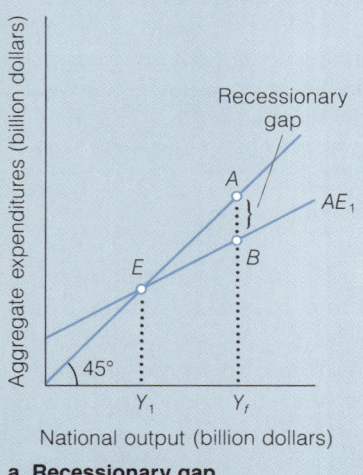

a. Recessionary gap

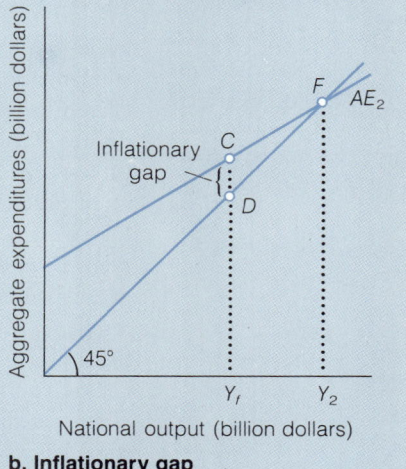

b. Inflationary gap

sponds to the vertical, or classical, portion of the AS curve introduced in Unit 3.6. Clearly, the equilibrium level of output at Y_1 is less than the full employment level of output at Y_f, meaning the economy is operating below full capacity and some factors of production are unemployed.

The reason the economy is operating below the full employment level of output is that aggregate expenditures are too low, as the recessionary gap in panel a indicates. The **recessionary gap** is the difference between actual aggregate expenditures and the level of aggregate expenditures needed to achieve full employment, if actual output is less than full employment output. The recessionary gap is the vertical distance between the aggregate expenditures line and the 45° line at the full employment level of output. In panel a this is the distance between points A and B. In essence, the recessionary gap indicates how much aggregate expenditures must increase in order to achieve full employment in the economy. Later in this unit we discuss how fiscal policy can be used to eliminate this gap.

The Inflationary Gap

In panel b of Figure 4.7.1 we see what happens if aggregate expenditures are greater than needed for full employment output. Once again full employment output is given by Y_f, but in this case aggregate expenditures are more than enough to obtain this level of output. In fact, if the economy was able to produce more output, the economy would be in equilibrium at Y_2. But the demand for output is greater than the available supply and, as with the market for a single good, this excess demand places upward pressure on the price level.

To see why this is so, let's define the inflationary gap, which is similar to, but opposite from, the recessionary gap. The **inflationary gap** is the difference between actual aggregate expenditures and the level of aggregate expenditures needed to achieve full employment, if actual output is greater than full employment output. In panel b the inflationary gap is seen as the vertical distance between the aggregate expenditures line and the 45° line, between points C and D. The inflationary gap exists because the demand for goods and services is greater than the supply.

FISCAL POLICY AND FULL EMPLOYMENT OUTPUT

From a graphical standpoint, eliminating recessionary and inflationary gaps is accomplished by shifts in the aggregate expenditures line. Figure 4.7.2 illustrates the appropriate shifts in each case. In panel a the recessionary gap can be eliminated by shifting the aggregate expenditures line up to $AE_1{'}$, where, in equilibrium, aggregate expenditures are equal to full employment output. In panel b the aggregate expenditures line must be shifted down to $AE_2{'}$ to close the inflationary gap and, in equilibrium, produce full employment output without inflationary pressures.

While graphically this process is very simple, the government has alternative fiscal policy tools that can be used to make these necessary shifts in the aggregate expenditures line. As mentioned earlier, the tools at the discretionary use of the government are government purchases and net taxation.

Government Purchases

Government purchases can eliminate a recessionary gap if they are increased by the amount of the recessionary gap. In this case the aggregate expenditures line shifts up to $AE_1{'}$ in panel a, and the gap is eliminated. For an inflationary gap, the government needs to reduce purchases by the amount of the inflationary gap, causing the aggregate expenditures line to shift down to $AE_2{'}$ in panel b.

While this is, from a graphical standpoint, a relatively simple procedure, in practice it is a little more involved, because we often do not know the size of the recessionary and inflationary gaps. However, we might know the full employment level of output and the size of the expenditures multiplier. For example, in panel a we might know that full

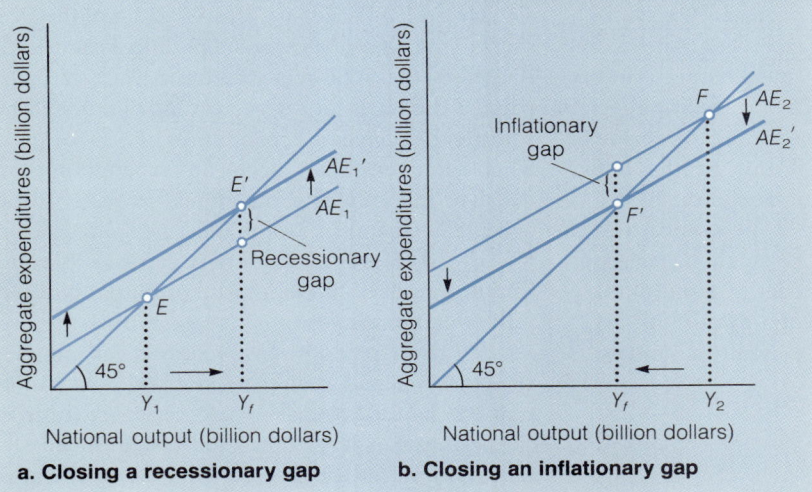

Figure 4.7.2

Fiscal Policy for Recessionary and Inflationary Gaps

The recessionary gap in panel a can be closed by using expansionary fiscal policy, which consists of increasing government purchases or decreasing net taxes (including an increase in transfer payments). The inflationary gap in panel b can be closed by using contractionary fiscal policy, which consists of decreasing government purchases or increasing net taxes (including a decrease in transfer payments).

employment output is $1400, but that the actual level of output is only $1200. If we also know that the expenditures multiplier is equal to 4, then we can compute the necessary increase in government purchases, in this case $50, to achieve full employment output.

Net Taxes

Using net taxes to achieve full employment is slightly more complicated than government purchases. First, to incease aggregate expenditures, net taxes must be decreased. Recall that a reduction in taxes leads to an increase in disposable income and, consequently, an increase in consumption. And second, a $1 decrease in taxes does not lead to an equivalent $1 increase in consumption and aggregate expenditures. If the MPC is equal to 0.75, consumption increases by only 75 cents, meaning that net taxes have to change by more than the size of the recessionary or inflationary gap. If the recessionary gap is $50, then taxes need to be reduced by $66.7, because with that level of additional income, households save 25 percent, or $16.7, and spend the remaining 75 percent, or $50.

The tax multiplier can be employed to compute the change in taxes, assuming that the necessary change in output is known. Let's say that the tax multiplier is equal to -3, which is the $-MPC$ (-0.75) times the autonomous expenditures multiplier (4). If the actual output is $200 less than full employment output, then taxes need to be decreased by $66.7 to achieve full employment output.

Furthermore, net taxes can be changed by changes in transfer payments. That is, the government can use transfer payments rather than government purchases to close an inflationary or recessionary gap. If we want to increase income by $200, we need to increase transfer payments by $66.7, since the tax multiplier is still equal to −3. An increase of $66.7 in transfer payments decreases net taxes by the same amount, and thus consumption increases by $50.

Note that the $200 gap can be closed by a smaller amount of government purchases than transfer payments. While $66.7 in transfer payments are needed to increase output by $200, only $50 in government purchases are needed, meaning it is $16.7 cheaper to reach full employment using government purchases rather than transfer payments. Government purchases are clearly more effective than transfer payments in closing both recessionary and inflationary gaps, simply because the expenditures multiplier is larger than the net tax multiplier. In short, $1 in government purchases generates more output in the economy than $1 in transfer payments. While part of the initial transfer payments are diverted to saving, all of the initial government purchases are used to purchase output.

The Balanced-Budget Multiplier

In comparing transfer payments and purchases, it should be pointed out that we cannot consider the tools of fiscal policy in isolation from each other. In particular, if the government tries to stimulate the economy toward full employment either through purchases or transfer payments, it must obtain the funds somewhere. Let's see what happens if the funds are derived through taxation.

Panel a of Figure 4.7.3 illustrates what happens if the government uses purchases to achieve

Figure 4.7.3
Balanced-Budget Multipliers

The balanced-budget multiplier for government purchases, depicted in panel a, is equal to 1. The increase in aggregate expenditures caused by government purchases is partially, but not entirely, offset by the reduction in consumption from higher taxes. The balanced-budget multiplier for transfer payments, depicted in panel b, is equal to zero. In this case consumption and aggregate expenditures decrease through taxes by the same amount that they increase through transfer payments.

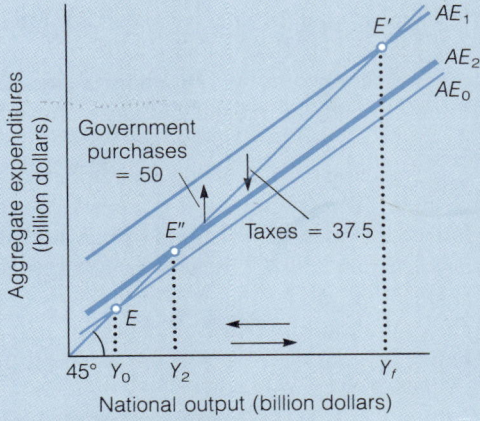

a. Government purchases

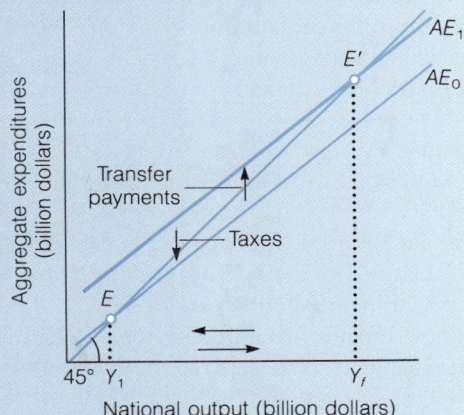

b. Transfer payments

full employment, then finances these purchases through additional taxes. Again the economy is operating below the full employment level of output based on the aggregate expenditures line AE_0. Suppose $50 in additional expenditures are needed to shift the aggregate expenditures line to AE_1 and achieve full employment.

If the government undertakes the required $50 in purchases, then the economy reacts accordingly, and full employment output is achieved at Y_f. However, if the government finances these purchases by raising taxes by the same $50, then disposable income and thus consumption expenditures decrease. Consumption expenditures fall by only $37.5 ($MPC \times \$50$), which shifts the aggregate expenditures line to AE_2, and a new equilibrium level of output is reached at Y_2.

Overall, what has happened to the economy? Full employment has not been achieved, since Y_2 is less than Y_f. However, the new level of output is above the original level of Y_1. In fact, we can determine the exact increase in output. Since government purchases increase by $50 and consumption decreases by $37.5, there is a net increase in autonomous aggregate expenditures of $12.5. Since the expenditures multiplier equals 4, we know that output has increased by $50 ($= \$12.5 \times 4$).

This is an interesting result. Output has increased by the amount of the original increase in government purchases and taxes. Indeed, whenever government purchases and taxes are increased by the same amount, the overall change in the economy's output is equal to this amount, because of the balanced-budget multiplier. The **balanced-budget multiplier** is the ratio of the change in output to changes in government expenditures that are matched by equal changes in taxes. The balanced-budget multiplier for government purchases is equal to 1.

We can see why the balanced-budget multiplier is equal to 1 by considering the circular flow. When government purchases are injected into the circular flow, the first round through the flow reflects the output and income generated by this initial expenditure. All subsequent rounds result from consumption expenditures induced by additional income. However, after the first round any additional income from the government purchases is canceled out by reductions in income from higher taxes. Therefore, the overall change in output in the economy is due exclusively to the *initial* government purchase.

The interesting aspect of the balanced-budget multiplier is that government purchases (and taxes) must change by the amount of the desired change in output. For example, if we are $200 below full employment, we must increase government purchases by $200.

But this is not the case if transfer payments rather than government purchases are used to achieve full employment, as illustrated in panel b of Figure 4.7.3. To increase aggregate expenditures to AE_1 from AE_0, transfer payments are increased by $66.7, which, as we saw earlier, leads to a $50 increase in consumption expenditures. Therefore, output increases to the full employment level at Y_f. However, to finance the transfer payments, taxes must be increased by an equal amount. If taxes increase by $66.7, consumption expenditures fall by $50, and the aggregate expenditures line falls back to AE_0. Aggregate expenditures do not change, and the level of output does not change from Y_0.

On the one hand, transfer payments are increased, causing net taxes to decline. But on the other hand, taxes are increased, causing net taxes to increase. Overall, net taxes *do not change*. Remember that in effect, taxes take funds from one household pocket, and transfer payments put them back into another household pocket. In more literal terms, the balanced-budget multiplier for transfer payments is equal to zero.

Since the balanced-budget multiplier for transfer payments is equal to zero, it is not possible to reach full employment by changing taxes and transfer payments equally. In the case of government purchases, full employment can be reached if purchases are increased enough. But it doesn't matter how much transfer payments are increased, because if taxes are increased by the same amount, output does not change.

Budget Deficits and Surpluses

This leads us to another important point. To eliminate a recessionary gap and reach full employment, the best alternative is to increase government purchases without an equal increase in taxes. And to eliminate an inflationary gap, the best alternative is to decrease government purchases without an equal decrease in taxes.

However, in the first case, if the government increases purchases without an equal increase in taxes, it is going to generate a deficit. In fact, an effective policy during recessionary times is to operate the government with a budget deficit. In this way the government is spending funds on goods and services, but it is not taxing away part of households' income that can also be used for spending on goods and services. During a recession it is even appropriate to reduce taxes at the same time government purchases are increased, so as to boost the aggregate expenditures line from both the government and household sectors. Indeed, a recessionary gap can best be eliminated by using expansionary fiscal policy. **Expansionary fiscal policy** is fiscal policy consisting of increases in government purchases and/or decreases in net taxes (including increases in transfer payments).

During inflationary times the government should undertake the exact opposite approach—increase taxes, reduce government purchases, and operate with a budget surplus. In this case aggregate expenditures are being curtailed by both a reduction in government purchases and a reduction in consumption from taxes. An inflationary gap can best be eliminated by using contractionary fiscal policy. **Contractionary fiscal policy** is fiscal policy consisting of decreases in government purchases and/or increases in net taxes (including decreases in transfer payments).

However, care must be exercised with budget deficits and surpluses. If the government operates with a budget deficit during inflationary times, aggregate expenditures are even greater, and inflationary pressures are more intense. And if the government operates with a budget surplus during a recession, aggregate expenditures are even less, and the recession is worsened.

FISCAL POLICY AND THE AGGREGATE MARKET

We can also use the aggregate market to see how fiscal policy stabilizes economic fluctuations. Recall from earlier discussions in this section that shifts in the aggregate expenditures line (when not caused by changes in the price level) lead to corresponding shifts in the aggregate demand curve. Therefore, the effect of expansionary and contractionary fiscal policy involving autonomous changes in government purchases and/or net taxes can be illustrated with the aggregate market presented in Figure 4.7.4.

Panel a depicts the Keynesian cross, where aggregate expenditures needed to achieve the full employment level of output at Y_f are AE. When aggregate expenditures are AE', a recessionary gap exists; when they are AE'', an inflationary gap exists. Expansionary fiscal policy can be used to shift the aggregate expenditures line from AE' to AE, and contractionary fiscal policy can be used to shift it from AE'' to AE.

The same mechanism is illustrated in panel b using the aggregate market. In this case full employment output is achieved if the aggregate demand curve is AD (corresponding with aggregate expenditures line AE). When aggregate demand is given by curve AD', then output is below the full employment level at Y_1, and expansionary fiscal policy can be used to shift the aggregate demand curve from AD' to AD.

Note that with expansionary fiscal policy the aggregate demand curve is moving through the intermediate range of the aggregate supply curve. Therefore, reaching full employment involves an

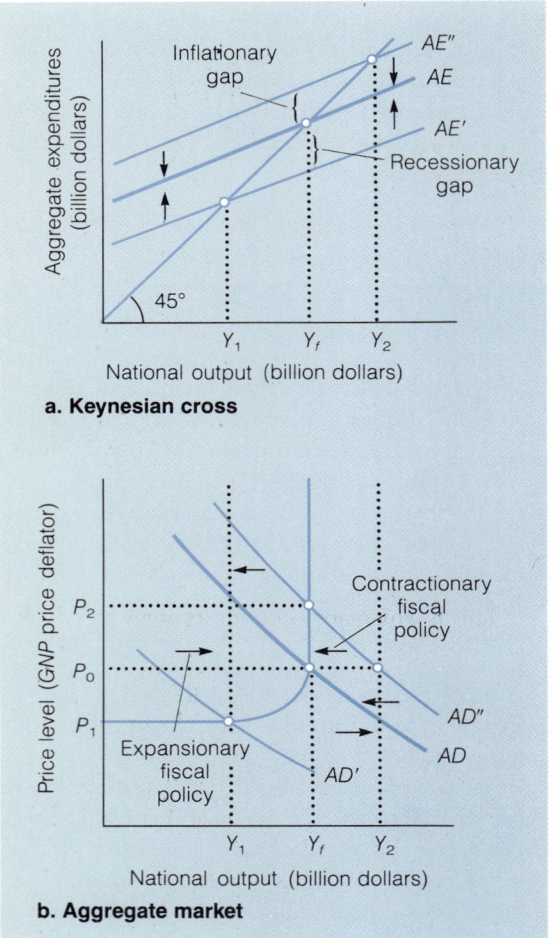

Figure 4.7.4

Fiscal Policy and the Aggregate Market

The government's use of fiscal policy can be illustrated using the aggregate market. With the Keynesian cross in panel a, expansionary policy is seen as an upward shift of the aggregate expenditures line toward AE, while contractionary fiscal policy is seen as a downward shift toward AE. With the aggregate market in panel b, expansionary policy is seen as a rightward shift of the aggregate demand curve from AD' to AD, while contractionary fiscal policy is seen as a leftward shift from AD'' to AD. Using the aggregate market forces us to consider how changes in the price level affect aggregate expenditures. Therefore, the government might need to shift aggregate expenditures more than the recessionary and inflationary gaps.

increase in the price level from P_1 to P_0. This means that the government will actually have to force the aggregate expenditures line to shift above AE, since the increase in the price level, through the real balance and interest rate effects, will cause it to shift back down.

At aggregate demand curve AD'' (corresponding to aggregate expenditures line AE'' if the price level is P_0), inflationary pressures exist in the economy. That is, if no action is taken, then the price level will increase from P_0 to P_2. This can be avoided if the government undertakes contractionary fiscal policy, causing the aggregate demand curve to shift leftward from AD'' to AD.

AUTOMATIC STABILIZERS

The fiscal policy we have discussed so far is discretionary fiscal policy, over which the government has a large degree of direct control and which can be systematically used to stabilize fluctuations of the business cycle. However, nondiscretionary parts of the government's budget, especially taxes and transfer payments, also stabilize business cycle fluctuations. Since cyclical fluctuations are stabilized automatically, with no direct discretionary control, taxes and transfer payments are regarded as automatic stabilizers. **Automatic stabilizers** are taxes and transfer payments that depend on the level of national output such that they automatically reduce the fluctuations of the business cycle with no discretionary action.

Let's see how nondiscretionary components of the government's budget can stabilize the business cycle. While the guidelines for nondiscretionary expenditures and taxes are established by the government, the actual levels are not. With nondiscretionary expenditures such as welfare payments, social security benefits, and unemployment compensation, the government sets the eligibility rules for the payments, and if someone qualifies, then they receive the funds. On the tax side of the budget, most taxes are nondiscretionary. The government establishes what is taxed, and at what rate, and then waits for the revenues to come in.

The interesting aspect of taxes and transfer payments is that both are realistically affected by the level of output in the economy. That is, as output increases, people pay more taxes and receive fewer welfare payments and social security benefits and less unemployment compensation. Since the government tends to collect more tax revenues and pay out less transfer payments as output increases, net taxes (the difference between taxes and transfer payments) typically increase at higher levels of output and decrease with lower levels of output.

In terms of the business cycle, net taxes increase as the economy enters into the expansionary phase. But as net taxes increase, disposable income and consumption expenditures increase less than they otherwise would. Therefore, the increase in output in the expansionary phase is not as large, and the peak of the business cycle is not as great as it would be without the automatic increase in taxes and decrease in transfer payments. By the same reasoning, if the economy is in the contractionary phase of the business cycle, the decrease in disposable income, consumption expenditures, and output is also not as large, and the trough in the business cycle is not as low.

HIGH EMPLOYMENT BUDGET

The role of automatic stabilizers brings into focus an important distinction between the government's actual budget and what is called the high employment budget. The **high employment budget** is the government budget that would exist if the economy were at full employment. In determining the appropriate fiscal policy to close inflationary and recessionary gaps, some economists argue that we should not consider the surplus or deficit from the actual budget but from the high employment budget.

When the economy is at full employment, automatic stabilizers reduce the amount of households' disposable income by decreasing transfer payments and increasing taxes. But such actions also affect the government's budget, because it makes fewer expenditures on transfer payments and receives more revenue from taxes. The opposite is true when unemployment is relatively high, because the government makes more transfer payments and receives less tax revenue. The operation of automatic stabilizers will turn a budget that is balanced with full employment into a budget with a deficit if there is high unemployment.

This is why many economists argue that looking at the actual budget is not a good indication of whether the government is undertaking the appropriate discretionary fiscal policy. Automatic stabilizers will tend to naturally generate a deficit with a recessionary gap, and a surplus with an inflationary gap. The high employment budget compensates for actions by the automatic stabilizers and gives a better indication of discretionary fiscal policy. And a high employment budget deficit is a better indication of expansionary fiscal policy, while a high employment budget surplus is a better indication of contractionary fiscal policy.

RECENT FISCAL POLICY

Although the fiscal policy prescriptions of Keynesian economics have been around since the 1930s, it was not until the 1960s that they were expressly implemented by the federal government to stabilize the economy. The first overt use of fiscal policy came in the form of a tax cut in February 1964. In the early 1960s the economy was recovering from the recessions of 1957 to 1958 and 1960 to 1961, which saw the unemployment rate reach 6.8 percent and 6.7 percent, respectively (the highest levels since the Depression). Economists and policymakers feared that another recession was around the corner.

To stimulate the economy, taxes for both individuals and corporations were reduced. The tax rates on personal income were permanently reduced from 18 to 91 percent to 14 to 70 percent, which reduced personal income taxes by $10 billion, or about 20 percent. The corporate tax rate was also reduced from 52 percent to 48 percent, reducing corporate taxes by $3 billion, or about 8 percent. This tax cut contributed to the longest sustained expansionary phase in recent history, lasting from February 1961 to December 1969, as shown in Table 3.7.1. Moreover, the unemployment rate, which was 5.7 percent in 1963, declined to 3.8 percent by 1966 and 3.5 percent by 1969.

The 1964 tax cut was hailed by Keynesian economists as the coming of age of Keynesian fiscal policy. However, two later uses of fiscal policy were not nearly as effective. In 1968, with the rate of inflation over 4 percent (the highest it had been since the early 1950s), policymakers feared that the economy was exceeding the full employment level of output. Therefore, a 10 percent tax surcharge on personal and corporate income was implemented, for one year. The intent of the tax was to reduce consumption, and thus aggregate expenditures, by reducing disposable income.

However, the tax was not effective in reducing inflation, which increased to over 5 percent in 1969 and 1970, and remained over 4 percent in 1971. There are two reasons why this fiscal policy did not achieve its desired results. First, because of the temporary nature of the tax, households reduced saving rather than consumption to pay for the tax, knowing they could resume saving when the tax was eliminated. Second, although taxes were increased, government spending and investment were also increased, offsetting the contractionary effect of the taxes.

A third implementation of fiscal policy occurred in 1975 in the form of another tax cut designed to stimulate the economy out of a recession entered in 1973. This tax cut consisted of a one-year reduction in personal income taxes paid in 1975, totaling $12 billion, and a rebate on 1974 personal income taxes totaling $8 billion. In spite of this attempt to stimulate the economy, the unemployment rate increased from 4.9 percent in 1973 to 8.5 percent in 1975, and remained over 7 percent until 1978. At the time this was the highest sustained unemployment since the Depression.

This tax cut, like the 1968 tax increase, was also ineffective. And like the 1968 tax increase, one reason for its ineffectiveness was its temporary nature. Households did not make the long-term changes in consumption needed to stimulate the economy. In addition, it should be noted that 1973 saw the first of the dramatic increases in the price of petroleum. Moreover, the Vietnam War ended in the early 1970s, causing reductions in military spending and increases in the civilian labor force.

The most recent major fiscal policy action occurred in 1981, with the Reagan administration's 25 percent tax cut, phased in over a three-year period. While the intent of the tax cut was *not* to stimulate aggregate expenditures in the short run, this appears to have happened. The tax cut aimed to stimulate the supply side of the economy by increasing the incentives to work harder and thus produce more output. But between July 1981 and November 1982 the economy was in the worst contractionary period since the Depression, with the unemployment rate near 10 percent. However, the tax cut, combined with increased government spending, helped stimulate the economy out of the recession, and by 1985 the unemployment rate had dipped to 7 percent.

IN SUMMARY

Fiscal Policy Applications of Keynesian Economics

- Fiscal policy is the discretionary use of government purchases and net taxes by the government to move the economy to the full employment level of output. Fiscal policy comes into play when aggregate expenditures do not achieve equilibrium at the full employment level of output. If aggregate expenditures are too low, then a recessionary gap is created. If aggregate expenditures are too great, then an inflationary gap is created. In both cases the government can use discretionary purchases and net taxation to increase or decrease aggregate expenditures appropriately.

- The balanced-budget multiplier for government purchases is equal to 1, which indicates that output increases by exactly the same amount as the increase in government purchases, if the purchases are financed through higher taxes. The balanced-budget multiplier for transfer payments is equal to zero, which indicates that there is no change in output if transfer payments and taxes are increased by the same amount.

- To close a recessionary gap, the government should use expansionary fiscal policy, increasing government purchases and reducing net taxes. Moreover, a budget deficit is appropriate during a recession. An inflationary gap can be closed with contractionary fiscal policy, reducing government purchases and increasing net taxes. In this case a budget surplus is most appropriate.

- In addition to the discretionary fiscal policy, the economy has automatic stabilizers built into the system with nondiscretionary expenditures and taxes. If taxes and transfer payments are affected by the level of income, they tend to reduce the peaks and troughs of the business cycle by taking away part of the additional disposable income in expansionary periods and by adding to disposable income in contractionary periods.

- The high employment budget is the government's budget that would exist if the economy was at full employment. It is based on the taxes collected and the expenditures made if the economy is at full employment. It is a better indication of discretionary fiscal policy because it compensates for the effect automatic stabilizers have on the budget.

- The first overt use of fiscal policy was the 1964 tax cut. It proved to be very effective and was considered a landmark for Keynesian economics. Two later uses of fiscal policy, a 1968 tax increase and a 1975 tax cut, were both less effective. However, in 1981 a 25 percent tax reduction by the Reagan administration had all of the indications of an effective use of expansionary fiscal policy, although that was not its intent.

QUESTIONS FOR STUDY AND ANALYSIS

1. Discretionary fiscal policy involves the use of government purchases and net taxes. While both can be used to change aggregate expenditures, and thus eliminate recessionary and inflationary gaps, they have differing effects on other parts of the economy and society. With this in mind, discuss some of the effects (both good and bad) that government purchases and taxes have on society. All things considered, is it better for society if a recessionary gap is eliminated with government purchases, taxes, or transfer payments? Explain. Is it better for society if an inflationary gap is eliminated with government purchases, taxes, or transfer payments? Explain.

2. Assume that the MPC is equal to 0.9. If the full employment level of output is $2000 and the actual level of output is $1500, what change in government purchases is necessary to close this recessionary gap? What change in net taxes is necessary to close this gap?

3. Explain why the balanced-budget multiplier for government purchases is equal to 1, but the balanced-budget multiplier for transfer

payments is equal to zero. In your answer consider the role of the MPC and the circular flow.

4. Under what circumstances is it appropriate to run a budget surplus? Under what circumstances is it appropriate to run a budget deficit?

5. How does the existence of automatic stabilizers in the economy affect the relative value of the expenditures multiplier? Explain.

6. Many people argue that the federal government should have a balanced budget. Considering that it has operated with a budget deficit for over a decade, how is the move to a balanced budget likely to affect economic activity?

REVIEW GLOSSARY

automatic stabilizers Induced components of the economy that dampen the fluctuations of the business cycle without discretionary action. The two most common types of automatic stabilizers are taxes and transfer payments. In both cases an increase in output leads to an increase in net taxes, which in turn leads to a decline in disposable income, consumption, and aggregate expenditures. The automatic stabilizers prevent output from increasing as much as it would if taxes and transfer payments did not depend on output.

balanced-budget multiplier The ratio of the change in output to a change in government expenditures that are matched by an equal change in taxes. The balanced-budget multiplier for government purchases is equal to 1. However, the balanced-budget multiplier for transfer payments is equal to zero.

contractionary fiscal policy Fiscal policy consisting of decreases in government purchases and/or increases in net taxes (including decreases in transfer payments).

expansionary fiscal policy Fiscal policy consisting of increases in government purchases and/or decreases in net taxes (including increases in transfer payments).

fiscal policy The use of the two components of the government's fiscal budget, government purchases and net taxation, to stabilize aggregate expenditures. Fiscal policy is one way the government can reduce the fluctuations in economic activity, limiting unemployment and inflation.

high employment budget The government budget that would exist if the economy were at full employment. The full employment budget estimates the tax revenues that will be collected and the expenditures that will be made (especially transfer payments) when the economy is at full employment. Since this budget eliminates the effect of automatic stabilizers, some economists argue its deficits and surpluses are a better indication of discretionary fiscal policy.

inflationary gap The difference between actual aggregate expenditures and the level of aggregate expenditures needed to achieve full employment, if actual output is greater than full employment output. An inflationary gap can be eliminated with contractionary fiscal policy.

recessionary gap The difference between actual aggregate expenditures and the level of aggregate expenditures needed to achieve full employment, if actual output is less than full employment output. A recessionary gap can be eliminated with expansionary fiscal policy.

SECTION INQUIRY

Balancing the Budget

In the past decade economists and policymakers have become increasingly concerned about the size of the federal government's budget deficit. This is due in large part to tremendous increases in the deficit in recent years. In 1979 the deficit was only $40 billion and less than 2 percent of *GNP*, as seen in Figure 4.4.1. However, by 1985 the deficit had grown to $212 billion and over 6 percent of *GNP*. Estimates for 1986 and 1987 place the deficit at $202 and $144 billion, respectively, showing a decline from the 1985 record but deficits that are still high by historical standards. Recent growth in the size of the deficit and the potential for future record high deficits have prompted many people to recommend an amendment to the U.S. Constitution requiring a balanced federal budget. While a balanced budget amendment to the constitution is unlikely to be approved in the foreseeable future, in 1985 Congress did pass the Gramm-Rudman Act, which calls for a balanced budget by the early 1990s. However, this act was declared unconstitutional by the Supreme Court in 1986.

Why is everyone so concerned about the federal deficit? Two basic problems associated with the federal deficit are cited by proponents of a balanced budget constraint. First, they argue that a large federal deficit prevents investment expenditures for capital goods and thus future economic growth. The deficit is financed by borrowing funds that households place into financial markets through saving. Since these funds are limited, government borrowing prevents investment borrowing for expenditures on capital goods. The deficit thus prevents the business sector from increasing the economy's stock of capital and inhibits future economic growth. Second, proponents of a balanced budget say that a large federal deficit leads to inflation because government purchases are greater than net taxes. Since government purchases add to aggregate expenditures while net taxes reduce aggregate expenditures through reduced consumption, a deficit means that the government spends more, through their purchases, *without* preventing households from spending less through an equal amount of taxes. A large deficit can thus overstimulate the economy and cause inflation.

QUESTIONS FOR DISCUSSION

1. In terms of the circular flow introduced in Section 3, Macroeconomic Foundations, discuss how an increase in the federal deficit could restrict investment expenditures for capital goods. What is likely to happen to the interest rate if government borrowing increases? Explain how this situation would affect investment borrowing.

2. If the federal government balanced its budget and eliminated a deficit that exceeds $100 billion, what do you think would happen to the level of national production? Explain. Considering the expenditure and tax multipliers, would it be best to balance the budget by decreasing government purchases or by increasing taxes? Explain.

3. Explain how a balanced budget constraint for the federal government would eliminate discretionary fiscal policy. What would happen to the peaks and troughs of business cycles with a balanced budget constraint?

4. Some opponents of a constraint forcing the government to balance the budget during the course of the year argue in favor of balancing the budget over the course of the business cycle instead. Discuss the pros and cons of a cyclically balanced budget versus an annually balanced budget. How would a cyclically balanced budget affect discretionary fiscal policy?

5. Some economists argue that the federal government should balance the high employment budget rather than the actual budget. Discuss the pros and cons of this recommendation. How would balancing the high employment budget affect discretionary fiscal policy?

SECTION 5

Money

In this section we turn our attention to another important cornerstone of macroeconomics—money. Obviously, we are well aware of the role money plays in our daily lives. We receive money in payment for income earned in the production of output, and we use money as payment for goods and services. In terms of the entire economy, money becomes significant as payment for goods, services, and resources exchanged in the economy. Without money, a particular good, service, or resource would have to be exchanged directly for another good, service, or resource, which would certainly hinder the day-to-day operation of the economy. In this section we examine both why and how money facilitates the exchange and production of output. Moreover, we discuss how the supply of money acts as a lubricant for the economy. If there is not enough money available, the economy begins to slow down and fall into the contractionary phase of the business cycle. However, if there is too much money available, the economy can head into the expansionary phase, with inflationary pressures on the price level.

In Unit 5.1, An Introduction to Money, our study of money begins by asking two simple questions. First, what are the functions of money? In answering this question, we quickly discover that the primary function of money is to assist in the exchange of goods and services. Second, what is money? While this may seem like a relatively simple question, money in fact has come in many different shapes, sizes, and forms. Even in today's economy no clear-cut definition of money exists, because various items are used as payment for goods, services, and resources.

Unit 5.2, Money Creation, takes us behind the scenes of what may appear to be a mysterious process. While we may think that all money is printed by the government, in this unit we find out that banks are actually able to "create" a large part of our money, not from thin air but through the use of fractional reserve banking.

Unit 5.3, The Federal Reserve System, sheds light on the mysterious process of money creation. In this unit we look at the Federal Reserve System, the nation's central banking authority, which oversees the banking system and the economy's supply of money. And we discuss how the Federal Reserve System, through the use of three regulatory tools known as monetary policy, is able to control banks' ability to create money.

Unit 5.4, The Money Market and Output Determination, discusses the crucial role of output determination. We examine exactly how the supply of money, controlled by the Federal Reserve System's monetary policy, affects the equilibrium level of national income and output. In essence, the monetary policy analyzed in this unit gives us an alternative to fiscal policy (discussed in Section 4) as a means of stabilizing business cycles and the fluctuations of economic activity.

Unit 5.5, Comparing Monetarist and Keynesian Policies, extends the analysis from Unit 5.4 into two separate views of the macroeconomy. While it would be nice if economists agreed on the role money plays in the economy, such is not the case. In fact, there are two relatively distinct groups of economists, monetarists and Keynesians, and each group views the role of monetary, and even fiscal, policy quite differently. In this unit we take a close look at the views expressed by these two groups of economists.

UNIT 5.1

An Introduction to Money

In this unit we begin our study of money and the role it plays in the macroeconomy. In particular, we examine the characteristics and functions of money. Quite simply, we want to know what money is and what it does. First, let's look at a general definition of money. **Money is anything that is generally accepted as payment in exchange for goods and services.** Although this definition gives us very little information on exactly what money is (since it could be anything), it tells us a great deal about what money does. In essence, money is used to facilitate the exchange of goods and services. This unit discusses why this is important to any economy, especially one as complex as in the United States.

The first topic in this unit is the nature and functions of money. While money makes it easier to exchange goods and services, it has other functions as well. We then look at different types of money, including various forms of money that have been used in the past. Finally, we review the current definitions of money for the United States economy.

FUNCTIONS OF MONEY

Although money is important in the exchange of goods and services, this is not its only function. In fact, money has four important functions: It is used as a medium of exchange, a standard unit of account, a store of value, and a standard of deferred payment. Let's look at each function.

Medium of Exchange

The most important function of money is as a medium of exchange. Money serves as payment for the goods, services, and resources exchanged in the economy. Consumers use money as payment for goods and services they buy from firms. Firms use money as payment for the factor services they hire from the households. In terms of the circular flow introduced in Unit 3.1, the physical flow of goods, services, and resources between the various sectors of the economy in one direction is offset by the flow of payments in the other direction. And money makes these payments, and the process of exchange, much easier.

To illustrate this, consider what the economy would be like without money, where every good, service, or resource would have to be exchanged directly for another good, service, or resource. For example, labor would be exchanged directly for food, automobile repair services for dental checkups, educational services for movie tickets, and so on. But in an economy without money, two people are not likely to exchange goods unless each has the good that the other wants. People would be spending so much time trying to find a trading partner that actual production would be affected. In short, without money more resources would be used in the *exchange* of goods and services and less in their *production*. But with money, exchanges are much easier. Since money can be used to buy any good, everyone is willing to accept it in payment for the good, service, or resource they are selling.

Standard Unit of Account

A second important function of money is as a standard unit of account. An economy that uses money as a medium of exchange naturally tends to state all prices in terms of the monetary unit. For example, a shirt might be priced at $10, a package of notebook paper at $1, and a movie ticket at $5. Each price tells a buyer how much money must be given up in exchange for the good, making it relatively easy for consumers to decide which goods to buy with the amount of available money.

But again, let's consider what would happen in an economy without money, where people would trade one commodity for another. Every price would be stated in terms of the amount of another good that would have to be given up, meaning a shirt would sell for ten packages of notebook paper, and a movie ticket for only five packages of paper. However, a shirt would also sell for two movie tickets, a movie ticket for one-half of a shirt, and a package of notebook paper for either one-tenth of a shirt or one-fifth of a movie ticket. With money we don't need to keep track of prices in each of these alternative units, so people can spend less time on exchange and more time on production.

Store of Value

A third important function of money is as a store of value. Value means the ability to buy goods and services that provide consumer satisfaction. In many cases we want to store the value of our current income until some time in the future. If you give up $100 worth of consumption today, you would like to have $100 worth of consumption tomorrow.

Money generally represents a good store of value over a relatively short period of time; a $5 bill will maintain its value for several weeks. However, the ability of money to store value depends on the price level. If the price level is rising during inflationary times, a unit of money is able to buy fewer goods and services, and thus it stores less value as time passes.

Standard of Deferred Payment

The last function of money is as a standard of deferred payment, which is a logical extension of its function as a standard unit of account. Many exchanges in the economy occur over a period of time. For example, consumer goods are purchased on credit, or a worker provides two weeks of work before being paid. In each case the payment for the commodity is deferred. For written contracts and unwritten agreements, the economy needs a standard for these deferred payments. Since money is the standard unit of account, it naturally becomes the standard for the deferred payments. If the price of an automobile is stated as $10,000, then it is natural for a loan contract to also specify the monthly payments in dollars.

CHARACTERISTICS OF MONEY

Now that we have an understanding of what money *does*, let's direct our attention back to what money *is*. There are five characteristics usually associated with money: general acceptance as payment, durability, ease of divisibility, ease of transportation, and difficulty of duplication. While an item does not need to have all five of these characteristics to be effectively used as money, the more it does have, the better.

Generally Acceptable We have already alluded to the characteristic of general acceptability, which is without question the most important characteristic of money. If no one in the economy is willing to accept an item as payment for goods and services, then it cannot be used as a medium of exchange and is no longer money.

Durable Money must also be a durable item since it is used and reused for exchange many times throughout the economy. If it is not durable, then it is not an effective store of value because most people will not accept as payment something that deteriorates in their hands before they can use it.

Divisible It also helps if the item is easily divisible, making it possible to state prices more precisely and allowing people to buy exactly the amount of a good that is desired. Consider what would happen if the smallest denomination in the economy was a $10 bill. A consumer would have to buy a minimum of twenty cans of soft drink that sold for 50 cents each or ten packages of notebook paper that sold for $1 each.

Transportable Transportability is also an important feature of money. Because money is used as a medium of exchange, buyers must be able to transport the money to the sellers of the goods and services. Obviously, money that can be easily carried in pockets (such as coins) does a better job of facilitating exchange than money that must be carried in large trucks (such as blocks of granite).

Difficult to Counterfeit Finally, money should be difficult to duplicate or counterfeit, because money that is easily duplicated can quickly lose its function as a medium of exchange. People will be reluctant to accept money in payment if there is a good chance that the money is counterfeit. No one wants to be stuck with counterfeit money that cannot be used to buy other goods and services.

These five characteristics can apply to a wide variety of different items. As a matter of fact, throughout history many different types of money have been used. In the colonial days of North America, trappers and explorers used beaver pelts and other types of furs as money, exchanging them at a trading post for necessary supplies. In prisoner-of-war camps during the Second World War, allied prisoners used cigarettes as money. On the tiny Micronesian island of Yap, large circular stones up to twelve feet in diameter have been used as money. And at different periods of time gold, silver, and precious gems have all been used as money.

TYPES OF MONEY

While the variety of money types is only bounded by the imaginations and necessities of an economy, we can classify money into two groups, commodity money and fiat money. Let's look at each.

Commodity Money

Commodity money is any money that has value in use in addition to its value in exchange. Beaver pelts, cigarettes, precious metals, and gems are all examples of commodity money. In each case the money can be used to facilitate exchange *or* it can be used to directly satisfy consumer wants as a commodity. Beaver pelts are used to make hats and coats. Cigarettes obviously are smoked. And gold, silver, and gems are used to make jewelry and other desirable goods. But they all have also been used as money at one time or another.

Fiat Money

The second basic type of money is fiat money. **Fiat money** is any money that has value in exchange but little or no value in use. The currency and coin issued by most governments today constitutes fiat money. The currency issued ($1, $5, and $10 bills) is worth very little as a commodity. When we consider that a $100 bill has the same paper content as a $1 bill, it is clear that paper currency has no practical value as a commodity. The same is true for most coins. The common metals such as copper and nickel currently used to make coins have less commodity value than their value in exchange.

Although the use of fiat money may seem like a risky way to run an economy, it is not as ludicrous as it appears. Money has value in exchange precisely because everyone in the economy is willing to accept it in payment for goods and services. There is no reason why money itself must provide value as a consumption good as long as it is generally accepted in exchange. Then it becomes just as valuable as an equivalent amount of gold, silver, or beaver pelts.

MONEY IN THE U.S. ECONOMY

Let's now turn our attention to the types of money currently used in the U.S. economy. Although we have been discussing money in terms of currency and coins, it is surprising to discover that these represent only a small fraction of the total money in the United States. Furthermore, note that there is not a single, all-encompassing, definition of money. In fact, we want to discuss the three most commonly used definitions of money: M1, M2, and M3.

M1: Currency and Checkable Deposits

The first, and narrowest, definition of money in the U.S. economy is **M1,** the total of currency held by the nonbank public and checkable deposits. Table 5.1.1 presents historical data for the M1 definition of money. **Currency** is the paper money and coins issued by the government. According to this definition, currency is money only if it is held by individuals, firms, and anyone else in the economy except banks, savings and loan associations, and credit unions, whose currency is out of circulation and cannot be used for exchange. While currency is what usually comes to mind when we think of money, even in this narrow M1 definition of money, currency represents less than one-fourth of the overall supply of money; the remaining three-fourths is checkable deposits. **Checkable deposits** are deposits at banks that can be withdrawn on demand, without prior notice. In other words, checkable deposits are common checking accounts, from which a deposit can be withdrawn by merely writing a check.

It is easy to see how currency fits the definition of money as a medium of exchange, but checkable deposits are included because they perform the same function as currency. In fact, a vast majority of the goods and services purchased in the economy are paid for by check, not by currency. People may pay for lunch at Burger King with a $5 bill, but they make their $300 car payment with a check.

Most checkable deposits contained in the M1 definition of money do not receive an interest on deposit. However, in the past decade interest-paying checkable deposits have increased significantly. The three most popular interest-paying checkable deposits are *NOW* (Negotiable-Order-of-With-

Table 5.1.1

The M1 Definition of Money, 1929 to 1985 (billions)

The M1 definition of the money supply has grown from $26.5 billion in 1929 to $593.9 billion in 1985. M1 consists of currency issued by the government and checkable deposits issued by banks (including *NOW* accounts, share drafts, and *ATS* services).

Year	M1	Year	M1	Year	M1
1929	$ 26.5				
1930	25.4	1950	$116.2	1970	$216.8
1931	23.6	1951	122.7	1971	231.0
1932	20.7	1952	127.4	1972	252.4
1933	19.5	1953	128.8	1973	266.4
1934	21.5	1954	132.3	1974	278.0
1935	25.6	1955	135.2	1975	291.8
1936	29.1	1956	136.9	1976	311.1
1937	30.3	1957	135.9	1977	336.4
1938	30.1	1958	141.1	1978	364.2
1939	33.6	1959	141.2	1979	390.5
1940	39.0	1960	142.2	1980	415.6
1941	45.4	1961	146.7	1981	441.9
1942	55.2	1962	149.4	1982	480.8
1943	72.3	1963	154.9	1983	509.1
1944	86.0	1964	162.0	1984	544.5
1945	99.2	1965	169.6	1985	593.9
1946	106.0	1966	173.8		
1947	113.1	1967	185.2		
1948	111.5	1968	199.5		
1949	111.2	1969	205.9		

Source: U.S. Bureau of Economic Analysis, *Survey of Current Business*, selected issues.

drawal) accounts, share drafts, and ATS (Automatic-Transfer-System) accounts. **NOW accounts** are interest-paying checkable deposits issued mainly by banks and savings and loans. By contrast, **share drafts** are interest-paying checkable deposits issued almost exclusively by credit unions. With an **ATS account** the bank automatically transfers funds from an interest-paying savings account to a non-interest-paying checking account whenever a check is written. ATS accounts were developed in the late

1970s because, prior to banking deregulation in 1980, checking accounts at banks could not pay an interest, but savings accounts could.

Regardless of which institution issues the accounts, they serve the same function as a non-interest-paying checkable deposit. In each case a buyer is able to purchase a good or service by issuing a check to a seller. Therefore, *NOW* accounts, share drafts, and *ATS* accounts are all part of the money supply. Figure 5.1.1 depicts how this first measure of money (M1) is divided between currency and checkable deposits, including both regular checking accounts and interest-paying checkable deposits.

Figure 5.1.1

Alternative Measures of the Money Supply, 1985

There are three common definitions of money in the United States. M1 includes currency held by the nonbank public and checkable deposits. M2 includes M1 and different types of near monies, such as time deposits and money market shares. M3 includes M2 and larger-denomination or longer-period types of near monies.

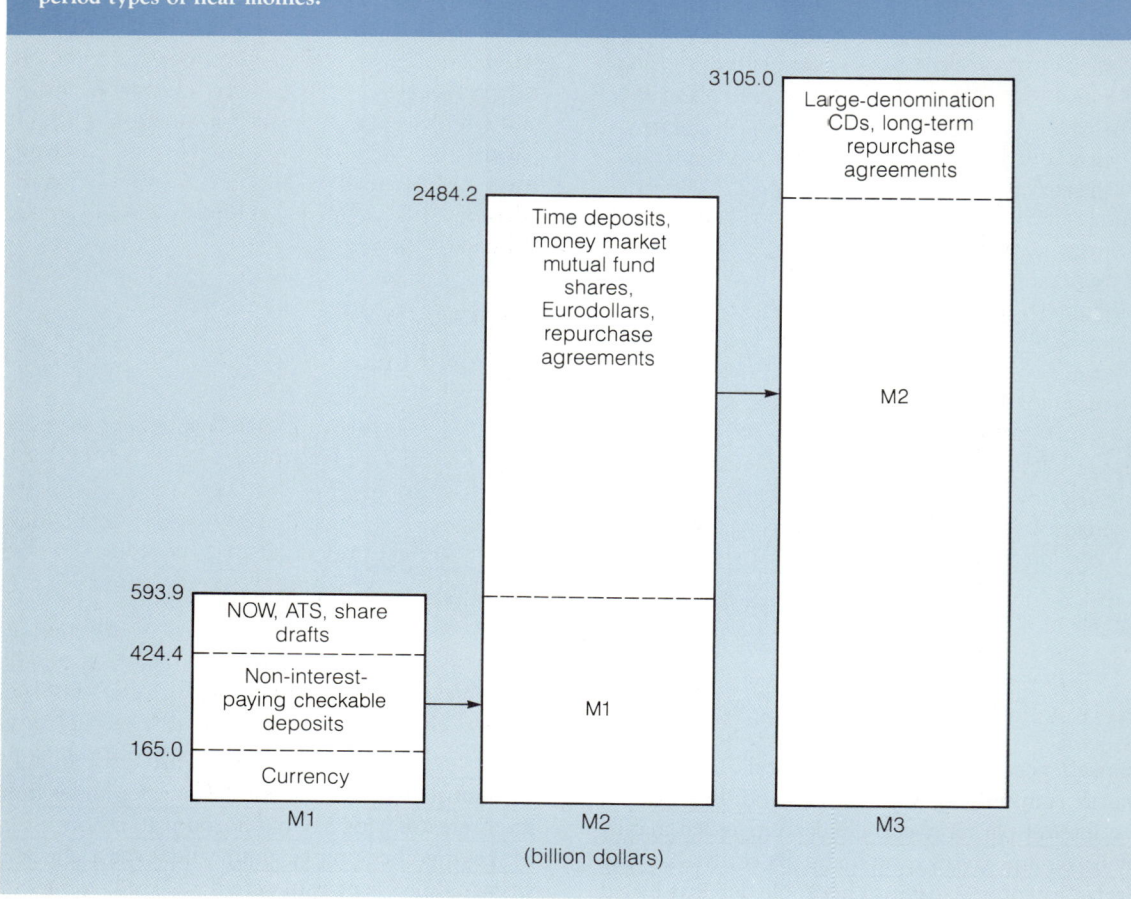

M2: M1 and Near Monies

Our second definition of money is **M2,** which is M1 plus other types of accounts that can be termed near monies. **Near monies** are financial assets that cannot be directly used to purchase goods and services but can be easily converted into currency or checkable deposits. Near monies are important when we consider the ability to buy goods and services. Although near monies are, strictly speaking, not money since they cannot be used as payment for a good, they can be quickly and easily converted into money, or M1.

The most important type of near money is a time deposit. In contrast to a checkable deposit, in which money can be withdrawn without notice, a time deposit in principle must be kept in the financial institution for a specified length of time. The most common type of time deposit is the savings account. Legally, a financial institution can require a thirty-day notice before withdrawal, though that requirement is rarely implemented. Other common types of time deposits are six-month or one-year certificates of deposit. With certificates of deposit, an interest penalty is imposed if the funds are withdrawn before the specified time period is up. While time deposits cannot be used to pay for goods and services, the funds can easily be converted to money to make a purchase.

Another important type of near money is a money market mutual fund share. A money market mutual fund is a financial instrument in which an intermediary buys government- or corporate-issued bonds. The intermediary then issues shares in the mutual fund, which can be easily converted to M1. Some money market mutual fund shares even have built-in check-writing capabilities.

Other types of near monies that are included in the definition of M2 are Eurodollars and repurchase agreements. Eurodollars are deposits held in foreign banks. While they are held in banks outside the United States, they can be easily and quickly transferred to U.S. banks. In fact, most Eurodollar accounts are transferred overnight between the United States and Europe, so that the funds are earning interest in Europe instead of lying dormant while banks in the United States are closed. Repurchase agreements are deposits placed in commercial banks overnight by firms to earn interest while everyone sleeps. Repurchase agreements are issued by financial institutions that need extra funds for a short period of time (overnight). Note that the relationship between M2 and M1 is also illustrated in Figure 5.1.1.

M3: M2 and Additional Near Monies

The third definition of money is M3. **M3 is M2 plus large-denomination certificates of deposit and longer-term repurchase agreements.** The large-denomination certificates of deposit include those for $100,000 or more. The longer-term repurchase agreements are for two days or longer, as compared with overnight. Both represent additional types of near monies. In the M3 definition, the funds are still convertible to money, but not quite as easily as the near monies included in M2. Note that the relationship between M3 and M2 is also illustrated in Figure 5.1.1.

IN SUMMARY
An Introduction to Money

- Money is anything that is generally accepted as payment in exchange for goods and services. Money has four basic functions in the economy: It is used as a medium of exchange, a standard unit of account, a store of value, and a standard of deferred payment.

- There are five important characteristics for an item to be used as money: It must be generally accepted as payment, durable, easily divisible, easily transported, and difficult to duplicate. While an item need not possess all the characteristics, the more it has, the better it can function as money.

- Money can be classified as either commodity money or fiat money. Commodity money is money that is desired as a commodity in addition to its use as money. Fiat money is money that has little or no value in use but only value in exchange. The money in the U.S. economy is fiat money.

- There are three common definitions of money for the U.S. economy. The narrowest definition is M1, which contains currency and checkable deposits (including standard checking accounts, *NOW* accounts, share drafts, and *ATS* services). The second is M2, which contains M1 and near monies such as savings accounts and money market mutual funds. The third definition is M3, which contains M2 and other types of near monies.

QUESTIONS FOR STUDY AND ANALYSIS

1. For each of the following items, indicate which of the four functions of money (medium of exchange, standard unit of account, store of value, or standard of deferred payment) is involved, and why?
   a. The dollar bill that has been in your pocket since last Tuesday
   b. The check you use to pay for your groceries
   c. A loan contract stipulating your monthly payments on the purchase of a new car
   d. A quarter placed in a soft-drink machine
   e. The price of a package of notebook paper
   f. Funds transferred from your checking account to your savings account

2. During the course of a typical week you probably use money in many different transactions. Discuss what your typical week would be like if you had no money for these transactions and had to rely exclusively on the direct exchange of goods.

3. The following list includes several items that have been, or could be, used for money. Discuss how each item fits the five characteristics of money (generally accepted, durable, easily divisible, easily transportable, and difficult to duplicate).
   a. Metal coins
   b. Beaver pelts
   c. Cigarettes
   d. Diamonds
   e. Gold
   f. Chewing gum wrappers
   g. Electronic entries in a computer network
   h. Giant stone wheels

4. Why would anyone be willing to accept fiat money, which has no intrinsic value, in payment for a good or service?

5. Why does the M1 definition of money exclude currency held by banks? Do you think M1 should include the currency held by banks? Explain.

6. Do you think interest-paying checking accounts (*NOW*, share drafts, and *ATS*) should be considered a part of the economy's money supply? Why or why not? Do you think typical savings accounts, certificates of deposit, or money market mutual fund shares should be considered part of the economy's money supply? Why or why not?

7. How well do bank credit cards, such as MasterCard and American Express, fulfill each of the four functions of money? Explain. Are credit cards money?

REVIEW GLOSSARY

ATS **(Automatic-Transfer-System) accounts** Accounts that automatically transfer funds between interest-paying savings accounts and checking accounts.

checkable deposits Deposits at banks that can be withdrawn on demand, without prior notice.

commodity money Any money that has value in use in addition to its value in exchange. In the past almost all money was commodity money, for example, gold, silver, and beaver pelts.

currency Paper money and coins issued by the government.

fiat money Any money that has value in exchange but little or no value in use. Currency and checkable deposits used as money in the U.S. economy are fiat money.

M1 The total of currency held by the nonbank public and checkable deposits. M1 is the narrowest definition of money.

M2 M1 plus such near monies as time deposits, money market mutual fund shares, Eurodollars, and repurchase agreements.

M3 M2 plus large-denomination certificates of deposit and longer-term repurchase agreements.

money Anything that is generally accepted as payment in exchange for goods and services. Money performs four basic functions in the economy: It is used as a medium of exchange, a standard unit of account, a store of value, and a standard of deferred payment. Money usually has the following characteristics: generally accepted as payment, durable, easily divisible, easily transportable, and difficult to duplicate.

near monies Financial assets that cannot be directly used to purchase goods and services but can be converted easily into currency or checkable deposits.

NOW **(Negotiable-Orders-of-Withdrawal) accounts** Checkable deposits at savings and loan associations and banks that pay an interest.

share drafts Checkable deposits at credit unions that pay an interest.

UNIT 5.2

Money Creation

In the last unit we discovered that money in modern economies is composed of more than just currency. In fact, according to the M1 definition of money, over three-fourths of the money in the economy is made up of checkable deposits at banks or other financial institutions. In this unit we examine checkable deposits in more detail, particularly how checkable deposits and thus money can be "created" through the day-to-day operations of the banking system. **Money creation is the process in which banks increase the amount of funds in checkable deposits by using reserves to make loans.**

What is interesting about this is that, by creating checkable deposits, banks can also increase the supply of money in the economy. This means that the federal government, which prints the paper money and mints the coins, has *direct* control over only a small part of the money supply. However, the government can *indirectly* control checkable deposits through the regulation of banks and the money creation process, as discussed in Unit 5.3.

To begin our study of money creation by the banking system, we look at a simplified, and somewhat embellished, account of how banking functions developed from the goldsmith profession. We then see how modern banks, operating much like the goldsmiths, are able to create deposits and thus increase the supply of money in the economy.

THE GOLDSMITH

The fable of the goldsmith has been passed down among economists from generation to generation to illustrate the process of money creation. While the following represents a simplified account of the history of the goldsmith profession, it does contain a grain of truth. However, we are not concerned as much with historical accuracy as with the banking process that is represented.

In the Beginning

Although goldsmithing was one of many "smithing" professions, including blacksmithing and silversmithing, the fact that goldsmiths used gold (the economy's money) as the raw material to fashion jewelry and other types of goods placed them in an interesting position. Not only was their product (jewelry) valuable but their raw material (gold) was, too. Since both raw material and product needed to be protected, a secure safe was needed.

The First Deposit

Goldsmiths' inherent need to keep their own gold secure led to a side operation—storing and protecting gold for other people. Storage and protection was necessary because the nature of gold made it awkward for people to carry all of their money with them all of the time, so they often turned to goldsmiths for safekeeping. In order to keep track of whose gold they had, goldsmiths simply issued a receipt for each deposit. When a depositor was ready to withdraw the gold, the receipt was simply exchanged for the specified amount of gold. The interesting aspect of this system was that the gold returned to each depositor was probably not the actual gold deposited. But as long as the amount was correct, no one really cared.

Gold Receipts as Money

The gold receipts issued by goldsmiths soon took on another function. Since the goldsmiths were holding the gold for many different people, anyone with a gold receipt could redeem it for the appropriate amount of gold; goldsmiths didn't care, and probably couldn't tell, if the person redeeming the gold receipt was the original depositor. This meant that people throughout a goldsmith's town were more than willing to exchange the *gold receipts* instead of the *gold* when purchasing goods and services. Before long, gold receipts, which were much easier to handle and carry than the gold, replaced the actual gold as the "money" in circulation. Who needed gold when gold receipts were accepted?

Gold Reserves and Loans

Since gold receipts were generally accepted as money in most towns, few people found it necessary to actually withdraw any of their gold from safekeeping. Indeed, such withdrawals were not very common, so that goldsmiths usually had a safeful of gold. In fact, let's say that the average goldsmith discovered that no more than 20 percent of the gold was withdrawn during any period of time.

This was an important realization. Goldsmiths discovered that they controlled a supply of gold that people were willing to pay to borrow. Indeed, goldsmiths found they could loan out 80 percent of the gold and no one would know the difference, as long as 20 percent was kept in reserve (in the safe) to cover withdrawals. This meant that for every five pounds worth of gold receipts in circulation, one pound of gold remained in the safe.

Creating Gold Receipts

Soon, however, the goldsmiths realized that they didn't actually need to loan out the gold itself. After all, since their receipts were used as money in the economy and were generally accepted as payment for goods and services, why bother loaning out the actual gold? People really didn't need the gold because gold receipts would work as well. Goldsmiths found that they could make loans simply using the gold receipts rather than the gold.

For example, if a goldsmith had receipts for 100 pounds of gold in circulation, only 20 pounds of gold had to be in the safe. But if the goldsmith had 100 pounds of gold in the safe, then receipts for 500 pounds of gold could be placed in circulation. As long as no more than 20 percent of the gold receipts were redeemed during any period, the goldsmith never had to pay out more than 100 pounds of gold. This meant the goldsmith could loan out receipts for 400 pounds of gold, to go with the receipts for 100 pounds of gold issued to the original depositors. The receipts for 500 pounds of gold were "backed up" by the 100 pounds of gold in the safe because no more than 20 percent of the gold receipts were exchanged for gold at any time.

This proved to be a profitable realization by goldsmiths. Instead of loaning out 80 pounds of the gold, they could loan out receipts for 400 pounds of gold, thereby earning five times the interest on receipts for 400 pounds of gold instead of 80 pounds.

Goldsmiths and the Money Supply

This fable has an important implication for the supply of money. Note that the goldsmith took 100 pounds of money (gold) and transformed it into 500 pounds of money (gold receipts), thus creating 400 pounds of money. This money creation was possible because goldsmiths discovered that only a fraction of the outstanding gold receipts had to be backed up with actual gold.

While this system of keeping only a fraction of the gold made it possible to create gold receipts and expand the money supply, the system was always on the verge of total disaster. Goldsmiths operated on the premise that only 20 percent of the gold receipts would be exchanged for gold. Therefore, if people tried to exchange 21 percent of the receipts, the entire system could collapse because the gold would not be available. For example, if receipts for 500 pounds of gold were in circulation, the goldsmith could pay out 100 pounds of gold but no more. The depositor who wanted to withdraw the 101st pound would place goldsmiths in very serious trouble.

Indeed, that 101st pound could topple the entire system. If only one person was unable to exchange a gold receipt for gold, the word would rapidly spread to all depositors and holders of gold receipts. Remember that the gold receipts were accepted as money only because everyone believed that they could exchange them at any time for an equal amount of gold. However, if they found out that even one gold receipt was not being honored, this belief would be shattered. People would not be willing to accept gold receipts as payment, making the receipts useless as money. Consequently, the total amount of money would decline from 500 pounds worth of gold receipts to the original 100 pounds of gold. As we see in Unit 5.4, this type of reduction in the money supply can have a disastrous effect on the economy (as well as on the goldsmiths' health).

MODERN BANKING AND MONEY CREATION

The fable of the goldsmiths reveals many of the important aspects of the modern banking system. Now let's look at today's banks and see how they perform the functions illustrated by the goldsmiths. The key to modern banking, like the key to the goldsmiths' operations, is fractional reserve banking. **Fractional reserve banking** is a system in which banks hold less than 100 percent of deposits as reserves. In the same way that the goldsmiths issued more gold receipts than the amount of gold in reserve, fractional reserve banking means banks can have more checkable deposits than the amount of their reserves. In fact, banks keep no more than between 3 and 20 percent of their deposits in reserves.

But what exactly is meant by reserves? For the goldsmiths, the concept of reserves was fairly simple—it was the amount of gold kept in the safe. For modern banks, reserves can take many forms. **Reserves** are the vault cash and deposits at the Federal Reserve System that banks use to complete day-to-day transactions. The first type of reserves is the actual currency kept in the bank vaults. During the course of a day, a bank needs currency to "cash" checks and otherwise pay out currency to its customers. In addition, it also receives cash deposits from its customers that it retains in its vaults. Even though the modern banking system is rapidly moving to a system of electronic funds transfers and accounting entries, a bank still needs to keep currency in its vaults.

A second type of reserves are deposits at the Federal Reserve System. In the next unit we discuss the Federal Reserve System and its role in the economy's banking system. For the moment, simply note that the Federal Reserve System operates as the "bank" for all of the commercial banks in the economy. Banks keep deposits in or receive loans from the Federal Reserve System in the same way that consumers keep deposits in or receive loans from commercial banks. In particular, the deposits from commercial banks enable the Federal Reserve System to act as a clearing house to process checks. This function, as we see shortly, is one reason that banks keep deposits at the Federal Reserve System.

The Process of Money Creation

To see how money is created by the banking system, let's see what happens when someone deposits money into a bank. We should point out that the term *bank* is used throughout this discussion to refer to all types of depository financial institutions, including savings and loan associations and credit unions.

Suppose you have been saving your coins for several years and decide to deposit them in a local bank. Figure 5.2.1 illustrates what happens to this initial deposit of $100 when it is converted into a checking account, or a checkable deposit, at the Urban National Bank. The left side of the figure shows how the assets of the bank are affected by the deposit. Since coins are currency, the bank's vault cash is increased by $100. The right side of the figure shows how the bank's liabilities are affected by the deposit. Since the coins are deposited in a checkable deposit, the bank's liabilities also increase by $100, the amount the bank owes to you. As with any transaction, the bank has an equal increase in assets and liabilities.

Since the bank is in business to earn a profit, which it does by making interest-paying loans, the additional $100 of vault cash comes in handy. Moreover, this bank, like the goldsmiths, practices

Figure 5.2.1
Balance Sheet of the Urban National Bank

The money creation process begins with an increase in a bank's reserves. For the Urban National Bank a deposit of $100 worth of coins increases the bank's vault cash, which are reserves, and its checkable deposits. Since the bank only needs to keep a fraction of the reserves to back up the $100 deposit, it transforms the rest into a loan. As it makes this loan, it creates a checkable deposit and thus also creates money.

Urban National Bank	
Assets	Liabilities
+ $100 Vault cash	+ $100 Deposit

fractional reserve banking and thus keeps only a fraction of the $100 deposit as vault cash, or reserves. Let's say that the bank, in the course of its business, keeps reserves equal to only 20 percent of its deposits.

At this point, let's distinguish between three different types of reserves. First, **legal reserves** are reserves (vault cash and deposits at the Federal Reserve System) that can be used to satisfy legal requirements. Although banks have several different types of financial assets, including bonds and government securities, such assets are riskier than vault cash and reserves at the Federal Reserve System. Legal reserves are the only financial assets that can be used to back up deposits.

Legal reserves are divided between required reserves and excess reserves. **Required reserves** are the minimum amount of reserves that a bank must hold to back up its deposits. As we discuss in the next unit, one way that banks are regulated by the Federal Reserve System is through control of the amount of required reserves. For now, assume that required reserves are reserves that the bank already uses to back up deposits and that cannot be used for new loans. The reserves that can be used to back up new deposits are excess reserves. **Excess reserves are the amount of legal reserves remaining after required reserves have been satisfied.** Excess reserves are the difference between legal reserves and required reserves.

Let's return to the initial $100 deposit of Figure 5.2.1. At this stage of the process the bank has $100 of legal reserves to back up the $100 of demand deposits. But since its required reserves are only $20, it has an extra $80 of excess reserves that can be used for a loan. Panel a of Figure 5.2.2 shows what happens when the Urban National Bank makes an $80 loan to a second consumer and in so doing creates an $80 checkable deposit. Since the $80 loan is an asset of the bank, there is an $80 increase on the left-hand side. However, there is an additional $80 liability on the right-hand side when the loan is deposited in the second consumer's checkable deposit.

At this point the bank still has $100 in vault cash, since there have been no checks written on either checkable deposit. However, suppose the second consumer spends the $80 by purchasing a used stereo from a third consumer. The third consumer then deposits this check into the Suburban State Bank, as depicted in panel b.

The Suburban State Bank has an immediate increase in its liabilities when the third consumer deposits the $80 check, but it also has an increase in its assets. The $80 check that is deposited represents a claim on the Urban National Bank. Thus, the Suburban State Bank has to send the check to the Urban National Bank, which will send it $80 in reserves. While this is, in principle, what happens, the actual mechanism is a little different.

As mentioned earlier, the Federal Reserve System acts as a clearing house for checks written on banks throughout the country. This is one reason that all banks keep deposits with the Federal Reserve System. When the Suburban State Bank receives this check written on an account at the Urban National Bank, it actually sends it to the Federal Reserve System, which then simply increases the reserves of the Suburban State Bank and reduces the reserves of the Urban National Bank. Since a single bank on a given day may receive checks written on hundreds of different banks, it is easier to send all of the checks to the Federal Reserve System than it is to send each check to a separate bank.

Note how the Urban National Bank has been affected by this transaction. Overall, its checkable deposits have increased by $100. On the asset side, it has $80 more in loans, and its reserves have had a net increase of $20. While vault cash (one form of reserves) increases by $100, deposits at the Federal Reserve System (the other form of reserves) decreases by $80.

Meanwhile, the Suburban State Bank has $80 in additional checkable deposits and $80 in additional reserves. But because it needs to keep only 20 percent of the $80 of new deposits as reserves, it can make a loan for 80 percent of $80, or $64. When it makes this loan, it does so by adding $64 to a checkable deposit.

Let's say the consumer who receives this loan purchases a good or service and writes a check in payment. This check is then deposited in the Farmers' Market Savings and Loan, which clears the $64 check through the Federal Reserve System. The $64 is added to the reserves of Farmers' Market Savings and Loan, and $64 is subtracted from the reserves of the Suburban State Bank, as depicted in panel c of Figure 5.2.2.

Since Farmers' Market Savings and Loan has $64 in additional reserves and $64 in additional deposits, it can make a loan of 80 percent of the $64 while retaining 20 percent in reserves. It makes a loan of $51.20 and adds $51.20 to a checkable deposit, which eventual finds its way to the City Employees' Credit Union. This process continues until there are no additional increases in deposits or reserves.

Figure 5.2.2 illustrates how the assets and liabilities of the first four banks involved in this process change. The Urban National Bank has an overall increase in checkable deposits of $100 and an

Figure 5.2.2
Money Creation

If banks keep 20 percent of their deposits as reserves, they can use the remaining 80 percent for loans. As they make the loans, checkable deposits and thus money are created. And when the checkable deposits are used for transactions, the reserves work their way through the banking system, creating additional checkable deposits along the way.

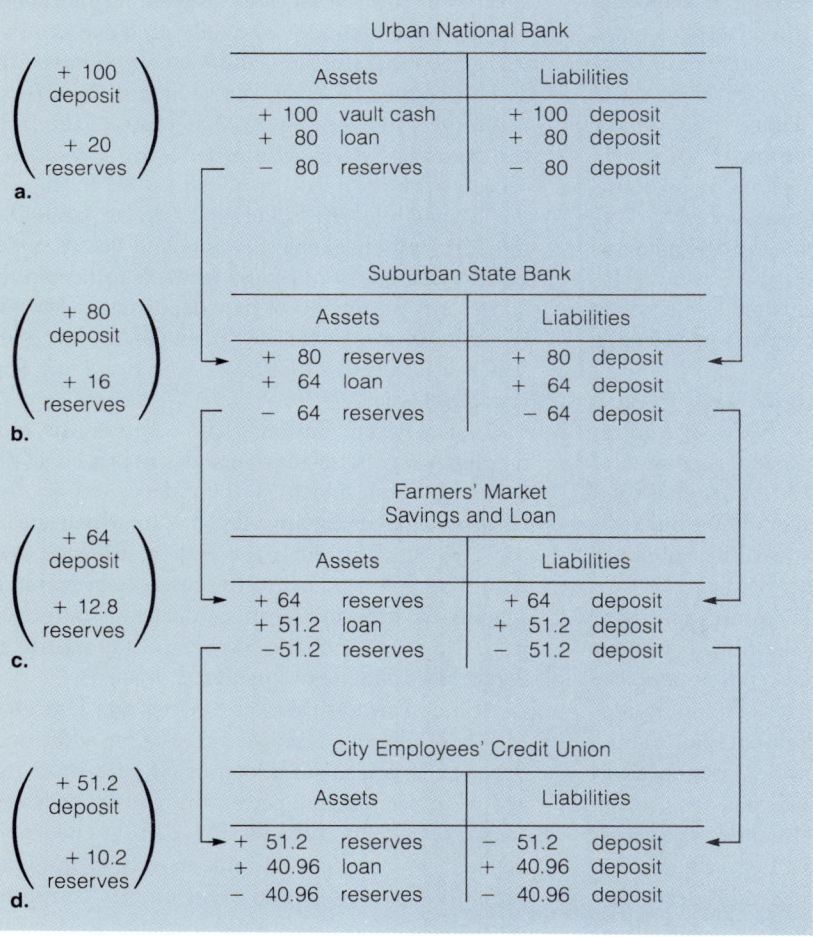

UNIT 5.2 • MONEY CREATION

Table 5.2.1

Changes in Deposits and Reserves

An injection of funds into the banking system leads to an increase in reserves and, subsequently, an increase in checkable deposits and the money supply as banks use the reserves to back up loans. If the Urban National Bank has an additional $100 in deposits and banks keep only 20 percent as reserves, the banking system creates a total of $500 in deposits.

Bank	Change in Deposits	Change in Reserves
Urban National Bank	$100.0	$20.0
Suburban State Bank	80.0	16.0
Farmers' Market Savings and Loan	64.0	12.8
City Employees' Credit Union	51.2	10.2
All other banks	204.8	41.0
Total	$500.0	$100.0

increase in reserves of $20. The Suburban State Bank has a net increase in deposits of $80 and a net increase in reserves of $16. The Farmers' Market Savings and Loan has a net increase in deposits of $64, while reserves increase by $12.80. The last of the four banks, the City Employees' Credit Union, has deposits that increase by $51.20 and reserves that increase by $10.20. Table 5.2.1 summarizes the changes in deposits and reserves for these four banks and for all other banks in the system.

If the change in deposits from every other bank in the system is added together, checkable deposits increase by a total of $500. By adding in the additional changes in reserves from the other banks, overall reserves increase by $100.

The Deposit Multiplier

Let's look at the overall change in deposits, which in this case increased by $500 simply because $100 was deposited into the Urban National Bank, thereby increasing its reserves by $100. Since banks hold only 20 percent of their deposits as reserves, the banking system, like the goldsmiths, is able to make loans equal to five times the amount of reserves. With $100 of reserves, the banking system can create $500 in deposits. In fact, knowing the percentage of deposits kept in reserves by the banking system allows us to determine the overall change in deposits without going through the step-by-step analysis just discussed.

We can determine the total change in deposits by using the deposit multiplier. The **deposit multiplier** is the change in deposits at banks divided by the initial change in reserves. For the percentage of deposits held in reserve (r), we can specify the deposit multiplier as

$$\text{deposit multiplier} = \frac{1}{r}$$

In our example the deposit multiplier equals 5 (1/0.2).

This deposit multiplier is important because it tells us how checkable deposits are affected by a change in reserves. And since checkable deposits are three-fourths of the economy's M1 supply of money, this indicates how the money supply is affected. In the next unit we examine how the Federal Reserve System can control the supply of money by influencing this money creation process.

IN SUMMARY

Money Creation

- Money creation is an important part of the supply of money because it is the process by which banks are able to create checkable

- deposits by using reserves to make loans. Since checkable deposits constitute a large part of the money supply, the government's ability to print currency and mint coins gives it direct control over just a fraction of the money supply.

- The money creation process can be illustrated by the fable of the goldsmiths. In this fable goldsmiths, whose initial function in the economy is to produce goods using gold, take on the functions of a bank. The goldsmiths first act as safekeepers for others' gold. But in doing so, the receipts issued to the depositors come to be used as money. Then the goldsmiths loan out the gold and find a greater profit in loaning out gold receipts than in the gold itself. The goldsmith fable indicates how money, in the form of gold receipts, can be created in spite of the fact that the goldsmiths hold only a fraction of the total amount of receipts in circulation.

- The modern banking system, like the goldsmiths, practices fractional reserve banking, in which the bank holds reserves equal to only a fraction of total deposits. With fractional reserve banking, a bank can make loans with the excess reserves it is not required to hold. And through this process of making loans with reserves, the banking system increases the amount of checkable deposits and thus the money supply. An easy way to determine the total amount of checkable deposits created with this process is with the deposit multiplier. The deposit multiplier is simply $1/r$, where r is the fraction of deposits kept in the form of reserves. If the deposit multiplier is 5, then each $1 of additional reserves leads to $5 of additional checkable deposits.

QUESTIONS FOR STUDY AND ANALYSIS

1. How does the general acceptability characteristic of money relate to the process of money creation? Explain.

2. Discuss how effectively the money creation process would work if all money was commodity money. Would it be possible to "create" commodity money? Is it necessary to have fiat money for the money creation process? Explain.

3. Explain how the money creation process is often on the brink of catastrophe. What does it take to destroy the general acceptability of money created through this process?

4. What role does fractional reserve banking play in the money creation process? Discuss how legal reserves, required reserves, and excess reserves each affect a bank's ability to create money.

5. What are the similarities between the deposit multiplier contained in the money creation process and the expenditures multiplier from Section 4? What are the similarities between r and MPS?

6. If banks hold 10 percent of their deposits in the form of reserves, what is the change in deposits if banks have $50,000 of excess reserves?

REVIEW GLOSSARY

deposit multiplier The change in deposits at banks divided by the initial change in reserves. The deposit multiplier is equal to $1/r$, where r is the fraction of reserves used to back up deposits.

excess reserves The amount of legal reserves remaining after required reserves have been satisfied. Excess reserves are the reserves that a bank can loan out.

fractional reserve banking A system in which banks hold less than 100 percent of deposits as reserves. In the United States banks keep between 3 and 20 percent of deposits as reserves.

legal reserves Reserves (vault cash and deposits at the Federal Reserve System) that can be used to satisfy legal requirements. Legal reserves do not include other financial assets, such as government securities.

money creation The process in which banks increase the amount of funds in checkable deposits by using reserves to make loans. Money creation is an important process in the economy because it means that the government has direct control over only part of the money supply.

required reserves The minimum amount of reserves that a bank must hold to back up its deposits. Required reserves are set by the Federal Reserve System.

reserves The vault cash and deposits at the Federal Reserve System that banks use to complete day-to-day transactions.

UNIT 5.3

The Federal Reserve System

Fractional reserve banking and the ability of banks to create money can lead to some devastating problems for the economy. Recall what happened to a goldsmith in the previous unit if an unusually large number of depositors tried to withdraw their gold. Even honest and reputable goldsmiths were forced out of business. The same type of thing can and has happened to otherwise sound and reputable banks. When a bank goes out of business, it takes with it the deposits that it has created, thus reducing the money supply. The Federal Reserve System was established in part to prevent these types of bank failures and in general to oversee the economy's banking system and supply of money.

We start by looking at the origin and history of the Federal Reserve System (which is commonly called the Fed) and discussing when and why it was created. Then we dissect the basic structure of the Fed to see how it is able to control the complex banking system that currently exists. And finally, we examine the three basic tools the Fed has for controlling the economy's supply of money: open market operations, reserve requirements, and the discount rate.

THE ORIGIN OF THE FEDERAL RESERVE SYSTEM

In the previous unit we saw that banks transform their excess reserves into loans in order to earn a profit. Any reserves that are not transformed into loans are earning no interest, so the bank is not making a profit. Banks therefore have a strong incentive to make loans and keep as few reserves as possible. But, as with the goldsmiths in the last unit, if only one depositor is unable to receive his or her funds, the entire bank can collapse.

In fact, this was a very common occurrence in the middle and late 1800s. Every so often a bank would make too many loans and would not be able to cover daily transactions or, for a variety of reasons, an unusually large number of depositors would want to make withdrawals. When a bank was unable to pay its depositors, customers often panicked, fearing that they would be unable to recover their funds. And when they tried to withdraw their deposits, the situation would grow even worse for the bank, and ultimately it would go out of business, taking with it all of the deposits that it had created.

During this time, the United States did not have a central banking authority to help a bank in this type of trouble. In many cases a troubled bank would borrow funds from another bank. However, this was often a futile effort, since a single bank would need all of the reserves of twenty or more banks to cover its outstanding deposits. When one bank tried to help another, the second bank often lost its reserves when the first bank went under.

Moreover, when one bank went out of business and hundreds of people lost their deposits, every other bank came under public scrutiny. Depositors at other banks often decided to withdraw their deposits "to be on the safe side." In the fractional reserve banking system, even the most cautious and best-managed banks found that they could not cover all withdrawals and often went out of business too.

Between 1837 and 1913 the United States did not have a central bank, and during this period the economy experienced several bank panics. **A bank panic is a situation in which numerous banks throughout the economy fail when they are unable to satisfy withdrawals of depositors.** As banks fail, deposits decline, the money supply declines, and the economy usually enters into a recession. We take a closer look at the mechanism behind the money supply and recessions in Unit 5.4.

One of the worst bank panics occurred in 1907 and motivated the federal government to form the Federal Reserve System in 1913. The purpose of the Fed was to establish order in the U.S. banking system through regulatory powers over banks and control of the nation's currency. Together with the Federal Depositors Insurance Corporation (FDIC), established in 1934, the Fed was set up to prevent the types of widespread bank failures that were common in the middle and late 1800s. The FDIC alone is a great help in guarding against bank failures by insuring the deposits of a bank. Since the FDIC guarantees that depositors will receive their funds even if a bank fails, people don't have to worry about withdrawing their deposits before a bank fails. And if they don't withdraw their deposits, then the bank doesn't fail. Moreover, in the event that there are an abnormally large number of withdrawals, the Fed is there to supply emergency funds to the bank and discourage even a hint of a bank failure.

More recently, this same type of bank panic has hit savings and loan associations. While most savings and loan associations are insured by the FSLIC (Federal Savings and Loan Insurance Corporation, a counterpart to the FDIC), some are not. In 1985 several savings and loans in Ohio went out of business, causing depositors to lose their funds and creating a panic throughout the state of Ohio. The situation became so severe that the governor of Ohio was forced to temporarily close the savings and loans throughout the state until the panic subsided.

STRUCTURE OF THE FEDERAL RESERVE SYSTEM

Now let's look at the structure of the Fed. Note that while the Fed represents the central bank for the economy and the federal government, it is not a single bank but numerous banks spread throughout the country. In fact, there are five essential components of the Federal Reserve System that we want to discuss: the Board of Governors, Federal

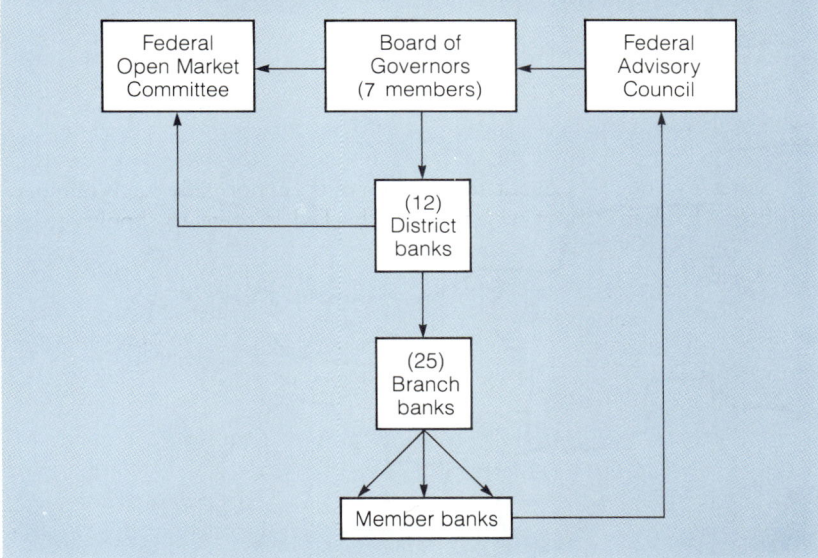

Figure 5.3.1

The Structure of the Federal Reserve System

The Board of Governors is the seven-member group overseeing the Federal Reserve System. Its policies are carried out by twelve district banks and twenty-five branch banks, which provide banking services for commercial banks. Presidents from five district banks join the seven governors on the Federal Open Market Committee, which controls the money supply. Presidents from twelve commercial banks make up the Federal Advisory Committee, which advises the Board of Governors.

Reserve Banks, member banks, the Federal Open Market Committee, and the Federal Advisory Council. The organizational structure of the Federal Reserve System is presented in Figure 5.3.1.

Board of Governors

The central ruling body of the Federal Reserve System is the **Board of Governors**. The Board of Governors is comprised of seven members, who are appointed by the president and approved by the Senate. Each member serves a fourteen-year term, with one term expiring every two years. To keep the Fed from becoming a political body, a president can thus appoint at most four members over an eight-year administration. As the name implies, the Board of Governors is responsible for setting policy for the money supply and the banking system.

Federal Reserve Banks

The **Federal Reserve Banks** are under the direct control of the Board of Governors. While the Board of Governors is appropriately located in Washington, D.C., the Federal Reserve Banks are scattered throughout the country. In fact, the Federal Reserve System is divided into twelve districts, each containing its own Federal Reserve Bank, which over-

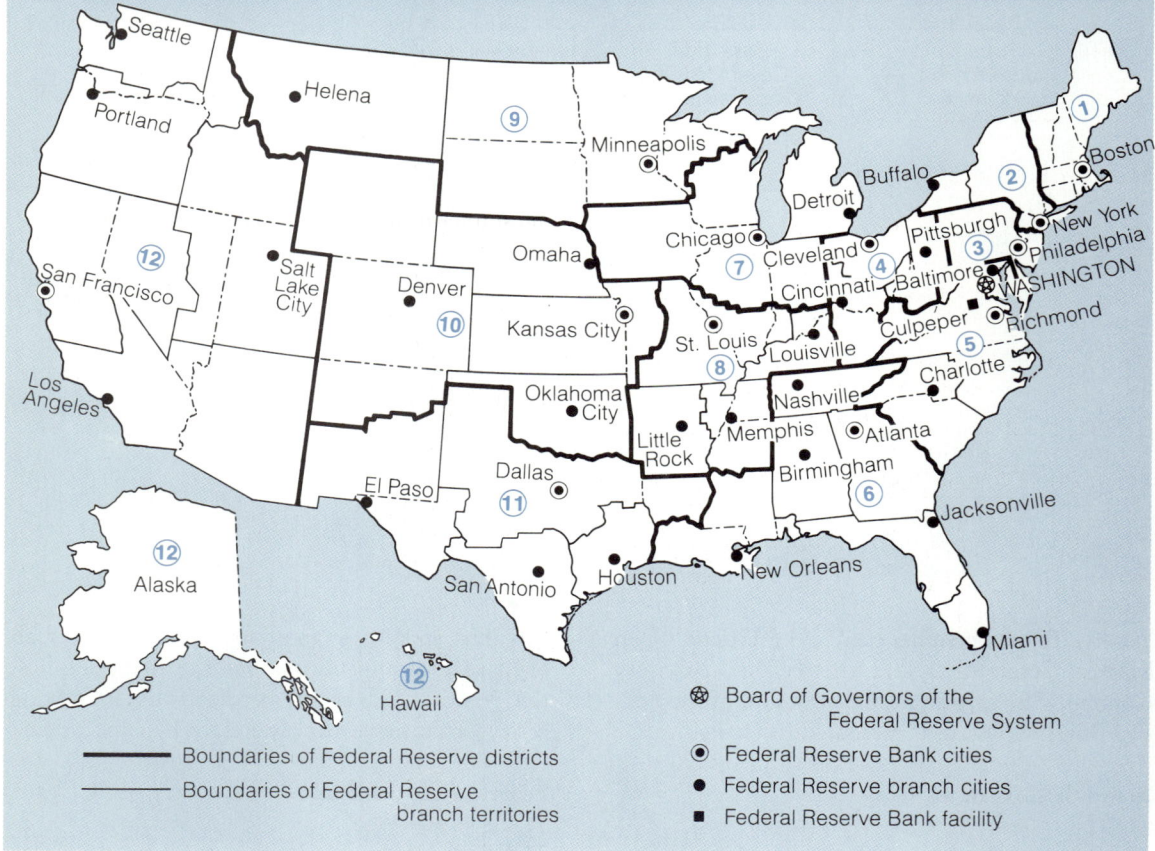

Figure 5.3.2

Federal Reserve Banks

The Federal Reserve System contains twelve district banks, which are centered in each of twelve districts throughout the country. Underneath the twelve district banks are twenty-five branch banks. The district and branch banks implement the monetary policies and regulations established by the Board of Governors. Moreover, they also provide a valuable check-clearing function for commercial banks. Source: Federal Reserve System, Board of Governors, *Federal Reserve Bulletin*, November 1985.

sees the operations of the commercial banks located within its district. While the Board of Governors sets the policy, the district banks have the responsibility of carrying it out. In addition to the twelve district banks, there are twenty-five branch banks scattered throughout the twelve districts. The locations of the Federal Reserve Banks are shown in Figure 5.3.2.

Each Federal Reserve Bank is actually owned by the commercial banks in its district, though they are not designed to earn a profit; any return greater than a specific rate is turned over to the U.S. Treasury. An important function of Federal Reserve Banks is to provide banking services to the commercial banks in their districts. If a commercial bank needs to borrow funds, it can do so at the local Federal Reserve Bank, though private individuals cannot. The district banks are also responsible for issuing the nation's currency, as most of us are probably aware. If you look at the top of a dollar bill, it says "Federal Reserve Note," meaning it is issued by and is backed by the Federal Reserve System. To the left of George Washington's picture is the indication of which of the twelve district banks issued the note.

Member Banks

The twelve district and twenty-five branch banks oversee the operation of commercial banks that are members of the Federal Reserve System. Not all commercial banks are officially members of the Fed. To see why this is the case, let's distinguish between two types of commercial banks, national and state. **National banks** are banks that are chartered by the federal government and are automatically members of the Federal Reserve System. It is easy to identify national banks because they often have the word *national* in their names. **State banks** are banks that are chartered by the government of the state in which they are located. State-chartered banks do not need to be official members of the Federal Reserve System, although about 10 percent are.

Before 1980 the distinctions between member and nonmember banks and between national and state banks were very important, mainly because member banks were directly regulated by the Fed and had to follow special regulations. But member banks also received more services than nonmember banks and usually at lower costs. This distinction was significant because the Fed had control over the deposits of the member banks but almost no control over the deposits of the nonmember banks. The Depository Institutions Deregulation and Monetary Control Act of 1980 changed this situation. This act essentially brought all financial institutions, including banks, credit unions, and savings and loan associations, under the control of the Fed. Today all banks and financial institutions are subject to the same regulations and control. Prior to 1980 NOW accounts at savings and loan associations and share drafts at credit unions (both of which are part of the M1 money supply) were becoming more widely used. But since they were issued by institutions beyond the control of the Fed, this reduced the ability of the Fed to control the overall money supply.

Federal Open Market Committee

The Federal Open Market Committee is one of the most important components of the Federal Reserve System. The **Federal Open Market Committee** consists of the seven members of the Board of Governors and five presidents from district Federal Reserve Banks. The president of the New York Federal Reserve Bank is always a member, and the remaining four positions are rotated among the presidents of the other eleven district banks.

The main function of the Federal Open Market Committee is to conduct open market operations. Later in this unit we see that open market operations comprise the Fed's most important tool in controlling the economy's supply of money. The main function of the Federal Open Market Committee is to control the money supply.

Federal Advisory Council

The last component of the Federal Reserve System is the Federal Advisory Council. The **Federal Advisory Council** is made up of the presidents from twelve commercial banks, one bank from each of the twelve districts. The function of the Federal Advisory Council is simply to advise the Board of Governors. They have no official powers, but they can let the Board of Governors know what the commercial banks think of their policies.

THE TOOLS OF MONETARY POLICY

While controlling the money supply is not the only function of the Fed, it has come to be its most important one. At this point we want to study exactly how the Fed controls the money supply. The ability to control the money supply is drawn from the tools of monetary policy. **Monetary policy is the discretionary control of the economy's money supply by the Federal Reserve System that is designed to affect the overall performance of the economy.** While both monetary policy and fiscal policy (examined in Unit 4.7) try to stabilize the fluctuations in the economy, fiscal policy does so through the federal government's expenditures and taxes, and monetary policy through the money supply.

The three tools of monetary policy that we want to discuss are open market operations, reserve requirements, and the discount rate.

Open Market Operations

The most important tool of the Fed for controlling the money supply is open market operations. **Open market operations are the buying and selling of U.S. government securities by the Federal Open Market Committee of the Federal Reserve System.** The Fed is able to increase the money supply by buying on the open market and decrease the money supply by selling on the open market. Figure 5.3.3 presents the monthly net change in open market accounts of the Federal Reserve System from 1983 to 1985. Here is how open market operations work. When the Fed buys government securities (the financial instrument used by the federal government to fund the public debt), it usually does so from commercial banks. To pay for the securities, it increases the amount of reserves the commercial banks have on deposit at the Fed. But recall from Unit 5.2 that when a bank has additional reserves, it can make loans, create checkable deposits, and thus expand the money supply. Therefore, buying on the open market is one way for the Fed to increase the money supply. However, when the Fed sells securities, the opposite happens. The commercial banks pay for the securities with the reserves they have on deposit with the Fed. With fewer reserves, the banks can make fewer loans and checkable deposits, and thus the money supply declines.

Open market operations are the Fed's most effective way of controlling the money supply, but they do not give the Fed complete control. Increasing commercial bank reserves by buying securities only makes it *possible* for banks to expand the money supply. If banks don't turn the reserves into loans and checkable deposits, then the money supply doesn't increase. And decreasing reserves by selling securities doesn't always mean that banks will decrease loans and checkable deposits. If banks are maintaining excess reserves, then the reduction in reserves will have little effect on the money supply.

Reserve Requirements

The second tool used by the Fed to control the money supply is reserve requirements. **Reserve requirements are the amount of reserves that the Federal Reserve System requires a bank to keep to back up its deposits.** The Fed requires that all banks maintain reserves, either as vault cash or deposits at the Fed, to back up its deposits. The reserve requirements are usually stated as ratios, meaning that a bank might need to keep reserves equal to 3 percent of its demand deposits. Table 5.3.1 presents the reserve requirement ratios for several different types of deposits at commercial banks.

The Fed uses reserve requirement ratios to control a bank's ability to create checkable deposits from reserves. Recall that the deposit multiplier studied in the previous unit is based on the percentage of deposits held in reserve ($1/r$). If banks use all of their excess reserves to make loans, then the percentage of deposits held in reserve is the reserve requirement ratio for checkable deposits established by the Fed. If the Fed decreases this reserve requirement ratio, then the deposit multiplier becomes larger, meaning that for a given

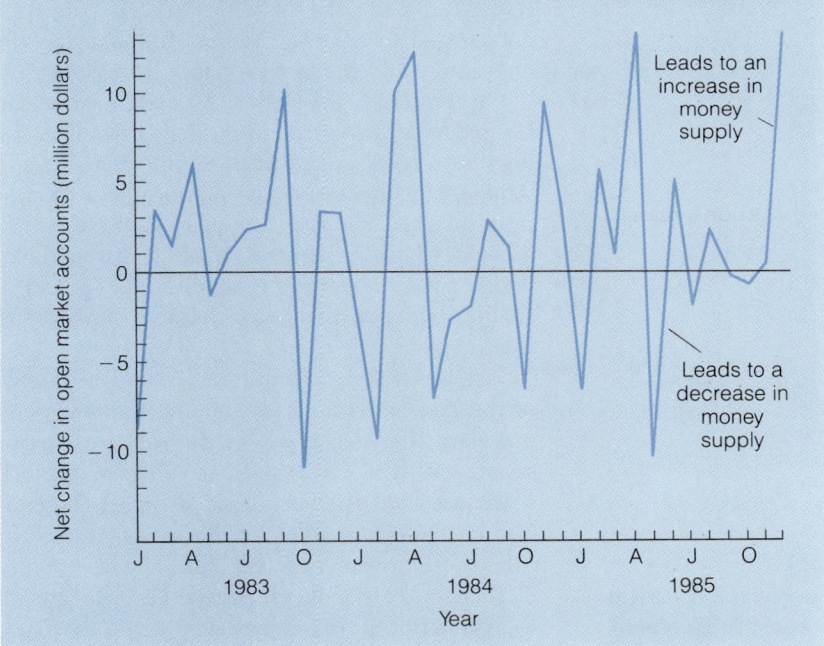

Figure 5.3.3

Open Market Operations, 1983 to 1985

The Fed's most important tool for controlling the money supply is open market operations. In months with positive open market operations (above the axis), the Fed was trying to increase the money supply. In months with negative open market operations (below the axis), the Fed was trying to decrease the money supply. Here we see monthly open market operations from 1983 to 1985. Source: Federal Reserve System, Board of Governors, *Federal Reserve Bulletin*, selected issues.

amount of reserves a bank can create more checkable deposits. Thus, the money supply increases. But if the Fed increases this reserve requirement ratio, then the deposit multiplier becomes smaller, meaning that with the same amount of reserves banks can create fewer deposits. Thus, the money supply declines.

The use of reserve requirements, like open market operations, represents an indirect method of controlling the money supply, and to be effective, the banks must have no excess reserves. Furthermore, the Fed does not like to change reserve requirements very often. Keep in mind that banks operate by using their excess reserves to make loans. If the Fed suddenly doubles the reserve requirement ratios, banks have to convert some of their

Table 5.3.1

Reserve Requirement Ratios, 1985

Reserve requirement ratios vary depending on the amount and type of deposits. The first $29.8 million of checkable deposits have a requirement of 3 percent, with 12 percent for anything greater. Nonpersonal time deposits of less than $1\frac{1}{2}$ years have a 3 percent requirement and no requirement for a longer period.

Type of Deposit	Reserve Requirement (percent)
Net transactions (checkable deposits)	
$0–29.8 million	3
Over $29.8 million	12
Nonpersonal time deposits	
Less than $1\frac{1}{2}$ years	3
Greater than $1\frac{1}{2}$ years	0

Source: Federal Reserve System, Board of Governors, *Federal Reserve Bulletin*, November 1985.

loans back into reserves, which may not be easy to do because many of the loans constitute commitments over relatively long periods of time. The bank can stop making new loans when existing loans are paid off, but if there are no loans being paid off, the bank is powerless.

The Discount Rate

The third major tool by which the Fed controls the money supply is the discount rate. The **discount rate** is the interest rate charged by the Federal Reserve System to banks for borrowed funds. Recall that the Fed acts as the bank for commercial banks. One function of the Fed is to loan funds to commercial banks, especially when commercial banks need reserves to satisfy depositors' withdrawals. The discount rate is the interest rate that the Fed charges for these borrowed reserves. Figure 5.3.4 presents the Fed's discount rate over the past several years.

If the Fed increases the discount rate, banks are discouraged from borrowing reserves, so fewer deposits are created and the money supply declines. If the Fed decreases the discount rate, banks are encouraged to borrow reserves, so more deposits are created and the money supply increases.

In principle, this is how the discount rate can be used to control the money supply. However, the discount rate is used even less often than reserve requirements because banks do not like to borrow from the Fed. The Fed is set up to loan reserves to a bank only as a last resort to keep it from going under. Since borrowing from the Fed is a sign of trouble, banks do everything that they can to avoid this.

However, the discount rate is used as a signal of the Fed's intentions. If the Fed wants to send out word that it is going to decrease the money supply with the other tools, it will raise the discount rate. At the very least, a higher discount rate encourages caution by the banks, who want to avoid borrowing from the Fed. The best way to do this is to keep some excess reserves, which leads to a reduction in the money supply.

MONETARY POLICY AND THE MONEY SUPPLY

Let's briefly discuss how these three tools of the Fed can affect the economy's money supply by looking at Figure 5.3.5. On the right-hand side of the figure is the money supply M1, consisting of currency and checkable deposits. On the left-hand side is cur-

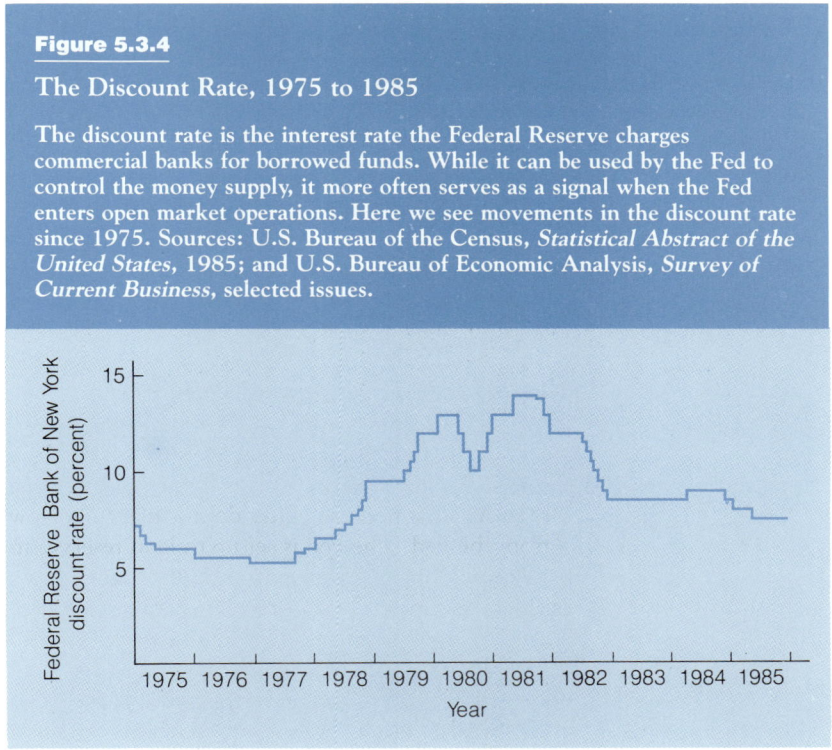

Figure 5.3.4

The Discount Rate, 1975 to 1985

The discount rate is the interest rate the Federal Reserve charges commercial banks for borrowed funds. While it can be used by the Fed to control the money supply, it more often serves as a signal when the Fed enters open market operations. Here we see movements in the discount rate since 1975. Sources: U.S. Bureau of the Census, *Statistical Abstract of the United States*, 1985; and U.S. Bureau of Economic Analysis, *Survey of Current Business*, selected issues.

rency and bank reserves, also called the monetary base. The **monetary base** is the currency held by the nonbank public and reserves held by banks. Unlike checkable deposits, which are only backed by a fraction of bank reserves, currency and reserves are backed 100 percent by government securities and other forms of financial assets held by the Federal Reserve System.

Figure 5.3.5 depicts the relationship between the monetary base and the money supply. While noting that currency is contained in both the monetary base and the money supply, let's direct our attention to the relationship between reserves and checkable deposits. Recall that checkable deposits are a multiple of reserves because of the deposit multiplier, which was introduced in the previous unit. This is where the tools of the Fed's monetary policy come into play.

Consider the following equation relating bank reserves to checkable deposits:

$$\text{checkable deposits} = \frac{1}{r} \times \text{bank reserves}$$

Bank reserves are expanded into checkable deposits through the operation of the deposit multiplier, $1/r$. The amount of checkable deposits in circulation depends on the size of the multiplier and the amount of bank reserves, both of which can be affected by the Fed. First, open market operations can increase or decrease bank reserves. Second, reserve requirements can change the value of r and the deposit multiplier. And third, the discount rate can also change bank reserves. However, the effectiveness of monetary policy does depend in large part on whether commercial banks "cooperate" and undertake the process of money creation.

Figure 5.3.5

The Money Supply and the Monetary Base

The monetary base includes currency held by the nonbank public and bank reserves. The money supply contains currency held by the nonbank public and checkable deposits. While currency is part of both the monetary base and the money supply, checkable deposits are related to reserves through the deposit multiplier and the money creation process. The amount of checkable deposits is equal to the deposit multiplier times the amount of reserves.

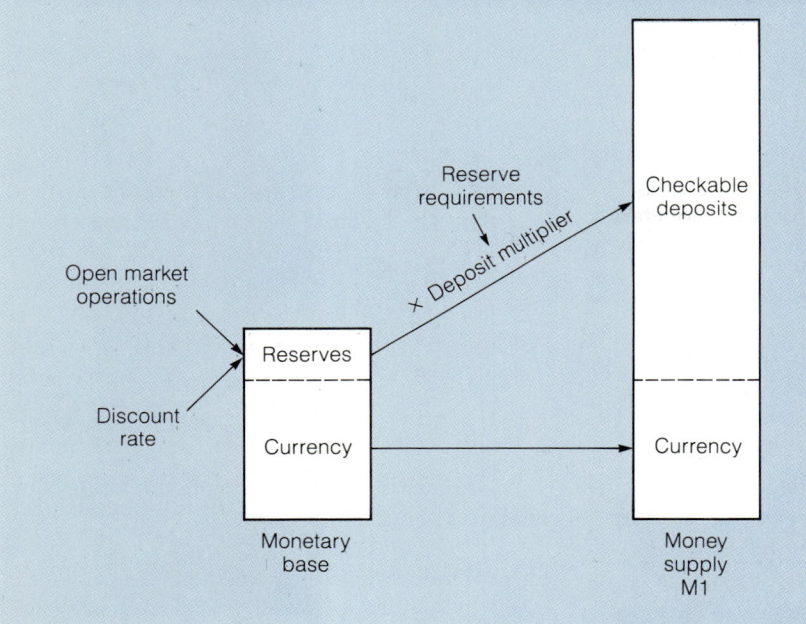

IN SUMMARY

The Federal Reserve System

- The Federal Reserve System is the central banking authority in the United States, responsible for regulating commercial banks and controlling the money supply. The Federal Reserve System was developed in response to the numerous and frequent bank panics that occurred in the 1800s. With fractional reserve banking, some banks were unable to satisfy the withdrawals of depositors, leading to a chain reaction of bank failures and a contractionary period in the economy. The Federal Reserve System (along with the Federal Depositors Insurance Corporation) was designed to prevent these types of bank panics by making sure that depositors' withdrawals could be met.

- The Federal Reserve System has five components. The Board of Governors is the policy-making body. The policies are carried out by twelve Federal Reserve district banks and twenty-five Federal Reserve branch banks. These Federal Reserve Banks provide banking functions to the commercial banks spread throughout the country. The Federal Open Market Committee, containing the Board of Governors and presidents from five district banks, decides on open market operations, which is the most important tool for controlling the money supply. The Federal Advisory Council, containing presidents of commercial banks, offers advice to the Board of Governors.

- Monetary policy is the discretionary control of the money supply, designed to affect economic activity. The three tools of monetary policy are open market operations, reserve requirements, and the discount rate. Open market operations involve the buying and selling of government securities. Reserve requirements represent the amount of reserves that a bank must keep to back up deposits. The discount rate is the interest rate charged to banks for borrowing from the Fed. If the Fed wants to increase the money supply, it can buy in the open market, lower reserve requirements, and lower the discount rate. If the Fed wants to decrease the money supply, it can sell in the open market, raise reserve requirements, and raise the discount rate.

QUESTIONS FOR STUDY AND ANALYSIS

1. In what way is the Federal Reserve System designed to prevent bank failures? Based on the cause of most bank failures, which do you think would be more effective in preventing bank failures, the Fed or the FDIC? Explain.

2. The Fed's discount rate is almost always 1 to 2 percentage points lower than the prime rate that commercial banks charge their best customers and several more percentage points lower than consumer loans from banks. Why don't individuals or corporations borrow funds from the Fed at the discount rate? What do you think might happen if the Fed got into the business of being a commercial bank?

3. Before 1980 national banks had to meet stricter requirements, but they also received added benefits from being members of the Federal Reserve System. However, after 1980 state and national banks had to meet the same requirements and received the same benefits. What do you expect will happen to the number of state banks in the country? Explain. What will this do to the Fed's ability to control the money supply?

4. Explain how the Federal Reserve System, through the use of open market operations, reserve requirements, and the discount rate, is able to affect the money creation process. Do these three tools of monetary policy give the Fed very good control of the money supply? Explain.

5. What are the appropriate actions in terms of open market operations, reserve requirements, and the discount rate if the Fed wants to increase the money supply? What if the Fed wants to decrease the money supply? If you were chairman of the Federal Reserve System, which of these three tools would you be more likely to use? Why?

6. What role does the monetary base play in the Fed's control of the money supply?

REVIEW GLOSSARY

bank panic A situation in which numerous banks throughout the economy fail when they are unable to satisfy the withdrawals of their depositors. The banks fail and take with them the deposits they created, leading to a reduction in the money supply and usually contributing to a contractionary period in the economy.

Board of Governors The policymaking and governing body of the Federal Reserve System, containing seven members appointed by the president. Each member is appointed to a fourteen-year term, with one term expiring every two years.

discount rate The interest rate charged by the Federal Reserve System to banks for borrowed funds. If the Fed increases the discount rate, the money supply decreases. If the Fed decreases the discount rate, the money supply increases.

Federal Advisory Council A council made up of twelve presidents of commercial banks, one from each district, that offers advice to the Board of Governors.

Federal Open Market Committee A committee of the Federal Reserve System containing the seven members of the Board of Governors, the president of the New York Federal Reserve Bank, and the presidents of four other district banks. The Federal Open Market Committee conducts open market operations, the main tool used by the Federal Reserve System to control the money supply.

Federal Reserve Banks The twelve district banks and twenty-five branch banks that carry out policy set by the Board of Governors. The Federal Reserve Banks are spread throughout the country and provide banking services for commercial banks.

monetary base The currency held by the nonbank public and reserves held by the banks.

monetary policy The discretionary control of the economy's money supply by the Federal Reserve System that is designed to affect the overall performance of the economy. The three tools of monetary policy are open market operations, reserve requirements, and the discount rate.

national banks Banks that are chartered by the federal government and are automatically members of the Federal Reserve System. Many national banks have the word *national* in their name.

open market operations The buying and selling of U.S. government securities by the Federal Open Market Committee of the Federal Reserve System. If the Fed buys securities, the money supply increases. If the Fed sells securities, the money supply decreases.

reserve requirements The amount of reserves that the Federal Reserve System requires a bank to keep to back up its deposits. If the Fed increases reserve requirements, the money supply decreases. If the Fed decreases reserve requirements, the money supply increases.

state banks Banks that are chartered by the government of the state in which they are located. Before 1980 state banks did not have to be members of the Federal Reserve System. However, today all banks, whether state or national, members or nonmembers, are subject to the same guidelines and regulations set by the Federal Reserve System.

UNIT 5.4

The Money Market and Output Determination

In the first three units of this section we studied what money is, how money is created by banks, and how the Federal Reserve System controls the money supply. But those units were only a foundation for the topic we are about to examine, money and the determination of national output. In this unit we discuss the role money plays in the economy and exactly how the Fed's monetary policy can be used to affect the level of national output.

First, we look at the money market to see how money demand and supply interact in determining the economy's interest rate. Recall that the interest rate has a significant effect on investment expenditures. Therefore, the interest rate determined in the money market affects investment and, consequently, aggregate expenditures and national output. The unit ends with a look at recent monetary policy.

MONEY DEMAND

The first aspect of the money market that we want to discuss is money demand. **Money demand is the quantity of money that the nonbank public wants to hold.** Keep in mind that when people hold money they are sacrificing the interest payments that could be earned. Even though NOW accounts and share drafts pay interest, other types of financial assets pay higher interest. But people do hold money for three basic reasons: for transactions, as a precaution, and for speculation.

Transactions Motive

The most important motive underlying the demand for money is the transactions motive. The **transactions motive is the desire to hold money to complete purchases of goods and services.** The transactions motive essentially states that people need money in order to buy goods and services.

Level of income is the key factor behind the transactions motive. A person who receives twice as much income is likely to make twice as many expenditures and thus need twice as much money to complete these transactions. This principle also applies to the overall economy. If national income in the economy increases, the amount of money demanded for transactions increases because expenditures are greater.

Another significant factor affecting the transactions motive for money is the interest rate. Note that most money (except NOW accounts and share drafts) pays no interest, so when people hold money instead of some other type of financial asset, they are foregoing the interest that could be earned. Even in the case of NOW accounts and share drafts, people could earn a higher interest with other types of assets. In other words, the interest rate reflects the cost of holding money. And like any other commodity, when the cost of money changes, the quantity of money demanded also changes. If the interest rate increases, the cost of holding money increases, and people want to hold less money and more of the financial assets that pay higher interest.

Precautionary Motive

The second motive underlying the demand for money is the precautionary motive. The **precautionary motive is the desire to hold money to undertake unexpected transactions.** Although many transactions are expected and people keep money to cover them, some transactions are unexpected. Examples of unexpected transactions include a car that breaks down, an illness in the family, and the "sale of the year" at the local department store; in each case people are making unplanned purchases of goods and services. While the actual transactions are not planned, many people set aside money to provide for such occasions. Money is retained for unexpected expenditures because of the precautionary motive.

The same two factors (income and the interest rate) that affect the transactions motive also affect the precautionary motive. If people have more income, they are likely to retain extra money. In addition, the interest rate also reflects the cost of holding money under the precautionary motive. If the interest rate is relatively high, then people are less likely to hold money for transactions that may or may not occur.

Speculative Motive

The third motive for holding money is the speculative motive. The **speculative motive** is the desire to hold money instead of interest-paying assets in anticipation of conditions in the financial market changing. The key to the speculative motive is that it is very easy to transfer funds from money to any other type of financial asset, but not so easy to transfer funds from one type of nonmoney asset to another. If people expect the interest rate to increase in the near future, they are likely to hold money instead of an interest-paying asset so that when (or if) the interest rate does increase, they can place the funds in the higher-interest-paying assets. But if their funds are tied up in an asset that pays a relatively lower interest, they might have problems transferring them to the higher-interest-paying assets.

Note that the speculative motive is closely tied to the interest rate. If the interest rate is relatively high, people are likely to feel that it won't go any higher, and they place their funds in the interest-paying assets. But if the interest rate is relatively low, then people are likely to hold their funds in money and wait for a higher interest rate.

The Money Demand Curve

Now let's plot the three motives of money demand onto the money demand curve. The **money demand curve** is a graphical representation of the relationship between the quantity of money demanded and the interest rate. Although money demand depends on both income and the interest rate, the money demand curve directs our attention to the interest rate because we ultimately want to see how the interest rate is affected by the Fed's monetary policy. But even though we concentrate on the interest rate, we do not ignore the role of income in money demand. To see how the interest rate and income affect the demand for money, let's look at Figure 5.4.1.

The horizontal axis measures the quantity of money demanded, and the vertical axis measures the interest rate. What we want to determine graphically is the relationship between the interest rate and the quantity of money demanded, holding everything else, including income, unchanged.

Figure 5.4.1

The Money Demand Curve

The money demand curve indicates the relationship between the amount of money the nonbank public wants to hold and the interest rate. If the interest rate is relatively high, people want to hold relatively little money, so the money demand curve has a negative slope. An increase in income shifts the money demand curve, because people want to hold more money at every interest rate.

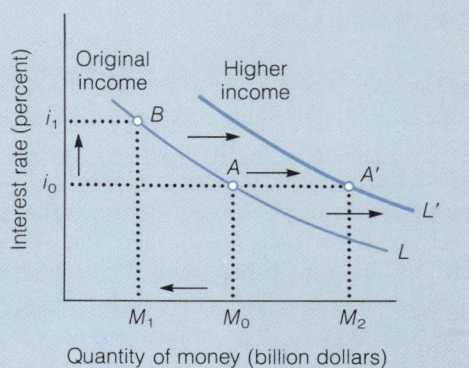

UNIT 5.4 ■ THE MONEY MARKET AND OUTPUT DETERMINATION

Let's start at point A on curve L, in which the interest rate is i_0 and the quantity of money demanded is M_0. What happens to the quantity of money demanded if the interest increases to i_1? First, we know that the higher interest rate increases the cost of holding money. Therefore, as a result of both the transactions and precautionary motives, people hold less money but more interest-paying financial assets. Furthermore, the speculative motive induces people to transfer funds to interest-paying assets. In short, all three motives indicate that the higher interest rate leads to a reduction in the quantity of money demanded, at point B.

Since a decline in the interest rate would have a comparable but reverse effect, clearly the quantity of money demanded and the interest rate are inversely related. If the interest rate increases, the quantity of money demanded declines. So the money demand curve L has a negative slope.

While we are primarily concerned with the interest rate, let's also see how the relationship between income and money demand is depicted in Figure 5.4.1. Recall that under the transactions and precautionary motives an increase in income causes an increase in the demand for money. If we keep the interest rate unchanged at i_0, we can see this relationship. At i_0, people with a relatively low level of income demand M_0 money, at point A. However, if the income increases, people now demand M_2 money, at point A'. In fact, at every interest rate, people demand more money if they have more income, so the money demand curve shifts from L to L'.

MONEY SUPPLY

In the previous unit we discussed almost everything that we need to know about the money supply. **Money supply** is the quantity of money that exists in the economy, or, officially, M1. The money supply is controlled by the Federal Reserve System through the three tools of monetary policy: open market operations, reserve requirements, and the discount rate. If the Fed wants to increase the money supply, it buys securities in open market operations, lowers reserve requirements, or lowers the discount rate. If the Fed wants to decrease the money supply, it does just the opposite.

Since the money supply is controlled by the Fed, it does not depend on the interest rate or the level of income. This makes it very easy to construct the money supply curve. The **money supply curve** is a graphical representation of the relationship between the quantity of money supplied and the interest rate. Figure 5.4.2 presents three alternative money supply curves.

Let's look first at the curve labeled M, which is a vertical line at the quantity of money M_0. This means the supply of money is M_0, regardless of the interest rate. However, if the Fed buys in open market operations, lowers reserve requirements, or lowers the discount rate, the supply of money in the economy increases. This is seen as a shift in

Figure 5.4.2

The Money Supply Curve

The money supply curve indicates the relationship between the amount of money in the economy and the interest rate. Since the supply of money is controlled by the Federal Reserve System, it is not affected by changes in the interest rate and is thus a vertical line. Contractionary monetary policy reduces the money supply, and expansionary fiscal policy increases the money supply.

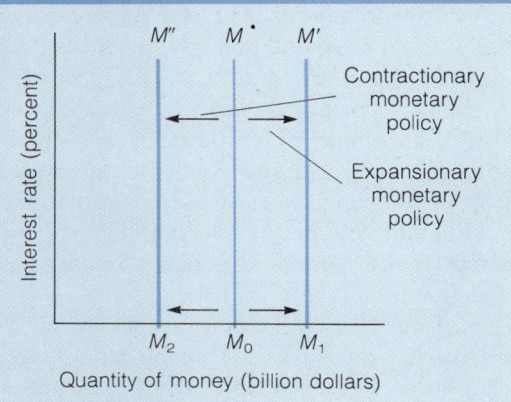

the money supply curve from M to M′. Once again the new quantity of money in the economy, M_1, does not change if the interest rate changes. If the Fed sells in open market operations, raises reserve requirements, or raises the discount rate, the money supply curve shifts to M″, in which case the quantity of money in the economy is M_2.

MONEY MARKET EQUILIBRIUM

Now let's combine the money demand and money supply into the money market. The **money market** is a market illustrating the interaction between the economy's demand for money and the available supply at different interest rates. The money market operates in the same manner as the market for every other commodity we have studied—on one side are people who want the commodity, on the other side are people who have it. And like the other markets, the money market is in equilibrium when the quantity of money demanded is equal to the quantity of money supplied. Figure 5.4.3 illustrates the money market.

The money market reaches equilibrium at point E, with the interest rate i_e and the quantity of money M_e. Of course the quantity of money in equilibrium *must* be M_e, since this is the amount that exists in the economy. The money market always reaches equilibrium by adjusting the quantity of money demanded until it is equal to the available supply.

Let's see what happens to the money market when it is not at equilibrium and the interest rate is not i_e. If the interest rate is above i_e, such as i_1, the quantity of money demanded (M_1) is less than the available supply (M_e), in which case there is a surplus of money in the economy. In other words, people in the economy have more money than they would like to hold because at the relatively high interest rate they are losing potential interest payments from other types of financial assets.

Since people are holding too much money, they try to get rid of it by exchanging it for interest-paying assets. Although many people can success-

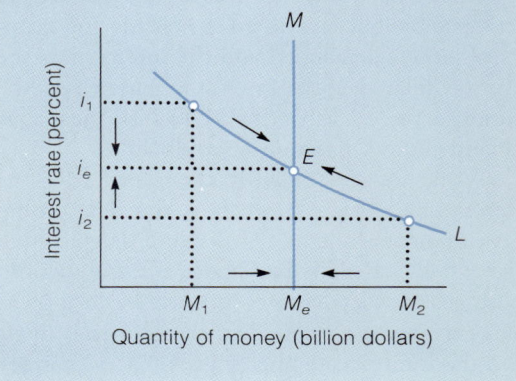

Figure 5.4.3

The Money Market

The money market represents the interaction between the demand for money and the supply. The interest rate adjusts in the money market to equate the quantity of money demanded with the available supply. If the interest rate is too high, it falls as people try to exchange their noninterest-paying money for interest-paying financial assets. If the interest rate is too low, it rises as people try to exchange their interest-paying assets for money.

fully trade their money for the other assets, everyone cannot do this because there is a fixed amount of money in the economy. In essence, if someone gets rid of their money, it winds up in someone else's pocket.

While it seems rather futile that in this situation everyone is trying to get rid of their money but merely ends up trading it around, this trading does have an important effect. Since the process involves trading money for interest-paying financial assets, people want less money, but they also want more interest-paying assets. In fact, people are so intent on acquiring interest-paying assets that they are willing to accept a lower interest rate. The issuers of these financial assets see that there is a greater demand for their commodity and they offer a lower interest rate.

What happens to the money market when the interest rate starts to decline? While the money supply does not depend on the interest rate, the money demand does. The quantity of money demanded increases as the interest rate declines, shown as a move down curve L in Figure 5.4.3. Moreover, as long as the quantity of money demanded is less than the supply, the interest rate declines. Once i_e is reached, demand is equal to the supply, and the interest rate doesn't change.

The opposite process takes place if the interest rate is below the equilibrium, such as i_2. In this case the demand for money is greater than the supply as people try to obtain more money by getting rid of their interest-paying assets. But since the supply of money in the economy is fixed, all they do is raise the interest rate. And as the interest rate increases, the quantity of money demanded falls and the shortage of money is eliminated, at point E.

THE MONEY MARKET AND NATIONAL OUTPUT

Now let's examine how the money market affects the economy's level of national output. The relationship between the money market and national output is tied to investment expenditures. Recall that the interest rate not only adjusts to obtain equilibrium in the money market but also relates to investment expenditures. If the interest rate changes, investment expenditures also change, meaning that the level of aggregate expenditures (as analyzed in Section 4, especially Unit 4.5) changes.

Figure 5.4.4 illustrates how the money market is related to the Keynesian cross studied in Section 4. Panel a depicts the money market, panel b the relationship between investment and the interest rate, and panel c the Keynesian cross. The equilibrium interest rate, i_e in panel a, is determined through the interaction of the demand and supply curves for money. Given the interest rate determined in the money market, the business sector must decide on the level of investment expenditures. In panel b the business sector decides to undertake investment expenditures I_e.

Once we have the level of investment expenditures, I_e, we can add these to the other expenditures to determine the equilibrium level of national output. In panel c the lowest line, $C + G$, represents total expenditures by the household and government sectors. By adding investment expenditures we obtain the line $C + G + I = AE$, which is the aggregate expenditures for the economy. With these aggregate expenditures the equilibrium level of output is Y_e.

Based on the mechanism presented in Figure 5.4.4, let's see how the Fed's monetary policy affects the economy, as demonstrated in Figure 5.4.5. Note that in panel a the money market, before the implementation of monetary policy, is in equilibrium at point E, where the money supply is M and the interest rate is i_e. If we trace the interest rate to panel b, we see that investment is I_e, which leads to aggregate expenditures of AE and output of Y_e in panel c.

Suppose that the Fed decides to increase the money supply by buying in the open market, lowering reserve requirements, or lowering the discount rate. Whichever tool is used, the result is to shift the money supply curve to M'. With this new supply of money, there is a surplus at the existing interest rate i_e. However, this surplus does not persist since the interest rate falls, and the money market reaches a new equilibrium at point F, with interest rate i_1.

In panel b the lower interest rate stimulates additional investment up to I_1. The new level of investment is reflected in panel c by an upward shift in the aggregate expenditures line from AE to AE'. Based on this new level of aggregate expenditures, the economy's output increases to Y_1. Overall, we see that an increase in the money supply leads to an increase in the economy's output.

But what are the implications of this? Recall that until now the only way for the government to increase aggregate demand has been through fiscal policy, either by increasing purchases or by reduc-

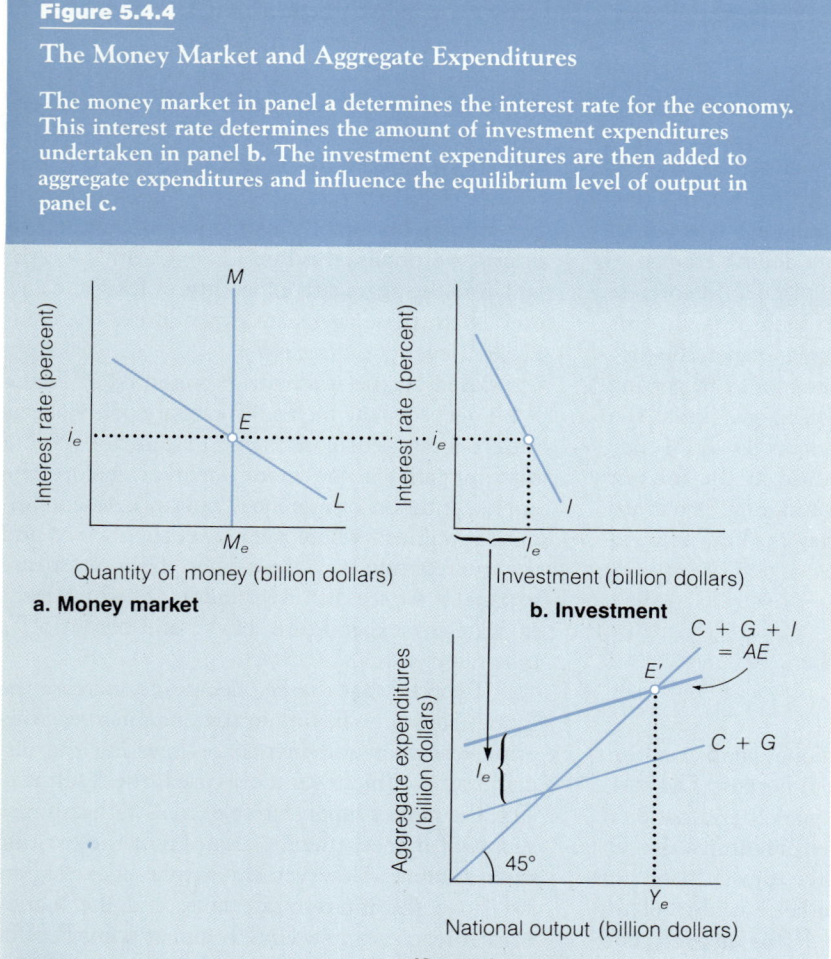

Figure 5.4.4

The Money Market and Aggregate Expenditures

The money market in panel a determines the interest rate for the economy. This interest rate determines the amount of investment expenditures undertaken in panel b. The investment expenditures are then added to aggregate expenditures and influence the equilibrium level of output in panel c.

ing net taxes. However, through the money market we see that the government can also increase aggregate expenditures by increasing the money supply, which is known as expansionary monetary policy. **Expansionary monetary policy** is monetary policy consisting of increases in the money supply through the use of open market operations, reserve requirements, and the discount rate. However, monetary policy, like fiscal policy, must take into account the actual level of output relative to the full employment level. If Y_e in panel c is at or above full employment output, the increase in the money supply merely increases the price level and introduces inflationary pressures into the economy. If Y_e is below full employment output, then the monetary policy can be used to stimulate the economy out of the trough of a business cycle.

A reduction in the money supply also affects

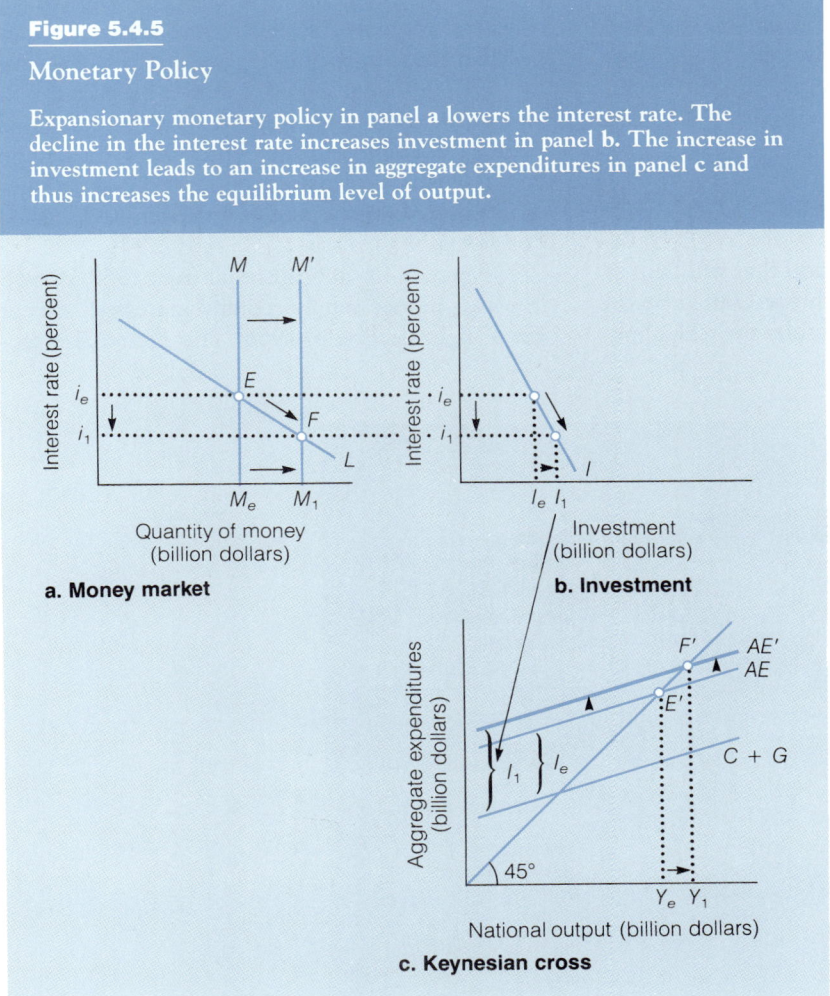

Figure 5.4.5

Monetary Policy

Expansionary monetary policy in panel a lowers the interest rate. The decline in the interest rate increases investment in panel b. The increase in investment leads to an increase in aggregate expenditures in panel c and thus increases the equilibrium level of output.

a. Money market

b. Investment

c. Keynesian cross

the economy through contractionary monetary policy. **Contractionary monetary policy** is monetary policy consisting of decreases in the money supply through the use of open market operations, reserve requirements, and the discount rate. If the Fed reduces the money supply, then the equilibrium level of output in panel c declines. Reducing the money supply constitutes appropriate policy if the equilibrium level is above the full employment level of output because it can reduce inflationary pressures in the economy.

As we consider reductions in the money supply, we can see why bank panics in the middle and late 1800s were so devastating to the economy. The failure of hundreds of banks over a short period of time caused a tremendous reduction in the money supply, which subsequently drove the economy into a recession. In fact, this is why the contractionary periods of business cycles were not called recessions, as they are today, but bank panics. Contractionary periods were invariably caused by a series of bank failures leading to a decrease in the money supply.

RECENT MONETARY POLICY

Figure 5.4.6 presents information that will help us to examine monetary policy in the United States since 1960. The upper line measures the real supply of money, which, like real GNP, is adjusted for inflation. More specifically, the real supply of money is M1 divided by the GNP price deflator. We want to look at the real supply of money because it tells us how many goods and services can be purchased with M1. The lower line, which we will examine in a moment, is a measure of the real interest rate, also adjusted for the rate of inflation, as discussed in Unit 3.5.

Figure 5.4.6 indicates that from 1960 to 1968 the real money supply steadily increased, except for a slight decline in 1966. This period also cor-

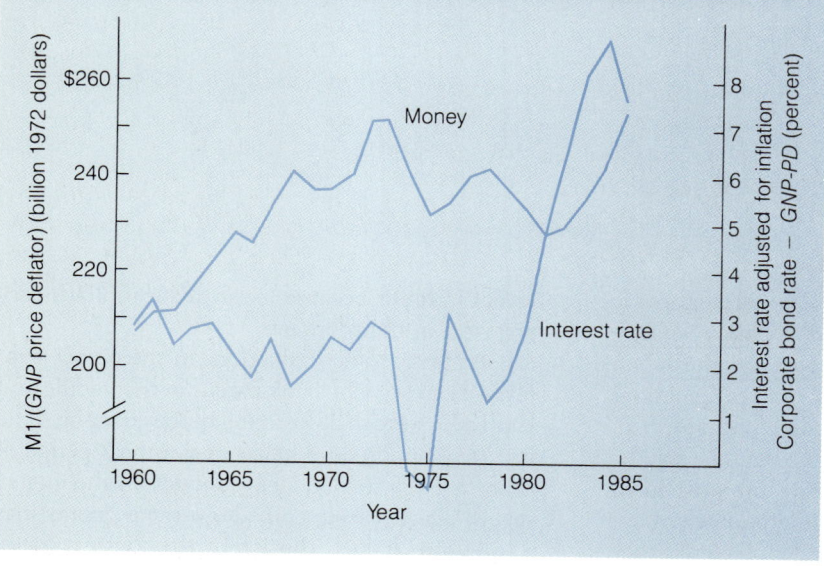

Figure 5.4.6

Recent Monetary Policy, 1960 to 1985

In the 1960s expansionary monetary policy contributed to the economy's longest expansionary period in history. However, in the early 1980s contractionary monetary policy, implemented to reduce inflation, contributed to the worst contractionary period since the Depression. The lower line in this diagram indicates how monetary policy affects the interest rate. If the money supply is increased (decreased), the interest rate falls (rises). Source: Calculated from U.S. Bureau of Economic Analysis, *Survey of Current Business*, selected issues.

responded with the longest peacetime expansionary period in history. In Unit 4.7 we saw that expansionary fiscal policy contributed to this increase; now we see that expansionary monetary policy also played an important role.

Following a brief contractionary period in 1970, the real money supply continued to increase until 1973. In 1974 and 1975 the real money supply took a sharp drop, not because of overt monetary policy on the part of the Fed but because of the sharp rise in the price level associated with the first major petroleum price increase. But since we are concerned with the purchasing power of the money supply, this increase in the price level had the same effect as contractionary monetary policy and caused the economy to dive into a recession from November 1973 to March 1975.

After a period of expansionary monetary policy, implemented in part to combat the recession of the mid-1970s, the Fed once again began to restrict the money supply in order to curb the high rates of inflation that existed during the late 1970s. This is indicated by the sharp decline in the money supply up to 1981. The restriction on the money supply in the early 1980s, while reducing the rate of inflation from 10 to 4 percent, also contributed to the worst contractionary period since the Depression, in 1981 and 1982.

The lower line in Figure 5.4.6 indicates how the real interest rate is affected by the money supply. Based on our analysis in Figure 5.4.5, an increase in the money supply reduces the interest rate; a decrease has the opposite effect. Note in this figure that when the money supply increases, the interest rate tends to decline the following year. Conversely, when the money supply declines, the interest rate tends to increase the following year. The change in the interest rate lags behind the change in the money supply because it takes time for the change to work its way through the economy. However, the change in the interest rate changes the level of investment, which affects aggregate expenditures and the level of national output.

IN SUMMARY

The Money Market and Output Determination

- The money market indicates how money supply and monetary policy affect the determination of equilibrium output in the economy. As with any market, the money market represents the combination of money demand and money supply. The interaction of demand and supply determines the equilibrium interest rate in the economy, which subsequently affects investment expenditures, aggregate expenditures, and output.

- The demand for money is motivated in three ways: the transactions motive, the precautionary motive, and the speculative motive. The combination of these three motives indicates that less money is demanded at higher interest rates and more money is demanded with more income. The curve graphing the relationship between the quantity of money demanded and the interest rate is the money demand curve.

- The supply of money is controlled by the Federal Reserve System and does not change as the interest rate changes. Therefore, the money supply curve, which depicts the relationship between the interest rate and the quantity of money supply, is a vertical line.

- The money market is in equilibrium when the demand for money is equal to the supply. This equilibrium is achieved by changes in the interest rate. The interest rate changes when demand and supply are not equal, causing people to hold too much or too little money. As they try to alter the amount of money they are holding, the interest rate changes.

- The money market affects the equilibrium level of national output through the interest rate and its effect on investment expenditures. If the interest rate changes, the level of investment and aggregate expenditures change. Thus, an increase in the money supply is an alternative to fiscal policy for stimulating the economy.

- Monetary policy in the 1960s contributed to the strong expansion during that decade. However, during the early 1980s contractionary monetary policy, implemented to reduce inflation, also sent the economy into the worst recession since the Depression of the 1930s.

QUESTIONS FOR STUDY AND ANALYSIS

1. Indicate whether each of the following items is related to the transactions, precautionary, or speculative motive for holding money, and why.
   a. You keep a folded up $5 bill in your wallet behind a picture of your Aunt Emma.
   b. You cash in several certificates of deposit and keep them in your checking account until the stock market looks like it is headed upward.
   c. You withdraw $25 from your savings account before spending the morning going to several flea markets and rummage sales.
   d. You keep $200 in your checking account from the first of the month until your car payment is due on the fifteenth.
   e. You cash in several certificates of deposit to buy your Aunt Emma a new backyard hot tub.

2. Explain what happens to the transactions, precautionary, and speculative motives for holding money if the interest rate declines. How does this affect the overall demand for money? What does this imply for the slope of the money demand curve? Are you likely to hold more or less money if the interest rate declines?

3. Some people argue that the supply of money actually depends on the interest rate, and that increases in the interest rate lead to an increase in the supply of money. In terms of the money creation process, do you think that this is a realistic possibility? Discuss whether or not you think banks might create more money at higher interest rates.

4. For each of the following items indicate how the equilibrium interest rate and quantity of money exchanged are affected, and why.
   a. The Fed buys in the open market.
   b. The discount rate is raised.
   c. Government purchases decline.
   d. Reserve requirements are lowered.
   e. Banks become more prudent and hold more excess reserves.

5. How does the buying and selling of interest-paying financial assets relate to the equilibrium mechanism for the money market?

6. If the Fed buys in the open market, lowers reserve requirements, or lowers the discount rate, what happens to the interest rate, investment, aggregate expenditures, and national output? Explain.

REVIEW GLOSSARY

contractionary monetary policy Monetary policy consisting of decreases in the money supply through the use of open market operations, reserve requirements, and the discount rate.

expansionary monetary policy Monetary policy consisting of decreases in the money supply through the use of open market operations, reserve requirements, and the discount rate.

money demand The quantity of money that the nonbank public wants to hold. There are three basic motives for holding money: transactions, as a precaution, and for speculation.

money demand curve A graphical representation of the relationship between the quantity of money demanded and the interest rate. An increase in income causes the money demand curve to shift to the right.

money market A market illustrating the interaction between the economy's demand for money and the available supply at different interest rates. The money market always achieves equilibrium by changes in the interest rate, adjusting the quantity of money demanded until it is equal to the available supply.

money supply The quantity of money that exists in the economy. The money supply is controlled by the Federal Reserve System through its monetary policy.

money supply curve A graphical representation of the relationship between the quantity of money supplied and the interest rate. The money supply curve is vertical.

precautionary motive The desire to hold money to undertake unexpected transactions. The precautionary motive is affected by income and the interest rate in exactly the same way as the transactions motive.

speculative motive The desire to hold money instead of interest-paying assets in anticipation of conditions in the financial market changing. The interest rate is the most important factor affecting the speculative motive. If the interest rate increases, people want to hold less money, because of the speculative motive.

transactions motive The desire to hold money to complete day-to-day purchases of goods and services. Two of the most important factors affecting the transactions motive are income and the interest rate. If income increases, people make more expenditures and thus need more money. If the interest rate increases, the opportunity cost of holding money increases, and people hold less money.

UNIT 5.5

Comparing Monetarist and Keynesian Policies

In the previous unit we saw how money affects the determination of income, though economists don't always agree on the nature of this effect or on the policies needed to control money and provide for economic well-being. **Keynesians** argue that fiscal policy is more effective than monetary policy for stabilizing economic fluctuations. Keynesians believe that money affects the economy's aggregate expenditures by changing the interest rate and thus investment expenditures. But **monetarists** argue that monetary policy is more effective in controlling economic fluctuations. Monetarists believe that money directly affects aggregate expenditures because people with more money are willing to buy more goods and services. In this unit we examine the differences between monetarists and Keynesians.

Although our comparison of monetarists and Keynesians concentrates on a discussion of the money supply and monetary policy, we should note that their differences extend into many areas of economic inquiry and even into opposing views of the world. After discussing the general characteristics of typical monetarists and Keynesians, we see how each group views both monetary and fiscal policy.

DIFFERENCES BETWEEN MONETARISTS AND KEYNESIANS

First, let's look at the philosophical and political differences between monetarists and Keynesians. The typical Keynesian tends to be politically liberal and to believe that government should play an important role in many areas of economic activity. A Keynesian generally supports transfer payments to the poor, antitrust legislation, and regulations to improve the quality of the environment. Philosophically, a Keynesian recognizes the importance of markets in the allocation of goods and services but also sees many imperfections in the market that require government intervention.

The typical monetarist tends to be politically conservative and to believe that government involvement in the economy is not only unnecessary but often creates more problems than it solves. Monetarists regard private markets as the best means of allocating goods and services, even though that system might contain imperfections. The motto of a monetarist is "The best government is the least government."

We should point out that these characterizations of monetarists and Keynesians are merely generalizations and not absolute categories. It is entirely possible that a monetarist could believe that environmental quality regulation is also needed. Likewise, a Keynesian might think that the imperfections in the private markets are relatively minor and require no government involvement.

Furthermore, we should note that when it comes to monetary and fiscal policy, many of the differences between monetarists and Keynesians are a matter of degree. Keynesians recognize that monetary policy is important but less so than fiscal policy; monetarists think the opposite way. Some economists in each group do hold extreme viewpoints, and they regard the policies of the other group as totally ineffective.

MONETARY POLICY

Political and philosophical differences aside, the big difference between monetarists and Keynesians lies in how each views the role of monetary policy. Keynesians think that monetary policy is generally ineffective in stimulating the economy out of the contractionary phase of the business cycle, even though reductions in the money supply can reduce inflationary pressures at full employment. By contrast, monetarists think that monetary policy is by far the best way to stimulate the economy.

The Keynesians' View of Monetary Policy

The Keynesians' view of monetary policy is essentially the one presented in the previous unit, especially in Figure 5.4.5. The main features of this argument are reviewed in Figure 5.5.1, which shows the money demand curve L in panel a and the investment curve I in panel b. If the initial money supply is M in panel a, then the initial interest rate is i_0, and the level of investment in panel b is I_0. Note that to simplify this analysis, we are ignoring the Keynesian cross. Since the change in the equilibrium level of output is based directly on the change in investment, we need go no further than panel b.

According to the Keynesians, an increase in the money supply to M' causes the interest rate to fall to i_1. The lower interest rate stimulates the level of investment to I_1, which increases aggregate expenditures and, subsequently, the level of national output. However, the Keynesians argue that the overall change in investment and thus national output is very small.

Their argument rests on the shapes of the money demand curve in panel a and the investment curve in panel b. First, they believe that the money demand curve is very sensitive to the interest rate. That is, a very small change in the interest rate leads to a relatively large change in the quantity of money demanded, which means that a relatively large increase in the money supply is needed to cause a small decrease in the interest rate. In panel a this would be seen as the relatively elastic money demand curve L. Second, they think that investment is not very sensitive to the interest rate. In this case it takes a relatively large decrease in the interest rate to cause an increase in investment. In panel b this is seen as the relatively inelastic investment curve I.

According to these two curves, monetary policy is relatively ineffective. A given increase in the

UNIT 5.5 ▪ COMPARING MONETARIST AND KEYNESIAN POLICIES

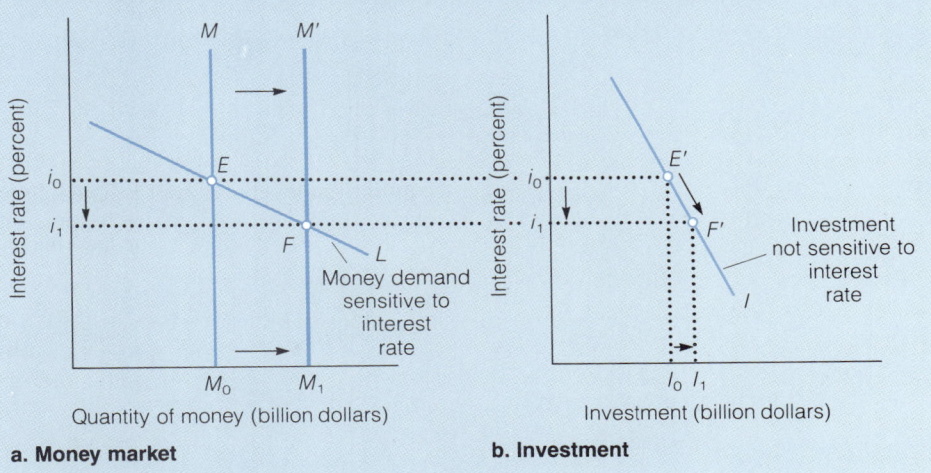

Figure 5.5.1

The Keynesians' View of Monetary Policy

Keynesians argue that the money demand curve in panel a is very sensitive to the interest rate and that the investment line in panel b is not very sensitive to the interest rate. This means that an increase in the money supply leads to a relatively small reduction in the interest rate and a correspondingly small increase in investment and aggregate expenditures. Therefore, Keynesians argue, monetary policy has very little effect on equilibrium output.

a. Money market

b. Investment

money supply causes a relatively small change in the interest rate because of the shape of the money demand curve. The relatively small change in the interest rate causes an even smaller change in investment because of the shape of the investment curve. And since there is very little change in investment, there is very little change in aggregate expenditures and national output. In short, Keynesians argue that monetary policy has a relatively small effect on equilibrium output.

The Monetarists' View of Monetary Policy

The monetarists' view of monetary policy comes in two stages. First, at the very least, they argue that the shapes of the money demand and investment curves are not like those described by the Keynesians. Second, they argue that the role of the interest rate and investment is not the primary way that monetary policy affects aggregate expenditures. Let's look first at the monetarist view of the interest rate and investment.

Figure 5.5.2 depicts the relative shapes of the money demand and investment curves according to the monetarists. In panel a the monetarist money demand curve is labeled L_m, in contrast to the Keynesian curve labeled L_k. Because the monetarists feel that demand for money is not very sensitive to the interest rate, L_m is more inelastic than L_k. In panel b the monetarist investment curve I_m is more elastic than the Keynesian curve labeled I_k because the monetarists feel that investment is very sensitive to the interest rate.

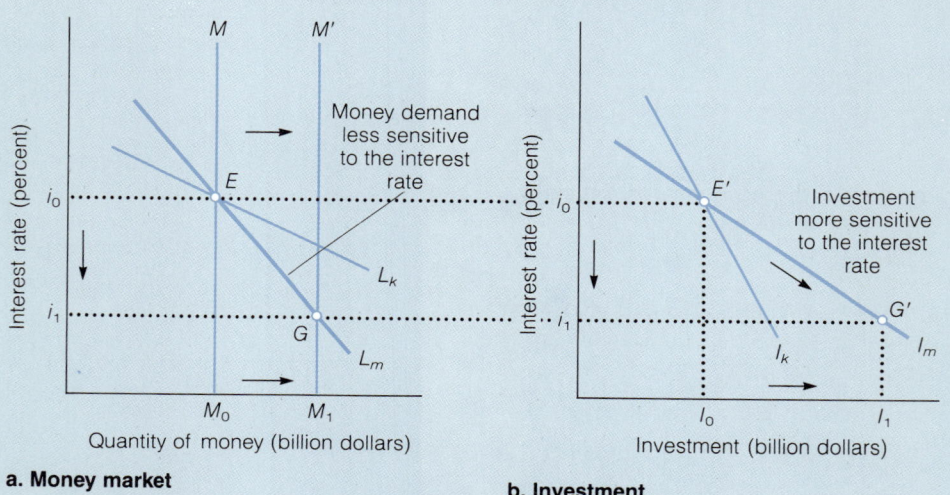

Figure 5.5.2

The Monetarists' View of Monetary Policy

Monetarists argue that the money demand curve in panel a is not very sensitive to the interest rate and that the investment line in panel b is very sensitive to the interest rate. This means that an increase in the money supply leads to a relatively large reduction in the interest rate and a correspondingly large increase in investment and aggregate expenditures. Therefore, monetarists argue, monetary policy has a large impact on equilibrium output.

a. Money market

b. Investment

These two new curves suggest that monetary policy is much more effective than the Keynesians think. In panel a the interest rate declines more than before, to i_1', and investment increases more than before, to I_1'. The increase in investment is greater because the interest rate has a larger decrease and because investment is more sensitive to changes in the interest rate. The overall effect is to increase aggregate expenditures and thus national output more under the monetarists' view than under the Keynesians' view.

The essential difference between Figures 5.5.1 and 5.5.2 is a matter of degree. In this analysis, aggregate expenditures are affected only by changes in investment. In Figure 5.5.1 investment and aggregate expenditures change very little, whereas in Figure 5.5.2 they change a lot more. However, the monetarists would argue that this type of effect is relatively unimportant. In fact, they would argue that there is a much more direct and fundamental relationship between the supply of money and aggregate expenditures that is not related to investment and the interest rate.

The Quantity Theory of Money

The monetarists' view of monetary policy is based on a relatively simple view of the economy, the equation of exchange. The **equation of exchange** relates the nominal value of goods and services to the money supply and the velocity of money. The equation of exchange can be specified as

$$M \times V = P \times Q$$

In this equation M is the supply of money, V is the velocity of money (which we will discuss in more detail shortly), P is the price level in the economy, and Q is the physical quantity of goods and services (real GNP).

Let's first consider the right-hand side of the equation, where $P \times Q$ is simply the nominal value of national production, or the market value of all transactions for currently produced final goods and services in the economy. However, the left-hand side of the equation is more important to us at the moment.

The money supply, M, comprises the total amount of money in the economy, or, officially, M1. This is the amount of money that people in the economy use as payment for final goods and services. Note that the money supply is much smaller than the total value of the transactions, meaning each dollar in the economy is used several times to complete different transactions over the course of a year.

The frequency with which money is used to pay for goods and services is its velocity. The **velocity of money** is the average number of times a dollar of money is used in transactions for final goods or services. In general, since the amount of money in the economy is less than the level of production, each dollar is used to complete several transactions. If GNP is equal to $3500 billion and the money supply is only $500 billion, then each dollar must be used seven times (= $3500/$500).

Figure 5.5.3 traces the velocity of money over the past several years. Here we see that the velocity of money generally declined up to the mid-1940s, reaching a low of 2, but since that time it has steadily increased, reaching a high of about 6.7 in 1983. This means that at one point an average dollar was used only twice a year, but now it is used nearly seven times a year.

The velocity of money is an important component of the monetarists' view of monetary policy.

Using the equation of exchange, the velocity calculation is merely a by-product of the money supply and nominal GNP. In fact, the velocity is calculated by dividing nominal GNP by the money supply ($V = PQ/M$). In this regard it is interesting but not very useful to the monetarists.

The velocity of money becomes important if the equation of exchange is transformed from a simply accounting identity into a theory. This theory is the quantity theory of money. The **quantity theory of money** is a theory that states a given percentage change in the money supply leads to an equal percentage change in nominal GNP. The equation of exchange is transformed into a theory by hypothesizing that the velocity of money is constant, which implies that a direct relationship between the money supply and nominal GNP exists.

Suppose that the velocity of money is equal to 7, the money supply is $500 billion, and nominal GNP is $3500 billion. If the velocity of money remains constant at 7, what happens if the money supply is increased by $100 billion? The extra $100 billion is used 7 times, and thus nominal GNP increases by $700 billion, to $4200 billion. However, if the economy is at full employment, the real GNP cannot increase, meaning any increase in GNP is reflected exclusively in a higher price level.

A quick glance at Figure 5.5.3 clearly indicates that the velocity of money is not constant, having changed from 2 to 7 over a period of forty years. However, the monetarists argue that the velocity of money is constant for a given structure of the economy. In the time period presented in Figure 5.5.3 there have been numerous structural changes in the economy that have affected the velocity of money. For example, the modernization of banking, the use of computerized tellers, and the ease of transferring funds between savings and checking accounts all increase the velocity of money. In essence, these structural changes mean people can hold smaller amounts of money (and larger amounts of interest-paying assets) to complete the same number of transactions. Each dollar is used a larger number of times, and the velocity is higher.

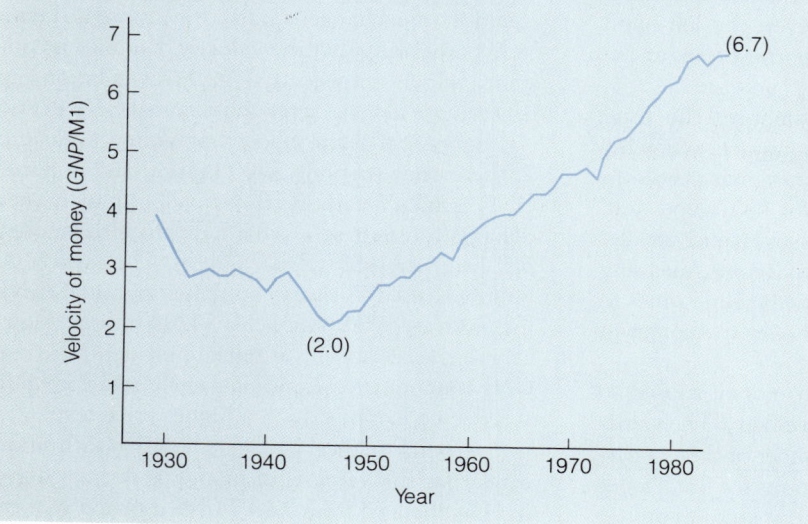

Figure 5.5.3

The Velocity of Money, 1929 to 1985

The velocity of money is the number of times during a year that each dollar is used to buy output. In the past few decades the velocity of money has generally increased, from a low of 2 in the 1940s to nearly 7 in recent years. Keynesians argue that the velocity is not stable and that the money supply thus has little effect on the economy's production. Monetarists argue that this change in velocity results from structural changes in the economy and that the velocity is otherwise stable. Source: Calculated from data in U.S. Bureau of Economic Analysis, *Survey of Current Business*, selected issues.

Using the quantity theory of money, monetarists argue that the money supply is directly linked to aggregate expenditures on output. That is, if the supply of money is increased, people are initially holding more money than they want. To get rid of this surplus of money, they spend it on goods and services. Note that this direct increase in aggregate expenditures is caused by an increase in money supply rather than a change in investment expenditures due to a change in the interest rate. As aggregate expenditures increase, nominal *GNP* also increases.

FISCAL POLICY

The monetarists and Keynesians not only disagree on the importance of monetary policy but they also disagree on the importance of fiscal policy. However, their disagreement is consistent. The Keynesians think that fiscal policy is very effective, whereas the monetarists believe it is ineffective. Now that we have discussed how both groups regard the role of monetary policy, let's examine how each side views the role of fiscal policy.

The Monetarists' View of Fiscal Policy

Recall that in the monetarists' view of the money demand and investment curves the quantity of money demanded is not very sensitive to changes in the interest rate, so the curve is relatively inelastic. This is seen by L_m in panel a of Figure 5.5.4. Furthermore, they believe that the investment curve is very sensitive to the interest rate, so the curve is relatively elastic, as shown by the curve labeled I_m in panel b.

Based on this set of curves, the monetarists say that fiscal policy is very ineffective in the economy. To see why, let's direct our attention to panel c, in which an initial equilibrium at point E' is given by the intersection of the aggregate expenditures line AE and the 45° line. This initial level of aggregate expenditures is based on investment I_0 in panel b, which derives from the interest rate i_0 in panel a. Note that the money demand curve L_m in panel a is based on the initial level of income Y_0.

Now let's see what happens if the government undertakes some expansionary fiscal policy by increasing government purchases, shown in panel c as a shift in the aggregate expenditures line to AE' and an increase in the level of output to Y_1. If the previous level of output at Y_0 was below full employment output, then the economy is expanding out of the trough of the business cycle, just as it should.

However, let's not forget the money demand curve. The money demand curve L_m in panel c is based on the initial level of output Y_0. But since output is a determinant of the money demand curve, L_m is no longer the relevant curve. The increase in output causes the money demand curve to shift to the right of L_m, which leads to a higher interest rate and, subsequently, a decrease in investment. The decline in investment then reduces aggregate expenditures and the equilibrium level of output, causing a leftward shift in the money demand curve, or a readjustment in the opposite direction.

Figure 5.5.4 depicts the final equilibrium of the economy after the numerous recurrences of this adjustment process are complete. The money demand curve L_m' in panel a corresponds to the equilibrium level of output Y_e in panel c. However, this level of output is based on the aggregate expenditures line AE″, which contains investment expenditures I_e. And this level of investment is based on the interest i_e determined by the money market.

For monetarists the comparison between the initial level of output, Y_0, and the new level, Y_e, is important. According to the monetarists, Y_e is much closer to Y_0 than it is to Y_1, meaning there is very little increase in output. This occurs because the increase in government purchases, which stimulates the economy, is offset by a decrease in investment expenditures. The investment expenditures are reduced because the stimulation of the economy causes higher interest rates.

This process is known as the crowding-out effect. The **crowding-out effect** is the process in which increases in government purchases lead to decreases in investment expenditures. In essence, the crowding-out effect says that government purchases of goods and services "crowd" business expenditures out of the aggregate market by driving up interest rates.

The monetarists argue that this crowding-out effect makes fiscal policy ineffective. Whether the initial shift in the aggregate expenditures line is caused by an increase in government purchases, an increase in transfer payments, or a reduction in taxes, the results are the same.

The Keynesians' View of Fiscal Policy

Now let's see how the Keynesians view the crowding-out effect. Note again that the two groups are not arguing over whether or not this process occurs but about the magnitude of the changes. Recall that the Keynesians see the money demand curve as very sensitive to the interest rate, as shown by the relatively elastic curve L_k in panel a of Figure 5.5.5. Furthermore, they regard the investment curve as not very sensitive to the interest rate, shown by the relatively inelastic curve I_k in panel b.

Figure 5.5.4
The Monetarist's View of Fiscal Policy

Monetarists argue that the steep money demand curve and the flat investment line make fiscal policy relatively ineffective. When fiscal policy stimulates the economy, the money demand curve in panel a is shifted, which increases the interest rate and reduces investment. Monetarists argue that the decrease in investment (crowding out) nearly offsets the increase in aggregate expenditures from fiscal policy.

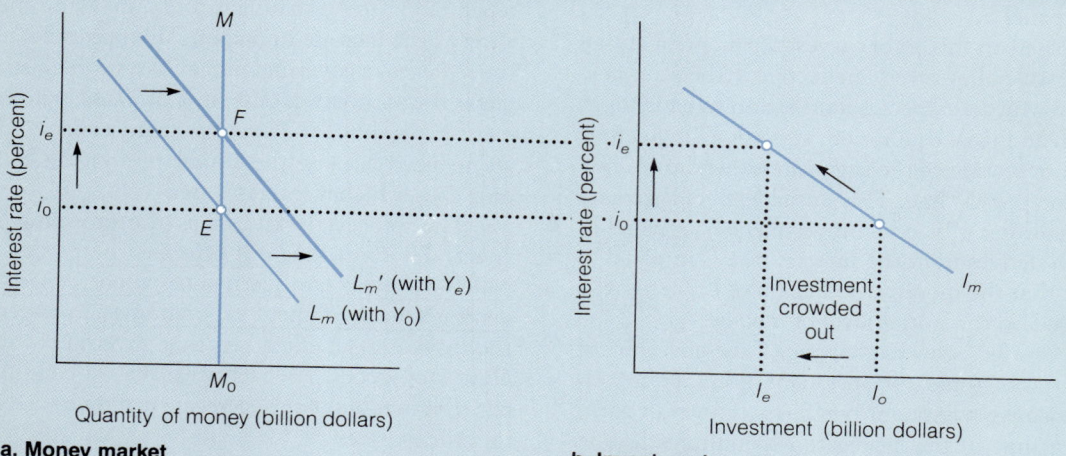

a. Money market

b. Investment

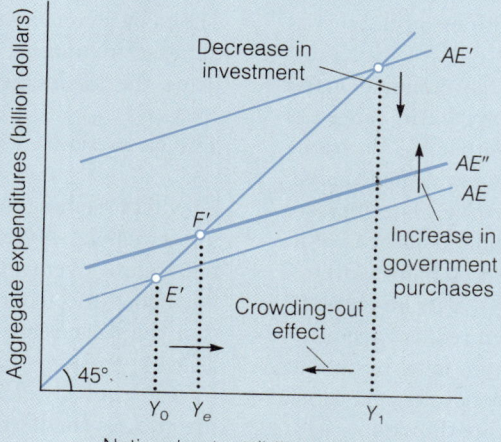

c. Keynesian cross

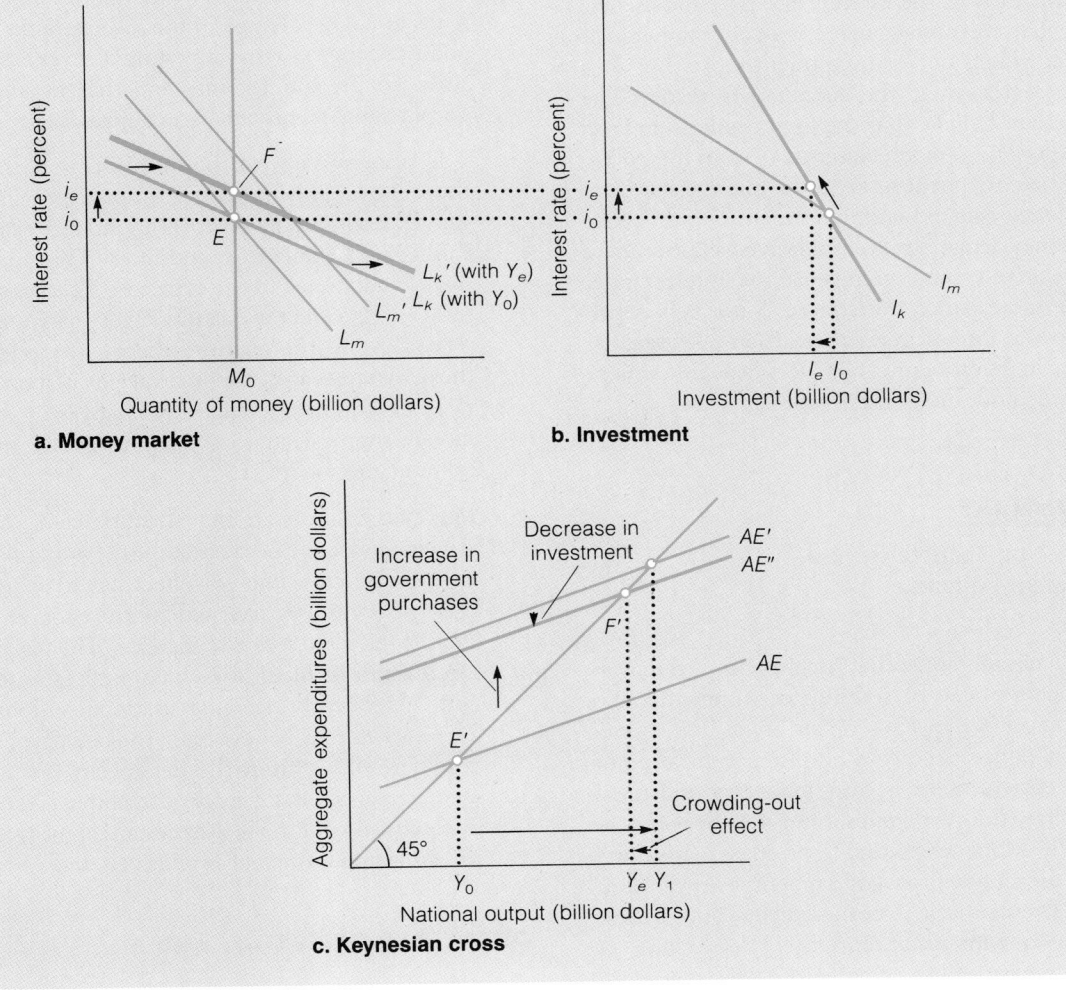

Figure 5.5.5

The Keynesians' View of Fiscal Policy

Keynesians argue that the crowding out of investment by fiscal policy is relatively insignificant. The economy's expansion has very little effect on the interest rate and thus investment because of the steepness of the money demand curve and the flatness of the investment line.

a. Money market

b. Investment

c. Keynesian cross

If we go through the process described for the monetarists' view of fiscal policy, we see that the increase in government purchases initially increases aggregate expenditures to AE', but because of the higher level of output the money demand curve shifts rightward, the interest rate increases, and investment is crowded out.

As before, the economy finally reaches equilibrium when aggregate expenditures are AE'', investment is I_e, the interest rate is i_e, and income is Y_e. The Keynesians agree with the monetarists that crowding out of investment exists but to a lesser degree than the monetarists think. The Keynesians believe that the final equilibrium level of output, Y_e, is much closer to Y_1 than it is to Y_0.

Their argument rests on the relative shapes of the money demand and investment curves. Since the money demand curve is relatively elastic, there is a relatively small change in the interest rate. Furthermore, since investment is not very sensitive to the interest rate, there is an even smaller change in investment. Thus, very little investment is crowded out under the Keynesian view.

IN SUMMARY

Comparing Monetarist and Keynesian Policies

- Keynesians argue that fiscal policy is the most effective way to stabilize economic fluctuations, whereas monetarists argue that monetary policy is best. While their central point of disagreement is over monetary and fiscal policy, the two groups differ in other areas as well. Monetarists tend to be conservative and to be opposed to government intervention. Keynesians tend to be more liberal and to favor government intervention. Their views of monetary and fiscal policy are consistent with their other beliefs.

- Keynesians state that monetary policy is not very effective because a given change in the money supply has very little effect on the interest rate. Furthermore, they regard investment expenditures as not very sensitive to the interest rate. Therefore, the Keynesians argue, the money supply is not likely to have a significant effect on investment, aggregate expenditures, and equilibrium national output.

- Monetarists hold the opposite viewpoint, stating that a given change in the money supply leads to a large change in the interest rate. In addition, they say that investment is very sensitive to the interest rate and that national output subsequently changes a great deal.

- The primary view of the monetarists is that the money supply has a direct impact on aggregate expenditures rather than an indirect effect through investment expenditures. This argument is contained in the equation of exchange ($MV = PQ$) and the quantity theory of money. According to the quantity theory of money, the monetarists argue that the velocity of money (V) is constant and that any changes in the money supply lead to equal changes in the nominal output (PQ).

- Monetarists also state that fiscal policy is relatively ineffective because of the crowding-out effect. The crowding-out effect occurs when fiscal policy is used to stimulate the economy, causing the interest rate to increase. The higher interest rate reduces investment expenditures and subsequently decreases national output. The monetarists believe that the decrease in output resulting from the decline in investment nearly offsets any increase in output caused by the fiscal policy. The Keynesians argue that the crowding-out effect is relatively small.

QUESTIONS FOR STUDY AND ANALYSIS

1. Why do you think monetarists tend to be conservatives while Keynesians tend to be liberals? Are the economic and political philosophies of both groups consistent? Explain.

2. Some monetarists argue that the Federal Reserve System has too much discretionary power and that the Fed's discretionary control of the money supply is often mistimed and usually worsens the peaks and troughs of the business cycle. The monetarists think that the money supply should grow at a constant rate without any discretionary changes by the Fed. Evaluate this position in light of the monetarists' view of money's role in output determination.

3. Indicate whether you think each of the following statements was made by a Keynesian or a monetarist, and why.
   a. Markets are the only way to allocate resources.
   b. The interest rate is one of the most important factors affecting investment.
   c. The interest rate is one of the most important factors affecting money demand.
   d. The velocity of money is very stable over time.
   e. Government involvement is needed in many areas of the economy.
   f. There is very little crowding out of investment by government purchases.

4. Under what circumstances can the equation of exchange be transformed into the quantity theory of money? Explain.

Keynesians Economists who argue that fiscal policy is more effective than monetary policy for stabilizing economic fluctuations.

monetarists Economists who argue that monetary policy is more effective than fiscal policy for stabilizing economic fluctuations.

quantity theory of money A theory that states a given percentage change in the money supply leads to an equal percentage change in nominal GNP. The quantity theory of money rests on the proposition that the velocity of money is constant.

velocity of money The average number of times a dollar is used in transactions for final goods or services. The velocity is computed by the equation $V = PQ/M$.

REVIEW GLOSSARY

crowding-out effect The process in which increases in government purchases lead to decreases in investment expenditures. The crowding-out effect occurs because the stimulation caused by government purchases leads to an increase in the interest rate, which reduces investment expenditures.

equation of exchange An equation relating the nominal value of goods and services to the money supply and the velocity of money. The equation of exchange is specified as $M \times V = P \times Q$.

SECTION INQUIRY

Return to a Gold Standard

In recent years many economists have argued in favor of returning to a gold standard for the money supply. There are three basic ways in which gold (or another type of commodity, for that matter) can be used as a standard for money. One way is to have the *gold* itself circulate as money. Another is to have *gold certificates,* representing an equal amount of gold locked away in storage, circulate as money. A third way is to establish a *price rule* between the monetary unit (dollars) and gold, in which the government agrees to buy and sell any gold at the established price. Whichever standard is used, the gold standard effectively means that the supply of money is based on the supply of gold. In the early 1970s the U.S. economy, which had operated under various forms of a gold standard since the 1800s, dropped the last bit of standard when it decided to stop buying and selling gold at a set price under a price rule standard.

But now there is a call to return to a gold standard. Proponents of a gold standard argue that it would promote stability in the economy by removing the destabilizing discretionary monetary policy they say is often undertaken by the Federal Reserve System. With a gold standard, the money supply is tied to the supply of gold, which tends to grow at a relatively constant rate. Proponents of the gold standard argue that under the current system the Fed often attacks a recession by increasing the money supply too much and too late, which leads to inflation. Then to fight inflation it reduces the money supply, again too much and too late, which leads to another recession. This discretionary control, rather than stabilizing the economy, actually worsens the instability of the business cycle. A gold standard would eliminate this instability by removing discretionary control of the money supply.

On the other hand, opponents of the gold standard argue that discretionary control of the money supply is still a necessary tool of the government. In particular, they argue that the money supply would be at the mercy of uncontrollable events or the actions of other countries. For example, discovering a major new gold mine could send the money supply soaring. Or if the supply of gold did not keep pace with overall growth in the economy's production capabilities, output could stagnate. In addition, other countries could stockpile gold and hold the U.S. economy ransom by threatening to increase the supply. And finally, opponents of a gold standard argue that the lack of discretionary control would make the government helpless in the event of devasting shocks to the economy, such as the increase in petroleum prices in the 1970s.

QUESTIONS FOR DISCUSSION

1. Discuss whether commercial banks would still be able to undertake the money creation process under a gold standard. Does it matter which way gold is used as a standard (actual gold, gold certificates, price rule)?

2. Using the analysis in Unit 5.4, illustrate why proponents of a gold standard say it will lead to stability and why opponents say it will lead to instability.

3. Discuss how the widespread use of electronic tellers and electronic banking would operate under each of the three alternative types of gold standard.

4. Considering the differences between Keynesians and monetarists, which group is most likely to favor a gold standard and which group is most likely to oppose it? Why?

SECTION 6

A Closer Look at Inflation

Throughout our study of macroeconomics the concept of inflation of the economy's price level has often cropped up. In our discussion of the business cycle we learned that the expansionary phase and the peak of a demand-driven business cycle is frequently associated with inflation. Furthermore, we saw that the contractionary phase of a supply-driven business cycle can also lead to inflation. In fact, our study of Keynesian economics indicates that any time aggregate expenditures for output are greater than the full employment level, inflation is likely to occur. Moreover, increases in the money supply can also overstimulate the economy and lead to inflation. In this section we examine the topic of inflation in detail. In particular, we want to see why it occurs and what we can do to control it.

Unit 6.1, The Causes of Inflation, looks at several reasons why inflation can occur. By applying the aggregate market introduced in Unit 3.6, we see that inflation is caused by a relative shift in the aggregate demand curve or the aggregate supply curve. Knowing this, we can identify the causes of inflation simply by identifying the determinants that shift each curve. In this regard we discuss how government spending,, taxation, the money supply, wages, and other factor costs can cause inflation.

Unit 6.2, Inflation and Unemployment, introduces an alternative but related way of viewing the causes of inflation. This unit examines the frequently observed relationship between inflation and unemployment known as the Phillips curve. The Phillips curve illustrates the tradeoff between inflation and unemployment—if one decreases, the other increases. However, when we take into consideration the role of inflationary expectations, we realize that this tradeoff is a short-run condition. In fact, the theory of rational expectations indicates that in the long run the rate of unemployment tends toward a natural level, independent of the rate of inflation.

Unit 6.3, Inflation Control Policies, concludes this section in the only logical way. Since the first two units deal with the nature and causes of inflation, we are directed here toward the question of control. We look at several policies that have been used, or at least recommended, to control inflation. These policies include contractionary fiscal and monetary policy, a balanced budget, wage and price controls, indexing, and various supply-side policies.

UNIT 6.1

The Causes of Inflation

In Unit 3.5 we discussed the nature and effects of inflation. In particular, we saw that inflation can lead to the redistribution of income and wealth and an overall reduction in real output. Before we examine different ways to reduce or eliminate inflation in the economy, we need to better understand the causes of inflation.

Our study of the causes of inflation in this unit centers around the aggregate market introduced in Unit 3.6. We begin with a discussion of the dynamics of inflation. Here we see that the price level increases when the aggregate demand curve shifts relatively more than the aggregate supply curve. With this in mind, we identify the determinants of the aggregate demand curve to see what causes it to shift. We then look at the determinants of the aggregate supply curve to see what might prevent national production from satisfying demand.

THE DYNAMICS OF INFLATION

The aggregate demand curve represents an ideal tool for examining the causes of inflation. As we saw in Unit 3.6, inflation can be caused by independent shifts in either the aggregate demand or aggregate supply curve, though realistically, both the aggregate demand and aggregate supply curves are constantly shifting over time. Therefore, to examine the causes of inflation, it is more instructive to look at *relative* shifts in the curves rather than *absolute* shifts. Figure 6.1.1 illustrates this point.

In the first year the price level is P_1 and national output is Y_1, determined by the intersection of curves AD_1 and AS_1. However, from one year to the next, both the aggregate demand and aggregate supply curves are likely to shift to the right. Suppose that

UNIT 6.1 • THE CAUSES OF INFLATION

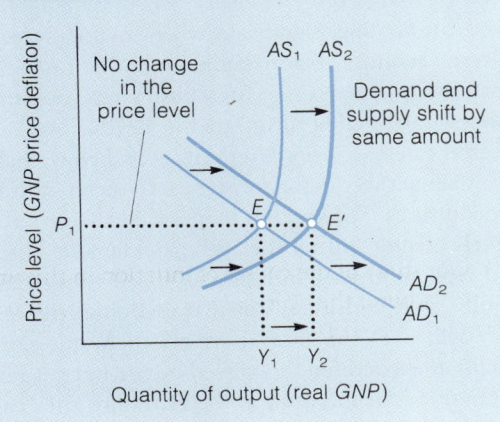

Figure 6.1.1

A Constant Price Level over Time

The aggregate demand and supply curves are constantly shifting over time. If both curves shift to the right by the same amount, then the price level remains constant.

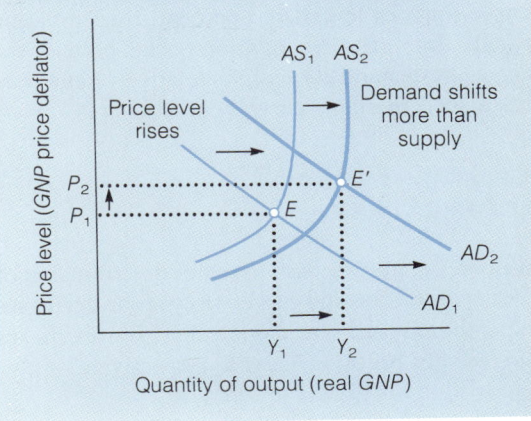

Figure 6.1.2

The Dynamics of Inflation

Inflation results when the aggregate demand and aggregate supply curves do not shift to the right by the same amount. In this case the aggregate demand curve shifts by 10 percent, but the aggregate supply curve shifts by only 5 percent, and the price level rises. Thus, inflation can be caused not only by a reduction in aggregate supply but also by a reduction in the relative rate of growth of aggregate supply.

both curves shift rightward by the same amount. The aggregate demand curve shifts to AD_2 and the aggregate supply curve shifts to AS_2; the intersection of these curves gives us national output equal to Y_2 and a price level equal to P_1. Note that the price level here does not change from the previous year because the aggregate demand curve shifts rightward the exact same horizontal distance as the aggregate supply curve. In other words, at price level P_1, 5 percent more output is demanded, but 5 percent more output is also produced. If the increase in output is the same as the increase in the demand for the output, then the price level does not change.

But what happens if the aggregate demand curve shifts relatively more than the aggregate supply curve, as in Figure 6.1.2? At the original price level P_1, aggregate supply increases by 5 percent as before, but aggregate demand now increases by 10 percent. When this happens, the price level increases to P_2. If the aggregate demand curve continues to shift relatively more than the aggregate supply curve, then the price level continues to rise and inflation sets in.

This analysis suggests that inflation is not necessarily caused by isolated shifts in either the aggregate supply or aggregate demand curves. In reality, inflation occurs if the aggregate demand curve shifts relatively more than the aggregate supply curve. On the one hand, if the determinants of aggregate demand change such that aggregate demand shifts more than aggregate supply, even though the aggregate supply also shifts rightward, then we have demand-pull inflation. **Demand-pull inflation** is inflation caused by increases in aggregate demand without comparable increases in aggregate supply. On the other hand, if the determinants of aggregate supply change such that it shifts relatively less than aggregate demand, then we have cost-push inflation. **Cost-push inflation** is inflation caused by increases in factor costs without comparable increases in the production of goods and services. Note that in both cases aggregate supply is shifting rightward but not as much as aggregate demand.

For example, suppose the economy has relatively equal shifts in both curves over a period of time, and the price level does not change. Assume that both curves shift by about 3 percent each year, which is the historical rate of growth of national output. But what happens if both the aggregate demand and aggregate supply curves do not shift by 3 percent? If the aggregate demand curve shifts by more than 3 percent or if the aggregate supply curve shifts by less than 3 percent, then inflation results. In both cases inflation occurs because the aggregate demand curve shifts relatively more than the aggregate supply curve.

DETERMINANTS OF AGGREGATE DEMAND

We can isolate two basic types of determinants of the aggregate demand curve—Keynesian aggregate expenditures and the money supply—which are discussed in Sections 4 and 5, respectively.

Keynesian Aggregate Expenditures

A change in aggregate expenditures can potentially shift the aggregate demand curve relatively more than the aggregate supply curve. Let's consider circumstances in which these expenditures can cause inflation.

Consumption Two of the determinants underlying changes in consumption expenditures that can cause inflation are interest rate and expectations. Lower interest rates lead to an increase in consumption because the prices of goods and services purchased with credit decline. Thus, inflation can occur if the interest rate begins to decline. And in considering the relationship between the nominal interest rate, the real interest rate, and inflation, we can see how consumption expenditures can cause inflation. If the *nominal* interest rate charged for borrowed funds doesn't change, but the rate of inflation increases, this means the *real* rate of interest actually declines. For example, suppose that you borrow $100 at 10 percent interest, so that the next year you owe $110. However, if the rate of inflation is 10 percent, this $110 has the same purchasing power as the $100 borrowed in the previous year. In effect, you are paying no interest on the borrowed funds, and the real interest rate is zero percent.

This becomes significant when inflation creeps into the economy before banks and other financial institutions have time to adjust their nominal interest rates, as occurred in the 1970s. The real interest rate can drop to zero, or even below, making it advantageous for consumers to increase their expenditures. But such an increase can cause a relatively greater shift of the aggregate demand curve and lead to further inflation in a self-reinforcing process that continues until the nominal interest rate overtakes the rate of inflation. While consumption expenditures increased by the interest rate might not start inflation in the economy, they can keep it going for a while.

Expectations can also play a significant role in inflation, as discussed in the next unit. Briefly, note that if households expect that the prices of goods and services will be higher in the future, they are likely to spend relatively more on consumption expenditures in the present. That is, expecting higher prices in the future can increase consumption expenditures, which then leads to a relatively greater shift in the aggregate demand curve, which causes inflation. In essence, the expectation of inflation is a self-fulfilling prophecy.

Investment Investment is related to inflation and the real interest rate in much the same way as consumption expenditures. If inflation catches lenders off guard such that the real interest rate is zero or below, then there is a relative increase in investment expenditures. This relative increase can then lead to further increases in the price level until lenders adjust the interest rate to overtake the rate of inflation. While investment expenditures, like consumption expenditures, might not cause inflation to begin, they can contribute to it.

Government Purchases and Net Taxes The government can also cause a relatively greater shift in the aggregate demand curve by increasing purchases or decreasing net taxes. Moreover, these two functions of the government cannot really be considered in isolation since net taxes generate the revenue used for purchases. In fact, the best way to view the government's net effect on aggregate demand is by considering its budget deficit or surplus. Recall that a deficit occurs when purchases are greater than net taxes, and a surplus occurs when net taxes are greater than purchases.

If there is a relative increase in government purchases or a decrease in net taxes, then the budget deficit increases (or at least the budget surplus is reduced), the aggregate demand curve shifts relatively more, and the price level increases. This suggests that increases in the deficit can lead to inflation.

The Money Supply

Increases in the money supply also cause the aggregate demand curve to shift to the right. If the money supply increases relatively more than the economy's ability to increase full employment output, then we have inflation.

Probably the best way to illustrate the relationship between the money supply and inflation is to look at the historical evidence. Figure 6.1.3

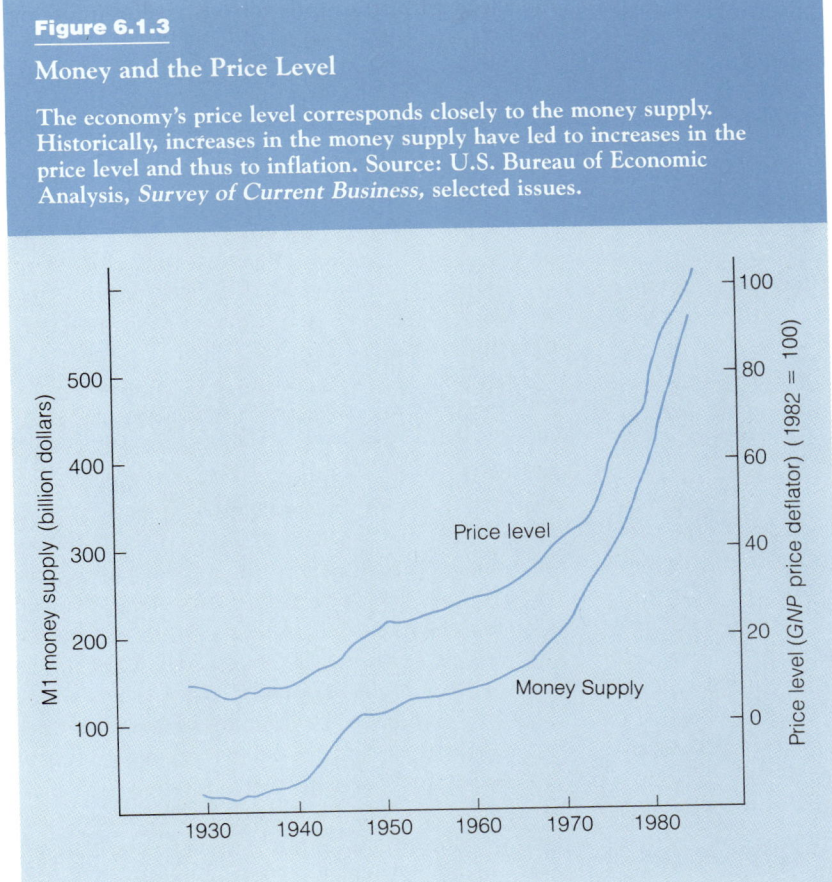

Figure 6.1.3

Money and the Price Level

The economy's price level corresponds closely to the money supply. Historically, increases in the money supply have led to increases in the price level and thus to inflation. Source: U.S. Bureau of Economic Analysis, *Survey of Current Business*, selected issues.

Table 6.1.1

Inflation and the Change in the Money Supply, Selected Countries, 1978 to 1983

A country's rate of inflation is closely tied to its annual change in money supply. Countries with low rates of inflation, such as Austria, Switzerland, and West Germany, also have relatively small changes in money supply. However, countries with high rates of inflation, such as Argentina, Brazil, and Israel, also have correspondingly large changes in money supply.

	1978–1979	1979–1980	1980–1981	1981–1982	1982–1983
Argentina					
Inflation	159.5	100.8	104.5	164.8	343.8
Money supply	131.4	115.8	53.9	195.7	287.7
Austria					
Inflation	3.7	6.4	6.8	5.4	3.3
Money supply	−6.1	7.4	3.7	3.1	12.0
Brazil					
Inflation	52.7	82.8	105.6	98.0	142.0
Money supply	53.2	76.4	65.1	75.4	87.6
Canada					
Inflation	9.1	10.2	12.4	10.8	5.8
Money supply	4.9	3.9	2.9	0.4	13.5
Greece					
Inflation	19.0	24.9	24.5	21.0	20.5
Money supply	19.7	20.3	18.3	24.8	12.5
Israel					
Inflation	78.3	131.0	116.8	120.4	145.6
Money supply	34.0	69.6	93.9	100.6	121.5
Mexico					
Inflation	18.2	26.4	27.9	58.9	101.9
Money supply	31.4	31.1	36.7	43.8	43.8
Switzerland					
Inflation	3.6	4.0	6.5	5.7	3.0
Money supply	8.9	−6.8	−2.2	4.3	10.8
United Kingdom					
Inflation	13.4	18.0	11.9	8.6	4.6
Money supply	12.2	4.4	10.2	8.2	4.6
West Germany					
Inflation	4.1	5.4	6.3	5.3	3.3
Money supply	7.2	2.4	0.9	3.2	10.3

Source: U.S. Bureau of the Census, *Statistical Abstract of the United States*, 1985.

depicts the money supply and the price level for the United States since 1929. Note that the growth of the money supply relates very closely to the increase in the price level. And this does not hold for just the U.S. economy. Table 6.1.1 lists the increase in the money supply and the rate of inflation for different countries at different times. In each case the rate of inflation is closely tied to the increase in the money supply.

DETERMINANTS OF AGGREGATE SUPPLY

A second group of factors can also cause inflation, in this case by shifting the aggregate supply curve. As we consider the dynamics of inflation, we particularly want to identify reasons why the aggregate supply curve would shift relatively less than the aggregate demand curve. Keep in mind that inflation can occur if the aggregate supply curve shifts rightward but relatively less than the aggregate demand or if the aggregate supply curve actually shifts to the left. There are three basic types of determinants of the aggregate supply curve—factor costs, factor quantities, and factor qualities—and each can lead to or contribute to inflation.

Factor Costs

Factor costs include wages, interest, rent, and profit paid to the four factors of production and also the costs of intermediate goods and raw materials. While the aggregate supply curve shifts because of increases in any of these factor costs, two in particular stand out in recent years, wages and petroleum prices.

Wages Labor can receive higher nominal wages for two reasons. First, when labor is more productive and thus contributes more to a firm's output, labor receives more of the firm's revenue. Second, when the price level in the economy is higher, nominal wages need to be increased to maintain a constant real wage. However, if labor is overcompensated, then the aggregate supply curve shifts to the left, or at least doesn't shift as far to the right, leading to even more inflation and even higher prices. Again, this process can be self-sustaining. Prices increase, leading to higher wages, which lead to higher prices, which lead to higher wages, and so on. This is often referred to as the wage-price spiral. The **wage-price spiral** is inflation caused by self-reinforcing increases in real wages and the price level. Note that the wage-price spiral does not occur if higher wages result exclusively from greater productivity. In this case the costs of production don't increase because real wages remain the same.

Petroleum Prices Another significant factor cost is the price of petroleum. While a price increase in any raw material can lead to inflation, the price of petroleum deserves special attention for two reasons. First, petroleum plays a part in the production and distribution of almost every type of output; very few other raw materials can make such a claim. As a raw material it is used in the production of plastics and a wide range of petrochemicals. And as fuel it is used in the transportation of almost every good and service produced in the economy. Therefore, the price of petroleum shows up in the production costs of most goods.

Second, the price of petroleum has already had a demonstrated effect on the economy during the 1970s, when the price of petroleum increased from a few dollars a barrel to over $30 a barrel. This price increase was in part responsible for the high rates of inflation in the 1970s. As the price of petroleum increased, the aggregate supply curve was prevented from shifting rightward, and national production thus was kept from increasing enough to satisfy aggregate demand. Note also that in the early 1980s the price of petroleum declined for the first time in a decade, and the rate of inflation was also at its lowest level in over a decade.

Factor Quantities

The second determinant of the aggregate supply curve is the quantities of the factors of production, which establish the full employment level of output, or the level of output corresponding to the vertical (classical) portion of the aggregate supply curve. If there are changes in the quantities of factors, then the full employment level of output changes and the aggregate supply curve shifts. Moreover, if factor quantities increase relatively less than the increase in aggregate expenditures, then the aggregate supply curve shifts relatively less than the aggregate demand curve.

Labor The most important factor of production is labor. Although the quantity of labor increases over time as a result of increases in the population and increases in the proportion of the population willing and able to work, in some cases the quantity of labor can actually decline. For example, during major wars the economy's labor force declines because a large number of young men and women enter the military and are not engaged in the production of goods and services for the domestic economy. A major war that continues for several years can prevent the full employment level of output from increasing or can even lead to reductions in full employment output. In either case inflation is likely to occur. The escalation of the Vietnam War in the late 1960s contributed to this type of inflation.

Capital The second factor of production that can lead to a relatively smaller shift in the aggregate supply curve is capital. In this regard let's consider the relationship among capital, investment, and depreciation. Investment represents the annual expenditures on capital goods used to increase the economy's capital stock. Depreciation represents the annual decline in the capital stock as it wears out in the production of goods and services. If the rate of investment slows down or the rate of depreciation increases, then the aggregate supply curve shifts relatively less. This process becomes particularly important when we recall one of the determinants of investment, the interest rate. An increase in the real interest rate can reduce investment and the growth of capital and cause a relatively smaller shift in the aggregate supply curve.

Factor Qualities

A third determinant of the aggregate supply curve is the quality of the factors of production. The full employment level of output depends not only on the quantity of factors but also on their quality. This means that a reduction in the quality of factors can lead to a relatively smaller shift in the aggregate supply curve and thus can cause inflation. In terms of quality, the two aspects that stand out are education, which is important to the quality of labor, and technology, which is important to the quality of capital. If the level of education declines, then the quality of labor is less, and the aggregate supply curve shifts relatively less. The aggregate supply curve is affected in the same manner if technology declines and the quality of capital is less.

IN SUMMARY
The Causes of Inflation

- A graph of the aggregate market indicates that inflation is caused by the relative shifts of the aggregate demand or aggregate supply curves. If there is a relatively smaller rightward shift of the aggregate supply curve or a relatively larger rightward shift of the aggregate demand curve, then inflation results.

- On the demand side, inflation can be caused by relative changes in the components of Keynesian aggregate expenditures, including changes in consumption expenditures, government purchases, net taxes, and investment expenditures. Of this group, government purchases and net taxes are most likely to begin a round of inflation, but consumption and investment can keep it going. Increases in the money supply can also cause inflation. Historically, the growth in the price level has matched the growth in the money supply.

- On the supply side, factor costs, especially wages and petroleum prices, are one potential cause of inflation. Relatively smaller decreases in the quantities and qualities of factors can also cause inflation. In terms of quantity, labor can be restricted in times of war and capital can be restricted by the lack of investment. In terms of quality, relative reductions in the levels of education and technology can lead to inflation.

QUESTIONS FOR STUDY AND ANALYSIS

1. Indicate which of the following items would tend to cause inflation through shifts in either the aggregate demand curve or the aggregate supply curve, and why.
   a. An increase in the number and length of labor strikes
   b. An increase in the federal deficit
   c. A decrease in the real interest rate
   d. An increase in government regulations
   e. A relative decrease in expenditures on education

2. Discuss two raw materials other than petroleum for which price increases could create a significant amount of inflation. Do you think either one has the inflation-causing potential of petroleum? Why or why not?

3. How would the crowding-out effect discussed in Unit 5.5 relate to the causes of inflation? Would the crowding-out effect lead to a relatively greater shift in the aggregate demand or a smaller shift in the aggregate supply? Explain. How might investment stimulated by inflation in the short run actually reduce inflation in the long run?

4. Many people argue that the consumer price index overstates inflation because it uses fixed quantities of goods and services. When the price of one good rises faster than the price of another good, people buy smaller quantities of the good with the higher price. However, the CPI assumes that the same quantity is being purchased and thus overstates the importance of its higher price in the overall price level. Note that most labor union contracts automatically adjust wages for increases in the price level using the *CPI*. In light of this information, discuss how the *CPI* relates to the wage-price spiral.

5. There has been growing concern in recent years over soil erosion in the agricultural heartland of the United States because the productivity of the soil has been reduced. Explain how soil erosion potentially could lead to inflation. Would this inflation be caused by shifts in the aggregate demand curve or the aggregate supply curve?

6. Based on your own experience, what do you think is (are) the primary cause(s) of inflation?

REVIEW GLOSSARY

cost-push inflation Inflation caused by increases in factor costs without comparable increases in the production of final goods and services.

demand-pull inflation Inflation caused by increases in aggregate demand without comparable increases in aggregate supply.

wage-price spiral Inflation caused by self-reinforcing increases in real wages and the price level. The wage-price spiral occurs because labor demands higher wages to compensate for higher prices. But if firms pay higher real wages, they compensate by increasing their prices, which leads to another round of wage increases and further price increases.

UNIT 6.2

Inflation and Unemployment

In this unit we discuss the relationship between inflation and unemployment, as embodied in the Phillips curve, which indicates that there is a tradeoff in the economy between inflation and the rate of unemployment. That is, high rates of inflation are associated with low rates of unemployment, and low rates of inflation are associated with high rates of unemployment. It is easy to relate the Phillips curve to the demand-driven business cycle discussed in Unit 3.7. When the economy is contracting, unemployment increases, but there is very little inflationary pressure on the price level. However, when the economy is expanding, unemployment decreases, and the price level increases as the economy reaches the full employment level of output.

To begin, we discuss the logic behind the Phillips curve. In particular, we see how the Phillips curve relates inflation and unemployment from the perspective of the aggregate market. We then examine historical evidence that initially supports but then contradicts this relationship. With these contradictions in mind, we look at an alternative way of relating inflation and unemployment based on inflationary expectations. And once again, we see how this relationship corresponds to the aggregate market.

THE PHILLIPS CURVE

The **Phillips curve** is a curve depicting the relationship between the rate of inflation and the unemployment rate. It was developed by the British economist A.W. Phillips in 1958 to describe

Figure 6.2.1

The Phillips Curve

The Phillips curve depicts the relationship between the rate of inflation and the rate of unemployment. It indicates that higher rates of inflation are associated with lower rates of unemployment. According to the Phillips curve, the economy can reduce unemployment and produce additional output at the expense of a higher rate of inflation.

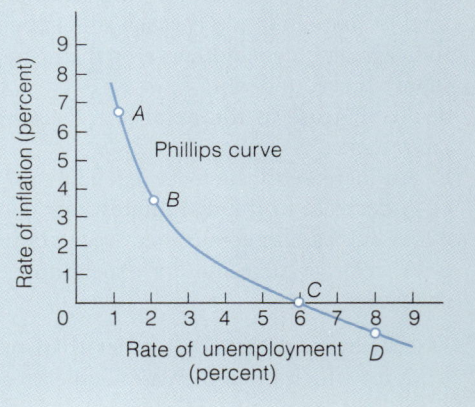

the relationship between wage increases and the unemployment rate in the United Kingdom, and it has since been adapted to relate inflation and the unemployment rate. Figure 6.2.1 depicts the Phillips curve relationship between inflation and unemployment. The vertical axis measures the rate of inflation in the economy, and the horizontal axis the unemployment rate for labor. The Phillips curve postulates that relatively high rates of inflation are associated with relatively low rates of unemployment, as shown by point A. However, reductions in the rate of inflation are accompanied by increases in the rate of unemployment, as indicated by a move down the Phillips curve to point B. Note that the Phillips curve cuts through the horizontal axis, meaning that the rate of inflation is zero if the rate of unemployment is high enough, point

C. Indeed, if the rate of unemployment is even higher, a negative rate of inflation, or a reduction in the price level, can exist, at point D.

The Phillips curve implies that the economy has a choice between inflation and unemployment. A low rate of unemployment in the economy means that a relatively high rate of inflation must be tolerated, at or near the full employment level of output. Furthermore, the way to eliminate inflation is to increase the rate of unemployment and go into a recession. The Phillips curve even suggests that the economy can permanently reduce unemployment if it is willing to live with inflation. On the surface this does not appear to be such a bad trade-off. With less unemployment the economy has a greater amount of goods and services. Since the costs of inflation basically constitute a redistribution of income and wealth, these costs can be addressed with income transfer policies. Moreover, the larger quantity of goods and services generated from reduced unemployment can be used to temper the adverse effects of redistribution.

In terms of the aggregate market, the logic behind the Phillips curve becomes evident. Figure 6.2.2 depicts the aggregate market for the economy in panel a and the corresponding Phillips curve in panel b. In panel a, with a given aggregate supply curve AS, a demand-driven business cycle is seen by shifts in the aggregate demand curve. If the aggregate demand curve is AD_1, then national output is Y_1 and the price level is P_1. But since Y_1 is less than the full employment level of output Y_f, there is unemployment in the economy corresponding to u_1 in panel b.

Figure 6.2.2
Aggregate Demand and the Phillips Curve

The aggregate market in panel **a** illustrates the basic relationship between unemployment and inflation contained in the Phillips curve in panel **b**. With a constant aggregate supply curve, leftward shifts in the aggregate demand curve reduce the price level and inflationary pressures but at the expense of higher unemployment.

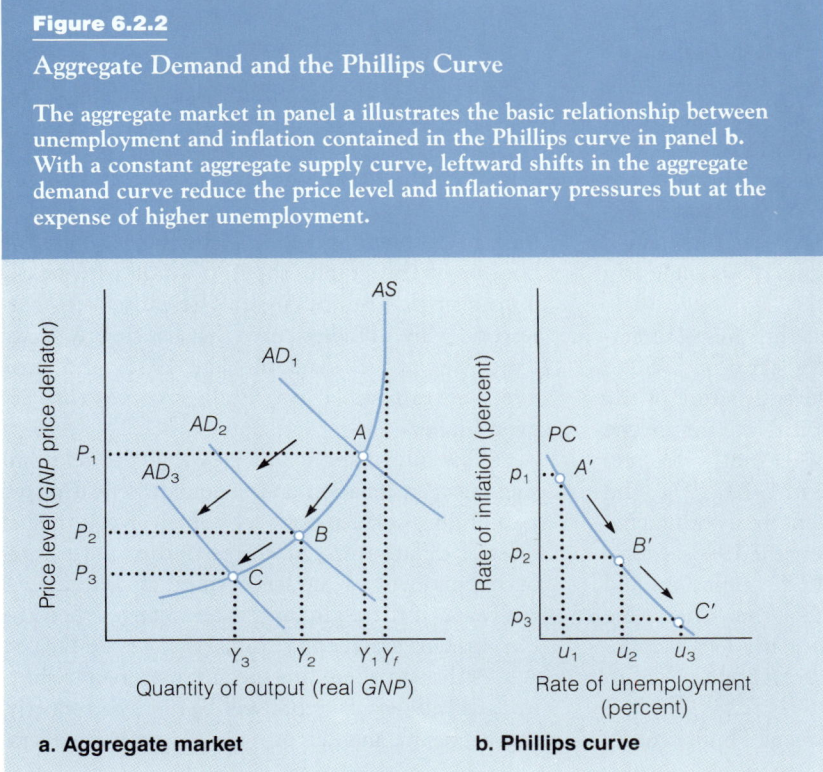

a. Aggregate market

b. Phillips curve

As the aggregate demand curve shifts to the left in the contractionary phase of a demand-driven business cycle due to a change in consumption, investment, net taxes, government purchases, or the money supply, less output is produced, and the unemployment rate increases in panel b from u_1 to u_2 to u_3. But along with the rising unemployment rate, there is a reduction in the inflationary pressures in the economy, indicated in panel a as a relative decline in the price level. If the direction of the shifts for the aggregate demand curve is reversed, then the expansionary phase of the demand-driven business cycle occurs. The unemployment rate declines as the economy moves closer to full employment, but the higher price level leads to greater inflationary pressures.

HISTORICAL EVIDENCE OF THE PHILLIPS CURVE

Figure 6.2.3 plots the actual rates of inflation and unemployment for the U.S. economy from 1959 to 1969, indicating that higher unemployment rates were accompanied by lower inflation rates. This type of information convinced most economists that a tradeoff between inflation and unemployment was necessary and unavoidable. Thus, what happened to the economy in the 1970s and 1980s came as a tremendous shock.

Figure 6.2.4, which depicts the rates of unemployment and inflation for each year from 1960 to the present, paints a very different picture of the unemployment/inflation tradeoff. Note that in the 1970s a simple tradeoff between inflation and unemployment does not exist. In 1970, 1971, and 1973, inflation and unemployment were both higher than in several of the years during the 1960s. Moreover, in 1976, 1977, and 1978, inflation and unemployment were both higher than they were in the early 1970s. And into the early 1980s, inflation and unemployment were both higher than in the late 1970s.

To put this in perspective, several Phillips curves

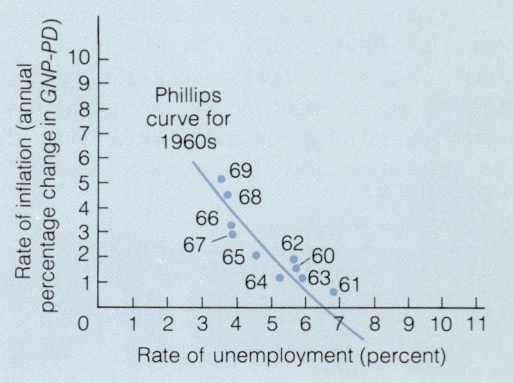

Figure 6.2.3

The Phillips Curve for the 1960s

During the 1960s the Phillips curve relationship was very stable. If the rate of unemployment during a given year was relatively high, then the rate of inflation was relatively low. If the rate of unemployment was relatively low, then the rate of inflation was relatively high.

have been superimposed in Figure 6.2.4. Near the bottom of the graph, the 1960s fall very neatly onto a single Phillips curve. The early 1970s correspond with a Phillips curve that lies slightly above the 1960s curve. And the late 1970s and early 1980s correspond to two Phillips curves that are even higher.

This information indicates that the relationship between inflation and unemployment depicted by a Phillips curve is not very stable. That is, higher rates of inflation might correspond to lower rates of unemployment under certain circumstances. However, if these circumstances change, then the Phillips curve evidently shifts.

Although there are specific reasons for shifts in the Phillips curve that will be discussed shortly, the aggregate market provides us with a general

UNIT 6.2 • INFLATION AND UNEMPLOYMENT

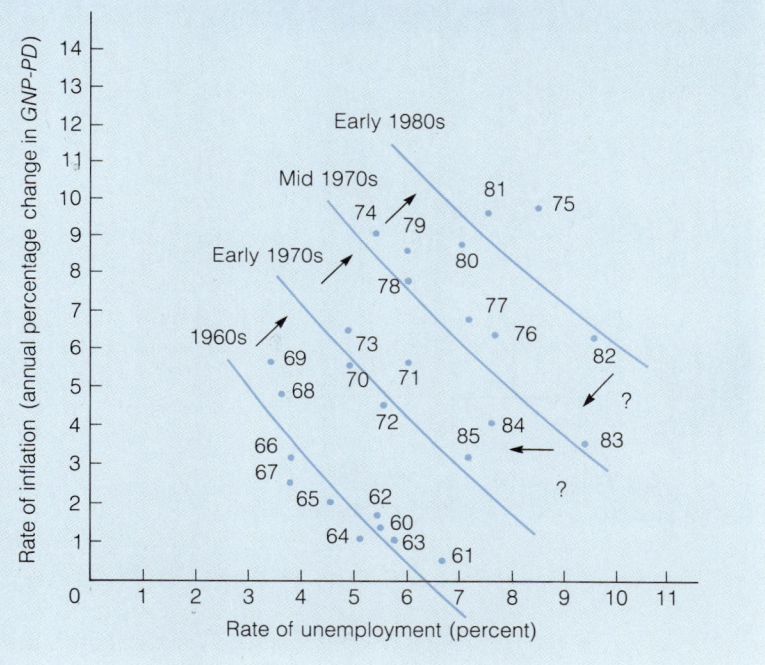

Figure 6.2.4

The Phillips Curves for the 1970s and 1980s

While the Phillips curve relationship during the 1960s was very stable, this changed during the 1970s and 1980s. In the early 1970s higher unemployment was associated with higher, not lower, inflation. The same can be said about the late 1970s and early 1980s. In effect, the Phillips curve shifted vertically during the 1970s and 1980s.

explanation. Recall that while the tradeoff between inflation and unemployment can be explained with shifts in the aggregate demand curve, that curve represents only half of the aggregate market. The reason for a shift in the Phillips curve can be found in the aggregate supply curve. If shifts in the aggregate demand curve lead to movements along a given Phillips curve, then shifts in the aggregate supply curve might lead to shifts in the Phillips curve.

AGGREGATE SUPPLY AND THE PHILLIPS CURVE

The relationship between shifts in the aggregate supply curve and the Phillips curve is illustrated in Figure 6.2.5. Panel a depicts the aggregate market, and panel b the Phillips curve tradeoff between inflation and unemployment. For the initial aggregate supply curve AS_1, the level of output is Y_1 and

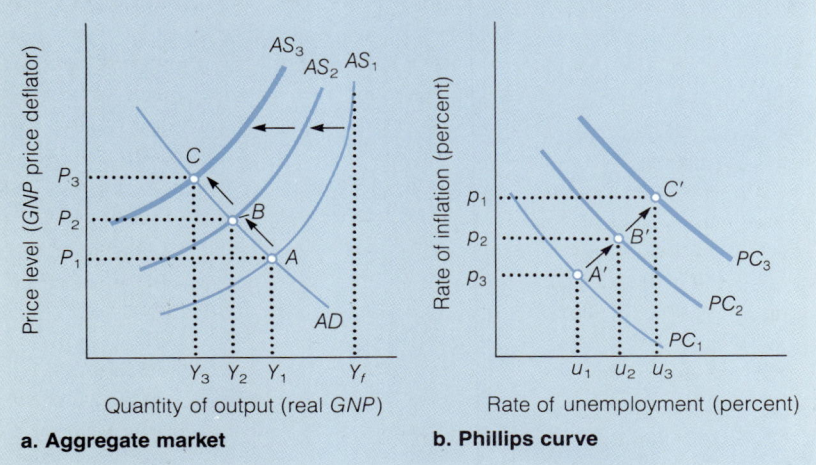

Figure 6.2.5

Aggregate Supply and the Phillips Curve

If movements along a Phillips curve are based on shifts of the aggregate demand curve, then shifts in the Phillips curve are based on shifts of the aggregate supply curve. Panel a illustrates how leftward shifts in the aggregate supply curve lead to inflationary pressures with higher price levels and higher unemployment. This corresponds with rightward shifts in the Phillips curve, in which higher rates of inflation are associated with higher rates of unemployment.

a. Aggregate market

b. Phillips curve

the price level is P_1. Given that the full employment level of output in the economy is Y_f, then point A in panel a corresponds to point A' on Phillips curve PC_1 in panel b, with unemployment u_1 and inflation p_1.

Now let's see what happens if the aggregate supply curve shifts to AS_2, in which case the aggregate market reaches equilibrium at point B, with output Y_2 and price level P_2. This shift increases the unemployment rate *and* places greater inflationary pressures on the price level, so point B in panel a corresponds with point B' on Phillips curve PC_2 in panel b. If the aggregate supply curve shifts to AS_3, then point C in the aggregate market corresponds to point C' on Phillips curve PC_3. As we saw in Unit 3.7, the leftward shift of the aggregate supply curve leads to stagflation, which in Figure 6.2.5 causes the Phillips curve to shift up.

Recall that there are several reasons for leftward shifts in the aggregate supply curve, including the cost, quantities, and qualities of the factors of production. Any of these determinants can lead to the shifts illustrated in Figure 6.2.5. However, at this point we want to focus on the role that inflationary expectations play in shifting the aggregate supply and Phillips curves.

INFLATIONARY EXPECTATIONS

Expectations of future inflation in the economy are a significant determinant of the aggregate supply curve. If expectations change, then the aggregate supply curve shifts. The pivotal role in this process is played by labor because the wages paid to labor represent an important factor cost underlying the aggregate supply curve. Moreover, labor is made up of consumers who are affected by the price level and inflation when they purchase goods and services.

Expectations and the Real Wage

Before we discuss how labor's expectations are related to the aggregate supply curve and inflation, let's distinguish between the nominal wage and the real wage. The **nominal wage** is the monetary value of the wage payment. If a worker's wage is $5 per hour, then after one hour of work the worker obviously receives the equivalent of a $5 bill. But knowing that the worker receives a $5 bill tells us nothing about the ability to buy goods and services. For example, a $5 nominal wage is quite different when the price of a loaf of bread is $5 then when the price of a Mercedes-Benz is $5. Therefore, it is often more instructive to look at the real wage.

The **real wage** is the purchasing power of the nominal wage payment. The real wage indicates the quantities of goods and services the nominal wage is able to buy. From an operational standpoint, the real wage is the ratio of the nominal wage payment and the economy's average price level. For example, if the nominal wage increases by 10 percent (from $10 to $11) but the price level also increases by 10 percent (from 1.0 to 1.1), then the real wage does not change. If the nominal wage increases by 10 percent while the price level increases by 7 percent, then the real wage actually increases by 3 percent. Since nominal wages have increased more than prices, more goods and services can be purchased.

The connection between the real wage and expectations can be seen in the following scenario. If labor expects the rate of inflation to be only 4 percent for a given year, then it sees no change in its real wage if the nominal wage also increases by 4 percent. But if the nominal wage increases by 6 percent, then labor acts as though the real wage increases by 2 percent since only 4 percent inflation is expected.

Expectations and the Aggregate Market

Let's see how this process is reflected in the aggregate market. In Figure 6.2.6 the aggregate market is initially in equilibrium at point A, determined

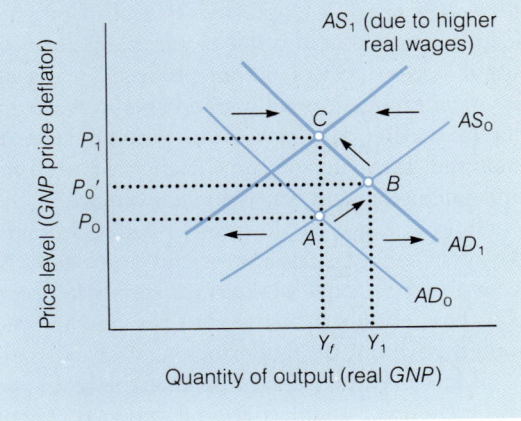

Figure 6.2.6

Expectations and the Aggregate Market

An important factor underlying shifts in the aggregate supply curve is inflationary expectations. If labor expects relatively low rates of inflation, it is willing to produce more output when producers pay a relatively high nominal wage. This can lead to an increase in output to Y_1, which is greater than the full employment level of output. But when labor realizes that inflation is actually greater than expected, it demands higher nominal, and thus real, wages, and the aggregate supply curve shifts up accordingly.

by the intersection of AS_0 and AD_0. The price level is P_0 and the level of output is Y_f, the full employment level of output. But what happens if the aggregate demand curve shifts to the right because of expansionary fiscal or monetary policy?

Recall from our study of the aggregate market in Unit 3.6 that a rightward shift of the aggregate demand curve at the full employment level of output can only lead to an increase in the price level, with no change in the level of output. In other words, the aggregate supply curve for the quantity Y_f would be vertical. This is not the case here. The aggregate supply curve AS_0 has a positive slope as a result of labor's inflationary expectations. Let's see why.

The rightward shift in aggregate demand means more goods and services are being demanded at higher prices. In response to this, firms try to increase production by obtaining more factors of production, especially labor. To obtain more labor, the firms offer higher nominal wages. While workers clearly know their nominal wages are increasing, they may not expect the increase in the price level that results from the increase in aggregate demand. Therefore, they assume that their real wage will also be greater and offer a larger quantity of labor. The increase in the quantity of labor means the economy is able to increase production to Y_1, and the AS curve has a positive slope.

But how can the economy produce Y_1 output when Y_f is the full employment level of output? Keep in mind that the full employment level of output is the level of output produced when all factors of production willing and able to work are employed; this does not mean that all labor is employed. In particular, some frictional and structural unemployment still persists even when the economy is at full employment. Frictional unemployment concerns us most at this point since it occurs because some workers are simply between jobs. The jobs are available, but the unemployed workers have not yet found them.

If labor erroneously thinks that the real wage has increased, then frictional unemployment declines because the frictionally unemployed worker has a greater incentive to find an available job. However, the decrease in frictional unemployment is only temporary. Once labor realizes that the price level has increased along with the nominal wage, then frictional unemployment returns to its former level. Frictionally unemployed workers will not make the extra effort to find jobs once it is clear the real wage has not actually risen.

In fact, labor is only willing to produce the greater level of output Y_1 if it actually receives the real wage it previously thought it was getting. For example, suppose that nominal wages increase by 5 percent and the price level also increases by 5 percent. If labor does not expect the price level to increase, it accepts a 5 percent increase in the *nominal* wage, thinking it is getting a 5 percent increase in the *real* wage. This increase in the nominal wage causes production to increase to Y_1. But when labor adjusts its expectations and realizes that the price level also increased by 5 percent, then it is only willing to produce Y_f. And if it is to continue producing Y_1, then an additional 5 percent increase in nominal wages is required, for a total increase in the nominal wage of 10 percent and a real wage increase of 5 percent.

But this actual increase in the real wage causes the aggregate supply curve in Figure 6.2.6 to shift from AS_0 to AS_1 because the real wage is a factor cost and thus a determinant of the aggregate supply curve. With this shift in the aggregate supply curve, the economy reaches a new equilibrium at point C, with price level P_1 and output Y_f.

What Figure 6.2.6 illustrates is the difference between short-run equilibrium and long-run equilibrium in the economy. In the short run the economy can be in equilibrium at some output greater or even less than Y_f as it moves along a short-run aggregate supply curve, such as AS_0. Here, the economy does not produce the full employment level of output because labor has imperfect expectations of inflation and thus provides a quantity of labor that is based on a misperception of the real wage. But in the long run the economy produces output equal to Y_f, where labor's expectations correspond with the actual rate of inflation and the quantity of labor provided corresponds to the actual real wage.

Figure 6.2.7 depicts these two basic types of aggregate supply curves. The curve LRAS is the long-run aggregate supply curve, which is unresponsive to changes in the price level and is completely vertical at the full employment level of output. The three positively sloped curves, $SRAS_1$, $SRAS_2$, and $SRAS_3$, are the short-run aggregate supply curves, each of which is based on a different expected rate of inflation.

Expectations and the Phillips Curve

Let's now return to the Phillips curve and see how expectations come into play. The tradeoff between inflation and unemployment contained in a Phillips curve is based on a given expected rate of infla-

tion. The **expected rate of inflation** is the rate of inflation that people in the economy expect to occur in the future. The expected rate of inflation depends in part on the rate of inflation in recent years, and in part on anticipated changes in the determinants of aggregate demand and supply that affect the price level. For example, if inflation has been 2 percent for the past several years, then people are likely to expect that the rate of inflation will continue at 2 percent in the future unless they anticipate government policies that will stimulate the economy beyond full employment output. For whatever reason, when expectations change, the Phillips curve shifts.

Figure 6.2.8 illustrates the Phillips curve if the expected rate of inflation is zero, curve PC_0. This does not create a problem if the rate of inflation actually is zero, at point A on the curve. In particular, if labor thinks that prices will not rise and they do not rise, then the real wage it thinks it is receiving is the actual real wage received. Here, the economy is at full employment.

But as we saw earlier, full employment is associated with a certain level of unemployment. Suppose that the level of unemployment that occurs at full employment is 5 percent, consisting of frictional and structural unemployment, which is often referred to as the natural rate of unemployment. The **natural rate of unemployment** is the rate of unemployment that occurs when the economy is at full employment.

Let's consider what happens if the actual rate of inflation is not the same as the expected rate of inflation. Perhaps unexpected expansionary fiscal or monetary policy is used to increase output above the full employment level by reducing unemployment below the natural rate. In the short run, with these unanticipated policies, the economy moves up the existing Phillips curve PC_0 from point A to point B. The economy is trying to increase output and reduce unemployment at the expense of inflation.

At point B people think inflation is zero, but it is actually 3 percent. As we saw before, labor is fooled into working more and producing more out-

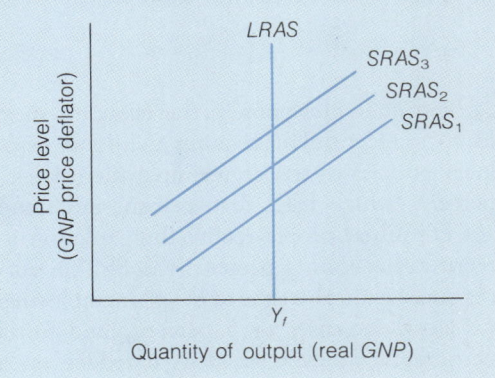

Figure 6.2.7

Long-Run and Short-Run Aggregate Supply Curves

In the short run, when labor has incorrect inflationary expectations, the aggregate supply curves are positively sloped. However, in the long run, when the expected rate of inflation is equal to the actual rate of inflation, the aggregate supply curve is vertical at the full employment level of output.

Figure 6.2.8

Expectations and the Phillips Curve

If the expected rate of inflation differs from the actual rate of inflation, the economy moves along a short-run Phillips curve. However, when the expected rate of inflation changes, then the Phillips curve shifts. When the expected rate of inflation is equal to the actual rate, then the economy is at the natural rate of unemployment.

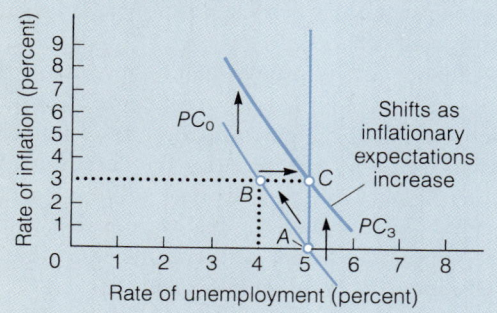

Figure 6.2.9

Expectations and Accelerating Inflation

If the economy tries to permanently reduce the unemployment rate below its natural level by increasing the rate of inflation, then accelerating inflation occurs. If the economy tries to maintain a 4 percent unemployment rate, the Phillips curve continues to shift upward as people adjust inflationary expectations to the actual rate of inflation. Therefore, higher and higher rates of inflation are needed to maintain 4 percent unemployment.

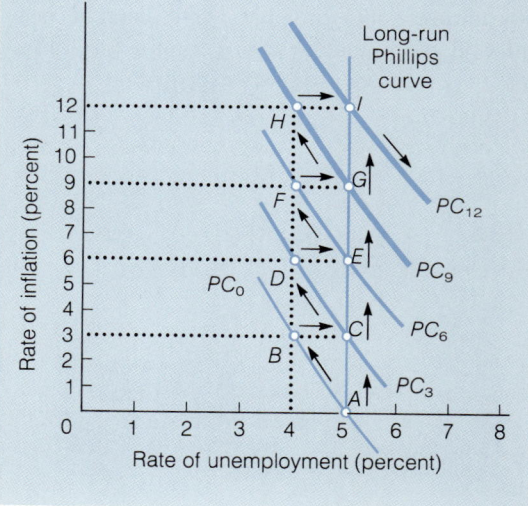

put. The reduction in frictional unemployment reduces the rate of unemployment to 4 percent, at point B, but this cannot last. Once people realize that the rate of inflation is 3 percent rather than zero, nominal wages increase and the Phillips curve shifts to PC_3 as the result of a corresponding shift in the aggregate supply curve. The economy then moves to point C, where the expected rate of inflation and the actual rate of inflation are equal once again.

The tendency of the economy to move back to the natural rate of unemployment can create accelerating inflation if the government tries to maintain unemployment below the natural level. Figure 6.2.9 illustrates how this can occur. If the government, through expansionary fiscal and/or monetary policy, reduces the unemployment rate to 4 percent, then the rate of inflation increases to 3 percent, at point B. However, as people adjust to this rate of inflation, the Phillips curve shifts to PC_3, and unemployment in the economy moves back to 5 percent. This requires additional expansionary policies to reduce unemployment back to 4 percent, which leads to 6 percent inflation at point D. When people realize that inflation is 6 percent rather than 3 percent, the Phillips curve shifts once again, this time to PC_6. Unemployment once again increases to 5 percent, and further expansionary policy is needed to reduce unemployment. As this process continues, the lower level of unemployment can only be maintained if the rate of inflation continues to reach higher and higher levels.

RATIONAL EXPECTATIONS

This problem of accelerating inflation, which the U.S. economy experienced in the 1970s, and the role played by expectations underlies an important school of thought developed during this period. Rather than viewing expectations as adaptive over a period of time, this school of thought considers expectations to be rational. **Rational expectations** are expectations people have concerning future rates of inflation, and other economic variables, that are based on anticipated government policies and other conditions in the economy. The idea underlying rational expectations is that people are generally aware of what fiscal and monetary policies the government plans to undertake and how these policies affect the economy. That is, if the government stimulates the economy at full employment with expansionary monetary policy, people rationally expect inflation to result.

Proponents of rational expectations argue that people in general will not be fooled into moving along any of the short-run aggregate supply curves in Figure 6.2.7 or the negatively sloped Phillips curves in Figure 6.2.9. Since these curves are based on incorrect expectations of the rate of inflation, the economy can move along them only if the government implements policies totally unexpected by the public or if other unexpected shifts in the aggregate demand or supply curves occur (such as abrupt changes in petroleum prices or export demand). With rational expectations and no unexpected shocks, the economy remains on the vertical aggregate supply curve *LRAS* in Figure 6.2.7 and the vertical long-run Phillips curve in Figure 6.2.8.

From a policy perspective the rational expectations view implies that discretionary fiscal and monetary policies designed to reduce unemployment below its natural rate will be totally ineffective. In fact, as we saw in Figure 6.2.9, such policies can lead to accelerating rates of inflation. The question is what the economy should do with 12 percent inflation and 5 percent unemployment at point *I*? In the next unit we look at several alternative policies to address this question.

IN SUMMARY

Inflation and Unemployment

- The Phillips curve depicts the tradeoff between the rate of inflation and the unemployment rate. If inflation is relatively high, the employment rate is relatively low. This suggests that the economy can have relatively low rates of employment by increasing the rate of inflation. The Phillips curve can be seen with the aggregate market by shifts in the aggregate demand curve. If the aggregate demand curve shifts to the left, unemployment increases but inflationary pressures are reduced. If the aggregate demand curve shifts to the right, unemployment decreases but inflationary pressures are increased. The Phillips curve is consistent with demand-driven business cycles.

- Through the late 1960s the Phillips curve was relatively stable. However, in the 1970s and 1980s the simple tradeoff between inflation and unemployment broke down. In this decade higher rates of inflation were associated with higher rates of unemployment rather than lower rates. The lack of tradeoff after 1970 can be explained by shifts in the aggregate supply curve. That is, a given Phillips curve is based on a given aggregate supply curve, and when the aggregate supply curve shifts, the Phillips curve also shifts.

- Although the aggregate supply curve can shift because of changes in factor costs, quantities, or qualities, it can also shift because of changes in expectations of inflation. If labor expects inflation will be relatively low in the future, then it will supply more effort based on these expectations. If labor's expectations are too low, then its real wage is less than expected, and it has supplied too much effort, which translates into a relatively low unemployment rate. However, when it realizes that its expectations are incorrect and adjusts its efforts accordingly, then unemployment returns to its natural level. Thus, the rate of unemployment tends to its natural level as long as the expected rate of inflation is equal to the actual rate, regardless of the level of inflation. This means that a long-run Phillips curve is vertical at the natural rate of unemployment.

QUESTIONS FOR STUDY AND ANALYSIS

1. A hypothetical rate of inflation over a ten-year period is given in the following table:

Year	'90	'91	'92	'93	'94	'95	'96	'97	'98	'99
Inflation	2.1	6.0	−3.2	0.1	4.2	−1.1	2.1	0.2	−4.0	5.3

   a. Based on this information, what do you expect the rate of inflation to be in the year 2000? Why?
   b. What do you expect the rate of inflation to be for the ten years following this period? Why?

2. Another hypothetical rate of inflation over a ten-year period is given as follows:

Year	'90	'91	'92	'93	'94	'95	'96	'97	'98	'99
Inflation	4.3	6.0	5.2	6.1	7.2	5.6	8.9	6.6	7.0	8.3

   Based on this information, what is the expected rate of inflation in the year 2000? Why? How does this compare with your answer to question 1a? Explain why your answer is different or why it is the same.

3. In terms of Figure 6.2.1, what do you think was the expected rate of inflation in the United States during the 1960s? Explain.

4. If the expected rate of inflation is 10 percent, do you think contractionary fiscal policy can effectively reduce the actual rate of inflation to zero? If this occurs, what is likely to happen to the unemployment rate?

5. What do you expect the rate of inflation to be one year from now? Why? If you are certain that you will be 3 percent more productive next year, what percentage increase in your wage will you request?

6. Using the short-run Phillips curve, policymakers and economists in the 1960s thought we could have a permanent decrease in the unemployment rate by increasing the rate of inflation. However, expansionary fiscal policy did not work. Considering the natural rate of unemployment, what are some alternative methods of permanently reducing the rate of unemployment without accelerating inflation? Discuss these methods.

REVIEW GLOSSARY

expected rate of inflation The rate of inflation that people in the economy expect to occur in the future. Changes in the expected rate of inflation lead to shifts in the short-run Phillips curve, and a separate Phillips curve exists for each expected rate of inflation.

natural rate of unemployment The rate of unemployment that occurs when the economy is at full employment. The natural rate of unemployment is primarily composed of frictional and structural unemployment. In the long run the rate of inflation does not affect the natural rate of unemployment, and the long-run Phillips curve is vertical at the natural rate of unemployment.

nominal wage The monetary value of the wage payment.

Phillips curve A curve depicting the relationship between the rate of inflation and the unemployment rate.

rational expectations Expectations people have concerning future rates of inflation and other economic variables that are based on anticipated government policy and other conditions in the economy. Rational expectations form the basis of a school of thought developed in the 1970s that argues that only unexpected shocks to the economy will cause changes in the full employment level of output.

real wage The purchasing power of the nominal wage payment. It is found by dividing the nominal wage by the price level.

UNIT 6.3

Inflation Control Policies

Now that we have looked at the causes and effects of inflation, let's discuss what can be done to control inflation, which became a major issue in the 1970s. Though inflation has always been a part of the economy, such periods in the past were typically offset at some point by stable or even declining prices. While prices were relatively stable in the early 1960s, the last time prices actually declined was in the mid-1950s. This prolonged period of inflation culminated with the double-digit inflation of the 1970s and prompted a variety of inflation control policies. Our objective in this unit is to look at several of these policies to see how effectively they can be used to control inflation.

Our starting point is contractionary fiscal and monetary policy, which leads us to a discussion of the effects of a balanced budget and constant growth of the money supply on inflation. Then we look at the use of wage and price controls (and guidelines), which have been implemented several times in the U.S. economy, most recently by the Nixon and Carter administrations. And finally, we consider indexing and the role it can play in controlling inflation, and we examine several supply-side policies, ranging from tax reductions to deregulation.

CONTRACTIONARY FISCAL AND MONETARY POLICY

The discussion of Keynesian economics in Unit 4.7 suggested that the prescribed method of eliminating an inflationary gap is with contractionary fiscal policy. **Contractionary fiscal policy** is fiscal policy consisting of decreases in government purchases and/or increases in net taxes (including decreases in transfer payments). Simply stated, if aggregate expenditures are greater than the full employment level of output, then the economy has inflationary pressures. The way to control the inflation is to reduce aggregate expenditures until they are equal to the full employment level of output.

There is similar logic behind the use of contractionary monetary policy to control inflation. **Contractionary monetary policy** is monetary policy consisting of decreases in the money supply through the use of open market operations, reserve requirements, and the discount rate. Monetary policy can also be used to reduce aggregate expenditures until they are equal to the full employment level of output. Contractionary monetary policy is politically more palatable than contractionary fiscal policy, which involves reducing spending or increasing taxes. Historically, politicians have been thrown out of office for trying such measures. By contrast, monetary policy indirectly affects aggregate expenditures through increases in the interest rate and reductions in investment.

However they differ in method, fiscal and monetary policy both try to control inflation through shifts in the aggregate demand curve. This may be appropriate if the inflation is caused by increases in aggregate demand. However, in the 1970s inflation was caused by increases in factor costs, directly through higher petroleum prices and indirectly through higher wages resulting from changes in inflationary expectations. If inflation is caused by shifts in the aggregate supply curve, then contractionary fiscal and monetary policy can create further problems.

Based on the analysis in the previous unit, let's see how contractionary fiscal and/or monetary policy works. Recall that in Figure 6.2.9 the economy had 12 percent inflation and 5 percent unemployment; this is the situation in Figure 6.3.1 as well. Panel a depicts the aggregate market corresponding to 12 percent inflation and 5 percent unemployment. Since 5 percent is the natural rate of unemployment, the aggregate demand curve AD_0 and the short-run aggregate supply curve AS_0 intersect at the full employment level of output Y_f. Panel b depicts the short-run Phillips curve PC_{12} that corresponds to a 12 percent expected rate of inflation. And since the expected inflation is the same as the actual inflation, the economy is at point A' on the long-run Phillips curve.

How does the economy react if contractionary fiscal and/or monetary policy is implemented? In panel a we see a leftward shift in the aggregate demand curve to AD_1, which in the short run leads to equilibrium at point B on the original short-run aggregate supply curve. At point B the level of output falls to Y_1, meaning unemployment in the economy increases. Although the relative price level falls, indicating a reduction in inflationary pressures, labor is still operating based on the original expected rate of inflation. Therefore, when firms reduce the nominal wage, labor sees this as a decline in the real wage and thus is willing to produce less output. Only when labor is convinced that the price level and rate of inflation have fallen will the aggregate supply curve shift to AS_1. With this shift in the aggregate supply curve, the economy reaches equilibrium at the full employment level of output and with less inflationary pressure in the economy.

In panel b we can see the same process using the Phillips curve. The economy begins with 12 percent inflation and 5 percent unemployment at point A'. The contractionary fiscal and/or monetary policy causes the rate of unemployment to increase in the short run as the economy moves to point B' on curve PC_{12}. At B' the rate of inflation declines to 4 percent. When people adjust their expectations and are convinced that the rate of inflation will remain at 4 percent, the short-run Phillips curve shifts to PC_4. The economy then moves back to the long-run Phillips curve at point C', with inflation equal to 4 percent and unemployment equal to 5 percent.

In principle, contractionary fiscal and/or monetary policy thus reduces inflation simply by holding it down long enough to convince people that the inflation has been reduced so that they adjust their inflationary expectations. This is accomplished with the contractionary policy by throwing the economy into a recession and forcing the

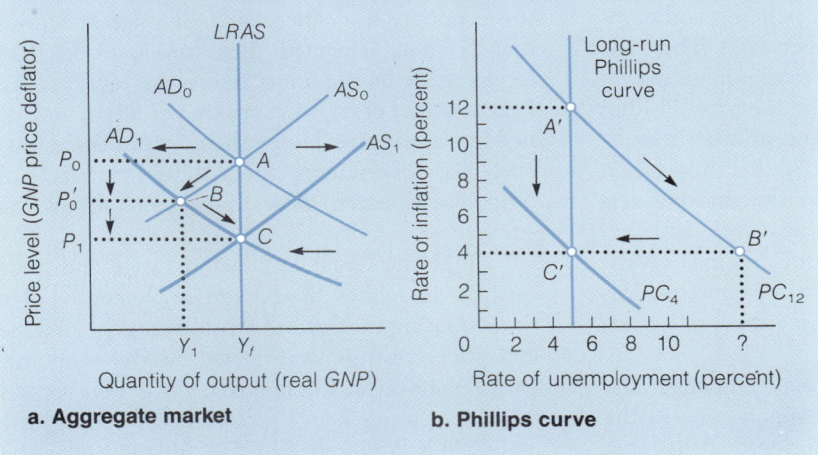

Figure 6.3.1

Contractionary Fiscal and Monetary Policy

While contractionary fiscal and monetary policy is most suited to demand-pull inflation, it can also be used to reduce inflationary expectations and shift the Phillips curve down. But to be effective, contractionary policy must reduce output and increase unemployment for a prolonged period of time. This moves the economy down a short-run Phillips curve, decreases the actual rate of inflation, and eventually decreases inflationary expectations.

a. Aggregate market

b. Phillips curve

unemployment rate to increase. What still has to be answered is how much of a recession is necessary? How much must the unemployment rate be increased? And how long does the economy need to remain in a recession before people adjust their expectations?

In the 1980s contractionary policy was used to reduce inflation. As a result, the unemployment rate increased from 7 to over 10 percent and the rate of inflation declined from 14 to 4 percent. However, four years after the rate of inflation declined, the unemployment rate had fallen only to 7 percent, still a few percentage points above the natural rate, indicating that inflationary expectations fell but not by as much as the decline in inflation. Indeed, even with several years of relatively low inflation, it might take only a few months of higher inflation to increase inflationary expectations, mainly because the 1970s increased everyone's sensitivity to inflation.

BALANCED BUDGET AND CONSTANT GROWTH OF THE MONEY SUPPLY

Two policies related to contractionary fiscal and monetary policy—a balanced budget and constant growth of the money supply—should also be considered as methods to control inflation. The balanced budget policy would prevent the federal government from operating with a budget deficit—the government would be able to spend no more than it received in tax revenues. In the same way that a balanced budget eliminates discretionary fiscal policy, the recommendation to have a constant growth of the money supply is designed to eliminate discretionary monetary policy. This second proposal would allow the money supply to grow at a constant rate based on the historical growth of real GNP.

Both of these policies are designed to prevent rather than merely reduce inflation. They are based on the idea that the government, through its discretionary fiscal and monetary policies, is the primary cause of inflation (and recessions). Thus, the best way to avoid inflation is to eliminate discretionary policies. In terms of the long-run Phillips curve discussed in the previous unit and the business cycles studied in Unit 3.7, this proposition has some merit. In Unit 3.7 we saw that business cycles are often tied to the political cycle and government expenditures during and after major wars. And in the previous unit we saw the consequences of trying to maintain unemployment below its natural level.

Proponents argue that a balanced budget and constant growth of the money supply prevent the time lags in implementing discretionary policy that often worsen inflation and recessions. For example, the time required to collect and process information measuring the levels of output and inflation merely indicates where the economy was several months ago. And once the government recognizes that discretionary policy is needed, it might take several more months before the policy is formulated and implemented by all of the appropriate legislative and administrative bodies. Keep in mind that after administrative and/or legislative committees decide what type of fiscal policy to implement, it must be passed by Congress and enacted by the administrative branch. Although monetary policy has shorter time lags than fiscal policy, there are still delays before the Federal Reserve System is able to change the money supply. Indeed, because of these lags, when contractionary policy is finally implemented, it might actually be time to implement expansionary policy, and vice versa.

WAGE AND PRICE CONTROLS/GUIDELINES

Another way to curb inflation is through wage and price controls and guidelines. **Wage and price controls/guidelines** are legally established (controls) or voluntary (guidelines) maximum limits on prices and wages. These controls and guidelines essentially constitute price ceilings (discussed in Unit 2.5) designed to keep firms from raising their prices as a means of preventing the overall price level in the economy from increasing. If wage and price *controls* are implemented, then firms and labor must legally abide by the limits, subject to legal action. But wage and price *guidelines* are voluntary and are not legally enforceable by the government. However, the government can withhold contracts or otherwise threaten those that do not follow the guidelines.

Since the Great Depression, wage and price controls/guidelines have been implemented five times. During the Second World War general wage and price controls were levied on the economy. During the Korean War limited controls were applied to a selected number of goods and services. In the early 1960s President John F. Kennedy initiated a set of guidelines (officially termed guideposts) that were continued by President Lyndon B. Johnson. In 1971 President Richard M. Nixon implemented widespread controls that lasted until 1974. And most recently, President Jimmy Carter established a set of wage and price guidelines in 1978.

The principle underlying wage and price controls/guidelines is very simple—control inflation by preventing prices from rising. In terms of prices, the maximum price firms can charge is typically set as the highest price charged in recent months. If firms cannot raise their prices, then the economy has no inflation.

Control of wages also plays an important role since wages are the largest single cost of production for most firms. If wages increase, then firms have to raise their prices or eventually go out of business. However, wages are attributable to both higher prices and increased productivity. Under wage and price controls/guidelines, wage increases and the maximum wage paid are tied to labor productivity. If productivity increases 3 percent while the price level increases by 4 percent, the wage controls/guidelines allow for wages to increase by 3 percent. Since production is greater, firms do not need to increase prices to cover the higher labor costs.

Proponents of wage and price controls/guidelines argue that inflation results mainly from the market power possessed by large firms, labor unions, and resource suppliers, who artificially raise prices and create inflation. Controls and guidelines must therefore be used to prevent higher prices and inflation. They also argue that controls and guidelines can limit inflationary expectations. In the previous unit we saw that if people expect higher rates of inflation, then the short-run Phillips curve rises accordingly. By using controls and guidelines, the government can convince the public that prices will not continue to rise, and thus inflationary expectations will be revised downward.

Furthermore, wage and price guidelines are politically more feasible than contractionary fiscal and monetary policy. While this is not really an argument in favor of controls, it certainly helps explain why they are implemented. The general voting public is more likely to vote for the politician who proposes to legally prevent big business, big labor, and unscrupulous resources suppliers from raising prices than for the politician who proposes to raise the public's taxes, reduce the benefits they obtain from government spending, and limit the amount of money in the economy.

In spite of their political popularity, wage and price controls/guidelines have historically been ineffective in controlling inflation. While controls such as the ninety-day freeze imposed by President Nixon in 1971 can be effective in the short run, long-run inflation is not controlled, and other problems are created.

One problem is the disruption of the allocation of resources. As we saw in Unit 2.5, the use of price ceilings leads to a shortage because buyers are not able to get enough of the good at the ceiling price. Shortages are accompanied by problems of rationing and a need to determine who gets how much of the good. The rationing can be done on a first-come-first-serve basis—remember the long lines at gasoline stations in the mid-1970s. Or it can be accomplished by issuing ration coupons, as in the Second World War.

In some cases price ceilings also lead to black markets, where buyers and sellers agree to exchange the good above the legal price. Black markets can greatly reduce, and even nullify, the effects of inflationary control. Indeed, the prices charged in the black markets might be even higher than the original price, meaning the wage and price controls actually worsen inflation.

Another problem created by wage and price controls/guidelines is that they can worsen future rates of inflation as well as inflationary expectations. If the controls/guidelines are implemented for a relatively short period of time, perhaps six months or a year, then firms and labor can simply wait until the controls/guidelines are lifted because prices and wages can then be increased enough to compensate for the lower wages and prices received when the controls/guidelines were operating. And if the public thinks that wages and prices will be increased after the controls/guidelines are lifted, then inflationary expectations will remain high and even increase.

And finally, firms can find ways to legally avoid wage and price controls. For example, the quantity and/or quality of an existing product can be reduced and sold at the controlled price. If the price of an automobile, candy bar, or rental apartment cannot be increased, then firms can use cheaper materials in the automobile, shrink the size of the candy bar, and let the quality of the apartment deteriorate through lack of maintenance.

INDEXING

Indexing is a policy that aims to limit the adverse effects of inflation rather than to control inflation itself. **Indexing** is the adjustment of nominal values to changes in the price level. Recall from Unit 3.5

that one of the primary problems with inflation is the redistribution of wealth and income. With pure inflation all nominal values, including prices, wages, income, and money, increase equally, and there are no distribution effects. Through the use of indexing, wages, social security payments, and other nominal values can be tied to the rate of inflation. For example, a union contract need not specify the actual wage paid to labor over the next three years but can compute wage increases based on the rate of inflation. If inflation is 5 percent, then employees receive a 5 percent cost-of-living adjustment in addition to any raise given for increased productivity. Indexing of this type has been implemented for social security payments and income taxes. With income taxes, the tax rate reflects the rate of inflation, thus preventing people from paying a larger portion of their income in taxes simply because they have more nominal income.

The main problem with indexing is that it tends to build inflation into the economy, because every union contract and government payment contains provisions for inflationary increases. This tends to enhance inflationary expectations and makes it even more difficult to reduce the expected rate of inflation and shift down the Phillips curve. In addition, indexing cannot be universally applied, and people who hold money or receive nominal payments that are not indexed still lose out.

SUPPLY-SIDE POLICIES

The inflationary period of the 1970s was almost as significant to our study of macroeconomics as the Depression of the 1930s. The 1930s sparked the realization that aggregate demand was related to the stability of the economy. And in the forty years that followed, the demand side of the economy received almost all of the attention. However, in the 1970s attention was focused on the supply side of the economy and supply-side economics. **Supply-side economics** is a body of economic thought emphasizing control of aggregate supply rather than aggregate demand. In the 1970s we saw that business cycles can be supply-driven as well as demand-driven. And in the decade that followed the first supply shock created by higher petroleum prices, many policies have been recommended to deal with the stagflation that characterized this period.

Taxes and Incentives

A major thrust of supply-side policies to control inflation has to do with incentives. In particular, supply-side proponents argue that the relatively high marginal tax rates in our progressive tax system reduce the incentive of labor to work and earn more income. Workers are willing to supply their labor based on the amount of net income remaining after taxes. If their marginal tax rate is 50 percent, then they are able to keep only $500 for an additional $1000 earned and are therefore only willing to put forth $500 worth of effort. If the marginal tax rate is higher, people retain less after-tax income and are willing to put forth less additional effort.

The same type of incentive reduction exists for firms and their investment in capital. When firms' earnings are taxed at relatively high marginal rates, then the return from an investment is reduced, and they have less incentive to invest in capital goods.

If labor is willing to work less and firms are willing to invest in fewer capital goods, then the economy has fewer factors of production. This means that the full employment level of output is reduced, and the aggregate supply curve shifts to the left. The supply-side policy to remedy this is to reduce the tax rates paid by labor and firms investing in capital goods, thus shifting the aggregate supply curve to the right and leading to an increase in full employment output and a reduction in inflation.

This relationship between taxes and incentives is often embodied in the Laffer curve. The **Laffer curve** is a curve depicting the relationship between tax rates and the tax revenue received by the government. A typical Laffer curve is presented in Figure 6.3.2. The horizontal axis mea-

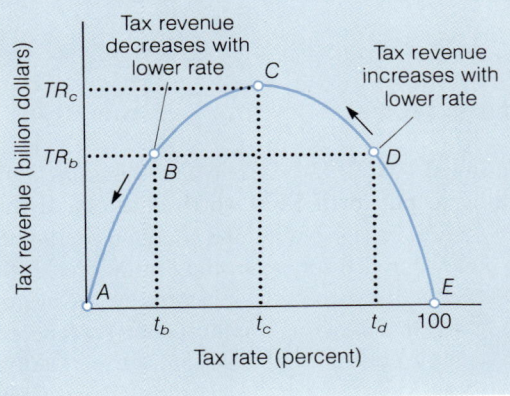

Figure 6.3.2

The Laffer Curve

The Laffer curve depicts the relationship between the tax rate and tax revenue received by the government. If the tax rate is zero percent, then no revenue is collected. If the tax rate is 100 percent, then no revenue is collected because people lose the incentive to work. Somewhere in between, at t_c, is the tax rate that brings in the most amount of tax revenue.

sures the tax rate, and the vertical axis the total tax revenue received by the government.

The shape of the Laffer curve reflects a fundamental principle about taxes. If the tax rate is zero, then the government collects no tax revenue, at point A. But if the tax rate is 100 percent, at point E, the government also collects no tax revenue because at that rate of taxation no one will work.

However, somewhere between a zero percent and 100 percent tax rate is the optimal tax rate, the rate that generates the highest amount of tax revenue. In Figure 6.3.2 this tax rate is t_c. If the tax rate is less than t_c, perhaps t_b, then the government can increase its revenue by *raising* the tax rate. But if the tax is greater than t_c, perhaps t_d, then the government can increase tax revenue by *lowering* the tax rate.

The reason for the changes in tax revenue is tied to incentives and the full employment level of output. At point D the tax rate is so high it is reducing incentives to produce goods and services. A reduction in the tax rate increases the incentives and leads to an increase in production. Greater production in turn leads to an increase in tax revenue because more economic activity is subject to that tax rate. According to this argument, a 25 percent reduction in tax revenue resulting from a decrease in the income tax rate would be offset by more than a 25 percent increase in revenue coming from the increase in income.

The main problem with this analysis is that no one is quite sure where we are on the Laffer curve. Those in favor of decreased taxes argue that we are to the right of point C; others argue that we are to the left of point C. While it is too early to tell for sure, the relative decline in tax revenue resulting from President Reagan's tax cut in the early 1980s would indicate that we are still to the left of point C.

Transfer Payments and Incentives

Supply-side policies also apply to transfer payments and their effects on incentives. As we see in Unit 11.5 transfer payments to the poor tend to reduce the incentive to work as welfare payments and benefits are typically reduced by close to 100 percent of any income earned. If someone has the choice between earning $5000 a year by working or receiving $5000 a year in transfer payments, it simply doesn't pay to work. This means fewer people are working, and less output is produced. Supply-side policies would eliminate the disincentives created by transfer payments by allowing recipients to keep a larger percentage of additional income.

Government Regulation

A third area of concern from the supply-side is government regulation. Here it is argued that government regulation, as discussed in Unit 12.4, leads to a reduction in output for a variety of reasons. Government regulation tends to increase the production costs of goods and services, reduces the productivity of factors, limits competition in an industry, and creates a multitude of different administrative inefficiencies, all of which affect the full employment level of output. The supply-side policy is therefore to reduce government regulation.

Although this argument has merit, note that most government regulations are established for specific reasons. That is, some regulations reduce environmental pollution, others protect the safety of workers, and still others protect the health and safety of consumers. While these regulations cost the economy in terms of lost output, they also provide benefits, though it is not clear whether the costs of regulation outweigh the benefits.

Other Supply-Side Policies

A final set of policies that deal with the supply-side of the economy should be noted, though they are not necessarily embraced by those who argue in favor of the conservative, supply-side policies of the Reagan administration.

As with the supply-side policies already discussed, these policies are concerned with the full employment level of output and the natural rate of unemployment. While the term *natural* is used to refer to this rate of unemployment, it does not mean that that rate cannot be changed. The natural rate of unemployment, as we saw earlier, is based on frictional and structural unemployment in the economy. Frictional unemployment can be reduced temporarily by increasing the real wage and thus the incentive to find a job. But frictional unemployment can also be reduced permanently by increasing the efficiency of the job market. In other words, increasing the availability of information to workers and firms helps match up workers to jobs and reduce frictional unemployment.

Structural unemployment can also be reduced, leading to a reduction in the natural rate of unemployment. Since structural unemployment represents the mismatching of workers' skills to the skills required by the job, the obvious policy is to retrain or reeducate workers or both. If changes in the structure of the economy means there are more computer programming jobs and fewer automobile assembly jobs, then some autoworkers should be retrained as computer programmers. Indeed, an increase in education typically leads to an increase in the quality of the labor force. And since labor is more productive, the full employment level of output is greater. Furthermore, education can also lead to technological achievements and thus increase the quality of other factors of production.

IN SUMMARY
Inflation Control Policies

- Contractionary fiscal and monetary policy is one approach for controlling inflation. However, since such policy operates on the aggregate demand curve, it is most effective for controlling demand-pull inflation. If the inflation is caused by shifts in the aggregate supply curve, then contractionary fiscal and monetary policy can reduce inflation only by sending the economy into a deep recession.

- An alternative approach for controlling inflation is to eliminate discretionary control of both fiscal and monetary policy. This involves a balanced budget to eliminate discretionary fiscal policy and a constant growth in the money supply to eliminate discretionary monetary policy. This approach is based on the proposition that inflation as well as unemployment and contractions of the businesss cycle is caused by discretionary policy. Therefore, the economy is stabilized by eliminating these discretionary actions.

- Wage and price controls/guidelines have been used in various forms on several occasions since the 1940s. They are controls if they are legally mandated and guidelines if they are voluntary. This approach to controlling inflation is usually ineffective. Since the controls/guidelines are temporary, firms and labor simply wait to raise prices and wages until the controls are lifted, so the control of inflation is only temporary at best. Moreover, this approach, like any price ceiling, creates inefficiencies and shortages throughout the economy.

- Indexing is a method of automatically adjusting nominal values to reflect changes in the price level. This is easily done for income taxes, wages, and transfer payments but less easily done for other nominal values. It is used to avoid the distribution effects caused by inflation rather than control inflation itself.

- Several supply-side policies recognize the importance of the aggregate supply curve in inflation. The main policies deal with taxes, transfer payments, and government regulations. In each case they are designed to increase incentives for the factors of production and thus lead to an increase in the supply of output. Other supply-side policies also include increasing factor qualities through education or reducing frictional unemployment through more efficient labor markets.

QUESTIONS FOR STUDY AND ANALYSIS

1. How long does the rate of inflation need to be at or near zero before you would expect no inflation in the coming year? Why?

2. Are Keynesians or monetarists more likely to recommend wage and price controls/guidelines? Why? Can wage and price controls/guidelines be used effectively to control inflation? If so, what must be taken into consideration when they are implemented?

3. Explain how indexing can be used to reduce inflationary expectations.

4. If inflation is caused by shifts in the aggregate demand curve, what is the best inflation control policy? Explain.

5. If inflation is caused by shifts in the aggregate supply curve, what is the best inflation control policy? Explain. Does your choice of policy change if the shift in the aggregate supply curve is caused by inflationary expectations as opposed to a change in the quantity, quality, or cost of a factor? Explain.

6. How effectively do you think demand-pull inflation can be controlled if the Keynesian aggregate expenditures are controlled but money supply is not? Explain.

REVIEW GLOSSARY

contractionary fiscal policy Fiscal policy consisting of decreases in government purchases and/or increases in net taxes (including decreases in transfer payments). Contractionary fiscal policy can effectively control demand-pull inflation but can create additional problems if inflation is caused by shifts in the aggregate supply curve.

contractionary monetary policy Monetary policy consisting of decreases in the money supply through the use of open market operations, reserve requirements, and the discount rate. Contractionary monetary policy can effectively control demand-pull inflation but can create additional problems if inflation is caused by shifts in the aggregate supply curve.

indexing The process of automatically adjusting nominal values to changes in the price level. Indexing tries to avoid the distribution effects described in Unit 3.5 rather than actually control inflation. Unfortunately, not all nominal values can be indexed, and indexing tends to build inflation into the economic system, making it difficult to eliminate with other policies.

Laffer curve A curve depicting the relationship between tax rates and tax revenue received by the government. The Laffer curve indicates that the government receives no tax revenue if the tax rate is either zero or 100 percent. If the rate is 100 percent, no one has the incentive to work, and thus there is nothing to tax. Somewhere between zero and 100 percent is the tax rate that generates the most tax revenue for the government.

supply-side economics A body of economic thought that emphasizes policies aimed at the aggregate supply side of the economy rather than the aggregate demand side. The most notable supply-side policies deal with incentives through reduction of tax rates, restructuring of transfer payments, or reduction of government regulation.

wage and price controls/guidelines Legally established (controls) or voluntary (guidelines) maximum limits on prices and wages. Whether the controls/guidelines are mandatory or voluntary, they lead to shortages of goods and services and a misallocation of resources. While they are politically more feasible than reducing the money supply or government spending or increasing taxes, they are also less effective.

SECTION INQUIRY

Inflation and Productivity

The stagflation of the 1970s was quite a shock, not only to the economy but also to the economics profession. Most economists did not think it was possible to have high rates of *both* inflation *and* unemployment at the same time. This led to a great deal of soul searching by economists as they tried to comprehend the supply side of the aggregate market. And, as might be expected with this soul searching, a number of potential causes for the stagflation were identified. One potential cause that continued to receive discussion into the 1980s was the productivity of labor.

Labor productivity, or the amount of output produced per unit of labor, has historically increased about 3 percent each year. While contractionary phases of the business cycle during the 1950s and 1960s occasionally saw productivity increase at only 1 to 2 percent per year, expansionary phases saw it increase more than 4 percent per year, making up for these relatively low rates. And during the two plus decades directly after World War II, productivity *never* declined. However, in 1969 and 1970 productivity increased by less than 1 percent. Furthermore, in 1974, 1979, 1980, and 1982 productivity actually declined. In 1974 workers produced less per hour than they did in 1973. In fact, between 1969 and 1985 productivity increased on average a little over 1 percent per year, reaching over 3 percent in only two of the seventeen years.

Some economists argue that the lack of growth in labor productivity contributed in large part to the high rates of inflation and unemployment during the 1970s. From the late 1940s through the 1960s, labor productivity increased 3 percent each year, leading to a 3 percent increase in the economy's ability to produce output. Very little inflation existed during this period because aggregate expenditures also increased at about 3 percent each year. However, buyers grew accustomed to buying 3 percent more output each year, and when productivity leveled off in the 1970s, aggregate expenditures did not, leading to higher prices and inflation. Several potential explanations exist for lower growth in productivity during the 1970s, including the price and availability of petroleum, reduced investment expenditures on capital goods, and high tax rates.

QUESTIONS FOR DISCUSSION

1. Using the aggregate market, demonstrate and discuss how a relatively smaller shift in the aggregate supply curve, caused by a decline in the relative growth of labor productivity, can lead to inflation.

2. Based on our discussion of the causes of inflation in Unit 6.1, determine which factor would most likely lead to a reduction in the growth of labor's productivity. Which do you think accounted for the reduction in labor productivity growth during the 1970s? Explain.

3. If the lack of growth in productivity was the main cause of inflation during the 1970s, which policy or policies would be most effective in controlling inflation? Explain. How effective would discretionary fiscal and monetary policies be in reducing this type of inflation?

4. If labor's productivity has increased by 3 percent per year for twenty-five years and consequently employers increased labor's real wage by 3 percent per year, what real wage will labor expect to receive in the following year? What is likely to happen if productivity increases by only 1 percent in the following year?

Growth Rates of Labor Productivity

Year	Percent Growth in Productivity
1948	4.2
1949	1.6
1950	8.1
1951	4.4
1952	3.0
1953	3.8
1954	1.7
1955	2.8
1956	0.7
1957	2.7
1958	3.2
1959	3.3
1960	1.7
1961	3.5
1962	3.6
1963	4.0
1964	4.3
1965	3.0
1966	2.8
1967	2.7
1968	2.7
Average: 1948–68	**3.2**
1969	0.1
1970	0.7
1971	3.2
1972	3.2
1973	2.0
1974	−2.1
1975	2.0
1976	2.8
1977	1.7
1978	0.8
1979	−1.2
1980	−0.3
1981	1.5
1982	−0.4
1983	2.6
1984	2.1
1985	0.3
Average: 1969–85	**1.1**

Source: *Economic Report of the President*, 1986.

PART III

Microeconomics: Output Markets

An economy is not a monolithic structure but is composed of many separate parts, like a forest that contains many trees and bushes of different sizes and shapes. While it is important to study the forest as a whole, each tree also has a story to tell. The same is true for an economy. Where our study of macroeconomics in Part II concentrated on the operation of the entire economy, our study in Part III of the microeconomy, or the individual parts, provides us with even more insight into the economy.

The study of microeconomics cannot begin without acknowledging the contributions of Alfred Marshall (1842–1924). If Adam Smith is the father of modern-day economics, then Alfred Marshall is the father of modern-day microeconomics. Marshall was trained in mathematics, which he applied to the study of economics. He was a professor at Cambridge University in England when his masterwork, *Principles of Economics,* was published in 1890. This book went through eight editions and served as the major textbook in economics for over thirty years.

However, *Principles of Economics* was not only a textbook; it also formed the cornerstone of the economics discipline. In this book Marshall developed a method of studying economics and analyzing economic problems that relied heavily on the use of diagrams, especially demand and supply curves, to represent economic principles. He also employed the concept of elasticity, *ceteris paribus* assumptions, and an understanding of the difference between long-run and short-run effects in the study of markets.

Part III of this text presents many of the basic ideas of microeconomics developed by Alfred Marshall and applies them to the study of output markets. In particular, we want to understand how output markets function. Output markets for goods and services are crucial to an economy because they are used to exchange most of the goods and services received by consumers. It is no understatement that this exchange constitutes the basic objective of an economic system. Thus, the study of microeconomics is intimately concerned with the efficient provision of goods and services to consumers.

However, the microeconomic study of output markets goes beyond the operation of the market. It also examines what lies behind that operation. In Section 2 we studied *how* the market operates, but we did not explain *why* it operates the way it does. Indeed, until now we have accepted the laws of demand and supply at face value. This is no longer necessary because the microeconomic study of output markets also is a study of the individual decisions by buyers and sellers that underlie the laws of supply and demand. In this way we can explain why higher prices induce buyers to demand less and sellers to supply more.

In fact, this study of individual decisions by buyers and sellers comprises the foundation of microeconomics, which essentially states that all activity in the economy is based on individual decisions. The total output in the economy depends on individual decisions by buyers concerning how much of which goods to buy and by sellers concerning how much of which goods to produce. In this sense our study of the economy is much like the study of the human body. Doctors can measure temperature, pulse, and rate of respiration to check a patient's health. However, only when doctors understand more about the parts of the human body for example, how a human cell functions, can they more effectively treat the patient. Likewise, an understanding of the operation of individual consumers, firms, and markets can help society increase the production of goods and improve the allocation of resources.

SECTION 7

A Closer Look at Demand

In Unit 2.2 the demand side of the market was introduced. The most important principle to emerge from our initial study of demand was the inverse relationship between price and quantity demanded, or the law of demand. The importance of the law of demand to economics in general and to our study of the economy in particular cannot be understated. Markets are formed by the combination of demand and supply, and they have the primary responsibility for allocating goods, services, and resources. Thus, an understanding of demand and of the law of demand is essential to a comprehension of the process of the economy's allocation.

In this section we look behind the law of demand to see why price and quantity demanded are inversely related. And since market demand consists of the combined demand of every buyer in the market, our starting point is the individual consumer. After all, an essential feature of demand in our market-oriented economy is the reliance on individual decisions.

Unit 7.1, Consumer Behavior, begins our in-depth examination of demand with a look at consumers. We see who they are and, more importantly, how they decide which goods to buy. In particular, this unit introduces the concept of utility underlying consumer behavior and demand and discusses how consumers choose between goods based on the additional utility provided.

Unit 7.2, Utility and Demand, takes the theory of consumer behavior introduced in Unit 7.1 one step further. In this unit the law of diminishing marginal utility is introduced, and we examine how it can be used to explain the inverse relationship between price and quantity demanded contained in the law of demand.

Unit 7.3, Indifference Curves and Demand, looks at the law of demand in a related but slightly different way. In Units 7.1 and 7.2 our discussion is centered around the hypothetical measurement of utility. However, in this unit we examine the indifference curve, which relies only on relative comparisons of utility and not on absolute measurements. But our conclusions that price and quantity demanded are inversely related is unchanged.

Unit 7.4, Applications of Consumer Demand, illustrates how the principles of consumer behavior can be used to explain and understand some recent events. We see how the relative price of diesel fuel affects the type of automobile purchased, why liquor industry sales have declined, why some people earn a lower interest rate on their savings, and how the price of a personal foul in college basketball can affect play. While this final example falls outside the realm of economics, it illustrates that the principles of consumer behavior introduced in this section really constitute principles of human behavior.

UNIT 7.1

Consumer Behavior

One of the essential features of a market and a market-oriented economy is the role of individual choice. This is particularly evident on the demand side of the market. The market demand for a good consists of the combined demand of every individual willing and able to buy the good. Each individual decides how much of the good to buy at each price, or whether to buy at all.

In this unit we examine what underlies an individual's decision to purchase a good by discussing three topics. First, we look at consumers, the individuals who make the decisions to buy the goods and services. Second, the concept of utility, on which decisions are based, is introduced. And third, applying the concept of utility, we look at how consumers choose between two goods.

The theory of consumer behavior introduced in this unit can help each of us understand our own behavior a little better. Although we are mainly concerned with the demand for goods and services, this theory can also be applied to other decisions, thereby making us better and more knowledgeable citizens as well as consumers.

THE CONSUMER

We begin our study of demand by looking at the consumer. A **consumer** is a person or household that purchases goods and services used for the satisfaction of wants and needs. In many cases consumers are individuals buying goods and services for their personal satisfaction, as when you buy an ice cream cone or a car. You are also a consumer if you purchase the good for someone else, as when you pay for a friend's ticket to a movie or buy your parents an anniversary present.

Note that in our definition the term *household* is synonymous with *consumer*. Many goods and services that are purchased by one member of a household are used to satisfy the wants and needs of other members in the household. For example, a family of four may have only one wage earner, but any food, clothing, shelter, and transportation is obtained for the entire household. And in this definition an individual merely comprises a one-person household.

However, just being an individual or a household as opposed to a business or a government does not necessarily make someone a consumer. What makes consumers unique is that the goods and services purchased are used to satisfy wants and needs. Although businesses buy goods and services, they do so in order to produce other goods and services. The same is true for governments, except that the types of goods and services provided are a little different and are not usually sold in markets. Any satisfaction of wants and needs resulting from purchases by businesses and governments, such as a business lunch or an army general's chauffeured limousine, is secondary.

UTILITY

Consumers buy a lot of different goods and services, and the types of goods and services purchased change over time. With the variety of goods and services available in the economy, how do consumers decide which ones to buy? To answer this, let's turn our attention to the concept of utility, which forms the basis for consumer choices.

Utility is the satisfaction of wants and needs obtained from the consumption of goods and services. Consumers purchase goods and services in order to satisfy wants and needs. For example, food is bought to satisfy hunger, and housing to provide protection from the weather. *Utility* is the term used in economics to identify the satisfaction received by people through the consumption of goods, though the terms *welfare*, *well-being*, and *happiness* convey the same meaning.

Keep in mind that utility is derived from the satisfaction of wants *and* needs. On the one hand, you may want an ice cream cone more than a polio vaccine, but you may need the polio vaccine more than you want the ice cream cone. In this case the utility gained from the polio vaccine is greater than the utility gained from the ice cream cone. On the other hand, utility is not based solely on the usefulness of a good. A hammer may be very useful, but on a hot summer day you may receive more utility from an ice cream cone. In short, the satisfaction of both wants and needs is important to utility.

Total Utility and Utility Maximization

Since utility is derived from the consumption of goods and services, it follows that the more goods that are consumed, the higher is the consumers' total utility. **Total utility** is the total level of satisfaction of wants and needs obtained from the consumption of goods and services.

In terms of consumer behavior, the idea is to obtain the highest possible level of utility. In economics we work under the assumption that consumers make choices that they expect will give them the most utility, or utility maximization. **Utility maximization** is the process of obtaining the highest level of utility through the consumption of goods and services.

While the assumption of utility maximization underlies our analysis of consumer behavior in the next three units, this assumption should be viewed as a motivating goal for consumers and not as a concrete law. Consumers do not necessarily maximize utility. In fact, consumers may never maximize utility. However, in terms of the theory of consumer behavior it is important only that they try to maximize utility. Obviously, given a choice, most people would rather have a higher level of utility. And when a consumer has a choice between two goods, the one providing the higher level of utility is chosen if possible.

Let's look at an example that illustrates total utility and utility maximization. While it is not possible to actually measure the level of utility a consumer derives from a good, for the sake of argument let's assume that we can. In Unit 7.3 we take a more realistic view of consumer behavior, one that does not require the measurement of utility. But for now, suppose that you are connected to a measuring device that determines the level of utility obtained from spending a day at the beach. Table 7.1.1 presents the hypothetical utility levels that might be obtained.

As expected, you receive no utility if no time is spent at the beach. If you spend one hour, you obtain a total utility of 10; if you spend two hours, you obtain a total utility of 18. Total utility continues to increase until five hours are spent at the beach. If you spend six or more hours at the beach, your level of utility actually declines because the wind, sand, and sun eventually take their toll. Therefore, given a choice, you would spend five hours at the beach since this provides you with a utility level of 30, the highest possible level. If you spend any more or less time at the beach, your utility level is lower.

Constrained Utility Maximization

Constrained utility maximization is the process of obtaining the highest possible level of utility under the given circumstances when the highest overall level of utility cannot be reached. In some cases you may not be able to spend the amount of time that generates the highest level of utility. For example, the beach may close after four hours, preventing you from reaching your utility-maximizing number of hours. Or you may be with a friend who wants to stay only two hours, or perhaps eight hours. If your friend is driving, you may have no choice in the matter.

There is another, more important, reason why you may not be able to spend five hours at the beach and maximize utility. If there is a charge for each hour spent at the beach, then you may not be able to buy five hours because of limited income. For example, if the beach charges $2 per hour and you have only $6 of income to spend, then you are prevented from staying longer than three hours. Indeed, the combination of price and income is crucial in our study of consumer behavior and demand.

Note that whether you are constrained by price and income or by the actions of a friend, you still attempt to maximize utility. You may not be able to spend five hours at the beach, but you will try to obtain the most utility under the circumstances. If the beach closes after four hours, then you will stay all four hours rather than leaving after two. Or if price and income prevent you from buying five hours of beach time, then you buy three hours rather than only one or two.

Most of the time, consumers are faced with price and income constraints. Very seldom is someone able to consume as much of a good as they

Table 7.1.1
Hypothetical Utility of a Trip to the Beach

Utility is the satisfaction derived from the consumption of goods and services. Here, utility increases for the first five hours on the beach but declines after that. Thus, utility can be maximized by spending five hours at the beach.

Hours at the Beach	Total Utility
0	0
1	10
2	18
3	24
4	28
5	30
6	28
7	24
8	18

want, which simply represents an expression of the economic problem of scarcity discussed in Unit 1.2, and which suggests that consumers, like economies, have to make choices. If people cannot have all that they want, they have to decide what they want most. This is why the study of utility is so important—it tells us how much a good is worth to a buyer.

Marginal Utility

Although total utility is very informative, a more useful concept for an economist is marginal utility. **Marginal utility** is the additional utility derived from consuming an additional unit of a good. Marginal utility is specified as

$$\text{marginal utility} = \frac{\text{change in total utility}}{\text{change in quantity}}$$

Notice in Table 7.1.2 that your first hour at the beach gives you 10 units of utility. Utility is zero if no time is spent at the beach, and it increases to 10 with the first hour, meaning the marginal utility obtained from that first hour is 10. Spending a second hour at the beach raises total utility to 18 units, but the additional utility derived from the second hour by itself is only 8. The utility attributable to each additional hour spent at the beach is listed in the third column in Table 7.1.2.

Marginal utility provides very useful information, because it indicates what each additional unit is worth. If the third hour provides you with 6 units of utility, this is its value to you. If you are given a choice between spending the hour at the beach or consuming some other good, you stay at the beach unless the marginal utility of the other good is equal to or greater than 6 units (assuming the price is the same for both).

In this way utility forms the basis for consumer choices. Consumers weigh the additional utility that can be obtained from one good against that obtained from another good. But consumers also decide how much of a good to purchase based not only on the price of the good but also on their willingness to buy it.

Table 7.1.2

Hypothetical Marginal Utility of a Trip to the Beach

Marginal utility is the additional utility obtained from an additional unit of a good. In fact, marginal utility indicates what each good is worth to the consumer. Here, the first hour at the beach provides 10 units of utility, the second hour 8 units, and so on. A consumer decides how much of a good to consume by comparing its marginal utility with its price and the marginal utility of other goods.

Hours at the Beach	Total Utility	Marginal Utility
0	0	
1	10	10
2	18	8
3	24	6
4	28	4
5	30	2
6	28	−2
7	24	−4
8	18	−6

THE CHOICE BETWEEN TWO GOODS

To see how consumers decide which goods to purchase, let's set up a simple example. Suppose you have $20 of income to spend on entertainment for the month, and the entertainment goods available are movies and basketball games. Table 7.1.3 lists the total and marginal utility that you might derive from both goods. The price per movie is $4 and the price per basketball game is $2. How many movies and how many basketball games will you buy?

The answer is easy if you have an unlimited amount of income, which in this case is anything

Table 7.1.3

Hypothetical Utility of Movies and Basketball Games

If the price of a movie is $4 and the price of a basketball game is $2, the consumer spends $20 of income by going to three movies and four basketball games. With this combination of goods, the last dollar spent on each good generates the same marginal utility. This combination provides the highest possible level of utility that can be obtained with $20.

Movies	Total Utility (TU)	Marginal Utility (MU)	MU/P (P = $4)	Basketball Games	Total Utility (TU)	Marginal Utility (MU)	MU/P (P = $2)
0	0			0	0		
		20	5			12	6
1	20			1	12		
		16	4			10	5
2	36			2	22		
		12	3			8	4
3	48			3	30		
		8	2			6	3
4	56			4	36		
		4	1			4	2
5	60			5	40		
		−4	−1			2	1
6	56			6	42		
						−2	−1
				7	40		

over $38. With $38 or more, utility can be maximized at 102 by going to five movies (a utility of 60) and six basketball games (a utility of 42). In fact, with $38, you can even go to six movies and seven basketball games. However, this combination actually provides a total utility of only 96 (56 + 40).

However, since you have a limited amount of income, $20, it is not possible to go to five basketball games and six movies. If you decide to spend all $20 on movies, then you can go to five movies at $4 each. Alternatively, if you decide to go to basketball games instead, you can attend ten games at $2 each. But because utility declines with the seventh game (the team is in last place), there is no reason to go to more than six games, spending $12 and leaving $8 for two movies.

Let's look closely at these two alternatives. If you go to five movies and no basketball games, you receive 60 units of utility, whereas with six basketball games and two movies you receive 78 units of utility (42 + 36). But are there other options that provide more than 78 units of utility?

Suppose you decide to go to three movies instead of two. To do this you need an extra $4, so you give up two basketball games. If four basketball games and three movies are selected, this option provides 84 units of utility (36 + 48), which is the best of the three alternatives so far.

Can you obtain a greater level of utility with your $20? If four movies rather than three are selected, then you can go to only two basketball games, and total utility is 78 (56 + 22). In fact, it is not possible to spend $20 on any combination of movies and basketball games that provides more than the 84 units of utility derived from four games and three movies. Therefore, you have reached a constrained utility maximization.

We can also see why you can do no better by looking at the marginal utility received from each good. The third movie provides 12 units of additional utility. The fourth basketball game provides 6 units of additional utility. But remember, movies are twice as expensive as basketball games. If twice as much income is spent on a good, then it should provide twice as much utility. If we divide the marginal utility of each good by its price, we obtain the numbers listed in the fourth and eighth columns in Table 7.1.3. For the third movie you receive 3 units of utility for each dollar spent, and for the fourth basketball game you also receive 3 units of utility for each dollar spent.

Suppose you did *not* receive the same marginal utility for the last dollar spent on each good. In this case expenditures can be altered to increase your utility. For example, let's say you go to two movies and six games. Four units of utility are received for the last dollar spent on the second movie and 1 unit of utility is received for the last dollar spent on the sixth basketball game. Since movies are providing more marginal utility than basketball games, you are better off going to more movies and fewer games.

With the utility maximization combination of movies and basketball games, a consumer *cannot* trade one good for the other and be any better off. This is **consumer equilibrium,** which exists when the last dollar spent on each good provides the same additional utility. This illustrates an important relationship, the **rule of consumer equilibrium,** which states that the ratio of marginal utility to price is the same for all goods. This rule is specified as

$$\frac{\text{marginal utility of good 1}}{\text{price of good 1}} = \frac{\text{marginal utility of good 2}}{\text{price of good 1}}$$

This states that a consumer has allocated expenditures to receive the highest possible utility. Although we have only dealt with two goods, this relationship holds for any number of goods. A consumer maximizes utility when the marginal utility per dollar spent is the same for all goods.

This approach to consumer behavior is designed to give us insight into the choices made by consumers. However, it doesn't mean that consumers sit down with paper and pencil and perform the types of calculations involved in Table 7.1.3 before they purchase any goods. But consumers do consider the three factors discussed here—the satisfaction received from goods, the price of the goods, and available income.

For example, when you walk up to a candy machine with enough money for only one candy bar, you have to make this type of choice. You may not think about the marginal utility, but you probably consider whether you feel more like eating a Snickers bar or a Hershey bar. Or if you shop for an automobile, you probably compare the quality of one car with another in terms of appearance, performance, fuel economy, and "rightness" for you. But comparisons of quality are not made without regard to the price and the amount of available income. One car may be twice as good as another, but you probably won't buy it if it costs more than twice as much.

We even make these types of choices in areas that would be considered outside the realm of typical economic activity (outside of market transactions). We vote for political candidates that we think will do the best job, which usually means they reflect our own philosophy and interests. We make choices between grades, work, recreation, and any number of other activities based on the benefits provided by each, together with what each will cost in terms of time and effort. In short, the decision-making process of consumers is fundamentally the same as that of voters at the polls or students in a classroom. Consumers are people too.

IN SUMMARY

Consumer Behavior

- The demand for goods and services is based on the individual decisions of consumers. A consumer is a person or household that purchases goods and services for the satisfaction of wants and needs. It is important to know how the consumer behaves in order to understand what lies behind the demand for goods and services.

- Utility is the degree of satisfaction received from the consumption of goods and services. Two important concepts are total utility, which is the total level of satisfaction received, and utility maximization, the process by which the consumer tries to obtain the highest possible level of utility. However, in many cases consumers are faced with a constrained utility maximization, in which the highest possible level of utility cannot be achieved. A third important concept relating to consumer behavior is marginal utility, which is the additional satisfaction received from consuming an additional unit of a good or service.

- Consumer equilibrium is reached when the last dollar spent on each good provides the same marginal utility. This is demonstrated by the rule of consumer equilibrium, which states that consumers equate the ratio of marginal utility and price for all goods. If this rule is satisfied, the consumer cannot achieve a higher level of utility with the given level of income and has reached the point of utility maximization.

QUESTIONS FOR STUDY AND ANALYSIS

1. Discuss whether each of the following acts is performed by a consumer or some other participant in the economy, such as government or business.
   a. Your instructor buys a notebook from the university bookstore to prepare class lectures.
   b. You buy a notebook from the university bookstore to take class notes.
   c. Your instructor buys lunch from the university cafeteria after class is over.
   d. A prospective employer, on campus for interviews, takes you to lunch at the university cafeteria.
   e. Your instructor, who is an old friend of your prospective employer, buys her a T-shirt with the university logo on it from the university bookstore.
   f. Your prospective employer gives your instructor a sample of her company's product, which happens to be an IBM personal computer.

2. For each of the following pairs of goods, indicate which of the two goods gives you the most utility, and why.
   a. A softball bat or a pair of dancer's tights
   b. A hot fudge sundae or a screwdriver
   c. A roll of 35mm camera film or a Cabbage Patch doll
   d. A Space Invaders video game cartridge or a biology textbook
   e. A year's subscription to *Time* magazine or a ticket to a Rolling Stones concert
   f. A three-piece pin-striped suit or a party with your five closest friends

3. Suppose you are given the following utility information for two goods:

A	Total Utility	B	Total Utility
0	0	0	0
1	10	1	20
2	18	2	36
3	24	3	48
4	28	4	56
5	30	5	60
6	30	6	60

   a. Compute the marginal utility for each good.
   b. If each good sells for $1, how many units of each would you buy if you had $6 of income? What if you had $9 of income? What if you had $20 of income?
   c. Based on your purchases with $6 of income, what is the ratio of the marginal utility of good A to its price? What is the ratio of the marginal utility of good B to its price?
   d. If income is $6, and the price of good B increases to $2 while the price of good A remains

at $1, how would you allocate your expenditures?

4. In the 1984 Olympics, Carl Lewis won four gold medals in track and field events, equaling the record set by Jesse Owens in 1936. However, in his quest for four gold medals he drew a great deal of criticism from sporting fans and the media. After easily winning his first gold medal in the 100-meter sprint, and knowing that he still had two events left in the following days, he sought to win his second gold medal in the long jump. In winning the long jump, he took only two out of a possible seven jumps. His first jump, which won the competition, was a foot farther than the second place finisher. His explanation for taking only two jumps was to conserve his energy for the remaining two events.

a. Based on the theory of consumer behavior, do you think Carl Lewis was maximizing utility by taking only two jumps? What would have been the marginal utility of a third or fourth jump, knowing that he had essentially won the gold on the first jump?

b. If another competitor had jumped farther, midway through the competition, do you think he would have taken any of his remaining jumps?

c. Now let's compound the story a little more. The world record in the long jump at this time was set in 1968. Carl Lewis was the only jumper to have come within a foot of the mark after it was set, and his best jump was about four inches short of the record. Many people felt that the Olympics was the best time for him to try to break this long-standing record. Based on this, do you think he was maximizing utility by taking only two jumps? Explain.

REVIEW GLOSSARY

constrained utility maximization The process of obtaining the highest possible level of utility under the given circumstances when the highest overall level of utility cannot be reached.

consumer A person or household that purchases goods and services used for the satisfaction of wants and needs.

consumer equilibrium The condition that exists when the last dollar spent on each good provides the same additional utility. In consumer equilibrium, consumers allocate their income between the purchase of different goods such that they cannot increase their level of utility. With consumer equilibrium a consumer has maximized utility.

marginal utility The additional utility obtained from the consumption of an additional unit of a good. It is specified as the change in total utility divided by the change in quantity. Marginal utility tells us what each additional unit of a good is worth to a consumer.

rule of consumer equilibrium The rule that states that the ratio of marginal utility to price is the same for all goods.

total utility The total satisfaction of wants and needs obtained from the consumption of goods and services.

utility The satisfaction of wants and needs obtained from the consumption of goods and services.

utility maximization The process of obtaining the highest level of utility from the consumption of goods and services.

UNIT 7.2

Utility and Demand

Demand is based on consumers' willingness and ability to buy goods and services. Our initial look at demand in Unit 2.2 indicated that price is the most important factor affecting demand. And the relationship between price and quantity demanded—the law of demand—is embodied in the demand curve. In this unit we want to see why the quantity demanded of a good is inversely related to the price, and why this relationship holds. Indeed, the law of the demand comprises one of the fundamental principles of economics, a principle upon which our understanding of markets, market-oriented economies, and allocation is based.

First, this unit builds on the theory of consumer behavior introduced in the previous unit. By applying the utility approach to consumer decisions, we examine how a change in the price of a good affects the quantity that a consumer is willing and able to buy. Our extension of the utility approach begins with the law of diminishing marginal utility, which helps illuminate the law of demand. We then look at a simple example illustrating why a consumer changes the quantity of a good purchased if the price changes. And finally, we look at two applications of utility and demand, consumer surplus and the diamond/water paradox.

THE LAW OF DIMINISHING MARGINAL UTILITY

The **law of diminishing marginal utility** is a principle stating that as more and more of a good is consumed, eventually each additional unit of the good provides less and less additional utility. Recall the example of the day spent at the beach in Unit 7.1. Table 7.2.1 reproduces the total and marginal utility obtained from spending up to seven hours at the beach. In this table we are concerned with the relationship between the number of hours spent at the beach and the marginal utility.

The first hour provides 10 units of utility, the second provides 8 units, the third provides 6 units, and so on. Note that each additional hour at the beach provides less additional utility because of the law of diminishing marginal utility.

But why does this law hold? In short, the fifth hour adds only 2 units of utility, while the first hour adds 10 units, because you have already spent four hours at the beach. Marginal utility declines as you slowly become satiated with the beach. After swimming, suntanning, playing volleyball, and so on, you become hot and tired, and you begin to run out of things to do.

Table 7.2.1

Hypothetical Marginal Utility of a Trip to the Beach

The law of diminishing marginal utility indicates that marginal utility declines as more of a good is consumed. While the first hour at the beach provides 10 units of utility, the second hour provides only 8, the third provides 6, and so on. Eventually, if enough of the good is consumed, marginal utility can even become negative, as in the sixth, seventh, and eighth hours.

Hours at the Beach	Total Utility	Marginal Utility
0	0	
1	10	10
2	18	8
3	24	6
4	28	4
5	30	2
6	28	−2
7	24	−4
8	18	−6

UNIT 7.2 • UTILITY AND DEMAND

The law of diminishing marginal utility can be seen in the consumption of almost any type of food. Is the fifth slice of pizza, the fourth cheeseburger, or the eighth chicken drumstick as tasty as the first? The law is also seen in the consumption of nonfood goods. If you own seven pairs of slacks or jeans, each probably provides nearly equal utility, since a different pair can be worn each day of the week. But the eighth and ninth pairs probably provide less utility than the other seven. And would the second Mercedes-Benz provide as much additional utility as the first?

The law of diminishing marginal utility also suggests why so many fads pass from the scene so quickly. Just in recent years, disco, Star Wars, breakdancing, Cabbage Patch dolls, and the careers of any number of aspiring entertainers have followed this pattern of diminishing marginal utility.

When fads begin, they have limited exposure, and what little is seen provides relatively high marginal utility. But as a fad becomes more widespread and exposure to it increases, its marginal utility declines. That's why in the late 1970s, after two years of disco dancing, disco clothes, and disco movies, people began to organize "Death to Disco" campaigns. By this time the marginal utility was apparently negative for many people.

Furthermore, when a fad has had an abundance of exposure, and its marginal utility is extremely low, society is ready for a new fad. And a new fad can easily grip the entire country because, when that fad is first introduced, it has limited exposure, and its marginal utility is relatively high compared to the old fad.

UTILITY AND THE LAW OF DEMAND

The concept of utility can also help explain why price and quantity demanded are inversely related. Table 7.2.2 presents the total and marginal utilities for two goods, movies and basketball games, that

Table 7.2.2

The Effect of Price on the Demand for Movies and Basketball Games

If the price of a movie declines from $4 to $2 and the price of a basketball game and the level of income do not change, the consumer increases the number of movies attended from three to five. The lower price leads to an increase in the quantity of movies demanded.

Movies	Total Utility (TU)	Marginal Utility (MU)	MU/P (P = $4)	MU/P (P = $2)	Basketball Games	Total Utility (TU)	Marginal Utility (MU)	MU/P (P = $2)
0	0				0	0		
		20	5	10			12	6
1	20				1	12		
		16	4	8			10	5
2	36				2	22		
		12	3	6			8	4
3	48				3	30		
		8	2	4			6	3
4	56				4	36		
		4	1	2			4	2
5	60				5	40		
		−4	−1	−2			2	1
6	56				6	42		
							−2	−1
					7	40		

are purchased with $20 of income. If the price of a movie is $4 and the price of a basketball game is $2, consumer equilibrium is achieved by going to three movies and four basketball games, as discussed in the previous unit.

But suppose that the price of a movie declines from $4 to $2. What happens to the consumer equilibrium, and more importantly, what happens to the quantity of movies demanded? To answer this, you need to know the marginal utility received for the last dollar spent on each good. Before the price change, you received three units of utility for the last dollar spent on each good. But now that the price of a movie has declined, you receive twice as much utility for the last dollar spent on the third movie.

The fifth column of Table 7.2.2 lists the ratio of marginal utilities to the price of movies when the price is $2. Since the price is half as much, the ratio in column five is twice the ratio in column four. Based on the rule of consumer equilibrium, you maximize utility by going to five movies and five basketball games. If this choice is made, the marginal utility–price ratio for both goods is 2, the entire $20 is spent, and a higher level of utility cannot be reached.

How has the change in the price of movies affected the quantity of movies demanded? At $4 you chose three movies, but at $2 you chose five movies. The decrease in the price leads to an increase in the quantity of movies demanded. Keep in mind that throughout this analysis only the price of movies has changed, and not income or the price of the other good, basketball games. Recall that prices of other goods and income constitute two of the five determinants of demand discussed in Unit 2.2. The other three determinants also remained unchanged. Tastes and preferences, and expectations, which are reflected in the marginal utilities of the goods, remained unchanged. And of course the number of buyers has not changed since we are only concerned with the single buyer. Thus, we have identified the basic law of demand. Holding other factors unchanged, the quantity demanded has increased due to a decline in the price.

Indeed, the law of demand can be explained by the law of diminishing marginal utility. A lower price enables a consumer to buy additional units of a good that provide relatively less marginal utility. If the price does not fall, the consumer has no desire to buy the extra units. And if the price rises, the consumer has to give up units of a good that do not provide sufficient utility. But note that while the law of diminishing marginal utility is sufficient to explain the law of demand, it is not necessary, as we see in Unit 7.3.

INCOME AND SUBSTITUTION EFFECTS

The utility approach to demand indicates the two ways a change in price can affect the quantity demanded, the income effect and the substitution effect. The **income effect** is a change in quantity demanded that results because a change in price gives the buyer more real income, even though money income remains unchanged. If the price of a good decreases, a buyer can purchase the same quantity and spend less, leaving additional income for the purchase of this good, or even other goods. For a normal good, a larger quantity is purchased, and for an inferior good, a smaller quantity is purchased. However, the income effect of an inferior good is almost always outweighed by the substitution effect.

The **substitution effect** is a change in quantity demanded that results because the price of the good changes relative to the prices of other goods. A lower price makes the good cheaper relative to other goods. Consumers tend to purchase more of the lower-priced good and less of other goods. If the price of steak decreases relative to the price of chicken, consumers are likely to substitute steak for chicken. This is the substitution effect, and unlike the income effect, a price decrease *always* leads to an increase in the quantity demanded.

The income and substitution effects reinforce each other for normal goods because a lower price increases real income and makes the good relatively cheaper. This is stated in the inverse relationship between price and quantity found in the law of demand. However, the income effect of an inferior good works in the opposite direction of the substitution effect, because an increase in income causes a decrease in the demand for an inferior good. Inferior goods are rare, and it is even rarer that the income effect of an inferior good is enough to offset the substitution effect.

Let's return to our example of the demand for movies. When the price of movies is cut in half, the marginal utility–price ratio for movies doubles, which means it is not equal to the unchanged marginal utility–price ratio for basketball games. One way to reestablish equality is to reduce the marginal utility of movies, which can be accomplished by going to more movies. And since the price has declined, real income has increased, and it *is* possible to go to more movies without affecting the number of basketball games that can be attended, even though you still have only $20. Going to more movies to bring the marginal utility–price ratio to its original level is the result of the income effect.

However, the marginal utility–price ratios can also be equalized by increasing the marginal utility of the other good. This is accomplished here by going to fewer basketball games and letting the law of diminishing marginal utility work in the other direction. But if fewer games are attended, some additional income is available for more movies. Thus, a decision to go to fewer basketball games and more movies is the result of the substitution effect.

CONSUMER SURPLUS

The relationship between marginal utility and demand helps us understand the concept of consumer surplus. **Consumer surplus is the difference between the price buyers are willing to pay for a good (based on the marginal utility received) and the actual price paid.** Consumer surplus occurs when buyers pay a single price for each quantity consumed, yet receive different amounts of utility. Figure 7.2.1, which displays a typical demand curve, illustrates how this works. Each point along the demand curve reflects the price a consumer is willing and able to pay for the corresponding quantity. However, the price is merely a reflection of the relative marginal utility received from each unit of the good.

Suppose the market price for the good is $6, and the consumer buys 10 units. The consumer does not buy an eleventh unit because it does not provide $6 worth of additional utility. However, the first 10 units provide *at least* $6 worth of additional utility, and the tenth unit provides *exactly* $6 worth of utility. Although the consumer is willing to pay more than $6 for each of the first nine units, which all provide more than $6 worth of utility, the consumer pays $6 for all 10 units, since that is the market price. The difference between what the consumer is willing to pay for each unit of the good and the actual price paid is the consumer surplus.

While the consumer is willing to pay $15 for the first good purchased, it is purchased for $6, for a difference of $9. Thus, the consumer comes out ahead. The second unit is valued by the consumer at $14, but again is purchased for $6, giving the consumer a surplus of $8. If we add the surpluses gained on each unit purchased, we have the total surplus received by the consumer. In general, consumers' surplus is seen as the entire area beneath the demand curve and above the price.

DIAMOND/WATER PARADOX

Consumer surplus can shed light on what has been called the **diamond/water paradox, which is based on the observation that water, which is more useful than diamonds, has a lower price.** This apparent paradox illustrates the difference between marginal and total utility. In spite of water's importance to life on this planet, its price is relatively low. But diamonds, which provide only limited utility, are quite expensive. Because life could exist without diamonds, but not without water, it seems para-

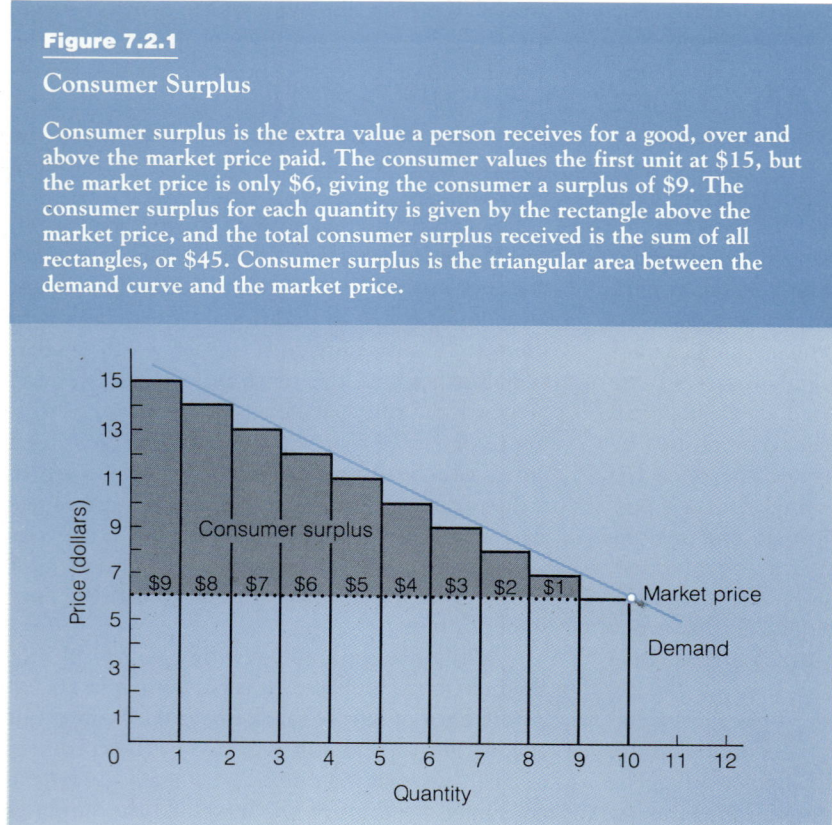

Figure 7.2.1

Consumer Surplus

Consumer surplus is the extra value a person receives for a good, over and above the market price paid. The consumer values the first unit at $15, but the market price is only $6, giving the consumer a surplus of $9. The consumer surplus for each quantity is given by the rectangle above the market price, and the total consumer surplus received is the sum of all rectangles, or $45. Consumer surplus is the triangular area between the demand curve and the market price.

doxical that water is so much cheaper than diamonds.

This apparent paradox can be resolved by looking at the difference between marginal and total utility. Clearly, water provides more total utility. Considering that three-fourths of the human body is water, the *total* utility provided to over 5 billion people is enormous, especially when compared to the *total* utility provided by diamonds.

But can the same be said about the relative *marginal* utility of water and diamonds? Note that because of the availability of water, and thus the amount consumed, an extra glass provides very little marginal utility. Indeed, the law of diminishing marginal utility is operating full force with water.

But diamonds are much less available than water, so the law of diminishing marginal utility has a much smaller effect. In short, people are willing to pay more for diamonds than water because diamonds provide a greater marginal utility.

Figure 7.2.2 presents demand curves for diamonds and water. The demand curve for diamonds is very close to the axes, indicating limited demand, and the market price is quite high, indicating a limited supply. The demand curve for water lies far away from the axes, indicating widespread use and overall importance to life. However, the tremendous supply of water keeps the price very low.

Note also that for diamonds the consumer surplus is very small, as indicated by the shaded area

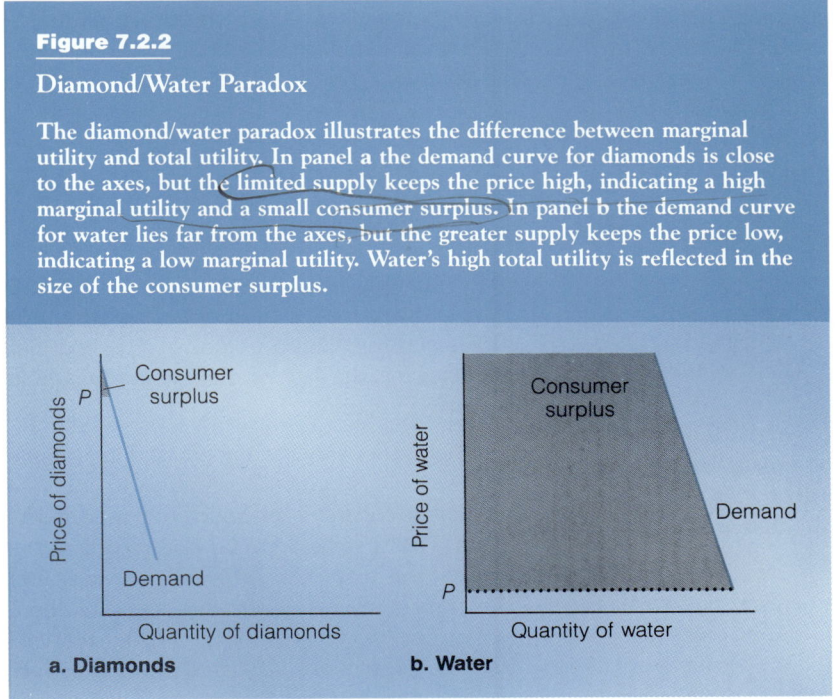

Figure 7.2.2

Diamond/Water Paradox

The diamond/water paradox illustrates the difference between marginal utility and total utility. In panel a the demand curve for diamonds is close to the axes, but the limited supply keeps the price high, indicating a high marginal utility and a small consumer surplus. In panel b the demand curve for water lies far from the axes, but the greater supply keeps the price low, indicating a low marginal utility. Water's high total utility is reflected in the size of the consumer surplus.

above the price in panel a. Water, however, has an enormous consumer surplus, as indicated by the shaded area in panel b. The consumer surplus for each good depends on total utility, whereas the price reflects the marginal utility of the last unit consumed. The price of water is low not because of its total utility but because the available supply lets people consume enough to decrease the marginal utility.

To illustrate this, consider two alternatives. First, suppose you live in a typical suburban house connected to a municipal water supply that is both abundant and inexpensive. How much water would you trade for a one-carat diamond? Ten gallons? A hundred gallons? A thousand gallons? Keep in mind that a hundred gallons is the equivalent of a long, soothing shower. Are you willing to give up a shower in exchange for a one-carat diamond?

Second, suppose you are stranded in the middle of an African desert, carrying a backpack full of diamonds, but no water. How many of those diamonds would you give up for a glass of water? A backpack full of diamonds probably satisfies the wants and needs of almost anyone walking through a hot desert. The marginal utility of the last diamond is very small (if not negative due to the extra weight). However, with no water, the marginal utility of one glass is very high.

The diamond/water paradox illustrates a fundamental lesson of economics. The market price of a good depends on the marginal utility received by consumers. Consumers buy a good if it provides a degree of satisfaction that is at least as much as the price paid. And the last unit sold in the market provides the last consumer with a marginal utility that is the same as the price of the good. However, demand, and thus marginal utility, comprises only one side of the market, because marginal utility alone does not determine the price of a good. Remember that price is determined jointly by demand and supply. In Section 8, A Closer Look at Supply, we examine what lies behind supply, which, together with marginal utility, determines the market price of a good.

IN SUMMARY
Utility and Demand

- The law of diminishing marginal utility states that as more of a good is consumed, each additional unit provides less utility than the previous unit. In other words, marginal utility decreases as quantity increases.

- The negative slope of the demand curve can be explained by the law of diminishing marginal utility. Lower prices induce consumers to purchase additional units, which provide less marginal utility. Through the income and substitution effects, consumers demand larger quantities at lower prices.

- Consumer surplus is a measure of the additional utility received by consumers over and above the price paid for the good. Although consumers pay the same price for the first good purchased as the last, the marginal utility of the first good is greater than that of the last because of the law of diminishing marginal utility. Consumer surplus is seen on the demand curve as the area between the demand curve and the market price.

- The difference between marginal and total utility is illustrated by the diamond/water paradox. Water has a high level of total utility, but water's availability makes its marginal utility, and market price, relatively low. Diamonds have a low level of total utility, but their limited supply makes the marginal utility of an additional diamond quite high. This reflects the extent to which the law of diminishing marginal utility affects water, but not diamonds.

QUESTIONS FOR STUDY AND ANALYSIS

1. How many pieces of pizza can you eat before you know the law of diminishing marginal utility is working? Can you think of any goods not affected by the law of diminishing marginal utility? Explain.

2. A high school in Richmond, Indiana, came up with an economic incentive to increase school attendance. It decided to pay each student with a perfect attendance record at the end of the year $100. With no reward in the previous year, only 37 students attended school every day. However, with the $100 incentive, 200 of the school's 1700 students had perfect attendance records. In addition, overall attendance in the school was up from 92 to 95 percent, and 22 students who had failed classes because of poor attendance before the incentives were offered did not miss a day of classes after.
   a. Explain how this incentive affected the rule of consumer equilibrium for the two goods, attending school and not attending school.
   b. What happened to the price of not attending school after the $100 incentive was established?
   c. What happened to the demand for not attending school after the $100 incentive was established?
   d. Due to the success of this program, which increased attendance more than expected, the school decided to offer jobs with local merchants, rather than cash payments, the following year. How do you think this affected the rule of consumer equilibrium? What do you think happened to attendance in the following year?

UNIT 7.2 • UTILITY AND DEMAND

3. Suppose you are given the following utility information for two goods:

A	Total Utility	B	Total Utility
1	120	1	200
2	220	2	360
3	300	3	480
4	360	4	560
5	400	5	600
6	420		

a. If each good sells for $20, how many units of each would you buy to maximize utility if you had $200 of income?

b. Now suppose that the price of good B increases to $40, while the price of good A remains at $20. In this case, if you still have $200 of income, how many units of each good would you buy? How has the increase in the price of good B affected the quantity of good B demanded?

c. What happens to the quantity of good A when the price of good B increases? What has happened to the relative prices of A and B? What has happened to real income after the price of good B increases? Would you say that good A is a normal or inferior good?

4. Assume that the demand curve is specified as

$$Q_d = 10 - 2P$$

where Q_d is the quantity demanded and P is the price. If the market price is $2, what is the consumers' surplus of the last unit purchased? If the market price increases to $3, what is the consumers' surplus of the last unit purchased? Would you expect consumers' surplus to be more or less at a higher price? Explain.

REVIEW GLOSSARY

consumer surplus The difference between the price buyers are willing to pay for a good (based on the marginal utility received) and the actual price paid. For a typical demand curve, consumer surplus can be seen as the triangular area between the market price and the demand curve.

diamond/water paradox This apparent paradox is based on the observation that water, which is much more useful than diamonds, has a lower price. If price is related to utility, how can this occur? The paradox is cleared up by an understanding of marginal utility. Water provides a greater amount of total utility, but the vast supplies of water available make its marginal utility quite low. Diamonds provide much less total utility, but the limited supplies keep the marginal utility, and the price, very high.

income effect The change in quantity demanded that results because a change in price gives a buyer more real income, even though money income remains unchanged. The change in real income can affect the quantity demanded of the good experiencing the price change in one of two ways. For a normal good the income effect causes quantity demanded to move in the opposite direction of the price. For an inferior good the income effect causes the quantity demanded to move in the same direction as price.

law of diminishing marginal utility A principle stating that as more of a good is consumed, eventually each additional unit of the good provides less additional utility. That is, marginal utility begins to decrease. Although marginal utility is still positive, each subsequent unit is valued less than the previous one. The law of marginal utility helps explain the negative slope of the demand curve.

substitution effect The change in quantity demanded that results because the price of the good changes relative to the prices of other goods. A price decline makes the good relatively more attractive, inducing consumers to substitute this good for other goods. The substitution effect always causes quantity demanded and price to move in opposite directions.

UNIT 7.3

Indifference Curves and Demand

In Unit 7.2 we looked at a simple explanation for the law of demand based on the law of diminishing marginal utility. Unfortunately, that analysis contained a basic flaw—that it is possible to measure the absolute level of a person's utility. However, we can also explain the law of demand without using such an unrealistic assumption. In this unit an alternative, and slightly more sophisticated, method of looking at the demand curve is presented.

More specifically, this analysis is based on two dimensions of demand, the *willingness* of consumers to purchase goods and services, which is embodied in indifference curves, and the *ability* of consumers to purchase goods and services, which is reflected in the budget line. After discussing each dimension of demand, we combine the indifference curves with the budget line. This allows us to graphically illustrate the choice a consumer makes between two goods, paralleling the discussion in Unit 7.1. And finally, we examine how a demand curve can be obtained directly from indifference curves and budget lines.

INDIFFERENCE CURVES

At the heart of the analysis in this unit lies indifference curves. An **indifference curve** is a curve depicting the different combinations of two goods that provide the same level of satisfaction. An indifference curve simply tells us if consumers like one set of goods as much as another set. A simple, yet very powerful, assumption reflected in indifference curves is that consumers are able to choose between one of three options. If a consumer is presented with a choice between any two goods, A and B, he or she can indicate that A is preferred to B, that B is preferred to A, or that A and B are preferred equally. To illustrate the concept behind an indifference curve, let's look at a simple example.

Suppose you go to a party and the host asks if you would prefer a soft drink or a beer. You can respond to this offer in one of three ways. First, you can state a preference for the soft drink. Second, you can state a preference for the beer. Or third, you can say that it really doesn't matter and that both are equally preferred, in which case you are indifferent between a soft drink and a beer.

Assume that you express a preference for the soft drink. However, the host does not stop with one offer, but asks for preferences on a whole range of options, including alternative bundles of beer and soft drinks. For example, do you prefer two beers and one soft drink or one beer and two soft drinks? With persistent questioning, the host comes up with four different combinations of beer and soft drinks, listed in Table 7.3.1, that you like equally well. Apparently you are just as happy with ten beers and one soft drink (bundle A) as with one beer and four soft drinks (bundle D). Indeed, there are four different bundles of beer and soft drinks that provide you with the same level of utility.

Of course, your preferences are based on utility. You have indicated that the same level of utility is received from ten beers and one soft drink as from one beer and four soft drinks—you are equally satisfied with any of the four bundles in Table 7.3.1. But note that nowhere have you been asked to state *how much* utility is obtained from each bundle, merely to compare one bundle with another. Because we are concerned in this unit only that a consumer can state the relative preferences between two bundles of goods, we do not need to measure utility in any absolute way, as we did in the previous two units.

These four bundles of beer and soft drinks form the basis of the indifference curve in Figure 7.3.1. If the four bundles in Table 7.3.1 are plotted on a graph and connected with a line, a curve showing

Table 7.3.1

Hypothetical Preferences for Two Goods

To maintain the same level of satisfaction, a consumer will give up some of one good (beer) only if he or she receives more of another good (soft drinks). If a consumer is equally satisfied with ten beers and one soft drink (bundle A) or one beer and four soft drinks (bundle D), then the consumer is indifferent between these two bundles of goods, and both bundles lie on the same indifference curve.

Bundle	Beer	Soft Drinks
A	10	1
B	6	2
C	3	3
D	1	4

Figure 7.3.1

Indifference Curve

An indifference curve indicates the different bundles of two goods that provide the same level of satisfaction. Since bundles A, B, C, and D lie on the same indifference curve, they are equally preferred. Bundle E, above the indifference curve, is more preferred, and bundle F, below the curve, is less preferred.

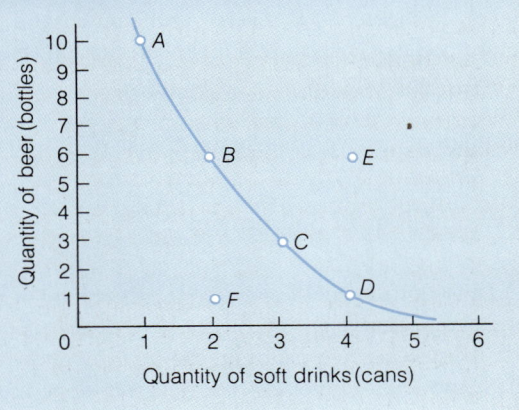

your indifference between bundles of beer and soft drinks is identified. You are equally satisfied with any bundle of beer and soft drinks that lies on this indifference curve. You are indifferent if the host offers ten beers and one soft drink (bundle A) or six beers and two soft drinks (bundle B).

The indifference curve in Figure 7.3.1 indicates three things about the relative preferences for beer and soft drinks. First, it tells us every bundle that is equally preferred to ten beers and one soft drink, the bundles that lie on the indifference curve.

Second, it tells us every bundle of beer and soft drinks that is more preferred than ten beers and one soft drink, for example, bundle E, which lies above and to the right of the indifference curve. Bundle E, containing six beers and four soft drinks, is more preferred than any bundle on the curve, including bundle A, because bundle E contains more beers and more soft drinks than bundle C. Since bundle E is more preferred than C and C is liked the same as A, then E must be more preferred than A.

Third, indifference curves tell us that every bundle that lies below the indifference curve is less preferred than every bundle on the curve. Bundle F, which contains only one beer and two soft drinks, is clearly less preferable than bundle C, and every other bundle on the indifference curve.

Properties of Indifference Curves

Indifference curves have two important properties. First, an indifference curve is negatively sloped. If you have more soft drinks, then you must have less beer to remain indifferent between two bundles of goods. Since you receive utility from both goods, the combination of more of one good and the same or more of the other good provides you with more satisfaction. But to be on the same indifference curve, any two bundles must give the same level of utility and satisfaction. Underlying the negative slope of an indifference curve is the tradeoff between two goods. If you want to remain equally satisfied, then you are willing to give up a certain amount of one good only if more of another good is received.

A second important property deals with the relative positions of two indifference curves. An **indifference map** is a graph of two or more indifference curves, as depicted in Figure 7.3.2. If there are two indifference curves for a consumer, the highest curve is associated with a higher utility level. In Figure 7.3.2, every bundle on curve II is more preferred, and gives more satisfaction, than every bundle on curve I. In fact, there is a whole array of indifference curves, and the higher the indifference curve, the greater the level of utility.

Marginal Rate of Substitution

As mentioned previously, the negative slope of an indifference curve reflects the tradeoff between goods that is necessary to maintain the same level of satisfaction. More precisely, the negative slope indicates the degree to which a consumer is willing to substitute one good for another, or the marginal rate of substitution. The **marginal rate of substitution** is the rate at which consumers are willing to trade one good for another and maintain the same level of utility.

Let's return to Table 7.3.1 to see what we mean by the marginal rate of substitution. Recall that you are equally satisfied with ten beers and one soft drink or with six beers and two soft drinks, meaning you are willing to substitute four beers for one additional soft drink. Thus, the marginal rate of substitution between bundles A and B is equal to 4, or more precisely, four beers per soft drink, and is also equal to the absolute value of the slope between corresponding bundles A and B on the curve in Figure 7.3.1. If you continue to trade beer for soft drinks, moving from bundle B to bundle C, you are willing to give up three beers for one soft drink, for a marginal rate of substitution of 3.

Figure 7.3.2
Indifference Map

Higher indifference curves provide a higher level of utility. Every point on indifference curve II provides more satisfaction than every point on indifference curve I. Two or more indifference curves constitute an indifference map.

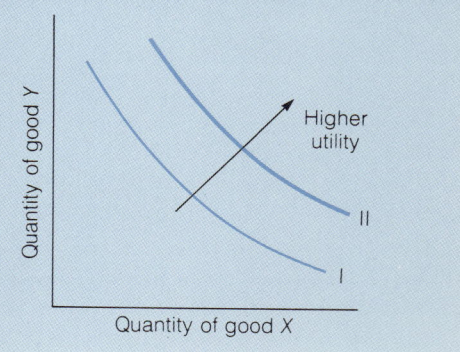

Between bundles C and D you are willing to trade two beers for one soft drink, giving a marginal rate of substitution of 2. In each case the tradeoff keeps you at the same level of utility.

Another interesting feature of the marginal rate of substitution is that it is not only equal to the absolute value of the slope of the indifference curve but is also equal to the ratio of marginal utilities of the two goods. If you are willing to give up four beers for one soft drink, that means a soft drink must be worth four times as much as one beer, and the marginal utility of soft drinks is four times the marginal utility of beer. The marginal rate of substitution can also be specified as

$$\text{marginal rate of substitution} = \frac{\text{marginal utility of soft drinks}}{\text{marginal utility of beer}}$$

Decreasing Marginal Rate of Substitution

Note that as beer is traded for soft drinks, moving from bundle A to bundle D, the marginal rate of substitution decreases from 4 to 2. This decrease not only gives the indifference curve its distinctive shape but also reflects an important characteristic of the marginal rate of substitution. The **decreasing marginal rate of substitution** states that as more of one good is traded for another, the marginal rate of substitution between the two goods declines. Moving from left to right on the indifference curve, the slope is initially very steep, then flattens out.

For example, with bundle A you have a lot of beer (ten), but very few soft drinks (one). The additional utility obtained from one less beer is relatively lower than that obtained from one more soft drink. It is no wonder you are willing to give up four beers for one soft drink, because even if four beers are given up, you still have six beers left. Each beer is worth relatively little when you have a lot of them.

But at bundle C, you have only three beers, so each is relatively more valuable. And with this bundle you also have three soft drinks, so the law of diminishing marginal utility has started to affect soft drinks. Here you are willing to give up only two beers for an additional soft drink. The marginal rate of substitution decreases from bundle A to bundle C because of relative changes in the marginal utilities of both goods. However, we should point out that it is not necessary to use the law of diminishing marginal utility to explain the decrease in the marginal rate of substitution. All that is needed is the changes in the *relative* marginal utilities of both goods.

Although we have been hypothetically talking about beer and soft drinks, a decreasing marginal rate of substitution can be seen between any two goods. Take for example the marginal rate of substitution between environmental quality and gross national product (GNP). If a country has a relatively large GNP, it doesn't value additional production as much as it values a cleaner environment. The United States in the early 1970s enacted a lot of legislation that tried to improve the quality of the environment. But in doing so, the economy sacrificed the production of goods and services.

However, in the early 1980s there was a movement in the opposite direction as the country sacrificed environmental quality in order to increase economic production. This change in attitude resulted from the stagnant economy of the 1970s as well as from improvements in environmental quality. In essence, with relatively more environmental quality, and relatively less production, the environment was not as valuable, but GNP was more so.

THE BUDGET LINE

While the indifference curve measures the willingness of consumers to buy goods and services, the budget line measures their ability. A **budget line** illustrates the alternative combinations of two different goods that can be purchased with a given income based on the prices of the two goods. Unfortunately, most of the goods and services people consume are not offered free of charge, so they must consider not only their willingness to buy goods but also consider their ability, as determined by income and prices.

Let's return once again to our case of the choice between two goods, beer and soft drinks. This time we want to know how much of each you are *able* to buy. Assume that you have $5 to spend, the price of beer is $1, and the price of a soft drink is 50 cents. All potential options are plotted in Figure 7.3.3.

If you buy nothing but beer, the most you can purchase is five bottles (bundle U), found by dividing income ($5) by the price ($1). If you spend all $5 on soft drinks, you can purchase ten cans (bundle Z). But there is no reason for you to be restricted to all of one good or the other—some of each can be purchased, for example four beers and two soft

Figure 7.3.3
Budget Line

The budget line presents all combinations of two goods that a consumer is able to buy, given a certain income and based on the prices of the two goods. If income is $5, the price of beer $1, and the price of soft drinks 50 cents, the consumer faces the budget line presented here. At most, five bottles of beer (bundle U) or ten cans of soft drink (bundle Z) can be purchased. Alternatively, such combinations as four bottles of beer and two soft drinks (bundle V) or three bottles of beer and four soft drinks (bundle W) can be purchased. The consumer can buy any combination lying below the line, but none that lie above.

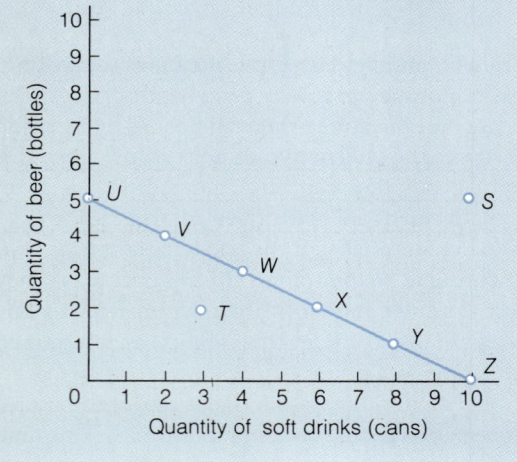

drinks (bundle V), three beers and four soft drinks (bundle W), and so on.

The line plotted in Figure 7.3.3 is the budget line, and it gives the options available to you based on your existing budget. It is also a budget constraint because no goods that lie above the line can be purchased. It is not possible to buy ten beers and five soft drinks (bundle S), since this bundle costs more than the $5 of income available. You could purchase any bundle of beer and soft drinks lying below the line, such as two beers and three soft drinks (bundle T), but since there are no other goods to buy with the income, there is no reason to spend less than $5 on these two.

A budget line represents one of the fundamental truths in economics—we cannot have everything that we want. In fact, the budget line limits the consumer in the same way that the production possibilities frontier limits the entire economy. In both cases the ability to provide goods and services for consumption is restricted, for the economy because of limited resources, for the consumer because of limited income.

The Slope of the Budget Line

The most important feature of the budget line in Figure 7.3.3 is the slope. The numerical value of the slope is $-\frac{1}{2}$, which, by no coincidence, is equal to the negative of the ratio of the two prices. The slope of the budget line in our ongoing example is specified as

$$\text{slope} = -\frac{\text{price of soft drinks}}{\text{price of beer}} = -\frac{\$0.50}{\$1} = -\frac{1}{2}$$

Why does the ratio of prices give us the slope of the budget line? Recall that one option on the budget line is five beers and no soft drinks. However, if you give up one beer, $1 of income (the price of one beer) is freed up to be spent on soft drinks. Since soft drinks are 50 cents each, two soft drinks can be purchased. Thus, one beer is given up to get two soft drinks. The change in beer divided by the change in soft drinks (which is the definition of slope) is $-\frac{1}{2}$.

A Price Change

If the market price for one of the goods changes, how is the budget line affected? Suppose that instead of paying 50 cents for each soft drink, you now pay $1 per can. You can no longer spend all $5 on soft drinks and buy ten cans; at most you can buy only five soft drinks.

With the change in the price of soft drinks,

Figure 7.3.4

A Price Change

A price change causes the budget line to shift. If the price of soft drinks increases from 50 cents to $1 a can, the budget line rotates from A to B, because the consumer can buy only five cans of soft drink instead of ten. The higher price also changes the slope of the line. After the price change, the consumer gives up one bottle of beer and can buy only one more soft drink. Before the price change, one less beer bought two more soft drinks.

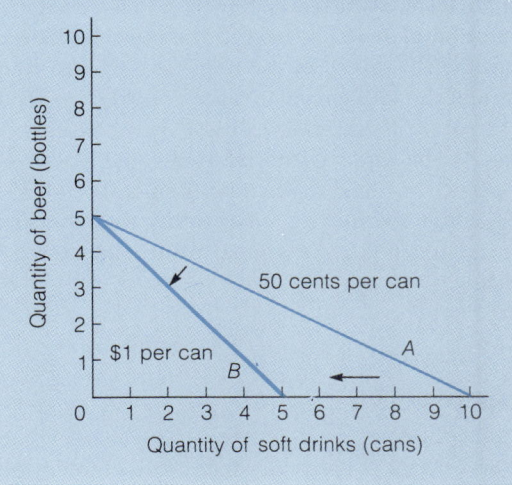

the market tradeoff between beer and soft drinks also changes. Instead of buying one less beer and two more soft drinks, one less beer gets you only one more soft drink. The slope of the budget line changes from $-\frac{1}{2}$ to -1. In Figure 7.3.4 the new budget line, line B, is more steeply sloped and intersects the soft drink axis at five cans instead of ten. Note, however, that line B still intersects the beer axis at five bottles. Since income remains $5 and the price of beer is $1, you can still spend all income and buy five bottles of beer. A change in the price of one good does not change the maximum quantity of the other good that can be purchased.

THE CHOICE BETWEEN TWO GOODS

Having discussed the two components necessary to our analysis, indifference curves and the budget line, we now combine them in Figure 7.3.5 to determine the quantities of beer and soft drinks that you are both willing and able to buy and that will provide you with the highest possible level of utility. The bundle that attracts our immediate attention is bundle M, where the budget line and indifference curve I intersect. Note that while an intersection in economics is usually an equilibrium, in this case it is not.

Bundle M, which consists of approximately $3\frac{3}{4}$ beers and $2\frac{1}{2}$ soft drinks, is on the budget line, meaning you are spending all available income. Unfortunately, your income is not being spent as wisely as it could be, because greater utility can be obtained by buying a different bundle of beer and soft drinks. For example, if three beers and four soft drinks (bundle N) are purchased, you are better off. Since bundle N lies above indifference curve I, a higher level of utility can be obtained with the same level of income. With indifference curves, an intersection is *not* a point of equilibrium.

We find the equilibrium by identifying the bundle on the budget line that gives the highest level of utility. The only way for this to occur is if the budget line is tangent to an indifference curve. At this equilibrium, if we move to the right or to the left, we also move to a lower indifference curve. Picture a perfectly smooth ball just touching an inclined plane; that is the point of tangency that we are looking for.

If you move down the budget line to bundle O on indifference curve II, you have reached this point of tangency. Curve II is the highest indifference curve (and the highest level of utility) that can be reached with the given budget line. If you move away from bundle O, you are buying a bundle that lies below curve II. Therefore, bundle O constitutes **consumer equilibrium**, the condition that exists when the last dollar spent on each good provides the same additional utility. You will have no

Figure 7.3.5

Consumer Equilibrium

Consumer equilibrium is reached with the tangency between the budget line and an indifference curve, at point O. If the slopes of the budget line and the indifference curve are not the same, such as at point M, the consumer is not in equilibrium. It is possible to buy more of one good and less of the other, and increase utility. If the consumer moves away from point M to point N, a higher indifference curve is reached. At point O, if the consumer moves to the right or left, a lower indifference curve is reached.

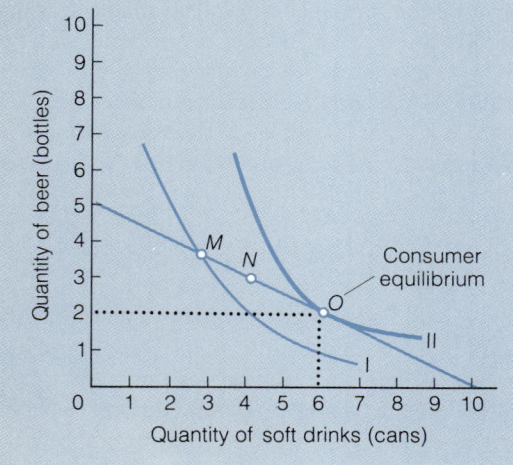

However, more important than the numerical value of the slopes is what each slope represents. The slope of the budget line is equal to the negative of the ratio of the prices, and the slope of the indifference curve is equal to the negative of the marginal rate of substitution, which is the same as the ratio of marginal utilities. Therefore, at bundle O, the ratio of the prices is equal to the ratio of marginal utilities, or

$$\frac{\text{price of soft drinks}}{\text{price of beer}} = \frac{\text{marginal utility of soft drinks}}{\text{marginal utility of beer}}$$

This is simply a variation of the rule of consumer equilibrium discussed in Unit 7.1. However, this variation allows us to extend the interpretation of the rule. In this form the rule states that in equilibrium the relative value placed on the two goods (the ratio of marginal utilities) by a consumer is exactly the same as the relative value placed on them by the market (the ratio of prices). Again, it is not the absolute marginal utility that concerns us but the relative marginal utility, and relative prices.

THE DEMAND CURVE

Now we want to know how many cans of soft drinks are bought if the price changes. Panel a in Figure 7.3.6 depicts the original consumer equilibrium, at bundle O. It also shows a second budget line based on a soft drink price of $1 per can. The two budget lines are identical to the ones presented in Figure 7.3.4. With the new, steeper budget line you can no longer buy two beers and six soft drinks, and bundle O is no longer consumer equilibrium. The new consumer equilibrium is at the tangency between indifference curve III and the new budget line, at bundle P. At bundle P, four cans of soft drink and one bottle of beer are purchased. The quantity of soft drinks purchased is reduced simply because the price is higher; income, the price of beer, and tastes and preferences for the two goods remain unchanged.

reason to switch from this consumption pattern once reaching bundle O. As long as income, prices of both goods, and preferences remain unchanged, you will buy two beers and six soft drinks.

The tangency at bundle O is extremely important. Since the budget line and the indifference curves are tangent, their slopes are equal. We know that the slope of the budget line is $-\frac{1}{2}$, so at bundle O, the slope of the indifference curve must also be $-\frac{1}{2}$, meaning you are not only willing but also able to trade one beer for two soft drinks in the market.

In our study of marginal utility in Unit 7.2 we concluded the inverse relationship between price and quantity can be explained with the law of diminishing marginal utility. Consumers buy a larger quantity at a lower price because each additional unit provides less additional utility. While decreasing marginal utility makes a great deal of intuitive sense, we cannot measure utility, and we do not know the actual utility an additional good provides.

However, with indifference curves we don't *need* to know the actual amount of utility, because indifference curves are based on relative preferences. All we need to know is that A is preferred to B. It does not matter that A provides twice as much, or twenty times as much utility, as B, only that it provides relatively more utility.

IN SUMMARY

Indifference Curves and Demand

- An analysis of demand combines the two fundamental aspects of demand, the willingness and the ability to buy goods and services. Willingness is embodied in the indifference curve, and ability in the budget line.

- An indifference curve shows different bundles of goods that give the consumer the same level of utility. Indifference curves also illustrate how much of one good a consumer is willing to give up in exchange for another good. This tradeoff between goods is specified in the marginal rate of substitution, which is equal to the ratio of marginal utilities of the two goods. The marginal rate of substitution is also the negative of the slope of the indifference curve.

- The ability to buy goods is embodied in the budget line. The slope of the budget line is the negative of the ratio of the prices of the two goods. The budget line indicates the ability of a consumer to trade two goods in the market.

- By combining indifference curves with the budget line, the quantities of two goods a con-

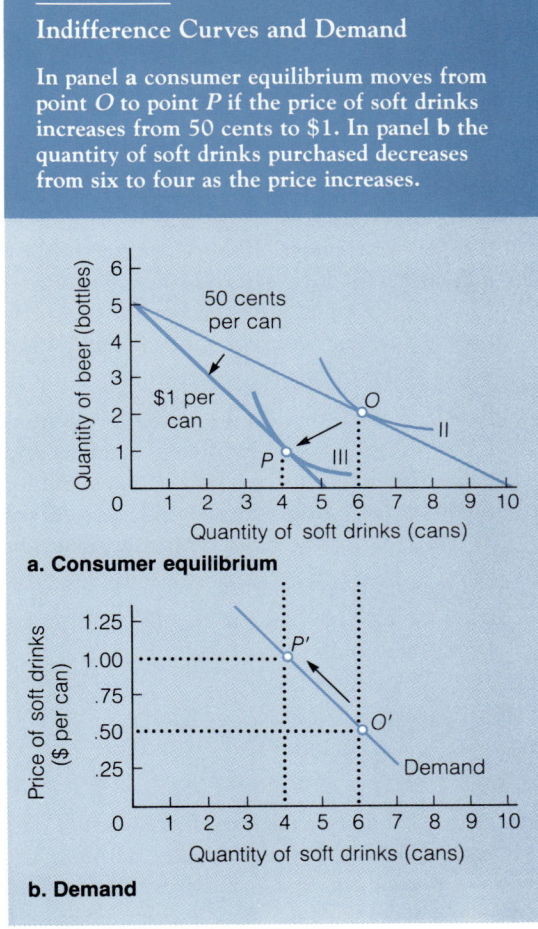

Figure 7.3.6

Indifference Curves and Demand

In panel a consumer equilibrium moves from point O to point P if the price of soft drinks increases from 50 cents to $1. In panel b the quantity of soft drinks purchased decreases from six to four as the price increases.

a. Consumer equilibrium

b. Demand

Panel b plots the original quantity of soft drinks demanded at the original price, bundle O'. Also plotted is the quantity of soft drinks demanded at the higher price, bundle P'. If we change the price of soft drinks further, we can find additional points on the demand curve, in the same way we found P' and O'. Connecting all the points gives us the demand for soft drinks. Note that the higher price of soft drinks leads to a decrease in the quantity demanded. Indifference curves have allowed us to demonstrate the basic law of demand.

sumer would buy can be determined. Consumer equilibrium is reached at the tangency between the budget line and the highest indifference curve that it touches. At this tangency the slope of the indifference curve is the same as the slope of the budget line. This means that the ratio of marginal utilities is equal to the ratio of prices. It further indicates that the consumer is in equilibrium after reaching a point at which the consumer's ability to trade one good for the other is exactly the same as the consumer's willingness to do so.

- By changing the price of one good, the effect on the quantity of the good demanded is reflected in the negative slope of the demand curve. As expected, a higher price leads to a smaller quantity demanded.

QUESTIONS FOR STUDY AND ANALYSIS

1. Assume you have the following information concerning the preferences of a consumer:

Bundle	Good A	Good B
S	6	1
T	4	2
U	2	3
V	1	4
W	6	3
X	4	4
Y	2	5
Z	1	6

a. Suppose the consumer prefers bundles S, T, U, and V equally, and also prefers bundles W, X, Y, and Z equally. Draw the indifference curves underlying the consumer's preferences. Is bundle S preferred to bundle Z? Explain.
b. Is it possible for bundles W and X to be equally preferred at the same time bundles X and S are equally preferred? Explain.
c. Which indifference curve gives the most utility?

2. **a.** Let's say that you have $100 to spend on two goods, textbooks and pizza. If textbooks sell for $20 each, and pizza for $10 each, plot your budget line. What is the slope of the budget line? Is it possible for you to buy five textbooks and five pizzas? What about two textbooks and six pizzas?
b. Draw your budget line if the price of pizza increases to $15. Now could you buy two textbooks and six pizzas? If you bought two textbooks, how many pizzas could you buy? What is the slope of the new budget line?

3. Based on the situation presented in question 2 from Unit 7.2, use indifference curves and budget lines to illustrate how the demand for the good "not attending school" was affected by the $100 incentive for perfect attendance.

4. Using indifference curves, examine the situation facing Carl Lewis in the 1984 Olympics as outlined in question 4 in Unit 7.1.

REVIEW GLOSSARY

budget line The alternative combinations of two different goods that can be purchased with a given income based on the prices of the two goods. The consumer can purchase any bundle that lies beneath the budget line but none that lies above it. The budget line reflects the ability of a consumer to purchase goods and services.

consumer equilibrium The condition that exists when the last dollar spent on each good provides the same additional utility. The point at which the consumer has allocated available income to achieve the highest level of utility. In indifference curve analysis this is where the budget line is tangential to the indifference curve. At this point the ratio of prices is equal to the ratio of marginal utilities. This means that the willingness of the consumer to trade one good for the other is exactly the same as the ability to trade the two goods in the market.

decreasing marginal rate of substitution A principle that states as more of one good is traded for another, the marginal rate of substitution between the two goods declines. Moving from left to right along an indifference curve, the slope begins very steep, then flattens out.

indifference curve A curve depicting the different combinations of two goods that provide the same level of satisfaction. An indifference curve is based on the relative preferences for the two goods by a consumer.

indifference map A graph of two or more indifference curves. Higher indifference curves are associated with higher levels of utility.

marginal rate of substitution The rate at which consumers are willing to trade one good for another and maintain the same level of utility. The marginal rate of substitution is equal to the ratio of marginal utilities of the two goods and also to the negative of the slope of the indifference curve.

UNIT 7.4

Applications of Consumer Demand

In the previous three units we examined several of the principles and concepts behind consumer behavior. We saw how utility—the satisfaction of wants and needs—underlies consumers' choices between two goods. We also saw that the law of diminishing marginal utility helps explain the law of demand.

In this unit we look at some specific examples that illustrate the principles of consumer behavior. First, we discuss the choice between buying diesel fuel or regular gasoline, and how that choice is affected by an increase in the relative price of diesel fuel. Second, we see that sales in the liquor industry have declined in recent years as the result of consumers making the same types of choices. Third, we enter the financial world of savings accounts, credit unions, and certificates of deposit to see why some savers are willing to accept a lower interest rate on certain types of savings. Finally, we discuss the penalty for a personal foul in college basketball, which represents a less obvious application of consumer behavior.

THE RELATIVE PRICE OF DIESEL FUEL

The choice between diesel fuel and regular gasoline represents a simple illustration of consumer behavior. Historically, diesel fuel has been a few cents cheaper than regular gasoline, which has encouraged some consumers to buy diesel-powered automobiles. Recall from the rule of consumer equilibrium introduced in Unit 7.1 that the lower price relates to the marginal utility derived from its use.

This is specified as

$$\frac{MU \text{ of diesel}}{\text{price of diesel}} = \frac{MU \text{ of gasoline}}{\text{price of gasoline}}$$

In spite of the relatively lower price of diesel fuel, consumers purchased relatively few diesel-powered automobiles. The reason for this is reflected in the relative marginal utility of diesel as opposed to regular gasoline. For example, diesel-powered automobiles are slightly more difficult to start than automobiles powered by regular gasoline, especially on cold mornings. Also, diesels use a glow plug, rather than a spark plug, which takes a few seconds to warm up before it ignites the fuel. And last, diesel fuel is not as readily available as regular gasoline. Since diesel fuel was originally used to power trucks, the first diesel-powered domestic automobiles had to be refueled at truck stops. While diesel fuel is more widely available in the 1980s than it was in the 1970s, it is still harder to find than regular gasoline. In short, the marginal utility of diesel is less than the marginal utility of regular gasoline.

However, in the mid-1980s, diesel fuel lost its relative price advantage over regular gasoline. Based on our study of consumer behavior, we can see how this affects the demand for diesel fuel. If the price of diesel increases, the marginal utility–price ratio on the left-hand side of the rule of consumer equilibrium is decreased.

Consumer equilibrium can be reachieved either by increasing the marginal utility of diesel or by decreasing the marginal utility of gasoline. The marginal utility of diesel can be increased by purchasing fewer diesel-powered automobiles and consuming less diesel fuel, thus letting the law of diminishing marginal utility work in reverse. Alternatively, a decrease in the marginal utility of gasoline results from buying more gasoline and letting the law of diminishing marginal utility take effect. However, consumers would buy more gasoline as a substitute for diesel fuel after switching from diesel-powered to gasoline-powered automobiles.

Either way, an increase in the relative price of diesel fuel clearly encourages consumers to purchase more gasoline-powered and fewer diesel-powered automobiles. However, there is an interesting point that needs to be made about this conclusion. Note that while the price of diesel went from being absolutely less than the price of gasoline to absolutely more, the conclusion is the same when only the relative price of diesel increases, even though it remains absolutely less than the price of gasoline. It is the increase in the relative price of diesel that encourages consumers to buy more gasoline-powered and fewer diesel-powered automobiles.

THE SLUMP IN LIQUOR INDUSTRY SALES

Consumer behavior can also affect sales in the liquor industry. In the early 1980s, sales in the liquor industry began to decline. Our understanding of consumer demand theory can help explain why this happened. But first, let's look at some relevant information.

The liquor industry as discussed here includes hard liquors—bourbon, vodka, scotch, and so on—but not beer and wine. This is important because liquor is taxed differently than other alcoholic beverages. For example, liquor taxes were about $10.50 per gallon in the early 1980s and on the rise, while the tax on a comparable amount of wine was only 17 cents. Also, a nationwide public service campaign stressing the problems of drinking and driving was initiated in the early 1980s, and the public's attitude toward drinking and driving began to change. Drunk driving laws were more strictly enforced, and penalties became more severe.

Based on our knowledge of utility and consumer behavior, why would these factors reduce liquor sales? The rule of consumer equilibrium for liquor and other beverages can be specified as

$$\frac{MU \text{ of liquor}}{\text{price of liquor}} = \frac{MU \text{ of other beverages}}{\text{price of other beverages}}$$

In this case, other beverages include beer, wine, soft drinks, and even Perrier water. In this example we are looking for the choice consumers make between liquor and these other beverages.

Obviously, higher taxes cause the price of liquor to rise, which then throws the consumer out of equilibrium. The ratio on the left-hand side of the equation becomes less than the ratio on the right-hand side. The ratios can be equalized by increasing the marginal utility of liquor and/or decreasing the marginal utility of other beverages. By employing the law of diminishing marginal utility, the marginal utility of liquor is increased by consuming a smaller quantity; the marginal utility of the other beverages is decreased by consuming larger quantities. In essence, the higher price of liquor encourages consumers to buy less liquor and more of the other beverages.

What effect does the campaign against drinking and driving have on liquor sales? Changing attitudes on the part of consumers, including greater expectations of being caught and more severe penalties for drinking and driving, affects the marginal utility of liquor. The utility provided by a drink is less if the chances of spending the night in jail are greater. Thus, changing attitudes and expectations reduce the marginal utility of liquor, and along with it, the left-hand side of the rule of consumer equilibrium. This throws the consumer out of equilibrium, just as the higher price does. The consumer can reachieve equilibrium in the same way as before, by reducing the quantity of liquor purchased and/or increasing the quantity of other beverages (especially nonalcoholic beverages) purchased.

THE CHOICE OF SAVINGS ACCOUNTS

The same principles of consumer behavior that indicate why consumers buy less liquor and more of other beverages also underlie savings decisions. Today, there are a number of different ways to save funds, ranging from standard passbook savings accounts to high-interest money market accounts. The variation in ways to save is accompanied by a variation in the interest rate paid. For example, the standard passbook account at a bank pays $5\frac{1}{4}$ percent, while a certificate of deposit at the same bank pays 8 to 10 percent.

What does the variation in interest rates mean to the saver? Basically, a saver is paying a higher price by saving at a lower interest rate. For example, if a consumer saves $1000 for one year at 5 percent, $50 of interest is received. If the same $1000 is saved at 10 percent, $100 in interest is received. In other words, it costs $50 to save at the lower interest.

Why then would anyone keep money in a passbook account that earns $5\frac{1}{4}$ percent when they could earn a higher interest elsewhere? Let's look at the rule of consumer equilibrium as it applies to a savings account and certificate of deposit. It can be specified as

$$\frac{MU \text{ of savings account}}{\text{price of savings account}} = \frac{MU \text{ of certificate of deposit}}{\text{price of certificate of deposit}}$$

If the price of a savings account is greater than the price of a certificate of deposit, people will use a savings account only if it provides relatively more marginal utility.

A key difference between a savings account and a certificate of deposit contributes to relative differences in marginal utilities. A certificate of deposit is for a fixed period of time, and a savings account is not. With a savings account, a saver is free to withdraw money at any time, whereas with a certificate of deposit, the saver agrees to keep the money in the bank for a specific length of time, usually a minimum of six months. If the money is withdrawn early, then the higher interest rate is forfeited.

Thus, savings accounts are much more accessible—the money can be withdrawn when it is needed. In fact, with the widespread use of electronic tellers, savers can gain access to savings accounts at any time, day or night, for emergencies, for impulse buying, or to supplement normal purchases near the end of the month. Because this can't be done with a certificate of deposit, savers are willing to sacrifice the higher interest rate in order to have ease of access.

Can the interest rate differentials of other types of savings accounts also be explained in this manner? For example, credit unions pay one to two percentage points higher than the passbook savings account at a bank. Despite that, savers are willing to pay an effectively higher price (receive a lower interest rate) at banks than at credit unions because of convenience. Many banks provide a wider range of financial services, including loans, checking accounts, and electronic tellers, than credit unions, although credit unions are closing the services gap.

Money market accounts usually pay even more interest than certificates of deposit and specify no minimum length of deposit. But do the high interest rates compensate for relatively lower marginal utilities? The feature that separates a money market account from other types of accounts is a variable interest, which can fluctuate from day to day. With a savings account or certificate of deposit, the interest rate doesn't change. Therefore, savers with money market accounts don't know what the interest will be in a year, unlike the holder of a one year certificate of deposit. Savers who don't care to watch the day-to-day movements of the interest rate and worry about the best time to withdraw the money are willing to pay a higher price, and receive a lower interest rate, with certificates of deposit.

THE PRICE OF A PERSONAL FOUL

An essential feature of the theory of consumer behavior is that it can be applied to all areas of human behavior. For this reason we now turn our attention to a slightly different type of example, the penalty for a personal foul in college basketball.

Just before the beginning of the 1983–84 college basketball season, the National Collegiate Athletic Association (NCAA) changed one of the rules governing play by awarding two free throws to any player on the receiving end of a personal foul in the last few minutes of a game. Before the rule change, the player was usually awarded a one-and-one, so named because a second free throw was awarded only if the first was made, and two free throws were awarded only if the personal foul was judged by the referee to be intentional.

In automatically awarding two free throws for a personal foul, the NCAA was applying basic economic principles. The free throws awarded to one team was the price paid by the other team for committing the foul. The NCAA felt that awarding two free throws rather than the one-and-one would make the price higher and reduce the incentive and thus number of fouls. This is simply the law of demand.

Unfortunately, after the rule was changed, more fouls rather than fewer were committed in the closing minutes of the game. In particular, more intentional fouls were committed, resulting in potential and actual harm to the player being fouled, so the NCAA changed the rule halfway through the season.

But what went wrong? Does the law of demand not apply to basketball players in the final minutes of a game? These questions can be answered by recognizing that the choice players (and coaches) make concerning fouls in a basketball game is the same type of choice consumers make between the purchase of two goods.

Prior to the rule change the player had a choice between three options in the closing minutes of the game: not to commit a foul, to commit an intentional foul, or to commit an unintentional foul. The important distinction is between an intentional and unintentional foul. The intentional foul is committed by grabbing the opponent. The unintentional foul is usually committed in an attempt to steal the basketball or block a shot. The real problem after the rule change was the increase in the number of intentional fouls.

The rule of consumer equilibrium, in which

the two "goods" are intentional fouls and unintentional fouls, can be specified as

$$\frac{MU \text{ of intentional foul}}{\text{price of intentional foul}} = \frac{MU \text{ of unintentional foul}}{\text{price of unintentional foul}}$$

After the rule change the price of an intentional foul remained unchanged at two free throws. However, the price of an unintentional foul increased from a one-and-one to two shots, meaning the ratio on the right-hand side of the rule of consumer equilibrium declined. As in the other examples, equilibrium can be reachieved by a combination of an increase in the marginal utility of the unintentional foul (by committing fewer unintentional fouls) and/or a decrease in the marginal utility of the intentional foul (by committing more intentional fouls).

Here is where the NCAA ran into its problem. The relative price of the intentional foul declined, encouraging an increase in intentional fouls. After the rule change the penalty was the same for the intentional as the unintentional foul. But recall what the rule of consumer equilibrium tells us about the marginal utilities prior to the rule change. Since the price of the intentional foul was relatively higher, the marginal utility was also relatively higher.

An intentional foul, by its very nature, is designed to keep the opponent from scoring. However, the unintentional foul may not prevent a score. Thus, the utility provided by an intentional foul is greater than an unintentional foul. It is no wonder that more intentional fouls were committed when the price became relatively lower.

IN SUMMARY

Applications of Consumer Demand

- The theory of consumer behavior can be used to explain some recent events. First, the rule of consumer equilibrium indicates what is likely to happen when the price of diesel fuel rises relative to the price of gasoline. The higher price of diesel induces consumers to raise the marginal utility of diesel and/or lower the marginal utility of gasoline by switching from diesel-powered to gasoline-powered automobiles.

- The theory of consumer behavior also explains why sales in the liquor industry declined. Higher taxes on liquor caused the price to increase and disturbed the consumer equilibrium. Furthermore, strict enforcement of drunk driving laws lowered the marginal utility of liquor. Consumer equilibrium was reestablished by switching from liquor to other beverages.

- The theory of consumer behavior suggests why some savers are willing to accept a lower interest rate from a passbook savings account than from certificates of deposit. The lower interest, which means savers are paying a higher price, can be charged because passbook accounts provide a greater marginal utility through accessibility and convenience. Other differences in interest rates can also be explained by similar reasoning.

- The consumer behavior theory can even be applied to areas that go beyond the workings of a typical market. College basketball players (and their coaches) make the same type of choice between intentionally or unintentionally fouling their opponent as consumers make when buying a good. As the relative price of an intentional foul in basketball declines, the quantity demanded increases.

QUESTIONS FOR STUDY AND ANALYSIS

1. Based on the analysis of the relative prices of diesel and gasoline, explain what would happen to the rule of consumer equilibrium, and the relative prices and quantities of diesel-powered and gasoline-powered automobiles, under each of the following circumstances:

a. The fuel efficiency of diesel-powered automobiles increases by 50 percent.
b. The prices of both gasoline and diesel decline by 10 percent.
c. A tax is imposed on gasoline.
d. Stricter emission control devices are required on all automobiles, but they are more costly for gasoline-powered automobiles.

2. Based on the analysis of the liquor industry, discuss how each of the following situations would affect the rule of consumer equilibrium and the relative prices and quantities of liquor and nonliquor beverages:
a. The legal age to buy beer is raised from eighteen to twenty-one years, while the legal age to buy liquor remains at twenty-one.
b. A nonalcoholic wine is introduced.

3. Based on the analysis of savings behavior, discuss how each of the following situations would affect the rule of consumer equilibrium and the savings patterns for consumers:
a. The tax-exempt status of credit unions is revoked, making them pay taxes like banks.
b. Savings and loan associations are allowed to offer all of the services carried by banks.
c. Banks allow customers to make all financial transactions between accounts by phone rather than using an electronic teller, but credit unions still require face-to-face transactions.

4. How would the marginal utility of a personal foul and the number of fouls committed be affected if a team were awarded two shots *and* the ball? Explain.

5. Government taxation has an important effect on consumer decisions because so many different types of taxes are levied on activity in the economy. The federal income tax is levied on income, the social security tax on wage income (but not other sources of income), sales taxes on goods sold (but not services), corporate income tax on corporate profits, property taxes on the value of houses and land, and the inheritance tax on the transfer of wealth from one generation to the next. Explain how the following changes in each of these taxes would affect consumers' decisions in the economy:
a. The federal income tax rate is doubled.
b. The social security tax on wages is extended to include income earned by capital, land, and entrepreneurship in addition to the wage income earned by labor.
c. Sales taxes are extended to include services as well as physical goods.
d. The corporate income tax is eliminated.
e. The property tax is changed such that it taxes only the value of land but not the value of any buildings on the land or improvements made to the land.
f. The tax on inheritances is increased by 50 percent.

SECTION INQUIRY

Consumer Demand for Television Programming

Due to recent technological advancements, consumers have several different ways to receive television programming. Most consumers receive television signals in the conventional manner, broadcast through the airwaves of the atmosphere. That is, the major networks send their programming signals to local network affiliates, who then transmit them to home television sets. All a consumer needs to receive these signals is a television set (and possibly an outdoor antenna). However, this method of receiving television programming is usually limited to a few channels, including the network affiliates and some independent stations.

Consumers also have a second way to receive television programming, cable television. In this case, a local cable company connects a cable between each television and a central transmitter. The cable is able to carry a wide variety of different channels, including local television stations (network affiliates and independent stations); optional commercial-free channels (Home Box Office, The Disney Channel, Showtime); large, independent "superstations" (WTBS, WGN); and special-interest channels (ESPN, Cable News Network, MTV). While the variety of programs and the quality of reception is typically much better with cable than without, cable companies also charge a monthly fee, which varies, depending on the number and type of channels received. However, in spite of the fee, nearly half of the households in the United States receive cable television.

In the last several years consumers have found a third way to receive television programs, satellite dishes. This method of reception is possible because the widespread use of cable television coincided with technological advances in satellite communications. In fact, most of the cable channels transmit their programs to local cable companies across the country by bouncing their signals off satellites orbiting overhead. Home Box Office, WTBS, MTV, and the others transmit their signals to the satellites, which send the signals back to earth to be received by large satellite dishes owned by the cable companies. The cable companies pay a fee for the signals, which is recovered when they charge a fee to households for the cable services. When this technology was first developed, the dishes used to receive the satellite transmissions were so expensive they could be purchased only by companies that were generating income from the monthly service fees. However, technological advances brought the price of satellite dishes into the affordable range for moderate-income families. Many consumers thus have begun using satellite dishes to receive programs directly from the satellites instead of going through the local cable company and paying the monthly fee. With satellite dishes, the variety of programs and the quality of reception are even better than with cable.

However, since the satellite dish owners do not pay for their reception or for monthly cable services, the cable companies and the cable channels have become concerned about lost revenue. Many cable channels therefore have begun to scramble their transmissions. The only way satellite dish owners can receive a clear transmission is with a descrambler, which is rented by the cable channel for a monthly fee approximately the same as that charged by the local cable companies.

QUESTIONS FOR DISCUSSION

1. Discuss how the decision to have cable television services rather than receiving only the signals broadcast by local stations fits the rule of consumer equilibrium. How does the marginal utility of cable television compare to the marginal utility of receiving signals only from local stations? How do the prices of these two goods compare?

2. Discuss how the decision to have satellite dish reception rather than cable television services

fits the rule of consumer equilibrium. How did the marginal utility of satellite reception compare to the marginal utility of cable television before satellite transmissions were scrambled? How did they compare after the satellite transmissions were scrambled? How did the prices of the two goods compare before and after the signals were scrambled?

3. Does the demand for television programming discussed here fit the law of demand? Why or why not? How do you think the demand for satellite dish reception was affected when the cable channels began scrambling their signals? Explain how this relates to the law of demand.

SECTION 8

A Closer Look at Supply

In Unit 2.3 the supply side of the market was introduced. The most significant principle to emerge from that study was the law of supply, which stated that price and quantity supplied are directly related. The law of supply rates with the law of demand as one of the key principles of economics; each is equally important to the market and the allocation of goods, services, and resources.

In the previous section we studied the forces behind the law of demand to see why higher prices induce consumers to demand a smaller quantity. In this section we take an analogous look behind the law of supply, concentrating again on individual decisions. However, in this case the individual decisions are made by firms rather than households.

Unit 8.1, The Firm, begins our in-depth examination of supply with a look at the organizations responsible for producing and supplying goods and services in the market. We also study the basic legal forms of the firm. This unit introduces the concept of profit maximization, which is assumed to be the primary motivating force for firms. And finally, we preview four types of market structures: perfect competition, monopoly, monopolistic competition, and oligopoly. These market structures are further discussed in Unit 8.4 of this section and in Section 9, Monopoly and Imperfect Competition.

Unit 8.2, Production, presents the first layer of the foundation underlying decisions made by individual firms and the law of supply. In this unit we look at the principles governing the short-run production of a good, the most important principle being the law of diminishing marginal returns. The law of diminishing marginal returns is to the law of supply what the law of diminishing marginal utility is to the law of demand.

Unit 8.3, The Costs of Production, looks at the second layer of the foundation for the law of supply—the costs a firm incurs in the short-run production of a good. Moreover, we see that the costs incurred by the firm are based on the principles of production introduced in Unit 8.2. And the law of diminishing marginal returns plays the central role in determining short-run costs.

Unit 8.4, Perfect Competition and Supply, uses the principles underlying the costs of production in the short run to look at the supply decisions of a perfectly competitive firm. In this unit we pull together everything we know about short-run production to identify the direct relationship between price and quantity supplied. In particular, we see that the direct relationship is based on the law of diminishing marginal returns. A perfectly competitive firm is the ideal type of firm to use in answering this question, because it has no influence over the price, unlike the other three types of firms discussed in Section 9.

Unit 8.5, Problems in the Supply of Agricultural Goods, applies the principles of cost and production to the industry that comes closest to perfect competition. In this unit we look at the farm problem that has affected agricultural production in the last several decades. In particular, we look at the government's agricultural policy to see how it affects agriculture and the economy's allocation of resources.

UNIT 8.1

The Firm

The market supply of a good is based on the combined supply of every firm willing and able to sell the good. As the consumer is the central figure in the demand for a good, the firm is the central figure in the supply of a good. To fully understand the supply side of the market, and the law of supply, it is necessary to study the operation of the firm.

In this unit we begin our study of supply and the behavior of the firm by examining the firm itself. We start with a functional definition of the firm that applies conceptually to both profit-seeking and nonprofit organizations. We discuss three specific legal forms of the firm: proprietorship, partnership, and corporation. We then look at the four basic types of market structures: perfect competition, monopoly, monopolistic competition, and oligopoly. And finally, we turn our attention to four different objectives that motivate, or could motivate, the behavior of a firm: profit maximization, sales maximization, pursuit of social objectives, and pursuit of personal objectives.

THE FIRM

A **firm** is an organization that combines resources for the production of goods and services. This definition emphasizes that a firm derives its status from its functional role in the economy and not from any particular characteristics that it might possess. In this sense, not only profit-seeking private business but also some nonprofit organizations and government agencies can be considered firms. For example, the Postal Service, the Tennessee Valley Authority, and the Army Corps of Engineers are all government firms, and the Red Cross, the

YMCA, and the American Cancer Society are all nonprofit firms.

Note the similarity between the function of a firm and the role an entrepreneur plays in the economy—both combine resources for the production of goods and services. This similarity is not coincidental. In fact, the firm simply constitutes the organization used by the entrepreneur to combine labor, capital, and land in the production process.

This brings us to an important distinction between a firm and a plant. A **plant** is the physical capital at a particular location used for the production of goods and services. Common examples of plants are factories, office buildings, and farms. A plant comprises part of the capital organized by the firm and thus represents but one of the factors of production. A firm may have more than one plant, for example the production facilities of General Motors scattered across the United States. Alternatively, a single plant can be part of the capital organized by more than one firm, for example an automobile plant owned jointly by General Motors and Toyota.

LEGAL FORMS OF THE FIRM

In the United States there are three different legal types of firms—proprietorship, partnership, and corporation—each of which can produce certain goods better than the others. As we will see, the distinctions between types of firms and the goods they produce can ultimately influence the structure of the market.

Proprietorship

The **proprietorship** is a firm owned and operated by a single person, which is why this type is often called a sole proprietorship. Here, the owner is the boss, making all decisions, receiving all profits, and responsible for all losses.

In many cases the proprietorship also provides or owns a large share of the factors of production, including labor, buildings, land, and equipment. Agricultural production represents a good example of proprietors in action, since 95 percent of all farms in the United States are proprietorships. The farmer typically owns the land, tractors, and buildings and does a great deal of the work. At the end of the year the farmer also collects the income or incurs the loss.

Partnership

A partnership has much in common with a sole proprietorship, the main difference being the number of owners. A **partnership** is a firm that is owned and operated by two or more people. Each partner generally shares in the risks, profits, and liabilities of the firm. The responsibilities can also be divided, with one partner in charge of management, another in charge of production, a third in charge of accounting, and so on. The division of responsibility could extend to one partner operating the firm and a limited partner providing only financial capital. Partnerships depend on mutual trust between partners—each partner must rely on the others for the success or failure of the firm. In many cases the partnership might be only as strong as the weakest link.

Corporation

The corporation is vastly different from either a partnership or proprietorship. A **corporation** is a firm that is also a distinct legal entity that exists separately from its owners. Corporations are usually chartered by state governments and are subject to any and all laws. Because a corporation is a separate entity from its owners, it can sell ownership shares, commonly called stocks. In a partnership, where the partners are the owners, whenever a new owner is brought in, a new partnership must be legally created. The ability of a corporation to sell stock allows it to raise far greater amounts of financial capital than a partnership. Keep in mind also that the shareholder in a corporation risks only the initial amount invested in the firm.

Advantages and Disadvantages of Each Form

Proprietorships have the advantages, and disadvantages, associated with relatively small, owner-operated firms. Since the firm and the owner are essentially one and the same in a proprietorship, this type of firm is more easily managed than partnerships and corporations. However, the limited resources available to the owner necessarily restrict the size of a proprietorship. Partnerships can be a little larger than proprietorships because they have access to the resources of numerous partners. Indeed, some legal and accounting partnerships have over fifty partners. Corporations have access to the most resources because of their ability to sell ownership to thousands of shareholders. Furthermore, by law the shareholders in a corporation have **limited liability,** meaning they risk only the amount of their initial investment. By contrast, the owner of a proprietorship has **unlimited liability,** meaning that any of the owner's personal assets can be used to pay the firm's liabilities. Unlimited liability also holds for partnerships, the only exception being for limited partners, who, like corporate shareholders, risk only their initial investment. Also, the profits earned by proprietorships and partnerships are treated as personal income by the government and taxed only once, whereas corporate profits are taxed first as corporate income and then a second time as dividend income.

FIRMS IN THE UNITED STATES

Table 8.1.1 lists recent data on the legal form of firms in the United States. Note that 76 percent of all firms in the United States are proprietorships. Corporations comprise only 16 percent of all firms, and partnerships about 8 percent. However, the number of proprietorships, partnerships, and corporations alone does not reveal the importance of each to the economy. In terms of percentage of

Table 8.1.1
Legal Forms of the Firm, 1981

Proprietorships outnumber partnerships and corporations by a wide margin, accounting for 76 percent of all firms in the country. However, since proprietorships cannot raise as much financial capital, they are limited in size and thus account for only 8 percent of sales. By contrast, corporations comprise only 16 percent of the firms but account for 88 percent of sales.

Type of Firm	Number of Firms (thousands)	Percentage of Total	Total Sales (billions)	Percentage of Total
Proprietorship	12,330	76	$ 488	8
Partnership	1,300	8	258	4
Corporation	2,557	16	5,599	88
Total	16,187	100	$6,345	100

Source: U.S. Bureau of the Census, *Statistical Abstract of the United States, 1982–83.*

total sales, corporations dominate with 88 percent of sales, compared to 8 percent for proprietorships and 4 percent for partnerships.

Even though proprietorships outnumber corporations, they account for a much smaller percentage of sales. Since proprietorships are owner-operated and are less able to accumulate large amounts of financial capital, they are necessarily small operations. But corporations can attract a large amount of financial capital, which enables them to produce a large volume of output.

As Table 8.1.1 suggests, the unlimited liability of partnerships makes them less attractive than either proprietorships or corporations. Fewer than 10 percent of the firms in the United States are based on the enormous trust that partners must hold for each other. Entrepreneurs either accept all risk and rewards alone, in a proprietorship, or they completely separate themselves from the day-to-day management of the firm in a corporation. Few entrepreneurs are willing to gamble their personal wealth on the decisions of others in a partnership. In fact, many of the partnerships in Table 8.1.1 are limited partnerships.

A breakdown of firms according to industry indicates that differences in the three types of firms make each more suited for the production of different types of goods. Before looking at this breakdown, we should point out that an **industry** is a group of firms that produces similar products or sells output in the same market. Table 8.1.2 presents information concerning nine of the broadest types of industries in the economy, from agriculture to services. Note that because agriculture is much more suited to proprietorships than any other industry, over 90 percent of the firms in the agricultural industry are proprietorships.

Other industries, such as mining, services, construction, transportation and public utilities, and retail trade are also dominated, though to a lesser degree, by proprietorships. For example, in the mining industry are independent petroleum drillers; in services, many doctors, dentists, and lawyers; in construction, self-employed contractors, primarily of residential housing; in transportation, the independent trucker; and in retail trade, the mom and pop type of operation, whether a grocery store, a macrame shop, or a computer store.

Partnerships are most prevalent in the finance, insurance, and real estate industry. Although partnerships account for only 8 percent of all firms, they account for 28 percent of firms in this industry. The importance of partnerships to the finance, insurance, and real estate industry emphasizes the role trust plays in partnerships. This industry contains financial brokers, accountants, and other professionals who depend on the trust of their customers. If the customers are convinced the partners trust each other, they are more likely to trust the firm.

Corporations are most prevalent in manufacturing and wholesale trade, controlling slightly over 50 percent of each industry. Manufacturing generally requires a large amount of capital and thus a large initial investment. Such financial resources are best raised through the corporate structure. Wholesale trade, especially by firms with a nationwide or even statewide distribution, also requires a large amount of financial capital for buildings, warehouses, and initial inventory.

MARKET STRUCTURES

The legal form of the firm affects the size of the firm because of the amount of financial capital that can be raised. Proprietorships and partnerships tend to be smaller than coprorations for this reason. Recall also that different industries tend to attract different types of firms. As we look more closely at the structure of industries in this section and the next, we see that markets with smaller firms behave differently than markets with larger firms.

We define **market structure** as the way in which an industry is organized. An industry composed entirely of small firms reacts differently in the market than an industry composed of large firms. The differences are great enough that we are able to

Table 8.1.2

Industrial Division of Firms, 1981

The differences in proprietorships, partnerships, and corporations make them appropriate for different types of industries. Agriculture, retail trade, and services tend to be dominated by proprietorships, since very little capital is required. However, corporations show up in industries that require more capital, such as manufacturing and wholesale trade.

Industry	Number of Proprietorships (thousands)	(percent)	Number of Partnerships (thousands)	(percent)	Number of Corporations (thousands)	(percent)
Agriculture, forestry and fishery	3762	95	125	3	83	2
Mining	97	65	28	19	24	16
Construction	1097	77	75	5	250	18
Manufacturing	236	47	30	6	237	47
Transportation, communication, and public utilities	415	77	20	4	104	19
Wholesale trade	315	51	32	5	266	44
Retail trade	1986	75	173	6	505	19
Finance, insurance, and real estate	1058	50	577	28	471	22
Services	3654	81	239	6	603	13

Source: U.S. Bureau of the Census, *Statistical Abstract of the United States*, 1982–83.

identify four distinct types of market structures—perfect competition, monopoly, monopolistic competition, and oligopoly—which can be laid out on a spectrum, as in Figure 8.1.1. At the far left the market is divided into a large number of firms. As we move to the right, the number of firms in the market falls, until there is only one firm at the far right. Also, the size of the firms, relative to the total market, increases from left to right.

Along this spectrum, perfect competition lies at the extreme left, with a large number of relatively small firms. At the other extreme lies monopoly, an industry containing only one relatively large firm. In between lie monopolistic competition and oligopoly.

Perfect Competition

Perfect competition is an ideal market structure characterized by a large number of small firms, identical products sold by all firms, freedom of entry and exit into the industry, and perfect knowledge of prices and technology. An important feature of a perfectly competitive firm is that it is a **price taker,** meaning it has no influence on the market price. While agriculture probably comes as close as any industry to being perfectly competitive, this market structure is an ideal model and no industry is truly perfectly competitive. For example, agriculture has neither perfect information of prices and technologies nor free entry and exit.

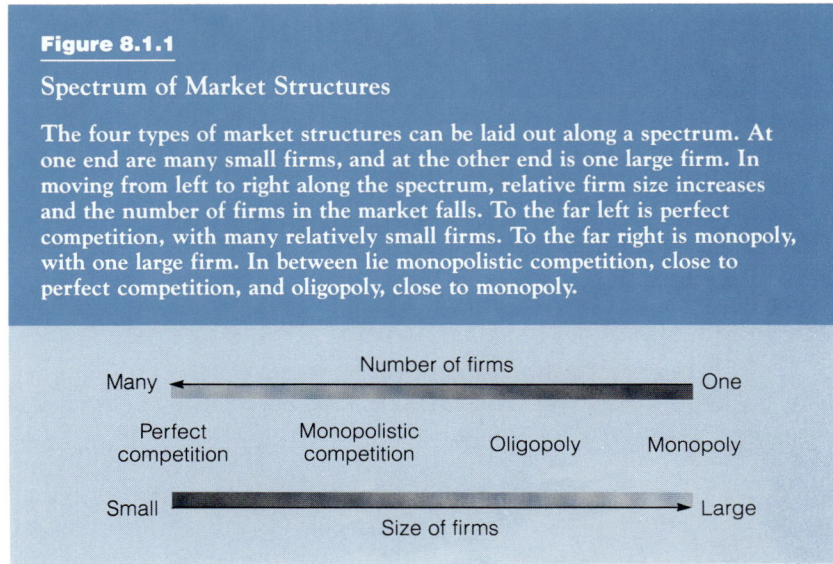

Figure 8.1.1

Spectrum of Market Structures

The four types of market structures can be laid out along a spectrum. At one end are many small firms, and at the other end is one large firm. In moving from left to right along the spectrum, relative firm size increases and the number of firms in the market falls. To the far left is perfect competition, with many relatively small firms. To the far right is monopoly, with one large firm. In between lie monopolistic competition, close to perfect competition, and oligopoly, close to monopoly.

Monopoly

Monopoly is a market structure characterized by a single firm supplying all output in the market. Before the breakup of AT&T in 1984, the telephone industry was a perfect example of a monopoly. Since the early 1900s, anyone who wanted phone service in the United States had to buy it from AT&T. Even after the breakup of AT&T, the regional divisions of AT&T—Southwestern Bell, Bell Atlantic, Pacific Telesis, and so on—maintain a degree of monopoly over local phone service in their area. Monopolies are still quite widespread, particularly in the public utilities such as electricity, water, and natural gas. A monopoly, unlike a perfectly competitive firm, is a **price maker,** meaning the firm can influence the market price.

Monopolistic Competition

Monopolistic competition is a market structure characterized by a large number of small firms, similar but not identical products, freedom of entry and exit, and imperfect information. Monopolistic competition lies toward the far left of the market structure spectrum, possessing many of the properties of perfect competition but with some significant differences. Like perfect competition, in monopolistic competition a large number of relatively small firms can enter or exit the industry quite easily. However, unlike perfect competition, monopolistically competitive firms do not sell identical products. Each product is similar but different enough that buyers know which firm is selling it. For example, IBM and Apple both sell computers that perform essentially the same functions but have slightly different features. They are differentiated products. Since monopolistically competitive firms sell differentiated products, each firm is a price maker, like a monopolist. Although perfect competition does not exist in the real world, monopolistic competition is widespread in the economy.

Oligopoly

Oligopoly is a market structure characterized by a small number of relatively large firms supplying most of the output in the market. While monopolistic competition is much like perfect competition, oligopoly is more like monopoly. An oligopolistic industry is characterized by a few relatively large firms. The main difference between oligopoly and monopoly is that oligopoly has two or more large firms rather than only one. Oligopolistic firms are also price makers and have an influence on the market price. Common examples of oligopolistic industries are steel and automobiles, where most of the output is produced by a handful of firms.

OBJECTIVES OF THE FIRM

While each of these four market structures have distinct characteristics, they also share one common attribute. To an economist, the primary objective of any firm, whether it is perfectly competitive, monopolistic, monopolistically competitive, or oligopolistic, is to maximize profits. These four types of firms differ not in their objectives but rather in the organization of their industry.

Although profit maximization constitutes the objective throughout our study of the firm and supply, firms in fact occasionally forego profit in pursuit of other objectives. For example, a firm might try to maximize sales rather than profit. Or it might pursue social objectives, such as a clean environment. Alternatively, the division of ownership and management for large corporations might lead managers to seek personal objectives rather than profit.

Profit Maximization

Profit maximization is the process of obtaining the highest possible level of profit through the production and sale of goods and services. A firm seeks to maximize profit if it decides to undertake an act when revenue exceeds cost and not undertake the act when cost exceeds revenue. Profit, which is discussed in more detail in Unit 10.1, is the difference between revenue and cost. In Unit 8.4 and all of Section 9, the primary decision of the firm with which we are concerned is a marginal change in production. The profit maximization objective implies that a firm marginally increases output if the additional revenue received from the sale of the output is greater than the additional cost of production. Since revenue increases more than cost, the firm's profit also increases, and the firm continues to increase production until profit can go no higher.

Sales Maximization

For many firms, large and small, the day-to-day working objective is **sales maximization,** the process of obtaining the highest possible level of sales. Clearly, sales lead to higher revenues and potentially to higher profit. But sales themselves can motivate a firm's behavior, even though they do not add to profit. Many firms and managers obtain a great deal of prestige from the overall level of sales and the size of the firm. A midlevel executive is more likely to gloat to a rival that his or her firm has twice the sales than that the firm earns twice the profit. A larger market share, through higher sales, can also enhance the economic and political power of a firm. For example, the president of Chrysler has more political and economic power than an Iowa farmer, even if the farmer makes a profit while the Chrysler stockholder does not.

Pursuit of Social Objectives

After achieving some acceptable level of profit, a firm may also focus on a **social objective,** an objective that exists when firms forego higher profits to pursue social goals. Such objectives might involve public service messages, support for the arts, or pursuit of a clean environment. While social objectives are at the expense of profit in the short run, this may not be true in the long run. If the socially responsible activities enhance the reputation and good-will of the firm, sales and profit might very well increase eventually. In fact, the act of giving up profit for the sake of socially responsible activities might even constitute an investment, in the same way the purchase of a piece of machinery is an investment. That is, the firm can use its profit to either purchase a piece of machinery or enhance the firm's social standing (and thus sales) by pursuing social objectives. In each case the firm is using short-run profit to obtain more profit in the longer run.

Pursuit of Personal Objectives

The division between management and ownership in corporations allows managers to pursue personal objectives in addition to, and sometimes at the expense of, profit. **Personal objectives** are the objectives of corporate managers when they forego profit to the firm in order to improve their own working environment, power base, or political goals. Managers keep their jobs if they produce an acceptable level of profit for the shareholders. But once they achieve this level, they can pursue activities that enhance their own personal well-being. In some cases this might involve sales maximization and the accompanying prestige, as mentioned before. In other cases managers might seek to establish their own empires within the corporate structure. The greater the division between ownership and management is, the more freedom management has to pursue its own personal objectives. The shareholder sees only the bottom line on the dividend statement, and the owners do not know how much greater dividends could have been. For example, if management decides to build a new executive washroom rather than expand an existing and profitable production operation, then dividends are high but less than they could have been.

NATURAL SELECTION

Each of these three non-profit-maximizing objectives—sales maximization, pursuit of social objectives, and pursuit of personal objectives—undoubtedly influences the production decisions of firms throughout the economy. All firms do not seek to maximize profit at all times. And even if firms do try to maximize profits, ignorance or incompetence might prevent them from doing so. In light of this, why do economists insist on assuming that firms maximize profit?

The objective of the profit maximization can be justified by borrowing the concept of natural selection from biology. Briefly, the concept of natural selection means that organisms best suited to their environment are the ones that naturally tend to survive and reproduce. In the context of economics, **natural selection** is the process in which the firms that are best suited to the economic environment naturally tend to survive. If a proprietor lacks a "business sense" and fails to make a profit, he or she does not remain in business. If the separation of ownership and management enables managers to pursue their own personal objectives at the expense of profit, then the firm suffers. Obviously, the firms with lower profits, and thus lower dividends, lose shareholders to more profitable firms. The lack of shareholders inhibits future expansion relative to the more profitable firms. And eventually the firm goes bankrupt. Therefore, while profit maximization may not be the only objective of a firm, the firms that directly, indirectly, or inadvertently increase profit are more likely to survive.

IN SUMMARY

The Firm

- The firm is the economic organization used by entrepreneurs to bring together resources for the production of goods and services. The firm is a functional entity. The characteristics of the firm are not important; what is important is what the firm does—combine resources to produce goods and services.

- The three legal forms of the firm are proprietorship, partnership, and corporation. The proprietorship is an owner-operated business, in which the proprietor supplies many of the resources, takes all risks, and reaps all rewards.

- The partnership is a jointly-owned firm, where two or more partners share risks and rewards equally. Partnerships are necessarily based on trust, since any decision made by one partner can cost the other partners their personal possessions. The corporation is a legal entity owned by a large number of shareholders, each with limited liability. This enables the corporation to raise more financial capital than either proprietorships or partnerships.

- Although proprietorships account for 76 percent of all firms in the United States, they produce only 8 percent of all output. Corporations account for only 16 percent of all firms, but their larger size enables them to produce 88 percent of all output. Partnerships comprise 8 percent of all firms and produce 4 percent of output.

- Four types of market structures studied in economics are perfect competition, monopoly, monopolistic competition, and oligopoly. Markets are distinguished mainly by the number and size of firms in the industry and by the differences in the product sold. In perfect competition a large number of relatively small firms exist, but in a monopoly only one large firm exists. Monopolistic competition and oligopoly lie between these two extremes.

- In profit maximization, marginal changes in output are based on marginal changes in revenue and cost. While economists state that the primary object of a firm is to maximize profit, other objectives can also come into play, such as sales maximization, pursuit of social objectives, and pursuit of personal objectives of management. However, natural selection of the most profitable firms tends to favor those that directly or indirectly maximize profits.

QUESTIONS FOR STUDY AND ANALYSIS

1. Would you consier a public library a firm? If so, what good or service does it produce? Can you think of any privately owned, profit-oriented firms that produce a comparable product? Explain.

2. Explain why proprietorships might be more suited to perfect competition and monopolistic competition, while corporations might be more suited to oligopoly and monopoly.

3. For each of the following types of firms discuss whether its owners/operators are more likely to pursue profit maximization, sales maximization, social objectives, personal objectives, or a combination of two or more.
   a. General Motors
   b. A small Idaho potato farmer
   c. Exxon
   d. A legal firm with five partners
   e. A large brewery in which all corporate stock is privately owned by a single family
   f. A former secretary of state who is currently a private consultant to the government

4. For each of the items in question 3, evaluate which ones are more likely to maximize profit through natural selection.

REVIEW GLOSSARY

corporation A firm that is also a distinct legal entity that exists separately from its owners. It is usually owned jointly by a large number of shareholders. Unlike partnerships and proprietorships, corporate shareholders have limited liability and can lose only their initial investment. This feature of corporations allows them to raise large amounts of financial capital.

firm An organization that combines resources for the production of goods and services. The firm is used by entrepreneurs to bring together otherwise unproductive factors. It is functionally defined and can be profit oriented, nonprofit, privately owned, or government controlled.

industry A group of firms that produces similar products or sells output in the same market.

limited liability The condition that exists when an owner of a firm is only responsible for his or her initial investment in the firm. This means the owner's personal property, unrelated to the firm's operation, cannot be used to satisfy the firm's obligations.

market structure The way in which an industry is organized. A market can be structured with only one firm or with several thousand. Each firm can have a great deal of control over the market price or no control at all.

monopolistic competition A market structure characterized by a large number of small firms, similar but not identical products, freedom of entry and exit, and imperfect information.

monopoly A market structure characterized by a single firm supplying all output in the market.

natural selection The process in which the firms that are best suited to the economic environment naturally tend to survive. This is an argument used to support the profit maximization assumption. It states that firms may pursue other objectives, but the firms that tend to maximize profit, either on purpose or by accident, are the ones that survive in the industry.

oligopoly A market structure characterized by a small number of relatively large firms supplying most of the output in the market.

partnership A firm that is owned and operated by two or more people. The risks and rewards of a partnership are shared equally by each partner unless one of the partners is a limited partner.

perfect competition An ideal market structure characterized by a large number of small firms, identical products sold by all firms, freedom of entry and exit into the industry, and perfect knowledge of prices and technology.

personal objective An objective of corporate managers that exists when they forego profit to the firm in order to improve their own working environment, power base, or political goals.

plant The physical capital at a particular location used for the production of goods and services.

price maker A firm that can influence the market price.

price taker A firm that has no influence on the market price.

profit maximization The process of obtaining the highest possible level of profit through the production and sale of goods and services. This represents the objective of a firm in which decisions are based exclusively on obtaining the most profit possible. Profit maximization is used as the underlying assumption in the economic analysis of a firm's output decision.

proprietorship A firm owned and operated by a single person. The proprietor takes all risks and receives all rewards. Quite often in a proprietorship, the owner also supplies most of the factors of production.

sales maximization The process of obtaining the highest possible level of sales.

social objective An objective that exists when firms forego higher profit to pursue social goals.

unlimited liability The condition that exists when the owner of a firm is personally responsible for any and all of the firm's debts. This means the owner's personal property, unrelated to the firm's operation, can be used to satisfy the firm's obligations.

UNIT 8.2

Production

The function of a firm is to transform resources into goods and services. An unproduced automobile is nothing more than piles of iron ore, rubber, bauxite, and petroleum, unusable by anyone needing transportation. Only after the firm combines the resources in a specific way is the automobile produced.

In this unit we examine the basic principles underlying the production of goods and services. We begin with an overview of the act of production, which conceptually entails the transformation of resources. We then make an important analytical distinction between a variable input and a fixed input and between the short run and the long run. With these concepts in hand, we look at the principles of short-run production in the last half of the unit. In particular, we identify and study the relationships between the total, average, and marginal product and a variable input. And finally, we discuss the law of diminishing marginal returns, the key relationship in the unit. Indeed, the principles of short-run production contained in this unit are crucial to our study of supply because the quantity of output supplied by a firm at the market price depends on the cost of producing it, which depends on the principles of production.

PRODUCTION

Our starting point is the act of production. **Production** is the process of transforming resources, through changes in structure, location, or time, into goods and services used for the satisfaction of wants and needs. An essential feature of the act of production is the relationship between inputs and outputs. Obviously, an output is the good or service being produced. An **input** is a resource or factor of production used in the production of a good or service. The basic process of production involves turning inputs that provide little or no satisfaction into outputs that provide more satisfaction.

In the act of production, the transformation of resources can occur in one of three ways. The transformation can involve a change in structure, such as processing iron ore into steel; a change in location, such as the shipment of goods across country; or a change in the time the good is consumed, illustrated by the storage of goods. A good is desired by consumers only if it is the correct form, at the right location, at the proper time. Suppose you demand a hamburger on the corner of Sixth and Western at noon. Your demand is not satisfied if the hamburger is not physically prepared. Neither is your demand satisfied if the hamburger is prepared but waits on the corner of Seventh and Western. Your demand is also unsatisfied if you are ready to eat at noon but the hamburger was prepared at 2:30 the day before.

Fixed and Variable Inputs

The inputs used in a production process can be classified as either fixed or variable. A **variable input** is an input whose quantity can be changed in the time period under consideration. A **fixed input** is an input whose quantity cannot be changed in the time period under consideration. For example, in terms of automobile production over a two-month period, the size of the factory is fixed. Two months is not long enough to expand the existing factory or to build a new one. But it is very easy to change the number of workers within a two-month period. Thus, labor represents a variable input and the factory, a fixed input.

Short Run and Long Run

The distinction between fixed and variable inputs is related to the time period under consideration. Although we often consider labor the variable input and capital the fixed input, this is not always the

UNIT 8.2 • PRODUCTION

case. A firm can build several factories if the time period is two decades, making capital a variable input. However, for a shorter time period, such as two hours, even labor is a fixed input.

For this reason we make a distinction between two periods, short run and long run. The **short run** is a period in which at least one input is variable and at least one input is fixed. The **long run** is a period in which all inputs are variable. The difference between short run and long run depends not simply on time but also on the nature of the industry. If the automobile industry needs two years to build a factory, then the short run is any time less than two years, and the long run is any time greater than two years. For another production process, such as a roadside vegetable market, if a new stand can be constructed in one week, then the short run is less than a week, and the long run is greater than a week.

THE PRINCIPLES OF SHORT-RUN PRODUCTION

The simplest case of short-run production involves one variable input and one fixed input. The use of a single variable input lets us isolate the relationship between the input and the output. To see this relationship, let's look at a simple example: the production of pizzas in a small pizza parlor. The fixed input is capital, including the pizza parlor and the associated equipment, and the variable input is the amount of labor used to prepare and serve pizza to the customers. Since we are concerned with short-run production, let's keep the fixed input, the size of the pizza parlor, unchanged.

Total Product and the Total Product Curve

The question is how many pizzas can be produced for different quantities of labor, the variable input? Suppose one person working an eight-hour day in the pizza parlor can produce 20 pizzas, two workers can produce 50 pizzas, three workers can produce 75 pizzas, and four workers can produce 95 pizzas.

Table 8.2.1

Hypothetical Production of Pizzas

In the short run, as more of a variable input is added to a fixed input, total production increases. Marginal product is the additional output attributable to each additional unit of the variable input. In this example the first unit of labor adds 20 pizzas to production, the second unit adds 30 pizzas, and so on. Average product is the total product divided by the quantity of labor. In this case the average product for two workers is 25 pizzas, for five workers it is 22 pizzas, and so on.

Amount of Labor	Total Product (pizzas)	Marginal Product (pizzas)	Average Product (pizzas)
0	0		0
		20	
1	20		20
		30	
2	50		25
		25	
3	75		25
		20	
4	95		23.8
		15	
5	110		22
		10	
6	120		20
		5	
7	125		17.9
		0	
8	125		15.6

Table 8.2.1 presents this hypothetical schedule for the production of pizzas. The second column lists the total product. **Total product** is the total quantity of output produced by a firm with the given quantity of inputs.

In Figure 8.2.1 we see a graphical representation of the relationship between pizza production and labor, which is the total product curve. The **total product curve** is a curve depicting the relationship between total product and the variable input. If 2 units of labor are used, the curve tells us that a total of 50 pizzas are produced; if 6 units are used, 120 pizzas are produced. The curve continues to rise until the eighth unit of labor is used, meaning an increase in the quantity of the variable input leads to an increase in the quantity of output.

Note that the slope over the entire range of the curve in Figure 8.2.1 is positive, meaning output increases with additional units of labor. With a few units of labor, the slope is rather steep, but as more units of labor are added, the slope becomes flatter. And when eight units of labor are employed, the total product curve has a slope of zero. To see why the total product curve is shaped in this way, let's turn our attention to one of the more important concepts we study in economics, marginal product.

Marginal Product

Marginal product tells us the contribution each unit makes to production by the firm. **Marginal product is the change in total product resulting from a change in a variable input, holding all other inputs unchanged.** It is specified as

$$\text{marginal product} = \frac{\text{change in total product}}{\text{change in variable input}}$$

Note in Table 8.2.1 that 20 pizzas are produced with 1 unit of labor, or one worker, but 50 pizzas are produced with 2 units, or two workers. Because one additional worker produces 30 additional pizzas, the second unit of the variable input has a marginal product of 30 pizzas. Keep in mind that labor is the only variable input, and we are holding the quantity of capital (the pizza parlor) fixed. The marginal product attributable to each additional unit of labor is listed in the third column of Table 8.2.1.

Average Product

As the name suggests, **average product is the quantity of total product produced per unit of variable input, holding all other inputs unchanged.** It is specified as

$$\text{average product} = \frac{\text{total product}}{\text{variable input}}$$

The average product of pizza production is listed in the fourth column of Table 8.2.1. Average product increases at first, reaching a high of 25 pizzas per unit of labor for both the second and third worker, but it starts to fall after the third unit of labor. The pattern displayed by average product, which mirrors the pattern found in marginal product, results from the key principle of short-run production, the law of diminishing marginal returns.

THE LAW OF DIMINISHING MARGINAL RETURNS

In the short run, all production processes succumb to the law of diminishing marginal returns. The **law of diminishing marginal returns is a principle stating that as more and more of a variable input is combined with a fixed input, eventually the mar-**

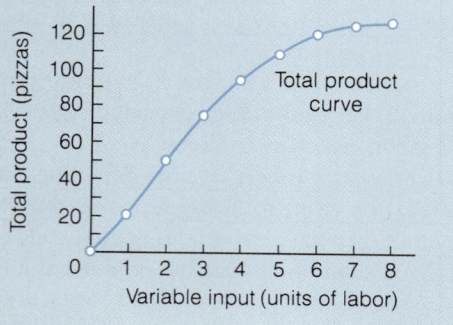

Figure 8.2.1

Total Product Curve

The quantity of output produced depends, in the short run, on the quantity of the variable input. The total product curve drawn here indicates that if 2 units of labor are used, then 50 pizzas are produced, and 6 units lead to the production of 120 pizzas.

ginal product of the variable input declines. For example, imagine what would happen if the law of diminishing marginal returns did not hold for corn production. Suppose Iowa corn farmers could add additional variable inputs, such as labor, seeds, and fertilizer, to a fixed amount of land *without* a decline in marginal product. They could grow all of the corn needed in the United States on one acre of land simply by adding the necessary amounts of variable inputs. In fact, they would not even need an acre of land, but only a flower pot. Clearly, this is not possible. There is a limit to the total product that can be obtained with a fixed input because the capacity of the fixed input is eventually reached.

The law of diminishing marginal returns is reflected in the decrease in marginal product in the third column of Table 8.2.1. After the second unit of labor is added, each additional worker adds less additional output. The marginal product of the third worker is less than the second, and the marginal product of the fourth is less than the third.

Let's look at the production of pizzas to see why. When one person operates the pizza parlor, he or she must perform every function needed to produce and sell the pizza including making the pizza, operating the cash register, cleaning tables, and washing dishes. Therefore, only 20 pizzas are produced. However, when a second worker is added, these functions can be divided up, with one person making the pizza and the second person performing the other jobs. This division of tasks makes both workers more productive, and thus the second worker is responsible for the production of an additional 30 pizzas.

However, a third worker contributes only 25 additional pizzas to total production. Since in this example we assume all units of labor are identical, the decrease in production cannot be attributed to a lack of competence. Rather, the reduction in marginal product with the third unit of labor is due to the law of diminishing marginal returns. This law applies because the amount of capital is fixed. The size of the pizza parlor is fixed. The third, fourth, and fifth workers have to use the existing amount of fixed capital. The parlor has limited oven space, floor space, and tables with which to produce and serve pizzas to the customers. While the addition of more workers generally enables production to increase, the workers actually contribute relatively less and less. In fact, the addition of the eighth worker contributes nothing to output, and the marginal product is zero. The marginal product of the ninth unit could even be negative, causing total product to fall.

The Relationship Between Total Product and Marginal Product

Marginal product is simply the slope of the total product curve. The slope of the total product curve is defined as the change in total product divided by the change in labor, which is the definition of marginal product.

To see why this relationship exists, let's turn our attention to the slope of the total product curve. Panel a of Figure 8.2.2 reproduces the total product curve from Figure 8.2.1. Panel b depicts the relationship between labor and marginal product. The marginal product increases for the first 2 units of output, until the law of diminishing marginal returns sets in and the marginal product curve declines. The curve hits the horizontal axis when marginal product is zero, with 8 units of labor. Note that marginal product is plotted at the midpoints between two quantities of the variable input in panel b because marginal product represents a change from one quantity to the other. For example, the marginal product of the second unit is 30 and is plotted accordingly between the first and second unit of labor.

If we look closely at the total product curve in panel a of Figure 8.2.2, we can see that marginal product increases over the same quantity of inputs as the slope of the total product curve. And after the law of diminishing marginal returns sets in and marginal product declines, the slope of the total product curve also becomes flatter. When the total product curve flattens out, with a zero slope at the eighth unit, marginal product is also zero.

Figure 8.2.2

Marginal Product Curve

The marginal product curve is the slope of the total product curve. With the first 2 units of labor, the slope of the total product curve increases as marginal product becomes greater. After the second unit of labor, the slope of the total product curve becomes flatter, and marginal product falls. For the eighth unit of labor, marginal product is zero, and the total product curve levels off.

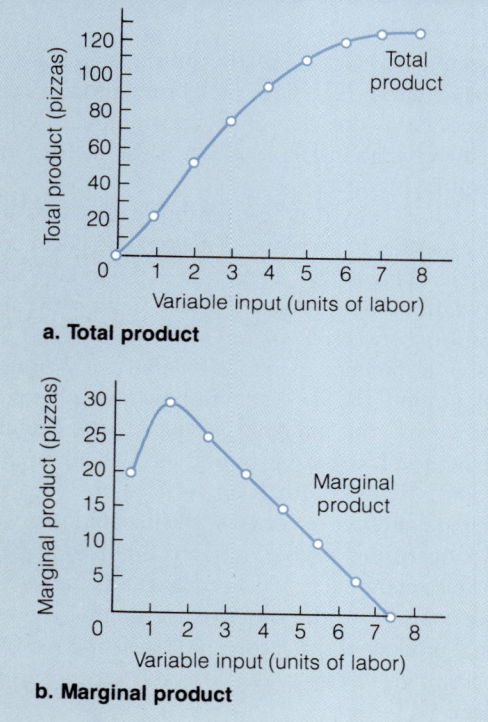

Figure 8.2.3

Marginal and Average Product Curves

When the marginal product curve is above the average product curve, the average product curve is rising. When the marginal curve is below the average product curve, the average product curve is falling. When the marginal product curve intersects the average product curve, the average product curve is at its peak and is not changing.

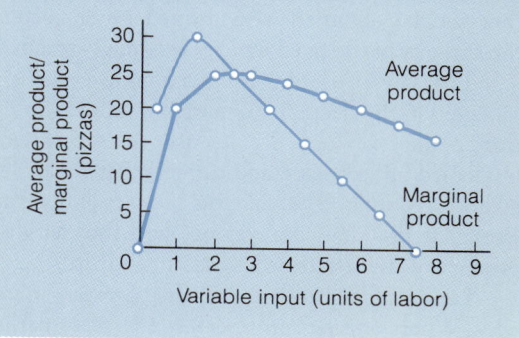

The Relationship Between Average Product and Marginal Product

An important relationship also exists between average product and marginal product. In fact, the decrease in the average product that occurs after the third unit of labor, as seen in Table 8.2.1, is a consequence of the law of diminishing marginal returns.

When marginal product is greater than average product, average product is increasing. When marginal product is less than average product, average product is decreasing. When marginal product is equal to average product, average product is not changing. Since the law of diminishing marginal returns causes the marginal product to decline, it indirectly causes the average product to decline as well.

In Figure 8.2.3, the marginal product and average product values from Table 8.2.1 are plotted to illustrate how average product is related to diminishing returns. The curve that peaks first, and highest, is the marginal product curve. Note in Table 8.2.1 that marginal product reaches a high of 30 for the second unit of labor, while average product reaches a high of only 25 for the second and third units of labor. Note also that the marginal product curve cuts the horizontal axis where the marginal product is zero, at the eighth unit of labor, and that further increases in labor might even lead to a negative marginal product. However, the average product is never negative. A negative average product means output is negative, which is impossible.

IN SUMMARY

Production

- Production of goods and services involves the transformation of inputs in structure, location, or time. If a good or service does not satisfy the buyer's physical form, place, and time, it cannot be consumed.

- Inputs can be classified as either fixed or variable. The quantity of a variable input can be changed in the time period under consideration, but the quantity of a fixed input cannot be. The short run is a time period in which at least one input is variable and one input is fixed. The long run is a time period in which all inputs are variable.

- Three important measures of production are total product, marginal product, and average product. Marginal product is the additional output resulting from an additional unit of the variable input. Average product is the total product per unit of input.

- The law of diminishing marginal returns states that as additional units of a variable input are added to a fixed input, eventually the marginal product will fall. The law of diminishing returns is directly responsible for the decline in marginal product and indirectly responsible for the decline in average product.

QUESTIONS FOR STUDY AND ANALYSIS

1. Suppose you are given the following information relating total product and quantity of labor in the short run:

Labor	Total Product
0	0
1	50
2	110
3	180
4	240
5	290
6	330
7	360
8	380
9	390
10	390

    a. Compute the marginal and average product for each quantity of labor.
    b. At what quantity of labor does diminishing marginal returns begin?
    c. At what quantity of labor is average product at its highest?
    d. At what quantity of labor is marginal product zero?
    e. At what quantity of labor is average product zero?

2. Discuss how each of the following acts of production involve transformation of structure, location, and/or time.
    a. Furniture shipped across the country by a moving company
    b. A professional football game
    c. Production of an automobile
    d. A u-store-it self-service storage center
    e. Watching television

3. Explain how the law of diminishing marginal returns affects the time you spend studying for class. What are the fixed and variable inputs? Do you think the marginal product of studying is ever zero? Explain.

4. a. Complete the following table with the information given.

Labor	TP	MP	AP
0	0		
1		5	
2			7.5
3		15	
4	42		
5	51		
6			9.5
7	60		
8		0	

b. At what quantity of labor are average product and marginal product equal?

c. Compute the slope of the total product curve. How does it compare to marginal product?

d. For quantities of labor greater than two, how are the marginal product and average product curves related? Why?

5. Would a firm ever operate in the range of output in which marginal product is increasing? Explain. Would it ever operate in the range of output in which marginal product is negative? Explain.

6. Can you think of a production process in which the law of diminishing marginal returns does not operate? If so, why not?

7. Based on your knowledge of hospitals and the principles of production, answer the following questions:
a. What good and/or service does a hospital produce?
b. What period of time would be considered the short run for a hospital? Why? What are the fixed and variable inputs for a hospital in this short-run period?
c. Which of the four market structures best characterizes hospitals in your city or town? Explain.

REVIEW GLOSSARY

average product The quantity of total product produced per unit of variable input, holding all other inputs unchanged.

fixed input An input whose quantity cannot be changed in the time period under consideration.

input A resource or factor of production used in the production of a good or service.

law of diminishing marginal returns A principle stating that as more and more of a variable input is combined with a fixed input, eventually the marginal product of the variable input declines.

long run A period of time in which all inputs are variable.

marginal product The change in total product resulting from a change in a variable input, holding all other inputs unchanged.

production The process of transforming resources, through changes in structure, location, or time, into goods and services used for the satisfaction of wants and needs.

short run A period of time in which at least one input is variable and one input is fixed.

total product The total quantity of output produced by a firm with the given quantity of inputs.

total product curve A curve depicting the relationship between total product and the variable input. The slope of the total product curve is the marginal product of the variable input.

variable input An input whose quantity can be changed in the time period under consideration.

UNIT 8.3

The Costs of Production

The second layer of the foundation underlying supply is the costs of production. The costs incurred by a firm in the production of goods and services are based on the principles of production identified in the previous unit, particularly the law of diminishing marginal returns. After we examine the costs of production in this unit, we see in Unit 8.4 that the law of supply depends on the law of diminishing marginal returns.

To begin, we discuss the fundamental concept of opportunity cost, first introduced in Unit 1.5. In particular, we see that the accounting costs used by firms for their record keeping are not necessarily the opportunity costs used in economics. We then look at the components of total costs incurred by a firm in short-run production, including total variable cost and total fixed cost. Because in our study of supply average costs are more useful than total costs, we focus on three types of average cost: average total cost, average variable cost, and average fixed cost. And finally, we look at the most important measure of cost, marginal cost.

OPPORTUNITY COST

In economics, when we speak of cost we mean opportunity cost. **Opportunity cost** is the highest value of goods or other benefits given up when a good is produced or any action is taken. The production of other goods is foregone because the resources used to produce one good are not available to produce the others.

The opportunity cost of using a factor of production is the value of output the factor could have contributed to the alternative production process, or the marginal product of the factor. For example, suppose a worker in the clothing industry decides to take an hour off from work to help out in the family's computer store. What is the opportunity cost of this hour of labor? If the worker contributes one pair of jeans selling for $10 a pair, then the opportunity cost of working in the family's computer store is $10.

As we see in Part IV, a profit-motivated business operating in a perfectly competitive labor market tends to pay labor the value of its marginal product. This means the opportunity cost of labor is equal to the wage rate. To simplify matters in this unit, we equate the wage rate with the opportunity cost of labor. The other factors of production—land, capital, and entrepreneurship—also have opportunity costs, equal to the factor payments of rent, interest, and profit. But why is profit, the revenue remaining after costs are paid, considered an opportunity cost?

Economic and Accounting Costs

To see how profit can be an opportunity cost, let's first examine the difference between accounting costs and economic costs. **Economic costs** are the opportunity costs incurred in production. **Accounting costs** are the explicit costs incurred in production that involve direct payments for the inputs. While these two definitions seem similar, there is one important distinction. The accounting costs used by a firm in its profit and loss statement include all explicit expenditures for inputs used in production, which for the most part represent the opportunity costs of the inputs. However, in many cases a firm incurs implicit opportunity costs that do not involve direct payment.

For example, the clothing worker who helps out in the family computer store has an opportunity cost of $10 per hour. If no explicit payment is made to the worker, then this is an implicit opportunity cost. The cost may not be explicitly entered into the firm's books, but it is an opportunity cost of operating the store nonetheless.

Accounting, Normal, and Economic Profits

The most important implicit opportunity cost in economics is profit. We need to distinguish between three types of profits: accounting profit, normal profit, and economic profit. An **accounting profit** is computed by subtracting the explicit accounting costs from the revenue received by the firm. This is the type of profit familiar to most people. However, one very important implicit opportunity cost is almost never included as an accounting cost, normal profit. **Normal profit** is the profit that can be earned by the entrepreneur in an alternative production process. An entrepreneur in one industry is foregoing profit that could be earned in another industry, in the same way a laborer is foregoing the wage from another job. Thus normal profit is an opportunity cost. The third type of profit is economic profit. **Economic profit** is the difference between all opportunity costs (including a normal profit) and the revenue received by a firm. Economic profit is what remains after all factors of production are paid their opportunity cost. Keep in mind that throughout the remainder of this unit the discussion of the costs of production includes a normal profit.

TOTAL COST

Total cost is the sum of total variable costs and total fixed costs. Total cost can be separated into total variable costs and total fixed costs. **Total variable costs** are costs that change as the quantity of output changes. If no output is produced, there is no variable cost. Thus, variable cost is closely associated with variable inputs. As a rule of thumb, the purchase of a variable input by the firm constitutes a variable cost. If a firm alters the existing quantity of labor used to produce a good, variable cost also changes.

Total fixed costs are costs that do not change with the quantity of output. Fixed costs are incurred whether or not any output is produced. Thus, fixed cost is closely associated with fixed inputs. A fixed input, like capital, in the short run must be compensated for, regardless of the level of output. If the entrepreneur takes out a loan to build a factory, the loan payments must be met whether 10 or 10,000 units of output are produced.

Total Variable Cost and Total Product

As mentioned before, the total variable cost of production is related to variable inputs. If we have only one variable input, such as labor, we can demonstrate the relationship between variable cost and the variable input. Panel b of Figure 8.3.1 depicts a total product curve similar to the curve for pizza production in Figure 8.2.1. Panel a depicts the total variable cost curve.

First, note that the vertical axes of both panels measure quantity of output. The horizontal axis of panel b measures the quantity of labor in units per day, but the horizontal axis of panel a is slightly different in that it measures the quantity of labor multiplied by the wage rate, which we assume is constant. The value of the wage times the quantity of labor used to produce the good represents the variable cost. In this example labor is the only variable input, and the only way to produce more output is to hire more labor.

Panel a is a little unorthodox in the way total variable cost is measured along the horizontal axis. The farther left we go on the horizontal axis, the greater is the total variable cost. Now look at panel b. If 4 units of labor are hired, 7 units of the output are produced. The variable cost of producing the 7 units of output if the wage is $50 per unit and 4 units of labor are hired is $200 (= 4 units × $50 per unit).

Here is how we get from panel b to panel a. At 4 units of labor and 7 units of output, measured on the vertical axes of both panels, we extend over to the point directly above $200 of total variable

UNIT 8.3 • THE COSTS OF PRODUCTION

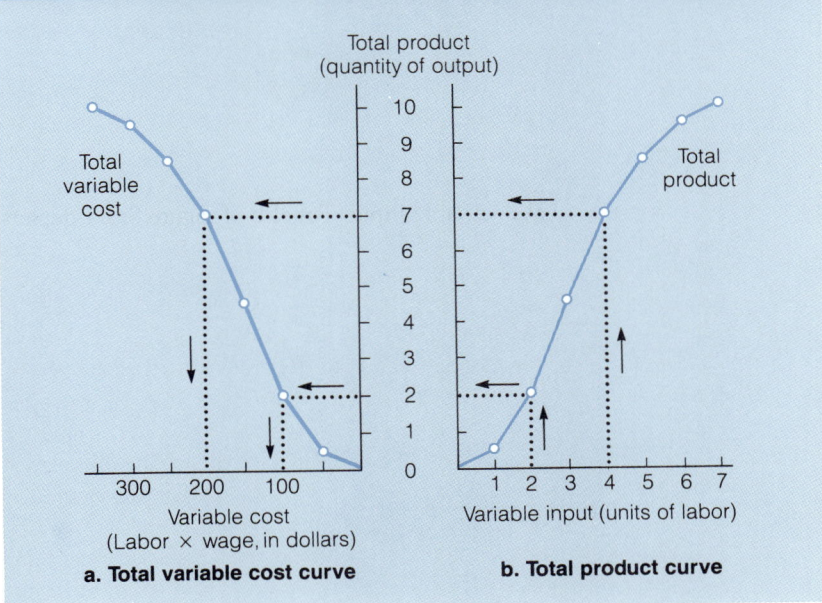

Figure 8.3.1

Total Variable Cost and Total Product Curves

The total variable cost curve is derived from the total product curve. The horizontal axis in panel b measures the quantity of labor, whereas the horizontal axis in panel a measures the cost of the labor (wage × labor). If the wage rate is $50 per unit, and 4 units of labor lead to 7 units of output, the variable cost of the output is $200. The total variable cost curve is the mirror image of the total product curve.

a. Total variable cost curve

b. Total product curve

cost on the horizontal axis of panel a. This is the point on the total variable cost curve that tells us that the production of 7 units leads to $200 in variable cost. Now take another point on the horizontal axis of panel b, such as 2 units of labor. Two units of labor result in 2 units of output, so the variable cost is $100 (= 2 units × $50 per unit).

In short, all of the combinations of variable cost and quantities make up the total variable cost curve. These combinations are listed in the first two columns of Table 8.3.1. Note that zero output leads to zero total variable cost. If no output is produced, then no variable inputs are hired. Note also that panel a is the mirror image of panel b, the main difference being that panel a measures the *quantity* of labor, while panel b measures the *cost* of labor. The total variable cost curve is also presented in a more conventional manner in Figure 8.3.2.

Total Fixed Cost

While variable cost incurred by a firm in the production of output is extremely important, the firm also incurs fixed cost unrelated to the quantity of output produced. The firm pays fixed cost whether

Table 8.3.1

The Costs of Production

Total variable cost depends on the costs of the variable inputs. The quantity of output can be increased only by increasing the quantity of the variable input and thus variable cost. Total fixed cost is related to fixed inputs and does not vary with the quantity of output. Total cost is simply the sum of the total variable and the total fixed cost. Marginal cost is the additional cost (either total cost or total variable cost) incurred for each additional unit of output produced.

Quantity	Total Variable Cost (TVC)	Total Fixed Cost (TFC)	Total Cost (TC)	Marginal Cost (MC)
0	$ 0	$100	$100	
1	60	100	160	$60
2	100	100	200	40
3	125	100	225	25
4	140	100	240	15
5	150	100	250	10
6	170	100	270	20
7	200	100	300	30
8	240	100	340	40
9	290	100	390	50
10	350	100	450	60

10,000 units of output or 10 units of output are produced. In the short run the firm pays fixed cost even if no output is produced.

What type of fixed cost does a firm pay no matter how much output is produced? Recall that fixed cost is associated with fixed inputs, in much the same way that variable cost is related to variable inputs. However, fixed cost often contains costs unrelated to a specific fixed input, unlike variable cost. Some examples of fixed cost are interest on borrowed funds, rent on land, normal profit, insurance premiums, and property taxes. All fixed cost must be paid as long as the firm is in business in the short run. The only way to avoid fixed cost is to get out of the business, which entails selling off all capital, and thus causing the quantity of fixed inputs to fall to zero (no business, no capital). However, when this happens, the firm is no longer in the short run, since capital has now become a variable input.

The horizontal line in Figure 8.3.2, which represents a total fixed cost curve, illustrates everything that we have said about total fixed cost. Note that fixed cost is unchanged even when the quantity of output varies. And even if no output is produced, the firm still pays total fixed cost, equal to $100.

The Total Cost Curve

Now let's put total variable cost and total fixed cost together. The sum of total variable cost and total

Figure 8.3.2

Total Cost Curves

The total fixed cost curve is a horizontal line on which fixed cost is the same for every quantity of output. The total cost curve is found by vertically adding the total variable cost curve to the total fixed cost curve. At 4 units of output, total fixed cost is $100 and total variable cost is $140, for a total cost of $240.

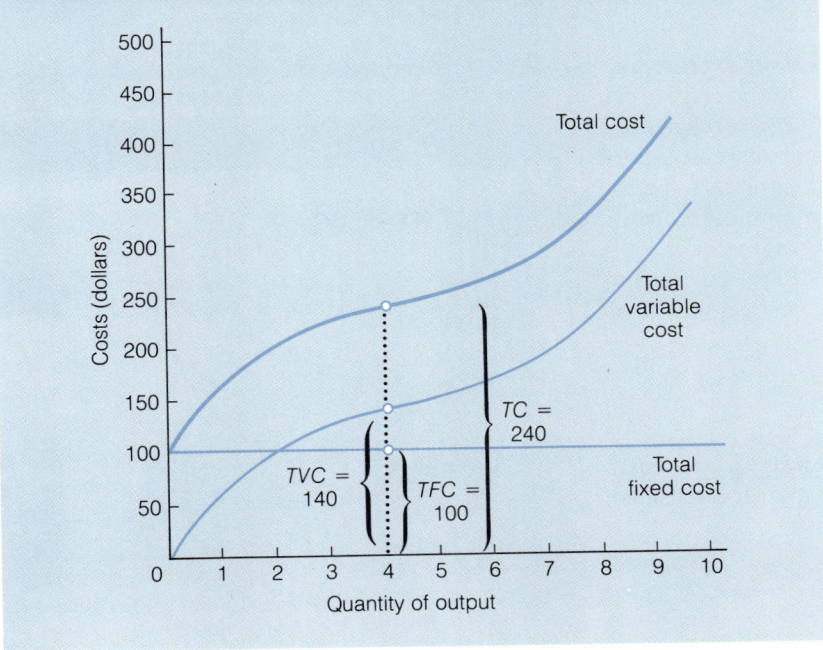

fixed cost in the second and third columns of Table 8.3.1 is total cost, listed in the fourth column. To determine total cost, merely combine the cost that varies with output (total variable cost) with the cost that does not vary with output (total fixed cost). This is specified as

total cost = total variable cost + total fixed cost

Graphically, we can construct the total cost curve in the same way. If we vertically add the total variable cost and total fixed cost curves in Figure 8.3.2, we obtain the total cost curve. For a particular quantity of output, perhaps 4 units, the variable cost is $140. Fixed cost is $100, as it would be for every quantity of output, meaning the total cost of producing 4 units of output is $240, which lies on the third curve in Figure 8.3.2. If we identify the sum of the variable cost and the fixed cost for every quantity of output and plot the value on the graph, we end up with the total cost curve.

Note that when all three curves are plotted together, the total cost curve has the same shape as the total variable cost curve. In fact, the vertical distance between the total cost and total variable cost curves is exactly the same at every quantity of output. This distance between the total cost and total variable cost curves represents the total fixed cost, which is always the same. Furthermore, the slope of the total cost curve is exactly the same as the slope of the total variable cost curve at every quantity of output, which becomes important in the discussion of marginal cost. But first, let's look at the average costs of production.

AVERAGE COST

Three important measures of cost are average variable cost, average fixed cost, and average total cost. Each measure of average cost is related to, and derived from, a corresponding total cost. Average cost is determined by dividing the corresponding total cost by the quantity of output to obtain the per unit cost of each output. In essence, we are looking at the variable cost needed per unit of output, fixed cost needed per unit, and per unit total cost.

Average Variable Cost

The first measure of cost is **average variable cost**, total variable cost per unit of output. It is specified as

$$\text{average variable cost} = \frac{\text{total variable cost}}{\text{quantity}}$$

The average variable cost curve in Figure 8.3.3 is noticeably U-shaped, meaning that average variable cost is initially high, then falls, and later begins to increase again. In a moment we see how the U-shape of the average variable cost curve is based on the law of diminishing marginal returns.

Average Fixed Cost

The second curve in Figure 8.3.3 is average fixed cost. Note that it is not U-shaped, but looks more like a ski slope. **Average fixed cost** is total fixed cost per unit of output. It is specified as

$$\text{average fixed cost} = \frac{\text{total fixed cost}}{\text{quantity}}$$

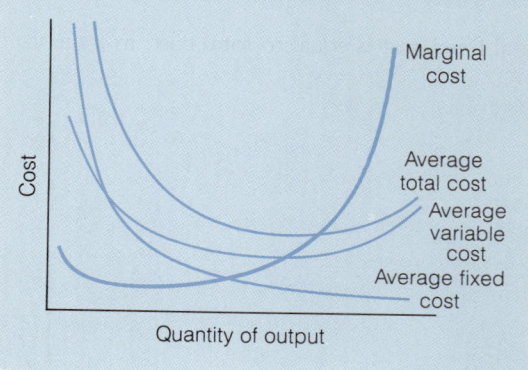

Figure 8.3.3

Marginal and Average Cost Curves

The curves of average variable cost and average total cost are both U-shaped, whereas the curve of average fixed cost is always negatively sloped. The difference between average total cost and average variable cost curves is average fixed cost. Marginal cost is below both average total and average variable cost curves when they decline, and above them when they rise. The intersection of the marginal cost curve with the average variable and total cost curves is the minimum point on the respective curve.

The average fixed cost curve has a negative slope, unlike the average variable cost curve, which has both negatively and positively sloped segments. Average fixed cost starts out relatively high, but as quantity increases, average fixed cost becomes less.

The reason for the shape of the average fixed cost curve is relatively simple. Remember that total fixed cost does not depend on quantity of output. Rent, insurance premiums, and property taxes are incurred whether 10 units or 10,000 units are produced. But if we compute the average fixed cost for 10 units, the per unit cost is much higher than if we compute it for 10,000 units. For example, if total fixed cost is $50,000, then the average fixed cost of producing 10 units is $5000 per unit, whereas the average fixed cost of producing 10,000 units is

$5 per unit. Clearly, the average fixed cost is less with a larger output.

Average Total Cost

The second U-shaped curve in Figure 8.3.3 is average total cost. **Average total cost** is total cost per unit of output. It is specified as

$$\text{average total cost} = \frac{\text{total cost}}{\text{quantity}}$$

While dividing total cost by quantity is one way to calculate average total cost, it is not the only way. If we know the variable cost per unit and the fixed cost per unit, then we also know the total cost per unit. In the same way that total variable cost plus total fixed cost is equal to total cost, average variable cost plus average fixed cost is equal to average total cost.

For a given quantity of output in Figure 8.3.3, average fixed cost added to average variable cost equals average total cost. The average total cost curve is the vertical addition of the average fixed cost and the average variable cost curves. The vertical distance between the average total cost and average variable cost curves is average fixed cost, in the same way that the vertical distance between the total cost and total variable cost curves is total fixed cost. However, unlike total cost and total variable cost, the slopes of the average total cost and average variable cost curves are not the same.

Note that the vertical distance between the average total cost and average variable cost curves is very large at small quantities of output but smaller at larger quantities of output. And at very large quantities of output, the two curves almost touch. Recall that the vertical distance is average fixed cost, so as the quantity of output increases, average fixed cost, and thus the vertical distance, declines.

MARGINAL COST

The last, and most important, measure of cost is marginal cost. **Marginal cost** is the change in total cost resulting from a change in the quantity of output. It is specified as

$$\text{marginal cost} = \frac{\text{change in total cost}}{\text{change in quantity}}$$

In the same way that marginal product is the slope of the total product curve, marginal cost is the slope of the total cost curve. Marginal cost tells us how much total cost increases for each unit increase in output, as illustrated in Table 8.3.1. Marginal cost in the fifth column is found by taking the change in total cost in the fourth column.

Marginal cost tells us even more. As output increases, total cost and total variable cost both increase because the variable input is increased. Since there is no change in total fixed cost, the change in total cost is exactly the same as the change in total variable cost. Thus, marginal cost can also be specified as the change in total variable cost resulting from a change in the quantity, or

$$\text{marginal cost} = \frac{\text{change in total variable cost}}{\text{change in quantity}}$$

If marginal cost is the slope of the total cost curve, then marginal cost must also be the slope of the total variable cost curve. And this means that the slopes of the total variable cost and total cost curves are the same, which is exactly what we concluded when we first discussed total cost and total variable cost.

THE LAW OF DIMINISHING MARGINAL RETURNS

The law of diminishing marginal returns affects not only short-run production by a firm but also the costs of production in the short run. As the marginal product of the variable input decreases, the firm must hire increasingly more units to get the same increase in output. The costs of hiring the variable input are reflected in the short-run production costs. Let's see how the law of diminishing marginal returns affects the short-run costs of production.

Suppose that we want to increase the quantity of output from 5 to 6 units. The only way to do this in the short run is to increase the quantity of the variable input and, subsequently, variable cost. Let's further suppose that the marginal product of labor is $\frac{1}{2}$, meaning to increase output from 5 to 6, 2 more units of labor are needed. If the wage is $5, total variable cost and total cost both increase by $10.

Now let's see what happens if we increase output from 10 to 11 units, which also requires additional labor. However, the marginal product of labor has fallen from $\frac{1}{2}$ to $\frac{1}{3}$ because of the law of diminishing marginal returns, so that 3 more units of labor are needed to increase output from 10 to 11 units. The cost now increases by $15 instead of $10. Total cost and total variable cost increase more from 10 to 11 units than from 5 to 6 units as a result of the law of diminishing marginal returns.

Look at what has happened to the total variable cost and total cost curves. At 5 units of output the increase in cost is only $10, but at 10 units of output the increase is $15. The marginal cost and thus the slopes of the total variable cost and total cost curves are becoming greater at larger quantities of output. The law of diminishing marginal returns implies that a firm needs increasingly greater amounts of the variable input to increase production, because each individual unit is less productive.

What about the average curves? Note again in Figure 8.3.3 that the marginal cost curve intersects both the average variable cost and average total cost curves at their minimum points. In addition, both of these average curves fall when the marginal cost curve lies below and rise when the marginal cost curve is above, the same type of relationship that we saw between marginal product and average product.

It is the marginal cost curve that makes the average variable cost curve at first decrease (because the marginal curve is below it), then subsequently increase (because the marginal curve is above it). Since the marginal cost curve increases, and thus rises above the average variable cost curve, the shape of the average variable cost curve is indirectly affected by the law of diminishing marginal returns.

What about the average total cost curve? Is it U-shaped for the same reason? Yes and no. The average total cost curve is U-shaped for two reasons, since average total cost represents the sum of both average variable cost and average fixed cost. Average total cost is relatively high at small quantities of output because both average variable cost and average fixed cost are high. When average fixed cost and average variable cost both decrease, average total cost declines right along with them.

As output increases, average fixed cost continues to decline, but average variable cost starts to increase. The initial increase in average variable cost is not enough to offset the continuing decrease in average fixed cost. But eventually, average variable cost increases more than average fixed cost declines, and thus average total cost increases. At relatively large quantities of output, average total cost increases due to marginal cost and the law of diminishing marginal returns.

IN SUMMARY

The Costs of Production

- The total opportunity cost of producing goods and services is based on the alternative production foregone by all of the factors, including the entrepreneur. Normal profit is an important, and often overlooked, opportunity cost. Accounting profit is usually not equal to economic profit because it also includes normal profit.

- Total variable cost is the cost of using variable inputs, enabling the total variable cost curve to be obtained from the total product curve. Variable cost is zero when no output is produced since no inputs are hired.

- Total fixed cost is related to fixed inputs and must be paid in the short run whether or not any output is produced. The only way to avoid

UNIT 8.3 • THE COSTS OF PRODUCTION

fixed cost is to go out of business, moving the firm from the short run to the long run.

- Total cost is the sum of total variable cost and total fixed cost. The total cost curve is obtained by vertically adding the total fixed cost curve to the total variable cost curve. Because total fixed cost is constant, the slopes of the total cost and total variable cost curves are the same.

- Average variable cost, average fixed cost, and average total cost are the per unit costs of producing output. Average total cost is the sum of average variable cost and average fixed cost. The average total cost curve can be found by vertically adding the average fixed cost curve to the average variable cost curve.

- Marginal cost is the additional cost incurred from producing an additional unit of output. Since the only cost that varies with output is variable cost, marginal cost is based on the change in either total cost or total variable cost.

- The manner in which costs vary with output (the shapes of the cost curves) depends on the law of diminishing marginal returns. This law, by decreasing the marginal productivity of the variable input, increases the cost of producing more output.

QUESTIONS FOR STUDY AND ANALYSIS

1. Assume that a professor of engineering decides to leave his job paying $40,000 per year and start a housing construction firm. After one year of operation his firm reports an accounting profit of $25,000. The profit was computed by subtracting $170,000 in operating expenses from $195,000 for the sale of two houses. The operating expenses included explicit payments for building materials and three laborers hired to help build the houses. The professor did not pay himself a wage during the year.
   a. Based on the information given so far, what was the total opportunity cost for the first year of the firm's operation? What important opportunity cost did the professor omit in computing the firm's accounting profit?
   b. Now let's also assume that every other house sold in the professor's housing market earned its builder exactly $5000 in profit. Based on this new information, what was the firm's normal profit for the two houses sold? With this new information, what was the firm's total opportunity cost during the year? What was the professor's economic profit?

2. Suppose you have the following information concerning a single variable input (labor) and the quantity of output. Furthermore, suppose that the wage rate is $10 per unit of labor. Construct the total product curve and the total variable cost curve with this information.

Labor	Output
0	0
1	3
2	10
3	15
4	18
5	20

3. a. Fill in the missing information in the following table:

Q	TVC	TFC	TC	AVC	AFC	ATC	MC
0	0	10					
1	20						
2	30						
3	35						
4	45						
5	60						
6	80						
7	105						
8	130						
9	170						
10	210						

   b. Construct the total cost, total variable cost, and total fixed cost curves.

c. Construct the average total cost, average variable cost, average fixed cost, and marginal cost curves.

4. If the law of diminishing marginal returns did not operate such that the marginal product of the variable input is always the same, how would the shapes of the marginal cost, average variable cost, average fixed cost, and average total cost curves be affected? Explain.

REVIEW GLOSSARY

accounting cost An explicit cost incurred in production that involves direct payment for the input.

accounting profit The difference between revenues and explicit accounting costs. Accounting profit generally appears on the firm's profit and loss statement, but it is not the economist's concept of profit.

average fixed cost Total fixed cost per unit of output. It is found by dividing total fixed cost by the quantity of output. The average fixed cost curve is negatively sloped, as average fixed cost decreases with larger quantities of output.

average total cost Total cost per unit of output. It is found by dividing total cost by the quantity of output. Average total cost is also the sum of average variable cost and average fixed cost. Average total cost decreases with small quantities of output because both average variable and average fixed costs decrease. However, average total cost begins to increase only when the increase in average variable cost is greater than the decrease in average fixed cost.

average variable cost Total variable cost per unit of output. It is found by dividing total variable cost by the quantity of output. The average variable cost curve is U-shaped. With small quantities of output, average variable cost decreases; with larger quantities, it increases. The increase is due to the law of diminishing marginal returns.

economic cost An opportunity cost incurred in production.

economic profit The difference between all opportunity costs of production (including a normal profit) and the revenue received by the firm.

marginal cost The change in total cost, or total variable cost, resulting from a change in the quantity of output. Marginal cost is the slope of both the total cost and total variable cost curves and increases due to the law of diminishing returns. When marginal cost is below either average variable or average total cost, the average curve is decreasing. When marginal cost is above either average variable or average total cost, the average curve is increasing. When marginal cost is equal to either average variable or average total cost, the average curve is at its minimum.

normal profit The profit that can be earned by an entrepreneur in an alternative production process. Like wages, rent, and interest, normal profit is an opportunity cost of production.

opportunity cost The highest value of goods or other benefits given up when a good is produced or any action is taken.

total cost The total opportunity cost of producing goods and services. Total cost is the sum of the total variable cost and the total fixed cost.

total fixed cost A cost that does not change as the quantity of output changes. Total fixed cost is closely related to fixed inputs. In the short run, fixed cost must be paid, regardless of the quantity of output produced.

total variable cost A cost that changes as the quantity of output changes. Total variable cost is closely related to variable inputs. Variable cost can be avoided in the short run by not producing output.

UNIT 8.4

Perfect Competition and Supply

A firm has two considerations when supplying goods and services—the costs of producing the good and the revenue received from the sale of the good. As we saw in Unit 8.3, the short-run costs of production are based on the law of diminishing marginal returns. But the revenue received by a firm for selling the good depends on the type of market structure in which it is operating.

In this unit we study perfect competition, the simplest of the four market structures. The key feature of perfect competition is that each firm is a price taker, with no control over the price. Perfectly competitive firms determine the quantity of output to produce based on the existing market price. If the market price changes, the firm re-evaluates its level of output. Thus, we examine how the output supplied by a perfectly competitive firm responds to the price by identifying its supply curve.

We begin by reviewing the characteristics of perfect competition. We then discuss how these characteristics affect the revenue received by a firm from the sale of its output. The revenue side of the firm's production decision is combined with the costs of production, and we determine the firm's profit-maximizing level of output. And finally, we see how the perfectly competitive firm responds to price changes, which lets us obtain the firm's supply curve.

NATURE OF PERFECT COMPETITION

Perfect competition is an ideal market structure characterized by a large number of small firms, identical products sold by all firms, freedom of entry and exit into the industry, and perfect knowledge of prices and technology. Although perfect competition represents the simplest, most idealistic, and thus most unrealistic market structure, it is instructive nonetheless. If economists were allowed to create their own world, it would be based on perfect competition because it allows us to see the *best* way to allocate society's scarce resources. Knowing this, we can look at the real world and see how far away we are from this ideal. Let's look at the four features that make perfect competition an idealized market structure.

Large Number of Small Firms

A perfectly competitive industry has a large number of firms, each of which is small relative to the size of the market. This insures that no single firm in a particular industry can influence the market price—if one firm decides to stop producing output, the market is not affected. The agricultural industry reflects this feature. If a farmer reduces wheat production by 20 percent, the wheat market, including the price, is unchanged because the farmer accounts for only a small fraction of total wheat production.

Identical Product

All firms in a perfectly competitive market sell the same product. Therefore, it is impossible for the buyer to determine which perfectly competitive firm produces a given product. Again, in the agricultural industry, a buyer cannot determine if the wheat purchased came from farmer A or farmer B, nor does it really matter since the wheat is the same.

Freedom of Entry and Exit

Perfectly competitive firms are free to enter and leave the industry at will, unimpeded by government restrictions or other barriers. While some firms incur high start-up costs or need government licenses to enter into an industry, this is not the case for a perfectly competitive firm. Likewise, a perfectly competitive firm is not prevented from leaving an industry, as are most government-regulated public utilities.

Perfect Knowledge

In perfect competition, buyers are perfectly aware of suppliers' prices, so that one firm is not able to sell their good at a higher price than other firms. Not only do buyers have perfect knowledge but every supplier knows the price of every other supplier, meaning they do not sell the good at a lower price. Perfect knowledge also extends to technology and information about production processes. All firms in a perfectly competitive industry have the same production techniques.

THE PERFECTLY COMPETITIVE FIRM'S DEMAND

The rather restrictive features of perfect competition insure that the perfectly competitive firm faces only one type of demand curve, a horizontal, or perfectly elastic, curve. Since the perfectly competitive firm is completely aware of the market price, there is no reason for it to sell any output below that price.

To illustrate the demand facing a perfectly competitive firm, let's look at agricultural production by a farmer. Keep in mind that while no industry in the real world meets all of the characteristics of perfect competition, agriculture comes closer than any, especially in terms of demand. Figure 8.4.1 depicts the demand curve facing our hypothetical perfectly competitive firm (farmer) in the production of wheat. The overall market for wheat in panel a determines the market equilibrium price of wheat, a price set by the unrestrained forces of demand and supply. The market-clearing price P_e exists for all farmers in the perfectly competitive industry. And since they are small relative to the market, they can produce and sell all of the wheat they want at the equilibrium price. Panel b depicts the demand curve for the perfectly competitive firm's output, a horizontal, perfectly elastic demand

Figure 8.4.1

The Perfectly Competitive Firm's Demand Curve

The demand curve facing a perfectly competitive firm is perfectly elastic at the market equilibrium price P_e. The firm can sell all of the output that it wants at the equilibrium price since it is a relatively small part of the market. Panel b depicts the demand curve facing a perfectly competitive firm.

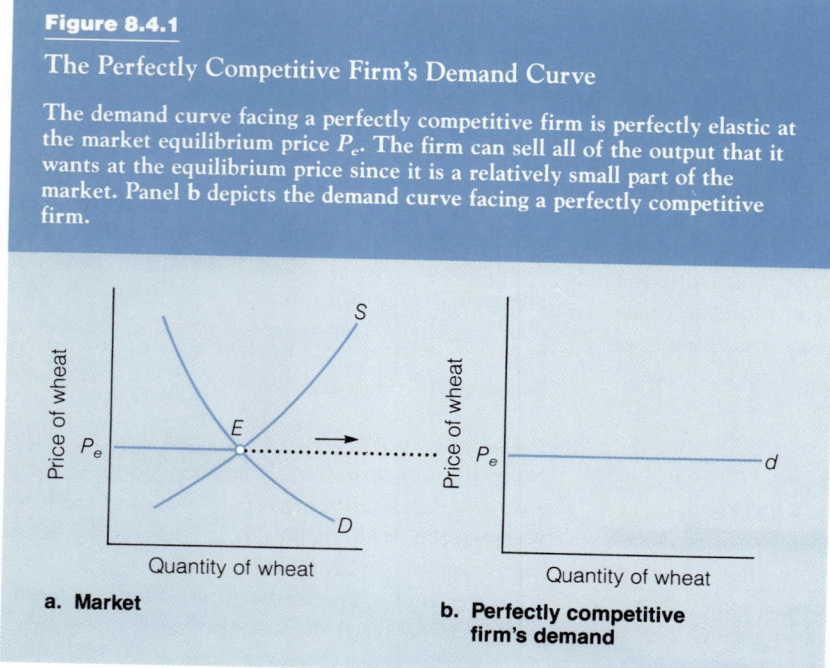

a. Market

b. Perfectly competitive firm's demand

UNIT 8.4 • PERFECT COMPETITION AND SUPPLY

Table 8.4.1

Perfect Competition and Revenue

The price received by a perfectly competitive firm for selling its output is the same at every quantity. For this reason the market price is also the perfectly competitive firm's average revenue and marginal revenue.

Quantity of Wheat (bushels)	Price and Average Revenue	Total Revenue	Marginal Revenue
1	$5	$ 5	$5
2	5	10	5
3	5	15	5
4	5	20	5
5	5	25	5
6	5	30	5
7	5	35	5
8	5	40	5
9	5	45	5
10	5	50	

Figure 8.4.2

Total, Average, and Marginal Revenue Curves

The total revenue curve for a perfectly competitive firm is depicted in panel a. It is a straight line coming from the origin. The marginal and average revenue curve for the firm is identical to the firm's demand curve. Since price is constant, the firm's average and marginal revenue is equal to the market price.

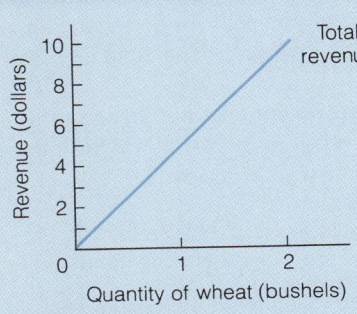

a. Total revenue

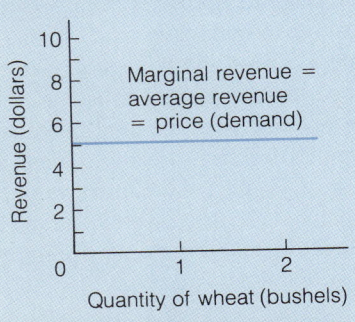

b. Marginal and average revenue

curve, also at price P_e. But note that the perfectly competitive firm is a price taker and has no influence over the market price.

Let's look at the total revenue received by the farmer for sale of wheat. **Total revenue** is the revenue received by a firm for the sale of its output, calculated as price times quantity. We know the farmer can sell all of the output produced at the market price. Therefore, if the market price of wheat is $5, the farmer who sells one bushel of wheat receives $5, the farmer who sells two bushels of wheat receives $10, and so on. Column three of Table 8.4.1 presents the total revenue received by the farmer for selling different quantities of wheat at $5.

The relationship between quantity of output produced and total revenue is plotted in panel a of Figure 8.4.2. Here, the total revenue curve is a straight line coming out of the origin, whose slope is constant because the price is constant. Since no revenue is received if no output is sold, the total revenue curve comes from the origin.

Two other measures of revenue are also important to the firm, average revenue and marginal revenue. **Average revenue** is revenue received per unit of output sold, which is the price of the good. It is specified as

$$\text{average revenue} = \frac{\text{total revenue}}{\text{quantity}}$$
$$= \frac{\text{price} \times \text{quantity}}{\text{quantity}}$$
$$= \text{price}$$

In Table 8.4.1, average revenue is determined by dividing total revenue in column three by the quantity sold in column two. Note that average revenue is $5, regardless of the quantity of wheat sold. If each bushel sells for $5, then the average revenue is $5, which is the market price at all quantities.

Marginal revenue is the change in total revenue resulting from a change in the quantity of output sold. It is specified as

$$\text{marginal revenue} = \frac{\text{change in total revenue}}{\text{change in quantity}}$$

If the farmer increases output from two to three bushels, total revenue increases from $10 to $15, and if the farmer increases output from five to six bushels, total revenue increases from $25 to $30. Marginal revenue in both cases is $5. In fact, marginal revenue is $5 for any change in output and is constant because the price is constant.

Average revenue and marginal revenue for a perfectly competitive firm are both equal to the price. Panel b of Figure 8.4.2 illustrates the combined marginal and average revenue curve, which is also the firm's demand curve, as presented in panel b of Figure 8.4.1.

SHORT-RUN OUTPUT

In our perfectly competitive economy, the farmer considers not only the revenue received from sale of the good but also the cost of production. If the revenue is greater than the cost, the farmer receives an economic profit, which, as we assume, represents the main objective of any firm.

Total Cost and Total Revenue

Let's look first at the total cost and total revenue of production. Figure 8.4.3 combines a total revenue curve similar to the one in Figure 8.4.2, with a total cost curve, as introduced in Unit 8.3. By comparing total revenue received from the sale of

Figure 8.4.3

Short-Run Output—Total Revenue and Total Cost

The perfectly competitive firm produces output where the difference between total revenue and total cost (economic profit) is the greatest. This is seen as the vertical distance between the total revenue and total cost curves, or the peak of the profit curve, with both occurring at q_e.

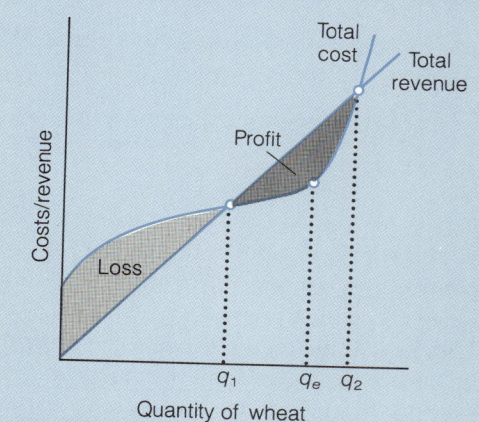

a. Total revenue and total cost curves

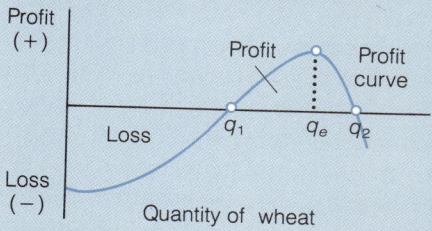

b. Profit curve

wheat with the cost of production, we can determine the level of economic profit received by the farmer and the most profitable quantity of wheat to produce.

First, note in panel a that our hypothetical perfectly competitive farmer receives an economic profit by producing more than q_1 and less than q_2. Both quantities are points of intersection between the total cost and total revenue curves, meaning that the total cost of production is equal to total revenue. At both quantities, the farmer is earning a normal profit (which is included in the total cost of production), but economic profit is zero. In other words, the revenue received is exactly enough to cover the costs of production. These are called breakeven outputs. **Breakeven output is the quantity of output in which total revenue is equal to total cost, such that a firm earns a normal profit, but no economic profit.**

Any quantity between q_1 and q_2 generates a positive economic profit, because in this range of production the total revenue curve lies above the total cost curve. For any quantity less than q_1 or greater than q_2, the total revenue curve lies below the total cost curve, and the farmer is unable to cover the cost of production. Clearly, the farmer wants the level of production in the range between q_1 and q_2 that gives the greatest profit. In terms of Figure 8.4.3, this comprises the greatest vertical distance between the total revenue and total cost curves, at q_e, the profit-maximizing level of output.

This is seen more clearly in panel b of Figure 8.4.3, which presents the profit curve. A **profit curve is the relationship between economic profit and the quantity of output.** It is the vertical distance between the total revenue and total cost curves, at each quantity of output. Between q_1 and q_2, the profit curve lies above the horizontal axis, and economic profit is positive. At quantities less than q_1 and greater than q_2, the profit curve lies below the horizontal axis, and economic profit is negative. The farmer receives the highest level of profit at q_e, where the profit curve is at its peak.

We must point out a particularly significant feature about the profit-maximizing quantity q_e. Not only is the distance between the total cost and total revenue curves the greatest but the slopes of the two curves are also the same. At quantities less than q_e, the total cost curve is flatter than the total revenue curve. At quantities greater than q_e, the total cost curve is steeper than the total revenue curve. If the slope of the cost curve is less than the revenue curve to the left and greater to the right, it must be the same at q_e.

Marginal Cost and Marginal Revenue

An alternative approach to determining our perfectly competitive farmer's optimum level of output is found by looking at marginal revenue and marginal cost. Figure 8.4.4 reproduces a set of average and marginal cost curves such as the ones introduced in Unit 8.3, including average variable cost, average total cost, and marginal cost. Although the average fixed cost curve is omitted to simplify the graph, we can still identify average fixed cost as the difference between average total and average variable cost.

The perfectly competitive farmer's demand curve, horizontal line P_e, is included. Recall that the farmer's demand curve is also its marginal revenue and average revenue curve. At all quantities of output, price is equal to both marginal and average revenue.

Our perfectly competitive farmer maximizes profit by equating price and marginal cost at q_e. Let's take an incremental approach to the farmer's production decision to see why this occurs. Suppose the farmer decides to produce q_1. Since price equals average total cost, total revenue equals total cost, and the farmer receives a normal profit but no economic profit. But what happens if the farmer decides to produce slightly more than q_1? To answer this, we need to look at marginal cost and marginal revenue. Since marginal revenue is equal to the price at every unit of output, we can compare price to marginal cost. At q_1, marginal cost is less than price, so the additional cost of producing one more unit is less than the additional revenue received. For the farmer it is wise to increase production from

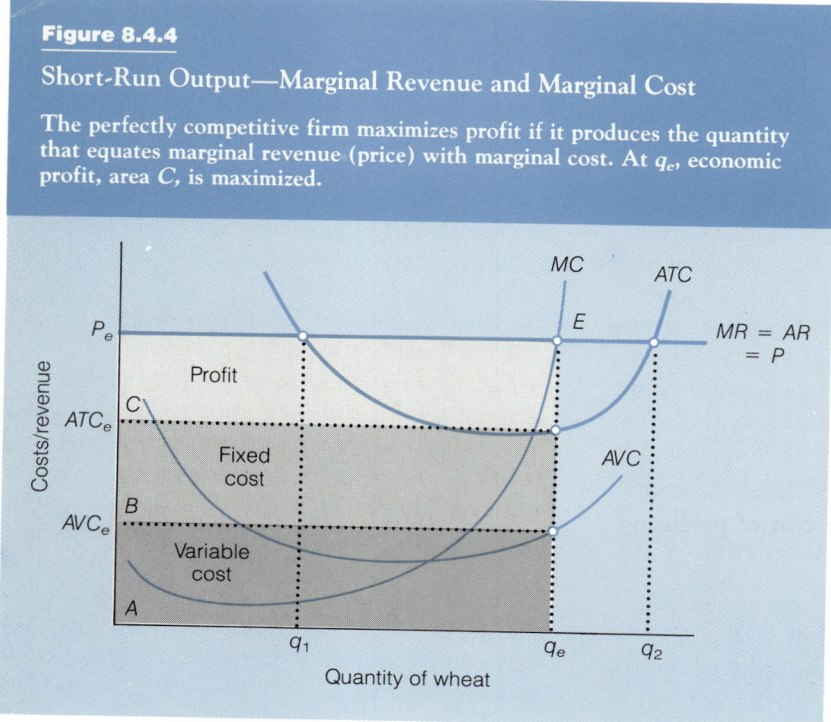

Figure 8.4.4

Short-Run Output—Marginal Revenue and Marginal Cost

The perfectly competitive firm maximizes profit if it produces the quantity that equates marginal revenue (price) with marginal cost. At q_e, economic profit, area C, is maximized.

q_1. If revenue rises more than cost, then profit is increasing. As long as marginal revenue is greater than marginal cost, profit increases.

The farmer can continue to increase production until q_e is reached. At q_e, the marginal cost curve intersects the marginal revenue (price) curve. If production is increased more than q_e, then the marginal cost is greater than marginal revenue, and profit falls. Therefore, the optimum quantity of output for the firm is q_e, where the level of profit for the firm is maximized. Note that the equilibrium quantity for a perfectly competitive firm occurs when price equals marginal cost.

This is the same equilibrium quantity determined with total revenue and total cost in Figure 8.4.3. Recall that at q_e in Figure 8.4.3 the slopes of the total revenue and the total cost curves are the same. The slope of the total revenue curve is marginal revenue, or the price. The slope of the total cost curve is marginal cost. Thus, at quantity q_e, marginal cost is equal to the price.

There is yet more information to be gained from Figure 8.4.4. Since price is greater than average total cost, the farmer makes an economic profit. We can determine that level of profit from the graph. First, we need to calculate the farmer's total revenue by multiplying price times quantity; this is seen in the graph as the large rectangular area OP_eEq_e.

What does the farmer do with the revenue received? This can be determined by dividing the large rectangle in Figure 8.4.4 into three smaller areas, labeled A, B, and C. One use is to cover variable cost, which is reflected in the average variable cost curve, AVC_e. Total variable cost is AVC_e times q_e, or area A. Next, the farmer pays fixed cost, which is given by area B. This leaves us, and the farmer, with area C. Subtracting total cost (A + B) from total revenue (A + B + C) gives us economic profit (C). At no other quantity of output, given price P_e, is area C greater.

PRICE AND AVERAGE COST: MINIMIZING LOSSES

Our perfectly competitive farmer does not necessarily make an economic profit in the short run. Even when price is set equal to marginal cost, the farmer may be faced with minimizing losses rather than maximizing profits. The farmer does not make an economic profit if the price is less than the average total cost because the cost of producing each unit is less than the average revenue received for each unit. But even though the farmer incurs a loss, output can continue to be produced in the short run. Whether a firm continues to produce output or shut down in the short run depends not on average total cost but on average variable cost.

Price Greater Than Average Variable Cost

Let's look at one of two possibilities. Figure 8.4.5 illustrates a situation in which price is less than average total cost but greater than average variable cost. In this case the farmer produces q_e of output, where marginal revenue equals marginal cost. However, since price is less than average total cost, the farmer incurs a loss. But that loss is preferable to the next best alternative, which is producing no output.

What are the losses to the farmer if q_e is produced? Total revenue is given by the area X + Y, while total cost is given by the larger area X + Y + Z. Thus, the loss incurred by the farmer is equal to area Z. Can the farmer do any better by not producing output? For any output produced, the farmer must pay variable cost plus fixed cost, whereas if no output is produced, then only fixed cost has to be paid.

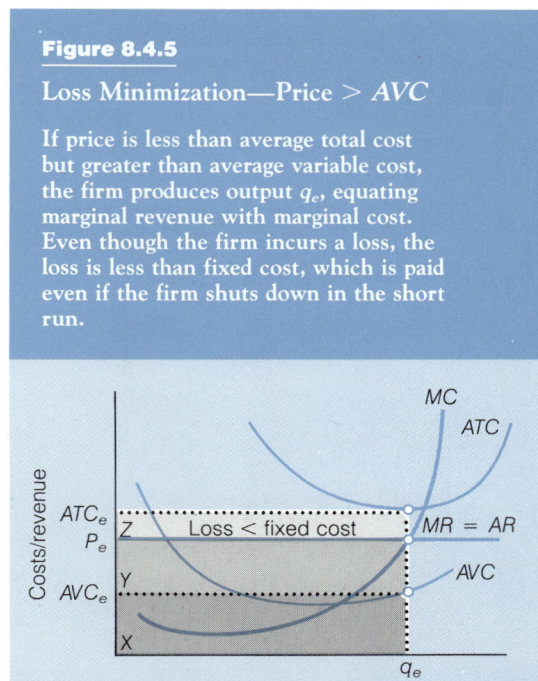

Figure 8.4.5

Loss Minimization—Price > AVC

If price is less than average total cost but greater than average variable cost, the firm produces output q_e, equating marginal revenue with marginal cost. Even though the firm incurs a loss, the loss is less than fixed cost, which is paid even if the firm shuts down in the short run.

The total variable cost of producing q_e is equal to area X in Figure 8.4.5, but total revenue is equal to the area X + Y. Therefore, the farmer is able to cover all variable costs incurred in the production of q_e, with some left over to pay part of the fixed cost. If no output is produced, then there is no revenue to pay any of the fixed cost. The farmer is better off in this case by producing q_e rather than not producing at all. In other words, as long as price is above average variable cost, a firm minimizes losses by producing output where price equals marginal cost.

Price Less Than Average Variable Cost

What if price falls below average variable cost, as in Figure 8.4.6. Under these circumstances the

Figure 8.4.6

Loss Minimization—Price < AVC

If price is less than average variable cost, the firm shuts down production in the short run. If q_e output is produced, the loss is greater than fixed cost.

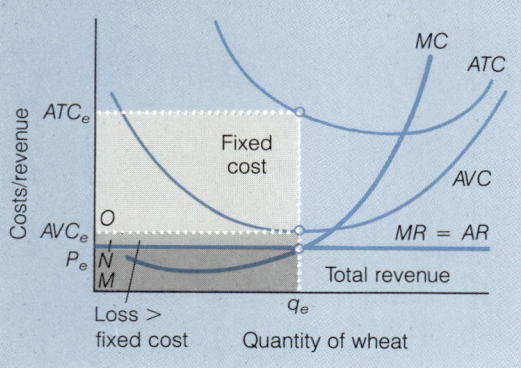

farmer shuts down in the short run to wait for better times and a higher price.

In Figure 8.4.6 the price is P_e, the farmer produces q_e where price equals marginal cost, and the farmer receives revenue equal to area M. However, this level is not enough to cover total variable cost, area M + N, let alone any part of the total fixed cost, area O. By producing output q_e, the farmer incurs a loss equal to the area N + O. But if the farmer produces no output at all, the loss incurred is fixed cost, area O.

Table 8.4.2 summarizes the four alternatives facing a firm in the short run. If total revenue equals total cost, a perfectly competitive firm is at a breakeven output and is earning only a normal profit. However, profit maximization is obtained when the firm sets price (marginal revenue) equal to marginal cost. Positive economic profits are received if total revenue is greater than total cost, or alternatively if price is greater than average total

Table 8.4.2

Short-Run Production Alternatives for a Perfectly Competitive Firm

A perfectly competitive firm maximizes profit at the quantity of output in which marginal cost equals marginal revenue. It receives a positive economic profit if price is greater than average total cost. If price is less than average total cost but greater than average variable cost, it still continues to produce in the short run even though it incurs a loss. However, if price is less than average variable cost, then the firm shuts down in the short run.

Total Revenue and Total Cost	Marginal Revenue and Marginal Cost	Price and Average Cost	Production Alternative
TR = TC		P = ATC	Breakeven
TR > TC	MR = MC	P > ATC	Profit maximization
TR < TC		P < ATC	Loss minimization
	MR = MC	P > AVC	Continue production
		P < AVC	Shut down

cost. When total revenue is less than total cost, the firm is faced with minimizing losses. If price is greater than average variable cost, even though price is less than average total cost, the firm minimizes losses by producing the quantity that equates marginal revenue to marginal cost. However, if price is less than average variable cost, then the firm minimizes losses by shutting down production in the short run.

THE PERFECTLY COMPETITIVE FIRM'S SUPPLY CURVE

We have reached two conclusions necessary to identify a firm's supply curve. First, a firm produces the quantity of output that equates price and marginal cost. Second, a firm shuts down production if price is less than average variable cost.

In Figure 8.4.7 a market price of P_1 leads a firm to produce and supply q_1 output, even though it incurs a short-run loss. If the price increases to P_2, the firm increases production to q_2. Higher prices result in greater quantities produced and supplied to the market. However, if the price falls below P_0, then the firm shuts down and supplies no output.

The segment of the marginal cost curve that lies above the average variable cost curve is the perfectly competitive firm's supply curve. This is because the firm produces the quantity of output that sets price equal to marginal cost. If the price falls below the average variable cost curve, output falls to zero.

The firm's supply curve is positively sloped because marginal cost increases with output. However, we saw in Unit 8.3 that the marginal cost curve is positively sloped due to the law of diminishing marginal returns, implying that a firm has to hire increasingly greater amounts of variable inputs to produce an additional unit of output.

The analysis of perfect competition has yielded a basic explanation for the positive slope of the

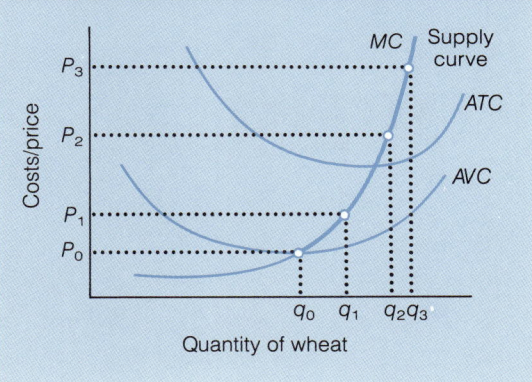

Figure 8.4.7

The Perfectly Competitive Firm's Supply Curve

The perfectly competitive firm's supply curve, in the short run, is the segment of its marginal cost curve lying above average variable cost. If the price is greater than P_0, the firm produces the quantity that equates price with marginal cost. If the price is below P_0, the firm shuts down in the short run.

supply curve. In the short run, if a firm is to supply more output, it must hire more inputs. However, even if the prices of inputs do not change, the marginal cost of the firm is greater because each additional unit of input is relatively less productive. The variable inputs are less productive in the short run because one or more inputs are fixed. Therefore, less output is produced by each additional input, and more inputs are needed. This increases the cost of supplying additional quantities and means the firm supplies more only if it receives a higher price.

It is a short step from positively sloped supply curves for each perfectly competitive firm to a market supply curve that is also positively sloped, as in Unit 2.3. If the quantity supplied by each firm increases at higher prices, then the quantity supplied by the entire market also increases at higher prices.

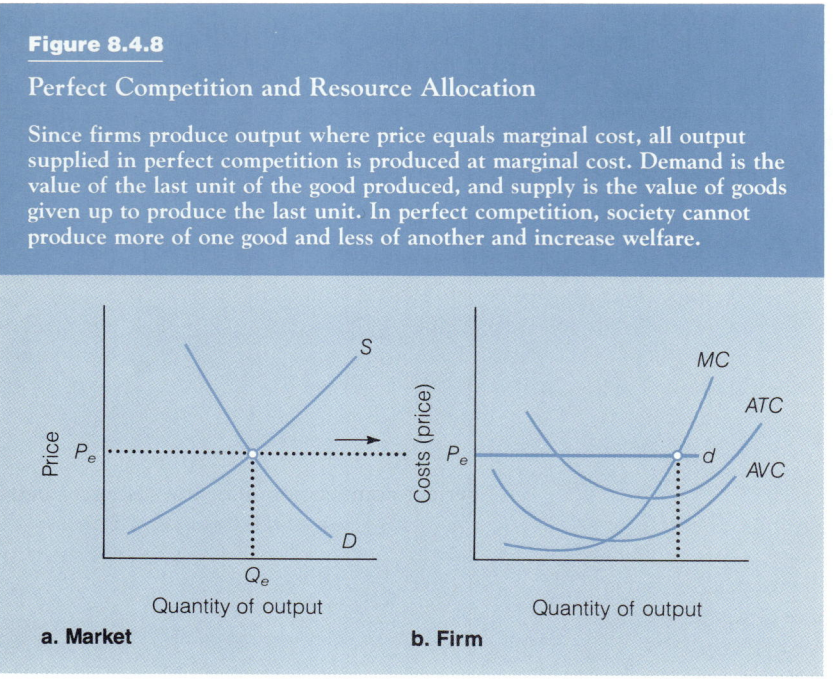

Figure 8.4.8

Perfect Competition and Resource Allocation

Since firms produce output where price equals marginal cost, all output supplied in perfect competition is produced at marginal cost. Demand is the value of the last unit of the good produced, and supply is the value of goods given up to produce the last unit. In perfect competition, society cannot produce more of one good and less of another and increase welfare.

PERFECT COMPETITION AND RESOURCE ALLOCATION

Why do economists prefer perfect competition to other market structures? The economic problem facing any society is to allocate scarce resources for the ultimate satisfaction of unlimited wants and needs. And perfect competition performs this task better than any alternative market structure, which is one reason it is called "perfect."

Panel a in Figure 8.4.8 depicts a typical market, and panel b shows the cost curves of a perfectly competitive firm. The free operation of the market in panel a results in a market clearing price of P_e. This price reflects the value of the equilibrium quantity Q_e to the demanders. Consumers are willing to pay P_e because that is the level of satisfaction obtained from that last unit of the good.

In terms of the supply side of the market, particularly the firm's cost of production, the perfectly competitive firm in panel b produces the quantity that sets marginal cost equal to the price. For this firm the quantity is q_e. Since all firms in the industry operate the same way and set price equal to marginal cost, the market quantity Q_e is supplied at the marginal cost of production.

What does marginal cost represent? It represents the marginal opportunity cost of producing each additional unit of output. Recall that the opportunity cost is the value of alternative production given up to produce this good. The supply curve represents the marginal value of other goods *not* produced in order to produce Q_e. And the demand curve represents the marginal value consumers place on the last unit of the good produced. Under perfect competition these two are equal. The marginal value of goods given up is the same as the marginal value of the last unit of the good produced.

This mean's society's welfare cannot be improved by producing more of one good and less of another. Suppose that the value of the good produced is more than the value of goods given up, that society values one good more than alternative goods. It benefits society in this case to produce more of the greater-valued good and less of others. Essentially, society is able to obtain a good with a higher value by giving up goods with lower value. This is like trading a nickel for a dime.

But with perfect competition this trade is not possible. Society cannot produce more of one good and less of another to become any better off. Society's welfare can be no higher because resources are efficiently allocated. In Section 9 we see that none of the other three market structures leads to this efficient allocation.

IN SUMMARY

Perfect Competition and Supply

- Perfect competition is an idealized market structure characterized by a large number of small firms, an identical product, perfect knowledge of prices and technology, and freedom of entry and exit.

- The demand for a perfectly competitive firm's output is perfectly elastic. The demand curve is horizontal because the firm can sell all of the output it wants at the existing market price and has no reason to sell for less. The market price for the perfectly competitive firm's output is also average revenue and, more importantly, marginal revenue.

- In the short run the firm produces the quantity of output that gives it the greatest level of profit. This is determined as the greatest distance between the total cost and total revenue curves. This equilibrium quantity is the peak in the profit curve. The optimum level of output is also determined by looking at the firm's marginal cost and marginal revenue. Since the market price is the firm's marginal revenue, it maximizes profit by setting price equal to marginal cost.

- In the short run the perfectly competitive firm minimizes losses by producing output if the price is greater than average variable cost. However, it stops producing if the price falls below average variable cost.

- The marginal cost curve of a perfectly competitive firm is the firm's supply curve. It is positively sloped due to the law of diminishing marginal returns. The market supply, being the combination of individual firms' supplies, is also positively sloped.

- Perfect competition allocates resources better than any other market structure. It is not possible in perfect competition to produce more of one good and less of another and make society better off.

QUESTIONS FOR STUDY AND ANALYSIS

1. Discuss how each of the industries listed below matches up to the four characteristics of perfect competition.
   a. The breakfast cereal industry, in which four firms—Kelloggs, General Mills, General Foods, and Quaker Oats—produce the majority of the thirty-plus different brands of cereal on the market
   b. Consolidated Edison Co. of New York, which is a public regulated utility and the only supplier of electricity to the city of New York
   c. Insurance sales representatives in any city with a population over 200,000
   d. Wheat producers in the Midwest
   e. Television broadcasting in the United States, consisting of the three major networks and all cable channels
   f. Retail grocery sales in Wyoming, which has 250 stores statewide

2. Using the following information, complete the table and determine the profit-maximizing quantity of output for this perfectly competitive firm.

Q	TC	MC	Price	MR	AR	TR	Profit
0	10	—	10				
1		6					
2		4					
3		5					
4		7					
5		10					
6		14					
7		19					
8		25					
9		32					

3. Use the information given and calculated in question 2 to address each of the following:
   a. Construct the total cost and total revenue curves. Identify the profit-maximizing quantity of output in the diagram.
   b. Construct the total profit curve and identify the profit-maximizing quantity of output.
   c. Construct the marginal cost and marginal revenue curves. Identify the profit-maximizing quantity of output.

4. a. For the following relationship between total cost and quantity, compute the profit-maximizing level of output at each of these market prices: $5, $10, $15, $20, $25.

Quantity	0	1	2	3	4	5	6	7
Total cost	$10	20	25	27	32	39	49	61
Quantity		8	9	10	11	12	13	14	15
Total cost		$76	93	113	135	160	190	230	280

b. Does the firm incur a loss at any of the prices? Does the firm shut down production at any of the prices?
c. Construct the firm's supply curve using the information from this problem.

5. If a farmer says that it is not worth the extra cost to harvest his corn because the price is too low, which of the production alternatives listed in Table 8.4.2 has he decided to undertake?

6. Assume that you start a house construction firm and find that the cost of building your first house is $50,000, but you can sell it for $60,000. Will you build a second house? What is the marginal cost of the first house? What is the marginal revenue? Now suppose that you continue to build houses and discover that the cost of building your fifth house of the year is $75,000 but that it sells for only $60,000. Based on this information, how many houses would you plan to build next year? Why?

REVIEW GLOSSARY

average revenue The revenue received per unit of output sold, which is the price of the good.

breakeven output The quantity of output in which total revenue is equal to total cost such that a firm earns a normal profit but no economic profit.

marginal revenue The change in total revenue resulting from a change in the quantity of output sold. For a perfectly competitive firm, marginal revenue is equal to price.

perfect competition An ideal market structure characterized by a large number of small firms, identical products sold by all firms, freedom of entry and exit into the industry, and perfect knowledge of prices and technology.

profit curve A curve depicting the relationship between economic profit and the quantity of output. A perfectly competitive firm produces the quantity that gives the highest level of economic profit. This is at the greatest distance between the total revenue and total cost curves and the peak of the profit curve.

total revenue The revenue received by a firm for the sale of its output, calculated as price times quantity. For a perfectly competitive firm, the total revenue curve is a straight line coming from the origin.

UNIT 8.5

Problems in the Supply of Agricultural Goods

Agricultural production comes as close as any industry to the ideal of perfect competition. Recall that perfect competition is characterized by a large number of small firms, identical product, freedom of entry and exit, and perfect knowledge. The agricultural industry has a large number of relatively small firms; the products are essentially identical, regardless of the farmer; there is a great deal of freedom to enter and exit the production process of any specific product; and most farmers are kept well informed by local farm reports and university extension programs.

In this unit we focus on production by the agricultural industry. To begin, we look at the **farm problem,** the situation in which relatively low and unstable farm incomes are caused by low or unstable agricultural prices. We examine the farm problem as it relates to agricultural production in both the short run and the long run. And finally, after we discuss why the farm problem exists, we look at agricultural policies the government has used to address the problem: price floor, price subsidy, and supply restriction.

THE FARM PROBLEM

The farm problem is a combination of two separate but related problems. The **short-run problem** is the fluctuation of farm incomes caused by fluctuations in agricultural prices. The **long-run problem** is the continuous decline in farm incomes caused by the continuous decline in agricultural prices, and it is potentially more serious.

The Short-Run Problem

Agricultural production in the short run is characterized by demand and supply that are relatively price inelastic, and also by relatively unstable determinants of demand and supply. The combination of relatively low price elasticities of demand and supply and wide shifts in both demand and supply curves creates a great deal of instability in agricultural markets in the short run.

For example, once a crop is planted, there is very little a farmer can do about price changes. If the price remains greater than average variable cost, the crop can be harvested and sold at the new price or held in storage for a higher price after it is harvested. If the price is less than average variable cost, the crop can be plowed under and not harvested at all. This tends to make the price elasticity of supply relatively low in the short run. The price elasticity of demand for most agricultural products is also relatively low, due in large part to our limited capacity to consume food and to the perishable nature of the products. We can consume only so much bread, beef, and milk, regardless of the price. And while price reductions might encourage us to stock up our freezers, cupboards, and basements, the products are still relatively perishable in the short run.

Some of the determinants of demand and supply tend to fluctuate widely from year to year. On the supply side, weather is probably the most variable factor underlying supply. In some years there is not enough rain, causing the loss of crops because of drought, or driving input costs higher because additional irrigation is needed. In other years the weather is nearly perfect, raining in exactly the right amounts at exactly the right times. Thus, the variability of the weather causes wide shifts in the supply curve.

Changes in agricultural exports cause equally wide shifts in the demand curve. International political conditions can rapidly change, leading to an increase or decrease in U.S. exports and the number of buyers in the agricultural markets. The weather in other countries can also lead to changes in demand for U.S. exports by affecting the supplies of agricultural products in those countries.

What happens to the supply curve in a year with ideal weather? Because of relatively inelastic demand, a good growing season usually means a bad year for farmers. Figure 8.5.1 presents the market for wheat, with demand curve D and supply curve S, based on a normal growing season for wheat. Given these demand and supply conditions, the market equilibrium price is $5 per bushel, and 10 million bushels are exchanged. However, if the weather is nearly perfect during the growing season, the supply curve shifts to S'. This means the

Figure 8.5.1

The Short-Run Problem—Supply Fluctuations

One aspect of the short-run problem is fluctuations in supply. While an increase in supply may seem beneficial to farmers, it can actually lead to an overall decrease in farmers' income. Because the demand for agricultural products is inelastic, the decrease in price is greater than the increase in the quantity exchanged in the market.

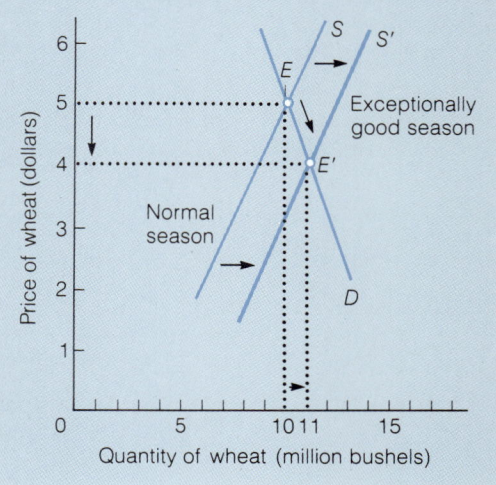

new market equilibrium is at E', with the price at $4 and 11 million bushels exchanged.

Note that the ideal growing season for wheat is bad for the farmers. The price falls from $5 to $4, but the quantity sold increases from 10 to only 11 million bushels. In a normal season the total revenue received by farmers is $50 million ($5 × 10 million bushels). However, the ideal growing season generates only $44 million ($4 × 11 million bushels) in revenue because the percentage increase in quantity demanded is less than the percentage decline in the price. This is the case whenever demand is price inelastic. Indeed, if the price declines enough, some farmers may incur a loss or even shut down in the short run. By contrast, if wheat has an extremely poor growing year, the supply curve shifts to the left, and the revenue received by farmers typically increases.

Now let's turn to shifts in the demand curve. Figure 8.5.2 illustrates how the market for wheat might be affected if the Soviet Union decides to cancel all purchases of U.S. wheat. The demand curve shifts from D to D', and the price of wheat falls from $5 to $4. In this case there is no doubt about how the total revenue received by farmers is affected. Less wheat is sold at a lower price, and total revenue declines.

However, if the price declines enough, the farmer may once again be faced with the short-run decision between producing at a loss or shutting down entirely. Recall that a firm continues to produce at a loss if price is less than average total cost but greater than average variable cost. But if price drops below average variable cost, the firm is better off producing no output because fixed costs still have to be paid in the short run.

For the farmer, fixed cost includes the rent, interest, and taxes related to the use of land and capital and, after the crop is planted, the costs of planting. In fact, the variable costs facing the farmer are the costs of harvesting the crop. If the price is so low the farmer cannot cover the costs of harvesting, then the crop is left in the field, whereas if harvesting costs are covered, then the farmer will harvest and sell the crops.

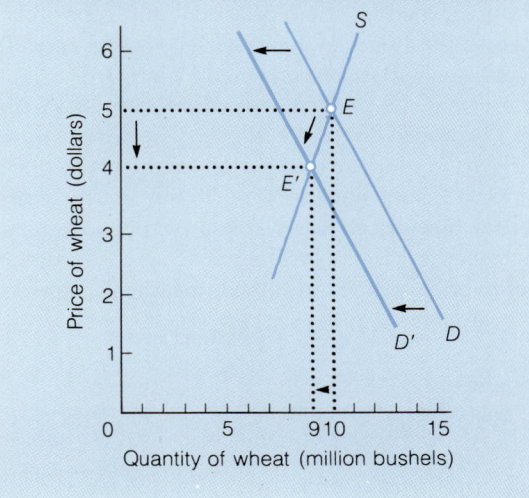

Figure 8.5.2

The Short-Run Problem—Demand Fluctuations

Another aspect of the short-run problem is fluctuations in demand. A decrease in demand clearly reduces the price and the quantity exchanged in the market, and farmers' incomes necessarily decline.

What makes short-run fluctuations in agricultural prices particularly important is the direct link between prices and farmers' incomes. While factor incomes in all industries are tied to the output prices, as we see in Section 11, most are not as obvious as in agriculture. Although the price of an automobile affects the wage paid to an autoworker, the effect is less direct and not immediately seen.

It is for this reason that the short-run fluctuations in farmers' incomes has stimulated so many government policies for the agricultural industry. The short-run problem in the agricultural industry is not necessarily any worse than comparable problems in the housing, manufacturing, or services industries, but it *is* more obvious.

The Long-Run Problem

In the short run, fluctuations in the determinants of demand and supply and the inelasticity of demand and supply lead to variability in farmers' revenues. However, in the long run the trend is toward lower prices and thus lower farmers' incomes. This long-run trend is shown in the parity price ratio. The **parity price ratio** is the ratio of prices received by farmers to prices paid by farmers. It illustrates what has happened to prices of agricultural goods relative to the prices of consumer goods and agricultural inputs that are purchased by farmers.

Figure 8.5.3 presents the parity price ratio from 1910 through the early 1980s. The period from 1910 to 1914 is the base period for the parity price ratio and is set equal to 100; the subsequent years reflect how prices received and paid change relative to the base year. Note that since 1950 the parity price ratio has declined, meaning the prices paid by farmers have increased relatively more than the prices received. Herein lies the long-run problem. Agricultural prices received by farmers are increasing at a slower rate than other prices; in other words, agricultural prices are declining relative to other prices.

We can single out two basic reasons for this long-run problem, relatively large increases in agricultural productivity and relatively small increases in demand for agricultural products. Since the beginning of the twentieth century, technological advances have spurred a tremendous increase in agricultural productivity. Mechanization, seed varieties, fertilizers, pesticides, and production techniques have all been improved to the point that crop yields have increased manyfold. This has led to a relatively large rightward shift in the supply curve, such as the shift from S to S' in Figure 8.5.4.

The demand for agricultural products has also shifted rightward over this period of time. For

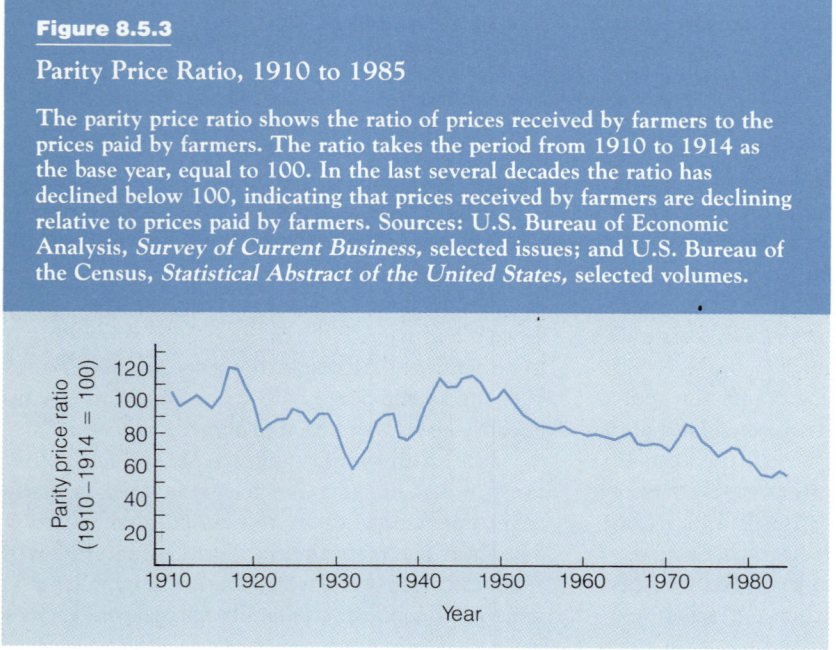

Figure 8.5.3

Parity Price Ratio, 1910 to 1985

The parity price ratio shows the ratio of prices received by farmers to the prices paid by farmers. The ratio takes the period from 1910 to 1914 as the base year, equal to 100. In the last several decades the ratio has declined below 100, indicating that prices received by farmers are declining relative to prices paid by farmers. Sources: U.S. Bureau of Economic Analysis, *Survey of Current Business*, selected issues; and U.S. Bureau of the Census, *Statistical Abstract of the United States*, selected volumes.

UNIT 8.5 • PROBLEMS IN THE SUPPLY OF AGRICULTURAL GOODS

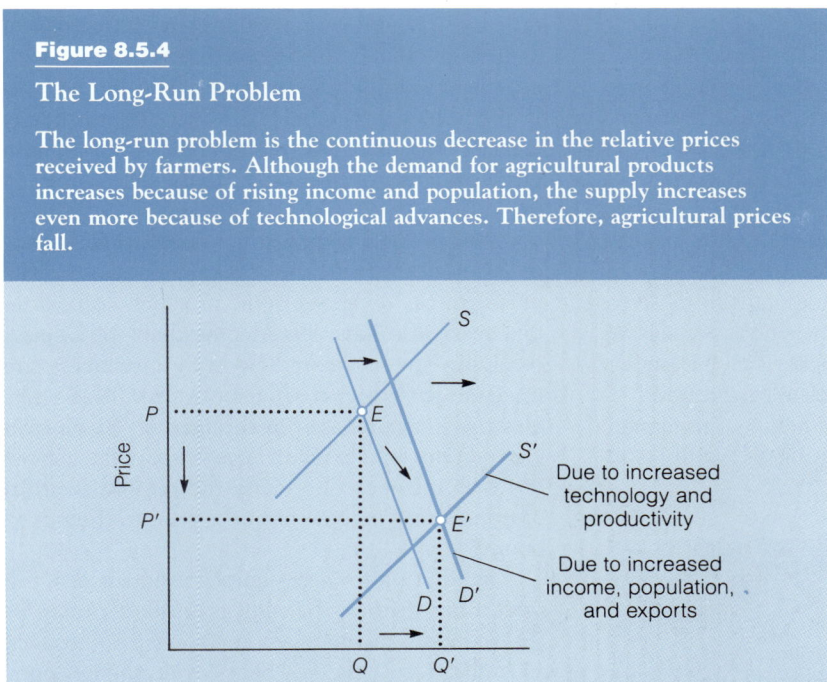

Figure 8.5.4

The Long-Run Problem

The long-run problem is the continuous decrease in the relative prices received by farmers. Although the demand for agricultural products increases because of rising income and population, the supply increases even more because of technological advances. Therefore, agricultural prices fall.

example, increases in population and the opening of export markets have led to an increase in the number of buyers in the market. In addition, since 1910 incomes of buyers have also increased substantially, causing a rightward shift of the demand curve. However, even with all of these determinants of demand working together, the shift in the demand curve in Figure 8.5.4 from D to D' is relatively less than the shift in the supply curve. Therefore, market equilibrium moves from point E to E', and the market price falls from P to P'.

The income elasticity of demand is primarily responsible for the relatively small shift in the demand curve. Recall that the income elasticity of demand constitutes the relative change in demand resulting from a change in income. And agricultural products are relatively unresponsive to changes in income. As people receive more income, they tend to spend a smaller proportion on food. For example, a person who eats three meals a day is not likely to eat six meals if income doubles or nine meals if income triples. While more income may be spent to buy higher quality food, most additional income will be used to buy other types of goods.

AGRICULTURAL POLICIES

Three basic types of agricultural policies have been aimed at the farm problem: price floor, price subsidy, and supply restriction. In each case the policies are designed to raise farmers' incomes by indirectly raising prices received by the farmers.

Price Floor

A **price floor** is a legally established minimum price above the market equilibrium, as discussed in Units 2.5 and 2.7.

Figure 8.5.5 depicts a price floor. If the market price of wheat is $4, the government might establish a price floor at $5 in an effort to raise farmers' incomes. However, as the price is increased from $4 to $5, the quantity demanded falls from 10 to 9 million bushels. In addition, since farmers are willing to supply 11 million bushels at the higher price, a surplus of 2 million bushels is created.

Farmers sell 9 million bushels in the market for the $5 price floor, generating $45 million in revenue. The government then buys the surplus of 2 million bushels for $5, providing farmers with another $10 million in revenue. The total revenue of $55 million generated by the price floor is clearly greater than the $40 million ($4 × 10 million bushels) of revenue generated in the unconstrained market.

One problem with the price floor involves equity considerations. First, the government buys the surplus with tax revenues, some of which come from taxpayers who have less income than the farmers receiving the payment. Second, consumers are forced to pay a higher price for the 9 million bushels of wheat purchased in the market. Since food expenditures tend to take a larger share of the income of lower income consumers, the possibility arises of transferring income from the poor to the not so poor.

In addition to these equity considerations, the price floor distorts the allocation of resources in the economy. Farmers are encouraged to produce 11 million bushels of wheat, even though consumers are willing to buy only 9 million bushels, which means that too many resources are being devoted to the production of wheat. Furthermore, once the government buys the wheat, it must store it or dispose of it in some manner. While stockpiles of agricultural commodities provide insurance against worldwide food shortages resulting from droughts or wars, the government has to do something about stocks that become too large, perhaps giving food away to foreign countries or to poor people in the United States. This could reduce the export or domestic demand for agricultural products and lead to an even greater surplus in subsequent years. That is, the government might inadvertently compete with farmers by supplying some of the 9 million bushels demanded in Figure 8.5.5.

Price Subsidy

One way to prevent the surplus generated with a price floor is to use a price subsidy. A **price subsidy** is the difference between the market price and a specified target price. With price subsidies, farmers

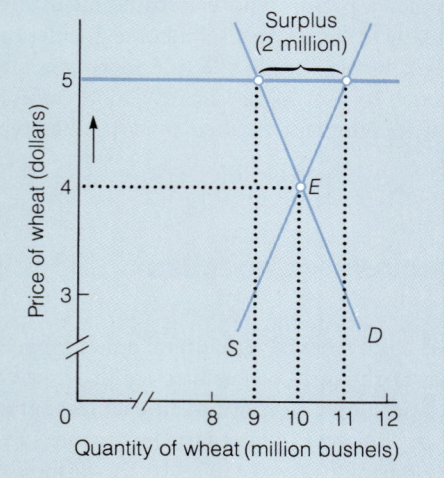

Figure 8.5.5

Agricultural Price Floor

A price floor set at $5, above the market equilibrium price of $4, leads to a surplus of 2 million bushels of wheat. Farmers produce 11 million bushels, selling 9 million on the market and the remaining 2 million to the government. Thus, farmers' total income is $55 million, compared to $40 million without the price floor.

are free to sell all that they can in the market, and the government pays them the difference between the market price and the target price. The target price resembles the price floor in that it is the price established to maintain farmers' incomes. Figure 8.5.6 illustrates how the price subsidy operates.

Once again, the unconstrained market equilibrium is at $4 and 10 million bushels. However, the target price, which is the price determined as the minimum needed by farmers to maintain incomes, is $5. The government agrees to pay farmers the difference between the price received for selling the good and this target price. This essentially means farmers are guaranteed $5 for each bushel of wheat produced.

Under these circumstances, if farmers receive $5 per bushel, they produce 11 million bushels. Once they try to sell the 11 million bushels, they find that buyers are willing to pay only $3 per bushel. But because the government will pay them the other $2 per bushel as the price subsidy, the farmers are not worried.

The result of this policy is that consumers come out ahead. They receive 11 million rather than 10 million bushels and pay $3 rather than $4. Farmers again receive $55 million in revenue, so they are just as well off as they were with the price floor. However, the taxpayers, through the government, bear the burden of the price subsidy because they pay farmers $2 per bushel for 11 million bushels, or a total of $22 million, compared to the $10 million paid by the government for a comparable number of bushels under the price floor.

In terms of equity, there is a redistribution from taxpayers to both farmers and consumers. And from an efficiency standpoint, too many resources are still being allocated to the production of this good.

Supply Restriction

The last of the three types of policies directed at the farm problem also prevents the surplus created by a price floor. With a **supply restriction,** farmers are induced to reduce the supply of output. Usually, supply restriction programs take the form of paying

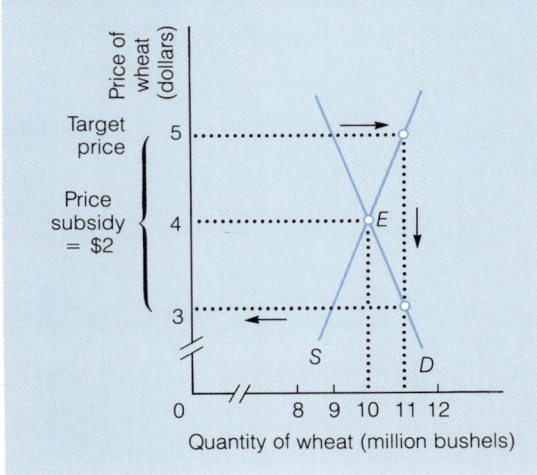

Figure 8.5.6

Price Subsidy

If a target price is set at $5, farmers produce 11 million bushels of wheat. However, consumers are only willing to pay $3 per bushel for this quantity, so the government must pay farmers $2 for each of the 11 million bushels sold. The price subsidy represents the difference between the target price and the market price, or $2. Farmers' incomes are $55 million with the subsidy and only $40 million without.

farmers to remove land from agricultural production. The operation of supply restriction policies is illustrated in Figure 8.5.7, where the unconstrained market equilibrium again is at $4 and 10 million bushels, and the desired price is $5. With a supply restriction program, the government tries to induce farmers to shift the supply curve from S to S'. If the supply shifts to S', then the market can reach equilibrium at $5, with 9 million bushels exchanged. The farmers receive $45 million from the sale of the crop, plus whatever the government pays them for taking land out of production.

As with the price floor, the supply restriction programs cause consumers to pay a higher price for

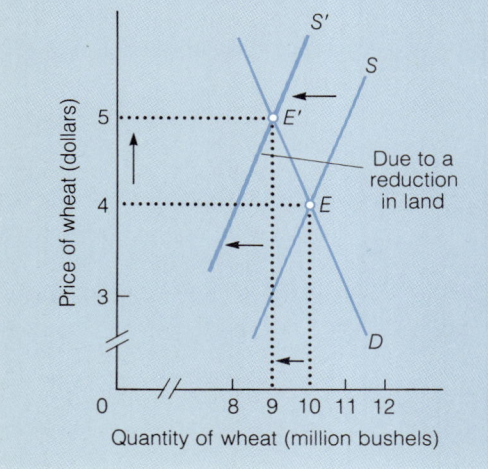

Figure 8.5.7

Supply Restriction

The intent of supply restriction programs is to shift the market supply from S to S'. This is usually accomplished by a reduction in the quantity of land used to produce agricultural products. Shifting the supply curve to S' raises the market price to $5 and reduces the quantity exchanged to 9 million bushels. However, farmers receive additional income through government payments to reduce the quantity of land.

a smaller quantity of the good. In addition, taxpayers, through the government, are paying the farmers to restrict the supply. And again there is an inefficient allocation of resources, but this time combined with unemployment of the land. Productive land is idled, and the economy is operating inside its production possibilities frontier.

Another kink in supply restriction programs is that they may be ineffective. The purpose of these programs is to shift the supply curve for the crop by reducing the quantity of one of the inputs, in this case land. However, there are typically no restrictions on the other inputs. Therefore, farmers can use greater amounts of labor, capital, fertilizers, and pesticides on the remaining amount of land, which can cause the supply curve to shift rightward, away from S' in Figure 8.5.7. In fact, with the additional income from the payment and the incentive of the higher price, there is no doubt that farmers try to increase the production on the smaller amount of land.

Thus, even though the supply curve is shifted to S', it is not likely to remain at S' very long, meaning the price will drop below $5 and defeat the purpose of the program. The government then has to pay farmers to remove even more land from production. Of course, the law of diminishing marginal returns will put a stop to this process after a while, when the farmers are unable to squeeze any more output from the land. But in the process of reaching that point, there is an inefficient allocation.

AN EVALUATION OF AGRICULTURAL POLICIES

All three of the agricultural policies—price floor, price subsidy, and supply restriction—distort the allocation of resources and lead to a redistribution of income among people in the economy. Since the ultimate objective of the agricultural policies is to do just that—redistribute income—there is no point in involving the market. Farmers' incomes can be maintained by a simple, straightforward government transfer payment through existing welfare programs. Moreover, since this would be geared toward the farmers who are truly in need of assistance, it would eliminate the problem of relatively wealthy farmers receiving government subsidies.

In addition to a direct welfare system, another potential policy should not be overlooked. The long-run aspect of the farm problem results because farmers' productivity is increasing relatively faster than the demand for the goods. This means that the proportion of the economy's employment in agriculture is shrinking, and less labor is required to produce the same amount of output. Therefore, farm incomes remain relatively low because the amount of labor does not decrease. Even though one farmer can do the work of two, two farmers continue to produce output.

In this light, it might be appropriate to encourage a shift of labor from agriculture to other industries in the economy, though this is certainly easier said than done. Agricultural production is as much a way of life as it is an industry. And shifting labor from agriculture to manufacturing or services usually involves moving labor from rural to urban settings, with all of the accompanying cultural changes. This long-run solution to the farm problem would thus also involve education, training, and cultural readjustment.

IN SUMMARY

Problems in the Supply of Agricultural Goods

- Agricultural production comes as close as any industry to the ideal of perfect competition. But the agricultural industry is affected by the farm problem. The farm problem is reflected in farmers' relatively low or unstable incomes resulting from relatively low or unstable agricultural prices.

- The farm problem is really a combination of a short-run and a long-run problem. The short-run problem is the wide fluctuations in agricultural markets, prices, and thus farmers' incomes. The long-run problem is the continuous decline in relative agricultural prices and thus farmers' incomes.

- The government has sought to address the farm problem with three different policies: price floor, price subsidy, and supply restriction. A price floor, as discussed in earlier units, is a legally established minimum price. A price subsidy is the difference between a target price and the market price. A supply restriction is the inducement to reduce the supply of output, usually by planting less land to crops. While each of these policies increases farmers' incomes, they also lead to a misallocation of resources.

QUESTIONS FOR STUDY AND ANALYSIS

1. Discuss whether each of the following situations would improve or worsen the farm problem. Also indicate whether it is more likely to affect the short-run or long-run aspect of the farm problem.
   a. A new export treaty signed with the Soviet Union that doubles the amount of grain that they will buy next year
   b. A steady increase in consumers' income over a three-decade period
   c. A new type of fertilizer that increases corn and soybean yields by 30 percent
   d. Excellent weather in almost every country that produces and exports grain
   e. A short-term drop in consumers' income due to a recession
   f. A moderate drought in the Midwest

2. Part of the farm problem can be attributed to its characteristics as a competitive industry. In particular, farmers have virtually no control over the market price. Thus, if the market price falls in the short run, farmers produce until price falls below average variable cost. However, agriculture is not the only industry that can experience this type of problem. For each of the industries listed below, discuss whether or not you think it might have a short-run problem comparable to the short-run farm problem, and why.
   a. Automobile industry
   b. Housing construction
   c. Drycleaning services
   d. Airline industry

3. Assume that the market for wheat is given by the following demand and supply schedules:

Price per Bushel	Quantity Demanded	Quantity Supplied
	(thousand bushels)	
$8.00	550	700
7.50	560	680
7.00	570	660
6.50	580	640
6.00	590	620
5.50	600	600
5.00	610	580
4.50	620	560
4.00	630	540
3.50	640	520
3.00	650	500
2.50	660	480
2.00	670	460

a. What is the market equilibrium price and quantity? What is the total revenue received by farmers for the sale of the wheat?

b. If a price floor is established by the government at $7.00 per bushel, how much of a surplus is created? How much does it cost the government to buy the surplus? How much revenue do farmers receive for the sale of the wheat at the legal price floor? What is the farmers' total revenue?

c. Suppose that a price subsidy program is used, with a target price of $7.00 per bushel. What is the quantity of wheat supplied by farmers? What is the price buyers are willing to pay in the market? What is the price subsidy per bushel of wheat? How much does it cost the government for this program? What is the farmers' total revenue?

d. If farmers can produce 50 bushels of wheat per acre, how much land must they keep from production if the government wants to raise the market price to $7.00 per bushel?

4. The payment-in-kind (PIK) was an agricultural policy used by the Reagan administration to boost farmers' incomes and eliminate large surpluses of agricultural products. An article in *Newsweek* described how it worked:

> Under the program, farmers who agreed to take some of their land out of production were paid by the government out of surplus stocks. The administration says the program was a great success: 80 million acres were idled, stockpilers got some breathing room, prices rose a bit and farmers got some extra money in their pockets.
>
> Critics say PIK has been the administration's biggest agricultural disaster, a $12 billion boondoggle. Most farmers took only their poorest land out of production, so harvests have not dropped dramatically. ("A Bumper Crop of Subsidies," *Newsweek*, 25 July 1983, p. 60)

a. Which of the three types of agricultural policies discussed in this unit would best describe the PIK program? Why?

b. From this account would you say that the PIK program was effective or ineffective in raising farmers' incomes? How has the program affected the allocation of resources in the economy?

c. Although the costs of the program are reported at $12 billion, what other opportunity costs are not considered?

d. If you were advising the secretary of agriculture and the president, outline a program that you would recommend to address the farm problem.

REVIEW GLOSSARY

farm problem A situation in which farmers have relatively low or unstable incomes caused by low or unstable agricultural prices.

long-run problem The continuous decline in farm incomes caused by the continuous decline in agricultural prices.

parity price ratio The ratio of prices received by farmers to prices paid by farmers. The parity price ratio illustrates the continuous decline in relative agricultural prices.

price floor A legally established minimum price above the market equilibrium. A price floor is one policy used to address the short-run farm problem, but it leads to a surplus of agricultural products and an inefficient allocation of resources.

price subsidy The difference between the market price and a specified target price. A price subsidy also leads to an inefficient allocation of resources.

short-run problem The fluctuation of farm income caused by fluctuations in agricultural prices.

supply restriction A policy in which farmers are induced to reduce output. This policy usually takes the form of restricting the amount of land used for agricultural production. However, with no limits on nonland inputs, the supply of agricultural production may be reduced less than planned.

SECTION INQUIRY

The Supply of Airline Services

In 1978 the Airline Deregulation Act established an important milestone for the supply of airline services. Between 1938 and 1978 airline services in the United States was regulated by the Civil Aeronautics Board (CAB). The CAB determined the prices airlines could charge and granted permission for new airlines to enter the industry or for existing airlines to establish new service between cities. During this period airlines were not allowed to compete with each other by lowering the prices, but they were allowed to compete by offering a wide range of services, such as more comfortable seats, better meals, and in-flight movies. Although the CAB established prices and limited entry into the industry, which helped insure profits for the airlines, the airlines were also required to meet other regulations established by the CAB, such as offering unprofitable flights between relatively small cities.

However, the 1978 Airline Deregulation Act changed all of this. The CAB no longer determined prices charged by airlines, allowing airlines the freedom to establish their own prices. In addition, the CAB lost the power to grant entry into the industry, meaning that nearly anyone with an airplane could enter the industry as long as they satisfied Federal Aviation Administration safety requirements. In fact, the Airline Deregulation Act legislated the CAB out of existence in 1985.

After 1978 the airline industry experienced both very good times and very bad times. For the first few years airline profits boomed as airlines lowered rates and attracted new customers. The boom was also due in part to rapid growth in national economic activity. When the economy is prosperous, people tend to demand more airline services. However, in the early 1980s the industry took a downturn. Since the CAB no longer restricted entry into the industry, many optimistic entrepreneurs saw the profits earned by the existing airlines and decided they wanted a piece of the pie as well. In addition, several existing smaller airlines expanded their services to compete directly with the larger airlines, something that was seldom allowed by the CAB. And finally, the national economy also took a nosedive into a recession, which meant that the demand for airline services also fell. The increased competition, lower prices, and reduced demand sent several airlines into financial turmoil. Braniff went in and out of bankruptcy several times. Continental, Delta, and Eastern all had financial problems. Many airlines went out of business, some merged with other airlines, and most cut back their services.

QUESTIONS FOR DISCUSSION

1. Which of the four types of market structures—perfect competition, monopoly, monopolistic competition, or oligopoly—do you think best fits the airline industry prior to deregulation in 1978? Explain. Which do you think best fits the airline industry now, after deregulation?

2. What are the fixed and variable inputs in the short-run production of airline services? Is the production of airline services affected by the law of diminishing marginal returns? Why or why not?

3. Based on your answer to Question 2, discuss the shapes of an airline's average and marginal cost curves. Does the marginal cost of airline services increase? Explain.

4. Considering the short-run production alternatives for a firm, discuss why several airlines incurred a loss and kept operating, while others shut down completely or went bankrupt after the airline industry was deregulated.

SECTION 9

Monopoly and Imperfect Competition

In our study of supply in Section 8 we saw that perfect competition leads to an efficient allocation of resources. However, market structures in the real world are not perfectly competitive, but rather are monopolistic and imperfectly competitive. Unfortunately, real world market structures do not allocate resources as efficiently as perfect competition. In this section we look at the three market structures that more closely resemble the actual operation of the economy: monopoly, monopolistic competition, and oligopoly. By studying these market structures and comparing them with the perfectly competitive ideal, we can see how efficiently the economy actually allocates resources.

Unit 9.1, Market Power, provides an introduction to monopoly and imperfect competition with a look at market power. Market power embodies the fundamental difference between perfect competition and the other three market structures. On the one hand, a perfectly competitive firm has no ability to influence the market, and thus has no market power. On the other hand, each of the three market structures studied in this section—monopoly, monopolistic competition, and oligopoly—have some degree of market power. This unit defines market power, discusses how firms obtain it, and illustrates how it affects the demand for a firm's product.

Unit 9.2, Monopoly, looks at the market structure that is the complete opposite of perfect competition. We examine how the market power of a monopoly, being the only firm in the market, leads to an inefficient allocation of resources. In addition, we see that a monopolist's market power prevents it from having a short-run supply curve like a perfectly competitive firm's curve.

Unit 9.3, Natural Monopolies and Public Utilities, looks at a special type of monopoly—a natural monopoly. A natural monopoly occurs when the costs of production make it most efficient for a single firm to produce all output in the market. Most public utilities that generate electricity, distribute natural gas, or provide telephone services are natural monopolies. In this unit we discuss why natural monopolies exist and look at some alternative methods for regulating the prices charged by public utilities.

Unit 9.4, Monopolistic Competition, introduces the first of the two market structures referred to as imperfect competition. The interesting feature of monopolistic competition is that it has characteristics of both perfect competition and monopoly. In this unit we see how a firm with these apparently contradictory characteristics undertakes the production of its output.

Unit 9.5, Oligopoly, discusses the second of the two imperfectly competitive market structures and takes a brief look at the diversity of oligopolies. We look at some of the types of behavior common to oligopolistic industries. Then we examine two alternative methods of explaining some of the behavior, the kinked demand curve and collusion.

Unit 9.6, Controlling Imperfect Competition with Antitrust Legislation, looks at three pieces of legislation that have influenced the structure of markets in the United States. In the study of monopoly, monopolistic competition, and oligopoly, one point stands out—firms with market power inefficiently allocate resources. In this unit we see how the government has sought to correct inefficiencies caused by market power through the use of antitrust legislation.

Unit 9.7, Market Power in the Health Care Industry, concludes this section by applying the principles of production studied in the previous six units to the health care industry. In this unit we see how market power contributes to the relatively higher prices of health care services. And we see that third party payments by insurance companies and the government also lead to the higher prices.

UNIT 9.1

Market Power

Perfect competition allocates the economy's goods, services, and resources more efficiently than any alternative market structure. However, in the real world, allocation is performed not by perfect competition, but by one of the other three market structures: monopoly, monopolistic competition, and oligopoly. This unit begins our study of these three market structures with a look at market power.

Market power represents the one crucial difference between perfect competition and the other three market structures. A perfectly competitive firm has no market power, because it has no control over price. By contrast, in monopoly, monopolistic competition, and oligopoly, varying degrees of market power, and corresponding degrees of control over price, are exhibited. As we see in Units 9.2, 9.4, and 9.5, this market power leads to an inefficient allocation of resources. Here, we relate the concept of market power to monopoly, monopolistic competition, and oligopoly.

We start by reviewing the characteristics of monopoly, monopolistic competition, and oligopoly, particularly as each differs from perfect competition. After we study these characteristics, the concept of market power is defined and discussed. We then focus on two reasons why market power exists, barriers to entry and product differentiation. The unit concludes by looking at how market power generally affects the demand curve facing a firm.

CHARACTERISTICS OF MONOPOLY, MONOPOLISTIC COMPETITION, AND OLIGOPOLY

Recall that perfect competition is a market structure characterized by a large number of relatively small firms, identical products, freedom of entry and exit, and perfect information concerning prices and technology. How do the other three market structures compare to the perfectly competitive ideal?

Monopoly

<u>Monopoly is a market structure characterized by a single firm supplying all output in the market.</u> Monopoly and perfect competition lie at opposite ends of the spectrum of market structures. A perfectly competitive firm is but one of many in the market producing the same product. Since the products are identical, each is a perfect substitute for all others. But a monopolist is the only firm in the market, which means there are no other firms producing an identical product. At best, a monopolist produces a product with only a limited number of highly imperfect substitutes. Perfect competition and monopoly also differ in terms of entry and exit. While perfectly competitive firms are free to enter and exit an industry, a monopolistic industry has barriers preventing or limiting the entry of other firms. Not only are other firms prevented from entering the market, but in some cases, such as government-regulated public utilities, a firm is even prevented from leaving the market.

Monopolistic Competition

<u>Monopolistic competition is a market structure characterized by a large number of relatively small firms, similar but not identical products, freedom of entry and exit, and imperfect information.</u> Like perfect competition, monopolistic competition features a large number of small firms with freedom of entry and exit. However, unlike perfect competition, monopolistically competitive firms sell products that are similar, but not necessarily identical. In some cases the products are physically different, and in other cases the differences are based on buyers' perceptions. Furthermore, monopolistically competitive firms do not necessarily have perfect information. Note that while monopolistic competition has the competitive characteristics of

perfect competition, most notably a large number of small firms, each firm in the market also acts a little like a monopolist, because of the slight differences in products.

Oligopoly

Oligopoly is a market structure characterized by a small number of relatively large firms supplying most of the output in the market. Where monopolistic competition resembles perfect competition, oligopoly resembles monopoly. In fact, the main difference between monopoly and oligopoly is the number of firms in the market—monopoly has exactly one firm in the market, oligopoly two or more. The number of firms in an oligopolistic market is limited by the same barriers that restrict entry into a monopolistic market, meaning oligopoly has neither freedom of entry and exit nor a large number of small firms. However, firms in an oligopolistic market can produce identical products, as in perfect competition, or differentiated products, as in monopolistic competition.

MARKET POWER

Market power is the ability of a firm to control or influence the price and/or quantity exchanged in the market. A perfectly competitive firm has no market power and is not able to influence the market price or quantity exchanged. As we saw in Unit 8.4, a perfectly competitive firm is a price taker, meaning it sells its output at the price determined by the market. And since each firm's output represents such a small part of the total market, changes in output have no effect on the market quantity exchanged.

The other three market structures are price makers and have differing degrees of market power. Each is able to exert some control over the price and quantity. Obviously, a monopoly has a great deal of market power, because a monopoly *is* the market. Whatever price the monopolist charges is the price buyers must pay for the product. And with control of the price, the monopolist can control the quantity sold by moving up and down the market demand curve. Note, however, that a monopolist cannot control both price and quantity. A supplier might control the price, but buyers still decide how much to buy. Or the monopolist might control the quantity supplied, and see the price buyers are willing to pay.

This relationship between demand and market power indicates that a firm producing a product with relatively few substitutes has more market power. If a monopoly raises the price, buyers have a very limited number of substitute goods to choose from, so they either buy the monopolist's good or do without. For example, if electricity is supplied by a monopolist, buyers can either purchase it or sacrifice the benefits of electricity. Although natural gas, coal, fuel oil, liquid propane, wind energy, and solar power can be substituted for electricity, none provides exactly the same type of services.

In monopolistic competition each firm produces a good with many relatively close substitutes. A monopolistically competitive firm can raise the price of its good, just like a monopolist, but if the price is raised too much, buyers switch to similar goods produced by other firms in the market. For example, if Pepsi-Cola raises its price, many buyers will buy Coca-Cola instead. The availability of substitutes means monopolistically competitive firms have much less market power than monopolies.

The market power of oligopolistic firms falls in between monopoly and monopolistic competition. Since there are a small number of firms in the market, buyers have fewer available substitutes. But in many cases the substitutes are identical, such as steel or petroleum, or the substitutes are very close, such as automobiles or tires. The availability of a small number of close substitutes gives oligopolistic firms an interesting type of market power, which depends on actions taken by the other firms in the market. For example, if there are only two firms in the market and both raise their prices together, then they effectively act as a single monopoly, giving each a great deal of market power. However, if only one firm raises its price, it has much less market power, since buyers will switch to the other good.

BARRIERS TO ENTRY

One reason that firms are able to obtain and keep market power is through barriers to entry. A **barrier to entry** is an institutional, technological, or economic restriction on the entry of firms into an industry. The four most important barriers to entry that contribute to the market power found in monopoly, monopolistic competition, and oligopoly are government franchise, patent, resource ownership, and decreasing average cost.

Government Franchise

A **government franchise** is the legal right granted to a firm to produce and/or sell a good in a particular market, subject to government control. In many cases franchises are created to limit the number of firms in the industry. For example, most public utilities are monopolies established by government franchises. For public utilities, the franchise prevents two or more firms from duplicating the large amount of capital needed to provide the good, which, as we discuss in Unit 9.3, means one firm can produce the good at a lower cost than two or more firms. The government franchise also gives the government the authority to oversee the activities of the firm, which usually takes the form of price regulation.

However, the government does not have to award a franchise to a single firm but can also use franchises to establish an oligopoly. For example, some towns have awarded franchises to two firms for the provision of cable TV services, thus creating an oligopoly.

Sometimes, firms are granted a license rather than a government franchise. A **license** is the legal right granted to a firm to produce and/or sell a good in a particular market, but with less government control than a franchise. A license is usually used to control product quality and set industry standards, and not to directly regulate the price. For example, liquor stores, barbershops, and taxicab services are all licensed to maintain quality standards. Licensing of this type generally leads to oligopolies or monopolistically competitive industries.

Patent

A **patent** is the exclusive control of an invention awarded to its inventor for a period of seventeen years. Government patents allow the inventor to reap the rewards of his or her creativity and innovativeness. But a patent can also give the patent holder exclusive ownership of an input, which creates market power. If a single firm holds the patent, then a monopoly can result. For example, the patent on the telephone helped create the AT&T monopoly. However, a patent can also create an oligopoly if two or more firms are allowed to produce the good, or if two or more firms have similar patents used to produce similar goods.

Resource Ownership

In the same way that a patent can lead to market power, market power can be created through exclusive ownership of any resource. Such resources as nickel, bauxite (used to produce aluminum), and petroleum have been, at one time or another, almost completely controlled by a single firm. Even today, the DeBeers Company of South Africa has a monopoly because of its control of the world's diamond mines. And resource ownership is responsible for many oligopolies. Petroleum, uranium, and bauxite are all resources that are currently controlled by a small number of firms in oligopolistic markets.

Decreasing Average Cost

One key source of market power is decreasing average cost. If an industry requires a production process that is very capital intensive, then average costs may decrease over the relevant range of production. For example, the generation of electricity, provision of telephone services, and distribution of natural gas are three goods that require a great deal of capital. The relatively high fixed costs in these industries tend to dominate variable costs at small quantities of output, leading to a decreasing average total cost curve. If the market demand is small relative to this section of the average total cost curve, then one firm can produce the output cheaper than two, and a monopoly is created. If two firms divide up the market, each produces at a higher average total cost.

In Figure 9.1.1 the monopoly is seen at the far right of the diagram as curve C. Up to 20,000 units of output, average total cost of a monopoly is decreasing, because the nature of the good requires substantial fixed cost. Market demand D falls within this range of output.

However, if production of the good requires less fixed cost, then the market demand curve may not lie in the decreasing portion of average total cost. For example, the average total cost curve of a typical perfectly competitive or monopolistically competitive firm might reach a minimum average total cost at 100 units of output, as indicated by curve A. The technology needed to produce goods in perfect or monopolistic competition is not capital intensive, and firms do not have high fixed cost. Here, since each firm produces around 100 units, about 200 firms are needed to satisfy market demand. This is one reason that perfectly competitive and monopolistically competitive industries are composed of a large number of small firms.

A third case is illustrated by curve B, which depicts the market structure of an oligopoly.

Figure 9.1.1
Decreasing Average Cost and Market Structures

Decreasing average cost can determine the type of market structure. For market demand of around 20,000 units, a monopoly is created if one firm can satisfy the market in the decreasing portion of average total cost (curve C). However, if one firm has decreasing average cost up to 10,000 units (curve B), then two firms can satisfy the market, and an oligopoly is created. By comparison, the average total cost curve for either a perfectly or monopolistically competitive firm is curve A. If each firm has decreasing average total cost up to 100 units, then 200 firms are needed to satisfy the market.

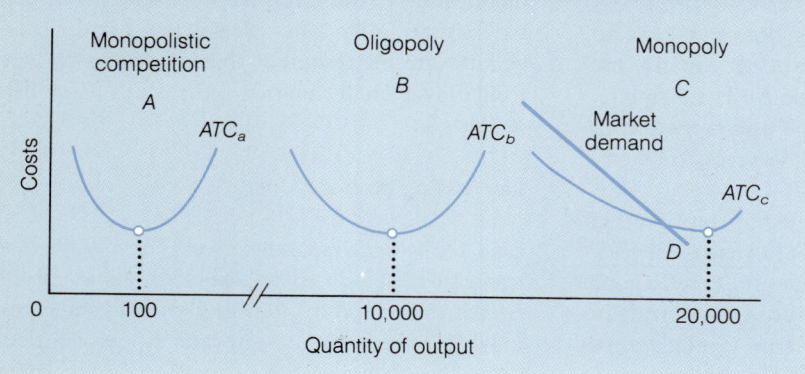

Decreasing average cost exists up to 10,000 units of output, or about one-half of the market demand. Each firm has more fixed cost than monopolistic competition, but not enough to generate a monopoly, so two firms divide the market in half. In other cases, if the production technology is such that average total cost decreases up to only 5000 units, then the market can be supplied by four firms. In this way decreasing average total cost can lead to an oligopoly.

Other Barriers to Entry

There are other barriers that can prevent the entry of firms into an industry. For example, new firms might have higher start-up costs than existing firms, and thus be forced to charge a higher price. This places the new firm at an immediate disadvantage. In addition, existing firms might have an established brand, with brand-name recognition. But a new firm, lacking brand-name recognition, would have to incur higher advertising costs than existing firms in order to achieve equal recognition. Any increase in the new firm's cost hinders its ability to compete with existing firms.

PRODUCT DIFFERENTIATION

Market power also derives from product differentiation. **Product differentiation is a real or perceived difference between goods, such that buyers are willing to pay different prices.** Product differentiation makes each good slightly different from other goods, which means they are not perfect substitutes. Recall that market power is based partly on the number of available substitutes and how closely they resemble each other. The existence of many perfect substitutes, as in perfect competition, means a firm has no market power. However, if a firm has only imperfect substitutes for its product, then it has some degree of market power. Products can be differentiated in three ways: physical difference, perceived difference, and support services.

Physical Difference

First, the good can be physically different. A Toyota Corolla is definitely not a Cadillac Eldorado. Coca-Cola does not taste like Dr. Pepper or Seven-Up. The physical distinction can be based on quality, durability, size, shape, or appearance, whatever makes the good functionally different. Most monopolistically competitive and oligopolistic firms try to physically differentiate their products.

Perceived Difference

However, if physical differentiation isn't possible, the firms often try to influence buyer perception. If buyers *think* one product is different from another, it does not matter whether or not a physical difference actually exists. Buyers who think Chevrolets are better than Fords are willing to pay more for Chevrolets. If Chevrolets actually are better than Fords, then they are also willing to pay more. Coca-Cola may taste the same as Pepsi-Cola, but if buyers think Coca-Cola is better, then it will be reflected in their demand. Indeed, the perception of product differences is very important in monopolistic competition and oligopoly. Because advertising and packaging affect buyers' perceptions of the product, firms in both types of market structures bombard the public with advertising. It's irrelevant whether the product actually is "new" and "improved" as long as the buyer thinks it is.

Support Services

A third way products are differentiated is through support services. Every grocery store in town may sell "Flaked Corn Crunchies," but some buyers go to the one that gives green stamps, and others go to the one with carry-out service. In both cases the physical product is the same, but the support services vary. In the years before high gasoline prices, gasoline stations engaged extensively in this type of competition. Advertisements told buyers how friendly, clean, cooperative, and enthusiastic each "service" station was. Hardly a week passed that one station or another was not offering free glasses, tune-ups, maps, or silverware with each tankful of gasoline. But the product was not physically different, nor was it perceived to be; only the support services varied.

MARKET POWER AND DEMAND

Market power does something very important for a firm—it generates a downward-sloping demand curve. This is true for monopoly, monopolistic competition, and oligopoly. In each case the firm can sell a larger quantity of output only if it lowers the price. If the firm tries to raise the price, the quantity demanded is reduced.

Figure 9.1.2 illustrates how the demand curve facing an individual firm is affected by the market power of the firm. For a perfectly competitive firm, the demand curve PC is perfectly elastic at the market price. The perfectly competitive firm, with no market power, has no control over the price, and thus can sell its output only at the market price P_e. However, if a firm has a small degree of market power, as would be the case for a monopolistically competitive firm, then the demand curve MC is no longer perfectly elastic, although it is still highly elastic. At the opposite extreme to perfect competition, monopoly has a great deal of market power, since demand curve M is the market demand curve. This curve illustrates the relative elasticity of a demand curve for a monopoly with a great deal of market power. In essence, the more market power a firm has, the less elastic is its demand curve.

Figure 9.1.2

Demand Curves and Market Power

The market power of a firm affects the relative elasticity of its demand curve. A perfectly competitive firm, with no market power, has a perfectly elastic demand curve. However, as a firm's market power increases, the elasticity of its demand curve declines. The demand curve for a monopoly, with a great deal of market power, has relatively low elasticity.

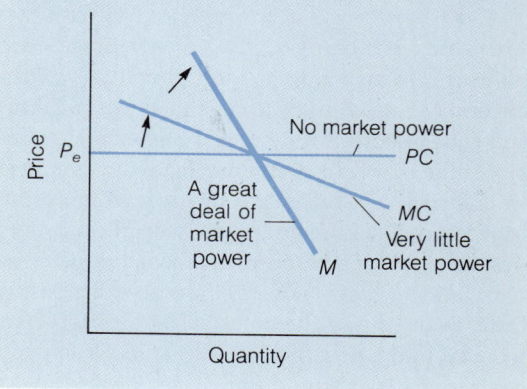

IN SUMMARY
Market Power

- Monopoly, monopolistic competition, and oligopoly differ from perfect competition in one important respect. Unlike perfect competition, each of these other three market structures has some degree of market power. Where perfect competition cannot influence the market price and/or quantity sold, monopoly, monopolistic competition, and oligopoly can.

- Monopoly is a market structure in which one firm supplies all output. It lies at the other end of the market structure spectrum from perfect competition. Monopolistic competition is similar to perfect competition, except that each firm sells a slightly different product. Oligopoly is very similar to monopoly, except there are two or more large firms in the industry rather than just one.

- Market power is the ability of a firm to control or influence the price and/or quantity exchanged in the market. Market power is graphically seen as a downward-sloping demand curve for a firm's output. A perfectly competitive firm has a horizontal demand curve, and thus no market power. Market power can result from barriers to entry and product differentiation.

- There are four barriers to entry that contribute to a firm's market power: government franchise, patent, resource ownership, and decreasing average cost. Each of these barriers limits the number of firms in an industry, thus increasing the ability of the remaining firms to control the market.

- Product differentiation is the real or perceived differences in products produced by two different firms. It can be caused by physical differences, perceived differences, or support services. In each case a buyer is willing to pay a higher price just because a particular firm is selling the product.

- The relative elasticity of the demand curve facing a firm depends on the degree of market power the firm has. Firms with relatively more market power tend to have demand curves with relatively less elasticity. In contrast to a perfectly competitive firm that faces a perfectly elastic demand curve, a monopolistically competitive firm faces a very elastic demand curve, and monopoly faces a relatively less elastic demand curve.

QUESTIONS FOR STUDY AND ANALYSIS

1. Why does the availability of close substitutes affect a firm's market power? Name three goods typically produced by monopolies. What substitutes exist for each? Are they close substitutes?

2. Listed below are several industries in which each firm has a fair degree of market power. One way the firms may have obtained (and retained) market power is through product differentiation. For each industry discuss the ways in which firms have differentiated their products. Try to be as specific as possible, and feel free to refer to specific companies.
   a. Automobiles
   b. Personal computers
   c. Toothpaste
   d. Carbonated soft drinks
   e. Airlines
   f. Beer
   g. Designer jeans

3. For each of the industries listed in question 2, discuss how barriers to entry might have contributed to the market power of each firm.

4. Biotechnology, which is based on the development of new substances and drugs through genetically modified organisms, is a new and growing field. Substances developed through gene splicing can be patented under a 1980 Supreme Court ruling. Directly after this ruling the Patent and Trademark Office was flooded with patent applications by the 300 companies working in the area of gene splicing.
   a. When the products developed by biotechnology research are finally sold on the market, what type of market structure is likely to develop?
   b. If most of the patents are likely to be very similar, with each one only slightly different from the others, how much market power is each firm likely to have?
   c. Under what conditions would the gene-splicing patents lead to an oligopoly? In your answer consider the role of research and development costs. Also consider that billions of dollars worth of potential sales are likely to be involved.

5. Discuss which of the following sports organizations is likely to have more market power and why.
   a. The Boston Celtics
   b. An intramural basketball team
   c. The National Football League
   d. Your school's athletic department
   e. The United States Football League
   f. The National Collegiate Athletic Association

REVIEW GLOSSARY

barrier to entry An institutional, technological, or economic restriction on the entry of firms into an industry.

government franchise The legal right granted to a firm to produce and/or sell a good in a particular market, subject to government control. Usually a government franchise sets up a single firm as a monopoly in a market. Public utilities are commonly franchised by the government.

license The legal right granted to a firm to produce and/or sell a good in a particular market, but with less government control than a franchise. A license is similar to a government franchise. However, a license usually does not stipulate control over the pricing activities of the firm, whereas a government franchise usually does.

market power The ability of one firm to control or influence the price and/or quantity exchanged in the market. Market power exists if the firm faces a downward-sloping demand curve. This allows a firm to choose the quantity of output or price.

monopolistic competition A market structure characterized by a large number of relatively small firms, similar but not identical products, freedom of entry and exit, and imperfect information.

monopoly A market structure characterized by a single firm supplying all output in the market. The good produced by a monopoly has very few close substitutes.

oligopoly A market structure characterized by a small number of relatively large firms supplying most of the output in the market.

patent The exclusive control of an invention awarded to its inventor for a period of seventeen years.

product differentiation The real or perceived differences between goods, such that buyers are willing to pay different prices.

UNIT 9.2

Monopoly

Recall that a **monopoly** is a market structure characterized by a single firm supplying all output in the market. The study of monopoly indicates how a firm behaves if it has complete market power, in contrast to a perfectly competitive firm, which has no market power. Also, in this unit groundwork is laid for studying monopolistic competition in Unit 9.4 and oligopoly in Unit 9.5, both of which fall between perfect competition and monopoly on the spectrum of market structures.

We begin by identifying the demand curve facing a monopoly. We then look at the short-run level of output produced by a monopolist if it seeks to maximize profit. Note that a monopolist has the same objective (profit maximization), and makes the production decision in the same manner (comparing marginal revenue to marginal cost), as a perfectly competitive firm. In fact, the primary difference between a monopolist and a perfectly competitive firm is the slope of the demand curve. For a perfectly competitive firm the demand curve is horizontal; for a monopolist the demand curve is negatively sloped.

This is a significant difference, as will be shown when we discuss the monopolist's supply curve and its influence on resource allocation. First, the negatively sloped demand curve means the monopolist does not have a supply curve. And second, the slope of the demand curve causes the monopolist to inefficiently allocate resources. Let's begin with a look at real world monopolies.

REAL WORLD MONOPOLIES

While there are several examples of monopoly markets in the economy, there are relatively few *good* examples. Because monopolies do not efficiently allocate resources, the government has expended a great deal of effort to eliminate them from the economy, as discussed in more detail in Unit 9.6, Controlling Imperfect Competition with Antitrust Legislation.

Although the government has made a concerted effort to eliminate monopoly markets from the economy, one type remains, public utilities. In fact, public utilities, which produce electricity, distribute natural gas, provide telephone and cable TV services, and supply municipal water, have more than escaped the antimonopoly efforts of the government. Public utilities are promoted, regulated, and even operated by the government; we find out why in Unit 9.3, Natural Monopolies and Public Utilities. Regardless of why public utilities are treated differently, they represent the most widespread example of monopoly markets in the economy.

Once we get past public utilities, there are few good examples of monopoly markets left. Perhaps the best example of a monopoly presently in operation is the DeBeers Company, which controls the world's diamond mines and, consequently, the supply of diamonds. It is not a U.S. company, which helps explain why it has not been broken up by the U.S. government. A hundred years ago, J. D. Rockefeller and Standard Oil controlled most of the petroleum in the United States. But this monopoly was broken up by the government. Alcoa Aluminum had a monopoly in aluminum production in the mid-1900s because of its control over bauxite, the resource used to produce aluminum. But this monopoly was also broken up by the government. Indeed, monopolies in the production of sugar, electrical equipment, and tobacco have all been broken up by the government in the past century.

THE MONOPOLIST'S DEMAND

The monopolist's demand *is* the market demand. Since the monopolist is the only seller in the market, it faces a downward-sloping market demand curve as it sells its product. Compare this to the perfectly competitive firm, which faces a perfectly elastic, horizontal demand curve. Figure 9.2.1

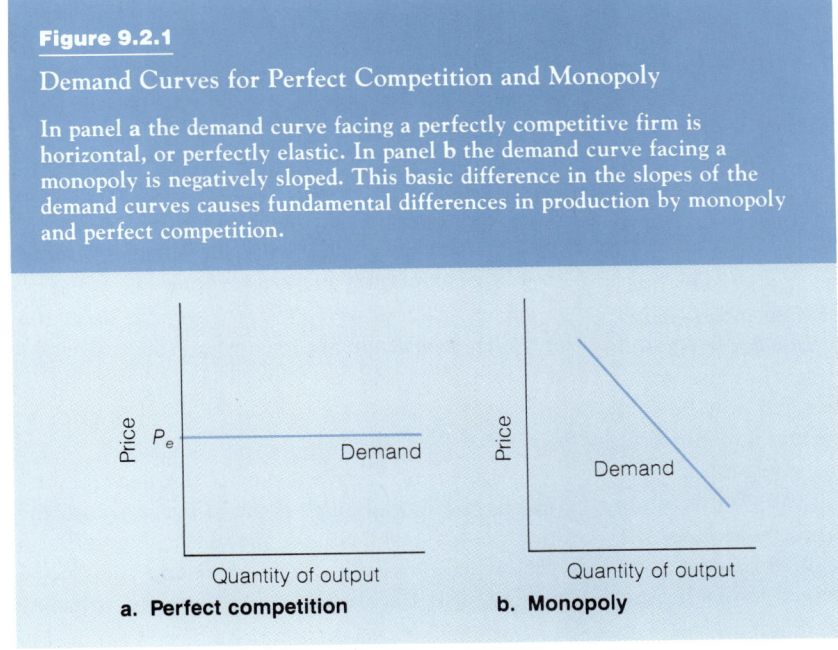

Figure 9.2.1

Demand Curves for Perfect Competition and Monopoly

In panel a the demand curve facing a perfectly competitive firm is horizontal, or perfectly elastic. In panel b the demand curve facing a monopoly is negatively sloped. This basic difference in the slopes of the demand curves causes fundamental differences in production by monopoly and perfect competition.

a. Perfect competition

b. Monopoly

depicts a perfectly competitive firm's demand curve in panel a and a monopolist's demand curve in panel b. Note that the monopolist must decrease the price in order to sell more output, whereas the perfectly competitive firm can sell all output at the existing market price. Herein lies the fundamental difference between perfect competition and firms with market power.

Recall from Unit 2.6 that the availability of substitutes is an important determinant of the price elasticity of demand. For the perfectly competitive firm, perfect substitutes are available, and thus the demand curve is perfectly elastic. For the monopolist only a few imperfect substitutes are available, and thus the demand curve is much less elastic.

Let's now look at a numerical example of a monopolist's demand. Assume that a single firm, Monopco, obtains complete control of the market for food sold on your campus. The first two columns of Table 9.2.1 list a demand schedule facing Monopco for the sale of pizza. Since Monopco's demand is also the market demand for pizza, price and quantity are inversely related. As the price declines from $10.50 to $4.50, the quantity demanded increases from zero to twelve pizzas.

If one pizza is sold for $10, the monopolist receives $10 of total revenue. If two pizzas are sold for $9.50 each, total revenue is $19. The third column of Table 9.2.1 lists the total revenue received by the monopolist for each quantity of pizza sold. Note that total revenue reaches a maximum of $55 for ten and eleven pizzas.

Figure 9.2.2 presents the total revenue curve for Monopco. Recall that the total revenue curve for a perfectly competitive firm is a straight line, because the price is the same for all pizzas. However, the monopolist's total revenue curve is not a straight line, but a curved line, because for a monopolist additional quantities can only be sold at lower prices. In Figure 9.2.2 revenue increases up to the tenth pizza, remains constant for the eleventh pizza, then declines for the twelfth pizza.

The average revenue received by Monopco is the market price. If three pizzas are sold for $9 each, the average revenue received for each pizza

Table 9.2.1

The Monopolist's Revenue

Since a monopolist is constrained by the market demand, the price received declines as more output is produced and sold. Therefore, the marginal revenue received by a monopolist also declines as more output is produced. Since a monopolist must lower the price on all output to sell one more unit, marginal revenue is less than price.

Quantity of Pizza	Price and Average Revenue	Total Revenue	Marginal Revenue
0	$10.50	$ 0	
1	10.00	10	$10
2	9.50	19	9
3	9.00	27	8
4	8.50	34	7
5	8.00	40	6
6	7.50	45	5
7	7.00	49	4
8	6.50	52	3
9	6.00	54	2
10	5.50	55	1
11	5.00	55	0
12	4.50	54	−1

is $9. The equality of price and average revenue is seen by calculating average revenue as

$$\text{average revenue} = \frac{\text{total revenue}}{\text{quantity}}$$
$$= \frac{\text{price} \times \text{quantity}}{\text{quantity}} = \text{price}$$

The equivalence between average revenue and price means the monopolist's demand curve is also the monopolist's average revenue curve. Figure 9.2.3 presents the average revenue/demand curve for a monopolist. Recall that the demand curve facing

Figure 9.2.2

The Monopolist's Total Revenue Curve

The total revenue curve for a monopolist is not a straight line, but a curve that flattens with larger quantities of output. Eventually, total revenue reaches a peak (here at ten and eleven pizzas), then begins to decline.

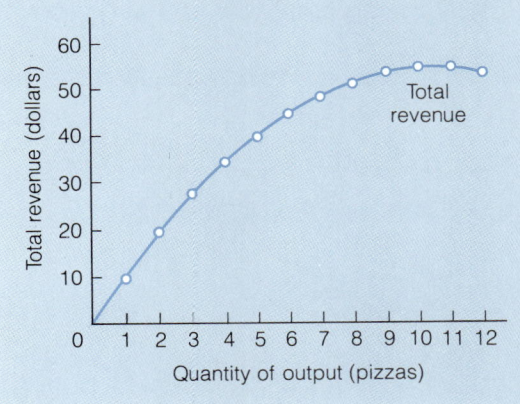

Figure 9.2.3

The Monopolist's Demand Curve

The demand curve facing a monopolist is the market demand curve and also the average revenue curve. Since the average revenue curve is downward sloping, the marginal revenue curve lies below it. Marginal revenue is always less than price (and average revenue) for the monopolist. In order to sell an additional unit of output, the monopolist reduces the price on all units sold. Thus, revenue increases from the price of the extra unit sold but decreases because of the lower price on all other units.

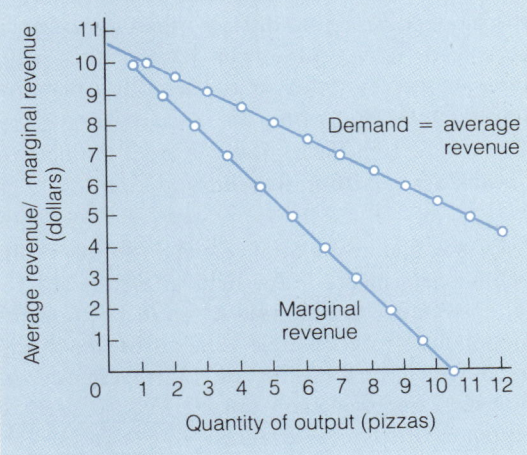

the perfectly competitive firm is not only its average revenue curve but also its marginal revenue curve. Is this also the case for the monopolist?

Marginal revenue is not equal to average revenue and price for a monopolist, as indicated by Figure 9.2.3. The mathematical relationship between average and marginal quantities states that a marginal curve lies below the average curve if the average curve is declining. Since the average revenue/demand curve declines (due to the law of demand), the marginal revenue curve of a monopolist must lie below the average revenue curve.

But other than the mathematical relationship between average and marginal quantities, why is a monopolist's marginal revenue less than average revenue? Let's look at the fourth column in Table 9.2.1, which lists the marginal revenue for each additional pizza. Note that the second pizza adds $9 to revenue, even though the price of the second pizza is $9.50. Why the difference?

If the monopolist sells one pizza, the price is $10. However, if the monopolist wants to sell a second pizza, the price is reduced to $9.50, for both pizzas. The sale of the second pizza for $9.50 adds $9.50 to the monopolist's revenue. But since the monopolist decreases the price on the first pizza from $10 to $9.50, $0.50 of revenue is lost on the first pizza. The net increment in total revenue is $9.50 − $0.50 = $9. The downward-sloping demand curve facing a monopolist means additional output changes revenue in two ways. First, revenue is increased by the sale of an additional unit. But second, revenue is decreased by the decline in the price on all other units. Because the price of the additional unit is also average revenue, marginal revenue is less than average revenue.

SHORT-RUN OUTPUT

The production objective of a monopolist is no different than that of a perfectly competitive firm—to produce the quantity of output that generates the highest level of economic profit. The monopolist weighs the cost of producing the good against the revenue received from its sale. To study the monopolist, we need to combine its revenue with its costs of production. The costs of production for the monopolist are no different than the costs for a perfectly competitive firm; both market structures are subject to the law of diminishing marginal returns in the short run.

Total Cost and Total Revenue

Let's look first at the total cost and revenue of the monopolist. Figure 9.2.4 depicts a standard total cost curve, as discussed in Unit 8.3, and the monopolist's total revenue. The quantities of output in which the total cost and total revenue curves intersect are **breakeven output,** the quantity of output in which total revenue is equal to total cost, such that the firm earns a normal profit, but no economic profit. Thus, economic profit is zero. At Q_1 and Q_2, total cost is equal to total revenue. At either quantity the monopolist receives a normal profit, since normal profit is part of cost. However, the monopolist wants to make the largest economic profit possible, just like a perfectly competitive firm.

Any quantity of output between Q_1 and Q_2 generates a positive economic profit. The maximum profit is obtained at Q_e, where the distance between the total revenue and total cost curves in panel a is the greatest. The difference between total revenue and total cost is given by the profit curve in panel b. The **profit curve** is a curve showing the relationship between profit and output. Up to

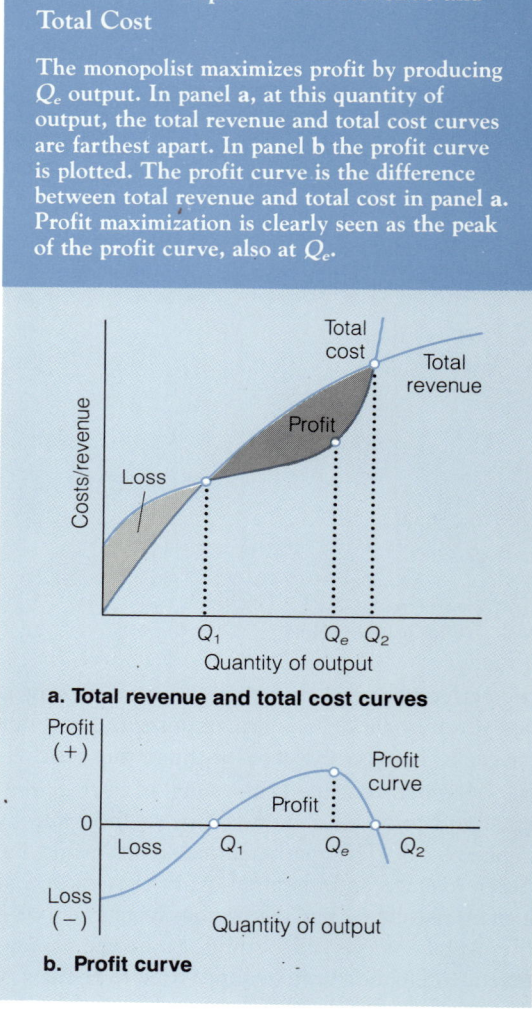

Figure 9.2.4

Short-Run Output—Total Revenue and Total Cost

The monopolist maximizes profit by producing Q_e output. In panel a, at this quantity of output, the total revenue and total cost curves are farthest apart. In panel b the profit curve is plotted. The profit curve is the difference between total revenue and total cost in panel a. Profit maximization is clearly seen as the peak of the profit curve, also at Q_e.

a. Total revenue and total cost curves

b. Profit curve

Q_1, the profit curve lies below the horizontal axis, meaning economic profit is negative. At quantities greater than Q_1, the first breakeven point, economic profit is positive, and continues to increase to Q_e. Further increases in quantity reduce profit until the second breakeven point, Q_2, is reached. Therefore, Q_e is the short-run profit-maximizing output for the monopolist.

Figure 9.2.5

Short-Run Output—Marginal Revenue and Marginal Cost

The monopolist maximizes profit by producing the quantity of output that equates marginal revenue and marginal cost. This quantity is Q_e, where the marginal revenue curve intersects the marginal cost curve. Economic profit is indicated by area C.

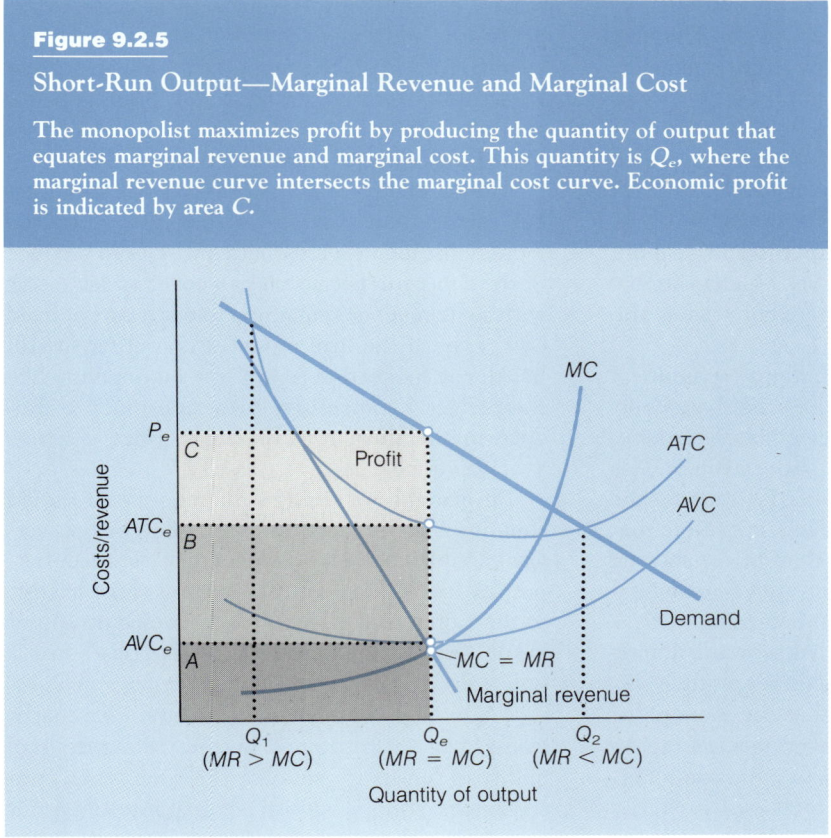

Marginal Cost and Marginal Revenue

The second approach to determining the monopolist's profit-maximizing level of output is based on marginal revenue and marginal cost. In many cases the marginal approach provides additional insight into the output decision, because while we might be able to determine the quantity of output using the total curves, we cannot easily see the price charged by the monopolist.

Figure 9.2.5 depicts a standard set of production cost curves, and the demand and marginal revenue curves for the monopolist. If the demand curve is downward sloping, the marginal revenue curve lies below it. Therefore, at every quantity of output, price is greater than marginal revenue.

The problem facing the monopolist in Figure 9.2.5 is to determine the quantity of output that provides the highest level of economic profit. If production is increased from Q_1, how is economic profit affected by the changes in output, based on marginal cost and marginal revenue? As output increases from Q_1, the marginal cost of production is relatively low, as shown by the marginal cost curve, but marginal revenue is relatively high, and profit is increasing. Thus, an extra unit of output adds more to revenue than it adds to cost.

As long as marginal revenue is greater than marginal cost, it is profitable to increase production. Only when the monopolist reaches Q_e is it no longer profitable to increase the quantity of output. If output is increased above Q_e, the additional cost becomes greater than the additional revenue, the marginal cost curve lies above the marginal revenue curve, and the level of profit is reduced. The profit-maximizing level of output, Q_e, occurs where marginal cost equals marginal revenue.

Note the similarity between perfect competition and monopoly. The monopoly maximizes profit by equating marginal cost to marginal revenue. Likewise, for the perfectly competitive firm, profit is maximized at the quantity in which marginal cost is equal to marginal revenue, but price is also equal to marginal revenue.

But price is not equal to marginal revenue for the monopolist. What price does the monopolist charge for Q_e? Once the monopolist determines the profit-maximizing level of output, the price is given by the demand curve. For Q_e output, the market is willing to pay P_e for each unit. Note that since marginal revenue is less than price, and the monopolist equates marginal revenue to marginal cost, marginal cost is also less than price. This is the case for any firm that faces a downward-sloping demand curve and seeks to maximize profit.

Figure 9.2.5 also reveals that the monopolist in this case makes a positive economic profit. At Q_e, average variable cost is AVC_e, and total variable cost is area A. Average total cost is ATC_e, and total cost is area A + B, with area B being total fixed cost. Therefore, total revenue received by the monopolist is the area A + B + C, which is equal to P_e times Q_e. The difference between total revenue and total cost is area C, economic profit.

Minimizing Losses

So far our examples have been very generous to the monopolist by providing an economic profit. However, a common misconception about monopoly is that it always makes an economic profit. While a monopolist tends to make more profit than a perfectly competitive firm, it can in fact incur a loss, or even be forced to stop producing in the short run, just like a perfectly competitive firm. Recall that the monopolist is constrained by the market demand for its product. If the price buyers are willing and able to pay for the good is less than average total cost, the monopolist, like any other firm, has a negative profit. If the price is below average variable cost in the short run, the monopolist shuts down, as shown by Figure 9.2.6.

In panel a price is less than average total cost but greater than average variable cost. Here, the monopolist incurs a loss, but continues to produce in the short run because it can cover variable cost with some revenue remaining to pay a part of fixed cost. Even if the firm produces no output, it still has to pay fixed cost. Again, the monopolist, like the perfectly competitive firm, continues to produce in the short run as long as price is above average variable cost.

In panel b we see that the monopolist should shut down in the short run if price falls below average variable cost. If the monopolist produces output, its loss is fixed cost plus part of variable cost, so the monopolist is better off producing no output at all. By shutting down, the monopolist's loss is only equal to fixed cost.

A monopolist *cannot* charge any price that it wants, but is constrained by the willingness and ability of buyers to purchase the good. As a consequence, monopolists are not guaranteed a profit and, in the short runs can lose money or even be forced to shut down.

THE MONOPOLIST'S SUPPLY CURVE

The most important result from the study of perfect competition was the identification of the firm's supply curve. We saw that the perfectly competitive firm's marginal cost curve *is* its supply curve. Is the monopolist's marginal cost curve also its supply curve?

In the first place, keep in mind that the monopolist does not produce output by equating price and marginal cost. For the monopolist, price is always greater than marginal cost. Thus, the short-run price and quantity combination for the monopolist does not lie on the marginal cost curve, as it

Figure 9.2.6

Loss Minimization

A monopolist is not guaranteed an economic profit. In panel a, if the demand curve lies below the average total cost curve, and price is less than average total cost but greater than average *variable* cost, the monopolist continues to produce output. However, in panel b, if the demand curve lies below the average variable cost curve, then price is less than average variable cost. In this case the firm shuts down production and incurs a loss equal to fixed cost.

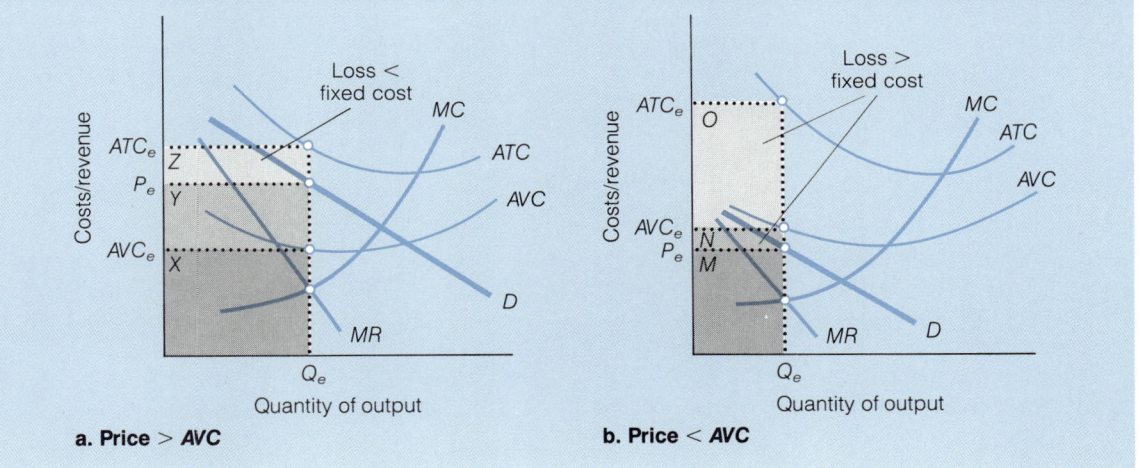

a. Price > AVC

b. Price < AVC

does for the perfectly competitive firm. For this reason the monopolist's marginal cost curve cannot be its supply curve.

Indeed, not only is the marginal cost curve not the monopolist's supply curve, but the monopolist does not even have a supply curve. For the monopolist to have a supply curve, it must have a one-to-one relationship between price and quantity. That is, if the price increases, the quantity supplied must also increase. This is not necessarily the case for a monopoly.

For example, in panel a of Figure 9.2.7 the monopolist produces Q_e output. But the price charged for Q_e can be either P_1 or P_2, depending on the market demand curve. If the demand curve shifts or changes shape, the monopolist can sell the same output at a different price. Or the monopolist can sell different quantities at the same price, as illustrated in panel b. Here, due to a shift in the demand curve, the monopolist sells both Q_1 and Q_2 at P_e.

In short, there is no way to isolate a relationship between price and the quantity supplied for a monopolist. If a perfectly competitive firm receives a higher price, it increases output. This is not true for a monopolist. We have no way of knowing whether a higher price leads to more, less, or the same amount of production.

Figure 9.2.7
Monopoly and the Supply Curve

A monopolist does not have a supply curve. A monopolist can sell the same quantity at different prices, as in panel a, or a different quantity at the same price, as in panel b. Because the monopolist's output decision depends on the market demand, a single relationship between price and quantity supplied does not exist.

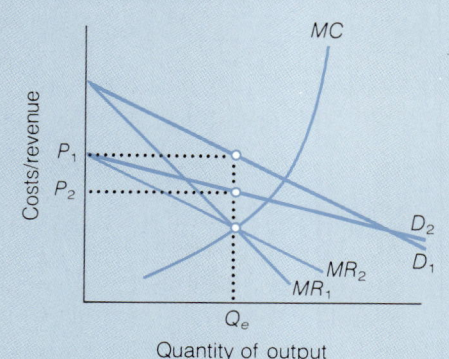

a. Same quantity, different price

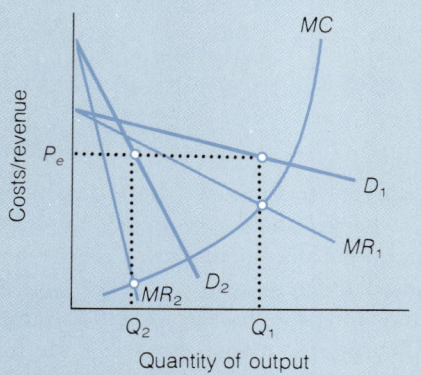

b. Same price, different quantity

Figure 9.2.8
Monopoly and Resource Allocation

The monopolist produces less output and charges a higher price than perfect competition. The monopolist produces Q_m output, where marginal revenue equals marginal cost, and sells it at P_m. By comparison, perfect competition produces Q_c, where price P_c equals marginal cost.

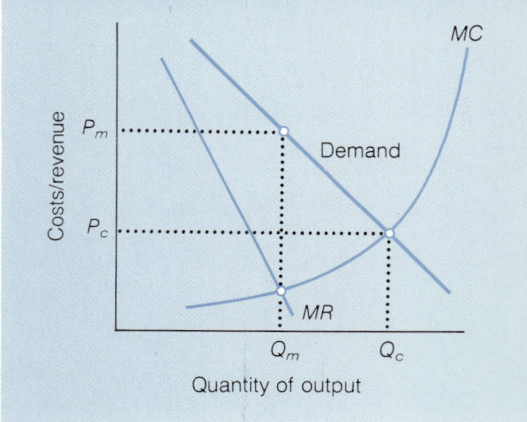

MONOPOLY AND RESOURCE ALLOCATION

In terms of the allocation of resources, a monopoly generally produces less output and sells it for a higher price than is the case in perfect competition. Figure 9.2.8 presents the profit-maximizing level of output and price for a monopolist, and the comparable output and price for perfect competition.

The monopolist produces output where marginal cost equals marginal revenue, at Q_m, and sells it for P_m. By contrast, in perfect competition output is produced where price equals marginal cost, at Q_c and P_c in Figure 9.2.8. The price charged by the monopolist is higher, and the quantity produced is lower, than perfect competition.

The higher price and lower quantity is one reason economists do not like monopolies. A second reason is that a monopoly misallocates resources. For a monopoly, price is *always* above marginal cost. The market price indicates not only how much buyers are willing and able to pay for the last unit of the good, but also the value buyers place on the last unit of the good. Marginal cost is the opportunity cost of foregone production, and indicates the value of other goods given up in order to produce the last unit.

In perfect competition, price is equal to marginal cost, and the value of the last unit of a good produced is equal to the value of goods given up in its production. Thus, it is not possible to produce more of one good and less of another in order to increase society's welfare. But for a monopoly, price is always greater than marginal cost, and the value of the last unit produced is greater than the value of goods not produced. Society can be better off by producing more of the monopolist's good, and less of other goods. Unfortunately, the monopolist allocates too few resources to the production of its good.

IN SUMMARY

Monopoly

- Monopoly is a market structure in which one firm supplies all output. It lies at the other end of the market structure spectrum from perfect competition. An important factor for a monopoly is the number of close substitutes that exists for the product. A monopoly has only a few imperfect substitutes.

- The demand curve for a monopolist's output is the market demand curve for the good, because the monopolist is the only producer in the market. The most important difference between monopoly and perfect competition is the downward-sloping demand curve facing the monopolist, as opposed to the horizontal demand curve of perfect competition.

- The monopolist produces the output that maximizes profit, just like a perfectly competitive firm. This output is determined where the difference between total revenue and total cost is the greatest, or where marginal revenue equals marginal cost.

- A monopolist is not guaranteed an economic profit. If price is less than average total cost but greater than average variable cost, the monopolist continues to produce output but at a loss. If price falls below average variable cost, the monopolist shuts down production. This is exactly the same for perfect competition.

- Unlike perfect competition, the marginal cost curve is not the monopolist's supply curve. The monopolist does not have a supply curve in short-run production. It is not possible to isolate a relationship between price and quantity supplied for the monopolist. A higher price can cause the monopolist to increase, decrease, or not change output.

- Monopoly produces less output and sells it at a higher price than perfect competition. Since price (the value of the good produced) is above marginal cost (the value of goods not produced), the monopoly misallocates society's scarce resources. Society is better off if monopolies produce more output.

QUESTIONS FOR STUDY AND ANALYSIS

1. Do you think major league baseball is a monopoly? In your answer consider the closeness and availability of substitutes. Also consider that major league baseball is an organization of twenty-six teams that are divided into two separate leagues. While each league has a separate president, all teams must answer to

the commissioner of baseball, who in turn answers to the owners of the twenty-six teams.

2. Suppose a monopolist faces the following demand schedule for electricity.

Price	$ 1	2	3	4	5	6	7	8	9	10
Quantity	100	90	80	70	60	50	40	30	20	10

a. Draw its total revenue, average revenue, and marginal revenue curves.
b. Explain why the marginal revenue curve lies below the demand curve for a monopolist. Use the marginal revenue curve to explain why the total revenue curve is not a straight line.

3. Assuming that the DeBeers Company of South Africa has a virtual monopoly on diamond mining, discuss whether there are too many or too few diamonds produced.

4. Some people argue that the American Medical Association, through its ability to control entry into medical school and the licensing of doctors, has a monopoly on medical services. Do you agree or disagree? Why?

5. Suppose you have the following information for a monopolist.

Q	TC	MC	Price	MR	AR	TR	Profit
0	10	—	10				
1		6	9				
2		4	8				
3		5	7				
4		7	6				
5		10	5				
6		14	4				
7		19	3				
8		25	2				
9		32	1				

a. With the information in this table, determine the profit-maximizing quantity of output and price.
b. How much profit does the monopolist earn? Is the monopolist able to cover variable and fixed cost? Will it produce or shut down in the short run?
c. Draw graphs of the total cost, total revenue, and profit curves.

6. Assume that the market demand from question 5 changes, and the new demand schedule is given by the following:

Price	$20	19	18	17	16	15	14	13	12	11
Quantity	0	1	2	3	4	5	6	7	8	9

a. What is the profit-maximizing quantity of output and the corresponding price?
b. How much profit does the monopolist earn? Is the monopolist able to cover variable and fixed cost? Will it produce or shut down in the short run?
c. Draw graphs of the total cost, total revenue, and profit curves.

7. Can a monopolist charge any price that it wants? Explain.

REVIEW GLOSSARY

breakeven output The quantity of output in which total revenue is equal to total cost, such that the firm earns a normal profit, but no economic profit.

monopoly A market structure characterized by a single firm supplying all output in the market. The good produced by a monopoly has very few substitutes.

profit curve A curve showing the relationship between profit and output.

UNIT 9.3

Natural Monopolies and Public Utilities

In the real world, one type of monopoly stands out, the public utility. A **public utility** is either a heavily regulated private business or a government-operated enterprise that supplies an essential good. The types of essential goods or services supplied by public utilities include water, electricity, natural gas, telephone service, sewage disposal, and, in more recent times, cable TV. In this unit we look at public utilities to see *why* they are heavily regulated or government-operated.

The study of public utilities goes hand in hand with the study of natural monopolies, because almost every public utility is a natural monopoly. As we see in the following discussion, natural monopolies are so named because a single firm "naturally" tends to dominate the market, thus forming a monopoly. After we examine the nature of a natural monopoly, we focus on its pricing behavior. Here, we discuss two pricing schemes that have been proposed, or actually used, by government-regulated public utilities, average cost pricing and marginal cost pricing.

THE NATURAL MONOPOLY

A **natural monopoly** is an industry in which a single firm has decreasing average cost over the range of market demand. Public utilities share one important characteristic—they all require a lot of capital. For example, to generate electricity, capital in the form of steam turbines, nuclear reactors, or hydroelectric dams is required; to distribute the electricity, even more capital in the form of wires, cables, poles, transformers, and booster stations is also needed. Thus, public utilities tend to be very capital intensive, because of the technological requirements for producing the good.

The heavy reliance on capital by public utilities means total fixed cost constitutes a large portion of total cost, which puts public utilities in a rather unique position. As they increase output, average fixed cost declines. If fixed cost outweighs variable cost, then the decline in average fixed cost for a large volume of output causes average total cost to fall even after diminishing marginal returns set in. Decreasing average cost means public utilities can produce increasingly larger quantities of output at lower prices. Most public utilities operate in the decreasing portion of the average total cost curve most of the time.

This is illustrated in Figure 9.3.1. Up to Q_o, average total cost is decreasing due to declining average fixed cost. While all firms have this segment of decreasing average total cost, market demand for the public utility is satisfied at a quan-

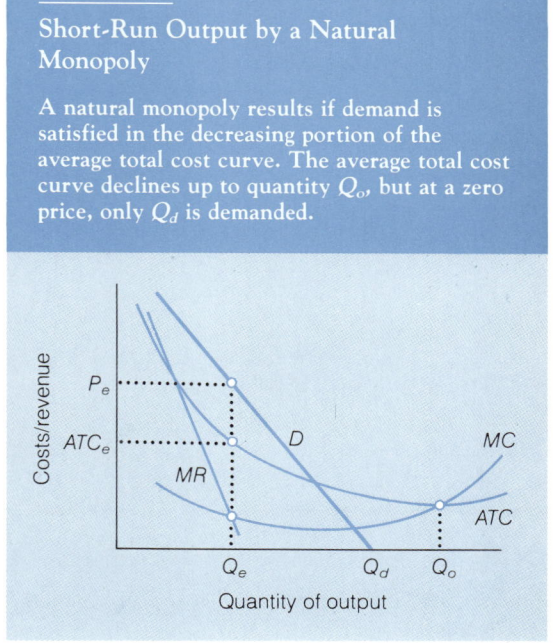

Figure 9.3.1

Short-Run Output by a Natural Monopoly

A natural monopoly results if demand is satisfied in the decreasing portion of the average total cost curve. The average total cost curve declines up to quantity Q_o, but at a zero price, only Q_d is demanded.

455

tity *less* than Q_o. This is indicated by the relative position of the demand curve. In this market the largest quantity that demanders are willing to buy, even at a zero price, is Q_d. Over the entire range of market demand the firm experiences decreasing average total cost.

When a natural monopoly produces a good that society feels is essential, it is either regulated by government or the government takes over direct production. Electricity, natural gas, and telephone services are all privately owned industries that are regulated natural monopolies. Some natural monopolies, such as sewage disposal, trash collection, inner city mass transportation, and the postal service, are operated directly by the government. For natural monopolies the government intervenes to prevent an increase in price and a reduction in the quantity of a necessary good.

Decreasing Average Cost

Why does decreasing average cost make a market naturally tend towards a monopoly? Suppose the total market demand is divided in half, with each of two firms providing exactly one-half of all output demanded at every price. This will illuminate first how one firm can produce output at a lower average cost than two firms, and second how one firm can charge a lower price than two separate firms.

Panel a of Figure 9.3.2 presents the price decision of a monopolist if the demand curve it faces,

Figure 9.3.2

Price Competition and Natural Monopoly

If a natural monopoly is divided into two separate firms, each produces output at higher average total cost than the single firm. In panel b each of two firms has demand curve D_1, exactly one-half of market demand. However, if one firm monopolizes the market, as in panel a, it can produce output at a lower average cost than the other firm.

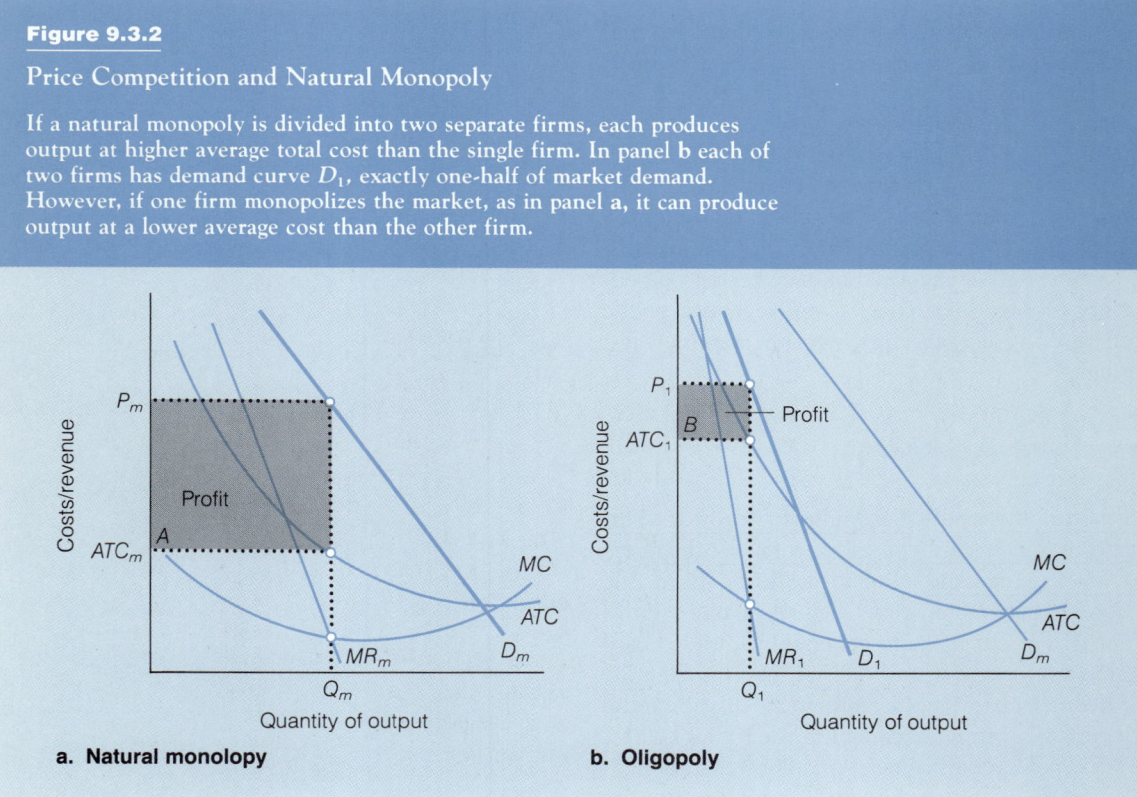

a. **Natural monolopy**

b. **Oligopoly**

D_m, is also the total market demand. It incurs an average cost of production equal to ATC_m and charges a price equal to P_m. Panel a is essentially a duplication of Figure 9.3.1.

In panel b the demand curve is divided in half to illustrate the profit-maximizing price for the formerly monopolistic firm if it now shares the market with another firm in an oligopolistic market. The relevant demand curve facing the firm is now D_1 rather than D_m, and MR_1 is now the firm's marginal revenue curve. Under these circumstances, by maximizing profit the firm incurs average total cost equal to ATC_1, and its price is P_1.

Clearly, the firm is better off being the only firm in the market. Its profit, area A in panel a, is bigger than the profit in panel b, area B. Moreover, the price charged by the monopolist in panel a is lower, as is the average cost of producing the good. But is there any reason that the market depicted here will naturally tend to the situation in panel a rather than panel b?

Price Competition

Panel b in Figure 9.3.2 is based on the proposition that both firms share the market demand equally, incurring the same average cost and charging the same price. This means a buyer is just as likely to buy from either firm. But what happens if one firm gets a larger share of the market than the other firm? Because the firm produces a larger quantity, it moves farther down the average cost curve.

Since both firms are producing the same good, buyers tend to buy from the firm with the lower price. This means that the firm with a slightly larger share of the market quickly obtains a much larger share of the market. And as the firm's share of the market grows, its average cost continues to decline as it moves down its average cost curve.

However, the other firm does not stand by while it rapidly loses its customers, but rather tries to match the price decreases offered by the firm with the larger market share. But if the smaller firm continues to have a smaller share of the market, it incurs higher average cost, and can't keep matching the lower price offered by the larger firm. While the larger firm can reduce its price until it equals average total cost (which still gives the firm a normal profit), if the smaller firm matches this price, its price is less than its average total cost, and it incurs a loss.

In the short run the smaller firm will try to ride out the loss, hoping to increase its market share, and thus reduce average cost. But the larger firm can reduce the price until it is lower than the average variable cost of the smaller firm, so the smaller firm has to shut down in the short run.

In either case the smaller firm is forced out of the market. As long as market demand places one firm in the decreasing portion of the average total cost curve, the market naturally tends toward a single firm. If two or more firms try to satisfy demand, one firm eventually obtains a larger share of the market, and is able to produce at a lower cost. This firm can dominate the market, and thus becomes a monopoly producer. That is why we call an industry with decreasing average total cost a "natural" monopoly.

Note that during the time the firms are competing against each other, the buyers benefit greatly. Prices decrease, and each firm does everything in its power to attract additional customers, even sacrificing economic profit in order to reduce the price. But after one firm dominates the industry, the price competition is over, and the remaining firm behaves like the monopolist it is, raising prices and reducing output.

An Example of Price Competition in the Airline Industry

To illustrate the nature of price competition, let's look at recent developments in the airline industry. Although the airline industry is not a natural monopoly, in recent years it has exhibited the type of competitive activity that we have just discussed, primarily because, like public utilities, airlines are very capital intensive.

Before the airline industry was deregulated in 1978, the government regulated the price, so there was no way for airlines to engage in price competition. However, after deregulation there was a free-for-all in the airline industry. Airlines cut fares, offered discounts, and otherwise lowered prices in every conceivable manner. In each case airlines lowered the price to attract more customers, *and* to more fully utilize their capital. In other words, they were trying to lower average cost.

The result of this price-cutting activity was that Braniff and Laker went bankrupt, and Continental, American, Delta, and Eastern, to name just a few, encountered serious financial difficulties. Part of the airlines' financial troubles were undoubtedly due to the general downturn of the economy in the early 1980s. However, a large share resulted from the price competition and the weeding-out process typical when natural monopolies are established.

The trucking industry went through a similar process after it was deregulated in 1980. The trucking industry was another capital intensive industry that did not need to worry about prices before deregulation. However, they did engage in price competition after deregulation, and several firms went bankrupt.

REGULATORY PRICING

Once a natural monopoly emerges from this type of price competition, it can adjust its price and quantity to profit-maximizing levels. This means the price charged is higher and the quantity produced is less than in perfect competition. To prevent this inefficient allocation of resources, the government usually becomes involved in either the regulation of the monopoly or the direct production of the good. In Unit 12.4 we discuss some of the government agencies involved in the regulation of public utilities. At this point let's look at two alternative methods proposed and/or used to regulate public utilities, marginal cost pricing and average cost pricing.

Marginal Cost Pricing

One major problem with monopolies is that price is greater than marginal cost. Since buyers are willing to pay more for the good than it costs, too little of the good is produced, and resources are misallocated. One way to rectify this is through marginal cost pricing. **Marginal cost pricing** is a pricing policy for public utilities in which price is set equal to marginal cost. This pricing policy is illustrated in Figure 9.3.3.

If public utilities use marginal cost pricing, they set the price equal to the cost of producing the last unit of output. Graphically, this is seen as the intersection of the demand and marginal cost curves. In Figure 9.3.3, with marginal cost pricing, the public utility charges P_{mc} for each unit produced.

Unfortunately, marginal cost pricing of public utilities leads to additional problems. Since the

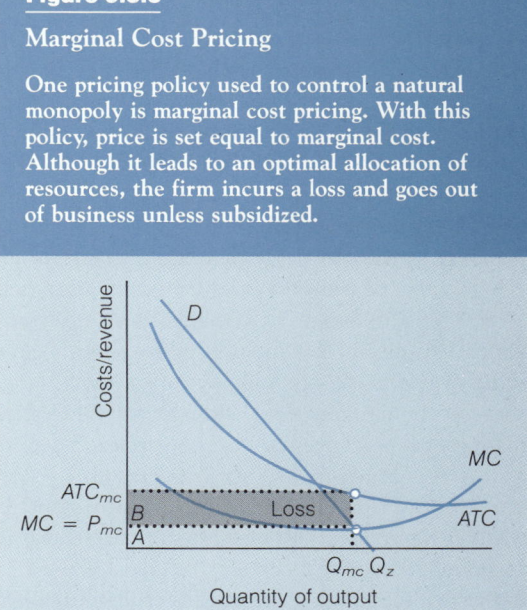

Figure 9.3.3
Marginal Cost Pricing

One pricing policy used to control a natural monopoly is marginal cost pricing. With this policy, price is set equal to marginal cost. Although it leads to an optimal allocation of resources, the firm incurs a loss and goes out of business unless subsidized.

firm operates in the decreasing portion of the average total cost curve, marginal cost lies below average total cost. If price is set equal to marginal cost, price is less than average total cost, and the firm incurs a loss. In Figure 9.3.3, marginal cost pricing generates total revenue to the firm equal to area A. But the total cost of production is equal to area A + B, so the firm incurs a loss equal to area B.

While the firm can continue to operate in the short run as long as price is above average variable cost, in the long run the firm goes out of business. If it is not making a normal profit, investors switch to firms that do make a normal profit. Therefore, marginal cost pricing alone is not a viable solution to an uncontrolled natural monopoly.

However, the attractive feature of marginal cost pricing is that it produces an optimal quantity of the good, and efficiently allocates resources. If marginal cost equals price, then buyers value the last unit of this good as much as any alternative good that can be produced with the same resources.

One way to overcome the limitations of marginal cost pricing is to subsidize the firm. If the firm incurs a loss equal to area B with marginal cost pricing, a subsidy equal to this loss enables the firm to receive a normal profit and operate profitably in the short run. Thus, the firm does not have to go out of business in the long run.

But who pays the subsidy? If the buyers of the product pay the subsidy, and this subsidy is connected directly to the quantity purchased, then the price of the good is essentially driven up, the buyers move up the demand curve, and the quantity demanded is reduced. Prices are greater than marginal costs and resources are inefficiently allocated once again. One alternative is to pay the subsidy from the government's general revenues raised through taxation.

This raises a question of equity. Why should people not buying the product subsidize people who are? If society feels the good is a necessity and that everyone should be able to have it, then a subsidy is in order. But if the good is that much of a necessity, it should be sold for a zero price, such that quantity Q_z is consumed, thus allowing everyone wanting and needing the good to get it. A subsidy is then given to the firm in order to cover cost, which, by the way, is how most government agencies operate. Any government agency that does not sell its output in a market, yet provides a service to the public, is essentially charging buyers a zero price. The cost of the services is then subsidized from general revenues.

However, this alternative also misallocates resources. The marginal cost of producing Q_z is greater than the value of the goods received. Any governmental good provided free of charge is overproduced.

Average Cost Pricing

A second pricing policy, the one most frequently used in the price regulation of public utilities, is average cost pricing. **Average cost pricing is a pricing policy for public utilities in which price is set equal to average cost.** Average cost pricing is illustrated in Figure 9.3.4 for a natural monopoly.

In order to maintain the profitability of the firm, price is set equal to average total cost at a breakeven quantity so that total revenue equals total cost, and economic profit is zero. In Figure 9.3.4, under average cost pricing, the price is P_{ac} and the firm produces Q_{ac} output. The firm makes a normal profit and can continue production in both the short and long run. The normal profit received by the firm is usually referred to as a "fair rate of return," which is the basic criterion applied in the regulation of most public utilities.

However, at Q_{ac} the marginal cost of producing the output is less than the price—there is not enough of the good being produced. Although the effects of average cost pricing are preferable to an uncontrolled monopoly, a misallocation of resources still results. Only when quantity Q_{mc} is produced are resources allocated efficiently.

Average cost pricing can also lead to other inefficiencies in public utilities. For example, because regulatory agencies guarantee public util-

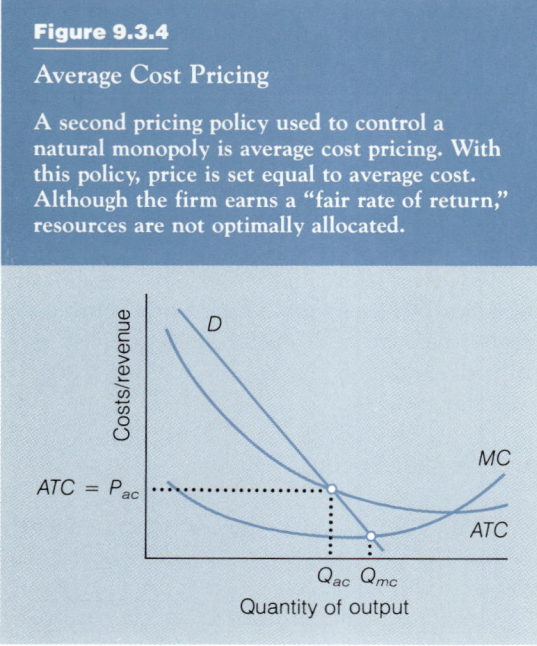

Figure 9.3.4

Average Cost Pricing

A second pricing policy used to control a natural monopoly is average cost pricing. With this policy, price is set equal to average cost. Although the firm earns a "fair rate of return," resources are not optimally allocated.

ities a price that covers the average cost of production, including a normal profit, public utilities are not overly concerned with reducing the costs of production. If they do reduce costs, the regulatory agency simply reduces the price accordingly. In fact, average cost pricing encourages public utilities to increase costs through the purchase of capital goods, high executive salaries, or generous fringe benefits. If these costs are related to the production of the good, then the regulatory agency includes them in the price. But the expenses are often for inputs that contribute very little to production and whose marginal product may be very close to zero, and much less than its cost. As we see in Section 11, a profit-maximizing firm does not use an input if its contribution to production is less than its cost. However, regulated public utilities are not concerned with maximizing profit, since the regulatory agency guarantees them nothing more or less than a normal profit.

IN SUMMARY

Natural Monopolies and Public Utilities

- Goods that require a substantial amount of capital, and thus have a large proportion of fixed cost, tend to be natural monopolies. If one firm can satisfy the total market demand and remain in the decreasing segment of the average total cost curve, then it naturally tends to dominate the market, driving out all competitors.

- Because of this tendency, natural monopolies are either regulated public utilities or are operated directly by the government. This is particularly true if the firm produces a good or service society feels is essential.

- Marginal cost pricing is one way to regulate the price charged by public utilities. For the efficient allocation of resources, the firm needs to charge a price equal to the marginal cost of production. However, since average total cost is decreasing, marginal cost is less than average total cost. This means price is less than average total cost, and the firm incurs a loss. This can be avoided if the firm receives a subsidy equal to the loss, but a subsidy raises questions of equity.

- Alternatively, with average cost pricing, public utilities can charge a price equal to average total cost. This insures a normal profit for the firm. Most public utilities are regulated with this pricing policy. However, average cost pricing fails to efficiently allocate resources, since price is greater than marginal cost.

QUESTIONS FOR STUDY AND ANALYSIS

1. After the energy crises hit the United States in the early 1970s, many people began looking into wind-powered generation of electricity. Some wind generators can produce up to 60

kilowatts of electricity, enough to operate a large house. By contrast, most electricity is currently produced by large generators with capacities measured in the millions of kilowatts.

a. How does wind-powered generation of electricity compare with public utility generation of electricity? Would you consider wind-powered generation of electricity a public utility? Why or why not?

b. If wind-powered generation is developed throughout the country (or at least in the Midwest, where it's relatively windy), how would this affect the natural monopoly nature of electricity generation?

2. Some people argue that price competition, such as that experienced by the airline industry, eliminates inefficient and poorly managed firms. Based on the discussion of natural monopolies and decreasing average costs, do you agree or disagree with this argument? Explain.

3. Discuss whether it would be better overall to regulate a public utility with marginal cost pricing or average cost pricing. What are the advantages and disadvantages to society of each method?

natural monopoly An industry in which one firm has decreasing average cost over the range of market demand. If this type of industry produces an essential good, it is usually heavily regulated or operated directly by the government.

public utility A heavily regulated private business or a government-operated enterprise that supplies an essential good or service. Public utilities are very capital intensive, meaning the average cost of one firm declines over the range of market demand. In this case one firm naturally tends to take over the market.

REVIEW GLOSSARY

average cost pricing A pricing policy for public utilities in which price is set equal to average cost. Average cost pricing insures that the firm earns a normal profit, sometimes called a "fair rate of return." However, average cost pricing does not lead to an optimal allocation of resources, because price is not equal to marginal cost.

marginal cost pricing A pricing policy for public utilities in which price is set equal to marginal cost. Marginal cost pricing, while optimally allocating resources, means the firm incurs a loss. For the firm to remain in operation, it needs a subsidy.

UNIT 9.4

Monopolistic Competition

As discussed in Unit 9.1, **monopolistic competition** is a market structure characterized by a large number of relatively small firms, similar but slightly different products, freedom of entry and exit, and imperfect knowledge. It has the characteristics of both perfect competition and monopoly. Monopolistic competition has a large number of small firms, like perfect competition, but each one acts a little like a monopolist.

Monopolistic competition is prevalent throughout the retail selling industry. For example, while the petroleum extraction and refining aspects of energy production do not constitute monopolistic competition, the retail sale of gasoline does. A large number of relatively small firms, each with a slightly different product (if only perceived as such), sell gasoline.

In this unit we compare monopolistic competition to perfect competition in terms of both characteristics and output decisions. We begin by discussing the differences between monopolistic competition and perfect competition. Then we look at the demand curve facing a monopolistically competitive firm, and its short-run output decision. Finally, we try to identify the monopolistically competitive firm's supply curve, and then evaluate its ability to allocate resources. Throughout this unit we see that monopolistic competition is not as efficient at allocating resources as perfect competition, but is more efficient than monopoly.

CHARACTERISTICS OF MONOPOLISTIC COMPETITION

Recall that perfect competition is characterized by a large number of small firms that sell the same product and have complete freedom to enter and leave the industry. In addition, firms and buyers have perfect knowledge of alternative prices and technology. Monopolistic competition is also characterized by a large number of small firms, each with freedom of entry and exit. However, unlike perfect competition, monopolistically competitive firms do not sell identical products. At least in the minds of the buyers, there is **product differentiation,** which is real or perceived differences between goods, such that buyers are willing to pay different prices. The possibility of perceived, but not physical, product differences implies that there is not necessarily perfect information in monopolistic competition.

These four characteristics of monopolistic competition—large number of small firms, similar but slightly different products, freedom of entry and exit, and potentially imperfect information—make it behave in some ways like a perfectly competitive firm, but in other ways like a monopolist. The large number of small firms and the similar nature of the product mean each firm faces a highly elastic demand curve for its product and has very little market power. But the slight differences between products give each firm a little bit of a monopoly, because the goods produced by different firms are extremely close, but not perfect, substitutes. In monopolistic competition some buyers are willing to pay a little more for a good, solely because it is produced by one particular firm.

THE MONOPOLISTICALLY COMPETITIVE FIRM'S DEMAND

The demand curve facing a monopolistically competitive firm is very elastic, but not perfectly elastic, the determining factor being the number and closeness of substitutes. Every firm in the industry produces a very similar product, but each product is slightly different from the other. For example, you may be willing to pay a penny more for gasoline sold by "Econoco" because the attendant has a nice smile. But if the price is 2 cents more, then you buy from "Monopco" instead.

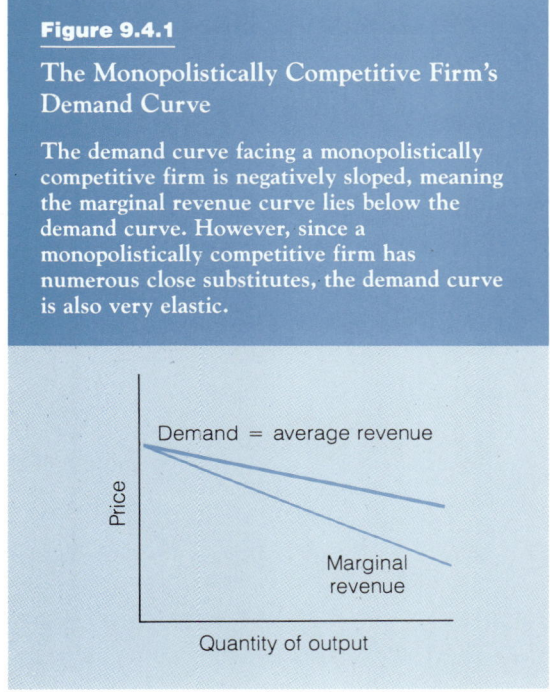

Figure 9.4.1

The Monopolistically Competitive Firm's Demand Curve

The demand curve facing a monopolistically competitive firm is negatively sloped, meaning the marginal revenue curve lies below the demand curve. However, since a monopolistically competitive firm has numerous close substitutes, the demand curve is also very elastic.

Figure 9.4.1 illustrates a typical demand curve facing a monopolistically competitive firm. Although the curve is negatively sloped, it is relatively elastic. The negative slope implies that if the monopolistically competitive firm wants to sell more output, it must lower the price.

The monopolistically competitive firm's average revenue curve is also its demand curve. Moreover, the marginal revenue curve lies below the average revenue/demand curve, meaning price is greater than marginal revenue for every quantity produced. However, since the demand curve is highly elastic, the difference between price and marginal revenue, which is related to the price elasticity of demand, is relatively small. The more elastic demand is, the smaller the difference between price and marginal revenue is. At the extreme, in perfect competition, the demand curve is perfectly elastic and price equals marginal revenue.

Figure 9.4.2 depicts two demand curves with different price elasticities. In panel a the demand curve for monopolistic competition is relatively elastic. The vertical distance between the demand and marginal revenue curves is equal to the difference between price and marginal revenue; here it is relatively small. However, in panel b the demand curve for a monopolist is relatively less elastic, so the vertical distance between the two curves is greater, and the difference between price and marginal revenue is greater.

SHORT-RUN OUTPUT

Since both monopolist and monopolistically competitive firms face negatively sloped demand curves, the short-run production decision by a monopolistically competitive firm is almost identical to that of a monopolist. To maximize profit, the firm selects the quantity of output that equates marginal cost and marginal revenue. In fact, any firm, whether perfectly competitive, monopolistic, or monopolistically competitive, that wants to maximize profit must equate marginal cost with marginal revenue.

Figure 9.4.3 illustrates the monopolistically competitive firm's output decision. Based on the standard set of U-shaped cost curves and the downward-sloping demand curve, the firm produces q_e output, determined by the intersection of the marginal revenue and marginal cost curves. Since price P_e is greater than average total cost, the firm receives an economic profit equal to area B.

Like a monopolist, and unlike a perfectly competitive firm, price is above marginal cost. In fact, except for the more elastic demand curve, Figure 9.4.3 is identical to Figure 9.2.5, which depicts the short-run output decision of the monopolist. The downward-sloping demand curve of the monopolistically competitive firm means it determines price and output in exactly the same way as a monopolist. Hence, each monopolistically competitive firm has its own little monopoly.

Figure 9.4.2
Marginal Revenue, Average Revenue, and Elasticity

The price elasticity of demand affects the difference between marginal and average revenue. In panel a, a monopolistically competitive firm faces a relatively elastic demand curve, so the difference between marginal and average revenue is relatively small. In panel b, a monopolist faces a less elastic demand curve, in which the difference between price and quantity is much greater.

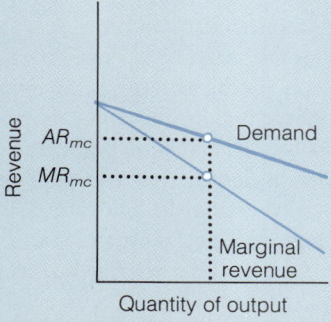

a. Monopolistic competition

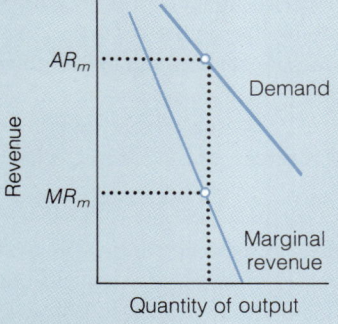

b. Monopoly

Figure 9.4.3
Short-Run Output in Monopolistic Competition

In the short run a monopolistically competitive firm maximizes profit by equating marginal revenue to marginal cost, at quantity q_e. With the demand curve given here, the firm earns an economic profit equal to area B. The output decision by a monopolistically competitive firm is nearly identical to the monopolist, the only difference being the elasticity of the demand curve.

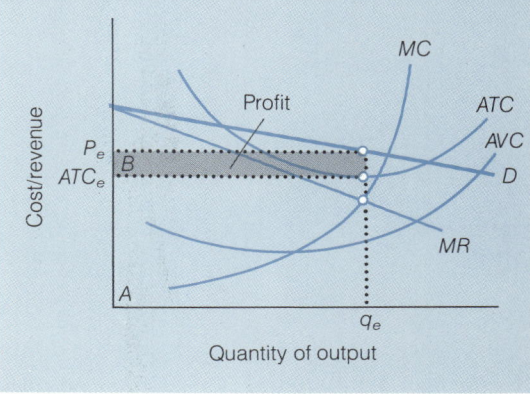

Profit and Loss in the Short Run

In the short run neither perfect competition nor monopoly is guaranteed economic profits. Monopolistic competition is no different. If price is below average total cost, the monopolistically competitive firm incurs a loss. If price is below average variable cost, the firm is better off by shutting down production in the short run.

Figure 9.4.4 presents three important alternatives for the monopolistically competitive firm. In panel a the demand curve is tangent to the average total cost curve, meaning total cost is exactly equal to total revenue and the firm is earning a zero economic profit. Keep in mind that it is still earning a normal profit. In panel b price is less

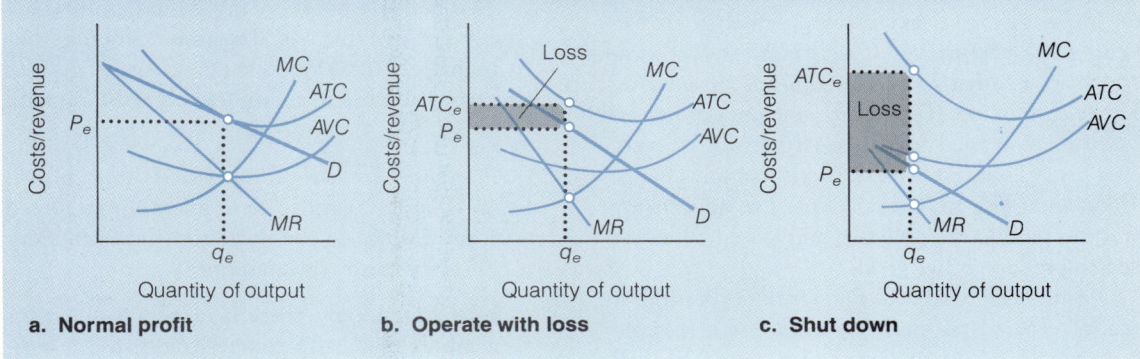

Figure 9.4.4

Profit and Loss in Monopolistic Competition

In the short run a monopolistically competitive firm is not guaranteed an economic profit. In panel a the firm earns only a normal profit, and no economic profit. In panel b the firm incurs a loss, but continues to produce in the short run because the loss is less than fixed cost. In panel c the firm incurs a loss greater than fixed cost if it produces q_e output. If the demand curve lies below the average variable cost curve, the monopolistically competitive firm shuts down in the short run.

a. Normal profit b. Operate with loss c. Shut down

than average total cost but greater than average variable cost. The firm incurs a loss, but should continue to produce because the loss is greater if the firm stops production. In panel c price is below average variable cost, and the firm shuts down production in the short run.

The Supply Curve

The similarity between monopoly and monopolistic competition extends to the firm's supply curve. The monopolistically competitive firm does not have a supply curve. Whenever a firm faces a downward-sloping demand curve, price is not equal to marginal cost. Therefore, equilibrium price and quantity do not lie on the firm's marginal cost curve, and the marginal cost curve is not the firm's supply curve. If the demand curve facing the firm shifts, it is possible that the monopolistically competitive firm, like the monopolist, will sell the same quantity at a different price, or a different quantity at the same price. Price and quantity produced by the firm need not be directly related.

MONOPOLISTIC COMPETITION AND RESOURCE ALLOCATION

With its monopolistic tendencies, how does monopolistic competition compare to perfect competition? First, since buyers are willing to pay more for the last unit of the good than it costs to produce, price is higher than marginal cost, leading to a misallocation of resources. This is the same problem we saw with the monopolist. Any firm that faces a downward-sloping demand curve misallocates resources, and does not produce enough output.

However, the misallocation is a matter of

degree. Since the relatively elastic demand in monopolistic competition means the difference between price and marginal cost is relatively small, the misallocation is much less than with monopoly. In fact, a firm with a very elastic demand comes very close to allocating resources the same as a perfectly competitive firm. The more elastic demand is, the more efficient the allocation is.

There is another aspect of resource allocation and monopolistic competition. In order to differentiate their products, monopolistically competitive firms advertise extensively, which increases the firm's cost. However, if all firms in the industry engage in advertising, each firm has little or no change in demand. The advertising undertaken by one firm is canceled out by the advertising of every other firm. Thus, costs increase without any change in demand. The resources devoted to advertising serve no productive purpose, and would be better used to produce other goods.

Firms also attempt to differentiate their products in terms of physical features, which leads to an increase in product variety and quality. Although the economist's world of perfect competition would be ideally efficient in the allocation of resources, it would also be very dull. There would be one type of car, house, clothing, video game, and soft drink. Product differentiation stimulated by monopolistic competition gives us a choice. Evey now and then, consumers would like to have a Michelob, a Dr. Pepper, and a car-wash with a tankful of gasoline rather than a Budweiser, a Coca-Cola, and self-service.

IN SUMMARY

Monopolistic Competition

- Monopolistic competition is a market structure with a large number of relatively small firms, freedom of entry and exit, slightly different products, and imperfect information. Product differentiation gives each firm a little bit of a monopoly.

- The demand curve facing a monopolistically competitive firm is downward sloping, but highly elastic. Due to the negative slope, the marginal revenue curve lies below the demand curve, like a monopoly.

- A monopolistically competitive firm can earn an economic profit, incur a loss, or be forced to shut down in the short run, like a monopolist or a perfectly competitive firm.

- Like a monopoly, there is no supply curve for a monopolistically competitive firm. Whenever a firm faces a negatively sloped demand curve, the firm has no supply curve.

- A monopolistically competitive firm charges a higher price and produces less output than a perfectly competitive firm. However, the lack of market power and the relatively elastic demand curve means the misallocation is not as great as a monopoly.

QUESTIONS FOR STUDY AND ANALYSIS

1. Discuss the following statement: "Advertising serves a vital economic function by providing the consumer with information about important product differences." In the context of monopolistic competition, do you agree or disagree with this statement? Explain.

2. Compare a monopolistic competitive firm with a perfectly competitive firm and a monopolist.

What is the short-run supply curve for a monopolistically competitive firm?

3. Magazine publishing might be considered a monopolistically competitive industry. Take for example magazines dealing exclusively with computers.

    a. How are computer magazines differentiated? Does this allow some magazines to charge a higher price than others? (Feel free to check out magazine prices at your local bookstore or newsstand.) Would the owner of an IBM personal computer be willing to pay a higher price for a magazine called *PC World* (for IBM PC owners) or *Macworld* (for Apple Macintosh owners)?

    b. How does the computer magazine publishing industry fit the characteristics of monopolistic competition?

    c. Now consider another form of magazine publishing, the weekly news magazines. This part of publishing is dominated by *Time*, *Newsweek*, and *U.S. News & World Report*. How does the news magazine industry fit the characteristics of monopolistic competition?

4. Explain why lawyers are more likely to be monopolistically competitive than doctors.

REVIEW GLOSSARY

monopolistic competition A market structure characterized by a large number of relatively small firms, similar but slightly different products, freedom of entry and exit, and imperfect information. This means each firm has a small degree of market power. A monopolistically competitive firm faces a downward-sloping demand curve and thus behaves much like a monopolist.

product differentiation Real or perceived differences between goods such that buyers are willing to pay different prices.

UNIT 9.5

Oligopoly

The last of the four major types of market structures is **oligopoly,** a market structure characterized by a small number of relatively large firms supplying most of the output in the market. The small number of firms gives each a substantial degree of market power, but also generates mutual interdependence between firms. While an oligopolistic firm has control over its price and output, the price and output of one firm also influences the price and output of the other firms in the industry.

There is a great deal of diversity in the types of oligopolistic industries in the economy. For example, the steel industry contains one large, dominant firm and several smaller firms, whereas the automobile industry contains several firms of nearly equal size. A third alternative is the petroleum industry, which has a handful of relatively large firms and many smaller firms. In addition to the size and number of firms, oligopolistic industries are also characterized by the type of product produced. Some oligopolistic industries produce a differentiated product (as in the automobile industry), others an undifferentiated product (as in the steel industry).

In this unit we begin by looking at the degree of concentration in oligopolistic U.S. industries, indicating how much output is produced by the largest firms in the industry. Next, we look at the type of behavior displayed by oligopolistic firms. Then we examine price rigidity in oligopolies, using the kinked demand curve. And finally, we discuss collusion and cartels, in which oligopolistic firms join together to monopolize a market.

OLIGOPOLY AND CONCENTRATION IN U.S. INDUSTRIES

One way to see if an industry is more or less oligopolistic is to look at the concentration of output. If a few firms produce most of the output in an industry, the industry is very likely an oligopoly. Table 9.5.1 presents concentration ratios for several major industries in the United States for 1972 and 1977. A **concentration ratio** is the percentage of total output in an industry that is produced by a given number of the largest firms. The four-firm and the eight-firm concentration ratios are two common measures. The four-firm concentration ratio indicates the share of the total industrial output produced by the four largest firms, the eight-firm ratio the share of the output produced by the eight largest firms.

Table 9.5.1

Concentration Ratios for Selected Industries

Concentration ratios provide an indication of the degree of market power in an oligopolistic industry. For the first five industries listed here, over 80 percent of output is produced by the eight largest firms in the industry. However, even if the eight largest firms account for only 22 percent of output, as with the bottled and canned soft drink industry, that industry still has many characteristics of an oligopoly.

Industry	1972 Four-Firm	1972 Eight-Firm	1977 Four-Firm	1977 Eight-Firm
Motor vehicles and car bodies	93	99	93	99
Guided missiles and space vehicles	62	88	64	94
Tires and inner tubes	73	90	70	88
Photographic equipment and supplies	74	85	72	86
Aircraft	66	86	59	81
Soaps and other detergents	62	74	59	71
Blast furnaces and steel mills	45	65	45	65
Electronic computing equipment	51	63	44	55
Petroleum refining	31	56	30	53
Pharmaceutical preparations	26	44	24	43
Bread, cake, and related products	29	39	33	40
Meat packing plants	22	37	19	37
Periodicals	26	38	22	35
Newspapers	17	28	19	31
Bottled and canned soft drinks	14	21	15	22

Source: U.S. Bureau of the Census, Census of Manufacturing, 1977, Concentration Ratios in Manufacturing, MC77-SR-9.

Note in Table 9.5.1 that the auto industry in the U.S. is almost totally dominated by the four largest firms, which in 1977 accounted for 93 percent of all automobile sales. Photographic equipment and tires are produced in industries in which the four largest firms control about 70 percent of the market. The eight-firm concentration ratio indicates that the eight largest firms in these three industries, plus the aircraft and guided missile industries, have over 80 percent of sales.

Between 1972 and 1977 the concentration ratios in most of the industries presented in Table 9.5.1 have tended to decline. Only four industries (guided missiles and space vehicles; bread, cake, and related products; newspapers; and bottled and canned soft drinks) have shown an increase in both concentration ratios.

The fifteen industries depicted in Table 9.5.1 tend to be oligopolistic. Even the bottled and canned soft drink industry, in which the eight largest firms have only 22 percent of output, has oligopolistic characteristics. However, the oligopolistic nature of an industry generally declines as the concentration of output declines. In fact, as we saw in Unit 8.1, a spectrum of market structures exists. In the real world there is no clear dividing line between oligopoly and monopolistic competition. As a concentration ratio becomes increasingly smaller, the industry tends to take on more of the characteristics of monopolistic competition and less of oligopoly. While we try to classify the real world into different market structures, keep in mind that there are a lot of gray areas; such is the case for the industries listed in Table 9.5.1.

OLIGOPOLISTIC BEHAVIOR

The concentration of production by a small number of firms in an industry causes oligopolies to behave differently than any of the other three market structures. There are four aspects of oligopolistic behavior we should note: mutual interdependence, price rigidity, nonprice competition, and mergers and collusion.

Mutual Interdependence

The first and foremost behavioral difference is **mutual interdependence,** in which each firm makes its decisions based on the reaction of other firms in the industry. Since there are few firms in an industry, each is extremely aware of its competitors. For example, Ford Motor Company does not make a decision that affects price or quantity without General Motors, Chrysler, and American Motors knowing about it, because any action taken by Ford also affects the other automobile companies. Competition in oligopoly is much like competition at a track meet. The winner of the 100 meter dash triumphs not by setting a world record, but by reaching the finish line before everyone else. So it is with competition in oligopoly. The share of the market held by General Motors is not based simply on its own performance, but also on the performance of the other firms. General Motors may have the best car it has ever produced, but if Ford produces one a little better, General Motors might still lose part of its market.

Price Rigidity

Second, oligopolistic firms are characterized by **price rigidity,** in which prices in the industry change very little over time. The mutual interdependence of oligopolistic firms is reflected in relatively rigid prices, so that a price increase by one firm is unlikely to be duplicated by the others. For example, if General Motors raises the price of its cars and Ford does not, Ford attracts some of General Motors's customers with its relatively lower price. By contrast, a price decrease by one firm will likely be matched by the others, because if they do not lower their price, then they lose some of their market share.

This makes it a no-win situation for oligopolistic firms when they try to change the price. If a firm lowers its price, so does the rest of the industry, and the firm attracts very few new customers. And if it raises its price, it loses its customers to other firms in the industry. In short, an oligopolistic firm has very little incentive to change its price.

Nonprice Competition

Because price competition is futile, most oligopolistic firms try to attract additional customers by engaging in **nonprice competition,** which is any type of behavior designed to increase a firm's demand without changing the price. Common examples of nonprice competition in oligopolies include advertising, product differentiation, and barriers to entry.

Advertising is one of the most widespread types of nonprice competition used by oligopolies. Advertising attempts to shift a firm's demand curve rightward by differentiating the product, providing information, or even changing the tastes and preferences of consumers. When Coca-Cola advertises that "Coke is it," it is not trying to attract customers based on a lower price but rather to differentiate its product from other soft drinks and alter consumer tastes and preferences. When the automobile companies advertise their new models, they provide the consumer with information, but they seldom mention the price.

An oligopoly also tries to increase demand through physical product differences, such that its product is actually better than the competitors'. For many years IBM has been able to stay at the forefront of the computer industry through the research and development of new products. Firms in the pharmaceutical industry also spend a lot on the development of new drugs in order to stay ahead of competition. In fact, most of the oligopolistic industries listed in Table 9.5.1 devote many resources to research and product development.

And last, an oligopoly can seek to increase its share of the market by trying to establish, or increase, barriers to entry. A firm might try to influence legal barriers, such as government franchises, licenses, patents, and import restrictions. For example, suppose a new television station tries to enter a local, oligopolistic market containing three existing stations. To do so, it must obtain a license from the government. Meanwhile, each of the three existing stations is telling the licensing agency exactly why a fourth station is not needed in the market. Another example of imposing a barrier to entry is when Chrysler lobbies Congress for import restrictions on foreign automobiles.

An oligopolistic firm might also try to influence technological barriers to entry. If IBM has several new innovations in the computer industry, it can release them one at a time to limit its competition. For example, it might release the first innovation and wait until its competitors incorporate this innovation in their computers. Then it releases the second innovation, which makes its competitors' computers outdated. And once competitors gear up to incorporate the second innovation, IBM releases its third. This process can continue indefinitely, making it very difficult for new firms to enter the industry because they are always one step behind.

Mergers and Collusion

Oligopolies also engage in mergers and collusion. A **merger** is when two or more firms legally combine to form a larger firm. **Collusion** is the secret agreement between two or more firms to use their market power to control market price and quantity or limit competition. With intense competition, oligopolistic firms are often inclined to shake hands and cooperate with each other. In some cases this may take the form of mergers between firms, in which one firm gobbles up its competition.

Under the Reagan administration in the early 1980s, oligopolistic firms were not discouraged from merging as they had been under previous administrations. Several big mergers resulted, including one between Gulf and Standard Oil and another between Getty and Texaco in the petroleum industry. Other notable mergers were undertaken by Rupert Murdoch's publishing empire and by American Express. Mergers between oligopolistic firms in the same industry tend to reduce competition and increase the market power of the resulting firm.

Dominant firms in an industry may also collude, secretly agreeing to set an industrywide price or control the quantity of output. As we discuss in Unit 9.6, collusion is illegal in the United States, but on the international scale, cartels such as OPEC constitute legal organizations. A **cartel** is a formal written agreement, usually between nations, designed to control the price and production in an industry or limit competition. A cartel operates in much the same way as colluding firms, though cartels are quite legal and operate very much in the open. If General Motors, Ford, Chrysler, and American Motors meet to fix the price of automobiles, they definitely would not want anyone to know (since they would all be subject to government prosecution). However, the news media report on every meeting openly held by OPEC.

THE KINKED DEMAND CURVE

The price rigidity common to many oligopolistic industries is reflected in the demand facing an oligopolistic firm, which is based on the fact that the market is shared by a few large firms in the industry. Recall that when one oligopolistic firm lowers its price, all other firms are likely to follow suit rather than risk losing a share of the market to the firm with the lower price. Thus, the demand curve facing the firm if it lowers the price is very inelastic. Since all firms in the industry lower the price, the total industry demand is greater, but each firm retains the same share of the market. However, when the firm raises its price, other firms will probably not follow suit, and the firm will lose a share of the market. Thus, the demand curve facing the firm if it raises its price is very elastic.

This type of interdependence between oligopolistic firms leads to a kinked demand curve, as depicted in Figure 9.5.1. A **kinked demand curve** is a demand curve with two distinct segments, one that is very elastic and one that is very inelastic. The demand curve DD reflects the relatively inelastic demand faced by the firm if it maintains its market share. Demand curve $D'D'$ is the relatively elastic demand curve facing a firm if it loses its market share to other firms in the market.

Figure 9.5.1

The Kinked Demand Curve

The mutual interdependence between oligopolistic firms is seen in the kinked demand curve. If a firm increases its price above P_e, other firms do not. Thus, its demand curve is relatively elastic along segment $D'E$ as it loses part of the market. If the firm lowers its price, the other firms also lower theirs. The demand curve below P_e is relatively inelastic along segment ED. Due to the kink at point E, the marginal revenue curve is discontinuous at q_e.

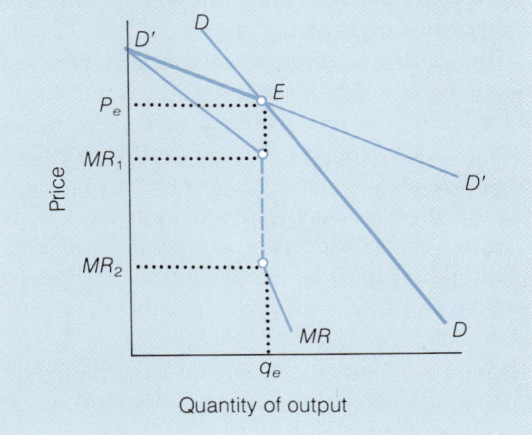

The actual demand curve facing the firm is a combination of DD and $D'D'$. For price increases above P_e, $D'D'$ is the relevant curve. For price decreases below P_e, DD is the relevant curve. The composite demand curve $D'ED$ is the kinked demand curve facing an oligopolistic firm.

Figure 9.5.1 also depicts the corresponding, and unusual-looking, marginal revenue curve for the firm. Note the discontinuous portion of the curve at quantity q_e. At this quantity there is an entire range of marginal revenue values, from MR_1 to MR_2. The marginal revenue curve also has two distinct segments. Above MR_1, the marginal revenue curve is based on the elastic segment of the demand curve, $D'E$, and is relatively flat. Below MR_2, the marginal revenue curve is based on the inelastic segment of the kinked demand curve, ED, and is relatively steep.

The kinked demand curve indicates why oligopolistic firms tend to have relatively rigid prices. Unfortunately, it doesn't explain how prices are established in the first place. With this in mind, let's use the kinked demand curve to look at an oligopolistic firm in the short run. Figure 9.5.2 duplicates a kinked demand curve and the associated marginal revenue curve. If the marginal cost for the firm is MC_1, marginal cost intersects marginal revenue at point A, and the equilibrium price and quantity are P_e and q_e, respectively.

But if a new union wage contract increases marginal cost to MC_2, the firm still produces at P_e and q_e, with the new marginal cost curve intersecting the marginal revenue curve at point B. For any marginal cost curve lying between MC_1 and MC_2, the firm produces q_e output at price P_e. This gives the oligopolistic firm a great deal of price rigidity. There must be relatively large changes in marginal cost before the firm alters short-run output and price.

While the kinked demand curve explains the price rigidity observed in oligopolistic markets, it does not explain why the kink is at P_e rather than another price. For example, suppose the marginal cost shifts above MC_2, such that a new equilibrium price is reached, above P_e. What happens if marginal cost shifts back below MC_2? Does the price fall back to P_e, or is a new kink established at the new price?

If the new price exists for a long enough period of time, a new kink is likely to be established. But how long must the new price prevail for this to happen? Without knowing the answer to this question, we have to be satisfied with the limited insight that the kinked demand curve provides. If a price exists for a relatively long time in an oligopolistic industry, then the kinked demand curve explains why the price remains rigid. However, no further

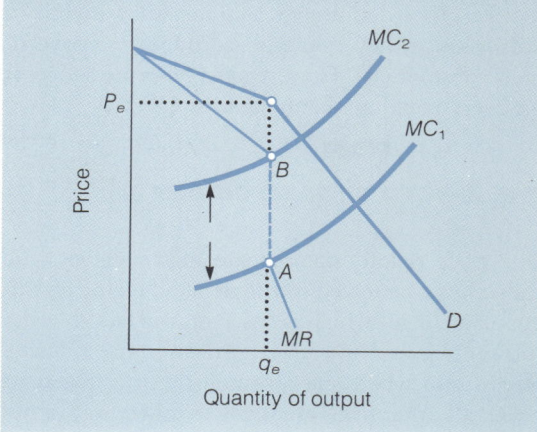

Figure 9.5.2

Price Rigidity in Oligopoly

If an oligopolistic firm faces a kinked demand curve, its price and output are not sensitive to changes in production cost. The marginal cost curve can lie anywhere between MC_1 and MC_2, and the firm produces the same output at the same price. The resulting price rigidity is often observed in oligopolies.

inferences of oligopolistic behavior can be made from the kinked demand curve.

COLLUSION AND CARTELS

Oligopolistic firms often benefit from cooperating rather than making independent decisions. In fact, mutual interdependence and the intense competition that exist in oligopoly often result in collusion or cartels, the primary difference between the two being the secretive nature of collusion and the open nature of the cartel. But whether cartel or collusion, the intent is the same—the firms seek to limit production and raise the price. Often, collusion is undertaken by several of the largest firms

Figure 9.5.3

Collusion and Cartel

The mutual interdependence between oligopolies encourages collusion and cartels. If the two oligopolistic firms in panels a and b decide to collude, they can obtain monopoly profits. They set industry output and price based on the equality of marginal revenue and marginal cost for the industry, at quantity Q_c and price P_c. The industry output is divided between each firm, q_1 in panel a and q_2 in panel b, by equating marginal revenue to the firm's marginal cost.

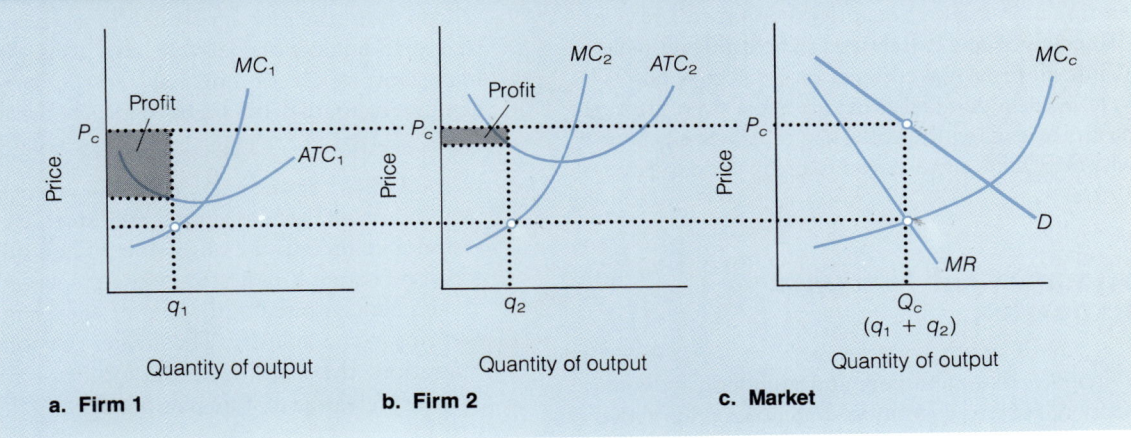

a. Firm 1   **b. Firm 2**   **c. Market**

in the industry in order to drive out smaller competitors.

Figure 9.5.3 illustrates how an oligopolistic industry with two firms sets price and quantity through collusion. Panels a and b depict the cost curves of the two firms, and panel c the industry marginal cost curve, MC_c. This curve represents the horizontal addition of MC_1 and MC_2, and reflects the total output produced by both firms at each marginal cost. Panel c also depicts the market demand and associated marginal revenue curves.

The collusion in Figure 9.5.3 is undertaken in order to increase the economic profit of both firms. Here, if the firms collude and operate like a monopolist, they can achieve the highest level of profit. This profit is obtained by equating the industry's marginal cost curve, MC_c, to marginal revenue, at quantity Q_c. Acting like a monopolist, the colluding firms charge price P_c. The market quantity is divided between both firms, such that q_1 plus q_2 equals Q_c. Both firms sell their output for P_c, and economic profit is indicated by the shaded areas in panels a and b.

Note that although both firms are receiving an economic profit, this is not always the case. It is possible that one of the colluding firms ends up producing at a level where price is less than average total cost. However, in the short run the firm continues to produce if price is greater than average variable cost (as with any other firm), and the other colluding firms cover the losses.

Even though industrywide profit is greater under

collusion than otherwise, each individual firm can actually make more profit if it breaks away from the other, as long as the price is kept at P_c. If the firm in panel a produces output greater than q_1, and sells it for slightly less than P_c, it increases profit since marginal cost is less than the price. Each firm in a collusive agreement has this incentive. But the incentive exists only if the other firms continue to charge the higher price. If firms lower their price, then they are no longer charging the monopolistic price and producing the profit-maximizing monopolistic quantity. It is for this reason that collusion and cartels tend to be highly unstable. While all firms make higher profits if they all collude, each individual firm can make even greater profits by leaving the collusion. This helps explain why the OPEC cartel began to break up in the mid-1980s.

OLIGOPOLY AND RESOURCE ALLOCATION

Oligopoly, like monopoly and monopolistic competition, reduces quantity and increases price above perfect competition. Thus, oligopoly also misallocates resources by devoting too few to the production of the good. But once again, misallocation is a matter of degree. Monopolistic competition allocates resources better than oligopoly, and oligopoly better than monopoly. However, the mutual interdependence of oligopoly produces great incentives to collude and act like a monopolist, worsening the allocation of resources. And the more market power a firm has, the greater the misallocation.

The disadvantage of resource misallocation aside, oligopolies do have some advantages. In particular, the size of oligopolistic firms enables them to undertake research and development more easily than monopolistic competition. Indeed, the competition is so fierce in oligopoly that each firm is usually looking for ways to gain an advantage. Since the advantage often cannot be gained through price competition, some firms turn to product innovations or technological advances designed to reduce production cost. However, there are no guarantees that oligopolistic firms will undertake more research and development than other types of firms.

IN SUMMARY
Oligopoly

- Oligopoly is a market structure characterized by a small number of relatively large firms. An important aspect of oligopoly is the large amount of mutual interdependence between firms.

- In the United States many of the most common industries, such as automobile, steel, cigarette, and aircraft, are oligopolies. Their oligopolistic nature is indicated by the proportion of sales concentrated in the four or eight largest firms in the industry. The greater the concentration, the more likely the top firms are to have a great deal of market power.

- Oligopolies have four important characteristics of behavior: mutual interdependence, price rigidity, nonprice competition, and mergers and collusion.

- The kinked demand curve is one explanation of oligopolistic behavior. While it explains price rigidity, it does not explain how the price is determined in the first place. Collusion by oligopolistic firms occurs when two or more firms get together to secretly raise price, reduce output, and act like a monopolist. A cartel is an open, written, and legal agreement, usually between nations, designed to control price and output.

- Oligopoly, like all imperfect competition, misallocates resources by charging a higher price and selling less output than under perfect competition. However, the mutual interdependence encourages oligopolies to worsen the allocation of resources by acting like a monopolist.

QUESTIONS FOR STUDY AND ANALYSIS

1. When the deregulation of the airline industry in 1978 sent the airlines into brutal competition, United Airlines had a hidden advantage. Its Apollo reservation system was widely used by both travel agents and other airlines, but since United controlled the Apollo system, it was able to list its own flights first and more prominently than competitors' flights. In addition, there were allegations that United rewarded travel agents who booked United flights and punished agents who booked competitors' flights. By controlling the Apollo system, United also knew when competitors lowered their fares, even before customers found out. It was even alleged that United delayed entering new, lower rates for competitors while it promptly lowered its own. (Source: "The Not-So-Friendly Skies," *Newsweek*, 13 February 1984, p. 72).
   a. How did United use the Apollo reservation system to increase its market power through product differentiation?
   b. In what way did United use Apollo as a barrier to entry?

2. IBM, which has long been the leader in the computer industry, tends to introduce a new generation of computers, or some other major innovation, at the same time its competitors introduce their new machines to the market. In 1984 AT&T entered the market for personal computers and was viewed by many as a major competitor for IBM. However, the day after AT&T introduced its new machine, IBM introduced a more advanced version of its personal computer, containing the latest in computer technology.
   a. Do you think the timing between IBM's announcement and AT&T's entrance in the personal computer market was a coincidence? Why or why not?
   b. In what ways does this illustrate the mutual interdependence in the personal computer industry?
   c. How do you think the introduction of IBM's new computer affected sales of AT&T's new computer?

3. The misallocation of resources is an important disadvantage of the oligopolistic market structure. However, oligopoly also provides valuable benefits to an economy. For example, an oligopoly is able to take advantage of decreasing average cost. In addition, the intense competition between firms in an oligopolistic industry encourages research, product development, and innovation. Overall, do you think oligopoly is beneficial or detrimental to the economy? Explain.

4. Why are oligopolies more likely to collude than any other market structure? Why is collusion undesirable from society's perspective?

5. Would you expect OPEC to be more stable with relatively high petroleum prices and a shortage of petroleum, or with relatively low petroleum prices and a surplus of petroleum? Explain.

6. Based on the concept of mutual interdependence, explain why General Motors behaves more like the University of Michigan football team than it behaves like a General Motors automobile dealership. Feel free to refer to the Ohio State football team if you want.

REVIEW GLOSSARY

cartel A formal, written agreement, usually between nations, designed to raise the price and decrease production in an industry or limit competition. OPEC is the most famous cartel.

collusion The secret agreement between two or

more firms to use their market power to control market price and quantity or limit competition.

concentration ratio The percentage of total output in an industry that is produced by a given number of the largest firms. The most common concentration ratios are for the four and eight largest firms. Higher concentration ratios mean the market is dominated to a greater degree by the largest firms.

kinked demand curve A demand curve with two distinct segments, one that is very elastic and one that is very inelastic. The kinked demand curve is often used to explain price rigidity in oligopoly.

mergers When two or more firms legally combine to form a larger firm.

mutual interdependence A behavior in which each firm makes its decisions based on the reaction of other firms in the industry. This is one of the most important behavioral aspects of oligopoly. With a small number of firms, each is well aware of its competition. One firm cannot change price, promote a sale, or alter production without response from the other firms.

nonprice competition Any type of behavior designed to increase a firm's demand without changing the price. Because of price rigidity, oligopolies usually engage in nonprice competition, such as advertising, product differentiation, or barriers to entry, in order to gain a larger share of the market.

oligopoly A market structure characterized by a small number of relatively large firms supplying most of the output in the market. Oligopoly is very similar to monopoly, except monopoly has only one firm, while oligopoly has two or more.

price rigidity A behavior of oligopolies in which prices in the industry change very little over time.

UNIT 9.6

Controlling Imperfect Competition with Antitrust Legislation

In this unit we continue our study of market structures in general, and imperfect competition in particular, with a look at antitrust legislation. **Antitrust legislation** is a series of laws designed to prevent the monopolistic actions that reduce competition and lead to an inefficient allocation of resources. Antitrust legislation deals directly with the types of resource allocation inefficiencies discussed in the previous five units.

Antitrust legislation comprises a significant part of the study of market structures. Over the past hundred years, since the first piece of antitrust legislation was passed in 1890, legal rules have been established that influenced the structure of real world markets. In the late 1800s, many markets were monopolized by a single firm, but today, due in large part to antitrust legislation, few monopolies exist aside from public utilities.

In this unit we look at the three key pieces of antitrust regulation: the Sherman Act (1890), the Clayton Act (1914), and the Federal Trade Commission Act (1914). These laws provide the government, and individuals, the basis for recourse if industries seriously misallocate resources. But before we examine the actual legislation, let's discuss why oligopoly is the market structure most likely to require antitrust action. We can then see the ways in which oligopolies obtain and misuse their market power.

MARKET STRUCTURES

In the United States, markets range from the near perfect competition of agriculture to the natural monopolies of public utilities. Along this spectrum lie different industries with differing degrees of market power. For example, monopolistic competition in retail trade has less market power than the oligopolistic automobile industry.

All forms of imperfect competition operating in the real world tend to misallocate resources. However, all types of imperfect competition do not misallocate resources in the same way, or to the same degree. Whereas monopolistic competition charges a price and produces output very close to perfect competition, an uncontrolled monopoly leads to the most inefficient allocation of any market structure. Oligopoly falls between these two.

If possible, society wants to prevent resource misallocation. The potential of natural monopolies for resource misallocation is so great and so obvious that they are usually regulated through government franchises and established as public utilities. Since monopolistic competition does not constitute a serious threat to the allocation process, it is often not worth the trouble to correct. By contrast, the natural tendency for oligopoly to collude, merge, and restrict competition makes it a prime target for government regulation. When an oligopolistic industry tries to operate like a monopoly, it worsens the resource allocation, necessitating some type of government involvement.

However, being an oligopoly is not sufficient grounds in itself for government action. All oligopolies do not try to restrict trade, or try to act like monopolies, and the inadvertent misallocation of resources is not a crime. But the government has determined that intentionally trying to monopolize an industry is indeed a crime. Therefore, at the point where firms in an industry have "too much" market power, the government steps in, although exactly when it should step in is the subject of considerable debate. Some feel that even monopolistic competition is too monopolistic, while others feel that the cost of trying to de-monopolize monopolistic competition is much greater than the cost of any resource misallocation. And some economists argue that even the most monopolistic of the oligopolies cause only insignificant resource misallocation, and thus are not worth the bother.

MARKET POWER AND ITS MISUSE

As we saw in Unit 9.5, oligopolistic industries have the tendency to cooperate, and thus increase their market power. However, it was not the existence of market power but its misuse that stimulated the development of the antitrust legislation studied in this unit. Market power can be misused in several ways, each of which is very likely to arouse the interest of the antitrust division of the Justice Department (one of the main agencies that enforces this legislation).

Collusion

As we saw in the last unit, **collusion** is the secret agreement between two or more firms to use their market power to control market price and quantity or limit competition. The secretiveness of collusion results in large part from its illegal status. The firms involved usually have no formal agreement or written document, because they want no incriminating evidence lying around. Probably the biggest case of collusion occurred in the electrical equipment industry between 1920 and 1950, when nearly thirty different firms were involved in fixing prices on twenty different types of products, ranging from small circuit breakers to large turbine generators.

Mergers

Collusion of this type is not the only way oligopolistic firms try to act like monopolists. In many cases, several firms simply join together to form a larger firm through a merger. A **merger** is when two or more firms legally combine to form a larger firm. Mergers by themselves are not only quite legal but also quite common. However, mergers that limit competition in an industry come under the provisions of the antitrust legislation. Therefore, we need to distinguish between three types of mergers.

A **conglomerate merger** is a merger between two firms in unrelated industries. For example, if a restaurant chain merges with a steel mill, a conglomerate merger results, because the firms are in two separate industries. ITT and Transamerica are noted conglomerates that were formed through mergers of this type. A conglomerate merger seldom affects competition, and is not likely to concern the Justice Department.

However, a **horizontal merger** is a merger between two firms in the same industry and is very likely to interest the Justice Department if it tends to lessen competition. The two most notable mergers in the early 1980s were horizontal mergers between Gulf and Standard Oil and between Getty and Texaco. Horizontal mergers have the most potential for limiting competition, because as the number of firms in the market declines, the remaining firms (or firm) have greater market power. J. D. Rockefeller formed the Standard Oil Trust in the late 1800s through numerous mergers with competing firms, and before it was broken up in 1911, Standard Oil controlled over 90 percent of the petroleum market. During this same period, horizontal mergers were used extensively to obtain market power in the sugar, railroad, tobacco, and steel industries.

Vertical mergers are less likely to reduce competition than horizontal mergers, but the potential exists. A **vertical merger** is a merger between two firms in different stages of the production of the same good. For example, many newspapers over the years have merged with timber companies to insure a supply of newsprint. Likewise, automobile companies merge with steel mills, and petroleum extraction firms merge with refineries. Though vertical mergers do not necessarily limit competition in an industry, they are scrutinized when they are likely to reduce competition in one stage of production or distribution. If a major retail clothing chain is acquired by a major clothing manufacturer, competition could be reduced if the clothing chain is forced to sell only the clothes manufactured by its new owner, thus severely limiting the outlet for competing manufacturers.

Other Methods of Monopolization

In addition to open legal mergers, firms have found other ways of combining to increase their market power. For example, a trust was another method used by Rockefeller to form Standard Oil in the late 1800s from many smaller firms. A **trust** is a legal entity established to act on the behalf of others. As a general rule, trusts are not illegal. Anyone can establish a financial trust for their children. However, in the late 1800s and early 1900s, trusts were set up for several firms in the same industry. The trusts then acted on behalf of the companies and operated just like a monopoly. The American Tobacco trust was another trust established at this time to increase market power. Trusts of this type were directly designed to monopolize the industry, and they actually stimulated the legislation studied in this unit, which is why it is called antitrust legislation.

Another, less formal, method of combining firms in the same industry is through the use of interlocking directorates. **Interlocking directorates** is the term used when two or more firms in the same industry have one or more board of directors in common. Since the board of directors runs a firm, two legally distinct firms can essentially operate as one with interlocking directorates.

Predatory Behavior

In some instances one firm might actually set out to "destroy" its competitors. This can take the form of destroying the competitor's product right on store shelves, or undertaking espionage, bribery, and blackmail, or any other conceivable practice to eliminate competition. However, in many cases the firm simply undertakes **predatory pricing,** in which prices are reduced below average total cost in order to undercut the price of a competitor and take away its customers. This type of predatory pricing, while similar to the price competition discussed under natural monopolies, can be extremely cutthroat, particularly when a larger firm is trying to drive out a smaller competitor. The larger firm, with more resources, can stand short-run losses much better than the smaller firm. The larger firm might cut the price in the market served by the smaller firm and finance short-run losses with revenue from other markets. Once again, Standard Oil provides an example of predatory pricing. During its monopolistic reign, it made extensive use of undercutting its competition, either to force them out of business or to make them join the Standard Oil Trust.

Exclusive Agreements and Tying Contracts

A firm might also try to restrict competition by obtaining exclusive agreements with retailers or distributors. An **exclusive agreement** between producer and dealer means the dealer only sells the producer's product, and the producer does not supply any other dealer in the same market. While the intent of exclusive agreements is to let one dealer specialize in one product, it can restrict competition by preventing competitors from gaining access to retail outlets. For example, an ice cream manufacturer might reduce competition by signing an exclusive agreement with a retail grocery chain. If the grocery chain is relatively large, this agreement can limit the retail outlets of competing ice cream manufacturers. Note that excluisive agreements can reduce competition in much the same way as vertical mergers.

Related to exclusive agreements are **tying contracts,** in which a producer makes the sale of one good conditional on the purchase of another good. Tying contracts allow a producer with substantial market power in one market to extend control to other markets. For example, in the 1930s, IBM forced customers who used their punch card tabulating machines to purchase their punch cards, thus extending their market power in tabulating machines to the market for punch cards. IBM already held the market power in tabulating machines because of patents. And although many firms were able to make punch cards that would work in the tabulation machine, through tying contracts IBM was able to dominate this market as well.

ANTITRUST LEGISLATION IN THE UNITED STATES

Over the last hundred years the government has passed numerous pieces of legislation and fought hundreds of court cases dealing with misuses of market power. Three pieces of legislation stand out: the Sherman Act (1890), the Clayton Act (1914), and the Federal Trade Commission Act (1914). Together with two important amendments, the Celler-Kefauver Act (1950) and the Wheeler-Lea Act (1938), these three acts form the foundations of the antitrust activity occurring over this period of time.

Sherman Act (1890)

The first major piece of legislation in the United States dealing with monopolistic business was the Sherman Act, which resulted from the "public-be-damned" business practices of the robber barons in the late 1880s. During this time several major trusts and monopolies were established in the oil, steel, sugar, tobacco, meat, and linseed oil industries, which were overrun by predatory pricing, monopolizing trusts, and mergers producing large firms that controlled 80 to 90 percent of an industry.

The **Sherman Act (1890),** the first antitrust legislation in the United States, outlawed monopolies, trusts, and any conspiracy to restrain trade. Enforcement of the law in the courts was initiated by the federal government or any private party injured by the firm. If the firm was found guilty under the Sherman Act, penalties included fines, jail terms, and injunctions for breaking up the firm.

In fact, this law was used to break up the Standard Oil Trust in 1911.

As the first piece of antitrust legislation, the Sherman Act was imperfect in many ways, but it did lay the foundation for later legislation. One important flaw in the act was vague wording. For example, although it outlawed the restraint of commerce, it did not specify exactly what this meant, thus permitting a great deal of interpretation on the part of each new presidential administration. A firm did not know if its practices this year would be illegal next year. A second flaw was inadequate provisions for enforcement. Since all enforcement came through the courts, the only way a potential offender could be forced to comply with the act was through criminal proceedings. At this time there was no agency devoted to antitrust policy that had the ability to levy fines and pursue enforcement outside of the judicial system, which made enforcement cumbersome and time consuming. These two flaws prompted passage of both the Clayton Act and the Federal Trade Commission Act in 1914.

Clayton Act (1914)

In response to some of the flaws with the Sherman Act, the **Clayton Act,** which outlawed such specific monopolistic practices as price discrimination, exclusive agreements and tying contracts, mergers, and interlocking directorates, if they substantially reduced competition, was passed in 1914. The primary objective of the Clayton Act was to outlaw specific practices that led to the monopolization of an industry. While the Sherman Act prosecuted monopolies *after* they surfaced, the Clayton Act was designed to *prevent* monopolies from emerging. Four practices were outlawed in this act. Price discrimination, in which a firm charges two different prices in different markets for the same good, was outlawed if it substantially reduced competition unless it was justified by differences in cost, quality, or quantity sold. Exclusive agreements and tying contracts and mergers were also outlawed if they substantially reduced competition. And interlocking directorates were specifically outlawed whether or not there was any evidence of reduced competition.

Even though the Clayton Act addressed some of the flaws contained in the Sherman Act, other flaws remained. For example, except for interlocking directorates, the practices outlawed in the act had to substantially lessen competition, though it was not clear from the act how to determine if competition was substantially lessened. In addition, the Clayton Act specifically exempted labor unions. Some people argue that labor unions should be subject to antitrust action because, if Standard Oil, as the sole supplier of a resource (petroleum), is subject to the Clayton Act, then a labor union, as the sole supplier of a resource (labor), should also come under its power. And last, mergers were outlawed only if the merger occurred through the purchase of corporate stock. But after the act was passed, firms stopped buying each other's corporate stock; instead, one firm simply purchased all of another firm's capital assets. For example, before the Clayton Act, U.S. Steel could increase its market power by merging with another steel company through the purchase of its corporate stock. However, after the Clayton Act, U.S. Steel could accomplish the same goal by purchasing all of the other firm's capital. The other firm might continue to legally exist, but there was nothing physically left of it. This type of "merger" was not outlawed by the Clayton Act.

However, in 1950 the Celler-Kefauver Act was passed to clarify and strengthen the antimerger portion of the Clayton Act. The **Celler-Kefauver Act,** an amendment to the Clayton Act, specifically outlawed the acquisition of the capital assets of one firm by a competitor.

Federal Trade Commission Act (1914)

The second act passed in 1914 to compensate for inadequacies of the Sherman Act was the Federal Trade Commission Act, which set up the agency of the same name (FTC). Under the Sherman Act, even business felt there was too much uncertainty.

They wanted an agency set up that would clarify which practices were illegal and which were not. In addition, some felt that the Sherman Act allowed the courts to take authority away from Congress and establish their own criteria as to what constituted restraint of trade and what did not. Proponents of the Federal Trade Commission Act felt that these criteria should be established by an agency under the jurisdiction of the Congress. Thus, the **Federal Trade Commission Act** established the FTC as a separate agency to investigate business practices that might lead to restraint of trade, set standards for unfair competition, and levy fines against offenders. And in 1938 the **Wheeler-Lea Act** extended the powers of the FTC to investigate unfair and deceptive business practices and prevent false advertising. Thus, today the FTC has evolved into a consumer protection agency in addition to its original role as a "trust buster."

AN EVALUATION OF ANTITRUST LEGISLATION

How well has antitrust legislation worked in the United States? The three major pieces of legislation discussed here set the basic guidelines for antitrust action. In modern times oligopolistic industries are constantly aware of potential antitrust action. For example, General Motors, Ford, Chrysler, and American Motors would probably not even consider a merger; a hundred years ago this might not have been true. Indeed, many of the monopolistic trusts of the late 1800s were formed through mergers of this type.

However, while antitrust legislation has helped to create the guidelines under which firms operate, enforcement of the legislation still depends on the existing political administration. The Reagan administration, unlike previous administrations, has *not* discouraged mergers between competitors in the same market. The Justice Department under the Reagan administration also dismissed an important antitrust suit against IBM that had been in the works for over a decade. In addition, the Reagan administration has reduced government funding for the FTC and the Antitrust Division of the Justice Department, making it difficult to enforce antitrust legislation.

While we have touched on the highlights of antitrust legislation, we should note that it is a complex and controversial area of study. In the real world it is often difficult to determine if a firm is misusing its market power. The courts over the past hundred years have devoted a great deal of attention to determining exactly what constitutes unfair competition because no one is certain exactly when "healthy" competition between two firms becomes "unfair" competition.

IN SUMMARY

Controlling Imperfect Competition with Antitrust Legislation

- Oligopoly is the market structure most likely to come under antitrust regulation in the United States. Monopolistic competition does a relatively good job of resource allocation. And natural monopoly, if uncontrolled, is so obvious in its misallocation that it is generally franchised and directly regulated by the government. But oligopoly has a strong tendency to collude and worsen the allocation of resources. Thus, it is the market structure most often subjected to antitrust legislation.

- Firms can be prosecuted under antitrust laws not because they have market power but because they misuse it. The most common misuses of market power are collusion, mergers, trusts, interlocking directorates, predatory pricing behavior, exclusive agreements, and tying contracts. Any one of these acts is likely to bring the scrutiny of the government.

- The Sherman Act (1890) was the first law dealing with monopolistic activity in the United States. It outlawed monopoly trusts and collusion but was vague and required enforcement through the courts. It was successfully used to break up the Standard Oil Trust in 1911.

- The Clayton Act (1914) was designed to overcome some of the failings of the Sherman Act. In particular, it specifically outlawed several practices that lead to restraint of trade, including price discrimination, exclusive agreements and tying contracts, mergers, and interlocking directorates. While interlocking directorates between firms in the same industry were outlawed, the other three practices were illegal only if they substantially reduced competition.

- The Federal Trade Commission Act (1914) was also designed to overcome some of the shortcomings of the Sherman Act. It established the Federal Trade Commission (FTC) as an agency to investigate monopolistic business practices and levy fines against offenders.

- It is not clear how well these three pieces of legislation have affected monopolistic practices in the United States. Undoubtedly, they have been a deterrent in the corporate boardrooms around the country. Many large firms do not want the scrutiny of the federal government and shy away from any action that might seem anticompetitive.

QUESTIONS FOR STUDY AND ANALYSIS

1. Collusion and antitrust behavior have not been completely eliminated from the economy. For example, in recent years Air Florida, together with three foreign airlines, was accused of colluding to fix the prices of air fares for flights between Central American countries and the United States. Part of the accusation stated that Air Florida agreed not only to increase fares but also to do away with special reduced rate fares.

   a. What misuses of market power were employed by Air Florida?
   b. Why would the airlines be subject to antitrust actions because they conspired to do away with reduced rate fares? Is "not giving a discount" the same as "raising the price"? Why or why not?

2. Under what circumstances would a conglomerate merger come under the jurisdiction of antitrust legislation?

3. How does predatory pricing, outlawed by antitrust legislation, differ from the price competition seen in the formation of a natural monopoly in Unit 9.3?

4. IBM has long been the dominant firm in the computer industry, especially in mainframe computers. Mainframe computers are the big systems used by universities and businesses that can simultaneously handle a hundred or so users. Because IBM has been the dominant firm, other firms that produce mainframes and peripheral equipment (printers, disk drives, terminals, and so on) must be compatible with IBM's machines and software. For this reason IBM's competitors are referred to as plug compatible manufacturers (PCMs). In other words, you can literally plug any competitor's peripheral equipment into an IBM mainframe. However, in spite of this compatibility, it is not easy to compete with IBM. It seems as though IBM lowers its prices or introduces innovations when the PCM competitors start to increase their sales.
   a. How much market power does IBM have? A little? A lot? What roles are played by barriers to entry or product differentiation or both in IBM's market power?
   b. Would you say IBM is misusing its market power? If so, in what way?
   c. Would you consider IBM's pricing policies predatory pricing or just healthy competition in the computer industry? Explain.

REVIEW GLOSSARY

antitrust legislation A series of laws designed to prevent monopolistic actions that reduce competition and lead to an inefficient allocation of resources.

Celler-Kefauver Act (1950) This act amended the Clayton Act by specifically outlawing the acquisition of capital assets of one firm by a competitor. The Clayton Act merely made mergers by the acquisition of stock illegal.

Clayton Act (1914) This act outlawed such specific monopolistic practices as price discrimination, exclusive agreements and tying contracts, mergers, and interlocking directorates if they substantially reduced competition.

collusion The secret agreement by two or more firms to use their market power to control price and quantity or limit competition.

conglomerate merger A merger between two firms in unrelated industries.

exclusive agreement An agreement between a producer and dealer where the dealer agrees to sell only the producer's product, while the producer agrees not to supply any other dealer in the same market.

Federal Trade Commission Act (1914) This act set up the Federal Trade Commission (FTC) as a separate agency to implement antitrust action, including investigating business practices that might lead to restraint of trade, setting standards for unfair competition, and levying fines against offenders.

horizontal merger A merger between two firms in the same industry.

interlocking directorates The term used when two or more firms in the same industry have one or more board of directors in common.

merger When two or more firms legally combine to form a larger firm.

predatory pricing The process of reducing prices below average total cost in order to undercut the price of a competitor and take away its customers.

Sherman Act (1890) The first antitrust legislation in the United States, which outlawed trusts and any conspiracy to restrain trade. Although used to break up the Standard Oil Trust in 1911, it is vaguely written.

trust A legal entity established to act on the behalf of others. While trusts are not illegal in general, they were used extensively in the late 1880s to give monopoly power to one firm in an industry.

tying contract A contract in which the producer makes the sale of one good conditional on the purchase of another good.

vertical merger A merger between two firms in different stages of the production of the same good.

Wheeler-Lea Act (1938) This act extended the powers of the FTC to investigate unfair and deceptive business practices and false advertising.

UNIT 9.7

Market Power in the Health Care Industry

An interesting application of market power is found in the provision of health care. Recall that **market power is the ability of a firm to control or influence the price and/or quantity exchanged in the market**. The health care industry has come under close scrutiny in the past decade because the percentage of gross national product spent on health care has increased, and the prices of health care have risen faster than prices of other goods. This has led some people to blame the market power held by doctors and the American Medical Association (AMA) for the higher costs of health care. In this unit we examine the provision of health care services to see what its market power is and if this is responsible for the higher costs.

First, we discuss the prices of and expenditures on health care in the United States and the rise in prices of health care relative to other goods and services. We then look at the structure of the health care industry and the sources of its market power. We see that the demand side of the market, particularly insurance companies and the government, is also responsible for higher health care prices. And finally, we consider policies for improving the allocation of resources in the health care industry.

RECENT TRENDS IN HEALTH CARE

Recent trends in the expenditures on health care services are presented in Table 9.7.1. Note that in 1950, total expenditures were $12.7 billion, which comprised 4.4 percent of gross national product.

However, by 1983 expenditures on health care had risen to $355 billion, or 10.8 percent of gross national product. Even though the economy's total production of goods and services increased in these three-plus decades, a greater share of resources has been devoted to the production of health care.

In part, this additional production has meant greater health care services for each member of the economy. The far right column of Table 9.7.1 lists the increase in expenditures on health care per person from $82 in 1950 to over $2000 in 1988. On the positive side, these additional expenditures have increased life expectancy to over seventy-five years, and reduced death rates from 10 people per 1000 in 1950 to $8\frac{1}{2}$ people per 1000 in 1987.

However, on the negative side, these additional expenditures have been caused in part by higher prices, which have made health care unaffordable for poorer members of the economy. Table 9.7.2 presents the relative prices of health care over the past three-plus decades.

The middle column of Table 9.7.2 lists the consumer price index (CPI) for all goods and services purchased by urban consumers, and the far right column lists the medical care component of the CPI. In 1967, the base year for the CPI, both indices were equal to 100. In 1985 the CPI for all goods and services was 322.2, while the CPI for medical care was 403.1. Clearly, since 1967 the prices of medical care have risen faster than the prices of other goods and services. And this relatively rapid increase in the price of health care concerns many people who feel that the market power of the health care industry is being used to charge higher prices for its output. In terms of the structure of the health care industry, are there grounds for this concern?

THE STRUCTURE OF THE HEALTH CARE INDUSTRY

The production of health, like the production of any good or service, requires the four factors of production (labor, capital, land, and entrepre-

Table 9.7.1

Health Care Expenditures in the United States, 1950–1988

Health care expenditures have risen not only in absolute levels since 1950 but also relative to other expenditures. They have increased from 4.4 percent of *GNP* to nearly 11 percent. Moreover, per capita expenditures have risen from $82 per person to over $2000 per person.

Year	Expenditures (billions)	Percent of *GNP*	Per Capita
1950	$ 12.7	4.4	$ 82
1955	17.7	4.4	105
1960	26.9	5.3	146
1965	41.7	6.0	211
1970	74.7	7.5	358
1975	132.7	8.6	604
1976	149.7	8.7	674
1977	169.2	8.8	755
1978	189.3	8.8	839
1979	215.0	8.9	938
1980	249.0	9.5	1075
1981	285.8	9.7	1195
1982	322.3	10.5	1337
1983	355.4	10.8	1459
1985*	419.5	10.5	1693
1988*	552.4	10.9	2171

*Estimated
Source: U.S. Health Care Financing Administration, *Health Care Financing Review*, August 1985.

neurship). However, the central role in the production of health care, as with the production of many other services, is played by labor, which in this case is the doctor.

Doctors

All types of doctors, physicians, dentists, and so on, play the primary role in the production of health care. Indeed, the health care services purchased by the patients revolve around doctors' knowledge and skill. Hospital services, prescription drugs, and nursing services are all dependent on doctor services. To practice medicine and provide health care services in the United States, a doctor must first receive medical training (either in domestic medical schools or in foreign schools) and then be licensed and certified by a state licensing board.

Hospitals

A second component in the structure of the health care industry is hospitals. Hospitals provide physicians with the facilities to produce a wide variety

Table 9.7.2

Relative Prices of Health Care Services, 1950 to 1985

One reason that health care expenditures have risen relative to *GNP* is that health care prices have also risen faster than other prices. Since 1950 the Consumer Price Index has risen by about 350 percent, but health care prices have risen by over 650 percent during the same period.

Year	Consumer Price Index (CPI)	Medical Care Prices
1950	72.1	53.7
1955	80.2	64.8
1960	88.7	79.1
1965	94.5	89.5
1967	100.0	100.0
1970	116.3	120.6
1975	161.2	168.6
1980	246.8	265.9
1981	272.4	294.5
1982	289.1	328.7
1983	298.4	357.3
1984	311.1	379.3
1985	322.2	403.1

Source: U.S. Bureau of Economic Analysis, *Survey of Current Business*, selected issues.

of health care services, ranging from major operations to continuous patient observation. Keep in mind that while hospitals offer services to patients, these services are provided under the authority of doctors, who purchase the services on behalf of patients.

Medical Schools

A third component of the health care industry is medical schools. Presently, about 120 medical schools in the United States are certified by the American Medical Association to train doctors. However, numerous medical schools in other countries throughout the world also train doctors, and the number and percentage of foreign-trained doctors has steadily increased over the last decade.

American Medical Association

A fourth component of the health care industry is the American Medical Association (AMA). On the surface the AMA is a professional association much like those found in many other professions. For example, economists belong to the American Economic Association, philosophers to the American Philosophical Association, and petroleum geologists to the American Association of Petroleum Geologists. However, the AMA represents much more than a collection of doctors who get together and trade operating room anecdotes. The AMA is the ultimate authority and power in the medical profession, with the authority to accredit medical schools in the United States. If a medical school does not have AMA accreditation, or loses this accreditation, then it is essentially unable to train doctors. Furthermore, the AMA plays a significant role in the licensing of doctors by each state. If a doctor performs unethically, then the doctor can be decertified and must discontinue the practice of medicine.

MARKET POWER

At first glance the health care industry would seem to be a prime candidate for a competitive industry. At present, about a half million doctors are practicing in the United States and the production by each doctor is small relative to the total production of health care, meaning this industry should be relatively competitive. Moreover, most doctors generally produce a slightly different product, based on both the type of services offered (such as pediatrics, internal medicine, obstetrics, and radiology) and the quality of the service. Therefore, we would expect that each individual doctor would tend to have a small amount of market power, making the health care industry monopolistically competitive.

Sources of Market Power

However, the structure of the health care industry creates more market power than is initially apparent, and this is attributable in large part to the AMA. Market power is generated in the health care industry in four basic ways: length of training, medical school admissions, state licensing, and limited information.

Length of Training It takes a minimum of eight years to train a doctor, including four years of college and four years of medical school. However, a doctor must also undergo one to two years of internship, and perhaps several more years of specialized training. The length of training required before a doctor can begin practice (and earn the resulting income) constitutes a serious barrier to the free entry of labor resources into the health care industry. By contrast, most unskilled and semiskilled occupations require very little training, and thus pose no significant barriers to entry. Furthermore, other skilled professions, such as accountants, economists, engineers, teachers, and lawyers, require only four to eight years of training.

Medical School Admissions Another barrier to entry is provided by admissions to medical schools. Before a doctor can enter the health care industry and begin the production of health care services, he or she must receive medical training. For example, if the number of applicants accepted to medical school is controlled this year, then the number of doctors operating eight, ten, or twelve years in the future can be controlled as well. As mentioned earlier, the AMA has a great deal of control over admissions to medical schools through their authority to accredit the schools. Thus, the AMA also has a degree of indirect control over the supply of doctors in the economy.

State Licensing Although the AMA can control the number of doctors trained in domestic medical schools, they cannot control the number trained in foreign medical schools. However, before a doctor can begin the practice of medicine, he or she must be licensed by the state. Because the AMA has a large amount of input into state licensing, it can also exert influence over the supply of doctors that are trained by foreign medical schools not accredited by the AMA.

Limited Information A fourth source of market power in the health care industry is limited information. Up to the early 1980s doctors were prevented from advertising their prices, which restricted the information available to patients. In fact, the AMA considered it unethical to advertise prices, and actually decertified and prevented from practicing medicine doctors who violated this code of behavior. Therefore, a patient was usually unaware of the prices charged for services until after the services were provided, making it very difficult to shop around for the best buy in medical care. Often, the prices for the same service, such as an office call, can differ by a large amount for doctors in the same city. In the early 1980s doctors were allowed to undertake a small amount of advertising.

Justification for the Sources of Market Power

Each of these four sources of market power contributes to the misallocation of resources. As with any industry that has a great deal of market power, market power in the health care industry means that prices are higher and output is less than in a more competitive industry. However, the health care industry argues that the length of training, medical school admissions, and state licensing are necessary to maintain a high quality of health care services. Obviously, no one would want open-heart surgery performed by a plumber whose training consisted of faithfully watching "General Hospital" and "Ben Casey" reruns. By the same token, others argue that while quality control is important, each year many well-qualified applicants are denied admission to medical school.

THE DEMAND FOR HEALTH CARE

Market power is one reason that prices in the health care industry have risen relatively more than in other industries. However, there are other reasons for the relatively higher prices underlying the demand for health care, the most important factor being the payments made by insurance companies and the government. In the 1950s patients directly paid about one-half of all expenditures on health care in the United States, but by the 1980s this had declined to only about one-fourth. The remaining three-fourths of the expenditures came from third parties. **Third party payments** are payments made to sellers on behalf of buyers by parties that do not directly receive the benefits from the payments. Third party payments in the health care industry come primarily from insurance companies and the government.

In general, insurance companies exist to spread the risks and uncertainty associated with an activity or event. In terms of health care, insurance companies spread the risk associated with accidents and illnesses. Because people don't know if they will have an illness or accident, they are willing to pay a small amount each year in exchange for the insurance company's agreement to pay for the health care should such an event occur. The key feature of insurance is that the recipient of the health care services does not pay the full price of the services at the time the services are received. The nature of insurance is to shift the burden of payment to everyone who might be affected by illness or accident. Therefore, people who do not receive the health care services end up paying for those who do.

The same is true for government payments for health care, which currently account for about one-half of all health care expenditures. If the government (or actually, taxpayers) pays for part of the health care services received by a patient, then this recipient is paying only a portion of the price of these services. The two most notable programs underlying government payments for health care are Medicare, which provides or pays for health care services for the poor, and Medicaid, which pays for health care services for the elderly. Essentially, both programs assist in the health care for people who would otherwise be unable to afford it.

While third party payments have beneficial aspects, they can also contribute to higher prices for health care services and lead to an inefficient allocation of resources. Figure 9.7.1, which depicts an individual's demand curve for health care, illustrates how this can occur. If a patient is required to pay the full costs of health care, price P_1, then the quantity q_1 is demanded. Note that q_1 could be equal to zero, in which case the price of health care services is so high that the patient is unable

Figure 9.7.1

Individual Demand and Third Party Payments

If third parties pay a portion of the health care services purchased by an individual, this has the same effect as a decrease in the price. Here, if buyers pay P_2, which is one-fourth of the total price, P_1, then the quantity demanded increases from q_1 to q_2.

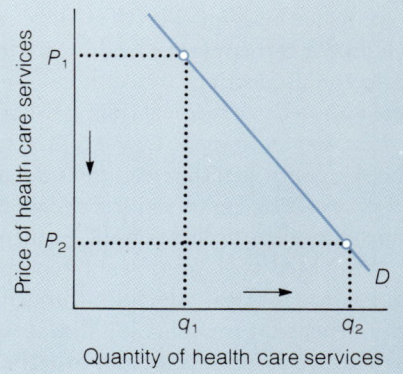

to purchase them, which is one justification for third party payments. Few people could afford the price of open-heart surgery without the help of insurance.

But what if third parties pay three-fourths of the health care costs, meaning the price actually paid by the patient is P_2, which is only one-fourth of P_1. Since the price paid by the patient is lower, according to the law of demand, the quantity demanded by the patient increases to q_2. While third party payments help people who are otherwise unable to pay for health care services, they also cause the quantity demanded by everyone else to increase. Over the last three decades the portion of the health care costs paid directly by patients has declined, which has caused an increase in the quantity of health care services demanded.

Figure 9.7.2 illustrates how this affects the overall market for health care services. The demand curve labeled D reflects the health care services demanded by patients if they pay 100 percent of the health care costs. However, if third parties pay three-fourths of the costs of health care, then the effective demand curve is D'. For each quantity demanded, the patient pays the price given by curve D, while third parties pay the difference between curves D and D'.

Now let's determine the quantity of health care services demanded with and without the third party payments. Without third party payments, equilib-

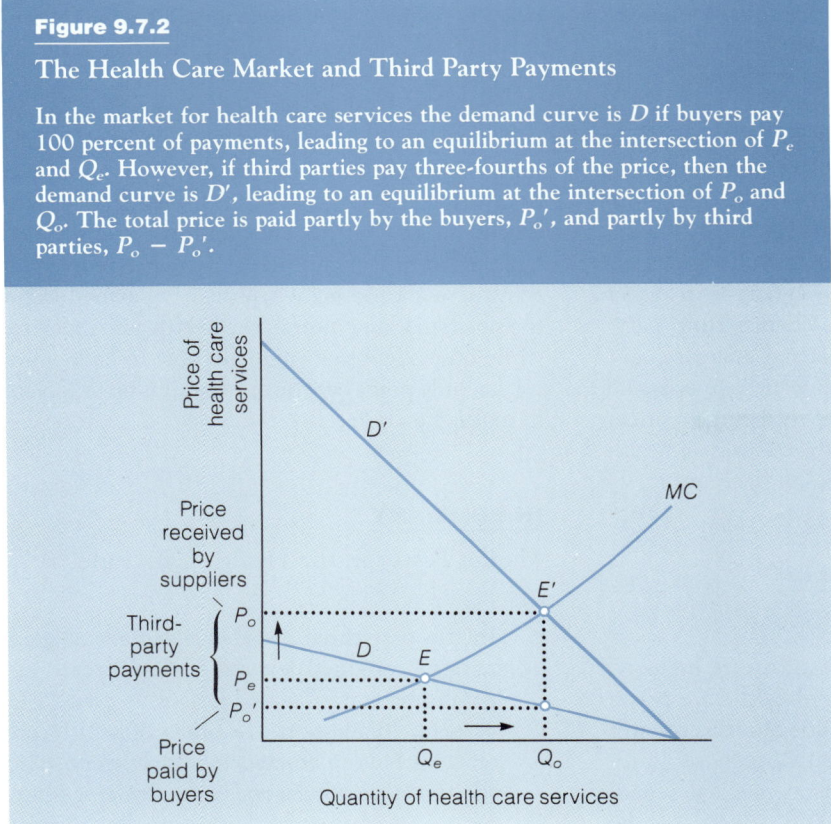

Figure 9.7.2
The Health Care Market and Third Party Payments

In the market for health care services the demand curve is D if buyers pay 100 percent of payments, leading to an equilibrium at the intersection of P_e and Q_e. However, if third parties pay three-fourths of the price, then the demand curve is D', leading to an equilibrium at the intersection of P_o and Q_o. The total price is paid partly by the buyers, P_o', and partly by third parties, $P_o - P_o'$.

rium in the health care market is found at the intersection of the demand and supply curves, at point E, where the price is P_e and the quantity is Q_e. This price and quantity provide an efficient allocation of resources because the price buyers are willing to pay for the last unit is equal to the costs of producing the last unit (given by the supply curve).

If third parties pay three-fourths of the costs of health care services, then the health care market achieves equilibrium at the intersection of D' and the supply curve, at point E'. At this point the total price of health care services is P_o and the quantity exchanged is Q_o. While the suppliers of the health care services receive P_o, part of this is paid by the patients, P_o', and part is paid by third parties, $P_o - P_o'$. In this case the price of health care and the quantity produced are both greater than if patients pay all health care costs. Moreover, more resources are being allocated to the production of health care services than is necessary under an efficient allocation.

Note the assumption that the firms supplying the health care services have no market power. But if we assume more realistically that the suppliers of health care services have some degree of market power, then our conclusions are changed only slightly. Recall that market power leads to a higher price and a smaller quantity, whereas third party payments lead to a higher price but a larger quantity. The combination of third party payments and market power definitely leads to a higher price, though it is not clear whether the quantity of health care services provided increases or declines.

POLICIES FOR CONTROLLING HEALTH CARE PRICES

Based on our analysis of the health care industry, two approaches for controlling health care prices come to mind. First, the amount of market power in the health care industry can be reduced by relaxing the restrictions placed on medical school admissions, state licensing, and advertising by doctors. In this way the "firms" in the health care industry can become more competitive. Second, the share of costs paid directly by patients can be increased, thus reducing the share of third party payments and moving the health care market closer to an efficient allocation of resources.

While both of these approaches would tend to hold down the prices of health care and improve the allocation of resources, they should not be implemented blindly. Medical school admissions, licensing practices, and advertising restrictions do maintain quality standards in the health care industry, restricting the potential for imposters and incompetents to enter the health care field. Furthermore, third party payments help provide health care services, including both government assistance for the poor and insurance for unforeseen and costly illnesses and accidents, to people who could not afford them otherwise. Should people be prevented from obtaining adequate health care simply because they cannot afford to pay?

As with many problems in economics, we are faced with a difficult choice. Do we want relatively high health care costs and an inefficient allocation of health care services, or do we want to maintain quality in the health care industry and provide widespread health care services? Some people feel that there are too many third party payments and too much market power in the health care industry, while others feel that there are not. In economics we can only point out the options; it is up to society to make the choice.

IN SUMMARY
Market Power in the Health Care Industry

- In the past three decades the share of gross national product devoted to health care expenditures has increased from 4 percent to 11 percent. In addition, the prices of health care services have increased relatively more than the prices of other goods and services. Many people are concerned that we are devoting too

- many resources, and paying too high a price, for health care services.

- The central component of the health care industry is the doctor, whose skills and training form the basis for most health care services. Hospitals, which contain much of the necessary capital, represent another important component. Medical schools provide the training for doctors. And the American Medical Association is the ultimate authority and power in the health care industry.

- One potential cause of higher prices and an inefficient allocation of resources is market power. The health care industry can obtain market power in at least four ways: length of training of doctors, controlled admissions to medical schools, controlled licensing of doctors, and limited availability of information on doctors' fees and prices.

- A second potential cause of higher prices is third party payments for health care services. Third party payments, including payments by insurance companies and the government, mean recipients of the health care services pay only a fraction of the total costs. Therefore, they tend to demand a larger quantity.

- The health care industry illustrates a basic tradeoff seen throughout economics. A more efficient allocation of resources at lower prices is possible, but this is likely to limit the availability of health care services and prevent poorer people from obtaining the services.

QUESTIONS FOR STUDY AND ANALYSIS

1. Explain how each of the following actions is likely to affect the allocation of health care resources and their prices.
   a. Foreign-trained doctors are prevented from practicing in the United States.
   b. The federal government reduces the amount of funds allocated to both Medicare and Medicaid.
   c. Insurance companies agree to pay 100 percent of all health care costs over $200, where they currently are paying only 80 percent.
   d. The American Medical Association is dissolved.

2. One proposed method of controlling the increase in health care costs is to make more extensive use of paramedics, nurses, and doctor's aides, who can provide some, but not all, of the services currently provided by doctors. In essence, a patient would have a choice between skill levels as well as different prices. Discuss how this program would likely affect the health care industry.

3. If the health care industry was perfectly competitive, then it would have a large number of relatively small firms, freedom of entry and exit, perfect information, and identical products. Discuss the pros and cons of a perfectly competitive health care industry.

4. If the health care industry was monopolistically competitive, then it would have imperfect information and slightly different products, together with a large number of small firms and freedom of entry and exit. Discuss the pros and cons of a monopolistically competitive health care industry.

REVIEW GLOSSARY

market power The ability of a firm to control or influence the price and/or quantity exchanged in the market. Many people suggest that the health care industry derives a great deal of market power from the American Medical Association.

third party payments Payments made to sellers on behalf of buyers by parties that do not directly receive the benefits from the payment. In the health care industry, third party payments are primarily made by insurance companies and the government.

SECTION INQUIRY

Market Power in the World Petroleum Market

Large increases in the prices charged for petroleum by OPEC (Organization of Petroleum Exporting Countries) in the 1970s made the terms *market power* and *the energy industry* synonymous in the minds of many. If we look at the situation in the world's petroleum production in the early 1970s, we can see how the thirteen countries of OPEC were able to exercise their market power. OPEC was able to increase the price of petroleum from $2.60 to $11 per barrel in 1973 because they accounted for over half of the world's petroleum production (55.7 percent). And even though their share of the world's petroleum market had declined slightly (to 49.5 percent), OPEC still maintained sufficient market power to begin raising the price of petroleum again in 1979, eventually reaching a high of $34 per barrel in 1981.

During the 1970s the OPEC cartel was able to raise these prices and keep them relatively high by agreeing to limit their production. Each country agreed on a production quota and happily counted the revenues. However, as often happens with cartels that do not have a complete monopoly in the market, OPEC had a fatal flaw. As they reduced production, the rest of the world did not. In fact, the high prices established by OPEC encouraged increased petroleum production throughout the world, which slowly eroded OPEC's market power. For example, between 1973 and 1983 China doubled its production of petroleum, Mexico increased its production by nearly six times, and the United Kingdom went from a negligible amount of production to about 5 percent of the world's total.

Decreased production by OPEC together with increased production from other countries meant an overall decline in OPEC's market power. By 1985 OPEC accounted for less than 30 percent of the world's energy production. Decreased market power combined with the natural tendency for each member of a cartel to undercut the price of other members led to a drastic decline in petroleum prices in 1986. In early 1986 prices declined from $28 per barrel to $10 per barrel. And during this price decline members of OPEC were unable to agree on a strategy to cut production or raise the price to previous levels, in large part because they simply lacked the same degree of market power they once held.

QUESTIONS FOR DISCUSSION

1. Considering the numerous sources of market power, what would you say contributed to OPEC's market power in the early 1970s? Which sources of market power deserted OPEC in the 1980s? Explain. If you had been in charge of OPEC, what would you have done to maintain its market power?

2. Discuss whether the world's petroleum market has any of the characteristics of a natural monopoly.

3. Discuss whether you think the world's petroleum market is more oligopolistic or monopolistically competitive. Has this situation changed from the 1970s to the 1980s? Explain.

4. Some people argue that the petroleum firms in the United States should be subject to antitrust legislation since the eight largest firms account for over 50 percent of domestic production. Evaluate this proposition in light of the fact that the United States imports about 40 percent of all petroleum it uses from other countries.

Distribution of World Oil Production (percent)

Year	OPEC	Canada	Mexico	United Kingdom	United States	China	Soviet Union	Other
1973	55.7	3.2	0.8	0.0	16.5	2.0	15.2	6.6
1974	55.0	3.0	1.0	0.0	15.7	2.4	16.1	6.8
1975	51.4	2.7	1.3	0.0	15.8	2.8	18.2	7.7
1976	53.6	2.3	1.4	0.4	14.2	2.9	17.7	7.4
1977	52.4	2.2	1.6	1.3	13.8	3.1	17.9	7.6
1978	49.6	2.2	2.0	1.8	14.5	3.5	18.6	7.8
1979	49.5	2.4	2.3	2.5	13.7	3.4	18.3	7.9
1980	45.2	2.4	3.3	2.7	14.4	3.6	19.8	8.7
1981	40.5	2.3	4.1	3.2	15.3	3.6	21.3	9.6
1982	35.4	2.4	5.2	3.9	16.2	3.8	22.5	10.6
1983	33.1	2.6	5.1	4.3	16.4	4.0	22.7	11.8
1984	32.4	2.7	5.1	4.7	16.4	4.2	21.9	12.6
1985	30.1	2.7	5.1	4.8	16.7	4.6	22.1	13.9

Source: Calculated from information in *Monthly Energy Review*, Energy Information Agency, May 1986.

PART IV

Microeconomics: Resource Markets

Economics concerns itself with such topics as the satisfaction of consumers' wants and needs, the growth of the economy's total output, and the efficient distribution of output. One of the most important topics is the distribution of factor payments, which economists have discussed and debated since the modern study of economics began two hundred years ago.

This concern with the distribution of factor payments is not one of idle academic curiosity but rather one that grew out of the harsh realities of society that existed when economics matured as a discipline. It is no coincidence that most of the founding fathers of economic thought were English. Keep in mind that the England of the 1700s and 1800s was in the middle of an industrial revolution and was witness to a serious split between different groups in society. The laborers who worked in the factories were being paid bare subsistence wages, while the entrepreneurial factory owners and landowners were becoming wealthier.

This social and economic division was an important motivating force for the study of economics at this time. Economists wanted to know the underlying reasons for the observed distribution of payments to the factors and also what they could do about it. While some economists wanted simply to justify the observed distribution, others wanted to show why the distribution was wrong. However, as with other areas of economics that begin as normative economics, the study of factor payments quickly turned into positive economics.

The most important and influential economist to deal with this problem was David Ricardo (1772–1823). Ricardo was an astute and successful businessman who became wealthy at a relatively young age. However, after reading Adam Smith's *The Wealth of Nations*, he also became fascinated with the study of economics. Indeed, he was so caught up in the study that he retired from his business in 1814 to devote all his time to economics and subsequently published *Principles of Political Economy and Taxation* in 1817. This book contained not only his theories explaining the distribution of factor payments but also the entire range of economic principles developed up to that time. While his work was theoretical and scholarly, he was anything but an ivory tower academician. Much of his work was aimed directly at the various social problems facing England at that time. In fact, he even held a seat in Parliament, where he proposed many political and economic reforms.

Part IV of this text focuses on the markets used to exchange the economy's resources. In this study we employ some of the microeconomic principles developed in our study of output markets in Part III, together with many important principles developed by Ricardo and his contemporaries. Through this examination of resource markets we see how and why factor payments are distributed. Moreover, we see how an efficient allocation of resources can be achieved through the efficient operation of resource markets.

SECTION 10

The Factor Market

Our study of microeconomics up to this point has focused on output markets used to exchange the economy's goods and services. However, to produce goods and services, firms require a wide variety of inputs from the four factors of production: labor, capital, land, and entrepreneurship. In this section we turn our attention to the markets used to exchange these factors of production—the factor markets. While firms play the role of supplier in the output markets, they play the role of demander in the factor markets.

There are many similarities between output and factor markets. On the one hand are the buyers, willing and able to purchase a good or factor; on the other hand are the sellers, willing and able to supply a good or factor. However, factor markets also have some unique features. For example, demanders in factor markets (the firms) require factors only as inputs in the production process. Whereas consumers receive satisfaction from goods and services demanded in output markets, firms receive no satisfaction from the factors they demand in the factor markets. The demand for a factor exists only as long as there is a demand for the firm's product. Moreover, on the supply side of the factor market, some factor suppliers do receive satisfaction from selling their services. In particular, the suppliers of labor and entrepreneurship are people who receive satisfaction, in one form or another, from the production process.

Unit 10.1, Factor Demand, introduces the demand side of the factor market. In this unit we see that the demand for a factor of production is a derived demand and is based on the use of the factors in the production of a good or service. If no one demands the good or service, then there is no demand for the factor of production. We also discuss the role of the law of diminishing marginal returns in factor demand.

Unit 10.2, Factor Supply, looks at the supply side of the factor market. In particular, this unit discusses the considerations of owners in supplying their factors of production. While there are many similarities underlying the supply of the four factors, this unit concentrates on the significant differences.

Unit 10.3, Factor Market Equilibrium, combines factor demand and factor supply to determine the factor market equilibrium. In particular, we see that factor markets, like product markets, can be influenced by the market power of one or more participants. Thus, this unit looks at monopsony, monopoly, and bilateral monopoly because in all three cases market power plays an important role in equilibrium determination.

Unit 10.4, The Effect of Unions on the Labor Market, applies the concepts and analysis from the first three units in this section to the labor market. Labor, in addition to being the most important factor of production in the economy, also provides an informative study of factor market power. In particular, this unit examines labor unions and their effect on the labor market.

UNIT 10.1

Factor Demand

In this unit we investigate the demand side of the factor market. While the demand for factors of production is very similar to the demand for goods and services, important differences do exist. Most notably, the demand for factors derives not from the factors themselves but from the goods and services that they produce.

Marginal productivity theory is also discussed in this unit. This theory builds on the law of diminishing marginal returns, introduced in Section 8, and on the concept of derived demand. That is, the quantity of a factor demanded depends in part on the factor itself and in part on the demand for the output being produced. And finally, we discuss the three most important determinants of factor demand: product price, technology, and prices of other factors.

DERIVED DEMAND

Keep in mind that the demand for factors of production differs from the demand for goods and services. Consumers demand goods and services, and that demand is based on the satisfaction the consumers receive from the goods. By contrast, firms demand factors of production and receive no direct satisfaction from the factors they demand. The factors of production are demanded by firms only because the factors are used to produce the goods and services desired by consumers. And if consumers have no demand for the goods and services produced by the firm, then the firm has no demand for the factors of production. Therefore, the demand for a factor of production is a derived demand. **Derived demand** is the demand for a factor of production resulting from the demand for the good or service it produces.

Derived demand points out two important aspects of factor demand. First, factor demand is based on the demand for the good being produced. If the demand for the good or service changes, then the demand for the factor of production also changes. Second, factor demand is based on the principles of production. The production techniques available to a firm determine the quantity of a factor required to produce the amount of goods and services demanded. If a farmer's production function indicates that fifty pounds of fertilizer are required to produce a hundred bushels of corn on an acre of land, then fifty pounds of fertilizer are demanded for every hundred bushels of corn produced. If production technology changes such that the farmer can produce a hundred bushels of corn with less fertilizer, then less fertilizer is demanded.

MARGINAL PRODUCTIVITY THEORY

Both of these aspects of derived demand are embodied in marginal productivity theory. **Marginal productivity theory** states that the demand for a factor of production is based on the marginal product of the factor and its marginal revenue. To see how marginal productivity theory explains the demand for factors of production, let's look at an example.

Suppose that Ireland's Ice Cream Delights employs one variable factor (labor) and one fixed factor (capital) in the short-run production of its output. Table 10.1.1 presents the quantity of ice cream delights produced by Ireland for different quantities of labor. The third column lists the marginal product of the variable factor, which up to this point has been called marginal product. Now let's be more precise and call it marginal physical product. **Marginal physical product** is the change in the quantity of output resulting from a change in the quantity of a factor. Note that marginal physical product is expressed in physical units of the output and is subject to the law of diminishing marginal returns. If more than the second unit of labor is used, the marginal physical product declines.

Assume that this is a perfectly competitive firm, able to sell all of its ice cream delights for $2 each. The fourth column of this table lists the revenue generated from the sale of the additional output in the third column, or the marginal revenue product. **Marginal revenue product** is the change in revenue received by the firm resulting from a change in the quantity of an factor. Marginal revenue product is calculated as

$$\text{marginal revenue product} = \text{marginal revenue} \times \text{marginal physical product}$$

For a perfectly competitive firm, price equals marginal revenue, so marginal revenue product also equals price times marginal physical product. However, this is only true for a firm that sells output in a perfectly competitive market.

Table 10.1.1 indicates that the marginal revenue product is $40 for the first unit of labor, $60 for the second unit and so on. Ireland is extremely interested in the additional revenue generated by each additional unit of factor because the revenue generated by the factor influences the units demanded.

However, Ireland also needs to know the cost of labor, which is discussed in more detail in the next unit. For now, suppose that each unit of labor costs the firm $40. In this case, how many units does Ireland demand? The first unit of labor costs Ireland $40, but this unit also generates $40 in additional revenue, which is acceptable. The second unit can also be hired for $40, but it generates $60 in revenue, which increases Ireland's profit by $20. The third unit of labor also increases Ireland's profit, as the marginal revenue product is $50 while the cost of the factor remains at $40. The fourth unit adds $40 to both revenue and cost, but the fifth unit costs $40 and adds only $30 to revenue. Therefore, Ireland is agreeable to hiring up to and including the fourth unit but not the fifth.

In short, if a firm seeks to maximize profit, it hires factors up to the point where the marginal revenue product is equal to the cost of the factor.

Table 10.1.1

Derivation of Marginal Revenue Product (MR = P = $2)

Marginal revenue product is the additional revenue generated by hiring an additional unit of input. It is found by multiplying the marginal physical product of an input by the marginal revenue obtained from selling the output. In this case, since marginal revenue is equal to price, the marginal revenue product in the fourth column is obtained by multiplying the price (= $2) times the marginal physical product in the third column.

Quantity of Labor	Quantity of Ice Cream Delights	Marginal Physical Product (MPP)	Marginal Revenue Product MR (= P) × MPP
0	0		
1	20	20	$40
2	50	30	60
3	75	25	50
4	95	20	40
5	110	15	30
6	120	10	20
7	125	5	10

If it hires fewer units, profit can be increased. If it hires more units, profit declines.

Factor Demand Curves

We are now ready to look at the demand curve for a factor of production. Figure 10.1.1 plots the marginal revenue product and units of labor from Table 10.1.1. Note that the shape of the marginal revenue product curve in Figure 10.1.1 reflects the law of diminishing marginal returns. Up to the second unit of labor, marginal revenue product increases, but after that it declines because the law of diminishing marginal returns sets in.

Recall from Table 10.1.1 that the firm hires 4 units of the factor if the cost of each factor is $40 (point A). When the cost of each factor is $30, the firm hires 5 units (point B), because the fifth unit adds exactly $30 to revenue. If the cost of each unit is $20, the firm hires 6 units (point C). The downward-sloping portion of the marginal revenue product curve in Figure 10.1.1 is the firm's demand curve for the factor.

But why does only the downward-sloping portion comprise the firm's demand curve? Why doesn't the firm hire one unit of labor on the upward-sloping portion if the price is $40? Clearly, in the upward-sloping portion of the marginal revenue product curve, an additional unit of a factor adds more to revenue than the previous unit. While the factor pays for itself in the upward-sloping portion, the firm can always do better by adding the next unit. This portion of the marginal revenue product curve is not part of the demand curve for the factor

Figure 10.1.1

Marginal Revenue Product and Factor Demand

A profit-maximizing firm hires a factor until the price of the factor is equal to the marginal revenue product. Thus, the marginal revenue product curve is also the firm's demand curve for the factor. Since the marginal revenue product curve is negatively sloped due to the law of diminishing marginal returns, the factor demand curve is also negatively sloped.

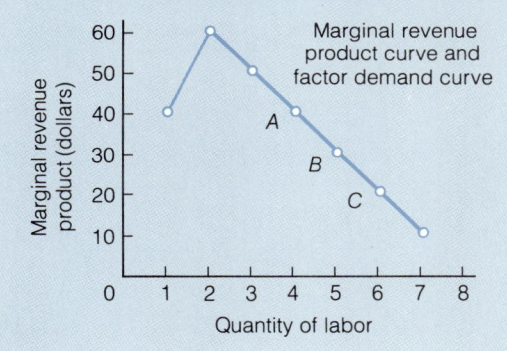

because the firm never stays there but rather always moves further along the curve.

The Law of Diminishing Marginal Returns

The importance of the law of diminishing returns to the demand curve for a factor of production must be emphasized. The law of diminishing marginal returns causes marginal revenue product to decline, which means the factor demand curve has a negative slope. Therefore, firms hire larger quantities of the factor only if the price of the factor declines. Since each factor is less productive and thus adds less to revenue, the firm can hire more only if the cost is lower.

DETERMINANTS OF FACTOR DEMAND

The three most important **determinants of factor demand** are product price, technology, and price of other factors. A change in any of these three determinants causes the factor demand curve to shift. As with the demand curve in an output market, a change in one of the determinants causes a change in demand, while a change in the price of the factor causes a change in the quantity demanded.

Product Price

If the price of the product sold by the firm increases, the demand curve for the factor shifts rightward, whereas if the price of the product decreases, the demand curve shifts leftward. Figure 10.1.2 illustrates a rightward shift in the factor demand resulting from an increase in the product price. For the perfectly competitive firm, the product price is equal to marginal revenue, and so the marginal revenue product is directly affected. However, even if the firm is not perfectly competitive, a change in the product price affects the firm's marginal revenue and thus the marginal revenue product.

Suppose that the product price of a perfectly competitive firm is $1 and the marginal physical product is 2, meaning the marginal revenue product is $2. Therefore, the firm hires the factor if the cost is also $2, at point A in Figure 10.1.2. However, if the price of the good rises to $2 while the marginal product remains at 2, the marginal revenue product is now $4 (point A'). If the cost per factor is $2, the firm can hire additional units even though they cause the marginal physical product of the factor to fall. The firm is not concerned exclusively with the marginal *physical* product but with the additional revenue the factor generates for the firm, which is the marginal *revenue* product. At point B' the marginal product is 1, but the marginal revenue product is $2. An increase in the product price and in the marginal revenue product allows a greater amount of the factor to be hired at each factor cost.

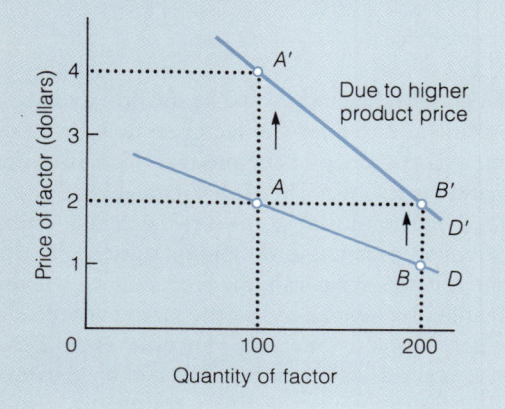

Figure 10.1.2

Factor Demand and Product Price

An increase in the price of a product causes the demand curve for the factor used in its production to shift rightward. Even though the marginal physical product of the factor does not change, the higher price means the factor generates greater marginal revenue.

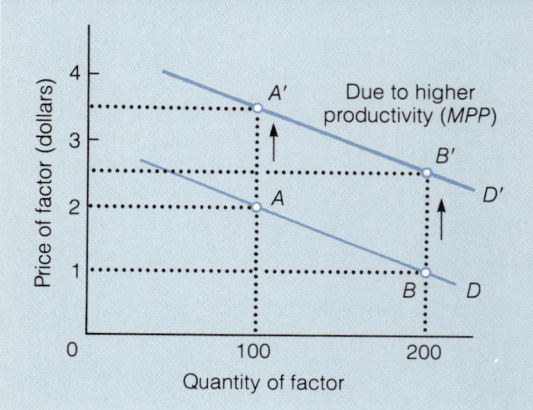

Figure 10.1.3

Factor Demand and Technology

An advancement in the level of technology associated with the use of a factor shifts the factor demand curve rightward. The improved technology increases the factor's marginal physical product at every quantity of the factor.

For example, if the price of automobiles increases because of an increase in their demand, automobile companies demand more labor but at the same wage, or price of labor. The additional labor may be less productive, based on the law of diminishing marginal returns, but it still generates the same marginal revenue due to the higher price of automobiles.

Technology

An increase in the level of technology also causes the demand curve for a factor to shift rightward, as Figure 10.1.3 illustrates by increasing the productivity of the factor. The marginal physical product of the factor increases and, with no change in the price of the good, the marginal revenue product also increases. The higher marginal revenue product means the firm can hire a greater number of units at the same factor cost. For example, technological advances have been making computers more productive over the past decade. Businesses that use computers in the production of their goods demand more computers, even if the price of their product and the price of computers does not change.

Prices of Other Factors

A change in the price of one factor of production can cause a shift in the demand curve for another factor used to produce the output. For example, an increase in the price of farmland causes the demand curve for fertilizer to shift leftward, as illustrated in panel a of Figure 10.1.4. If the price of land rises, less land is used in the production of agricultural products, and the marginal physical prod-

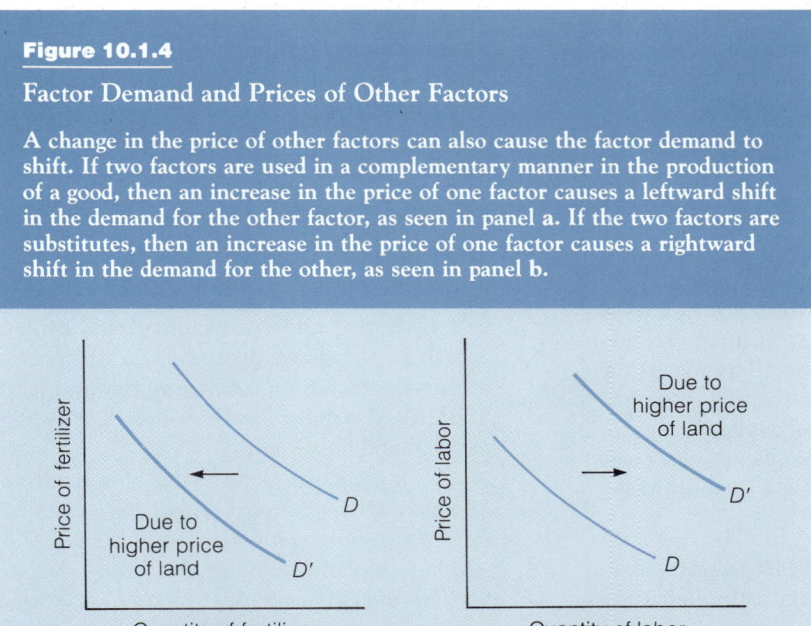

Figure 10.1.4

Factor Demand and Prices of Other Factors

A change in the price of other factors can also cause the factor demand to shift. If two factors are used in a complementary manner in the production of a good, then an increase in the price of one factor causes a leftward shift in the demand for the other factor, as seen in panel a. If the two factors are substitutes, then an increase in the price of one factor causes a rightward shift in the demand for the other, as seen in panel b.

a. Demand for fertilizer—complements

b. Demand for labor—substitutes

uct of a given quantity of fertilizer is also less. If the price of the output is unchanged, the marginal revenue product of fertilizer is less, and the firm demands less at the existing cost of fertilizer.

An increase in the price of one factor can also cause the marginal physical product and marginal revenue product of another factor to rise, which leads to a rightward shift in the demand curve for the other factor. For example, the increase in the price of land can lead to a substitution of labor for land. The farmer might use less land, hiring additional labor to work the land more intensely. In this case the marginal revenue product of labor rises and the demand curve for labor shifts rightward, as illustrated in panel b of Figure 10.1.4.

For example, an increase in the price of trucks leads to a decrease in the quantity of trucks used by a delivery company such as United Parcel Service (UPS). Obviously, UPS has a smaller demand for truck drivers if it has fewer trucks; this would also be depicted by panel a. By contrast, an increase in the price of trucks might cause UPS to use fewer trucks and more airplanes in deliveries, in which case the demand for airplanes by UPS shifts rightward, as depicted in panel b.

IN SUMMARY

Factor Demand

- The demand for factors of production is a derived demand. Factor demand depends on the demand for the goods and services produced by the firm employing the factors.

- Marginal productivity theory states that the demand for factors of production is based on the marginal revenue of the factor and its marginal physical product. Marginal revenue product is the amount of revenue generated by an additional unit of a factor. It is the marginal revenue received from the sale of the product times the marginal physical product of the factor.

- A firm hires a factor up to the point where the cost of the factor is equal to the marginal revenue product of the last factor. This means the downward-sloping portion of the marginal revenue product curve is the demand curve for the factor. The factor demand curve is downward sloping because of the law of diminishing marginal returns.

- The three most important determinants of factor demand are product price, technology, and prices of other factors. A change in any of these determinants causes a shift in the factor demand curve, while a change in the price of the factor causes a change in the quantity of the factor demanded.

QUESTIONS FOR STUDY AND ANALYSIS

1. Why is the demand for factors of production a derived demand? What is the difference between marginal product, discussed in Unit 8.2, and marginal physical product?

2. **a.** Calculate the marginal revenue product for the following factors if the firm sells its output for $5 each.

Quantity of factor	0	1	2	3	4	5	6	7	8
Quantity of output	0	40	75	105	130	150	165	175	160

   b. Construct the demand curve for the factor.
   c. Construct the demand curve for the factor if the price of the firm's output falls to $3. How does it compare to the factor demand curve drawn in question 2b?
   d. How many units of the factor are hired by the firm if the factor cost is $75 per unit and the price of the output is $5? What if the price of the output is $3?

3. Evaluate this statement: According to marginal productivity theory, every unit of labor is paid its contribution to production.

4. For each of the following situations, explain which of the determinants of factor demand causes the factor demand curve for farm labor to shift. Also indicate which direction the factor demand curve shifts.
   a. An increase in export sales of agricultural products to the Soviet Union.
   b. An increase in the amount of land used to produce agricultural product.
   c. The development of a new fertilizer that increases crop yields by 50 percent.

5. Do you think your instructor assigns grades based on marginal productivity? Explain.

6. In many colleges throughout the country, newly hired Ph.D.'s (especially in engineering and business) receive higher salaries than established faculty members. Is this consistent with marginal productivity theory? Why or why not?

REVIEW GLOSSARY

derived demand The demand for a factor of production resulting from the demand for the good or service it produces. Factor demand is a derived demand.

determinants of factor demand There are three determinants of factor demand: product price, technology, and prices of other factors. An increase in both the product price and technology causes a rightward shift in the factor demand curve. An increase in the price of another factor can cause either a rightward or a leftward shift in the factor demand curve.

marginal physical product The change in the quantity of output resulting from a change in the quantity of a factor. Marginal physical product is always stated in physical units.

marginal productivity theory A theory stating that the demand for a factor of production is based on the marginal product of the factor and its marginal revenue.

marginal revenue product The change in the revenue received by a firm resulting from a change in the quantity of a factor. To maximize profit, a firm hires a factor to the point where the cost of the factor is equal to the marginal revenue product. The demand curve for a factor is the downward-sloping portion of the marginal revenue product curve. The law of diminishing marginal returns causes the factor demand curve to have a negative slope.

UNIT 10.2

Factor Supply

Aspects of factor supply are as diverse as the factors themselves. Note, for example, differences between the supply of tractors, the supply of migrant workers, and the supply of land in New York City. However, similarities in the supply of these factors do exist as well. Both the similarities and the differences are examined in this unit.

We begin by looking at the three types of supply that concern factor markets. The first type is the supply *by* a firm, the second is the total market supply of a factor, and the third is the supply *to* a firm. The differences in each type of supply influence not only how we view the factor market but also how we look at the concept of marginal factor cost, the cost to a firm of hiring another unit of a factor. We then focus on differences between the supplies of labor, capital, land, and entrepreneurship that affect factor supply. This discussion brings us to one of the key aspects of factor supply, mobility, both geographic and occupational.

MARKET AND FIRM SUPPLY

Each of the three types of supply mentioned previously—supply by a firm, market supply, and supply to a firm—should be discussed as they relate to factor markets.

Supply by a Firm

Supply by a firm is the range of quantity an individual firm is willing and able to sell, at alternative prices. Indeed, many factors of production are produced in much the same way as consumer goods and services. For example, the pickup truck used by a farmer to transport hay around the farm is produced in exactly the same way as the pickup truck owned by a suburban family. Keep in mind that the principles underlying the production of goods and services also underlie the production of many factors. An individual supplier of a factor of production offers a larger quantity at a higher price as the marginal cost of production increases.

Typically, the total supply of a factor is composed of several individual suppliers. However, it is also possible that a factor market is dominated by a single supplier, just as an output market can be dominated by a single firm. A market characterized by a single firm supplying all the output is a **monopoly**.

Market Supply

The **market supply** of a factor is the total supply of every seller willing and able to sell a good (or factor), at alternative prices. While the market supply for many factors of production adheres to the general principles of supply, sometimes the market supply for a factor of production does not change, so that the quantity supplied is totally unresponsive to changes in price. For example, in the United States there are only 3.5 million square miles of land area. Nor is it possible to increase the quantity of land in downtown New York City.

Supply to a Firm

A fixed market supply does not necessarily mean the supply to an individual firm is also fixed. **Supply to a firm** is the range of quantities of a factor that a firm is able to buy, at alternative prices. Note that the supply of a factor to a single firm is not the same as the total market supply. For example, the market supply for land in the United States is fixed, but a single farm can increase the quantity of land it uses. Likewise, anybody can buy land in New York City if they are willing to pay a high enough price. In essence, an individual firm can always obtain more of a factor by bidding a higher price, even though the market supply is fixed.

However, in some cases a firm is the only buyer of a factor. A **monopsony** is a market that is characterized by a single buyer of the good or factor. An example of a monopsony is the company town, where all labor in a town is hired by a single firm. Although monopsony resembles monopoly, there is one important difference. A monopoly is a market with only one seller, whereas a monopsony is a market with only one buyer. Unlike output markets, factor markets are prone to having monopolies, monopsonies, or both.

In Unit 10.4 we see that many labor markets have only one buyer (the firm) and one seller (the labor union). In fact, many of the monopolies discussed in the context of output markets in Section 9 were based on monopolies in factor markets. For example, Rockefeller's Standard Oil Trust in the late 1800s was built on a monopoly in the petroleum market, a resource used to make gasoline and other outputs. And the DeBeer's diamond empire represents a monopoly of diamond resources, which is a resource used in the production of outputs such as jewelry.

MARGINAL FACTOR COST

In terms of the factor supply to an individual firm, the quantity purchased by a firm depends not only on the factor's marginal productivity but also on the cost of the factor, particularly the marginal factor cost. **Marginal factor cost** is the additional cost of hiring an additional unit of a factor. If the firm can hire all of the labor it needs for $5 per hour, then the marginal factor cost is constant at $5 per hour. However, if the firm must pay a higher price to hire larger quantities of a factor, then the marginal factor cost is not constant.

For example, suppose a firm can hire 1 unit of labor for $5 but has to pay $6 for 2 units of labor. While the price of the second unit is $6, the marginal factor cost is $7. Since the firm has to pay $6 for both units, it is paying the first unit $1 more than if it hired only the first unit. Thus, the marginal factor cost of the second unit is the $6 price paid the second unit plus the extra $1 paid to the first unit. Note that the marginal factor cost of the second unit of labor is greater than the price, because the price of the factor increases. In fact, any time the price of a factor increases with the quantity purchased, the marginal factor cost is greater than the price.

This relationship is very similar to the relationship between price and marginal revenue for a monopolistic firm, and for very similar reasons. Since the price changes on all units purchased, the marginal factor cost (or marginal revenue) is not equal to the price. In the case of a rising factor price, marginal factor cost is greater than the price, and in the case of falling output price, marginal revenue is less than the price.

FACTOR SUPPLY CURVES

We can distinguish between three different types of factor supply curves as illustrated in Figure 10.2.1.

In panel a, a perfectly inelastic market supply curve is presented. As the price rises, the quantity supplied does not change. Such a curve reflects the fixed quantity of land in many urban areas and also represents the short-run supply of doctors since the production of doctors requires several years of training. Another example is the short-run supply of labor in a small town before people have time to move in or out. The inelastic supply curve is almost always representative of the market supply for a factor rather than the supply of the factor to a particular firm.

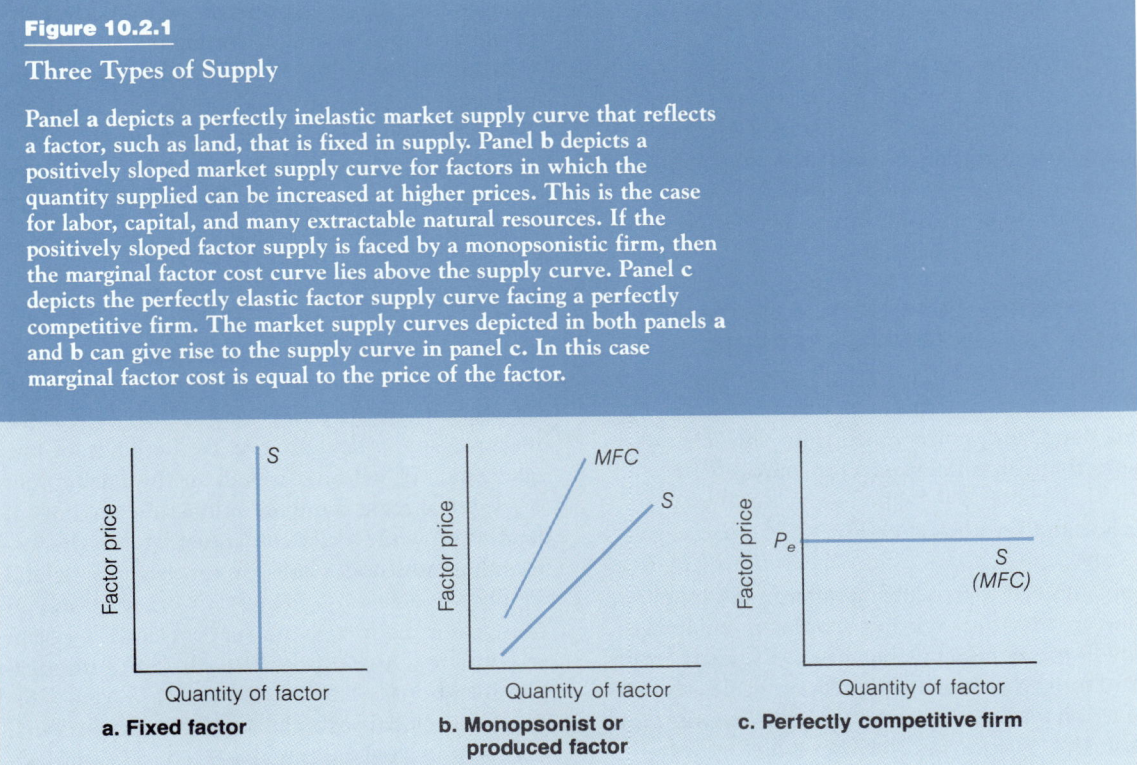

Figure 10.2.1
Three Types of Supply

Panel a depicts a perfectly inelastic market supply curve that reflects a factor, such as land, that is fixed in supply. Panel b depicts a positively sloped market supply curve for factors in which the quantity supplied can be increased at higher prices. This is the case for labor, capital, and many extractable natural resources. If the positively sloped factor supply is faced by a monopsonistic firm, then the marginal factor cost curve lies above the supply curve. Panel c depicts the perfectly elastic factor supply curve facing a perfectly competitive firm. The market supply curves depicted in both panels a and b can give rise to the supply curve in panel c. In this case marginal factor cost is equal to the price of the factor.

a. Fixed factor

b. Monopsonist or produced factor

c. Perfectly competitive firm

However, panel b presents a positively sloped factor supply curve that could represent either the market supply or the supply to a single firm. If the marginal cost of producing the factor rises with larger quantities, as with most capital goods, skilled labor, and the extraction of many natural resources, then the market supply for a factor will have a positively sloped supply curve. But this is also the supply curve facing the firm if the market is monopsonistic. The marginal factor cost is greater than the price at each quantity, so the marginal factor cost curve lies above the supply curve.

Panel c presents the last of the three alternatives. If the firm operates in a perfectly competitive factor market and is able to buy all of the factor it needs at the same price, then the factor supply curve facing the firm is perfectly elastic. Since the price is the same for every factor, the marginal factor cost is equal to the price of the factor, meaning the supply curve is also the marginal factor cost curve.

Either the perfectly inelastic market supply curve in panel a or the positively sloped supply curve in panel b can lead to the perfectly elastic supply curve in panel c. But the *structure* of the factor market determines whether a firm faces a positively sloped (b) or horizontal (c) supply curve.

DIFFERENCES IN LABOR, CAPITAL, LAND, AND ENTREPRENEURSHIP

Each of the four factors of production—labor, capital, land, and entrepreneurship—has characteristics that can influence factor supplies.

Labor and Entrepreneurship

Labor and entrepreneurship differ from capital and land in that they are not inanimate equipment, buildings, or minerals but involve human effort. And for this reason people receive utility and satisfaction while they are on the job. Keep in mind that this satisfaction can be either positive or negative. For example, while a coal miner might not like his or her job, a professional golfer may derive a great deal of personal satisfaction while on the job.

Indeed, with labor and entrepreneurship we cannot separate the person from the factor of production. When firms hire a unit of labor, they get the person too. In this sense, the supply of human resources depends on more than just the price. Different people prefer different types of jobs and thus are willing to sell their services at different prices. For example, many professional athletes have said that money is secondary to playing the game. A public school teacher may feel the same. By contrast, sanitation workers, coal miners, and assembly line workers may require a higher price because the job is dangerous, boring, or dirty.

Capital

The most important characteristic of capital in terms of supply is that it is a produced factor of production and thus follows the principles underlying the production of any good. In the short run the production of capital is dependent on the law of diminishing marginal returns. Everything that was said about the supply of output in Section 8 also applies to the supply of capital.

Land

The characteristic of land that distinguishes it from the other three factors is its essentially fixed supply. Of course there are exceptions to this, such as the reclamation of land in the Netherlands or the emergence of volcanic islands in the Pacific, but on a global scale these are minuscule amounts of land. And while a city can annex land in the surrounding area and a country can expand its land supply through wars, treaties, or other means, in these cases the increase in supply is usually not in response to a higher price but is based on political considerations.

On a global scale the supply of many natural resources in the land can also be considered fixed. There is only a finite quantity of petroleum, coal, bauxite, and other mineral resources in the land, and the total quantity of air and water is likewise fixed. But the fixity of natural resources must be qualified. While the natural resources are fixed on a global scale, they *are* responsive to price. In a sense, as capital or other goods are produced, natural resources can be produced, through exploration. Petroleum and molybdenum can enter into the market supply only if suppliers know they exist. Thus, exploration is an important part of their production and is guided by the principles of production. This means additional quantities of natural resources are supplied at higher cost because of the law of diminishing marginal returns, which affects exploration just as it affects the production of a capital good.

MOBILITY

Mobility is the movement of factors from one production process to another and represents a significant aspect of factor supply. There are two important types of mobility that we want to discuss. The first is geographic mobility. **Geographic mobility** is the movement of factors from one geographic area to another. For labor, capital, and entrepreneurship, mobility is extremely important. Labor is willing and able to travel from one part of the country to another in search of higher wages and better working conditions. Likewise, investors of financial capital can send their funds to any firm anywhere in the country in search of higher interest. Factories and other physical capital can be produced anywhere in the country with these funds, and entrepreneurs can move their production to the part of the country with the highest profit potential.

By contrast, land has limited geographic mobility, particularly in terms of its accessibility and natural resources. Obviously, by its very nature, land has no geographic mobility. For example, an acre of land in upstate New York cannot be moved to downtown Manhattan to improve its accessibility. Natural resources do have some limited geographic mobility. Mineral resources can be moved after they are extracted, but before that time they are immobile. In addition, a hydroelectric dam must be located where the water flow is adequate.

A second type of mobility is occupational mobility. **Occupational mobility** is the movement of factors from one occupation to another, which can affect the supply of a factor to a single industry. For example, unskilled or semiskilled labor is relatively mobile between occupations. A janitor can easily become an assembly line worker in an automobile factory. And industries that employ relatively low skilled workers face a labor supply that is relatively elastic because of high occupational mobility. But industries that employ skilled labor face relatively inelastic factor supply curves because of low occupational mobility. It is difficult for a medical doctor to become a nuclear physicist, and vice versa. The training and skill required in both occupations limit mobility for each.

Entrepreneurs probably have the highest occupational mobility of any factor. Their managerial skills and risk-taking ability usually extend beyond the production of any particular good. For example, William Simon was the secretary of the treasury *and* president of the United States Olympic Committee. Lawrence O'Brien was the chairman of the Democratic party *and* the commissioner of the National Basketball Association. It is not unusual for a corporate executive in one industry to move to a completely different industry.

Occupational mobility is also important for capital. Factory and equipment designed for one production process cannot be easily shifted into the production of another good. Once again, the more specialized the capital, the lower its occupational mobility is. Where a personal computer has a high degree of mobility between occupations, a wheat combine does not.

Land and natural resources have the greatest occupational mobility of any of the factors (excluding perhaps entrepreneurship). Any piece of land can be used as the site for almost any type of production process. An acre of land can be changed from farmland to residential use to factory use with very little trouble. It is easier and faster to build a doctor's office on an acre of farmland than it is to train a farmer to become a doctor. Natural resources also have a great deal of occupational mobility. A barrel of petroleum can quickly be diverted from the trucking industry to manufacturing. Note, however, that this mobility is high until the resources are processed. Once petroleum is transformed into plastic used to manufacture cars, it cannot be used to make gasoline for the trucking industry.

IN SUMMARY

Factor Supply

- There are three different types of factor supply. One is the supply of a factor *by* an individual firm, the second is the market supply, and the third is the supply of a factor *to* a firm. If there is only one supplier of a factor in a market, then the supplier is a monopoly. If there is only one buyer in a factor market, then the buyer is a monopsony.

- Marginal factor cost is the additional cost of hiring an additional unit of a factor. Marginal factor cost is equal to the price of the factor if the price does not change. However, if the price of the factor increases with additional units, then the marginal factor cost is greater than the price.

- If the total market supply of a factor is fixed, the supply curve is perfectly inelastic. However, for a factor that can be produced, like a consumer good, the market supply is positively sloped because of the rising marginal cost of production. If only one firm is buying the factor, then the marginal factor cost curve for the monopsonist lies above the market supply curve. The supply curve facing a perfectly competitive firm is perfectly elastic at the market price. In addition, the market price is the marginal factor cost.

- With labor and entrepreneurship the person cannot be separated from the factor, unlike land and capital. Thus, the satisfaction received from the job is an important aspect of supply. Furthermore, land is a fixed factor, while capital and many natural resources of the land can be produced.

- The mobility of factors affects the supply in a single market. The two important types of mobility are geographic mobility from one area to another and occupational mobility from one production process to another. Financial capital is extremely mobile. Labor is geographically mobile, but occupational mobility depends on the skill level of the worker. Physical capital is relatively immobile between geographic areas and occupations. And land is relatively mobile between occupations but not between geographic areas.

QUESTIONS FOR STUDY AND ANALYSIS

1. How does the supply by a firm differ from the supply to a firm? Under what conditions is the supply by a firm the same as the market supply? Under what conditions is the supply to a firm the same as the market supply?

2. Explain why marginal factor cost can be greater than the factor price.

3. Under what circumstances is the market supply curve perfectly inelastic? Under what circumstances is the supply curve to a firm perfectly elastic? When is the market supply not perfectly inelastic? When is the supply curve to a firm not perfectly elastic?

4. How do the differences between labor, capital, land, and entrepreneurship affect the supply of each?

5. For each of the following pairs of factors, indicate and discuss which has greater geographic

mobility and which has greater occupational mobility.
a. Medical doctor or service station mechanic
b. Farmland or farmer
c. Semitrailer or bulldozer
d. Pine tree or chief executive officer of Gulf and Western Industries

REVIEW GLOSSARY

geographic mobility The movement of factors from one geographic area to another.

marginal factor cost The additional cost of hiring an additional unit of a factor. If the price of a factor does not change, marginal factor cost is equal to the price. If the price of factor increases with additional units, marginal factor cost is greater than the price. If the supply of a factor is fixed, the supply curve is perfectly inelastic.

market supply The total supply of every seller willing and able to sell a good (or factor), at alternative prices. If a single firm supplies all of the factor to a market, a monopoly exists.

mobility The movement of factors from one production process to another.

monopoly A market characterized by a single firm supplying all of the output in the market.

monopsony A market structure characterized by a single buyer of the good or factor.

occupational mobility The movement of factors from one occupation to another.

supply by a firm The range of quantities that an individual firm is willing and able to sell, at alternative prices.

supply to a firm The range of quantities of a factor that a firm is able to buy, at alternative prices.

UNIT 10.3

Factor Market Equilibrium

In the previous two units we studied first the demand and then the supply of factors of production. In this unit we combine the two as they relate to the operation of the factor market. Keep in mind that a perfectly competitive factor market operates in the same way as any of the other perfectly competitive markets studied in this text. If there is a surplus, the price falls; if there is a shortage, the price rises. However, factor markets in the real world are not perfectly competitive, and like the product markets we looked at in Section 9, market power also plays an important role in factor markets.

Along this line we investigate four basic structures of factor markets: perfect competition, monopsony, monopoly, and bilateral monopoly. The perfectly competitive market serves as a benchmark with which to compare the other market structures. In monopsony, buyers have a large degree of market power, whereas in monopoly, sellers exercise more market power. In bilateral monopoly, market power is shared by both sides of the factor markets. And as we might expect, the market power prevents the market from achieving the perfectly competitive equilibrium and also distorts the allocation of resources in the economy.

PERFECT COMPETITION

Recall that **perfect competition** is a market structure characterized by a large number of small firms, identical products sold, freedom of entry and exit, and perfect knowledge. Perfect competition in a factor market means each buyer of a factor faces a perfectly elastic supply curve. A firm is able to buy as much as it needs at the market price of the factor. For example, a small firm hiring only a few employees in a major urban labor market tends to approximate this type of market structure, hiring as many employees as it wants at the existing wage.

Figure 10.3.1 illustrates the overall market for a factor in perfect competition, and the supply facing a single firm. Panel a depicts the factor market. The factor market demand is the total of every firm demanding the factor and comprises the horizontal addition of all marginal revenue product curves. The factor supply curve has a positive slope, indicating that the total supply is not fixed, though our analysis does not change if the factor is fixed in supply. The intersection of the market supply and demand curves gives us the factor market equilibrium for the quantity exchanged N_e and the equilibrium factor price w_e.

The equilibrium factor price w_e most concerns a single firm hiring the factor in a perfectly competitive market. Because the firm is able to hire as much of the factor as it wants at that same factor price, the supply curve for the factor is perfectly elastic at w_e, as seen in panel b.

The firm hires the factor up to the point where the marginal revenue product generated by the factor to the firm is equal to the factor price, which is also the marginal factor cost. In panel b the equilibrium quantity is n_e, at which quantity the cost of the last factor is equal to the additional revenue generated by the last factor. If the firm hires one more or one less unit, it has less profit. But since the firm hires the factor in a perfectly competitive market, the factor price w_e is also the marginal factor cost, meaning the firm equates marginal factor cost with the marginal revenue product. By contrast, all other factor market struc-

Figure 10.3.1

A Perfectly Competitive Factor Market

In a perfectly competitive factor market, each individual firm takes as a given the factor price w_e determined in the market, seen in panel a. It then hires the quantity of the factor until the price is equal to the marginal revenue product, seen in panel b as quantity n_e.

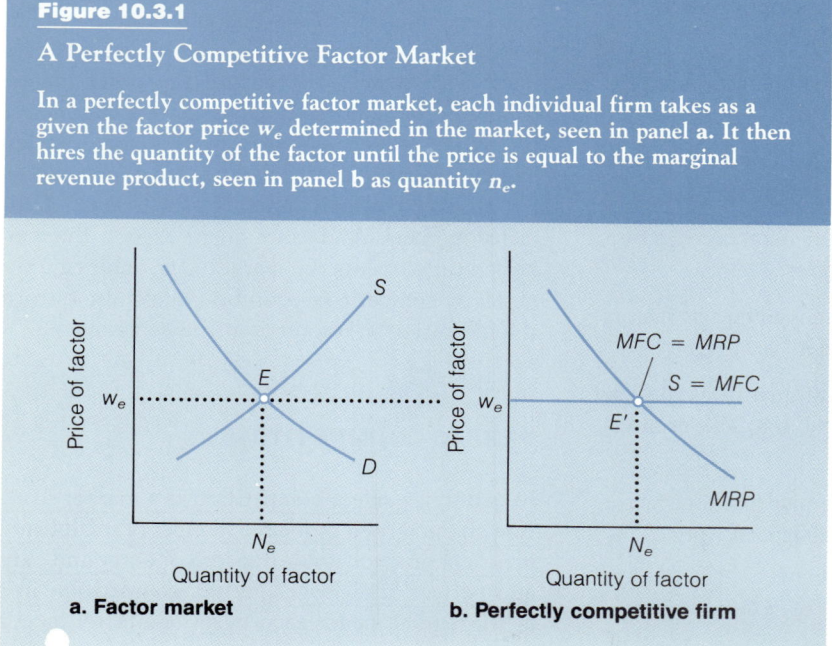

a. Factor market

b. Perfectly competitive firm

tures equate marginal revenue product with marginal factor cost rather than price.

MONOPSONY

A monopsony lies at the other end of the spectrum of factor market structures from perfect competition. A **monopsony** is a market characterized by a single buyer of a good or factor. An example of a monopsony is the company town, in which there is one major employer. If anyone in the town wants to work, they must seek employment with this firm and only with this firm. Prior to the formation of the United States Football League, the National Football League was a monopsonistic employer of professional football talent in the United States. If a college player wanted to play professional football, he had to play with the NFL.

Figure 10.3.2 illustrates the equilibrium for a monopsonistic employer. Note that the marginal revenue product curve for the factor purchased by the monopsonist, as for the perfectly competitive firm, is negatively sloped, reflecting the law of diminishing marginal returns. But the supply curve facing the firm is different from the one in Figure 10.3.1.

The supply curve for the factor in Figure 10.3.2 is the market supply. Since it is positively sloped, the marginal factor cost curve lies above the supply curve. If the monopsonistic firm hires an additional unit of the factor, it pays all units more. Thus, the marginal factor cost for the additional unit is greater than its price.

For the firm to maximize profit, it hires the factor until the marginal revenue product is equal to the marginal factor cost. As with the perfectly competitive firm, if the marginal factor cost is less than the marginal revenue product, the monopsonist can increase profit by hiring more of the factor. If marginal factor cost is greater than marginal revenue product, it can increase profit by hiring less of the factor.

In Figure 10.3.2 marginal factor cost and marginal revenue product are equal at point A, and

Figure 10.3.2

Monopsony

Since a monopsonist is the only firm hiring the factor, its factor supply curve is the market supply curve for the factor. The market supply is positively sloped, meaning the marginal factor cost is greater than the price of the factor. To maximize profit, the firm hires the factor up to the quantity that equates marginal factor cost to marginal revenue product, N_{ms}. It then pays the factor w_{ms}. A monopsonist hires less of the factor and pays a lower price than would be the case in a perfectly competitive market.

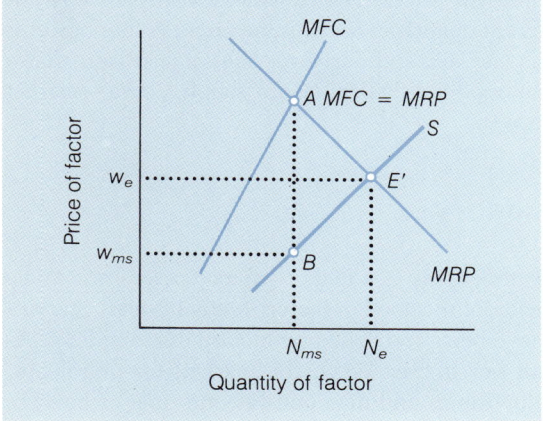

N_{ms} units of the factor are hired. However, at N_{ms}, the factor price is w_{ms}, which is less than the marginal revenue product at that quantity. Each unit of the factor is generating more revenue to the firm (marginal revenue product) than it is receiving as payment for its services (factor price). Figure 10.3.2 suggests that, contrary to popular belief, professional athletes are underpaid, since they are probably paid less than their marginal revenue product.

In short, a factor market with only one buyer hires fewer units of the factor and pays each less than is the case in perfect competition. In panel a of Figure 10.3.1 perfect competition reaches equilibrium at the intersection of the supply and demand curves. The equilibrium in Figure 10.3.2 that corresponds to a perfectly competitive outcome is point E', the intersection of the supply and marginal revenue product curves. Here, the marginal revenue product curve plays the role of the market demand curve.

The intersection of the supply and marginal revenue product curves is at a higher factor price and larger quantity than the monopsonistic equilibrium, meaning the firm hires too little of the factor and pays each less than in perfect competition. Furthermore, note that a monopsonist buyer does not generate a demand curve for the factor. Because of market power, a monopsonist can pay different prices for the same quantity, or buy different quantities at the same price. A monopsonist has no demand curve for the same reason that a monopolistic seller has no supply curve—market power.

MONOPOLY

A **monopoly** is a market characterized by a single seller of the good or factor. Many resource markets have been controlled by monopolist suppliers. As we saw in Section 9, the markets for petroleum, aluminum, and diamonds at one time or another were controlled essentially by a single resource supplier. Moreover, labor unions have continually sought to monopolize various types of skilled labor, ranging from plumbers and electricians to actors and movie directors. And although the American Medical Association (AMA) claims otherwise, it has near monopolistic control over the supply of doctors in the United States. Recall that the AMA controls admissions to medical school and that every doctor must be certified by the AMA before he or she can practice.

Figure 10.3.3 illustrates the market equilibrium when a monopolist is in charge of the factor supply. The equilibrium is no different than that found when a monopolist is the sole supplier of a consumer good or service. The monopolist equates marginal revenue from the sale of the factor to the

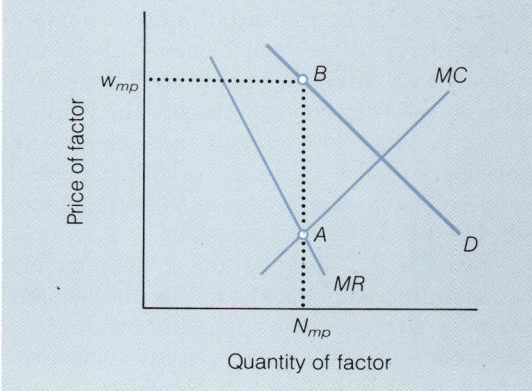

Figure 10.3.3
Monopoly

A monopoly in a factor market operates in the same way as a monopoly in an output market. It supplies the factor up to the quantity that equates marginal revenue to marginal cost, which is quantity N_{mp}. It then charges a price w_{mp}. A labor union is a good example of a monopoly supplier.

marginal cost of production; this equality is achieved at N_{mp} units of the factor. The monopolist then charges each buyer a price of w_{mp} and maximizes profit in the sale of the factor.

Keep in mind that in factor markets, as in product markets, the price charged by a monopolist is higher and the quantity produced is less than in perfect competition. Basically, everything stated about monopoly in Unit 9.2 also applies here, including the observation that the monopolist seller does not have a supply curve.

BILATERAL MONOPOLY

When a monopolistic supplier comes face to face with a monopsonistic buyer, a bilateral monopoly results. A **bilateral monopoly** is a market with one seller and one buyer. For example, if employees in a company town are unionized, a bilateral monopoly is created. Another example of a bilateral monopoly is the National Basketball Association and the National Basketball Association Players Union. In this case the union represents the sole supplier of the factor and the league represents the sole buyer of the factor. And in each of the other major professional sports (football, baseball, and hockey) the players union negotiates with the league for the services of the players. A bilateral monopoly is also approximated if a major union supplies the labor to a major manufacturing firm. For example, the United Auto Workers, as the monopolistic supplier, and General Motors, as the monopsonistic buyer, closely resemble a bilateral monopoly.

Figure 10.3.4 illustrates a bilateral monopoly. For the monopsonist the marginal factor cost curve lies above the market supply curve, as in Figure 10.3.2. For the monopolist the marginal revenue curve from the sale of the factor lies below the market demand curve, as in Figure 10.3.3. Note that the monopsonist's marginal revenue product curve assumes the role of the market demand curve for the monopolist since the monopsonist does not generate a demand curve. Likewise, the monopolist's marginal cost curve assumes the role of the market supply curve for the monopsonist since the monopolist does not generate a supply curve.

In a bilateral monopoly the buyer and seller are forced to negotiate the factor price and the

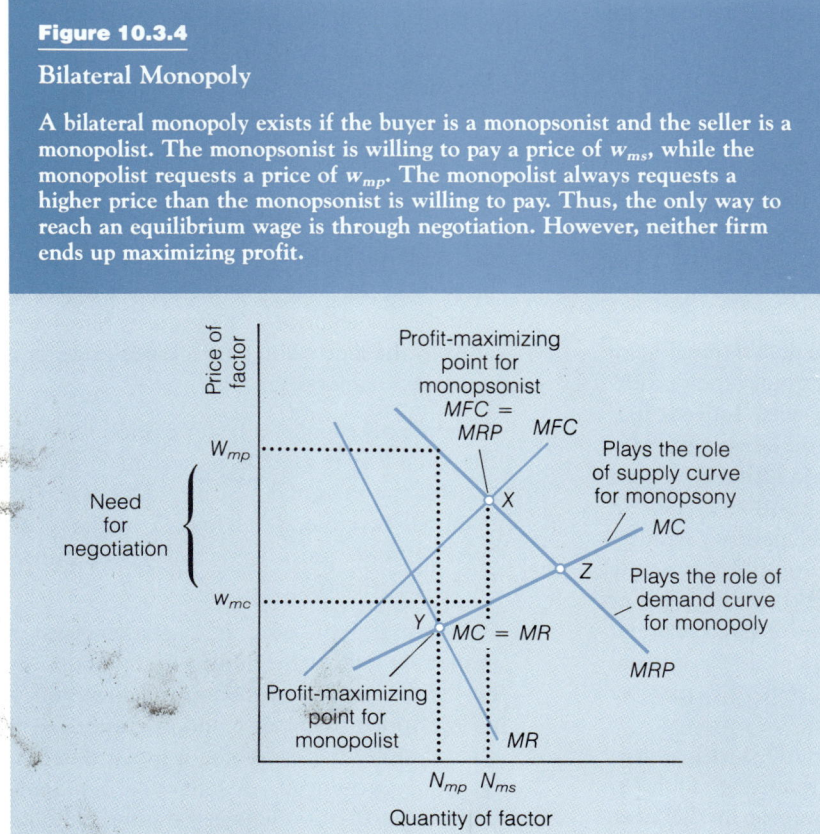

Figure 10.3.4

Bilateral Monopoly

A bilateral monopoly exists if the buyer is a monopsonist and the seller is a monopolist. The monopsonist is willing to pay a price of w_{ms}, while the monopolist requests a price of w_{mp}. The monopolist always requests a higher price than the monopsonist is willing to pay. Thus, the only way to reach an equilibrium wage is through negotiation. However, neither firm ends up maximizing profit.

quantity of the factor exchanged. The monopsonist equates the marginal factor cost to its marginal revenue product curve at intersection point X, with N_{ms} units of the factor exchanged. At N_{ms}, the monopsonist is willing to pay a factor price of w_{ms}.

But the monopolist equates marginal revenue to marginal cost, at point Y and quantity N_{mp}. At N_{mp}, the monopolist is willing to sell the factor for a price of w_{mp}. Note that the price the monopsonist is willing to pay for the factor is less than the price the monopolist wants to receive for the factor. In addition, the quantity the monopsonist is willing to buy is not the same as the quantity the monopolist is willing to sell. While the quantities the two sides of the market are willing to trade *could* be equal, the price is never the same because the monopsonist always offers a lower price than the monopolist desires.

In this case, since they do not agree on the price and may not agree on the quantity, the only avenue left is negotiation. A simple exchange of goods is not obtained by the normal forces of supply and demand. The two sides of the market have to agree on a price somewhere between w_{mp} and w_{ms} and at the same time agree on a quantity between N_{mp} and N_{ms}. Whether the final price and quantity in the market are closer to the monopolist's or the monopsonist's depends on the relative market power of each.

One conclusion that can be drawn from Figure 10.3.4 is that both sides cannot obtain their profit-maximizing point at the same time. Indeed, it is more likely that neither firm will be able to maximize profit. A second conclusion is that the quantity of the factor exchanged is less than in perfect competition. The perfectly competitive equilibrium is obtained at the intersection of the supply and demand curves, point Z. While the price of the factor resulting from negotiations in a bilateral monopoly can be less than, greater than, or equal to the price in perfect competition, the quantity exchanged is always less.

Thus, in labor union negotiations with a firm, employment is necessarily less than it would be in perfect competition. And as we see in the next unit, a labor union's primary objective of increasing the wages of employees does not necessarily occur in a bilateral monopoly. Often, a union is formed in response to a monopsonistic factor market, such as shown in Figure 10.3.2. In this case the union is able to raise wages above the monopsonistic situation through negotiations in bilateral monopoly. If the union is as strong as the monopsonistic employer, then the wage might be increased up to the perfectly competitive level.

IN SUMMARY

Factor Market Equilibrium

- There are four basic structures for factor markets: perfect competition, monopsony, monopoly, and bilateral monopoly. In perfect competition the factor supply curve to a firm is perfectly elastic at the market price. The firm hires enough units of the factor to equate the marginal factor cost (market price) with the marginal revenue product.

- With monopsony the firm also hires enough units to equate the marginal factor cost to the marginal revenue product. However, for a monopsony the marginal factor cost is greater than the market price. A monopsony hires fewer units of the factor and pays a lower price than in perfect competition.

- A monopoly supplies a factor of production in the same way it supplies a consumer good. It equates the marginal cost of production with marginal revenue. It charges a higher price and sells fewer units of the factor than in perfect competition.

- A bilateral monopoly is a market with a monopoly selling the factor and a monopsony buying the factor. The monopsony always offers a lower price than the monopoly wants. It is also possible that each side wants a different quantity exchanged. A bilateral monopoly requires negotiation between the two sides, as a single equilibrum price and quantity is not achieved. Both sides are not able to maximize profit at the same time. While the negotiated price can be less than, greater than, or equal to the perfectly competitive price, the quantity exchanged is always less than in perfect competition.

QUESTIONS FOR STUDY AND ANALYSIS

1. What is the difference between a monopsonist and a monopolist? Explain.

2. How is a bilateral monopoly related to monopoly and monopsony? What is the profit-maximizing level of exchange in a bilateral monopoly? Why is it necessary for the two sides of a bilateral monopoly to negotiate?

3. Suppose a firm has the following marginal revenue product schedule:

Labor	1	2	3	4	5	6	7	8	9
MRP	$7	6	5	4	3	2	1	0	0

If the firm is perfectly competitive, and the market price for labor is $6, how much labor is hired?

4. Suppose the firm in question 3 is a monopsonist with the following market supply schedule:

Labor	1	2	3	4	5	6	7	8	9
Price	$1	2	3	4	5	6	7	8	9
MFC	$1	3	5	7	9	11	13	15	17

a. How much labor does the firm hire if it seeks to maximize profit?
b. What price is the monopsonist in question 4a willing to pay labor?

5. Explain why United Auto Workers and General Motors fit the model of a bilateral monopoly.

6. Discuss whether the markets for each of the following factors is more likely to have perfect competition or be a monopoly, a monopsony, or a bilateral monopoly.
   a. Reporters in a city with only one newspaper
   b. Fast food workers in a large city
   c. A doctor in a small town
   d. Land that is the proposed site of a new shopping center
   e. A high first-round draft choice in any professional sport
   f. Ceramic tiles used as a heat shield for the space shuttle

REVIEW GLOSSARY

bilateral monopoly A market with one seller and one buyer. The two sides of a bilateral monopoly must negotiate the price and quantity exchanged. The monopsonist offers a lower price than the monopolist wants. The quantities could be equal but need not be. Both sides are not able to maximize profit at the same time. The quantity exchanged is always less than in perfect competition.

monopoly A market that is characterized by a single seller of the good or factor. The demand curve facing a monopolistic firm is the market demand for the factor. The monopolist maximizes profit by equating marginal cost to marginal revenue. A monopolist sells fewer units of the factor and charges a higher price than is the case in perfect competition.

monopsony A market that is characterized by a single buyer of the good or factor. The supply curve facing a monopsonistic firm is the market supply for the factor. A monopsonist maximizes profit by equating marginal factor cost to marginal revenue product. A monopsonist hires fewer units of the factor and pays a lower price than is the case in perfect competition.

perfect competition A market structure characterized by a large number of small firms, identical products sold by all firms, freedom of entry and exit into the industry, and perfect knowledge of prices and technology. The most important feature of perfect competition for factor markets is that each firm faces a perfectly elastic supply curve for the factor. In this case a perfectly competitive firm hires enough of the factor to equate the market price to the marginal revenue product.

UNIT 10.4

The Effect of Unions on the Labor Market

In this unit we focus on a specific application of labor markets by analyzing the role of labor unions. A **labor union** is an organization of workers formed to negotiate with employers over wages, working conditions, and fringe benefits. Labor unions are designed to obtain market power in the labor market through the control of the supply of labor. Labor unions originated in the 1700s and 1800s in response to both dismal, and often dangerous, working conditions and low wages. Today, labor unions have limited membership, but they remain an important social institution and a viable force in economic and political activity. In this unit we look at the role labor unions play in the U.S. economy and see how they affect the labor market.

We begin by distinguishing between craft and industrial unions and assessing the extent of union membership in the United States. We then discuss the types of activities typically undertaken by labor unions, most notably collective bargaining and strikes. Using this information as a framework, we briefly review the history of the development of labor unions in the United States. And finally, we analyze the four basic ways unions can affect a labor market: through a craft union, through an industrial union, by stimulating demand, and by affecting a nonunion labor market.

TYPES OF LABOR UNIONS

Two types of labor unions have evolved over the past two hundred years, craft unions and industrial unions. A **craft union** is a labor union composed of workers in the same occupation. For example, the carpenters, meat cutters, and plumbers unions represent three of the largest craft unions in the United States. Each union is comprised of workers in the same occupation, regardless of the type of industry involved or the product produced. A member of the carpenters union could be employed in the construction of a house in Detroit or the production of furniture in Atlanta.

An **industrial union** is a labor union composed of workers in the same industry. Each union is centered around a particular industry and type of product, regardless of the occupations involved. Several notable examples of industrial unions are the United Auto Workers, the Steelworkers, and the International Ladies Garment Workers. The United Auto Workers union contains workers in every facet of automobile production, though most industrial unions tend to contain workers in unskilled and semiskilled occupations.

The umbrella organization of most unions in the United States, the AFL-CIO, contains both craft and industrial unions. In fact, the American Federation of Labor (AFL) began as a collection of craft unions, and the Congress of Industrial Organizations (CIO) began as a collection of industrial unions.

UNION MEMBERSHIP IN THE UNITED STATES

Currently, about 20 percent of the U.S. civilian labor force belongs to one union or another. Figure 10.4.1 depicts the trend in total union membership since 1900. Note that until the 1930s, generally less than 10 percent of the civilian labor force belonged to labor unions in large part because of government, judicial, and business hostility directed toward labor unions. However, in the 1930s the dramatic increase in union membership indicated a change in attitude. From the mid-1940s to the present, union membership has averaged between 20 and 25 percent of the labor force, although membership in recent years has declined.

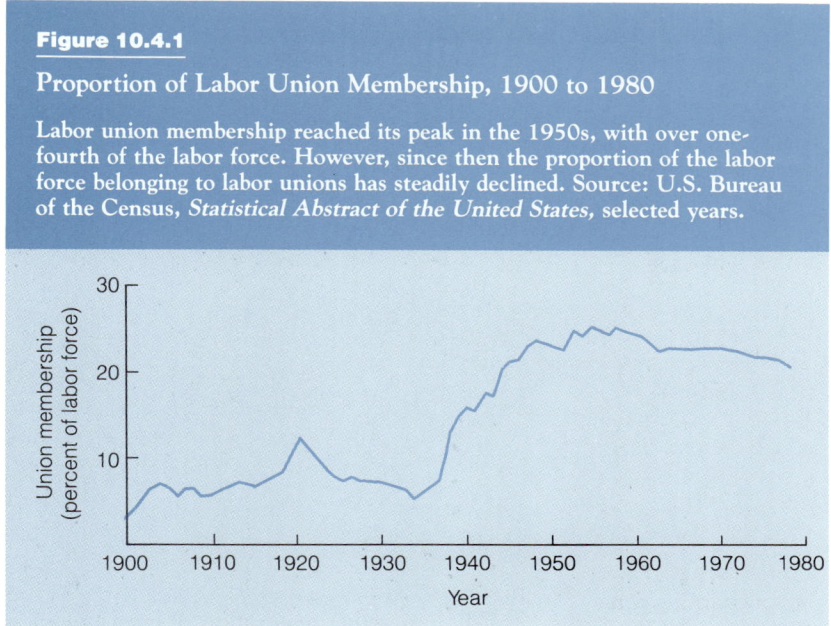

Figure 10.4.1

Proportion of Labor Union Membership, 1900 to 1980

Labor union membership reached its peak in the 1950s, with over one-fourth of the labor force. However, since then the proportion of the labor force belonging to labor unions has steadily declined. Source: U.S. Bureau of the Census, *Statistical Abstract of the United States*, selected years.

Most goods produced in the United States are affected in one way or another by labor unions. Table 10.4.1 lists the twenty-five largest unions in the United States. At the top of this list is the Teamsters Union, which contains most of the nation's truck drivers, followed by teachers, autoworkers, steelworkers, carpenters, retail clerks, clothing and textile workers, communication workers, plumbers, musicians, and so on. Clearly, unions are involved in the production of many different goods and services.

ROLE OF LABOR UNIONS IN THE LABOR MARKET

Labor unions are generally concerned with three objectives: higher wages, better working conditions, and job security. Labor unions pursue these objectives through a variety of avenues, particularly collective bargaining and strikes. However, unions also exert a great deal of effort maintaining or increasing union membership.

Collective Bargaining

The most important function of a labor union is to allow every member in the organization to negotiate with employers as a group. **Collective bargaining** is the negotiation between employers and employees to develop a contract or agreement applicable to all workers in an industry or occupation. This type of negotiation can deal with all aspects of labor-management relations, including wages, fringe benefits, vacations, grievance procedures, promotion and layoff procedures, and even the time allowed for the daily necessities. Sometimes labor and management cannot reach an agreement on the various conditions of employment. In order to prevent a strike, labor and man-

Table 10.4.1

Membership in Labor Unions, 1968 to 1980 (in thousands)

Even though labor union employment constitutes only about 20 percent of the labor force, unions are involved in almost every phase of the economy's production. The industries with unions range from transportation (Teamsters) to teaching (National Education Association) to musicians.

Rank	Union	1968	1972	1976	1980
1	Teamsters	1755	1855	1889	1891
2	National Education Association	NA	1166	1887	1684
3	Automobile workers	1473	1394	1358	1357
4	Food and commercial workers	1052	1162	1209	1300
5	Steelworkers	1352	1400	1300	1238
6	State and county employees	364	529	750	1098
7	Electrical workers	897	957	924	1048
8	Carpenters	793	820	820	784
9	Machinists	903	758	917	754
10	Service employees	389	484	575	650
11	Laborers	553	600	627	608
12	Communications workers	357	443	483	551
13	Teachers	165	249	446	551
14	Clothing and textile workers	569	539	502	455
15	Engineers, operating	350	402	420	423
16	Hotel and restaurant workers	459	458	432	400
17	Plumbers	297	228	228	352
18	Garment, ladies, workers	455	428	365	323
19	Musicians	283	315	330	299
20	Paperworkers	328	389	300	275
21	Government employees	295	293	260	255
22	Postal workers	166	239	252	251
23	Mine workers	NA	213	277	245
24	Electrical workers	324	290	238	233
25	Letter Carriers	20	220	227	230

Source: U.S. Bureau of the Census, *Statistical Abstract of the United States*, 1982–83.
NA—not available.

agement have two options, mediation and arbitration.

Mediation If a collective bargaining agreement cannot be reached between labor and management, the first alternative is usually mediation. **Mediation** is the intervention of a third party (usually the government) in the collective bargaining process, offering nonbinding guidance and solutions. A mediator tries to find areas of agreement and compromise between labor and management, but nothing the mediator does is binding on either party. In essence, this form of intervention represents simply a helping hand. Either labor or management, or even the government, can call in the third party mediator if collective bargaining talks are not working.

Arbitration A second alternative to a breakdown in collective bargaining is arbitration. **Arbitration** is the intervention of a third party in the collective bargaining process, making legally binding and enforceable judgments. An arbitrator acts much like a judge, and the resulting decisions must be obeyed by both labor and management. While arbitration is sometimes used to reach a collective bargaining agreement, it is most frequently applied in the interpretation of an existing agreement. If there are questions by either labor or management concerning promotions, layoffs, wages, or any other provisions of an existing agreement, an arbitrator is often called in to make a settlement.

Strikes

If collective bargaining fails to produce an agreement between labor and management, in spite of mediation and arbitration, a labor union might resort to a strike. A **strike** is an agreement between workers or members of a labor union to temporarily stop working. Apart from preventing a firm from producing output, the purpose of a strike is to get the employer's attention. Strikes have had varying degrees of success throughout the history of labor unions. Strikes were primarily responsible for obtaining labor union recognition in the early 1800s, and were thus labor's most effective weapon. However, in more recent times, the strike by air traffic controllers in the early 1980s was crushed when all of the striking air traffic controllers were fired by the government.

The firm has its own version of the strike, the lockout. A **lockout** occurs when management refuses to admit workers to their jobs. Quite literally, the firm locks the door. Lockouts have been used by management at various times to prevent a threatened strike by labor.

Means of Maintaining Membership

Labor unions are, and always have been, concerned about union membership. A labor union wants to represent all workers, either in an occupation or industry, because it has bargaining power only if it has control of the supply of labor. Ideally, a labor union would like to be a monopolist in the labor market. Labor unions have used a variety of methods to directly control the supply of labor in an occupation or industry.

One of the earliest methods of control was the closed shop. A **closed shop** exists when a firm is allowed to hire only union members, giving a union complete control over the supply of labor to any firm. However, closed shops were declared illegal by the Taft-Hartley Act (1947). An alternative to the closed shop is the union shop. A **union shop** exists when a firm is free to hire union or nonunion workers, with the stipulation that the worker must join the union once hired. While union shops are legal in many states, some states have right-to-work laws. A **right-to-work law** does not allow any type of compulsory union membership to be written into a collective bargaining agreement. Right-to-work laws effectively outlaw union shops. Under right-to-work laws a firm must have an **open shop**, which exists when employment is unrelated to union membership.

A BRIEF HISTORY OF LABOR UNIONS IN THE UNITED STATES

Labor unions have had a turbulent and often bloody history in the United States. The first milestone in U.S. labor history occurred in 1799, only twenty-three years after the Declaration of Independence was written and Adam Smith's *Wealth of Nations* was published, when the first collective bargaining, between Philadelphia shoemakers and their employers, took place. While craft unions existed before this time, there had been no collective bargaining between workers and management.

In the early days of labor-management negotiations, or what is more aptly termed labor-management conflicts, unions were held in low regard. In fact, unions were often accused, and found guilty, of restraint of trade when they tried to collectively raise workers' wages. Simply being a member of a labor union, without going on strike or taking any other actions, was sufficient cause to be found guilty of conspiring to restrain trade. However, this changed slightly with the second milestone in U.S. labor history, in 1842.

Commonwealth v. Hunt In the case of Commonwealth v. Hunt, the Massachusetts Supreme Court in 1842, declared that unions were not illegal organizations, a reversal of the existing interpretation of the laws. This meant a worker could join a labor union without fear of being thrown in jail. However, the court also said that while unions were legal, the activities of a union were not necessarily legal, which was the equivalent of making it legal to own a gun, but not to shoot anyone. Basically, any activity that disrupted the flow of goods, including strikes, carried the risk of legal action against its perpetrator.

Printers Union In 1852 the first permanent national craft union was formed by printers. Before 1852 most labor unions were autonomous craft unions centered in one city or another. For example, the shoemakers union in Philadelphia was unconnected to the shoemakers union in Boston. But the formation of the national printers union in 1852 was the first of many national unions formed over the following two decades. Clearly, a national union had much more market power than a local union, because it controlled more of the labor in a particular occupation.

American Federation of Labor The trend toward the formation of national unions led to the organization of the American Federation of Labor (AFL) in 1886. The AFL began as a voluntary association of national craft unions. While other attempts were made to establish an umbrella organization for labor, such as the Knights of Labor, only the AFL has managed to survive until today. The primary reason cited for its continued existence is its philosophy of working within the existing structure of the economy rather than trying to change the fundamental underlying institutions, as many of the other umbrella organizations did.

Sherman Act In 1890 the Sherman Act was passed by Congress. This act was designed to prevent abuses of market power by business firms and monopolies, as discussed in Unit 9.6. However, management and the courts also applied the Sherman Act to labor unions. While the Sherman Act was not intended to be used against unions, it was vaguely written and represented a serious setback for labor unions around the turn of the century.

Clayton Act It wasn't until 1914 that the Clayton Act was passed to rectify this situation by clarifying the vagueness of the Sherman Act. While the Clayton Act dealt primarily with monopolistic practices of firms, it did contain a section that specifically excluded labor unions from antitrust action.

The Clayton Act also made it difficult to use injunctions in labor disputes. An **injunction** is a court order requiring a person, union, or company to refrain from a particular activity. The intent of an injunction in everyday use is to prevent an action by one person that might harm another person.

However, the courts gave a generous interpretation to the term *detrimental harm*. According to the courts a firm was "detrimentally harmed" if it was prevented from producing and selling its product as a result of strikes or other labor union activities. Indeed, before the Clayton Act was passed, management found it very easy to obtain legal injunctions restricting the activities of unions. The courts and judges, to put it simply, were primarily on the side of management until the 1930s. The Clayton Act made it legal to issue an injunction only to prevent irreparable property damage, not merely to halt a loss of production.

United Mine Workers Another major milestone was the formation of the United Mine Workers Union, one of the first industrial unions, in 1890. Up to this time all *national* unions were craft unions. Craft unions could control the supply of labor in an occupation with relative ease, since all of its members had a certain level of skill or expertise. It was difficult to replace a shoemaker on strike, because few potential replacements had the necessary skills. However, industrial workers were primarily unskilled laborers, and if they went on strike, another unskilled worker could easily be found as a replacement. Thus, industrial unions were more difficult to form than craft unions. Even though other industries, such as the garment and brewery industries, became unionized after the mine workers, this was the exception rather than the rule for several decades.

Norris-LaGuardia Act In 1932 the Norris-LaGuardia Act was passed, foreshadowing the improved climate for labor under the Roosevelt administration. The Norris-LaGuardia Act improved on the Clayton Act by making it more difficult to use injunctions against labor unions. In addition, the Norris-LaGuardia Act outlawed what were called yellow-dog contracts. A **yellow-dog contract was an agreement signed by workers before they were hired, saying they would not join a union.** Since workers could not legally join a union, yellow-dog contracts made it extremely difficult for unions to organize the employees of a company.

National Industrial Recovery Act A year later, in 1933, the National Industrial Recovery Act (NIRA) was passed by the Roosevelt administration. This act specifically allowed workers to organize and bargain collectively without employer interference. While the act was declared unconstitutional in 1935, it gave a tremendous boost to labor unions, and helped increase membership.

National Labor Relations Act In response to the NIRA being declared unconstitutional, the National Labor Relations Act (NLRA) was passed in 1935 to strengthen and extend the labor aspects of the NIRA. In particular, the NLRA outlawed such unfair labor practices by employers as refusing to negotiate with a union representing a majority of the workers. It also set up the National Labor Relations Board to oversee labor activities.

Congress of Industrial Organizations In 1938 several industrial unions that were expelled from the AFL formed the Congress of Industrial Organizations (CIO). At this time industrial unions and craft unions were divided over politics, philosophy, and even age differences between members. The differences stemmed mainly from the fact that craft unions contained skilled workers, while industrial unions contained unskilled workers. This split between the AFL and CIO lasted for nearly twenty years. After its split from the AFL, the CIO made a strong push to unionize many industries that had no unions. Most notable were the automobile, steel, and rubber industries, which helped establish the CIO as a major labor organization.

Taft-Hartley Act During the Roosevelt administration, from 1933 to 1945, unions were regarded in a positive light. Not only did Congress enact favorable legislation, but unions also benefited from rulings in a variety of court cases. However, in 1947 the tide changed with the passage of the Taft-Hartley Act. Many people felt that unions had become too powerful during the 1930s and early 1940s, and the Taft-Hartley Act was passed to limit some of this power. In particular, it established provisions outlawing unfair labor practices by *labor*, to counterbalance earlier legislation outlawing unfair labor practices by *firms*. This act also set up provisions to decertify a union if workers no longer wanted it to represent them. In addition, the act allowed individual states to pass right-to-work laws, effectively enabling states to outlaw union shops, which were commonly used at that time to increase union membership.

The AFL-CIO Merger The final milestone in U.S. labor history was the merger of the AFL and CIO in 1955. After nearly two decades, many of the differences that split the CIO from the AFL no longer existed. The distinctions between craft and industrial unions were not as clear in 1955 as they had been in the 1930s. The AFL-CIO as it now stands is the umbrella organization for most unions in the United States.

CRAFT UNIONS

How can labor unions use their market power to affect the labor market? Let's first see how craft unions affect the labor market. The key characteristic of a craft union is its ability to control the overall supply of labor in a particular occupation. Typically, every member in a craft union agrees to offer less labor at the existing price, or the same labor at a higher price.

In essence, the craft union can shift the supply curve leftward from S to S', as illustrated in Figure 10.4.2. If the perfectly competitive market equilibrium is at point E, the labor market equilibrium resulting from the entry of a craft union is point E'. The wage rate increases from w_e to w_{cu}, and the quantity of labor employed decreases from N_e to N_{cu}.

Keep in mind that this form of control by a craft union is effective only if the demand curve is inelastic. In that case the percentage increase in

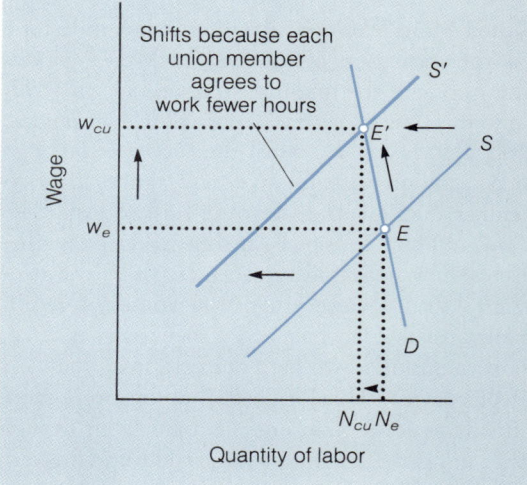

Figure 10.4.2

Craft Unions

Craft unions control wages and the labor market by controlling the supply of workers. Since there are few substitutes for the specialized craft workers, unions can raise wages and reduce the quantity supplied by each member. If the demand for this type of labor is inelastic, then the total income received by each member increases. This type of union control is seen as a shift in the supply curve from S to S'.

the wage rate is greater than the percentage decline in the number of hours worked, and the total wages received by craft union members increase. If each member of the union decreases the amount of hours supplied equally, then each receives a higher total income. But if the demand curve is elastic, then the total amount of wages falls, and the members of the union are actually worse off.

The demand curve is more inelastic if the skills of the craft union members are rather unique, with few close substitutes, for examples plumbers, carpenters, and musicians. Each of these occupations is the basis for a rather large, and effective union. If all plumbers decide to work half as many hours, at three times the previous wage, the best alternative is do-it-yourself home repairs, which for most people is an imperfect substitute.

INDUSTRIAL UNIONS

Industrial unions wield a different type of power in the labor market than craft unions. Recall that industrial unions contain unskilled and semiskilled members, meaning many close substitutes exist for the worker who tightens lugbolts on cars in a General Motors plant. Compared to a musician, the amount of skill required by an assembly line worker is relatively low. Therefore, an industrial union cannot control the supply of labor in an industry in the same way a craft union controls the supply of labor in an occupation.

An industrial union seeks to set a minimum wage for the industry, as illustrated in Figure 10.4.3. Once again, the perfectly competitive equilibrium in the labor market is at point E, with the wage w_e and employment N_e. However, through their control of the labor market, which is based on their membership, an industrial union can establish a minimum wage at w_{iu}. The members of the union, by means of strikes and collective bargaining, simply agree not to work at any wage below w_{iu}.

Note the effect this has on the labor supply curve. The industry can hire any quantity of labor it wants at w_{iu}, until it hires N_{nu}. In other words, the supply curve of labor is perfectly elastic at the minimum union wage over this range of labor. However, beyond N_{nu}, at point F, the supply curve takes on its positive slope.

The labor market equilibrium based on this supply curve is at point E', the market wage is the union minimum, w_{iu}, and the quantity of labor hired is N_{iu}. Here, the wage is higher and the quantity of employment is less, the same result obtained with craft unions in Figure 10.4.2. However, an important difference is that each member of the craft union remains employed but simply works fewer

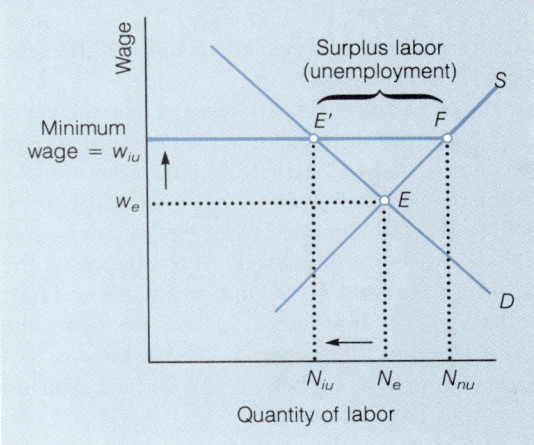

Figure 10.4.3

Industrial Unions

Industrial unions are not able to control the supply of labor as easily as a craft union. Therefore, they try to establish a minimum wage, rather than shifting the supply curve. As with any minimum wage, the wage of w_{iu} causes a surplus in this market equal to the distance from E' to F.

hours, whereas with industrial unions, some workers are unemployed. At the wage w_{iu}, a surplus of labor exists because of the unskilled nature of industrial union jobs. At the higher wage, nonunion workers are willing to switch from another industry to this one, which is easy to do since little training or skill is required. As a result, unemployment occurs in the labor market for industrial workers.

STIMULATING DEMAND

In both preceding cases unions have generated higher wages, but at the expense of employment. For the craft unions this is acceptable as long as each member receives an increase in total income. However, the minimum wage established by an industrial union creates unemployment in the labor market. An alternative method of increasing the wage would certainly be more desirable for both types of unions. If unions can generate an increase in the demand for the labor, they reap the benefits of both higher wages *and* greater employment.

Figure 10.4.4 illustrates the labor market if the demand for labor shifts rightward. Once again, the original equilibrium is at point E and the new equilibrium is at point E'. The wage increases from w_e to w_o, and the quantity of labor employed increases from N_e to N_o.

How might the union cause the demand curve to shift rightward? Recall that the demand for labor is a derived demand. Anything causing an increase in the demand for the product produced by members of the labor union causes the demand curve for labor to shift from D to D'. For this reason the autoworkers union favors import quotas or tariffs on foreign cars. If fewer foreign cars are sold in the United States, the demand for domestic cars is increased, and along with it the derived demand for autoworkers.

However, there are other means of shifting the demand curve from D to D'. One is an improvement in technology. Better technology increases the marginal product, marginal revenue product, and thus the demand for labor. Likewise, an increase in the quantity of capital, brought about by relaxing the law of diminishing returns, can also increase the marginal product of labor.

Another means of increasing the demand for labor is often referred to as featherbedding. **Featherbedding** is the practice of artificially increasing the number of workers employed. Featherbedding occurs if a union requires a certain number of workers on a job even though the job can be completed with fewer workers. For example, the musicians union might require a certain number of musicians in an orchestra, even though it would sound the same with one less trumpet player. Featherbedding causes the demand curve for labor to artificially shift from D to D'.

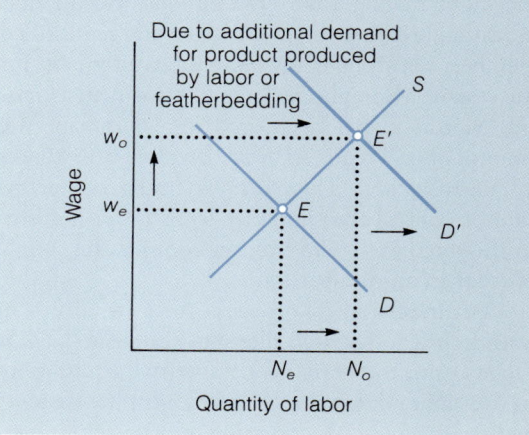

Figure 10.4.4

Stimulating Demand

Unions can have the best of both worlds, higher wages and higher employment, if the demand for labor shifts rightward. Such a shift is caused by an increase in the demand for the product. Unions can also try to increase labor demand through featherbedding.

HOW A UNION AFFECTS A NONUNION LABOR MARKET

The existence of a labor union in one market can also affect a labor market without a union, as Figure 10.4.5 illustrates. Panel a depicts a unionized labor market, in which the union causes a higher wage and a lower employment than is the case in perfect competition. With no union in the market in panel a, the equilibrium wage in both panels is the same; w_e equals w_o. However, if the union establishes a minimum wage at w_u, unemployment is created in the unionized market. What happens to the unemployed workers? They leave the market in panel a and enter the market in panel b, causing the supply curve in panel b to shift from S_{nu} to S_{nu}'. The rightward shift of the supply curve in turn causes the wage in the nonunionized labor market to fall from w_o to w_{nu}.

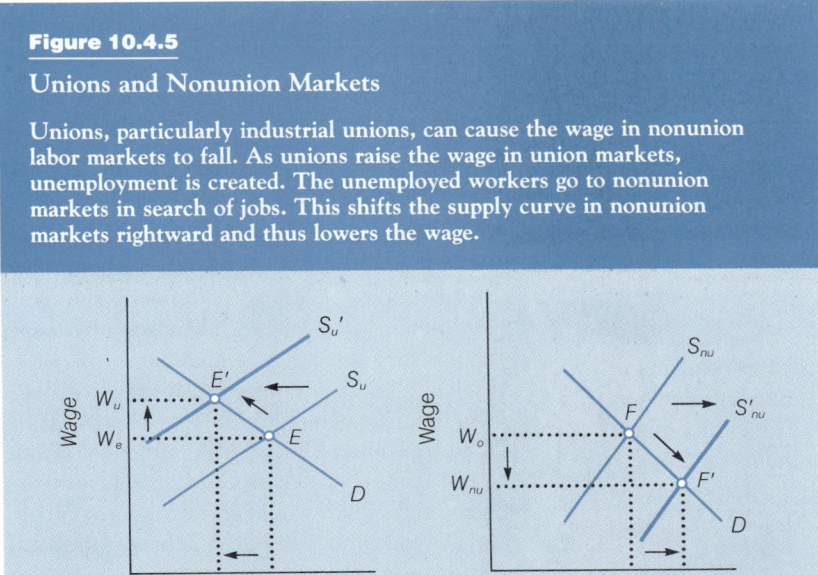

Figure 10.4.5

Unions and Nonunion Markets

Unions, particularly industrial unions, can cause the wage in nonunion labor markets to fall. As unions raise the wage in union markets, unemployment is created. The unemployed workers go to nonunion markets in search of jobs. This shifts the supply curve in nonunion markets rightward and thus lowers the wage.

a. Union labor market

b. Nonunion labor market

IN SUMMARY

The Effect of Unions on the Labor Market

- A labor union is an organization of workers that tries to improve its members' economic and working conditions. The two basic types of unions are craft unions, containing workers in the same occupation, and industrial unions, containing workers in the same industry. While union membership has fluctuated, it is currently about 20 percent of the labor force.

- One important function of a labor union is collective bargaining with employers. If collective bargaining fails, labor and management might resort to mediation, where a third party helps to reach a nonbinding agreement, or arbitration, in which the third party imposes a legally binding agreement. If this process fails to produce an agreement, then a union may go on strike. Sometimes management uses a lockout to prevent a threatened strike.

- Labor unions have tried various means of maintaining membership, including closed shops and union shops. However, in states with right-to-work laws, only open shops are allowed.

- From the first recorded collective bargaining agreement in 1799 to the Roosevelt administration in the 1930s, labor unions fought an uphill battle against employers. However, beginning in 1932 with the Norris-LaGuardia Act, unions were acknowledged as legitimate representatives of labor by the government. This lasted until the Taft-Hartley Act, limiting the power of unions, was passed in 1947.

- Craft unions affect the labor market by restricting the supply of labor. The rightward shift in the supply curve causes the wage to increase and the quantity of labor employed to fall. Industrial unions affect the labor market by establishing a minimum wage, which increases the wage of those employed but causes unemployment in the labor market. With craft unions the decrease in employment can be spread over all members, but industrial unions generally cause the unemployment burden to fall on a few.

- Labor unions can have a higher wage, and prevent unemployment, by shifting the demand curve for labor to the right. This shift increases employment and the wage. The shift is made possible by increasing the demand for the product using the labor, improving technology, adding more capital, or featherbedding.

- The existence of a union in one market can decrease the wage in a nonunionized market. The unemployment created in a unionized market goes to the nonunionized market, shifting the supply curve rightward, and decreasing the wage.

QUESTIONS FOR STUDY AND ANALYSIS

1. Explain which actions/policies the Postal Workers Union is more likely to favor and why.
   a. Increase in the price of postage stamps
   b. Increased use of United Parcel Service
   c. A proposal to reduce the number of hours each postal employee works
   d. A minimum wage for postal employees

2. The following news item appeared in a recent issue of *Business Week*:

   Only a year ago, just before the breakup of American Telephone & Telegraph Co., the Communications Workers of America waged a bitter strike against the Bell System. Now the union may spend as much as $4 million to help market AT&T's long-distance service. (Source: "The Communications Workers Are Selling AT&T's Line," *Business Week* [13 August 1984]: 61.)

   Explain why the Communications Workers union had this turnaround after AT&T became more competitive in the sale of its long-distance services.

3. The American Medical Association steadfastly denies that it is in any way a labor union. However, the AMA sets admission standards for medical schools and licenses physicians before they can practice medicine.
   a. If the AMA is considered a union, explain whether it operates more like a craft or an industrial union. If the AMA wanted to become a full-fledged union, what essential feature of physicians' labor would allow them to do this?
   b. Do you think the AMA achieves the same results as a union? How and why?

4. Why do you think the percentage of the labor force that is unionized has declined in recent times? Explain.

5. Compare the climate for labor unions in the United States before 1933 with that from 1933 to 1947. What do you think the climate is like for unions today?

6. Since the 1970s labor unions have begun to organize workers in traditionally nonunion occupations and industries. Schoolteachers, nurses, police, university professors, and air traffic controllers are a few examples. And when negotiations break down, the unions threaten to go on strike as they would in the automobile industry. However, many of these newly unionized areas provide public services that people consider essential. People are not adversely affected if they have to wait an extra month to buy an automobile. But if fire fighters are on strike when a house catches fire, the results are catastrophic. For this reason most federal, state, and local governments have outlawed strikes by public employees. This is why the federal government fired the air traffic

controllers when they went on strike in the early 1980s.

a. While strikes are the most effective tool of unions in negotiations, discuss whether or not you think strikes are appropriate when labor provides an essential service, such as police protection.

b. If strikes are illegal for public employees, what alternative negotiation technique should unions use? Why?

c. Should federal, state, and local governments be legally forced to negotiate with unions? What role should a third party arbitrator or mediator play in these negotiations?

REVIEW GLOSSARY

arbitration The intervention of a third party in the collective bargaining process, making legally binding and enforceable judgments.

closed shop A firm that is allowed to hire only union members.

collective bargaining The negotiation between employers and employees to develop a contract or agreement applicable to all workers in an industry or occupation. Collective bargaining is the most important function of a labor union.

craft union A labor union composed of workers in the same occupation.

featherbedding The practice of artificially increasing the number of workers employed.

industrial union A labor union composed of workers in the same industry.

injunction A court order requiring a person, union, or company to refrain from a particular activity.

labor union An organization of workers formed to negotiate with employers over wages, working conditions, and fringe benefits.

lockout The refusal of management to admit workers to their jobs.

mediation The intervention of a third party in the collective bargaining process, offering nonbinding guidance and solutions.

open shop A firm that is free to hire union or nonunion workers, with no stipulation of union membership.

right-to-work laws A law that does not allow any type of mandatory union membership to be written into a collective bargaining agreement.

strike An agreement between workers or members of a labor union to temporarily stop working.

union shop A firm that is free to hire union or nonunion workers, with the stipulation that the worker must join the union once hired.

yellow-dog contract An agreement signed by workers before they are hired, saying they will not join a union.

SECTION INQUIRY

Comparable Worth

Today women account for about 44 percent of the U.S. economy's labor force. However, on average women receive only about 60 percent of the wage received by men. There are several potential reasons for this wage differential. Female workers may have lower skill or educational levels that prevent them from obtaining higher-paying jobs. In addition, female workers take more temporary, and thus lower-paying, jobs as they enter and leave the labor force in the process of raising children or assuming other family responsibilities. Moreover, female workers may be secondary wage earners, with the wage of the male worker the primary source of income for the family. However, the lower wage received by women may also be due to discrimination.

According to Title VII of the Civil Rights Act, discrimination against female workers based on sex is illegal. This basically means that it is illegal to pay female workers a lower wage than male workers for doing the same job. A female automobile mechanic should receive the same wage as a male mechanic. In addition, some people argue that discrimination can also occur between comparable jobs in different occupations. That is, some jobs with *comparable worth* do not have comparable pay. Proponents of the concept of comparable worth argue that discrimination is possible because some occupations, such as nurse, secretary, receptionist, and waiter, are dominated by women. While all workers in each occupation receive similar wages, these wages are lower than occupations dominated by men, even though both occupations require the same amount of skill, effort, and responsibilities.

Implementing the concept of comparable worth would entail that jobs be rated according to their worth. Wages paid for each job would then be based on the rating points received in the evaluation. Those jobs with equal ratings, and thus comparable worth, would receive equal pay.

QUESTIONS FOR DISCUSSION

1. How does the term *comparable worth* relate to marginal revenue product? Does the fact that two occupations require equal effort, ability, and responsibilities necessarily mean the marginal product is equal? Explain.

2. What role does the supply of labor play in the wage received by a worker in a particular occupation? How does the supply of labor enter into the computation of comparative worth? Explain.

3. What role does labor mobility (or immobility) play in the wage differentials between male- and female-dominated occupations? If immobility between occupations is a problem, how much immobility would you say is voluntary and how much involuntary (due to discrimination)?

4. Many of the higher-paid male-dominated occupations (truck drivers and warehouse workers, for example) are unionized, while many of the lower-paid female-dominated occupations (for instance, nurse and secretary) are not. Explain the role market power might play in the wage differentials between male and female occupations.

SECTION 11

The Distribution of Factor Incomes

In the last section we examined how the factors of production are exchanged through the factor markets. In this section we concentrate on the payments received by the factors and their resulting factor income. In particular, we discuss the functional distribution of factor income to the four factors of production in the form of wages, interest, rent, and profit. We also examine the personal distribution of income to individuals in the economy.

Income is not distributed equally to all members of an economy. Workers who are more productive receive higher wages. And entrepreneurs who take the most risks and produce the goods most desired by consumers receive the highest profits. Differential factor payments attract the most productive factors to the goods and services demanded most by consumers, which makes the economy more efficient and increases the well-being of society. However, the unequal distribution of income has both advantages and disadvantages. For example, the lack of income restricts the opportunities available. Moreover, the lack of productive ability on the part of the mentally or physically disabled does not mean they deserve no income. In addition, if most of the income is distributed to the rich, then the poor are likely to be politically rebellious.

Unit 11.1, Wages, looks at the factor payments made to labor. Because labor constitutes the largest contributor to the production of goods and services, wages are an important component of factor income. In this light we investigate the nature and causes of wage differentials to see why all labor is not paid the same.

Unit 11.2, Interest, examines the factor payments made to capital. In this unit we distinguish between physical and financial capital. And we also discuss how physical and financial capital are related and what the role of the interest rate is in this relationship.

Unit 11.3, Rent and Profit, looks at the factor payments to both land and entrepreneurship. Land and entrepreneurship payments are combined in this unit for an important reason. Here, we see that economic profit received by entrepreneurs is the same as economic rent received by owners of land.

Unit 11.4, Income Distribution, examines the personal distribution of income. In this unit we identify several methods of measuring the distribution of income, including income classes, the Lorenz curve, and the Gini coefficient. We also see why income is unequally distributed and what the advantages and disadvantages of a more equal distribution of income are.

Unit 11.5, Poverty, concludes the section with a study of the people on the low end of the income distribution spectrum. We discuss the definition of poverty and how poverty is measured. We also examine two alternative policies designed to reduce poverty, guaranteed income and the negative income tax. And finally, we take a brief overview of poverty programs that have been tried in the United States.

UNIT 11.1

Wages

A **wage** is the payment for the use of labor resources. Wages can take many forms, including the simple hourly wage paid to unskilled, semi-skilled, and skilled workers and salaries paid to professionals, managers, and executives. The only difference between salaries and hourly wages is that salaries are typically paid on a monthly or annual basis rather than hourly. However, both represent payments for labor services.

In many cases part of labor's wages are not paid directly to labor, for example, employer contributions to employee medical, dental, and retirement plans. Other forms of indirect wages are social security contributions paid by the employer, expense accounts, incentive bonus plans, and myriad other fringe benefits.

Our study of wages begins with a look at wage differentials, which are different wage payments to different workers. We see how wage differentials can be eliminated through the operation of efficient labor markets. Then we identify several reasons why wage differentials continue to exist in spite of the operation of the labor markets. And finally, we discuss in more detail two important reasons for continued wage differentials, human capital and the labor-leisure tradeoff.

WAGE DIFFERENTIALS

While it has been convenient throughout this text to refer to *the* labor market, in reality, there is not one single labor market in any economy, but rather a multitude of different labor markets. A market for autoworkers exists in Detroit, and another one for autoworkers in Kansas City. Any city has markets for unskilled workers, mechanics, retail salespersons, and postal workers. Markets exist for professional athletes, economists, and corporate presidents. And each labor market pays a different wage. For example, workers in manufacturing industries earn a different wage than workers in retail sales. Likewise, a corporate executive earns a different wage than a university professor.

We study these wage differentials for two reasons. First, we can analyze the economic forces that operate to eliminate wage differentials between two markets. Second, we can see a variety of reasons why wage differentials are likely to remain and contribute to an unequal distribution of income.

The Elimination of Wage Differentials

To illustrate the economic forces that eliminate wage differentials, let's look at the two markets presented in Figure 11.1.1. In panel a the market for computer programmers has a relatively high wage, w_1, determined by the intersection of the market supply and demand curves. In panel b the market for school teachers has a relatively low equilibrium wage, w_2. The difference between w_1 and w_2 com-

Figure 11.1.1

Wage Differentials

A wage differential between two labor markets can be eliminated by labor mobility. If the wage in one market is higher than the wage in a second market, labor moves from the second market to the first. The supply curve in the second market shifts leftward, raising the wage, while the supply curve in the first market shifts rightward, lowering the wage. If there are no constraints on labor mobility, this process continues until the wages in both markets are equal.

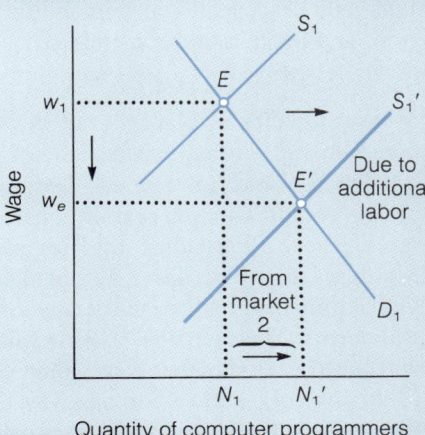

a. Market for computer programmers

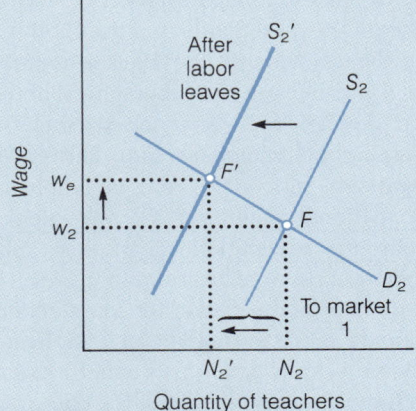

b. Market for teachers

prises the wage differential the markets try to eliminate.

In the second market, N_2 teachers are employed at the wage w_2. However, the relatively higher wage w_1 paid to computer programmers attracts some teachers from the second market. The number of teachers willing and able to work in the second market declines, causing the supply curve in that market to shift leftward from S_2 to S_2', while simultaneously causing the supply curve for computer programmers to shift rightward from S_1 to S_1'.

In general, workers from the second market go to the first market as long as w_1 is greater than w_2. This adjustment process stops only when the wages in both markets are equal to w_e. This wage is obtained when $N_2 - N_2'$ teachers go from the second market to the first. Thus, $N_2 - N_2'$ is equal to $N_1' - N_1$. The number of teachers leaving the second market is identical to the number of computer programmers entering the first market.

Labor Mobility

The key to the adjustment process that eliminates wage differentials is labor mobility. As discussed in Unit 10.2, there are two types of mobility, geographic and occupational. **Geographic mobility** is the movement of factors from one geographic area to another. If panel b in Figure 11.1.1 depicts the labor market in the rural South after the Civil War, and panel a the urban North, the adjustment process from panel b to panel a entails geographic mobility. Geographic mobility represents an extremely significant force in the elimination of wage differentials.

Occupational mobility is also an important force. **Occupational mobility** is the movement of factors from one occupation to another, often involving retraining or education. If panel a in Figure 11.1.1 depicts the market for computer programmers, and panel b the market for schoolteachers, the mobility from panel b to panel a entails more than moving from one part of the country to the other. Only when the schoolteachers are retrained as computer programmers do the supply curves shift as indicated.

The Existence of Wage Differentials

Although labor mobility works to eliminate wage differentials between various parts of the country and various occupations, differentials still exist. Table 11.1.1 presents examples of wage differentials in the United States. In terms of the average hourly wage in eight different industries, the construction industry has the highest wage at $12.26 per hour, and the retail trade industry the lowest wage at $5.97 per hour. Obviously, the differential between these two industries is quite dramatic.

Table 11.1.1 also illuminates some relatively dramatic differentials between broad occupational categories. Note that on a weekly basis, managers and administrators earn over twice as much as service or farm workers. For example, in 1981, managers and administrators earned an average of $407 per week, whereas service workers earned $192 per week and farm workers only $179 per week. The significance of these differentials is that they have persisted for a long time. Managers and administrators were earning more than service workers in 1961, and they will probably earn more in 2001.

Wage differentials persist for six basic reasons: worker quality, personal preferences, geographic immobility, occupational immobility, discrimination, and institutional constraints.

Worker Quality All labor is not the same. Labor comes in various shapes, sizes, and qualities, with differences based on manual dexterity, physical ability, coordination, appearance, personality, and intelligence. Professional athletes such as Dan Marino, Larry Bird, Dave Winfield, and Wayne Gretzky are paid high wages because of their physical talents. Their physical talents explain not only why they receive higher wages than the General Motors factory worker but also why they receive higher wages than other athletes in their respective sports. Likewise, the charming sales representative, witty junior executive, and energetic new reporter are all likely to receive higher relative wages.

Table 11.1.1

Wage Differentials

Wage differentials exist for workers in different industries and different occupations. Among industries the wage ranges from $5.97 per hour in retail trade to $12.26 in construction. Among occupations the wage ranges from $179 per week for farmworkers to $407 for managers and administrators.

Industry (1985)	Wage (per hour)
Mining	$11.95
Construction	12.26
Manufacturing	9.52
Transportation	11.38
Wholesale trade	9.26
Retail trade	5.97
Finance, insurance, and real estate	7.93
Services	7.95

Occupation (1981)	Wage (per week)
Professional and technical	$377
Managers and administrators	407
Salesworkers	306
Clerical workers	233
Craft workers	352
Transportation equipment operatives	303
Nonfarm laborers	238
Service workers	192
Farm workers	179

Sources: U.S. Bureau of the Census, *Statistical Abstract of the United States*, 1982–83, and U.S. Bureau of Economic Analysis, *Survey of Current Business*, March 1986.

Differential worker quality occurs for two reasons. First, people are born physically different. Some people are naturally faster, prettier, or taller than others. World class sprinters, fashion models, and centers in the National Basketball Association are typically born and not made. Second, through training and education, the quality of workers can be improved. This process is referred to as human capital, and will be discussed in more detail later in this unit.

Personal Preferences The person cannot be separated from the factor of production. For this reason, labor receives some form of satisfaction (good or bad) while on the job. Some jobs are enjoyable, and others are not, and the more enjoyable jobs are likely to pay a lower wage. A coal miner needs a higher wage than a shoe store salesclerk to compensate for the unpleasant and dirty working conditions in the mines. Likewise, an accountant needs a higher wage than an economist to compensate for the drudgery of accounting. Some people are willing to work for a lower wage simply because they like the job.

Geographic Immobility While geographic mobility is an important mechanism in the elimination of wage differentials, there are barriers to geographic mobility. One is the cost of moving. For example, the cost of moving a family from New York to California is several thousand dollars. While this may be insignificant to the Broadway star who has recently signed a new film contract, it can prevent the clerk at the local convenience store from making the move.

People might be hesitant to move to a new labor market because it means leaving friends and family, especially if they have no friends or family in the new labor market. Differing cultures can also be a barrier to labor mobility. The native of New York City may think twice about moving to Goodland, Kansas, with its population of 20,000.

Occupational Immobility As with geographic mobility, there are also barriers to changing occupations. Seniority and fringe benefits can reduce the incentive to change occupations. For example, it is unlikely that a schoolteacher who has twenty years of service and is a few years from retirement will retrain to become a computer programmer.

Discrimination Wage differentials can also persist because of discrimination. Some employers are willing to pay a premium for certain types of workers, meaning that women, blacks, and various ethnic minorities often receive lower wages than white males.

Institutional Constraints The existence of institutional constraints can also cause wage differentials to persist. The two most notable institutional constraints are the legally imposed minimum wage and the market power of labor unions. Recall that a labor union's primary objective is to raise the wages of its members, at which unions have been quite successful. Industries that are highly unionized tend to have higher wages than nonunionized industries. A minimum wage can also contribute to wage differentials because all unskilled or semiskilled jobs are not subject to the minimum wage.

HUMAN CAPITAL

One reason for the continued existence of wage differentials is human capital. **Human capital is the training and education received by labor that improves its ability to produce goods and services.** Human capital can range from the formal education received by a medical student to the on-the-job training received by a carpenter's apprentice. After receiving the human capital, the doctor or carpenter is able to produce either a higher value or a larger quantity of goods and services with the same effort.

Investment in Human Capital

An important analogy can be drawn between physical capital and human capital. A firm constructs a new factory or buys a new piece of equipment because it expects the capital to generate a profit. The firm incurs a large cost in the present, anticipating that the initial cost will be more than recovered in the future. This is the nature of investment—you give up something today, hoping you get back more tomorrow. The same is true for human capital—you are willing to incur the expense of a college education because you expect a higher income in the future.

Figure 11.1.2 illustrates the investment in human capital. Suppose that you are graduating

Figure 11.1.2

Investment in Human Capital

The decision to invest in human capital is similar to a firm's decision to build a new factory. The investor decides if future returns from higher earnings are greater than the initial costs. Here, a college student foregoes $10,000 of earnings for each year of college. In addition, the student pays $10,000 per year in out-of-pocket costs for tuition and books. However, a college education leads to a higher income, path B, than without the education, path A.

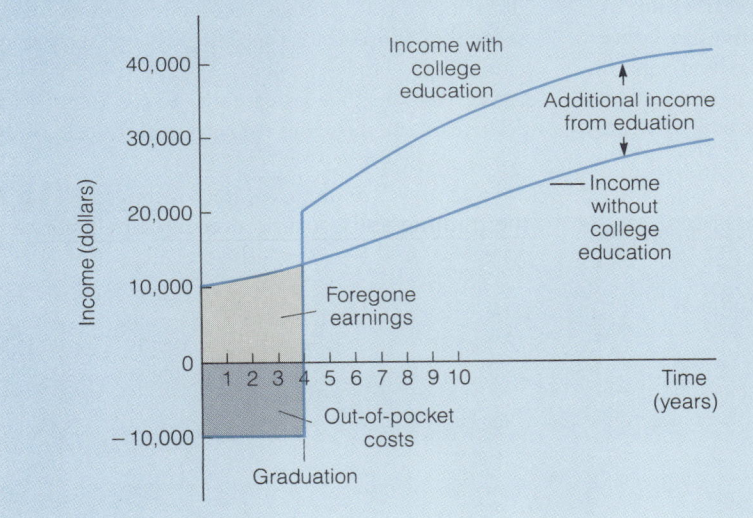

from high school and have two options. The first option, path A, is to take a job for $10,000 a year, foregoing a college education. The second option, path B, is to enter college and invest in human capital, thus foregoing the immediate employment and initial wage of $10,000. Furthermore, by following path B, you incur out-of-pocket costs for tuition and books, also amounting to $10,000 the first year. The sum of the foregone earnings and the out-of-pocket costs represents the total opportunity costs, the shaded areas between paths A and B. These opportunity costs are analogous to the costs of constructing a factory or the purchase price of a piece of equipment and constitute your initial investment.

However, upon graduation your income path with the college education lies above your income path without the college education. Because of your investment in human capital, you expect to earn a higher income. However, it is important to know how much higher the income will be after the investment. Suppose you incur $80,000 in foregone earnings and out-of-pocket costs for 4 years of college, but then have an annual increase in income of only $100. In this case your investment in human capital is probably not a good idea, because it would take several hundred years to recover the initial investment. However, if your annual increase in income is $20,000, then the investment makes more sense, because your investment is recovered in only a few years.

To see if the investment is worthwhile, we need to compare the initial investment with the extra income earned. If the $80,000 initial investment generates $10,000 in additional income each year until retirement, it is probably worthwhile. In fact, you might even be willing to invest a larger amount, perhaps several years of medical school and internship. The extra income generated by your investment in human capital is the area between curves A and B after graduation. If this area is larger than your initial investment (shaded area), then the investment is worthwhile.

Education and Income

The additional income generated by an investment in education is illustrated in Figure 11.1.3. Each curve represents a different level of education. Clearly, the additional years of schooling raise the level of income at all age groups. With 8 years of education or less, average income reaches its highest level of $25,000 for those fifty-five to sixty-four years of age. However, with 9 to 12 years of education, the same age group earns $32,000; with 13 to 16 years of education this group earns $38,500;

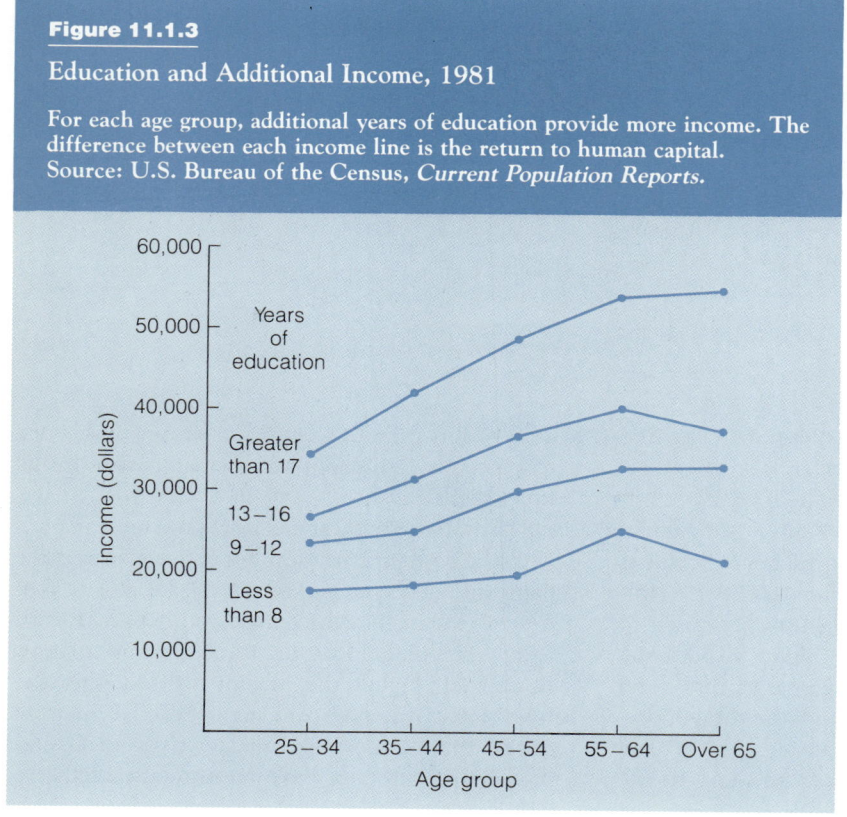

Figure 11.1.3

Education and Additional Income, 1981

For each age group, additional years of education provide more income. The difference between each income line is the return to human capital.
Source: U.S. Bureau of the Census, *Current Population Reports*.

and with over 17 years of education this age group earns almost $53,000 of income. The difference between income earned by the same age group for different levels of education is primarily due to human capital. In fact, the area between any pair of curves essentially comprises the additional income from education and human capital.

THE LABOR-LEISURE TRADEOFF

Since the person and the factor cannot be separated, time spent by labor working is time *not* spent in leisure activities. In this sense, every worker faces an important tradeoff between leisure and the goods and services that can be purchased with the income earned from working. If you decide to work less and engage in leisure activities, you earn less income. But if you spend more time working and purchase more goods, then you have less leisure time.

This tradeoff has an important effect on the supply of labor. Suppose you earn a relatively low wage. If your wage increases, you are likely to increase the quantity of labor supplied. If the wage is low, you give up relatively little income to take out a few extra hours in leisure. In fact, your hourly wage rate can be considered the price of an hour of leisure. If your wage rate is $2 an hour, then the price you pay to take an hour off from work is $2. By comparison, a two-hour movie that charges $4 for admission has the same price per hour.

However, if your wage rate increases, this increases the price of leisure. You are less likely to take off an extra hour if it costs $5 than if it only costs $2. Therefore, at higher wages you are likely to buy less leisure, and offer more hours of labor. This is seen in Figure 11.1.4 as an increase in wages from w_1 and w_2 leading to an increase in the quantity of labor supplied fron N_1 to N_2.

However, there is more to the supply of labor than the price of leisure. Labor generates the income you use to buy goods and services. As your wage increases and you supply more labor, your income also increases. And with this income you are able

Figure 11.1.4

The Backward-Bending Labor Supply Curve

Due to the tradeoff between labor and leisure, the supply curve for labor can be negatively sloped at relatively high wages. At low wages labor is likely to increase supply in order to receive additional income to buy goods and services. However, at higher wages labor is likely to supply less labor. In essence, labor is spending the additional income that could be earned by working on greater amounts of leisure.

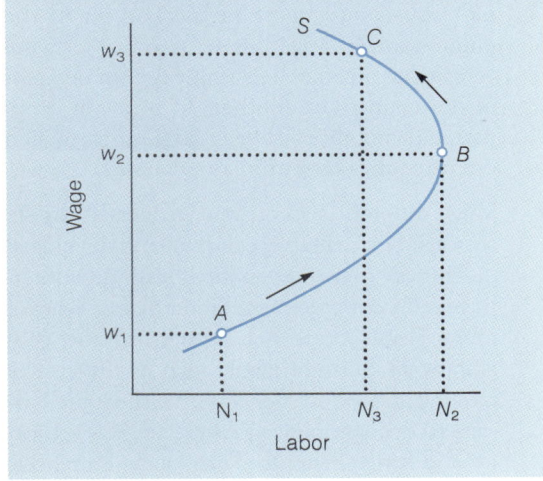

to buy more of all goods and services except one, leisure. At some point the goods and services you can buy with the extra income are not as valuable as the extra leisure time you give up.

Even though the price of leisure increases with the wage, you may decide to work less and buy more leisure time. In essence, an increase in the wage gives you an increase in income, which you can spend either on more goods and services or on leisure time. If you have a high wage and are already purchasing a large quantity of goods and services, the extra income is more likely to be spent on leisure.

This is shown in Figure 11.1.4 by the segment of the labor supply curve above wage w_2. As the wage increases from w_2 to w_3, the quantity of labor supplied decreases from N_2 to N_3. This supply curve is called the **backward-bending labor supply curve**, which is positively sloped at relatively low wages and negatively sloped at relatively high wages.

IN SUMMARY
Wages

- Wages vary in different labor markets. Labor mobility is an important mechanism in the elimination of wage differentials. In terms of geographic mobility, labor moves from one part of the country to another. In terms of occupational mobility, labor changes jobs, which often requires retraining or education.

- Wage differentials continue to persist for six reasons. First, there are natural and developed differences in worker quality. Second, workers have different preferences for different types of jobs. Third, there are barriers to the geographic mobility of labor, such as the cost of moving and family ties. Fourth, there are barriers to occupational mobility, such as seniority and fringe benefits. Fifth, some employers discriminate against minorities or women, paying lower wages. Sixth, there are institutional constraints preventing wages from adjusting, such as labor unions and minimum wage legislation.

- Human capital is the investment by labor on training and education, which increases productivity and income. Like physical capital, there is an investment in human capital if the future income generated is greater than the initial investment cost.

- Unlike other factors of production, labor gives up leisure time while on the job. Therefore, there is a tradeoff between the amount of labor supplied and the time taken in leisure. This tradeoff leads to a positively sloped labor supply curve at relatively low wage rates but a negative, backward-bending slope at higher wage rates.

QUESTIONS FOR STUDY AND ANALYSIS

1. Suppose you have two very attractive job offers after graduating from college. Both positions are identical except for the salary and location. The first position pays $20,000 a year, while the second pays $15,000.
   a. Based only on this information, which position would you take?
   b. If you are also told that the first position is in Hawaii while the second is in Montana, which position would you take?
   c. Now suppose you are told that the cost of living in Hawaii is twice as high as in Montana. Which position would you take?

2. Historically, the average wage earned by women has been less than the average pay earned by men. In 1983 a woman's average wage was only 63 percent of a man's average wage. Discuss how each of the reasons for wage differentials—worker quality, worker preferences, geographic immobility, occupational immobility, discrimination, and institutional constraints—might contribute to this difference.

3. Assume that four different occupations have the following annual wages: doctor—$80,000; economist—$40,000; schoolteacher—$20,000; maintenance worker—$10,000. Furthermore, a doctor requires twelve years of college, an economist eight years, a schoolteacher four years, and a maintenance worker none. The cost of each year of college is $5000.
   a. What is the human capital return on the first four years of college? The second four years? The third four years?

    b. What is the total cost of becoming a teacher? How many years does it take before the return on the human capital of being a schoolteacher pays for the initial investment?
    c. What is the total cost of becoming an economist? In your answer be sure to include the opportunity cost of foregone earnings that could be earned after four years of college (the schoolteacher's salary). How many years does it take before the return on the human capital of being an economist pays for the initial investment?
    d. What is the total cost of becoming a doctor? In your answer be sure to include the opportunity cost of foregone earnings that could be earned after four and eight years of college. How many years does it take before the return on the human capital of being a doctor pays for the initial investment?
    e. Under these conditions, which occupation would you choose? Why?

4. During the Oklahoma oil boom of the late 1970s and early 1980s, the automobile industry centered in Detroit had serious financial difficulties. During this period a large number of families moved from Michigan to Oklahoma. Explain why.

5. At what annual wage would your labor supply curve begin to bend backwards? Why?

6. Explain why mineworkers earn higher wages than retail salesworkers.

REVIEW GLOSSARY

backward-bending labor supply curve A labor supply curve that is positively sloped at relatively low wages and negatively sloped at relatively high wages. The backward-bending labor supply curve is based on the tradeoff between time spent on the job and leisure time.

geographic mobility The movement of factors from one geographic area to another.

human capital The training and education received by labor that improves its ability to produce goods and services. The investment in human capital is much like the investment in physical capital. An investment in human capital is made if there is a large enough increase in future income to offset the initial investment cost.

occupational mobility The movement of factors from one occupation to another.

wage The payment for the use of labor resources. The wage is the payment to labor based on its contribution to the production of goods and services. Wages can be either direct payments to labor or indirect payments for fringe benefits and taxes.

UNIT 11.2

Interest

Capital plays a part in the production of almost every kind of good and service. Recall that capital includes all synthetic resources used in production, ranging from a General Motors assembly factory to a doctor's stethoscope. In this unit we turn our attention to the market for capital goods. In particular, we see how **interest, which is the payment for the use of financial capital**, is also considered a payment for the use of physical capital.

As discussed in previous units, the term *capital* refers to both physical and financial capital. Though physical and financial capital are distinct, they are related. Note that financial capital is used by firms to fund the production of physical capital. It is this relationship between financial and physical capital that we want to study in this unit.

To begin, we look at investment in physical capital, particularly the decision behind the purchase of a piece of capital, and we examine the role the interest rate plays in this decision. In fact, the interest rate ties together the market for capital goods and the financial market for funds to buy the capital goods. The unit ends with a discussion of several common interest rates in different financial markets, and we see four important reasons for differences in interest rates.

INVESTMENT IN PHYSICAL CAPITAL

When a firm is deciding on the purchase of a capital good, it faces a basic choice. It can either buy the capital good and receive the additional profit that is generated, or it can take the funds that would be used to buy the good, loan them out through the financial markets, and receive the revenue generated from the interest. The interest rate has a direct bearing on this decision.

For example, suppose L. L. Manzer's Copycenter is considering the purchase of a new copier that copies twice as fast as the old machine but that costs $20,000. Should Manzer's Copycenter buy the machine?

To answer this, let's look more closely at what factors enter into this decision. The existing copier can make about 50,000 copies each year. Thus, if each copy sells for 5 cents, the machine generates $2500 of revenue. The new machine is able to double that figure, generating $5000 of revenue. Assuming the costs of operating both machines are the same, replacing the old machine with the new one adds an extra $2500 of profit a year.

Manzer's Copycenter happens to have $20,000 of profit that has accumulated over previous years, meaning the firm does not have to borrow from the bank to finance the copier. In this case the firm can either buy the copier or invest the funds. It could put the $20,000 in the bank, or otherwise invest in one of several financial markets, and earn the market rate of interest, perhaps 10 percent per year. Thus, the $20,000 would earn $2000 per year in interest. But if the funds are used to buy the copier, they earn $2500 per year. Clearly, the firm is better off buying the copier, because more revenue is earned.

In a nutshell, this is the investment decision facing a firm. It can purchase the physical capital, which generates additional earnings and profit. Or it can use the funds in another manner, such as investing in the financial market, which generates interest earnings.

Sources of Funds

In the previous example Manzer's Copycenter just happened to have $20,000 lying around that could be used to buy the copier. While firms very often use profits earned in previous years for investment in capital, other ways to finance the purchase of capital exist. The three basic ways of funding investment are through retained earnings, borrowing, and the sale of stock.

Retained Earnings Manzer's Copycenter used retained earnings to finance the copier. <u>Retained earnings are profits earned by a firm that are not distributed to shareholders or owners in the form of dividends</u>. Retained earnings constitute a substantial source of investment funding. Because a firm has to decide whether the purchase of physical capital or investment in financial markets will provide the highest possible return, it compares the interest earnings in the financial markets with the additional profit generated by the physical capital.

Borrowed Funds A second source of funding for capital is borrowing. When a firm borrows from the bank, it agrees to pay back the amount borrowed, plus an interest payment. If Manzer's Copycenter borrows $20,000 from the bank, at 10 percent annual interest it pays $2000 per year on the borrowed funds. The interest payment then becomes an additional cost of buying and operating the new copier. Since the copier generates $2500 in revenue and the borrowed funds cost $2000, the firm still increases profit by $500 per year. As long as the extra revenue generated by the purchase of the capital is greater than the interest payment, the investment in the capital is profitable. But again, note that the firm compares the revenue earned from the physical capital to the interest payment.

Funds from the Sale of Stock Firms also raise funds for the purchase of capital goods by selling stock, or ownership shares in the firm. We should point out that the sale of stock in this case is newly issued stock, not the existing stock that is exchanged daily in the stock markets. When an owner of IBM stock sells his or her stock to someone else, IBM does not receive any additional funds. Only when IBM issues new stock, not previously owned, does it receive additional funds.

A potential buyer of the stock issued by the firm must decide if the stock will earn more than another investment alternative. Keep in mind that the earnings received by the owner of the stock include annual dividends paid by the company and the future price of the stock if it is sold, both of which depend on the earnings generated by the physical capital purchased with the funds. If the capital generates a great deal of earnings, the firm is more profitable and is able to pay higher dividends. Likewise, the profitability of the firm attracts additional buyers of the stock, causing the price, and value, of the stock to rise. The alternative to buying the stock again is investment in the financial market. The potential buyer of the corporate stock must compare the direct interest earnings in the financial market with the indirect earnings generated by the physical capital.

The Role of the Interest Rate

With any of the three sources of funding for physical capital, the interest rate plays an important role. In each case the earnings generated from the physical capital are compared to the earnings generated in the financial market. If the physical capital earns more, then the capital is purchased. However, if the interest earnings are higher, then the capital is not purchased.

Let's return to our example of Manzer's Copycenter. What happens if the interest rate in the financial market increases to 15 percent per year? Manzer's Copycenter can put the retained earnings in the financial market and receive $3000 ($= 0.15 \times \$20,000$) in interest per year. In this case the financial market generates more earnings than the copier, and the firm is better off not buying the copier. The higher interest rate has turned a profitable investment into an unprofitable one. The same result also occurs if the other two sources of funding are used.

THE FINANCIAL MARKET

Investment in physical capital is closely tied to the financial market. The **financial market** <u>is the market used to exchange an assortment of financial</u>

capital. While there are a number of different types of financial markets, we are combining them into one financial market in order to simplify this analysis. Like any market, the financial market comprises the interaction of the demand and supply of financial funds.

Demand for Funds

The demand for funds in the financial market comes from two main sources. The first, which we have alluded to already, is for investment in physical capital. The second is the demand for funds by consumers. Consumers borrow funds to buy goods and services today rather than waiting until a later date when they have saved enough of their income. Consumers are willing to pay a higher price (by including the interest payment) for current consumption. The total cost of a $10,000 automobile, purchased with funds borrowed at 10 percent over a four-year period, is over $12,000. Moreover, if the interest rate increases, the total cost of the car also increases. Thus, according to the law of demand, fewer cars, and consequently fewer funds, are demanded at higher interest rates.

In terms of funds demanded to purchase capital goods, how much are firms willing to pay for the borrowed funds? Again, we use Manzer's Copycenter as an example. Based on the $2500 profit generated by the new copier, we know that the investment is made if the interest rate is 10 percent, but not if it is 15 percent. What is the highest interest the firm is willing to pay for funds to buy the copier?

Very simply, if the interest payments are less than $2500 per year (which is the profit generated by the copier), then the copier is a good investment. An interest payment of $2500 per year works out to a 12.5 percent interest rate. Thus, Manzer's Copycenter demands $20,000 of funds if the interest rate is 12.5 percent or less. The same type of analysis applies for other firms contemplating an investment in capital. Although each firm is likely to have a different maximum interest rate they are willing to pay (since different revenue is likely generated by each capital good), each firm shares one thing in common. If the interest rate becomes too high, a firm will not purchase the capital good, and the amount of funds demanded will decrease. In Figure 11.2.1 the negatively sloped demand curve D for the financial market depicts this inverse relationship between the interest rate and the demand for funds.

Supply of Funds

The supply of funds, like the supply of any good, depends on opportunity cost. In the financial market the opportunity cost represents the alternative uses of the funds. As previously mentioned, one

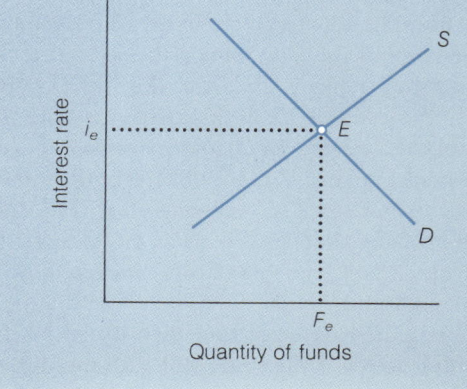

Figure 11.2.1

The Financial Market

The demand for funds is inversely related to the interest rate. At higher interest rates, consumers and firms demand less funds because the cost of the funds is higher. The supply of funds is positively related to the interest rate. At higher interest rates, consumers supply more savings and firms supply more retained earnings. As with any market, equilibrium is reached at the intersection of the demand and supply curves.

source of supply is retained earnings of firms. The opportunity cost of retained earnings placed in the financial markets is the revenue that can be generated with physical capital. If the interest rate increases, firms find their physical capital relatively less profitable and decide to supply more funds to the financial market.

Another source of funds is consumer saving. Consumers place part of their income in banks or other financial institutions in return for the interest payment; the higher the interest rate the more saving. When consumers save part of their income, they are giving up current consumption. As mentioned earlier, consumers are often willing to pay more for current consumption. If consumers are willing to pay an interest to borrow funds for current consumption, this also means they are willing to forego current consumption *only* if they receive an interest payment. That is, consumers who save part of their income, and thus give up some current consumption, must receive an interest payment. It follows that as the interest rate increases, consumers are willing to supply more funds. The positively sloped supply curve S for funds in the financial market in Figure 11.2.1 reflects an increase in the quantity of funds supplied by both consumers and firms at higher interest rates.

FINANCIAL MARKET EQUILIBRIUM AND CAPITAL

Note that the financial market in Figure 11.2.1 operates like any other market. If the supply of funds is greater than the demand, the interest rate falls. If the demand for funds is greater than the supply, the interest rate rises. At the intersection of the supply and demand curves (point E), the interest rate i_e leads to the same quantity of funds demanded and supplied, F_e.

How then does this relate to physical capital? As we move up the demand curve, the higher interest rate eliminates the investments by some firms whose capital goods earn less than the interest rate. Therefore, at the equilibrium interest rate i_e, firms are demanding funds that earn a return at least equal to i_e. The last dollar of funds demanded by a firm is for capital goods that earn exactly i_e. In fact, each firm continues to demand funds until the last capital good purchased is exactly equal to the market interest rate. Otherwise, they are not maximizing profit.

This means that the return received by firms on the last unit of their capital goods is exactly the same as the interest rate in the financial market. Moreover, firms use the revenue generated by the physical capital to pay for the funds borrowed in the financial market. The funds placed by consumers in the banks and other financial institutions are used for the purchase of capital goods. The interest paid to the financial institutions by the firms is in turn paid to the consumers (after banks cover their costs). It is for this reason that interest is considered the payment for capital.

INTEREST RATE DIFFERENTIALS

As stated earlier, there are actually a variety of financial markets and a variety of different interest rates. Table 11.2.1 presents several of the most common interest rates.

The first rate listed is the prime lending rate. The **prime lending rate** is the interest rate charged on short-term loans by banks to their best customers. The banks' best customers are usually major corporations, who have the highest credit ratings, and who are certain to repay the loan. Another common interest rate is the 30-year conventional mortgage, which is used to finance home-buyers. Both the prime lending rate and the mortgage rate are interest rates charged when consumers or firms, as demanders, borrow funds from the bank.

The other interest rates listed are paid when funds are borrowed from consumers or firms, who are suppliers of funds. However, in these cases the bank is only acting as the intermediary between demanders and suppliers. A **certificate of deposit** is a certificate for funds deposited in a bank or financial institution for a specific time period and

Table 11.2.1

Selected Interest Rates, January 1986

Interest rates vary for different financial markets and depend on who does the borrowing and lending. If large corporations borrow from banks, they pay the prime lending rate. If consumers borrow from a bank to buy a house, they pay the mortgage rate. However, if banks borrow from corporations, they might pay the rate on $100,000 CDs, and if they borrow from consumers, they might pay the rate for savings or NOW accounts.

Name	Interest Rate (percent)
Prime lending rate	9.5
30-year conventional mortgage	10.4
$100,000 certificates of deposit (CD)	
3-month	7.8
Treasury bill discount rate	
6-month	7.14
3-month	6.98
Savings	5.5
Negotiable orders of withdrawal (NOW)	5.25

Source: U.S. Bureau of Economic Analysis, *Survey of Current Business*, March 1986; and Federal Reserve System, Board of Governors. *Federal Reserve Bulletin*, March 1986.

rate of interest. A **treasury bill** is a financial note issued by the federal government. The federal government uses treasury bills to borrow funds for financing the federal deficit.

Table 11.2.1 lists just seven of the numerous interest rates that exist in the U.S. economy. But even these seven interest rates show a great deal of variation. The $100,000 certificates of deposit pay 7.8 percent, whereas the 30-year conventional mortgages pay 10.4 percent, a difference of only four percentage points. By contrast, the interest paid on a passbook savings account (5.5 percent) is far less than that paid on installment purchases and credit cards (up to 21 percent). There are four basic reasons for interest rate differentials: risk, length of maturity, liquidity, and administration costs.

Risk

If a loan has a higher degree of uncertainty of repayment, the interest rate is also higher. Thus, the prime lending rate applies only to a near riskless loan. Since the loan is to the bank's best customers, there is little doubt that the loan will be repaid. But suppose a bank makes loans with only a 50 percent chance of being repaid; that is, for one hundred loans of this type, the bank can count on repayment of only fifty. The bank would have to include a risk premium in the interest rate charged the borrowers. The amount of the risk premium would be large enough that the bank would earn the same amount of interest whether it made a loan with a 100 percent chance of repayment at the prime lending rate or a 50 percent chance of repayment at the higher interest rate.

Length of Maturity

Because of the uncertainty in financial markets, the longer the period of the loan, the higher the interest rate. No one knows what the interest rate will be next year. Suppose a bank makes a two-year loan at a 10 percent interest rate and the interest rate increases to 15 percent next year. Since the bank is committed to the 10 percent interest, it cannot reloan those funds at 15 percent and thus loses potential revenue. This uncertainty means longer loans carry a higher interest rate, just in case the interest rate happens to rise in the future. That's why a 6-month treasury bill has a higher interest rate than a 3-month treasury bill.

Liquidity

Liquidity is the ease of turning funds into currency or transferring them from one financial market to another. Funds that are more liquid have a lower interest rate, because suppliers of funds are willing to give up part of their interest if they are able to transfer the funds more easily. This is why passbook savings accounts pay 5.5 percent interest, while certificates of deposit pay 10 percent. Savers can withdraw funds very easily from passbook savings accounts but not so easily from certificates of deposit.

Administration Costs

Financial institutions charge a higher interest to borrowers than to lenders. A bank charges its best customers 10 percent with the prime lending rate. However, it is only willing to pay others up to 8 percent for $100,000 certificates of deposit. A large part of this difference is due to administration costs. After all, banks and other financial institutions are providing a valuable service to the economy by collecting funds and making them available to borrowers. To perform this service, they have to cover their costs, and make a normal profit.

IN SUMMARY

Interest

- A firm has three basic sources of funds that can be used to purchase capital goods: retained earnings, borrowed funds, and funds from the sale of stock. For each source a comparison is made between the revenue generated by the capital and the interest earnings in the financial market. The firm purchases the capital if it generates more revenue than the interest payment.

- The financial market determines the interest rate through the interaction of demand for funds and the supply of funds. The demand comes from firms that need funds to buy capital, or consumers unwilling to wait to buy consumer goods. The supply of funds comes from retained earnings and consumer savings. While demand is inversely related to the interest rate, supply is directly related to the interest rate. In equilibrium the interest rate is equal to the rate of return on the capital goods for each firm.

- There are a variety of different financial markets, each with its own interest rate. Differences in interest rates result from the degree of riskiness of the loan, the length of time before the loan is paid off, the ease of transferring the funds from one market to another (liquidity), and the administration costs incurred by the financial institution.

QUESTIONS FOR STUDY AND ANALYSIS

1. Suppose your firm is thinking about building a new factory. Your best estimate is that the firm will generate between $200,000 and

$250,000 of additional profit each year. The cost of the factory is $3 million.

a. If the interest rate is 10 percent, would you recommend that the firm should or should not build the factory?

b. What would you recommend if the interest rate fell to 5 percent?

c. What if the interest rate is 10 percent, but you have found a way to cut the cost of building the factory in half, to $1.5 million?

2. Why is a saver willing to accept a lower interest rate on a standard savings account than on a certificate of deposit? Explain.

3. Considering the financial market, why do we say that the interest is the indirect payment for the use of capital?

4. Explain why the demand for funds is inversely related to the interest rate. Explain why the supply of funds is directly related to the interest rate.

5. Why is the interest rate charged by a shady loan shark likely to be more than that charged by your local bank?

REVIEW GLOSSARY

certificate of deposit A certificate for funds deposited in a bank or financial institution for a specific period of time and rate of interest.

financial market The market used to exchange an assortment of financial capital. The demand for funds in the financial market comes from the demand by firms for capital goods and by consumers for consumer goods. In both cases higher interest rates reduce the quantity of funds demanded. The supply of funds comes from firms' retained earnings and consumers' savings and increases at higher interest rates. The financial market is in equilibrium at the intersection of the demand and supply curves.

interest The payment for the use of financial capital. In the operation of the financial market, interest is also considered the factor payment to physical capital.

liquidity The ease of turning funds into currency or transferring them from one financial market to another.

prime lending rate The interest rate charged by banks to their best customers on short-term loans.

retained earnings The profits earned by a firm that are not distributed to shareholders or owners in the form of dividends. The firm invests its retained earnings where the highest returns can be made, either in the financial market or by purchasing capital.

treasury bill A financial note issued by the federal government.

UNIT 11.3

Rent and Profit

Land and entrepreneurship initially may seem to be the most dissimilar of the four factors of production. While land constitutes the raw materials and natural resources of the earth, entrepreneurs are the risk-taking individuals who guide the production process. However, the payments to both factors—rent and profit—share one characteristic. Each is likely to receive a payment over and above its opportunity cost. While for land this payment is called economic rent and for entrepreneurs it is called economic profit, they are fundamentally the same type of payments. In this unit we examine the payments to land and entrepreneurship to indentify which part is an opportunity cost and which part is not.

To begin, we look at the nature of land and its productive function in the economy to determine whether the payment of rent represents an opportunity cost. We then examine entrepreneurship in terms of the three types of profit discussed before: accounting, normal, and economic. In addition, we see that economic profit, while not an opportunity cost, can have an important effect on resource allocation as a reward for innovation and risk.

LAND AND SPACE

Land is the term used in economics when referring to the naturally occurring resources. Land comprises the resources found on, above, and below the surface, including the trees, vegetation, wildlife, and water on the surface, the air, climate, and weather above the surface, and the minerals, fossil fuels, and soil nutrients beneath the surface. The naturally occurring resources of land are the raw materials used to produce consumer goods.

Without timber, petroleum, iron ore, and other minerals, there would be no goods. Land also supplies the economy with the space needed to locate economic activity and carry out the production of goods and services.

Take for example the business of professional football (or any other major sport). First, the production of football entertainment requires several acres on which to operate and play the game. At the very least, a playing field 130 yards long and $53\frac{1}{3}$ yards wide is needed. Since professional football is a spectator sport, space is also needed for the fans. This usually consists of a stadium seating 60,000 to 100,000 people and parking spaces for the fans' automobiles.

While professional football, airports, and amusement parks are three obvious examples of activities that require a great deal of space for production, all activities require some space. Some activities can be produced in a room with only a hundred square feet of space, such as providing legal services or writing a book.

Keep in mind that when one activity is using the space, another activity cannot. Even though some activities share space, such as a sports stadium used by football in the fall and baseball in the summer, they do so at different times. Land used to house a computer research and development laboratory cannot be used to grow oranges. Thus, the land on which most productive activities take place has an opportunity cost.

Land often must be accessible to be productive. **Accessibility** is the location of the activity of land relative to other activities. Not only does the production of professional football require a stadium with parking, it also needs to be relatively close to fans. It is very difficult to attract a sufficient number of fans in western Kansas to make a professional football team profitable, which is why most major sporting activities are located in or near large cities.

Many other activities are also dependent on accessibility. A doctor, dentist, lawyer, or anyone else providing a service must be located near consumers desiring the service. This is also true for any firm in retail trade that sells goods to consumers. In other cases an activity needs accessibility to the inputs used to produce its goods. For example, steel mills must locate near iron ore and coal deposits, and petroleum refining near oil fields.

However, the need for space and the need for accessibility are often not compatible. Many different activities find it profitable to locate in the middle of a city, but each activity requires space. Thus, some activities that want to locate in the middle of a city are unable to find the space to do so.

THE SUPPLY OF LAND

The total supply of land is fixed, particularly in terms of using land for space. There is only so much space. Although the supply of natural resources is also fixed, it is not quite the same as the supply of space. The supply of most natural resources can still be increased *if* the price rises. For example, exploration and the use of more expensive extraction techniques can increase the supply of many minerals and fossil fuels. Therefore, natural resources that are not fixed in supply follow the same principles of production discussed in Section 8. But what interests us in this unit is the market for a good with a fixed supply, such as the total supply of land.

THE MARKET FOR LAND

Figure 11.3.1 illustrates a market with a perfectly inelastic supply curve for land, labeled S. The quantity of land supplied is fixed at L_e, as is the amount of land in most major cities. The demand curve for land is labeled D, and reflects a demand similar to that for any factor of production. Firms demand land based on its contribution to production. If the land contributes more revenue to the firm, the firm is willing to pay a higher price in the form of rent.

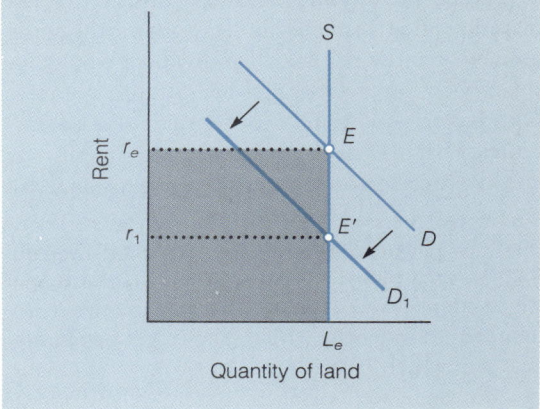

Figure 11.3.1

Economic Rent and the Land Market

If land is fixed in supply, the amount of rent received by land is determined by the demand for land. If the demand is given by curve D, then economic rent per acre is r_e. However, if the demand falls to D_1, then rent falls to r_1. In both cases the supply of land is L_e.

Two items are significant in the demand for land. One is its accessibility. An acre of land that is more accessible to the customers and inputs of a certain firm generates more revenue for that firm. For example, a football stadium located between Dallas and Fort Worth generates more revenue than a football stadium located on the outskirts of Garden City, Kansas. The Dallas Cowboys football team is willing to pay $20 million for its stadium, but the Garden City Junior College football team is not willing to pay nearly that much.

Another significant aspect in the demand for land is its natural characteristics. Land with greater natural fertility and soil composition generates more revenue for the farmer. Obviously, a farmer is willing to pay more rent for more fertile land.

Equilibrium in the land market is determined in the same way as equilibrium in any market. If the quantity supplied is greater than the quantity demanded, the rent falls. If the quantity demanded is greater than the quantity supplied, the rent rises. In Figure 11.3.1 the land market equilibrium is at point E, and the equilibrium rent is r_e. In addition, the equilibrium quantity of land exchanged has to be L_e, because there is only L_e quantity of land in the market. Since the supply is fixed, this quantity is supplied at any rent. In fact, if the demand for land shifts to D_1, the quantity of land exhanged at equilibrium point E' remains at L_e. The only difference is that the rental payment decreases to r_1.

RENT

Rent is the payment for the use of land in the production of goods and services. In Figure 11.3.1 the rent per unit of land is r_e. However, the total rent received by the owners of land is the shaded area, $L_e \times r_e$.

While this representation of rent seems straightforward, the term needs some clarification. Like many terms, rent has one meaning in common usage and another, related but different, meaning in economics. To many people the term *rent* brings to mind the payment to a landlord for the use of an apartment, or the payment for the services of a steam carpet-cleaning system. However, to distinguish the term *rent* as it applies to economics, it is known as economic rent. **Economic rent is the payment to a factor of production over and above its opportunity cost.** The opportunity cost of a factor is the payment it can earn in the next best alternative. Paying a factor its opportunity cost thus represents the minimum payment needed to keep the factor in a particular activity. If it is paid any less, it moves to the next best alternative. If the factor receives payment greater than the opportunity cost, this is an economic rent.

If land is fixed in supply, then all rent that it earns is economic rent. The economic rent earned by land is the shaded area in Figure 11.3.1. It is not necessary to pay the land a rent of r_e to keep it in the market, because if the demand falls to D_1, the same quantity of land is exchanged at the lower rent r_1.

Economic Rent Is a Residual

The payment of rent to land is a residual. That is, firms pay land what they can afford after all other opportunity costs are paid. Suppose a firm is located in the middle of city and has a great deal of sales simply because there are a lot of people around. Its profits are high, and it is able to pay high rent on the land. But if the same firm is located on the outskirts of the city, its sales, profits, and rental payments are less.

This means that a firm with a profitable product, or a firm that sells its product at a relatively high price, can afford to pay more rent. The amount of the rent results from the profitability of the product. A common misconception is that high rents cause the price of a product to be high. Whenever a new store or shopping center opens with slightly higher prices than existing stores, people invariably feel that the higher prices are needed to pay the rent on the new building. This is not the case. The rent is affordable only because buyers are willing to pay higher prices for the store's goods.

A single firm rightfully considers the rent on the land an opportunity cost of producing its product. For a particular firm or industry the supply of land is *not* fixed; one firm can increase its quantity of land by bidding it away from another production process. In this sense, there is an opportunity cost to a particular piece of land, but the total supply of land is fixed, and thus there is no opportunity cost.

Resource Allocation and Rent

If the total supply of land is fixed, and the same quantity is supplied at any rent, then does rent serve any purpose in the allocation of resources? Let's first look at the argument that rent serves no purpose in the allocation of resources. If rent is a residual and is determined by the demand for the

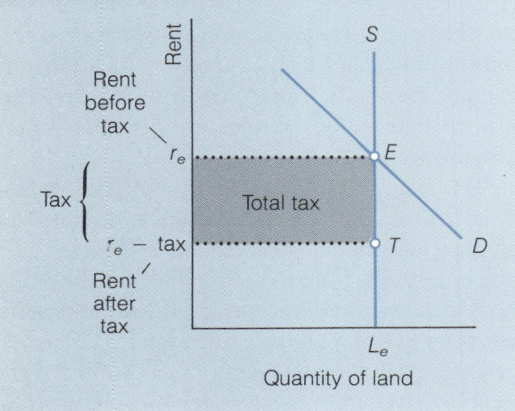

Figure 11.3.2

Economic Rent and the Single Tax

A tax placed on a fixed supply does not affect the quantity supplied. It has been suggested that a single tax levied on all land could be used to generate enough revenue to operate the government.

output, then the same quantity of land is supplied regardless of the rent, and higher rents do not lead to greater supplies.

To illustrate this point, let's see what happens if a tax is placed on all land. A tax of this nature, which is often called a single tax, was first proposed by Henry George, a nineteenth-century economist. A **single tax** is a tax levied on only one item, used to raise all of the revenue needed by the government. Henry George argued that all of the funds needed to operate the government could be raised by taxing the economic rent on land, and nothing else. Figure 11.3.2 illustrates how a single tax on land affects the land market.

The pretax rent per acre is r_e. The single tax is levied on all land, which reduces the after-tax rent to r_e − tax. But demanders continue to pay r_e, while suppliers receive only r_e − tax. The difference is the tax paid to the government. Henry George argued that an appropriate tax rate could be found such that the total amount of taxes received (shaded area) was sufficient to operate the government. Moreover, he argued that the tax would not distort the allocation of resources. The land market exchanges L_e before and after the tax. The only effect is that the government collects part of the economic rent originally received by landowners.

While this argument is appealing to many people who watch wealthy landlords become wealthier without putting forth effort, economic rent does have an allocative function. In the simple example of the land market just discussed, land has no alternative uses. In reality, there is an alternative use of land—removing the land from the market and letting it sit idle. If 50 percent of the rent on land is taxed away, landowners might continue to supply the same quantity of land. However, if 90, 95, or 99 percent of the rent is taxed, the land may be removed entirely from the market.

Economic Rent for Other Factors

Economic rent is the payment over and above the opportunity cost of a factor. Although we have concentrated on the economic rent received by land, any factor of production can receive economic rent. For example, Figure 11.3.3 illustrates the labor market for janitors, who can also receive an economic rent. The supply curve is positively sloped, meaning a higher wage attracts additional janitors into the market. The supply curve depicts the opportunity cost of each janitor. Some have a relatively low opportunity cost, and are willing to work for a relatively low wage. Others have a relatively high opportunity cost, and thus need a higher wage.

The market reaches equilibrium at wage w_e, the wage the last janitor needs to receive, equal to his or her opportunity cost. However, every janitor in the market receives the wage w_e. The difference between the opportunity cost (the supply curve) and the wage is the economic rent received by janitors, which is the shaded area in Figure 11.3.3. Thus, janitors, factory workers, and even economists receive some economic rent if their supply curve is positively sloped.

PROFIT

Economic profit and economic rent are essentially the same. Economic profit is the profit earned by a firm when total revenue is greater than the opportunity costs of production. It is the payment over and above the normal profit of an entrepreneur. Normal profit is the entrepreneur's opportunity cost, making economic profit the entrepreneur's economic rent.

However, entrepreneurs may not be able to keep all of the economic profit received by their firms. The other three factors—labor, capital, and land—may be able to obtain part of the economic profit as their own economic rent as a result of monopolistic power in the sale of their factors.

Economic profit is the total of all revenue over and above the opportunity costs of all factors. Economic rent is that part of economic profit obtained by the individual factors. If a firm earns an economic profit, one or all of the factors of production end up with economic rent. Along this line let's review the three basic types of profit—accounting, normal, and economic—briefly noting that **profit is the payment for the use of entrepreneurship.**

Accounting profit is the difference between a firm's revenue and its explicit accounting costs. Accounting profit is reported by a firm on its profit and loss statement. However, the explicit accounting costs of a firm usually omit an important opportunity cost, normal profit. **Normal profit** is the profit that can be earned by an entrepreneur in an alternative production process. Subtracting all opportunity costs, including normal profit, from a firm's total revenue gives the firm's economic profit. **Economic profit** is the difference between all opportunity costs, including a normal profit, and the revenue received by a firm. While normal profit is an opportunity cost, economic profit is a residual, and unearned. Normal profit is the minimum required to keep an entrepreneur producing the good. Economic profit is the same as economic rent.

However, no clear-cut difference between economic profit and normal profit exists. For example,

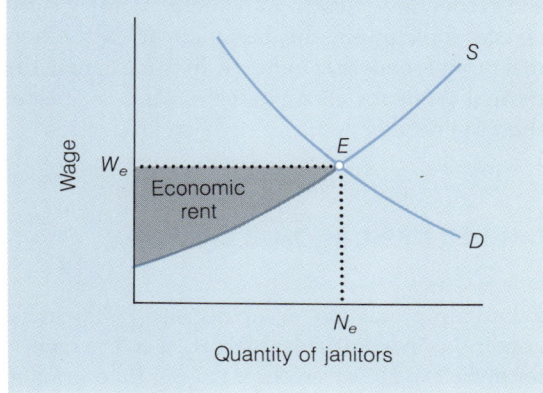

Figure 11.3.3

Economic Rent and Other Factors

Any factor of production can receive economic rent if the price received by a factor is greater than its opportunity cost. Here, some janitors can receive economic rent if the market wage is greater than the lowest wage that would keep them on the job.

the production of corn and soybeans employs similar inputs. The similarity in the industries makes it easy for entrepreneurs to switch from one industry to another. The same labor, capital, land, and entrepreneurship can be used to produce either product.

Assume that half of the farmers produce soybeans and the other half produce corn, and every farmer earns the same profit. Thus, the normal profit for farmers producing corn is the profit earned by the farmers producing soybeans, and vice versa. Since all farmers are earning the same profit, none is earning an economic profit.

But what happens if the demand for soybeans increases, perhaps as a result of a technological breakthrough that utilizes soybeans in the production of microcomputers? The demand for soybeans, the price of soybeans, and the profit received by soybean producers all increase. Soybean producers are earning an economic profit, because the profit earned by soybean producers is greater than the next-best alternative, corn production.

Meanwhile, the normal profit, or opportunity cost, of the farmers still producing corn has just gone up. Each farmer can now earn more profit by producing soybeans instead of corn. The farmer who continues to produce corn is losing the profit that can be earned in soybean production. Keep in mind that the economic profit earned in the production of soybeans is part of the normal profit for the production of corn. When one industry earns an economic profit, this becomes part of the normal profit for another industry. In this example the normal profit for corn production is now greater than the normal profit for soybean production.

CAUSES OF ECONOMIC PROFIT

Economic profit can occur because of favorable conditions in a particular market, as in the market for soybeans. However, three reasons for economic profit—risk, innovation, and monopoly power—have the greatest effect on the allocation of resources.

Risk Profits

Risk is the possibility of gain or loss, and it is an important dimension of entrepreneurial activity. When an entrepreneur combines the other three factors to begin the production of a good, no one is certain of the success of the venture. In 1983 several entrepreneurs came together and formed the United States Football League. They invested millions of dollars hiring coaches, players, and other personnel, leasing stadiums, and purchasing equipment and uniforms. The venture was based on the hope that sports fans would be willing to watch football in the spring. Prior to 1983, high school, college, and professional football had been played in the fall.

If the entrepreneurs are right, they will earn a great deal of economic profit. However, if they are wrong, they could lose millions of dollars. The economic profits are earned, in part, as a reward for the risk undertaken by the entrepreneurs. Each entrepreneur could have invested his or her funds in an enterprise with less risk and earned a normal profit.

Innovation Profits

Economic profit is also earned through innovation. **Innovation** is the introduction of a new product or production process. The founders of Apple Computers have earned enormous economic profit as a result of innovation. When Steven Jobs and Steve Wozniak introduced the Apple computer in the mid 1970s, it represented the first attempt to market personal microcomputers. They were not totally responsible for inventing the microcomputer (although they did have a hand in it), but they were responsible for putting it on the market.

Innovation profits are earned with the introduction of any successful product. Some examples of entrepreneurs or firms that have earned innovation profits include Henry Ford for the mass-produced Model-T automobile, Wham-O for the Frisbee, and Colonel Harlan Sanders for "finger lickin' good" Kentucky Fried Chicken. In each case the entrepreneurs who first introduced the innovation reaped economic profits. However, for every example of innovation profits there are hundreds of examples of innovations that failed, accompanying economic losses of untold magnitude.

Monopoly Profits

Economic profit also derives from the market power of firms. In Section 9 we discussed how monopoly and other imperfectly competitive firms can earn economic profits. Note that a firm with market power can earn economic profit *without* innovation and risk. Any firm facing a downward-sloping demand curve can receive monopoly profits if the demand for the product is sufficient.

RESOURCE ALLOCATION AND ECONOMIC PROFIT

Economic profit plays an important role in the allocation of resources. If firms in one industry earn an economic profit, other firms are encouraged to enter. Economic profit might result because the demand for a good increases, which signals firms in other industries to produce the good that is more desired by consumers.

Economic profit also provides an incentive to existing and potential entrepreneurs. If entrepreneurs have the expectation of earning large economic profits, then they are encouraged to undertake risk and develop new ideas and products. Indeed, if entrepreneurs in the past had expected to receive nothing more than normal profits, we might still be driving covered wagons, living in log cabins, and wearing flour-sack clothes.

However, when economic profit is caused by monopoly power, no incentive exists for innovation, risk, or an improved allocation of resources. Monopoly profits, unlike risk and innovation profits, do not lead to a more efficient allocation of resources or an improved standard of living.

REAL WORLD PROFITS AND THE REWARD TO ENTREPRENEURS

In the real world we can easily identify accounting profits earned by firms. However, accounting profits are usually not closely related to economic or normal profits. There are problems in trying to identify entrepreneurs. Are entrepreneurs the corporate stockholders, the top-level managers, or someone else? Without identifying the entrepreneurs, it is extremely difficult to determine normal profit. If we do not know who they are, then we do not know their opportunity cost.

In many cases accounting profit is the payment to owners of capital, for example, corporate stockholders, who are also the owners of the firm's capital. Of course, there is risk involved when investors buy corporate stock. The day after an investor buys stock, demand for the firm's product may vanish, the firm might face a devastating product liability suit, or the entire economy might fall into a depression. While shareholders are rewarded for this risk, does this constitute an entrepreneurial risk? Likewise, many factory workers also face the risk of physical injury on their jobs, and are usually rewarded for this risk. But is this an economic profit payment for an entrepreneurial risk?

The problems involved in measuring economic and normal profits makes this a much-debated topic. While most people agree that entrepreneurs should be rewarded for their activities, the serious arguments usually start when the level of profits are discussed. Entrepreneurs need to earn a normal profit, but a normal profit in one industry may not be equal to the normal profit in another industry. In addition, while risk and innovation profits may stimulate technological advancement and economic growth, can risk and innovation profits be separated from monopoly profits? If IBM receives economic profits, are they due to risk and innovation or to market power?

IN SUMMARY
Rent and Profit

- As a factor of production land provides the raw materials used to produce goods. Land also provides the space needed to locate economic activity. An important aspect of this location is the accessibility of an activity to other activities.

- The fixed supply of land means the same quantity is exchanged at every rent. Therefore, the rent on land is determined only by the demand for the land. The demand is based on the accessibility offered by the land, in addition to any important natural characteristics. Economic rent is the payment to a factor over and above its opportunity cost. Economic rent is a residual payment, made after all opportunity costs are paid. Thus, a firm with a profitable product can afford to pay a high rent. Since rent is a residual, some people have proposed a single tax on land, which could be used to raise the funds needed to operate government. However, if the tax is too high, the land may be completely removed from the market.

- All factors can earn an economic rent if their payment is greater than their opportunity cost. In fact, the economic profit earned by a firm is the same as economic rent. The economic profit is paid to one or more of the four factors of production as economic rent.

- There are three types of profit: accounting, normal, and economic. Accounting profit is the difference between a firm's explicit costs and revenue that is reported on the profit and loss statement. Normal profit is the profit that could be earned in the next-best production process, and is an opportunity cost. Economic profit is the difference between a firm's revenue and its opportunity cost, including a normal profit. An economic profit in one industry may be a normal profit for a related industry.

- There are three basic reasons for the existence of economic profit: risk, innovation, and monopoly power. Entrepreneurs earn economic profit because they are willing to take the risk of producing a good or service. They can also earn economic profit by implementing an innovation. And last, they can earn an economic profit by acquiring a degree of monopoly power.

- Risk and innovation are important in the allocation of resources, because both encourage development of new products or technological change. Monopoly profits, if they are created from barriers to entry, do not benefit the allocation of resources.

- Real world accounting profit is not easily identifiable as either economic or normal profit. Since entrepreneurship is often difficult to identify, it is equally difficult to determine the payment for entrepreneurship.

QUESTIONS FOR STUDY AND ANALYSIS

1. The market for videocassette tapes grew rapidly in the 1980s with the widespread use of videocassette recorders. It wasn't long before movie companies released their movies on tape (of course, after the movies had played at the local theaters). However, consumers tended to buy some movies, and only rent others. If consumers were likely to buy a movie, the purchase price was around $40, but if the movie was more likely to be rented, then the purchase price was around $80. (The cost of renting each tape was between $1 and $5.)
   a. Why do you think the prices were different for rental movies and purchase movies?
   b. Do you think the purchase price of the movie determined the rental rate, or vice versa? Why?

2. Explain why labor union members are likely to earn an economic rent.

3. In 1983, Lee Iacocca, the chairman of the board of Chrysler, earned $650,000 in compensation. Would you say he was earning any economic rent? If you also knew that the top twenty-five highest paid executives earned over $2.3 million in 1983, would you say that he was earning an economic rent?

4. If you are renting an apartment off-campus, would you being willing to pay more for an apartment one mile or ten miles from campus? Explain the role accessibility plays in your choice.

REVIEW GLOSSARY

accessibility The location of an activity or parcel of land relative to other activities.

accounting profit The difference between a firm's revenue and its explicit accounting costs.

economic profit The difference between all opportunity costs of production, including a normal profit, and the revenue received by a firm. Economic rent and economic profit are essentially the same. Economic profit is the revenue earned by a firm over and above all opportunity costs. Economic rent is the payment to a factor over and above its opportunity cost. Economic profit can be divided up as economic rent to the four factors of production.

economic rent The payment to a factor of production over and above its opportunity cost. A factor, like land, that is fixed in its supply earns nothing but an economic rent. Economic rent is a residual paid after all of the opportunity costs are paid. Firms with a more profitable product can pay a higher rent. High rent does not cause the price of a product to be high.

innovation The introduction of a new plant or production process.

normal profit The profit that can be earned by an entrepreneur in the next-best production process. In practice, the distinction between normal profit and economic profit is not clear-cut.

profit The payment for the use of entrepreneurship.

rent The payment for the use of land.

risk The possibility of gains or losses.

single tax A tax levied on only one item, used to raise the revenue needed by the government. A single tax on land does not alter the amount of land exchanged, and thus does not affect the allocation of resources. However, if the single tax on land is too high, landowners might remove their land from the market.

UNIT 11.4

Income Distribution

In the previous three units we examined the payments (wages, interest, rent, and profit) to the four factors of production. The distribution of income to the factors, or factor payments, is important to the allocation of resources. In this unit we examine the distribution of factor incomes in terms of the amount received by people rather than factors of production.

We start by identifying the difference between the personal and functional distributions of income. We then look at three alternative measures of the personal distribution of income: income classes, the Lorenz curve, and the Gini coefficient. After documenting the existence and degree of income inequality in the United States, we look at several causes of income inequality. And finally, we discuss two crucial goals of an economy, equity and efficiency. From an equity perspective we see the case for an equal distribution of income. Then, from an efficiency perspective we look at the case against an equal distribution of income.

PERSONAL AND FUNCTIONAL INCOME DISTRIBUTIONS

The total income earned by all factors of production in the United States in 1985 was over $3 trillion. If we look at how this income is distributed to each of the four factors of production, we are looking at the functional distribution of income. The **functional income distribution** is the distribution of income to factors of production, based on their contribution to output. The functional income distribution to the factors of production is an important component in the efficient allocation of resources.

However, the distribution of income can also be viewed in terms of the personal distribution. The **personal distribution of income** is the manner in which income is distributed to members of the economy. Here, we are not concerned with the percentage of national income received by labor, capital, land, and entrepreneurship, but with the percentage of income received by the poorest 20 percent of the population or the richest 10 percent.

The personal distribution of income is related to, and depends on, the functional distribution of income. A person whose only factor is labor is likely to receive less income than a person who has control over capital and land as well as labor. In addition, the ownership of factors is closely related to a person's position in the personal distribution of income. Labor tends to be on the lower end of the personal income distribution scale, whereas people who also have capital, land, and entrepreneurship tend to be on the higher end.

Each of these types of income distribution tells us something different. The personal income distribution indicates how income is divided among people; the functional income distribution indicates how income is divided among factors. This distinction is crucial because many people have command over, and earn income from, more than one factor of production. For example, laborers may earn interest on savings, or profit dividends on corporate stock owned through pension plans, in addition to wage income. And landowners and entrepreneurs may not only collect rent and profit but also earn a salary for labor.

Keep in mind that the functional distribution of income tells us if income is efficiently distributed to the factors of production, while the personal distribution of income tells us how equally income is distributed among members of the economy. Therefore, if the economy is trying to obtain maximum output with the available resources, then efficiency and the functional distribution of income take precedence. But if society is more concerned with the well-being of *each* member, regardless of their contribution to production, then the personal distribution of income takes precedence. In this text we have been concerned almost exclusively with efficiency. We now turn our attention to equality and the personal distribution of income.

MEASURES OF THE DISTRIBUTION OF INCOME

A number of methods of measuring the personal distribution of income have been developed, including income classes, the Lorenz curve, and the Gini coefficient. Each method can give a slightly different picture of the distribution, but no method gives a complete description.

Income Classes

The first method of measuring the personal distribution of income is based on the share of income earned by different income classes. Table 11.4.1 lists the percentage of money income received by nine different income classes and also the percentage of households in each income class. Note for example that 13.2 percent of all households earn less than $5000 of income and that 1.1 percent of all households earn over $75,000.

To get an idea of how the distribution of income changes over time, we can keep an eye on the percentage of households in each of these nine income classes. But a fuller understanding of the income distribution depends also on the percentage of income earned by each class. For example, the lowest income class (less than $5000) contains 13.2 percent of the households but earns only 1.9 percent of the income. By contrast, the highest income group (over $75,000) contains only 1.1 percent of the households but earns 5.6 percent of the income.

In each income class the combination of the percentage of households and the percentage of income earned gives us a picture of the income distribution. For example, if in the lower income classes the percentage of households increases and the percentage of income earned decreases, then the income is distributed more unequally. A larger share of the population is earning a smaller share

UNIT 11.4 ■ INCOME DISTRIBUTION

Table 11.4.1

Income Classes and the Distribution of Income, 1982

One way to examine the distribution of income is with income classes. This table lists the percentage of households and the percentage of income earned for each of nine income classes. If income were equally distributed, then the percentage of households and income would be the same for all classes.

Income Class	Households (percent)	Income (percent)
Less than $5000	13.2	1.9
$5000 to $9999	16.4	6.2
$10,000 to $14,999	15.9	10.0
$15,000 to $19,999	14.0	12.4
$20,000 to $24,999	12.0	14.1
$25,000 to $34,999	15.6	23.3
$35,000 to $49,999	8.3	17.3
$50,000 to $74,999	3.1	9.2
More than $75,000	1.1	5.6

Source: U.S. Bureau of the Census, *Current Population Reports*.

Table 11.4.2

Population Classes and the Distribution of Income, 1947 and 1984

Another way to examine the distribution of income is with population classes. In this table the population is divided into equal groups, with 20 percent in the first group, 20 percent in the second group, and so on. If income were equally distributed, then the percentage of income earned by all five groups would be equal to 20 percent. The greater the deviation from 20 percent, the more unequal the distribution. According to this table the distribution of income has become slightly more unequal between 1947 and 1984.

	Percentage of Income	
Population Class	1947	1984
Lowest fifth	5.0	4.7
Second fifth	11.9	11.0
Third fifth	17.0	17.0
Fourth fifth	23.1	24.4
Highest fifth	43.0	42.9

Source: U.S. Bureau of the Census, *Current Population Reports*.

of the income. By the same token, the income is also distributed more unequally if in the higher income classes a smaller percentage of households earns a larger percentage of income.

However, measuring the distribution of income in terms of absolute income classes can be misleading. In times of inflation the money income of households can increase along with higher prices, without any increase in well-being. The number of people earning less than $5000 may decrease, and the number earning more than $75,000 may increase, which would seem to indicate a more equal distribution of income. However, since prices are higher, real income is unchanged.

One solution is to adjust real income to compensate for increases in prices. However, a more common method is to divide the income classes in a slightly different manner. Instead of the absolute income earned by households, we can look at relative income. For example, we can divide all households into five equal groups, as in Table 11.4.2.

Here, each class has the same number of households. The first class contains the 20 percent of households with the lowest incomes. The next class contains the 20 percent of households with the next lowest incomes. This continues until we reach the fifth class, which contains the 20 percent of households with the highest incomes. Since we

Figure 11.4.1

The Lorenz Curve

The Lorenz curve illustrates the cumulative percentage of income earned by the cumulative percentage of households. The 45° line represents a perfectly equal distribution of income. The right-angled axes represent a perfectly unequal distribution. This diagram shows the Lorenz curve for 1984.

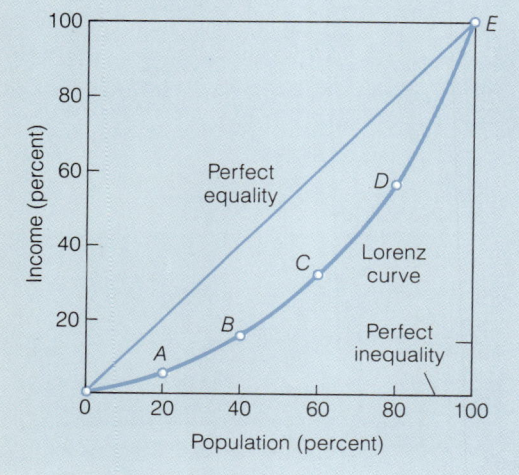

are looking only at relative income (there is always a highest and lowest 20 percent), changes in money income due to inflation become irrelevant.

As Table 11.4.2 indicates, in 1984 the households in the lowest income class earned only 4.7 percent of the income, while households in the highest income class earned 42.9 percent of the income. A perfectly equal distribution of income exists when each income class earns exactly 20 percent of the income. If the poorest 20 percent of the households earns 20 percent of the income, and the richest 20 percent of the households also earns 20 percent of the income, then both must earn the same income. The closer each class comes to 20 percent of the income, the more equal is the distribution of income.

For example, in 1947 the lowest 20 percent earned 5 percent of the income, while the highest 20 percent earned 43 percent of the income. In 1984 the lowest and the next-to-the-lowest groups had a smaller percentage of the income, while the fourth highest group had a larger percentage, indicating that the income distribution in 1984 tended to be less equal than the distribution in 1947.

The Lorenz Curve

A second method of measuring the personal distribution of income is the Lorenz curve. Tables of income classes, such as those in Tables 11.4.1 and 11.4.2, can be informative but sometimes hard to read. This is especially true if we want to look at more than five income classes. For this reason the personal distribution of income is often presented in the form of a graph called the Lorenz curve. The **Lorenz curve** is a curve depicting the cumulative percentage of income earned by the cumulative percentage of households. Figure 11.4.1 presents a Lorenz curve.

The horizontal axis measures the percentage of households, and the vertical axis, the percentage of income. Thus, point A tells us that the lowest 20 percent of the households earns only 4.7 percent of the income. Point B tells us that the lowest 40 percent of households (including the first 20 percent) earns 15.9 percent of the income. Point C is the lowest 60 percent, earning 33 percent of the income, and point D the lowest 80 percent, earning 57.3 percent of the income. And at point E, in the upper right-hand corner, 100 percent of the households earns 100 percent of the income.

The position of the Lorenz curve provides a graphic illustration of the equality of the personal income distribution. The straight 45° line connecting the origin to point E is the line of perfect equality. If every person in the economy receives the same income, then 20 percent of the households receives 20 percent of the income. Likewise, 40 percent of the households receives 40 percent of the income. The Lorenz curve, *if* income is equally distributed, is this straight 45° line.

But suppose one person in the economy received all income. In this case 99+ percent of the households receives no income, and the remaining person receives 100 percent of the income. In this case of perfect inequality, the Lorenz curve would be the right-angled axes.

With these boundaries of perfect equality and perfect inequality, we can easily see how equally the income is distributed. If the Lorenz curve is closer to the 45° line, income is more equally distributed. If the Lorenz curve is closer to the lower right-hand corner of the figure, income is less equally distributed.

The Gini Coefficient

The **Gini coefficient** is a numerical measure of the inequality of the distribution of income. The Gini coefficient captures the distribution of income in a single measure. The best way to see how the Gini coefficient is calculated is by looking at the Lorenz curve, as presented in Figure 11.4.2. The area between the 45° line and the Lorenz curve is labeled A; the area between the Lorenz curve and the axes is labeled B. The Gini coefficient is calculated as the ratio of area A to area A + B.

If area A is relatively small, then the Lorenz curve is very close to the 45° line, and the income distribution is relatively equal. Thus, the numerical value of the Gini coefficient is relatively small. A perfectly equal distribution of income exists if the Gini coefficient is equal to zero.

But if area A is relatively large, nearly equal to the entire triangle A + B, then the Lorenz curve approaches the right angle formed by the two axes. In this case the Gini coefficient approaches the value of 1, reflecting an unequal distribution of income.

Table 11.4.3 presents the Gini coefficient for the United States for selected years since 1947. The Gini coefficient indicates that income has become less equally distributed in the United States in recent times. In 1947 the Gini coefficient was

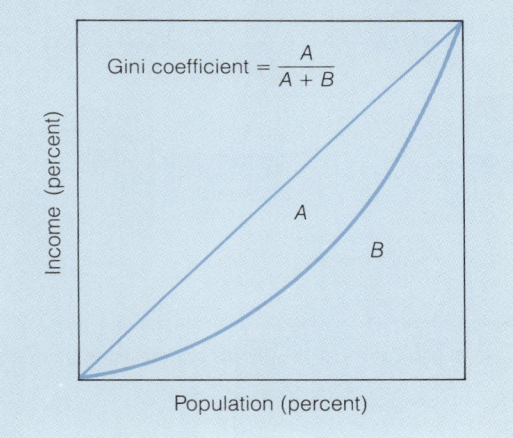

Figure 11.4.2

The Lorenz Curve and the Gini Coefficient

The Gini coefficient is a single number used to measure the distribution of income. It is the ratio of the area between the Lorenz curve and the 45° line, area A, to the entire triangular area between the 45° line and the axes, area A + B. The Gini coefficient ranges from 1 (perfect inequality) to zero (perfect equality).

0.376, and in 1982 it was 0.381. However, as recently as 1977, the Gini coefficient was as low as 0.364.

CAUSES OF INCOME INEQUALITY

In the past several decades the personal distribution of income has become less equal. We can begin to understand why this has occurred by looking at several factors that lead to an unequal distribution of income.

Natural Ability One of the most important reasons that people earn different levels of income is

Table 11.4.3

The Gini Coefficient, 1947 to 1982

The Gini coefficient is a third indicator of the distribution of income. A larger value of the coefficient indicates a more unequal distribution of income. Note that the Gini coefficient generally declined from 1947 through the early 1970s, but in the late 1970s and early 1980s it began to increase, reflecting greater inequality of income distribution.

Year	Gini Coefficient
1982	0.381
1977	0.364
1972	0.360
1967	0.348
1962	0.362
1957	0.351
1952	0.368
1947	0.376

Source: U.S. Bureau of the Census, *Current Population Reports*.

natural ability. Some workers are better at their jobs than others because they are naturally more intelligent, physically stronger, or more ingenious. A salesperson may receive a higher commission simply because he or she has more charisma or a nicer personality. A junior executive may rise through the ranks faster, and earn more income, as a result of natural ability. Professional athletes receive high salaries based in large part on their natural physical abilities.

Human Capital A second reason for differences in income and the resulting income inequality is human capital. Some people are better at their jobs, and more productive, because they have invested in training and education. For example, an accountant receives more income than an unskilled laborer due to human capital.

Personal Preferences Another reason some people earn less income than others is due to their personal preferences. One person may prefer a lower-paying job because it has fewer responsibilities, is less hectic, and provides more leisure time. A second person may not care about these amenities, preferring to have a higher-paying job, with all of the goods and services that can be purchased with the income. Some people would rather work long hours, while others would rather spend more time with their family.

Inherited Wealth Some people receive higher incomes than others due to inherited wealth. This wealth, in the form of productive capital and land, can generate a great deal of income. Note that the income is not earned because the current owner has any natural abilities or human capital but was created by the abilities of others.

Discrimination Discrimination based on a person's ethnic background or sex can also lead to differences in income. In the United States many ethnic groups have been knowingly or unwittingly discriminated against. Blacks, Indians, and women still tend to receive less income than white males performing the same jobs.

Market Power The ability to control the supply of a factor is another cause of income differences. If labor unions successfully control the supply of workers in a particular industry or occupation, then these workers receive higher incomes than non-union workers. If the American Medical Association controls the supply of doctors through admissions to medical schools, then doctors receive higher incomes. Controlling the supply of any mineral resource, of land in a city, or of an important piece of capital equipment can lead to higher incomes for the factor owners if they exercise their market power.

Luck Luck can also play a part in income distribution. Some people simply happen to be at the right place at the right time. For example, the young comedian who gets the big break because a network executive has a flat tire in front of the nightclub where the comedian is performing is obviously lucky. The college graduate who enters the job market just as the economy is starting a period of rapid growth is also lucky. Being born a year earlier or a year later might mean unemployment.

EQUITY AND EFFICIENCY

An equal distribution of income is generally desirable. Keep in mind, however, that there are advantages and disadvantages to a more equal distribution of income.

The Case for an Equal Distribution

An unequal distribution of income can lead to unequal opportunities for people in an economy. A person with less income is less able to invest in human capital through training and education, which will tend to limit the amount of income earned in the future. Likewise, investment in other productive factors, such as land and capital, is less likely for people with lower incomes. An unskilled worker earning $5000 a year cannot buy a hundred shares of IBM stock selling for $100 per share. Thus, an unequal distribution tends to be perpetuated if there is no outside involvement (such as through government transfers of income).

A case can be made for an equal distribution of income based on the satisfaction received from an additional dollar of income. The marginal utility received for an extra dollar of income is less for someone with a relatively high income than for someone with a relatively low income. Thus, the loss in utility from a dollar taken from a rich person is less than the gain in utility from the poor person. In this case a more equal distribution of income leads to an increase in society's overall utility.

A good case can also be made for an equal distribution of income on political grounds. Income inequality often leads to political unrest and turmoil. Throughout history, people with very low incomes have revolted against those with higher incomes. If poor peasants who are unable to feed their families on a regular basis witness conspicuous consumption by a few members of the society, they are likely to use force to increase their own incomes.

The Case Against an Equal Distribution

An argument against an equal distribution of income is also based on the concept of equity. Briefly, this argument states that people with varying natural abilities and preferences for work and leisure should not receive the same income. If one person works harder and contributes more to the production of output, then he or she should receive a higher income. An equal distribution of income is not equitable if every person in the economy does not have the same ability.

Another argument against an equal distribution of income is based on efficiency. An unequal distribution of income also provides incentives. If a person knows that harder work leads to a higher income, then the economy has provided an important incentive. The opportunity for relatively high incomes from capital (both physical and human), land, and entrepreneurship also provides incentives for development of these factors. An aspiring doctor will not spend eight years in school, and additional years as an intern, in order to earn the minimum wage. Nor will a person forego current consumption and purchase of capital goods if there is no chance of additional income.

While a more equal distribution of income generally benefits society, it is usually not desirable to have a perfectly equal distribution of income. For any economy the *best* distribution of income is a Gini coefficient that lies somewhere between zero and 1, though no one really knows what value the coefficient should have. Most people would agree that an income distribution in which 1 percent of the population receives 99 percent of the income is not desirable. But what incentives would exist for innovation, investment in physical and human capital, and extra work if everyone in the economy could expect to receive no more than $10,000?

IN SUMMARY

Income Distribution

- The functional distribution of income represents the payment to factors of production based on their contribution to output. The personal distribution is simply the income received by people. The functional distribution is important in terms of the efficiency of production. The personal distribution is important in terms of the well-being of people.

- The personal distribution of income can be viewed in three ways. The first divides people into different income classes. The second is the Lorenz curve, which graphically illustrates the degree of income inequality. The third is the Gini coefficient, which captures the degree of income inequality in a single number.

- An unequal distribution of income results from several factors: natural ability, human capital, personal preferences, inherited wealth, discrimination, market power, and luck.

- There are pros and cons to an equal distribution of income. A more equal distribution is desirable because it gives every member of society equal opportunities. It can also increase the overall utility of society, and prevent political turmoil. However, an equal distribution of income can also be inequitable, since some people have more ability and desire to work harder. In addition, the chance of a relatively high income provides incentives to invest in human and physical capital, land, and entrepreneurship.

QUESTIONS FOR STUDY AND ANALYSIS

1. The following table lists hypothetical distributions of income between five income classes for two different countries, the United States and China.

Population Class	Percentage of Income	
	United States	China
Lowest fifth	5.0	2.0
Second fifth	10.0	8.0
Third fifth	15.0	10.0
Fourth fifth	25.0	20.0
Highest fifth	45.0	60.0

   a. Which country has the more equal distribution of income? Why?
   b. Construct the Lorenz curves for each country.
   c. Based on the Lorenz curves, which country has the more equal distribution of income? Why?
   d. Assume that the distribution of income in China is altered, as the following table indicates.

Population Class	Percentage of Income
Lowest fifth	2.0
Second fifth	8.0
Third fifth	20.0
Fourth fifth	30.0
Highest fifth	40.0

   Now which country has the more equal distribution of income? Why? (To answer this question, construct a new Lorenz curve.)

2. Evaluate whether each of the following is likely to make the distribution of income more or less equal. Also, indicate which of the causes of income inequality is operating on the income distribution.
   a. An increase in the amount of government funds spent for public education

b. A lower tax rate on inherited wealth
c. The elimination of labor unions
d. Tougher antidiscrimination legislation
e. An influx of illegal aliens from Mexico

3. Explain why a society with a perfectly equal distribution of income might be an exceedingly dull society.

4. Many developing countries throughout the world are concerned with their income distribution. However, some people argue that an unequal distribution of income can eventually benefit the country. Discuss how an unequal distribution of income can be both good and bad for a developing country.

REVIEW GLOSSARY

functional distribution of income The distribution of income to factors of production, based on their contribution to output. The functional distribution of income is an important component in the efficiency of production.

Gini coefficient A numerical measure of the inequality of distribution of income. The Gini coefficient is calculated as the ratio of the area between the Lorenz curve and the 45° line to the area of the entire triangle beneath the 45° line. The Gini coefficient can range between zero, for perfect equality, and 1, for perfect inequality.

Lorenz curve A curve depicting the cumulative percentage of income earned by the cumulative percentage of households. With a Lorenz curve the 45° line represents a perfectly equal distribution of income and the right angle formed by the axes represents a perfectly unequal distribution of income. The distribution of income is more equal the closer the Lorenz curve is to the 45° line and the farther it is from the right-angled axes.

personal distribution of income The distribution of income to people in the economy. The personal distribution of income indicates the well-being of people in the economy.

UNIT 11.5

Poverty

In one sense the function of an economy is to eliminate poverty. Recall that an economy allocates resources toward the production of the goods and services used to satisfy wants and needs. The better an economy performs this function, the more satisfied its members are. But if people are left wanting some of the necessities of life, then they are in a state of poverty. **Poverty is the condition in which people do not have the basic necessities of life, and lack the income to buy them.** Even the U.S. economy, which does a relatively good job of producing and allocating goods and services, has widespread poverty. While the United States produces $4 trillion worth of goods and services a year, over 10 percent of the population remains in poverty.

In this unit we first examine the concepts of absolute and relative poverty, and then discuss the measurement of poverty. Next, we look at two types of antipoverty policies, the guaranteed income and the negative income tax. And we conclude the unit with a brief discussion of several poverty programs that the government has used in recent years to reduce poverty.

ABSOLUTE AND RELATIVE POVERTY

It is easy to say that poverty results from the lack of income. The difference between a poor person and a rich person is the amount of income each has. Thus, to move someone from the lower end of the income distribution to the upper end, simply increase their income.

However, another aspect of poverty warrants more discussion. Poverty exists if people lack the basic necessities of life. But how we define the basic necessities of life can give us two different views of poverty, an absolute view and a relative view.

In one sense the basic necessities of life constitute the food, clothing, shelter, and fuel required to sustain physiological functions. In this case poverty exists if a person does not have enough income to purchase these absolute necessities. The **absolute poverty level** is the condition in which people do not have the income to buy an absolute amount of the basic necessities of life. It would seem easy enough to specify the amount of income needed to bring someone up to the absolute level of poverty. First, identify the minimum number of calories, square feet of shelter, amount of clothing, and Btu's of fuel that will sustain life, then determine the total income required to buy these goods. This would be the absolute level of poverty.

However, there are problems with this approach. For example, the minimum number of calories needed can be obtained with a variety of different foods, ranging from dogfood to beef Wellington. Should the level of poverty be defined as the amount of income needed to buy dogfood? In the United States few people would regard dogfood as an appropriate way of obtaining the minimum daily requirement of calories.

But in some countries, being able to eat *any* food, including dogfood, might be acceptable. In this sense poverty depends on the relative circumstances of a society. A person considered poor in the United States might be considered middle class in other countries. A basic necessity of life in the United States is different than in other countries. And because of the relative nature of basic necessities, the **relative poverty level** is the condition in which people do not have the income to buy a relative amount of the basic necessities of life.

For example, people in the United States who cannot afford a refrigerator are considered poor, whereas in other countries a refrigerator is purchased only by the wealthy. This difference is based, in large part, on differences in technology and the structure of the economy. In the United States less than 5 percent of the population works on farms, and 95 percent must purchase their food from others. Therefore, a refrigerator is necessary to store and preserve the food. But in a country where 70 to 80 percent of the population works on farms, a refrigerator for storage is not necessary, because people can grow their own food.

Poverty and the Distribution of Income

The relative poverty level also depends on people's perception of their own income relative to that of others. Suppose a person has an increase in income, and thus a greater command over goods and services. In this case we can argue that the person is better off, and more satisfied. But what if everyone else also has more income? If the person remains in the bottom 5 percent of the income distribution, he or she may not be any more satisfied. And even though there is absolutely more income, the level of satisfaction is the same.

The distribution of income, as a relative measure, provides an indication of the degree of poverty in the economy. In general, the more unequal the distribution is, the larger the degree of poverty is. In particular, if we view poverty from a relative perspective, the lowest 5 percent of the population is going to feel poorer the farther they are from the upper 5 percent.

The Poverty Line

While it is difficult to settle on an ideal definition of poverty, it is important to have a working definition. In the United States the government identifies the official poverty line. The **poverty line** is a measure of the income needed by a family based on family size, location, and characteristics of the head of the household. The official poverty line in the United States is based on an absolute measure of poverty, found by estimating the minimum daily food requirements and determining the amount of income required to buy the food.

For example, a family containing one person requires less income to meet the basic necessities of life than does a family of eight. Furthermore, the family of eight does not need eight times the income of the family of one. In addition, if the head of the household is over sixty-five years old,

Table 11.5.1

The Official Poverty Line for Selected Groups, 1984

The threshold poverty level varies for people of different ages and family sizes. A single person over sixty-five is in poverty with income less than $4979. However, a family of nine is in poverty with income less than $21,247.

Size of Family	Poverty Threshold
One person	$ 5,278
Under 65	5,400
Over 65	4,979
Two persons	6,762
Head Under 65	6,983
Head Over 65	6,282
Three persons	8,277
Four persons	10,609
Five persons	12,566
Six persons	14,207
Seven persons	16,096
Eight persons	17,961
Nine persons or more	21,247

Source: U.S. Bureau of the Census, *Current Population Reports*.

Figure 11.5.1

Percentage of Population Below the Poverty Line, 1960 to 1984

The percentage of the population below the poverty line declined from 22 percent in 1959 to 11 percent in 1973. While it remained around 11 to 12 percent during most of the 1970s, it rose sharply beginning in 1980. Source: U.S. Bureau of the Census, *Current Population Reports*, selected issues.

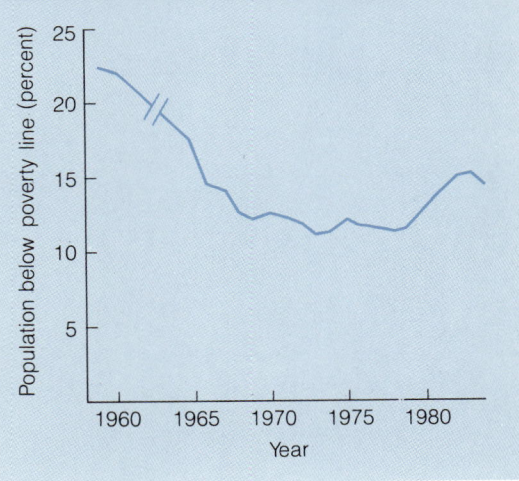

less income is required for the basic necessities. Table 11.5.1 presents the poverty line for families with different characteristics.

Poverty in the United States

Based on the official poverty line, Figure 11.5.1 depicts the trend in poverty over the past several years. Note that in 1960 about 22 percent of all families in the United States were below the poverty line, before President Johnson declared the famous "War on Poverty" in 1964. Through the rest of the 1960s the percentage of families below the poverty line decreased. However, this decline leveled out in the 1970s, and took a sharp upturn in the early 1980s, so that in 1984 the percentage of poor families was as large as it was in the mid-1960s.

While Figure 11.5.1 depicts the extent of poverty for all families in the United States, some groups are more likely to be poor than others. Table 11.5.2 gives the percentage of people below the poverty line for different groups. For example, slightly over 14 percent of all people are below the poverty line, but only 11.5 percent of whites are poor, while nearly 34 percent of blacks are poor. Furthermore, families with female heads have over

Table 11.5.2

Percentage Below the Poverty Line for Selected Groups, 1984

The percentage of people below the poverty line varies for different socioeconomic groups. While 14.4 percent of the total population is below the poverty level, only 11.5 percent of whites are below that level. Blacks and Hispanics have 33.8 and 28.4 percent below the poverty level, respectively.

Group	Percentage of Group Below Poverty Line
Total population	14.4
White	11.5
Black	33.8
Hispanic	28.4
Male	12.8
Female	15.9
Female head of household	34.5
Over 65	12.4
Under 18	21.5

Source: U.S. Bureau of the Census, *Current Population Reports*.

34 percent below the poverty line. In addition, people over 65 and people under 18 tend to have a larger than average share below the poverty line.

ANTIPOVERTY POLICIES

The elimination of poverty can be approached in a number of different ways. If the basic view of poverty is that people do not have enough income, the most direct approach is to give poor people more spendable income. A second method is to provide incentives to work through negative income tax policies.

Guaranteed Income

One method of reducing poverty is the guaranteed income approach. **Guaranteed income** is a policy that insures everyone receives a minimum amount of income, regardless of income earned. The operation of this method is depicted in Figure 11.5.2. The horizontal axis measures the amount of income earned by a person; the vertical axis measures the amount of income received, which includes earned income plus any welfare payments from the government. If this person receives no welfare payments, then the amount of income earned is exactly the same as the amount received, which falls on the 45° line coming from the origin. But suppose that the poverty line for this person is $5000. In essence, the government guarantees that this person receives $5000 of income, meaning if the person does not work and earns no income, the government pays the full $5000. However, if the person works a little bit and earns $3000, the government pays $2000. With this policy every person in the economy earns at least $5000, and no one is below the poverty line.

This particular method of eliminating poverty has one major drawback. Everyone receives $5000 whether they work and earn all $5000 or do not work and receive $5000 as welfare payments. If poor people value leisure time, they will probably choose not to work, because their level of income is the same in either case. Thus, this method of eliminating poverty provides enormous incentives *not* to work. Anyone who can earn at most $5000 by working is better off not working. Furthermore, those earning $5500 might be encouraged to stop working completely. They lose $500 of income, but gain all of their leisure time.

And what happens if they stop working? First, they do not produce goods and services, so the overall level of goods and services produced in the economy declines. Second, the more people receiving welfare payments, the greater the amount of funds needed to support this program. Obviously, if twice as many people are paid $5000, the government needs twice as much money, which it raises

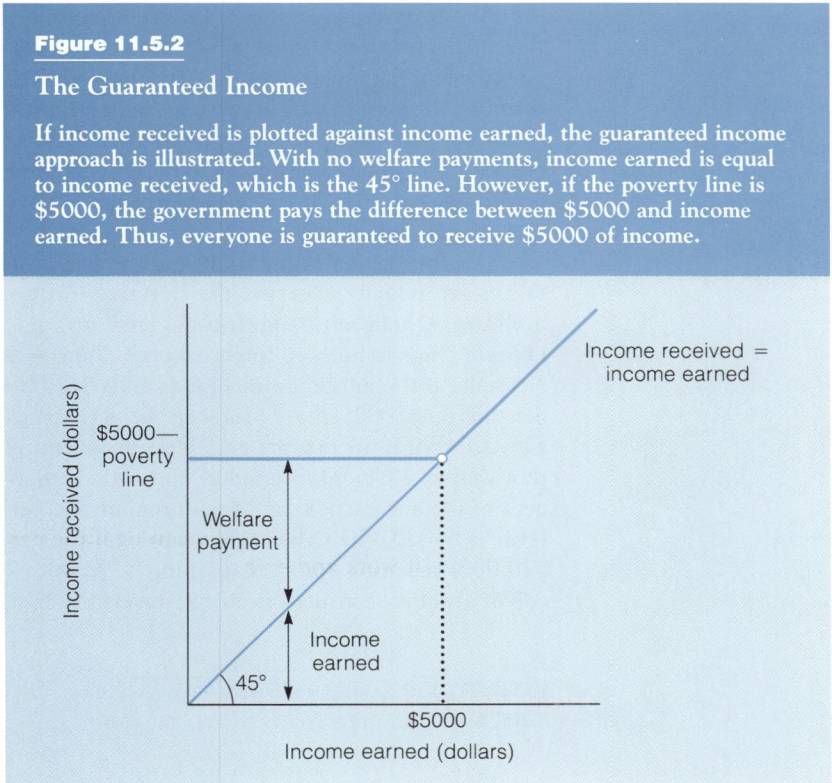

Figure 11.5.2

The Guaranteed Income

If income received is plotted against income earned, the guaranteed income approach is illustrated. With no welfare payments, income earned is equal to income received, which is the 45° line. However, if the poverty line is $5000, the government pays the difference between $5000 and income earned. Thus, everyone is guaranteed to receive $5000 of income.

by taxing the people who are working. And since fewer people in the economy are working, and more money is needed, each person who is working has to pay a higher tax.

The fundamental problem with the guaranteed income method is the lack of incentives. Even if a person works harder and obtains an increase in earned income from $2000 to $3000, total income is unaffected. Essentially, every dollar of income earned up to $5000 is effectively taxed at a 100 percent rate.

Negative Income Tax

An alternative to guaranteed income is the negative income tax. The **negative income tax** is a policy in which public assistance payments are reduced by a fraction of additional income earned. The negative income tax reduces the incentive problems in the guaranteed income method by letting people keep additional money for working, rather than taking it all away. As the name implies, the negative income tax is set up much like the standard income tax system, but in reverse.

For example, a minimum income level of $5000 is established, so that everyone, whether or not they earn income, receives at least $5000. If they earn no income, as shown in Table 11.5.3, the government pays them the entire $5000, just like with the guaranteed income method. However, if the recipient earns $1000, the guaranteed income method reduces welfare payments by an equal $1000; the negative income tax does not.

Table 11.5.3

The Negative Income Tax

The negative income tax is designed to provide incentives for people to earn income in addition to welfare payments. In this table the negative tax rate is 50 percent, meaning welfare payments are reduced by 50 percent of income earned. By contrast, the guaranteed income approach reduces welfare payments by 100 percent of income earned.

Income Earned	Welfare Payments	Total Income
$ 0	$5,000	$ 5,000
1,000	4,500	5,500
2,000	4,000	6,000
3,000	3,500	6,500
4,000	3,000	7,000
5,000	2,500	7,500
6,000	2,000	8,000
7,000	1,500	8,500
8,000	1,000	9,000
9,000	500	9,500
10,000	0	10,000

If the recipient earns $1000, welfare payments are reduced by only a fraction of that amount. In the example shown in Table 11.5.3, welfare payments are reduced by $500, meaning for each extra dollar earned, welfare payments are reduced by 50 cents. In essence, the negative income tax rate is 50 percent. Since the negative income tax rate is 50 percent, people still have an incentive to earn additional income and, consequently, produce goods and services. In addition, a recipient who earns $1000 only receives $4500 from the government, and not the full $5000. As recipients work more, the total amount paid by the government is actually reduced.

As we move down Table 11.5.3, we can see that higher levels of earned income reduce the welfare payment but increase the total income received. At the bottom of the table, we see that if $10,000 is earned, the welfare payment is zero, which is the breakeven point. Note that if the breakeven point is too high, people who are nowhere near poverty can receive welfare payments.

This breakeven point is affected by both the minimum income level and the negative income tax rate. A high minimum income level or a low tax rate tends to push up the breakeven point. For example, if the minimum income level is $10,000 instead of $5000, the breakeven level rises to $15,000. But if the tax rate is 25 percent, meaning that welfare payments are reduced by only 25 percent of income earned, and the minimum income level is $5000, then the breakeven level rises to $20,000, meaning someone earning $19,000 receives a welfare payment from the government.

POVERTY PROGRAMS IN THE UNITED STATES

The United States has many programs designed to reduce poverty by supplying both money and in-kind payments (such as food, housing, or medical services) to the poor. The most notable money payment is through Aid to Families with Dependent Children (AFDC). The AFDC program began in 1935 under the provisions of the Social Security Act, which itself was responsible for setting up the Social Security system and many of the poverty programs discussed here. The AFDC was originally designed to aid widows not covered by Social Security; it now provides public assistance to female heads of households below the poverty line. Over half of the funds supporting this program are supplied by the federal government, with the remainder coming from state and local governments. The program is administered by the states, meaning the states establish eligibility guidelines and benefits. Therefore, eligibility criteria and benefits can vary from state to state.

The second most important money payment is through the Supplemental Security Income (SSI) program for the blind, aged, and permanently disabled, which was also established by the Social Security Act of 1935. Until 1972 it was administered much like AFDC, with funds coming from all levels of government and the states administering the program. However, after 1972 the federal government took over the program to standardize benefits and guidelines.

The biggest program providing in-kind benefits to the poor is Medicaid. Medicaid was set up in 1965 by an amendment to the Social Security Act of 1935 and pays for medical services for the poor. In general, anyone receiving public assistance is eligible for Medicaid. In fact, many states provide Medicaid to people who are not on public assistance but who are close to the poverty line. As with AFDC, the federal government provides over half of the funds, while state governments administer the program and establish guidelines.

Food stamps is the second most important in-kind poverty program, providing the means to purchase food. While a food stamp program existed between 1939 and 1943, the current program was established in 1961. For the first two decades of the program, food stamp eligibility guidelines were looser than other programs, but in 1980 these guidelines became more restrictive. The federal government provides all of the funding for the food stamps themselves and part of the costs of administering the program. State governments provide the remainder of the administrative costs and also administer the program.

While other programs also aid the poor, these four account for over 80 percent of the support to the poor. Table 11.5.4 summarizes recent funding for the four programs.

Our discussion of poverty programs should mention several other programs that indirectly affect the poor. Most notable is Old Age, Survivors, and Disability Insurance (OASDI), which is part of the Social Security program. The OASDI program is *not* based on poverty, although these payments represent an important source of income for poor people. The Social Security system is based not on income but on prior earnings and taxes paid into the system. As a matter of fact, a retired millionaire can collect from OASDI. However, even though payments are not made based on the degree of poverty, this program provides more income assistance to the poor than any other program.

Unemployment insurance and veteran's benefits comprise two other programs that provide money payments to people who are not necessarily poor. However, an unemployed worker is more likely to be below the poverty line than an employed worker. Medicaid is another benefit not based on poverty but still providing a source of assistance for

Table 11.5.4

Expenditures on Poverty Programs in the United States, 1983

The two largest money payment programs aimed at people in poverty are Aid to Families with Dependent Children and Supplemental Security Income, accounting for $25 billion in 1983. The two largest in-kind payment programs are Medicaid and food stamps, accounting for about $44 billion in 1983.

Program	Expenditure (billions)
Money payments	
Aid to Families with Dependent Children (AFDC)	$ 15.4
Supplemental Security Income (SSI)	10.1
In-kind payments	
Medicaid	35.0
Food stamps	9.2
Other miscellaneous payments	57.5
Total	127.2

Source: U.S. Bureau of the Census, *Statistical Abstract of the United States*, 1985.

poor people in the form of payments for medical services for people over sixty-five. And both poor and nonpoor people benefit from Medicare.

Indeed, Social Security, unemployment insurance, veterans' benefits, and Medicare all provide valuable benefits to the poor. However, unlike AFDC, SSI, Medicaid, and food stamps, they are not designed specifically for the poor, and thus are less effective in helping the poor.

AN EVALUATION OF POVERTY PROGRAMS

How effective are the programs designed specifically for the elimination or reduction of poverty? The biggest problem facing each of these poverty programs discussed is administration. Most of the programs have difficulty in getting the money or benefits into the hands of the people with the greatest need. There is also the potential for a great deal of overlap between programs, so that a recipient can live quite comfortably from combined payments. However, while overpayments may occur in some cases, other times a recipient may receive too few benefits. In addition, due to the number and diversity of programs and the complex bureaucracy that administers the system, some recipients have found it possible to receive illegal benefits by claiming extra children or not reporting earned income.

In a nutshell, poverty is the lack of income. One way to eliminate poverty is to give people more income, or at least the basic necessities that they buy with the income; this is the basis of antipoverty programs in the United States. However, the lack of income is only a symptom of poverty, and maintaining the income levels of poor people represents a short-term solution. An alternative approach is to attack the causes of poverty, to eliminate poverty in the long run.

In Unit 11.4 we discussed the basic causes of income inequality: natural ability, human capital, personal preference, inherited wealth, discrimination, market power, and luck. In addition to creating a more unequal distribution of income, each can also lead to poverty. Some of these causes are beyond anyone's control, since very little can be done to improve a person's natural ability or luck. But several of the other causes can be addressed directly in an attempt to eliminate poverty. The most obvious is human capital. Providing education and training can improve a person's income earning ability, and thus eliminate poverty. And discrimination can be controlled through antidiscrimination programs aimed in part at reducing the poverty of blacks and other ethnic groups.

IN SUMMARY

Poverty

- Poverty exists when someone does not have enough income to afford the basic necessities of life. Absolute poverty level is when people do not have the income to buy absolute levels of food, clothing, and shelter. Relative poverty level depends on society and the existing technology.

- The poverty line is an absolute measure of the income needed by a family, based on different characteristics. In the United States the percentage of people below the poverty line declined from the mid-1960s until 1980. Since 1980 this percentage has increased. In addition, some groups in society are more likely to be below the poverty line than others.

- One way to reduce poverty is with a guaranteed income. If people earn less than the poverty line, then they receive a welfare payment from the government. However, this approach reduces the incentive to work if someone makes less than the guaranteed income. An alternative approach is the negative income tax, which provides incentives to work even if someone makes less than the guaranteed income.

- In the United States four programs provide over 80 percent of the assistance directed to the poor. Aid to Families with Dependent Children and Supplemental Security Income provide direct payments to the poor. Medicaid and food stamps provide in-kind medical services and food. Other programs such as Social Security and Medicare provide assistance to the poor, even though this is not their main purpose.

QUESTIONS FOR STUDY AND ANALYSIS

1. In the United States in 1984 the official poverty line for a single-person household was $5278. However, in the same year the average income per person in numerous other countries—Egypt, Bolivia, Thailand, Kenya, and India, to name just a few—was less than $1000. In this light, how can anyone say that there is poverty in the United States?

2. Suppose you are in charge of poverty programs in the kingdom of Econovaria. You have five people below the official poverty line of $6000. The incomes earned by the poorest ten people in the kingdom are given in the following table:

Person	Income
1	$ 1,000
2	2,000
3	3,000
4	4,000
5	5,000
6	6,000
7	7,000
8	8,000
9	9,000
10	10,000

a. If you use the guaranteed income method, such that the income of everyone below the poverty line is raised to $6000, what is the total amount of welfare payments in the kingdom? In answering this question, assume that everyone continues to work as before.
b. What is the total amount of payments if everyone earning less than $6000 of income stops working and receives nothing but the government payment?
c. Now let's say you want to try the negative income tax method. Each person is guaranteed $6000 as before, but now the subsidy is reduced by 60 percent of income earned over $6000. The tenth person, earning $10,000, is at the breakeven point and receives no payment. What is the total amount of payments? How does this compare to question 2b?
d. Will the guaranteed income or negative income tax method be better for your kingdom? Why?

3. Of the four major poverty programs, only the Supplemental Security Income program is controlled entirely by the federal government. The other three programs are administered by state governments, so eligibility guidelines and benefits differ between states. A poor person in Mississippi does not receive the same benefits as a poor person in California.
a. In terms of the absolute and relative levels of poverty, evaluate the suitability of state administration of poverty programs.
b. If we apply the concept of geographic mobility (discussed in Units 10.2 and 11.1) to welfare recipients and potential recipients, what is likely to happen in states with the highest benefits? The lowest benefits?

4. Currently, untold numbers of illegal immigrants are coming into the United States. Because of their illegal status they typically do not show up in the "official" measures of unemployment or poverty. There is a proposal in Congress to legalize all illegal immigrants already in the country, but to severely restrict and punish future illegal immigrants. How would this proposal affect the official measure of poverty in the United States? How is it

likely to affect the number of welfare recipients in the country?

5. If you were the president of the United States, what policy or policies would you undertake to address the poverty problem? What are the pros and cons of this policy or policies?

REVIEW GLOSSARY

absolute poverty level The condition in which people do not have the income to buy an absolute amount of the basic necessities of life.

guaranteed income A policy that insures everyone receives a minimum amount of income, regardless of income earned.

negative income tax A policy in which public assistance payments are reduced by a fraction of additional income earned.

poverty The condition in which people do not have the basic necessities of life and lack the income to buy them.

poverty line A measure of the income needed by a family based on family size, location, and characteristics of the head of the household.

relative poverty level The condition in which people do not have the income to buy a relative amount of the basic necessities of life.

SECTION INQUIRY

Minimum Wage for Teenagers

When the Reagan administration came into power in 1981, it proposed the establishment of a minimum wage for teenagers that was below the existing minimum wage of $3.35 per hour. President Reagan proposed that the minimum wage for teenagers be $2.50 per hour. The main reason for the lower minimum wage can be seen by examining the unemployment rates in the United States. For example, as seen in Table 3.4.1, in 1985 the overall unemployment rate in the economy was 7.2 percent. Yet for white teenagers between sixteen and nineteen the rate was around 15 percent, and for nonwhite teenagers the unemployment rate was around 40 percent. The unemployment rate for teenagers is typically two to three times the overall rate. Some people argue that the existing minimum wage of $3.35 per hour is largely responsible for the high teenage unemployment rates.

The argument for a lower teenage minimum wage goes something like this. The teenage unemployment rate is high because businesses cannot afford to hire teenagers, who have relatively low skills, training, and education, at the existing $3.35 minimum wage. A lower minimum wage would make it possible to employ low-skilled teenagers and reduce the high teenage unemployment rates.

However, there is a great deal of opposition to a lower minimum wage for teenagers. Labor unions argue that business will simply hire teenagers at the lower minimum wage to replace adults who currently earn the higher wage. Unions also fear that a lower minimum wage for teenagers is a step in the direction of lowering the minimum wage for all workers, something they have fought long and hard to prevent. Still others believe that a lower minimum wage is simply another way to discriminate against disadvantaged youths, many of whom are black, by paying them less than everyone else.

QUESTIONS FOR DISCUSSION

1. Based on the alternative reasons for wage differentials, discuss the pros and cons of paying teenagers a different wage than adults.

2. If the lower minimum wage for teenagers is effective, leading to a reduction in the teenage unemployment rate, how would the personal distribution of income be affected? Explain. If the jobs "created" for teenagers simply replaced the jobs of older, higher-paid workers, how would the personal distribution of income be affected? Explain.

3. Is a lower minimum wage for teenagers an effective way to reduce poverty? Explain. Is a minimum wage in general an effective way to reduce poverty? Explain. In your answers consider the role of unemployment.

PART V

Selected Topics in Economics

In our study of economics through the first four parts of this text, we have identified the fundamental principles of economics, ranging from the laws of demand and supply in the market to the multiplier in the macroeconomy. But in Part V we sit back and look at several special applications of these economic principles. As a group, the topics presented in Part V deal with actual problems facing the U.S. economy, today and into the future.

The first problem we discuss is the role of the government in the production of goods and the allocation of resources. We have seen various ways that the market-oriented economy fails to efficiently allocate resources. And the typical recommendation to alleviate inefficient resource allocation has been some type of government involvement—a tax here, a regulation there. However, these taxes and regulations represent economists' idealized solutions, designed to achieve an efficient allocation of resources. As we see in Section 12, Government and Allocation, the government has inefficiencies of its own and does not always implement the economists' ideals.

If we combine these inefficiencies of the government with the feeling of many people that the government is already too involved in the market economy, we have a lively debate over the role of the government. As we see in the first section of Part V, the government does play a necessary and important role in the economy. The debate revolves around what degree of government involvement is appropriate. While we won't get a definitive answer to that question, we will get some valuable insight.

A second problem, one that is likely to become increasingly more important in the years to come, concerns the natural environment. In the 1960s and early 1970s our society became acutely aware of the problems of pollution; in the mid-to-late 1970s we were awakened to the issue of energy depletion. In the first half of the 1980s, due to pollution control laws and a surplus of petroleum, these problems were overshadowed by the federal deficit, inflation, unemployment, and other more immediate concerns. However, as we see in Section 13, The Natural Environment, problems of pollution and energy shortages are likely to resurface in the decades ahead.

We discuss a third area of interest, the world economy, in Section 14. As we move toward the year 2000, it becomes clear that our national economy is merely one part of an overall world economy. And the interdependence between national economies of the world will become even greater as the twenty-first century approaches. In this section we examine the role of trade between nations in the allocation of resources. People are becoming increasingly more concerned about Asian and European imports into our economy. However, in this section we see that international trade usually benefits both countries.

In our study of the world economy we are also concerned with the growth and development of individual countries. This topic takes on significance as many developing countries strive to obtain greater economic and political power in the world economy. In the decades ahead, some of the less developed countries will likely try to increase their standards of living using the type of economic power displayed by the OPEC countries in the 1970s.

In Part V, our final topic deals with the structure of economic systems in countries throughout the world. And like the other topics in this part, we do not study this out of idle academic curiosity. The differences in economic systems and their accompanying political systems has been at the bottom of most political turmoil in the world since the Second World War. While the economies of the United States, Canada, and Western European countries are market-oriented, Russia, China, and Eastern European countries rely much more on government in their economies. The philosophical and political differences in each type of economy are likely to lead to conflict throughout the remainder of this century and into the next. In Section 15, Alternative Economic Systems, we examine alternatives to the market-oriented economy.

SECTION 12

Government and Allocation

The government involves itself in the economy in many ways. In this section we look at three ways in particular that the government is involved in output markets: direct production of goods and services, taxation, and regulation. Most markets efficiently allocate resources; when they do not, there is usually a call for some type of government intervention. However, in this section we see that the government does not necessarily allocate resources efficiently itself.

Unit 12.1, Public Choice, begins our study of government and production by examining the principles underlying government decision making. While private decision making through the markets can be imperfect, public decision making by the government has imperfections of its own. This unit looks at the principles of public choice to provide reasons for these imperfections.

Unit 12.2, The Market Failure of Public Goods, discusses the characteristics of public goods and how they differ from goods exchanged in markets. In this unit we learn that public goods become public goods because they will not be produced by the private markets. We see how the characteristics of public goods affect their demand, and why they usually require direct production by the government.

Unit 12.3, Principles of Taxation, looks at the basic concepts underlying taxation. Since public goods cannot be exchanged in markets, the government cannot sell them directly. This means it must find another way to finance their production. The most common method is through taxation. However, as we see in this unit, taxation can also lead to inefficiencies in allocation.

Unit 12.4, Government Regulation of Economic Activity, examines a handful of the most important regulatory agencies that oversee production and the markets. In this unit we discuss the imperfections in the market that stimulate a need for government regulation. We also look at some problems and inefficiencies created by government regulation.

UNIT 12.1

Public Choice

We know that some degree of government involvement occurs in any market-oriented economy. Government involvement ranges from direct government regulation of firms and markets (as discussed in Units 2.5, 9.6, 12.2, 12.4, and 13.3) to indirect control of the macroeconomy through fiscal and monetary policies (as discussed in Units 4.7, 5.4, and 6.3). In these units the problems of the market-oriented economy were relatively easy to pinpoint, as was the necessary action by the government. And if we had an ideal government (one that responded perfectly to the dictates of economists), this current discussion would be irrelevant. Unfortunately, governments do not always implement the policies that generate an efficient allocation of resources.

Therefore, in this unit we undertake a study of government decision making to see why governments do not necessarily behave according to economic ideals. This study of government decision making is often referred to as public choice. **Public choice is the study of collective decisions made by groups of individuals.** Government decisions are usually made by groups of people, ranging from voters to legislators to committees. By contrast, decisions in private markets are typically made by individual buyers and sellers.

Our study of public choice begins by focusing on the pivotal role played by the politician, or political entrepreneur. We then examine four principles of voting behavior: the median voter, rational ignorance, logrolling, and the voting paradox. And finally, we look at special interest groups and their role in the voting process.

THE POLITICAL ENTREPRENEUR

Politicians, or political entrepreneurs, play the central role in collective decision making by the government. Politicians are often called political entrepreneurs because their function in the government resembles that of the business entrepreneur in business. Recall that business entrepreneurs bring together the resources needed for production of goods and services; for them the risk of production is profit and loss. For political entrepreneurs the risk of production is more or less votes at election time. Clearly, while the business entrepreneur seeks to stay in business, the **political entrepreneur** seeks to obtain reelection and remain in office.

Political entrepreneurs are primarily responsible for most decisions affecting resource allocation. This ranges from Congress deciding on the division of federal expenditures between national defense and social programs to county commissioners deciding on the division of expenditures between salaries and road improvements.

Political entrepreneurs face only one important constraint on their action, the voters. To remain in office, political entrepreneurs need to obtain a majority of the votes at election time. This implies political entrepreneurs are not necessarily going to do what is best for the entire population. First, they are going to make decisions that satisfy voters rather than nonvoters. Moreover, they are going to make decisions that satisfy the majority of the voters, which is usually not the majority of the population.

While political entrepreneurs *can* undertake decisions that lead to an efficient allocation of resources, there is no particular reason to assume they will. For example, a representative from an agricultural state will support agricultural programs if farmers benefiting from the programs are more likely to vote than consumers affected by the higher food prices. By the same reasoning, the representative of an industrial state will support tariffs and quotas on imported cars if the autoworkers are more likely to vote than the consumers suffering from the higher prices.

THE PRINCIPLE OF THE MEDIAN VOTER

Political entrepreneurs have the incentive to satisfy only a majority of the voting population. To see how they can do this, let's examine the principle of the median voter. The **principle of the median voter** states that the median voter determines the outcome of a decision made by majority rule. The median voter casts the deciding vote when there are an equal number of voters on either side. For example, suppose five people are voting on funds for public education. The first voter favors $5 billion, the second voter $10 billion, the third voter $15 billion, the fourth voter $50 billion, and the fifth voter $75 billion. In this case, the third voter, who favors $15 billion, is the median voter, because two voters want higher expenditures and two voters want lower expenditures. Note that the median voter does not necessarily favor the average amount of the five proposed expenditures; the median voter is simply the voter in the middle.

The principle of the median voter also applies to the spectrum of political philosophies. If five candidates are running for office, one liberal, one moderate, and three far-right conservatives, then the median candidate is the more moderate of the three conservatives.

Figure 12.1.1 provides an illustration of how the principle of the median voter operates. In panel a the horizontal line measures the amount of expenditures on public education. For the sake of simplicity, assume that there are 101 voters and that each voter wants to spend $1 billion more on education than the previous voter. Thus, the first voter wants to spend nothing on education, the second voter wants $1 billion, the third voter $2 billion, and so on, until the 101st voter, who wants to spend $100 billion. In this case the median voter wants to spend $50 billion on education.

Now suppose there are two candidates running for election. Candidate D wants to spend $75 billion on education, while candidate R wants to spend $25 billion. This situation is depicted in panel a. Under these circumstances every voter wanting more than $50 billion in expenditures

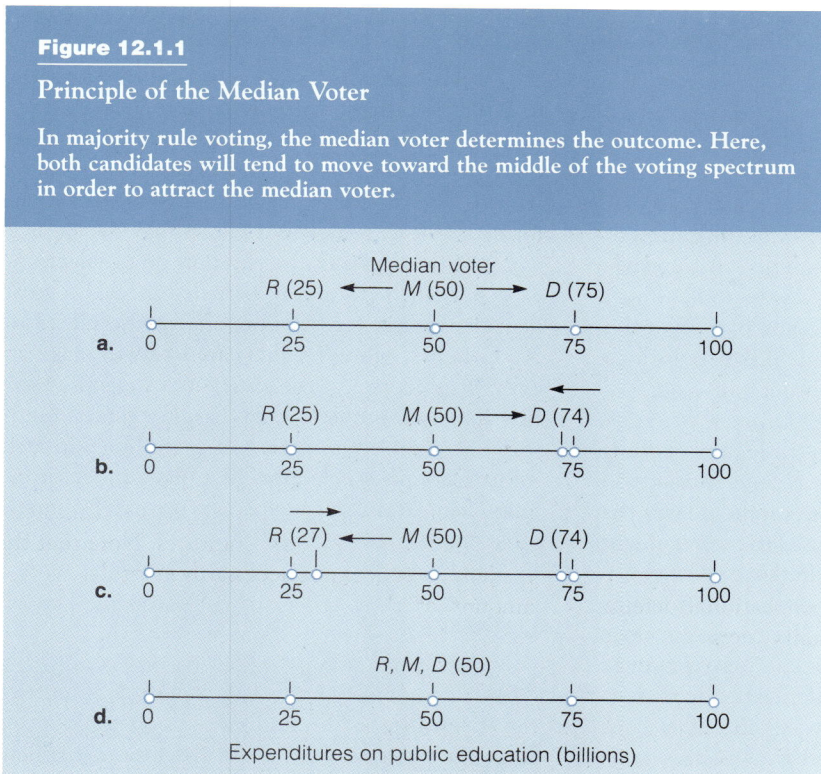

Figure 12.1.1

Principle of the Median Voter

In majority rule voting, the median voter determines the outcome. Here, both candidates will tend to move toward the middle of the voting spectrum in order to attract the median voter.

votes for candidate D, and every voter wanting less than $50 billion votes for candidate R. Each person votes for the candidate who is closest to their own desired amount. Therefore, whoever the median voter favors (it could be either candidate) wins the election.

This fact is not lost on the two candidates. Candidate D proposes to spend a slightly lower amount ($74 billion), and is now more attractive to the median voter (by $1 billion) than candidate R. So the median voter chooses candidate D, and thus determines the outcome of the election, as illustrated in panel b.

However, if candidate R proposes to spend $27 billion, then the median voter favors R, as indicated in panel c. This process continues as each candidate moves closer and closer to the median voter's position. Eventually, the candidates will propose the same amount of expenditures as that desired by the median voter, as seen in panel d. In this case it doesn't matter which candidate the median voter chooses, but the median voter still determines the outcome of the election.

Keep in mind that there is nothing special about the median voter's desire to spend $50 billion on public education. In fact, the amount need not, and probably does not, represent the most efficient allocation of resources on public education. The only reason this amount is ultimately spent is that it is desired by the median voter.

VOTING AND RATIONAL IGNORANCE

The fundamental act of voting is similar to consumer behavior in the market. In the economic market people "vote" with their income, registering their preferences for particular goods and services. In the political market each person has one vote, and can vote yes or no with no indication of the intensity of the preference. The only alternative to voting yes or no is to not vote at all. Thus, voters decide to vote based on a comparison of the benefits and costs of voting, much like choosing a dentist or purchasing a new automobile.

Voters benefit from voting in three ways. First, voters receive satisfaction from the feeling of doing their public duty. Second, they receive satisfaction from the thought of helping the candidate win the election. If the election is close, the voter might feel his or her vote made the difference. And third, the voter might receive direct satisfaction from any goods or services provided by the candidate once elected, for example, lower taxes, an improved transportation system, or a balanced budget.

Voting has costs as well as benefits. First, the voter spends time in the process of voting, time that cannot be used in another activity. Second, the voter incurs transportation costs traveling to and from the voting place. These costs of voting are real, tangible, and immediately incurred by the voter. By contrast, the benefits are less obvious and may never even develop. People are more likely to vote if an election result is in doubt or the candidates promise numerous benefits, because the benefits to the voter are more obvious.

Information is another important aspect of voting. The act of obtaining information about the candidates and issues can also be considered a consumer good. Voters have to determine if the benefits of obtaining information are worth the costs. The time spent in, and resource costs of, gathering and intelligently analyzing information concerning candidates and issues are not trivial. The benefit of information is a more intelligent voting choice. And like the benefits of voting, the benefits of gathering information about the election depend on the closeness of the election and a sense of public duty.

Often, the voter may feel it is not worthwhile to gather information. **Rational ignorance** is a state in which a voter or consumer decides not to gather information because the costs exceed the benefits. In other words, the voter decides to remain uninformed. But in some cases voters may decide it is worthwhile to gather information on an election, especially if they stand to benefit (or lose) a great deal depending on the outcome of the election. For example, schoolteachers are likely to make an effort to understand the issues in an election setting limits on property taxes used for school funding. Likewise, environmentalists are likely to seek information in an election that pits a proenvironmentalist candidate against an antienvironmentalist candidate.

LOGROLLING

Another important principle of voting is logrolling. **Logrolling** is the trading of votes to obtain a favorable outcome on a specific decision. Explicit logrolling is commonplace in most legislative bodies, where two legislators agree to vote for each other's proposed legislation in order to assure passage of both. Although logrolling can lead to the provision of inefficient public goods and programs, it can also lead to an efficient outcome that otherwise might not be obtained. Let's look at two examples.

Logrolling can lead to the provision of a public good that benefits society, and that otherwise might not be produced. Figure 12.1.2 illustrates the relative intensity of preferences that three legislators have for two programs or, more generally, the change in each legislator's welfare. Nancy strongly favors a tax increase ($+10$) and slightly opposes a farm subsidy (-1). Gary strongly favors a farm subsidy ($+10$) and only slightly opposes a tax increase (-1). And George strongly opposes both programs, as indicated by the -5s.

If the two programs are put to a simple major-

Figure 12.1.2

Logrolling—Efficient Outcome

Logrolling occurs if Nancy votes for Gary's program, on the condition that Gary votes for Nancy's program. An efficient outcome can result from the logrolling if proponents more intensely favor the programs than opponents oppose them.

	Nancy	Gary	George	Net change in society's welfare
Tax increase	+10	−1	−5	+4
Farm subsidy	−1	+10	−5	+4

ity vote, both lose, since two of the three legislators oppose each program. But if the programs are implemented, the net effect on society can be seen by adding up the relative preferences. In both cases society has a net increase of 4 units, because one of the voters more strongly favors a program than the other two oppose it. However, the simple majority voting system means society loses this potential gain in welfare.

Indeed, logrolling can lead to programs that benefit society. For example, Gary is willing to vote for Nancy's program (tax increase) if Nancy votes for Gary's program (farm subsidy). Since Nancy and Gary only slightly oppose the other program, they are willing to vote for it on the condition that their own pet program is passed. Both Nancy and Gary have a net gain of +9 if both programs pass, and society is better off.

Logrolling can just as easily lead to programs that do not benefit society. Figure 12.1.3 presents a set of programs and preferences similar to those in Figure 12.1.2. However, in this case George more intensely opposes both programs, as indicated by the −10s. The sum of the preference intensities indicates that the net change in society's welfare is −1 for both programs. However, if logrolling occurs, Gary and Nancy are still willing to vote for the other's program, and both receive a majority. Here, there is no guarantee that logrolling either helps or hurts society. Logrolling could just as easily lead to an inefficient allocation of resources as to an efficient allocation.

While these two examples have used explicit logrolling, very often implicit logrolling takes place in the voting process of legislative bodies. With explicit logrolling, Gary and Nancy trade votes on separate programs. However, implicit logrolling can occur if the two separate programs are combined into one. For example, a bill introduced in Congress might contain the provisions for both a tax increase and a farm subsidy. If Gary wants the farm subsidy, he has to vote for the bill, and thus impli-

Figure 12.1.3

Logrolling—Inefficient Outcome

Logrolling can also lead to an inefficient outcome if opponents more intensely oppose the programs than proponents favor them. In this example, Nancy and Gary trade votes as before. However, the net effect of each program is a decrease in society's welfare.

	Nancy	Gary	George	Net change in society's welfare
Tax increase	+10	−1	−10	−1
Farm subsidy	−1	+10	−10	−1

citly votes for the tax increase. Likewise, if Nancy wants the tax increase, she votes for the bill, implicitly voting for the farm subsidy. As a result, both programs pass. For a legislator, implicit logrolling can be very beneficial, because no official support for the other program is exhibited. Gary can always tell his constituency that he really didn't want the tax increase but had to vote for it because it was "unavoidably" included in the bill with the farm subsidy.

THE VOTING PARADOX

A basic principle of consumer behavior is the transitivity of preferences. That is, if a consumer prefers good A to good B and good B to good C, then good A is also preferred to good C. However, for group decision making there is a good chance that group preferences are not transitive. For example, a group might decide it prefers A to B and B to C, but then prefers C to A. This is the **voting paradox, which is the possibility that group decision making leads to an intransitive ranking of preferences.**

Figure 12.1.4 illustrates a situation in which three voters (Nancy, Gary, and George) are deciding between three alternative programs: tax increase, farm subsidy, and import quotas on foreign cars. The ranking of preferences of the three voters for the three programs is depicted.

Nancy prefers a tax increase, thinks a farm subsidy is okay, but does not like import quotas. Thus, Nancy ranks the three programs one, two, and three, accordingly. Gary has his own preferences for the three programs. His pet program, a farm subsidy, is rated at the top. Import quotas is the next choice, followed by a tax increase. George likes import quotas the most, then a tax increase, and a farm subsidy.

How does the group jointly rank the three programs? Let's compare any two programs. If the group votes between a tax increase and a farm subsidy,

Figure 12.1.4

Voters' Paradox

If three voters rank their preferences for three different programs as indicated here, comparisons based on two programs at a time will lead to an intransitive ranking. In this case a tax increase is preferred to a farm subsidy by the group. And since a farm subsidy is preferred to import quotas, a transitive ranking would mean a tax increase is also preferred to import quotas. However, a comparison of these two programs indicates that the group prefers import quotas to a tax increase.

Program	Voter Nancy	Voter Gary	Voter George
Tax increase	1	3	2
Farm subsidy	2	1	3
Import quota	3	2	1

Nancy definitely prefers a tax increase and Gary definitely prefers a farm subsidy. But although George's first choice is import quotas, he prefers a tax increase to a farm subsidy. In a choice between a tax increase and a farm subsidy, the group selects a tax increase by a two to one vote based on George's preference for a tax increase over a farm subsidy.

Now what if a farm subsidy and import quotas are compared? Once again, a farm subsidy is Gary's first choice and import quotas is George's first choice. But Nancy prefers a farm subsidy to import quotas, so a farm subsidy is selected by the group over import quotas. If the group prefers a tax increase to a farm subsidy and a farm subsidy to import quotas, it seems logical to think it prefers a tax increase to import quotas. However, this is not the case.

If the group has a choice between a tax increase and import quotas, it selects import quotas over a tax increase. Once more, Nancy prefers a tax increase and George prefers import quotas. But Gary now has the deciding vote, and he prefers import quotas to a tax increase. Thus, the group votes for import quotas. The intransitive preferences displayed by the group constitute the voting paradox.

Of course, the example in Figure 12.1.4 is contrived. If any of the voters changed their preferences, then the voting paradox need not occur. For example, if Gary prefers a tax increase to a farm subsidy, then the programs would have a consistent and transitive ranking: tax increase, import quotas, and a farm subsidy. But the example does illustrate that the voting paradox is possible. And given the fact that most legislative bodies have members representing different constituencies, each with their own priorities, the voting paradox is very likely to occur from time to time.

The voting paradox suggests that political decisions can depend on the order in which they are made. If the group decides to enact only two of the programs (due to limited funds), and votes for a tax increase, a farm subsidy, and import quotas in that order, then import quotas will not be enacted, even though import quotas may be as preferred as either of the other two programs. The voting paradox also indicates the complex nature of group decision making. If an individual expressed the intransitive preferences indicated by the group, we would say he or she was irrational. But in terms of their decision making, each member of the group in this example is entirely rational (or at least, no member has displayed any irrational tendencies in this voting pattern).

SPECIAL INTEREST GROUPS

Special interest groups play an important role in group decision making by the government. A **special interest group** is a group of people who are intensely interested in an issue because they are more affected by it than the general public is. The formation of a special interest group is related to the principle of rational ignorance. As we saw with the principle of rational ignorance, voters tend to seek out information in the elections that are likely to affect them the most. They are also more likely to vote, and even campaign, for their position. However, people less affected by an issue are less concerned, less likely to become informed, and also less likely to vote. This means that politicians, as political entrepreneurs seeking reelection, will try to satisfy special interest groups, since the special interest groups are more likely to vote than the general public.

Due to differences in socioeconomic and occupational characteristics, most people fall into some type of special interest group that can be significantly affected by a single issue. For example, college students represent a special interest group concerning an increase in tuition, autoworkers concerning import quotas on foreign cars, environmentalists concerning toxic wastes, and the military concerning defense spending.

Special interest groups have a significant effect on any group decision. A special interest group intensely supports its side of an issue, because it has the most to gain or lose by the outcome. But the rest of society, which by definition is *not* part of the special interest group, is less affected by the issue. Therefore, the rest of society might implement the principle of rational ignorance, and thus play a relatively small role in the collective decision.

For example, a budget reduction at a state-supported university would most adversely affect faculty, students, and staff. In response, they might form a special interest group and propose an increase in state taxes. If taxes are increased, each taxpayer pays higher taxes. But their additional taxes are small relative to the adverse effect on the faculty, students, and staff if the university budget is reduced.

Another example has to do with the import restrictions on foreign automobiles. The automobile companies in the United States have a lot to gain or lose from this restriction. Unrestricted imports mean greater competition for domestic automobile companies; restricted imports mean less competition and potentially higher economic profits. The restriction of imports also means higher prices for automobile buyers. However, while automobile prices might increase by a few hundred dollars, automobile companies stand to gain or lose millions of dollars, and thus are more intensely interested in the restrictions than the buyers are.

The role of special interest groups in government decision making in the United States cannot be overemphasized. The existence of special interest groups could very well be most responsible for the government's misallocation of resources. In an economy as complex as in the United States, a large number of special interest groups is unavoidable, with each group wanting the government to reallocate resources in a different manner. Everyone—worker, student, consumer, employer, investor, taxpayer—is a member of one or more special interest groups.

Indeed, even government agencies constitute special interest groups in terms of government funding. A given agency has the most to gain or lose by the allocation of government funds. For example, the military is likely to lobby Congress and the president with a great deal of intensity if it has something to gain or lose from a particular piece of legislation affecting allocation of government funds. Thus, large, powerful government agencies are likely to stay large and powerful by virtue of their roles as special interest groups.

IN SUMMARY

Public Choice

- Public choice is the study of the manner in which decisions to allocate resources are made by government. While the market is primarily based on individual decisions, the government is operated by joint decisions. The joint decisions do not necessarily lead to an efficient allocation of resources.

- Politicians are entrepreneurs, much like business entrepreneurs. The successful business entrepreneur stays in business. The successful political entrepreneur stays in office. The politician is likely to satisfy special interest groups that take an intense interest in the election at the expense of the general public.

- The principle of the median voter illustrates why majority rule might not be optimal for society. This principle indicates that the median voter determines the outcome of an election, because politicians seek to satisfy the median voter.

- Voters can be considered as consumers in the voting process. They vote as long as the benefits of voting exceed the costs. Information on the election is also a consumer good. The voter gathers information as long as the benefits exceed the costs. Rational ignorance occurs if the voter decides not to be informed because the costs are greater than the benefits.

- Logrolling is the practice of trading votes to obtain support for a specific proposal. Logrolling can lead to an efficient decision that would not otherwise be made. However, it can also lead to an inefficient decision. Logrolling represents either the explicit trading of votes for distinct programs or the implicit combining of several programs into one decision.

- The voter paradox indicates that majority rule can sometimes lead to intransitive preferences by the group of voters. That is, if the voters prefer A to B and B to C, this implies they should prefer A to C. However, it is possible that they will prefer C to A. This intransitivity means decisions may very well depend on the order in which they are made.

- Voters gather more information on issues and elections that affect them the most. In this way special interest groups become well informed on specific decisions, and have a much greater impact on the decision than the less-informed general public. The special interest group stands to gain or lose a lot by the decision, while the general public is affected very little.

QUESTIONS FOR STUDY AND ANALYSIS

1. Evaluate the following statement: Politicians are crooks.

2. Suppose you are given the following information concerning voting preferences for four people: A, B, C, and D. The positive numbers indicate support and the negative numbers indicate opposition.

Program	Voter			
	A	B	C	D
X	− 1	+ 5	+ 10	− 1
Y	+ 10	− 2	− 1	− 10
Z	− 5	− 10	− 5	+ 10

   a. Which of the three programs is socially desirable? That is, which will lead to a net increase in the welfare of the voters?
   b. Which of the three programs is likely to pass due to logrolling? Are any of the programs unable to pass through logrolling? Of the programs passed through logrolling, which benefit society and which do not?

3. Some people argue that the proliferation of government regulations in the 1970s was caused by special interest groups. Explain how the actions of government agencies (as special interest groups) and nongovernment special interest groups could lead to an increase in government regulations. If you want, use specific examples of government regulations, special interest groups, or government agencies.

4. In the 1980s there was a movement to reduce government regulation. Explain how special interest groups could have affected this decision. If you want, use specific examples, such as airline, trucking, or natural gas deregulation or the reduction in environmental quality standards.

5. Describe a situation within the last year in which you employed the principle of rational ignorance.

6. Based on the principle of the median voter, why might resource allocation decisions deter-

mined by a majority vote lead to an inefficient outcome? Is there any reason to think majority voting would lead to an efficient outcome?

7. Under what circumstances would government decision making be better than private decision making? Under what circumstances would private decision making be better than government decision making?

REVIEW GLOSSARY

logrolling The practice of trading votes to obtain a favorable outcome on a specific decision. Logrolling can lead to an efficient decision that would not otherwise be made, but it can also lead to inefficient decision. Implicit logrolling occurs when two programs are combined into one.

political entrepreneur A politician whose primary goal is to obtain reelection and remain in office.

principle of the median voter A principle that states the median voter determines the outcome of a decision made by majority rule. The proposal of the median voter is the only proposal to find a majority.

public choice The study of collective decisions made by groups of individuals.

rational ignorance The state in which a voter or consumer decides not to gather information because the costs exceed the benefits.

special interest group A group of people who are intensely interested in an issue because they are more affected by it than the general public is.

voting paradox The possibility that group decisions lead to intransitive rankings of programs. The voting paradox implies that group decisions may very well depend on the order in which they are made.

UNIT 12.2

The Market Failure of Public Goods

The provision of public goods is one of the more important functions performed by the government. In this unit we see that because certain types of goods are *not* efficiently produced through the markets, the government must become directly involved in their production. In this unit we introduce public goods and illustrate how they are different from private goods that are efficiently exchanged in markets.

A public good is a good that cannot be efficiently produced and allocated by private markets. By its very nature, once a public good is produced, everyone in the economy consumes the good, whether or not they pay to have it produced. Since everyone can have it *without* paying, no one in the economy is willing to pay for the good, making it unlikely that enough of a public good will be privately produced. Only if the government forces everyone to pay for the public good through taxation will enough of the public good be produced.

To begin, we look at the characteristics of private goods and public goods to see why one can be handled efficiently by private markets and the other cannot. Then we determine the optimal production of a public good, which further illustrates why a market fails in its allocation. And finally, we examine benefit-cost analysis, the technique most often used by the government in deciding if a public good should be produced.

WHAT MAKES A PUBLIC GOOD?

Public goods are inherently different from private goods. It is easy to name a wide variety of private goods that are efficiently exchanged through markets, for example, personal computers, notebooks, and donuts. By contrast, national defense, city parks, education, and highways are all examples of public goods. What is it about public goods that makes them different from private goods?

Goods have two notable dimensions. First, goods can be rival or nonrival in consumption. If a good is rival in consumption, it means the use of the good by one consumer prevents its use by another consumer. When one person eats a donut, someone else is prevented from eating it. If a good is nonrival in consumption, it means the use of the good by one consumer does not prevent its use by another. The fact that one person is protected from enemy attack by our national defense does not prevent others from *also* being protected.

Second, the owners of goods have the ability to exclude nonpayers. A car dealer can exclude people from consuming an automobile by hiding the keys and keeping the car locked in the showroom. But it is not possible to exclude anyone from benefiting from the protection of national defense, short of expelling them from the country. By the very nature of national defense, anyone living within the country is automatically protected. Figure 12.2.1 presents four possible types of goods based on these two dimensions.

Private Goods

In the upper left-hand corner of Figure 12.2.1 are private goods. A **private good** is a good that is rival in consumption, and nonpayers can be excluded from consumption. Pure private goods can be efficiently exchanged in markets because of these two characteristics. The exclusion of nonpayers means a supplier can prevent potential buyers from using the good unless they are willing to pay an accept-

Figure 12.2.1

Characteristics of Goods

Goods can be rival or nonrival in consumption and owners may or may not be able to exclude nonpayers. Private goods are characterized by rival consumption and the ability to exclude nonpayers. Pure public goods are characterized by nonrival consumption and the inability to exclude nonpayers. Near public goods are characterized by nonrival consumption but the ability to exclude nonpayers. Common property goods are characterized by rival consumption and the inability to exclude nonpayers.

	Rival in consumption	Nonrival in consumption
Able to exclude nonpayers	Private good (apples, automobiles)	Near public good (television signals, radio signals)
Not able to exclude nonpayers	Common property good (parks, oceans)	Pure public good (police protection, clean environment)

able price. Rival consumption means that the use of the good by one person imposes an opportunity cost on other potential users. Examples of private goods include a wide variety of goods produced in the economy, ranging from apples to zippers.

Public Goods (Pure)

In the lower right-hand corner of Figure 12.2.1 are public goods. A **public good (pure)** is a good that is nonrival in consumption, and nonpayers cannot be excluded from consumption. Public goods generally need to be produced with government involvement. Because it is not possible to exclude anyone from using a public good, any supplier trying to sell a public good has a great deal of difficulty. Once the good is produced, everyone benefits. There is no reason for anyone to buy the good, since everyone benefits without paying.

Public goods are also nonrival in consumption, meaning the use of the good by one person does not impose an opportunity cost on other potential users. Thus, after a public good is produced, society incurs no additional cost if another person uses the good. The birth of a new baby in the United States does not impose a cost on everyone else already protected by national defense.

Note that for public goods there is no way to exclude nonpayers. Furthermore, there is no reason to exclude nonpayers, since their use imposes no opportunity cost on anyone else. Common examples of public goods are police protection, national defense, and a clean environment.

Common Property Goods

In the lower left-hand corner of Figure 12.2.1 are common property goods. A **common property good** is a good that is rival in consumption, but nonpayers cannot be excluded from consumption. The use of a common property good by one person imposes an opportunity cost on all other potential users. However, the inability to exclude nonpayers from the use of a common property good means it is difficult to do anything about these costs.

For example, our oceans are a common property good. Every country in the world has the freedom to use the oceans. However, some of the users impose a cost on others, as is quite evident in the fishing industry. Obviously, fish caught by one fisherman cannot be caught by another. Furthermore, if too many fish are caught, their reproduction can be inhibited, reducing future fish populations and imposing further costs on all future fisherman. This is the situation facing whales today. Russia and Japan, among others, have caught so many whales that they are an endangered species and could become extinct in the near future. And the reason for this is the inability to exclude anyone from catching whales.

Problems resulting from overuse of a common property good stem primarily from lack of clear ownership. Although fishing in the ocean can lead to problems, fishing in a privately owned pond does not. The owner of a pond can prevent nonpayers from fishing by putting up a fence. And if fishing begins to threaten the stock of fish in the pond, the owner can keep people from using it. By contrast, no one has the authority to exclude potential users from the ocean, because no one can claim clear ownership. This ownership problem also affects other common property goods such as air, rivers, and city parks and underlies many of the pollution problems we discuss in Section 13.

Near Public Goods

In the upper right-hand corner of Figure 12.2.1 are near public goods. A **near public good** is a good that is nonrival in consumption, but nonpayers can be excluded from consumption. The main difference between a pure public good and a near public good is the ability to exclude nonpayers. With a near public good, nonpayers can be excluded, though there is no reason why they should be excluded. The use of a near public good by one person imposes no opportunity cost on any other users. Thus, the efficient allocation of public goods illustrated later in this unit applies to near public goods exactly as it applies to pure public goods.

A common example of a near public good is the transmission of television signals. Once the signal is sent from the transmitting tower, it makes no difference how many people receive it. The clarity of the signal is the same for all. However, nonpayers can be excluded by scrambling the signal and charging for a descrambling device. An alternative method of excluding nonpayers is to transmit the signal over a cable. Cable TV companies can exclude nonpayers by simply disconnecting the cable.

THE FREE RIDER PROBLEM

The inability to exclude nonpayers from consuming a pure public good leads to the free rider problem. The **free rider problem** occurs when a person consumes a public good without contributing to the costs of production. Recall that anyone can consume a public good whether or not he or she pays to have it produced. For example, a visitor to a city can enjoy the benefits of a local park without having paid for its construction. And even the most ardent opponents of military activity are protected by a country's national defense.

The nonexclusive characteristic of public goods means people will choose not to pay if they are given a choice. If people have a choice between spending $500 on national defense and $500 on a set of golf clubs, most will buy the private good. The consumer who buys the golf clubs has both the golf clubs *and* the protection of national defense, whereas the consumer who pays the $500 for national defense has only national defense. As long as everyone else in the country pays for the national defense, the nonpayer is a free rider.

If the production of public goods is left to the market, the free rider problem prevents an efficient level of production. Since everyone would prefer to consume the good without paying for its production, no one voluntarily pays to have it produced. Therefore, a public good is not privately produced through the market. Of course, the possibility exists that a few people might try to privately produce the good and sell it on the market. But the quantity produced is less than the quantity that everyone would like to have, and too many people will consume the good as free riders. This means producers are unable to raise enough revenue to cover the costs of producing a sufficient quantity.

THE DEMAND FOR PUBLIC GOODS

Let's see how the characteristics of public goods are reflected in demand. Keep in mind that private goods are rival in consumption, meaning the consumption by one person prevents the consumption by another. To determine the total demand for a private good, we need to add up the quantities every individual demands at a given price, or horizontally add the demand curves in panel a of Figure 12.2.2.

But this is not the way to determine the total demand for a public good. Since public goods are nonrival in consumption, two people can consume the same public good at the same time. Adding up the quantities, or horizontally adding demand curves, is thus not appropriate for public goods. For public goods we are not interested in the quantity sold at a given price but in the value of the quantity produced, which requires **vertical addition,** the process of adding two curves vertically by adding the total value every buyer places on the quantity of the good.

For example, how does a city decide if it is feasible to build a new park? In general, it would have to determine if the people of the city wanted the park, or alternatively, how much the people would value the park. Note that we are given a particular quantity, one park, and we need to determine its value to the demanders. Each person in the city may place a very small value on the park. What is the value of a Sunday afternoon stroll? Fifty cents? A dollar? However, the *combined* value placed on the park by everyone in the city might be quite large.

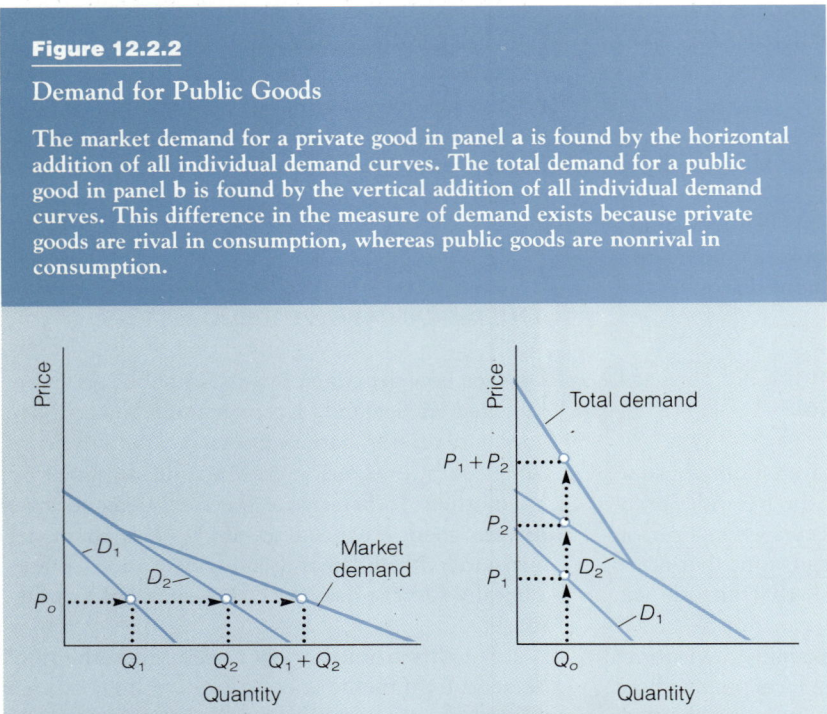

Figure 12.2.2

Demand for Public Goods

The market demand for a private good in panel a is found by the horizontal addition of all individual demand curves. The total demand for a public good in panel b is found by the vertical addition of all individual demand curves. This difference in the measure of demand exists because private goods are rival in consumption, whereas public goods are nonrival in consumption.

a. Demand for private good

b. Demand for public good

Panel b of Figure 12.2.2 illustrates how the demand for a public good is determined. For a given quantity Q_o, the value placed on it by consumer 1, which is P_1, is read from demand curve D_1. In other words, if Q_o were placed on the market, consumer 1 would be willing to pay a price of P_1. But consumer 2 is willing to pay P_2 for Q_o of the good. If there are only two consumers of the good, the value of the good is the sum of P_1 and P_2. In panel b the demand for a public good constitutes the vertical addition of all individual demand curves. Note that the vertical addition occurs because the good is nonrival in consumption. Only when the consumption by one person prevents the consumption by another do we horizontally add demand curves.

OPTIMAL PRODUCTION OF PUBLIC GOODS

Once we determine the demand for a public good, it is simple to determine the optimal quantity of production. The optimal quantity of production occurs where the value provided by the last unit is equal to the opportunity cost of producing the last unit. Recall that this is how the optimal quantity of output is determined in a market. The only difference between private and public goods in this case is how the value of the last unit produced is determined. In a private market it is the value each buyer *separately* places on the last unit. For a public good it is the value placed on the last unit by everyone *combined*.

UNIT 12.2 • THE MARKET FAILURE OF PUBLIC GOODS

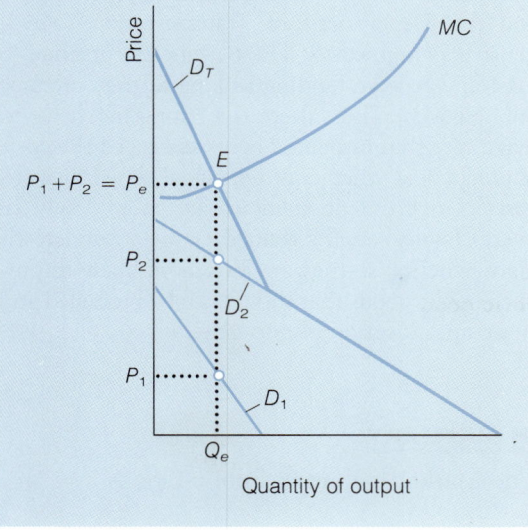

Figure 12.2.3

Efficient Production of a Public Good

The efficient production of a public good is found by the intersection of the total demand curve and the marginal cost curve. In this sense it is the same as a private good. However, the difference is that the demand curve is found through the vertical addition of all individual demand curves. Unlike private goods, the marginal cost of production of a public good is greater than the highest price any individual buyer is willing to pay.

Figure 12.2.3 illustrates how the quantity of a public good is determined. The demand curve D_T is obtained by vertically adding every individual demand curve. The marginal cost curve MC is a standard marginal cost curve, and indicates the opportunity cost of producing an additional unit of the public good. The production of a public good is generally the same as the production of a private good.

The optimal quantity of the public good is determined by the intersection of the marginal cost and demand curves, point E. The demand curve tells us the sum of all marginal values placed on the public good by consumers. The marginal cost curve tells us the value society places on other goods given up in the production of this good. At point E, society can be no better off by increasing or decreasing the quantity of this good. Once the optimal quantity (Q_e) is determined, it is simply a matter of generating the necessary tax revenue to cover the costs of production (P_e), a subject that is discussed in detail in Unit 12.3.

Figure 12.2.3 not only tells us how to determine the optimal production of a public good, it also indicates why this good would not be produced privately. To produce the optimal quantity Q_e, the marginal cost of the last unit is P_e, which is equal to the combined value every user places on that quantity. What would happen if someone tried to sell Q_e at a price of P_e through a market? For that quantity, the first user is willing to pay, at most, P_1, which is clearly less than P_e. Likewise, the second user is only willing to pay P_2, also less than P_e. Unlike a private market, no one is individually willing to pay enough to cover the costs of producing Q_e.

In fact, the marginal cost curve lies above the demand curves for both individuals at all points. The highest price any one person is willing to pay is less than the marginal cost of producing any quantity of the good. No one is willing to buy this good in the market.

BENEFIT-COST ANALYSIS

In practice, the production of public goods does not always occur as shown in Figure 12.2.3. Remember that public goods need to be produced by the government because private markets are unable to obtain equilibrium, at point E. But how does the government determine the optimal quantity Q_e? For many public goods it is not a matter of quantity, but simply of determining if the good should be produced at all. For example, a city decides if it should build a park or not. The government decides whether or not to construct a highway between two cities.

The technique most often used to determine if a public good is produced is benefit-cost analysis. **Benefit-cost analysis** is a technique that compares the benefits obtained from a public good with the costs of production. Benefit-cost analysis, on the surface, is simple enough. The benefits consumers obtain from the public good are compared to the costs of production. If the benefits are greater than the costs, the good should be produced for an efficient allocation of resources. If the benefits are less than the cost, the good should not be produced.

However, in practice, it is usually not that simple. Most of the time the costs of producing a public good are easily identified, since they are essentially the same as the costs of producing a private good. But the benefits are often hard to measure. Recall that public goods are not traded in the market, so their value is not readily apparent. By contrast, the value of a private good is the price consumers actually pay in the market. With a public good, the value must be determined in some other way. If you merely ask people how much they value a good, they may under- or overestimate it. For example, if they think their future taxes will be tied to the value they place on the good, then they might underestimate the value. Alternatively, they might overestimate the value if they think this will insure the production of the good. They may want the good, but they are not willing to pay a great deal for it.

Another problem in assessing the benefits of a public good exists. Most public goods are investments. The cost are incurred at one time, but the benefits of the good accrue over a long period of time. For example, a city park built in 1990 will be enjoyed by consumers in 2000, 2010, and later. Many of the future consumers are not even born at the time the park is built. Clearly, it is difficult to calculate the value that an unborn population will place on a public good.

However, in spite of the problems surrounding benefit-cost analysis, it represents the best technique available for determining if public goods should be produced. If properly used, it can assist the government in resource allocation decisions. However, if improperly used, it can lead to a serious misallocation of resources. If benefits are overestimated, then a public good is produced that should not be. If benefits are underestimated, then a public good that should be produced is not.

Several government agencies are deeply involved in the production of public goods, such as the Army Corps of Engineers (which constructs artificial lakes and waterways, among other things) and the Department of Transportation (which constructs highways). These agencies continue to exist and receive funding as long as they produce public goods. Thus, there is a strong incentive to make sure that estimated benefits exceed the costs of production, whether or not actual benefits exceed costs. Government agencies are more likely to overestimate benefits than they are to underestimate benefits, so they are also more likely to produce public goods that should not be produced and cause misallocation of resources.

IN SUMMARY

The Market Failure of Public Goods

- An important function of the government is the provision of public goods. Public goods are goods that would not be produced if it were left up to private markets. People can consume public goods without paying for them, so the government needs to finance their production through taxation.

- Goods can be characterized in two ways. First, goods can be rival or nonrival in consumption. A good is rival if the consumption by one person prevents the consumption by another. Second, owners of goods can have the ability to exclude nonpayers. Private goods are characterized by rival consumption and exclusion of nonpayers. Pure public goods are characterized by nonrival consumption and the inability to exclude nonpayers. Common property goods are characterized by rival consumption but the inability to exclude nonpayers. Near public goods are characterized by nonrival consumption but the ability to exclude nonpayers.

- The free rider problem results from the inability to exclude nonpayers. Everyone can consume a public good at the same time, whether or not they pay. If consumers have the choice, they would rather not pay for the good, but continue to consume it. Thus, they get a free ride from those who do pay for the public good. The free rider problem means the private market is unable to adequately supply a public good.

- The demand curve for a public good is obtained by vertically adding the demand curves of every individual consumer. This is different from a private good, in which the market demand is obtained by horizontally adding all individual demand curves.

- The efficient production of a public good is determined by identifying the intersection of the demand curve and the marginal cost curve. This is essentially the same as the efficient production of a private good. The intersection indicates the quantity at which the opportunity cost of goods given up equals the value of the last unit of the good produced.

- Benefit-cost analysis is the technique often used to determine if a public good should be produced. It is a simple comparison between the costs of producing the good and the benefits obtained. While there are many problems in estimating the benefits of public goods, benefit-cost analysis remains a useful technique.

QUESTIONS FOR STUDY AND ANALYSIS

1. Based on Figure 12.2.1, classify each of the following goods as private, pure public, common property, or near public. Explain your choice in each case.
   a. A 300,000 acre national park in Alaska
   b. A country club
   c. A satellite transmission of a Home Box Office movie
   d. A class lecture by your economics instructor
   e. A refrigerator shared by four students in the same dormitory room
   f. A pair of blue jeans
   g. A swimming pool
   h. The Statue of Liberty

2. Explain why the optimal production of a near public good is determined in the same manner as that of a pure public good.

3. The music industry has characteristics of a public good. For example, songs played on the radio or television can be enjoyed without the consumer paying to buy a record. However, the consumer might indirectly pay by buying the products of the firm that runs the commercials.
   a. Even considering the indirect payment through advertised products, explain how the music industry can have a free rider problem.
   b. Have you ever been a free rider in the music industry? Explain.
   c. Given that the music industry has numerous free riders and that the music industry is profitable, how do you think the price of a record compares to its opportunity cost of production?

4. Suppose you use benefit-cost analysis to evaluate the production of national defense. List the various types of benefits and costs that you would need to consider in this analysis. How easy or difficult do you think it would be to measure each?

5. In what way would reducing pollution (or producing a clean environment) be considered a public good?

6. Why is it necessary to vertically add the demand curves for public goods, while the demand curves for private goods are horizontally added?

REVIEW GLOSSARY

benefit-cost analysis A technique that compares the benefits obtained from a public good with the costs of production.

common property good A good that is rival in consumption, but nonpayers cannot be excluded from consumption.

free rider problem A situation in which a person consumes a public good without contributing to the costs of production. This problem exists for public goods because nonpayers cannot be excluded. It also means that the market is unable to efficiently produce and exchange public goods.

near public good A good that is nonrival in consumption, but nonpayers can be excluded from consumption.

private good A good that is rival in consumption, and nonpayers can be excluded from consumption.

public good (pure) A good that is nonrival in consumption, and nonpayers cannot be excluded from consumption.

vertical addition The process of adding two curves vertically by adding the total value every buyer places on the quantity of the good. While the total demand curve for a private good is found by horizontally adding all individual demand curves, the total demand curve for a public good is found by vertically adding all individual demand curves.

UNIT 12.3

Principles of Taxation

In this unit we look at the principles of taxation. Taxes are levied by governments to finance their operations. As we saw in the previous unit, the provision of public goods is undertaken by the government because of market inefficiencies. Since public goods cannot be sold through markets, the government must finance their production with tax revenues. However, imposing taxes on the economy can in turn cause inefficiencies in resource allocation. In this unit our main goal is to see how taxation affects the efficient allocation of resources.

First, we introduce a few of the basic principles of taxation. We then consider the equity effects of taxation. Although we are concerned with taxes that are efficient, we also want taxes that are fair and equitable, especially since the provision of public goods is only one of the reasons governments levy taxes. As we saw in Unit 11.4, a more equitable distribution of income is desirable. An inequitable tax defeats this purpose. We then discuss the inefficiencies created when a tax is levied on a freely operating market. And finally, we look at several types of taxes used by different levels of government in the United States.

A FEW BASICS

First, we need to explain a few of the basic concepts of taxation. The standard way of computing a tax is given in the following equation:

tax = tax rate × tax base

The **tax base** is the object of taxation, consisting of income, expenditures, personal property, or a variety of other possibilities. Usually, the tax base is a monetary measure, such as the amount of income. However, it can also be physical units, such as the number of tires sold or members in a household. The **tax rate** is the amount of tax applied per unit of the tax base. Sometimes the tax base is specified as a monetary value. An ***ad valorem tax*** *is a tax that is levied on the monetary value of the tax base*. A 3 percent sales tax or a 30 percent income tax are common examples of *ad valorem* taxes. Alternatively, the tax base can be specified as a physical quantity. A **per unit tax** is a tax that is levied on the physical quantity of the tax base. A per package tax on cigarettes is an example of a per unit tax.

Although income constitutes only one of many different tax bases, examining the percentage of income paid in various taxes can be instructive. For example, a sales tax is based on expenditures for goods and services. While expenditures and income are usually closely related, they need not be the same. Thus, we might want to determine the percentage of income that is paid in sales taxes. The relationship between taxes and income can be proportional, regressive, or progressive.

A **proportional tax** is a tax in which the proportion of income paid in tax is the same for all levels of income. In other words, a proportional tax exists if a person earning $1000 pays $50 in tax and a person earning $100,000 pays $5000 in tax. Each person pays 5 percent of his or her income. A **regressive tax** is a tax in which the proportion of income paid in tax decreases for higher levels of income. For example, if a lower-income person pays 5 percent of his or her income in the tax ($50 out of $1000), but a higher-income person pays only 1 percent ($1000 out of $100,000), then the tax is regressive. A **progressive tax** is a tax in which the proportion of income paid in tax increases for higher levels of income. A progressive tax exists if the lower-income person pays 5 percent and the higher-income person pays 10 percent ($10,000 out of $100,000). Figure 12.3.1 depicts proportional, regressive, and progressive taxes.

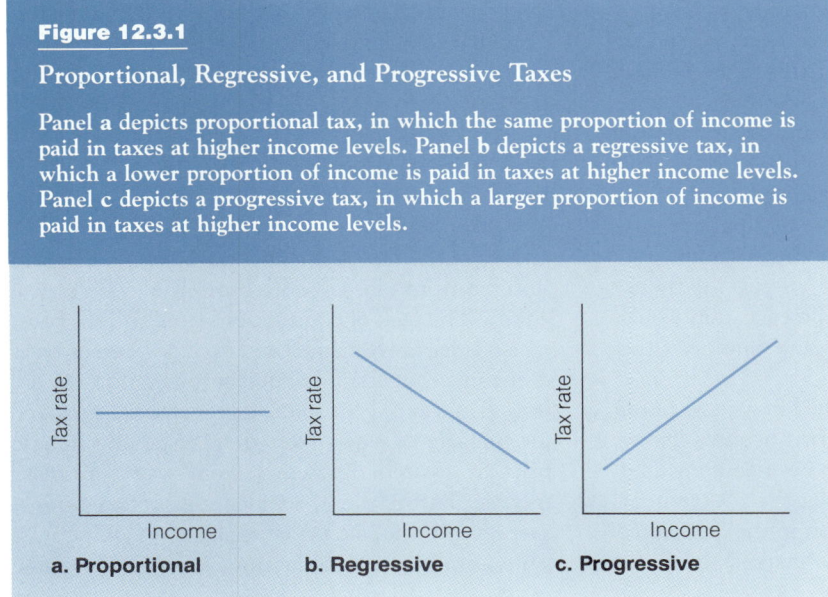

Figure 12.3.1

Proportional, Regressive, and Progressive Taxes

Panel a depicts proportional tax, in which the same proportion of income is paid in taxes at higher income levels. Panel b depicts a regressive tax, in which a lower proportion of income is paid in taxes at higher income levels. Panel c depicts a progressive tax, in which a larger proportion of income is paid in taxes at higher income levels.

TAXATION AND EQUITY

As mentioned at the beginning of this unit, governments also levy taxes and raise revenue to make the distribution of income more equitable. Therefore, the equity effects of taxation cannot be ignored. In this context, let's look at two basic principles of taxation, the benefit principle and the ability-to-pay principle.

The Benefit Principle

The **benefit principle** states that taxes are based on the benefits received. According to this principle of taxation, the people who receive the most benefits from the government pay the most taxes. This principle appeals to an economist by making the government perform like a market and promoting allocative efficiency.

However, problems arise in implementing the benefit principle. In the first place, the provision of public goods is undertaken by the government precisely because the market is inefficient. Since public goods are nonexclusive in consumption, beneficiaries can continue to consume the good whether or not they pay taxes. Because of the free rider problem, beneficiaries have every reason in the world to hide their true benefits if the benefit principle of taxation is used.

In addition, many government programs and public goods are designed specifically for people unable to pay for the benefits received, most notably the poverty and income redistribution programs. The poor are eligible for the programs precisely because they are unable to pay for them. Furthermore, goods such as public education would be available only to higher-income families if the benefit principle were used.

The benefit principle is applied in specific cases, for example, toll roads and hunting licenses. However, if the benefit principle can be effectively used for a good, you might ask whether the government should be involved in its provision in the first place. If the government can effectively "market" the good, then maybe its production and allocation should be left to the private market system.

The Ability-to-Pay Principle

If the people benefiting do not pay for the programs and public goods, then who should pay? The **ability-to-pay principle** states that taxes are based on the ability of people to pay. One interpretation of the ability-to-pay principle is that people with more income pay more taxes. However, income may not be the best indicator of ability-to-pay. Financial and physical wealth is also an important consideration. In general, ability-to-pay might be based on a person's wealth or command over income earning resources, including labor, capital, land, and entrepreneurship.

The ability-to-pay principle has two components. **Vertical equity** is a principle stating that people with different ability to pay pay a different tax. This means if some people earn more income, they should pay more taxes. **Horizontal equity** is a principle stating that people with the same ability to pay pay the same tax. For example, two families of four that earn $20,000 should each pay the same tax. Together, vertical and horizontal equity simply mean equals should be treated equally and unequals should be treated unequally.

TAX REFORM AND THE FEDERAL INCOME TAX SYSTEM

Critics of the federal income tax system argue that it suffers from a lack of both horizontal and vertical equity. The lack of equity stems from the tax base, which is narrowly defined and excludes various types of income that could be subject to taxation but are not. For example, capital gains income received for the sale of assets over their original purchase price is treated differently from wage or salary income. Furthermore, a wide range of deductions, such as interest paid on mortgage loans, is permissible. Since these deductions are not available equally to everyone, people with the same ability-to-pay do not pay the same taxes, which violates horizontal equity.

To see how horizontal equity is violated, assume there are two families with the same incomes who live in identical houses with equal monthly payments. However, one family is buying its house, and its monthly payment is to the mortgage company; the second family is renting its house, and its payment goes to the owner of the house, who in turn makes the mortgage payment. In this case the family buying the house can deduct the mortgage interest from its income (usually a substantial portion of the monthly payment). But the other family cannot, even though it may be indirectly making the mortgage payment. While both families have equal incomes, the family that deducts the mortgage interest pays less income tax. Thus, when deductions are unequally available to people with equal incomes, the horizontal equity principle is violated. Moreover, vertical equity can also be violated when various deductions enable people with higher incomes to pay less tax than people with lower incomes.

In 1986, Congress began discussing some major reforms of the income tax system. The reforms sought to create a more comprehensive tax base by eliminating some deductions and applying a broader definition of income. While the thrust of the reforms was to reduce horizontal and vertical inequities, it is not likely that all inequities will be eliminated from a tax system as complex as ours.

TAXATION AND EFFICIENCY

We are concerned not only with equity but also with the efficiency of taxation. Keep in mind that one of the basic reasons for taxation is the provision of public goods by the government that are not efficiently allocated by markets. However, generating revenue through taxation to pay for the public goods can lead to additional inefficiencies of resource allocation. Without more study, there is no way of knowing which inefficiency is worse. In this unit we can at least look at the inefficiencies caused by taxation to see how they might be reduced.

Taxation has two fundamental effects, the revenue effect and the reallocation effect. The **revenue effect** is the process of raising revenue from a tax to carry on the operations of the government. In terms of financing public goods, this is the desired effect. It is also the desired effect from most taxes levied by federal, state, and local governments. The second effect, of reallocating resources, may not be the desired effect, but it is almost always present in a tax. The **reallocation effect** is the reallocation of resources caused by changes in relative prices due to a tax. The reallocation effect occurs because a tax invariably leads to a relatively greater change in the price of one good, service, or resource than another. As we saw in our study of demand in Section 7, a change in relative prices leads to a change in relative quantities purchased, which ultimately leads to a change in the allocation of resources. One way of looking at the reallocation effect is through changes in incentives. If one good is taxed more than another, then buyers have less incentive to buy that good.

These two effects can be illustrated with the federal income tax. While the federal income tax is designed to raise revenue, it also provides people with less incentive to earn income. The best way to earn less income is to withhold resources from productive activities. Labor has less incentive to work, investors have less incentive to purchase capital, and entrepreneurs have less incentive to organize production. This doesn't mean they have *no* incentive; it only means they have *less* incentive.

These two effects can also be illustrated with speeding fines. While a speeding fine is designed to reduce the amount of speeding, it also raises revenue. Speeding fines are intended to reallocate resources by providing incentives to drive slower, thus forcing drivers to use less gasoline and more labor (time).

If the main function of a tax is the reallocation effect—to discourage the use of a good, such as smoking, pollution, or speeding—then ideally it should generate *no* revenue. If no tax revenue is generated, then no one is paying the tax "penalty" for consuming or producing the good. But if the main function of a tax is the revenue effect, then it should distort the allocation of goods and resources as little as possible. The government does not want to generate revenues from a tax base that can be easily taxed out of existence with disincentives from the reallocation effect.

We can think about the effect of taxation on allocative efficiency in terms of the substitution and income effects, as discussed in Section 7. A substitution effect, where one good is substituted for another, results if the relative prices of goods change. That is, if a tax affects one good and not another, there is a substitution between the goods, and thus the reallocation effect. By contrast, an income effect, where more or less of a good is purchased as income changes, does not change the allocation of resources. This means an ideal tax system would affect income but not relative prices, with income effects but no substitution effects.

This is not as easy as it may seem. One alternative might be to tax all goods equally, which would lead to an equal change in the price of each good, thus preventing substitutions. However, problems arise in trying to define a good. Are services, such as legal and medical, included? If not, they would become relatively cheaper than physical goods, leading to a substitution effect. Would the inclusion of every good and service purchased by consumers prevent substitution effects? Not necessarily, since income can also be saved. Recall that if the prices of all goods and services increase, people would have a greater incentive to save.

A second alternative is simply to place a tax on all income, thus preventing a substitution effect and giving nothing but an income effect. But again, problems arise in trying to define income. If only wage income is taxed, people will try to substitute nonwage income for wage income. If all monetary income, regardless of source, is taxed, people will tend to substitute nonmonetary income for monetary income. That is, people will tend to work less but enjoy more leisure time, a form of non-monetary income.

Indeed, it is very difficult to eliminate every substitution effect caused by a tax. But we can try to find the taxing plan that has the fewest substitution effects. As a general rule, it is better to tax all goods rather than only specific goods. It is also better to include services in the tax base. And the best approach is to tax all income.

TAX INCIDENCE AND WELFARE LOSS

The simplest way to see how taxes affect resource allocation is through a single market. In Units 2.5 and 2.7 we looked at the incidence of taxation in a market. **Tax incidence** is the division of a tax between buyers and sellers. At this point we want to use the analysis of tax incidence to see how taxes affect resource allocation.

Tax incidence can be measured by determining who ultimately pays the tax. For example, many states and cities levy sales taxes on consumer expenditures for goods. Although the sales taxes are charged to stores based on the value of their sales, no one would argue that the stores pay the tax. After all, if the sales tax is 5 percent, the store merely adds an extra 5 cents to each dollar of goods sold. But this figure is not quite accurate, because the sales tax may very well lead to a decline in total sales for the store, causing the store to end up paying part of the tax.

Figure 12.3.2 illustrates the incidence of a tax. The market equilibrium prior to the tax is given by the intersection of the demand and supply curves at point E. The original quantity is Q_e and the initial price is P_e. If a tax is levied on the good sold in this market, the new equilibrium is achieved at point E', and the quantity exchanged declines to Q_t. The price paid by demanders is P_t and the price received by suppliers, after the tax is paid, is P_s. The tax is the difference between P_t and P_s, equal to the distance AE' at quantity Q_t.

In this case, and in general, the tax incidence is divided between buyers and sellers. Buyers pay

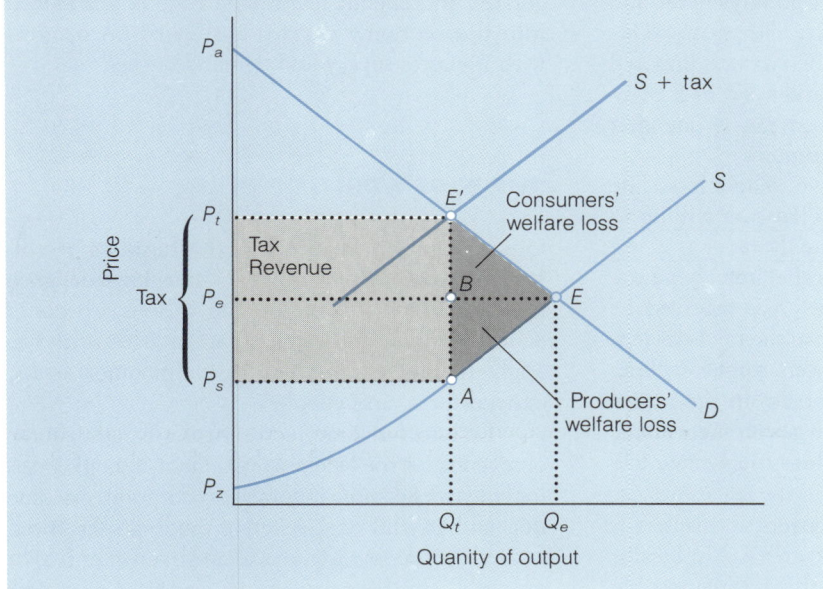

Figure 12.3.2

Tax Incidence and Welfare Loss

Tax incidence is the division of taxes between buyers and sellers in a market. Buyers pay a higher price and sellers receive a lower price after the tax than they did before. However, a tax also generates a welfare loss as buyers and sellers lose a greater amount of consumers' and producers' surplus than the tax revenue received by the government.

the difference between P_t and P_e, equal to the distance BE'. Sellers pay the difference between P_e and P_s, equal to the distance AB. In extreme circumstances, if the demand or supply curve is perfectly elastic or inelastic, only one side of the market pays the entire tax. Unit 2.7 discusses tax incidence and elasticity in more detail.

In this unit we are concerned with the efficiency aspects of the tax. While we know that both buyers and sellers are paying part of the tax, the problem is that the total amount of tax collected by the government is less than what buyers and sellers are giving up. Let's first look at the buyers.

At the original price, P_e, buyers are willing to pay up to P_a for the good. The difference between the price actually paid and the price the buyer is willing to pay is **consumers' surplus.** The total consumers' surplus for all buyers is the triangular area beneath the demand curve but above the price paid by buyers, area P_aEP_e.

After the tax is levied, the price paid by buyers increases to P_t, and the consumers' surplus decreases to the area of the smaller triangle, $P_aE'P_t$. Clearly, buyers have lost some consumers' surplus as a result of the tax. But part of the lost consumers' surplus actually goes to the government as the tax. The buyers' share of the tax is equal to the area $P_tE'BP_e$. However, if we add the buyers' share of the tax to the consumers' surplus after the tax, we still come up short of the original amount of consumers' surplus. We have not yet accounted for the shaded triangle $E'BE$.

The triangular area $E'BE$ is the welfare loss from the tax. **Welfare loss** is the difference between the reduction in consumers' and producers' surplus and the tax revenue. It doesn't go anywhere, and it's not paid to anyone; it simply disappears. This is an inefficiency that results when a tax is imposed on an efficiently operating market. From a revenue-raising perspective, the best tax is one that keeps this welfare loss to a minimum.

Sellers as well as buyers have welfare loss. The difference between the price sellers are willing to accept and the price they actually receive is the **producers' surplus.** Here, it is the area above the supply curve and beneath the price received by sellers, which is area P_zEP_e before the tax is levied. After the tax is levied, the producers' surplus declines to area P_zAP_s. Part of the decrease in producers' surplus is the tax paid to the government, area P_sABP_e. The remaining triangle is the welfare loss by suppliers, area ABE.

The combined losses by buyers and sellers is the total welfare loss from the tax, area $E'AE$. Ideally, taxes have no welfare loss, but this is only possible in certain circumstances. Figure 12.3.3 presents four alternative markets. Note that in each market either the supply or demand curve is perfectly elastic or inelastic.

In panel a the demand curve is perfectly inelastic; buyers pay the entire tax, and there is no welfare loss. In panel c the supply curve is perfectly inelastic; the sellers pay the entire tax, and there is no welfare loss. In both panels a and c no welfare loss occurs because the quantity exchanged after the tax is the same as before the tax. Thus, the tax with the least effect on resource allocation and efficiency is the one levied on goods that are either perfectly inelastic in demand or supply.

By contrast, panel b illustrates a market with a perfectly elastic supply curve. Note that the buyers pay the entire tax, as in panel a. However, the buyers also incur a welfare loss, equal to the shaded triangle. Panel d illustrates a perfectly elastic demand curve, and the entire tax is paid by the sellers. In addition, the sellers now incur a loss in welfare from the tax.

The more elastic the demand and supply curves are, the greater the distortion in the market is. This means the quantity exchanged is much less after the tax is levied, and the total welfare loss is greater. In general, less inefficiency is introduced into the economy if taxes are levied on markets with inelastic supply and demand curves.

THE WIDE WORLD OF TAXES

Governments have been in the business of collecting taxes for a long time, and they have designed a wide variety of taxes on the various aspects of economic life. These taxes can be categorized to apply to one of four tax bases: income, assets, expenditures, and people.

Taxes on income represent the biggest source of revenue for the federal government. Income taxes include the personal income tax, corporate income tax, and payroll tax. Assets provide a substantial tax base for most state and local governments. For example, the property tax is used as a source of funding for many local schools. Expenditure taxes are also very important at the state and local level. The general sales tax on the purchase of goods is an example of an expenditure tax. At the federal level many excise taxes are levied on the sale of specific goods, such as tires, cigarettes, and alcohol. The last tax base, people, is no longer used in the United States, though in the past it was common to place a head tax on citizens, where every person paid the same tax. The closest we come to a head tax now is the itemized deduction for each member of a household on the federal income tax form. But this really constitutes a negative tax, whereby the recipient receives a reduction in taxes.

Figure 12.3.4 depicts the distribution of several major taxes. At the federal level, in panel a, the personal income tax is by far the most impor-

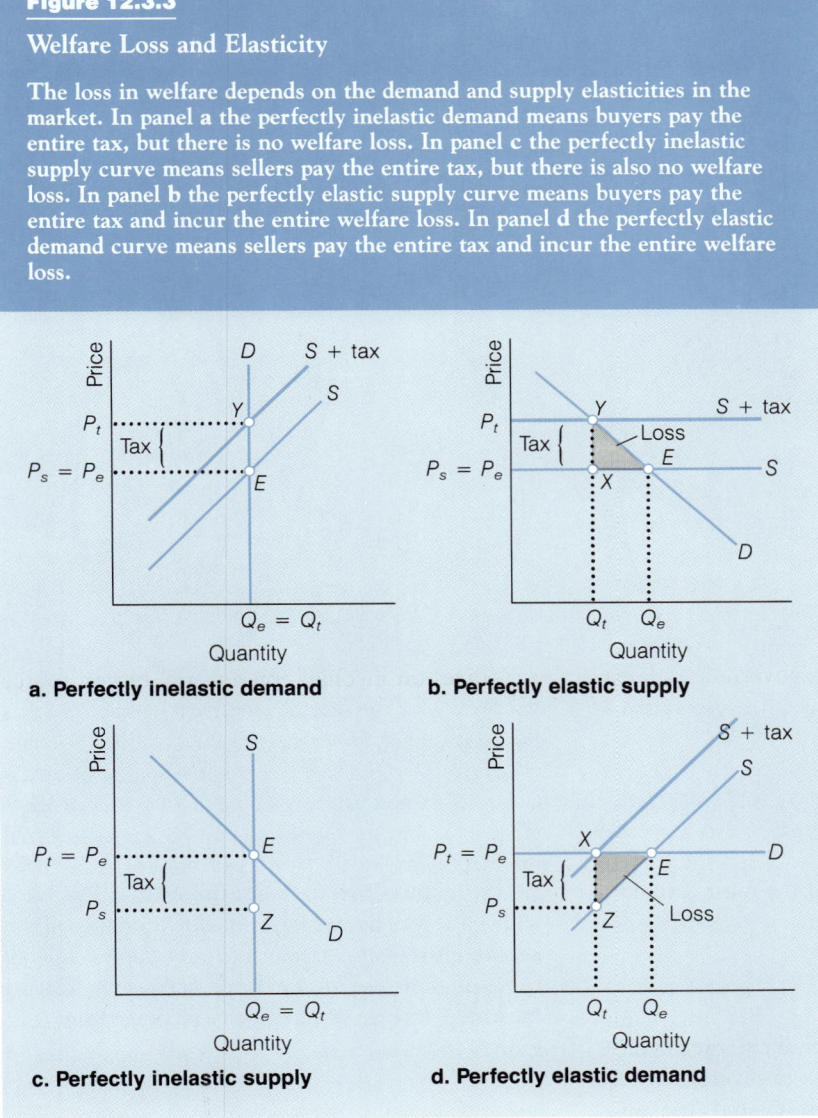

Figure 12.3.3

Welfare Loss and Elasticity

The loss in welfare depends on the demand and supply elasticities in the market. In panel a the perfectly inelastic demand means buyers pay the entire tax, but there is no welfare loss. In panel c the perfectly inelastic supply curve means sellers pay the entire tax, but there is also no welfare loss. In panel b the perfectly elastic supply curve means buyers pay the entire tax and incur the entire welfare loss. In panel d the perfectly elastic demand curve means sellers pay the entire tax and incur the entire welfare loss.

tant source of revenue, accounting for about 45 percent of all revenue received by the federal government. Social insurance, which is a tax on wage income, is the second largest source of revenue, with about 38 percent.

For state and local governments, in panel b, almost equal shares of revenue come from sales taxes, property taxes, and grants from the federal government. Note that the grants from the federal government are merely part of the taxes paid to the federal government but then shifted to the state and local governments for spending. Let's take a

Figure 12.3.4

Federal and State and Local Tax Revenues, 1984

The federal government receives nearly 50 percent of its revenues from personal income taxes. The second largest source is the payroll tax for social insurance. State and local governments receive almost equal amounts from sales and excise taxes, property taxes, and grants from the federal government.

a. Federal
- Indirect business taxes (7.9%)
- Social security (37.5%)
- Corporate income (8.9%)
- Personal income (44.7%)

b. State and local
- Income (14.3%)
- Grants (18.5%)
- Other (28.3%)
- Property (18.3%)
- Sales (20.6%)

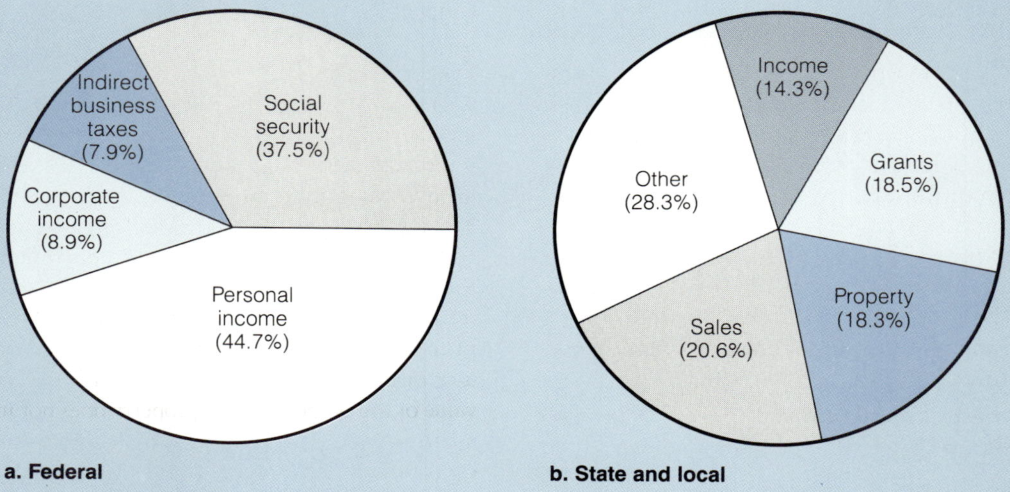

more detailed look at several of the most common taxes used in the United States.

Personal Income Tax

As mentioned earlier, the personal income tax represents the largest single source of revenue of the federal government, and many states and cities also have personal income taxes. At the federal level the personal income tax, on the surface, is progressive. That is, the tax rate increases for higher levels of income. However, deductions and a variety of loopholes make the actual tax rate less progressive than the official tax rate.

As a tax base, personal income is a good measure of a person's ability-to-pay. However, as long as the income tax code continues to allow for a wide variety of deductions, taxable income will not accurately reflect command over resources. It leads to inefficiencies, as we have seen, by creating incentives to earn nonmonetary income rather than money income.

Payroll Tax

The most common payroll tax is the Social Security tax, which people generally think is shared equally by employees and employers. Currently, employees pay about 7 percent of their wage income, up to $40,000, in Social Security, and employers then match the payment of the employee. However, in reality, the employer considers its share of the tax part of the wage paid to the employee.

For example, an employee earns $1000 a month in wages, of which 7 percent, or $70, is paid by the employee as the Social Security tax. The employer also contributes $70. The total wage paid by the employer is actually $1070, the $1000 wage plus the $70 Social Security payment. The employer will continue to employ the worker as long as he or she generates at least $1070 to the firm. But if the worker contributes only $1000 in production, the employer will be losing profit. In this sense the employee actually pays all $140 of the Social Security tax.

The Social Security tax creates disincentives to earn wage income, and more incentives to earn income from the other factors of production—land, capital, and entrepreneurship—which are not subject to the tax. By increasing the price of labor relative to other factors, the Social Security tax also creates incentives for firms to substitute the other factors for labor in the production of goods and services.

Corporate Income Tax

The corporate income tax is a tax on the accounting profits of a corporation. First, note that the tax is on accounting profits, and not on economic profits, which means part of the tax is undoubtedly on normal profits. This in turn implies that it is a tax on an opportunity cost of production, which is the equivalent of taxing a firm for buying raw materials or labor.

Second, note that the income from partnerships and proprietorships is not subject to the corporate income tax but is taxed as personal income. However, some corporate profits are actually taxed twice, first by the corporate income tax, and subsequently as dividends by the personal income tax.

Sales and Excise Tax

Sales and excise taxes are similar, with one notable difference. Sales taxes are levied on a wider number of goods, while excise taxes are levied on specific goods. For example, a city might levy a sales tax on all food sold in the city; an excise tax would be one placed on the sale of a single good, such as alcohol.

Sales taxes tend to be regressive. People with lower incomes tend to spend a larger fraction of their income on commodities covered by sales taxes, such as food and clothing. By contrast, people with higher incomes tend to spend more income on services, investments, savings, and other goods not covered by sales taxes.

Property Tax

A property tax is a tax on the value of land and its improvements. The value of land usually derives from its location (for example, downtown Manhattan), intrinsic quality (for example, prime agricultural land), and any capital improvements on the land. A house, building, barn, or other improvement increases the value of the land, and thus the amount of the tax. One of the biggest, and most controversial, problems is assessing the value of the property. Most property does not involve a current market transaction, making it difficult to determine the "market value" of the property. Thus, two identical properties may pay different taxes because one has been on the market, with a recent market value, and the other has not, a violation of the horizontal equity principle.

IN SUMMARY

Principles of Taxation

- The amount of a tax is specified as the tax rate times the tax base. Tax rates can be *ad valorem*, in which the tax base is stated as the value, or per unit, in which the tax base is stated as a physical quantity. With respect to income, taxes can be either proportional, regressive, or progressive, depending on whether the proportion of income paid in taxes stays the same, decreases, or increases as income increases.

- One way to apply an equitable tax is with the benefit principle, where people benefiting from a government program or public good pay the tax. However, the benefit principle cannot be applied to most areas of the government because it is difficult to determine who benefits and how much.

- The ability-to-pay is the most commonly accepted principle of taxation. It states that taxes are paid by people based on their ability to pay. The ability-to-pay principle is usually extended to vertical and horizontal equity. With vertical equity, people with more paying ability pay more. With horizontal equity, people with the same paying ability pay the same.

- Taxation has two effects. The first is the revenue effect, which raises revenue for government operations and provision of public goods. The second is the reallocation effect, which provides incentives for changing consumption patterns. If the main purpose of a tax is to raise revenue, then the tax should affect consumption, and the allocation of resources, as little as possible.

- Tax incidence is generally divided between both buyers and sellers in a market. However, buyers and sellers usually give up more than the total amount of the tax revenue collected by the government. Buyers lose consumers' surplus and sellers lose producers' surplus over and above the amount of the tax. This combined welfare loss is greater if demand and supply are more elastic. In general, there is less distortion of an efficient resource allocation if taxes are levied in markets with relatively inelastic demand and supply.

- There are four basic tax bases: income, assets, expenditures, and people. The first three are commonly used in the United States, while the last one is not. The federal government obtains nearly half of its revenue from the personal income tax. Other important sources of revenue at the federal level are the Social Security payroll tax, the corporate income tax, and excise taxes. State and local governments obtain revenue from property taxes, sales taxes, income taxes, and grants from the federal government.

QUESTIONS FOR STUDY AND ANALYSIS

1. The following table lists expenditure and income information for four income groups:

Class	Total Income	Wage Income	Dividend Income	Other Income	Expenditures on Food
I	$ 10,000	$10,000	$ 0	$ 0	$ 5,000
II	20,000	15,000	2,000	3,000	8,000
III	50,000	30,000	10,000	10,000	10,000
IV	100,000	50,000	30,000	20,000	15,000

   a. Is a 15 percent tax on total income proportional, regressive, or progressive? Explain.
   b. Is a 15 percent tax on nondividend income proportional, regressive, or progressive? Explain.
   c. Is a 3 percent sales tax on food expenditures proportional, regressive, or progressive? Explain.
   d. Is a 40 percent tax on corporate income, including dividends, proportional, regressive, or progressive? Explain.
   e. Is a 7 percent payroll tax on wage income proportional, regressive, or progressive? Explain.

2. In question 1, which of the five taxes best meets the ability-to-pay equity principle of taxation? Why?

3. Rank the following markets in order of smallest to largest welfare loss to society.
   a. The market for gasoline (refer to Unit 2.7)
   b. The market for land in downtown New York City
   c. The market for corn

4. Many states have used lotteries over the past several years as a means of raising revenue.

The lotteries usually work in the following manner. Tickets with a combination of numbers or letters are sold for a nominal amount, usually between 50 cents and $1. The state takes a share of the revenue, and the remainder is used to pay off the lucky winner or winners. However, a lucky winner may not be produced during each periodic drawing, meaning the pot is increased until a winner is found. In recent years lottery pots have been in the millions of dollars, creating some rather ecstatic winners. The states can also be pretty happy at receiving billions of dollars in revenue from lotteries.

  a. Would you expect a lottery, as a tax, to be proportional, regressive, or progressive? Why?
  b. Evaluate a lottery in terms of the benefit principle. Evaluate it in terms of the ability-to-pay principle.
  c. What type of welfare loss, if any, is caused by a lottery?

5. Explain why it is desirable to have either the revenue effect or the reallocation effect, but not both.

REVIEW GLOSSARY

ability-to-pay principle A principle that states taxes are based on the ability of people to pay.

ad valorem tax A tax that is levied on the monetary value of the tax base.

benefit principle A principle that states taxes are based on the benefits received. The benefit principle is difficult to apply because the degree of benefit people obtain from government programs and public goods is not easily measured.

consumers' surplus The difference between the price buyers are willing to pay for a good (based on the marginal utility received) and the actual price paid. Buyers lose more in consumers' surplus than their share of the tax.

horizontal equity A principle that states people with the same ability to pay should pay the same tax.

per unit tax A tax that is levied on the physical quantity of the tax base.

producers' surplus The difference between the price suppliers are willing to accept for a good (based on the costs of production) and the price actually received. Sellers also lose more in producers' surplus than their share of the tax.

progressive tax A tax in which the proportion of income paid in tax increases for higher levels of income.

proportional tax A tax in which the proportion of income paid in tax is the same for all levels of income.

reallocation effect The reallocation of resources caused by changes in relative prices due to a tax. An ideal tax designed to raise revenue has no reallocation effect.

regressive tax A tax in which the proportion of income paid in tax decreases for higher levels of income.

revenue effect The process of raising revenue from a tax in order to carry on the operations of the government.

tax base The object of taxation.

tax incidence The division of a tax between buyers and sellers. In general, both buyers and sellers pay part of a tax levied on a market.

tax rate The amount of tax applied per unit of the tax base.

vertical equity A principle that states people with different ability to pay should pay a different tax.

welfare loss The difference between the reduction in consumers' and producers' surplus and the tax revenue. Welfare loss is greater if the demand and supply curves are more elastic.

UNIT 12.4

Government Regulation of Economic Activity

One of the most controversial areas of government involvement in the economy is regulation. **Government regulation** is the process of controlling business activities through laws and administrative rules. Other units in this text concentrate on specific types of regulation. For example, Unit 9.3 looks at price regulation of natural monopolies, Unit 9.6 covers regulation of market structures, and Unit 13.3 studies pollution control regulation. But this unit presents an overview of all types of government regulation, concentrating on the advantages and disadvantages of regulation in general.

Government regulation affects almost every phase of economic activity. Laws and rules control the types of products produced, how they can be sold, what prices can be charged, how inputs are combined in their production, and how much waste materials can be discharged. Indeed, government regulation is so widespread that it can directly affect the allocation of resources in many ways. Our main goal in this unit is to see how government regulation can alter the allocation of resources, for better or worse.

First, we identify the most prominent government regulatory agencies and see what they regulate. Then we discuss the arguments for and against government regulation, to see how it can improve or worsen the allocation of resources.

A SHORT LIST OF REGULATORY AGENCIES

A complete discussion of all regulatory agencies would require more space than is available in this unit. However, we can take a brief look at several of the most important and notable government agencies, dividing them into two types, industry and social.

Industry Regulatory Agencies

Industry regulation is the regulation of an entire industry. Many of the most prominent regulatory agencies deal with the regulation of individual industries, such as the airline, trucking, and communications industries. Industrial regulatory agencies include the Interstate Commerce Commission, the Federal Communications Commission, the Civil Aeronautics Board, and the Federal Energy Regulatory Commission.

Interstate Commerce Commission (ICC) The Interstate Commerce Commission, formed in 1887 by the Interstate Commerce Act, is in charge of almost all interstate transportation, including trucking, railroads, buses, water carriers, and pipelines. The key exceptions are pipelines transporting oil, water, and natural gas and trucks transporting agricultural products. Until 1980 the ICC had the power to limit the number of firms in each of the transportation industries, and authority to regulate prices. However, in 1980 the Motor Carrier Act was passed, which deregulated the trucking industry, and thus substantially lessened the ICC's control over it. In the same year, the Staggers Rail Deregulation Act also went into effect, which reduced the regulation of the railroad industry.

Federal Communications Commission (FCC) The Federal Communications Commission, formed in 1934 by the Federal Communications Act, has authority over telephone and telegraph communications, and the power to regulate and license radio and television stations. The FCC is currently relaxing its control over the radio and television industries by allowing more stations and a wider range of broadcasting frequencies than in the past.

Civil Aeronautics Board (CAB) The Civil Aeronautics Board was established in 1938 by the Civil Aeronautics Authority Act. Until 1985 it had the authority to regulate the number of firms and the prices in the airline industry. However, in 1978 the Airline Deregulation Act was passed to phase out the CAB by 1985. Even though it is no longer around, the CAB is included here because it was one of the more important regulatory agencies in its time, and because it exemplifies some of the problems of regulation that are discussed later.

Federal Energy Regulatory Commission (FERC) The Federal Energy Regulatory Commission was technically formed in 1977 by the Department of Energy Organization Act. However, it took over for the Federal Power Commission, which was established in 1920. The FERC regulates the interstate transportation of electricity, natural gas, and petroleum.

Social Regulatory Agencies

<u>Social regulation</u> is the regulation of specific activities, regardless of industry. Social regulation deals primarily with three areas—health, safety, and the environment—and thus almost always cuts across industrial classifications. When the FCC establishes the number of hours that can be devoted to prime time television programming, this affects only firms in the television industry. However, if a social regulatory agency establishes a regulation affecting worker safety, it applies to all industries. Social regulatory agencies include the Food and Drug Administration, the Environmental Protection Agency, the National Highway Traffic Safety Administration, the Occupational Safety and Health Administration, and the Consumer Product Safety Commission.

Food and Drug Administration (FDA) The Food and Drug Administration was officially established in 1931 by the Food, Drug, and Cosmetic Act. However, prior to this act the Bureau of Chemistry in the Department of Agriculture performed many of the FDA's regulatory functions. The FDA has wide-ranging authority, from protecting the public from unsafe and ineffective drugs to regulating the purity of food. It also has authority over product packaging and cosmetics and can even ban products and prevent their sale.

Environmental Protection Agency (EPA) The Environmental Protection Agency was formed in 1970 by the Clean Air Amendments. A major extension of its power came from the Water Pollution Control Amendments in 1972. The EPA has the authority to protect and improve the quality of the natural environment. It controls pollution of the air, water, and land by establishing and enforcing pollution emission standards. Pollution control legislation is discussed in more detail in Unit 13.3.

National Highway Traffic Safety Administration (NHTSA) The National Highway Traffic Safety Administration was formed in 1970 by the Highway Safety Act. It took over for the National Highway Safety Agency, which was created in 1966. It is the branch of the Department of Transportation that sets and enforces safety standards for motor vehicles, such as the use of seat belts and padded dashboards. It is also in charge of the 55 mile per hour speed limit and regulates fuel economy.

Occupational Safety and Health Administration (OSHA) The Occupational Safety and Health Administration was formed in 1970 by the Occupational Safety and Health Act. Its primary responsibility is to establish standards for workplace safety and health. However, it is also involved in education and training programs concerning worker safety and health.

Consumer Product Safety Commission (CPSC) The Consumer Product Safety Commission was established by the Consumer Product Safety Act in 1972. As its title implies, it is charged with the authority to regulate the safety of consumer products. This includes setting and enforcing a variety of standards for safety and product labeling. It also has the authority, like the FDA, to ban products.

REASONS FOR REGULATION

The agencies just discussed regulate everything from the number of television stations in a city to the labels on breakfast cereal. And keep in mind that this is only a small list of the most important regulatory agencies. Given the large number of regulatory agencies, there must be some pretty good reasons for government regulation. Indeed, government regulation has the highest of goals, to protect the public interest. **Public interest** is simply the well-being of the consuming public. The public interest can be threatened in three ways: market power, externalities, and imperfect information.

Market Power

In Section 9, we extensively discussed **market power, which is the ability of a firm to control or influence the price and/or quantity exchanged in the market.** Recall that market power leads to a misallocation of resources, particularly a higher price charged and a lesser quantity produced. Thus, it is in the public interest to control market power. The misallocation of resources caused by market power is the basic reason for almost all industry regulation, especially the regulation of natural monopolies.

The FCC, ICC, CAB, and FERC all have (or *had* in the case of the CAB) the authority to control the price, so as to prevent the type of competitive, predatory pricing that can occur in the emergence of a natural monopoly. In addition, most industry regulatory agencies control the number of firms in the industry, in order to prevent the duplication of capital that causes higher average costs of production.

Externalities

Another important reason to protect the public interest through government regulation is the existence of externalities. An **externality** is a cost or benefit that affects someone not directly involved in the production or exchange of a good, and that is incurred without compensation. In most cases government regulation is concerned with the cost side of an externality, or an external cost. An external cost exists when an opportunity cost of production is not paid by the producer. For example, pollution represents a sizable external cost. If a firm discharges toxic waste in a river and downstream users are adversely affected, then they incur an opportunity cost. However, the firm does not compensate the downstream users for their opportunity cost the way it compensates labor for its opportunity cost. Because all of the costs of production are not included, the price charged for the product is too low. Thus, buyers demand too much of the good, overproduction occurs, and resources are misallocated.

Figure 12.4.1 illustrates how an external cost affects a market. The private market is indicated by the demand curve D and supply curve S, leading to equilibrium at point E. However, supply curve S reflects only the costs of production incurred by the firm; it does not include the external costs caused by pollution. But S' is based on *all* opportunity costs of production, including the costs incurred by the firm and the external costs from the pollution. In this case an efficient allocation of resources is given by point E', where the value of the last unit of the good produced is equal to the opportunity costs of producing the last unit. Left alone, the market charges a lower price and produces a larger quantity than the efficient allocation.

The EPA is the main regulatory agency dealing with pollution externalities. It does this by regulating the quantities and types of pollution dis-

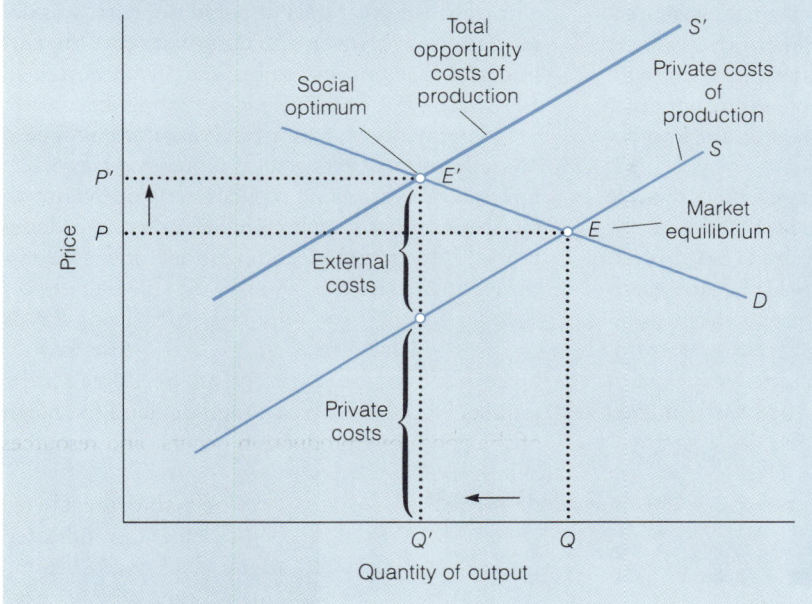

Figure 12.4.1

Externalities

A market that considers only the private costs of production reaches equilibrium at point E, the intersection of demand curve D and supply curve S. If there is an opportunity cost external to a market, then the supply curve based on all opportunity costs is S', and the market should operate at point E'. Left alone, the market does not efficiently allocate resources.

charged into the natural environment. Externalities, pollution, and methods of regulation are discussed in more detail in Section 13.

Imperfect Information

A third way the public interest can be threatened is through imperfect information. Consumers buy hundreds of different types of goods each year and cannot possibly become knowledgeable about each good. The main source of information on any one good usually comes from advertising by the producing firm, whose interest generally lies in selling the product and not necessarily in providing complete and accurate information. Thus, a pharmaceutical drug might have harmful side effects, a food additive might be carcinogenic, and ground "beef" might contain ground horsemeat, although consumers are led to believe otherwise. In other cases the firms might not be intentionally trying to deceive consumers. The firms might also have imperfect information if it is not profitable for them to find out more about the product they are producing.

A misallocation of resources occurs if consumers have imperfect information, as Figure 12.4.2 illustrates. If consumers have imperfect information about the good, their demand curve is D, leading to a market equilibrium at point E. However, if consumers have complete information concerning the side effects or true quality of the good, then the demand curve is D'. That is, at any given price, people are willing to buy less of the good, or for each quantity, buyers are willing to pay a lower price. With complete information, the market equilibrium is point E'. The market price is lower and a smaller quantity is exchanged than with imperfect information. The lack of information leads to an overproduction of this good and a misallocation of resources.

Many of the social regulatory agencies provide consumers with information; the CPSC heads the list, followed by the FDA and the NHTSA. In fact, the EPA became well known when it began reporting mileage estimates on new automobiles as part of its regulation of automobile pollution emissions.

REASONS AGAINST REGULATION

In spite of the many compelling reasons for regulation, the late 1970s and early 1980s saw a strong push against regulation. A major issue in Ronald Reagan's 1980 presidential campaign, and one that earned him a great deal of public support, was deregulation. Moreover, the deregulation of the airline and trucking industries actually occurred in 1978 and 1980, before Reagan took office.

Opponents of government regulation argue it has fallen short of its goal of protecting the public interest. Government regulation is criticized on four basic grounds: higher production costs, reduced productivity, reduced competition, and administrative inefficiencies.

Figure 12.4.2

Imperfect Information

Where buyers have imperfect information concerning hazards or side effects of a product, the demand curve is D and the market equilibrium is point E. However, if buyers have complete information, the demand curve is D' and the market equilibrium is point E'.

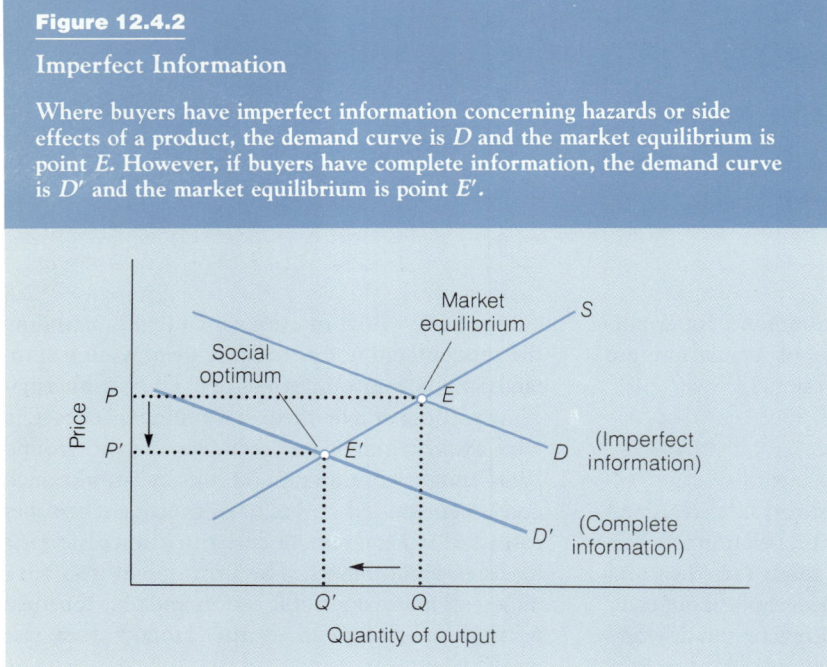

Production Costs

One of the biggest criticisms leveled at government regulation, especially social regulation, is that it increases production costs. For example, in order to comply with EPA standards for water pollution discharge, firms have to purchase and install pollution control devices, which leads to higher production costs. Likewise, standards set by OSHA to insure worker health and safety also cause higher production costs.

However, the main problem is not so much the costs themselves as the costs relative to the benefits received from the regulations. For example, the costs of reducing the first 95 percent of the pollution in the environment are about the same as reducing the remaining 5 percent. The question becomes whether the benefits received from the last 5 percent are worth the costs. Many people argue that they are not.

Productivity

A second criticism is that government regulation reduces productivity and the incentive for innovation and technological advances. For example, prices in the railroad industry are controlled in order to insure that each firm receives a normal profit (to the best of the regulating agency's ability). This provides very little incentive for a firm in the railroad industry to invest in technological innovation. If it generates an innovation that reduces production costs or increases labor productivity, such as a fuel-efficient, automated train, the regulatory agency will simply lower the price to insure a normal profit.

Innovation in socially regulated industries can also be reduced. For example, the FDA must test and certify every new pharmaceutical drug produced, a process that takes about seven years. A firm might spend several years developing a drug, then wait seven more years, while the FDA tests it, only to find out that it cannot be sold. Clearly, a firm has less incentive to invest in the development of new drugs if it must wait seven to ten (or more) years before receiving a return. The same is true for firms regulated by the Consumer Product Safety Commission, only for those firms more uncertainty is involved. Drug firms know their products must be tested and approved by the FDA. However, testing for other consumer products is not automatic. For example, after developing a product, a firm may begin to receive sales orders and gear up for production, at which point the CPSC might determine that the product is unsafe. The firm loses its product development costs as well as its initial marketing and production costs.

Competition

A third criticism, that government regulation can reduce competition in an industry, is directed especially at industrial regulation by agencies such as the FCC and the ICC. One of the main reasons for deregulation of the airline and trucking industries was to increase competition. Some people feel that regulatory agencies are actually captured by the industry they regulate, such that the industry turns into a legal cartel.

In fact, a regulatory agency could set up a legal cartel in three ways. First, the regulatory agency has the legal authority to set prices and limit the number of firms in the industry, which, as we saw in Unit 9.5, is exactly what a cartel tries to do. By controlling price and the number of firms, a cartel like OPEC uses its market power to increase profits for each individual member. When a regulatory agency acts in this way, it is reducing competition, and actually working against the public interest.

Second, the capture of a regulatory agency by an industry depends on the expertise required by the regulatory commissions. To effectively regulate an industry, a regulator must be very knowledgeable about its operation. And the people most knowledgeable about an industry are those who work in it, which suggests that many commission members may have worked for one of the firms being regulated at some time in the past. Furthermore, since commissioners serve limited terms, they are likely to work for one of the firms in the industry sometime in the future too. Thus, a commissioner, with his or her long-run interests in mind, tends to act more on the behalf of the industry than the consuming public.

Third, the capture of a regulatory agency by an industry takes place because of the role of the industry as a special interest group. The industry is directly affected by regulatory decisions, and therefore has ample reason to strongly plead its case before the commission. By contrast, the consumers of the good produced by the industry form no special interest group. The industry's good, whether it is electricity, transportation services, or communications, is only one of many goods purchased by consumers. Consumers lack the time, organization, and financial resources to present their case to the regulatory agency. This means that, combined with the lack of information-gathering resources on the part of the agency, the industry provides most of the information used in its own regulation.

Administrative Inefficiencies

The last of the four major criticisms of government regulation focuses on administrative inefficiencies. The administration of regulations can lead to a misallocation of resources in five general ways: inflexible rules, time lag, paperwork, ineffective rules, and special interests of the regulatory agency.

Inflexible Rules Rules and regulations are often inflexible and not easily changed to address different situations in the economy or changes in relevant markets. For example, an OSHA regulation for accessibility to toilet facilities makes sense in a field filled with migrant workers (there must be a facility within a few miles of each worker). However, it is an absurd regulation when applied to a single Montana rancher, miles from nowhere. Another inflexibility appears in the price regulation of industries, which does not allow for quick changes in prices to meet changes in production costs or market conditions. For example, a regulated airline industry cannot lower its prices when a downturn in the economy reduces air travel. Likewise, a regulated electric company cannot immediately raise rates to cover higher input costs.

Time Lag The time lag for regulatory action also leads to administrative inefficiency. Recall that the FDA can take up to seven years to approve a new drug. In addition, the time lag for testing other consumer products can cause inefficiencies if a product is banned after many of the costs of production have been incurred. The time lag also contributes to the inflexibility of rate regulation just discussed. A regulatory agency must conduct a public hearing every time a firm requests a change in price; for large public utilities, this can take several months, or years.

Paperwork A regulated firm can be swamped by government paperwork. For example, an automobile firm has to fill out forms indicating compliance with regulations set by the EPA, NHTSA, OSHA, and a score of other agencies we have not even discussed. Resources used to fill out forms cannot be used to produce automobiles.

Ineffective Rules Administrative inefficiency also results from ineffective rules and regulations, especially if the cost of the rule outweighs the benefits. For example, a regulation to pave the shoulders of a highway might save ten lives each year. However, in money terms the costs of this regulation could be several billion dollars. In addition, as many or more lives might be lost in other industries that provide materials used to pave the shoulders. Another example is the rule forcing a coal-fired generator in Wyoming to reduce pollution emissions. Since Wyoming is not densely populated and has very little pollution, the generator has negligible external costs. Thus, a rule forcing it to reduce pollution has little effect on the level of pollution, but can be very costly.

Special Interests of Agency As we saw in Unit 12.1, the regulatory agency represents a special interest group in terms of its own funding. As with any government agency, it has the incentive to grow and increase its power and funding. For a regulatory agency, growth is measured by the extent of its regulatory power. It has the incentive to generate more rules and regulations for its existing "clientele" and to bring new firms and products under its authority.

AN EVALUATION OF GOVERNMENT REGULATION

Government regulation has a definite role in the economy. This is particularly evident in high risk areas, such as nuclear energy and toxic substances. While a profit-maximizing firm might make decisions that are ultimately in the public interest, the consequences can be catastrophic if it doesn't. Regulation is also needed to contend with market power, externalities, product safety, and imperfect information.

The question is not whether government regulation is necessary, but how much is necessary. Normative arguments for and against government regulation tend to be long-winded and highly emotional. For example, environmentalists argue that the very existence of the planet is in jeopardy without regulation. Libertarians blame regulation for everything from inflation to the moral degradation of society. While many of the arguments may have merit, a more precise way to evaluate the pros and cons of government regulation is needed. For this we can turn to benefit-cost analysis, introduced in Unit 12.2. Although benefit-cost analysis has been used for many years in the evaluation of public goods, it has only recently been used, by academic researchers, to evaluate government regulation. No systematic evaluation of regulation has been performed by the government. Only when this is done can we determine the "right" amount of government regulation. At the present, we can merely say that there is probably too much regulation in some areas, but not enough in others.

IN SUMMARY

Government Regulation of Economic Activity

- The government becomes involved in the economy through government regulation, the process of controlling business activity. The numerous agencies used for government regulation fall into one of two categories, industry regulatory agencies and social regulatory agencies. Industry regulation is the regulation of an entire industry, especially of the number of firms and the price. Social regulation concentrates on specific activities, regardless of which industry is affected.

- The three primary reasons for government regulation are market power, externalities, and imperfect information. Without regulation of market power, industries would tend to charge a higher price and reduce the quantity of output produced. Externalities such as environmental pollution are one reason for social regulation. Externalities lead to an inefficient allocation of resources if left uncorrected. Imperfect information also causes a need for social regulation. Consumers as well as producers may be unaware of the true nature and costs of a good.

- The four main arguments against government regulation are higher production costs, reduced productivity, reduced competition, and administrative inefficiencies. Government regulation can increase the costs of production more than the benefits obtained by the public from the regulation. Regulation can also inhibit technological advances, and thus reduce productivity. In addition, an industry regulatory agency can be captured by the industry it regulates, effectively establishing a legal cartel that reduces competition. And last, administrative inefficiencies resulting from inflexible rules, time lag, paperwork, ineffective rules, and the special interests of the regulatory agency can diminish the benefits of government regulation.

QUESTIONS FOR STUDY AND ANALYSIS

1. The Consumer Products Safety Commission (CPSC) has recently become concerned with the safety of amusement park rides. In the past, its authority to regulate these rides has been limited to the movable rides found in state fairs or other traveling carnivals. The CPSC would also like to regulate stationary rides found in amusement parks throughout the country.
   a. Which of the three public interest reasons do you think the CPSC is using to argue for more regulation of the amusement rides industry?
   b. Opponents of the regulation argue that it would create unneeded controls and put an impossible, impractical load on the six hundred CPSC inspectors. Which of the arguments against regulation are the opponents using?
   c. Evaluate CPSC's motives for stronger regulation in terms of the agency as a special interest group.
   d. Do you think the amusement rides industry should have more regulation? Why or why not?

2. In its move to loosen regulations on the broadcast industry, the FCC increased the number of television and radio stations a single firm could own from seven to twelve. How do you think this will affect competition in the broadcast industry? How is this likely to affect the market power of each firm?

3. Considering the reasons for regulation (the benefits) and the reasons against regulation (the costs), outline how you would evaluate the effectiveness of a regulation requiring all automobile bumpers to withstand a 10 mile per hour rather than a 5 mile per hour collision. That is, determine what types of benefits and costs you would include in a benefit-cost analysis. Indicate how easy (or difficult) it would be to actually estimate each of the benefits and costs.

4. Discuss whether the airline industry was more likely to be in favor of or opposed to the deregulation that occurred in 1978. Explain.

5. It has long been known that subliminal messages can be broadcast in such a way that people subconsciously get the message without being consciously aware of it. Though the FCC has prevented the use of subliminal messages in advertising, they can have other uses. Retail stores have been using subliminal signals to tell shoppers not to steal. Another potential use is to give a subliminal message to surgery patients telling them that they are feeling better.
   a. Do you think subliminal signals should be regulated? Why or why not?
   b. Which of the reasons in favor of regulation are most appropriate in this case? Which of the reasons against regulation do you think most apply?
   c. What are the potential benefits from regulation of the signals? What are the potential costs of regulation? Do you think the benefits outweigh the costs, or vice versa? Explain.

REVIEW GLOSSARY

externality A cost or benefit that affects someone not directly involved in the production or exchange of a good, and that is incurred without compensation.

government regulation The process of controlling business activities through laws and administrative rules.

industry regulation The regulation of an entire industry.

market power The ability of a firm to control or influence the price and/or quantity exchanged in the market.

public interest The well-being of the consuming public.

social regulation The regulation of specific activities, regardless of industry.

SECTION INQUIRY

A Flat Rate Tax

An essential feature of the government's involvement in the economy is its powers of taxation. Taxation provides the resources the government uses to produce public goods, establish and enforce regulation, and generally undertake its administrative operations. However, the important question is how best to raise the government's revenue. The federal government, which is subject to the most scrutiny, currently has a complex progressive tax structure. In principle, people with higher incomes pay higher tax rates. In 1986 these rates ranged between 11 and 50 percent. However, the amount of income earned and the amount subject to taxation is often quite different because of a wide variety of deductions, including mortgage interest, state and local taxes, medical expenses, individual retirement accounts, and business-related entertainment, to name just a few. These various deductions, because they are often more readily available to people with higher incomes, mean that the tax system is less progressive in practice than in principle.

There are numerous other criticisms of the federal income tax system. First, some people argue that the progressive nature of the income tax reduces the incentive to earn more income. In particular, people are discouraged from working harder and investing in new capital since in the highest bracket they can keep only 50 percent of what they earn. Second, others argue that the complexity of the tax system causes too many of the economy's resources to be wasted in the process of paying (or trying not to pay) taxes. For example, tax lawyers and accountants who spend their time identifying ways to avoid paying taxes are not engaged in the production of other goods and services. Third, with the variety of deductions, people with the same ability to pay do not necessarily pay the same taxes, distorting efficiency throughout the economy.

For these reasons, many people have suggested that the federal government should implement a flat rate tax. That is, everyone would pay the same percentage of all income in taxes, with no deductions. If the rate is 10 percent, everyone would pay 10 percent of their income in taxes. People would have no reductions in incentives to earn more income, resources would not be wasted on tax avoidance, and everyone with the same ability to pay would pay the same tax. It is estimated that a flat rate tax of 12 percent on all income would raise enough revenue to operate the federal government.

QUESTIONS FOR DISCUSSION

1. The current federal income tax system, with its wide range of deductions from income, is so complex in part because each deduction appeals to one or more special-interest groups. In light of this, discuss the probability that a flat rate tax, with no deductions, will be implemented.

2. Discuss the role that logrolling might have played in establishing the current system of deductions.

3. Explain how the principles of horizontal and vertical equity can be violated under the current tax system.

SECTION 13

The Natural Environment

The naturally occurring resources of the land provide our economy with crucial productive inputs in the form of minerals, fossil fuels, and soil nutrients. The natural environment also directly provides the economy with consumption goods. For example, the Grand Canyon, a forest, or a clear lake constitute naturally occurring goods that satisfy consumers without processing or production. Naturally occurring goods are consumed and valued in the same way as an automobile, frozen pizza, or designer shirt.

In this section we see that the natural environment is often subject to external effects. That is, the production of conventional goods and services can lead to opportunity costs not paid by producers or consumers of the good. These unpaid opportunity costs often take the form of damage to the natural environment. Because the market system fails to consider these external opportunity costs, the result is an inefficient allocation of resources and a reduction in the quality of the environment.

Unit 13.1, The Market Failure of Externalities, presents a theoretical discussion of the costs and benefits that occur outside the normal operation of the market. We also see how and why externalities prevent an efficient allocation of resources in the economy.

Unit 13.2, The Costs of Pollution, applies the externality concept to an analysis of pollution in the natural environment. In this unit we look at several forms of air and water pollution. And we introduce the materials balance concept, which shows that pollution is not just a failing of economic markets but an inherent part of all human activity.

Unit 13.3, Pollution Control Policies, discusses several ways that environmental pollution can be reduced. The most important method is the Pigouvian tax, which can be used to internalize an external cost into the operation of a market. We conclude this unit by looking at current environmental legislation in the United States.

Unit 13.4, The Economics of Energy Resources, examines an important group of raw materials provided by the natural environment, energy resources. In this unit we see that our three main sources of energy (petroleum, natural gas, and coal) all comprise exhaustible resources, meaning any of the resources used today cannot be used tomorrow. We also discuss how government policies of the 1970s worsened our energy problems during that decade. We conclude with a brief examination of several alternatives to fossil fuels, including nuclear fission, solar and geothermal energy, and nuclear fusion.

UNIT 13.1

The Market Failure of Externalities

Although markets efficiently allocate resources most of the time, in cases of natural monopoly, market power, public goods, or imperfect information, a market does not efficiently allocate resources. In this unit we examine another important case of market failure, externalities, where the market price does not fully represent either the opportunity costs of producing a good or the value placed on the good by consumers. Since the price is too low or too high, too much or too little of the good is produced, and resources are inefficiently allocated.

We begin by examining the concept of externalities itself. In particular, we see how an externality occurs when there are either costs or benefits that affect people who are not directly involved in the production or exchange of a good. We then see how a market operates with and without externalities, thereby illustrating how externalities lead to an inefficient allocation. And finally, we discuss the two basic reasons for externalities, the production of joint goods and common property goods.

WHAT IS AN EXTERNALITY?

An **externality** is a cost or benefit that affects someone not directly involved in the production or exchange of a good, and that is incurred without compensation. An externality represents a cost or benefit that exists beyond the normal operation of a market. For example, automobile emissions, and the resulting air pollution in a major city, are an externality. People are harmed by the air pollution, and thus incur an opportunity cost, but no market exists to compensate them for the harm incurred. It is an externality because the cost is external to a market.

A contrasting example is provided by a meat packing plant, where the act of processing the meat fills the plant with a distasteful odor. While the odor is not harmful, the air inside the plant resembles the polluted air of a city. The workers inside the plant incur an opportunity cost due to the unpleasant odor. That is, they would be happier if the odor wasn't there. However, the odor inside the plant is not an externality, because it is not external to the market for workers. In order to hire employees, the meat packing plant must pay a higher wage than a comparable production process that doesn't have the odor. Thus, the labor market operates to compensate the workers for the opportunity costs incurred by the odor. The same cannot be said of the residents of a city and air pollution.

The existence of an externality means that the market price does not fully represent the opportunity costs of production or the value from consumption. If the externality is on the cost side, the difference is between the overall opportunity costs incurred by society and the opportunity costs paid for by the firm. If the externality is based on a benefit, the difference is between the value received from the good by the consumers who buy it and the overall value received by everyone consuming it. To see how these differences occur, let's examine the costs of production and the benefits from consumption.

Private, External, and Social Costs

When an externality is associated with the opportunity costs of production, there is a difference between the opportunity costs incurred by society and the opportunity costs incurred by a firm. This difference can be illustrated by a simple example. A pulp and paper processing mill located on the bank of a river uses timber products in the production of paper products. In the course of production the mill maximizes profit, hiring all inputs to the quantity that equates marginal factor costs and marginal revenue product. The costs of the inputs hired, including the entrepreneur, are the private costs of producing the product. A **private cost** is the cost incurred explicitly or implicitly by the firm. Wages are a good example of an explicit private cost; normal profit is a good example of an implicit private cost. But whether implicit or explicit, *the firm* incurs the cost. Therefore, the firm always has an eye on the private costs of production. If these costs change, the firm will likely reevaluate the quantity of output produced to maintain maximum profits. Moreover, buyers of the product must cover the private costs of production or the firm will have to shut down operations.

To complicate matters, suppose in the course of producing the paper goods, the mill creates a useless organic waste. The mill has several options to handle the waste. First, it can pay someone to collect and remove the waste. Second, it can process the waste in some manner that makes it useful, which might entail additional inputs and production. Or third, it can simply pour the waste into the river.

The first option is totally unsatisfactory from the mill's point of view. Paying someone to take the waste away increases the mill's cost, but adds nothing to revenue, and thus diminishes profit. The second option has promise. If the mill can produce a useful product with the additional stages of production, it can generate additional revenue. But the additional revenue must be greater than the additional cost. In this case the additional stages of production fall under the principles of production discussed in Section 8 and do not concern us here.

It is the third option that most concerns us in this unit. Note that it costs the mill virtually nothing to pour the waste into the river. The mill might need to build some pipes to transport the waste, but the marginal cost of dumping the waste is very little when compared to the alternative of paying someone to remove it.

What if the mill decides on this third option? Pouring organic waste into a river is not necessarily a bad act. In many cases the natural capacity of the river can absorb the waste, in much the same way a dead fish or plant is absorbed by the river. However, if too much waste is poured into the river, then the natural capacity of the river can be exceeded, making it uninhabitable for fish, unfit to drink, and aesthetically displeasing.

Dumping the waste into the river can have additional consequences. Suppose a soft drink bottling company is located downstream from the paper mill, so that the water flowing past the paper mill subsequently passes the bottling company. Furthermore, the bottling company uses water from the river in the production of soft drinks. While the bottling company is equipped to remove the small amounts of impurities found in the water in its natural state, it cannot handle the polluted water from the paper mill upstream. Thus, the bottling company must take extra steps in order to clean up the water before using it in the soft drinks.

The production of paper by the mill upstream causes the firm downstream to pay higher costs in the production of soft drinks. However, the additional costs incurred by the bottling firm have absolutely no effect on the paper mill, which bases all output decisions on its own private costs of production. The costs imposed on the downstream bottling company are an external cost to the paper mill. An **external cost** is a cost that affects someone not directly involved in the production or exchange of a good, and that is incurred without compensation.

How does an external cost compare to a private cost such as the wages paid to labor? Labor incurs an opportunity cost in the production of paper by the mill. A worker must drive to the factory and spend valuable time working that could be used fishing, playing golf, or reading a book. Through the operation of the labor market, the worker agrees to incur the personal opportunity cost in exchange for the wage payment. However, the bottling company downstream has not reached such an agreement with the paper company. Because the costs incurred by the bottling company are outside the operation of the market, they are "external" costs.

Although private costs guide the operation of the firm, we are concerned here with more than the individual firm. An efficient allocation of resources depends on the overall opportunity costs of production. The external costs must be considered together with the private costs before we can determine if an efficient allocation of resources exists. This is where social cost comes in. A **social cost** is the total opportunity cost of production, or the sum of private and external costs.

Private, External, and Social Benefits

In addition to private costs and external costs, there are also private benefits and external benefits. A **private benefit** is the value placed on a good by its buyers. An **external benefit** is the value placed on a good by consumers who do not buy the good. An external benefit, analogous to an external cost, exists when a someone not directly involved in the production or exchange of a good benefits from the good without paying for it. To illustrate, suppose the paper mill, for some obscure and non-profit-maximizing reason, decides to clean up its waste before pouring it into the river. Because of this action, the river actually becomes cleaner than in its natural state. The bottling company downstream incurs less cost in purifying the water it uses than it would have if the river were in its natural state, so it can sell soft drinks at a lower price. This constitutes an external benefit to the soft drink consumers. And as with the external cost, no market transaction is involved.

Another example of an external benefit is a homeowner with a well-kept yard. The well-kept yard not only makes the house more attractive and raises its value, it also raises the property values of every house in the neighborhood. Once again, no market transaction takes place between the other property owners and the homeowner with the attractive yard. Remember that the efficient allocation of resources dictates that we consider not only the private benefits received from the production of a good but also the overall social benefits. A **social benefit** is the total benefit received from a good, or the sum of private and external benefits. In general, most public goods, including education, national defense, and public parks, are goods that involve external benefits. Unit 12.2 discusses the external benefits of public goods in more detail.

Two Sides of an Externality

An important feature of an externality was alluded to in earlier discussions. An externality, whether it is an external cost or benefit, requires *two* participants. The act of pouring organic waste into the river is not an externality as long as no one is harmed. And cleaning up the river is not an externality if no one receives the benefits. An externality requires one participant to undertake the action, and a second participant to be affected by the action. If no one is harmed or helped, then there is no externality.

The two sides of an externality are important from a policy point of view. Recall from the water pollution example that the river has a natural ability to cleanse itself of organic waste. Normally, the farther we go downstream from the point the waste enters the river, the cleaner is the river. Suppose the paper mill has been located on the river for several years and that it chose this particular location because it was several miles from the nearest user of the water. Therefore, it was able to pour the waste into the river and let the natural capacity of the stream clean the water before any users were harmed.

But now the bottling company locates a few hundred yards downstream from the paper mill. The water is unusable by the bottling company, and an externality exists. Given this additional information, it is difficult to portray the paper mill as the perpetrator of the externality, because the externality was not created until the bottling company appeared on the scene. Note that the quality of the water was the same before the bottling company started operations as it was after. But before the bottling company entered the picture, no one was harmed.

In fact, this sequence of events commonly occurs around major airports. Because of land requirements and the amount of noise created by the planes, an airport tends to locate on the outskirts of cities. However, as a city grows over time, houses locate closer and closer to the airport. The noise created by the planes eventually becomes an externality, and the homeowners complain accordingly. However, it is hard to find fault with the airport, even though it is causing the external opportunity costs. The noise was always there, but the externality began only when the homeowners moved in.

OPTIMAL PRODUCTION WITH EXTERNALITIES

The existence of externalities in the production of a good means the market fails to efficiently allocate resources, unlike an efficiently operating market in which all costs are private costs.

The Efficient Market

As we know, a market reaches equilibrium at the intersection of the demand and supply curves, point E in Figure 13.1.1. The equilibrium price is P_e and the equilibrium quantity is Q_e. The supply curve is based on the private costs of production. If there are no external costs in this market, then the supply curve fully reflects the social cost of producing this good.

Let's review the interpretation of the demand and supply curves in this light. The demand curve indicates the marginal value buyers place on the good produced. If a smaller quantity is produced, we move up the demand curve to a higher price, indicating that buyers place a higher marginal value on the good. At the equilibrium quantity, the price P_e is the marginal value placed on unit Q_e of the good.

The supply curve, with no external costs, reflects the marginal opportunity costs of producing the good and indicates the marginal value of

Figure 13.1.1

The Efficient Market

If all opportunity costs are incurred by producers, then the market equilibrium represents an efficient allocation of resources. In this case the market price P_e fully covers all opportunity costs of producing the last unit of the good. Society cannot be better off by increasing or decreasing the quantity of this good produced.

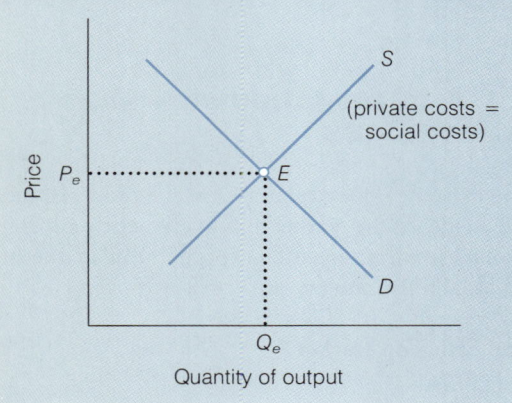

Figure 13.1.2

A Market with External Costs

A market with external costs does not efficiently allocate resources, because the market price does not cover all opportunity costs of production. Since supply curve S_s contains all opportunity costs, the efficient allocation of resources is given by Q_s rather than Q_e.

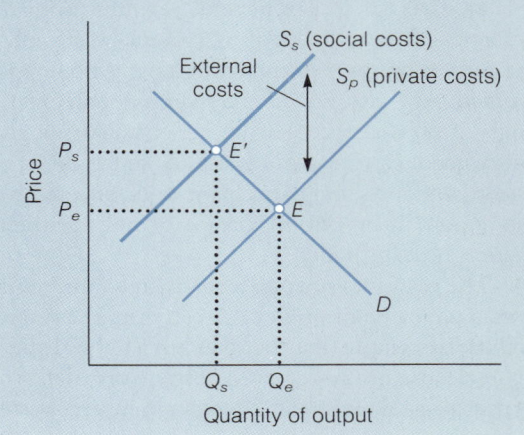

other goods given up in order to produce this good. At the equilibrium, the marginal value of goods not produced is also equal to P_e. A freely operating market, which is allowed to reach point E, leads to an equilibrium quantity in which the marginal value of the last unit produced is exactly equal to the marginal value of goods not produced. It is not possible for society to produce more or less of this good and increase the overall level of welfare.

The Market with External Costs

But the market is different if externalities exist. In Figure 13.1.2 the market is affected by an external cost, which means the market supply curve S_p is based only on the private costs of production, found by horizontally adding the marginal cost curves for all firms. The intersection between the market, or private, supply curve and the demand curve is point E and is identical to point E in Figure 13.1.1. The equilibrium quantity is Q_e and the price is P_e.

The existence of an external cost means the private supply curve omits some of the opportunity costs incurred in the production of this good. The supply curve S_s includes all opportunity costs, or social costs. The vertical distance between S_p and S_s is equal to external costs.

At market equilibrium E, the price paid by buyers covers only the private marginal costs of production, and not external costs. Recall that opportunity costs are the marginal value of other goods given up in the production of this good, including external costs. Only in this case some production is foregone without compensation, but is foregone nonetheless.

At market equilibrium quantity Q_e, the marginal value of the good produced is less than the marginal value of all goods given up. This means the economy is better off if it produces less of this good, and more of other goods. In fact, only at point E' is the marginal value of the good produced equal to the marginal value of other goods not produced. Point E', the intersection of the demand curve and the social cost supply curve, is the social optimum quantity of production. Only at Q_s production are resources efficiently allocated.

The existence of external costs means the market produces too much of the good. In doing so it inefficiently allocates resources to the production of this good that could be used to produce other goods. Furthermore, the market price is too low. The market price P_e does not cover all opportunity costs. Only at price P_s are all social costs paid entirely by the buyers.

The Market with External Benefits

With external benefits, participants outside of the market benefit from the good produced. Figure 13.1.3 illustrates how external benefits are depicted in the market. While external costs show up on the side of the supply curve, external benefits show up on the side of the demand curve. As we know, the market demand curve is based on the benefits received by buyers. If buyers receive more benefits, they are willing to pay a higher price. The demand curve D_p is based only on the benefits received by participants in the market. A demand curve based on all social benefits, both private and external, would be D_s.

The private market, containing only private benefits, reaches equilibrium at point E, the same equilibrium point E as in the previous two figures. Likewise, at this equilibrium the price is P_e and the quantity is Q_e. However, at the quantity Q_e, the market is omitting external benefits, the difference between curves D_s and D_p. In other words, the beneficiaries of the good (both in the market and out) are willing to pay more than P_e for Q_e. The market is not producing enough of this good, and an inefficient allocation of resources exists.

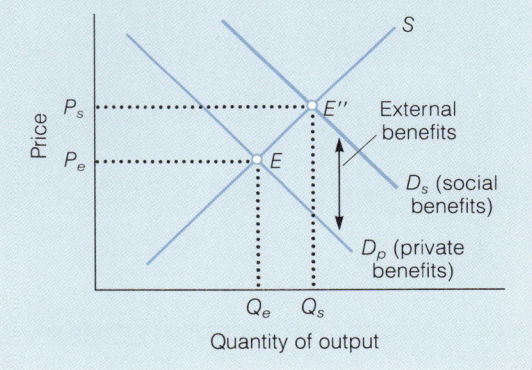

Figure 13.1.3

A Market with External Benefits

A market with external benefits also fails to efficiently allocate resources. In this case the market price does not reflect the total benefits of everyone consuming the good. Since the demand curve D_s is based on the benefits received by all consumers, the efficient allocation of resources is given by Q_s rather than Q_e.

Only at the intersection of the supply curve S and the social demand curve D_s, at point E'', are resources allocated efficiently. At this point the quantity produced is Q_s and the price is P_s. In addition, the marginal value of the last unit of the good produced is equal to the marginal value of goods not produced. In general, if an external benefit exists, the market does not produce enough of the good, and it charges a price that is too low.

TWO REASONS FOR EXTERNALITIES

Externalities exist for two basic reasons. One is the production of joint goods; the other is the production of common property goods. In Figure 13.1.4 (which is similar to Figure 12.2.1) goods are characterized by two dimensions—rivalry in consump-

Figure 13.1.4

Externalities and the Characteristics of Goods

Externalities can be caused by the joint production of a private good and a pure public good or near public good. Alternatively, an externality can result from the use of a common property good due to the lack of clear ownership.

	Rival in consumption	Nonrival in consumption
Able to exclude nonpayers	Private good	Near public good
Not able to exclude nonpayers	Common property good	Pure public good

tion and excludability of nonpayers. **Private goods are rival in consumption, and nonpayers can be excluded.** **Public goods are nonrival in consumption, and nonpayers cannot be excluded.**

What does this have to do with externalities? First, externalities often result from joint production, but not just any kind of joint production. If the production of a private good also results in the production of a public good or near public good, an externality usually results. Recall that a **near public good** is one in which consumption is nonrival, but nonpayers can be excluded.

An example of an externality that results from jointly produced goods is the water pollution scenario described earlier in this unit. The paper company was engaged in the production not only of paper but also of organic waste. Or more precisely, the joint product it actually produced was a polluted river. This is an example of a near public good being produced jointly with a private good. The paper is the private good, and the water pollution is the near public good. The water pollution is near public because it is nonrival in consumption, yet consumers can, to a degree, be excluded by erecting a fence or otherwise keeping them away from the river. The pollution is nonrival because one user who pumps polluted water from the stream, for the most part, does not prevent others from pumping polluted water.

Air pollution is an example of an externality in which the joint product is more of a pure public good. Air pollution is nonrival, like water pollution, but its ability to exclude consumers is much less. The only way to keep people from consuming polluted air is to force them to leave the area. In fact, most cases of pollution are external costs created by the production of a private good jointly with a public or near public good.

The second important reason for an externality is the existence of common property goods. **Common property goods are rival in consumption, but nonpayers cannot be excluded.** For the most part, common property is owned by large groups of people, which actually means that no one in particular has specific ownership and control. For example, clean air can be considered a common property good. Officially, the air belongs to everyone in the country. But practically speaking, no one really owns the air, not in the sense that a car is privately owned.

For many years clean air has been considered the common property of everyone, so that anyone who wanted to emit smoke, soot, or anything else into the air was free to do so. Furthermore, it was, and still is, very difficult to keep anyone from emitting pollution into the air, or to exclude nonpayers. However, clean air is rival in consumption, even though the air is able to cleanse itself of small amounts of pollution. At some point, if too much smoke is emitted into the air, people are prevented from breathing.

At this point let's clear up what may seem to be an inconsistency. Can air be an example of a good that is both rival and nonrival in consumption? In this last example air is depicted as a common property because it is rival in consumption. However, a few paragraphs earlier air pollution is depicted as an example of a public good because it is nonrival in consumption.

To solve this apparent contradiction, note that the air itself is rival, since one use (pollution) precludes another use (breathing). By contrast, air pollution is a nonrival good. The fact that one person is harmed by air pollution does not keep someone else from also being harmed.

The characteristics of a common property resource lead to an externality because no one actually owns the good. If someone tried to dump waste into a privately owned car or backyard, the owner would seek immediate action. If the dumper did not adequately compensate the owner, the owner would likely take the dumper to court for compensation. With private property, an owner can legally seek and obtain compensation.

But suppose someone is polluting the air on federal land in Alaska. While in principle, a resident of Arizona, as a U.S. citizen, is part owner of the Alaskan air, there is no easy way to obtain compensation, either through the markets or the courts. A worker can withhold labor from the market if compensation is not received, but since no one really owns the air, no one can withhold the air from the market.

IN SUMMARY

The Market Failure of Externalities

- Externalities are uncompensated benefits or costs that occur beyond the normal operation of the market. While private costs and benefits guide decisions in the market, the efficient allocation of resources depends on social costs and benefits. Social costs and benefits are the sum of private costs (benefits) and external costs (benefits). An externality can occur only if two parties are involved. One party generates the externality and a second party bears the cost or receives the benefit from the externality.

- A market without externalities reaches equilibrium when the value of the last unit of the good produced is equal to the value of goods not produced. This is an efficient allocation of resources because society's welfare cannot be increased. However, if the market has external costs, the market obtains equilibrium where the value of the good produced is less than the value of goods not produced. Society's welfare can be increased by producing less of this good and more of others. With an external benefit, equilibrium is reached when the value of the good produced is greater than the value of goods not produced. In this case society's welfare can be increased by producing more of this good and less of another.

- There are two important reasons for externalities. The first is the joint production of a public or near public good together with a private good. Air and water pollution are examples of public or near public goods that are produced with private goods. The second is the existence of common property goods. The lack of private ownership of the resource allows anyone to emit waste.

QUESTIONS FOR STUDY AND ANALYSIS

1. Explain how each of the following can lead to, or cause, an externality. Indicate whether an external cost or benefit is generated. Also indicate whether the externality is associated with a common property good, public good, and/or near public good.
   a. An oil spill off the coast of California
   b. Agricultural research undertaken by a university
   c. Contributions by the Rockefeller Foundation to the opera
   d. Illegally copying and selling videocassette tapes of major motion pictures
   e. Harmful exhaust emissions from automobiles in a large city

2. The following table presents the important relationships between private costs and benefits, external costs and benefits, and the quantity of output produced. Note that the private costs and benefits are simply the prices on the supply and demand curves. In light of this information, answer each of the following questions.

Quantity	Private Cost	Private Benefit	External Cost	External Benefit
1	$10	$70	$20	$40
2	20	60	20	40
3	30	50	20	40
4	40	40	20	40
5	50	30	20	40
6	60	20	20	40
7	70	10	20	40

   a. If you ignore the external costs and benefits, what is the market equilibrium price and quantity?
   b. If you include only the external costs, what is the socially optimum quantity of output? How does it compare with your answer to question 2a?
   c. If you include only the external benefits, what is the socially optimum quantity of output? How does it compare with your answer to question 2a?
   d. If both external costs and benefits are included, what is the socially optimal quantity of output?

3. If a major shopping center is located next to an existing cattle feedlot (complete with its unmistakable odor), why is an externality created? Who causes the externality? Explain.

4. Explain why a monopolistic market structure (as discussed in Unit 9.2) would be better than perfect competition when an external cost exists.

5. Why would an externality exist if labor is unknowingly exposed to a substance with long-term health effects on the job?

6. The new field of biotechnology and genetic engineering promises to generate technological advances and product innovations that will increase the economy's productivity and overall well-being. However, as with any new technology, it also has the potential to generate external costs. A recent example was seen with a new type of frost-free bacteria that was genetically engineered to prevent frost from forming on potatoes or other crops. While the benefits from using this type of bacteria are enormous, the potential for external costs is equally great.
   a. How might this type of bacteria cause an external cost? Who is most likely to incur the external cost?
   b. Is it possible that the bacteria could lead to an external benefit? Explain.
   c. If you were the federal government, would you allow this type of bacteria to be used? Why or why not?

REVIEW GLOSSARY

common property good A good that is rival in consumption, but nonpayers cannot be excluded from consumption. A common property good can also lead to an externality because people cannot be prevented from using the good, but the use by one prevents the use by another.

external benefit The value placed on a good by consumers who do not buy the good.

external cost A cost that affects someone not directly involved in the production or exchange of a good, and that is incurred without compensation.

externality A cost or benefit that affects someone not directly involved in the production or exchange of a good, and that is incurred without compensation. An externality occurs outside the operation of a market.

near public good A good that is nonrival in consumption, but nonpayers can be excluded from consumption.

private benefit The value placed on a good by its buyers.

private cost A cost incurred explicitly or implicitly by a firm. Private costs guide the production decisions of the firm.

private good A good that is rival in consumption, and nonpayers can be excluded from consumption.

public good A good that is nonrival in consumption, and nonpayers cannot be excluded from consumption. Many externalities occur when a private good is jointly produced with a public or near public good.

social benefit The total benefit received from a good, or the sum of private and external benefits.

social cost The total opportunity cost of production, or the sum of private and external costs.

UNIT 13.2

The Costs of Pollution

Externalities, and particularly external costs, are prevalent throughout the economy. Many externalities create serious distortions in the allocation of resources, and some lead to adverse health affects and even loss of life. In this unit we see that some of the most serious externalities result from pollution of the natural environment. **Pollution** is the artificially generated waste that is emitted into the natural environment.

Recall that an externality always involves two parties, the generator of the externality and the receiver. If no one is harmed, there can be no external cost. In this context, all pollution does not cause externalities. For example, automobile emissions represent a primary source of air pollution. If a car is driven in a city with over a million people, these people are potentially harmed by the pollution. But if the same car is driven through the sparsely populated plains of western Kansas, there are very few people to harm.

In this unit we focus on pollution, and on the various ways society has found to emit pollution into the natural environment. But keep in mind that our ultimate concern is with the external costs created by the pollution and the resulting impact on the allocation of resources. We begin by examining the pollution associated with the natural environment's two common property goods, air and water. Then we discuss some of the more important policy considerations of air and water pollution. And finally, we look at the materials balance concept, which indicates that pollution is not restricted to a few isolated markets.

WATER POLLUTION

Water pollution is the discharge of waste materials into rivers, streams, lakes, or oceans. The waste materials range from organic domestic sewage to highly complex synthetic chemicals. The three main sources of pollution consist of deposits from urban sewage treatment plants, waste materials from various types of industries, and runoff from agricultural land.

Domestic Sewage

The most prevalent source of organic water pollution is domestic sewage from urban areas. Organic materials are often referred to as degradable pollution. Degradable pollution is organic materials that can be broken down by the natural capacity of the environment. Degradable pollution is different from other types of pollution, in that the natural environment has the ability to cleanse itself of organic materials. The organic materials are broken down to simpler nutrient materials, and then enter back into the natural food chain.

However, this does not mean that degradable pollution is harmless. As the cleansing process occurs, the water can be aesthetically unpleasing and potentially unhealthy. Moreover, if too much organic waste is deposited into the water, its natural capacity for cleansing can be exceeded, in which case the water becomes totally unfit for any life. Essentially, the body of water has been killed. Fortunately, if no inorganic wastes are present, even the death of a body of water can be reversed over time.

An important dimension of degradable pollution is time, or alternatively, distance. As organic waste enters a standing body of water, the quality of the water is initially reduced; then over time the quality improves back to its initial state. In looking at a river or other running water, the distance from the point of deposit of organic waste follows a similar pattern. A short distance from the deposit the water quality is low; farther downstream the quality improves to its natural state. This dimension of degradable water pollution is significant because if no one is adversely affected over the time period or distance of low water quality, then no external costs are incurred.

Industrial Waste

Factories are also a major source of water pollution. Industries that often use the water as a waste depository include pulp and paper, chemical, petroleum refining, food processing, and metal processing. The diversity of industries responsible for this type of waste means the waste materials are also diverse. Although many factories deposit degradable organic waste, such as from pulp and paper and food processing, other factories deposit more complex, and potentially more harmful, nondegradable, and persistent, pollution. Nondegradable pollution is simple inorganic materials that cannot be broken down by the natural capacity of the environment. Persistent pollution is complex synthetic materials that remain in the natural environment for a long time. Nondegradable pollution, which usually consists of heavy metals or simple compounds containing heavy metals, is not broken down by the natural processes of the environment. Common examples of nondegradable pollution include mercury, lead, chromium, and cadmium. Persistent pollution usually consists of highly complex chemical compounds, such as pesticides, polychlorinated biphenyls, and vinyl chloride, which can break down to simpler compounds, but over a much long time period than organic waste.

Both the simplicity of inorganic nondegradable pollution and the complexity of synthetic persistent pollution means each remains in the environment, virtually unchanged, for long periods of time. This allows the pollution to work its way up the food chain, becoming more concentrated and harmful as it goes. For example, a relatively small fish, such as a minnow, might contain a low concentration of mercury. But, if minnows are the food supply for a larger fish higher up in the food chain, the larger fish acquires a higher concentration of mercury. The larger fish can digest all of the minnow except the nondegradable mercury. If it eats ten minnows, it absorbs ten times the mercury of one minnow. If it eats one hundred minnows, it absorbs one hundred times the mercury, and so on. If humans then eat the larger fish, they receive an even higher concentration of mercury, which doesn't break down, but remains in the body. And many of these simple inorganic chemicals and complex synthetic materials can be extremely toxic when concentrated. While most of the nondegradable inorganic materials appear naturally in the environment, they are not concentrated until used in the production of goods and services.

Agricultural Runoff

Runoff from agricultural land is caused by exposed agricultural soil that is eroded away by heavy rains. The eroded soil entering rivers and lakes pollutes the water in two ways. First, the soil itself is dissolved in the water, giving the water a muddy appearance and making it difficult for the plant and animal life in the water to maintain normal functions. Second, agricultural runoff often includes a variety of degradable organic soil nutrients and persistent synthetic chemicals used in agricultural production. Not only can the synthetic agricultural chemicals be toxic, such as pesticides but also the organic nutrients can exceed the natural capacity of a body of water to absorb them. By volume, water pollution from agricultural runoff is greater than any of the other sources of pollution.

An important distinction between pollution from agricultural runoff and domestic or industrial waste should be made. Agricultural runoff is nonpoint source pollution. **Nonpoint source pollution** is pollution that does not originate at a distinct, identifiable source, unlike domestic and industrial waste, which is called point source pollution. **Point source pollution** is pollution that can be traced to a specific point of origin. Agricultural runoff comes from the millions of acres of agricultural land in the United States. If a pesticide is discovered in a river, it is next to impossible to determine the farm of origin. However, domestic and industrial wastes are deposited into a stream at particular points, and the pipes coming from the sewage treatment plants and factories are usually quite evident.

AIR POLLUTION

Air pollution is the discharge of waste materials into the air. The primary source of air pollution is emissions from internal combustion engines, though factory smokestacks and power plants also contribute. In addition, wind erosion of agricultural land can also cause significant air pollution from time to time.

Automobile Emissions

Emissions from automobiles represent the biggest source of air pollution in cities. Internal combustion engines emit various types of pollution, such as hydrocarbons, nitrogen oxides, carbon monoxide, and sulfates. The emissions can have a variety of adverse effects, most notably respiratory problems and cancer. Under the right circumstances, automobile emissions contribute to the production of photochemical oxidants, or smog.

Air pollution from automobiles has two significant aspects. First, automobile emissions resemble runoff from agricultural land in that it is difficult, if not impossible, to trace the pollution to any specific source. Second, the emissions from a concentration of automobiles have a far greater impact than emissions from any one automobile. For example, emissions from an automobile in western Kansas are negligible, because any pollution is rapidly dispersed into the atmosphere. But the same emissions in New York City, combined with all of the other emissions, contribute to higher concentrations of pollution in the atmosphere. Therefore, the external costs of pollution from a single automobile are much greater.

Smokestacks and Power Plants

Factories and power plants that burn fossil fuels emit particulate matter, sulfur dioxide, and nitrogen oxides, all of which contribute to respiratory problems, among other things. While automobiles are nonpoint source pollution, smokestacks are point source pollution. It is easy to see smoke coming from a smokestack. An important dimension of smokestack pollution is distance. Obviously, pollution is highly concentrated near the point of emission, but farther away the pollution gradually disperses, and becomes potentially less harmful.

Wind Erosion

Wind erosion of agricultural land blows dust, and accompanying agricultural chemicals, into the air. The particulate matter suspended in the air can lead to respiratory problems. As anyone who has experienced a dust storm in the plains ranging from Texas to North Dakota knows, this form of air pollution is not very pleasant.

POLICY CONSIDERATIONS

In our discussion of pollution, several important considerations for pollution control policies surface. First, we must reemphasize that pollution and external costs do not go hand in hand. If no one is harmed by organic waste in a river, then there is no externality. Thus, one way to reduce the external costs of pollution is to separate polluters from those potentially harmed by pollution. For example, people with respiratory problems should not live in urban areas with air pollution.

Second, degradable, nondegradable, and persistent pollution cannot be controlled by the same policies. It is important to control the amount of degradable pollution that enters a body of water over a period of time. As long as the capacity of the natural environment is not exceeded, the problems caused by organic waste are not too severe. But the total amounts of nondegradable and persistent pollution must be taken into account, regardless of when they were emitted into the environment. It is not enough to limit the amount emitted into the environment each year. We must also consider how much was emitted last year and the year before, and how much will be emitted ten years in the future. Nondegradable and persistent pollution stay in the environment a long time; some pollution never leaves at all.

Third, nonpoint source pollution cannot be dealt with in the same way as point source pollution. Point source pollution usually involves a small number of polluters along a given river or in a given city, and it is not difficult to monitor or regulate each one. By contrast, nonpoint source pollution involves a large number of polluters, making it difficult to police each one. Trying to determine which of the nonpoint source polluters is responsible for the pollution is virtually impossible.

A fourth important policy consideration involves the difference between air and water. Since water is confined to rivers, streams, lakes, and oceans, pollution control policies can be applied to a limited geographic area. In particular, if a river is cleaned up at one point, it stays clean downstream. But air is not confined, and cannot be dealt with on only a limited geographic basis. For example, the particulate matter thrown into the atmosphere when Mount St. Helens erupted in the state of Washington was carried as far east as the Great Plains.

These considerations make it difficult to design a perfect pollution control policy. At best, one policy cannot be used for all types of pollution. Furthermore, one policy may not be effective at all times for the same type of pollution. In Unit 13.3 we see how existing and proposed policies address the problems of pollution.

THE MATERIALS BALANCE CONCEPT

The most important topic in our discussion of pollution may be the materials balance concept. **Materials balance** is a principle stating that the amount of material taken from the environment equals the amount returned. The materials balance concept is based on the simple fact that all economic activity and the production of goods and services necessarily involve the use of natural resources. The economy cannot avoid tampering with the natural environment. Production, by its very nature, necessitates the transformation of raw materials. We extract millions of tons of minerals and fossil fuels from the ground for the production of goods, but what comes out of the natural environment must eventually return.

Figure 13.2.1 depicts the interaction between the economy and the natural environment. The first phase of production, the extraction of raw material from the environment, takes place in the box on the far left. The raw materials are transformed by the firms and sold to the households as consumer goods. Until now, the production and transformation of raw materials are the phases of the economy that have attracted most of our attention.

However, in the course of production, firms send waste products back to the natural environment. For example, only a fraction of the iron ore extracted is used to make steel; the rest is waste material. In addition, households also send waste products back to the environment. For example, the box containing the breakfast cereal goes into the trash when empty. These residuals from both firms and households are shown in the lower loop in Figure 13.2.1. Moreover, all of the materials removed from the environment must eventually return. The automobile might be used for ten years or more, but eventually it is junked. The tuna salad sandwich made last week will probably stay in the refrigerator for another month, but sooner or later it will have to be thrown out, returning to the environment with the rest of the trash.

Indeed, everything eventually returns to the

Figure 13.2.1

The Materials Balance Concept

The materials balance concept states that all raw materials removed from the natural environment eventually return as waste materials. In this diagram the raw materials are extracted from the environment and used to make goods and services for consumers. The lower loop indicates that these materials eventually return to the environment as residuals. One way to reduce the amount of residuals is through recycling, as shown in the upper loop. Another way is to increase the usable life of goods to keep them from returning to the environment.

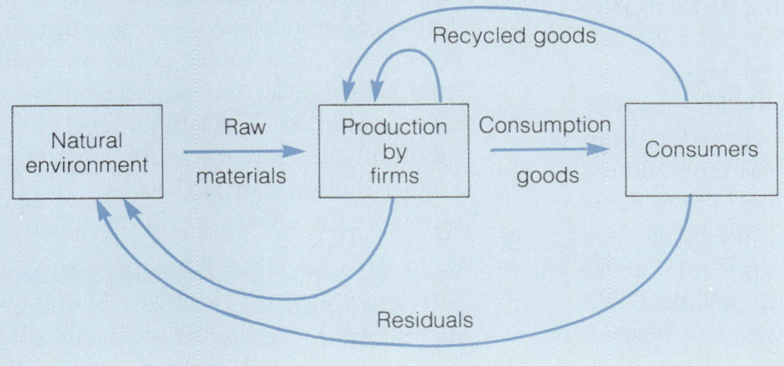

natural environment, as the materials balance principle states. Over a short period of time, the extractions from the environment are greater than the returns because of the amount of material kept for productive use in the economy. That is, the car and the tuna salad sandwich remain out of the natural environment until they have outlived their productive usefulness.

The materials balance concept tells us one simple fact—if we take a lot from the environment, we put a lot back. This means that pollution, and any resulting externalities, are not just a minor flaw in an otherwise perfectly operating market system. Pollution potentially affects every market, because the production of every good in some way involves materials that will eventually return to the environment.

A remedy for this problem is suggested by the materials balance concept. Quite simply, if the economy extracts less material, and produces fewer goods, less pollution returns to the environment. Barring this, the economy can produce goods that remain in the economy longer, thus requiring less material in the future. Alternatively, the waste material can be recycled back into the production of other goods rather than being returned to the environment. **Recycling is the process of reusing waste materials in the production of goods and services rather than using natural resources.** Recycling is indicated by sending waste into the upper loop in Figure 13.2.1 rather than the lower loop. More recycled materials mean fewer new materials need be removed from the environment. Recycling not only reduces pollution today but it also reduces it tomorrow.

The materials balance concept implies something crucial to the control of individual sources of pollution. As long as waste is created and not recycled, it must be returned to the environment in some form. If we prevent pollution from going into the air, the pollution might just be dumped into the water. Or potential water pollution might be collected and burned, causing air pollution. Pollution control policies must consider all types of air and water pollution collectively. If not, then reducing one type of pollution may very well increase another type.

IN SUMMARY

The Costs of Pollution

- Pollution is a major source of external costs in the economy. Pollution in the environment can have a variety of adverse effects. However, pollution alone is not enough to create external costs. If no one is harmed by the pollution, then there are no external costs.

- Water pollution results from domestic sewage, industrial waste, and agricultural runoff. Organic domestic sewage is degradable, meaning the natural environment has the ability to absorb the waste. Industrial waste and agricultural runoff often contain nondegradable and persistent pollution. Nondegradable pollution consists primarily of metals, and simple compounds containing metals, that cannot be broken down and absorbed by the environment. Persistent pollution results from complex synthetic chemicals that also remain in the environment for long periods of time. Unlike domestic and industrial waste, in which pollution originates from distinct points, agricultural runoff is usually considered nonpoint source pollution.

- Air pollution results from automobile emissions, industrial smokestacks, and power plants. Automobile emissions, like agricultural runoff, are nonpoint source pollution. Pollution from smokestacks and power plants is point source pollution. The various types of air pollution usually cause respiratory problems, and some pollution can lead to cancer or other serious health effects.

- Pollution control policies must take four factors into consideration. First, pollution does not necessarily cause an external cost, and action is needed only if an external cost occurs.

Second, degradable, nondegradable, and persistent pollution require different policies. Third, nonpoint source pollution cannot be controlled in the same manner as point source pollution. Fourth, the natural differences between water and air require different policies for pollution control.

- The materials balance concept indicates that any raw materials removed from the environment eventually return as waste materials and pollution. Materials balance implies that pollution is not a fluke of a few markets, but a natural result of economic production. It also suggests that pollution can be reduced by recycling materials and making goods that last longer. In addition, this concept indicates that air and water pollution problems must be solved collectively.

QUESTIONS FOR STUDY AND ANALYSIS

1. Explain why pollution does not necessarily create an external cost.

2. What important differences exist between degradable, nondegradable, and persistent pollutions that need to be considered for pollution control policies? Explain.

3. What important differences exist between air and water pollution that need to be considered for pollution control policies? Explain.

4. Discuss each of the following in light of the materials balance concept.
   a. Externalities in a communist country, such as the Soviet Union
   b. A 5-cent deposit on all beverage containers
   c. A five-year warranty on new automobiles versus a two-year warranty
   d. Growth in the economy's production of goods and services

5. Ozone is one form of air pollution that, on the surface, seems like it should be harmless. After all, ozone is merely oxygen. But that is like saying hydrochloric acid is nothing but hydrogen and chlorine. Ozone is formed by lightning or when the sun's rays cause a chemical reaction between hydrocarbons and nitrogen oxides (produced by burning coal or other fossil fuels). Ozone can cause damage to various agricultural crops.
   a. Who is most likely responsible for generating the externality in this case? Who is incurring the external cost?
   b. Would you consider this a point source or nonpoint source pollution? Why?

REVIEW GLOSSARY

air pollution The discharge of waste materials into the air. The major sources of air pollution are automobile emissions, smokestacks, and power plants.

degradable pollution Organic waste that can be broken down by the natural capacity of the environment. Water can usually cleanse itself of organic waste if its capacity is not exceeded.

materials balance A principle that states the amount of material taken from the environment equals the amount of material returned. The total amount of pollution depends on the amount of material removed from the environment.

nondegradable pollution Simple inorganic materials that cannot be broken down by the natural capacity of the environment.

nonpoint source pollution Pollution that does not originate at a distinct, identifiable source.

persistent pollution Complex synthetic materials that remain in the natural environment for a long time.

point source pollution Pollution that can be traced to a specific point of origin.

pollution The artificially generated waste that is emitted into the natural environment. Pollution does not create an external cost if no one is harmed.

recycling The process of reusing waste materials in the production of goods and services rather than using natural resources. Recycling materials reduces pollution by returning less waste today, and reducing the need for raw materials tomorrow.

water pollution The discharge of waste materials into rivers, streams, lakes, or oceans. The three most common sources of water pollution are domestic sewage, industrial waste, and agricultural runoff.

UNIT 13.3

Pollution Control Policies

In this unit we look at several policies that have been used or proposed for pollution control. While in the two previous units it may have seemed that the economy is at the mercy of externalities and environmental pollution, this does not need to be the case. Indeed, policies can be implemented that control pollution and achieve an efficient allocation of resources. For these policies the key word in dealing with an externality is internalization. **Internalization** is the process of making participants in the market consider externalities associated with the production of a good. To alleviate the resource misallocation caused by an externality, the market must consider the additional costs or benefits created by the production of the good.

To illustrate the concept of internalization, we first look at the most commonly prescribed policy for dealing with an external cost, a Pigouvian tax. We then look at other policies, including government regulation, negotiation, markets for pollution permits, charges and standards, and moral suasion. And finally, we discuss existing environmental legislation in the United States.

PIGOUVIAN TAX

A market with an external cost is depicted in Figure 13.3.1. Note that the market produces at point E, but that the efficient allocation of resources is at point E'. How can we get from E to E'? One way to internalize the external cost is to increase the private costs of production. That is, suppliers are forced to incur private costs of production equal

Figure 13.3.1

Pigouvian Tax

The key to controlling an external cost is through internalization. This is demonstrated with a Pigouvian tax, in which producers pay a tax equal to the marginal external costs. In this way producers pay all opportunity costs of production, and the private supply curve coincides with the social supply curve.

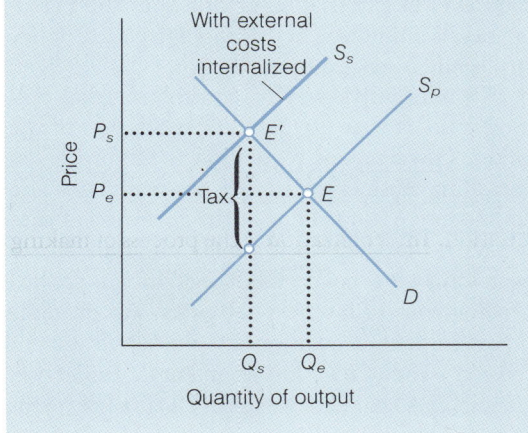

to P_s at quantity Q_s. If they incur higher costs of production, they are no longer able to supply output at market equilibrium price P_p.

This process of internalization can be achieved by charging the producers a tax, equal to the marginal external cost at quantity Q_s. In fact, one way to internalize an external cost is to place a tax on the producers that is exactly equal to the marginal external cost. By increasing private costs with a tax, the private supply curve effectively shifts to the position of the social supply curve. As a result, the market reaches equilibrium at E' rather than E. A **Pigouvian tax** is a tax placed on producers to internalize an external cost, and is named after the economist who first studied externalities, A. C. Pigou.

Note, however, a very important point. The external cost, or pollution itself, is not totally eliminated. If the market produces quantity Q_s, the difference between curves S_p and S_s is the internalized external costs. Because this difference is not zero, some pollution continues to occur. In many cases, especially organic degradable pollution, it is not efficient to reduce the level of pollution to zero.

A market with external benefits can be handled in a similar manner. However, instead of being taxed, producers are given a subsidy. The subsidy causes them to produce a larger quantity at a lower price, thus leading to an increase in production and the amount purchased by consumers. Recall that a market with external benefits misallocates resources by producing too little of the good. A subsidy remedies this misallocation.

ALTERNATIVE POLLUTION CONTROL POLICIES

While a Pigouvian tax can lead to an optimum allocation of resources, it has one major drawback. It is often difficult to determine the actual amount of external costs incurred, and thus the appropriate level of the tax. Thus, while a Pigouvian tax is ideally the best tax, it is often hard to implement. Five other policies can also be used to internalize an externality: government regulation, negotiation, permit market, charges and standards, and moral suasion.

Government Regulation

Sometimes government regulation may be more appropriate than a Pigouvian tax. Figure 13.3.2 depicts a market that might exist for a nondegradable or persistent pollution. The market achieves equilibrium at point E, as in Figure 13.3.1. However, the external costs from the pollution are much greater. In fact, curve S_s, which contains both private and external costs, lies everywhere above the demand curve. The highest price anyone is willing to pay for the good is P_m. However, the lowest

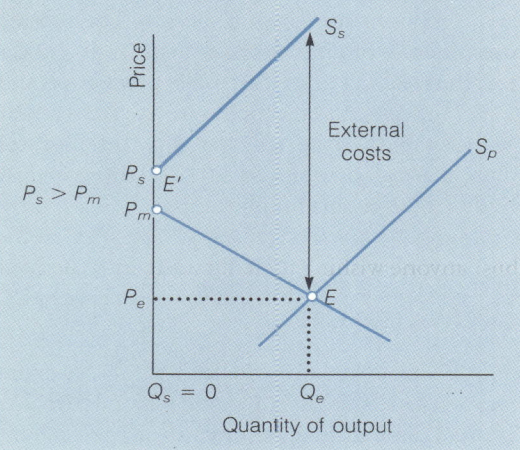

Figure 13.3.2

A Case for Government Regulation

Government regulation is the best policy if the social opportunity costs of production are greater than the highest price consumers are willing to pay. In this case the optimal level of production is zero, and it is easier for the government to ban the good than to try to establish the correct Pigouvian tax.

opportunity cost, private and external, incurred in producing the good is P_s, which is greater than P_m. In terms of the graph, the demand and social supply curves do not intersect, which means the optimum quantity of the output is zero.

Is this a realistic possibility? Take for example a highly toxic nondegradable pollution, such as beryllium, the most toxic nonradioactive substance known. Its nondegradability can cause both short- and long-term external costs. The toxicity of the pollution means people can suffer a great deal, up to the point of losing their life. Thus, the continued existence of beryllium in the environment means countless numbers of people can be harmed, today, tomorrow, and indefinitely into the future. In this context it does not seem unreasonable to think that S_s might lie everywhere above the demand curve, especially if the good generating the pollution is valued relatively little by buyers, even though it is valued enough to be produced in the private market.

For a market such as depicted in Figure 13.3.2, a Pigouvian tax may be inappropriate. If a tax is levied equal to the external cost, no production occurs, because buyers are unwilling to pay enough to have the good produced. While it may be clear that optimal quantity of production is zero, the exact level of external costs, and thus the Pigouvian tax, is unknown. In this case the easiest policy is to legally restrict output to zero.

An alternative way to control external pollution costs is with government regulation of the market. **Government regulation** is the process of controlling business activities through laws and administrative rules. That is, the government simply says no production is legally allowed. As we saw in Unit 12.4, government regulation is applied in many areas of business activities. An example of government regulation of the environment occurred when the Environmental Protection Agency (EPA) banned the use of DDT, a hazardous pesticide. The EPA felt that the external costs from DDT were greater than the value of goods produced. Indeed, with persistent and nondegradable pollution the best alternative is usually to ban it using government regulation.

However, government regulation is often inappropriately used. For example, banning a degradable pollution is usually not optimal for society. In addition, government regulation may be inefficient in reaching the social optimum. Suppose we determine that the social optimum is 25 percent less production than the market equilibrium. With government regulation, a common approach is to force every supplier in the market to reduce production by 25 percent, even though this is likely to be inefficient. Differences in technology, management, and production costs mean society is better off if some suppliers cut back by more than 25 percent and some by less. In some cases government regulation involves precise specification of the equipment or technology to be used, for example, the catalytic converter on automobiles. But this type of regulation prevents firms from seeking the most efficient way to reduce pollution. In general, the socially optimum quantity of production can be reached more efficiently, with lower opportunity costs, through the use of Pigouvian taxes than government regulation.

Negotiation

An interesting alternative to government regulation is negotiation between the parties involved in the externality. **Negotiation** is the act of agreement between an affected party and the generator of an externality. For example, suppose you have a neighbor with an annoying barking dog. One way to solve the problem, short of calling the dog pound, is by negotiation. If you value the cost of annoyance at $10 per hour, you are equally satisfied if the dog barks and you receive $10 per hour or the dog does not bark at all. By negotiation, you and your neighbor agree that whenever the dog barks, the dog's owner pays you $10 per hour. Through negotiation, the externality has been internalized. To avoid paying the $10, the owner reduces the amount of barking by the dog to the socially optimal level. Moreover, the dog catcher, and the government, are kept out of the process.

However, there is a problem with using negotiation for the widespread contol of environmental externalities. For negotiation, all of the parties involved must get together. And in terms of most external costs, the harmed parties are numerous and widely dispersed. For example, how many people are adversely affected by air pollution in Los Angeles? Moreover, the generators of externalities are also widely dispersed for nonpoint source pollution. How can any reasonable negotiation occur between automobile drivers and people harmed by air pollution in the Los Angeles area? In short, negotiation is ineffective for environmental externalities that involve more than a few people, which means the dog catcher, or the government, has to be called in.

Pollution Permit Market

Establishing a market for pollution permits is an effective means of controlling pollution through market forces and internalizing an external cost. The **pollution permit market** is a policy in which transferrable permits allowing polluters to discharge waste into the environment are issued by the government. The market for permits works in this way. Suppose the government determines that a river has the natural capacity to absorb a hundred tons of organic waste per day. Permits are issued that allow one ton of waste per day; if a firm has ten permits, then it can dispose of ten tons of waste per day. These permits can be bought and sold by any firm or city wishing to dump organic waste into the river. Like any other input, the firms needing the waste disposal capacity of the river the most are willing to pay the highest price for the permits. Thus, anyone wishing to dump waste into the river must pay the price of the permits, which internalizes the external costs, forcing firms to consider the cost of pollution in their production decisions.

However, the market for pollution permits has drawbacks of its own. Permits are not very effective if the pollution is discharged into a common property resource like the air. Since nonpayers cannot be excluded from using a common property resource, it would be difficult to prevent polluters without permits from discharging pollution. Enforcement would also be difficult for nonpoint source pollution. Since the source of nonpoint pollution cannot be determined, there is no way of knowing if the polluter has the proper permits.

Charges and Standards

The charges and standards approach is similar to the use of marketable permits. The **charges and standards** approach is a policy that controls pollution by adjusting taxes on pollution discharges to meet a desired level of pollution. One problem with the permits approach is the need to establish the number of permits. Even though the capacity of the river may be incorrectly measured, or may change over time, once the permits are owned by firms, it is difficult to get them back or reduce their number.

The charges and standards approach can avoid this problem. Once the capacity of the river is set, a tax is levied on waste discharges. After a period of time, the actual level of waste is compared with the desired level. If the actual level is too high, the tax is raised. If it is too low, the tax is reduced. With this continuous adjustment of the tax, the desired level of pollution is achieved. Furthermore, once the desired level is reached, and it turns out to be unsatisfactory, the tax can be altered to reach a new level of pollution. The biggest potential problem with the charges and standards approach is the potential for large changes in the tax rate. If the tax rate is changed abruptly and often, firms will find it difficult to comply, especially since firms often need to install new equipment to reduce pollution. It is inefficient to force firms to install new equipment every few weeks.

Moral Suasion

A final policy is moral suasion. **Moral suasion is a policy based on convincing people or firms to voluntarily reduce pollution.** For example, if air pollution has been especially bad over a city for several days, with no relief in sight, the mayor might ask people to keep from driving their cars. Moral suasion is strictly voluntary, and unenforceable, usually playing on the spirit and goodwill of the party generating the pollution. However, it is only effective for short periods of time, and only in crisis conditions. If a major smog alert is declared, people will voluntarily stop driving for a few days. But if the alert continues for a longer period, the moral suasion quickly becomes ineffective.

ENVIRONMENTAL LEGISLATION

Current legislation and policies dealing with environmental pollution rely almost exclusively on the use of government regulation. The first piece of legislation dealing with pollution was the Refuse Act of 1899, which regulated the discharge of waste into navigable waters and was used to control pollution in limited circumstances. We now operate under two major sets of legislation, one dealing with air pollution and the other with water pollution.

Water Pollution

After the Refuse Act of 1899, the next piece of legislation was the Water Pollution Control Act, passed in 1948 and amended and strengthened over the next twenty years. The most recent legislation was the Water Pollution Act Amendments, passed in 1972.

This series of legislative acts, especially the 1972 Water Pollution Act Amendments, set out the following policy for water pollution control. First, the federal government established waste discharge limits for individual sources of pollution. Second, the federal government has the ability to issue discharge permits. Third, dischargers were required to have the "best practicable" pollution technology by 1977 and the "best available" technology by 1983. Fourth, a system of subsidizing and regulating municipal sewage treatment plants was established. The 1972 Water Pollution Act Amendments also gave the power of enforcement to the Environmental Protection Agency, which was established in 1970.

Air Pollution

The first legislation dealing with air pollution was the Air Pollution Control Act of 1955. Additional amendments and legislation were also passed in subsequent years, the most important being the Clean Air Amendments of 1970.

Like water pollution legislation, air pollution legislation uses government regulation and the establishment of emission standards. The essential provisions of air pollution control contained in the legislation are as follows. First, emission standards were set for automobiles. Second, emission standards were set for specific types of pollution for specific industries. Third, in many instances the type of technology used to control pollution was specified. The 1970 Clean Air Amendments also established, and gave powers of enforcement to, the Environmental Protection Agency.

An Evaluation of Environmental Legislation

Current environmental legislation has reduced both air and water pollution. However, this legislation relies almost exclusively on direct government regulation, which suggests that we don't have the level of pollution associated with an efficient allocation of resources. In fact, the stated objective of the legislation is to eliminate discharges into the environment. As we discussed earlier in this unit, except in the case of extremely toxic and hazardous pollutants, an efficient allocation of resources involves some level of pollution. If environmental legislation is carried to the extreme of its stated objective, then we will clearly have an inefficient allocation.

IN SUMMARY

Pollution Control Policies

- The basic process for correcting an externality, and efficiently allocating resources, is internalization. If the market is forced to consider the external cost, then it reaches equilibrium at the socially optimal quantity. One way to internalize an external cost is with a Pigouvian tax equal to the value of the external cost.

- The optimal level of pollution is usually not zero, especially for degradable pollution. However, nondegradable and persistent pollution may very well have an optimal level of production at zero.

- In addition to the Pigouvian tax, five policies can be used to control pollution. Government regulation can be used to completely ban a pollution, reduce the quantity discharged, or specify technologies used to control pollution. Negotiation can be used for very small groups in order to internalize the external cost. A market for permits establishes a maximum level of pollution and allows polluters to use and exchange the permits. Charges and standards also set a level of pollution, then use taxes to achieve this level of pollution. Moral suasion is an effective short-run policy aimed at convincing polluters to cut back in times of severe crises.

- Current environmental legislation is based almost exclusively on the use of government regulation. Emission standards for air and water pollution are set for automobiles, different industries, and different types of pollution.

QUESTIONS FOR STUDY AND ANALYSIS

1. What is the best policy for controlling each of the following types of pollution? Explain why it is best and also indicate any important considerations in controlling each type.
   a. Radioactive waste
   b. Automobile emissions in New York City
   c. Automobile emissions during the Los Angeles Olympics
   d. Automobile emissions in any town with fewer than five thousand people
   e. Organic waste from a meat processing plant
   f. Persistent agricultural pesticides from agricultural runoff
   g. Your neighbor's loud stereo
   h. Domestic sewage discharged into a river by a small number of cities

2. The following table presents the important relationships between private costs, private benefits, external costs, and the quantity of output produced. Note that the private costs and benefits are the prices on the supply and demand curves. In light of this information, answer each of the questions below.

Quantity	Private Cost	Private Benefit	External Cost
1	$10	$90	$20
2	20	80	20
3	30	70	20
4	40	60	20
5	50	50	20
6	60	40	20
7	70	30	20

a. What is the equilibrium achieved by the market?
b. What is the socially optimal quantity of output?
c. Given that the market is affected by the external costs, what is the value of the Pigouvian tax that would internalize the externality?
d. With government regulation, what quantity of output would you set for the market?

3. In light of the materials balance concept discussed in the previous unit, what type of policy or policies should be implemented to internalize all external costs?

4. Based on your own experiences, would you say that we have an "optimal" quantity of pollution, too much, or too little?

REVIEW GLOSSARY

charges and standards A policy that controls pollution by adjusting taxes on pollution discharges to meet a desired level of pollution. This policy gives policymakers a greater degree of flexibility than the pollution permit market.

government regulation The process of controlling business activities through laws and administrative rules. Government regulation controls pollution by banning pollution, reducing the amount that can be discharged, or specifying technologies that can be used.

internalization The process of making participants in a market consider externalities associated with the production of a good.

moral suasion A policy based on convincing people or firms to voluntarily reduce pollution. Moral suasion is only effective in controlling pollution in short-run crises by appealing to the goodwill of the polluters.

negotiation The act of agreement between an affected party and the generator of an externality. Negotiation is only effective if a small number of people are involved in the externality.

Pigouvian tax A tax placed on producers to internalize an external cost.

pollution permit market A policy in which transferrable permits allowing polluters to discharge waste into the environment are issued by the government. This policy uses market forces to achieve an efficient level of pollution.

UNIT 13.4

The Economics of Energy Resources

The natural environment provides us with the raw materials used in the production of goods and services—timber for houses, iron ore for automobiles, water for daily consumption, and so on. In this unit we focus on a specific group of raw materials, energy resources. Energy resources, including petroleum, coal, natural gas, uranium, and solar and geothermal power, are used in every phase of the production and consumption of goods and services. Without energy, raw materials could not be physically transformed into finished products. For example, we could not extract iron ore from the ground, smelt it into steel, shape it into automobile parts, assemble the parts, or drive the automobile off the assembly line.

The overwhelming importance of energy resources became obvious in the 1970s, when energy prices in general, and petroleum prices in particular, increased dramatically. Higher prices, combined with artificially imposed shortages, made us question the future availability of these energy resources.

We begin by looking at the production and current use of energy resources in the United States and throughout the world. We then examine the principles underlying the supply of energy resources. With this in mind we see how recent government policies affect the markets for petroleum and natural gas. And finally, we discuss several alternative energy sources.

ENERGY RESOURCES IN THE UNITED STATES

The U.S. economy uses about 70 quadrillion (70,000,000,000,000,000) Btu's of energy per year, meaning that each person in the United States is, on average, using about 800 trillion Btu's per day, or 150,000 Btu's per second. To put this in perspective, note that a 60 watt light bulb uses about 200 Btu's of energy, and it takes about 300,000 Btu's to heat an average house for one day. Of course, most of this energy is not used directly by consumers to light living rooms or heat houses, but indirectly by consumers in the production and transportation of goods and services.

As Figure 13.4.1 illustrates, energy consumption in the United States, while rising through the first seven decades of the 1900s, has declined through the first half of the 1980s. Increases in energy consumption throughout most of the 1900s reflect increases in the production of goods and services. The decline in the 1980s was caused partly by an economic recession and partly by conservation practices stimulated by rising prices in the 1970s. As economic production increases in the last half of the decade, energy consumption is also likely to increase once again.

Figure 13.4.2 presents basic sources of energy that provide us with most of the 70 quadrillion Btu's of energy used in the United States. Petroleum provides 42.0 percent of all energy consumed, natural gas 24.6 percent, and coal 23.2 percent, for a total of almost 90 percent of all energy consumed in the United States. Of the remaining 10 percent, 5.1 percent comes from hydroelectric power, 4.8 percent from nuclear power, and 0.2 percent from such diverse sources as geothermal, solar, and biomass energy.

To put the United States energy market into perspective, let's compare its levels of energy production and consumption to those of other countries. Table 13.4.1 lists the top ten energy-consuming nations in the world, in terms of all major energy types converted to a petroleum equivalent. At the top of the list is the United States, consuming the equivalent of 34 million barrels of petroleum each day. The Soviet Union is right behind, with 24 million barrels per day; no other country uses more than 10 million barrels per day.

It should come as no surprise that the United States uses more energy than other countries, since it has both a large population base and a highly

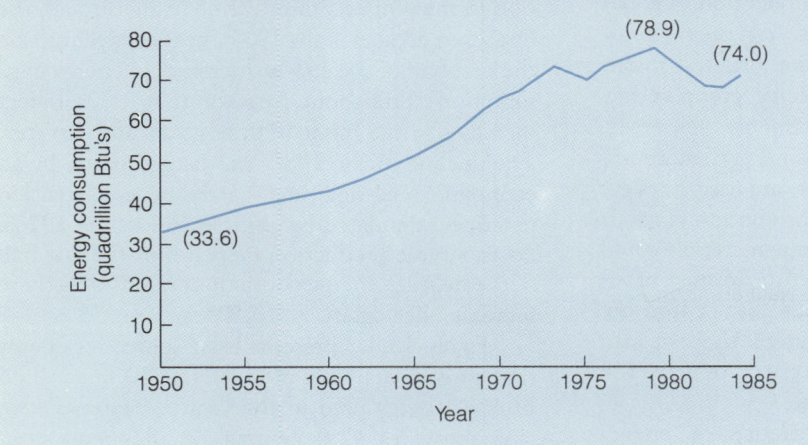

Figure 13.4.1

Energy Use in the United States, 1950 to 1984

Total energy use in the United States has increased throughout most of the century. Until the 1980s the economy has needed increasingly greater amounts of energy to produce more output. However, in the 1980s energy use declined, in part due to an economic recession and in part due to the relatively high energy prices of the 1970s. Source: U.S. Bureau of the Census, *Statistical Abstract of the United States*, selected years.

industrialized economy. The large populations of the Soviet Union and China mainly account for their extensive use of energy, whereas the highly industrialized economies of Japan and West Germany explain their high rank on the list of energy-consuming nations.

The other side of the world energy market is shown in Table 13.4.2, which lists the top ten energy-producing nations. Once again, the United States, the Soviet Union, and China occupy the top three spots. Not only do these countries consume a lot of energy but they produce a lot as well. However, while Saudi Arabia, Mexico, and Kuwait are three of the top ten energy producers, they are nowhere near the head of the list of energy consumers. By contrast, Japan, France, and Italy are among the top ten energy consumers but fall way down on the list of energy producers.

THE SUPPLY OF FOSSIL FUELS

The three main sources of energy—petroleum, natural gas, and coal—are similar in that they are all fossil fuels. Because only a limited quantity was produced and during specific conditions in prehistoric times, the supply of fossil fuels follows different principles than the supply of other types of goods and services.

All natural resources, including energy resources, can be classified into two groups, renewable and exhaustible. **Renewable resources** are resources that can be increased by the natural forces of the environment. Plant life, animal life, clean water, clean air, and sunshine are all examples of renewable resources. In each case the natural processes of the environment work to replenish the supplies of each resource. **Exhaustible resources**

Figure 13.4.2
Sources of Energy, 1984

Petroleum is the main source of energy in the United States, contributing about 42 percent of all energy used, followed by natural gas with 25 percent, and coal with 23 percent. Hydroelectric power contributes 5 percent, nuclear fission 5 percent, and other sources less than 1 percent.

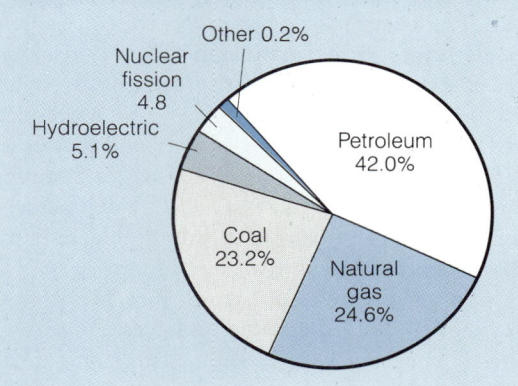

Table 13.4.1
Energy Consumption in Selected Countries, 1983

The United States is the top energy-consuming nation in the world, followed by the Soviet Union and China. High energy consumption occurs primarily in a country that is populous or highly industrialized.

Country	Energy Consumption (thousand barrels per day petroleum equivalent)
United States	34,914
Soviet Union	24,376
China	9,191
Japan	7,132
West Germany	5,117
Canada	4,238
United Kingdom	3,893
France	3,791
Italy	2,699
Poland	2,419

Source: Central Intelligence Agency, Directorate of Intelligence, *Handbook of Economic Statistics*, 1985.

are resources that are not increased by the natural forces of the environment. Petroleum, natural gas, and coal are all examples of exhaustible resources. The amount of each resource is fixed, since each was created by conditions that no longer exist on the planet. Many other types of nonenergy resources, especially minerals, also constitute exhaustible resources.

The Extraction of Exhaustible Resources

With renewable resources we are concerned with the amount of the resource that is generated, or replenished, over a period of time. If the amount replenished each year is less than society uses, then the resource can be used indefinitely into the future. For example, if timber producers harvest ten trees a year from a forest, but ten new trees reach maturity each year, then the company can continue this rate of production forever. With a renewable resource, the question facing society is how much to use each year. Keep in mind that for many renewable resources, the amount used today has no effect on the amount that can be used tomorrow. Clearly, the sunshine that falls today has no bearing on the amount of sunshine falling on the planet in the future.

However, this is not the case for exhaustible resources. The petroleum extracted from the ground and used to power an automobile this year cannot be extracted and used next year. Thus, the central issue for exhaustible resources is whether to use them today or use them tomorrow.

Suppose the current price of petroleum is $30 per barrel and the interest rate is 10 percent. If the producer extracts one barrel today and invests the $30 revenue at 10 percent, then by next year this $30 has grown to $33. Thus, if the price expected by the producer next year is less than $33, it is better to extract the petroleum this year and invest the funds at 10 percent. But if the producer expects a price greater than $33 next year, it is better to wait and extract the petroleum next year.

At this point the analysis takes an interesting turn. Producers who do not expect the price to rise extract more of the petroleum today. But if producers extract more today, this increase in supply will force the current price to decrease. Moreover, with less petroleum left in the ground for future extraction, the future supply will be less, causing the future price to increase. Under competitive conditions the price of the exhaustible resource rises at a rate equal to the rate of interest.

This result takes on significance in terms of the depletion of exhaustible resources. At current rates of consumption, we can use up many of the planet's exhaustible resources, including the fossil fuels, within the next fifty years. However, if the prices of these resources rise, then the rate of consumption will decline, leading to a prolonged use of the resources. The higher prices also make it feasible to develop new and (currently) more expensive energy sources.

Exploration and the Supply of Exhaustible Resources

The higher price of an exhaustible resource has another notable effect on its supply. As with the supply of other goods, the higher price leads to an increase in the quantity supplied. And even though fossil fuels are exhaustible, the higher price makes it possible to find and extract resources from more expensive sources.

Figure 13.4.3 depicts the type of supply curve facing petroleum, natural gas, and coal. Unlike the production of manufactured goods, the supply of fossil fuels usually comes in distinct steps. If the price is only P_1, then the cheapest and most easily

Table 13.4.2
Energy Production in Selected Countries, 1984

The United States is also the top energy-producing nation in the world, again followed by the Soviet Union and China. However, Saudi Arabia, Mexico, and Kuwait join the top ten as producers, while Japan, France, and Italy drop out.

Country	Energy Production (thousand barrels per day petroleum equivalent)
United States	33,066
Soviet Union	30,004
China	10,700
Canada	5,117
Saudi Arabia	5,091
United Kingdom	4,325
Mexico	3,862
Poland	2,525
West Germany	2,507
Kuwait	2,397

Source: Central Intelligence Agency, Directorate of Intelligence, *Handbook of Economic Statistics*, 1985.

For example, a petroleum producer has the option of either pumping petroleum from the ground today and selling it at current prices or pumping the petroleum in the future and selling it at future market prices. If the producer expects higher prices in the future, then it seems reasonable to wait. However, the decision involves more than just the relative prices. The producer can use the revenue received from the sale of the petroleum either to purchase physical capital or to invest in financial capital. As we saw in Unit 11.2, interest represents the payment for the use of the funds; this means that for the supplier to wait, the future price must be higher than the current price *plus* any interest received.

Figure 13.4.3

The Supply Curve of Fossil Fuels

The supply curve of fossil fuels tends to have distinct steps as more proven resources are identified through exploration. At relatively low prices, the least expensive, and easiest to locate, sources are used. However, as the price rises, more expensive sources are identified and supplied.

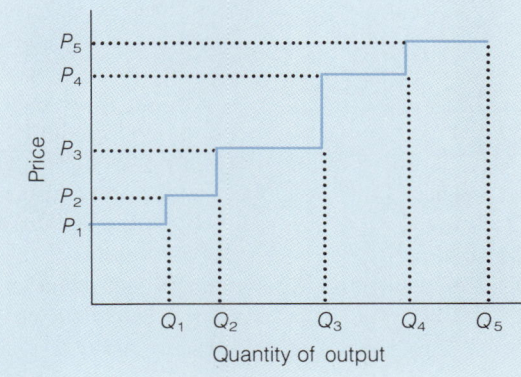

obtained resources are supplied, those within a few hundred feet of the surface. However, as the price rises to P_2, P_3, and P_4, petroleum producers can afford to drill deeper wells, and coal miners can afford to dig deeper mines. The higher prices also make it feasible to drill offshore oil wells, process oil shale, use more advanced and expensive secondary and tertiary extraction methods on existing wells, and employ more expensive machinery for strip mining.

This suggests that exploring for resources plays an important role in supplying fossil fuels. Although the total quantity of exhaustible resources, by their very nature, is fixed, the supply available to the economy for the production of goods and services is not necessarily fixed. Thus, the economy depends on locating proven reserves of a resource. **Proven reserves** are sources of an exhaustible resource that have been identified as economically usable. For example, a source of fossil fuel is a proven reserve once it has been discovered and it has been determined that the fuel can be profitably extracted under existing costs and prices. While some sources of fossil fuels can become proven reserves with nothing more than changes in prices and costs, exploration is ultimately needed to increase proven reserves and the supply of fossil fuels.

RECENT ENERGY POLICIES

The 1970s were marked by shortages of petroleum and natural gas and significant increases in energy prices. The price increases resulted in large part from the market power exerted by the Organization of Petroleum Exporting Countries (OPEC), which controls about 70 percent of the world's petroleum reserves. Before 1973, OPEC was willing to sell its petroleum for a few dollars a barrel. However, in 1973 and 1979, OPEC increased prices, so that by 1980 the price was over $30 per barrel.

While OPEC's market power certainly led to higher prices, existing government policies helped create significant shortages of both petroleum and natural gas. In 1973, when petroleum prices first increased, both petroleum and natural gas were subject to price controls. A price ceiling on natural gas had been in place since a 1954 Supreme Court decision in the case of Phillips Petroleum v. Wisconsin. In addition, petroleum prices had been controlled, along with all other prices, under President Nixon's wage and price controls of 1971. After all other price ceilings were removed, the price ceiling on petroleum was extended in order to shelter consumers from the price shocks caused by OPEC's price increase.

However, as we saw in Units 2.5 and 2.7, price ceilings create shortages. If the prices of petroleum and natural gas had been allowed to rise without restraint through the 1970s, shortages of gasoline and natural gas would not have resulted. Moreover, the price ceiling on petroleum actually increased our dependence on imported petroleum, leading to even more severe shocks from later price increases, as shown in Figure 13.4.4.

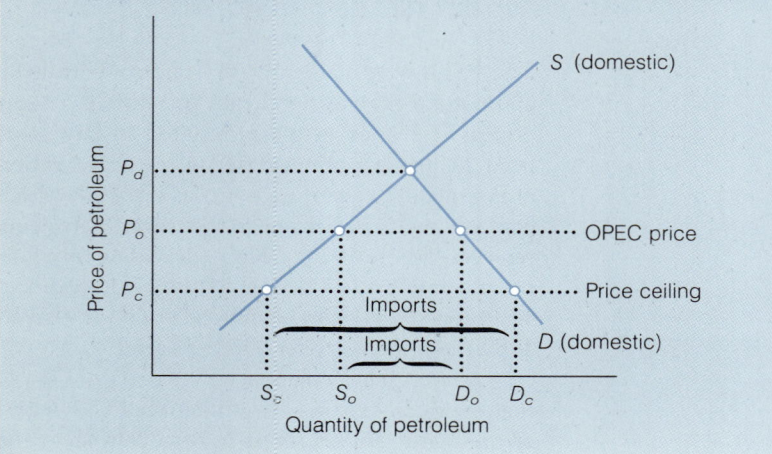

Figure 13.4.4

A Price Ceiling on Petroleum

When the price of petroleum began to rise in the early 1970s, government price controls held it below the price set by OPEC. Therefore, domestic supply was less, and domestic demand was greater, at the lower price than it would have been at the OPEC price. This meant that we imported more petroleum and were hurt more severely by price increases during the later part of the 1970s.

Figure 13.4.4 illustrates the domestic market for petroleum in the United States. The demand curve for petroleum is D, and the supply curve for domestically produced petroleum is S. For the United States to satisfy domestic demand entirely from domestic production, the price would have to be P_d, above the price established by OPEC. Without a price ceiling in the market, our domestic economy would import the difference between domestic demand D_o and domestic supply S_o. This is consistent with the principles of international trade discussed in Unit 14.1.

However, in the early 1970s, when the government maintained a price ceiling on petroleum below the OPEC price at P_c, the quantity of imports began to increase after the first price increase in 1973. Since the ceiling price was below the OPEC price, the domestic quantity supplied was less, at S_c, and the domestic quantity demanded was greater, at D_c. Thus, when OPEC increased prices again in 1979, the U.S. economy was importing almost 50 percent of all petroleum used in the United States. This price increase had a more devastating effect on the economy than it might have otherwise.

The analysis in Figure 13.4.4 can also be applied to shortages of natural gas. However, with natural gas we did not have a ready supply of imports, so during the 1970s many people simply did without during the cold winters.

Of course, the price ceilings on both petroleum and natural gas were kept in place during the 1970s for good reasons. The government wanted to prevent poor people from paying exorbitantly high prices for needed energy. However, the resulting misallocation of resources created widespread problems, many of which have yet to work their way through the economy. As we discussed in Units 2.5 and 2.7, when poor people have to pay higher energy prices, it is generally better to address the equity problems created through some form of direct subsidy or welfare payment than through price controls.

ALTERNATIVE ENERGY RESOURCES

The problems of rising prices and shortages that existed for petroleum and natural gas during the 1970s focused attention on alternative energy sources. People became intrigued by nuclear fission, solar power, geothermal energy, nuclear fusion, and other alternatives to the three basic fossil fuels.

Nuclear Fission

As we saw in Figure 13.4.2, nuclear fission accounts for about 5 percent of all energy consumption in the United States. Nuclear fission energy uses uranium-powered nuclear reactors to heat steam, which is then used to drive electric turbines to generate electricity. Coal and natural gas are the fossil fuels most commonly used to generate electricity.

After the atomic age began, at the end of the Second World War, nuclear energy appeared to be the ultimate energy source for the future. Some people in the 1950s even projected that electricity generated from nuclear energy would be so efficient that consumers would not be charged for its use.

However, it is becoming increasingly evident that nuclear energy is not economically competitive with other forms of electricity generation. While the variable costs of generating a kilowatt hour of electricity from nuclear energy are lower than other sources, the fixed costs of constructing a nuclear reactor make it more expensive. The construction costs of a nuclear generator have increased substantially in the last decade, to between $2 and $4 billion, because of government licensing and regulations, delays, higher input costs, and mismanagement. These costs alone remove any cost advantage nuclear energy has over coal or natural gas for the generation of electricity.

However, the existence of other costs that are often not paid by the firm or the customer make nuclear energy even more costly to society. First, the costs of disassembling or permanently shutting down a nuclear reactor have never been totally determined. Once a reactor outlives its useful life, it must be shut down. Part of the reactor itself becomes radioactive in the course of operation, and these radioactive materials have to be disposed of. Some people estimate that the costs of disassembling a reactor are equal to, or greater than, the costs of construction. Second, a safe and effective method of permanently disposing of the used fuel, which is highly radioactive and thus extremely deadly, has yet to be found; the costs of disposing of this waste have not been incorporated into the price charged to customers. Third, the federal government insures nuclear reactors up to $560 million in damages in the event of an accident. The firms generating electricity from the nuclear energy do not pay the costs of this insurance, and thus they are not reflected in the prices paid by buyers.

Solar Energy

A second alternative source of energy, which received a great deal of attention in the 1970s, is solar energy. Solar energy includes several alternatives that all originate with the sun, such as photovoltaic generation of electricity, solar water and space heating, passive solar heating, and wind energy. While the photovoltaic generation of electricity is based on new and developing technology, the other three employ relatively simple technology. In solar water and space heating, the sun heats water, which in turn is used directly as hot water or indirectly to heat the space inside a house. Passive solar heating is even simpler. It is based on constructing structures such that the sun shines through the right windows at the right time of the day to heat the inside. Wind energy, which uses the force of the blowing wind to generate electricity or pump water, has been around for a long time. A hundred years ago, farmers and ranchers on the Great Plains used windmills to pump water from the ground. And Holland is noted for its uniquely shaped windmills, used for centuries to grind grain.

The main drawback to solar energy is the cost. While there are no fuel costs for using solar energy, the costs of equipment and maintenance make the various types of solar energy competitive with fossil fuels only in limited circumstances. The wind in the Great Plains and the sunshine in the Southwest make solar energy feasible in these areas. However, photovoltaic generation of electricity remains one or two technological advances away from practical use. The most feasible source of solar energy remains passive solar heating. It is just as easy to build a house with south-facing windows as with north-facing ones. But south-facing windows heat the inside of a house in the winter time, while north-facing windows do not.

Geothermal Power

Another alternative to fossil fuels is the use of geothermal energy, which is steam produced by heat deep beneath the earth's surface. Geothermal energy can be, and has been, effectively used to power turbines to generate electricity. The main problem with geothermal power is its general lack of availability. Geothermal steam from the earth simply does not occur on a widespread basis.

Nuclear Fusion

The last alternative is nuclear fusion, the process in which hydrogen atoms are "fused" together to form helium and more complex atoms, giving off heat and energy in the process. Note how nuclear *fusion* differs from nuclear *fission*, in which uranium and other radioactive materials are "split" apart. Actually, nuclear fusion represents another form of solar energy, since the sun's energy derives from the process of fusing atoms together. Because nuclear fusion uses the abundantly available hydrogen atom as its fuel, it could provide a vast source of energy.

Unfortunately, the technology needed to harness nuclear fusion has not been completely developed.

IN SUMMARY
The Economics of Energy Resources

- The U.S. economy uses an enormous amount of energy each year. The three major sources of energy—petroleum, natural gas, and coal—are all fossil fuels. Petroleum accounts for over 40 percent of all energy used, while natural gas and coal account for just under 25 percent each.

- The most important feature of these three fossil fuels is that they are all exhaustible, because each was formed through natural processes that no longer occur. While renewable resources can be used for an indefinite period, exhaustible resources used today cannot be used tomorrow. This means that under competitive conditions the prices of these energy resources will rise in the future as they become more limited in supply. The higher prices will then lead to a reduction in demand.

- While the supplies of exhaustible resources are ultimately fixed, the proven reserves of each can be increased through exploration. As the price of an exhaustible resource increases, it becomes economically feasible to discover and use sources that are more difficult and costly to supply.

- Energy policies in the United States tended to worsen energy shortages in the 1970s. Price ceilings on petroleum and natural gas prevented prices from rising to equilibrium levels, thus creating or worsening shortages of both.

- The four most commonly discussed alternatives to fossil fuels are nuclear fission, solar energy, geothermal power, and nuclear fusion. Nuclear fission has lost most of its comparative cost advantages, and has many costs that are external to its production. Solar energy is also at a cost disadvantage to most forms of fossil fuel, except in a few circumstances. Geothermal power has limited potential, since it is available in only limited areas. And nuclear fusion still lacks the technology needed for practical application.

QUESTIONS FOR STUDY AND ANALYSIS

1. In terms of the decision to extract an exhaustible resource, would you expect more or less of the resource to be extracted today if the interest rate increased? Explain.

2. Now that the price ceilings on petroleum and gasoline have been lifted, do you think that the energy crisis, stimulated by OPEC, that we saw in the 1970s can be repeated? Explain.

3. Based on the law of demand and the proposition that the price of an exhaustible resource rises over time as its availability becomes limited, explain why we are never likely to completely "run out" of petroleum. What is likely to happen to the economic feasibility of using nuclear and solar energy before we exhaust our supply of exhaustible fossil fuels?

REVIEW GLOSSARY

exhaustible resource A resource that cannot be increased by the natural forces of the environment. Common examples of exhaustible resources are petroleum, coal, natural gas, and various types of minerals.

proven reserves Sources of an exhaustible resource that have been identified as economically usable.

renewable resource A resource that can be increased by the natural forces of the environment. Common examples of renewable resources are plant and animal life, clean air and water, and solar energy.

SECTION INQUIRY

The Limits to Growth

In 1972 a book titled *The Limits to Growth* was published under the auspices of an organization called the Club of Rome. This book made some startling projections about the future of civilization. It projected that continued economic and population growth would exhaust the world's supply of natural resources and pollute the natural environment to deadly levels. The result, if growth were left unchecked, would be widespread death, disease, and famines. The world's population, which is over 5 billion, would decline to only a fraction of this level by the beginning of the twenty-first century.

At the time this book was published it sparked controversy everywhere. Critics argued that the projections failed to consider numerous economic principles. First and perhaps most important and fundamental, many economists argued that the projections failed to consider the effect that shortages of natural resources, especially exhaustible fossil fuels and minerals, would have on their prices and subsequently the effect that rising prices would have on the demand for the natural resources. In particular, they argued that higher prices would lead to conservation of the resources and substitution of other resources that became relatively cheaper. Second, critics argued that the projections failed to adequately consider the possibility of future technological advances that would provide solutions for many of the projected problems.

Many critics of *The Limits to Growth* cited similar projections made by the economist and theologian T. R. Malthus in the late 1800s. He argued that population growth would exceed the world's capacity to increase the production of food, leading to widespread starvation. However, Malthus, writing in the early stages of the Industrial Revolution, failed to anticipate the beneficial effects technological advances would have on the world's ability to increase food production. Many critics thus argue that *The Limits to Growth* is merely a restatement of the projections originally made by Malthus, with the same oversights.

However, events in the 1970s seemed to bear out the projections made in *The Limits to Growth*. Petroleum prices increased from around $3 to over $30 per barrel, along with prices for other natural resources. Several countries experienced shortages in the production of food, including the United States and the Soviet Union. The U.S. economy and other economies throughout the world seemed to stagnate, with little or no increases in national production. Meanwhile, population growth continued unabated in most of the less-developed countries in Latin America, Africa, and Asia. But as the world moved into the 1980s, these problems did not seem as severe. Petroleum prices fell, and economic growth rebounded. In addition, actions by the Environmental Protection Agency led to reduced pollution and a cleaner natural environment in the 1980s than during the 1960s. Whether the good times of the 1980s are a refutation of the limits to growth or merely a temporary pause before the catastrophe begins, no one really knows.

QUESTIONS FOR DISCUSSION

1. Discuss environmental pollution problems resulting from continued population and economic growth in terms of the materials balance concept. With this in mind, how could the world squeeze more growth out of the world's resources without creating devastating pollution problems?

2. Explain how taxes could be used to avoid the pollution problems associated with growth.

3. How are the projected problems and potential solutions of worldwide pollution dependent on the type of pollution discharged (degradable, nondegradable, or persistent)?

4. What types of policies would be most effective in preventing the worldwide pollution problems projected in *The Limits to Growth*?

5. Explain how prices can prevent the total exhaustion of an exhaustible resource. With alternative but more expensive energy sources, such as solar, geothermal, wind, and nuclear power, are we likely to exhaust our supply of petroleum? Explain.

SECTION 14

The World Economy

In recent years it has become evident that the U.S. economy merely comprises one part of an overall world economy. The OPEC petroleum price shocks, Japanese imports, and Soviet grain sales have affected, and been affected by, the U.S. economy. The production decisions of many firms, the economywide unemployment rate, and the market power in various industries are all influenced by activities in other countries. To better understand our role in the world economy, we take up two distinct topics, international trade and economic development.

Unit 14.1, International Trade, is the first of two units that takes a detailed look at the net exports component of aggregate expenditures. In particular, we see why one country exports goods to, and imports goods from, other countries. We examine the key principle in the study of international trade, the principle of comparative advantage. This principle helps explain why a country with the ability to produce a wide variety of goods decides to produce a limited number and import the rest.

Unit 14.2, International Finance, offers another dimension to the study of the trade between nations. In this unit we see that international trade differs from trade within a country because different countries use different currencies. When goods and services flow between countries in one direction, the payments flow in the other direction. Since the payments involve different currencies, the exchange of goods between countries also leads to the exchange of currencies.

Unit 14.3, Economic Growth, is the first of two units dealing with the nature and causes of economic growth in countries throughout the world. In this unit we expand our initial discussion of economic growth presented in the study of production possibilities in Unit 1.5. First, we identify the basic nature of economic growth. Then we examine the various causes of economic growth, which include increases in the quantity and quality of the factors of production, especially labor and capital. Furthermore, we see how saving, investment, education, and research contribute to the growth of the economy.

Unit 14.4, Economic Development, extends our discussion of economic growth of modern industrial economies in Unit 14.3 to the many countries throughout the world that have maintained relatively low levels of development. In particular, we discuss the difference between economic growth and economic development. And we look at some of the problems that are unique to developing countries and the solutions for those problems.

UNIT 14.1

International Trade

In the 1970s many people in the United States received their introduction to the realities of international trade when OPEC tripled the price of crude petroleum. In the 1980s our focus has turned toward competition from foreign imports, such as Japanese automobiles and steel. Keep in mind, though, that international trade has been going on for centuries. Marco Polo traveled to the Orient in search of trade. Later, Christopher Columbus inadvertently discovered North America while trying to trade with the Far East. And the Spanish, French, and English explorers of the sixteenth and seventeenth centuries were all motivated by the desire for trade.

In this unit we look at some of the principles underlying international trade. First, we review and define several concepts relating to the trade between nations by examining existing patterns of international trade. We then turn our attention to the most important principle of international trade, the principle of comparative advantage, which explains why a country would choose to import goods it is able to produce. While the principle of comparative advantage indicates why countries trade, we also need to analyze the international market to see how much countries trade. And finally, we look at tariffs, the most common means of restricting trade between countries.

PATTERNS OF INTERNATIONAL TRADE

A few definitions are necessary to provide some background on international trade in the world. First, <u>international trade is the exchange of goods across national boundaries</u>. And recall from Unit 3.1 the terms used for the goods and services that are traded across national boundaries are exports and imports. **Exports** are domestically produced goods purchased by other countries. **Imports** are goods purchased from other countries by the domestic economy. For example, the United States exports automobiles to Saudi Arabia and imports petroleum from Saudi Arabia, while Saudi Arabia imports automobiles from the United States and exports petroleum. One country's import is another country's export.

In our discussion of national production and the circular flow in Section 3, we found it convenient to discuss net exports, the difference between exports and imports. In the context of international trade, net exports are also called the balance of trade. The **balance of trade** is the relationship between a country's exports and imports. In fact, a **balance of trade surplus** is when a country exports more goods and services than it imports, and net exports are positive. And a **balance of trade deficit** is when a country imports more goods and services than it exports, and net exports are negative.

Table 14.1.1 illustrates the importance of international trade to several countries. Even the United States, with its vast supplies of natural resources, capital, and labor, engages in a significant amount of international trade. Although our net exports amount to only around 1 percent of gross national product, we import about 10 percent of the goods and services purchased in the country and export about 10 percent of our total production. However, for several other Western industrialized countries—the United Kingdom, West Germany, France, Italy, and Canada—international trade comprises up to one-fourth of total

Table 14.1.1

Patterns of International Trade, 1983

While the United States generally has less than 10 percent of *GNP* either exported or imported, many other countries are more heavily involved in international trade. Canada, France, Italy, United Kingdom, and West Germany are all around 20 percent on both imports and exports.

Country	Exports Total (billions)	Exports Percentage of *GNP*	Imports Total (billions)	Imports Percentage of *GNP*
Canada	$ 76.7	23.5	$ 65.1	19.9
China	24.0	7.0	18.4	5.4
France	94.9	18.4	105.4	20.5
Italy	72.7	20.5	80.4	22.6
Japan	147.0	12.7	126.4	10.9
Soviet Union	91.6	5.0	80.4	4.4
United Kingdom	91.6	20.4	100.2	22.3
United States	200.5	6.1	269.9	8.2
West Germany	169.4	25.8	152.9	23.2

Source: Central Intelligence Agency, Directorate of Intelligence, *Handbook of Economic Statistics*, 1984.

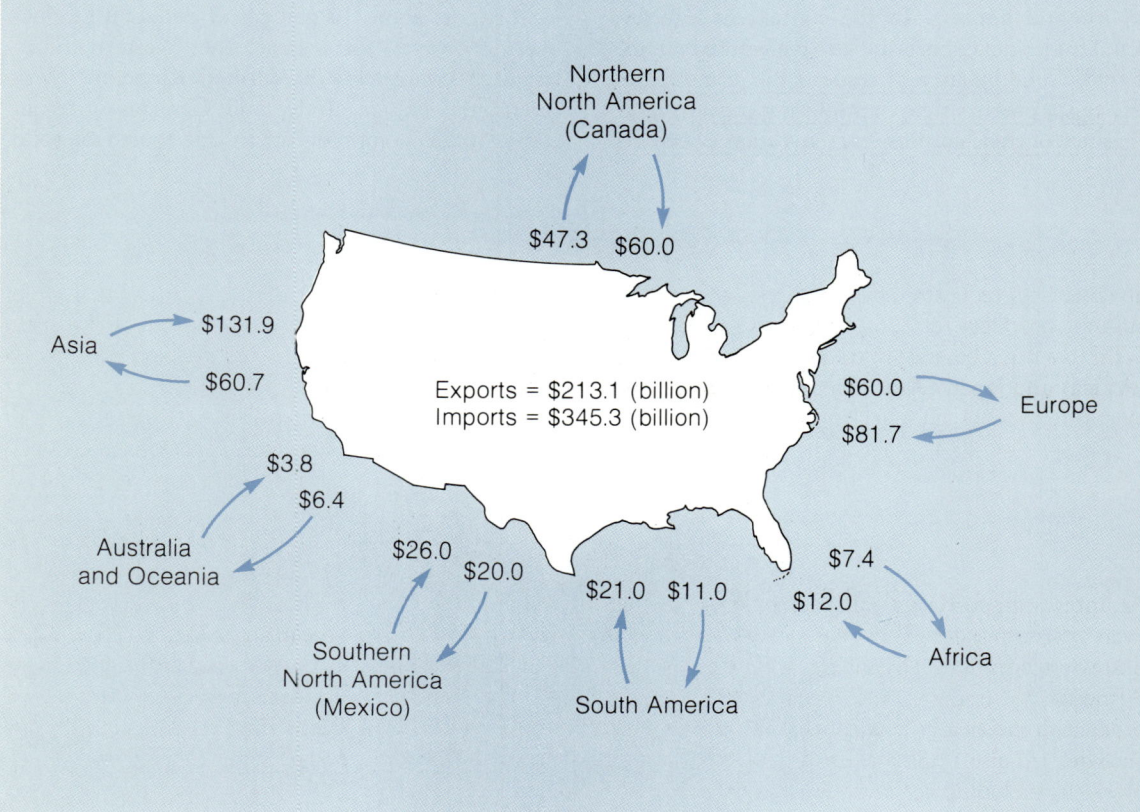

Figure 14.1.1

Trade Between the United States and the Rest of the World, 1985

The United States engages in international trade with many different countries. Our biggest trading partners include Japan, West Germany, Canada, England, and the countries of OPEC. With some countries we have a balance of trade surplus, in which we export more than we import. However, with other countries we have a balance of trade deficit, in which we import more than we export. Source: U.S. Bureau of Economic Analysis, *Survey of Current Business,* March 1986.

production. And for OPEC nations, international trade represents almost half of total production.

Figure 14.1.1 illustrates the extent of U.S. trade with other countries. As you might expect, a great deal of our imports come from OPEC countries (Africa), Japan (Asia), Canada, and Europe. OPEC and Canada sell us petroleum, Japan sells us electronics and automobiles, and Europe supplies us with a wide range of manufactured goods. Meanwhile, we export not only a large amount of man-

Table 14.1.2

The Principle of Comparative Advantage

The principle of comparative advantage states that countries can engage in trade even though one country does not have an absolute advantage in the production of any goods. Here, Lageonia is able to produce more of both goods than the Republic of Hansen with the same quantity of labor. However, the Republic of Hansen has a comparative advantage in the production of silicon chips. For each chip it produces it gives up only 2 pounds of peanuts, whereas Lageonia must give up 3 pounds of peanuts for each chip produced.

Country	Chocolate-Covered Peanuts Per Unit of Labor	Silicon Chips Per Unit of Labor
Lageonia	30 pounds	10 chips
Republic of Hansen	10 pounds	5 chips

ufactured goods but also an ample supply of agricultural products to Europe, Canada, and Asia. While we run a balance of trade deficit with OPEC (Africa) and Japan (Asia), we have a surplus with most of our other trading partners.

COMPARATIVE ADVANTAGE

An interesting feature of international trade is that even a country as large and productive as the United States engages in a significant amount of trade. Although we import some goods that we cannot produce domestically, such as cacao, bananas, and bauxite, we also import many goods that we can produce, including automobiles, electronic equipment, and petroleum. To see why this happens, let's look at the principle of comparative advantage. The **principle of comparative advantage** states that trade between nations is beneficial to both if there is a difference in relative opportunity costs. In other words, we import some types of goods simply because another country can make it cheaper than we can.

For example, two countries, Lageonia and the Republic of Hansen, are able to produce the same two goods, chocolate-covered peanuts and silicon chips used in computers. To simplify, assume that the only factor used to produce both goods is labor. Table 14.1.2 lists the amount of chocolate-covered peanuts and silicon chips that can be produced with one unit of labor.

In Lageonia a unit of labor can produce 30 pounds of peanuts or 10 silicon chips. However, a unit of labor in the Republic of Hansen can produce 10 pounds of peanuts or 5 silicon chips. Note that Lageonian labor is more productive than labor in the Republic of Hansen for both goods, which means it has an absolute advantage. A country has an **absolute advantage** if it can produce more output than another country with the same factors of production. Lageonia might have an absolute advantage over the Republic of Hansen for several reasons. Perhaps Lageonia is more industrially developed. Or maybe it employs better technology in the production of both goods. Or it might have a more abundant supply of the natural resources (peanuts, chocolate, and silicon) needed to make the goods.

Since Lageonia has an absolute advantage and can effectively produce both goods cheaper (with less labor) than the Republic of Hansen, it is easy to see why the Republic of Hansen would want to enter into trade. The Republic of Hansen can buy both goods more cheaply from Lageonia that it can make them itself (that is, if the costs of transporting the goods are negligible). But why would Lageonia want to trade with the Republic of Hansen if it can produce both goods more cheaply (in terms of labor used) than if it buys them from the Republic of Hansen? Note that it is not the absolute advantage in the production of goods that is important to international trade, but the comparative advantage. Lageonia can benefit from trade with the Republic of Hansen because of the principle of comparative advantage.

One unit of labor in Lageonia can produce 30 pounds of chocolate-covered peanuts or 10 silicon chips. If a unit of labor is used to produce silicon chips, this means it is not producing peanuts. Thus, Lageonia gives up 30 pounds of peanuts for every 10 silicon chips produced, meaning the opportunity cost for each silicon chip produced is 3 pounds of peanuts. By contrast, the opportunity cost per silicon chip in the Republic of Hansen is only 2 pounds of peanuts. Even though the Republic of Hansen needs to use more labor to produce the same amount of silicon chips, it gives up fewer chocolate-covered peanuts than Lageonia. In other words, the Republic of Hansen incurs a lower opportunity cost for each silicon chip produced. It is relatively more productive (compared to the alternative of producing peanuts), even though it is absolutely less productive, per unit of labor.

Since a unit of labor in Lageonia can produce 30 pounds of peanuts or 10 silicon chips, every pound of peanuts produced in Lageonia means it is giving up $\frac{1}{3}$ silicon chip. But for the Republic of Hansen, every pound of chocolate-covered peanuts produced means it is not producing $\frac{1}{2}$ silicon chip. Since $\frac{1}{3}$ is smaller than $\frac{1}{2}$, Lageonia gives up fewer silicon chips in the production of peanuts than the Republic of Hansen. This means that Lageonia has a comparative advantage in the production of peanuts.

This is why Lageonia can also benefit from trade with the Republic of Hansen. In Lageonia each silicon chip costs 3 pounds of peanuts. However, in the Republic of Hansen, each silicon chip costs only 2 pounds of peanuts, which is quite a bargain for Lageonia. Instead of producing silicon chips domestically, it can produce peanuts and trade them for silicon chips produced in the Republic of Hansen. If Lageonia produces the silicon chips domestically, it gives up 3 pounds of peanuts for each chip. However, if it takes those 3 pounds of peanuts to the Republic of Hansen, it can use them to buy $1\frac{1}{2}$ silicon chips.

And by the same token, the Republic of Hansen benefits from trade with Lageonia. In the Republic of Hansen each pound of peanuts costs $\frac{1}{2}$ silicon chip. However, the cost in Lageonia is only $\frac{1}{3}$ chip. If the Republic of Hansen produces 10 silicon chips at home, it can take them to Lageonia and trade them for 30 pounds of chocolate-covered peanuts, when the most it could produce domestically is 20 pounds.

In short, each country is better off by trading with the other. Lageonia has a comparative advantage in the production of chocolate-covered peanuts, and should specialize in that, while the Republic of Hansen has a comparative advantage, and should specialize, in the production of silicon chips. Each country can then trade the good they produce for the good they don't produce, at a lower cost than if they tried to produce it themselves.

THE INTERNATIONAL MARKET

The study of comparative advantage indicates why two countries engage in international trade, but not *how much* they will trade. Figure 14.1.2 presents the international market for silicon chips, in which the only two countries in the market are Lageonia and the Republic of Hansen.

Panel a depicts the domestic market for silicon chips in Lageonia. If the country does not engage in international trade, it reaches equilibrium at the intersection of the demand and supply curves, point L, with the equilibrium price P_L. In terms of our

Figure 14.1.2

The International Market

In panel a the domestic price of silicon chips in Lageonia, without international trade, is greater than the domestic price in the Republic of Hansen, in panel c. If the price in panel a declines from P_L, Lageonia is willing to import silicon chips based on the excess demand curve in panel b. If the price rises above P_H in panel c, the Republic of Hansen is willing to export silicon chips, based on the excess supply in panel b. The international market in panel b achieves equilibrium at the intersection of the excess demand and supply curves. The quantity Q_e is imported by Lageonia and exported by the Republic of Hansen.

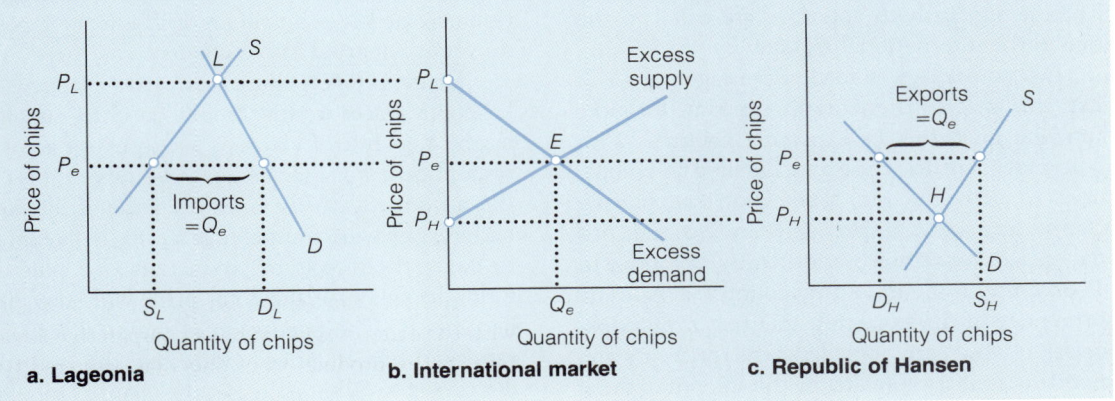

a. Lageonia
b. International market
c. Republic of Hansen

previous analysis from Table 14.1.2, P_L corresponds to the opportunity cost of silicon chips, which was 3 pounds of chocolate-covered peanuts.

Based on our analysis of comparative advantage, we have good reason to think that Lageonia will import silicon chips, but we want to know how much. To do this, let's determine the quantity of silicon chips Lageonia imports if the price falls below P_L. At lower prices the quantity demanded increases and the quantity supplied decreases, creating an excess demand. The horizontal difference between the demand and supply curves for Lageonia is the excess demand curve plotted in panel b. The excess demand curve indicates the quantity of silicon chips Lageonia is willing to import at different prices.

Panel c depicts the domestic market for silicon chips in the Republic of Hansen. If the Republic of Hansen does not engage in international trade, it reaches equilibrium at point H. The equilibrium price P_H corresponds to the opportunity cost of silicon chips in Table 14.1.2 for 2 pounds of peanuts.

Since the Republic of Hansen is likely to export silicon chips, the amount can be determined by the excess supply curve in panel b. The excess supply curve is the horizontal difference between the supply and demand curves for the Republic of Hansen as the price rises above P_H. The excess supply curve tells us the quantity of silicon chips that Lageonia is willing to export at different prices.

Once we know the quantity that the Republic of Hansen is willing to export, and the quantity that Lageonia is willing to import, it's a simple matter to determine the price equating both. The intersection of the excess demand and supply curves in panel b is equilibrium in the international market. At P_e the quantity the Republic of Hansen is willing to export is equal to the quantity Lageonia is willing to import, Q_e.

In panel a domestic production in Lageonia is S_L and domestic consumption is D_L; the difference between the two constitutes imports. In panel c domestic production in the Republic of Hansen is S_H and domestic consumption is D_H; the difference between these two constitutes exports. Moreover, the quantity of exports from the Republic of Hansen is equal to the quantity of imports to Lageonia. Furthermore, in equilibrium the opportunity costs of production in both countries are equal to the price in the international market, P_e.

Two points can be made from Figure 14.1.2. First, this analysis is essentially the same for more than one importing or exporting country. With additional countries, the excess demand and supply curves would be the total of all countries exporting or importing goods, respectively. And second, this analysis ignores transportation costs. The price of silicon chips in the importing country is the same as the price in the exporting country. If the transportation costs are included, the price in the importing country is greater by the amount of these additional costs.

Figure 14.1.2 illustrates quite clearly the winners and losers from international trade. Consumers in the importing country benefit, and producers in the importing country do not. In the importing country, consumers get more of the good at a lower price. However, domestic producers sell less of their good, also at a lower price. By contrast, producers in the exporting country benefit, and consumers do not. In the exporting country, producers sell more at a higher price, and consumers get less, but still at the higher price.

This helps explain why so many political problems are associated with international trade. In importing countries, producers are against international trade. For example, the U.S. automobile industry does not want Japanese imports, but U.S. consumers stand to benefit from the imports. Conversely, U.S. farmers are very much in favor of wheat sales to the Soviet Union, while consumers of bread in the United States pay higher prices as a result. This implies that although trade between nations benefits both nations, the benefits are not equally distributed throughout. Someone gains and someone loses, even though the gains are greater than the losses.

TARIFFS

Because producers in importing countries are usually hurt by imports, they often encourage the government to restrict or prevent imports. The most common method is a tariff. A **tariff** is a tax imposed on goods imported into a country.

Figure 14.1.3 illustrates what happens if Lageonia places a tariff on silicon chips supplied by the Republic of Hansen. The pretariff equilibrium price is P_e, and the quantity imported is Q_e. But a tariff effectively raises the price of the good because importers must charge a price high enough to cover their costs of production (P_e) plus the tariff. In this case the total price with the tariff becomes P_t. The imposition of the tariff, and the resulting higher price, decreases the quantity demanded to D_t but increases the quantity supplied by domestic producers to S_t. This reduces the quantity of imports to Q_t, which is exactly the intent of the tariff.

However, in addition to reducing imports, a tariff reduces the overall welfare of society. First, since consumers pay a higher price for a smaller quantity, they are prevented from consuming the quantity between D_t and D_L. In fact, they lose the consumers' surplus equal to the triangular area labeled D, beneath the demand curve. This is one part of the welfare loss to society.

Another part of society's welfare loss can be seen by examining the higher price paid by consumers. Consumers pay more for the quantity D_t, equal to the rectangular area $A + B + C$. Part of this additional payment goes to the government as revenue from the tariff, labeled area C. Since the tariff revenue is merely a transfer from consumers to the government, it does not represent a loss to society.

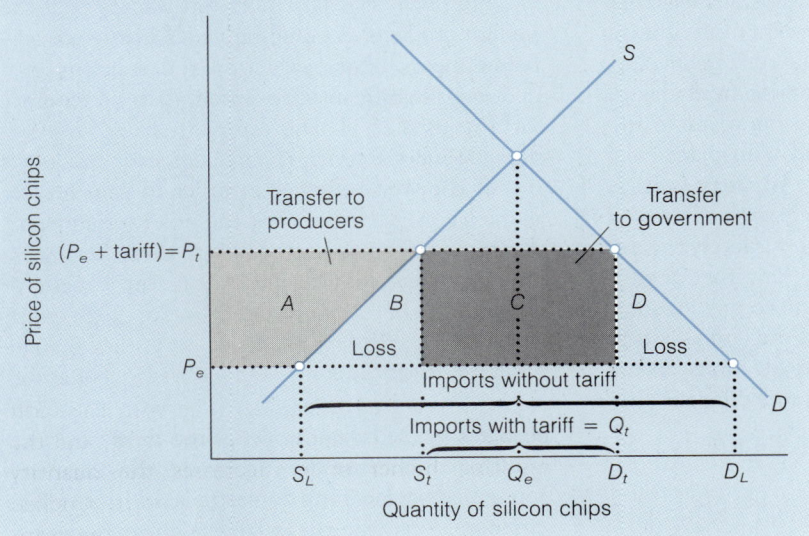

Figure 14.1.3

Tariffs and the International Market

A tariff is a tax on imports that raises the price paid by domestic consumers as well as the price charged by domestic producers. Domestic consumers pay a higher price for a smaller quantity of output, thus losing area D. Domestic producers are encouraged to be inefficient, using more costly factors, which results in a welfare loss of area B.

Consumers also have a transfer to domestic producers. Since producers receive the higher price P_t, they increase the production to quantity S_t. However, for the quantity between S_L and S_t, the price received is greater than the costs of production. The producers receive a producers' surplus equal to area A, which is a transfer from the consumers but not a loss to society.

This leaves us with area B. As domestic producers increase production, opportunity costs increase. The opportunity costs of production at S_t are greater than the pretariff opportunity costs at S_L. In fact, the opportunity costs with the tariff are greater than the opportunity cost of the exporting country, which is still equal to P_e. Thus, domestic producers are incurring higher opportunity costs than necessary, which represents an inefficiency. Area B is a loss to society due to the inefficient use of resources. And the total loss to society from the tariff becomes the combination of areas B and D. The question is whether the benefits derived from a tariff are worth the inefficiency and misallocation of resources.

AN EVALUATION OF ARGUMENTS IN FAVOR OF TARIFFS

Over the years, several arguments have been developed to justify tariffs on imported goods. However, none are very convincing, especially considering the adverse impact tariffs have on the allocation of resources. Let's look at these arguments.

Infant Industry

A relatively new industry in a developing country is often less efficient than foreign competitors because the industry has had little time to develop skilled management, exploit efficient technologies, or take advantage of decreasing average costs. Domestic producers often argue for a tariff limiting imports until the industry has had time to develop. Unfortunately, the lack of competition from imports often keeps the industry from becoming more efficient. Moreover, once the tariff is in place, it is difficult to determine when the industry is ready to go out on its own and compete with the rest of the world. If the domestic industry is likely to have a comparative advantage in the long run, then it would be better for the government to provide some other type of subsidy or support. And if the country has no conceivable comparative advantage in the industry, then it is better off producing another good.

Employment

Another argument often used is that tariffs maintain employment where foreign competition is taking jobs away from domestic workers. However, in this case the tariff is used to support an inefficient industry. Total domestic production would be greater if the workers were trained for jobs in which the country did have a comparative advantage. Instead of placing a tariff on the imported good, the country is better off if the government implements some type of job-training program.

Retaliation, Foreign Subsidies, and Dumping

Another argument is that other countries engage in trade restrictions that hurt domestic producers, so trade restrictions should be placed on imports from these countries. However, this type of retaliation only compounds the inefficiencies, and it can lead to further retaliation from the other country.

It is also argued that foreign countries subsidize their businesses, giving them an unfair advantage over domestic producers. If this is the case in the long run, then the importing country should take advantage of the foreign country's generosity. If it wants to export goods at a lower price, then let it. Domestic consumers benefit, and domestic producers can switch to a domestic industry with a comparative advantage.

However, if it is a short-run subsidy or if the foreign producer is dumping goods in the country below the costs of production and domestic production is significantly disrupted, then a temporary tariff is justified. This is especially true if the foreign producer is trying to force domestic producers out of the world market in order to gain greater market power. However, if there is no significant disrupton of domestic production, then the domestic consumers should simply reap the benefit of lower prices.

Cheap Foreign Labor

It is also argued that tariffs should be imposed on some goods because they are produced with cheap foreign labor, meaning domestic labor is unable to compete. First, the cheap labor is cheap because it is less productive. Second, cheap labor means the other country has a comparative advantage in goods using labor as a resource. We are better off buying goods made with this cheap labor and specializing in goods in which we have a comparative advantage.

THE COSTS OF TRADE RESTRICTIONS

Although tariffs have historically been the most common means to restrict trade between countries, other forms of trade restrictions are also used. Another common form of trade restriction is an import quota, in which a country limits the quantity of a good imported into the country. A good example of import quotas occurred in the early 1980s, when Japan placed voluntary quotas on the shipment of automobiles into the United States.

In Figure 14.1.3 we saw that a tariff increases

the price of an imported good to domestic consumers. A restriction on the quantity of imports has a similar effect. Robert W. Crandall of the Brookings Institute tried to determine the additional price domestic consumers paid for U.S. automobiles as a result of the trade restrictions. For the years 1981 to 1983 he estimated, in three different ways, that the price of automobiles was about $350 to $400 greater with the import quotas than they would have been without the quotas.* Considering that about 6 million automobiles were sold in each of the three years studied, it is easy to see that the total costs to domestic consumers was substantial during this period. The question becomes whether the costs to the domestic consumer are worth the gains received by the domestic automobile industry from the reduction in competition.

IN SUMMARY

International Trade

- International trade is the exchange of goods between nations. Although the importance of international trade has been highlighted in recent years by the imbalances in petroleum and automobile imports into the United States, international trade has been around as long as countries have been around.

- The balance of trade is the relationship between goods one country buys from another (imports) and goods one country sells to another (exports). A surplus exists if exports are greater than imports, and a deficit exists if exports are less than imports.

- The most important principle in international trade is the principle of comparative advantage. One country has an absolute advantage over another if it is technologically more efficient in the production of all goods. A comparative advantage occurs if one country has lower relative opportunity costs of producing a good, and the comparative advantage exists even without an absolute advantage. With comparative advantages both countries can benefit from international trade.

- The international market equates the excess demand for goods from one or more countries (imports) with the excess supply from others (exports). The equilibrium price in the international market equates imports and exports. At this price the opportunity costs of domestic production in the importing country are equal to the opportunity costs of production in the exporting country. While both countries can be better off with trade, the benefits are not evenly distributed within each country. In the importing country, consumers benefit, while producers are harmed. In the exporting country, producers benefit, while consumers are harmed.

- A tariff is a tax placed on an imported good. A tariff distorts the allocation of resources. It increases the price paid by domestic consumers, leading to a welfare loss. It also increases the quantity supplied by domestic producers but creates inefficiency because the opportunity costs of production are greater than the imported goods. There are several arguments made in favor of tariffs: to protect infant industries, to maintain employment, and to avoid unfair competition due to cheap labor and foreign subsidies.

QUESTIONS FOR STUDY AND ANALYSIS

1. Suppose you have the following information concerning labor productivity in two countries, Frankton and Jadlowvonia. Labor is the only factor used in both countries to produce automobiles and cantaloupes. The numbers given in the table indicate the automobiles or cantaloupes produced by a unit of labor in each country.

---

*"Imported Quotas and the Automobile Industry: The Costs of Protectionism," *The Brookings Review,* Summer 1984, pp. 8–16.

Country	Automobiles	Cantaloupes
Frankton	1	300
Jadlowvonia	5	200

a. What is the opportunity cost of an automobile in Frankton? In Jadlowvonia? What is the opportunity cost of a cantaloupe in Frankton? In Jadlowvonia?
b. Which country has an absolute advantage in the production of automobiles? Cantaloupes?
c. Which country has a comparative advantage in the production of automobiles? Cantaloupes?

2. Suppose we have two countries (A and B) willing to engage in the exchange of a good. The domestic demand and supply schedules are given by the following equations. Note that $D_{a,b}$ is the quantity demanded for each country and $S_{a,b}$ is the quantity supplied at price $P_{a,b}$. (*Hint:* Solve this problem by graphing the demand and supply curves.)

Country A
$P_a = 100 - 5D_a$
$P_a = 0 + 5S_a$

Country B
$P_b = 200 - 5D_b$
$P_b = 0 + 20S_b$

a. If there is no trade between the two countries, what is the equilibrium price and quantity in each?
b. Which country will import the good and which will export?
c. What is the equilibrium price and quantity imported/exported in the international market? (*Hint:* Construct the excess demand and supply curves.)

3. Under what circumstances would a tariff be most appropriate? Explain.

4. If a tariff is imposed on Japanese automobiles imported into the United States, who is helped and who is hurt? Why? How?

5. In terms of the circular flow, discussed in Unit 3.1, and Keynesian economics, discussed in Section 4, would a balance of trade surplus or deficit increase the amount of national output in the circular flow? Explain.

REVIEW GLOSSARY

absolute advantage A condition in which one country can produce more output than another country with the same factors.

balance of trade The relationship between a country's exports and imports.

balance of trade deficit The balance of trade when a country imports more goods than it exports, and net exports are negative.

balance of trade surplus The balance of trade when a country exports more goods than it imports, and net exports are positive.

exports Domestically produced goods purchased by other countries.

imports Goods purchased from other countries by the domestic economy.

international trade The exchange of goods across national boundaries.

principle of comparative advantage A principle stating that trade between nations is beneficial to both if there is a difference in the relative opportunity costs. This principle means that even a country without an absolute advantage in the production of goods can engage in trade.

tariff A tax imposed on goods imported into a country. A tariff increases the price paid in the importing country and reduces the quantity imported.

UNIT 14.2

International Finance

In the previous unit we were concerned with the flow of goods and services between countries, or international trade. However, as this output flows in one direction, payment for the output flows in the other. In fact, trade between nations, unlike trade within a nation, almost always involves an exchange of different currencies. A consumer might pay for an imported good with domestic currency, but somewhere along the line, the foreign producer of the good must receive its own currency.

In this unit we examine this exchange of currency between countries. First, we discuss how international trade necessitates the exchange of currency, which takes place in the foreign exchange market. We also see that other reasons besides international trade lead to the exchange of currency. We then turn our attention to the price of currency, or the exchange rate, and the determinants of the exchange rate. And finally, we relate the concept of balance of payments to the concept of balance of trade introduced in the previous unit.

INTERNATIONAL TRADE AND FOREIGN EXCHANGE

Recall that international trade leads to the exchange of currencies. For example, General Motors is glad to accept U.S. dollars as payment for an automobile purchased by a Kansas wheat farmer because it can use the U.S. dollars to pay its factors of production. But what if the Kansas wheat farmer buys a Honda imported from Japan? The local Honda car dealer will undoubtedly accept U.S. dollars, as will the wholesaler who imports the car from the Japanese manufacturer. But the Japanese manufacturer must receive Japanese yen when selling to the importer because all of the Japanese autoworkers, landowners, suppliers of intermediate goods, and capital owners want yen. Clearly, the Japanese factors of production do not want to buy food or pay their rent with U.S. dollars. Likewise, General Motors, which also sells automobiles in England, West Germany, France, and Japan, is certainly not going to pay its workers in British pounds, German marks, French francs, or Japanese yen. Somewhere along the line, U.S. dollars must be converted to Japanese yen.

Suppose the wholesaler importing the Honda sells it to dealers for U.S. dollars but pays the Japanese manufacturer in yen. Therefore, the importer needs to convert U.S. dollars received from this sale into Japanese yen. In other words, the importer has a demand for Japanese yen and is willing to buy it with U.S. dollars. This means that when one country imports goods from another, it also demands the foreign country's currency.

This is also the case if a Japanese autoworker buys bread made with U.S. wheat. While the Japanese autoworker pays for the bread with Japanese yen, ultimately the Kansas farmer is paid for the wheat with U.S. dollars. When Japan imports U.S. wheat, it has a demand for U.S. dollars. Figure 14.2.1 illustrates the relationship between the exchange of goods between countries and the subsequent need for the exchange of currencies.

The upper half of the diagram depicts the flow of goods from Japan to the United States. Initially, the goods are purchased with U.S. dollars, but they are subsequently exchanged for Japanese yen. The lower half of the diagram depicts the flow of goods from the United States to Japan. Once again, they are initially paid for with domestic Japanese yen but ultimately exchanged for U.S. dollars.

The exchange of U.S. dollars for Japanese yen occurs in the foreign exchange market, which is the focus of this unit. **Foreign exchange** is the term one country uses in reference to all currency other than its own. Therefore, the **foreign exchange market** is the market in which countries trade

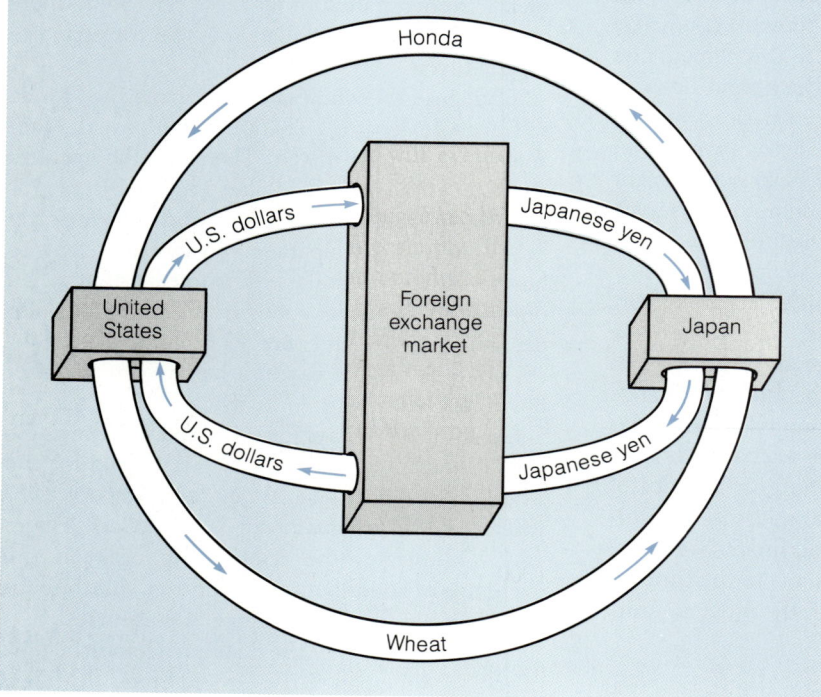

Figure 14.2.1

International Trade and Foreign Exchange

Underlying the exchange of goods and services between nations is the exchange of currency. Since countries use different currencies, when one country exchanges goods with another, one currency must be exchanged for the other. If the United States buys a good from Japan, the buyers pay for the good with U.S. dollars, but Japanese producers need to be paid in Japanese yen, requiring the exchange of dollars for yen.

domestic currency for foreign currency. It is where Japan trades yen for dollars, the United States trades dollars for yen, France trades francs for deutsche marks, and England trades pounds for pesos.

THE FOREIGN EXCHANGE MARKET

A market for the exchange of currency is slightly different from many other markets we have seen in this text. In most markets, currency is exchanged for goods, making it easy to determine which side of the market is supplying the good and which is demanding it. But in the foreign exchange market, currency is exchanged for currency, which implies not only that two markets are contained in one but also that the two markets are really mirror images of each other. To see why this is the case, let's look at the market for Japanese yen.

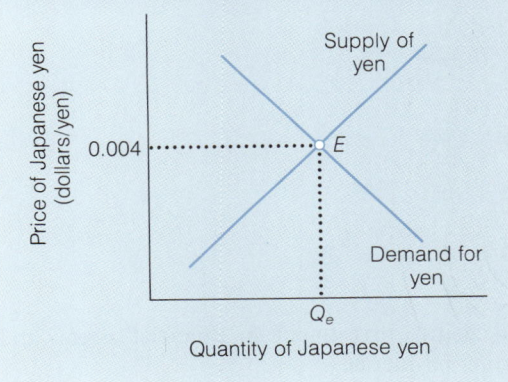

Figure 14.2.2

The Foreign Exchange Market

The foreign exchange market is the market in which countries trade domestic currency for foreign currency. A country demands foreign currency in order to pay for goods imported from other countries. If the price of foreign currency rises, then the price of imports rises, and the demand for foreign currency falls. An increase in the exchange rate increases the supply of foreign currency because foreign countries are willing to supply more of their currency for our currency.

The Demand for Foreign Exchange

We have already seen that Japanese yen are demanded by the United States in order to buy Japanese goods; this demand for yen can be embodied in a demand curve like the one depicted in Figure 14.2.2. As with any good, the price of yen is expressed in terms of dollars per yen on the vertical axis. As the price increases, the quantity of yen demanded declines. Why?

Suppose the price per yen is $0.004. That is, one yen costs four-tenths of a cent, or $1 buys 250 yen. At this price of yen, a Honda that costs 2.5 million yen in Japan (ignoring transportation costs) costs $10,000 in U.S. currency. But if the price of yen doubles to $0.008 per yen, the $1 can buy only 125 yen. This means that the Honda now costs $20,000 in the U.S. currency. Since the yen is demanded in order to buy imports from Japan, an increase in the price of yen leads to an increase in the price of the Japanese imports. And when the price of a good increases, the quantity of the good demanded declines, as does the quantity of yen demanded. Therefore, the demand curve for yen has a negative slope.

The Supply of Foreign Exchange

In exchange markets, the supply of a currency really represents the other side of demand. Recall what happened when Japan bought wheat from the United States. To pay the U.S. farmers, Japan needed U.S. dollars, which it obtained by exchanging Japanese yen. In effect, as Japan demanded U.S. dollars, it offered Japanese yen in supply. The demand for one currency in the foreign exchange market is always accompanied by the supply of another.

In Figure 14.2.2 the supply curve of yen is positively sloped because as the price of yen increases, Japan is willing to exchange more yen for dollars. For example, suppose that wheat sells for $4 per bushel in the United States. If the price of yen is $0.004, then each bushel of wheat costs 1000 yen. But if the price of yen increases to $0.008, then each bushel of wheat now costs only 500 yen. Therefore, Japan demands more wheat. To pay for the wheat, Japan supplies more yen, and exchanges them for more U.S. dollars.

Two Markets in One

The market for yen in this example is the mirror image of the market for dollars. As the United States demands yen, it supplies dollars. As Japan demands dollars, it supplies yen. Panel a of Figure 14.2.3 depicts the market for yen. Assume once again that the price per yen is $0.004 per yen and the quantity of yen exchanged is 100,000. Panel b depicts the market for dollars, in which the price

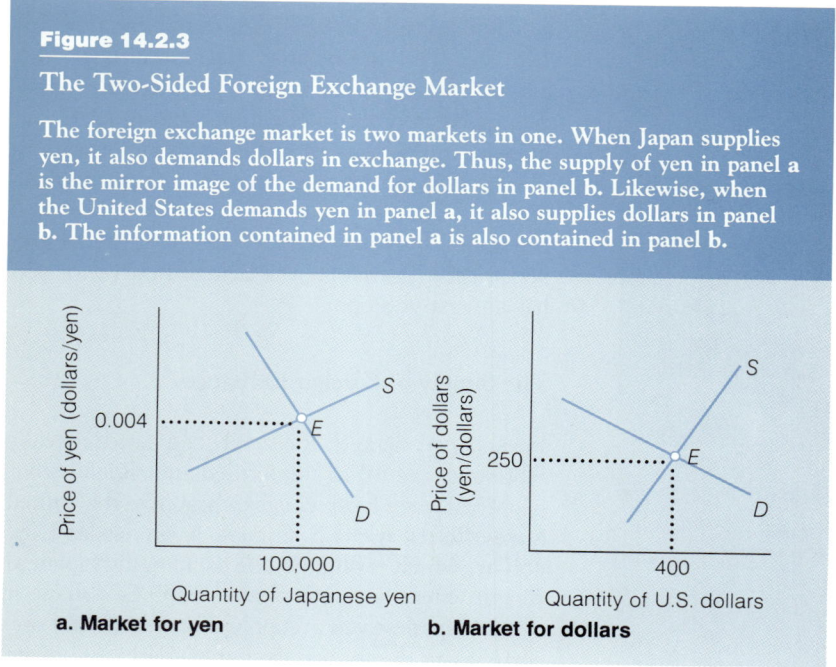

Figure 14.2.3

The Two-Sided Foreign Exchange Market

The foreign exchange market is two markets in one. When Japan supplies yen, it also demands dollars in exchange. Thus, the supply of yen in panel a is the mirror image of the demand for dollars in panel b. Likewise, when the United States demands yen in panel a, it also supplies dollars in panel b. The information contained in panel a is also contained in panel b.

a. Market for yen

b. Market for dollars

is 250 yen per dollar, or precisely the inverse of the price of yen. If four-tenths of a cent buys 1 yen, then $1 buys 250 yen. The quantity of dollars exchanged in panel b is 400. In essence, $400 are exchanged for 100,000 yen. The ratio of the two quantities is the price (0.004 = $400/100,000 yen and 250 = 100,000 yen/$400). All of the information in panel a, the market for yen, is also contained in panel b, the market for dollars.

Additional Sources of Foreign Exchange Demand and Supply

International trade constitutes an important part of a foreign exchange market. While selling exports and buying imports requires the exchange of one currency for another, at least three other reasons exist for demanding a foreign currency (and also supplying domestic currency): investment in physical capital, investment in financial assets, and transfer payments.

If General Motors builds an assembly plant in West Germany, it needs German marks to pay construction workers, buy raw materials, and so on. Thus, any foreign investment in physical capital requires the country's currency, in the same way that importing goods requires the country's currency. Likewise, the purchase of financial assets such as stocks and bonds in another country requires foreign exchange. A German resident who wants to buy IBM stock on the New York Stock Exchange would find it necessary to use U.S. dollars rather than deutsche marks. Also, the transfer of money from people and businesses in one country to another creates a demand for foreign currency. For example, if you send your Swedish Uncle Swen $100, he will exchange it for Swedish kronor. Transfers of currency between people in different countries resemble the purchase of goods in their effect on the demand for foreign exchange. The only difference is that no goods or services are received for the payment.

THE EXCHANGE RATE

What we have been calling the price of currency in previous discussions is more commonly known as the exchange rate. The **exchange rate** is the price of one currency in terms of another, so called because it is the rate at which one currency is exchanged for another.

Table 14.2.1 lists the exchange rates between the U.S. dollar and several other currencies. The exchange rates indicate the amount of each currency that can be purchased for $1. The inverse of each number gives the price, stated in dollars, for each currency. For example, $1 in U.S. currency can be purchased for 0.7225 British pounds, and a Swiss franc can be sold to the bank for $0.44 (the inverse of 2.2962).

At this point, two concepts should be defined as they relate to the exchange rate. The first is appreciation. **Appreciation** occurs when one unit of a currency can buy more of another currency. If every exchange rate in Table 14.2.1 is cut in half, then the U.S. dollar appreciates with respect to the other currencies because the price of each currency is less and a dollar can buy more of each. When a currency appreciates, it becomes easier (cheaper) to buy imports from the other countries. Therefore, appreciation of currency is not necessarily good for the domestic economy, even though it makes goods cheaper for consumers. Since more goods are imported, there are fewer exports and thus a lower GNP.

A currency can also depreciate. **Depreciation** occurs when one unit of a currency can buy less of another currency. If every number in Table 14.2.1 doubles, then the U.S. dollar depreciates with respect to the other currencies, because a dollar can buy less of each currency. Imports are relatively more expensive, but exports to the other countries are relatively cheaper. Therefore, a depreciating currency is more desirable to domestic producers even though consumers have fewer imports.

Every time one currency appreciates, another currency necessarily depreciates. If the exchange rate for a British pound rises from $1.39 to $1.50, the U.S. dollar depreciates with respect to the pound, while the pound appreciates with respect to the dollar. Many times, one currency depreciates with respect to a second currency but appreciates with respect to a third.

Table 14.2.1

Exchange Rates of Foreign Currencies and U.S. Dollars, August 1985

The exchange rate indicates the price of one currency in terms of another currency, in this case between U.S. dollars and other currencies. In August 1985, the price of $1 in U.S. currency was 0.7225 British pounds, 8.5323 French francs, or 1873.51 Italian lira. The inverse of each rate indicates the price, in dollars, for one unit of each foreign currency.

Currency	Exchange Rate per U.S. Dollar
British pound	0.7225 pounds
Canadian dollar	1.3575 dollars
Chinese (PR) yuan	2.9093 yuan
French franc	8.5323 francs
Irish pound	1.1143 pounds
Italian lira	1873.51 lira
Japanese yen	237.46 yen
Mexican peso	339.78 pesos
Norwegian krone	8.2487 kroner
Swedish krona	8.3106 kronor
Swiss franc	2.2962 francs
West German deutsche mark	2.7937 marks

Source: Federal Reserve System, Board of Governors, *Federal Reserve Bulletin*, November 1985.

A second pair of concepts we need to consider are floating and fixed exchange rates. A **floating exchange rate** is an exchange rate determined by the forces of supply and demand in the foreign exchange market. A **fixed exchange rate** is an exchange rate set by the government. A floating exchange rate, like any other unrestricted price, reaches equilibrium at the intersection of the supply and demand curves. But what are the determinants that cause the foreign exchange market to move to a new equilibrium?

The Determinants of the Exchange Rate

Three of the most important factors affecting a floating exchange rate are purchasing-power parity, interest rate, and performance of the economy.

Purchasing-Power Parity In the long run, exchange rates are primarily determined by equality in the purchasing power of each country's currency. Suppose that the United States and Canada both export wheat throughout the world. The price of wheat in the United States is $4, and the price of wheat in Canada is 5 Canadian dollars. Under these circumstances, if the exchange rate is anything other than $0.8 per Canadian dollar (which is $\frac{4}{5}$), then one country is able to sell wheat in the world market at a lower price.

For example, if the exchange rate is $0.5 per Canadian dollar, then the price of Canadian wheat is $2.50 in U.S. dollars. The lower exchange rate makes Canadian wheat relatively cheaper than U.S. wheat. Therefore, someone planning to buy U.S. wheat for $4 is better off trading the $4 for 8 Canadian dollars and buying 1.6 bushels of Canadian wheat at 5 Canadian dollars per bushel. By contrast, an exchange rate above $0.8 makes U.S. wheat relatively cheaper. Note that in the long run, the exchange rate is equal to the ratio of prices in the two countries. If the price of wheat in the United States increases from $4 to $4.50, then the exchange rate increases to $0.90 per Canadian dollar (4.5/5).

Purchasing-power parity indicates that exchange rates in the long run are determined by relative prices. In particular, the exchange rate changes when the rate of inflation in one country is substantially higher than in another. If the rate of inflation in the United States is 8 percent per year, and in West Germany it is 5 percent, the exchange rate (dollars per mark) should increase by 3 percent per year.

Interest Rate A second determinant that is more important for short-run changes in the exchange rate are relative interest rates. If the interest rate in the United States increases relative to the interest rate in Japan, Japanese investors find it more profitable to buy financial assets in the United States, thus increasing the demand for U.S. dollars relative to Japanese yen. Likewise, U.S. investors find it less profitable to invest in Japanese financial capital, which also increases the demand for dollars relative to yen. As a result, the dollar appreciates relative to the yen, and the exchange rate in yen per dollar increases.

Economic Performance A country's currency depreciates if its economy is growing relatively faster than other economies in the world. A growing economy demands more imports from other countries and more foreign exchange; thus, its currency depreciates. However, growth in foreign countries means they demand more of our domestic exports, which causes our country's currency to appreciate in response to the increased demand.

BALANCE OF PAYMENTS

The **balance of payments** is the relationship between the demand for and the supply of a country's currency. The demand includes currency used to purchase the country's exports, to invest in the country's physical and financial capital, and for transfers into the country. The supply is based on imports purchased from other countries, investments in other countries, and transfers to other countries. The balance of payments is based on all economic transactions between one country and other countries that involve the exchange of currency.

If a country has a floating exchange rate, determined by the forces of supply and demand, then demand and supply are equal. However, if it has a fixed exchange rate, set by the government, then demand and supply need not be equal. A fixed exchange rate can lead to a balance of payments deficit or surplus.

If the exchange rate is fixed above the equilibrium rate, the **balance of payments deficit** means the quantity of currency supplied is greater than the quantity demanded. This is illustrated in Figure 14.2.4. The equilibrium exchange rate between dollars and pounds is $1.40. If the actual exchange rate is $1.50, there is a balance of payments deficit. However, note that usually when the supply in a market is greater than the demand, a surplus exists. Why then is this considered a deficit?

The supply of pounds in Figure 14.2.4 is the amount of pounds people in England are exchanging for other currencies. They trade British pounds for yen to buy Japanese Hondas, for dollars to invest in U.S. factories, and for francs to send to relatives living in France. The demand for pounds is the amount of pounds other countries need in order to buy British goods, invest in British factories, and transfer to British residents. Here, more pounds are offered for sale than are purchased, which is where the fixed exchange rate comes in.

The quantity of currency sold must equal the quantity demanded. For the government to maintain the fixed exchange rate above the equilibrium rate, it must buy up any of its currency not demanded by foreigners, or currency equal to the amount AB in Figure 14.2.4. It pays for this currency with stocks of foreign currency or gold that it keeps as reserves. As long as it fixes the exchange rate above the equilibrium rate, it continues to lose reserves and incur a deficit, not of currency but of reserves that are being used to buy up the extra currency.

A **balance of payments surplus** exists when the demand for the country's currency is greater than the supply. England has a balance of pay-

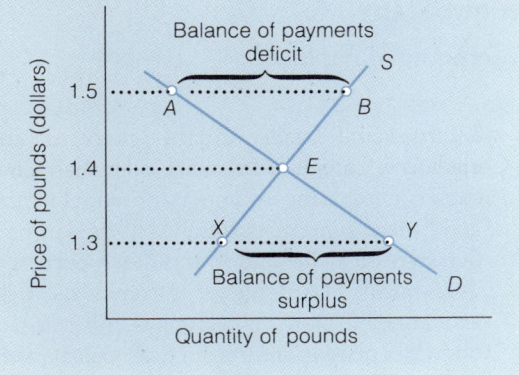

Figure 14.2.4

Balance of Payments Deficits and Surpluses

A balance of payments deficit occurs when the exchange rate is fixed above the market exchange rate. If a country fixes the exchange rate above equilibrium, it must buy a larger amount of foreign currency relative to the amount of domestic currency demanded by foreign countries. Since foreign countries do not want the domestic currency, the foreign currency must be purchased with gold or financial assets. A deficit of payments is created as financial assets flow out of the country. With a balance of payments surplus financial assets are flowing into the country, since the exchange rate is fixed below the market equilibrium.

ments surplus if it fixes the exchange rate below the equilibrium rate at $1.30. Since demand is greater than supply, to equalize transactions and keep the exchange rate fixed, the government needs to sell British pounds. In return, it builds up its reserves of other currencies or gold, thus running a surplus.

While the balance of trade represents an important component in the balance of payments, it is only part of the foreign exchange market. When imports are greater than exports, a country is running a balance of trade deficit. If no investments, transfers, or other transactions take place, a balance of payments deficit will also occur. But the relationship ends there.

A balance of trade surplus or deficit simply depends on the flow of goods between countries, and a country's exports need not equal its imports. The balance of payments is determined by the exchange rate. Recall that a floating exchange rate keeps demand and supply in the foreign exchange market equal. A balance of payments surplus or deficit occurs because of a fixed exchange rate. Therefore, with a floating exchange rate, a balance of trade surplus or deficit can occur without a balance of payments deficit or surplus. Likewise, a fixed exchange rate invariably leads to a balance of payments deficit or surplus, regardless of the balance of trade.

IN SUMMARY
International Finance

- International trade usually involves the exchange of two different currencies. Consumers purchasing an import initially buy the good with domestic currency, but foreign producers need to be paid in their own currency. This means the domestic currency must be exchanged for foreign currency. This transaction takes place in the foreign exchange market.

- In the foreign exchange market, currency is exchanged for currency. Thus, the demand for one currency is related to the supply of the other. If the price of a currency goes up, the quantity demanded falls and the quantity supplied rises. The market for one currency is the mirror image of the market for the other currency.

- International trade is an important reason for the exchange of currency. Three other notable reasons are investment in foreign physical capital, investment in foreign financial capital, and transfers to foreign residents.

- The exchange rate is the price of one currency in terms of another. One currency appreciates if it can buy more of another and depreciates if it can buy less of another. A floating exchange rate is determined by market forces. A fixed exchange rate is determined by the government. A floating exchange rate is determined in the long run by purchasing-power parity. In the short run the exchange rate is influenced by relative interest rates and relative growth rates between economies.

- The balance of payments is the relationship between the demand and supply of a country's currency. If the government fixes the exchange rate, it can have a balance of payments deficit or surplus. A deficit exists if supply is greater than demand, causing the country to lose part of its reserves of gold and foreign currency. A surplus exists if demand is greater than supply, causing the country to increase its reserves. A surplus or deficit does not occur with a floating exchange rate.

QUESTIONS FOR STUDY AND ANALYSIS

1. Explain how international trade is related to the exchange of currency. Can international trade occur without the exchange of currency? (Recall the purchase of Manhattan by the Dutch.)

2. How can a fixed exchange rate cause balance of payments problems? How would a floating exchange rate eliminate these problems?

3. Suppose the exchange rate between U.S. dollars and Swedish kronor is 12.5 cents per krona. That is, 1 krona costs 12.5 cents, or $1 in U.S. currency can buy 8 kronor.
   a. If the price of a U.S. computer is $2000, according to purchasing-power parity, what should be the price, in kronor, of a Swedish computer?
   b. If the interest rate in the United States is 10 percent but it increases from 10 to 15 per-

cent in Sweden, what is likely to happen to the exchange rate?

c. If the growth rate of output is 5 percent in Sweden but the United States is in a recession and the growth rate is −2 percent, what is likely to happen to the exchange rate?

d. If the exchange rate increases to 15 cents per krona, which currency appreciates and which depreciates?

4. Who benefits when the dollar appreciates in value? Who loses when the dollar appreciates in value?

5. In terms of Keynesian economics, as discussed in Section 4, which is more likely to increase national output, depreciation or appreciation of domestic currency? Explain.

REVIEW GLOSSARY

appreciation When one currency can buy more of another currency.

balance of payments The relationship between the demand for and the supply of a country's currency. A fixed exchange rate can lead to a balance of payments deficit or surplus.

balance of payments deficit When the quantity of currency supplied is greater than demand. A balance of payments deficit causes a country to lose reserves.

balance of payments surplus When the quantity of currency demanded is greater than supply. A balance of payments surplus causes a country to gain reserves.

depreciation When one currency can buy less of another currency.

exchange rate The price of one currency in terms of another.

fixed exchange rate An exchange rate determined by the government.

floating exchange rate An exchange rate determined by the forces of supply and demand. A floating exchange rate is primarily determined by three factors. The first is purchasing-power parity, which states that exchange rates are determined in the long run by relative rates of inflation. The second is the interest rate, which states that relative interest rates influence the exchange rate in the short run. The third is economic performance, which states that relative rates of economic growth affect the exchange rate in the short run.

foreign exchange The term one country uses in reference to all currency other than its own.

foreign exchange market The market in which countries trade domestic currency for foreign currency. In the foreign exchange market, since currency is exchanged for currency, each currency has its own market. However, the market for one currency is the mirror image of the market for the other.

UNIT 14.3

Economic Growth

In this unit we return to a topic that was first introduced in Unit 1.5, economic growth. **Economic growth is the continuous increase in the economy's ability to produce goods and services over time.** Quite simply, economic growth occurs when the economy's full employment level of output is increased; the importance of this growth cannot be overemphasized. With economic growth, the economy has more goods and services available for the satisfaction of consumers' wants and needs, which is the economy's primary function. In essence, economic growth means that the economy is getting closer to solving the economic problem of scarcity.

First, we consider the nature of economic growth, as embodied in outward shifts of the production possibilities frontier and rightward shifts of the aggregate supply curve. We also discuss why economic growth does not necessarily mean a country is better off. We then turn our attention to the causes of economic growth. In particular, we isolate the two basic dimensions of the factors of production—quantity and quality—and see how these dimensions relate to labor, capital, and land. And finally, we examine the costs associated with economic growth.

THE NATURE OF ECONOMIC GROWTH

Recall that economic growth involves the continual outward shifting of the production possibilities frontier over time, as depicted in panel a of Figure 14.3.1. The production possibilities frontier is the boundary indicating the amount of output that can be produced if the factors of production are fully employed. As this frontier shifts outward from A to B to C, the economy is able to produce more output. This is the basic process of economic growth.

However, economic growth is only a reflection of the ability to produce output and does not indicate the amount of output actually produced. As we saw throughout Part II, actual production also depends on aggregate demand; this is more clearly reflected by the aggregate market depicted in panel b. As the aggregate supply curve shifts rightward from AS_a to AS_b to AS_c, the full employment level of output increases from Y_a to Y_b to Y_c, and economic growth occurs. However, note that the actual level of output remains at Y_1 if aggregate demand does not change.

Even if aggregate demand is sufficient to take advantage of the economy's increased production, this does not mean people are better off or closer to solving the economic problem. Although the total availability of goods and services is important, the number of people using the output to satisfy wants and needs must also be considered.

In this light, we need to make a distinction between real GNP and per capita real GNP. Real GNP is the gross national product of the economy after adjusting for inflation. Or more specifically, **real GNP is the total market value of all final goods and services produced in the economy in a given period of time, expressed in constant dollars. Per capita real GNP is the average real gross national product per person in the economy.** Per capita real GNP is found by dividing real GNP by the number of people in the economy and is often referred to as the standard of living.

In terms of the economic problem, per capita real GNP is more informative than real GNP. For example, if real GNP increases by 5 percent each year over a ten-year period, the economy is clearly experiencing economic growth. However, if the population of the economy also increases by 5 percent over this period, there is no change in per capita real GNP. In effect, the additional production is claimed by the additional members of the economy. On average, no one in the economy would have any more goods and services today than he or she did ten years ago. While the overall econ-

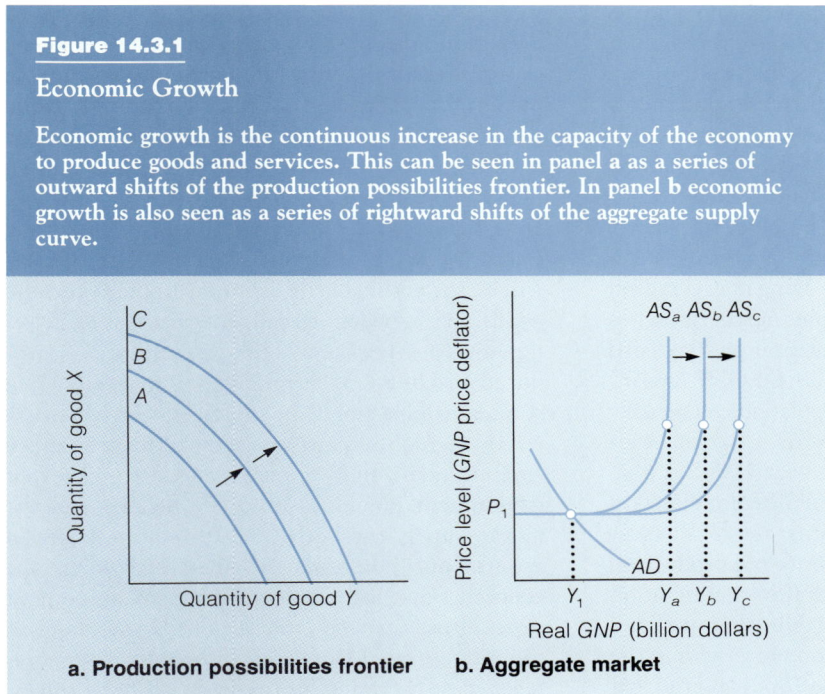

Figure 14.3.1

Economic Growth

Economic growth is the continuous increase in the capacity of the economy to produce goods and services. This can be seen in panel a as a series of outward shifts of the production possibilities frontier. In panel b economic growth is also seen as a series of rightward shifts of the aggregate supply curve.

a. Production possibilities frontier

b. Aggregate market

omy has grown, people are no closer to solving the economic problem.

However, if real GNP increases by 5 percent while the population increases by only 2 percent, then per capita real GNP increases by 3 percent. This means that, on average, people in the economy have more goods and services available to solve the economic problem and a higher standard of living. In terms of economic growth, keep in mind that growth contributes to a higher standard of living but does not necessarily guarantee one.

THE SOURCES OF ECONOMIC GROWTH

The two basic sources of economic growth are quantity and quality of the factors of production. The production possibilities frontier and aggregate supply curve can shift because the economy has a larger amount of labor (including entrepreneurship), capital, and/or land. In addition to the quantity of the factors, increases in the quality of the factors is also an important source of economic growth.

Factor Quantities

Economic growth can occur because there are more factors of production in the economy. Within this context, there are seven items associated with economic growth that we want to consider: population, labor force participation, investment, saving, social overhead capital, exploration, and land reclamation. The first two factors affect the quantity of labor, the next three affect the quantity of capital, and the last two affect the quantity of land.

Population An economy with a larger population has potentially more labor, and thus more output can be produced. A country's population can increase in two ways, natural increases and immigration. Natural increases occur when more people are being born than are dying. Obviously, natural increases in population do not immediately contribute to economic growth because the newly arrived members of the country are young children. Moreover, those who are dying may very well have been part of the labor force. Furthermore, as the population increases, a greater output is needed to maintain the same per capita real *GNP*, meaning that natural increases in population *can* actually worsen an economy's attempt to solve the economic problem.

But immigration can have a different effect on the economy. While immigrants are of all ages, many are able to quickly enter into the production of output. Population increases from immigration often lead to increases in available labor and thus economic growth. Indeed, economic growth in the United States through all of the 1800s and the first half of the 1900s was spurred in large part by immigrants from Europe.

Labor Force Participation Although the size of the population contributes to the size of the labor force, as we saw in Unit 3.4, the entire population is not part of the economy's labor force. Historically, less than half of the population of the United States has been engaged in the production of goods and services. Those who are not part of the labor force are either too young or too old, are in the military, in hospitals, or in prisons, or simply choose not to work. Students and homemakers comprise the two largest groups of people who choose not to engage in the production of the economy's output.

In fact, if students and homemakers enter the labor force, then economic growth occurs, without an increase in the population. Traditionally, women have devoted their efforts to maintaining households, but in more recent times they have become more active members of the labor force, contributing significantly to the economic growth in recent years. Figure 14.3.2 presents the labor force participation rates for men and women over the past several decades. While the participation rate for men in the labor force has declined somewhat, the participation rate for women has increased noticeably.

Investment The greater the quantity of capital (factories, equipment, and structures), the greater will be the ability of the economy to produce more goods and services. Recall one of the key determinants of investment—the interest rate—introduced in Unit 4.3. A relatively low interest rate stimulates investment in capital goods, whereas a relatively high interest rate reduces investment in capital goods. In Sections 4 and 5 we saw that government purchases (and the deficit) and the money supply can both affect the interest rate. If government purchases are increased when the economy is at full employment, then investment expenditures can be crowded out by increases in the interest rate. Moreover, if the money supply is reduced or prevented from increasing fast enough, then investment also decreases because of the higher interest rate. Where earlier we were primarily concerned with the short-run effects on the economy of reduced output, here we focus on how the lack of investment inhibits long-run economic growth.

Saving In our study of the production possibilities frontier in Unit 1.5, we saw the tradeoff an economy experiences between consumption and capital goods. In essence, if the economy wants to have more capital in the future to shift the production possibilities frontier, then it must give up some consumption goods in the present. Based on our study of Keynesian economics in Section 4, we can state this process in slightly different terms. The amount of consumption that is given up by the economy represents nothing other than saving, which is channeled through financial markets and used by businesses for investment expenditures on capital goods.

If the economy is operating at or above full employment and it is fully utilizing its capital stock,

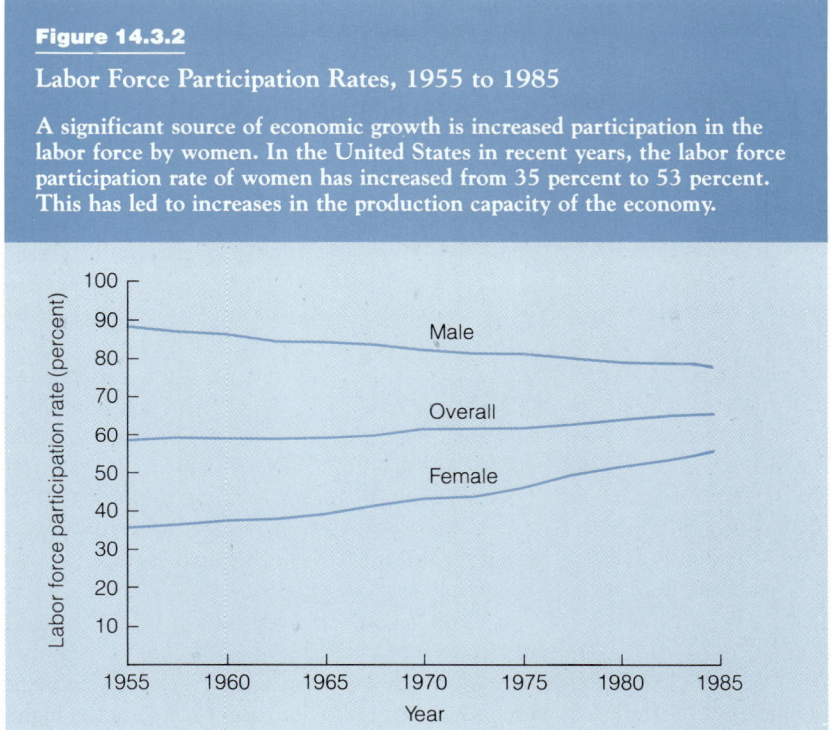

Figure 14.3.2

Labor Force Participation Rates, 1955 to 1985

A significant source of economic growth is increased participation in the labor force by women. In the United States in recent years, the labor force participation rate of women has increased from 35 percent to 53 percent. This has led to increases in the production capacity of the economy.

then the funds provided by additional saving can be used to increase the amount of capital and thus provide more of the output demanded. However, if the economy is operating below full employment, the additional saving can actually inhibit economic growth. Because the economy is not fully utilizing the existing capital stock, it does not need additional capital.

The differential impact of saving is illustrated in Figure 14.3.3. For aggregate demand AD_1, the economy is operating below full employment. An autonomous increase in saving means the aggregate demand curve shifts to the left, and the level of output decreases from Y_1. However, for aggregate demand AD_2, the economy is operating at full employment. The additional saving, while shifting the aggregate demand to the left, also shifts the aggregate supply curve to the right by allowing investment in the capital.

Social Overhead Capital In terms of the economy's stock of capital, we also need to consider social overhead capital. <u>Social overhead capital is the government-produced or government-subsidized portion of the economy's capital stock, consisting of transportation systems, water and sewage systems, energy and communication systems, and educational systems.</u> Social overhead capital incudes highways, railroads, airports, schools, universities, hydroelectric dams, and municipal sewage and water systems, each of which typically requires substantial amounts of capital. As discussed in Unit 9.3, because private firms are usually unable to profitably produce these types of goods and services, the

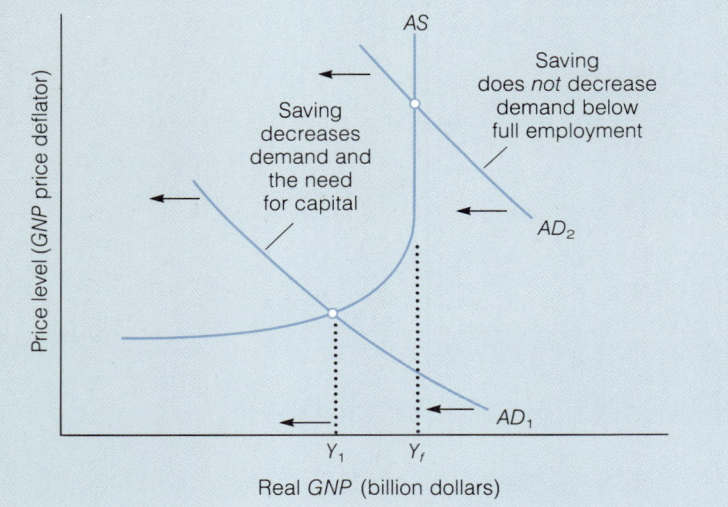

Figure 14.3.3

Aggregate Demand and Economic Growth

If the aggregate demand curve is AD_1, and the economy has unemployment, then additional saving is not needed for investment since existing production capacity is unused. Increased saving merely reduces aggregate demand and output. However, if the aggregate demand curve is AD_2, the economy is at full employment, and additional saving is needed to increase the production capacity of the economy. In this case, economic growth occurs.

government either directly produces the output or heavily subsidizes private firms to do so. This means that the government is involved in purchasing the necessary capital, which is financed through taxes.

Social overhead capital stimulates economic growth by making the rest of the economy's capital stock (the part that is privately owned and operated) more productive. For example, private manufacturers would certainly be less productive without streets, highways, and railroads on which to ship output to buyers. Likewise, electricity and communication, water, and sewage systems are necessary for the production of most goods and services. While additional social overhead capital does not guarantee economic growth, the lack of this capital is almost always a restrictive factor.

Exploration Without the raw materials provided by the land, the economy cannot produce material goods. Increases in output and economic growth can be obtained through increases in raw materials, but first, the natural resources must be located. The exploration for natural resources involves the same type of tradeoff as between consumption goods and capital goods. Exploration uses factors of production that cannot be used to produce consumption goods, meaning saving can also be channeled into exploration for minerals, fossil fuels, and other natural resources, in addition to being used for investment expenditures on capital goods.

Exploration for resources can also involve the discovery of new, unknown land. For example, most of the Spanish, English, French, and Dutch explorers of the 1400s through the 1600s went to North America, South America, Australia, and other places in search of raw materials (especially gold). The raw materials they discovered helped fuel the economic growth of Europe during this colonial period. And in the United States during the 1800s, the westward movement from the original thirteen colonies led to the discovery of vast resources, including productive agricultural land, grazing land, coal, and petroleum, that helped stimulate economic growth through most of the 1900s.

Land Reclamation The quantity of land can be increased through land reclamation. This process can range from land reclaimed from the sea through the use of dikes in the Netherlands to jungles cleared of vegetation in Brazil. Whatever the means, the result is more land to use in the production of output.

Factor Qualities

Factor qualities (especially the productivity of the factors) represent another important source of economic growth. Note that the *quality* of a factor increases if the same *quantity* is able to produce more output. Over the past hundred years, the quality of factors has made a major contribution to economic growth, especially in terms of technology and human capital.

Technology The level of technology determines how the economy combines its existing factors in the production of output. Technology essentially constitutes the current knowledge concerning the production of goods and services. In many cases the technology is embodied in the capital goods. For example, an aluminum alloy might be discovered that is lighter and stronger than steel. Capital goods such as trucks or airplanes are made using this new aluminum alloy rather than steel. Since these vehicles are lighter, they use less fuel, and thus produce more output with the same quantity of factors. Technology often involves combining factors in different ways. For example, agricultural production might be increased if more water and less fertilizer is applied to a crop.

Technological innovations and inventions have been a tremendous source of economic growth in the past hundred years. It is hard to imagine what our economy would be like today without inventions like the telephone, steam engine, radio, and computer. And increases in technology spread in a multiplicative fashion. How many technological developments have been made possible because of the speed and computational ability of the computer, or because of the existence of Edison's light bulb?

Human Capital A final item that affects the quality of the factors is human capital. <u>**Human capital is the training and education received by labor that improves its ability to produce goods and services**</u>. Earlier, we saw that technology is embodied in physical capital. By analogy, formal education or on-the-job training is embodied in labor as human capital. Through human capital, the same quantity of labor is able to produce more output, resulting in economic growth.

THE COSTS OF ECONOMIC GROWTH

In our discussion so far, economic growth has been cast in a generally favorable light, mainly because it is beneficial to the economy. Economic growth provides the goods and services used for the satisfaction of wants and needs, and thus moves the economy closer to solving the economic problem. However, economic growth is not without its costs. In fact, many people feel that the costs of growth, after some point, are greater than the benefits received. Four of the most important costs of economic growth are reduced consumption, pollution, resource depletion, and changes in lifestyles.

Reduced Consumption

Recall that many of the sources of economic growth involve investment in capital goods, social overhead capital, exploration, or human capital. But with any type of investment, the economy is foregoing current consumption as factors are diverted away from the production of consumption goods. And some people argue that the reduction in current consumption is too high a price to pay for the future consumption that results from the economic growth.

These arguments revolve around two basic points. First, the investment may not actually pay off in economic growth, as sometimes argued with the development of nuclear energy or space exploration. And because any investment gambles resources on uncertain future returns, some people argue that we should get the most out of life today and worry about the future when it gets here. Second, the people foregoing the consumption today will not be the people benefiting from the increased consumption in the future. Why should a childless, retired couple help support the education of schoolchildren since they are unlikely to benefit in any way from this education?

Pollution

As discussed in Unit 13.2, the discharge of waste products into the natural environment, or pollution, is an inherent part of the production. And when economic growth leads to greater production, it also leads to more pollution. Pollution is a problem because it generally reduces the level of society's welfare. While the production of output leads to the satisfaction of wants and needs, the pollution leads to the dissatisfaction of wants and needs. Some people argue that further economic growth reduces welfare through pollution more than it increases welfare through output.

Resource Depletion

Economic growth requires the raw materials extracted from the land in the production of goods. But as these materials are extracted, less remains for future production. If we use up the resources today, then we are depriving future generations of goods and services. It is argued therefore that less economic growth today will insure a longer period of future satisfaction for the human species.

The concept of resource depletion is directed particularly toward irreplaceable natural environments. That is, in many cases economic growth leads to the destruction of natural areas that can never be duplicated and the extinction of different species of plant and animal life. When these natural resources are destroyed, present and future generations lose the satisfaction that they might otherwise have had. Nor do we know what value future generations will place on these natural resources. For example, if the bacteria used to discover the polio vaccine had become extinct before this vaccine was discovered, society would probably have less welfare today. Likewise, a seemingly innocent plant may become a source of energy, a cure for cancer, or a new type of food. But if it becomes extinct, we may never know.

Changes in Lifestyles

And finally, economic growth invariably leads to changes in lifestyles. Some people argue that these changes in lifestyles and the loss of traditional cultural values are not worth the economic growth obtained. For example, the introduction of the automobile and other improvements in transportation have had a tremendous impact on the structure of the family. In the past, family members were unable to travel very far from home, so many generations of a family often lived close together. Now, with improved transportation, family members can easily spread throughout the country, and thus lose interaction and family ties. Another example is the family farm. With improvements in agricultural production, it is very difficult to profitably operate a small family-owned farm, so the lifestyle associated with the family farm can also be lost. Changes in lifestyles, while important in this country, are even more significant in many developing countries, where people have lived for hundreds of years of relatively unchanged lifestyles. People in these countries often value their existing lifestyles more than any increased satisfaction achieved through economic growth.

IN SUMMARY

Economic Growth

- Economic growth is the process of continuously increasing the economy's ability to produce goods and services. This is seen as either an outward shift in the production possibilities frontier or a rightward shift in the aggregate supply curve. However, economic growth only reflects the economy's capacity to produce output. Actual production also depends on aggregate demand.

- Economic growth is measured by real gross national product. However, real GNP does not necessarily indicate whether the economy is closer to solving the economic problem. Even though output increases, an increase in the size of the population might mean that the output per person is the same or even less. It is also instructive to look at per capita real GNP, or the standard of living.

- Economic growth can result from an increase in the quantities of the factors of production. Two sources of economic growth that affect the quantity of labor are increases in population and the labor force participation rate. Three sources that affect the quantity of capital are investment expenditures, saving, and social overhead capital. And two sources that affect land are exploration and land reclamation.

- A second important category of sources of economic growth is the quality of the factors of production. One source is the level of technology. A second source is human capital. Each of these sources leads to increases in the quality of the factors of production.

- Economic growth benefits the economy mainly by providing more goods and services, thus moving the economy closer to solution of the economic problem of scarcity. However, economic growth is not without its costs. The four most important costs of economic growth are reduced consumption in the present, pollution of the environment, depletion of resources, and changes in lifestyles.

QUESTIONS FOR STUDY AND ANALYSIS

1. What is the relationship between economic growth, real GNP, per capita real GNP, and the economic problem?

2. For each of the following items, indicate which of the sources of economic growth based on factor quantities is involved, and why. Also indicate whether the item leads to more or less economic growth.
   a. Women resume their traditional roles as housewives and mothers.
   b. The average propensity to consume declines.
   c. There is an increase in the amount of funds used for highway construction.
   d. The Great Lakes are drained and used as farmland.
   e. The federal government eliminates tax deductions currently available for the purchase of capital goods.
   f. Transfer payments to the poor are reduced.
   g. The interest rate declines.

3. For each of the following items, indicate which of the sources of economic growth based on factor qualities is involved, and why. Also indicate whether the item leads to more or less economic growth.
   a. Several of the best Soviet scientists defect to the United States.
   b. The salary paid to public schoolteachers is reduced.
   c. A new, inexpensive energy source for powering automobiles is discovered.
   d. NASA, the space agency, decides to make

an all-out effort to put a manned colony in space.

4. An important aspect of economic growth is reduced consumption today for more consumption tomorrow. Discuss whether or not you think it is appropriate for people to reduce their standard of living today so that people in the future can have a higher standard of living.

5. Discuss the role that the crowding-out effect, discussed in Unit 5.5, plays in economic growth.

6. Do you think economic growth is an effective way to control inflation? Explain.

REVIEW GLOSSARY

economic growth The continuous increase in the economy's ability to produce goods and services over time. Economic growth is seen as outward shifts in the production possibilities frontier and as rightward shifts in the aggregate supply curve. It is measured by changes in real GNP.

human capital The training and education received by labor that improves its ability to produce goods and services. Human capital leads to economic growth by increasing the quality of labor.

per capita real *GNP* The average real gross national product per person in the economy. Per capita real GNP is a better indicator of the economy's ability to solve the economic problem for each of its members. It is often used to indicate the standard of living.

real *GNP* The total market value of all final goods and services produced in the economy in a given period of time, expressed in constant dollars. Increases in real GNP can indicate if the economy is experiencing economic growth. However, real GNP does not necessarily indicate if people in the economy are better off or closer to solving the economic problem.

social overhead capital The government-produced or government-subsidized portion of the economy's capital stock, consisting of transportation, water and sewage, energy and communication, and educational systems. Social overhead capital is a necessary foundation for growth, but it is usually not profitably produced by private firms.

UNIT 14.4

Economic Development

In this unit we focus on the problems of economic development, particularly the lack of economic development that exists in many countries throughout the world. While the United States and other industrialized countries have experienced phenomenal rates of economic growth and development, many other countries have not. This disparity becomes a problem because millions of people throughout the world suffer low standards of living simply because they were born in the wrong country. Furthermore, the countries with lower levels of development are very aware that they are not enjoying the standards of living in other countries, which creates political turmoil and even war.

We begin by looking at the nature of economic development, and comparing it to economic growth. After examining the relative levels of development of countries throughout the world, we identify a series of key problems facing the less developed countries. And finally, we discuss several solutions that have been proposed to increase economic development.

THE NATURE OF ECONOMIC DEVELOPMENT

In this unit we are concerned with economic development rather than the more narrowly defined economic growth. **Economic development is the continuous increase in society's overall level of welfare over time**, whereas economic growth is the continuous increase in the economy's ability to produce goods and services over time. While economic growth represents an important part of economic development, it is not the only part. Economic growth means there are more goods and services available to satisfy people's wants and needs, but it does not necessarily mean a country is more developed. First, the production of goods and services provides only part of the satisfaction received by people. People also receive satisfaction from lifestyles, family ties, cultural traditions, and environmental quality, among other things. Second, total production does not indicate how much is available for each person. This is partly remedied by looking at per capita real output, which indicates the amount of goods and services available to each person in the economy. But even per capita real output does not accurately reflect the distribution of output. If output becomes more unequally distributed, even though per capita real output increases, then the overall level of welfare may be unaffected or may even decline.

ECONOMIC DEVELOPMENT THROUGHOUT THE WORLD

While economic growth and development are not synonymous, we are limited in our ability to measure economic development. Although per capita real output is an imperfect indicator of the level of economic development, it does provide a general indication.

Table 14.4.1 lists the per capita real *GNP* for selected countries throughout the world. Note the enormous range of values. At one extreme are the United States, Canada, France, Sweden, Switzerland, and West Germany, with per capita output of over $10,000 per year. At the other extreme are countries such as Bangladesh, Burma, Ethiopia, and Nepal, with per capita output of less than $200 per year. The different per capita outputs indicate that people in the United States have access to almost one hundred times more goods and services than people in Bangladesh have. This difference is reflected not only in the quantity of goods but also in their quality. For example, in the United States a person might prepare breakfast with several different electrical appliances, whereas a person in

Table 14.4.1

Per Capita Real *GNP* in Selected Countries, 1982

A major difference between MDCs and LDCs is the level of per capita real *GNP*. The United States, Canada, France, Sweden, Switzerland, and West Germany had per capita real *GNP* of over $10,000 in 1982. By contrast, Bangladesh, Burma, Ethiopia, and Nepal had per capita real *GNP* of less than $200.

Country	Per Capita Real *GNP* (1981 dollars)
More-developed countries	
United States	$12,482
Austria	8,686
Belgium	9,691
Canada	10,610
Czechoslovakia	9,001
France	10,531
Japan	9,774
Sweden	13,516
Switzerland	15,030
United Kingdom	8,954
West Germany	11,031
Less-developed countries	
Bangladesh	133
Burma	167
Egypt	621
Ethiopia	142
India	235
Indonesia	536
Kenya	374
Nepal	161
Pakistan	344
Sri Lanka	297
Uganda	813

Source: U.S. Bureau of the Census, *Statistical Abstract of the United States*, 1985.

Bangladesh might prepare breakfast over an open fire. The U.S. resident then commutes in the family car down a modern highway to work in a high-rise office building; the Bangladesh resident takes the ox cart down the dirt road to work in the fields.

Many other countries lie between the extreme levels of economic development embodied by the United States and Bangladesh. For purposes of discussion, however, it is convenient to separate the countries of the world into two types, less-developed countries and more-developed countries. A **less-developed country (LDC)** is a country with a relatively low standard of living and level of development. In general, most of the labor in LDCs is employed in the agricultural sector; very little labor is used to produce manufactured goods or services. By contrast, a **more-developed country (MDC)** is a country with a relatively high standard of living and level of development. In most MDCs a large portion of the population lives and works in cities, producing manufactured goods and services, and very little labor is employed in the agricultural sector. In fact, many of the more advanced MDCs tend to devote increasingly smaller shares of labor to manufactured goods and larger shares to services.

As with any two-tiered classification system, some overlap is possible. For example, many of the oil-rich countries, including Kuwait, Saudi Arabia, and the United Arab Emirates, have achieved relatively high levels of per capita output, matching many MDCs. But in other ways they resemble LDCs in their level of development.

Any classification difficulties aside, LDCs share many of the same problems. In this unit we focus on the problems of these LDCs. In particular, we want to see why many LDCs that seemed on the verge of higher levels of development for several decades have failed to do so.

PROBLEMS OF LDCs

Several distinct problems associated with LDCs result from the lack of economic development, which in turn restricts further development. These problems relate to population, income distribution, agricultural production, and capital.

Population

LDCs usually have a rapid rate of population growth, especially when compared to MDCs. Note in Table 14.4.2 that the annual rates of population growth for several MDCs are around 1 percent or less, whereas the rates of population growth for several LDCs are 3 percent or more.

While this difference may not seem significant, let's consider what would happen to two countries with equal population but differing rates of population growth, as illustrated in Table 14.4.3. In year zero both countries have equal populations of 100 people, but the rate of population growth in country A is 1 percent, while the rate of growth in country B is 3 percent. For the first few years little difference in population exists; in the first year country A has 101 people and country B has 103. But after 5 years, country A has 105 people and country B has 116 people. After 10 years country B has 24 more people, after 15 years it has 40 more people, and after 35 years country B has nearly twice as many people as country A.

The relatively high rates of growth in LDCs have a significant impact on the level of development. In country A real output needs to grow at only 1 percent each year to maintain a constant level of real per capita output. Any growth in output greater than 1 percent means each person in the country has more goods and services available, so development is likely to be greater. However, in country B real output needs to grow at 3 percent per year just to maintain a constant level of per capita output. In other words, the rate of economic growth must be greater in country B than country A just for B to maintain an equal standard of living.

The growth of population indicates why many LDCs are in big trouble. Not only are they less developed than other countries, but they have to work three times as hard (in terms of economic growth) to become more developed. However, once

Table 14.4.2
Population Growth Rates Throughout the World, 1980–1983

Another important difference between MDCs and LDCs is the rate of population growth. The rate of population growth in MDCs is typically 1 percent or less. However, in most LDCs the rate of growth is 2 to 3 percent.

Country	Population Growth Rate (percent)
More-developed countries	
United States	0.9
Austria	1.4
Belgium	0.1
Canada	1.1
Czechoslovakia	0.4
France	0.5
Japan	0.7
Sweden	0.1
Switzerland	0.4
United Kingdom	0.0
West Germany	0.0
Less-developed countries	
Bangladesh	3.1
Burma	2.5
Egypt	2.8
Ethiopia	1.7
India	2.1
Indonesia	2.1
Kenya	4.1
Nepal	2.5
Pakistan	3.3
Sri Lanka	1.8
Uganda	2.5

Source: U.S. Bureau of the Census, *Statistical Abstract of the United States*, 1985.

Table 14.4.3

A Comparison of Relative Population Growth Rates

Different rates of population growth mean countries need different rates of increase in production to maintain their standards of living. Country A needs to increase production by only 1 percent each year to keep per capita real *GNP* constant. Anything greater than 1 percent contributes to greater welfare. However, country B needs to increase production by 3 percent each year just to keep per capita real *GNP* constant.

Years	Country A—1 Percent Growth	Country B—3 Percent Growth
0	100.0	100.0
1	101.0	103.0
2	102.0	106.9
3	103.0	109.3
4	104.1	112.6
5	105.1	115.9
10	110.5	134.4
15	116.1	155.8
20	122.0	180.6
25	128.2	209.4
30	134.8	242.7
35	141.7	281.4
40	148.9	326.2

development does begin to take hold in a country, then the rate of population growth typically declines.

The greater population growth in LDCs than in MDCs is reflected in the demographic transition. The **demographic transition** is the process in which a country goes from a low rate of population growth to a high rate, then back to a low rate as the country develops. To see how the demographic transition works, consider the birth rate and the death rate. The **birth rate** is the number of people born per thousand population. In essence, the birth rate indicates how much the population is being increased through births. The **death rate** is the number of deaths per thousand population. The death rate indicates how much the population is being reduced by deaths. Immigration aside, the population of a country obviously increases if the birth rate is greater than the death rate. The relationship between birth and death rates plays the key role in the demographic transition.

Figure 14.4.1 illustrates this relationship. In panel a the vertical axis measures the birth and death rates in a country, and the horizontal axis measures the level of development in the country over time. Note at the far left of panel a that the birth and death rates are both very high and nearly equal, meaning the rate of population growth of the country in panel b is relatively low. The high death rate results from the general lack of medical care, the inability to prevent famine and disease, and numerous other related reasons. The high birth rate derives in part from the need for labor to work the fields.

This situation continues to exist up to t_1, when the death rate begins to decline. The decline in the death rate, without a comparable decline in the birth rate, means the population begins to rapidly increase. In this portion of the demographic transition the introduction of new technology, such as medicine, lowers the death rate but attitudes concerning large families in the agriculture setting have not changed. Moreover, in this stage large families are still valuable because most of the population continues to work in agriculture.

As development moves to level t_2, the death rate is relatively low, and the birth rate begins to decline. But the birth rate is still greater than the death rate, and the rate of growth in population in panel b is still relatively high. The birth rate declines as the population moves to urban areas and finds that large families are no longer needed to work the farms. Furthermore, the cultural attitudes concerning large families slowly change.

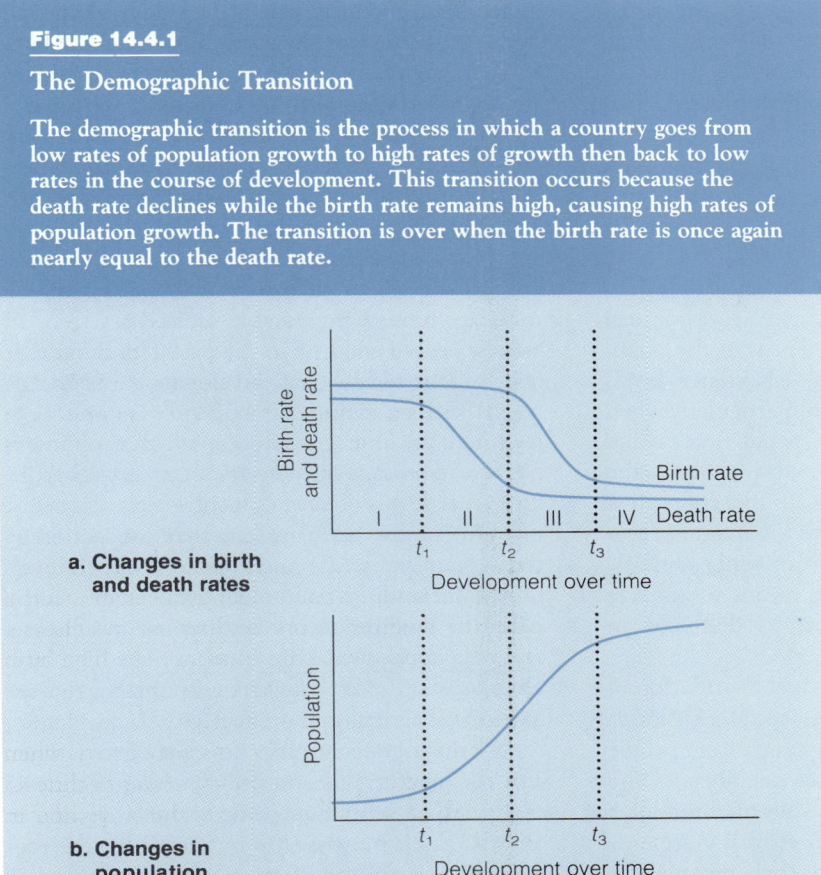

Figure 14.4.1

The Demographic Transition

The demographic transition is the process in which a country goes from low rates of population growth to high rates of growth then back to low rates in the course of development. This transition occurs because the death rate declines while the birth rate remains high, causing high rates of population growth. The transition is over when the birth rate is once again nearly equal to the death rate.

a. Changes in birth and death rates

b. Changes in population

Finally, at t_3 the demographic transition is complete. The birth rate has fallen to nearly the level of the death rate, and the rapid increase in population is over. Beyond t_3 the economy has reached the level of an MDC.

The problem facing most LDCs today is that they are in the phase of the demographic transition with low death rates and high birth rates. The birth rate is not likely to decline until a given country becomes more developed. Unfortunately, it cannot become more developed as long as the increased population continues to eat up increases in output brought about by economic growth. Although the MDCs throughout the world have already undergone this demographic transition, there is no guarantee that LDCs will follow the same pattern. In fact, they could be caught indefinitely in phase II, between t_1 and t_2.

Income Distribution

LDCs also usually have problems with the distribution of income. The nature and measurement of the distribution of income is discussed in detail in

Unit 11.4. In this unit we discuss *why* the distribution of income, or the manner in which income is distributed to members of the economy, is a problem for LDCs. If income is equally distributed, then everyone in the economy receives the same amount of income. If income is unequally distributed, then some members of the economy receive more income than others. Typically, LDCs have a less equal distribution of income than most MDCs.

An unequal distribution of income can lead to three types of problems. First, it can create political unrest and instability. If nine-tenths of the population are living at a minimal subsistence level, they can be driven to revolution, particularly when the remaining one-tenth of the population, which receives most of the income, also controls the political and economic systems. In this context, it is easy to see why LDCs embrace a communist philosophy of development, which prescribes revolution by the working class as a means to achieve higher levels of development, as discussed in Section 15.

Second, an extremely unequal distribution of income inhibits investment in capital. Although investment in capital generally comes from people with more income, if only a few members of the country have all of the income, they might indulge in personal consumption rather than investment. That is, the wealthy might use their incomes for large houses, imported automobiles, servants, and the latest in consumer goods rather than investing in factories or other productive capital.

Third, an unequal distribution often perpetuates itself. Those members of the economy with income are able to invest in physical and human capital, which generates even more income. However, those members without income cannot invest in the physical and human capital and thus are less able to raise their own levels of income.

Agricultural Production

A third problem associated with economic development in LDCs is reflected in the production of agricultural goods, which plays a key role in the development process. In many LDCs, families have to grow all of their own food merely to sustain themselves. Because the technology of agricultural production is very low, it takes five people to grow enough food to feed five people. Agricultural production is not able to supply food to people engaged in the production of other goods.

However, once the technology of agricultural production is improved, then five people working in agriculture might be able to feed six, ten, or twenty people engaged in the production of other goods. This means that development necessarily begins with agriculture. If a country is not able to feed nonagricultural workers, then the country is not able to produce the nonagricultural goods needed for higher levels of development.

One of the main reasons that production in the agricultural sector might be constrained, even though increases in technology are available, is the system of land tenure. A **land tenure system** is a system of land ownership in a country. The land tenure system often provides very little incentive to increase agricultural productivity by developing or adopting new technology. In some LDCs farmers rent the land and receive only a minimal amount of the output, with most going to the landlords. In other LDCs the ownership of land is highly fragmented, meaning one farmer has several tracts of land dispersed throughout the area; the farmer can waste a lot of time simply traveling back and forth between the separate tracts of land. Moreover, each tract is so small that it is impossible to apply more advanced production techniques involving tractors and other machinery.

Capital

A fourth problem experienced by most LDCs is the lack of capital. In Unit 14.3 we discussed the importance of capital to economic growth. The economic development of a country also depends on capital, not only physical capital, both privately owned and social overhead, but also human capital. All LDCs must forego current consumption in order to produce more capital and thus generate more output in the future.

Moreover, in terms of the demographic transition, if the rate of population growth is high, then development and per capita output is likely to be relatively low. But with very little output per person, then the average propensity to save is also very low, if not negative. And saving is needed for investment in these alternative forms of capital. Without additional capital, economic growth is relatively low, and per capita output increases very little (if at all) due to the population growth. Moreover, population growth is not likely to slow down until the birth rate drops from an increased level of development.

POLICIES FOR LDCs

Two basic types of policies can be applied to increase the level of development of LDCs. First, the rate of growth of output can be stimulated such that per capita output increases despite high rates of population growth. This policy is based on the proposition that the increased level of development will be reinforced through reductions in the birth rate. Second, the growth of population can be confronted directly. In this way, increases in total output will lead to greater increases in per capita output and development.

Technology Transfer

The first specific policy involves the transfer of existing technology from MDCs to LDCs so that the LDCs can improve their productivity and thus increase the level of per capita output. The problem with this particular approach is that the technology sent from the MDCs may not be appropriate for the LDCs. The technology developed in one country is designed for resources and factors of production that may not exist in the LDCs.

For example, because wheat production in the United States is based on large amounts of relatively flat land and a limited amount of labor, production techniques have been developed that depend on a lot of capital and very little labor. This type of production technology cannot be directly transfered to an LDC that has small tracts of land, hilly terrain, and an abundance of labor. Where in the United States one farmer can easily work eighty acres of land, in many LDCs eighty farmers might be working eighty acres of land. The use of the U.S. production techniques would put seventy-nine farmers out of work, which would be appropriate only if other industries wanted to employ them. Such is usually not the case.

The key concept in the transfer of technology is appropriate technology. **Appropriate technology is technology that is suited to the factors of production and resources of a particular country.** The transfer of an inappropriate technology in many cases can be worse than the transfer of no technology at all.

Direct Aid

Another policy to assist LDCs is direct aid, or transfer payments, in the form of medicine, funds, food, or other consumer goods. In the short run this policy might benefit a country in a crisis situation, such as a famine. However, in the long run this type of aid is likely to help very little, and in fact, it might even worsen the situation. This is especially true if the aid reduces the death rate without affecting the birth rate. With an increase in the growth rate of the population, the LDC might get stuck in the middle of the demographic transition.

Education and Training

A third policy is education and training, in which MDCs transfer human capital to the LDCs. This policy is crucial to the development of a country, regardless of what other policies are undertaken. Even the transfer of appropriate technology may be ineffective if people in the LDC do not know how to use the technology.

The biggest problem with education and training, like technology, is that it too may be inappropriate. For example, it is better to train someone in agronomy than astronomy. While astronomy may become important if the LDC gets to the stage of space exploration, in the meantime, someone trained to plant the crops most suitable for different types of soils is far more valuable. Likewise, a highly trained theoretical economist is less useful than one trained in urban planning, a lawyer is less useful than a mechanic, and so on.

Birth Control

The last policy is directed not at increasing the production of output but at population growth. With this policy, techniques of birth control and information on family planning are applied in an attempt to reduce the birth rate. The actual tools used to reduce the birth rate range from free contraceptives and abortions to taxes based on the number of children in the family. In many cases policies aimed at birth control are not very effective because children in LDCs represent a significant source of labor for the farm and also provide security for parents when the parents are no longer able to care for themselves.

IN SUMMARY
Economic Development

- Economic development, or rather the lack of economic development, is a serious problem in many countries throughout the world. While the United States and other industrialized countries have relatively high levels of development, other countries do not. This can lead to, and has led to, various political and economic conflicts.

- Economic development is not the same as economic growth. While economic growth is an increase in real GNP, economic development is an increase in the overall level of society's welfare. Economic development depends not only on per capita real output but also on cultural tradition, lifestyles, family ties, the natural environment, and the distribution of income.

- The problems experienced by LDCs include high rates of population growth, unequal distributions of income, low levels of agricultural productivity, and the lack of capital. The high rates of population growth are reflected in the demographic transition. The demographic transition indicates that the death rate declines before the birth rate, leading to relatively high rates of population growth as a country develops. The high rates of population growth make it very difficult to continue to increase the level of development.

- The income distribution in most LDCs is also highly unequal, leading to political problems and constraints on economic growth. Another problem is low levels of agricultural productivity, caused by the lack of technology and inefficient land tenure systems. A final problem is the lack of capital. Because an LDC has very little income, very little saving can be used for investment in capital.

- Policies for aiding LDCs include the transfer of technology, direct aid, education and training, and birth control. Technology transfer is helpful if it is appropriate technology, suited for the factors of production and resources in the LDCs. Direct aid is usually of little help except during crisis conditions, such as famines. Education and training is also very helpful, but like technology, it must be suited for the conditions in the LDCs. And birth control, aimed at limiting growth of the population, can be helpful for LDCs caught in the middle of the demographic transition.

UNIT 14.4 ▪ ECONOMIC DEVELOPMENT

QUESTIONS FOR STUDY AND ANALYSIS

1. Discuss three aspects of your daily life that are largely unrelated to your income or the quantities of goods and services you buy. Would you consider these important parts of your overall level of welfare? Explain.

2. Assume that you are a leader in an LDC that is caught in the middle of the demographic transition. Discuss the policies that you would implement to alleviate the problem of a high population growth rate.

3. Explain why the agricultural sector and agricultural production is the key to economic development for LDCs. What role does a country's land tenure system play in economic development?

4. Why is appropriate technology in the United States inappropriate technology for some LDCs? Discuss whether or not the following items are likely to be appropriate for most LDCs.
   a. Nuclear energy used to produce electricity
   b. Improved seed varieties
   c. An automobile factory
   d. A computerized communications network

REVIEW GLOSSARY

appropriate technology Technology that is suited to the factors of production and resources in a particular country. The direct transfer of technology used in an MDC may be unusable in an LDC because the factors of production and resources are different.

birth rate The number of people born per thousand population.

death rate The number of people dying per thousand population.

demographic transition The process in which a country goes from a low rate of population growth to a high rate then back to a low rate as the country develops. The demographic transition occurs because the death rate declines at an earlier level of development than the birth rate.

economic development The continuous increase in society's overall level of welfare over time. Economic development and economic growth are not the same. While economic growth contributes to development through the provision of additional goods and services, it is only one part of development. Per capita real GNP, rather than total real GNP, is a better measure of development, but it is also imperfect.

land tenure system A system of land ownership in a country. The land tenure system in an LDC can often inhibit development by preventing needed increases in agricultural productivity. This can occur because the farmers are not the owners and thus do not receive profits from increased production. Alternatively, this can occur because ownership of the land is fragmented, with one farmer owning several small pieces of land scattered many miles apart.

less-developed country (LDC) A country with a relatively low standard of living and level of development.

more-developed country (MDC) A country with a relatively high standard of living and level of development.

SECTION INQUIRY

The Third World Debt

A major problem facing many less-developed countries (LDCs) in the last half of the 1980s and into the 1990s is the repayment of borrowed funds. While LDCs have been borrowing funds from MDCs, especially the United States, since the 1940s, the energy problems during the 1970s accelerated borrowing on the parts of many countries. Higher energy prices together with generally stagnant economies forced many LDCs to obtain loans to purchase the petroleum vital to their economic activity. However, in the 1980s many of the LDCs had difficulty paying the interest charges, let alone repaying the loans themselves.

A notable example came in August 1982, when Mexico almost defaulted on $65 billion of debt, mainly to banks in the United States. If Mexico had failed to repay this debt, several of our largest banks could have been destroyed, and shocks would have reverberated throughout the entire U.S. banking system. Fortunately, a short-term agreement was worked out in 1982, and a longer-term agreement for repayment of Mexico's debt was worked out in 1984. However, several other countries, including Argentina, Brazil, Chile, Peru, and Venezuela, could be facing loan repayment problems in the years to come.

What can these countries do to repay their loans? The basic problem in most cases is that they simply do not have enough funds. They do not have the funds because their domestic economies are not exporting enough goods to other countries and they are importing too many goods. They are thus not bringing in enough foreign currency to pay foreign lenders. One solution is to devalue their domestic currency relative to other currencies. When their currency is devalued, it makes their exports less expensive and other countries' imports more expensive. The resulting balance of trade surplus can contribute to a balance of payments surplus, giving the country the foreign currency needed to pay the loans.

Unfortunately, devaluing the domestic currency generally creates severe problems for the domestic economy. Prices of goods and services increase, inflicting hardships on the domestic population. And labor often demands higher wages because of the higher prices. However, to keep the currency devalued, the country must prevent wages from increasing. This is often done with authoritarian sanctions, which can lead to political instability. Yet short of defaulting on the loans and creating financial panic throughout the world, there seems little else that can be done.

QUESTIONS FOR DISCUSSION

1. Explain how a balance-of-trade deficit made it necessary to borrow funds from MDCs in the first place.

2. Considering the various determinants of the exchange rate, discuss how a country with debt problems could devalue their currency without running a balance-of-trade surplus. Do any of these solutions seem plausible for less-developed countries? Explain.

3. Discuss why less-developed countries are more likely to get caught in this time of debt problems than more-developed countries.

SECTION 15

Alternative Economic Systems

In this text we have focused, first and foremost, on the market-oriented economy in the United States, simply to gain an understanding of how our economy operates. Now we need to examine other types of economic systems used throughout the world. Although most of the Western industrialized countries in Europe and North America rely predominately on markets for the allocation functions of the economy, other countries containing a large share of the world's population rely primarily on government decisions in the allocation process. In this section we discuss alternatives to the market-oriented economic system.

Unit 15.1, An Introduction to Economic Systems, looks at the different methods that can be used to address the three basic questions of allocation: What is produced? How is it produced? For whom is it produced? We identify three types of systems in this unit: capitalism, socialism, and communism. And we examine how these systems differ, and what the pros and cons of each are.

Unit 15.2, Marxian Economics, focuses on one of the most dominant economic, sociological, and philosophical views of the world. In this unit we look at the economics of Karl Marx, on which the socialist and "communist" economic systems throughout the world are based. We examine Marx's view of history as a struggle between economic classes, and see what this implies for the future of capitalism.

Unit 15.3, The Soviet Economy, discusses the first of the two major countries in the world that have tried to apply the philosophy of Marx to an operating economic system. In this unit we get a feel for how well the Marxian philosophy has worked. We see that while the Soviet economy, which is structured around a central planning system, can generate relatively high rates of economic growth for the economy, it also creates an inefficient allocation of resources.

Unit 15.4, The Chinese Economy, discusses the second of the two major countries that have applied Marx's philosophy. While the Soviet Union is the first country to adopt the Marxian principles, China is the most populous. Here, we see a country that initially tried to adopt the Soviet central planning system, but gradually shifted toward a more decentralized approach, relying more heavily on markets.

UNIT 15.1

An Introduction to Economic Systems

When we began our study of economics in Section 1, we saw that every economy and society is faced with the fundamental economic problem of scarcity. And every economy, regardless of political philosophy, must address the three basic questions of allocation: What goods should be produced? How should the goods be produced? Who receives the goods that are produced? Our initial study indicated that most economies in the world today answer these three questions using a mixture of markets and government decisions.

While a wide variety of economic systems exists throughout the world, they are bound together by several threads of similarity. To understand these similarities, we first look at the two basic characteristics of economic systems, ownership of resources and decision making. In terms of these two characteristics, we then isolate the three main types of economic systems: capitalism, socialism, and communism. We discuss other considerations of the various economic systems, including the role of market and command economies, market socialism, political communism, and the welfare state. And finally, we examine the convergence hypothesis, which speculates that capitalism and socialism are becoming, and will continue to become, more alike.

TWO CHARACTERISTICS OF ECONOMIC SYSTEMS

To begin, note that an **economic system** is an organized method of producing and distributing goods, services, and resources in a society that answers the three basic questions of allocation: What to produce? How to produce? For whom to produce? The two basic characteristics that we need to identify as we look at alternative economic systems are ownership of resources and decision making.

Ownership of Resources

Resources can be privately owned and controlled, by firms or individuals, or government owned and controlled. A third alternative is also possible, collective ownership, in which a group of individuals jointly own a resource. An example of this is the ownership of a factory by its workers. In one sense collective ownership might be considered another type of government ownership (or vice versa), in that the government is really the collective group containing everyone in the country. However, in practice, the difference between collective and government ownership is substantial. In terms of ownership, the most important resources are capital and land. However, in the extreme, some economic systems might profess and even operate as if labor were also owned by the government.

Decision Making

Decision making consists of answering the three questions of allocation. These questions can be answered by decisions made by the individuals through the operation of markets or by government decisions. A third alternative, related to collective ownership of resources, is the collective decision making by groups of individuals. While the three alternative means of decision making often correspond with the three alternatives of ownership, this need not be the case. We see examples later in this unit of systems with a mixture of ownership and decision making.

In considering the decision-making process, keep in mind the role played by incentives. In a market-oriented economy, buyers and sellers receive either positive or negative incentives, provided by the markets and based on the prices of the goods, services, and resources. For example, producers supply more because the price of a good is higher, thus responding to the positive incentive of additional profit. Or buyers demand less at a higher price because they have the negative incentive of spending limited income. And even though decisions are made by individuals through the markets, the government can influence these incentives by levying taxes, providing subsidies, or otherwise manipulating the prices. Whether the incentives provided in the market-oriented economy are positive or negative, they are almost always economic incentives.

An economic system based on government decisions also operates by providing incentives to individuals. In some cases economic incentives might be used. For example, a central government might decide that a farmer needs to produce a thousand bushels of wheat. If this amount is produced, then the farmer might receive a cash bonus or additional material goods. But if this quota is not reached, then the farmer might receive lower wages or fewer material goods. However, the government might also provide noneconomic (or moral) incentives, such as imprisonment, physical harm, social status, political power, and so on. Noneconomic incentives can also be positive or negative.

THREE ALTERNATIVE ECONOMIC SYSTEMS

Based on these two criteria (ownership of resources and decision making), we can identify three basic types of economic systems: capitalism, socialism, and communism.

Capitalism

Capitalism is an economic system that is primarily based on private ownership of resources and allocative decisions made through markets. Our economic system in the United States is based on capitalism. Most, though not all, resources are privately owned, and the three questions of allocation are answered mainly through the market. As in many other areas of economics, capitalism is a matter of degree. A capitalistic economic system does not mean the government owns no resources, nor does it mean that the government makes no allocative decisions. But with capitalism the government involvement is relatively small, while private ownership and market orientation is relatively large.

Socialism

<u>Socialism is an economic system that is primarily based on government ownership of resources and allocative decisions made by the government</u>. The central feature of socialism is the government involvement in both the ownership of resources and the decision-making process. At the extreme, a total socialistic economic system would mean all resources would be owned by the government. Moreover, all productive, consumption, and allocative decisions would be made by the government, state and local as well as federal.

While this would represent an extreme case of socialism, in practice many countries in the world operate with socialistic economic systems that have something less than total government involvement. As we see in Unit 15.3, even the Soviet Union, which is a functioning socialistic economy, allows some private ownership of resources and individual production decisions. Like capitalism, socialism is a matter of degree. Some economies extend socialistic control only as far as government ownership (or nationalization) of a few key industries, such as transportation, steel production, or automobile production.

Communism

<u>Communism is an economic system that is primarily based on collective ownership of resources and allocative decisions made by groups of individuals</u>. First let's note that communism is not a functioning economic system in the world today but an idealized economic system developed by Karl Marx. As we see in the next unit, Marx believed that natural economic forces would ultimately cause capitalism to be replaced, first by socialism and then by the idealized state of communism. Marx's communism is an economic system in which no one privately owns resources, but all resources are jointly owned by society. Furthermore, all workers produce as much as they can but only consume what they need. In this economic system there would be no need for the government because all wants and needs would be satisfied.

While many countries in the world today profess some form of communism, in reality they have socialistic economies, as indicated by the government ownership of resources and government decision making. While the countries may argue that the government is only acting collectively on behalf of the people, the government nevertheless owns the resources and makes the decisions.

OTHER CONSIDERATIONS

With these three basic economic systems in mind, let's consider some additional aspects of how an economy answers the three questions of allocation. First, we want to see how our discussion in Unit 1.3 of market and command economies relates to these economic systems. Second, we want to examine the differences between economic systems and political systems. And third, we want to see how a welfare state relates to our discussion thus far.

Market and Command Economies

In Unit 1.3 we introduced two basic methods of allocation, the market economy and the command economy. Recall that a **market economy** <u>is an economy that relies on markets for the allocation of resources</u>. And a **command economy** <u>is an economy that relies on the government for the allocation of resources</u>. Note how closely these two methods of allocation are related to capitalism and socialism, respectively. But there are also slight differences.

Although by definition capitalism is characterized by private ownership of resources and decision making through markets, the main criterion that separates capitalism from socialism is ownership. A capitalistic system need not use markets to allocate goods, services, and resources; the government could make all allocative decisions. However, in capitalistic economies, markets comprise the logical way to make allocative decisions. While market allocation need not result from private ownership of resources, it almost always does. At this point it is only necessary to recognize that the government could force some other type of decision-making system on the economy, although that would be very difficult.

By definition, socialism is based on government ownership and decision making. But once again, the distinguishing feature of socialism is government ownership of resources. And since government ownership logically implies that the government makes decisions on what to do with the resources, socialism usually corresponds with a command economy. However, in socialistic economies, both the government and markets can make allocative decisions.

Indeed, **market socialism** is an economic system based on government ownership of resources and allocative decisions made through markets. An important feature of market socialism is how it makes use of incentives. Rather than employing non-economic moral incentives, such as the threat of punishment, market socialism uses economic incentives, such as higher or lower prices. In effect, the government owns the railroads, steel mills, or automobile factories, but it sells the goods and services in the market as any firm would do. With capitalism (or market capitalism) the stock of a corporation is owned by thousands of individuals. With market socialism the "stock" of a corporation is owned by the government. Yugoslavia is a prime example of an economy that practices market socialism. And mainland China, in recent years, has moved toward market socialism.

Political Systems

Political systems should be distinguished from economic systems. As we saw earlier, an economic system comprises a method of answering the three questions of allocation. A political system is a method of governing a group of people. The United States has a representative democracy, where every citizen past a certain age has the right to vote for government leaders. An essential feature of a representative democracy is the freedom of choice, both in choosing leaders and in civil liberties. Other political systems, such as totalitarian dictatorships, restrict this freedom of choice.

Two points should be made concerning political and economic systems. First, some economic systems tend to go better with certain political systems. For example, the freedom of choice in a representative democracy is well suited to the individual decision making and private ownership of resources in capitalism. That is, the individual decides how much bread to buy at the market price, how much labor to supply at the existing wage, and which candidate to vote for in the election. By the same token, socialism is more compatible with some form of totalitarian government. If the government tells people how much bread to buy or how many hours to work, it is a short step to telling them where to live, with whom they can associate, and how to live their lives.

Second, any economic system can, in principle, function within any political system. While capitalism and markets tend to be found in democratic governments and socialism tends to be found in totalitarian governments, this need not be the case. Government ownership of resources does not always lead to government restriction of other aspects of one's life. For example, with market socialism the government owns the resources but people have the freedom to buy and sell goods through markets. And the private ownership of resources and decision making through markets in capitalism can also exist under a dictatorship. In this case markets might be used for allocation, but civil and individual liberties in other aspects of life are restricted.

This brings us to an important distinction between economic communism and political communism. As proposed by Karl Marx, economic communism represents the ideal economic system, as the ultimate replacement for socialism. Recall that there are no practicing communistic economic systems in the world today. This means that the Soviet Union, East Germany, Cuba, and all the other "communist" countries are communistic not based on their economic system, which is in fact socialistic, but based on their political system.

Welfare State

A **welfare state** is a country that places a great deal of emphasis on equity and the minimum level of individual welfare. A welfare state is simply a country that is highly concerned with the welfare of the poorest segment of society, usually at the expense of increased production in the economy. In this regard, any economic system can be a welfare state. Although many people erroneously associate a welfare state exclusively with socialism, a welfare state is not necessarily socialistic. Government control of resources and allocation might make it easier to redistribute income or wealth to the poor, but this can also be accomplished in a capitalistic system, without eliminating private ownership of resources or the majority of allocative decisions through markets. The best example of a welfare state is Sweden, which is much less socialistic than the Soviet Union.

THE CONVERGENCE HYPOTHESIS

Our discussions of capitalism and socialism suggest that the real world contains no *pure* forms of either economic system. No economy relies exclusively on either markets or the government for allocative decisions. In addition, no economies exist in which all resources are owned exclusively by either individuals or the government. Rather, the economies in the world have differing degrees of government and private involvement. There are no purely capitalistic economies or socialistic economies (let alone communistic economies). All economies are a mixture, to varying degrees, of socialism and capitalism.

This mixture results for some very important reasons. First, capitalism and markets are not infallible in their allocative decisions. As we have seen at various times in our study of economics, markets do not always efficiently allocate resources. At these times the government needs to step in and either acquire direct ownership of resources and the production activity or at least become heavily involved in the decision-making process.

By the same token, socialism and command economies cannot effectively undertake the entire allocation process either. As many socialistic countries are discovering, the forces of demand and supply are very strong. In our examination of price ceilings in Unit 2.5, we saw that market forces are very likely to generate a black market. It is not only difficult but also extremely unwise to try to suppress these market forces. Thus, even a socialistic economy would find it appropriate to use markets.

Some argue that this is an indication of the convergence hypothesis. The **convergence hypothesis** is a hypothesis that states common economic forces will eventually make capitalism and socialism indistinguishable from each other and form a new type of economic system. This new economic system will blend the government controls and the broad centralized decision making in socialism with the freedom of choice and extensive use of markets in capitalism. While there are indications that this may be occurring in countries like the United States and the Soviet Union, it is still too early to tell.

While the pressures leading to convergence may be operating on the economies throughout the world, the role of culture and social attitudes cannot be ignored. People in the United States have grown up believing in the Constitution and the economic teachings of Adam Smith, which are reflections of their political and economic freedoms, and they react quickly and intensely to threats to either freedom. And for most people the ideals of socialism constitute a threat. By contrast, in the Soviet Union people have grown up believing in Karl Marx and the problems and eventual downfall of capitalism. It is equally difficult for them to accept many of the principles of markets and other economic activity that are associated with the capitalistic system. If this convergence hypothesis is correct, these attitudes might not prevent, but they might at least delay, the convergence.

This process of delay has become most apparent in the 1980s. Under the Reagan administration, a concerted effort has been made to move away from government involvement in markets and the economy, as indicated by the deregulation of the airline and trucking industries, the breakup of AT&T, and the reduction of various social regulatory programs. Meanwhile, the Soviet Union has made efforts to reduce the use of illegal markets for goods that are officially controlled by the government, such as denim blue jeans. In both countries these actions represent movements away from convergence. Only time will tell if this divergence is temporary or permanent.

IN SUMMARY

An Introduction to Economic Systems

- Every economy in the world must answer the three questions of allocation: What to produce? How to produce? For whom to produce? The two main characteristics that distinguish economic systems are ownership of resources and type of decision making. Resources can be owned privately, governmentally, or collectively. Decision making can be undertaken through markets, by the government, or collectively by groups of individuals.

- Based on these two characteristics, we can identify three basic economic systems: capitalism, socialism, and communism. Capitalism is based on private resource ownership and decision making through markets. Socialism is based on government resource ownership and decision making. Communism is based on collective ownership and decision making.

- While private ownership and market decision making often go together, as do government ownership and government decision making, this need not be the case. Capitalism can exist in a command economy. Likewise socialism can exist in a market economy as market socialism. In addition, while some economic systems go better with particular political systems, the various systems are not mutually exclusive. Democracy and capitalism work well together, as do socialism and political communism. And finally, a welfare state is a country that tries to increase the minimum level of welfare of everyone and equalize the income distribution. A welfare state can exist under any economic system.

- The convergence hypothesis states that capitalism and socialism will eventually become indistinguishable. This hypothesis is based on the proposition that a necessary role exists for both markets and the government in the allocation of resources. While a socialistic economy may try to ignore the market forces, and a capitalistic economy may try to prevent government intervention in the markets, according to this hypothesis every economy will eventually have similar mixes of markets and government. There was a movement toward convergence until the 1980s. But in the 1980s the United States returned to greater reliance on markets, and the Soviet Union to less reliance.

QUESTIONS FOR STUDY AND ANALYSIS

1. In a representative democracy such as in the United States, is government decision making and ownership of resources the same as in a country like the Soviet Union, which practices political communism? Explain.

2. Is it possible to effectively and completely separate ownership of resources from decision making? Discuss whether market socialism and government decision making with private ownership are viable economic systems. That is, can they continue to exist in the long run?

3. Under what circumstances would an economic system based on a mix of private and government ownership and control, as implied by the convergence hypothesis, lead to an improvement in the current allocation of resources under either capitalism and socialism? Do you think that these circumstances are realistic?

4. Can a welfare state be more effective (in providing for the welfare of poor people) in capitalism or socialism? Explain.

REVIEW GLOSSARY

capitalism An economic system that is primarily based on private ownership of resources and allocative decisions made through markets. While capitalism almost always uses markets for allocative decisions, the distinguishing feature of capitalism is the private ownership of resources. Capitalism is the economic system of many industrialized countries, including the United States.

command economy An economy that relies on the government for the allocation of resources. While socialism usually contains a command economy, this need not be the case. Socialism in some countries operates effectively by using markets for allocative decisions.

communism An economic system that is primarily based on collective ownership of resources and allocative decisions made by groups of individuals. While capitalism and socialism actually operate in the real world, communism is an ideal economic system developed by Karl Marx. In this system there is no government, and everyone works according to his or her ability and is paid according to need.

convergence hypothesis A hypothesis that states common economic forces will eventually make capitalism and socialism indistinguishable from each other and form a new type of economic system. According to the convergence hypothesis, both markets and the government are needed in the ownership and allocation of resources. And whether an economic system begins as capitalism or socialism, it will eventually have the same mix of markets and government involvement.

economic system An organized method of producing and distributing goods, services, and resources in a society that answers the three basic questions of allocation: What to produce? How to produce? For whom to produce? Alternative economic systems can be classified based on ownership of resources and type of decision making. Ownership of resources can be private, government, or collective. Decision making can be undertaken by markets, by governments, or collectively.

market economy An economy that relies on markets for the allocation of resources. While capitalism often contains a market economy, this need not be the case. Capitalism could use the government for allocative decisions. However, capitalism and markets are much more compatible.

market socialism An economic system based on government ownership of resources and decisions made through markets. Many socialist countries blend government and market decision making. However, Yugoslavia is a good example of a country with government ownership that relies heavily on markets for allocation.

socialism An economic system that is primarily based on government ownership of resources and allocative decisions made by the government.

Socialism is an economic system used by many "communist" countries, including the Soviet Union and China. Throughout the world, numerous types of socialistic economic systems exist, each a little different from the others.

welfare state A country that places a great deal of emphasis on equity and the minimum level of individual welfare. A welfare state can exist under any type of economic system, even though it is often erroneously equated with socialism. Sweden is a good example of a welfare state.

UNIT 15.2

Marxian Economics

In our world economy it is possible to trace the alternative economic systems to two founding fathers. Capitalism and market-oriented economies have their origins in the works of Adam Smith; the socialistic economies have their origins in the works of Karl Marx. Even though we live in a capitalistic economy, on which this text has focused, the widespread existence of socialistic economies requires that we investigate the economics of Karl Marx. **Marxian economics** is a body of economic thought developed by Karl Marx, based on the propositions that the conflict between opposing economic groups and the surplus value that is not paid to labor will eventually lead to the downfall of capitalism.

First, we look at the background of Karl Marx, which reveals that his philosophy, ideas, and theories were the outgrowth of classical economics in the 1800s. Then we discuss Marx's basic view of the world—a constant struggle between competing groups—as contained in the concept of dialectic materialism. And finally, we look at Marx's basic theory of economics, and see why Marx felt that labor was being exploited by owners of capital, and why this would ultimately lead to the downfall of capitalism.

THE BACKGROUND OF MARXIAN ECONOMICS

An understanding of Marxian economics depends in part on the economic and historical setting in which it was developed. Karl Marx (1818–1883) lived and wrote during the formative years of classical economics. In fact, he studied the works of Thomas Robert Malthus (1766–1834) and David

Ricardo (1772–1823), two major contributors to classical economics, and he was a contemporary of John Stuart Mill (1806–1873), another great classical economist. In this regard, Marx himself would best be classified as a classical economist.

Thus, Marx developed his economic view of the world based on the classical economic theory of the time. The key aspect of that theory was the idea that labor would receive only a subsistence wage in the long run. The **subsistence wage** is the wage needed by labor in order to provide enough food just to maintain life. The prediction by classical economists of a long-run equilibrium at the subsistence wage for labor earned economics the title of the dismal science. But that prediction also contributed to the development of Marxian economics as Marx sought to explain this subsistence wage and the consequences of its persistence.

Another component in the development of Marxian economics was the economic setting during the 1800s. The industrial revolution in Europe that began in the late 1700s was in full swing as Marx observed his world. And what he saw were disgusting and dangerous conditions in factories, with labor working long hours for very low wages. Moreover, the owners of capital were becoming very wealthy in a very short time, at the expense of labor. Under these circumstances it is easy to see how Marx concluded that capital owners and entrepreneurs, who performed intangible and hard-to-observe functions in the production of output, were exploiting the workers, who apparently performed all of the actual work.

It is also interesting to consider the personal plight of Karl Marx. In his life he was expelled by several countries, and persecuted by police for his radical socialist writings and ideas. Furthermore, he continued to live in poverty until he died. Perhaps he chose to live in poverty as an extension of his views on capitalism and wealth. Or perhaps his poverty also contributed to his views. That is, maybe he saw the wealth of the capitalist owners and felt, with some degree of envy, that their wealth was wrong and unjustified. But keep in mind that both his closest friend, Friedrich Engels, and his wife were from wealthy families; thus it seems evident that Marx could have obtained the "good" life if he so desired.

MARX'S VIEW OF THE WORLD

Marx saw the history of civilization as a continuous struggle between competing groups. In Marx's time the two competing groups were the capitalists and the workers. In Marx's terminology the capital owners and the entrepreneurs were the **bourgeois**, and the workers were the **proletariat**. According to Marx, the struggle between the bourgeois and the proletariat was only one in a long line of struggles between competing groups throughout history, a struggle he referred to as dialectic materialism. **Dialectic materialism** is the process in which opposing economic groups, through their inherent conflicts, lead to structural changes in society. To understand the concept of dialectic materialism more fully, let's break the term down.

First, materialism refers to the idea that economic forces are the basis for social change. That is, people are basically motivated by many of the economic forces discussed in this text, such as the pursuit of wants and needs. Dialectic stems from the ideas of Georg Hegel, a philosopher Marx studied in the early 1800s. According to Hegel, **dialectic** is the process of change in which one concept (thesis) brings forth a competing concept (antithesis) and which together generate a new concept (synthesis). In this process, as illustrated in Figure 15.2.1, the original thesis is challenged by the antithesis. And as the two concepts collude, they form the synthesis, which takes the best parts of each earlier concept. This process continues, because once the synthesis is formulated, it then becomes the new thesis, which brings forth a new antithesis; together, they generate a second synthesis. Note that this type of process also forms the basis for scientific investigation. In economics, for example, the classical theory was the thesis and the

Figure 15.2.1

The Dialectic

According to the philosopher Hegel, the dialectic is the process in which a thesis generates its antithesis, and together they lead to a synthesis. Marx applied this dialectic to the process of economic change throughout history, where the thesis and antithesis were two conflicting economic groups. The synthesis was the formation of a new economic group together with a new economic system.

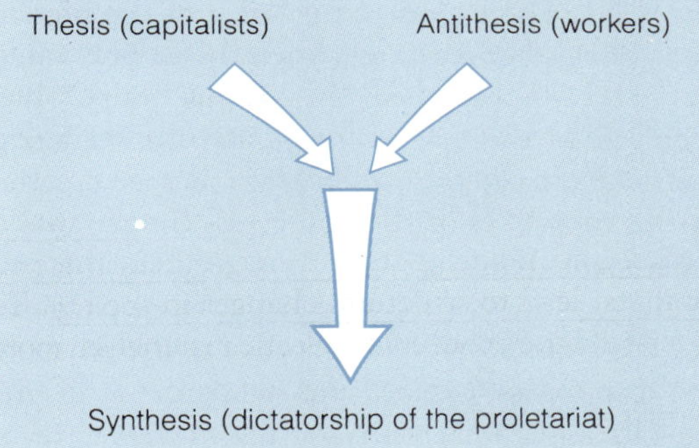

Thesis (capitalists)   Antithesis (workers)

Synthesis (dictatorship of the proletariat)

Keynesian theory was the antithesis. The Keynesian theory studied in Section 4 is not the actual theory originally developed by John Maynard Keynes, but is a synthesis of ideas from Keynes, the classical economists, monetarists, and proponents of several other theories that have gone through this dialectic process.

In Marx's view of the world, the thesis was one group in society, the antithesis was another group, and the synthesis was the development of a group that was characteristic of a new economic structure. For example, the feudal system of Europe in the Middle Ages was replaced by the capitalistic system through the dialectic process. The two competing groups were the feudal lords and the serfs (or peasants) who worked the land owned by the lords. The inherent conflict between the lords and the serfs was set in motion by the development of the merchant class, the forerunners of the capitalists. And when the merchant class and capitalists developed, the feudal system was replaced by capitalism.

But according to Marx, the capitalistic system that took over also contained an inherent struggle between the capital owners and the workers. Marx believed that workers were exploited by the capitalists and did not receive all of the revenue generated by their productive activities. In Marxist theory, such a conflict eventually leads to a revolution by the workers in which capitalism is toppled and a dictatorship of the proletariat is established in its place. The **dictatorship of the proletariat** is a state of socialism in which workers have taken over control of resources and temporarily given this control to the government. But note that this stage of socialism is only temporary.

With the downfall of capitalism, the workers receive all of the fruits of their output, which enables the satisfaction of human wants and needs. At this point, there is no longer a need for the government, and as it disappears, communism becomes the economic system. Under Marx's communism the key phrase is "from each according to his abilities, to each according to his needs." In other words, people produce whatever they can and receive only what they need. Communist countries professing Marxian ideals argue that they are still in the transitional stage of socialism, preparing for the movement to the final and ultimate stage, communism. However, some countries, for example the Soviet Union, have been in this stage for a long time, with no sign of the government disappearing.

MARX'S ECONOMIC THEORY

To see why Marx argued that capitalism would be replaced by socialism, and then communism, let's look into his economic theory. The best place to start is with the concept of surplus value.

Surplus Value

According to Marx, **surplus value** is the value of the output produced over and above the wages paid to labor. Marx felt that the value of a commodity should be determined entirely by the effort of labor. That is, since labor does the actual production, and transforms unusable raw materials into goods desired by people, it creates any and all value contained in a good. By contrast, note that our modern view of value is based on both the production of the good and the demand by buyers. As discussed in Section 2, the value of a good, or its price, is determined by the interaction of supply (containing the costs of production, including labor *and* the other factors of production) and demand (based on the satisfaction buyers receive from the good). Marx, however, totally ignored the demand side of value determination, and attributed all value determination to the supply side, particularly to labor.

According to Marxist theory, the other factors of production do not contribute to the value of output. In the first place, land is a gift of nature, and does nothing to contribute to production. In particular, the owners of land do nothing to add to value, since they simply sit back and receive the rental payments on the land. This view of land is consistent with the view held by most classical economists at that time.

The Marxist view of entrepreneurs is quite different from other economists. From Adam Smith on, classical economists saw the entrepreneur as the key to the economy because entrepreneurs bring together the other factors of production. However, Marx regarded profit received by entrepreneurs as unearned, since they contributed nothing to value. Marx simply did not acknowledge the entrepreneurial function.

Marx did recognize that capital contributes to production by adding to the value of a good. But he also argued that capital is nothing more than stored labor. That is, capital contributes to production, but capital itself is originally produced by labor. Therefore, production by capital is only indirect production by labor, and any value added by capital is really added by the labor that produced the capital. In essence, labor creates *all value*.

Here is where the seeds of revolution are planted. While labor creates all value, it does not receive all value that is created, but is paid only a subsistence wage. And one reason labor is paid no more than a subsistence wage is due to the pool of unemployed labor maintained in the economy. If one worker is unhappy with the subsistence wage, another worker is always willing to take the job. As a result of maintaining the wage at the subsistence level, the revenue labor receives in wages is less than the total revenue generated in the sale of the good. The excess of the value of the product over what labor receives is then the surplus value.

And who receives this surplus value? It is received by the entrepreneurs and the owners of the land and capital, which Marx lumped together as the capitalists or the bourgeois. Since none of these contributes to value, yet receives the payments of rent, interest, and profit, these payments are the surplus value of labor's activity. In short, the capitalists exploit the workers. And this exploitation is what motivates the workers to revolt and establish socialism in place of capitalism.

Concentration of Wealth

Another important aspect of Marx's theory is the increased concentration of wealth and capital among the capitalists, which they are able to accumulate in two ways. First, they generate more surplus value than they can use for purchases of consumer goods. Thus, they can continue to take part of their surplus value, create more capital, and expand their abilities to exploit labor by extracting even greater amounts of surplus value.

Capitalists also obtain greater concentrations of wealth through the business cycle. According to Marx, during each contractionary phase of a business cycle, some of the smaller capitalists are forced out of business, and have to join the ranks of the proletariat. But this means when the expansionary phase returns, fewer capitalists are left to take advantage of the increased production and further capital accumulation. As the business cycles continue, fewer capitalists are left, and the concentration of wealth becomes greater and greater.

AN EVALUATION OF MARXIAN ECONOMICS

In the decline of capitalism Marx saw several things occurring. First, he thought that a continual exploitation of workers would lead to more unemployment and misery. Second, he predicted an increasing concentration of wealth and greater market power. Third, he foresaw more severe business cycles contributing to the unemployment of labor and the concentration of wealth. And fourth, he predicted increasing numbers of revolutions by the workers as they overthrew the capitalistic system.

For the United States in the last half of the 1800s and the first half of the 1900s, some of Marx's predictions appeared to be coming true. Until the beginning of the twentieth century, workers continued to work long hours with very little pay in factories that were dangerous and unhealthy. Furthermore, the "robber barons" of the late 1800s, including J. D. Rockefeller, established powerful monopolies in oil, sugar, and steel, among other industries. The Great Depression of the 1930s was by far the worst contractionary phase and trough of a business cycle yet experienced, and certainly increased the misery of the workers. And the bloody and intense struggles between labor and factory owners during the formation of labor unions throughout this period could easily be interpreted as the beginnings of a proletarian revolution in the United States.

Indeed through the first part of the 1900s, it is hard to argue that Marx was wrong in his predictions. Until the Depression, capitalism seemed poised to fall. However, since the 1940s economic conditions in the United States have changed significantly. In particular, the wages paid to labor have increased steadily and significantly, such that wages today are far above the subsistence level. And while market power in some industries has been increasing in recent years, wealth itself has become more equally distributed. That is, more people are becoming capital owners and entrepreneurs, rather than fewer. Furthermore, business cycles have become less intense and severe. And most of the political revolutions of recent years have been supported, and even caused by, the external influence of Marxist countries such as the Soviet Union, Cuba, and China. These revolutions have been anything but a spontaneous uprising of the workers.

But where did Marx go wrong? First, Marx, like other classical economists, failed to recognize the role of technological change, which has made it possible to increase the standard of living of the workers. Workers with an improved standard of living have very little incentive to revolt. Second, Marx was wrong in his belief that labor is the only source of value. All of the factors on the supply side, and consumers on the demand side, contribute to the value of a good. The realization that entrepreneurs, land owners, and capital owners deserve payments for their contributions to production, also reduces the motive for revolution of the workers. Third, Marx didn't take into account the adaptability of society, and the potential for cooperation among competing groups. That is, when working conditions are bad, labor unions form to improve the conditions by working with capital owners. And if market power becomes concentrated, antitrust laws are passed to reduce this power.

IN SUMMARY

Marxian Economics

- Marxian economics is a body of economic thought developed by Karl Marx. It is based on the proposition that the conflict between opposing economic classes leads to structural changes in society. In particular, the conflict between capital owners and labor in the capitalistic system will eventually lead to the replacement of capitalism with socialism.

- Marx developed his theory of economics as an outgrowth of classical economics. In particular, his theories revolved around the subsistence wage. The idea that the wage always tends toward the subsistence level is what stimulates the conflict between workers and capital owners and subsequently leads to the overthrow of capitalism by the workers.

- Marx viewed the history of civilization as a continuous struggle between two conflicting economic groups, a process he termed dialectic materialism. In general, dialectic is the process of change in which one concept (thesis) brings forth a competing concept (antithesis), and together they generate a new concept (synthesis). For Marx, the thesis and antithesis were competing economic groups that lead to the emergence of a new economic group and a new structure of society.

- Under capitalism, Marx foresaw the proletariat (labor) overthrowing the bourgeois (capital owners and entrepreneurs) and establishing the dictatorship of the proletariat to replace capitalism. The dictatorship of the proletariat is replaced by communism when the government is no longer needed, and the economy operates based on the principle of "from each according to his abilities, to each according to his needs."

- A central theme of Marxian economics is the concept of surplus value, which is the value of output over and above the wage paid to labor. Marx felt that labor was the only productive factor, and thus was the only source of value for a good. But since labor does not receive all of the value of a good, surplus value is obtained by capital owners, land owners, and entrepreneurs. The extraction of this surplus value motivates labor, under Marx's view, to revolt against the bourgeois.

- Since the Second World War, Marx's predicted downfall of capitalism has not materialized. Until the time of the Great Depression, it looked as though some of his predictions were coming true. However, in the latter part of the twentieth century his predictions do not hold. Marx failed to consider increases in wages resulting from technological advances, he erroneously attributed all value to labor, and he didn't consider the ability of society to adapt to problems generated by capitalism.

QUESTIONS FOR STUDY AND ANALYSIS

1. Discuss a situation in which you have used the dialectic process to synthesize an idea or way of looking at the world. What is the thesis, antithesis, and synthesis in this example?

2. Some people argue that a democracy is more compatible with Marx's ideal state of communism than it is with market-oriented capitalism. Do you agree or disagree with this? Explain.

3. Marx argues that labor is the source of all value. Make a convincing argument that labor is not the source of all value. Moreover, refute the contention that the owners of capital and land do not personally contribute to the production of output with their own physical effort, and thus should not be rewarded.

4. Marx claimed that capitalism, in its advanced stages, would generate the conflict that would ultimately lead to its downfall. With this in mind, explain why the two biggest examples of Marxian-dominated countries, the Soviet Union and China, became socialistic in the earliest stages of capitalism.

5. If Karl Marx had lived in the latter part of the 1900s, do you think his theory would have been different? How and why?

REVIEW GLOSSARY

bourgeois   Marx's term for capital owners and entrepreneurs.

dialectic The process of change in which one concept (thesis) brings forth a competing concept (antithesis), and which together generate a new concept (synthesis). Marx applied this concept to structural changes in society, in which the thesis in capitalism is the capitalists and the antithesis is labor. The synthesis generated leads to the establishment of socialism.

dialectic materialism The process in which opposing economic groups, through their inherent conflict, lead to structural changes in society. Marx attributed society's movement through distinct stages, including feudalism, capitalism, socialism, and communism, to this process of dialectic materialism.

dictatorship of the proletariat A state of socialism in which workers have taken control of resources and temporarily given this control to the government. In Marx's view of the development of society, this was an intermediate stage that would subsequently be replaced by communism.

Marxian economics A body of economic thought developed by Karl Marx, based on the propositions that the conflict between opposing economic groups and the surplus value not paid to labor will eventually lead to the downfall of capitalism.

proletariat Marx's term for the working class.

subsistence wage The wage needed by labor in order to provide enough food just to maintain life. According to Marx, the subsistence wage would lead workers to revolt against the owners of capital.

surplus value The value of output produced over and above the wages paid to labor. According to Marx, labor was the only source of production, and thus the only factor that created the value of output. Surplus value plays an important role in the downfall of capitalism, because capital owners and entrepreneurs exploit labor by taking this surplus value. This exploitation then motivates labor to revolt and replace capitalism with socialism.

UNIT 15.3

The Soviet Economy

In the previous two units we looked at the nature of socialistic economies and their origin in Marxian economics. In this unit and the next one, we look at two countries that have tried to develop economies that follow the Marxist doctrines. In Unit 15.4 we see how China has implemented this type of economy; here, we focus on the Soviet Union. The study of the Soviet economy is important for many reasons. The Soviet Union was the first country to adopt socialism under the philosophical direction of Marx. Also, the Soviet Union is one of the most politically and economically powerful countries in the world, and is likely to remain that way for many years to come.

We begin by examining the formation of the Soviet economy in 1917, when the revolution led by Vladimir Lenin established the communistic form of government. The nature of the present Soviet economy can only be understood in the context of its background. We then examine the current structure of the Soviet economy. In particular, we see how this government-controlled economy resorts to central planning as a means of answering the three questions of allocation. And last, we try to evaluate the performance of the Soviet economy in terms of growth, efficiency, and the economic problem.

THE BACKGROUND OF THE SOVIET ECONOMY

Prior to the communist revolution in 1917, Russia was ruled by a corrupt, repressive, and exploitative Tsarist monarchy. While capitalism in the United

States, England, and several western European countries was advancing very rapidly, Russia was still in the latter stages of a feudal system. Moreover, Russia had been at war with Germany since 1914. Because Russia was on the losing end of this war, internal political dissension was mounting. The country was ready for a revolution.

Lenin and the Revolution

The best place to begin in the study of the Soviet economy is with Vladimir Ilyich Lenin (1870–1924), the founder of the communistic form of government in the Soviet Union. Lenin was a lawyer, intellectual, and revolutionary who was exiled from Russia, along with many others, during the Tsarist regime. It was during his exile that he became intimately familiar with the works of Marx. As a follower of Marx's doctrines, he foresaw an inevitable growth of capitalism in Russia, with all of its accmpanying problems.

Although Lenin was a disciple of Marx, he developed his own special interpretation and application of Marxian ideas. According to Marx, countries with the most advanced capitalistic economies were supposed to be the most exploitative, and thus the first to be replaced by socialism and then communism. However, Russia was one of the least capitalistic economies in the world when the communist government took over in 1917. According to Marx's theories of economic development, Russia's highly agrarian economy was in the feudal stage of development, which was the stage *preceding* capitalism.

But according to Lenin, this was entirely appropriate. Marx and Lenin both argued that the only way capitalism could sustain itself was through imperialism, or taking control of lesser developed areas of the world. Imperialism provided the capitalist economies with a continuous source of supply of raw materials, subsistence labor, and demand for their output. In this way they could prevent the overthrow of capitalism by the proletariat. Therefore, Lenin felt that the best way to revolt against capitalism was through the liberation of imperialistically controlled areas. While Russia in the early 1900s only marginally fell into this category of imperialist control by capitalist economies, he felt this was as good a place as any to begin. Of course, his logic was undoubtedly influenced by the fact that he was from Russia.

So the stage was set for a revolution. In 1914, at the start of the First World War, the Tsarist government of Russia experienced costly defeats against Germany. This external war disrupted the internal economy, and also led to internal political turmoil. As such, in 1917 Lenin's Bolshevik party, which later became the official communist party, took control of the country from a moderate group that itself had overthrown the Tsarist government. Although Lenin quickly made peace with Germany, an internal civil war continued until 1921.

New Economic Policy

In an attempt to recover from the seven years of war and revolution, Lenin implemented the New Economic Policy. The **New Economic Policy (NEP) was an economic plan implemented in 1921 by Lenin that relied on market forces and private production**. The irony of the NEP lay in its reliance on market forces and private production to get the Soviet economy back into operation. The only socialistic/communistic aspect of the NEP was the government control of heavy industry, foreign trade, banking, and transportation. To compound this irony, the NEP was very effective, as indicated by the fact that the level of output quickly reached the level that existed before the war.

Stalin's Regime

However, Lenin died in 1924, and saw only part of the NEP go into effect. His place was taken by Joseph Stalin, who continued the NEP until 1928 but then began to implement a different strategy. Stalin controlled the Soviet Union until his death in 1953, and had a tremendous influence on the structure of today's Soviet economy. To put it bluntly, Stalin was a dictator. His three decades of control were politically bloody and economically full of hardship. During the Stalin years the complex and inefficient central planning process that is a trademark of the Soviet economy was developed.

Stalin's primary objectives were to increase the levels of industrial development, agricultural productivity, and military strength. To pursue these objectives, the central planning system diverted enormous quantities of resources toward investment in capital and production of military equipment, at the expense of consumer goods. The hardships for the people were both political and economic. Stalin did not tolerate political dissension, and thousands of people were imprisoned, tortured, and executed. And from an economic perspective, very few consumer goods and services were available. After his death, the severity of Stalin's rule was modified by subsequent Soviet leaders, including Khrushchev, Brezhnev, and Gromyko, but the effect of Stalin's policies was deeply imbedded into the economy.

THE STRUCTURE OF THE SOVIET ECONOMY

When Stalin took over the Soviet Union in 1924, he embarked on a course of rapid industrial growth. For this growth to take place, two things had to happen, as discussed in Section 14. First, the economy had to devote a large share of its productive capacity to the production of capital goods rather than consumer goods. And second, the agricultural sector had to produce enough output to feed workers in the nonagricultural industries. To satisfy these two conditions, Stalin created a planned economy, so that the government could direct resources to those parts of the economy that would provide the greatest industrial growth. That is, the planned economy dictated that resources be diverted to the production of capital goods and agricultural goods, instead of other types of consumption goods.

The Soviet Planned Economy

A planned economy is often, though not always, a feature of a socialist economy. A **planned economy** is an economy in which resources are allocated according to some preestablished plan. While a planned economy necessitates some degree of control over resources, this control can come directly in the form of government ownership, such as the case in socialism, or indirectly through laws, regulations, and restrictions on markets. At the macroeconomic level almost all countries in the world have some degree of planning. Even capitalistic countries such as the United States plan future levels of output, inflation, unemployment, and so on, and then try to achieve the plan through fiscal and/or monetary policy.

However, in the Soviet Union the planning is much more extensive, covering almost every phase of production in the economy. For example, while the government of the United States can influence the amount of investment in capital goods by using monetary policy to control the interest rate, the Soviet government can change the amount of investment simply by directing more or fewer resources into the production of capital goods.

The Soviet agency in charge of planning is the **Gosplan**. The Gosplan is at the top of an enormous bureaucratic planning system, which operates mostly in a one-way direction. The Gosplan establishes how much of each good will be produced, and how many resources are available for its production. Gosplan policy moves down through the bureaucratic hierarchy until it reaches the level of the individual enterprise—the factory, plant, or farm—that is the basic production unit in the planning system.

The Gosplan oversees this planning in three basic ways. The first function, long-range projections, is probably the least known. The Gosplan makes long-range projections, ranging between ten and twenty years, pertaining to population, natural resources, labor supplies, and technological development.

A second function of Gosplan is more widely known, the five-year plans. The **five-year plans** establish broad goals for the economy, and the aggregate levels of resources allocated to investment, consumption, scientific research, military expenditures, and so on. The first five-year plan was initiated in 1928. While they are called five-year plans, they have not always been five years in duration because of wars or changes in policy. However, since 1966 the five-year plans have continued on schedule, with the twelfth plan beginning in 1986.

While the five-year plans set the guidelines of the planning process, the one-year plans have more specific goals. The **one-year plans** specify the precise amounts of each resource that go to each enterprise and the minimum amounts of outputs that they have to produce. The one-year plans are established using the directives from the Gosplan, but they are also based on information supplied from the lower levels of the hierarchy. That is, the enterprises indicate their production capacities and the technological production relationships between resources and outputs. The Gosplan then specifies the quantities of resources each enterprise receives and establishes the minimum quotas for the production of output.

The implementation of one-year plans is a very complicated and involved process, requiring an enormous amount of information. In many cases the one-year plan may not be completed until the year for which it is intended is half over. And in other cases the one-year plan is never even finished. The one-year plans are also hindered by a great deal of incorrect information. Since the enterprise managers are rewarded, and punished, based on meeting and exceeding quotas specified in the one-year plans, it is in their interest to understate their production capacity and overstate the amount of resources required. And when they exceed these relatively low quotas, which are based on erroneous information, they are amply rewarded.

A central feature of the one-year plans is materials balance. For the Gosplan the **materials balance** equates the total amount of resources needed by all enterprises to the amount that is available. This can become extremely difficult when many of the resources are in fact intermediate goods. For example, if one intermediate good is used to produce a second intermediate good, the second intermediate good is used to produce a third intermediate good, and this third intermediate good is used to produce the first intermediate good, then making certain that the economy has a balance of materials becomes quite complicated. If the output quota in one industrty is set too low, then this can lead to a shortage in a second industry, which subsequently leads to shortages in a third industry, and which then compounds the original shortage and makes matters even worse.

This process reflects the basic system of production in the planned Soviet economy, which uses quotas and bonus incentives. If enterprise managers, or workers, meet the quota, then they are not punished. And if they exceed the quota, they are rewarded with a bonus. Unfortunately, the nature of the planning process, with the enormous amount of information required, leads to quotas that are typically specified in some physical units, such as tons of wheat or number of cars. But there is no way to incorporate quality, meaning that cars need not function, food might be inedible, and other goods might be totally worthless.

The Agricultural Sector

Another important feature of the Soviet economy is the agricultural sector. When Stalin took over in 1924, he recognized that increased agricultural production was needed to feed workers in nonagricultural production. But agricultural production was extremely low for three reasons. First, before the Revolution, Russia was primarily an agrarian country, with very low agricultural productivity. Second, agricultural productivity declined even more because both the war and the Revolution led to an enormous loss of life. Third, the push toward increased industrial development after Stalin took over encouraged many of the remaining farmers to migrate to the cities. Together, these actions left the farms with a very small labor force and extremely low agricultural productivity.

To increase agricultural output, one of the first tasks Stalin undertook was to establish collective farms. **Collective farms** are farms that are collectively operated by groups of farmers on land that is leased from the government. In essence, Stalin took the land from farmers, who then had to lease it back from the government. Moreover, the farmers were forced to sell most of their output to the government at extremely low prices, though they were free to consume or sell any remaining output at any price.

Collective farms still exist today, but they account for a relatively small part of agricultural production. Most output is produced on state farms. **State farms** are farms that are owned and operated by the government. On state farms the workers and managers are hired for a specific wage, and receive incentive bonuses based on output quotas. The state farms operate essentially the same as any factory in the industrial sector.

Households and Labor

The final relevant aspect of the Soviet economy is the households. Although households are prevented from owning productive capital, they have a great deal of freedom of choice in terms of owning consumer goods. Although prices and quantities of almost all goods are controlled, everyone is free to buy any goods that he or she can afford at the controlled prices. In this sense, households in the Soviet economy are much like households in the U.S. economy. However, while producers in the United States have the freedom to react to consumer desires by increasing the production of goods at relatively higher prices, government control in the Soviet Union prevents such actions. Moreover, neither prices nor quantities are necessarily reflective of the value Soviet consumers place on the goods, meaning extreme shortages often exist for some goods, and continuous surpluses for others. Finally, people are generally free to hold any job that they want. However, the government also tries to control these labor resources by paying higher wages in occupations that are most important and lower wages in those less important.

AN EVALUATION OF THE SOVIET ECONOMY

The planned Soviet economy has both good points and bad points. On the positive side, the planned economy allows a purposeful redirection of resources to promote economic growth. However, on the negative side, the planned economy is extremely inefficient. The amount of information required to efficiently operate an economy with 275 million people is staggering. To evaluate the performance of the Soviet economy, let's compare it to the U.S. economy in five different areas: economic growth, efficiency, stability, equity, and freedom.

Economic Growth

In terms of economic growth, the Soviet economy has done very well since it began operating its five-year plans in 1928. While the information is incomplete and very sketchy for the years before the Second World War, growth rates of gross national product have been estimated at around 5 to 7 percent. In more recent years the information is a little more accurate, even though the Soviet Union doesn't measure GNP the same way we do. Table 15.3.1 lists the growth rates for different periods from 1950 to 1980 for the Soviet Union and other selected countries in the world.

Note that the Soviet economy has consistently grown faster than the U.S. economy in every period except 1975 to 1980. And the Soviet growth is comparable to the other countries listed except for Japan. In this light, the Soviet Union's objective of high rates of growth has been realized. And this is not surprising, since they directed enormous amounts of resources toward the production of capital goods, and have otherwise overtly tried to stimulate economic growth.

Table 15.3.1

Growth Rates of *GNP* for Selected Countries, 1950 to 1980 (percent)

The Soviet Union has increased production as fast or faster than most capitalistic countries since 1950. The only exception is Japan. However, in the past decade the rate of growth in the Soviet Union has tended to fall off.

Country	1950–60	1960–65	1965–70	1970–75	1975–80
Soviet Union	5.7	5.0	5.2	3.7	2.7
United States	3.3	4.6	3.1	2.3	3.7
Canada	4.6	5.7	4.8	5.0	2.9
United Kingdom	3.3	3.1	2.5	2.0	1.6
Japan	2.9	10.0	12.2	5.0	5.1
West Germany	4.6	5.7	4.8	5.0	2.9

Source: Paul R. Gregory and Robert C. Stuart, *Comparative Economic Systems*, 2d ed. (Boston: Houghton Mifflin, 1985), pp. 480–481. Reprinted by permission.

However, in recent years the rate of growth in the Soviet economy has slowed, dropping below the U.S. growth rate. The growth rate of *GNP* has probably declined for two reasons. First, the early high rates of growth resulted partly from borrowing existing technology from the United States and other countries. But high growth rates cannot be maintained once all existing technology has been borrowed. Second, the high rates of growth have also resulted from migration of labor from rural to urban areas. The influx of labor in the urban areas has provided an increasing labor force for economic growth. However, without continual increases in agricultural productivity, the Soviet Union has not been able to continue to send additional labor to the cities.

In spite of the relatively high rates of economic growth, the per capita output in the Soviet economy still lags behind most capitalistic countries. Figure 15.3.1 presents the per capita *GNP* in 1982 for several countries. For example, per capita income in West Germany is over $11,000, in the United States it is over $12,000, and in the other countries presented it is over $8000. However, in the Soviet Union per capita *GNP* is just over $5000. While the high rates of economic growth have brought the level of per capita income closer to that of many capitalistic countries, the Soviet economy still has a long way to go.

Efficiency

The Soviet economy has not done nearly as well in terms of efficiency. We have already seen numerous ways that the planned economy leads to inefficiencies. First, inaccuracies in information, or errors in computations, lead to ripples of inefficiencies throughout the economy. Workers and enterprise managers have little incentive to produce useful, high quality products when they are only rewarded for quantities produced. Second, the size of the bureaucracy needed to operate the plan-

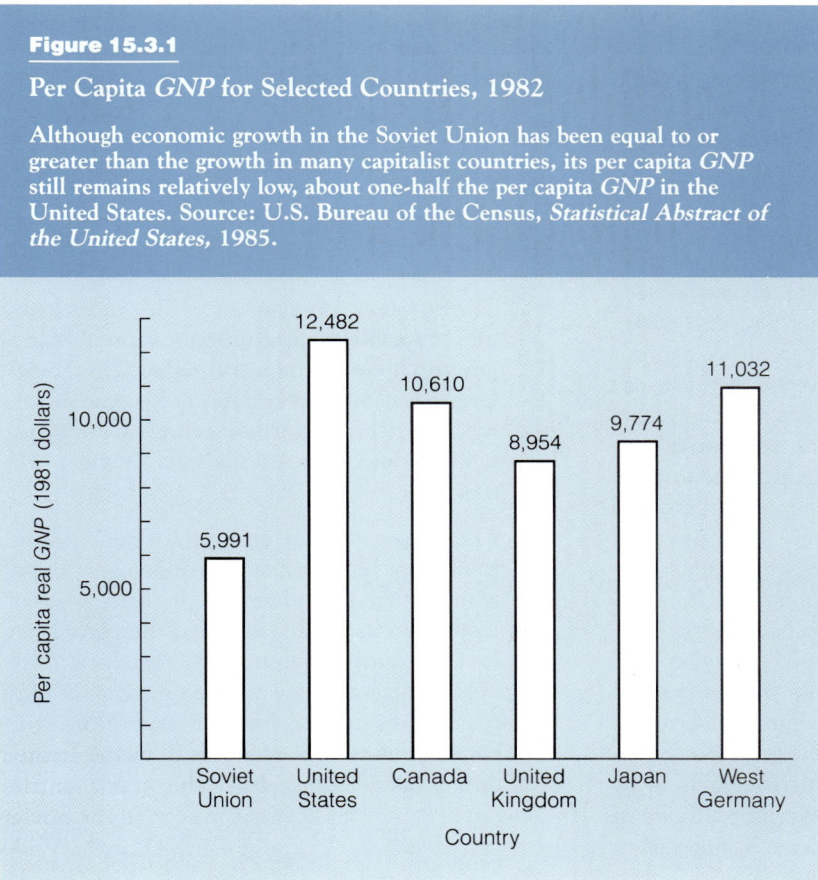

Figure 15.3.1

Per Capita *GNP* for Selected Countries, 1982

Although economic growth in the Soviet Union has been equal to or greater than the growth in many capitalist countries, its per capita *GNP* still remains relatively low, about one-half the per capita *GNP* in the United States. Source: U.S. Bureau of the Census, *Statistical Abstract of the United States*, 1985.

ning agencies uses valuable resources that cannot be used to produce goods and services. Third, inefficiencies are created because production does not reflect consumers' wants and needs. Thus, there are shortages of some goods and surpluses of others.

In the U.S. economy many (but not all) of these inefficiencies are handled by the markets. Market prices supply much of the information needed to allocate resources in the economy. A shortage of one good need not lead to shortages of other goods, since the price rises to reflect this shortage. And of course prices in the markets for consumer goods rise and fall to eliminate shortages and surpluses. Moreover, very few resources are used to maintain the market system, leaving more for the production of output.

Stability

One of our biggest concerns in Part II of this text was the stability of the economy. The U.S. economy has repeatedly traversed the phases of the business cycle, with periods of high and low unemployment. In this regard the Soviet economy performs much better than the U.S. economy. Since the economy is planned, employment is always maintained at its fullest levels, and everyone in the economy has a job. The only problem is that labor is often underemployed. While everyone is working, some are working in jobs that do not draw on all of their skills, or that are totally unrelated to their education, training, and ability.

Equity

A comparison of the distribution of income between the United States and the Soviet Union is tricky. First, the Soviet Union pays different occupations widely differing wages. The Soviet planners pay very high wages to the occupations that they deem most important, such as scientists, athletes, or educators. But the less desired occupations are paid very poorly. This by itself contributes to an unequal distribution of income. However, if we also consider that everyone in the country has free or low-cost access to education, health care, and housing, then the distribution tends to become a little more equitable. Moreover, there is no income earned from ownership of land or capital, which also tends to make the distribution more equitable. Overall, the distribution is about the same as in many capitalistic countries. However, this itself should be surprising, since one of the basic propositions of Marxist philosophy is that everyone is supposed to be treated equally.

Freedom

In terms of economic freedom, the Soviet economy does not do as badly as many people think. The restrictions on production are ever present, but individuals have a great deal of economic freedom. Recall that consumers can buy most goods that they want, subject to availability and price. However, while consumers might have more freedom than most of us would expect, they still do not enjoy the freedom that we experience in the United States. For example, in recent years Soviet officials have cracked down on many types of consumer goods, such as denim blue jeans, that have been illegally smuggled into the country. Although consumers have the freedom to buy whatever the Soviet planners determine is to be produced, this is all they can buy.

IN SUMMARY
The Soviet Economy

- The Soviet economy is one of the prime examples of socialism and the application of Marxian principles in the world today. The Soviet Union was the first country to become socialistic, in 1917, and it is also one of the major political and economic powers in the world today.

- The present Soviet economy represents the result of seventy years of development, but it is important to understand the early years of its formation. V. I. Lenin led the revolution in 1917, and established the socialistic form of government, following the principles of Karl Marx. His successor, Joseph Stalin, created the basic structure of the current Soviet economy during his three decades of rule.

- The current Soviet economy is a planned economy. The amount of each resource used in the production of each good is established by the Gosplan, the Soviet's central planning authority. The Gosplan oversees five-year plans that establish goals and allocations of resources to major aggregates. It also develops one-year plans that establish specific levels of each output for each enterprise. This planning process is a complicated and inefficient method of allocating resources.

- The agricultural sector of the Soviet economy contains collective farms and state farms. The collective farms are operated by groups of farmers on land leased from the government, and contribute very little to total agricultural production. State farms are owned and operated by the state, like any other enterprise in the economy. Most of the country's agricultural production comes from state farms.

- In comparison to the United States and other capitalistic economies, the Soviet Union has tended to grow as fast or faster. However, its growth began at a lower level of per capita income, and it still has a long way to go before it is as developed as other countries. The planning process in the Soviet economy is much less efficient than the market economy in the United States. However, the planned economy does lead to a more stabilized economy than in capitalistic countries. In terms of equity, it does better than other countries in its stage of development. And finally, the freedom in the Soviet economy is less than in other countries.

QUESTIONS FOR STUDY AND ANALYSIS

1. Compare and contrast the Soviet economy with Marx's concept of socialism. Discuss whether or not you think socialism in the Soviet economy is an intermediate stage in the move toward communism.

2. If you were in charge of the Soviet economy, what steps would you take to improve the efficiency of the planning system, assuming that you were not able to switch to a market economy?

3. In our capitalistic economy in the United States the cost of economic growth is reduced consumption, environmental pollution, resource depletion, and changing lifestyles. In the Soviet economy the cost of economic growth includes these factors, and inefficiency and loss of freedom. In light of the fact that the rate of economic growth has been higher in the Soviet Union than in the United States, do you think these additional costs are worth the additional growth? Explain.

REVIEW GLOSSARY

collective farm A farm that is collectively operated by groups of farmers on land that is leased from the government. Farmers on collective farms are forced to sell most of their output at very low prices to the government, but are free to sell any remainder in markets, keeping any profits that they receive. Collective farms were developed under Stalin's rule, but today account for only a small fraction of total agricultural production.

five-year plan A plan that typically, although not always, covers a five-year period. It contains aggregate levels of resources allocated to major activities in the economy, such as investment, consumption, military expenditures, and scientific research. The five-year plans are directed in only one way, from the Gosplan to the enterprise.

Gosplan The Soviet Union's central planning agency. It determines the quantities of each good that is to be produced, and how many resources are directed to each of the enterprises involved in its production.

materials balance Equating the amounts of resources required by all enterprises with the amounts that are available. Maintaining a materials balance is the most difficult task in the Soviet economy, and is the central objective in each one-year plan.

New Economic Policy (NEP) The economic plan implemented by Lenin in 1921 that relied on market forces and private production. The NEP was designed to speed up the recovery of the Russian economy after several years of external and internal wars. By 1928 the NEP increased output to the level existing before 1914.

one-year plan A plan that establishes the detailed flows of resources to each of the enterprises and the quantities of goods that have to be produced. The one-year plans set the specific goals for each enterprise and plant manager. Constructing one-year plans, unlike the five-year plans, involves large amounts of information from the enterprise level that indicate an enterprise's production capacity and resource requirements.

planned economy An economy in which resources are allocated according to a preestablished plan. While the socialist Soviet economy is a planned economy, planned economies need not be socialist, and vice versa. Even capitalist economies have some degree of planning at the macroeconomic level.

state farm A farm that is owned and operated by the government. State farms are operated in the same way as any other government enterprise. The workers receive wages and incentive bonuses if they surpass the established output requirements. State farms account for the majority of agricultural production.

UNIT 15.4

The Chinese Economy

In 1917 the Soviet Union became the first country to officially adopt Marxist doctrine. In 1949 China became the largest socialist country, in terms of population. While these two economies have many similarities, they also have many important differences. The similarities result from the fact that the Soviet economy was originally used as the blueprint for the Chinese economy. However, many of the differences result from the fact that China has three times the population of the Soviet Union in an area that is only half as large. In this unit our objective is to examine the origin, nature, and structure of the Chinese economy.

As we did in our study of the Soviet economy, we begin by looking at how the historical background of China relates to the establishment of its present economic system. Then we discuss the current structure of the Chinese economy, particularly in comparison to the Soviet economy. This is especially important in light of China's move toward greater reliance on markets and private ownership in 1984. And finally, we evaluate the performance of the Chinese economy using the same five criteria as in the previous unit: economic growth, efficiency, stability, equity, and freedom.

THE BACKGROUND OF THE CHINESE ECONOMY

Prior to 1949, China was as underdeveloped as almost any economy in the world, and its economy had been relatively stagnant for many centuries. This economic malaise was compounded by several years of war with Japan. Ironically, China during the time of Marco Polo around the 1300s was one of the most advanced civilizations in the world, providing the Western world with many discoveries and inventions. However, by the 1900s it had become one of the least developed countries in the world.

The level of development in China in 1949 was much less than the level of development in Russia in 1917. In Russia the seeds of capitalistic growth had already been planted and were beginning to blossom, which is what motivated Lenin to revolt. However, prior to the communist revolution in 1949, China had had very little industrial growth. In fact, the country was characterized predominately by agrarian peasants, much like any less-developed country today. In addition to the lack of private capital, there was also very little social overhead capital in the form of transportation, communication, or other public utilities.

Recall that the communist revolution in Russia actually did not occur in an advanced capitalistic country, as Marx had predicted it would. However, the revolution in Russia was still centered in the urban working class, which was according to Marxist philosophy. The irony of the Chinese revolution was even greater. The revolution in China, led by Mao Zedong (often spelled Tse-tung) (1893–1976), was powered by peasant farmers rather than urban workers. While this was not according to Marx's predictions, it did make a great deal of sense for China at this time. The peasant workers were mainly landless tenants working for wealthy and often absentee landlords. While there was no capitalism in sight at this time, the Marxian concept of labor exploitation was quite evident.

Before we look at the current structure of the Chinese economy, it would be very helpful to examine seven periods in the historical progression of the economy: consolidation, first five-year plan, the Great Leap Forward, recovery I, the Cultural Revolution, recovery II, and Four Modernizations.

Consolidation (1949–1952)

When Mao Zedong and the Communist Peoples Liberation Army successfully took control of China in 1949, they spent the next three years in consolidation. The agricultural land was taken from the landowners and turned over to the peasant farmers in order to set the stage for later collectivization of the farms. During the period from 1949 to 1953, China also nationalized the few industries that existed in the country at the time. While China set out to use the basic Soviet structure, it intended to implement this structure of centralized planning gradually; the period of consolidation laid the foundation for this implementation.

First Five-Year Plan (1953–1957)

In 1953 the first five-year plan was set into operation. In the first three years of this plan the shift from private industry to state planning began very gradually. However, this shift became more intense and rapid in the last few years of the plan, around 1956. The first five-year plan also established collective farms in the agricultural sector.

The Great Leap Forward (1958–1960)

At the end of the first five-year plan in 1958, Mao Zedong tried to put the development process into full gear with the Great Leap Forward. The intent of the **Great Leap Forward,** which lasted from 1958 to 1960, was to push the level of development in China ahead of the Soviet Union, the United States, and other countries throughout the world. This leap was to be accomplished in four ways. First, the role of peasants and small-scale industries was emphasized, which effectively meant that millions of farmers began producing steel in small backyard furnaces. Second, communes were introduced into the agricultural sector. Even though communes underwent gradual changes over time, they were the dominant means of production in the agricultural sector through the early 1980s. We will discuss communes in more detail later in this unit. Third, there was a great emphasis on water development. And fourth, the whole process was promoted with a level of advertising that resembled the religious intensity of the original revolution in

1949. In fact, the focus of the leap was more on ideology than on sound economic rationale.

Recovery I (1961–1966)

The Great Leap Forward ended in 1960, when it was clear that the program was a complete disaster. Total output in the country had fallen. The backyard steel furnaces were producing worthless pieces of scrap metal. Agricultural production also declined, because too many people left the agricultural sector to work in other industries. Thus, from 1961 to 1966 the key word was moderation. Until this time China had been following the Soviet plan that was based on strong centralized decision making, allocation of resources toward capital goods and away from consumer goods, and rapid industrialization. But in the recovery period after the Great Leap Forward, China redirected its attention toward improving agricultural production. In spite of this shift it was several years before the economy fully recovered from the Great Leap Forward.

The Cultural Revolution (1967–1969)

The period of moderation lasted until 1967, the beginning of the Cultural Revolution. **The Cultural Revolution was designed, among other things, to prevent a white-collar bureaucratic class from developing in the ranks of the army, the communist party, and the government.** During this period, anyone in the country who still possessed private wealth or operated private businesses was treated as a common criminal. In particular, there was a strong attempt to replace all economic incentives with noneconomic moral incentives. The Cultural Revolution was pursued with the same religious fervor that was seen during the Great Leap Forward, and it had the same disastrous effect on the economy. The Cultural Revolution created nothing short of chaos in China.

Recovery II (1970–1977)

The early-to-mid 1970s saw a period of recovery from the Cultural Revolution. This recovery began to fade in 1976, when two of China's moderate leaders died. Jou Enlai, a proponent of a moderate course for industrialization and development, died early in 1976; later in the same year Mao Zedong, the revolutionary leader, also died. A period of internal political struggles followed, during which time the famous "Gang of Four" were arrested. This is notable because the Gang of Four were proponents of continuing the Soviet course of development (strong central planning, heavy industrialization, limited consumption goods, and so on).

Four Modernizations (1978–1984)

In 1978, China embarked on the course of Four Modernizations, which once again reflected China's emphasis on ideology as much as economics. **Four Modernizations were aimed at modernizing the economy in four areas: industry, agriculture, science and technology, and the military.** Early in 1978 a ten-year plan was started that was to achieve these four economic goals. However, the ten-year plan was overly ambitious in its goals, and was replaced later in the same year with one-year plans. In 1982, China went back to a five-year plan that officially covered the period 1981 to 1985, but effectively operated from 1983 to 1984. Under the Four Modernizations the direction of the economy was pointed toward the development of light industry, agriculture, and social overhead capital. Moreover, decision making became more decentralized, and the incentives for agricultural production were enhanced. The period of Four Modernizations effectively ended in 1984, when China embarked on a bold new course that relied to a greater degree on markets.

THE STRUCTURE OF THE CHINESE ECONOMY

In 1984 China undertook a radical change in philosophical direction. It implemented a policy of greater reliance on markets for resource allocation and encouraged private ownership of resources and the accumulation of private wealth. This represented almost a complete break from Marxist philosophy.

How has the current structure of the Chinese economy incorporated the use of markets and private ownership into a centrally planned economy?

The Planned Economy

Recall that the Chinese economy was originally patterned after the Soviet economy, meaning that the emphasis was on central planning. The bureaucratic agency in charge of central planning is the **State Planning Commission,** comparable to the Soviet Union's Gosplan. The State Planning Commission oversees the allocation of resources and the establishment of production quotas for the various production activities. Even with the increased emphasis on markets and private ownership, the Chinese economy is still primarily a planned economy. In the industrial sector, most enterprises remain under government control and ownership, though they are becoming more and more autonomous. Indeed, many are able to set their own production goals, determine the types of goods produced, negotiate for their raw materials, and keep a portion of the profits that they generate. While this decentralization of decision making has been gradually increasing over the past several decades, the move toward markets in 1984 made it even more pronounced.

However, prices of many goods are still under government control. In particular, many key raw materials, such as petroleum, steel, and coal, remain controlled. Although enterprise managers have a great deal of freedom to produce and sell their output, they often have difficulty obtaining some of the required materials. In other areas of the economy, individuals are encouraged to set up privately owned, profit-motivated businesses. Since this move toward markets, small shops and businesses have emerged all over the country. And many entrepreneurs are becoming quite wealthy.

The Agricultural Sector

While China's industrial sector has expanded rapidly because of the move toward markets, agriculture still comprises the most important part of the Chinese economy. Prior to the switch to markets, the basic structure in the agricultural sector was the commune. A **commune** is a collectively operated farm composed of several brigades from different villages. A brigade is formed by the combination of several production teams within a village. Since 1979 the communes have been reduced in size and given greater autonomy and control. Moreover, individual farmers now have greater freedom to grow their own food and sell surpluses in the market. In fact, the use of markets, prices, and private ownership has been even more pronounced in the agricultural sector than in the industrial sector. State-owned and state-operated farms also exist in China. But unlike the Soviet Union, where they are the dominant form of agricultural production, state farms in China are used mainly as agricultural experiment stations, designed to test new seed varieties or develop new technologies.

Households

Since 1984 households have had tremendous increases in freedom of choice and opportunity. During the 1970s and before, individuals in China had even less freedom than people in the Soviet Union. They had very little choice of occupation, since this was determined by the government. Moreover, they had almost nothing to say about the types of goods produced. Like the Soviet citizens, people in China were only able to buy the goods available for whatever price the government set. But now, a Chinese individual can go as far as setting up a private business. Moreover, the variety and quality of goods is improving on a daily basis, as enterprise managers and privately operated businesses try to fulfill consumers' demands.

AN EVALUATION OF THE CHINESE ECONOMY

The Chinese economy from 1949 to the present has been characterized by periodic changes in ideological directions. But through all of this a gradual

Table 15.4.1

Growth Rates of *GNP* for Selected Countries, 1950 to 1980 (percent)

The rate of growth of *GNP* in China has generally exceeded the rates for capitalistic countries since 1950. However, China started the 1950s from a much lower level of *GNP* and needs even higher rates of growth to catch up to other countries in the coming decades.

Country	1950–60	1960–65	1965–70	1970–75	1975–80
China	7.9	4.0	7.1	7.0	6.2
Soviet Union	5.7	5.0	5.2	3.7	2.7
United States	3.3	4.6	3.1	2.3	3.7
Canada	4.6	5.7	4.8	5.0	2.9
United Kingdom	3.3	3.1	2.5	2.0	1.6
Japan	2.9	10.0	12.2	5.0	5.1
West Germany	4.6	5.7	4.8	5.0	2.9

Source: Paul R. Gregory and Robert C. Stuart, *Comparative Economic Systems*, 2d ed. (Boston: Houghton Mifflin, 1985), pp. 480–481. Reprinted by permission.

change has taken place in the underlying structure of the economy. In the early years virtually the entire Soviet approach to planning was adopted by the Chinese economy. But it became evident that modifications to the Soviet approach were needed. Since China lacked the social overhead capital, especially communication and transportation systems, highly centralized planning was just not possible. Therefore, China gradually moved to more and more decentralization. While it is too early to tell what effect the shift to markets in the latter half of 1984 will have on the economy, some early indications are instructive. As with the Soviet economy, let's consider five areas: economic growth, efficiency, stability, equity, and freedom.

Economic Growth

Recall that the primary objective in the introduction of socialistic planning into China was the rapid industrialization, and thus economic growth, of the country. Table 15.4.1 presents the growth rates for China, the Soviet Union, and the United States between 1950 and 1980. In this regard, the performance has been commendable. The rate of economic growth has been between 4 and 8 percent over this thirty-year period, compared to 5 percent for the Soviet Union and 3 to 4 percent in the United States. While Table 15.4.1 does not extend beyond 1980, there are indications that economic growth since the move toward markets has been even greater than between 1949 and 1980.

However, keep in mind that China began in 1949 from a very low level of development, so any increase in output becomes relatively significant. Moreover, since many of China's one-, five-, and ten-year plans during these three decades called for growth rates of 10 percent or more, the record is much less encouraging, especially considering that the intent of the Great Leap Forward was to increase

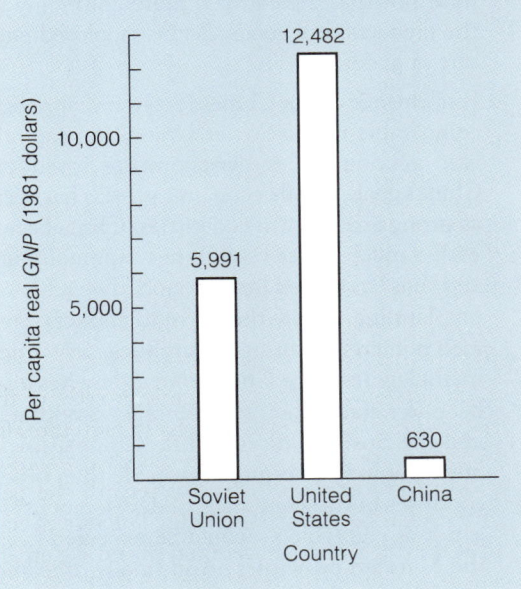

Figure 15.4.1

Per Capita *GNP*, for Selected Countries, 1982

Although economic growth in China has been equal to, or greater than, the growth in many capitalistic countries, its per capita *GNP* still remains extremely low. It is about one-twentieth the per capita *GNP* in the United States and one-tenth that of the Soviet Union. Source: U.S. Bureau of the Census, *Statistical Abstract of the United States*, 1985.

the level of development in China beyond that of the Soviet Union and United States. Figure 15.4.1 presents the per capita *GNP* for China, the Soviet Union, and the United States in 1982. Note that while the United States is over $12,000, and the Soviet Union is over $5000, the per capita output in China is only $630. If China is to reach, and surpass, the level of development in the Soviet Union or the United States, then it must grow much faster than it has in the past three decades.

Efficiency

While the efficiency in the Chinese economy is rapidly improving as it adopts greater reliance on markets, a great deal of inefficiency still exists. In particular, the enterprises that are still subject to strong central planning control remain inefficient, with continuing shortages of petroleum, coal, steel, and other raw materials. However, in the areas of the economy where profit motives and greater enterprise autonomy have been introduced, efficiency has improved noticeably. Without government control, enterprise managers know that they have to make it on their own, and that the sale of their output depends on its quality. The government will not step in and buy up worthless goods at a preestablished price. However, as with per capita *GNP*, while the efficiency is improving, it still has a long way to go.

Stability

The two major changes in ideology, the Great Leap Forward and the Cultural Revolution, have led to a great deal of instability since the communist revolution in 1949. While the Soviet Union has had a relatively smooth and stable period of growth since its revolution, this has not been the case in China. Even though China has not experienced the business cycles characteristic of capitalism, the Great Leap Forward and the Cultural Revolution were followed by two periods that would be best classified as severe depressions.

Equity

The distribution of income in China is much like the distribution in the Soviet Union. Very few people privately own any land or capital; thus, most income is still received from wages. In addition, many goods and services, such as education, health care, and housing, are provided free or at low subsidized prices for everyone. In both of these cases, the income distribution tends to be more equal. However, higher wages are paid to workers in the more-desired occupations, which tends to make the distribution less equal. Overall, the income distribution is more equal than in capitalistic countries in a similar stage of development. But as markets and private ownership become more widespread, and a portion of the economy accumulates private wealth, the equality of income distribution is likely to decrease.

Freedom

Prior to the redirection of the economy toward markets in 1984, the typical Chinese citizen probably had less economic freedom than his or her counterpart in the Soviet Union. The labor markets were government controlled, and the freedom of occupational choice was even less than in the Soviet Union, let alone the United States. While the typical citizen did have freedom to buy goods and services, the prices and quantities were controlled, and as in the Soviet Union, production did not reflect the goods most desired by the consumers. Furthermore, the low levels of individual income were a severe restriction on an individual's ability to buy goods. But, as in other areas, restrictions in China are loosening. While political freedom is still limited, economic freedom has certainly increased.

IN SUMMARY

The Chinese Economy

- Although the Soviet Union was the first country to adopt the socialist principles of Karl Marx, in 1949 China became the most populous country to do so. While China initially tried to adopt the Soviet central planning structure, differences between China and the Soviet Union have led to several changes. The most notable is the greater use of decentralized decision making.

- The development of the current Chinese economy is marked by several distinct periods. The three that stand out are the Great Leap Forward from 1958 to 1960, the Cultural Revolution from 1967 to 1969, and the Four Modernizations beginning in 1978. The first two periods were marked by chaotic disruption of the economy. The last period has led to greater decentralized decision making and, in 1984, to greater reliance on markets.

- Prior to the switch to markets in 1984, the Chinese economy was structured much like the Soviet economy. At the top of the planning system was the State Planning Commission, which directed various ten-, five-, and one-year plans, on down to the level of the individual enterprise. However, each enterprise now has a great deal more autonomy in the production of goods, factors employed, and sale of goods.

- Performance of the Chinese economy, although comparable to the Soviet Union and capitalistic economies, is disappointing based on China's goals. While economic growth has been as strong as most other countries, China began with a much lower level of per capita output, and thus has gained little ground. The reliance on planning, before the move to markets, created numerous shortages, surpluses, and other inefficiencies. The Chinese economy has also been less stable than the capitalist economies and the Soviet Union. While China's distribution of income is more equitable than other countries in the same stage of development, it is not as equitable as would be expected from the Marxian principles. And finally, freedom in China, before the move to markets, was much less than in the Soviet Union.

QUESTIONS FOR STUDY AND ANALYSIS

1. Discuss the similarities and differences between the Chinese economy and the Soviet economy.

2. Is it possible to have a centrally planned economy without well-developed transportation and communication systems? Explain.

3. Which country, China or the Soviet Union, do you think has done a better job of implementing Marxian philosophy?

4. In terms of economic growth, as discussed in Units 1.5 and 14.3, how is the emergence of an entrepreneurial group in China likely to affect future growth? Explain.

5. Evaluate China's move toward markets in terms of the convergence hypothesis discussed in Unit 15.1.

6. If you were a political leader in the Soviet Union, how would you feel about China's move toward markets? How do you think Karl Marx would feel about this philosophical change?

REVIEW GLOSSARY

commune A collectively operated farm composed of several brigades from different villages. Each brigade is composed of several production teams within a village.

Cultural Revolution The period between 1967 and 1969 in which China tried to replace material production incentives with moral incentives and purge the white-collar bureaucrats from the government. While this was not an economic program, it had a devastating impact on the economy.

Four Modernizations A program started in 1978 to modernize four areas of the economy: industry, agriculture, science and technology, and the military. This led to the development of light industry, agriculture, social overhead capital, more decentralized decision making, and eventually a shift toward greater reliance on markets.

Great Leap Forward The period between 1958 and 1960 in which China attempted to increase its level of development beyond that of the Soviet Union and other countries. It tried to accomplish this leap by emphasizing the role of peasants and small-scale industry. While the Great Leap Forward was promoted with all of the enthusiasm of a religious crusade, it was a complete economic disaster.

State Planning Commission China's central planning authority.

SECTION INQUIRY

Market Socialism in Yugoslavia

The best example of market socialism, in which the use of markets and individual decision making are combined with government ownership of resources, is seen in Yugoslavia. Yugoslavia has many of the features common in the planned socialist economy of the Soviet Union. There is a single official Communist party in control, the government owns most of the resources, and the central government issues five-year and one-year plans to establish output levels. However, this is where the similarity with the Soviet Union ends.

While there is only one official Communist party, there is actually a great deal of social diversity throughout the country. There are three official languages, six different regions, and five distinct ethnic groups. This diversity means that the Soviet Union's style of centralized planning, which was originally implemented in Yugoslavia in the 1940s and 1950s, was not very effective. The centralized planning has since given way to more decentralized control of economic decision making. Therefore, while the government owns many of the resources, the actual production operations are controlled at the local level. The individual enterprises are managed by the workers, councils are elected by the workers, and managers are hired by the councils. The local enterprises make almost all decisions about production levels, prices to charge, pay levels for the workers, and the division of any profits received by the enterprise. The output is then sold in either domestic or international markets.

This decentralized decision making also applies to the five-year and one-year plans. Unlike the Soviet plans, which establish output quotas and goals, the Yugoslav plans merely project anticipated levels of output in each industry based on information provided by the individual enterprises. The main function of the plans is to provide information to potential resource suppliers and buyers so that they can make decisions accordingly.

While the market-oriented nature of the Yugoslav economy eliminates much of the inefficiency evident in planned economies like that of the Soviet Union, other problems seen in economies like that of the United States are present. In particular, unemployment is more commonplace since the enterprise managers decide who to hire and fire independent of central government control. Also, since some very productive enterprises receive more profit and thus pay their workers higher wages, income is less equally distributed in Yugoslavia than in other socialist economies. Further, many of the enterprises are effectively monopolies since the government controls the startup of new enterprises, giving the enterprises market power that the managers are happy to exercise.

QUESTIONS FOR DISCUSSION

1. Discuss how the Yugoslav economy answers the three basic questions of allocation: What to produce? How to produce? For whom to produce? What are the pros and cons of market socialism compared to socialism and capitalism? Explain.

2. How do you think Karl Marx would feel about the Yugoslav economy? Does it fit in with his views of capitalism giving way to socialism and eventually to communism?

3. How does the Yugoslav economy fit in with the convergence hypothesis? In your answer consider the fact that Yugoslavia is one of the least developed countries in Europe. Does knowing this fact have an influence on your answer? Explain.

4. How does market socialism in Yugoslavia compare with the move toward markets in the Chinese economy? What role does decentralization play in each economy?

Selected Answers

UNIT 1.1

3. "If the interest rate increases, then consumer spending will decline." The logic behind this principle should be fairly obvious. If the interest rate increases, then fewer factories will be built. With fewer factories, consumers receive less income, and with less income, consumer spending declines. This question can be extended by asking students how they might go about testing this principle. It can also be used to preview some of the material to come in Part II, Macroeconomics: The National Economy.

4. Several factors that need to be held constant when testing this hypothesis are intelligence of the student, interest in the subject matter, attitude of the student, the instructor teaching the class, and the student's location in the classroom. This question can illustrate how difficult it is to actually test a hypothesis using data from the real world.

UNIT 1.2

1. There are two ways to eliminate the economic problem of scarcity. The first is to have unlimited rather than limited resources. If resources are unlimited, then no economic problem will exist, because everyone can obtain all of the goods they desire. This might be possible if we tap the vast resources of the universe, but even then we are limited by the available technology. The second is to have limited rather than unlimited wants; in this way the limited wants can be satisfied with the limited resources. The only way to produce limited wants is to change our basic nature. This might be possible with some type of genetic engineering. But no one really knows what makes us tick. Neither alternative seems possible in the foreseeable future.

5. **a.** If factors of production are divided into only two groups, capital and natural resources, labor can fall into either group. The key is whether the labor is "produced" in any way. An essential part in the production of labor would be training and education. As such, labor with acquired skills and education would be considered capital. Unskilled labor with no acquired skills

or education would be considered natural resources. Moreover, labor with natural talent or ability would also be considered natural resources.

b. Entrepreneurs could also fall into either group. Once again the key is to identify production. If entrepreneurs have a natural talent or ability for combining the other factors, then they are considered natural resources. However, if their entrepreneurial ability is learned or acquired, then they are considered capital.

UNIT 1.3

1. A political democracy is more compatible with a market economy than with a command economy. The key to the compatibility is freedom. In a market economy people have economic freedom. In a political democracy people have political freedom. While it is possible to combine the political freedom of a democracy with the lack of economic freedom of a command economy, freedom in one area is more compatible with freedom in another area.

2. A pure command economy is not a practical system for allocating resources. The main problem is the enormous amount of information needed to make all of the allocation decisions. Without the necessary information, the command economy would be very ineffective. For a pure command economy to be effective, the government would require information concerning nearly all aspects of our lives. To implement decisions in the command economy, the government would need almost total control of our daily lives, telling us what to buy and consume and where to live and work.

UNIT 1.4

1. **a.**

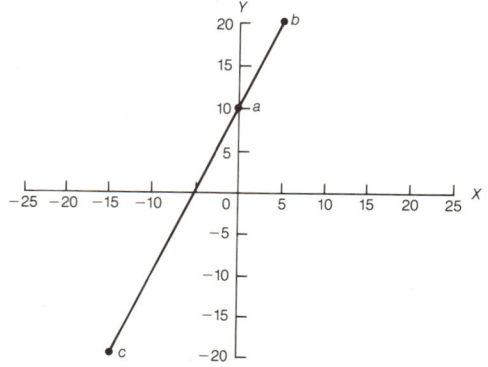

b. 2. Yes. Positive.
c. 10.
d. $Y = 10 + 2X$.
e. 14.

3. By abstracting from unneeded details we can identify relationships that link many different parts of our world. Abstraction can help us understand the laws of physics as they apply not only to common household objects but also to planetary bodies throughout the universe. We can also identify the economic principles that help explain the behavior of General Motors, a suburban housewife, or an economics student. Without the abstraction we might not see the important similarities underlying the obvious differences.

UNIT 1.5

2. Opportunity cost is the slope of the *PPF*. As the economy moves along the frontier, producing more of one good, the opportunity cost of the good represents the amount of the other good given up. If the economy is producing inside the frontier, then it can produce more of both goods. However, society still incurs an opportunity cost as labor gives up leisure time. The law of increasing opportunity cost means the slope of the *PPF* (moving from left to right) becomes steeper, giving the frontier its bowed-out shape.

4. **a.** The opportunity cost is 0.1 textbooks per YoYo in both cases.

b. The production possibilities does *not* reflect the law of increasing opportunity cost. Resources are equally suited to the production of either good. The same number of textbooks are given up whether YoYo production increases from 0 to 1000 or from 4000 to 5000.

c.

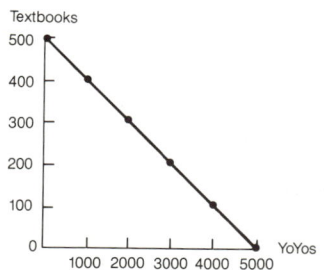

SELECTED ANSWERS

The slope is 0.1 textbooks per YoYo, or 10 YoYos per textbook. In this case there are no increasing opportunity costs. The *PPF* reflects constant opportunity costs.

UNIT 2.1

1. If the price of medical care increases faster than the price of food, we can expect a reallocation of resources between the production of food and medical care. For example, visualize a farmer selling off a few acres of farmland for the construction of a new hospital or nursing home. Since the price of medical care is relatively higher than food, the farmer can receive more income from selling the land to the hospital than from selling any food grown on the land. You could also envision the son or daughter of the farmer leaving the farm to enter medical school. Furthermore, if college students are interested in their potential income after graduation, an increase in the relative price of medical care over food will lead many students to choose biology (in preparation for medical school) over agronomy (in preparation for a career in farming).

UNIT 2.2

2. **a.** There would be a change in demand resulting from a change in the price of other good determinant of demand. In this case personal computers and software are complements, meaning a reduction in the price of computers leads to an increase in the demand for software, or a rightward shift in the demand curve.

    b. There would be a change in the quantity demanded resulting from a change in the price. If there are fewer software producers, then the price increases and the quantity demanded declines.

    c. There would be two separate effects. First, the tax break would reduce the price of software, leading to an increase in the quantity demanded. Second, the tax break would reduce the price of personal computers, causing the same increase in demand for software discussed in answer 2a.

    d. There would be a change in demand resulting from a change in the price of other good determinant of demand. In this case electricity and software are complement goods, both being used to operate the computer. An increase in the price of electricity would decrease the demand for software (as well as computers), which would be seen as a leftward shift in the demand curve.

    e. There would be a change in demand resulting from a change in the price of other good determinant of demand. In this case movies and software are substitute goods, meaning a decrease in the price of movies would lead to a decrease in the demand for software, or a leftward shift in the demand curve.

    f. There would be a change in demand resulting from a change in the tastes and preferences determinant of demand. In this case people do not want to use computers and computer software, meaning there would be a decrease in the demand for software, or a leftward shift in the demand curve.

    g. There would be a change in the quantity demanded resulting from a change in the price of software. Separating the manuals and selling them at a higher price effectively increases the price paid for the software.

3. Buyers, especially local residents, probably expected large crowds and higher prices at retail stores in the Los Angeles area during the Olympics. Because they expected to pay higher prices or face limited quantities due to the crowds, buyers increased demand before the Olympics began. However, once the Olympics were underway there was less demand than merchants anticipated, and in some cases less than normal.

UNIT 2.3

2. **a.** There would be a change in supply resulting from a change in the number of sellers determinant of supply. In this case, if Canadian producers are allowed to sell belts in the United States for the first time, there is an increase in the number of sellers and an increase the supply of belts, or a rightward shift in the supply curve.

    b. There would be a change in supply resulting from a change in the price of other good determinant of supply. In this case beef and leather belts are complements in production, meaning a decrease in the price of beef leads to a decrease in the supply of belts, or a leftward shift in the supply curve.

    c. There would be a change in supply resulting from a change in the technology determinant of supply. In this case improvement in the tanning machine leads to an increase in technology and an increase in supply, or a rightward shift in the supply curve.

    d. There would be a change in supply resulting from a change in the price of other good determinant of supply. In this case leather belts and leather boots are substitutes, since both use the same resources in production. As such, an increase in the price of boots would divert resources away from the production of belts, leading to a decrease in the supply of belts, or a leftward shift in the demand curve.

e. There would be a change in the quantity of belts supplied resulting from a change in the price of belts. In this case the price ceiling reduces the price of belts and thus decreases the quantity supplied.

f. There would be a change in the supply of belts resulting from a change in the expectations determinant of supply. In this case suppliers expect the price they receive for producing the belts to decline due to the tax to be imposed. As such, they try to supply more belts before the tax goes into effect, leading to an increase in the supply of belts, or a rightward shift in the supply curve.

g. There would be a change in the supply of belts resulting from a change in the factor cost determinant of supply. In this case the increase in wages leads to a decrease in supply, or a leftward shift in the supply curve.

4. The two determinants of supply that are operating here are technology and number of sellers. If technology increases, the supply of computers increases. If the number of sellers in the market increases, supply also increases. Combined, the two determinants lead to an increase in supply, or a rightward shift in the supply curve.

UNIT 2.4

1. **a.**

Price	Quantity Demanded	Quantity Supplied	Surplus or Shortage
$10	1000	100	+900
20	800	200	+600
30	600	300	+300
40	400	400	0
50	200	500	−300
60	0	600	−600

Equilibrium price = $40
Equilibrium quantity = 400

b.

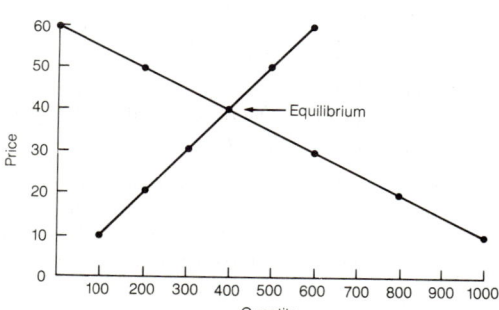

c. The equilibrium price is $30 and the equilibrium quantity is 600. The price declines and the quantity exchanged increases, which are the expected changes with an increase in supply.

4. **a.** There would be a rightward shift in the demand curve, or an increase in demand, caused by an increase in income. This is based on the assumption that automobiles are a normal good.

b. There would be a rightward shift in the supply curve, or an increase in supply, caused by an increase in the number of sellers in the market.

c. There would be a leftward shift in the demand curve, or a decrease in demand, caused by an increase in the price of other (complement) goods.

d. There would be a rightward shift in the demand curve, or an increase in demand, caused by an increase in the price of other (substitute) goods.

e. There would be a leftward shift in the supply curve, or a decrease in supply, caused by a change in sellers' expectations that the price will be higher in the future. In addition, there would be a rightward shift in the demand curve, or an increase in demand, caused by a change in buyers' expectations that the price will be higher in the future.

f. There would be a leftward shift in the demand curve, or a decrease in demand, caused by a decrease in the number of buyers in the market since fewer people will be able to drive at the higher minimum age.

g. There would be a leftward shift in the supply curve, or a decrease in supply, caused by an increase in factor prices as additional parts are installed on automobiles.

h. There would be a leftward shift in the demand curve, or a decrease in demand, caused by a decrease in the number of buyers in the market as people take up other forms of transportation.

UNIT 2.5

1. **a.** The equilibrium price is $50 and the equilibrium quantity is 60.

b. If a $60 price floor is established, a surplus of 20 units is created. If a $30 price floor is established, there will be no overall effect on the market because the price will rise back to the equilibrium level of $50.

c. If a $20 price ceiling is established, a shortage of 60 units is created. If a $70 price ceiling is established, there will be no overall effect on the market because the price will fall back to the equilibrium level of $50.

SELECTED ANSWERS

d. If a $20 tax is levied on the market, the quantity exchanged is 50 units. The price paid by buyers is $60. The after-tax price received by sellers is $40. The tax incidence is divided equally between buyers and sellers, with each paying $10.

3. The nonrefundable "finder's fee" is merely a method of increasing the price renters pay for the apartment. Because the price ceiling prevents the landlords from charging higher rent, they charge the finder's fee instead. This is essentially a black market operation, although for the most part a finder's fee is completely legal. While it does not violate the letter of a price ceiling law, it does violate the spirit of the law.

UNIT 2.6

4. If revenues increase in the spring term due to the higher tuition, this indicates that the short-run elasticity of demand for higher education is inelastic. This is probably because students are committed to finishing the academic year and have very little time to consider substitutes. However, the falling revenues in the following year indicate that the demand for higher education is elastic in the long run. The longer period of time enables students to reevaluate their plans, perhaps enrolling in another school or finding a full-time job.

5. At each of the three prices an increase in income from $5000 to $8000 leads to a reduction in the demand. The income elasticity of demand is negative, and this is an inferior good.

UNIT 2.7

1. A price floor can be effective if either demand or supply is perfectly inelastic. However, if either demand or supply is perfectly elastic, imposition of a price floor can cause some interesting results. If supply is perfectly elastic, a price floor above the equilibrium price will lead to an infinitely large increase in the quantity supplied, and consequently an infinitely large surplus of the good. If demand is perfectly elastic, buyers are not willing to buy any quantity of the good above the market equilibrium price. The price floor will cause the quantity demanded to drop to zero and will essentially destroy the market; because no goods will be exchanged.

6. More revenue can be raised for the county by taxing gasoline. Because both demand and supply for gasoline are inelastic, the quantity exchanged after the tax would be about the same as before the tax. If the tax was levied on cruises, the elastic demand would lead to a relatively large reduction in the quantity exchanged in the market.

UNIT 3.1

1. **a.** Because the insurance company is a part of the business sector, this computer purchase is an investment expenditure.

   b. Because the defense department is a part of the government, this computer purchase is a government purchase.

   c. Presumably, the economics instructor uses personal funds to purchase the computer, making this a consumption expenditure.

   d. This expenditure could be either consumption or government purchase, depending on whether the prime minister used his or her own funds to purchase the computer or whether it was purchased with government funds.

   e. Presumably, the secretary of defense uses personal funds to purchase this computer, making it a consumption expenditure. However, if the government purchases the computer, then it is a government purchase, even though it is used for personal reasons.

   f. Because the computer is purchased with state funds, this is a government purchase.

4. The amount of saving undertaken by the household sector supplies the financial markets with funds for loans to the government and business sectors. If households save more or less of their income, then there are greater or fewer funds that can be borrowed by the government (under the watchful eye of the president's budget director) and the business sector.

UNIT 3.2

3. **a.** Nominal GNP for each of the years is as follows: 1988—$10,000; 1989—$10,550; 1990—$20,000; 1991—$11,500.

   b. Real GNP in 1988 prices for each of the years is as follows: 1988—$10,000; 1989—$12,400; 1990—$14,500; 1991—$7600.

   c. The GNP price deflator, using 1988 as the base year, is as follows: 1988—100; 1989—85.08; 1990—137.93; 1991—151.13.

5. Because value added and the final sale price of a good are the same, it would not matter if the tax were placed on value added or on the final sale price. The resulting tax would be exactly the same.

UNIT 3.3

2. The two basic differences between personal income and national income are income earned but not received and income received but not earned.

   a. Part of national income, but not part of personal income. It is earned by the factors but not received by the households because it is paid to the government.

   b. Part of personal income, but not part of national income. It is not earned by the factors, but it is paid to the households as a transfer payment from the government.

   c. Part of both national income and personal income. It is earned by the factors and it is also received by the households.

   d. Part of national income, but not part of personal income. It is earned by the factors but not received by the households because it is retained by the business sector.

   e. Part of national income, but not part of personal income. It is earned by the factors but not received by the households because it is paid to the government.

   f. Part of both national income and personal income. It is earned by the factors and it is also received by the households.

4. An increase in taxes on any portion of the circular flow reduces the amount in subsequent portions of the flow. For example, an increase in indirect business taxes (sales and excise) reduces not only *NI* but also *PI* and *DPI*. An increase in the corporate profits tax reduces both *PI* and *DPI*. Because the factors of production in the household sector can claim all revenue received for national production, tax on any portion of this flow is a tax on household income.

   Indirect business taxes and corporate profits taxes are often called hidden taxes because they reduce the flow of income before it reaches the households. On the other hand, personal income taxes are paid after the income reaches the households. The household sector is more aware of paying taxes on income after they receive it than before.

UNIT 3.4

1. **a.** Seasonal unemployment. The referees are well aware that they will be working only during the basketball season, in the fall and winter months. During the spring and summer months their unemployment is best characterized as voluntary.

   b. Cyclical unemployment. The slowdown in business activity for airlines is irregular and never fully expected, unlike the regularity of seasonal unemployment. This is best characterized as involuntary unemployment.

   c. Structural unemployment. The coal miners are unemployed because the economy has shifted the types of goods it produces, no longer needing the skills possessed by the coal miners. This is best characterized as involuntary unemployment.

   d. Frictional unemployment. The programmer has left an existing job in search of another job. A job is available, but the worker has elected not to take it. This is best characterized as voluntary unemployment.

5. We are most concerned with unemployed labor because there is a greater potential for human suffering and personal hardship. For most people labor is the only factor of production they have to sell. If they are unemployed and cannot sell their labor, they do without income. However, most land and capital owners also have labor to sell, even if their land or capital is unemployed. In some circumstances land or capital owners have no labor, and their only income is from the land or capital, for example, an elderly invalid receiving petroleum royalty payments from a small tract of land in western Kansas. Such capital and land owners are much less common than unemployed factory workers.

UNIT 3.5

2. There are no adverse effects from pure inflation. If all nominal values increase by the same proportion, then all goods and services purchased before the inflation can be purchased after. Inflation becomes a problem only when all nominal values do not increase by the same proportion.

3. The real interest rate is determined by subtracting the rate of inflation from the nominal interest rate. If the nominal interest rate is 18 percent and inflation is 15 percent, the real interest rate is 3 percent ($= 18\% - 15\%$). If the nominal interest on the savings account is $5\frac{1}{4}$ percent, then the real interest is $-9\frac{3}{4}$ ($= 5\frac{1}{4}\% - 15\%$).

UNIT 3.6

1. If the economy is in the Keynesian range of the aggregate supply curve, then it has unemployment and is producing less than the full employment level of output. As such, the size of the circular flow is smaller than it would be at full employment. This means all of the segments of the circular flow, from national production to factor payments to national income to expenditures, are going to be smaller.

SELECTED ANSWERS

2. Aggregate expenditures are the total expenditures on *GNP* by the household, business, government, and foreign sectors. Aggregate demand is the range of aggregate expenditures at alternative price levels. The difference between aggregate expenditures and aggregate demand is much like the difference between quantity demanded and demand for a single good. Aggregate expenditures, similar to the quantity demanded for a single good, represent a specific amount at a specific price. Aggregate demand, similar to the demand for a single good, is the entire range of expenditures at different prices.

The aggregate demand curve is similar to the demand curve for a single good in that both are negatively sloped and relate price to demand. However, the main difference lies in the reason for the negative slope. For a single good, the demand curve is negatively sloped due to the income and substitution effects. The aggregate demand curve is negatively sloped due to the real balance and interest rate effects.

If the average price level in the economy increases, aggregate expenditures decline due to the real balance and interest rate effects. Through the real balance effect a higher price level lowers the value of financial assets of consumers (especially money), meaning households reduce consumption expenditures because they can afford to buy fewer goods and services. Through the interest rate effect a higher price level leads to an increase in the interest rate because it lowers the value of financial assets, which means households and businesses reduce consumption and investment expenditures, respectively.

UNIT 3.7

2. Demand-driven business cycles are caused by shifts in the aggregate demand curve. Supply-driven business cycles are caused by shifts in the aggregate supply curve. A demand-driven business cycle can be caused by changes in expenditures from the four basic sectors of the economy: consumption, investment, government purchases (and/or taxes), and net exports. Of the four, investment and government purchases (and/or taxes) are most likely to cause a demand-driven business cycle. A supply-driven business cycle is caused by changes in either the costs of production or the full employment level of output. For a complete supply-driven business cycle to occur a systematic leftward then rightward shift of the aggregate supply curve is needed. This type of shift is very common with the aggregate demand curve, but not so common with the aggregate supply curve.

4. The record high deficits during the early 1980s would put the economy into the expansionary phase of a business cycle, shifting the aggregate demand curve to the right. If the deficit were eliminated by a balanced budget constraint, then the aggregate demand curve would be shifted to the left because of reduced government purchases or increased taxes, and the economy would likely go into the contractionary phase of the business cycle.

UNIT 4.1

2. If the household sector decides to reduce the amount of income used for consumption and divert more to saving, aggregate demand will decrease and the economy can achieve equilibrium below the full employment level of output. This is especially true if investment expenditures do not increase as a result of the additional saving. If the business sector decides to reduce investment expenditures because they don't need additional capital goods, then equilibrium can also be achieved below full employment. If the government reduces purchases, for example after wars or simply based on other political factors, then similar results can be achieved. And finally, net exports can decline if the foreign sector decides to reduce purchases of exports, or if domestic consumers decide to increase imports.

UNIT 4.2

4. Because of the interest rate effect, higher interest rates during the 1970s caused a reduction in consumption. Higher interest rates increase the cost of purchasing goods with borrowed funds, which decreases the expenditures on goods that typically require borrowed funds (such as automobiles, furniture, and appliances).

5. A sudden increase in financial wealth can lead to either an increase or a decrease in consumption. If someone is saving for a specific reason, such as purchasing a new car, then the increase in wealth is likely to lead to an increase in consumption. At the very least, the person is closer to reaching the desired level of saving and will reduce the amount of current income diverted to saving, thus increasing consumption. Or the person might withdraw the funds and buy the new car, also increasing consumption. The increase in wealth can also reduce consumption in later periods if durable goods, such as cars, appliances, or furniture, are purchased. If the purchases are made this year, the person will not have to buy the goods later on, meaning fewer consumption expenditures will be made, and more income diverted to saving, in the future.

UNIT 4.3

2. **a.** At a 9 percent interest rate each $1000 borrowed would cost $90 per year. Projects 1 and 2 generate less than $90 per year and would not be profitable to undertake. However, projects 3 through 7 generate over $90 per year and would be profitable to undertake. The total investment for these five projects would be $5000.

   b. If the interest rate is raised to 14 percent, the annual interest payments will be $140 on each $1000 borrowed. As such, only projects 5, 6, and 7 would be profitable, since they generate more than $140 in revenue. The total amount of investments is now only $3000. The increase in the interest rate has reduced the investment expenditures by Keynes Communications Co. from $5000 to $3000.

5. With autonomous investment expenditures the slope of the aggregate expenditures line (C + I) is equal to the slope of the consumption function, which is the marginal propensity to consume. This occurs because investment is the same at every level of income; the aggregate expenditures line is thus parallel to the consumption function.

UNIT 4.4

1. **a.** This would be nondiscretionary. The state government sets the tax rates but has no control over the total amount of sales subject to the tax and thus the total tax revenue.

   b. For the most part these would be discretionary, because legislation would have to be passed each year for the appropriations. However, as with many federal agencies, a certain level of the appropriations would be automatic, making them somewhat nondiscretionary.

   c. These payments would be nondiscretionary. The guidelines for unemployment payments are set by law and the government has no control over the total number of people meeting the guidelines and thus the total amount of the payments to the unemployed.

   d. This revenue would be nondiscretionary, because the tax rates are set by the federal government, which has no control over the total income subject to the tax and thus the total tax revenues.

   e. For the most part these would be discretionary, because the municipal government would have to decide each year on the level of the appropriations.

5. A constitutional constraint to balance the budget would make government purchases nondiscretionary. While the federal government would still have to appropriate funds to the different agencies and branches of government, they could only spend the amount received in tax revenue. Because tax revenue is nondiscretionary, the total expenditures by the government are also nondiscretionary.

UNIT 4.5

1. **a.**

National Output	$2000	3000	4000	5000	6000	7000
Disposable Income	1000	2000	3000	4000	5000	6000
Consumption	2000	2500	3000	3500	4000	4500
Investment	1000	1000	1000	1000	1000	1000
Government Purchases	1500	1500	1500	1500	1500	1500
Aggregate Expenditures	4500	5000	5500	6000	6500	7000

   b. The equilibrium level of output is $7000, where aggregate expenditures equal national output.

   c. The equilibrium level of disposable income is $6000.

   d. The equilibrium level of consumption is $4500.

   e. The equilibrium level of saving is $1500, found by subtracting consumption ($4500) from disposable income ($6000).

   f. Yes. Leakages are equal to $2500 (= S + T = $1500 + $1000) and injections are equal to $2500 (= I + G = $1000 + $1500).

4. Changes in inventories warn firms to increase or decrease the level of production. If output is less than equilibrium, then aggregate expenditures are greater than production and inventories decline, signalling firms to increase production. If output is greater than equilibrium, then aggregate expenditures are less than production and inventories increase, signalling firms to reduce production.

UNIT 4.6

3. **a.** The equilibrium level of national output is $400, where aggregate expenditures (C + I + G = $250 + $50 + $100) are equal to national output.

   b. The new equilibrium level of national output is $600, where aggregate expenditures (C + I + G = $350 + $150 + $100) are equal to national output.

   c. The change in national output is $200. The expenditures multiplier is determined by dividing the change

SELECTED ANSWERS

in output by the change in investment (= $200 / $100 = 2).

d. The marginal propensity to save is equal to 0.5. As such, the value of the expenditures multiplier is 1/MPS = 1/0.5 = 2. Both values are the same.

6. If government officials had known the value of the expenditures multiplier, they could have determined the reduction in national output caused by a decline investment (assuming this information was known) and also how much government purchases would need to be increased to achieve full employment.

UNIT 4.7

2. If the $MPC = 0.9$, the expenditures multiplier is $1/(1 - MPC) = 1/(1 - 0.9) = 10$. To increase output by $500 from $1,500 to $2,000, government purchases need to be increased by $50. The tax multiplier is $-MPC/(1 - MPC) = -0.9/(1 - 0.9) = -9$. As such the needed increase of $500 in output can be achieved by decreasing net taxes by $55.56 ($500 = -55.56×-9).

4. It is appropriate to run a budget surplus with an inflationary gap. A budget surplus means government purchases are relatively low and taxes are relatively high, leading to contractionary fiscal policy. It is appropriate to run a budget deficit with a recessionary gap. A budget deficit means government purchases are relatively high and taxes are relatively low, leading to expansionary fiscal policy.

UNIT 5.1

3. **a.** Generally accepted, very durable, divisible down to a penny, easily carried in your pocket, relatively difficult to duplicate.

b. Generally accepted in limited geographic areas in the period of their main use, relatively durable, not very divisible, not very easily transportable, relatively difficult to duplicate (you might as well go catch the real thing).

c. Accepted in limited circumstances (POW camps), not very durable, divisible down to a single cigarette, easily carried in your pocket, relatively difficult to duplicate.

d. Generally accepted, extremely durable, not very divisible, relatively easy to transport, historically difficult to duplicate but becoming easier today.

e. Generally accepted, relatively durable, very divisible, relatively easy to transport small amounts, can be duplicated depending on the form it's in.

f. No widespread acceptance, not very durable, divisible to a single wrapper, easy to transport, very easy to duplicate.

g. Generally accepted, as durable as the equipment and technology that supports the network, divisible as much as anyone would care to do, very easy to transport across telephone lines, can be "duplicated" by computer pirates.

h. Accepted in limited areas, extremely durable, not very divisible, not easily transportable, difficult to duplicate in the limited areas where commonly used (since the needed stone is not there).

6. Interest-paying checking accounts are used just like non-interest-paying checking accounts, as payment for goods and services, and should be considered part of the money supply. Whether a bank pays an interest on the account has no bearing on whether it can be used as money. However, savings accounts, money market funds, and CDs should not be included in the narrow M1 definition of money because they cannot be directly used to purchase goods and services. In some cases it is important to know the total amount of funds that can be easily transferred into currency or checkable deposits to buy output; the M2 definition includes these near monies. However, we still need a definition of money that includes only items that can be directly used to pay for goods and services.

UNIT 5.2

4. Fractional reserve banking makes it possible for banks to create money. If banks kept 100 percent of all deposits as reserves, they could not make loans and would not be able to create additional deposits and money. Legal reserves are the reserves banks can use to satisfy Federal Reserve requirements, which include vault cash and deposits with the Fed. Required reserves are the amount of reserves that the Fed tells banks they must have to back up their deposits. The difference between legal and required reserves is excess reserves—the amount of reserves banks can use to back up new deposits made from loans in the money creation process.

6. Based on the deposit multiplier of $1/r = 10$ ($= 1/0.1$), the excess reserves create $500,000 ($= $50,000 \times 10$) in deposits.

UNIT 5.3

2. In the first place the laws governing the operation of the Federal Reserve System do not allow it to lend funds to the public. The Fed is set up only to make loans to commercial banks. If the Fed got in the busi-

ness of lending to the general public, it would hinder its role as the regulator of commercial banks. Unlike commercial banks, the Fed is not a profit-oriented business. It makes loans as part of its regulatory responsibilities and unlike commercial banks does not do it to make a profit.

4. Open market operations affect the money creation process by changing the amount of reserves, thus allowing banks to either increase or decrease deposits through the deposit multiplier and the money creation process. Reserve requirements directly affect the deposit multiplier underlying the money creation process. If the reserve requirements change, then banks' ability to create money is also changed. The discount rate also changes the amount of reserves banks have and thus affects the amount of deposits created with their reserves. All three of these tools are indirect methods of controlling the money supply, unlike the ability to print and issue currency. The Fed can provide the reserves or change the reserve requirements, but it is up to the banks to actually change the money supply.

UNIT 5.4

3. If the interest rate is relatively low, banks have relatively less incentive to make loans and create deposits and are probably less concerned about keeping excess reserves. However, as the interest rate increases, banks have more incentive to make loans, create deposits, and get rid of their excess reserves. Thus it is very likely that banks will create more money at higher interest rates, giving the money supply curve a positive slope.

4. **a.** The interest rate declines and the quantity of money exchanged increases, because buying in the open market shifts the money supply curve to the right.

   b. The interest rate increases and the quantity of money exchanged declines, because a higher discount rate shifts the money supply curve to the left.

   c. The interest rate increases and the quantity of money exchanged remains unchanged. This occurs because a decline in government purchases decreases the level of output in the economy, which shifts the money demand curve to the left.

   d. The interest rate declines and the quantity of money exchanged increases, because lower reserve requirements shift the money supply curve to the right.

   e. The interest rate increases and the quantity of money exchanged decreases. This occurs because an increase in excess reserves by banks means they are not creating as many deposits, and the money supply declines, which shifts the money supply curve to the left.

UNIT 5.5

2. The monetarist's view of money, especially the equation of exchange, supports the idea that the best policy is actually the least policy. That is, the money supply provides the means to purchase the economy's production. If there is too much money, inflation results. If there is too little money, a recession occurs. The best course of action is to constantly increase the supply of money to match the rate of growth of the economy's production capabilities (based on growth of labor, capital, and so forth).

3. **a.** Monetarist. They view markets as the best way to allocate resources and see little or no need for the government.

   b. Monetarist. They think that investment is very sensitive to the interest rate, which is why they argue that monetary policy is so effective.

   c. Keynesian. They think that money demand is very sensitive to the interest rate, which is why they argue that monetary policy is not very effective.

   d. Monetarist. According to the quantity theory of money, the velocity of money is a constant, giving money a direct influence on nominal GNP.

   e. Keynesian. They believe that markets have numerous imperfections that can only be corrected by government action.

   f. Keynesian. They believe that investment is reduced by expansionary fiscal policy, but that the reduction is very small.

UNIT 6.1

1. **a.** Aggregate supply. The labor strikes would increase the costs of production and/or reduce the full employment level of output, causing the aggregate supply curve to shift up and to the left.

   b. Aggregate demand. An increase in the federal deficit would result from increased government purchase and/or lower net taxes, causing the aggregate demand curve to shift to the right.

   c. Aggregate demand. A decrease in the real interest rate would increase investment expenditures, causing the aggregate demand curve to shift to the right.

   d. Aggregate supply. An increase in government regulations would increase the costs of production and/or reduce the full employment level of output, causing the aggregate supply curve to shift up and to the left.

   e. Aggregate supply. A decrease in education expenditures would increase the costs of production and/or reduce the full employment level of output, causing the aggregate supply curve to shift up and to the left.

4. If union wages are automatically adjusted using the *CPI*, inflation can be more severe due to the wage-price spiral. If the *CPI* overstates inflation, then wages are increased more than they need to be to keep up with inflation. As such, firms' costs of production increase more than necessary, forcing them to charge even higher prices. While using a more accurate measure of inflation would not prevent the wage-price spiral, using an inaccurate measure tends to worsen inflation.

UNIT 6.2

1. a. The average rate of inflation over this ten-year period is 0.33. Because inflation goes up and down with no clear pattern, there is no reason to expect it will be anything other than zero in the year 2000.

   b. By the same logic there is no reason to expect the rate of inflation will be anything other than zero for the following decade.

6. Alternative methods of reducing the natural rate of unemployment (that is, frictional and structural unemployment) center around improving the efficiency of the job market and the skills of the workers. Frictional unemployment can be reduced by providing more and better information to both the unemployed and employers or providing relocating expenses. Structural unemployment can be reduced by retraining programs or education.

UNIT 6.3

2. Keynesians are more likely to recommend wage and price controls/guidelines because they tend to favor more government controls of the economy than monetarists. Monetarists would likely argue for some less restrictive way to control inflation, such as constant growth of the money supply or a balanced budget.

   Wage and price controls/guidelines can be effectively used to control inflation if they are widespread and have no time limits on their use. In the past with temporary controls, workers and producers have simply waited until the controls were lifted, then raised wages and prices even more to compensate for the period of no increases. However, if there is no indication that the controls will be lifted, everyone will have to accept the fact that wages and prices won't increase.

6. The money supply provides the funds used for consumption, investment, and government purchases. Even though you try to control the Keynesian aggregate expenditures, an increase in the money supply will make it possible to increase aggregate demand and thus lead to demand-pull inflation. It is necessary to control both the money supply and aggregate expenditures to control demand-pull inflation.

UNIT 7.1

1. a. Your instructor would not be a consumer since the paper was purchased as part of his or her job. More than likely this would be a purchase by the government if the school is a state-funded institution.

   b. You would be a consumer since you are buying for your own use.

   c. Your instructor would be a consumer because this is not part of the job.

   d. Since this lunch is part of the interviewing process, the prospective employer would not be considered a consumer. More than likely, the employer's business is paying for the lunch.

   e. Your instructor would be a consumer in this case since the purchase is not part of the job.

   f. Your prospective employer would not be considered a consumer because once again the IBM computer would be purchased by the business.

4. a. Based on this information he was probably maximizing utility by taking only enough jumps to ensure his victory and allocating some of his time and energy for the other events.

   b. It is very likely that he would have taken another jump or two to ensure his victory in this event.

   c. Whether or not he was maximizing utility depends on his relative preferences for gold medals versus world records. It boils down to a comparison between the marginal value of breaking the world record during the Olympics and winning gold medals in the remaining two events. Of course this comparison is complicated by the fact that he could always try to break the record in later meets and that taking the extra jumps attempting to break the record would not necessarily prevent him from winning gold medals in the remaining two events.

UNIT 7.2

3. **a.** First, we need to determine the marginal utility for each good.

A	Marginal Utility	B	Marginal Utility
2	120	1	200
2	100	2	160
3	80	3	120
4	60	4	80
5	40	5	40
6	20		

With $200 of income you would buy 5 units of good A, providing a marginal utility of 40, and 5 units of good B, also providing a marginal utility of 40. The ratio of marginal utility to price is 40:20, or 2:1 for both goods.

b. With $200 of income you would buy 4 units of good A, providing a marginal utility of 60, and 3 units of good B, providing a marginal utility of 120. The ratio of marginal utility to price is 60:20 for good A and 120:40 for good B, or 3:1 for both goods. The higher price has reduced the quantity of good B demanded from 5 to 3 units.

c. The quantity of good A has also decreased, from 5 to 4 units. The relative prices of the two goods have gone from 1:1 to 1:2; good B is now relatively higher than it was. Real income has decreased due to the increase in the price of good B. Good A is a normal good because the reduction in income led to a reduction in the amount purchased.

4. If the price is $2, 6 units will be purchased. The consumers' surplus of the sixth unit is zero; the buyer is willing to pay exactly $2 for that unit. However, the total consumers' surplus for all goods is $9, which is the area between the demand curve and the market price. If the price is $3, 4 units will be purchased. The consumers' surplus of the fourth unit is also zero; the buyer is willing to pay exactly $3 for that unit. The total consumers' surplus in this case is $4. The consumers' surplus should decline at higher prices because the quantity demanded is less.

UNIT 7.3

1. **a.**

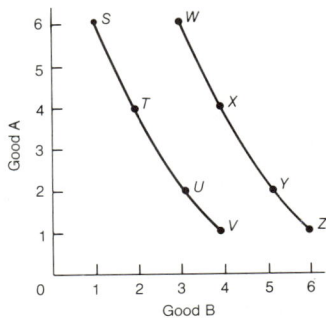

Bundle Z is preferred to bundle S because Z lies on a higher indifference curve than S. Moreover, bundle W, which is equally preferred to bundle Z, has the same amount of good A but two more units of good B, making both bundles W and Z more preferred than bundle S.

b. No, both sets of bundles cannot be equally preferred. Because bundle W has the same amount of good A but more of good B, W must be preferred to S.

c. The indifference curve with bundles W, X, Y, and Z provides the most utility, because it lies above the other curve.

3.

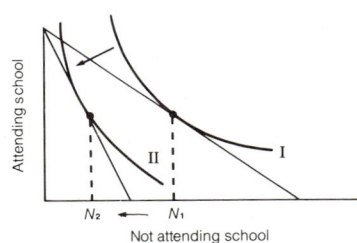

Because the price of not attending school increased, the budget constraint shifted toward the origin, leading to a reduction in the good "not attending school."

UNIT 7.4

2. **a.** The MU of nonliquor decreases. As such, the MU of nonliquor needs to increase and/or the MU of liquor needs to decrease, which can be accomplished by buying more liquor and less nonliquor.

b. The MU of nonliquor increases. As such, the MU of nonliquor needs to decrease and/or the MU of liquor needs to increase, which can be accomplished by buying more nonliquor and less liquor.

SELECTED ANSWERS

5. **a.** Consumers would try to earn less taxable income, and more income not subject to the income tax, to equal out the relative marginal utilities.

    b. There would be an increased incentive to earn wage income, and a reduced incentive to earn nonwage income, which is now subject to the tax, to equal out the relative marginal utilities.

    c. The relative price of physical goods would decline relative to services, meaning people would tend to buy relatively more goods and fewer services to equal out the relative marginal utilities.

    d. The relative price of earning profit would decline, meaning there would be an incentive to earn more profit to reduce its relative marginal utility.

    e. The relative price of buildings and improvements would decline, meaning there would be an increase in expenditures on them to reduce their marginal utility.

    f. The relative price of inheritances would be increased, meaning the economy would switch to some other method of transferring wealth between generations.

UNIT 8.1

2. Because proprietorships have access only to the personal wealth of the owner, they tend to be smaller than corporations, which can attract financial capital from thousands of investors. As such, for a given size of industry, more proprietorships would be needed to satisfy market demand, tending to make each one relatively small. The market would thus be characterized by perfect competition and monopolistic competition. Since corporations tend to be larger, fewer are needed to satisfy market demand, making them more suited to oligopoly and monopoly. Of course, corporations can be relatively small compared to the market, and proprietorships relatively large.

3. **a.** General Motors is likely to pursue all four objectives to varying degrees. While General Motors is certainly concerned about profit, it is also likely to try selling as many cars as possible. Moreover, because it is one of the largest corporations in the world, it is likely to try enhancing its good will by pursuing social objectives. In addition, many of the executives are likely to pursue their own personal goals from time to time, at the expense of the firm's profits.

    b. A small Idaho potato farmer is more likely to pursue profit maximization than any of the other three objectives, because he or she will benefit directly from the additional profit by any decisions made.

    c. Exxon, like General Motors, is likely to pursue all four objectives to varying degrees. While Exxon is no doubt concerned about profit, it is also likely to try selling as much gas as possible. Since it is one of the largest corporations in the world it is also likely to try enhancing its good will by pursuing social objectives. In addition, many of the executives are likely to pursue their own personal goals from time to time, at the expense of the firm's profits.

    d. In addition to profit maximization, this type of partnership is likely to see each partner pursuing personal objectives when possible. The main problem with profit maximization is that all five partners benefit from the work of one, giving each the incentive to let the others earn the profit while pursuing their own personal objectives.

    e. Profit maximization is probably high on the list of objectives for this firm, followed by sales maximization. However, depending on the personalities and beliefs of the family members, social objectives could also be an important objective.

    f. Personal objectives undoubtedly play an important role for this firm. However, as in any small proprietorship, profit maximization is likely to be extremely important, because the former secretary of state receives all of the income from the firm's activities.

UNIT 8.2

1. **a.**

Labor	Marginal Product	Average Product
0	—	0
1	50	50
2	60	55
3	70	60
4	60	60
5	50	58
6	40	55
7	30	51.4
8	20	47.5
9	10	43.3
10	0	39

    b. The fourth unit of labor has a lower marginal product than the third.

    c. The average product for both the third and fourth unit is 60.

    d. The marginal product is zero for the tenth unit.

    e. The average is never zero once the first unit is used. Average product can be zero only if total product is zero.

2. **a.** The act of transporting any good involves a change in location, because the good at the wrong location cannot provide consumer satisfaction.

  b. The entertainment services provided by a football game involve a change in structure, in particular, a change in the memories of the people watching the game.

  c. The production of an automobile, like the production of any manufactured good, involves a change in the structure of the raw materials.

  d. Any type of storage activity involves a change in time, making the goods available to the consumers at the proper time.

  e. Like the entertainment services of a football game, watching television involves a change in structure—the memories of the people watching.

UNIT 8.3

1. **a.** The total opportunity cost would include the professor's salary ($40,000) plus the operating expenses ($170,000), a total of $210,000. The professor forgot to include his foregone wage of $40,000 when computing accounting profit.

  b. The normal profit would have been $5000 for each of the two houses sold, a total of $10,000 for both houses. With this information the total opportunity costs for the firm were $220,000. The professor's economic profit was actually −$25,000 (= $195,000 − $220,000).

4. A constant marginal product would imply a horizontal marginal cost curve. As such, the average variable cost curve would also be horizontal and would lie directly over the marginal cost curve. That is, marginal cost and average variable cost would be equal at every quantity of output. However, average fixed cost would not be affected by the law of diminishing marginal returns and would continue to have a negative slope at all quantities of output. And because average total cost is the sum of average fixed cost and average variable cost (which is constant), the average total cost curve would be parallel to the average fixed cost curve and also negatively sloped at all quantities of output.

UNIT 8.4

1. **a.** There are only a handful of firms, the products are not very similar, there is probably limited freedom to enter and exit the industry, but each firm might have pretty good information on prices and production technologies.

  b. There is only one firm, which means there is no reason to discuss the similarity of products, there is no freedom to enter and exit the industry, and the firm probably has pretty good information.

  c. There are a large number of relatively small firms, each sells relatively similar but slightly differentiated products, there is a good deal of freedom to enter and exit the industry, and each representative probably has limited information concerning the prices of the other firms.

  d. There are a large number of relatively small firms, each sells an identical product, there is a good deal of freedom to enter and exit the industry, and each farmer probably has pretty good information concerning the market price and technology.

  e. There is a small number of relatively large firms, each sells relatively differentiated products, there is very little freedom to enter and exit the industry, and the firms probably have pretty good information concerning prices and technology.

  f. Although the firms might be small, each probably dominates its own local market, each firm also sells similar but slightly differentiated products, there is some freedom to enter the market but not a lot, and the firms probably have limited information concerning prices charged by the others.

4. **a.** First, identify marginal cost:

Quantity	0	1	2	3	4	5
Total Cost	10	20	25	27	32	39
MC	—	10	5	2	5	7

Quantity	6	7	8	9	10	11
Total Cost	49	61	76	93	113	135
MC	10	12	15	17	20	22

Quantity	12	13	14	15
Total Cost	160	190	230	280
MC	25	30	40	50

Then identify the outputs that equate marginal cost to price:
$5—4 units; $10—6 units; $15—8 units; $20—10 units; $25—12 units.

  b. The firm incurs a loss if the price is $5, where total revenue is $20 but total cost is $32. At all other prices the firm does not incur a loss. In all cases the price is greater than average variable cost, so the firm does not need to shut down in the short run.

c.

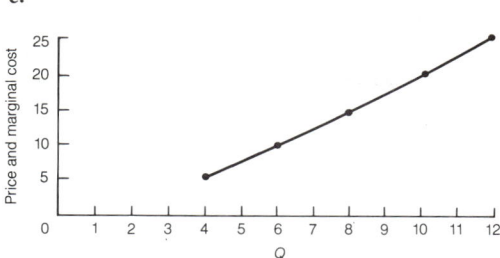

UNIT 8.5

1. **a.** This should definitely improve the farmers' situation by stimulating demand for agricultural production. Prices will increase and the quantity exchanged will also go up. This is most likely to improve the short-run problem.

   b. This should also improve the farmers' situation by stimulating demand for agricultural production. Prices will increase and the quantity exchanged will also go up. This is more likely to improve the long-run problem, but it probably won't hurt the short-run situation either.

   c. This is likely to worsen the farmers' situation by increasing productivity and shifting the supply curve to the right. Although the quantity exchanged will increase, prices are likely to fall. This will probably affect the long-run problem the most.

   d. This is also likely to worsen the farmers' situation by increasing production and shifting the supply curve to the right. Although the quantity exchanged will increase, prices are likely to fall. However, this will have an impact primarily on the short-run problem.

   e. This will worsen the farmers' situation by decreasing demand and shifting the demand curve to the left. Both the quantity exchanged and the price will decline. This will primarily affect the short-run problem.

   f. Except for those in the Midwest, who will be hit very hard by the drought, farmers will be helped because production will decrease, leading to a leftward shift in the supply curve. As such, the price will increase, even though the quantity exchanged will fall, the reduction in the quantity exchanged being borne by the Midwestern farmers. This will also primarily affect the short-run problem.

3. **a.** The equilibrium price is $5.50 and the equilibrium quantity is 600,000 bushels. The farmers' total revenue is $3,300,000.

   b. A surplus of 90,000 bushels is created if a price floor is set at $7.00. It would cost the government $630,000 to buy the surplus wheat. The farmers' total revenue is $4,620,000.

   c. Farmers supply 660,000 bushels at $7.00 per bushel. For 660,000 bushels buyers are willing to pay $2.50 per bushel. This means the subsidy per bushel is $4.50. In this case it costs the government $2,970,000. The farmers' total revenue is again $4,620,000.

   d. Farmers need to take 1800 acres out of production to achieve market equilibrium at $7.00 and 560,000 bushels exchanged. The farmers would have to reduce production by 90,000 bushels, the size of the surplus, which is equal to 1800 acres of land if yields are 50 bushels per acre (90,000 bushels = 50 bushels per acre × 1800 acres).

UNIT 9.1

1. If a firm produces a good with numerous close substitutes, then potential buyers can buy essentially the same good from several firms. However, if the good has no close substitutes, then one firm has the ability to control the price and/or quantity because it is the only firm supplying that particular good to buyers. If buyers switch to the less perfect substitutes, then they receive relatively less satisfaction.

    The most common types of goods typically produced by monopolies are public utility services, including electricity, natural gas, local telephone, water, sewage disposal, trash collection, and cable television. No very close substitutes exist for any of these goods. The best substitute for electricity is natural gas, and vice versa. The best substitute for local telephone services is mail or personal contact. There are no substitutes for water, sewage disposal, or trash collection.

4. **a.** Due to the ability to patent genetically modified organisms, either a monopolistically competitive or oligopolistic market structure is likely to develop.

   b. This information indicates that a monopolistically competitive market structure is more likely to occur unless a handful of firms can obtain most of the patents.

   c. Since research and development costs are likely to be relatively high, this could be an important barrier to entry into this market. Once firms have profitable patents, they can use their profits to develop new organisms or buy existing patents and add to their market power.

UNIT 9.2

2. **a.**

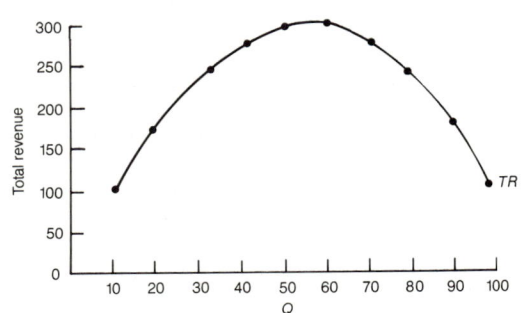

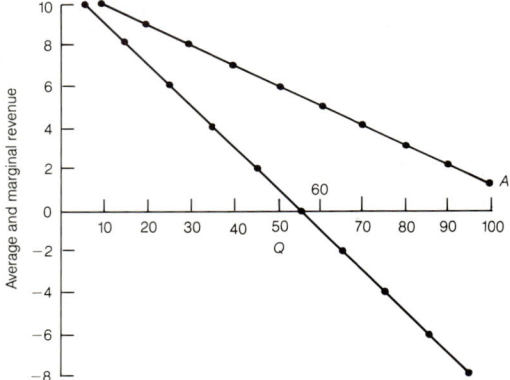

b. The marginal revenue curve lies below the demand curve for the monopolist because the demand curve is negatively sloped. The negative slope means that the monopolist must lower the price on all units to sell an additional unit of output. Although the monopolist receives additional revenue from the additional unit (equal to the price charged for the additional unit), it receives less revenue on all units up to that additional unit. The marginal revenue received by the monopolist for the additional unit is thus less than selling price (average revenue) of the additional unit. Since the demand curve is the monopolist's average revenue curve, the marginal revenue curve lies below the demand curve.

Since the marginal revenue curve is not constant but rather is negatively sloped, and marginal revenue is the slope of the total revenue curve, the total revenue curve is not a straight line with constant slope. In fact, the total revenue curve begins relatively steeply with relatively high and positive marginal revenue, then flattens out as marginal revenue falls, and finally becomes negatively sloped when marginal revenue is negative.

7. A monopolist is not able to charge any price that he wants, being constrained by the market demand curve. A monopolist can either set the price and let the buyers decide how much they want or set the level of production and let the buyers decide what price they are willing to pay. If the monopolist tries to increase the price too much, buyers will simply not buy the good.

UNIT 9.3

1. **a.** The primary difference between public utility and wind-powered generation of electricity is the amount of capital required and the subsequent fixed cost. Compared to generation by public utilities, very little capital is required to generate electricity with the wind. For this reason, wind-powered generation would not really be considered a public utility. Even though a necessary good is produced, there is no natural tendency for the industry to be monopolized because of decreasing average cost.

   b. The most important consideration is the relative cost of producing electricity by wind and by public utilities. If wind-powered production has a lower average cost, then it could take some of the output away from public utilities, causing them to move up their average cost curve and become even less competitive, eventually forcing them out of the market. This would mean the generation of electricity would be a relatively competitive market structure. However, if public utility generation has a lower average cost, then it could prevent wind-powered generation from taking any of the market, meaning the natural monopoly status of public utilities would be unaffected.

UNIT 9.4

1. If there are physical differences in the products produced by monopolistically competitive firms, then advertising does play an important role by giving buyers information needed to choose the products that best satisfy their needs. However, if the differences are only perceived by the buyers due to advertising itself, then the benefits of advertising are subject to question. While advertising definitely increases the costs of production and uses resources that cannot be used to produce other goods, there is no clear-cut benefit if the only effect is to mislead people about the good they purchase.

2. A monopolistically competitive firm is similar to a perfectly competitive firm in many ways. In both markets

SELECTED ANSWERS

a large number of relatively small firms exist, with freedom of entry and exit. However, monopolistically competitive firms sell slightly different products, and usually there is not perfect information. Because of product differentiation among monopolistically competitive firms, each one faces a downward-sloping demand curve, like a monopolist. While in monopolistic competition resources are misallocated, the misallocation is less than in a monopoly. In addition, a firm that faces a downward-sloping demand curve does not have a short-run supply curve for its output.

UNIT 9.5

4. The large number of relatively small firms in perfect competition and monopolistic competition makes it virtually impossible for them either to get together or to reach an agreement on market price and quantity acceptable to all. Think of the problems of getting 100,000 farmers together (secretly, of course) to establish a marketwide price and quantity and the share of the market to be produced by each farmer. And a monopoly has no need to collude with any other firm, since it has all of the market power to begin with. But oligopoly, with a small number of relatively large firms, can easily determine the market price and quantity and the share each firm will produce. Moreover, oligopolistic firms have a great deal to gain from cooperation rather than competition—monopolistic profits.

    In that collusion essentially transforms an oligopolistic market into a monopolistic market, it worsens the allocation of resources. The price is higher and the quantity produced is less with collusion than without.

6. General Motors is in direct competition with Ford and Chrysler, in much the same way that the University of Michigan football team is in direct competition with the Ohio State football team. During the annual Michigan–Ohio State matchup, it doesn't matter how well Michigan plays, it matters how well Michigan plays relative to Ohio State. Michigan can play their worst game of the year but still win by playing a little bit better than Ohio State. In the same way, General Motors can increase its sales and profits, not just by producing a better car but by producing one a little better than Ford and Chrysler. This type of head-to-head competition usually does not exist for a General Motors dealership, especially in a large city with twenty or more dealerships.

UNIT 9.6

2. In general, conglomerate mergers are not likely to come under the jurisdiction of antitrust legislation unless they substantially reduce competition in a particular industry. For example, if a conglomerate firm established by the merger of dozens of different firms in different industries already owned the largest firm in one particular industry and then acquired the second largest, this could substantially reduce competition. While this example might technically be considered a conglomerate merger, it also has the makings of a horizontal merger.

3. Nonpredatory price competition occurs when firms reduce prices corresponding with decreases in average cost. Predatory pricing occurs when firms reduce prices below average cost, intentionally incurring a loss in the short run to eliminate competition, but making up for the loss from other operations or with economic profit earned when the competition is eliminated. While firms in price competition also hope to eliminate other firms, they don't intentionally reduce prices below average cost to accomplish this goal.

UNIT 9.7

1. **a.** This would limit competition in the health care industry, increase the prices doctors charge, reduce the quantity exchanged, and lead to a less efficient allocation of resources.

   b. By reducing third party payments, the demand for health care would decline, leading to a reduction in the allocation of resources toward health care and reducing the price of health care.

   c. By increasing third party payments, the demand for health care would increase, there would be an increase in the allocation of resources toward health care, and the price of health care would increase.

   d. This would likely reduce many of the barriers to entry into the health care industry, leading to increased competition, an increase in allocation of resources toward health care, and a reduction in the price.

2. Without the use of lesser-skilled health care professionals, patients need to consult with, and pay the prices charged by, highly skilled doctors. For minor health problems, this means the economy is allocating too many resources to, and paying too much for, the production of the health care services. The use of different skill levels would improve this misallocation of resources. In fact, the health care industry already has varying skill levels that accomplish similar results. General practitioners give a preliminary diagnosis and

specialists provide more extensive diagnosis or treatment if needed; everyone with a headache need not see a neurosurgeon. And often a nurse or paramedic rather than a general practitioner can provide for patients' health care needs.

UNIT 10.1

2. **a.**

Quantity of Factor	0	1	2	3	4
Quantity of Output	0	40	75	105	130
MPP	—	40	25	30	25
MRP (Price = $5)	—	200	125	150	125

Quantity of Factor	5	6	7	8
Quantity of Output	150	165	175	160
MPP	20	15	10	5
MRP (Price = $5)	100	75	50	25

b.

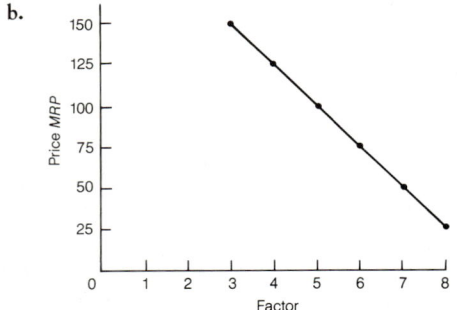

c.

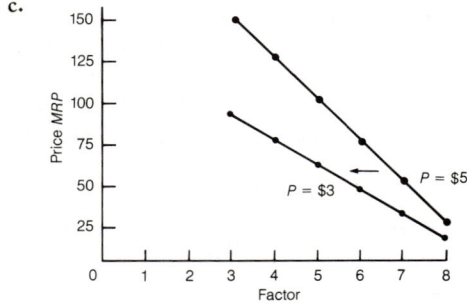

The factor demand curve based on the price of $3 is to the left of the factor demand curve based on the price of $5.

d. If each factor cost $75 and the price of the output is $5, then 6 units of the factor are hired, where the factor cost is equal to the marginal revenue product. If the price of output drops to $3, then 4 units of the factor are hired, again where factor cost is equal to the marginal revenue product.

4. **a.** Product price. An increase in sales will likely increase the price of agricultural products, leading to an increase in the marginal revenue product and consequently an increase in the demand for labor and a rightward shift in the demand curve.

b. Prices of other factors. If the increase in the amount of land used to produce agricultural products is due to a decrease in the price of land, and if labor and land are complements in production, then the demand for labor will increase, and the demand curve will shift to the right.

c. Technology. An increase in technology, such as the development of a new fertilizer, will increase the productivity and thus the marginal revenue product of the labor. As such, the demand for labor will increase, and the demand curve will shift to the right.

UNIT 10.2

2. Marginal factor cost can be greater than factor supply when the supply facing a firm is upward sloping. In this case, for the firm to hire more of the factor it must increase the factor price paid to all units. As such, the marginal cost of hiring the factor is greater than the factor price because it includes the additional cost to all other factors.

5. **a.** A medical doctor probably has greater geographic mobility, while the service station mechanic has better occupational mobility, since he or she has less training.

b. Farmland has a great deal of occupational mobility; it is very easy to switch an acre of farmland into another production process. However, the farmer has much greater geographic mobility, because he or she can go anywhere in the world, while the farmland must remain where it is.

c. A semi-truck has greater mobility; its basic function is to travel cross-country. Moreover, the semi-truck probably has better occupational mobility as well, because it is not nearly as specialized as a bulldozer.

d. A pine tree has a good degree of both occupational and geographic mobility; however, the chief executive officer of Gulf and Western probably has greater mobility in both areas.

UNIT 10.3

2. A bilateral monopoly is a market that consists of one buyer, a monopsonist, and one seller, a monopolist. No single price maximizes profits for both the mon-

SELECTED ANSWERS

opsonist and the monopolist. Moreover, there is no reason for both sides to maximize profits at the same quantity. Negotiation is necessary in bilateral monopoly because the profit-maximizing prices are different for both sides. As such, they must negotiate a price that is agreeable to both.

3. If the market price is $6, then the firm hires 2 units of labor such that MRP = price = $6. The first unit adds more ($7) to revenue than it costs, and the third unit adds less ($5).

UNIT 10.4

1. **a.** The union would favor this action, because it would increase the price of the product produced by the factor. The marginal revenue product of postal workers would increase, potentially leading to an increase in both wages and the number of workers hired.

    b. The union would not favor this action, because United Parcel Service is a substitute for the postal office. Increased use of UPS would probably mean reduced use of the post office and consequently less demand for postal workers.

    c. The union would not favor this action unless it was combined with an increase in the wage. However, because the postal union is more of an industrial union than a craft union, reduced hours alone would probably not increase the wage, meaning the union would not be likely to favor this action.

    d. The union would favor this action, because the main objective of unions has always been to establish and increase the minimum wages paid to its employees.

3. **a.** The AMA is more like a craft union than an industrial union, as shown by the fact that it is more concerned with the number of workers than with the wage paid. The AMA could become a full-fledged union because physicians are highly skilled workers.

    b. If the AMA is not a labor union, it has achieved many of the results usually desired by unions, especially higher wages. This has been made possible by the AMA's control of medical school admissions and physician licensing.

UNIT 11.1

2. Worker quality—while males have traditionally been expected to be the family breadwinner, females have traditionally been expected to raise the family and take care of the home. As such, the average skill and education level of males is higher than females, leading to higher-paying jobs for males.

    Worker preference—If women choose to raise a family rather than pursue a full-time career, they must often either work part-time at relatively low pay or leave the labor force for several years, sacrificing seniority and career advancement.

    Geographic immobility—Females tend to have less geographic mobility than males, thus restricting their ability to receive higher wages, precisely because they have lower wages to begin with. That is, a two-wage family, with the male earning more than the female, is more likely to follow the relocation needs of the higher-paid husband than the lower-paid wife. Thus, the husband gets a raise and the wife starts over in a new job.

    Occupational immobility—Females, because of their lower-wage status and relatively less education and training, tend to have greater occupational mobility. However, greater occupational mobility, especially at the low-paying end of the job spectrum, is not likely to equalize wage differentials between men and women.

    Discrimination—Discrimination, based on the sex of the worker, is undoubtedly a big reason women receive a lower average wage than men.

    Institutional constraints—Institutional constraints, such as labor unions and minimum wages, are not likely to contribute to the wage differential between men and women.

4. The oil boom led to higher wages in Oklahoma, while the slowdown in the automobile industry led to unemployment in Michigan. Many people therefore moved from the Michigan labor market to the Oklahoma labor market. This was simply an example of wage differential adjustment, as discussed in Figure 11.1.1, due to geographic and occupational mobility.

UNIT 11.2

1. **a.** If the interest rate is 10 percent, the interest payments on the $3,000,000 would be $300,000 per year. Because the factory is expected to return at most $250,000 per year, this would not be a good investment.

    b. If the interest rate fell to 5 percent, then the factory would be profitable because the interest payments on the $3,000,000 would now be only $150,000 per year, less than your lowest estimate of $200,000 per year in profit.

    c. In this case it would also be profitable to build the factory, because the interest payments would be $150,000 per year, less than your lowest estimate of profit per year.

3. The interest rate is the indirect payment for the use of capital, because in equilibrium firms borrow funds through the financial market until the return on the

last unit of capital is exactly the same as the return on the last dollar of funds borrowed. In essence, the return on the last unit of capital purchased is used to pay the interest on funds borrowed through the financial markets.

UNIT 11.3

1. **a.** The purchase price of rental tapes was higher because rental stores were willing to pay more. And they were willing to pay more because consumers were willing to rent the tapes. The amount rental stores were willing to pay to purchase the tapes depended on the amount consumers were willing to pay to rent them.

   b. The rental rate that consumers were willing to pay for the tapes determined the purchase price that rental stores were willing to pay. The higher the rental rate, the more stores would be willing to pay for the tapes.

3. Based on the earnings of executives in comparable positions, it is unlikely that Lee Iacocca earned an economic rent in 1983. In fact, $650,000 for the chairman of the board of any major corporation was probably a steal in 1983. It's very likely that Iacocca could have obtained another job with another company for more than $650,000. On the other hand, some of the executives paid over $2 million might have been receiving economic rent.

UNIT 11.4

2. **a.** More equal; human capital. Additional funds for education will likely increase the amount of human capital of the general population and thus equalize the amount of income received.

   b. Less equal; inherited wealth. A lower inheritance tax will allow people with more wealth and income to pass it down to subsequent generations. There will be less tax revenue to raise the incomes of the poorer members of society.

   c. More or less equal; market power. The elimination of labor unions could change the distribution in either direction. Without labor unions workers would tend to earn the same wage, leading to greater equality at the lower end of the income distribution. However, corporate owners are likely to have relatively more market power, allowing them to retain relatively more of the revenue received by business and increasing income inequality.

   d. More equal; discrimination. Since those discriminated against are most often at the low end of the income distribution, tougher antidiscrimination laws are likely to increase the relative income at the lower end and increase income equality.

   e. Less equal; human capital. Since the illegal aliens entering the country have few skills and relatively low levels of human capital, there will be an increase in the relative number of people at the lower end of the income distribution, thus making the distribution of income less equal.

4. An unequal distribution of income can be bad for the economy, because a small number of people might be living in aristocratic splendor while the rest of the society endures unspeakable hardships. The total welfare of the society can be very low with an unequal distribution of income. However, an unequal distribution of income can also be good for the economy if those members with the high levels of income invest part of their income in capital goods that will increase the productivity, and subsequently income, of the poorer members of the economy. Capital investment is more likely if a small number of people have a lot of extra income, over and above that needed for consumption, than if a large number of people each have a little bit of extra income.

UNIT 11.5

2. **a.** The total amount of welfare payments would be $15,000, distributed in the following manner: person 1—$5000; person 2—$4000; person 3—$3000; person 4—$2000; person 5—$1000.

   b. In this case the total amount of welfare payments would be $30,000, with $6000 paid to each of the five people earning less than $6000.

   c. The welfare payments for each person are given as follows:

Person	Income	Welfare Payment
1	$ 1,000	$5,400
2	2,000	4,800
3	3,000	4,200
4	4,000	3,600
5	5,000	3,000
6	6,000	2,400
7	7,000	1,800
8	8,000	1,200
9	9,000	600
10	10,000	0

   The total payments in this case are $24,300, less than the amount in question 2b.

   d. The negative income tax will probably be better for the kingdom because everyone will still have the

SELECTED ANSWERS

incentive to work, which is not likely with the guaranteed income.

4. If the illegal aliens currently in the country are suddenly "legalized," then they would find their way into the official poverty measure, leading to an increase in the "official" percentage of people below the poverty line. Moreover, the now-legal aliens would be able to officially obtain welfare payments, leading to an increase in the number of welfare recipients as well.

UNIT 12.1

2. **a.** Program x is the only one that will provide a positive net increase in welfare, a total change of +13. The other two programs will lead to welfare changes of −3 (y) and −10 (z).

   b. Programs x and y can both pass due to logrolling. In this case A would vote for x if B and C voted for y. Program z cannot find enough logrolling with either of the other two programs for passage. Of the two programs passed through logrolling, x benefits society, but y does not.

3. Special interest groups, whether government agencies or private groups, are more concerned about a particular activity or issue than the rest of society. Nongovernment special interest groups undoubtedly played an important role in government regulations implemented during the 1970s as they sought to increase environmental quality, improve occupational safety, prevent unsafe consumer products, and so forth. Moreover, government agencies also played a role in additional government regulations as they tried to extend their areas of jurisdiction and control and justify their existence and need for appropriations.

UNIT 12.2

2. The only difference between a near public good and a pure public good is the ability to exclude nonpayers. However, because both types are nonrival in consumption, there is no reason that nonpayers should be excluded from consumption. It is the nonrival nature of public goods, whether pure public or near public, that underlies the optimal level of production. Because they are nonrival, the market demand curves for both types are found by vertically adding individual demand curves. The ability to exclude nonpayers has no bearing on the optimal quantity of production.

3. **a.** A free rider can exist in the music industry if someone listens to the music but buys neither the records nor the products advertised on the radio or television.

   b. Almost everyone has been a free rider in the music industry at one time or another. Anyone who listens, either intentionally or inadvertently, to a song without buying the record or the products advertised is a free rider.

   c. If the music industry is profitable, then the price of a record is equal to or greater than its opportunity cost of production. Whether or not the music industry has free riders has no bearing on whether the price is more or less than production cost. What the free rider problem does mean is that a misallocation of resources exists. A handful of people are paying to have records produced, while others benefiting from the music do not pay. Thus, the price is lower and the quantity produced is less than it needs to be to achieve an optimal allocation.

UNIT 12.3

1. **a.** A 15 percent tax on total income is proportional because each of the four income groups pays 15 percent of its total income.

   b. The tax on nondividend income and the percentage of total income paid in tax for the four groups is I, $1500 (15 percent); II, $2700 (13.5 percent); III, $6000 (12 percent); IV, $10,500 (10.5 percent). This tax is regressive because higher-income groups have relatively more dividend income excluded from the tax, and thus they pay a relatively smaller proportion of total income in tax.

   c. The tax on food expenditures and the percentage of total income paid in tax for the four groups is I, $150 (1.5 percent); II, $240 (1.2 percent); III, $300 (0.6 percent); IV, $450 (0.45 percent). This tax is regressive because higher-income groups spend relatively less of their income on food, and thus they pay a relatively smaller proportion of total income in tax.

   d. The tax on corporate income and the percentage of total income paid in tax for the four groups is I, $0 (0 percent); II, $800 (4 percent); III, $4000 (8 percent); IV, $12,000 (12 percent). This tax is progressive because higher-income groups have relatively more dividend income on food, and thus they pay a relatively larger proportion of total income in tax.

   e. The tax on wage income and the percentage of total income paid in tax for the four groups is I, $700 (7 percent); II, $1050 (5.25 percent); III, $2100 (4.2 percent); IV, $3500 (3.5 percent). This tax is regressive because higher-income groups have relatively less wage income, and thus they pay a relatively smaller proportion of total income in tax.

5. The intent of the revenue effect is to raise revenue for government operations. The intent of the reallocation effect is to reduce the level of a particular activity. If the government wants to tax an activity, such as speeding, out of existence, then it does not want to receive any revenue from this tax. If it receives revenue, that means the activity still exists. On the other hand, if the government is trying to raise funds to operate, it does not want the reallocation effect to eliminate the activity. With no activity there are no funds.

UNIT 12.4

1. a. It is probably using the argument of imperfect information to justify regulating amusement park rides. If the rides are not as safe as users think, then demand for the rides is artificially high.

   b. The primary argument against regulation probably centers on administrative inefficiencies, especially the specific areas of time lag, paperwork, and ineffective rules.

   c. The CPSC undoubtedly has motives for extending its regulatory power to amusement park rides as part of its role as a special interest group. The CPSC must justify its appropriations each year to Congress. And one way to justify larger appropriations, which lead to more power and prestige for the administrators of the commission, is to extend its areas of regulation.

   d. Students are likely to answer both yes and no to this question. However, they should justify their answers by making a comparison of the costs and benefits of the regulation. That is, do the benefits of safer rides outweigh the costs of a greater regulatory burden, not only on the amusement rides industry but on society as a whole?

5. a. Subliminal messages undoubtedly need to be regulated. If used improperly, they could easily manipulate consumers into buying goods they neither want nor need.

   b. The two basic reasons for regulation of subliminal messages are imperfect information and externalities. Not only do people not know they are receiving the information but also they could be incurring a cost without compensation. The most applicable arguments against regulation probably concern higher production costs needed to meet regulations, reduced productivity if the subliminal messages are overly restricted, and administrative inefficiencies resulting from inflexible and ineffective rules.

   c. The potential benefit from the regulation of subliminal messages is a society not comprised of a bunch of mindless zombies following the instructions of the subliminal transmitters. The potential costs of the regulation are higher production costs needed to meet the regulations and reduced productivity if the regulations prevent transmissions in some areas that are highly beneficial, such as assisting the recovery of surgery patients.

UNIT 13.1

2. a. The equilibrium price is $40 and the equilibrium quantity is 4 units.

   b. The socially optimum quantity of output with external costs included would be 3 units, where the private benefits ($50) equal the private costs ($30) plus the external costs ($20). It is less than the quantity in question 2a.

   c. The socially optimum quantity of output with external benefits included would be 6 units, where the private benefits ($20) plus the external benefits ($40) equal the private costs ($60). It is greater than the quantity in question 2a.

   d. The socially optimum quantity of output with both external costs and benefits included would be 5 units, where the private benefits ($30) plus the external benefits ($40) equal the private costs ($50) plus the external costs ($20). It is greater than the quantity in question 2a.

4. An uncontrolled external cost misallocates resources because less of the good is produced and the price is lower than the socially optimal solution. However, due to its market power a monopolistic market structure produces less output at a higher price than perfect competition. Thus, a monopolistic market structure would tend to move in the direction of a higher price and less output needed for a social optimum. But the monopolistic market structure might also go too far, raising the price too high and restricting the quantity of output too much.

UNIT 13.2

1. Pollution, which only involves emitting waste material into the environment, does not create an external cost if no one is harmed. In many cases the natural capacity of the environment is able to dispose of the waste before anyone is harmed.

5. a. The main generator of this externality would be those who burn coal and other fossil fuels that provide the necessary materials for the formation of ozone. The external cost is incurred by the farmers growing the crops.

SELECTED ANSWERS

b. This is probably best considered a nonpoint source pollution, because coal and natural gas are used as fuel sources throughout the economy, not only in smokestacks but also in automobiles.

UNIT 13.3

1. **a.** Government regulation is probably best, because the total amount of waste is more important than the amount emitted in any given year.

   b. A charges and standards approach should be effective for this pollution. Drivers can pay a charge based on emissions found during annual inspections, and if pollution becomes worse or better, the charge can be raised or lowered.

   c. Moral suasion, asking people not to drive for a week or two, is probably the most effective policy for this situation.

   d. The best policy in this case is probably no policy at all, because the natural capacity of the environment should be sufficient to control the emissions.

   e. A Pigouvian tax, forcing the plant to internalize the externality, should be most effective here.

   f. Government regulation of the pesticides would likely be in order, because the total amount of the pesticides is more important than the amount emitted each year.

   g. Negotiation can probably be effectively used to prevent this externality.

   h. A pollution permits market can be an effective policy by issuing the permits for the total amount of pollution the river can handle, then letting the cities exchange the permits as they see fit.

3. The key to the materials balance approach is that all materials extracted from the natural environment eventually return as pollution. This means it is not possible to design a policy that deals with only air pollution or only water pollution. One alternative is to tax materials as they are withdrawn from the environment, as they will eventually return to the environment as pollution. However, since the costs have already been paid, there is little incentive to prevent residuals from returning. Moreover, this approach ignores the principle that all pollution does not lead to external costs if no one is harmed. Taxing the materials does not distinguish between pollution that harms and pollution that does not. The other, more sensible, alternative is to tax or otherwise control the emissions as they are returned to the environment. This provides incentives to keep materials in the economy longer, recycle waste, and use fewer raw materials. The alternative pollution control policies discussed in this unit basically follow this approach.

UNIT 13.4

2. Without the price ceilings, we are likely to import less petroleum because domestic production will be greater and domestic consumption less. As such, it is less likely that we would be as severely affected if OPEC raised its prices like it did in the 1970s. In fact, OPEC would probably not be able to implement the price increases it did in the 1970s as long as we imported less of their petroleum.

UNIT 14.1

2. **a.**

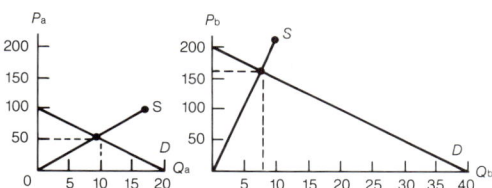

In country A the equilibrium price is 50 and the equilibrium quantity is 10. In country B the equilibrium price is 160 and the equilibrium quantity is 8.

b. Since country A has a lower price than country B, country B will import the good and country A will export the good.

c.

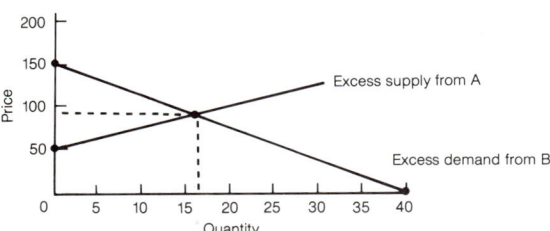

The equilibrium price is approximately 92 (92.3 to be exact) and the equilibrium quantity imported/exported is approximately 17 (16.92 to be exact).

4. A tariff on imported Japanese automobiles helps domestic automobile producers because they can charge a higher price and sell more output. It also helps Japanese consumers because Japanese automobile manufacturers are forced to sell more output at home at a lower price. However, this tariff hurts domestic consumers because they have to pay a higher price for a smaller quantity of the good. It also hurts Japanese automobile manufacturers because they sell less output.

UNIT 14.2

3. **a.** According to purchasing-power parity a computer that has a price of $2000 in the United States should have a price of 16,000 kronor in Sweden. If the price is less than 16,000 kronor, then someone in the United States can take $2000, trade for 16,000 kronor at the exchange rate of 8 kronor per $1, and have money left over.

   b. If the interest rate in Sweden increases from 10 to 15 percent, this is likely to attract investment dollars from the United States. That is, the demand for Swedish kronor will increase, leading to an increase in the exchange rate between dollars and kronor. The price of a krona will be greater than 12.5 cents, meaning the krona appreciates relative to the dollar.

   c. If Sweden's economy grows relatively faster than the U.S. economy, its import of U.S. goods relative to the U.S. import of Swedish goods will increase. As such, Sweden will demand more dollars, while the United States will demand fewer kronor, meaning the price of a krona will decline below 12.5 cents as it depreciates relative to the dollar.

   d. If the exchange rate between dollars and kronor increases to 15 cents per krona, this means $1 can buy fewer kronor (6.67 kronor per dollar) and 1 krona can buy more dollars. As such, the krona appreciates relative to the dollar and the dollar depreciates relative to the krona.

5. Since appreciation of U.S currency encourages imports and discourages exports, it will lead to a reduction in national output. However, depreciation of currency will have the opposite effect. It encourages exports because it makes the price of exported goods relatively cheaper and discourages imports because it makes the price of imported goods relatively higher. As such, depreciation of currency will lead to an increase in national output.

UNIT 14.3

2. **a.** Labor force participation rate. If women leave the labor market, the labor force participation rate will decline and less economic growth will result.

   b. Saving. If the average propensity to consume declines, the average propensity to save increases, meaning more funds will be available to purchase capital goods. While saving is the key source of economic growth, investment, social overhead capital, exploration, and land reclamation could all contribute to economic growth, depending on how the funds are used. However the funds are used, the additional saving is likely to lead to economic growth, taking into consideration the role of aggregate demand discussed in Figure 14.3.3.

   c. Social overhead capital. An increase in the amount of funds for highway construction will lead to an increase in the economy's social overhead capital, providing the way for additional economic growth.

   d. Land reclamation. Using the Great Lakes as farmland would be an example of land reclamation that likely would lead to additional economic growth.

   e. Investment. If tax deductions on capital goods are eliminated, the price of capital increases and the amount purchased through investment expenditures declines. This will lead to a reduction in economic growth.

   f. Labor force participation and saving. A reduction in transfer payments could affect economic growth through both labor force participation and saving. If the reduced transfer payments provide more incentives to join the labor force, then the labor force participation rate will increase, leading the additional economic growth. However, the reduction in transfer payments will also reduce disposable personal income and consequently the amount of saving in the economy, leading to a reduction in economic growth (again considering the role of aggregate demand).

   g. Investment, exploration, and saving. A decline in the interest rate is likely to affect several sources of economic growth. First, a lower interest rate will lead to an increase in investment and consequently an increase in economic growth resulting from the additional capital. Second, a similar effect is likely from exploration, which is essentially investment on natural resources rather than capital goods. However, a lower interest rate will encourage exploration. Third, a decline in the interest rate will discourage saving by households, meaning fewer funds will be available to finance investment expenditures, leading to a reduction in economic growth.

4. This is a good question for stimulating classroom discussion. Students are likely to take both sides of this issue. One argument is that people today should not reduce consumption and have a lower standard of living, because people tomorrow are likely to be much better off anyway. This is much like taking from the poor and giving to the wealthy. Another argument is that people today are better off because people yesterday reduced consumption and made their own sacrifices. As such, we are merely paying back to the future what we received from the past.

SELECTED ANSWERS

UNIT 14.4

3. Increased agricultural production is essential for an LDC to increase its level of development. With relatively low agricultural productivity, farmers are barely able to feed those working on the farm, with little or nothing left over for people working in nonagricultural areas such as manufacturing. However, with increased agricultural productivity, farmers can supply enough food to feed people in other industries, meaning the various types of goods and services associated with a higher level of development can be produced.

    A land tenure system can severely inhibit or reduce agricultural productivity. With an inefficient system of land ownership, less agricultural output will be produced, meaning fewer people can work in the nonagricultural industries that provide the goods needed for higher economic development.

4. Technology in the United States was developed based on the quantities and qualities of resources in that particular country. Most LDCs do not have the same mixes of labor, capital, and land that we have, making a lot of our technology inappropriate for LDCs.

    a. Inappropriate. While we may have the need for large, centrally located electricity generation, most LDCs would probably be better off with small-scale generators.

    b. Appropriate. One thing most LDCs need is better agricultural productivity, which can be achieved through technological advances such as this.

    c. Inappropriate. Most LDCs are probably more in need of factories that produce engines to pump irrigation water or small tractors than automobiles.

    d. Inappropriate. While computerized communications are very important for MDCs, LDCs are more in need of improved highways or railroads for shipping goods across the country.

UNIT 15.1

2. It is not possible to completely separate ownership of resources from decision making. Whoever owns the resources ultimately has control over how they are used. But the owners can give control of the resources to others, as corporations in capitalistic societies have done for the last century. It is possible to effectively separate ownership and decision making in a functioning economy. Market socialism can continue to operate as an economic system if the government, as the resource owner, allows markets to make the allocative decisions. On the other hand, private ownership with government decision making is likely to generate more conflict and is less likely to continue over a long period of time. This is because people are less prone to release control of their resources to the government than the government is to release control to the markets. This latter type of market structure would require some type of totalitarian control by the government.

4. There is no reason to think either economic system is necessarily more suited to be a welfare state. Government control in socialism allows the economy to direct resources to increased welfare of the poor better than the private control in capitalism. However, increased efficiency through the use of markets in capitalism tends to generate more overall welfare in the economy, making it possible to redirect more to the poor. But, there is less of a guarantee in capitalism that the redirection will actually take place.

UNIT 15.2

3. The best way to see if labor is the source of all value is to remove the other factors from the production process. Without land, there are no raw materials to process and produce goods. Without capital, including a simple screwdriver, labor's task would be much more difficult. Without entrepreneurs, labor would be idled because none of the other factors would be combined in the production process.

    Physical exertion is not the only type of effort needed in the production of goods and services. An entrepreneur who wheels and deals to get the right factors together at the right time could be expending much more effort than the worker on the assembly line. Moreover, the land or capital owner who thinks and plans the best use of the resource is also exerting effort. Thomas Edison said that invention was 99 percent perspiration and 1 percent inspiration. While labor contributes most of the perspiration, the inspiration provided by entrepreneurs, capital owners, and land owners is also needed to produce goods.

5. Karl Marx's economic theories were undoubtedly influenced by the times in which he lived. Adam Smith was influenced by government control over national economies when he wrote about the importance of free markets in *The Wealth of Nations*. John Maynard Keynes was influenced by the Depression of the 1930s when he developed his macroeconomic theory. And the supply-side theorists in the 1970s were influenced by the economic times. It is very difficult to predict how Marx's theory would have differed if he had lived in the late 1900s. He could have been a supply-sider or even a monetarist.

UNIT 15.3

1. The Soviet economy is a socialist economy based on government ownership of resources and decision making. The Soviet government controls all of the economy's basic resources except for labor. Moreover, with its central planning it makes all of the important allocative decisions. Over seven decades of socialism there is little evidence that the Soviet Union is moving toward Marx's ideal state of communism. Government resource control and ownership are as great as ever.

UNIT 15.4

1. The Soviet economy relies more on centralized planning. The Chinese economy may be more decentralized in part because it has more people, making it harder to control their actions, and in part because it was much less developed, especially in terms of communication and transportation systems, when it became a socialist country. And more recently, a big difference is China's increased reliance on markets.

4. An increase in entrepreneurs, like an increase in any of the other factors of production, is likely to increase economic growth in China. One reason is that the new entrepreneurs have incentives to produce more goods and services.

Glossary/Index

A

ability-to-pay principle The principle stating that taxes are based on the ability of people to pay. 600

absolute advantage The condition in which one country can produce more output than another country with the same factors. 659

absolute poverty level The condition in which people do not have the income to buy an absolute amount of the basic necessities of life. 566

accelerator theory of business cycles, 186–187

accessibility The location of an activity or parcel of land relative to other activities. 549–550

accounting cost An explicit cost incurred in production that involves direct payment for the input. 401

accounting profit The difference between a firm's revenue and its explicit accounting costs. Accounting profit generally appears on a firm's profit and loss statement, but it is not the economist's concept of profit. 402, 553

ad valorem **tax** A tax that is levied on the monetary value of the tax base. It is also a tax that is specified as a percentage of the price. 88–89, 599

aggregate demand The total demand by the household, business, government, and foreign sectors for final goods and services produced in the economy at alternative price levels. 170–172
   contraction and, 183–184
   determinants of, 318–321
   fiscal policy and, 257–258
   Phillips curve and, 325

aggregate demand curve A curve representing the relationship between aggregate demand for final goods and services and the average price level. 170–172, 176–177, 239

aggregate expenditures The total expenditures on final goods and services for all relevant sectors. 217, 218
   equilibrium with, 233–235
   government purchases and, 227–229
   Keynesian, 318–319
   money market and, 298
   multiplier and, 242–244
   net taxes and, 229

aggregate market The combined product markets for all final goods and services in the economy. The aggregate market combines the aggregate demand and aggregate supply curves to analyze equilibrium national production and the price level. 170–178
    business cycles and, 183–186
    expectations and, 329–331
    fiscal policy and, 257–258
    Keynesian cross and, 239–240
    multiplier and, 248
    shocks to, 175–178
aggregate supply The total amount of final goods and services produced in the economy at alternative price levels. 172–174
    contraction and, 185
    determinants of, 321–322
    expansion and, 185–186
    Phillips curve and, 327–328
aggregate supply curve A curve representing the relationship between the average price level and the quantity of final goods and services produced in the economy. The aggregate supply curve has three distinct segments—one that is vertical, one that is horizontal, and one that is positively sloped. The slope becomes vertical when all factors of production in the economy are fully employed. The slope becomes positive when the economy is getting close to full employment. The slope becomes horizontal when there is unemployment throughout the economy. 172–174, 177–178, 197, 331
agricultural goods, supply problems with, 423–431
agricultural policies, 427–431
    evaluation of, 430–431
    price floor, 428
    price subsidy, 428–429
    supply restriction, 429–430
agricultural runoff, 633
agriculture:
    in China, 721
    in less-developed countries, 690
    in Soviet Union, 712–713
Aid to Families with Dependent Children (AFDC), 570
Airline Deregulation Act of 1978, 433, 611
airline services:
    price competition and, 457–458
    supply of, 433–434
air pollution The discharge of waste materials into the air. The major sources of air pollution are automobile emissions, smokestacks, and power plants. 633–634, 642–643
Air Pollution Control Act of 1955, 642
allocation The process of distributing resources for the production of goods and services and of distributing goods and services for consumer use. 5–6
    economic system and, 697
    market and, 50–51
    methods of, 18–19
    monopolistic competition and, 465–466
    monopoly and, 452–453
    oligopoly and, 474
    perfect competition and, 420–421
    profit and, 555
    reallocation effect and, 601–602
    rent and, 551–552
    three questions of, 42–43
American Federation of Labor (AFL), 518, 522, 524
American Medical Association (AMA), 486, 487
antitrust legislation A series of laws designed to prevent monopolistic actions that reduce competition and lead to an inefficient allocation of resources. 476–482
Apple computers, 15
appreciation When one currency can buy more of another currency. 671
appropriate technology Technology that is suited to the factors of production and resources in a particular country. The direct transfer of technology used in a more-developed country may be unusable in a less-developed country because the factors of production and resources are different. 691
arbitration The intervention of a third party in the collective bargaining process, making legally binding and enforceable judgments. 521
AT&T, 5, 7, 389
ATS (automatic transfer system) accounts Accounts that automatically transfer funds between interest-paying savings accounts and checking accounts. 269–270
automatic stabilizers Taxes and transfer payments that depend on the level of national output such that they automatically reduce the fluctuations of the business cycle with no discretionary action. 258–259
automobile emissions, 633
autonomous government purchases Government purchases that do not depend on the current level of national income and output. 226, 230
autonomous investment expenditures Investment expenditures that do not depend on the current level of national income and output. 214
average cost, 406–407, 417–419
    decreasing, 439–441, 456–457
average cost pricing A pricing policy for public utilities in which price is set equal to average cost. Average cost pricing insures that the firm earns a normal profit, sometimes called a "fair rate of return." However, average cost pricing does not lead to an optimal allocation of resources because price is not equal to marginal cost. 459–460

average fixed cost Total fixed cost per unit of output, found by dividing fixed cost by the quantity of output. The average fixed cost curve is negatively sloped, as average fixed cost decreases with larger quantities of output. 406

average product The quantity of total product produced per unit of variable input, holding all other inputs unchanged. It is found by dividing total product by the quantity of the variable input. 396, 398–399

average propensity to consume (*APC*) The proportion of total income that is used for consumption expenditures, found by dividing consumption by disposable income. 205

average propensity to save (*APS*) The proportion of total income that is used for saving, found by dividing saving by disposable income. 205

average revenue The revenue received per unit of output sold, which is the price of the good. It is found by dividing total revenue by the quantity of output. 413–414, 464

average total cost Total cost per unit of output, found by dividing total cost by the quantity of output. Average total cost is also the sum of average variable cost and average fixed cost. Average total cost decreases with small quantities of output because both average variable and average fixed costs decrease. However, average total cost begins to increase only when the increase in average variable cost is greater than the decrease in average fixed cost. 407

average variable cost Total variable cost per unit of output, found by dividing variable cost by the quantity of output. The average variable cost curve is U-shaped. Average variable cost decreases with small quantities of output, then increases with larger quantities. The increase is due to the law of diminishing marginal returns. 406, 417–418

B

backward-bending labor supply curve A labor supply curve that is positively sloped at relatively low wages and negatively sloped at relatively high wages. The backward-bending labor supply curve is based on the tradeoff between time spent on the job and leisure time. 539, 540

balanced-budget multiplier The ratio of the change in output to a change in government expenditures that are matched by an equal change in taxes. The balanced-budget multiplier for government purchases is equal to 1. However, the balanced-budget multiplier for transfer payments is equal to 0. 255–257

balance of payments The relationship between the demand for and the supply of a country's currency. A fixed exchange rate can lead to a balance of payments deficit or surplus. 672–674

balance of payments deficit When the quantity of currency supplied is greater than demand. A balance of payments deficit causes a country to lose reserves. 672, 673

balance of payments surplus When the quantity of currency demanded is greater than supply. A balance of payments surplus causes a country to gain reserves. 673

balance of trade The relationship between a country's exports and imports. 657

balance of trade deficit The balance of trade when a country imports more goods than it exports, and net exports are negative. 657

balance of trade surplus The balance of trade when a country exports more goods than it imports and net exports are positive. 657

bank:
  Federal Reserve, 283–285
  national, 285
  state, 285
banking, 275–279
  fractional reserve, 275
  money creation and, 275–279
  reserves in, 276–277

bank panic A situation in which numerous banks throughout the economy fail when they are unable to satisfy the demands of their depositors. The banks then fail and take with them the deposits they created, leading to a reduction in the money supply and usually contributing to a contractionary period. 282

barrier to entry An institutional, technological, or economic restriction on the entry of firms into an industry. 439–441

benefit-cost analysis A technique that compares the benefits obtained from a public good with the costs of production. 596
  government regulation and, 617

benefit principle A principle that states taxes are based on the benefits received. The benefit principle is difficult to apply because the degree of benefit people obtain from government programs and public goods is not easily measured. 600

Berck, Peter, 109n

bilateral monopoly A market with one seller and one buyer. The two sides of a bilateral monopoly must negotiate the price and quantity exchanged. The monopsonist offers a lower price than the monopolist wants. The quantities could be equal but need not be. Both sides are not able to maximize profit at the same time. The quantity exchanged is always less than in perfect competition. 514–516

birth rate The number of people born per thousand population. 688, 692

black market A market that exchanges goods above the legally restricted maximum price. A black market is created by a price ceiling because some buyers are left without goods and are willing to pay a premium above the ceiling. 87–88

Board of Governors The policymaking and governing body of the Federal Reserve System, containing seven members appointed by the president. Each member is appointed to a fourteen-year term, with one term expiring every two years. 283

bourgeoisie Marx's term for capital owners and entrepreneurs. 704

breakeven output The quantity of output in which total revenue is equal to total cost such that a firm earns a normal profit but no economic profit. 415

budget A listing of all revenues and expenditures for a given period of time. 224–227
 balancing, 263, 337–338
 high employment, 259
 inflation control and, 337–338

budget deficit The situation that exists when the government's expenditures are greater than taxes. A recessionary gap can be more effectively eliminated by running a budget deficit. 224, 225, 257

budget line The alternative combinations of two different goods that can be purchased with a given income based on the prices of the two goods. The consumer can purchase any bundle that lies beneath the budget line but none that lies above it. The budget line reflects the ability of a consumer to purchase goods and services. 369–371
 price change and, 370–371
 slope of, 370

budget surplus The situation that exists when the government's expenditures are less than taxes. An inflationary gap can be more effectively eliminated by running a budget surplus. 224, 225, 257

business cycle The pattern of expansion and contraction of economic activity. Business cycles are the frequent but irregular fluctuations in national production in the economy. 180–190
 aggregate market and, 183–186
 alternative theories of, 186–187
 demand-driven, 183
 inflation and, 189–190
 since 1919, 181–182
 phases of, 181
 supply-driven, 183
 unemployment and, 188–189

business sector All of the privately owned firms engaged in the production of goods and services, including corporations, partnerships, and proprietorships. 117

business tax, indirect, 141, 142
buyers, number of, 59–60

C

capital The synthetic resources used to produce goods and services. Capital is a factor of production that has been previously produced. Unlike other types of material items, capital does not become a part of the product. 14
 factor supply and, 508
 human, 536–539, 681
 inflation and, 322
 in less-developed countries, 690–691
 social overhead, 679–680

capital consumption allowance The amount of capital stock worn out, or depreciated, in the production of goods and services. 137–138

capital goods:
 cost of, 217
 investment in, 542–543

capitalism An economic system that is primarily based on private ownership of resources and allocative decisions made through markets. While capitalism almost always uses markets for allocative decisions, the distinguishing feature of capitalism is the private ownership of resources. Capitalism is the economic system of many industrialized countries, including the United States. 697–698

cartel A formal, written agreement, usually between nations, designed to raise prices and decrease production or limit competition in an industry. OPEC is the most famous cartel. 471, 472–474

Carter, Jimmy, 338

Celler-Kefauver Act of 1950 This act amended the Clayton Act by outlawing mergers made through the acquisition of assets. The Clayton Act merely made mergers by the acquisition of stock illegal. 480

certificate of deposit A certificate for funds deposited in a bank or financial institution for a specific period of time and rate of interest. 545–546

ceteris paribus A Latin term meaning that all other factors are held unchanged. The *ceteris paribus* assumption is used to isolate the effect one economic factor has on another. Without this assumption, it would be difficult to determine cause and effect in the economy. 8–9

change in amount consumed A movement along the consumption function caused by a change in disposable income. 209

change in consumption A shift in the consumption function caused by a change in one of the determinants, such as interest rates, wealth, or

GLOSSARY/INDEX

expectations, and a change in autonomous consumption expenditures. 209–210
change in demand A shift of the entire demand curve resulting from a change in any of the determinants of demand. 55
change in quantity demanded The movement along a demand curve caused by a change in the price of the good. A change in quantity demanded can only result from a change in price. 54–55
change in quantity supplied The movement along a supply curve caused by a change in the price of the good. A change in the quantity supplied can only result from a change in the price of the good. 64–65
change in supply A shift in the entire supply curve resulting from a change in any of the determinants of supply. 64–65
changes in inventories The increases or decreases in the business sector's accumulated stocks of raw materials, intermediate goods, and final goods. Changes in inventories are an important part of the equilibrium mechanism for the macroeconomy. Inventories increase when the business sector is selling less than current production, and they decrease when sales exceed current production. If there are positive changes in inventories and inventories are increasing, then producers are signaled to reduce production. If there are negative changes in inventories and inventories are decreasing, then producers are signaled to increase production. The only time there are no changes in inventories is when aggregate expenditures are equal to national production. 235
characteristics of a market The three important characteristics of a market are type of commodity, geographic area, and period of time. 49
charges and standards A policy that controls pollution by adjusting taxes on pollution discharges to meet a desired level of pollution. This policy gives policymakers a greater degree of flexibility than the pollution permit market. 641–642
checkable deposits Deposits at banks that can be withdrawn on demand, without prior notice. 268
Chinese economy, 718–724
 background of, 718–720
 evaluation of, 721–724
 structure of, 720–721
circular flow The continuous and simultaneous flow of final goods and services and factors of production in exchange for the payments for the goods, services, and factors. The circular flow is the simplest yet most fundamental way of looking at the operation of the macroeconomy. 116–124, 147–150
 with financial markets, 119–120
 with foreign sector, 122–124
 with government, 120–122
 government purchases, 230
 investment, 218–219
 net taxes, 230–231
Civil Aeronautics Authority Act of 1938, 611
Civil Aeronautics Board (CAB), 433–434, 611, 612
Civil Rights Act, 530
classical economics A body of economic thought originating with the pioneering work of Adam Smith that built on the idea that freely operating markets would lead to production that always tended to the full employment level of output. 195–198
classical range The vertical segment of the aggregate supply curve. In this segment all factors of production are fully employed. The classical range occurs when the economy is on the production possibilities frontier. 172, 173
Clayton Act of 1914 This act outlawed such specific monopolistic practices as price discrimination, exclusive agreements and tying contracts, mergers, and interlocking directorates if they substantially reduced competition. 480, 522–523
Clean Air Amendments of 1970, 611, 642, 643
closed shop A firm that is allowed to hire only union members. 521
Club of Rome, 653
collective bargaining The negotiation between employers and employees to develop a contract or agreement applicable to all workers in an industry or occupation. Collective bargaining is the most important function of a labor union. 519–521
collective farm A farm in the Soviet Union that is collectively operated by groups of farmers on land that is leased from the government. Farmers on collective farms are forced to sell most of their output at very low prices to the government but are free to sell any remainder in markets, keeping any profits they receive. Collective farms were developed under Stalin's rule but today account for only a small fraction of total agricultural production in the Soviet Union. 713
collusion The secret agreement between two or more firms to use their market power to control market price and quantity or to limit competition. 470–471, 472–474, 477
command economy An economy that relies on the government for the allocation of resources. While socialism usually contains a command economy, this need not be the case. Socialism in some countries operates effectively by using markets for allocative decisions. 698–699
 pure, 20
commodity money Any money that has value in use in addition to its value in exchange. 268

common property good A good that is rival in consumption, but nonplayers cannot be excluded from consumption. A common property good can also lead to an externality because people cannot be prevented from using the good, but the use by one prevents the use by another. 592, 628–629

Commonwealth v. Hunt, 522

commune In China, a collectively operated farm composed of several brigades from different villages. Each brigade is composed of several production teams within a village. 721

communism An economic system that is primarily based on collective ownership of resources and collective decisions made by groups of individuals. While capitalism and socialism actually operate in the real world, communism is an ideal economic system developed by Karl Marx. In this system there is no government, and everyone works according to his or her ability and is paid according to need. 698. *See also* Soviet economy

comparable worth concept, 530

comparative advantage. *See* principle of comparative advantage

comparative statics The technique of comparing the equilibrium resulting from a change in a determinant with the equilibrium prior to the change. 76

competition:
   antitrust legislation and, 476–481
   monopolistic, 389, 437–438, 462–466
   nonprice, 470
   perfect, 388, 411–421, 511–513
   regulation and, 615–616

complements Two goods that are used together such that increase in the price of one good leads to a decrease in demand and a leftward shift in the demand curve of the other good. If demand of good 1 decreases as the price of good 2 increases, the goods are complements, or two goods with a negative cross price elasticity. 57, 98, 108

complements in production Goods that are produced jointly with the same resources. An increase in the price of one complement good leads to an increase in the supply of the other good and a rightward shift of the supply curve. 68

concentration ratio The percentage of total output in an industry that is produced by a given number of the largest firms. The most common concentration ratios are for the four and eight largest firms. Higher concentration ratios indicate the market is dominated to a greater degree by the largest firms. 468–469

conglomerate merger A merger between two firms in unrelated industries. 478

Congress of Industrial Organizations (CIO), 518, 523, 524

constrained utility maximization The process of obtaining the highest possible level of utility under the given circumstances when the highest overall level of utility cannot be reached. 352–353

consumer A person or household that purchases goods and services used for the satisfaction of wants and needs.
   expectations of, 58–59
   number of, 59–60
   tastes and preferences of, 58
consumer behavior, 350–379
consumer demand:
   applications of, 375–379, 381
   indifference curves and, 366–373

consumer equilibrium The condition that exists when the last dollar spent on each good provides the same additional utility. In consumer equilibrium, consumers allocate their income between the purchase of different goods such that they cannot increase their level of utility. With consumer equilibrium, a consumer has maximized utility. In indifference curve analysis this is where the budget line is tangential to the indifference curve. At this point the ratio of prices is equal to the ratio of marginal utilities. This means that the willingness of the consumer to trade one good for the other is exactly the same as the ability to trade the two goods in the market. 355, 371–372
   rule of, 355

consumer price index (CPI) An index of the prices of goods and services purchased by families in urban areas. The CPI is the most common measure of the price level and inflation. It is limited because it is based only on the prices of goods and services purchased by urban families in 1967. 161–163

Consumer Product Safety Act of 1972, 612

Consumer Product Safety Commission (CPSC), 612, 614, 615

consumer satisfaction, 6

consumer surplus The difference between the price buyers are willing to pay for a good (based on the marginal utility received) and the actual price paid. For a typical demand curve, consumer surplus can be seen as the triangular area between the market price and the demand curve. 361, 362, 603

consumption expenditures Expenditures by households for the purchase of final goods and services. 118–119, 203–211
   aggregate demand and, 318
   changes in, 209–210
   determinants of, 209

consumption expenditures *(continued)*
    disposable personal income and, 203–205
    investment and, 217–221
consumption function A line that depicts the relationship between consumption and disposable income. The slope of the consumption function is the marginal propensity to consume. 206–207, 208
consumption/saving schedule A table that illustrates the division of disposable income between consumption and saving. 204
contraction The declining phase of the business cycle, in which economic activity is falling. 181
    aggregate demand and, 183–184
    aggregate supply and, 185
contractionary fiscal policy Fiscal policy consisting of decreases in government purchases and/or increases in net taxes (including decreases in transfer payments). Contractionary fiscal policy can effectively control demand-pull inflation but can create additional problems if inflation is caused by shifts in the aggregate supply curve. 257, 335–337
contractionary monetary policy Monetary policy consisting of decreases in the money supply through the use of open market operations, reserve requirements, and the discount rate. Contractionary monetary policy can effectively control demand-pull inflation but can create additional problems if inflation is caused by shifts in the aggregate supply curve. 299, 336–337
convergence hypothesis The hypothesis stating that common economic forces will eventually make capitalism and socialism indistinguishable from each other and form a new type of economic system. According to the convergence hypothesis, both markets and the government are needed in the ownership and allocation of resources. And whether an economic system begins as capitalism or socialism, it will eventually have the same mix of markets and government involvement. 700
corporate income tax, 607
corporate profits, 142
corporation A firm that is also a distinct legal entity that exists separately from its owners. It is usually owned jointly by a large number of shareholders. Unlike partnerships and proprietorships, corporate shareholders have limited liability and can lose only their initial investment. This feature of corporations allows them to raise large amounts of financial capital. 385, 386
cost, 401–408
    accounting, 401
    average decreasing, 439–441, 456–457
    average fixed, 406–407
    average total, 407
    average variable, 406, 417–418
    economic, 401
    external, 624
    marginal, 406, 407, 415–417, 449–450
    marginal factor, 506–507
    opportunity, 37–39, 401–402
    price and, 417–418
    private, 623
    social, 624
    total, 402–406, 414–415, 448
    total fixed, 402, 403–404
    total variable, 402–403
cost-push inflation The inflation caused by increases in factor costs without comparable increases in the production of final goods and services. 185, 317–318
CPI. *See* consumer price index
craft union A labor union composed of workers in the same occupation. 518, 524–525
Crandall, Robert W., 665
cross price elasticity of demand The relative response of demand to a change in the price of another good. It is defined as the percentage change in the demand of good 1 divided by a percentage change in the price of good 2. 98, 108–109
crowding-out effect The process in which increases in government purchases lead to decreases in investment expenditures. The crowding-out effect results because the stimulation caused by government purchases leads to an increase in the interest rate, which reduces investment expenditures. 309
Cultural Revolution The period between 1967 and 1969 in which China tried to replace material production incentives with moral incentives and purge the white-collar bureaucrats from the government. While this was not an economic program, it had a devastating impact on the economy. 720
currency The paper money and coins issued by the government. 268. *See also* money
curve A line that does not have a constant slope, 29, 30
cyclical unemployment Unemployment created by the frequent but irregular declines in economic activity associated with business cycles. 153

D

death rate The number of people dying per thousand population. 688
decreasing marginal rate of substitution A principle that states as more of one good is traded for another, the marginal rate of substitution between the two goods declines. Moving from left to right along an

indifference curve, the slope begins very steep, then it flattens out. 369
degradable pollution Organic waste that can be broken down by the natural capacity of the environment. Water can usually cleanse itself of organic waste if its capacity is not exceeded. 632
   Pigouvian tax and, 639
demand The range of quantities of a commodity that buyers are willing and able to buy at different prices in a given period of time. 49, 52–60
   consumer, 366–379, 381
   cross price elasticity of, 98, 108–109
   decrease in, 77–78, 81, 82
   derived, 498–499
   determinants of, 56–60
   factor, 498–503
   farm problem and, 425
   income elasticity of, 97–98, 108
   increase in, 76–77, 80–82
   indifference curves and, 366–373
   law of, 52–53, 359–360
   market, 54, 55
   market power and, 442
   monopolistic competition and, 462–463
   monopoly and, 445–448
   of perfectly competitive firm, 412–414
   price elasticity of, 92–97, 106–108
   quantity demanded and, 55
   utility and, 358–364
   See also aggregate demand
demand curve A graphical representation of the law of demand. A demand curve has a negative slope due to the law of demand. 53–54
   aggregate, 170–172, 176–177, 239
   indifference curves and, 372–373
   kinked, 471–472
   market power and, 442
   of monopolistically competitive firm, 463
   for monopoly, 445, 447
   of perfectly competitive firm, 412
demand-driven business cycle A business cycle caused by changes in aggregate demand. 183
demand-pull inflation The inflation caused by increases in aggregate demand without comparable increases in aggregate supply. 185, 317
demand schedule A table that illustrates the alternative quantities of a commodity demanded at different prices. 52–53, 93
demographic transition The process in which a country goes from a low rate of population growth to a high rate, then back to a low rate as the country develops. The demographic transition occurs because the death rate declines at an earlier level of development than the birth rate. 688, 689

Department of Energy Organization Act of 1977, 611
deposit multiplier The change in deposits at banks divided by the initial change in reserves. The deposit multiplier can be specified as $1/r$, where r is the fraction of reserves used to back up deposits. 279
Depository Institutions Deregulation and Monetary Control Act of 1980, 285
depreciation When one currency can buy less of another currency. 671
depression. *See* Great Depression
derived demand The demand for a factor of production resulting from the demand for the good or service it produces. Factor demand is a derived demand. 498–499
determinants of consumption The three factors other than income that have the most important effect on consumption are the interest rate, wealth, and expectations. A change in any of these determinants leads to a change in autonomous consumption expenditures and a shift in the consumption (and saving) function. 209
determinants of demand The five key factors that affect market demand are income, prices of other goods, tastes and preferences, expectations, and the number of buyers in the market. 56–60
   expectations, 58–59
   income, 56–57
   number of buyers, 59–60
   prices of other goods, 57
   tastes and preferences, 58
determinants of elasticity The three key determinants of elasticity are availability of substitutes, time period of analysis, and proportion of budget. While the first two apply to the price elasticities of both demand and supply, the last applies primarily to the price elasticity of demand. 99–100
determinants of factor demand The three determinants of factor demand are product price, technology, and prices of other factors. An increase in both the product price and technology causes a rightward shift in the factor demand curve. An increase in the price of another factor can cause either a rightward or leftward shift in the factor demand curve. 501–503
determinants of investment Other than output and the interest rate, the four most important factors that affect investment are technology, cost of capital goods, government policies, and expectations. A change in these determinants causes either of the investment curves to shift. 216–217
determinants of supply The five most important factors that affect market supply are factor prices, technology, prices of other goods, expectations, and number of sellers in the market. 65–70
   expectations, 69

GLOSSARY/INDEX

determinants of supply (*continued*)
    factor prices, 65–66
    number of sellers, 69–70
    prices of other goods, 67–68
    technology, 66–67
dialectic The process of change in which one concept (thesis) brings forth a competing concept (antithesis), which together generate a new concept (synthesis). Marx applied this concept to structural changes in society, in which the thesis in capitalism is the capitalists and the antithesis is labor. The synthesis generated leads to the establishment of socialism. 704, 705
dialectic materialism The process in which opposing economic groups, through their inherent conflict, lead to structural changes in society. Marx attributed society's movement through distinct stages, including the feudal system, capitalism, socialism, and communism, to this process of dialectic materialism. 704
diamond/water paradox This apparent paradox is based on the observation that water, which is much more useful than diamonds, has a lower price. If price is related to utility, how can this occur? The paradox is cleared up by an understanding of marginal utility. Water provides a greater amount of total utility, but the vast supplies of water available make its marginal utility quite low. Diamonds provide much less total utility, but the limited supplies keep the marginal utility, and the price, very high. 361–364
dictatorship of the proletariat The state of socialism in which workers have taken control of resources and temporarily given this control to the government. In Marx's view of the development of society, this was an intermediate stage that would subsequently be replaced by communism. 705
diesel fuel, relative price of, 375–376
direct relationship. *See* positive relationship
discount rate The interest rate charged by the Federal Reserve System to banks for borrowed funds. If the Fed increases the discount rate, then the money supply decreases. If the Fed decreases the discount rate, then the money supply increases. 288, 289
discouraged workers Unemployed workers who have given up looking for employment because of their inability to find work. 154
discretionary expenditures Expenditures that must be periodically (annually) appropriated by legislative and political bodies. Discretionary expenditures give the government control over the total amount of the expenditures. 225
discrimination:
    income inequality and, 562
    wage, 530, 536

disguised unemployment Unemployment created when labor is engaged in the production of goods and services but is not being used to its full potential. 152–153
disposable personal income The income remaining after personal taxes are paid. Disposable personal income is found by subtracting taxes from personal income and represents the income that households can use for either consumption or saving. 146–147, 203–205
dissaving The process of spending more on consumption than is available in current disposable income. Dissaving is made possible by spending either past income from accumulated savings or future income through borrowing. 204
double counting The process in which the value of an intermediate good is counted once when it is sold to a firm and again when it is sold as the final good to a household. GNP measures only market transactions of final goods to avoid double counting. 127

E

economic cost An opportunity cost incurred in production. 401
economic development The continuous increase in society's overall level of welfare over time. Economic development and economic growth are not the same. While economic growth contributes to development through the provision of additional goods and services, it is only one part of development. 685–692
economic growth The process of increasing the economy's ability to produce goods and services. Economic growth can be achieved by increases in labor, land, capital, and technology. Economic growth is seen as outward shifts in the production possibilities frontier and as rightward shifts in the aggregate supply curve. It is measured by changes in real GNP, 22, 40–42, 676–683
    in China, 722–723
    costs of, 681–683
    nature of, 676–677
    sources of, 677–681
    in Soviet Union, 713–714
economic principle A hypothesis that has been tested many times and that consistently agrees with the real world. 9
economic profit The difference between all opportunity costs of production, including a normal profit, and the revenue received by a firm. Economic rent and economic profit are essentially the same. Economic profit is the revenue earned by a firm over and above

all opportunity costs. Economic rent is the payment to a factor over and above its opportunity cost. Economic profit can be divided up as economic rent to the four factors of production. 402, 553, 554–555

economic rent The payment to a factor of production over and above its opportunity cost. A factor (for example, land) that is fixed in its supply earns nothing but an economic rent. Economic rent is a residual paid after all of the opportunity costs are paid. Firms with a more profitable product can pay a higher rent. High rent does not cause the price of a product to be high. 551–552, 553

economics A social science that studies the allocation of resources to the production of goods and services used to satisfy consumers' unlimited wants and needs. As a social science, economics studies the behavior of society. But unlike other social sciences, economics concentrates its study on the economy. 5–9
  classical, 195–198
  Keynesian (*see* Keynesian economics)
  Marxian, 703–707
  normative, 9
  positive, 9
  study of, 7–9
  supply-side, 340–342

economic system An organized method of producing and distributing goods, services, and resources in a society that answers the three basic questions of allocation: What to produce? How to produce? For whom to produce? Alternative economic systems can be classified based on ownership of resources and type of decision making. Ownership of resources can be private, government, or collective. Decision making can be undertaken by markets or government or collectively. 696–701
  capitalism, 697–698
  characteristics of, 696–697
  Chinese, 718–724
  communism, 698
  Marxian, 703–707
  socialism, 698
  Soviet, 709–716
  Yugoslavian, 725–726

economist, world view of, 9–10

economy A system of production, distribution, and consumption of goods and services. 5
  Chinese, 718–724
  command, 698–699
  market, 698–699
  market-oriented, 21–23
  mixed, 20–21
  planned, 711–712, 721
  pure command, 20
  pure market, 19–20
  Soviet, 709–716
  Yugoslavian, 725–726

efficiency The process of obtaining the highest level of consumer satisfaction from the available resources. 6, 22

elastic The condition of elasticity in which the percentage change in quantity demanded (or supplied) is greater than the percentage change in price, and the absolute value of the price elasticity of demand (or supply) is greater than 1.0. An elastic curve is very responsive to changes in price. 95

elasticity A measure of the relative response of one variable to changes in another variable. In terms of the market, it is the relative response of quantity demanded, or supplied, to a change in price, income, or the price of another good. Elasticity is determined by the percentage change in quantity divided by the percentage change in the variable stimulating the change in quantity. 92–100
  cross price elasticity of demand, 98, 108–109
  determinants of, 99–100
  income elasticity of demand, 97–98, 108
  market and, 102–109
  price elasticity of demand, 92–97, 106–108
  price elasticity of supply, 98–99
  relative, 93
  slope and, 95, 96
  total expenditure and, 95–97
  welfare loss and, 605

employment:
  full, 21–22, 39
  underemployment, 39, 152–153
  See also full employment output; unemployment

energy:
  alternative sources of, 651–652
  consumption of, 647
  geothermal, 652
  income elasticity of demand for, 108
  nuclear, 651
  policies on, 649–651
  production of, 648
  solar, 651–652
  sources of, 647

energy resources, 645–652

Engels, Friedrich, 704

entrepreneurship The specialized type of human resource that assumes the risk of combining the other three factors in the production of a good. 15, 508, 555

environment:
  energy resources, 645–652
  market and, 622–629
  pollution of, 631–636
  pollution control policies and, 634, 638–643

Environmental Protection Agency (EPA), 611, 612–613, 614, 615, 616, 642, 654
environmental quality and GNP, 131
equation A formal statement showing the equality between two variables. 27
   of a straight line, 27–28
equation of exchange An equation relating the nominal value of goods and services to the money supply and the velocity of money. The equation of exchange is specified as $M \times V = P \times Q$. 306–307
equilibrium The state that exists when opposing forces exactly offset each other and there is no inherent tendency for change. In terms of the market, equilibrium is reached at the price at which the quantity supplied is exactly the same as the quantity demanded. In terms of the macroeconomy, equilibrium is reached when the expenditures on national output are exactly the same as the amount of national output produced. 72, 233–239
   with aggregate expenditures, 233–235
   factor market, 511–516
   with leakages and injections, 236–239
   market, 73
equilibrium price The price that equates the quantity demanded and supplied in the market. 73–74
equilibrium quantity The quantity exchanged between buyers and sellers in equilibrium. 74
equity The fairness with which income or wealth is distributed within a society. 23
   Chinese economy and, 723
   efficiency and, 563–564
   horizontal, 600
   Soviet economy and, 716
   vertical, 600
excess reserves The amount of legal reserves remaining after required reserves have been satisfied. Excess reserves are the reserves that a bank can loan out. 277
exchange rate The price of one currency in terms of another. 670–672
excise tax, 607
exclusive agreement An agreement between a producer and dealer in which the dealer agrees to sell only the producer's product, while the producer agrees not to supply any other dealer in the same market. 479
exhaustible resource A resource that cannot be increased by the natural forces of the environment. Common examples of exhaustible resources are petroleum, coal, natural gas, and various types of minerals. 646–647
expansion The growing phase of the business cycle, in which economic activity is increasing. 181
   aggregate demand and, 184–185
   aggregate supply and, 185–186

expansionary fiscal policy Fiscal policy consisting of increases in government purchases and/or decreases in net taxes (including increases in transfer payments). 257
expansionary monetary policy Monetary policy consisting of increases in the money supply through the use of open market operations, reserve requirements, and the discount rate. 298, 299
expectations:
   of buyers, 58–59
   consumption and, 209
   inflation and, 318, 329–333
   investment and, 217
   Phillips curve and, 331–333
   rational, 333
   of suppliers, 69
expected rate of inflation The rate of inflation that people in the economy expect to occur in the future. Changes in the expected rate of inflation lead to shifts in the short-run Phillips curve, and a separate Phillips curve exists for each expected rate of inflation. 331
expenditures multiplier The ratio of the change in national output to the change in autonomous consumption, investment, or government purchases. The expenditures multiplier is equal to 1/MPS, when consumption is the only expenditure that depends on output. 246
exports Domestically produced goods purchased by other countries. 122, 657
   net, 124
   See also international trade
external benefit The value placed on a good by consumers who do not buy the good. 624
external cost A cost that affects someone not directly involved in the production or exchange of a good and that is incurred without compensation. 624
externality A cost or benefit that affects someone not directly involved in the production or exchange of a good and that is incurred without compensation. An externality occurs outside the operation of a market. 22
   market failure of, 622–629
   optimal production with, 625–627
   reasons for, 627–629
   regulation and, 612–613

F

factor costs, 321
factor demand, 498–503
   determinants of, 501–503
   marginal revenue product and, 501

factor demand *(continued)*
    product price and, 501–502
    technology and, 502
factor demand curves, 500–501
factor market equilibrium, 511–516
factor markets Markets used to exchange the services of the factors of production. In factor markets the business sector is the demander and the household sector the supplier. In factor markets only the services of the factors are exchanged, not the factors themselves. 117
factor payments Payments made by firms for the services of the four factors of production. 119
factor prices, 65–66
factor qualities, 322, 681
factor quantities, 321–322, 677
factors of production The four basic factors used to produce goods in the economy are labor, capital, land, and entrepreneurship. 14–16
factor supply, 505–510
factor supply curves, 507–508
farm problem The situation in which relatively low and relatively unstable incomes are caused by low or unstable agricultural prices. 432–427. *See also* agricultural policies
featherbedding The practice of artificially increasing the number of workers employed. 526
Federal Advisory Council A council made up of twelve presidents of commercial banks, one from each Federal Reserve district, which offers advice to the Board of Governors. 285
Federal Communications Act of 1934, 610
Federal Communications Commission (FCC), 610–611, 612, 615
Federal Depositors Insurance Corporation (FDIC), 282
Federal Energy Regulatory Commission (FERC), 611, 612
Federal Open Market Committee A committee of the Federal Reserve System containing the seven members of the Board of Governors, the president of the New York Federal Reserve Bank, and the presidents of four other district banks. The Federal Open Market Committee conducts open market operations, the main tool used by the Federal Reserve System to control the money supply. 285
Federal Reserve Banks The twelve district banks and twenty-five branch banks that carry out the policy set by the Board of Governors. The Federal Reserve Banks are spread throughout the country and act as the banks for the commercial banks. 283–285
Federal Reserve System, 281–290
    Board of Governors of the, 283
    monetary policy and, 286–290
    money creation and, 276

    money supply and, 288–290
    origin of, 281–282
    structure of, 282–285
Federal Savings and Loan Insurance Corporation (FSLIC), 282
Federal Trade Commission Act of 1914 This act set up the Federal Trade Commission (FTC) as a separate agency to implement antitrust action, including investigating business practices that might lead to restraint of trade, setting standards for unfair competition, and levying fines against offenders. 480–481
fiat money Any money that has value in exchange but little or no value in use. 268
final goods Goods that are purchased for final use and not transformed and resold. 127
financial market The market used to exchange an assortment of financial capital. The demand for funds in the financial market comes from the demand by firms for capital goods and by consumers for consumer goods. In both cases higher interest rates reduce the quantity of funds demanded. The supply of funds comes from firms' retained earnings and consumers' savings and increases at higher interest rates. The financial market is in equilibrium at the intersection of the demand and supply curves. 119
    circular flow with, 119–120
    investment in, 543–545
firm An organization that combines resources for the production of goods and services. The firm is used by entrepreneurs to bring together otherwise unproductive factors. It is functionally defined and can be profit oriented, nonprofit, privately owned, or government controlled. 384–391
    industrial division of, 388
    legal forms of, 385–386
    market structures and, 387–390
    natural selection and, 391
    objectives of, 390–391
    supply by, 505–506
    supply to, 506
    in the United States, 386–387
fiscal policy The use of the two components of the government's fiscal budget, purchases and net taxation, to stabilize aggregate expenditures. Fiscal policy is one way the government can reduce the fluctuations in economic activity, reduce unemployment, and limit inflation. 251–260
    aggregate market and, 257–258
    contractionary, 257, 335–337
    expansionary, 257
    full employment output and, 253–257

GLOSSARY/INDEX

fiscal policy *(continued)*
  Keynesians on, 309–312
  monetarists on, 309, 310
  recent, 259–260
five-year plan In the Soviet Union, a plan that typically, although not always, covers a five-year period. It contains aggregate levels of resources allocated to major activities in the economy, such as investment, consumption, military, and scientific research. The five-year plans are directed in only one way, from the Gosplan to the enterprise. 712, 719
  in Yugoslavia, 725
fixed costs:
  average, 406–407
  total, 402, 403–404
fixed exchange rate An exchange rate determined by the government. 671
fixed input An input whose quantity cannot be changed in the time period under consideration. 394
floating exchange rate An exchange rate determined by the forces of supply and demand. A floating exchange rate is primarily determined by three factors. The first is purchasing-power parity, which states that exchange rates are determined in the long run by relative rates of inflation. The second is the interest rate, which states that relative interest rates influence the exchange rate in the short run. The third is economic performance, which states that relative rates of economic growth affect the exchange rate in the short run. 671
Food and Drug Administration (FDA), 611, 614, 615
Food, Drug, and Cosmetic Act of 1931, 611
food stamp program, 571
foreign exchange The term one country uses in reference to all currency other than its own. 667–672
  demand for, 668–669
  exchange rate, 670–672
  fixed, 671
  floating, 671
  international trade and, 667–668
  supply of, 669
foreign exchange market The market in which countries trade domestic currency for foreign currency. In the foreign exchange market, since currency is exchanged for currency, each currency has its own market. However, the market for one currency is the mirror image of the market for the other. 667–670
foreign sector Households, businesses, and governments located in other countries. 122–124
fossil fuels, supply of, 646–649
Four Modernizations In China, a program started in 1978 to modernize four areas of the economy: industry, agriculture, science and technology, and the military. This led to the development of light industry, agriculture, social overhead capital, more decentralized decision making, and eventually a shift toward greater reliance on markets. 720
fractional reserve banking A system in which banks hold less than 100 percent of deposits as reserves. In the United States, banks keep between 3 and 20 percent of deposits as reserves. 275
free good A good with an available quantity that is greater than its desired use. Free goods can be limited as long as people want less than is available. 13
free resource A resource with an available quantity greater than its desired use. Free resources can be limited as long as people want less than is available. 13
free rider problem The situation in which a person consumes a public good without contributing to the costs of production. This problem exists for public goods because nonpayers cannot be excluded. It also means that the market is unable to efficiently produce and exchange public goods. 593
frictional unemployment Unemployment created by imperfections in the labor market. 153
Friedman, Milton, 114
fuel oil, income elasticity of demand for, 108. *See also* fossil fuels
full employment The condition of the economy in which all available resources are used in the production of goods and services. Full employment exists when the economy is on the production possibilities frontier. It is generally considered to occur when 5 percent of the labor force is unemployed. 21–22, 39
full employment output The quantity of final goods and services produced by the economy when all factors of production are engaged in production. Full employment output occurs in the classical range of the aggregate supply curve. 172
  fiscal policy and, 253–257
  inflationary gap and, 253
  recessionary gap and, 252–253
functional income distribution The distribution of income to factors of production, based on their contribution to output. The functional distribution of income is an important component in the measure of efficiency of production. 557

G

gasoline, price elasticity of demand for, 106–107
General Theory of Employment, Interest, and Money, The (Keynes), 114, 194–195
geographic mobility The movement of factors from one geographic area to another. 509, 534, 536

geothermal energy, 652

Gini coefficient A numerical measure of the inequality of distribution of income. The Gini coefficient is calculated as the ratio of the area between the Lorenz curve and the 45° line to the area of the entire triangle beneath the 45° line. The Gini coefficient can range between 0, for perfect equality, and 1, for perfect inequality. 561, 562

GNP. *See* gross national product

***GNP* price deflator** (*GNP-PD*) A price index computed from the ratio of nominal *GNP* to real *GNP*. The *GNP* price deflator is an important method of measuring changes in the economy's average price level. Since the *GNP-PD* derives from gross national product, it is based on all final goods and services currently produced in the economy, thus avoiding limitations of the *CPI*. However, while the *CPI* is available every month, the *GNP-PD* is available only once every three months. 132–133, 163

gold, 273–275
gold standard, 314
good:
   agricultural, 423–431
   capital, 217, 542–543
   common property, 592, 628–629
   consumer choice of, 353–355, 367, 371–372
   final, 127
   inferior, 56, 97, 108
   intermediate, 127, 128
   near public, 592–593, 628
   normal, 56, 97
   private, 591–592, 628
   public, 22, 590–596, 628

Gosplan The Soviet Union's central planning agency, which determines the quantities of each good that is to be produced and how many resources are directed to each of the enterprises involved in its production. 711–712

government A political body exercising control and authority over a group of individuals. Governments allocate resources based on laws and the command of the government. 19
   antipoverty policies of, 568–572
   circular flow with, 120–122
   market and, 85–90
   See also tax

government budget. *See* budget

government franchise The legal right granted to a firm to produce and/or sell a good in a particular market, subject to government control. Usually a government franchise sets up a single firm as a monopoly in a market. Public utilities are commonly franchised by the government. 439

government policies:
   agricultural, 427–431
   antitrust, 476–482
   investment and, 217
   See also fiscal policy; monetary policy

government purchases Expenditures by the government for final goods and services. 122, 200
   aggregate expenditures and, 227–228, 318
   autonomous, 226, 230
   circular flow, 230–231
   fiscal policy and, 253–254
   output and, 226–227

government regulation The process of controlling business activities through laws and administrative rules. Government regulation controls pollution by banning products, reducing the amount of pollution that can be discharged, or specifying technologies that can be used. 610–617
   agencies for, 610–612
   competition and, 476–482
   evaluation of, 617
   inflation control and, 341–342
   pollution control and, 639–641
   reasons against, 614–617
   reasons for, 612–614

government sector The combination of all levels of government: federal, state, and local. 120

Gramm-Rudman Act, 263

graph A diagram of two or more lines, with each line representing the relationship between two variables. Graphs are a method of abstraction that helps isolate important economic principles. 25–32
   interpreting, 25–27
   misuse of, 31–32

Great Depression, 198–202
   as business cycle, 181, 182
   economic activity during, 199
   government purchases during, 200
   Keynesian view of, 200–202
   unemployment during, 199

Great Leap Forward The period between 1958 and 1960 in which China attempted to increase its level of development beyond that of the Soviet Union and other countries. China tried to accomplish this leap by emphasizing the role of peasants and small-scale industry. While the Great Leap Forward was promoted with all the enthusiasm of a religious crusade, it was a complete economic disaster. 719–720

gross national product (*GNP*) The total market value of final goods and services produced in the economy in a given period (usually one year). 126–136
   depreciation and, 137–138
   expenditures on, 133–136

gross national product (GNP) *(continued)*
  nominal, 132, 133
  per capita, 131
  per capita real, 676
  real, 131–133, 676
  welfare and, 130–131
guaranteed income A policy that insures everyone receives a minimum amount of income, regardless of income earned. 568–570

H

Hanke, S. H., 107n
health care industry, 484–490
Hegel, Georg, 704, 705
high employment budget The government budget that would exist if the economy were at full employment. 259
Highway Safety Act of 1970, 611
horizontal equity The principle stating that people with the same ability to pay should pay the same tax. 600
horizontal merger A merger between two firms in the same industry. 478
Hothakker, H. S., 107n, 108n
household sector All households and nonprofit organizations in the economy. 117
human capital The training and education received by labor that improves its ability to produce goods and services. Human capital leads to economic growth by increasing the quality of labor. The investment in human capital is much like investment in physical capital. An investment in human capital is made if there is a large enough increase in future income to offset the initial investment cost. 536–539, 681
hypothesis A prediction obtained directly from a theory that can be compared with observations in the real world. Hypotheses usually take the form "If A, then also B." 8

I

imports Goods purchased from other countries by the domestic economy. 122, 657. *See also* international trade
income:
  demand and, 56–57
  discrimination and, 530, 536
  education and, 538–539
  guaranteed, 568–570
  from interest, 542–547
  from land, 549–551
  national (*see* national income)
  personal, 146–147, 148, 203–205
  from profit, 553–555
  of proprietors, 144–145
  from rent, 141–142, 551–552
  from wages, 530, 532–540
income classes, 558–560
income distribution, 557–564
  causes of inequality in, 561–563
  functional, 557
  in less-developed countries, 689–690
  measures of, 558–561
  personal, 558
  poverty and, 566 (*see also* poverty)
income effect The change in quantity demanded that results because a change in price gives a buyer more real income, even though money income remains unchanged. The change in real income can affect the quantity demanded of the good experiencing the price change in one of two ways. For a normal good the income effect causes quantity demanded to move in the opposite direction of the price. For an inferior good the income effect causes the quantity demanded to move in the same direction as price. 53, 360–361
income elasticity of demand The relative response of demand to changes in income, defined as the percentage change in demand divided by the percentage change in income. 97–98, 108
income tax:
  corporate, 607
  negative, 569–570
  personal, 606
  tax reform and, 600–601
indexing The process of automatically adjusting nominal values to changes in the price level. Indexing tries to avoid the adverse distribution effects of inflation. Unfortunately, not all nominal values can be indexed, and indexing tends to build inflation into the economic system, making it difficult to eliminate with other policies. 339–340
indifference curve A curve depicting the different combinations of two goods that provide the same level of satisfaction. An indifference curve is based on the relative preferences for the two goods by a consumer. 366–369
  demand and, 366–373
  properties of, 367–368
indifference map A graph of two or more indifference curves. Higher indifference curves are associated with higher levels of utility. 368
indirect business taxes Taxes levied on business firms but indirectly paid by households through higher prices. Indirect business taxes are the difference between net national product and national income. 141, 142
industrial union A labor union composed of workers in the same industry. 518, 525

industrial waste, 632–633
industry A group of firms that produces similar products or sells output in the same market. 387, 388
industry regulation The regulation of an entire industry. 610–611
inelastic The condition of elasticity in which the percentage change in quantity demanded (or supplied) is less than the percentage change in price, and the absolute value of the price elasticity of demand (or supply) is less than 1.0. An inelastic curve is not very responsive to changes in price. 94
inferior good A good for which an increase in income causes a decrease in demand, or a leftward shift in the demand curve. If demand decreases as income increases, it is an inferior good, or a good with a negative income elasticity. 56, 97, 108
inflation An increase in the average price level. 161–168
  business cycle and, 189–190
  causes of, 316–322
  cost-push, 185, 317–318
  demand-pull, 185, 317
  dynamics of, 316–318
  effects of, 165–168
  expectations and, 329–333
  expected rate of, 331
  measures of, 161–164
  money supply and, 320
  productivity and, 344–345
  pure, 165
  unemployment and, 324–333
inflationary gap The difference between actual aggregate expenditures and the level of aggregate expenditures needed to achieve full employment if actual output is greater than full employment output. An inflationary gap can be eliminated with contractionary fiscal or monetary policy. 253, 254
inflation control policies, 335–342
  balanced budget, 337–338
  contractionary fiscal and monetary policy, 335–337
  indexing, 339–340
  supply-side policies, 340–342
  wage and price controls, 338–339
injection A nonconsumption expenditure on national product that is outside the main flow relating national product, factor payments, national income, and expenditures. 219–221
  equilibrium with, 236–239
  government and, 230
injunction A court order requiring a person, union, or company to refrain from a particular activity. 522–523
innovation The introduction of a new plant or production process. 554

input A resource or factor of production used in the production of a good or service. 394
  fixed, 394
  variable, 394
intercept (Y-intercept) The value of the variable on the vertical axis when the variable on the horizontal axis equals zero. The intercept is where the line cuts the vertical axis. 27
interest The payment for the use of financial capital. In the operation of the financial market, interest is also considered the factor payment to physical capital. 542–547
  in national income, 141
  net, 141
interest rate The charge for the use of borrowed funds over a period of time expressed as a percentage.
  consumption and, 209
  foreign exchange and, 672
  investment and, 214–215, 216
  nominal, 167
  prime, 545
  real, 167–168
  role of, 543
interest rate differentials, 545–547
interest rate effect The change in consumption and investment expenditures caused by a change in the interest rate. 171
  consumption and, 209
  Keynesian cross and, 239–240
interlocking directorates The term used when two or more firms in the same industry have one or more board of directors in common. 478
intermediate goods Goods that are transformed and ultimately resold. 127, 128
intermediate range The positively sloped segment of the aggregate supply curve. In this segment some but not all industries are at full employment. Therefore, national production can be increased, but the price level also increases. 172, 173
internalization The process of making participants in a market consider externalities associated with the production of a good. 638
international finance, 667–674
  balance of payments, 672–674
  foreign exchange, 667–672
international trade The exchange of goods across national boundaries. 122, 656–665
  balance of, 657
  comparative advantage in, 659–660
  foreign exchange and, 667–668
  market for, 660–662, 663
  patterns of, 656–659
  tariffs and, 662–665

intersection The point at which two lines cross, where the values of both variables are equal for the two relationships depicted in the graph. 29
Interstate Commerce Act of 1887, 610
Interstate Commerce Commission (ICC), 610, 612, 615
inventories, changes in, 235
inverse relationship. *See* negative relationship
investment expenditures Expenditures by firms for final goods and services. 213–221
   aggregate demand and, 318
   autonomous, 214
   business cycles and, 186–187
   on capital goods, 217, 542–543
   in classical economics, 197–198
   consumption and, 217–221
   determinants of, 216–217
   economic growth and, 678
   in financial market, 543–545
   interest rate and, 214–215, 216
   output and, 213–214, 216
   planned, 213
   rate of return on, 215
   realized, 213
   recent data on, 220, 221
involuntary unemployment Unemployment created when labor is willing and able to work but cannot find jobs. 152

J

Jobs, Steve, 15
Johnson, Lyndon B., 338

K

Kennedy, John F., 338
Keynes, John Maynard, 114, 194–195
Keynesian cross A graph containing the Keynesian aggregate expenditures line that is used to illustrate equilibrium between aggregate expenditures and national output. The Keynesian cross contains the essence of Keynesian economics. 235, 236
   aggregate market and, 239–240
   multiplier and, 243
Keynesian economics A body of economic thought, first developed by John Maynard Keynes, built on the idea that the aggregate demand for output is not necessarily equal to the economy's full employment level of output. 194–195
   fiscal policy applications of, 251–260
   on Great Depression, 200–202
Keynesian range The horizontal segment of the aggregate supply curve. In this segment factors of production are unemployed. 172, 173
Keynesians Economists who argue that fiscal policy is more effective than monetary policy for stabilizing economic fluctuations. 303–312
   on fiscal policy, 309–312
   monetarists vs., 303–304
   on monetary policy, 304–305
kinked demand curve A demand curve with two distinct segments, one that is very elastic and the other that is very inelastic. The kinked demand curve is often used to explain price rigidity in oligopoly. 471–472

L

labor The human resources used to produce goods and services. 14
   factor supply and, 508
   inflation and, 322
   productivity of, 344–345
   quality of, 534–535
   wages of, 530, 532–540
labor force The portion of the population that is willing and able to work, including those actively engaged in the production of goods and services and those who are unemployed. 154–155, 678
labor force participation rate The percentage of the population that is willing and able to work, and thus is a part of the labor force. 155–157
labor supply curve, backward-bending, 540
labor union An organization of workers formed to negotiate with employers over wages, working conditions, and fringe benefits. 518–527
   craft, 518, 524–525
   history of, 522–524
   industrial, 518, 525
   membership in, 518–519, 520
   nonunion labor markets and, 526–527
   role of, 519–521
Laffer curve A curve depicting the relationship between tax rates and the tax revenue received by the government. The Laffer curve indicates that the government receives no tax revenue if the tax rate is either zero or 100 percent. If the rate is 100 percent, no one has the incentive to work, and thus there is nothing to tax. Somewhere between zero and 100 percent is the tax rate that generates the most tax revenue for the government. 340–341
land The natural resource used to produce goods and services, including the land itself, the minerals and nutrients in the ground, the water, wildlife, and vegetation on the surface, and the air above. 15
   factor supply and, 508–509

land *(continued)*
  investment in, 549–551
  market for, 550–551
  supply of, 550
land tenure system A system of land ownership in the country. The land tenure system in a less-developed country can often inhibit development by preventing needed increases in agricultural productivity. This can occur because the farmers are not the owners and thus do not receive profits from increased production. Alternatively, this can occur because ownership of the land is fragmented, with one farmer owning several small pieces of land scattered many miles apart. 690
law of demand The principle stating that an inverse relationship exists between the price of a commodity and the quantity of the commodity that buyers are willing and able to purchase in a given period of time if other factors are held constant. One reason the law of demand holds is that buyers substitute similar goods that become relatively cheaper as the price of one good rises. A second reason is that buyers are constrained by the amount of income they have to spend on a good. 52–53
law of diminishing marginal returns The principle stating that as more and more of a variable input is combined with a fixed input, eventually the marginal product of the variable input declines. 396–399, 407–408, 501
law of diminishing marginal utility The principle stating that as more of a good is consumed, eventually each additional unit of the good provides less additional utility—that is, marginal utility begins to decrease. Although marginal utility is still positive, each subsequent unit is valued less than the previous one. The law of marginal utility helps explain the negative slope of the demand curve. 358–359
law of increasing opportunity cost The principle stating that the opportunity cost of producing a good increases as the economy moves along the production possibilities frontier and more of the good is produced. The production possibilities frontier is bowed away from the origin due to the law of increasing opportunity costs. The law of increasing opportunity cost holds because all resources are not equally suited to the production of all goods. 37–39
law of supply The principle stating that a direct relationship exists between the price of a commodity and the quantity of the commodity that suppliers are willing and able to supply in a given period of time if other factors are held constant. The law of supply holds because the cost of producing additional units increases. 62–63
LDC. *See* less-developed country

leakage A nonconsumption use of income that diverts funds away from the main flow relating national product, factor payments, national income, and expenditures. Saving is one important type of leakage in the economy. 219
  equilibrium with, 236–239
  government and, 230
legal reserves Reserves (vault cash and deposits at the Federal Reserve System) that can be used to satisfy legal requirements. Legal reserves do not include some types of financial assets, such as government securities, that could be used to back up demand deposits. 276
leisure time:
  GNP and, 131
  price of, 539
Lenin, Vladimir, 709, 710
less-developed country (LDC) A country with a relatively low standard of living and level of development. 686–692
  debts of, 694
  policies for, 691–692
  problems of, 686–691
liability, 386
license The legal right granted to a firm to produce and/or sell a good in a particular market but with less government control than a franchise. A license is similar to a government franchise. However, a license usually does not stipulate control over the pricing activities of the firm, whereas a government franchise usually does. 439
limited good A good that has a finite quantity. 13
limited liability The condition that exists when an owner of a firm is only responsible for his or her initial investment in the firm. This means the owner's personal property, which is unrelated to the firm's operation, cannot be used to satisfy the firm's obligations. 386
limited resource A resource that has a finite quantity. 13
Limits to Growth, The, 653–654
lines, 27–31
  intersection of, 29–30
  straight, 27–28
  tangency between, 31
liquidity The ease of turning funds into currency or transferring them from one financial market to another. 547
liquor industry sales, 376–377
lockout The refusal of management to admit workers to their jobs. 521
logrolling The practice of trading votes to obtain a favorable outcome on a specific decision. Logrolling can lead to an efficient decision that would not otherwise be made, but it can also lead to an

inefficient decision. Implicit logrolling occurs when two programs are combined into one. 584–586
long run A period of time in which all inputs are variable. 395
long-run farm problem The continuous decline in farm incomes caused by continuous declines in agricultural prices. 423, 426–427
Lorenz curve A curve depicting the cumulative percentage of income earned by the cumulative percentage of households. With a Lorenz curve the 45° line represents a perfectly equal distribution of income and the right angle formed by the axes represents a perfectly unequal distribution of income. The distribution of income is more equal the closer the Lorenz curve is to the 45° line and the farther it is from the right-angled axes. 560–561
loss minimization, 417–418
  in monopoly, 450, 451
  in perfect competition, 417–418

M

M1 The total of currency held by the nonbank public and checkable deposits, including standard checking accounts, NOW accounts, share drafts, and ATS accounts. 268–270
M2 M1 plus near monies, which include time deposits, money market mutual fund shares, Eurodollars, and repurchase agreements. 271
M3 M2 plus large-denomination certificates of deposit and longer-term repurchase agreements. 271
macroeconomics The branch of economics that studies the entire economy. Macroeconomics studies such topics as the total amount of output in the economy, the rate of inflation, and the number of unemployed workers. 6
Malthus, T. R., 653–654, 703
Mao Zedong, 719, 720
marginal cost The change in total cost or total variable cost resulting from a change in the quantity of output. Marginal cost is the slope of both the total cost and total variable cost curves and increases due to the law of diminishing returns. When marginal cost is below either average variable or average total cost, the average curve is decreasing. When marginal cost is above either average variable or average total cost, the average curve is increasing. When marginal cost is equal to either average variable or average total cost, the average curve is at its minimum. 406, 407, 415–417
marginal cost pricing A pricing policy for public utilities in which price is set equal to marginal cost. Marginal cost pricing, while optimally allocating resources, means the firm incurs a loss. For the firm to remain in operation, it needs a subsidy. 458–459
marginal factor cost The additional cost of hiring an additional unit of a factor. If the price of a factor does not change, marginal factor cost is equal to the price. If the price of factor increases with additional units, marginal factor cost is greater than the price. 506–507
marginal physical product The change in the quantity of output resulting from a change in the quantity of a factor. Marginal physical product is always stated in physical units. 499
marginal product The change in total product resulting from a change in a variable input, holding all other inputs unchanged. 396, 397–399
marginal productivity theory The theory stating that the demand for a factor of production is based on the marginal product of the factor and its marginal revenue. 499–501
marginal propensity to consume (*MPC*) The proportion of each additional dollar of income used for consumption expenditures, found by dividing the change in consumption by the change in disposable income. 205
  multiplier and, 246
  slope of aggregate expenditures line and, 217, 228
marginal propensity to save (*MPS*) The proportion of each additional dollar of income used for saving, found by dividing the change in saving by the change in disposable income. 205
  multiplier and, 246
  multiplier effect and, 245
marginal rate of substitution The rate at which consumers are willing to trade one good for another and maintain the same level of utility. The marginal rate of substitution is equal to the ratio of marginal utilities of the two goods and also to the negative of the slope of the indifference curve. 368, 369
marginal returns, law of diminishing, 396–399, 407–408, 501
marginal revenue The change in total revenue resulting from a change in the quantity of output sold. For a perfectly competitive firm, marginal revenue is equal to price. For firms with market power, marginal revenue is less than the price.
  for monopolistic competition, 464
  for monopoly, 449–450
  for perfect competition, 413, 414, 415–417
marginal revenue product The change in the revenue received by a firm resulting from a change in the quantity of a factor. To maximize profit, a firm hires a factor to the point where the cost of the factor is equal to the marginal revenue product. The demand curve for a factor is the downward-sloping portion of

the marginal revenue product curve. The law of diminishing marginal returns causes the factor demand curve to have a negative slope. 499, 500, 501

marginal utility The additional utility obtained from the consumption of an additional unit of a good. It is specified as the change in total utility divided by the change in quantity. Marginal utility tells us what each additional unit of a good is worth to a consumer. 353, 355
  law of diminishing, 358–359

market An organized exchange of commodities (goods, services, or resources) between buyers and sellers within a specific geographic area and in a given period of time. The market facilitates the exchange of a commodity between those who have it and those who want it. Markets allocate resources based on the individual decisions of buyers and sellers. 18–19, 48–51, 72
  as allocative mechanism, 50–51
  black, 87–88
  characteristics of, 49
  elasticity and, 102–109
  externalities and, 625–627
  factor, 117
  financial, 119, 543–545
  government and, 85–90
  ideal, 51
  international, 660–662, 663
  price and, 50
  product, 117
  pure market economy, 19–20
  tax on, 88–90
  See also aggregate market

market demand The total demand of every individual willing and able to buy the good. The market demand curve is found by horizontally adding all individual demand curves. 54, 55

market economy An economy that relies on markets for the allocation of resources. While capitalism often contains a market economy, this need not be the case. Capitalism could use the government for allocative decisions. However, capitalism and markets are much more compatible. 698–699

market equilibrium The state of the market that occurs when the demanders and suppliers come together and exchange a mutually agreeable quantity at a mutually agreeable price. Graphically, equilibrium is determined by the intersection of the demand and supply curves. 72–82
  determination of, 72–74
  factor, 511–516

market power The ability of buyers or sellers to control or influence the price and/or quantity exchanged in the market. Market power exists if a firm faces a downward-sloping demand curve. This allows the firm to choose the quantity of output and price. 22–23, 437–442
  demand and, 442
  in health care industry, 484–490
  misuse of, 477–479
  regulation and, 613
market shocks, 75–80
  decrease in demand, 77–78
  decrease in supply, 79–80
  increase in demand, 76–77
  increase in supply, 78–79

market socialism An economic system based on government ownership of resources and decisions made through markets. Many socialist countries blend government and market decision making. However, Yugoslavia is a good example of a country with government ownership that relies heavily on markets for allocation. 699, 725–726

market structure The way in which an industry is organized. A market can be structured with only one firm or with several thousand. Each firm can have a great deal of control over the market price or no control at all. 387–390
  antitrust legislation and, 476–482
  average cost and, 440
  monopolistic competition, 389, 437–438
  monopoly, 389, 437, 444–453
  oligopoly, 389–390, 438, 467–474
  perfect competition, 388, 411–421

market supply The total supply of every seller willing and able to sell a good or factor at alternative prices. The market supply curve is found by horizontally adding all individual supply curves. If a single firm supplies all of a factor in a market, a monopoly exists. 64, 65, 506
market value, 127
Marshall, Alfred, 348
Marx, Karl, 700, 703–707, 710

Marxian economics A body of economic thought developed by Karl Marx, based on the propositions that the conflict between opposing economic groups and the surplus value not paid to labor will eventually lead to the downfall of capitalism. 703–707
  background of, 703–704
  in China, 718–724
  evaluation of, 707
  in Soviet Union, 709–716

materials balance The principle stating that the amount of material taken from the environment equals the amount of material returned. The total amount of pollution depends on the amount of material

GLOSSARY/INDEX

removed from the environment. Also, in the Soviet Union's planned economy it is the process of equating the amount of resources required by all enterprises with the amount that is available. Maintaining a materials balance is the most difficult task in the Soviet economy and is the central objective in each one-year plan. 634–636, 712

mediation The intervention of a third party (usually the government) in the collective bargaining process, offering nonbinding guidance and solutions. 521

Medicaid, 571

mergers When two or more firms legally combine to form a larger firm. 470–471, 477–478
  conglomerate, 478
  horizontal, 478
  vertical, 478

microeconomics The branch of economics that studies parts of the economy. Microeconomics studies individual consumers, businesses, and industries that make up the economy. Macroeconomics and microeconomics are interdependent, although each views the operation of the economy from a different perspective, and both are essential to an understanding of how the economy functions. 6

midpoints formula A method of calculating elasticity that uses the average, or midpoint, price and quantity over the range of the change. 94

military spending, 45–46

Mill, John Stuart, 704

mixed economy An economy that relies on both markets and government for the allocation of resources. 20–21

mobility The movement of factors from one production process to another. 509–510
  geographic, 509, 534, 536
  occupational, 509, 534, 536

monetarists Economists who argue that monetary policy is more effective than fiscal policy for stabilizing economic fluctuations. 303–312
  on fiscal policy, 309, 310
  Keynesians vs., 303–304
  on monetary policy, 305–306

monetary base The currency held by the nonbank public and reserves held by banks. 288–290

monetary policy The discretionary control of the economy's money supply by the Federal Reserve System that is designed to affect the overall performance of the economy. The three tools of monetary policy are open market operations, reserve requirements, and the discount rate. 286–290
  contractionary, 299, 336–337
  discount rate and, 288, 289
  expansionary, 298, 299
  Keynesians on, 304–305

monetarists on, 305–306
money supply and, 288–290
open market operations and, 286, 287
recent, 300–301
reserve requirements and, 286–288

money Anything that is generally accepted as payment in exchange for goods and services. 265–271
  characteristics of, 267
  commodity, 268
  fiat, 268
  functions of, 265–267
  gold as, 273–275, 314
  near, 271
  price level and, 319
  quantity theory of, 306–308
  types of, 267–268
  in U.S. economy, 268–271
  velocity of, 307, 308

money creation The process in which banks increase the amount of funds in checkable deposits by using reserves to make loans. Money creation is an important process in the economy because it means that the government does not have total control over the money supply. 273–279
  modern banking, 275–279
  process of, 276–279

money demand The quantity of money balances that the public wants to hold. There are three basic motives for holding money: for transactions, as a precaution, and for speculation. 293–295

money demand curve A graphical representation of the relationship between the quantity of money demanded and the interest rate. An increase in income causes the money demand curve to shift to the right. 294–295

money market A model illustrating the interaction between the economy's demand for money and the available supply at different interest rates. The money market always achieves equilibrium by changes in the interest rate, adjusting the quantity of money demanded until it is equal to the available supply. 296–300
  aggregate expenditures and, 298
  national output and, 297–300

money supply The quantity of money that exists in the economy. The money supply is controlled by the Federal Reserve System through its monetary policy. 295–296
  inflation and, 319–321
  inflation control and, 337–338
  monetary policy and, 288–290

money supply curve A graphical representation of the relationship between the quantity of money supplied and the interest rate. 295–296

monopolistic competition A market structure characterized by a large number of relatively small firms, similar but slightly different products, freedom of entry and exit, and imperfect information. This means each firm has a small degree of market power. A monopolistically competitive firm faces a downward-sloping demand curve. Therefore, it behaves much like a monopolist. 389, 462–466
   antitrust legislation and, 476–482
   characteristics of, 437–438, 462
   demand and, 462–463
   profit and loss in, 464, 465
   resource allocation and, 465–466
   short-run output and, 463–465

monopolist's supply curve Because the monopolist faces a downward-sloping demand curve, its marginal cost curve, above the average variable cost curve, is not the supply curve. In fact, the monopolist does not have a supply curve. 450–452

monopoly A market structure characterized by a single firm supplying all output in the market. The good produced by a monopoly has very few close substitutes. The demand curve facing a monopolistic firm is the market demand for the factor. The monopolist maximizes profit by equating marginal cost to marginal revenue, but a monopolist sells fewer units of the factor and charges a higher price than is the case in perfect competition. 389, 437, 444–453
   antitrust legislation and, 476–482
   bilateral, 514–516
   demand and, 445–448
   factor market equilibrium and, 514–516
   factor supply and, 506
   natural, 455–460
   profit and, 554
   real world, 444–445
   resource allocation and, 452–453
   short-run output and, 448–450
   supply curve and, 450–452

monopsony A market that is characterized by a single buyer of the good or factor. The supply curve facing a monopsonistic firm is the market supply for the factor. A monopsonist maximizes profit by equating marginal factor cost to marginal revenue product. A monopsonist hires fewer units of the factor and pays a lower price than is the case in perfect competition. 506, 513–514

moral suasion A policy based on convincing people or firms to voluntarily reduce pollution. Moral suasion is effective in controlling pollution only in short-run crises. 642

more-developed country (MDC) A country with a relatively high standard of living and level of development. 686

Motor Carrier Act of 1980, 610

multiplier The ratio of the change in national output to the change in an autonomous component of aggregate expenditures. The multiplier indicates how national output is affected by a change in autonomous aggregate expenditures. 242–249
   aggregate market and, 248
   balanced-budget, 255–257
   deposit, 279
   expenditures, 246
   Keynesian cross and, 243
   in real world, 247
   tax, 246–247, 254–255
multiplier effect, 244–247

mutual interdependence A behavior in which each firm makes its decisions based on the reaction of other firms in the industry. This is one of the most important behavioral aspects of oligopoly. With a small number of firms, each is well aware of its competition. One firm cannot change price, promote a sale, or alter production without response from the other firms. 469

N

national banks Banks that are chartered by the federal government and are automatically members of the Federal Reserve System. A national bank often has the word *national* in its name. 285

National Highway Traffic Safety Administration (NHTSA), 611, 614, 615, 616

national income (NI) The income earned by the factors of production. National income can be viewed as national production valued at factor prices, while net national product (NNP) is national production valued at product prices. 119, 140–145
   components of, 141–145
   determination of, 232–240
   personal income vs., 147

National Industrial Recovery Act (NIRA) of 1933, 523
National Labor Relations Act (NLRA) of 1935, 523

national product The total value of final goods and services produced in the economy and sold through product markets. 119, 126–138
   gross, 126–136
   net, 136–138, 142

natural monopoly An industry in which one firm has decreasing average cost over the range of market demand. If this type of industry produces an essential good, it is usually heavily regulated or operated directly by the government. 455–460

natural rate of unemployment The rate of unemployment that occurs when the economy is at full employment. The natural rate of unemployment is primarily composed of frictional and structural unemployment. In the long run the rate of inflation does not affect the natural rate of unemployment, and the long-run Phillips curve is vertical at the natural rate of unemployment. 331

natural selection The process in which the firms that are best suited to the economic environment naturally tend to survive. This is an argument used to support the profit maximization assumption. It states that firms may pursue other objectives, but the firms that tend to maximize profit, either on purpose or by accident, are the ones that survive in the industry. 391

near monies Financial assets that cannot be directly used to purchase goods and services but can be easily converted into currency or demand deposits. 271

near public good A good that is nonrival in consumption, but nonpayers can be excluded from consumption. 592–593, 628

negative income tax The policy in which public assistance payments are reduced by a fraction of additional income earned. 569–570

negative (inverse) relationship A relationship that exists when the value of one variable increases as the value of the other variable decreases. 28

negotiation The act of agreement between an affected party and the generator of an externality. Negotiation is only effective if a small number of people are involved in the externality. 641

net exports Expenditures by the foreign sector on domestically produced final goods and services minus the expenditures by the three domestic sectors on foreign-produced goods and services. 124

net interest, 141

net national product (*NNP*) The total market value of all final goods and services produced in the economy in a given period of time, excluding the depreciation of capital. 136–138, 142

net taxes The difference between taxes and transfer payments. Net taxes are the amount of tax revenues remaining for government purchases after transfer payments are made. 227, 229
  aggregate demand and, 319
  circular flow and, 230–231
  fiscal policy and, 254–255

New Economic Policy (NEP) An economic plan implemented in the Soviet Union in 1921 by Lenin that relied on market forces and private production. The NEP was designed to speed up the recovery of the Russian economy after several years of external and internal wars. By 1928 the NEP increased the level of output to the level existing before 1914. 710

Nixon, Richard M., 338, 339

nominal *GNP* The total market value of all final goods and services produced in the economy in a given period of time, expressed in current dollars. 132, 133

nominal interest rate The interest rate actually paid on borrowed funds. 167

nominal wage The monetary value of the wage payment. 329

nondegradable pollution Simple inorganic materials that cannot be broken down by the natural capacity of the environment. 632
  government regulation and, 640

nondiscretionary expenditures Expenditures that depend on established laws and that must be made unless new laws are passed. Nondiscretionary expenditures limit the amount of control over the total amount of the expenditures. 226

nonpoint source pollution, 633

nonprice competition Any type of behavior designed to increase a firm's demand without changing the price. Because of price rigidity, oligopolies usually engage in nonprice competition, such as advertising, to gain a larger share of the market. 470

normal good A good for which an increase in income causes an increase in demand, or a rightward shift in the demand curve. If demand increases as income increases, it is a normal good or a good with a positive income elasticity. 56, 97

normal profit The profit that can be earned by an entrepreneur in an alternative production process. Like wages, rent, and interest, normal profit is an opportunity cost of production. In practice, the distinction between normal profit and economic profit is not clear-cut. 402, 553

normative economics A branch of economics that states the way the economy should operate. A normative statement is based on values and can be proved neither right or wrong. 9

Norris-LaGuardia Act of 1932, 523

NOW (negotiable-order-of-withdrawal) accounts Checkable deposits at savings and loan associations and banks that pay an interest. 268–269, 270

nuclear energy, 651, 652

O

objectives, 390–391
  personal, 391
  social, 390–391

occupational mobility The movement of factors from one occupation to another. 509, 534, 536

Occupational Safety and Health Act of 1970, 611

Occupational Safety and Health Administration (OSHA), 611, 615, 616

Old Age, Survivors, and Disability Insurance (OASDI), 571
oligopolistic behavior, 469–471
oligopoly A market structure characterized by a small number of relatively large firms supplying most of the output in the market. Oligopoly is very similar to monopoly except monopoly has only one firm, while oligopoly has two or more. 389–390, 438, 467–474
   antitrust legislation and, 476–482
   cartels, 471, 472–474
   collusion and, 470–471, 472–474
   concentration in U.S. industries and, 468–469
   kinked demand curve and, 471–472
   resource allocation and, 474
one-year plan In the Soviet Union, a plan that establishes the detailed flows of resources to each of the enterprises and the quantities of goods that have to be produced. The one-year plans set the specific goals for each enterprise and plant manager. Constructing one-year plans, unlike the construction of five-year plans, involves large amounts of information from the enterprise level that indicate an enterprise's production capacity and resource requirements. 712
   in Yugoslavia, 725
OPEC (Organization of Petroleum Exporting Countries), 7, 658–659
open market operations The buying and selling of U.S. government securities by the Federal Open Market Committee of the Federal Reserve System. If the Fed buys securities, then the money supply increases. If the Fed sells securities, then the money supply decreases. 286, 287
open shop A firm that is free to hire union or nonunion workers, with no stipulation of union membership. 521
opportunity cost The highest value of goods or other benefits given up when a good is produced or any action is taken. When the economy is on the production possibilities frontier, to produce more of one good it must produce less of another by reallocating resources. The value of other goods given up is the opportunity cost of increasing the production of a good. 37, 401–402
   law of increasing, 37–39
Osborne computers, 59
output:
   breakeven, 415
   determination of, 232–240
   government purchases and, 226–227
   investment and, 213–214, 216
   money market and, 297–300
   short-run (*see* short-run output)

P

paradox of thrift An analysis indicating that an increase in saving by the entire economy leads to a decline in output and a probable subsequent decrease in saving. 247–249
parity price ratio The ratio of prices received by farmers to prices paid by farmers. The parity price ratio illustrates the continuous decline in relative agricultural prices. 426
partnership A firm that is owned and operated by two or more people. All risks of a partnership are shared equally by each partner, unless one of the partners is a limited partner. 385, 386
patent The exclusive control of an invention awarded to its inventor for a period of seventeen years. 439
payroll tax, 606–607
peak The highest phase of the business cycle, in which the factors of production are at or near full employment. 181
per capita *GNP* The average gross national product per person in the economy. While per capita *GNP* indicates the amount of output that is available for each person in the economy, it doesn't indicate whether or not each person receives the output. 131
per capita real *GNP* The average real gross national product per person in the economy. Per capita real *GNP* is a better indicator of the economy's ability to solve the economic problem for each of its members. It is often used to indicate the standard of living. 676
perfect competition A market structure characterized by a large number of small firms, identical products sold by all firms, freedom of entry and exit into the industry, and perfect knowledge of prices and technology. 388, 411–421
   demand and, 412–414
   factor market equilibrium and, 511–513
   nature of, 411–412
   resource allocation and, 420–421
   revenue and, 413
   supply and, 411–421
perfectly competitive firm's supply curve The marginal cost curve above the average variable cost curve is the perfectly competitive firm's supply curve. Since the marginal cost curve, and thus the supply curve, for a perfectly competitive firm are positively sloped, the market supply curve is also positively sloped. The reason supply is positively sloped in the short run is the law of diminishing marginal returns. 418–419
perfectly elastic The condition of elasticity in which there is an infinitely large change in quantity demanded (or supplied) for a small percentage change in price and the absolute value of the price

elasticity of demand (or supply) is infinity. A perfectly elastic curve is extremely responsive to any changes in price and is depicted by horizontal demand and supply curves. 95

perfectly inelastic The condition of elasticity in which quantity demanded (or supplied) does not change regardless of the percentage change in price and the absolute value of the price elasticity of demand (or supply) is 0. A perfectly inelastic curve is not responsive to any changes in price and is depicted by vertical demand and supply curves. 95

persistent pollution Complex synthetic materials that remain in the natural environment for a long time. 632
   government regulation and, 640

personal distribution of income The distribution of income to people in the economy. The personal distribution of income indicates the well-being of people in the economy. 558

personal income The income received by households. Personal income is found by subtracting social security contributions, corporate income taxes, and undistributed corporate profits from and adding transfer payments to national income. 146–147, 148
   disposable, 146–147, 148, 203–205
   national income vs., 147
   tax on, 606

personal objective The objective of corporate managers that exists when they forego profit to the firm in order to improve their own working environment, power base, or political goals. 391

per unit tax A tax that is levied on the physical quantity of the tax base; a tax that is a fixed amount on each unit sold. 88, 89, 599

petroleum prices, 321

Phillips curve A curve depicting the relationship between the rate of inflation and the unemployment rate. 324–328
   aggregate demand and, 325
   aggregate supply and, 327–328
   expectations and, 331–333
   historical evidence of, 326–327

Pigouvian tax A tax placed on producers to internalize an external cost. 638–639

planned economy An economy in which resources are allocated according to a preestablished plan. While the socialist Soviet economy is a planned economy, planned economies need not be socialist, and vice versa. Even capitalist economies have some degree of planning at the macroeconomic level. 711–712, 721

planned investment Investment expenditures that firms would like to make over a period of time based on conditions in the economy. 213

plant The physical capital at a particular location used for the production of goods and services. 385

point source pollution Pollution that can be traced to a specific point of origin. 633

political cycles, 187

political entrepreneur A politician whose primary goal is to obtain reelection and remain in office. 582

pollution The artificially generated waste that is emitted into the natural environment. Pollution does not create an external cost if no one is harmed. 631–636
   of air, 633–634, 642–643
   degradable, 632
   economic growth and, 682
   nondegradable, 632
   nonpoint source, 633
   persistent, 632
   point source, 633
   of water, 632–633, 642

pollution control policies, 634, 638–643

pollution permit market A policy in which transferable permits allowing polluters to discharge waste into the environment are issued by the government. This policy uses market forces to achieve an efficient level of pollution. 641

population:
   economic growth and, 678
   GNP and, 131
   in less-developed countries, 687–689, 692

positive economics The branch of economics that tries to explain the way the economy actually operates. Positive economics is concerned with the process of testing hypotheses. A positive statement can be refuted by looking at the real world. 9

positive (direct) relationship The relationship that exists when the values of two variables increase together. 27

poverty The condition in which people do not have the basic necessities of life and lack the income to buy them. 565–572
   absolute, 566
   distribution of income and, 566
   government policies on, 568–572
   relative, 566
   in the United States, 567–568, 570–572

poverty line A measure of the income needed by a family based on family size, location, and characteristics of the head of the household. 566–567

poverty programs, 570–572

PPI. *See* producer price index

precautionary motive The desire to hold money to undertake unexpected transactions. The precautionary motive is affected by income and the interest rate in exactly the same way as the transactions motive. 293–294

predatory pricing The process of reducing prices below average total cost in order to undercut the price of a competitor and take away its customers. 478–479

price The amount of money or other commodity given up to buy a commodity in a market. While the price is usually in monetary units, it can also be in terms of another commodity. The price of a commodity provides information and incentives to both buyers and sellers. 50
- average cost and, 417–419
- demand and, 57
- of diesel fuel, 375–376
- equilibrium, 73–74
- factor, 65–66
- factor demand and, 501–502
- flexibility of, 195–197
- market and, 50
- supply and, 67–68

price ceiling A legally established maximum price below the market equilibrium. Rent controls and natural gas regulation are two examples of price ceilings. A price ceiling established below the market equilibrium price creates a shortage, or excess demand, the size of which depends on the elasticities of demand and supply. The more elastic demand and supply are, the greater the shortage is. 86–87, 104–105

price change, 370–371

price competition, 456, 457–458

price controls/guidelines, 338–339

price elasticity of demand The relative response of quantity demanded to a change in price, defined as the percentage change in quantity demanded divided by the percentage change in price. 92–97, 106–108

price elasticity of supply The relative response of quantity supplied to a change in price, defined as the percentage change in quantity supplied divided by the percentage change in price. 98–99

price floor A legally established minimum price above the market equilibrium. Minimum wages and agricultural price supports are two examples of price floors. A price floor established above the market equilibrium price creates a surplus, or excess supply, the size of which depends on the elasticities of demand and supply. The more elastic demand and supply are, the greater the surplus is. A price floor is one policy used to address the short-run farm problem, but such a policy leads to a surplus of agricultural products and an inefficient allocation of resources. 85–86, 102–103, 428

price level The average of all prices of goods and services in the economy. 161
- inflation and, 163–164, 317, 319
- measures of, 162, 164
- money and, 319

price maker A firm that can influence the market price. 389

price rigidity The behavior of oligopolies in which prices in the industry change very little over time. 469–470, 472

price rule, 314

price stability The condition in which the average level of prices in the economy does not change or changes very slowly. 22

price subsidy The difference between the market price and a specified target price. A price subsidy also leads to an inefficient allocation of resources. 428–429

price taker A firm that has no influence on the market price. 388

pricing:
- predatory, 478–479
- regulatory, 458–460

prime lending rate The interest rate charged by banks to their best customers on short-term loans. 545

principle of comparative advantage The principle stating that trade between nations is beneficial to both if there is a difference in the relative opportunity costs. This principle means that even a country without an absolute advantage in the production of goods can engage in trade. 659–660

principle of the median voter The principle stating that the median voter determines the outcome of a decision made by majority rule. The proposal of the median voter is the only proposal that finds a majority. 582–583

Principles of Economics (Marshall), 348

private benefit The value placed on a good by its buyers. 624

private cost A cost incurred explicitly or implicitly by a firm. Private costs guide the production decisions of the firm. 623

private good A good that is rival in consumption, and nonpayers can be excluded from consumption. 591–592, 628

producer price index (*PPI*) A price index based on the prices of selected raw materials and intermediate goods purchased by producers. While the *PPI* is not a measure of the economy's price level, it typically indicates whether the price level is likely to rise or fall in the near future. 163

producers' surplus The difference between the price suppliers are willing to accept for a good (based on the costs of production) and the price actually received. 604

GLOSSARY/INDEX

product:
   average, 396, 398–399
   marginal, 396, 397–399
   marginal physical, 499
   marginal revenue, 499, 500, 501
   total, 395–396, 397, 402–403
product differentiation Real or perceived differences between goods such that buyers are willing to pay different prices. 441–442, 462
production The process of transforming resources, through changes in structure, location, or time, into goods and services used for the satisfaction of wants and needs. 394–399
   complements in, 68
   costs of, 401–408, 615
   factors of, 14–16
   in GNP, 128–129, 130
   law of diminishing marginal returns and, 396–399, 407–408
   long-run, 395
   of public goods, 594–595
   short-run, 395–396, 418
   substitutes in, 67
production possibilities The alternative combinations of goods produced if the economy fully uses all resources. The production possibilities of an economy are limited because resources used to produce goods and services are limited. 34–37
   student example of, 34–35
   in U.S. economy, 35–36
production possibilities frontier (*PPF*) The curve that illustrates the alternative combinations of goods that can be produced with the existing quantity of resources and current level of technology. The economy can produce at any point on or inside the frontier, but it cannot produce at any point outside the frontier. 36–37, 40
productivity:
   inflation and, 344–345
   regulation and, 615
product markets Markets used to exchange final goods and services. In product markets the household sector is the demander, and the business sector the supplier. 117
profit The payment for the use of entrepreneurship. 553–555
   accounting, 402, 553
   economic, 402, 553–555
   innovation, 554
   monopoly, 554
   in national income, 142
   normal, 402, 553
   resource allocation and, 555
   risk, 554

profit and loss, 464, 465
profit curve A curve depicting the relationship between economic profit and the quantity of output. A perfectly competitive firm produces the quantity that gives the highest level of economic profit. This is at the greatest distance between the total revenue and total cost curves and the peak of the profit curve. 414, 415
profit maximization The process of obtaining the highest possible level of profit through the production and sale of goods and services. This represents the objective of a firm in which decisions are based exclusively on obtaining the most profit possible. Profit maximization is used as the underlying assumption in the economic analysis of a firm's output decision. 390
progressive tax A tax in which the proportion of income paid in tax increases for higher levels of income. 599
proletariat Marx's term for the working class. 704
   dictatorship of the, 705
property tax, 607
proportional tax A tax in which the proportion of income paid in tax is the same for all levels of income. 599
proprietorship A firm owned and operated by a single person. The proprietor takes all risks and receives all rewards. Quite often in a proprietorship, the owner also supplies most of the resources. 385, 386
proprietors' income, 144–145
proven reserves Sources of an exhaustible resource that have been identified as economically usable. 649
public choice The study of collective decisions made by groups of individuals. 581–588
public good A good that is nonrival in consumption, and nonpayers cannot be excluded from consumption. Many externalities occur when a private good is jointly produced with a public or near-public good. 22, 590–596, 628
   demand for, 593–594
   near, 592–593
   optimal production of, 594–595
   pure, 592
public interest The well-being of the consuming public. 612
public utility A heavily regulated private business or a government-operated enterprise that supplies an essential good or service. Public utilities are very capital intensive, meaning the average cost of one firm declines over the range of market demand. In this case one firm naturally tends to take over the market. 455–460
pure command economy An economy that relies

exclusively on the government for the allocation of resources. 20

pure inflation An equal proportional increase in all nominal values in the economy. With pure inflation there are no distribution or production effects. 165

pure market economy An economy that relies exclusively on markets for the allocation of resources. 19–20

Q

quantity demanded, change in, 54–55
quantity supplied, change in, 64–65
quantity theory of money A theory that states a given percentage change in the money supply leads to an equal percentage change in nominal GNP. The quantity theory of money rests on the proposition that the velocity of money is constant. 306–308

R

rate of return The additional profit generated by an investment expenditure over a period of time, expressed as a percentage. 215

rational expectations Expectations people have concerning future rates of inflation and other economic variables that are based on anticipated government policy and other conditions in the economy. 333

rational ignorance The state in which a voter or consumer decides not to gather information because the costs exceed the benefits. 584

Reagan, Ronald, 45, 614

real balance effect The change in consumption expenditures caused by a change in the purchasing power of financial wealth (real balance). 171
  consumption and, 209
  Keynesian cross and, 239–240

real GNP The total market value of all final goods and services produced in the economy in a given period of time, expressed in constant dollars. Increases in real GNP can indicate if the economy is experiencing economic growth. However, real GNP does not necessarily indicate if people in the economy are any better off or any closer to solving the economic problem. 131–133, 676
  per capita, 676

real interest rate The difference between the nominal interest rate and the rate of inflation. The real interest rate reflects the purchasing power of the nominal interest income. 167–168

realized investment Investment expenditures that business firms actually make over a period of time. 213

reallocation effect The reallocation of resources caused by changes in relative prices due to a tax. An ideal tax designed to raise revenue has no reallocation effect. 601–602

real wage The purchasing power of the nominal wage payments, found by dividing the nominal wage by the price level. 329

recessionary gap The difference between actual aggregate expenditures and the level of aggregate expenditures needed to achieve full employment if actual output is less than full employment output. A recessionary gap can be eliminated with expansionary fiscal or monetary policy. 252–253, 254

recycling The process of reusing waste materials in the production of goods and services rather than using natural resources. Recycling materials reduces pollution by returning less waste today and reducing the need for raw materials tomorrow. 636

Refuse Act of 1899, 642

regressive tax A tax in which the proportion of income paid in tax decreases for higher levels of income. 599

regulation. *See* government regulation
regulatory pricing, 458–460

relative poverty level The condition in which people do not have the income to buy a relative amount of the basic necessities of life. 566

renewable resource A resource that can be increased by the natural forces of the environment. Common examples of renewable resources are plant and animal life, clean air and water, and solar energy. 646

rent The payment for the use of land. 551–552
  economic, 551–551, 553

rental income, 141–142, 551–552

required reserves The minimum amount of reserves that a bank must hold to back up its deposits. 276–277

reserve requirements The amount of reserves that the Federal Reserve System requires a bank to keep to back up its deposits. If the Fed increases reserve requirements, then the money supply decreases. If the Fed decreases reserve requirements, the money supply increases. 286–288

reserves The vault cash and deposits at the Federal Reserve System that banks use to complete day-to-day transactions. 275–277
  excess, 277
  legal, 276
  required, 276–277

resource allocation. *See* allocation

resources The materials available to an economy for the production of goods and services. 5, 12–14
  economic growth and, 682
  energy, 645–647
  exhaustible, 646–647
  free, 13

GLOSSARY/INDEX

resources (*continued*)
  limited, 13
  ownership of, 439, 697
  renewable, 646
  scarce, 13–14
retained earnings The profits earned by a firm that are not distributed to shareholders or owners in the form of dividends. The firm invests its retained earnings where the highest returns can be made, either in the financial market or by purchasing capital. 543
revenue:
  average, 413–413, 464
  marginal, 413, 414, 415–417, 449–450, 464
  monopoly and, 446, 447
  perfect competition and, 413
  total, 413, 414–415, 448
revenue effect The process of raising revenue from a tax in order to carry on the operation of the government. 601
Ricardo, David, 704
right-to-work law A law that does not allow any type of mandatory union membership to be written into a collective bargaining agreement. 521
risk The possibility of gains or losses. 554
rule of consumer equilibrium The rule stating that the ratio of marginal utility to price is the same for all goods. 355

S

sales maximization The process of obtaining the highest possible level of sales. 390
sales tax, 607
saving The disposable income that is not used for consumption expenditures. 119
  in classical economics, 197–198
  consumption vs., 204–205, 210
  economic growth and, 678–679
saving function A line that depicts the relationship between saving and disposable income. The slope of the saving function is the marginal propensity to save. 207–209
savings accounts, 377–378
Say, Jean Baptiste, 195
Say's law The principle stating that supply creates its own demand. 195
scarce good A good with an available quantity less than its desired use. All scarce goods have limited availability. However, a limited good is scarce only if people want more than is available. 13–14
scarce resource A resource with an available quantity less than its desired use. Scarce resources are also called factors of production. 13–14

scarcity The condition that exists when there is an insufficient quantity of resources to produce all of the goods and services desired by people. The economic problem of scarcity has always faced humanity and always will. 5, 12–14
seasonal unemployment Unemployment created by relatively regular, or seasonal, declines in business activity. 153
sellers, number of, 69–70
sewage, 632
share drafts Checkable deposits at credit unions that pay an interest. 269
Sherman Act of 1890 The first antitrust legislation in the United States, which outlawed trusts and any conspiracy to restrain trade. Although used to break up the Standard Oil Trust in 1911, it is vaguely written. 479–480, 522
shortage A condition in the market in which the quantity demanded is greater than the quantity supplied at the existing price. A shortage causes the price to rise. 75
short run A period of time in which at least one input is variable and one input is fixed. 395
short-run farm problem The fluctuation of farm income caused by fluctuations in agricultural prices. 423–425
short-run output:
  monopolistic competition and, 463–465
  monopoly and, 448–450
  natural monopoly and, 455
  perfect competition and, 414–417
short-run production, 395–396, 418
single tax A tax levied on only one item, used to raise the revenue needed by the government. A single tax on land does not alter the amount of land exchanged and thus does not affect the allocation of resources. However, if the single tax on land is too high, landowners might remove their land from the market. 552
slope The change in the variable on the vertical axis divided by the change in the variable on the horizontal axis. 27, 30
  elasticity and, 95, 96
  negative, 28
  positive, 27
Smith, Adam, 2, 195
social benefit The total benefit received from a good, or the sum of private and external benefits. 624–625
social cost The total opportunity cost of production, or the sum of private and external costs. 624
socialism An economic system that is primarily based on government ownership of resources and allocative decisions made by the government. Socialism is an economic system used by many "communist"

countries, including the Soviet Union and China. Throughout the world, numerous types of socialistic economic systems exist, each a little different from the others. 698
  market, 699, 725–726
social objective The objective that exists when firms forego higher profits to pursue social goals, such as environmental quality or public safety. 390–391
social overhead capital The government-produced or government-subsidized portion of the economy's capital stock, consisting of transportation, water and sewage, energy and communication, and educational systems. Social overhead capital is a necessary foundation for growth, but it is usually not profitably produced by private firms. 679–680
social regulation The regulation of specific activities, regardless of industry. 611–612
Social Security Act of 1935, 571
Social Security tax, 606–607
solar energy, 651–652
Soviet economy, 709–716
  background of, 709–711
  evaluation of, 713–716
  structure of, 711–713
special interest group A group of people who are intensely interested in an issue because they are more affected by it than the general public. 587–588
speculative motive The desire to hold money instead of interest-paying assets in anticipation of conditions in the financial market changing. The interest rate is the most important factor affecting the speculative motive. If the interest rate increases, people want to hold less money because of the speculative motive. 294
stagflation The condition of the economy characterized by both a decline in economic activity and inflation. 185
Staggers Rail Deregulation Act of 1980, 610
Stalin, Joseph, 710–711
Standard Oil, 478, 479, 480
state banks Banks that are chartered by the government of the state in which they are located. Before 1980 state banks did not have to be members of the Federal Reserve System. Today all banks, whether state or national, members or nonmembers, are subject to the same guidelines and regulations set up by the Federal Reserve System. 285
state farm In China and the Soviet Union, a farm that is owned and operated by the government. State farms are operated in the same way as any other government enterprise. The workers receive wages and incentive bonuses if they surpass the established output requirements. State farms account for the majority of agricultural production. 713

State Planning Commission China's central planning authority. 721
statics, comparative, 76
straight line A line with a constant slope. 27–28, 29–31
strike An agreement between workers or members of a labor union to temporarily stop working. 521
structural unemployment Unemployment created by changes in the types of skills required in the production of goods and services. 153–154
subsistence wage The wage needed by labor in order to provide enough food just to maintain life. According to Marx, the subsistence wage would lead workers to revolt against the owners of capital. 704
substitutes Two goods that have similar uses, where an increase in the price of one good leads to an increase in demand and a rightward shift in the demand curve of the other good. If demand for good 1 increases as the price of good 2 increases, the goods are substitutes, or two goods with a positive cross price elasticity. 57, 98, 99, 108
substitutes in production Goods that are produced with the same resources such that resources used to produce one good cannot be used to produce the other. An increase in the price of one substitute good leads to a decrease in the supply of the other good and a leftward shift of the supply curve. 67
substitution:
  decreasing marginal rate of, 369
  marginal rate of, 368
substitution effect The change in quantity demanded that results because the price of a good changes relative to the prices of other goods. A price decline makes the good relatively more attractive, inducing consumers to substitute this good for other goods. The substitution effect always causes quantity demanded and price to move in opposite directions. 53, 360–361
sunspot theory of business cycles, 187
Supplemental Security Income (SSI), 571
suppliers, expectations of, 69
supply The range of quantities of a commodity that sellers are willing and able to sell at different prices in a given period of time. 49, 62–70
  of agricultural goods, 423–431
  of airline services, 433–434
  decrease in, 79–80, 81–82
  determinants of, 65–70
  factor, 505–510
  increase in, 78, 79, 80, 82
  law of, 62–63
  market, 64, 65, 506
  perfect competition and, 411–421
  price elasticity of, 98–99

GLOSSARY/INDEX

supply (*continued*)
  quantity supplied and, 64–65
  See also aggregate supply
supply by a firm The range of quantities that an individual firm is willing and able to sell at alternative prices. 505–506
supply curve A graphical representation of the law of supply, with a positive slope due to the law of supply. 63–64
  aggregate, 172–174, 177–178, 197
  of monopolistically competitive firm, 464
  of monopoly, 450–452
  of perfectly competitive firm, 419–420
supply-driven business cycle A business cycle caused by changes in aggregate supply. 183
supply restriction The policy in which farmers are induced to reduce output. This policy usually takes the form of restricting the amount of land used for agricultural production. However, with no limits on nonland inputs, the supply of agricultural production may be reduced less than planned. 429–430
supply schedule A table that illustrates the alternative quantities of a commodity supplied at different prices. 62–63
supply-side economics A body of economic thought that emphasizes policies aimed at the aggregate supply side of the economy rather than the aggregate demand side. The most notable supply-side policies deal with incentives through reduction of tax rates, restructuring of transfer payments, or reduction of government regulation. 340–342
supply to a firm The range of quantities of a factor that a firm is able to buy at alternative prices. 506
surplus The condition in the market in which the quantity supplied is greater than the quantity demanded at the existing price. A surplus causes the price to fall. 74–75
  consumer, 361, 362
surplus value The value of output produced over and above the wages paid to labor. According to Marx, labor was the only source of production and thus the only factor that created the value of output. Surplus value plays an important role in the downfall of capitalism, because capital owners and entrepreneurs exploit labor by taking this surplus value. This exploitation then motivates labor to revolt and replace capitalism with socialism. 706

T

Taft-Hartley Act, 523–524
tangency The point at which the slopes of two lines are the same and the values of the variables are the same. 30, 31

tariff A tax imposed on goods imported into a country. A tariff increases the price paid in the importing country and reduces the quantity imported. 662–665
tax, 88–90, 598–607
  ad valorem, 88–80, 599
  corporate, 607
  efficiency and, 601–602
  equity and, 600
  excise, 607
  flat rate, 619–620
  indirect business, 141, 142
  inflation control and, 340–341
  negative income, 569–570
  payroll, 606–607
  personal, 148, 606
  per unit, 88, 89, 599
  Pigouvian, 639
  progressive, 599
  property, 607
  proportional, 599
  regressive, 599
  sales, 607
  single, 552
  See also net taxes
tax base The object of taxation. 598–599
tax incidence The division of a tax between buyers and sellers. Generally, the tax is paid by both buyers and sellers in a market. However, the tax incidence is not necessarily divided equally between the two but depends on the price elasticities of demand and supply. The more elastic demand is, the larger the share paid by sellers is. The more elastic supply is, the larger is the share paid by buyers. 89–90, 105–106, 602–604
tax multiplier The ratio of the change in national output to the change in net taxes. The tax multiplier is equal to $-MPC \times 1/MPS$. The MPC indicates that only a fraction of the change in taxes leads to a shift in the aggregate expenditures line. The minus sign indicates that an increase in taxes leads to a decrease in aggregate expenditures and output. 246–247, 254–255
tax rate The amount of tax applied per unit of the tax base. 599
tax reform, 600–601
Taylor, Lester D., 107n, 108n
technology The economy's combined knowledge and information of alternative methods for using factors in the production of goods and services. An increase in the level of technology shifts the supply curve rightward. 66–67
  appropriate, 691
  economic development and, 691
  economic growth and, 681

technology (*continued*)
  investment and, 216–217
  supply and, 66–67
television programming, consumer demand for, 381
textbooks, used, 111
theory A set of general principles used to explain actions in the world. Economic theories abstract from the world in a way that is similar to the way a road map abstracts from the world. Both highlight important features and neither attempts total description. 8
third party payments Payments made to sellers on behalf of buyers by parties that do not directly receive the benefits from the payment. In the health care industry, third party payments are primarily made by insurance companies and the government. 488–490
Third World. *See* less-developed country
three questions of allocation The three questions every economy has to address are: What goods should be produced? How will the goods be produced with the available resources? Who will get the goods once they are produced? 42–43
thrift, paradox of, 247–249
timber, cross price elasticity of demand for, 108–109
total cost The total opportunity cost of producing goods and services. Total cost is the sum of total variable cost and total fixed cost. 402–406
  average, 407
  for monopoly, 448
  for perfect competition, 414–415
total cost curve, 404–406
total fixed cost A cost that does not change as the quantity of output changes. Total fixed cost is closely related to fixed inputs. In the short run, fixed cost must be paid, regardless of the quantity of output produced. 402, 403–404
total product The total quantity of output produced by a firm with the given quantity of inputs. 395–396, 397, 402–403
total product curve A curve depicting the relationship between total product and the variable input. The slope of the total product curve is the marginal product of the variable input. 395, 396, 402–403
total revenue The revenue received by a firm for the sale of its output, calculated as price times quantity. For a perfectly competitive firm, the total revenue curve is a straight line coming from the origin. 413
  for monopoly, 448
  for perfect competition, 414–415
total utility The total satisfaction of wants and needs obtained from the consumption of goods and services. 351–352
total variable cost A cost that changes as the quantity of output changes. Total variable cost is closely related to variable inputs. Variable cost can be avoided in the short run by not producing any output. 402–403
trade. *See* international trade
transactions motive The desire to hold money to complete day-to-day purchases of goods and services. Two of the most important factors affecting the transactions motive are income and the interest rate. If income increases, people make more expenditures and thus need more money. If the interest rate increases, the opportunity cost of holding money increases and people hold less money. 293
transfer payments Payments from one sector of the economy to another sector that do not result in current production. Transfer payments are income received by households but not earned. 146, 341
treasury bill A financial note issued by the federal government. 546
trough The lowest phase of the business cycle, in which many of the factors of production are unemployed. 181
trust A legal entity established to act on the behalf of others. While trusts are not illegal in general, they were used extensively in the late 1800s to give monopoly power to one firm in an industry. 478
tying contract A contract in which the producer makes the sale of one good conditional on the purchase of another good. 479

U

underemployment The condition of the economy that exists when resources are engaged in the production of goods and services but are operating below capacity or potential. Underemployment of resources also means the economy is operating inside the production possibilities frontier. 39, 152–153
underground economy, 192
unemployment The condition of the economy in which some available factors of production are not being used in the production of goods and services. When unemployment exists, the economy is producing inside the production possibilities frontier. 39, 152–158
  business cycles and, 188–189
  costs of, 157–158
  cyclical, 153
  disguised, 152–153
  frictional, 153
  during Great Depression, 199
  inflation and, 324–333
  involuntary, 152
  measurement of, 154–155
  natural rate of, 331

unemployment *(continued)*
  seasonal, 153
  structural, 153–154
  trends in, 155–157
  voluntary, 152
unemployment rate The percentage of the total labor force that is unemployed. 154–157
unions. *See* labor union
union shop A firm that is free to hire union or non-union workers, with the stipulation that once hired, the worker must join the union. 521
United Mine Workers union, 523
United States:
  energy resources in, 645–646
  factors of production in, 15–16
  firms in, 386–387
  mixed economy of, 20–21
  money in, 268–271
  oligopolies in, 468–469
  poverty in, 567–568, 570–572
U.S. Steel, 480
unit elastic A condition of elasticity in which the percentage change in quantity demanded (or supplied) is equal to the percentage change in price, and the absolute value of the price elasticity of demand (or supply) is equal to 1.0. A unit elastic curve is neutral in its response to changes in price. 95
unlimited liability The condition that exists when the owner of a firm is personally responsible for any and all of the firm's debts. This means the owner's personal property, which is unrelated to the firm's operation, can be used to satisfy the firm's obligations. 386
unlimited wants A characteristic of people such that they are never totally satisfied with the quantity and variety of goods and services. 16–17
utility The satisfaction of wants and needs obtained from the consumption of goods and services. 351–364
  law of demand and, 359–360
  marginal, 353, 355, 358–359
  total, 351–352
utility maximization The process of obtaining the highest level of utility from the consumption of goods and services. 351–352
  constrained, 352–353

V

value, surplus, 706
value added The increase in the value of a good at each stage of the production process. The value of a final good can be divided between the value that each stage of the production process adds to the good. 127–128
variable A quantity that can take on a series of different values. 26
variable costs:
  average, 406, 417–419
  total, 402, 403
variable input An input whose quantity can be changed in the time period under consideration. 394
velocity of money The average number of times a dollar is used in the transaction for a final good or service. The velocity is computed by the equation $V = PQ/M$. 307, 308
vertical addition The process of adding two curves vertically by adding the total value every buyer places on the quantity of the good. While the total demand curve for a private good is found by *horizontally* adding all individual demand curves, the total demand curve for a public good is found by *vertically* adding all individual demand curves. 593
vertical equity The principle stating that people with varying ability to pay should pay a different tax. 600
vertical merger A merger between two firms in different stages of the production of the same good. 478
voluntary unemployment Unemployment created when labor chooses not to take available employment, anticipating that better jobs can be found. 152
voting and rational ignorance, 584
voting paradox The possibility that group decisions lead to intransitive rankings of programs. The voting paradox implies that group decisions may well depend on the order in which they are made. 586–587

W

wage The payment for the use of labor resources. The wage is the payment to labor based on its contribution to the production of goods and services. Wages can be either direct payments to labor or indirect payments for fringe benefits or taxes. 532–540
  comparable worth concept and, 530
  discrimination and, 530, 536
  expectations and, 329
  flexibility of, 195–197
  inflation and, 321
  in national income, 141
  nominal, 329
  real, 329
  subsistence, 704

wage and price controls/guidelines Legally established (controls) or voluntary (guidelines) maximum limits on prices and wages. Whether the controls/guidelines are mandatory or voluntary, they lead to shortages of goods and services and a misallocation of resources. While they are politically more feasible than reducing the money supply or government spending or increasing taxes, they are also less effective. 338–339

wage differentials, 532–536
   elimination of, 533–534
   reasons for existence of, 534–536

wage-price spiral Inflation caused by self-reinforcing increases in real wages and the price level. The wage-price spiral occurs because labor demands higher wages to compensate for higher prices. But as firms pay higher real wages, they compensate by increasing their prices, which leads to another round of wage increases and further price increases. 321

water, price elasticity of demand for, 107–108

water pollution The discharge of waste materials into rivers, streams, lakes, or oceans. The three most common sources of water pollution are domestic sewage, industrial waste, and agricultural runoff. 632–633, 642

Water Pollution Control Act of 1948, 642
Water Pollution Control Amendments of 1972, 611, 642

Wealth:
   concentration of, 706–707
   consumption and, 209

Wealth of Nations, The (Smith), 2

welfare loss The difference between the reduction in consumers' and producers' surplus and the tax revenue. Welfare loss is greater if the demand and supply curves are more elastic. 604, 605

welfare state A country that places a great deal of emphasis on equity and the minimum level of individual welfare. Although it is often equated with socialism, a welfare state can exist under any type of economic system. Sweden is a good example of a welfare state. 700

Wheeler-Lea Act of 1938 The act that gave the FTC powers to investigate unfair and deceptive business practices and false advertising. 481

wind erosion, 634
workers, discouraged, 154
Wozniak, Steve, 15

Y

yellow-dog contract An agreement signed by workers before they are hired saying they will not join a union. 523

Yugoslavia, market socialism in, 725–726